The Court and the Constitution

LEADING CASES

Peter H. Russell
University of Toronto

Rainer Knopff
University of Calgary

Thomas M.J. Bateman
St. Thomas University

Janet L. Hiebert
Queen's University

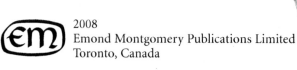

2008
Emond Montgomery Publications Limited
Toronto, Canada

Emond Montgomery Publications Limited
60 Shaftesbury Avenue
Toronto ON M4T 1A3
http://www.emp.ca

Printed in Canada on 100 percent recycled paper.

We acknowledge the financial support of the Government of Canada through the Book Publishing Industry Development Program (BPIDP) for our publishing activities.

Acquisitions and developmental editor: Mike Thompson
Marketing manager: Christine Davidson
Copy editor: Nancy Ennis, WordsWorth Communications
Proofreader: David Handelsman, WordsWorth Communications
Production editor: Jim Lyons, WordsWorth Communications
Text designer: Tara Wells, WordsWorth Communications
Cover designers: Stephen Cribbin & Simon Evers
Back cover photo: Mike Thompson

Library and Archives Canada Cataloguing in Publication

The Court and the Constitution : leading cases / Peter H. Russell ... [et al.].

Includes the text of The Constitution Act, 1867 and The Constitution Act, 1982.
ISBN 978-1-55239-275-1

   1. Canada—Constitutional law—Cases.   2. Canada. Supreme Court.
3. Judgments—Canada.   I. Russell, Peter H.

KE4216.3.C69 2008   342.71   C2008-901531-2
KF4482.C69 2008

Contents

PART ONE

The Division of Powers

A: THE PRIVY COUNCIL'S LEGACY

B: THE SUPREME COURT SINCE 1949

PART TWO
Rights and Freedoms

A: FUNDAMENTAL RIGHTS AND FREEDOMS IN THE B.N.A. ACT

B: THE CANADIAN BILL OF RIGHTS

C. THE CHARTER OF RIGHTS AND FREEDOMS

PART THREE

Aboriginal Rights

PART FOUR

Constitutional Change

APPENDIX 1

APPENDIX 2

Preface

This collection of leading Supreme Court of Canada decisions is rooted in previous collections dating to 1965. When Peter Russell's *Leading Constitutional Decisions* was first published, few political scientists in Canada were interested in the practice of judicial review and, more generally, the influence of courts on constitutional development and public policy. Law professors and historians dominated the field. Russell's book, however, attracted attention and underwent several subsequent editions, culminating in 1989 in *Federalism and the Charter: Leading Constitutional Decisions*, which he co-edited with F.L. Morton and Rainer Knopff.

The success of Russell's venture coincided with important developments in Canadian law and politics. By the 1960s, Canada was shedding its historical and cultural connection with Great Britain. British legal forms and traditions were losing some of their directing force. Civil libertarianism was gripping Canadian political and legal elites and Prime Minister Pierre Trudeau proposed to entrench a charter of individual rights into a patriated Canadian Constitution. In a bold move, Trudeau appointed the brilliant, Harvard-educated civil libertarian and jurist Bora Laskin to the Supreme Court of Canada in 1970, and, three years later, elevated Laskin to Chief Justice, over the heads of seven other more senior *puisne* justices. Laskin's American legal training was evident in his interest in civil liberties and in his view that law can be a vehicle of progressive social change. As Chief Justice of the Supreme Court, Laskin set the Court and Canadian law on a new course. Canadians henceforth became more familiar with the influence of courts and law on public policy.

What for decades were commonplaces in the study of American law and courts—judicial review is not straightforward legal decision making; courts are important political institutions; law is influenced by political culture, institutions, and political and ideological forces; courts exercise important policy-making power—were becoming more evident in Canada. Students of political science now appreciate the need to read the decisions of our high court in order to understand the complex role of the judiciary and law in the Canadian polity. Yet there has not been a comprehensive collection of high court decisions designed for Canadian political science students for almost 20 years. We think such a collection is overdue.

Of course, the *Canadian Charter of Rights and Freedoms*, in force since 1982, has decisively shown that constitutional interpretation is politically salient. *Charter* decisions expose different views of the relationship between courts and legislatures and different understandings of the transformative character of law. Such is the resonance of the *Charter* in law and political culture that many think the *Charter is* the Constitution. This is far from the case. The Supreme Court used both constitutional principles and the common law to protect individual rights long before the *Charter* was entrenched in 1982. Aboriginal rights are protected by section 35 of the *Constitution Act, 1982* and the Supreme Court has boldly gone where politicians have feared to tread. The *Constitution Act, 1982*, which includes the *Charter* but also much more, is but one of two major constitutional documents. The other is the *British North America Act*, passed by the British Parliament in 1867, which established Canada as a federal regime modelled on British parliamentary principles. In 1982, that *Act* was renamed the *Constitution Act, 1867,* but it remains a basic part of Canada's constitutional architecture. Canada is a deeply federal country and courts have played a major role in shaping that character. Further, Canadian parliamentary government is bound up with myriad conventions (or unwritten constitutional rules) whose force and legitimacy have nothing to do with their judicial enforceability. There is indeed much more to Canadian constitutional law than the *Charter.*

Understanding the history of constitutional interpretation is vital to understanding our present circumstances. Two examples will suffice. First, the Supreme Court frequently intones that the "*British North America Act* planted in Canada a living tree capable of growth and expansion within its natural limits." This metaphor allows the Court to interpret the Constitution not in terms of original meaning but in terms of the felt needs of the day as discerned by the justices. That metaphor comes from a 1929 decision on the eligibility of women to be members of the Senate and was made by the Judicial Committee of the Privy Council (JCPC), the British imperial legal body that possessed final interpretive authority over the Canadian Constitution until 1949.

Second, as environmental concerns attract more public attention and federal politicians are called on to act, the federal government may be tempted to undergird its constitutional authority to act in this amorphous area of public policy by reference to the "peace, order, and good government" (POGG) clause of section 91 of the *Constitution Act, 1867,* which in its origins was a significant grant of residual policy power to the federal Parliament. But the federal government would have to overcome precedents dating to the 19th century that limit the exercise of the POGG power to exceptional, even emergency, circumstances. Present predicaments are understandable in terms of historical legacies.

We have had to make many hard decisions about the cases constituting this collection. Naturally, the difficulty lay in what to exclude, not what to include. We have included decisions that broadly represent the sweep of high court decision making. We include "opinions" of the JCPC because that body was Canada's high court of appeal until 1949 and a major determinant of our constitutional law. We selected cases that acquired major jurisprudential force over time. In *Citizens Insurance Co. v. Parsons* (1881), for example, the JCPC limited the federal Parliament's capacious trade and commerce power to matters of interprovincial trade, making it difficult henceforth for the federal government to shape and direct the Canadian economy. We selected cases that contain political resonance. *Morgentaler v. The Queen* (1988) was a political bombshell that put to rest any lingering doubt that the Court would shy away from political questions in the age of the *Charter.* We also selected cases for their historical value: pre-*Charter* civil liberties decisions, for example, as well as decisions that influenced the nature and prospects of constitutional change.

The secondary literature on Canadian constitutionalism is now immense and students will be tempted to read that literature in place of the primary sources of constitutional law. This would be a mistake. No one would recommend reading about Plato over reading Plato himself. We suggest that it is important to read the primary data of Canadian constitutionalism—the decisions themselves—to develop the capacity to understand legal writing and to develop the critical skills of interpreting a decision for oneself. Knowing the primary data helps the student understand and assess the secondary literature more deeply. It is hard work, but it repays the investment. We lessen the burden by editing the decisions to manageable length and by including introductory notes to provide context.

Constitutional law is a moving target. Every decision contains the potential to steer jurisprudence in new directions. Personnel changes on the Court, new issues, emergencies, shifts in public opinion, politicians' use of the courts to advance their agendas, changes in the rules of Court, interest group participation in litigation—all these inject a complex dynamism into Supreme Court decision making, governance, and public policy. The revolution in electronic communications technologies—which the courts have largely embraced—only magnifies this dynamism. We have accommodated these developments by linking purchasers of this book to an Internet-based platform of both historic and current decisions to supplement this collection. Students have ample access to older decisions for research and to new decisions to understand the direction of change.

The editors of this volume represent four universities, three regions, three academic generations, and diverse political persuasions. Knopff and Hiebert studied under Russell; Bateman studied under Knopff. All have a keen interest in constitutional law and politics and all have published in the field. We value teaching and hope that this collection will help students discover what is interesting, important, deficient, and worthy in Canadian constitutionalism.

Our project is made possible by the enthusiastic support of Emond Montgomery Publications, and particularly Mike Thompson. Many thanks to him and the staff.

Website

This book is supplemented by an extensive password-protected website containing introductions and edited decisions for many additional Supreme Court of Canada cases not included in this book. Instructors who have selected this book for course use can contact an Emond Montgomery sales representative for more information at 1-888-837-0815, or visit www.emp.ca/university.

About the Authors

Peter H. Russell is Professor of Political Science at the University of Toronto. Rainer Knopff is Professor of Political Science at the University of Calgary. Thomas M.J. Bateman is Associate Professor of Political Science at St. Thomas University. Janet L. Hiebert is Professor of Political Studies at Queen's University.

Introduction

Many Canadians expressed shock and surprise when the Supreme Court of Canada was called upon in the spring of 1981 to determine the constitutionality of the federal government's plan to proceed unilaterally with its proposed restructuring of Canada's Constitution to establish fully domestic amending procedures and entrench a *Charter of Rights and Freedoms.* "Isn't it strange," they asked, "for the Court to be involved in such a *political* question?" This question reflected the fact that, at that time, Canadians had little understanding of the political significance of judicial interpretation of the Constitution. This is not surprising given the quiet, unheralded way in which judicial review became an important part of Canada's constitutional system.

It is in keeping with the nature of much of Canada's constitutional history that one of the most influential elements in its development—judicial interpretation of the *British North America (B.N.A.) Act*[1]—was accepted at the outset with little awareness of its full significance. The Fathers of Confederation were remarkably insensitive to the problems connected with judicial review under a federal constitution, despite the fact that American experience had, by 1867, shown the crucial importance of the Supreme Court in determining the extent of national and state powers. Section 101 of the *B.N.A. Act* granted to the federal Parliament the power to establish a "General Court of Appeal for Canada," but nowhere in the Constitution was there explicit recognition of the power of that court, nor of the Judicial Committee of the Privy Council (the English tribunal that was then the final court of appeal for British colonies), to determine the constitutional validity of federal or provincial legislation. Canadians never experienced a case like *Marbury v. Madison,*[2] in which Chief Justice Marshall successfully claimed for the United States' Supreme Court the role of constitutional arbiter with the power to strike down any act of government, national or local, that in the Court's view violated the terms of the Constitution. Yet it was precisely that power which, from the country's earliest days, the Canadian judiciary, without explicit acknowledgment and despite the incompatibility of judicial review with the traditional British theory of parliamentary sovereignty, assumed with respect to the *B.N.A. Act.*

Before the *Charter* era, Canadians were apt to look upon judicial review as a necessary ingredient of a federal state. But to those who accepted judicial review so readily in the 1870s and 1880s, especially to the jurists who manned the Judicial Committee of the Privy Council, the courts' power to assess the constitutional validity of legislation was as much a corollary of imperialism as of federalism. The *B.N.A. Act* was, after all, an act of the Imperial Parliament and, according to the *Colonial Laws Validity Act,* Dominion statutes were void if they

---

[1] In 1982, Canada's original Constitution, the *British North America Act, 1867,* was renamed the *Constitution Act, 1867.* Similarly, amendments to the Constitution, including the 1982 amendment, are now entitled the *Constitution Act,* followed by the year of enactment.

[2] 5 U.S. (1 Cranch) 137 (1803).

conflicted with British statutes. However, over time, with the waning of the imperial connection and the experience of so many controversies associated with the division of powers
between the federal and provincial legislatures, judicial review came to be seen as an imperative of federalism. Canadian judges, in rejecting the few attempts by legislatures to evade
judicial review, reasoned that the federal division of powers could be effectively destroyed
if a legislature could deny the right to challenge the constitutional validity of its actions in
the courts.[3]

The patriation of the Constitution in 1982 significantly broadened the basis of judicial
review in Canada. Section 52 of the *Constitution Act, 1982*[4] establishes, for the first time, an
explicit basis for the judicial veto of unconstitutional laws by declaring that the Constitution
of Canada is "the supreme law of Canada" and that "any law that is inconsistent with the
provisions of the Constitution is, to the extent of the inconsistency, of no force or effect."
More important, the addition of a *Charter of Rights and Freedoms* to the Constitution and
the recognition of Aboriginal and treaty rights widen the focus of judicial review from a
preoccupation with the powers of government to a concern for the rights of citizens and
Aboriginal peoples. Until the advent of the *Charter* and constitutional recognition of
Aboriginal rights—despite the inclusion in the original Constitution of clauses guaranteeing
rights to denominational education (section 93) and the use of English and French in certain
institutions (section 133), as well as the implicit entrenchment of rights inherent in an
independent judiciary (section 99) and parliamentary institutions (for example, section
17)—the prevailing theory was that the Constitution exhaustively distributes *all* the powers
of self-government to the provincial and federal legislatures.[5] Under a constitution that
contains a charter of rights and freedoms, and recognizes the rights of Aboriginal peoples,
this so-called exhaustion theory gave way to a theory which acknowledges that the Constitution entrenches rights of individuals and groups that limit the powers of legislatures,
whether federal or provincial.

However, the shift away from a regime of legislative supremacy has not been unqualified.
Section 33 of the *Charter* permits the federal Parliament and provincial legislatures to
include clauses in their legislation that, for five years at a time, insulate the legislation from
Charter challenge. The override can be applied to the political freedoms in section 2 of the
Charter, the legal rights in sections 7 to 14, and the equality rights in section 15. Although
the override clause (or "notwithstanding clause" as it is often called) has rarely been used

---

3   The fullest consideration of this issue was by Ontario's highest court, in *Ottawa Valley Power
    Vo. v. A.G. Ontario* (1937), O.R. 297. The Supreme Court of Canada briefly considered the
    matter in *B.C. Power Corp. v. B.C. Electric Co.*, [1962] S.C.R. 642.

4   The *Constitution Act, 1982* was made part of the Canadian Constitution by the *Canada Act
    1982*, an Act of the United Kingdom Parliament. It is the *Canada Act 1982* that patriated
    Canada's Constitution by establishing that it would no longer be amended in the United
    Kingdom. The *Constitution Act, 1982* contains the *Canadian Charter of Rights and Freedoms*, a
    section recognizing the rights of Aboriginal peoples, rules for amending the Constitution in
    Canada, and one small change in the division of powers. See case 45 for the Supreme Court's
    decision concerning the validity of the federal government's attempt to accomplish these
    changes without the support of most of the provinces.

5   For a classic statement of the theory, see the opinion of Justice Kerwin in *Saumur*, case 20.

as a deliberate means of insulating legislation from judicial review,[6] the very fact that it exists and enables elected governments to overturn decisions they believe are detrimental to their people's interests removes much of the anti-democratic sting from judicial decisions vetoing acts of the democratically accountable branches of government.[7] On the other hand, some Canadian constitutionalists view the clause as incompatible with a regime of constitutional rights, and at least two Canadian Prime Ministers, Brian Mulroney and Paul Martin, swore that they would never use it.

FROM THE JUDICIAL COMMITTEE TO THE SUPREME COURT

One reason Canadians were slow to realize the importance of judicial review is that, until 1949, their highest court of appeal in constitutional matters was a foreign tribunal, the Judicial Committee of the Privy Council. When the Supreme Court of Canada was established in 1875, efforts were made, notably by the Liberal Minister of Justice, Edward Blake, to limit, if not abolish, appeals to the Judicial Committee. But these efforts came to naught before the determined opposition of the British law officers and Sir John A. Macdonald's Conservative party, both of whom looked upon the appeal as an essential link of imperial union. In the 20th century, the agitation to abolish appeals was rekindled, in part by growing nationalist sentiment, but also, with increasing urgency, by those Canadians who resented what they regarded as the unduly rigid and decentralizing tenor of the Judicial Committee's treatment of Canada's Constitution. The enactment of the *Statute of Westminster* in 1931 opened the way for the Canadian Parliament to abolish appeals to the Privy Council. Although the federal Parliament's power to do this was challenged in the courts, it was finally confirmed by the Judicial Committee itself in 1947.[8] When the *Supreme Court Act* was at last amended in 1949 to make the Supreme Court supreme, in fact as well as in name, the most serious opposition came not from Anglo-Canadian imperial sentiment, but from advocates of provincial interests, particularly in Quebec, who by this time had come to believe that they had a vested interest in the Judicial Committee's line of constitutional interpretation.

There can be no doubt about the supremacy of the Judicial Committee up to the abolition of appeals in 1949. Before the Judicial Committee began rendering important decisions

---

6   The most prominent use of the override occurred when the Quebec government used it as a gesture of protest against the 1982 constitutional settlement, which it vehemently opposed. From 1982 to 1987, Quebec's National Assembly attached an override clause to all existing legislation. This blanket use of section 33 was found to be constitutional by the Supreme Court in its 1988 decision in the Quebec sign case (case 26). Following this case, the Bourassa government used the override again to fend off any court challenges to new legislation requiring French-only outdoor signs. For an account of the override's use and the controversy surrounding it, see Howard Leeson, "Section 33, The Notwithstanding Clause: A Paper Tiger?" in Paul Howe and Peter H. Russell, eds., *Judicial Power and Canadian Democracy* (Montreal and Kingston: McGill-Queen's University Press, 2001) 297-327.

7   For the theory behind the override, see Paul C. Weiler, "Rights and Judges in a Democracy: A New Canadian Version" (1984) 18 *University of Michigan Journal of Law Reform* 51.

8   Case 10.

on Canada's Constitution, the Supreme Court of Canada had an opportunity to act independently. In *Severn,*[9] one of the Court's first constitutional decisions, Chief Justice Richards supported a broad interpretation of the federal trade and commerce power by referring to the intentions of the framers of Canada's Constitution to avoid the problem of states rights that had plagued the United States. But the Supreme Court's centralist approach soon succumbed to the Privy Council's concern for maintaining a balanced federal system. Within a decade the Supreme Court accepted the reality of its subordinate position in the judicial hierarchy and remained, with few exceptions, a "captive court" until its emancipation in 1949. In the words of a scholar who was to become Chief Justice of the Court, "the task of the Supreme Court was not to interpret the constitution but rather to interpret what the Privy Council said the constitution meant."[10] The Court's recognition of its subservience to the Privy Council was reinforced by the tendency of Canadian litigants in some of the most important constitutional cases to bypass the Supreme Court altogether. Nearly half of the Privy Council's decisions on the Canadian Constitution (77 out of 159) came in cases appealed directly from provincial courts of appeal.[11]

When the Supreme Court took over as Canada's highest court of appeal, in theory it was free to strike out on an independent course of constitutional interpretation. In 1957, Justice Ivan Rand explained that the Supreme Court had the same power as the Judicial Committee to modify and refine interpretations of the Constitution.[12] But in practice, there were powerful constraints limiting the Supreme Court's freedom to set aside the constitutional handiwork of the Privy Council. Supreme Court justices were aware of provincial anxieties that the Court might turn out to be dangerously centralist and of the federal government's promise in 1949 that the abolition of Privy Council appeals would not lead to the jettisoning of the Privy Council precedents. Further, the concern in our legal culture for consistency and predictability was too ingrained, and the Privy Council's decisions far too extensive and prescriptive, to leave much scope, at least in the short run, for judicial pioneering.[13] Still, over time, the Supreme Court has given new shape and substance to Canada's constitutional law of federalism. It has done this not through dramatic overruling of Privy Council decisions, but by choosing among competing lines of precedents (for instance, on the peace, order, and good government power) and by applying established interpretive formulations to new fields of legislation (for instance, wage and price controls and environmental protection). In the civil liberties field, the Supreme Court has had virtually a free hand for the simple reason that the *Charter* raises issues that the Privy Council never pronounced on.

---

[9]   *Severn v. The Queen,* [1878] 2 S.C.R. 70.

[10] Bora Laskin, "The Supreme Court of Canada: A Final Court of Appeal of and for Canadians" (1951) 29 *Canadian Bar Review* 1038 at 1069.

[11] This enumeration is based on the compilation of cases in *Decisions of the Judicial Committee of the Privy Council Relating to the British North America Act, 1867 and the Canadian Constitution 1867-1954,* arranged by Richard A. Olmstead.

[12] *Re The Farm Products Marketing Act,* [1957] S.C.R. 198.

[13] But the Liberal government rejected a proposal supported by the Canadian Bar Association and the Conservative opposition that would have made Privy Council decisions binding on the Supreme Court.

We are now at a point in the development of Canada's constitutional law where the Supreme Court's jurisprudence surpasses in importance the work of the Judicial Committee. Still, the Privy Council's legacy will continue to be felt as an enduring ingredient of Canada's political culture. The core of that legacy is, above all, a tendency to look upon federalism as "a level of sovereign jurisdictional rivalry."[14] In endeavouring to preserve a division of powers appropriate for "classical federalism" and thereby resist the strongly centralizing tendencies of the constitutional text, the Judicial Committee developed an acute sensitivity to the competing claims of the provinces and the federal government. Despite periods of cooperative federalism, of province building, and of populist centralism, this atmosphere of competing jurisdictions is likely to remain a distinctive feature of the Canadian political system. Quebec alone would ensure that this is so. But Quebec is by no means the only province that jealously guards its jurisdiction. In a political environment in which the language of rights has become so pervasive, perhaps the most enduring feature of the Privy Council's constitutional interpretation is the honourable status it bestowed on provincial rights as one of Canada's fundamental constitutional values.[15]

The Judicial Committee's interpretation of the Canadian Constitution also generated a debate about the proper role of the courts in constitutional interpretation—a debate that has a timeless quality and that is highly relevant to the *Charter of Rights*.[16] This is another important reason for continuing to study the work of the Judicial Committee.

THE CHANGING ROLE OF CANADA'S SUPREME COURT

The significant role the modern Supreme Court has come to play as the judicial arbiter of Canada's federal Constitution was not anticipated in the years immediately following World War II. Of course, there was no constitutional bill of rights at that time and, so far as federalism was concerned, the emphasis was on instruments of "executive federalism" such as tax-sharing arrangements and shared-cost programs rather than on judicial interpretation or constitutional amendment as the principal means of developing the Constitution. Professor Donald Smiley expressed the prevailing view of constitutional observers in the 1950s and 1960s when he wrote that "[t]he federal aspects of the Canadian Constitution, using the latter term in the broadest sense, have come to be less what the courts say they are than what the federal and provincial cabinets and bureaucracies in a continuous series of formal and informal relations determine them to be."[17]

Undoubtedly there was a great deal of truth in this thesis. Politicians and administrators certainly played a more prominent role than judges in the postwar evolution of Canadian

---

14   F.E. Labrie, "Canadian Constitutional Interpretation and Legislative Review" (1949-50) 8 *University of Toronto Law Journal* 298.

15   See Robert C. Vipond, "Constitutional Politics and the Legacy of the Provincial Rights Movement in Canada" (1985) 18 *Canadian Journal of Political Science* 495.

16   See, for example, Frederick Vaughan, "Critics of the Judicial Committee: The New Orthodoxy and an Alternative Explanation," and Replies by Alan Cairns and Peter Russell (1986) 19 *Canadian Journal of Political Science* 495.

17   D.V. Smiley, "The Rowell-Sirois Report and Provincial Autonomy" (1962) 28 *Canadian Journal of Political Science and Economics* 54 at 59.

federalism. Supreme Court decisions on the Constitution in the two decades after 1949 were not as important as Privy Council decisions had been in the two decades before the war. Even so, the decline in the importance of judicial review tended to be exaggerated. Quantitatively, there was virtually no change in the frequency with which Canada's highest court was called upon to decide federalism issues: two or three such cases a year continued to be the norm. Qualitatively, some of these decisions had a significant impact on developments in the federal system during these years. The Court's approval of a system of intergovernmental delegation to administrative agencies[18] contributed to the so-called cooperative federalism that flourished for a while. Its 1967 decision giving Ottawa jurisdiction over offshore minerals[19] increased the federal government's bargaining power in a major field of federal–provincial combat and aroused provincial suspicions of the Supreme Court's fairness as a judicial umpire of Canadian federalism.

The veritable explosion of division-of-powers litigation that occurred in the 1970s demonstrated how wrong it was to write off the Supreme Court as an important player in the dynamics of Canadian federalism. Whereas the *Supreme Court Reports* for the first half of the 1970s contain only 9 decisions on the division of powers, the *Reports* for the last five years of the decade record 36 decisions on such issues—a fourfold increase. The trend continued into the 1980s. Forty-two federalism decisions are reported for the four-year period from 1980 to 1983—the period preceding the Court's first decision on the *Charter*.

This sudden increase in division-of-powers litigation reflected a more combative period in federal–provincial relations. Instead of waiting to reach accommodations through intergovernmental negotiations, governments were often inclined to test the limits of their constitutional powers by taking unilateral policy initiatives, hoping that they would withstand a court challenge. Provincial initiatives in the field of natural resources[20] and the Trudeau government's attempts at unilateral constitutional reform are leading examples.[21]

In its treatment of the division of powers in the 1970s and 1980s, the Supreme Court adopted a remarkably balanced approach—perhaps not as solicitous of provincial rights as the Judicial Committee or Quebec nationalists would want, but certainly less centralist than the Court tended to be in its first two decades as Canada's highest court.[22] A clear indication of this shift is the *Anti-Inflation Reference*,[23] where the Court's majority rejected the national concern approach to peace, order, and good government that it had embraced 14 years earlier in *Johannesson*.[24] In the 1970s, for the first time since 1949, the Supreme Court over-

---

[18] See case 44.

[19] *Reference re Offshore Mineral Rights of British Columbia*, [1967] S.C.R. 792.

[20] See case 14.

[21] See cases 45 and 46.

[22] For two scholarly analyses of the Court's balance, see Gilbert l'Ecuyer, *La Cour Supreme du Canada et la partage des Competences 1949-78* (Gouvernement de Québec: Ministre des Affaires Intergouvernementales, 1978), and Peter W. Hogg, "Is the Supreme Court of Canada Biased in Constitutional Cases?" (1979) 57 *Canadian Bar Review* 721.

[23] See case 13.

[24] See case 11.

ruled national legislation on federalism grounds.[25] True, there were some major provincial losses during this period—notably in the fields of natural resources and communications policy[26]—that generated public criticism of the Court by provincial premiers and demands for constitutional amendments to overcome the decisions. These provincial attacks on the Court put pressure on the justices to demonstrate their legitimacy as trustworthy arbiters of federal–provincial disputes. The fact that they were appointed by the federal government, without any formal participation of the provinces in the appointment process, probably added to this pressure. The balance the Court began to strike in adjudicating federalism issues—a balance highlighted in its decision in the *Patriation Reference*[27]—suggests that the justices were sensitive to their political environment.

The Supreme Court's success in establishing its credibility as a federal umpire has encouraged constitutional litigation on issues of federalism. An umpire who is perceived to be reasonably balanced is much more likely to be resorted to than one who is demonstrably biased. In Canada "whatever side you are on in a constitutional dispute over the division of powers, the record of balance makes it reasonable to believe you might win."[28] For a long time, the opposite was the case in the United States. This trend culminated in the *Garcia* case, where a majority of the United States Supreme Court took the position that challenges to Congressional legislation based on federalism grounds would no longer be dealt with by the courts; it would be the responsibility of the United States Senate to apply any states rights restrictions on Congress.[29] But after *Garcia*, the Rehnquist Court, bolstered by additional Republican appointments, began to reverse the dismissal of federalism as a protected constitutional value. In asserting the federal aspects of the Constitution, the United States has been catching up with Canada.[30]

At the same time that the Canadian Supreme Court was playing such an active role in deciding disputes over the powers of governments, an increasing number of its decisions dealt with the constitutional rights of citizens. Some of its decisions dealt so negatively with civil rights claims that they gave added impetus to the movement for a constitutional bill of rights. This is true of its decision in *Dupond*,[31] which put an end to the notion it had opened up in the *Alberta Press* case[32] and *Saumur*[33] that there was an implied bill of rights in Canada's founding Constitution; and its unwillingness, so evident in *Lavell and Bédard*,[34]

---

[25]   *McDonald v. Vapor Canada Ltd.*, [1977] 2 S.C.R. 655. For discussion and further examples, see case 15.

[26]   Besides case 14, other cases were *Public Service Board v. Dionne*, [1978] 2 S.C.R. 191, and *Central Canada Potash Co. Ltd. v. Government of Saskatchewan*, [1979] 1 S.C.R. 42.

[27]   Case 46.

[28]   Peter H. Russell, "The Supreme Court and Federal–Provincial Relations: The Political Use of Legal Resources" (1985) 11 *Canadian Public Policy* 161 at 164.

[29]   *Garcia v. San Antonio Metropolitan Transit Authority*, 105 S. Ct. 1005 (1985).

[30]   See Gerald Baier, *Courts and Federalism: Judicial Doctrine in the United States, Australia, and Canada* (Vancouver: University of British Columbia Press, 2006).

[31]   *A.G. Canada and Dupond v. Montreal*, [1978] 2 S.C.R. 770.

[32]   Case 19.

[33]   Case 20.

[34]   See case 21.

to give much weight to the statutory *Bill of Rights* gave added momentum to the movement in Canada to adopt a constitutional bill of rights. Yet, at the same time, in its treatment of constitutionally entrenched language rights,[35] the Court indicated that it was prepared to be quite "activist"[36] in giving a liberal interpretation of constitutional rights as restrictions on government power. Similarly, the Court's decision in the 1973 *Calder*[37] case resuscitated recognition of Aboriginal rights and helped pave the way for the recognition of Aboriginal and treaty rights in the *Constitution Act, 1982.*

In the 1970s, the Supreme Court's jurisdiction was changed in a way that greatly increased its exposure to issues of public law. Up until 1975, there was a right to appeal to the Supreme Court on a question of law from a provincial Court of Appeal or the Federal Court of Appeal in any suit involving $10,000 or more. Under this rule, the Court was obliged to expend much of its energy on run-of-the-mill private suits. In 1975, the monetary criterion was abolished and the Court became its own gatekeeper with the opportunity to choose most of the cases it hears on the basis of their public importance. Increasingly, the Supreme Court of Canada became primarily a public law forum. Most of its cases deal with public law issues. The advent of *Charter of Rights* and Aboriginal rights litigation has accelerated this trend. By the mid-1980s, constitutional cases accounted for nearly a quarter of the Court's caseload.[38] This means that the Canadian Supreme Court's docket has come to more closely resemble that of its American counterpart. Nevertheless, it still has a much wider range of responsibilities than its U.S. counterpart. As a "General Court of Appeal for Canada," the Supreme Court of Canada continues to serve as the final court of appeal in all matters of provincial law, which include judge-made common law and Quebec's *Civil Code.* In the United States, the highest state courts are the final courts of appeal in interpreting the laws and constitutions of the states.

Patriation of the Constitution in 1982 did not give Canada a new Constitution. The *Constitution Act, 1982* added three new elements to the *Constitution Act, 1867*: the Canadian *Charter of Rights and Freedoms,* a section dealing with the rights of the Aboriginal Peoples of Canada, and a formula for amending the Constitution in Canada. The first two of these elements have had an enormous impact on the role of the Supreme Court. The Court continues to play a role as umpire of the federal system, but its decisions on the rights of individuals and groups now far exceed in number its decisions on the powers of government. Since 1984, when the first *Charter* cases reached the Supreme Court, and the end of 2007, 22 percent of the cases decided by the Court have dealt with the *Charter*, 2 percent with Aboriginal rights, and 3 percent with federalism and other constitutional issues.[39] Very little use has been made of the formal amending process that was such an important part of the patriation package. The 616 constitutional decisions rendered by the Supreme Court in the

---

[35]   See case 27.

[36]   This term is defined below.

[37]   *Calder v. A.G. British Columbia* (1973), 34 D.L.R. (3d) 145 (S.C.C.); see also case 38.

[38]   Patrick Monahan, *Politics and the Constitution: The Charter, Federalism, and the Supreme Court of Canada* (Toronto: Carswell, 1987) c. 2.

[39]   The editors are grateful to Professor Peter McCormick of the University of Lethbridge for providing data on the Supreme Court's caseload.

1984-2007 period—492 on the *Charter*, 52 on Aboriginal rights, and 72 on federal division of powers and other constitutional matters (which together constitute 27 percent of the cases decided by the Court in this period)—have contributed much more to Canada's constitutional development than the five formal amendments to the Constitution that have been made under the new amending formula.[40]

Although the *Charter of Rights* came into force on April 17, 1982, it took two years for the first *Charter* cases to work their way up to the Supreme Court. From the very beginning, the Court seems to have had no doubt about the judiciary's *general mandate* with respect to the *Charter*. In *Skapinker*,[41] its first *Charter* decision, Justice Estey, writing for a unanimous court, made it clear that the justices were prepared to take the *Charter* seriously, to avoid a narrow and overly technical interpretation of its terms, and to strike down laws and practices of government found to be in conflict with it. In decisions that immediately followed, various members of the Court stated their conviction that the *Charter* brought with it, in the words of Justice Le Dain, a "new constitutional mandate for judicial review."[42]

The Supreme Court certainly started off on an extremely activist note. In 9 of the first 15 *Charter* cases it decided, the Court upheld the *Charter* claim—a very high success rate of 60 percent for *Charter* claimants. In this early group of cases, the Court struck down five pieces of legislation—two provincial laws and three federal laws.[43] In this initial period of *Charter* interpretation, the Court also read onerous procedural requirements into the refugee provisions of the *Immigration Act*,[44] took a very liberal approach to the test for excluding evidence obtained in violation of an accused's *Charter* rights,[45] and made it clear that, when a law is found to violate a *Charter* right, the onus would be on the offending government to demonstrate that its law is "justified in a free and democratic society."[46] It also repudiated the "political questions" doctrine employed by the U.S. Supreme Court. For the Canadian Supreme Court, no question was to be considered non-justiciable simply because of its contentious political nature.[47] But after this opening spurt, which ended in early 1986, the Court began to moderate its activism. Litigants claiming *Charter* rights were successful in

---

[40]   The first, and only, use of the amending formula procedure that requires the agreement of the federal Parliament and the legislatures of seven provinces with at least 50 percent of the population was the addition of some clarifying clauses to section 35 on Aboriginal rights. The other four amendments were passed under section 45 of the amending formula, which provides for amendments to constitutional provisions relating to individual provinces. This section was used to make changes in constitutional provisions relating to Prince Edward Island, New Brunswick, Quebec, and Newfoundland. For an account, see Peter H. Russell, *Constitutional Odyssey: Can Canadians Become a Sovereign People?*, 3d ed. (Toronto: University of Toronto Press, 2004) at 249.

[41]   *Law Society of Upper Canada v. Skapinker*, [1984] 1 S.C.R. 357.

[42]   *R. v. Therens*, [1985] 1 S.C.R. 613 at para. 48.

[43]   One of the federal laws that was overturned was the *Lord's Day Act*; see case 22.

[44]   *Singh v. Minister of Employment and Immigration*, [1985] 1 S.C.R. 177.

[45]   *R. v. Therens*, *supra* note 42.

[46]   *Hunter v. Southam*, [1984] 2 S.C.R. 145.

[47]   *Operation Dismantle v. The Queen*, [1985] 1 S.C.R. 441.

60 percent of the cases heard by the Supreme Court in the first two years, but their success rate soon plummeted after that. The average success rate for the first decade of Supreme Court *Charter* decisions was 33 percent.[48] A study of *Charter* cases dealt with by the Supreme Court in the period from 1991 to 2003 shows sharp fluctuations, with success rates ranging from a low of 20 percent in 1993 to a high of 65 percent in 2003.[49]

After the Court's initial honeymoon period with the *Charter*, the *Charter*'s complexity and the jurisprudential options in interpreting its very abstract terms began to sink in. Important differences of constitutional philosophy began to emerge within the Supreme Court. Whereas all but 2 of the Court's first 15 *Charter* decisions were unanimous, subsequently, dissents became much more frequent. While the frequency of dissenting opinions has continued to be significantly higher in *Charter* cases than in non-*Charter* cases,[50] nothing like the sharply defined voting blocs that are a feature of the U.S. Supreme Court's civil rights decision-making has developed in Canada's Supreme Court. Many dissents are the opinions of one or two justices. It has been possible to identify a few justices as most likely to be on the pro-claimant side or on the pro-government side of the Court in a split decision. For instance, in the early years of the *Charter*, Justice Wilson supported the *Charter* claimant in 56 percent of the cases, while Justice McIntyre, at the other end of the Court, did so in only 23 percent of the cases.[51] Most of the justices tend to be clustered in the middle and are difficult to predict. Donald Songer, an American scholar, is struck by the much higher degree of collegiality evident in the Canadian Supreme Court as compared with the American Supreme Court.[52]

The first 25 years of the *Charter* show that judicial culture, like political culture, is apt to be dynamic. Indeed, much as legal purists may be loath to admit it, interpreting the Constitution of a democratic people is as much a political as a legal task, and the justices that take on that task interact with the politics of their day. In doing so they are not insensitive to the sound and fury their decisions arouse. And we can be sure that there will be a lot of sound and fury. Whatever approach the Supreme Court takes—restrained, activist, or middle-of-the-road—it is bound to come in for heated criticism. In applying the *Charter*, it has dealt with issues on which there were strongly opposed interest groups and no clear social consensus—such as abortion, Sunday closing, public funding of religious education, pornography, same-sex marriage, and the future of medicare. The Supreme Court's involvement with these issues in the *Charter* era has given it a prominence in Canadian public affairs that it never had in the past.

---

[48]   F.L. Morton, Peter H. Russell, and Troy Riddell, "The Canadian Charter of Rights and Freedoms: A Descriptive Analysis of the First Decade, 1982-1992" (1995) 15 *National Journal of Constitutional Law* 1 at 5.

[49]   Daved Muttart, *The Empirical Gap in Jurisprudence: A Comprehensive Study of the Supreme Court of Canada* (Toronto: University of Toronto Press, 2007) at 92.

[50]   *Ibid.* at 109.

[51]   *Ibid.* at 38.

[52]   Donald R. Songer, *The Transformation of the Supreme Court of Canada: An Empirical Examination* (Toronto: University of Toronto Press, 2008) c. 8 (forthcoming). See also Peter McCormick, "Blocs, Swarms, and Outliers: Conceptualizing Disagreement on the Modern Supreme Court of Canada" (2004) 42 *Osgoode Hall Law Journal* 99.

Aboriginal rights cases did not become a significant part of the Supreme Court's docket until its decision in the 1990 *Sparrow* case.[53] In *Sparrow*, the Court espoused a liberal approach to section 35 rights that was encouraging to Aboriginal litigants. But its performance after that has become something of a roller-coaster ride. First came a series of decisions cutting back Aboriginal rights to what the Court considered were activities at the core of traditional cultures.[54] These were followed by its decision in *Delgamuukw*,[55] taking a much more liberal and dynamic view of Aboriginal land rights. Aboriginal groups, in trying to advance their interests and vindicate their rights, are often faced with a difficult choice between litigation and political negotiation. Litigation, though expensive, time-consuming, culturally alienating, and uncertain, sometimes appears as the only alternative to acquiescing in what is seen as a violation of Aboriginal or treaty rights. And sometimes, the Court's decisions, as in *Delgamuukw* and *Haida Nation*,[56] show that resorting to litigation can pay off with decisions that enhance the position of Aboriginal people in political negotiations. The Court's decisions on Aboriginal and treaty rights, like its *Charter* decisions, often arouse stormy political controversy. But the politics of Aboriginal rights are structured differently than the politics of the civil liberties issues dealt with in *Charter* cases. The non-Aboriginal public know very little about Aboriginal societies, the history of their treaty relations with Canada, or their colonial subjugation by the Canadian state. Supreme Court decisions upholding an Aboriginal right or a treaty right tend to catch the general public by surprise and are often portrayed in the media as unfairly benefiting a group that is said to be racially defined. The huge row over the Court's decision in the first *Marshall* decision[57] is a leading example. Its follow-up opinion in the second *Marshall* decision[58] indicates that the Court can be influenced by this kind of political backlash. On the Aboriginal side, there is still considerable doubt as to whether the non-Aboriginal judges of the Supreme Court can be trusted as custodians of Aboriginal peoples' rights. The Supreme Court and all Canadians have a long way to go in finding justice in relations with Aboriginal peoples. The Supreme Court's decisions are bound to be an important part of that journey.

Important as the Supreme Court's new post-1982 role has been in adjudicating *Charter* rights and Aboriginal rights, it has by no means eliminated the Court's role as the judicial umpire of Canada's federal system. Cases on the division of powers continue to come before the Court, though not in the numbers of the 1970s and early 1980s, but on subjects of great political importance. The two federalism decisions from the 1990s included in this volume—the *Canada Social Assistance Reference*,[59] dealing with welfare assistance and raising a crucial issue about intergovernmental relations, and *Hydro Québec*,[60] dealing with legislative

---

[53] Case 38.

[54] See Peter H. Russell, "High Courts and the Rights of Aboriginal Peoples: The Limits of Judicial Independence" (1998) 61 *Saskatchewan Law Review* 247.

[55] Case 39.

[56] Cases 39 and 42.

[57] Case 40.

[58] Case 41.

[59] Case 17.

[60] Case 18.

juridiction in relation to environmental protection—are good examples. In addition to these standard divison-of-powers cases, on three occasions the Court has been called upon to deal with the constitutional amending process itself. In these decisions—the *Patriation Reference*, the *Quebec Veto Reference*, and the *Quebec Secession Reference*—the Court has wrestled with questions fundamental to the constitutional structure of the country.

When you add all this up—the *Charter*, the rights of Aboriginal peoples, the federal division of powers, the fundamental nature of our federal union—it is easy to appreciate that the Court has emerged as a major branch of Canadian governance in the contemporary era. And bear in mind that it is still the final court of appeal in all areas of Canadian law—including commercial law, labour law, family law, criminal law, property law, and the law of contracts and torts. It is difficult to think of any other high court in the world that has as large a role in the governance of its country as the Supreme Court of Canada.

THE JUSTICES

The marked increase in the Supreme Court's political prominence has shone the spotlight of public interest much more sharply on the justices of the Supreme Court. There is much greater awareness among those who follow politics closely that the values and outlook of those who serve on the Court can have major policy implications. When justices retire from the Court, there is a great deal of media speculation on the leading candidates to fill the vacancy and any evidence of their philosophical or jurisprudential leanings. All of this has led to much more concern about how Supreme Court justices are selected and the absence of effective checks and balances in the appointing process.

The appointment of Supreme Court justices is governed by an ordinary Act of Parliament, the *Supreme Court Act*. Section 4 of the *Act* states that the Supreme Court shall consist of a chief justice and eight *puisne* judges, who shall be appointed by the Governor in Council.[61] Governor in Council means the federal Cabinet. In practice the Justice Minister and the Prime Minister select the judges. There are only two legal conditions regulating their selections: appointees must have 10 years' professional legal experience, and three of the nine justices must have had their professional experience in Quebec.

In addition to these two legal rules, there is a pattern of regional representation in making appointments that has hardened into a constitutional convention that three justices will be from Ontario, two from the Western provinces, and one from the Atlantic provinces. From 1979 to 1982, there were only two Ontario judges on the Court, but that is the only time since 1949, when the Court's numbers were increased from seven to nine, that the regional pattern has been modified. Conventions also seem to be developing with respect to justices from Western Canada that one will always be from British Columbia and that the replacement of a Prairie province justice will not come from the same province as the retiring judge. The legislative requirement of three judges from Quebec has an important functional rationale. Because the Supreme Court is the final court of appeal in cases involving Quebec's distinct system of civil law, it is essential to have at least three members of the court who

---

61   R.S.C. 1985, c. S-26, s. 4. *Puisne* is the Latin word for designating ordinary judges of a court. Originally, the Court had six justices, with a requirement that two must be from Quebec. One justice was added in 1927. In 1949, it became a nine-judge court, three of whom must be from Quebec.

have been educated in that system and have practised in it.[62] But aside from the Quebec provision, regional representation on the Supreme Court of Canada is strictly of symbolic significance. In no sense are the justices representative of their region or province.

The requirement of professional legal experience means that Supreme Court justices come to the Court either directly from legal practice or are "elevated" from the lower courts, almost always from a provincial Court of Appeal or the Federal Court of Appeal. It used to be that as many Supreme Court justices came directly from legal practice as from the lower courts, but in recent decades these kinds of appointments have become quite unusual. In the *Charter* era, only two Supreme Court appointees, Justices Sopinka and Binnie, have not had previous judicial experience.[63] The decisions of provincial or federal appellate judges being considered for appointment to the Supreme Court provide an accessible track record of their ability and approach as jurists and of how they have dealt with controversial constitutional matters.

Another significant development in Supreme Court appointments in the *Charter* era is the selection of women jurists. Justice Bertha Wilson, who was appointed in 1982, was the first woman to serve on the Supreme Court. Since then, six women have been appointed. Four of the nine justices at present serving on the Court are women, and one of them, Beverley McLachlin, is the Court's Chief Justice. On no other high court in the western world do women play such a prominent role. It is also notable that three of the Court's current incumbents—Justices Abella, Fish, and Rothstein—have Jewish backgrounds. Justices Sopinka and Iacobucci were the first two appointees who were not from the main ethnic streams of English and French Canada. No member of a visible minority has been appointed to the Court, nor—more tellingly, given the important role the Court plays as an adjudicator of Aboriginal rights—has the Court had an Aboriginal jurist.

The selection of Supreme Court justices has been a closed and unaccountable process in which authority is in the unfettered hands of the prime minister and the minister of justice. The justice minister, in effect, serves as the prime minister's chief talent scout, consulting with politicians, judges, and lawyers in the region in which a position is open and absorbing the efforts of lobby groups and fan clubs to promote particular candidates. Unlike appointing procedures in most other constitutional democracies, Canada's has no formal checks and balances on the leaders of the government of the day in selecting the judges who will apply the constitutional limits on government.[64] While partisan considerations have clearly influenced federal government appointments to provincial superior courts, provincial courts of appeal, and the Federal Court,[65] there is no strong evidence that partisan or ideological

---

[62] For an account of the Supreme Court's decision making with respect to Quebec's civil law, see Peter H. Russell, *The Supreme Court of Canada as a Bilingual and Bicultural Institution* (Ottawa: Queen's Printer, 1969).

[63] Donald R. Songer, *supra* note 52 at 46.

[64] For a discussion of appointing systems around the world, see Kate Malleson and Peter H. Russell, *Appointing Judges in an Age of Judicial Power: Critical Perspectives from Around the World* (Toronto: University of Toronto Press, 2006).

[65] See Peter H. Russell and Jacob S. Ziegel, "Federal Judicial Appointments: An Appraisal of the First Mulroney Government's Appointments and the New Judicial Advisory Committees" (1991) 41 *University of Toronto Law Journal* 4.

factors have influenced prime ministers in filling Supreme Court vacancies. Nevertheless, there is apprehension that in the *Charter* era, when Supreme Court appointments are recognized as having major policy implications, prime ministers may begin to emulate American presidents in appointing ideological soulmates to the Supreme Court.

Both the Meech Lake Accord and Charlottetown Accord contained proposals for reforming the system of appointing Supreme Court justices and entrenching the Court in the Constitution.[66] Both sets of proposals gave provincial governments the role of nominating bodies. The federal government would keep the power of appointment but would be required to select from names submitted by governments of the provinces.[67] It may be just as well that these proposals went down with the failure of these two efforts at mega constitutional reform. The approaches to Supreme Court reform in these mega constitutional exercises were driven entirely by an agenda of accommodating provincial demands and were insensitive to the new constitutionalism of post-patriation Canada, in which, as Alan Cairns has observed, the rights of citizens jostle with the powers of government.[68] But the demise of those proposals leaves Canada with the anomaly of a Constitution that provides rules for amending the Constitution with respect to the Supreme Court even though the Court itself is still not entrenched in the Constitution.[69]

Since the defeat of the Charlottetown Accord in the 1992 referendum, most of Canada's political leaders and citizens have had little appetite for constitutional reform. However, continuing criticism of federal judicial appointing has kept interest alive in reform of the Supreme Court appointing process that would not require constitutional amendment. In 2004, the House of Commons' Justice Committee conducted hearings on the Supreme Court appointing process. The Committee's majority report called for an advisory committee of MPs and provincial, judicial, legal, and lay members to develop a list of candidates for vacancies on the Court and submit to the justice minister a short list of the top-ranked candidates from which the government "may" select its appointee. After the appointment, the minister of justice would appear before the House Committee to explain how the government made its selection.[70]

---

[66]   For a discussion of these proposals, see Peter H. Russell, *supra* note 40.

[67]   In the Meech Lake proposals, the federal government would have to appoint a person nominated by the government of Quebec for Quebec vacancies, whereas other appointments could be nominees of any provincial government. The Charlottetown Accord added territorial governments to the nominating process.

[68]   Alan C. Cairns and Cynthia Williams, *Constitutionalism, Citizenship, and Society in Canada* (Toronto: University of Toronto Press, 1985) at 38.

[69]   Under section 41(*d*) of the *Constitution Act, 1982*, an amendment to the Constitition in relation to the composition of the Supreme Court requires the consent of the federal Parliament and the legislative assemblies of all the provinces. Other constitutional amendments in relation to the Supreme Court come under section 42(*d*) and require the consent of Parliament plus seven provinces, representing the 50 percent of the population rule.

[70]   House of Commons, Report of the Standing Committee on Justice, Human Rights, Public Safety, and Emergency Preparedness, "Improving the Supreme Court of Canada Appointments Process," May 2004.

In 2005, in filling the vacancy created by Justice Major, who had reached age 75, the mandatory age of retirement, the Martin Liberal government adopted a modified version of the parliamentary Committee's proposal. A nine-person Advisory Committee was appointed consisting of four MPs (one from each party), a retired judge chosen by the Canadian Judicial Council, a lawyer chosen by the law societies of the Prairie provinces (Justice Major was from Alberta), a representative of the three Prairie province governments, and two lay persons of "integrity and distinction" from the region chosen by Irving Cotler, the Minister of Justice.[71] But this Advisory Committee was given a truncated role in the nominating process. The Minister of Justice was the main nominator, submitting to the Advisory Committee the names of five to eight candidates that he had selected. The Committee, if it wished, could add a candidate with the Minister's approval, but its principal function was to assess the candidates on the Minister's list. The Advisory Committee operated entirely on a confidential basis. It was not allowed to interview candidates, so it had to assess them entirely on the basis of their record and consultations with lawyers and judges who knew them. In November, the Committee submitted the names of its three most highly rated candidates to the Minister of Justice.[72] The Justice Minister was then to recommend one of these three to Prime Minister Martin. If this person was not appointed, the Minister would offer an explanation to the House of Commons Justice Committee.

On the very day the Advisory Committee submitted its list, the Martin government was defeated on a confidence vote in the House of Commons, bringing on the January 2006 election. Thus, it remained for the Harper Conservative government that came to power after the election to complete the final stage of the process initiated by the Martin government. In February 2006, Justice Minister Vic Toews announced that Prime Minister Harper had chosen Justice Marshall Rothstein, a member of the Federal Court of Appeal, from the three names submitted by the Advisory Committee. But the Justice Minister then added a new wrinkle to the process: he announced that an *ad hoc* committee of MPs from all parties would interview the Prime Minister's choice. The committee conducted its interview on the afternoon of February 27 in a three-hour televised session.[73] The committee was directed not to ask questions about legal issues that might come before the Court and did not vote on the Prime Minister's choice. Justice Rothstein was officially appointed two days later.

The process stitched together for the appointment of Justice Rothstein is not likely to be a model for future appointments. Both the Liberal government's nominating process and the Harper government's appointing process were subject to a good deal of criticism. Instead of injecting some real checks and balances into the system, the government dominated both stages of the process. The Minister of Justice nominated the candidates that would get serious consideration and the *ad hoc* parliamentary committee could neither challenge the Prime Minister's selection nor ask questions that probed very deeply into his constitutional or jurisprudential thinking. Canada still has some way to go in finding a system that has the openness,

---

71 Information on the Advisory Committee and the new process, under the heading "Proposal to Reform the Supreme Court of Canada Appointments Process," was posted on the Department of Justice website in September 2005.

72 "Advisory panel drafts nominees list for top court" *The Globe and Mail* (22 November 2005).

73 "Nominee says he's no activist" *The Globe and Mail* (28 February 2006).

accountability, and political balance needed in appointing members of the Supreme Court, which has come to play such a vital role in Canada's constitutional democracy.

APPROACHES TO CONSTITUTIONAL INTERPRETATION

Constitutional documents require interpretation. Many of the important rules and principles of a constitution are expressed in broad and abstract language. This is to be expected. As legal documents, constitutions cannot be drafted like private contracts designed to govern a specific situation for a finite period of time. Constitutions are designed to endure, to provide a framework for the governance of a people into a future the framers of the constitution cannot foresee.[74] True, there are formal mechanisms for amending constitutions but they are ill-suited for the ongoing, detailed application of the constitution to the circumstances that arise in the unfolding life of the nation. The mechanism for carrying out this function is constitutional interpretation through the exercise of judicial review.

Some of the Fathers of Confederation felt that they had been so detailed and thorough in drafting the Constitution that there would be little need for interpretation. "We have avoided all conflict of jurisdiction and authority," boasted John A. Macdonald.[75] How wrong he was. Consider the terms on which power is divided between federal and provincial legislatures. The federal Parliament is to make laws for "the Peace, Order, and good Government of Canada" in all matters except those assigned exclusively to the provincial legislatures. The provincial legislatures have exclusive jurisdiction over "Property and Civil Rights," while the "Regulation of Trade and Commerce" is under exclusive federal jurisdiction. What do these phrases mean? More specifically, what do they mean when applied, say, to the regulation of industrial relations in an advanced industrial economy?

Consider, too, the terms of the *Charter of Rights.* That document, among other things, tells us, in section 7, that "Everyone has the right to life, liberty and security of the person and the right not to be deprived thereof except in accordance with the principles of fundamental justice." Now, just for starters, what does "Everyone" embrace—a foetus; a person applying to enter Canada as a refugee? Does "liberty" cover anything and everything each of us wants to do? Are social and economic security to be included under "security of the person"? And what on earth is "fundamental justice"? Philosophers have been wrestling with that question through the millennia. Then, bear in mind that whatever the rights in section 7 mean, they, like all of the rights and freedoms set out in the *Charter,* are subject to "such reasonable limits prescribed by law as can be demonstrably justified in a free and democratic society." These words too require more than a little interpretation.

These examples underline the fact that constitution making is always incomplete. In applying the general terms of a constitutional text to specific disputes, the judiciary adds flesh and blood to the bare bones of the constitution. Judicial decisions, above all those of the final court of appeal, become part of the law of the constitution. But not a fixed and unmoving part. As interpretations accumulate, they too contain doctrines and statements of general

---

[74]   For a classic statement of this idea, see the words of American Chief Justice John Marshall, adopted by the Supreme Court of Canada in *Law Society of Upper Canada v. Skapinker, supra* note 41, its first *Charter* decision.

[75]   *The Confederation Debates in the Province of Canada,* Carleton Library ed. (Toronto: McClelland & Stewart, 1963) at 44.

principle, which are interpreted and reinterpreted by ensuing generations of judges. Not that judges are the only participants in this ongoing process of constitution making. Occasionally, their interpretations may generate so much political discontent that they are reversed by formal constitutional amendments. Such was the case with the Privy Council decision denying the federal Parliament the power to establish a national unemployment scheme and the Supreme Court decisions denying the provinces the power to levy indirect taxes on their natural resources.[76] On a regular basis, the legislative and executive branches of government make decisions about the meaning of the Constitution, either in anticipation of being challenged in the courts or in response to successful court challenges.[77] In the *Charter* era, this kind of interaction between the political branches of government and the judiciary has come to be referred to (perhaps misleadingly) as a "dialogue."[78]

The cases in this volume contain a number of different approaches to the task of constitutional interpretation. However, one approach that will not be found is so-called literal interpretation. Sometimes the Judicial Committee's approach has been described as literalistic. This is a mistake. We can see this by examining its decision in the very first case in this book, *Citizens Insurance Co. v. Parsons*. The issue here was whether Ontario legislation regulating fire insurance contracts was a matter of "Property and Civil Rights in the Province," and thus within the province's constitutional powers, or whether it was a "Regulation of Trade and Commerce," and therefore beyond provincial powers. One will search the constitutional text in vain for a literal answer to this question. Literal interpretation was simply not an option.

The approach that the Judicial Committee took in *Parsons* and many other cases may more aptly be described as highly legalistic. Not surprisingly, the English judges who wrote these decisions applied to the *B.N.A. Act* the basic technique of interpretation they were accustomed to applying to any Act of Parliament. The key to this technique of statutory interpretation is to assume that the legislators were completely rational and logical (not always a very realistic assumption) and to adopt an interpretation that makes it possible to read the text in a logically coherent way. But this would only take the judges so far. They still had to go outside the text to obtain meanings for key terms such as "Property and Civil Rights" and "Trade and Commerce." Consider where they went in *Parsons*. Not to the debates and discussions of the Constitution drafters—English judges would never consider legislative debates in interpreting statutes. Instead they considered how these phrases had been used in other British statutes—the *Act of Union* (between England and Scotland) and the *Quebec Act*.

The Judicial Committee's style of opinion writing may seem exceptionally legalistic, but it would be a mistake to believe that its members had nothing but narrowly legal considerations on their minds when they interpreted Canada's Constitution. The Law Lords who staffed the Judicial Committee would often invoke the unwritten principles they identified

---

[76] See cases 8 and 14.

[77] See Janet Hiebert, *Charter Conflicts: What Is Parliament's Role?* (Montreal & Kingston: McGill-Queen's University Press, 2002), and James Kelly, *Governing with the Charter: Legislative and Judicial Activism and Framers' Intent* (Vancouver: University of British Columbia Press, 2005).

[78] See (2007) 45 *Osgoode Hall Law Journal* 1—the entire issue is devoted to a discussion of *Charter* dialogue.

as underlying the written law in justifying their decisions. Supreme Court justices, especially in the *Charter* era, do the same. This effort to base legal reasoning on fundamental principles that are understood as the normative justification of laws is an age-old feature of common-law jurisprudence in all fields of law.[79] The Judicial Committee's commitment to the notion of classical federalism as a fundamental principle of the Canadian Constitution underlies most of its opinions and occasionally breaks through the legalistic prose. An outstanding example occurred in the *Local Prohibition* case, where Lord Watson argued that the federal Parliament's general power must be interpreted narrowly so as not to encroach on provincial powers because "[t]o attach any other construction to the general power . . . would, in their Lordships' opinion, not only be contrary to the intendment of the Act, but would practically destroy the autonomy of the provinces."[80] A leading example of a Supreme Court of Canada decision that relies heavily on the justices' sense of the underlying principles of Canada's Constitution is the opinion of the Court in the *Quebec Secession Reference*.[81]

The Judicial Committee and the Supreme Court relied on different sources for finding underlying principles of Canada's Constitution. The Canadian justices in their first encounters with constitutional interpretation resorted not to British legal history but to Canadian political history. As noted above in *Severn*, Chief Justice Richards and his colleagues derived a broad, virtually unlimited scope for the federal trade and commerce power from *their understanding* of the intentions of the Fathers of Confederation. A century later, in the reference case on Senate reform, the Supreme Court of Canada looked to the Confederation Debates for evidence of the Founding Fathers' intentions with regard to the Senate.[82]

Many believe that basing constitutional interpretation on the framers' intentions is an attractive approach. It would seem to conform to common sense for judges in determining the meaning of any legal document to consider evidence of the original intent of those who drafted it. The legitimacy of judges striking down laws passed by democratically elected legislatures on the ground that they violate the Constitution would certainly be enhanced if the judges could show that their reading of the Constitution was based not on their own personal views but on the intentions of the Founding Fathers.[83] This has been a major reason for the appeal of the so-called interpretivist approach. But one serious difficulty with this approach is that it is often difficult to ascertain the intention of those who created the Constitution with regard to the question at issue in a constitutional case.[84] Consider again

---

[79]   For an analysis of the role of principle in judicial reasoning, see Paul Weiler, *In the Last Resort: A Critical Study of the Supreme Court of Canada* (Toronto: Carswell/Methuen, 1974).

[80]   Case 4.

[81]   Case 48.

[82]   Case 45.

[83]   In the United States, there is an important school of thought that believes this is the only legitimate approach to judicial review. For the leading exponent, see Raoul Berger, *Government by Judiciary* (Cambridge, MA: Harvard University Press, 1977). For a critique of this theory, see Michael Perry, *The Constitution, the Courts, and Human Rights* (New Haven, CT: Yale University Press, 1982).

[84]   For a discussion of these difficulties, see Clifford Ian Kyer, "Has History a Role to Play in Constitutional Adjudication? Some Preliminary Considerations" (1981) 15 *Law Society Gazette* 135.

the issue in *Parsons.* Do the events and debates leading to Confederation make it clear what the original intent was concerning jurisdiction over the regulation of insurance contracts? Certainly we can tell from John A. Macdonald's speeches that he favoured the widest possible scope for Dominion powers and cared not a whit for "provincial autonomy." But Macdonald was not the only Father of Confederation. He had colleagues in the political coalition that put the Constitution together, especially from the Maritimes and Quebec, who hoped that strong provincial governments with a significant role in economic regulation would develop under the new Constitution.

Modern constitutions are not the product of a single mind, or even a single, coherent political philosophy. Their key terms are usually the product of political compromise. That is certainly the case with the federal provisions of the *B.N.A. Act.* They were a compromise between political leaders like Macdonald, who wanted a single, unitary government for the new Canada, and other colonial politicians, who wished to retain significant powers in provincial capitals.[85] Similarly, in the 1982 additions to the Canadian Constitution, there was a compromise between those who favoured a strong entrenchment of rights and freedoms and those who wanted the least possible restriction on parliamentary supremacy. Constitutional provisions resulting from such compromises paper over important differences among the framers that will continue to be worked out in the political evolution of the nation—an evolution in which judicial interpretation will play a prominent role.

In interpreting the *Charter of Rights*, the Supreme Court indicated that it would give "minimal weight" to the statements of any particular participant in the negotiating, drafting, and adoption of the *Charter*, no matter how important or distinguished these individuals might be.[86] The history that the Supreme Court has considered in giving more precise meaning to the vague terms of the *Charter* has tended to be much broader and deeper than the discussion in Canada that preceded the *Charter*. The main thrust of the "purposive" approach to *Charter* interpretation, fashioned by Chief Justice Dickson in some early *Charter* cases,[87] is to inquire into the reasons a particular right or freedom came to be valued in the history of western civilization or in Canada's political life and thereby to identify the "interests" each right or freedom was meant to protect. While there would seem to be general agreement within the Court on this "purposive" approach, it is an approach that may not yield the same results for all who apply it.

Supreme Court of Canada judges have tended to be more explicit than were the English Law Lords of the Privy Council in considering the policy consequences of constitutional interpretation. This is clearly one result of the Canadianization of judicial review. Frequently, Supreme Court judges openly reflect on the possible effects of decisions on the capacity of government, national and local, for effectively handling a given problem. A leading example

---

[85]   For evidence that Quebec supporters of Confederation intended that provinces should have strong powers in the economic as well as the social and cultural spheres, see P.B. Waite, *The Life and Times of Confederation* (Toronto: University of Toronto Press, 1962) c. 10.

[86]   See *Reference re B.C. Motor Vehicle Act*, case 23 at para. 52. But note that, in *Attorney General of Quebec v. Association of Quebec Protestant School Boards*, [1984] 2 S.C.R. 66 (discussed in the introduction to case 27), the Court was willing to give much more weight to the *Charter's* political sponsors' objective of advancing the rights of linguistic minorities.

[87]   See *The Queen v. Big M Drug Mart Ltd.*, case 22.

is Justice Locke's opinion in *Johannesson*,[88] the first constitutional case decided by the Supreme Court after it became Canada's final court of appeal. A key part of Locke's justification for assigning to the federal government the power to determine the location of airports is his fear that a local veto over the location of airports would impede the development of the country. As many of the cases in this volume attest, assessing the reasonableness of legislative limits on *Charter* rights and freedoms has provided many more occasions for such policy analysis by the Court. All this increases the Court's political exposure and puts pressure on the Court to widen the kind of material it takes into account in considering the purposes and effects of challenged legislation.[89]

At one time it was fashionable for critics of the Privy Council to fault that body for failing "to adapt the constitution to the changing needs of the country."[90] The problem with that kind of thinking is its assumption that the changing needs of Canada are clear and self-evident, that there is some kind of objective method which right-thinking judges need only follow to give the Constitution just the twist that all Canadians are looking for. But, alas, we know that such assumptions are simplistic. It is not self-evident that Canada needs a uniform national system of environmental protection or that increasing the private sector of the health system would be harmful to the majority of Canadians. We should not expect the Court to give us answers to these questions, which, in some objective sense, are logically or legally necessary. All that we can reasonably expect is that the judges might persuade us that their decisions are based on considerations about our country and principles of governance that embody the wisdom of our collective experience.

The metaphor of the Constitution as a "living tree" has come into vogue in Canada to justify a more creative, less history-bound approach to constitutional interpretation. The metaphor was coined in 1930 by a member of the Judicial Committee, Lord Sankey, in an appeal from a Supreme Court of Canada decision holding that women were ineligible for appointment to the Senate because they were not "persons" according to the legal meaning of that word at the time of Confederation. Sankey rejected the Supreme Court's position.[91] He justified moving beyond the historical meaning of constitutional language by comparing the *B.N.A. Act* to "a living tree capable of growth and expansion within its natural limits."[92] The "living tree" analogy was used by the Supreme Court in 1979 to justify an expansive interpretation of the language guarantees in section 133.[93] The Supreme Court has continued to endorse the "living tree" approach in its interpretation of the *Charter of Rights and Freedoms*.[94] In the *B.C. Motor Vehicle Reference*, Justice Lamer, in explaining why the Court

---

[88]   Case 11.

[89]   See Peter W. Hogg, "Proof of Facts in Constitutional Cases" (1977) 26 *University of Toronto Journal* 386.

[90]   See Alan C. Cairns, "The Judicial Committee and Its Critics" (1971) 3 *Canadian Journal of Political Science* 301.

[91]   Case 43.

[92]   *Ibid.*

[93]   See *Attorney General of Quebec v. Blaikie*, discussed in the introduction to case 27.

[94]   Justice Estey referred to the "living tree" in *Law Society of Upper Canada v. Skapinker*, *supra* note 41, the Court's first *Charter* decision.

should give little weight to documentary evidence of the drafters' intentions, stated that "If the newly planted 'living tree' which is the *Charter* is to have the possibility of growth and adjustment over time, care must be taken to ensure that historical materials . . . do not stunt its growth."[95]

The "living tree" approach appeals to those who are optimistic about the policy-making capabilities of courts. However, it is important to bear in mind that when applied to constitutional rights and freedoms, this approach is likely to have quite different results than when it is applied to government powers. A broad and liberal interpretation of rights and freedoms will constrain government power and serve as a basis on which an "activist" judiciary may frequently overturn legislation and executive acts. On the other hand, a flexible and generous interpretation of the terms defining the federal division of legislative powers may result in much more judicial "self-restraint" in dealing with challenges to legislation.

The categories of "activism" and "self-restraint" are not to be confused with different modes of judicial reasoning. Activism refers to judicial vigour in enforcing constitutional limitations on the other branches of government and a readiness to veto the policies of those branches of government on constitutional grounds. Self-restraint connotes a judicial predisposition to make room within the Constitution for the policies of democratically accountable decision makers. The Judicial Committee of the Privy Council, although it tended to be relatively legalistic in its style of reasoning, became a fairly activist court under the leadership of Viscount Haldane, frequently striking down laws that violated its interpretation of the division of powers. By comparison, the Supreme Court, when it took over as Canada's highest court, was less legalistic in its reasoning and exercised more restraint with regard to enforcing the requirements of federalism on both levels of government.[96]

In cases involving the *Charter of Rights*, activism and self-restraint may come into play at two stages. The first step in every *Charter* case is to determine whether the challenged law or government action violates a right or freedom. If the Court finds no such violation, then that is the end of the case. However, if the first stage yields the opposite result, the court must go on to consider whether the encroachment on the right can be upheld under section 1 of the *Charter* as a reasonable limit prescribed by law as can be "demonstrably justified in a free and democratic society." At this stage judges must openly assess the policy considerations behind the legislative or government initiative. In applying section 1, the Supreme Court has made it clear that the onus is on government to justify its limit.

The wider and more liberally rights and freedoms are interpreted at stage one, the more frequently stage two will be reached.[97] This was a factor that clearly influenced the Court's ruling in the 1987 *Alberta Labour Reference* that the right to freedom of association in section 2(*d*) of the *Charter* did not embrace the collective bargaining rights of unions. Part of the majority justices' rationale for taking this position was their reluctance to see the judiciary

---

[95]   Case 23 at para. 53.

[96]   This is particularly evident in its willingness to find new areas of concurrence in which both levels of government could operate. See W.R. Lederman, "The Concurrent Operation of Federal and Provincial Laws in Canada" (1963) 9 *McGill Law Journal* 185.

[97]   Sujit Choudhry and Claire E. Hunter, "Measuring Judicial Activism on the Supreme Court of Canada: A Comment on Newfoundland (Treasury Board) v. NAPE" (2003) 48 *McGill Law Journal* 525.

involved in reviewing the judgment of the legislature as to the circumstances which justify restricting the right to strike.[98] Over the years, the Court has drawn away from restrictive interpretations of *Charter* rights. In 2007, in the *B.C. Health Services* case,[99] it reversed its 1987 position and ruled that section 2(*b*) protects collective bargaining rights. This trend moves the Court to basing more of its *Charter* jurisprudence on section 1.

Section 1 of the *Charter* creates jurisprudential options that are not available in interpreting constitutional guarantees in the American Constitution. The Bill of Rights in the Constitution of the United States does not contain any limiting clause, so that constitutionally protected rights can be limited only by building limits into the way these rights and freedoms are defined—something the U.S. Supreme Court has frequently done. Under the Canadian *Charter* there is the option of treating the rights and freedoms literally as embracing virtually everything the words can mean and leaving the possibility of setting limits on them entirely to section 1. Such an approach would maximize judicial scrutiny of legislative decisions. If, for instance, no limits are attached to the "right to liberty" in section 7, then virtually every government restriction on anything any of us wants to do would be a violation of a constitutional right and could be saved only by convincing the judiciary that it was justifiable under section 1. It is doubtful that any judge would want to go this far. Much of the Supreme Court's jurisprudence on section 7, the principles of fundamental justice section, and on section 15, the equality rights section, has concentrated on defining these rights, whereas in dealing with freedom of expression claims under section 2(*b*) it has tended to give an unlimited scope to forms of expression that come under this right and has concentrated its jurisprudence on section 1 limits on the right.

In the early *Charter* cases, Supreme Court justices had a greater degree of freedom than their successors enjoy. They also must have experienced a greater burden of decision as they applied their brushes to the blank canvas before them. For in those early cases they were dealing with constitutional concepts that were entirely novel to Canadian constitutional law. They received some help from the first approaches to these concepts in the lower courts. Also they considered how similar rights and freedoms had been dealt with in foreign jurisdictions—especially under the European Convention on Human Rights and by the United States Supreme Court, although, with regard to the latter, the court has shown more than a mild sense of Canadian nationalism. Justice La Forest expressed this well when he wrote that

> Canadian legal thought has at many points in the past deferred to that of the British; the *Charter* will be no sign of our national maturity if it simply becomes an excuse for adopting another intellectual mentor. American jurisprudence, like the British, must be viewed as a tool, not as a master.[100]

Peter McCormick reports that Canadian courts of appeal in the *Charter* era continue to cite more English precedents than American precedents.[101]

---

[98]   *Reference re Public Service Employee Relations Act, Labour Relations Act, and the Police Officers Collective Bargaining Act of Alberta*, [1987] 1 S.C.R. 313.

[99]   *Health Services and Support—Facilities Subsector Bargaining Assn. v. British Columbia*, 2007 SCC 27, case 37.

[100]   *Rahey v. The Queen*, [1987] 1 S.C.R. 588 at 639.

[101]   Peter McCormick, *Canada's Courts* (Toronto: James Lorimer, 1994) at 146.

As Supreme Court precedents accumulate, there will still be plenty of room for development. As befits the highest court of a sovereign nation, the Supreme Court has relaxed the strict rule of *stare decisis* according to which a court is bound to follow its own previous decisions. In *Paquette*,[102] decided in 1976 (a non-constitutional, criminal case), the Court for the first time explicitly departed from a position it had taken in an earlier case and, shortly afterward, in *McNamara Construction v. The Queen*,[103] it reversed one of the Supreme Court's earlier constitutional decisions. The Court's repudiation of its Bill of Rights jurisprudence in the early *Charter* cases constitutes its most dramatic change of direction.[104]

Flexibility and change will come not nearly so much from the explicit overruling of earlier precedents as from the various ways judges work with previous decisions. Judges will sometimes "distinguish" previous decisions they do not wish to follow as turning on facts different from those in the case at hand. Alternatively, judges are adept at giving a new twist to the *ratio decidendi* (reason for decision) of an earlier decision. An instructive example in this volume is the *Crown Zellerbach* case,[105] where the majority opinion provides yet another way of interpreting previous decisions on peace, order, and good government. Already we can see how the test for meeting the *Charter*'s standard of a reasonable limit established in *Oakes* is being applied differently by different judges and sometimes differently by the same judge.[106]

The real effect of the application of *stare decisis* is not to freeze the law of the Constitution in a fixed mould, but to structure judicial discretion. Earlier precedents establish boundaries within which judges manoeuvre. On a given point, there may be considerable room for choice between competing lines of cases. There are bound to be some ambiguities in the language of earlier decisions. But whatever course is taken, the reasoning of judges in Canada, as in all common-law countries, will normally be developed by reference to the "authority" of previous cases.

The various approaches discussed above represent different tendencies, not mutually exclusive alternatives. Even the most creative, policy-oriented, activist judge will not be indifferent to the constitutional text, will wish to make some sense of its internal structure and the accumulation of precedents interpreting it, and will have some sense of the limits on the judiciary's mandate to strike down the policies of the "popular" branches of government. By the same token, it is unlikely that we will find today a judge whose approach to judicial review is so traditional as to preclude any inquiry into the underlying principles of the Constitution and their practical implications for the governance of the country or who exudes an unqualified deference for the legislature and executive.

We urge students using this text to be wary of simplistic labelling of courts or judges. Read the judges' reasons and conscientiously assess them as exercises in practical reasoning about how best to apply Canada's constituent political principles.

---

[102]   *Paquette v. R.*, [1977] 2 S.C.R. 189.

[103]   [1977] 2 S.C.R. 654.

[104]   See, for example, *Big M Drug Mart*, case 22.

[105]   Case 16.

[106]   For a good example, see *RJR-MacDonald*, case 31.

PROCEDURES OF JUDICIAL REVIEW

Most constitutional cases begin at the trial court level. Typically, constitutional issues are raised either by the defendant in a criminal case, arguing that the police investigation or the law under which the accused is charged is unconstitutional, or by an individual or organization in a civil action, claiming that a government regulation to which they are subject is unconstitutional. Most of the trial courts in which these cases originate are provincial or territorial courts; some begin in the smaller, more specialized Federal Court.[107] The losing party in the trial court has a right of appeal to the provincial or territorial court of appeal or from the Federal Court to the Federal Court of Appeal. Except when a court of appeal is divided in a criminal case, a further appeal to the Supreme Court is possible only with the leave of the Supreme Court itself.

Reference cases provide another way of bringing constitutional questions before the courts. A reference case occurs when the federal government refers a question directly to the Supreme Court, or a provincial government refers a question directly to a provincial court of appeal. The reference case procedure is a distinctive feature of Canada's constitutional process that was built into the *Supreme Court Act*, which established the Court in 1875. Section 52 of the *Act* empowered the Governor in Council "to refer to the Supreme Court, for hearing and consideration, any matters whatsoever as he may think fit."[108] In practice, reference cases have been largely confined to assessing the constitutionality of statutes or proposed bills. Originally, the federal government's referral of provincial legislation to the Supreme Court was a means of obtaining judicial advice about whether provincial laws should be disallowed. However, this rationale has long been superseded. For example, in all the "New Deal" references of the 1930s, the federal government asked the Supreme Court to determine whether Parliament had exceeded its jurisdiction.[109] The provinces have adopted their own reference-case procedures under which they can refer their own or federal legislation to the provincial court of appeal. In these provincial reference cases, there is a right of appeal to the Supreme Court. The importance of this procedure as a means of challenging federal initiatives was dramatically demonstrated by the decisions of three provinces to have their provincial courts of appeal pronounce on the constitutionality of the Trudeau government's unilateral approach to constitutional change in 1980-81. This manoeuvre forced the Supreme Court to become a major player in the constitutional struggle.

The highest courts of both Australia and the United States have refused to answer questions put to them by governments on the ground that to give advice outside of adjudicating issues raised in the regular process of litigation is incompatible with the judicial role. Although in theory opinions in reference cases are merely advisory, in practice they are treated as binding.[110] They have been criticized as creating what the American jurist Felix Frankfurter once referred to as "ghosts that slay"—judicial precedents created out of hypo-

---

[107]   For a complete description of the Canadian court system, see Peter H. Russell, *The Judiciary in Canada: The Third Branch of Government* (Toronto: McGraw-Hill Ryerson, 1987).

[108]   *Statutes of Canada 1875*, c. 11, s. 52. This is now section 53 of the *Act*.

[109]   See cases 8 and 9.

[110]   See Barry L. Strayer, *The Canadian Constitution and the Courts*, 2d ed. (Toronto: Butterworths, 1983) c. 9.

thetical situations in which judges do not have the facts necessary to ascertain the actual effects of challenged laws.[111] However, the Court may refuse to answer questions it considers to be too abstract or hypothetical.[112]

Politicians have not shared the jurists' qualms about reference cases. They have found that the procedure has some practical advantages. When constitutional doubts are raised about an important legislative initiative, government may be anxious to obtain an opinion on its constitutionality without waiting months or years for the constitutional question to be raised in an ordinary case and work its way up to the Supreme Court. When federal and provincial governments are trying to coordinate their programs and jointly maximize their regulatory power, a reference case opinion can serve as a judicious guide to those who must draft the federal and provincial legislation.[113] Where jurisdiction is much more an object of federal–provincial rivalry, the referring of a question to the courts undoubtedly has the effect of throwing sensitive political issues into the laps of the judges, but there may still be a real advantage in submitting the resolution of the political conflict to the relatively dispassionate ways of the judicial process. The *Patriation Reference* is surely a case in point. In the *Manitoba Language Rights Reference*, the Supreme Court resolved an issue that the local politicians seemed incapable of handling through the legislative process.[114] Also, where there is serious doubt about the validity of major constitutional changes, as was the case before the 1980 *Senate Reference* and the 1981 *Patriation Reference*, it would seem wise to obtain a Supreme Court decision before they are put in place. Otherwise the legitimacy of the restructured institution and of the Constitution itself would be in question.

Reference cases figured more prominently in constitutional adjudication in the past than they do today. One-third of all constitutional cases decided by the Privy Council originated in questions referred to Canadian courts by federal or provincial governments. Among these were many of the most significant decisions concerning the division of legislative powers. Two-thirds of these cases were decided during the Privy Council's last three decades as Canada's final court of appeal. During this period, reference cases accounted for nearly all of its constitutional decisions. After the Court became truly supreme in 1949, reference cases continued to be a source of constitutional adjudication: 12 of the 36 constitutional cases decided by the Supreme Court in the 1950s originated in references. Since then, although reference cases have become much less frequent, some of the Court's most important decisions in the *Charter* era have come in reference cases.[115] Reference cases, which give governments a privileged access to the courts and permit them to frame the terms on which constitutional questions are considered, may seem less appropriate in *Charter* cases where the rights of citizens are pitted against the powers of government. In this regard, it was interesting to observe the Supreme Court's refusal in the summer of 1988 to postpone hearing an

---

[111] See Justice Laskin's objection to this feature of reference cases, in the *"Chicken and Egg" Reference*, case 12.

[112] See, for example, the Supreme Court's refusal to answer some of the questions put to it in the *Senate Reference*, case 45.

[113] A good example is *Re The Farm Products Marketing Act*, *supra* note 12.

[114] *Reference re Manitoba Language Rights*, [1985] 2 S.C.R. 347, discussed in the introduction to case 27.

[115] See cases 23, 35, 45, 46, 47, and 48.

appeal concerning the rights of a foetus brought by a citizen, Joe Borowski, until it had dealt with the federal government's new abortion legislation in a reference case.[116]

In recent years, constitutional litigation has become much more accessible to individual citizens. The Supreme Court has broadened the rules governing "standing"—that is, the right to stand before the court and challenge legislation. In the *Thorsen* and *McNeil* cases, the Supreme Court recognized the right of individuals to challenge laws that affect them only as members of large sections of the general public (for example, as taxpayers or moviegoers) and not directly as individuals.[117] In 1981, the Court went even further and granted Joe Borowski standing to challenge federal legislation permitting abortions, even though the legislation was totally inapplicable to him. In this case, Justice Martland on behalf of the majority set down the following rule on standing:

> To establish status as a plaintiff in a suit seeking a declaration that legislation is invalid, if there is a serious issue as to its validity, a person need only show that he is affected by it directly or that he has a genuine interest as a citizen in the validity of the legislation and that there is no other reasonable and effective manner in which the issue may be brought to the court.[118]

This rule, coming as it did just when the *Charter of Rights* was coming into force, makes it considerably easier for a Canadian citizen than it is for an American citizen to attack legislation in the courts. Still, as the decision in *Operation Dismantle*[119] indicates, there are limits to the kinds of issues that the Court considers to be justiciable.

Not only is constitutional litigation legally more accessible, but the rapid expansion of the legal profession, the development of legal aid, and the increased resources and organizational skills of special interest groups have also made it more accessible in a practical sense. It costs many thousands of dollars to take a constitutional challenge through the courts. At least three-quarters of all *Charter* cases arise when an accused person challenges some aspect of the criminal justice system. Nearly all of these challenges are supported through publicly funded legal aid. Challenges to non-criminal laws are facilitated by pressure groups and advocacy organizations willing to back an individual's grievance as a test case.[120] An influential network of legal academics in Canada's law schools enthusiastically embraced the *Charter* and formed close ties with rights-oriented advocacy groups.[121] Charles Epp has shown how the presence of this strong infrastructure for supporting *Charter* litigation in Canada is an important factor in explaining why the adoption of a constitutional bill of

---

[116] Transcript of Appeal Proceedings, October 3, 1988, Supreme Court of Canada, vol. I. For a discussion, see case 51 in Peter H. Russell, Rainer Knopff, and Ted Morton, eds., *Federalism and the Charter* (Ottawa: Carleton University Press, 1989).

[117] *Thorsen v. A.G. Canada,* [1975] 1 S.C.R. 138, and *Nova Scotia Board of Censors v. McNeil,* [1978] 2 S.C.R. 662.

[118] *Minister of Justice (Canada) v. Borowski* (1982), 1 W.W.R. 97 (S.C.C.).

[119] *Operation Dismantle v. The Queen,* [1985] 1 S.C.R. 441.

[120] See F.L. Morton, "The Political Impact of the Canadian Charter of Rights and Freedoms" (1987) 20 *Canadian Journal of Political Science* 31, and Gregory Hein, "Interest Group Litigation and Canadian Democracy" in Howe and Russell, eds., *supra* note 6 at 214-54.

[121] F.L. Morton and Rainer Knopff, *The Charter Revolution and the Court Party* (Peterborough, ON: Broadview Press, 2000).

rights has had greater effect in Canada than in other countries that have made similar changes in their constitutions.[122]

The federal government, which has entered many *Charter* cases to defend its laws against *Charter* challenges, has also funded the claimant side of rights litigation. In 1977, as part of the Trudeau government's promotion of coast-to-coast bilingualism, it established the Court Challenges Program (CCP) to fund minority language group challenges to provincial language policies.[123] In the *Charter* era, the CCP was extended to the funding of *Charter* litigants in language rights and equality rights cases.[124] The CCP also encouraged the organization of advocacy groups for prisoners' rights and ethnocultural rights. The program came under attack from those who resented the use of public funds to support the policy agenda of the groups it supported. In 1992, CCP was cancelled by the Mulroney government as part of a general cost-cutting policy. The CCP was restored by the Chrétien government only to be cancelled again by the Harper government in 2006.

Constitutional litigation in Canada, although it is usually initiated by private citizens, can quickly become a model of political combat for interest groups and governments. In contrast to the United States, where only the national government has the right to intervene in federal courts and then only when an act of Congress is challenged, in Canada, by legislation and custom, the provinces as well as the federal government are in most instances notified when their legislative powers are being tested in the courts and are given the right to become active parties in a case raising a constitutional issue. Non-governmental organizations can also be given intervener status to argue points that may not be developed by the parties themselves.[125] In the *Charter* case reviewing the validity of the funding of Catholic schools in Ontario, 24 such organizations were given intervener status.[126] It may seem paradoxical that in Canada, while the style of constitutional jurisprudence has been more legalistic than it tends to be in the United States, the interventions of governments and pressure groups, coupled with the reference case, expose judicial review much more directly to the contention of major political forces in the country.

Since 1975, when the Supreme Court gained a real measure of control over its docket, one of the Court's most important functions is selecting the cases it will hear. It discharges this function through panels of three judges. Up until 1988, every request for leave to appeal required a hearing (which is sometimes conducted by long-distance television). Now leave hearings occur only at the Court's discretion and are limited to the most difficult cases. For leave to be granted, two of the three judges on the panel must consider the issue raised in the case to be one that the Court should decide. As the volume of litigation in the country

---

[122] Charles R. Epp, *The Rights Revolution: Lawyers, Activists, and Supreme Courts in Comparative Perspective* (Chicago: University of Chicago Press, 1998).

[123] See Ian Brodie, "The Court Challenges Program" in F.L. Morton, ed., *Politics and the Judicial Process in Canada*, 3d ed. (Calgary: University of Calgary Press, 2002) 326-28.

[124] The minority-language groups involved in the litigation that brought the *Mahe* case to the Supreme Court were funded under the Court Challenges Program. See case 27.

[125] For a discussion of the recent changes in the rules governing private interveners, see Kenneth B. Swan, "Intervention and Amicus Curiae Status in Charter Litigation" in Robert Sharpe, ed., *Charter Litigation* (Toronto: Butterworths, 1987).

[126] *Reference re Bill 30, An Act to Amend the Education Act*, [1987] 1 S.C.R. 1148.

increases, the Court has had to become much more selective in granting leave. It is difficult for the Court to handle more than 100 cases a year. In recent years, its caseload has been below 100, and it has been granting leave in roughly 15 percent of the 500-600 applications for leave to appeal that it receives annually.[127]

This means that most cases, including most constitutional cases, go no higher than the intermediate appeal courts—the provincial courts of appeal and the Federal Court of Appeal. It is not the Supreme Court's function to correct mistakes made in the court of first instance. That is the primary purpose of the courts that hear the first appeal. The Supreme Court's function is to select those cases that raise difficult and contentious questions in all areas of law—not just constitutional law—and to write opinions on these that will guide lower courts and the lawyers who advise citizens and governments on their legal rights and duties.

After leave to appeal is granted, there will be an interval of several weeks or months before the case is heard by the Court. A quorum for hearing a case is five judges. Chief Justices have struggled to have all nine judges sit for at least the major constitutional cases. While that goal is almost always met, one still finds the occasional important constitutional case being decided by a seven-judge panel. This is usually caused by delays in filling vacancies on the Court.[128] Even-numbered panels are avoided to prevent ties, but, occasionally, an even number occurs when a justice who heard the appeal is forced by ill health to withdraw before a decision is reached. In the event of a tie vote, the appeal from the decision below is dismissed.

Before the hearing, judges will have an opportunity to examine the parties' written submissions. Each party submits a "factum," which should be a succinct, carefully organized statement of their arguments with references to all the authorities they are using to buttress their points.[129] The interveners submit factums highlighting the particular themes they wish to develop. The judges will also examine the record of the proceedings and opinions from the lower courts. Until recently there were virtually no limits on the time lawyers could take to make their oral arguments. Often cases were argued for many days, using up a great deal of court time. Lawyers rambled on for hours, often reading long passages from the law reports and contributing little to the lucidity or wisdom of the Court's decision making. In the fall of 1987, the Court issued a notice stating that henceforth it would expect to hear two cases a day—one in the morning and one in the afternoon—giving each side an hour to make its case. This makes hearings more like seminars, as they are in the U.S. Supreme Court, where the time allotted for each side is normally half an hour, and where the judges draw counsel out on the more problematic aspects of their arguments.

After the hearing, the justices hold a brief conference. Each judge, in reverse order of seniority, gives his or her views on the case. This is the same order as is used in the English

---

[127]   See Roy B. Flemming, *Tournament of Appeals: Granting Judicial Review in Canada* (Vancouver: University of British Columbia Press, 2004).

[128]   See, for example, *Chaoulli*, case 36.

[129]   Prior to the *Charter*, there was no limit on the length of factums, and they could run well over 100 pages. Beginning in the fall of 1987, the Court requested all parties coming before it to comply with a 40-page maximum.

House of Lords, but differs from the American Supreme Court, where the Chief Justice speaks first. Justice Wilson has explained that the practice is designed to reduce the risk of junior members feeling pressure to side with more senior judges, a risk she assures us no longer exists.[130] In any event, it does underline the fact that in the Court's decision making all judges, including the Chief Justice, formally have equal power and status. The conference discussion will indicate whether the justices are all in agreement (as is most often the case) on the basic outcome. Often, one member of the group will volunteer to draft the reasons for the decision. If not, the Chief Justice will ask someone to take this on. If the Court appears to be split, then writers for the majority and dissenting opinions will be designated.

Opinion-writing is the Supreme Court justice's most creative and challenging responsibility. Each justice will write only a handful of opinions each year, but the reasons he or she articulates as the justification for the Court's decision add important propositions to Canadian law, including the law of the Constitution. Each justice has the assistance of two or three "law clerks," the bright young law graduates who assist and who spend a year or two at the Court. The law clerks provide assistance in summarizing the issues involved in leave applications and researching background material salient to the cases their justices are working on. The lively conversations law clerks often have with their justices, and with one another, help to sharpen the analysis in the Court's final product. Also, at the opinion-writing stage, there will be a fair amount of interaction among the judges as drafts are circulated and commented on. When judges look at the reasons a colleague has drafted, the majority may begin to come apart, or at least one or more justices may be moved to write a concurring opinion expressing their own reasons for supporting the majority position. The Supreme Court has become far more collegial than it was in the past and nowadays it endeavours to produce a clear majority opinion. Indeed, in cases which are extraordinarily political, the authorship of the majority opinion is sometimes not disclosed and the opinion is simply attributed to "[t]he Court."[131]

The Court's judgment will not be released to the parties and the public until months, sometimes many months, after the hearing. These judgments are the Court's final product. Each judgment ends by dismissing or granting the appeal or by giving simple one-line or one-word answers to reference questions. But these "bottom lines"—who wins and who loses—are not the important part of Supreme Court judgments. What warrants collecting the leading decisions together here and engaging the student's interest are the reasons for the decisions. At the heart of each is some principle or rule about the powers of government or the rights of citizens that plays its part in the evolution of one of the world's oldest constitutional democracies.

In the *Charter* era, the Court's decisions in all areas of law, but above all in constitutional law, have come to attract a great deal of media attention. The Court has responded by making its decisions much more accessible to journalists. For cases of great public importance, it has released the report to journalists in a lockup several hours before the public release. This gives journalists some lead time to read the Court's judgment and prepare their news

---

[130]   Bertha Wilson, "Decision Making in the Supreme Court" (1986) 26 *University of Toronto Law Journal* 236.

[131]   Major examples are cases 45 and 47.

stories. Although there are now a handful of journalists who are able to grasp the significant aspects of the justices' reasoning, most of the media coverage tends to be shrill and superficial. A recent study of media coverage of Supreme Court decisions concludes that "[t]he glaring reality . . . is that the legal aspects of decisions were buried beneath an avalanche of political reporting."[132] As a result, Supreme Court decisions often have two lives—their legal life based on what the judges actually said and decided, and a political life based on the spin the media put on the decision. A good example of this is the Court's decision in *Chaoulli*, which newspaper headlines trumpeted meant the end of Canada's public medicare program.[133] Sometimes, the political understanding of a decision transcends its legal significance. Constitutional judicial review in a vibrant democracy such as Canada's is bound to be both a legal and political process. No one would think it strange today to find the Supreme Court of Canada involved in some very political questions.

---

[132]   Florian Sauvageau, David Schneiderman, and David Taras, *The Last Word: Media Coverage of the Supreme Court of Canada* (Vancouver: University of British Columbia Press, 2006) at 228.

[133]   Case 36.

PART ONE

The Division of Powers

A: THE PRIVY COUNCIL'S LEGACY

1

Citizens Insurance Co. v. Parsons;
Queen Insurance Co. v. Parsons, 1881

The constitutional issue in this case concerned the validity of the *Ontario Fire Insurance Policy Act*, which prescribed uniform conditions for all fire insurance contracts unless variations from the statutory conditions were properly indicated. Parsons, the respondent in the case, had taken actions against two fire insurance companies to obtain compensation for damages caused by fire in a warehouse insured by the companies. The companies' defence was that Parsons should not receive compensation because he had failed to observe conditions that had been written into the companies' policies or that were prescribed by the Ontario statute. Parsons's reply was that he was not bound by the conditions written into the contracts because they were not written on the contracts as variations from the statutory conditions in the manner prescribed by the *Ontario Fire Insurance Policy Act*. The companies' counsel attempted to counter this contention by arguing that the Ontario statute was *ultra vires*. The judgments of the Ontario Court of Appeal and the Supreme Court of Canada were both in favour of Parsons.

The Privy Council had heard six cases dealing with Canada's Constitution before this, but this is the first of its important decisions on the division of powers. The Privy Council's judgment, delivered by Sir Montague Smith, is important in terms of both the general approach to the interpretation of the *B.N.A. Act* and the construction of the federal trade and commerce power. The Judicial Committee treated the interpretation of the *B.N.A. Act* no differently than it would treat the interpretation of an ordinary statute. No reference was made to the historical context in which the constitution was drafted nor to the intentions of the Fathers of Confederation. Instead, the English judges tried to interpret the words of the *Act* in a way that would make the *Act* internally consistent. This meant that they felt obliged to attach some limits to broad terms like "trade and commerce." If this were not done, then a broad general power as an exclusive field of jurisdiction for one level of government would render meaningless more specific subjects in that same field assigned exclusively to the other level of government.

In this case the Judicial Committee declined to stretch trade and commerce as an exclusive field of federal jurisdiction so far as to prevent the provinces from regulating the contracts of a particular trade, such as the business of fire insurance, in a province. On the other hand, the Committee refused to interpret provincial jurisdiction over property and civil rights so narrowly as to exclude rights arising from contract. As a result, the *Ontario Act* was found constitutional as a law relating to property and civil rights in the province.

At the end of this opinion, Sir Montague Smith pointed to three kinds of laws that might be supported by the federal trade and commerce power: political arrangements in regard to trade requiring the sanction of Parliament (that is, international trade arrangements); regulation of trade in matters of interprovincial concern; and general regulation of trade affecting the whole Dominion. This definition of the parameters of the trade and commerce power, although not strictly necessary for the decision in this case, was returned to in many subsequent decisions. The consolidation in later cases of the doctrine that the trade and commerce power does not extend to intraprovincial, as distinguished from interprovincial, trade had the effect of excluding from the scope of that power all business or commercial transactions completed within a province. By thus excluding intraprovincial trade from federal jurisdiction, judicial review introduced into the Canadian Constitution a restriction on the federal commerce power similar to that which the United States' Constitution by express provision applies to the commerce power of its federal legislature. Ironically, though, the express restrictions in the American Constitution have proved to be far less of a barrier to the development of national economic policies than have the judicially created restrictions in Canada. ◠

CITIZENS INSURANCE CO. v. PARSONS;
QUEEN INSURANCE CO. v. PARSONS
(1881), 7 App. Cas. 96, I Olmsted 94 (Privy Council)*

Present: Sir Barnes Peacock, Sir Montague E. Smith, Sir Robert P. Collier, Sir Richard Couch, and Sir Arthur Hobhouse.

* Throughout this book, hearing and judgment dates are given whenever they were provided in the original law reports.

The judgment of their Lordships was delivered by

SIR MONTAGUE SMITH: The questions in these appeals arise in two actions brought by the same plaintiff (the respondent) upon contracts of insurance against fire of buildings situate in the province of Ontario, in the Dominion of Canada.

The most important question in both appeals is one of those, already numerous, which have arisen upon the provisions of the *British North America Act, 1867,* relating to the distribution of legislative power between the parliament of Canada and the legislatures of the provinces, and, owing to the very general language in which some of the powers are described, the question is one of considerable difficulty. Their Lordships propose to deal with it before approaching the facts on which the particular questions in the actions depend. . . .

The distribution of legislative powers is provided for by sects. 91 to 95 of the *British North America Act, 1867;* the most important of these being sect. 91, headed "Powers of the Parliament" and sect. 92, headed "Exclusive Power of the Provincial Legislature." . . .

The scheme of this legislation, as expressed in the first branch of sect. 91, is to give to the dominion parliament authority to make laws for the good government of Canada in all matters not coming within the classes of subjects assigned exclusively to the provincial legislature. If the 91st section had stopped here, and if the class of subjects enumerated in sect. 92 had been altogether distinct and different from those in sect. 91, no conflict of legislative authority could have arisen. The provincial legislatures would have exclusive power over the sixteen classes of subjects assigned to them, and the dominion parliament exclusive power over all matters relating to the good government of Canada. But it must have been foreseen that this sharp and definite distinction had not been and could not be attained, and that some of the classes of subjects assigned to the provincial legislatures unavoidably ran into and were embraced by some of the enumerated classes of subjects in sect. 91; hence an endeavour appears to have been made to provide for cases of apparent conflict; and it would seem that with this object it was declared in the second branch of the 91st section, "for greater certainty, but not so as to restrict the generality of the foregoing terms of this section" that (notwithstanding anything in the *Act*) the exclusive legislative authority of the parliament of Canada should extend to all matters coming within the classes of subjects enumerated in that section. With the same object, apparently, the paragraph at the end of sect. 91 was introduced, though it may be observed that this paragraph applies in its grammatical construction only to No. 16 of sect. 92.

Notwithstanding this endeavor to give pre-eminence to the dominion parliament in cases of a conflict of powers, it is obvious that in some cases where this apparent conflict exists, the legislature could not have intended that the powers exclusively assigned to the provincial legislature should be absorbed in those given to the dominion parliament. Take as one instance the subject "marriage and divorce," contained in the enumeration of subjects in sect. 91; it is evident that solemnization of marriage would come within this general description; yet "solemnization of marriage in the province" is enumerated among the classes of subjects in sect. 92, and no one can doubt, notwithstanding the general language of sect. 91, that this subject is still within the exclusive authority of the legislatures of the provinces. So "the raising of money by any mode or system of taxation" is enumerated among the classes of subjects in sect. 91; but, though the description is sufficiently large and general to include "direct taxation within the province, in order to the raising of a revenue for provincial purposes," assigned to the provincial legislatures by sect. 92, it obviously could not have been intended that, in this instance also, the general power should override the particular one. With regard to certain classes of subjects, therefore, generally described in sect. 91, legislative power may reside as to some matters falling within the general description of these subjects in the legislatures of the provinces. In these cases it is the duty of the Courts, however difficult it may be, to ascertain in what degree, and to what extent, authority to deal with matters falling within these classes of subjects exists in each legislature and to define in the particular case before them the limits of their respective powers. It could not have been the intention that a conflict should exist; and, in order to prevent such a result, the two sections must be read together, and the language of one interpreted, and, where necessary, modified, by that of the other. In this way it may, in most cases, be found possible to arrive at a reasonable and practical construction of the language of the sections, so as to reconcile the respective powers they contain, and give effect to all of them. In performing this difficult duty, it will be a wise course of those on whom it is thrown, to decide each case which arises as best they can, without entering more largely upon an interpretation of the statute then is necessary for the decision of the particular question in hand.

The first question to be decided is, whether the Act impeached in the present appeals falls within any of the classes of subjects enumerated in sect. 92, and assigned exclusively to the legislatures of the provinces; for it does not, it can be of no validity, and no other question would then arise. It is only when an Act of the provincial legislature *prima facie* falls within one of these classes of subjects that the further questions arise, *viz.*, whether, notwithstanding this is so, the subject of the Act does not also fall within one of the enumerated classes of subjects in sect. 91, and whether the power of the provincial legislature is or is not thereby overborne.

The main contention on the part of the respondent was that the Ontario Act in question had relation to matters coming within the class of subjects described in No. 13 of sect. 92, *viz.*, "Property and civil rights in the province." The Act deals with policies of insurance entered into or enforced in the province of Ontario for insuring property situate therein against fire, and prescribes certain conditions which are to form part of such contracts. These contracts, and the rights arising from them, it was argued, came legitimately within the class of subject, "Property and civil rights." The appellants, on the other hand, contended that civil rights meant only such rights as flowed from the law, and gave as an instance the status of persons. Their Lordships can not think that the latter construction is the correct one. They find no sufficient reason in the language itself, nor in the other parts of the *Act*, for

giving so narrow an interpretation to the words "civil rights." The words are sufficiently large to embrace in their far and ordinary meaning, rights arising from contract, and such rights are not included in express terms in any of the enumerated classes of subjects in sect. 91.

It becomes obvious, as soon as an attempt is made, to construe the general terms in which the classes of subjects in sects. 91 and 92 are described, that both sections and the other parts of the *Act* must be looked at to ascertain whether language of a general nature must not by necessary implication or reasonable intendment be modified and limited. In looking at sect. 91, it will be found not only that there is no class including, generally, contracts and the rights arising from them, but that one class of contracts is mentioned and enumerated, *viz.*, "18, bills of exchange and promissory notes," which it would have been unnecessary to specify if authority over all contracts and the rights arising from them had belonged to the dominion parliament.

The provision found in sect. 94 of the *British North America Act*, which is one of the sections relating to the distribution of legislative powers, was referred to by the learned counsel on both sides as throwing light upon the sense in which the words "property and civil rights" are used. By that section the parliament of Canada is empowered to make provision for the uniformity of any laws relative to "property and civil rights" in Ontario, Nova Scotia, and New Brunswick, and to the procedure of the courts in these three provinces, if the provincial legislatures chose to adopt the provisions so made. The province of Quebec is omitted from this section for the obvious reason that the law which governs property and civil rights in Quebec is in the main the French law as it existed at the time of the cession of Canada, and not the English law that prevails in the other provinces. The words "property and civil rights" are, obviously used in the same sense in this section as in No. 13 of section 92, and there seems no reason for presuming that contracts and the rights arising from them were not intended to be included in this provision for uniformity. If, however, the narrow construction of the words "civil rights," contended for by the appellants were to prevail, the dominion parliament could, under its general power, legislate in regard to contracts in all and each of the provinces and as a consequence of this the province of Quebec, though now governed by its own Civil Code, founded on the French law, as regards contracts and their incidents would be subject to have its law on that subject altered by the dominion legislature, and brought into uniformity with the English law prevailing in the other three provinces, notwithstanding that Quebec has been carefully been left out of the uniformity section of the *Act*.

It is observed that the same words, "civil rights," are employed in the *Act* of 14 Geo. 3, c. 83, which made provision for the Government of the province of Quebec. Sect. 8 of that Act enacted that His Majesty's Canadian subjects within the province of Quebec should enjoy their property, usages, and other civil rights, as they had before done, and that in all matters of controversy relative to property and civil rights resort should be had to the laws of Canada, and be determined agreeably to the said laws. In this statute the words "property" and "civil rights" are plainly used in their largest sense; and there is no reason for holding that in the statute under discussion they are used in a different and narrower one.

The next question for consideration is whether, assuming the *Ontario Act* to relate to the subject of property and civil rights, its enactments and provisions come within any of the classes of subjects enumerated in sect. 91. The only one which the Appellants suggested as expressly including the subject of the *Ontario Act* is No. 2, "the regulation of trade and commerce."

A question was raised which led to much discussion in the Courts below and this bar, *viz.*, whether the business of insuring buildings against a fire was a trade. This business, when carried on for the sake of profit, may, no doubt, in some sense of the word be called a trade. But contracts of indemnity made by insurers can scarcely be considered trading contracts, nor were insurers who made them held to be "traders" under the English bankruptcy laws; they have been made subject to those laws by special description. Whether the business of fire insurance properly falls within the description of a "trade" must, in their Lordships' view, depend upon the sense in which that word is use in the particular statute to be construed; but in the present case their Lordships do not find it necessary to rest their decision on the narrow ground that the business of insurance is not a trade.

The words "regulation of trade and commerce" in their unlimited sense are sufficiently wide, if uncontrolled by the context and other parts of the *Act*, to include every regulation of trade ranging from political arrangements in regard to trade with foreign governments, requiring the sanction of parliament, down to minute rules regulating particular trades. But a consideration of the *Act* shows that the words were not used in this unlimited sense. In the first place the collocation of No. 2 with classes of subjects of national and general concern affords an indication that regulations relating to general trade and commerce were in the mind of the legislature when conferring this power on the dominion parliament. If the words had been intended to have the full scope of which in their literal meaning they are susceptible, the specific mention of several of the other classes of subjects enumerated in sect. 91 would have been unnecessary; as, 15, banking; 17, weights and measures; 18, bills of exchange and promissory notes; 19, interest; and even 21, bankruptcy and insolvency.

"Regulation of trade and commerce" may have been used in some such sense as the words "regulations of trade" in the *Act of Union between England and Scotland* (6 Anne, c. 11), and as these words have been used in *Acts of State* relating to trade and commerce. Article V of the *Act of Union* enacted that all the subjects of the United Kingdom should have "full freedom and intercourse of trade and navigation" to and from all places in the United Kingdom and the colonies; and Article VI enacted that all parts of the United Kingdom from and after the Union should be under the *same* "prohibitions, restrictions, and *regulations of trade*." Parliament has at various times since the Union passed laws affected and regulating specific trades in one part of the United Kingdom only, without its being supposed that it thereby infringed the *Articles of Union*. Thus the *Acts* for regulating the sale of intoxicating liquors notoriously vary in the two kingdoms. So with regards to *Acts* relating to bankruptcy, and various other matters.

Construing therefore the words "regulation of trade and commerce" by the various aids to their interpretation above suggested, they would include political arrangements in regard to trade requiring the sanction of parliament, regulation of trade in matters of interprovincial concern, and it may be that they would include general regulation of trade effecting the whole dominion. Their Lordships abstain on the present occasion from any attempt to defined the limits of the authority of the dominion parliament in this direction. It is enough for the decision of the present case to say that, in their view, its authority to legislate for the regulation of trade and commerce does not comprehend the power to regulate by legislation the contracts of a particular business or trade, such as the business of fire insurance in a single province, and therefore that its legislative authority does not in the present case conflict or compete with the power over property and civil right assigned to the legislature of Ontario by No. 13 of sect. 92. . . .

The opinions of the majority of the Judges in Canada, as summed up by Ritchie, C.J., are in favour of the validity of the *Ontario Act*. In the present action, the Court of Queen's Bench and the Court of Appeal of Ontario unanimously supported its legality; and the Supreme Court of Canada, by a majority of three Judges to two, have affirmed the judgments of the provincial Courts. The opinions of the learned judges of the Supreme Court are stated with great fullness and ability, and clearly indicate the opposite views which may be taken of the Act, and the difficulties which surround any construction that may be given to it.

Taschereau, J., in the course of his vigorous judgment, seeks to place the plaintiff in the action against the Citizens Company in a dilemma. He thinks that the assertion of the right of the province to legislate with regard to the contracts of insurance companies amounts to a denial of the dominion parliament to do so, and that this is, in effect, to deny the right of that parliament to incorporate the Citizens Company, so that the plaintiff was suing a non-existent defendant. Their Lordships can not think that this dilemma is established. The learned Judge assumes that the power of the dominion parliament to incorporate companies to carry on business in the dominion is derived from one of the enumerated classes of subjects, *viz.,* "the regulation of trade and commerce," and then argues that if the authority to incorporate companies is given by this clause, the exclusive power of regulating them must also be given by it, so that the denial of one power involves the denial of the other. But, in the first place, it is not necessary to rest the authority of the dominion parliament to incorporate companies on this specific and enumerated power. The authority would belong to it by its general power over all matters not coming within the classes of subjects assigned exclusively to the legislatures of the provinces and the only subject on this head assigned to the provincial legislature being "the incorporation of companies with provincial objects," it follows that the incorporation of companies for objects other than provincial falls within the general powers of the parliament of Canada. But it by no means follows (unless indeed the view of the learned judge is right as to the scope of the words "the regulation of trade and commerce") that because the dominion parliament has alone the right to create a corporation to carry on business throughout the dominion that it alone has the right to regulate its contracts in each of the provinces. Suppose the dominion parliament were to incorporate a company, with power, among other things, to purchase and hold lands throughout Canada in mortmain, it could scarcely be contended if such a company were to carry on business in a province where a law against holding land in mortmain prevailed (each province having exclusive legislative power over "property and civil rights in the province") that it could hold land in that province in contravention of the provincial legislation; and, if a company were incorporated for the sole purpose of purchasing and holding land in the dominion, it might happen that it could do no business in any part of it, by reason of all the provinces having passed *Mortmain Acts*, though the corporation would still exist and preserve its status as a corporate body.

On the best consideration they have been able to give to the arguments addressed to them and to the judgments of the learned judges in Canada, their Lordships have come to the conclusion that the *Act* in question is valid. . . .

Russell v. The Queen, 1882

In the case of *Russell v. The Queen*, the Judicial Committee of the Privy Council was confronted for the first time with what has undoubtedly been the classic issue in the Canadian division of powers, the contest between the Dominion's "[p]eace, order and good government" power and the provinces' power in relation to "property and civil rights" and "all matters of a merely local or private nature in the province." Here, the Privy Council ruled the Dominion's temperance legislation *intra vires* on the ground that since the subject matter of the legislation did not belong to any of the classes of subjects assigned exclusively to the provinces, it must fall under the central Parliament's residuary power.

The direct challenge to the Dominion's *Canada Temperance Act* came from Charles Russell, who had been convicted under the *Act* of unlawfully selling liquor in Fredericton, New Brunswick. But the fate of Russell's appeal, the immediate issue of the case, was less important than the opportunity the case gave to the Privy Council to review the earlier decision of the Supreme Court of Canada in *City of Fredericton v. The Queen*,[1] ruling the *Canada Temperance Act intra vires*. The Supreme Court majority in that case sustained the *Act* under the trade and commerce clause of section 91, giving a broad interpretation of that power. In *Russell v. The Queen*, the Privy Council agreed with the Supreme Court of Canada that the *Act* was valid, but on the basis of Parliament's residuary power, not the trade and commerce power. While not repudiating the possibility of sustaining the legislation under section 91(2), Sir Montague Smith refused to endorse positively the Supreme Court's reasoning. This refusal was more in keeping with the narrower interpretation of section 91(2), which their Lordships had given the previous year in the *Parsons* case.

The Privy Council considered that the primary matter dealt with by the *Canada Temperance Act* was one relating to public order and safety and that any effect on property and civil rights was merely incidental. As in the *Parsons* case, the Judicial Committee was opposed to interpreting an exclusive power of one level of government (in this case, provincial jurisdiction over property and civil rights) so broadly as to sterilize a power assigned to the other level (the general authority of Parliament to make laws for the peace, order, and good government of Canada and Parliament's jurisdiction in relation to criminal law).

The Privy Council's use of the peace, order, and good government power in the *Russell* case as a constitutional basis for federal legislation proved to be highly exceptional as subsequent decisions considerably narrowed its scope. ⁓

---

1   (1880), 3 S.C.R. 505.

RUSSELL v. THE QUEEN
(1882), 7 App. Cas. 829, I Olmsted 145 (Privy Council)

Present: Sir Barnes Peacock, Sir Montague E. Smith, Sir Robert P. Collier, Sir James Hannen, and Sir Richard Couch.

The judgment of their Lordships was delivered by

SIR MONTAGUE SMITH: This is an appeal from an order of the Supreme Court of the Province of New Brunswick, discharging a rule *nisi* which had been granted on the application of the Appellant for a *certiorari* to remove a conviction made by the police magistrate of the city of Fredericton against him for unlawfully selling intoxicating liquors, contrary to the provisions of the *Canada Temperance Act, 1978.*

No question has been raised as to the sufficiency of the conviction, supposing the above-mentioned statute is a valid legislative *Act* of the Parliament of Canada. The only objection made to the conviction in the Supreme Court of New Brunswick, and in the appeal to Her Majesty in Council, is that, having regard to the provisions of the *British North America Act, 1867,* relating to the distribution of legislative powers, it was not competent for the Parliament of Canada to pass the *Act* in question.

The Supreme Court of New Brunswick made the order now appealed from in deference to a judgment of the Supreme Court of Canada in the case of *City of Fredericton v. The Queen.* In that case the question of the validity of the *Canada Temperance Act, 1878,* though in another shape, directly arose, and the Supreme Court of New Brunswick, consisting of six Judges, then decided, Mr. Justice Palmer dissenting, that the *Act* was beyond the competency of Dominion Parliament. On the appeal of the city of Fredericton, this judgment was reversed by the Supreme Court of Canada, which held, Mr. Justice Henry dissenting, that the *Act* was valid. (The case is reported in the third Supreme Court of Canada Reports, p. 505.) The present appeal to Her Majesty is brought, in effect, to review the last-mentioned decision.

The preamble of the *Act* in question states that "it is very desirable to promote temperance in the Dominion, and that there should be uniform legislation in all the provinces respecting the traffic in intoxicating liquors." The *Act* is divided into three parts. The first relates to "proceeding for bringing the second part of this *Act* into force"; the second to "prohibition of traffic in intoxicating liquors"; and the third to "penalties and prosecution for offenses against the second part."

The mode of bringing the second part of the *Act* into force, stating it succinctly is as follows: On a petition to the Governor in Council, signed by not less than one fourth in number of the electors of any county or city in the Dominion qualified to vote at the election of a member of the House of Commons, praying that the second part of the *Act* should be in force and take effect in such county or city, and that the votes of all electors be taken for or against the adoption of the petition, the Governor-General after certain prescribed notices and evidence, may issue a proclamation, embodying such petition, with a view to a poll of the electors being taken for or against its adoption. When any petition has been adopted by the electors of the county or city named in it, the Governor-General in Council may, after the expiration of sixty days from the day on which the petition was adopted, by Order in Council published in the *Gazette,* declare that the second part of the *Act* shall be in force and take effect in such county or city, and the same is then to become of force and take effect accordingly. Such Order in Council is not to be revoked for three years, and only on like petition and procedure.

The most important of the prohibitory enactments contained in the second part of the *Act* is s. 99, which enacts that, "from the day on which this part of this *Act* comes into force and takes effect in any county or city, and for so long thereafter as the same continues in force therein, no person, unless it be for exclusively sacramental or medical purposes, or for *bona fide* use in some art, trade, or manufacture, under the regulation contained in the fourth sub-section of this section, or as hereinafter authorized by one of the four next sub-sections of this section, shall, within such county or city, by himself, his clerk servant, or agent, expose or keep for sale, or directly or indirectly, on any pretense or upon any devise, sell or barter, or in consideration of the purchase of any other property give, to any other person, any spirituous or other intoxicating liquor, or any mixed liquor capable of being used as a beverage and part of which is spirituous or otherwise intoxicating."

Sub-sect. 2 provides that "neither any license issued to any distiller or brewer" (and after enumerating other licenses), "nor yet any other description of license whatever, shall in any [way] avail to render legal any act done in violation of this section."

Sub-sect. 3 provides for the sale of wine for sacramental purposes, and sub-sect. 4 for the sale of intoxicating liquors for medicinal and manufacturing purposes, these sales being made subject to prescribed conditions.

Other sub-sections provide that producers of cider, and distillers and brewers, may sell liquors of their own manufacture in certain quantities, which may be termed wholesale quantities, or for export, subject to prescribed conditions, and there are provisions of a like nature with respect to vine-growing companies and manufacturers of native wines.

The third part of the *Act* enacts (section 100) that whoever exposes for sale or sells intoxicating liquors in violation of the second part of the *Act* should be liable, on summary conviction, to a penalty of not less than fifty dollars for the first offense, and not less that one hundred dollars for the second offense, and to be imprisoned for a term not exceeding two months for the third and every subsequent offense; all intoxicating liquors in respect to which any such offense has been committed to be forfeited.

The effect of the *Act* when brought into force in any county or town within the Dominion is, describing it generally, to prohibit the sale of intoxicating liquors, except in wholesale quantities, or for certain specified purposes, to regulate the traffic in the excepted cases, and to make sales of liquors in violation of the prohibition and regulations contained in the *Act* criminal offenses, punishable by fine, and for the third or subsequent offense by imprisonment.

It was in the first place contended, thought not very strongly relied on, by the Appellant's counsel, that assuming the Parliament of Canada had authority to pass a law for prohibiting and regulating the sale of intoxicating liquors, it could not delegate its powers, and that it had done so by delegating the power to bring into force the prohibitory and penal provisions of the *Act* to a majority of the electors of counties and cities. The short answer to this objection is that the *Act* does not delegate any legislative powers whatever. It contains within itself the whole legislation on the matters with which it deals. The provisions that certain parts of the *Act* shall come into operation only on the petition of a majority of electors does not confer on these persons power to legislate. Parliament itself enacts the conditions and everything which is to follow upon the condition being fulfilled. Conditional legislation of this kind is in many cases convenient and is certainly not unusual, and the power so to legislate cannot be denied [the] Parliament of Canada, when the subject of legislation is within its competency. . . .

The general question of the competency of the Dominion Parliament to pass the *Act* depends on the construction of the 91st and 92nd sections of the *British North America Act, 1867*, which are found in Part VI of the statute under the heading, "Distribution of Legislative Powers."

The 91st section enacts, "it shall be lawful for the Queen by and with the advice and consent of the Senate and House of Commons to make law for the peace, order, and good government of Canada, in relation to all matters not coming within the classes of subjects by this *Act* assigned exclusively to the legislatures of the provinces; and for greater certainty, but not so as to restrict the generality of the foregoing terms of this section, it is hereby declared that (notwithstanding anything in this *Act*) the exclusive legislative authority of [the] Parliament of Canada extends to all matters coming within the classes of subjects next hereinafter enumerated"; then after the enumeration of twenty-nine classes of subjects, the section contains the following words: "and any matter coming within any of the classes of subjects enumerated in this section shall not be deemed to come within the classes of matters of a local or private nature comprised in the enumeration of the classes of subjects by his *Act* assigned exclusively to the Legislature of the Province."

The general scheme of the *British North America Act* with regard to the distribution of legislative powers, and the general scope and effects of ss. 91 and 92, and their relation to each other, were fully considered and commented on by this Board in the case of the *Citizens Insurance Company v. Parsons* (7 App. Cas. 96). According to the principle of construction there pointed out, the first question to be determined is whether the *Act* now in question falls within any of the classes of subjects enumerated in s. 92, and assigned exclusively to the Legislature of the Provinces. If it does, then the further question would arise, *viz.*, whether the subject of the *Act* does not fall within one of the enumerated classes of subjects in s. 91, and so does not still belong to the Dominion Parliament. But if the *Act* does not fall within any of the classes of subjects in s. 92, no further question will remain, for it cannot be contended, and indeed was not contended at their Lordship's bar, that, if the *Act* does not come within one of the classes of subjects assigned to the Provincial Legislatures, the Parliament of Canada had not, by its general power "to make laws for the peace, order, and good government of Canada," full legislative authority to pass it.

Three classes of subjects enumerated in s. 92 were referred to, under each of which, it was contended by the appellant's counsel, the present legislation fell. These were:

> 9. Shop, saloon, tavern, auctioneer, and other licenses in order to the raising of a revenue for provincial, local, or municipal purposes.
> 13. Property and civil rights in the province.
> 16. Generally all matters of a merely local or private nature in the province.

With regard to the first of these classes, No. 9, it is to be observed that the power of granting licenses is not assigned to the Provincial Legislatures for the purpose of regulating trade, but "in order to the raising of a revenue for provincial, local or municipal purposes."

The *Act* in question is not a fiscal law; it is not a law for raising revenue; on the contrary, the effect of it may be to destroy or diminish revenue; indeed it was a main objection to the *Act* that in the city of Fredericton it did in point of fact diminish the sources of municipal revenue. It is evident, therefore, that the matter of the *Act* is not within the class of subject No. 9, and consequently that it could not have been passed by the Provincial Legislature by virtue of any authority conferred upon it by that sub-section.

[Sir Montague E. Smith then pointed out that while national legislation such as the *Canada Temperance Act* might affect the sale or use of an article covered by a licence granted under subsection 9 of section 92, this in itself was not grounds for bringing the legislation under that subsection.]

Next, their Lordships cannot think that the *Temperance Act* in question properly belongs to the class of subjects, "Property and Civil Rights." It has in its legal aspect an obvious and close similarity to laws which place restrictions on the sale or custody of poisonous drugs, or of dangerously explosive substances. These things, as well as intoxicating liquors, can, of course, be held as property, but a law placing restrictions on their sale, custody, or removal, on the ground that the free sale or use of them is dangerous to public safety, and making it a criminal offense punishable by fine or imprisonment to violate these restrictions, cannot properly be deemed a law in relation to property in the sense in which those words are used in the 92nd section. What parliament is dealing with in legislation of this kind is not a matter in relation to property and its rights, but one relating to public order and safety. That is the primary matter dealt with, and though incidentally the free use of things in which men may have property is interfered with, that incidental interference does not alter the character of the law. Upon the same considerations, the *Act* in question cannot be regarded as legislation in relation to civil rights. In however large a sense these words are used, it could not have been intended to prevent the Parliament of Canada from declaring and enacting certain uses of property, and certain acts in relation to property, to be criminal or wrongful. Laws which make it a criminal offense for a man willfully to set fire to his own house on the ground that such an act endangers the public safety, or to overwork his horse on the ground of cruelty to the animal, though affecting in some sense property and the right of a man to do as he pleases with his own, cannot properly be regarded as legislation in relation to property or to civil rights. Nor could a law which prohibited or restricted the sale or exposure of cattle having a contagious disease be so regarded. Laws of this nature designed for the promotion of public order, safety, or morals, and which subject those who contravene them to criminal procedure and punishment, belong to the subject of public wrongs rather than to that of civil rights. They are of a nature which fall within the general authority of Parliament to make laws for the order and good government of Canada, and have direct relation to criminal law, which is one of the enumerated classes of subjects assigned exclusively to the Parliament of Canada. It was said in the course of the judgment of this Board in the case of the *Citizens Insurance Company of Canada v. Parsons* that the two sections (91 and 92) must be read together, and language of one interpreted, and, where necessary, modified by that of the other. Few, if any, laws could be made by the Parliament for the peace, order, and good government of Canada which did not in some incidental way affect property and civil rights; and it could not have been intended, when assuring to the provinces exclusive legislative authority on the subjects of property and civil rights, to exclude the parliament from the exercise of this general power whenever any such incidental interference would result from it. The true nature and character of the legislation in the particular instances under discussion must always be determined, in order to ascertain the class of subjects to which it really belongs. In the present case it appears to their Lordships, for the reasons already given, that the matter of the *Act* in question does not properly belong to the class of subjects "Property and Civil Rights" within the meaning of sub-sect. 13....

It was lastly contended that this *Act* fell within sub-sect. 16 of sect. 92—"Generally all matters of a merely local or personal nature in the province."

It was not, of course, contended for the appellant that the Legislature of New Brunswick could have passed the *Act* in question, which embraces in its enactments all the provinces; nor was it denied, with respect to this last contention, that the Parliament of Canada might have passed an *Act* of the nature of that under discussion to take effect at the same time throughout the whole Dominion. Their Lordships understand the contention to be that, at least in the absence of a general law of the Parliament of Canada, the provinces might have passed a local law of a like kind, each for its own province, and that, as the prohibitory and penal parts of the *Act* in question were to come into force in those counties and cities only in which it was adopted in the manner prescribed, or, as it was said, "by local option," the legislation was in effect, and on its face, upon a matter of merely local nature. The judgment of Allan C.J., delivered in the Supreme Court of the Province of New Brunswick in the case of *Barker v. City of Fredericton* (3 Pugs & Burb. Sup. Ct. New Br. Rep. 139), which was adverse to the validity of the *Act* in question, appears to have been founded upon this view of the enactments. The learned Chief Justice says: "Had this *Act* prohibited the sale of liquor, instead of merely restricting and regulating it, I should have no doubt about the power of the Parliament to pass such an *Act*; but I think an *Act*, which in effect authorizes the inhabitants of each town or parish to regulate the sale of liquor, and to direct for whom, for what purposes, and under what conditions spirituous liquors may be sold therein, deals with matters of a merely local nature, which, by terms of the 16th sub-section of sect. 92 of the *British North America Act*, are within the exclusive control of the local legislature."

Their Lordships cannot concur in this view. The declared object of Parliament in passing the *Act* is that there should be uniform legislation in all the provinces respecting the traffic in intoxicating liquors, with a view to promote temperance in the Dominion. Parliament does not treat the promotion of temperance as desirable in one Province more than in another, but as desirable everywhere throughout the Dominion. The *Act* as soon as it was passed became a law for the whole Dominion, and the enactments of the first part, relating to the machinery for bringing the second part into force, took effect and might be put in motion at once and everywhere within it. It is true that the prohibitory and penal parts of the *Act* are only to come into force in any county or city upon the adoption of a petition to that effect by a majority of electors, but this conditional application of these parts of the *Act* does not convert the *Act* itself into legislation in relation to a merely local matter. The objects and scope of the legislation are still general, *viz.*, to promote temperance by means of a uniform law throughout the Dominion.

The matter of bringing the prohibitions and penalties of the *Act* into force, which Parliament has thought fit to adopt, does not alter its general and uniform character. Parliament deals with the subject as one of general concern to the Dominion, upon which uniformity of legislation is desirable, and the Parliament alone can so deal with it. There is no ground or pretence for saying that the evil or vice struck at by the *Act* in question is local or exists only in one province, and that Parliament, under colour of general legislation, is dealing with a Provincial matter only. It is therefore unnecessary to discuss the considerations which a state of circumstances of this kind might present. The present legislation is clearly meant to apply a remedy to an evil which is assumed to exist throughout the Dominion, and the local option, as it is called, no more localises the subject and scope of the *Act* than a provision in an *Act* for the prevention of contagious diseases in cattle that a public officer should proclaim in what districts it should come in effect, would make the statute itself a mere local law for each of these districts. In statutes of this kind the legislation is general, and the provisions for the special application of it to particular places does not alter its character.

Their Lordships having come to the conclusion that the *Act* in question does not fall within any of the classes of subjects assigned exclusively to the Provincial Legislatures, it becomes unnecessary to discuss the further question whether its provisions also fall within any of the classes of subjects enumerated in s. 91. In abstaining from the discussion, they must not be understood as intimating any dissent from the opinion of the Chief Justice of the Supreme Court of Canada and the other Judges, who held that the *Act*, as a general regulation of the traffic in intoxicating liquors throughout the Dominion, fell within the class of subject, "the regulation of trade and commerce," enumerated in that section, and was, on that ground, a valid exercise of the legislative power of the Parliament of Canada. . . .

Liquidators of the Maritime Bank of Canada v. Receiver General of New Brunswick, 1892

While this case did not deal directly with the division of legislative powers, it did provide the occasion for Lord Watson to express a conception of Canadian federalism that underlies most of the Judicial Committee's decisions on the Canadian Constitution.

The immediate issue in the case was whether the Government of New Brunswick could use Crown prerogative as a basis for claiming priority over other creditors seeking to recover funds from the liquidators of the Maritime Bank. The federal government endeavoured to deny New Brunswick's claim on the ground that Confederation had severed any direct relationship between the Crown and a province and in this sense had made the provinces subordinate to the federal government.

Lord Watson, in dismissing this argument, denied that the *B.N.A. Act* was intended to produce a system in which provinces were subordinate to a central government. The conception of federalism he found in the *B.N.A. Act* was much closer to the definition of federalism found in classic constitutional texts than it was to Sir John A. Macdonald's conception of the purpose of Confederation. A.V. Dicey's *Introduction to the Law of the Constitution*, an influential English text that was first published in 1885, offered the following definition of federalism:

> A federal state is a political contrivance intended to reconcile national unity and power with the maintenance of "state rights." The end aimed at fixes the essential character of federalism. For the method by which Federalism attempts to reconcile the apparently inconsistent claims of national sovereignty and of state sovereignty consists of a formation of a constitution under which the ordinary powers of sovereignty are elaborately divided between the common or national government and the separate states.[1]

Compare this with the following statement of Sir John A. Macdonald from the Confederation Debates:

> The true principle of a Confederation lay in giving to the General Government all the principles and powers of sovereignty, and that the subordinate or individual states should have no powers but those expressly bestowed on them. We should thus have a powerful Central Government, a powerful Central Legislature, and a decentralized system of minor legislatures for local purposes.[2]

While the contrast between Macdonald's theory of confederation and the doctrine of classical federalism enunciated by the Privy Council is clear, it is important to bear in mind that Macdonald was only one of the Fathers of Confederation and he belonged to the group that was most skeptical about federalism. Other members of the political coalition that produced Confederation and forced Macdonald to accept federalism might not have been surprised or dismayed by the Privy Council's tendency to read classical federalism into the *B.N.A. Act*. ⌐

---

1 *Introduction to the Law of the Constitution*, 10th ed. (London: Macmillan, 1961) at 143.

2 P.B. Waite, ed., *The Confederation Debates in the Province of Canada*, Carleton Library ed. (Toronto: McClelland and Stewart, 1963) at 156.

LIQUIDATORS OF THE MARITIME BANK OF CANADA v. RECEIVER GENERAL OF NEW BRUNSWICK

(1892) A.C. 437, I Olmsted 263 (Privy Council)

Judgment: July 21, 1892.

Present: Lord Watson, Lord Hobhouse, Lord Macnaghten, Lord Morris, Sir Richard Couch, and Lord Shand.

The judgment of their Lordships was delivered by

LORD WATSON: This appeal is brought by special leave in a suit which followed upon a case submitted for the opinion of the Supreme Court of the province of New Brunswick, by the appellants, the liquidators of the Maritime Bank of the Dominion of Canada, in the interest of unsecured creditors of the bank, on the one side, and by the Receiver-General of the Province, claiming to represent Her Majesty, on the other. The only facts which it is necessary to refer to are these: that the bank carried on its business in the city of St. John, New Brunswick; and that, at the time when it stopped payment in March, 1887, the provincial government was a simple contract creditor for a sum of $35,000, being public moneys of the province deposited in the name of the Receiver-General. The case, as originally framed, presented two questions for the decision of the Court; but, owing to the condition of the bank's assets, the first of these has ceased to be of practical importance, and it is only necessary to consider the second, which is in these terms: "Is the provincial government entitled to payment in full over the other depositors and simple contract creditors of the bank?"

The Supreme Court of New Brunswick unanimously, and, on appeal, the Supreme Court of Canada with a single dissentient voice, have held that the claim of the provincial government is for a Crown debt to which the prerogative attaches, and therefore answered the question in the affirmative.

The Supreme Court of Canada had previously ruled, in *Reg. v. Bank of Nova Scotia* (9 App. Cas. 117), that the Crown, as a simple contract creditor for public moneys of the Dominion deposited with a provincial bank, is entitled to priority over other creditors of equal degree. The decision appears to their Lordships to be in strict accordance with constitutional law. The property and revenues of the Dominion are vested in the Sovereign, subject to the disposal and appropriation of the legislature of Canada; and the prerogative of the Queen, when it has not been expressly limited by local law or statute, is as extensive in Her Majesty's colonial possessions as in Great Britain. In *Exchange Bank of Canada v. The Queen* (11 App. Cas. 157), this Board disposed of the appeal on that footing, although their Lordships reversed the judgment of the Court below, and negatived the preference claimed by the Dominion

Government upon the ground that, by the law of the province of Quebec, the prerogative was limited to the case of the common debtor being an officer liable to account to the Crown for public moneys collected or held by him. The appellants did not impeach the authority of these cases, and they also conceded that, until the passing of the *British North America Act, 1867*, there was precisely the same relation between the Crown and the Dominion. But they maintained that the effect of the statute has been to sever all connection between the Crown and the provinces; to make the government of the Dominion the only government of Her Majesty in North America; and to reduce the provinces to the rank of independent municipal institutions. For these propositions, which contain the sum and substance of the arguments addressed to them in support of this appeal, their Lordships have been unable to find either principle or authority.

Their Lordships do not think it necessary to examine, in minute detail, the provisions of the *Act* of 1867, which nowhere profess to curtail in any respect the rights and privileges of the Crown, or to disturb the relations then subsisting between the Sovereign and the provinces. The object of the *Act* was neither to weld the provinces into one, nor to subordinate provincial governments to a central authority, but to create a federal government in which they should all be represented, entrusted with the exclusive administration of affairs in which they had a common interest, each province retaining its independence and autonomy. That object was accomplished by distributing, between the Dominion and the provinces, all powers executive and legislative, and all public property and revenues which had previously belonged to the provinces; so that the Dominion Government should be vested with such of these powers, property, and revenues as were necessary for the due performance of its constitutional functions, and that the remainder should be retained by the provinces for the purposes of provincial government. But, in so far as regards those matters which, by sect. 92, are specially reserved for provincial legislation, the legislation of each province continues to be free from the control of the Dominion, and as supreme as it was before the passing of the *Act*. In *Hodge v. The Queen* (9 App. Cas. 117), Lord Fitzgerald delivering the opinion of this Board, said: "When the *British North America Act* enacted that there should be a legislature for Ontario, and that its legislative assembly should have exclusive authority to make laws for the province and for provincial purposes in relation to the matters enumerated in sect. 92, it conferred powers not in any sense to be exercised by delegation from or as agents of the Imperial Parliament, but authority as plenary and as ample within the limits prescribed by sect. 92 as the Imperial Parliament in the plenitude of its power possessed and could bestow. Within these limits of subject and area, the local legislature is supreme, and has the same authority as the Imperial Parliament, or the Parliament of the Dominion." The *Act* places the constitutions of all provinces within the Dominion on the same level; and what is true with respect to the legislature of Ontario has equal application to the legislature of New Brunswick.

It is clear, therefore, that the provincial legislature of New Brunswick does not occupy the subordinate position which was ascribed to it in the argument of the appellants. It derives no authority from the Government of Canada, and its status is in no way analogous to that of a municipal institution, which is an authority constituted for purposes of local administration. It possesses powers, not of administration merely, but of legislation, in the strictest sense of that word; and, within the limits assigned by sect. 92 of the *Act* of 1867, these powers are exclusive and supreme. . . .

Attorney General of Ontario v. Attorney General of Canada (Local Prohibition Case), 1896

Competition between Ontario and the federal government to regulate the consumption and sale of liquor was a major source of constitutional litigation in the last two decades of the 19th century. As we have seen, a federal scheme for a system of local prohibition was upheld in the *Russell* case. In *Hodge v. The Queen*,[1] the Judicial Committee upheld an Ontario scheme for licensing taverns and retail liquor outlets. But two years later, the Privy Council, without giving reasons, ruled *ultra vires* a federal law (the *McCarthy Act*) that provided a scheme for the appointment of local liquor licensing commissioners across Canada.[2] The *Local Prohibition* case of 1896 raised the question whether a province could provide a system of local prohibition, at least for those districts that had not availed themselves of the provisions of the *Canada Temperance Act*.

This question first arose in private litigation in *Huson v. South Norwich*.[3] In that case, the Supreme Court, by a 3-to-2 majority, found Ontario's local prohibition scheme constitutional. But shortly after this decision, the federal government referred the question of the validity of the Ontario law, along with six more hypothetical questions, to the Supreme Court. In the interval between the *Huson* case and the reference case, Justice King replaced Justice Taschereau, with the result that the Supreme Court now found Ontario's local prohibition legislation unconstitutional. The Court's decision in the reference case represents the last manifestation of the early Supreme Court's allegiance to the centralist concepts of certain Fathers of Confederation. Justice Gwynne, for example, fortified his view that the prohibition of liquor sales fell under exclusive federal jurisdiction over trade and commerce by quoting George Brown in the Confederation Debates: "All matters of trade and commerce, banking and currency and all questions common to the whole people we have vested fully and unrestrictedly in the general government."[4]

On appeal, the Privy Council reversed the Supreme Court's decision in the reference case. The opinion, written by Lord Watson, had the effect of attenuating both the federal trade and commerce power and the federal Parliament's general power. By repudiating the Supreme Court's holding that the *Canada Temperance Act* was a proper exercise of the trade and commerce power, the Privy Council culminated its overruling of the early Supreme Court's tendency to assign virtually all aspects of trade and commerce exclusively to the federal Parliament. The Privy Council also held that the federal peace, order, and good government power did not exclude the provinces from enacting their own local prohibition laws. In reaching this conclusion, Lord Watson argued that the preservation of provincial autonomy required that Parliament's general power to legislate for the peace, order, and

---

1   (1883), 9 App. Cas. 177.

2   (1875-1893), Cassels, *Digest of Supreme Court Decisions* at 509.

3   (1895), 24 S.C.R. 145.

4   *Re Prohibitory Liquor Laws* (1895), 24 S.C.R. 170 at 207.

good government of Canada not have the same capacity as the federal enumerated powers to override provincial jurisdiction over matters of a local or private nature.

This distinction between peace, order, and good government and the enumerated powers (which are listed "for greater Certainty but not so as to restrict the Generality" of the general power) has been regarded as a serious diminution of the general power. Yet it should be noted that Lord Watson left what appears to be a potentially liberal test for the application of the general power when he stated that circumstances might transform local and private matters into matters of national concern and thus bring them under Parliament's power to make laws for the peace, order, and good government of Canada. In succeeding decisions, however, this test was restrictively applied by the Privy Council. ⌐

ATTORNEY GENERAL OF ONTARIO v. ATTORNEY GENERAL OF CANADA

[1896] A.C. 348, I Olmsted 343 (Privy Council)

Present: Lord Halsbury L.C., Lord Herschell, Lord Watson, Lord Davey, and Sir Richard Couch.

[The appeal was made by special leave from a judgment of the Supreme Court of Canada, 24 S.C.R. 170, on a reference to it of seven questions:]

1. Has a provincial legislature jurisdiction to prohibit the sale within the province of spirituous, fermented, or other intoxicating liquors?

2. Or has the legislature such jurisdiction regarding such portions of the provinces as to which the *Canada Temperance Act* is not in operation?

3. Has a provincial legislature jurisdiction to prohibit the manufacture of such liquors within the province?

4. Has a provincial legislature jurisdiction to prohibit the importation of such liquors into the province?

5. If a provincial legislature has not jurisdiction to prohibit sales of such liquors, irrespective of quantity, has such legislature jurisdiction to prohibit the sale by retail, according to the definition of a sale by retail either in statutes or in force in the province at the time of confederation, or any other definition thereof?

6. If a provincial legislature has a limited jurisdiction only as regards the prohibition of sales, has the legislature jurisdiction to prohibit sales subject to the limits provided by the several sub-sections of the 99th section of the *Canada Temperance Act*, or any of them (*Revised Statutes of Canada*, 49 Vict. c. 106, s. 99)?

7. Has the Ontario legislature jurisdiction to enact s. 18 of *Ontario Act*, 53 Vict. c. 56, intituled "*An Act to improve the Liquor Licence Acts*," as said section is explained by *Ontario Act*, 54 Vict. c. 46, intituled "*An Act respecting local option in the matter of liquor selling*"?

Sect. 18, referred to in the last of the said question, is as follows:

18. Whereas the following provision of this section was at the date of confederation in force as a part of the *Consolidated Municipal Act* (29th and 30th Victoria, chapter 51, section 249, subsection 9), and was afterwards re-enacted as sub-section 7 of section 6 of 32nd Victoria, chapter 32, being the *Tavern and Shop Licence Act of 1868*, but was afterwards omitted in subsequent consolidations of the *Municipal and the Liquor Licence Acts*, similar provisions as to local prohibitions being contained in the *Temperance Act of 1864*, 27th and 28th Victoria, chapter 18; and the said last-mentioned *Act* having been repealed in municipalities where not in force by the *Canada Temperance Act*, it is expedient that municipalities should have the powers by them formerly possessed; it is hereby enacted as follows:

The council of every township, city, town, and incorporated village may pass by-laws prohibiting the sale by retail of spirituous, fermented, or other manufactured liquors in any tavern, inn, or other house or place of public entertainment, and for prohibiting liquor altogether the sale thereof in shops and places other than houses of public entertainment. Provided that the by-law before the final passing thereof has been duly approved of by the electors of the municipality in the manner provided by the section in that behalf of the *Municipal Act*. Provided further that nothing in this section contained shall by construed into an exercise of jurisdiction by the Legislature of the province of Ontario beyond the revival of provisions of law which were in force at the date of the passing of the *British North America Act*, and which the subsequent legislation of this province purported to repeal.

Act 54, Vict. c. 46, referred to above, declares that s. 18 was not intended to affect the provisions of s. 252 of the *Consolidated Municipal Act, being Canada Act*, 29 & 30 Vict. c. 51.

A majority of the Supreme Court, after hearing counsel for the Dominion, the provinces of Ontario, Quebec, and Manitoba, and also, under s. 37, sub-s. 4, of the *Supreme and Exchequer Courts Act for the Distillers and Brewers Association of Ontario*, answered all the questions in the negative. Strong C.J., and Fournier J., while agreeing in a negative answer to questions 3 and 4, answered the remainder in the affirmative.

The judgment of their Lordships was delivered by

LORD WATSON: Their Lordships think it expedient to deal, in the first instance, with the seventh question, because it raises a practical issue, to which the able arguments of counsel on both sides of the Bar were chiefly directed, and also because it involves considerations which have a material bearing upon the answers to be given to the other six questions submitted in this appeal. In order to appreciate the merits of the controversy, it is necessary to refer to certain laws for the restriction or suppression of the liquor traffic which were passed by the legislature of the old province of Canada before the Union, or have since been enacted by the Parliament of the Dominion, and by the legislature of Ontario respectively.

[Lord Watson then reviewed the history of liquor legislation in Ontario. He related how the Ontario legislature came to pass the *Act* referred to in the seventh question. This *Act* aimed at restoring to Ontario municipalities the power of making bylaws prohibiting the sale of liquor. The right had been bestowed upon them in 1864, but had later been allowed to lapse by the Ontario legislature and was not in force when the *Canada Temperance Act of 1886*, which provided for prohibition at the option of localities, purported to repeal it.]

The seventh questions raises the issue, whether, in the circumstances which have just been detailed, the provincial legislature had authority to enact s. 18. In order to determine that issue, it becomes necessary to consider, in the first place, whether the Parliament of Canada had jurisdiction to enact the *Canada Temperance Act*; and, if so, to consider, in the second place, whether, after that *Act* became the law of each province of the Dominion, there yet remained power with the Legislature of Ontario to enact the provisions of s. 18.

The authority of the Dominion Parliament to make laws for the suppression of liquor traffic in the province is maintained, in the first place, upon the ground that such legislation

deals with matters affecting "the peace, order, and good government of Canada," within the meaning of the introductory and general enactments of s. 91 of the *British North America Act*; and, in the second place, upon the ground that it concerns "the regulation of trade and commerce," being No. 2 of the enumerated classes of subjects which are placed under the exclusive jurisdiction of the Federal Parliament by that section. These sources of jurisdiction are in themselves distinct, and are to be found in different enactments.

It was apparently contemplated by the framers of the *Imperial Act of 1867* that the due exercise of the enumerated powers conferred upon the Parliament of Canada by s. 91 might, occasionally and incidentally, involve legislation upon matters which are *prima facie* committed exclusively to the provincial legislatures by s. 92. In order to provide against that contingency, the concluding part of s. 91 enacts that "any matter coming within any of the classes of subjects enumerated in this section shall not be deemed to come within the class of matters of a local or private nature comprised in the enumeration of the classes of subjects by this *Act* assigned exclusively to the legislatures of the provinces." It was observed by this Board in *Citizens Insurance Company of Canada v. Parsons* (7 App. Cas. 108) that the paragraph just quoted "applied in its grammatical construction only to No. 16 of s. 92." The observation was not material to the question arising in that case, and it does not appear to their Lordships to be strictly accurate. It appears to them that the language of the exception in s. 91 was meant to include and correctly describes all the matters enumerated in the sixteen heads of s. 92, as being, from a provincial point of view, of a local or private nature. It also appears to their Lordships that the exception was not meant to derogate from the legislative authority given to provincial legislatures by those sixteen subsections, save to the extent of enabling the Parliament of Canada to deal with matters local or private in those cases where such legislation is necessarily incidental to the exercise of the powers conferred upon it by the enumerative heads of clause 91. . . .

The general authority given to the Canadian Parliament by the introductory enactments of s. 91 is "to make laws for the peace, order, and good government of Canada, in relation to all matters not coming within the classes of subjects by this *Act* assigned exclusively to the legislatures of the provinces"; and it is declared, but not so as to restrict the generality of these words, that the exclusive authority of the Canadian Parliament extends to all matters coming within the classes of subjects which are enumerated in the clause. There may, therefore, be matters not included in the enumeration, upon which the Parliament of Canada has power to legislate, because they concern the peace, order, and good government of the Dominion. But to those matters which are not specified among the enumerated subjects of legislation, the exception from s. 92, which is enacted by the concluding words of s. 91, has no application; and, in legislating with regard to such matters, the Dominion Parliament has not authority to encroach upon any class of subjects which is exclusively assigned to provincial legislatures by s. 92. These enactments appear to their Lordships to indicate that the exercise of legislative power by the Parliament of Canada, in regard to all matters not enumerated in s. 91, ought to be strictly confined to such matters as are unquestionably of Canadian interest and importance and ought not to trench upon provincial legislation with respect to any of the classes of subjects enumerated in s. 92. To attach any other construction to the general power which, in supplement of its enumerated powers, is conferred upon the Parliament of Canada by s. 91, would, in their Lordships' opinion, not only be contrary to the intendment of the *Act,* but would practically destroy the autonomy of the provinces. If it were once conceded that the Parliament of Canada has authority to make laws applicable to the whole Dominion, in relation to matters which in each province are substantially of local or private interest, upon the assumption that these matters also concern the peace, order, and good government of the Dominion, there is hardly a subject enumerated in s. 92 upon which it might not legislate, to the exclusion of the provincial legislatures.

In construing the introductory enactments of s. 91, with respect to matter other than those enumerated, which concern the peace, order, and good government of Canada, it must be kept in view that s. 94, which empowers the Parliament of Canada to make provision for the uniformity of the laws relative to property and civil rights in Ontario, Nova Scotia, and New Brunswick does not extend to the province of Quebec; and also that the Dominion legislation thereby authorized is expressly declared to be of no effect unless and until it has been adopted and enacted by the provincial legislature. These enactments would be idle and abortive, if it were held that the Parliament of Canada derives jurisdiction from the introductory provisions of s. 91, to deal with any matter which is in substance local or provincial, and does not truly effect the interest of the Dominion as a whole. Their Lordships do not doubt that some matters, in their origin local and provincial, might attain such dimensions as to effect the body politic of the Dominion, and to justify the Canadian Parliament in passing laws for their regulation or abolition in the interests of the Dominion. But great caution must be observed in distinguishing between that which is local and provincial, and therefore within the jurisdiction of the provincial legislatures, and that which has ceased to be merely local or provincial, and has become a matter of national concern, in such sense to bring it within the jurisdiction of the Parliament of Canada. An *Act*

restricting the right to carry weapons of offense, or their sale to young persons, within the province would be within the authority of the provincial legislature. But traffic in arms, or the possession of them under such circumstances as to raise a suspicion that they were to be used for seditious purposes, or against a foreign state, are matters which, their Lordships conceive, might be completely dealt with by the Parliament of the Dominion.

The judgment of this Board in *Russell v. Reg.* (7 App. Cas. 829) has relieved their Lordships from the difficult duty of considering whether the *Canada Temperance Act* of 1886 relates to the peace, order, and good government of Canada, in such sense as to bring its provisions within the competency of the Canadian Parliament. In that case the controversy related to the validity of the *Canada Temperance Act* of 1878; and neither the Dominion nor the provinces were represented in the argument. It arose between a private prosecutor and a person who had been convicted, at his instance, of violating the provisions of the Canadian *Act* within a district of New Brunswick, in which the prohibitory clauses of the *Act* had been adopted. But the provisions of the *Act* of 1878 were in all material respects the same with those which are now embodied in the *Canada Temperance Act* of 1886; and the reasons which were assigned for sustaining the validity of the earlier, are, in their Lordships' opinion, equally applicable to the later *Act.* It therefore appears to them that the decision in *Russell v. Reg.* must be accepted as an authority to the extent to which it goes, namely, that the restrictive provisions of the *Act* of 1886, when they have been duly brought into operation in any provincial area within the Dominion, must receive effect as valid enactments relating to the peace, order, and good government of Canada.

That point being settled by decision, it becomes necessary to consider whether the Parliament of Canada had authority to pass the *Temperance Act* of 1886 as being an *Act* for the "regulation of trade and commerce" within the meaning of No. 2 of s. 91. If it were so the Parliament of Canada would, under the exception from s. 92 which had already been noticed, be at liberty to exercise its legislative authority, although in doing so it should interfere with the jurisdiction of the provinces. The scope and effect of No. 2 of s. 91 were discussed by this Board at some length in *Citizens Insurance Co. v. Parsons* (7 App. Cas. 96), where it was decided that, in the absence of legislation upon the subject by the Canadian Parliament, the legislature of Ontario had authority to impose conditions, as being matters of civil right, upon the business of fire insurance, which was admitted to be a trade, so long as those conditions only affected provincial trade. Their Lordships do not find it necessary to reopen that discussion in the present case. The object of the *Canada Temperance Act* of 1886 is, not to regulate retail transactions between those who trade in liquor and their customers, but to abolish all such transactions within every provincial area in which its enactments have been adopted by a majority of the local electors. A power to regulate, naturally, if not necessarily, assumes, unless it is enlarged by the context, the conservation of the thing which is to be made the subject of regulation. In that view, their Lordships are unable to regard the prohibitive enactments of the Canadian Statute of 1886 as regulation of trade and commerce. . . .

The authority of the Legislature of Ontario to enact s. 18 of 53 Vict. c. 56, was asserted by the appellant on various grounds. The first of these, which was very strongly insisted on, was to the effect that the power given to each province by No. 8 of s. 92 to create municipal institutions in the province necessarily implied the right to endow these institutions with all the administrative functions which had been ordinarily possessed and exercised by them before the time of the Union. Their Lordships can find nothing to support that contention in the language of s. 92, No. 8, which, according to its natural meaning, simply gives provincial legislatures the right to create a legal body for the management of municipal affairs. Until confederation, the Legislature of each province as then constituted could, if it chose, and did in some cases, entrust to a municipality the execution of powers which now belong exclusively to the Parliament of Canada. Since its date a provincial legislature cannot delegate any power which it does not possess; and the extent and nature of the functions which it can commit to a municipal body of its own creation must depend upon the legislative authority which it derives from the provisions of s. 92 other than No. 8.

Their Lordships are likewise of opinion that s. 92, No. 9, does not give provincial legislatures any right to make laws for the abolition of the liquor traffic. It assigns to them "shop, saloon, tavern, auctioneer and other licences, in order to the raising of a revenue for provincial, local or municipal purposes." It was held by this Board In *Hodge v. Reg.* (9 App. Cas. 117) to include the right to impose reasonable conditions upon the licencees which are in the nature of regulation; but it cannot, with any show of reason, be construed as authorizing the abolition of the sources from which revenue is to be raised.

The only enactments of s. 92 which appear to their Lordships to have any relation to the authority of provincial legislatures to make laws for the suppression of the liquor traffic are to be found in Nos. 13 and 16, which assign to their exclusive jurisdiction, (1) "property and civil rights in the province," and (2) "generally all matters of a merely local or private nature in the province." A law which prohibits retail transactions and restricts the consumption of liquor within the ambit of the province, and does not effect transactions in liquor between persons in the province and persons in other provinces or in foreign countries, concerns property in the province which would be the subject matter of the transactions if they were not prohibited, and also the civil rights of persons in the province. It is not impossible that the vice of intemperance may prevail in particular localities within a province to such an extent to constitute its cure by restricting or prohibiting the sale of liquor a matter of a merely local or private nature, and therefore falling *prima facie* within No. 16. In that state of matters, it is conceded that the Parliament of Canada could not imperatively enact a prohibitory law adapted and confined to the requirements of localities within the province where prohibition was urgently needed. . . .

The question must next be considered whether the provincial enactments of s. 18 to any, and if so to what, extent came into collision with the provisions of the Canadian *Act* of 1886. In so far as they do, provincial [legislation] must yield to Dominion legislation, and must remain in abeyance unless and until the *Act* of 1886 is repealed by the Parliament which passed it.

[Lord Watson then examined the differences between the prohibitions authorized by section 18 of the *Ontario Act* and the prohibitions of the *Canada Temperance Act.*]

It thus appears that, in their local application within the province of Ontario, there would be considerable difference between the two laws; but it is obvious that their provisions could not be in force within the same district or province at one and the same time. . . .

If the prohibitions of the *Canada Temperance Act* had been made imperative throughout the Dominion, their Lordships might have been constrained by previous authority to hold that the jurisdiction of the Legislature of Ontario to pass s. 18 or any similar law had been superseded. In that case no provincial prohibitions such as are sanctioned by s. 18 could have been enforced by a municipality without coming into conflict with the paramount law of Canada. For the same reason, provincial prohibitions in force within a particular district will necessarily become inoperative whenever the prohibitory clauses of the *Act* of 1886 had been adopted by that district. But their Lordships can discover no adequate grounds for holding that there exists repugnancy between the two laws in districts of the Province of Ontario where the prohibitions of the Canadian *Act* are not and may never be in force. . . .

Their Lordships, for these reasons, give a general answer to the seventh question in the affirmative. They are of the opinion that the Ontario legislature had jurisdiction to enact s. 18, subject to this necessary qualification, that its provisions are or will become inoperative in any district of the province which has already adopted, or may subsequently adopt, the second part of the *Canada Temperance Act* of 1886.

Their Lordships will now answer briefly, in their order, the other questions submitted by the Governor-General of Canada. So far as they can ascertain from the record, these differ from the question which has already been answered in this respect, that they relate to matters which may possibly become litigious in the future, but have not as yet given rise to any real and present controversy. Their Lordships must further observe that these questions, being in their nature academic rather than judicial, are better fitted for the consideration of the officers of the Crown than of a Court of law. The replies to be given to them will necessarily depend upon the circumstances in which they may arise for decision; and these circumstances are in this case left to speculation. It must, therefore, be understood that the answers which follow are not meant to have, and cannot have, the weight of a judicial determination, except in so far as their Lordships may have occasion to refer to the opinions which they have already expressed in discussing the seventh question.

Answer to questions 1 and 2—Their Lordships think it sufficient to refer to the opinions expressed by them in disposing of the seventh question.

Answer to question 3—In the absence of conflicting legislation by the Parliament of Canada, their Lordships are of opinion that the provincial legislatures would have jurisdiction to that effect if it were shown that the manufacture were carried on under such circumstances and conditions as to make its prohibition a merely local matter in the province.

Answer to question 4—Their Lordships answer this question in the negative. It appears to them that the exercise by the provincial legislature of such jurisdiction in the wide and general terms in which it is expressed would probably trench upon the exclusive authority of the Dominion Parliament.

Answers to question 5 and 6—Their Lordships consider it unnecessary to give a categorical reply to either of these questions. Their opinion upon the points which the questions involve has been sufficiently explained in their answer to the seventh question.

5 In re Board of Commerce Act and Combines and Fair Prices Act, 1919, 1922

The federal legislation reviewed in this case was introduced after World War I to break up business combines and monopolies and to prevent the hoarding of basic necessities. Although the legislation was prompted by profiteering in scarce commodities that had developed after the war, it was cast in the form of permanent legislation.

The Privy Council viewed legislation limiting the commercial liberty of entrepreneurs as essentially an interference with the property and civil rights of the inhabitants of the provinces and hence subject to exclusive provincial jurisdiction. Viscount Haldane considered that the context in which the legislation was enacted did not amount to the "highly exceptional circumstances" that could transform such a subject into a matter of national concern, thus bringing it under the federal peace, order, and good government power. His reasoning amounted to the "emergency doctrine": only under special circumstances, such as war or famine, could a matter normally within section 92 become of such national importance as to be brought under the Dominion's general power. In this instance, he reported that their Lordships could find no evidence to indicate that such a "standard of necessity" had been reached.

Nor could the Judicial Committee be persuaded that the challenged legislation was a valid exercise of Parliament's trade and commerce power. Under Viscount Haldane's leadership, this power had reached its nadir. Sir Montague Smith's opinion in the *Parsons* case pointed to three kinds of trade that might be brought under the federal trade and commerce power—international, interprovincial, and general trade affecting the whole of Canada.[1] In 1915, in *John Deere Plow Co. v. Wharton*,[2] Haldane invoked the general trade aspect of trade and commerce to uphold federal legislation defining the rights and capacities of companies that had been incorporated by Parliament. But a year later, in the *Insurance Reference*, he showed how limited this third aspect of trade and commerce would be by denying that it could be used as a basis for regulating an entire business, such as insurance, throughout the Dominion.[3] Now, in the *Board of Commerce* case, Haldane explains his use of the commerce power in *John Deere Plow* as supplementing Parliament's exercise of its general residual power. Thus, aside from its possible application to international and interprovincial trade, the trade and commerce power at this stage had been assigned by judicial interpretation to a position in the division of powers inferior to all other heads of power: it was now regarded as essentially an auxiliary power incapable of serving on its own as a primary source of legislative capacity.

Viscount Haldane's opinion is also notable for the limit it imposed on federal jurisdiction in relation to criminal law. The criminal law power could be applied only to behaviour that "by its very nature belongs to the domain of criminal jurisprudence." While incest could meet this test, apparently postwar profiteering could not.

---

1 See case 1, above.

2 (1915), A.C. 330.

3 *Attorney General of Canada v. Attorney General of Alberta* (1916), 1 A.C. 589.

The six members of the Supreme Court of Canada had been evenly divided in this case. It is interesting to compare the opinion of Justice Anglin with that of the Judicial Committee. Justice Anglin found the federal legislation and the order authorized by it valid. Unlike the Privy Council, Justice Anglin relied on the "national dimensions" test of the peace, order, and good government power set out in the *Local Prohibition* case. In the 1916 *Insurance Reference,* however, the Privy Council had struck down the federal regulation, despite acknowledging that "the business of insurance is a very important one, which has attained to great dimensions in Canada." Clearly, some kinds of national dimension would justify legislation under peace, order, and good government and some would not. Justice Anglin could not have known that the Privy Council was about to make "special circumstances" of an emergency nature the test of the required degree of "national dimension." He found a plausible distinction between the *Canada Temperance Act* and the *Insurance Act* of 1910 in the fact that the former related to "public order, safety or morals," while the latter did not. In the case at hand, because he viewed profiteering as "an evil so prevalent and so insidious that . . . it threatens to-day the moral and social well-being of the Dominion,"[4] he could consider that the *Board of Commerce Act* dealt with a matter of national "public order," and on this ground invoke Parliament's general power to sustain the legislation. He also thought that it could be supported by the trade and commerce power and, in part, by the criminal law power (section 91 [27]). Justice Duff, on the other hand, rejected what he regarded as the dangerous notion that the Dominion, simply in order to deal with vicissitudes of national trade, could, under its general power, legislate in relation to matters otherwise subject to provincial jurisdiction. Such reasoning would "justify Parliament in any conceivable circumstance forcing upon a province a system of nationalization of industry."[5] These disagreements between the two judges on the Supreme Court and between Justice Anglin and the Privy Council provide a good illustration of how extralegal considerations can enter into the judiciary's determination of constitutional issues. ⌁

---

4   (1920), 60 S.C.R. 456 at 467.

5   *Ibid.* at 466.

IN RE THE BOARD OF COMMERCE ACT, 1919, AND THE COMBINES AND FAIR PRICES ACT, 1919
[1922] 1 A.C. 191, II Olmsted 245 (Privy Council)

Hearing: July 14, 15, 116, 1921; Judgment: November 11, 1922.

Present: Viscount Haldane, Lord Buckmaster, Viscount Cave, Lord Phillimore, and Lord Carson.

[This appeal was by special leave from the Supreme Court of Canada. The appeal related to the validity of two acts passed by the Parliament of Canada in 1919—namely, the *Board of Commerce Act* and the *Combines and Fair Prices Act*.]

The judgment of their Lordships was delivered by

VISCOUNT HALDANE: This is an appeal from the Supreme Court of Canada, before which were brought, under statute, questions relating to the constitutional validity of the *Acts* above mentioned. As the six Judges who sat in the Supreme Court were equally divided in opinion, no judgment was rendered. Davies, C.J., and Anglin and Mignault, JJ., considered that the questions raised should be answered in the affirmative, while Idington, Duff and Brodeur, JJ., thought that the first question should be answered in the negative and that therefore the second question did not arise. These questions were raised for the opinion of the Supreme Court by a case stated under s. 32 of the *Board of Commerce Act, 1919*, and were: (1) whether the Board had lawful authority to make a certain order; and (2) whether the Board had lawful authority to require the Registrar, or other proper authority of the Supreme Court of Ontario, to cause the order, when issued, to be made a rule of that Court.

The order in question was to the effect that certain retail dealers in clothing in the city of Ottawa were prohibited from charging as profits on sales more than a certain percentage on cost which was prescribed as being fair profit. The validity of this order depended on whether the Parliament of Canada had legislative capacity, under the *B.N.A. Act of 1867*, to establish the Board and give it authority to make the order.

The statutes in question were enacted by the Parliament of Canada in 1919, and were to be read and construed as one *Act*. By the first of these statutes, the *Board of Commerce Act*, a Board was set up, consisting of three commissioners appointed by the Governor-General, which was to be a Court of Record. The duty of the Board was to be to administer the second of the two statutes in question, the *Combines and Fair Prices Act*, called the *Special Act*. It was to have power to state a case for the opinion of the Supreme Court of Canada upon any question which, in its own opinion, was one of law or jurisdiction. It was given the right to inquire into and determine the matters of law and fact entrusted to it, and to order

the doing of any act, matter, or thing required or authorized under either *Act*, and to forbid the doing or continuing of any act, matter or thing which, in its opinion, was contrary to either *Act*. The Board was also given authority to make orders and regulations with regard to these, and generally for carrying the *Board of Commerce Act* into effect. Its finding on any question of fact within its jurisdiction was to be binding and conclusive. Any of its decisions or orders might be made a rule or order or decree of the Exchequer Court, or of any Superior Court of any Province of Canada.

The second statute, the *Combines and Fair Prices Act*, was directed to the investigation and restriction of combines, monopolies, trusts and mergers, and to the withholding and enhancement of the prices of commodities. By Part I the Board of Commerce was empowered to prohibit the formation or operation of combines as defined, and, after investigation, was to be able to issue orders to that effect. A person so ordered to cease any act or practice in pursuance of the operations of a combine, was, in the event of failure to obey the order, to be guilty of an indictable offence, and the Board might remit to the Attorney-General of a Province the duty of instituting the appropriate proceedings. By Part II the necessaries of life were to include staple and ordinary articles of food, whether fresh, preserved, or otherwise treated, and clothing and fuel, including the materials from which these were manufactured or made, and such other articles as the Board might prescribe. No person was to accumulate or withhold from sale any necessary of life, beyond an amount reasonably required for the use or consumption of his household, or for the ordinary purpose of his business.

Every person who held more, and every person who held a stock-in-trade of any such necessary of life, was to offer the excess amount for sale at reasonable and just prices. This, however, was not to apply to accumulating or withholding by farmers and certain other specified persons. The Board was empowered and directed to inquire into any breach or non-observance of any provision of the *Act*, and the making of such unfair profits as above referred to, and all such practices with respect to the holding or disposition of necessaries of life as in the opinion of the Board, were calculated to enhance their cost or price. An unfair profit was to be deemed to have been made when the Board, after proper inquiry, so declared. It might call for returns and enter premises and inspect. It might remit what it considered to be offences against this part of the *Act* to the Attorney-General of the Province, or might declare the guilt of a person concerned, and issue to him orders or prohibitions, for breach of which he should be liable to punishment as for an indictable offence.

The above summary sufficiently sets out the substance of the two statutes in question for the present purpose.

In the first instance the Board stated for the opinion of the Supreme Court of Canada, a case in which a number of general constitutional questions were submitted. That Court, however, took the view that the case was defective, inasmuch as it did not contain a statement of concrete facts, out of which such questions arose. Finally, a fresh case was stated containing a statement of the facts in certain matters pending before the Board, and formulating questions that had actually arisen. These related to the action of certain retail clothing dealers in the city of Ottawa. An order was framed by the Board which, after stating the facts found, gave directions as to the limits of profit, and a new case was stated which raised the questions already referred to.

In these circumstances the only substantial question which their Lordships have to determine is whether it was within the legislative capacity of the Parliament of Canada to enact the statutes in question.

The second of these statutes, the *Combines and Fair Prices Act*, enables the Board established by the first statute to restrain and prohibit the formation and operation of such trade combinations for production and distribution in the Provinces of Canada as the Board may consider to be detrimental to the public interest. The Board may also restrict, in the cases of food, clothing and fuel, accumulation of these necessaries of life beyond the amount reasonably required, in the case of a private person, for his household, not less than in the case of a trader for his business. The surplus is in such instances to be offered for sale at fair prices. Certain persons only, such as farmers and gardeners, are excepted. Into the prohibited cases the Board has power to inquire searchingly, and to attach what may be criminal consequences to any breach it determines to be improper. An addition of a consequential character is thus made to the Criminal Law of Canada.

The first question to be answered is whether the Dominion Parliament could validly enact such a law. Their Lordships observe that the law is not one enacted to meet special conditions in war time. It was passed in 1919, after peace had been declared, and it is not confined to any temporary purpose, but is to continue without limit in time, and to apply throughout Canada. No doubt the initial words of s. 91 of the *British North America Act*, confer on the Parliament of Canada power to deal with subjects which concern the Dominion generally, provided that they are not withheld from the powers of that Parliament to legislate, by any of the express heads in s. 92, untrammelled by the enumeration of special heads in s. 91. It may well be that the subjects of undue combination and hoarding are matters in which the Dominion has a great practical interest. In special circumstances, such as those of a great war, such an interest might conceivably become of such

paramount and overriding importance as to amount to what lies outside the heads in s. 92, and is not covered by them. The decision in *Russell v. The Queen* ((1882), 7 App. Cas. 829), appears to recognize this as constitutionally possible, even in time of peace; but it is quite another matter to say that under normal circumstances general Canadian policy can justify interference, on such a scale as the statutes in controversy involve, with the property and civil rights of the inhabitants of the Provinces. It is to the Legislatures of the Provinces that the regulation and restriction of their civil rights have in general been exclusively confided, and as to these the Provincial Legislatures possess quasi-sovereign authority. It can, therefore, be only under necessity in highly exceptional circumstances, such as cannot be assumed to exist in the present case, that the liberty of the inhabitants of the Provinces may be restricted by the Parliament of Canada, and that the Dominion can intervene in the interests of Canada as a whole in questions such as the present one. For, normally, the subject matter to be dealt with in the case would be one falling within s. 92. Nor do the words in s. 91, the Regulation of trade and commerce, if taken by themselves, assist the present Dominion contention. It may well be, if the Parliament of Canada had, by reason of an altogether exceptional situation, capacity to interfere, that these words would apply so as to enable that Parliament to oust the exclusive character of the provincial powers under s. 92.

In the case of Dominion companies their Lordships in deciding the case of *John Deere Plow Company v. Wharton* ([1915] A.C. 330, 339, 340), expressed the opinion that the language of s. 91, head 2, could have the effect of aiding Dominion powers conferred by the general language of s. 91. But that was because the regulation of the trading of Dominion companies was sought to be invoked only in furtherance of a general power which the Dominion Parliament possessed independently of it. Where there was no such power in that Parliament, as in the case of the *Dominion Insurance Act*, it was held otherwise, and that the authority of the Dominion Parliament to legislate for the regulation of trade and commerce did not, by itself, enable interference with particular trades in which Canadians would, apart from any right of interference conferred by these words above, be free to engage in the Provinces ([1916] 1 A.C. 588). This result was the outcome of a series of well-known decisions of earlier dates which are now so familiar that they need not be cited.

For analogous reasons the words of head 27 of s. 91 do not assist the argument for the Dominion. It is one thing to construe the words "the criminal law, except the constitution of courts of criminal jurisdiction, but including the procedure in criminal matters," as enabling the Dominion Parliament to exercise exclusive legislative power where the subject matter is one by which its very nature belongs to the domain of criminal jurisprudence. A general law, to take an example, making incest a crime, belongs to this class. It is quite another thing, first to attempt to interfere with a class of subject committed exclusively to the Provincial Legislature, and then to justify this by enacting ancillary provisions, designated as new phases of Dominion criminal law which require a title to so interfere as basis of their application. For analogous reasons their Lordships think that s. 101 of the *British North America Act*, which enables the Parliament of Canada, notwithstanding anything in the *Act*, to provide for the establishment of any additional Courts for the better administration of the laws of Canada, cannot be read as enabling that Parliament to trench on provincial rights, such as the powers over property and civil rights in the Provinces exclusively conferred on their Legislatures. Full significance can be attached to the words in question without reading them as implying such capacity on the part of the Dominion Parliament. It is essential in such cases that the new judicial establishment should be a means to some end competent to the latter.

As their Lordships have already indicated, the jurisdiction attempted to be conferred on the new Board of Commerce appears to them to be *ultra vires* for the reasons now discussed. It implies a claim of title, in the cases of non-traders as well as of traders, to make orders prohibiting the accumulation of certain articles required for everyday life, and the withholding of such articles from sale at prices to be defined by the Board, whenever they exceed the amount of the material which appears to the Board to be required for domestic purposes or for the ordinary purposes of business. The Board is also given jurisdiction to regulate profits and dealings which may give rise to profit. The power sought to be given to the Board applies to articles produced for his own use by the householder himself, as well as to articles accumulated, not for the market but for the purposes of their own processes of manufacture by manufacturers. The Board is empowered to inquire into individual cases and to deal with them individually, and not merely as the result of applying principles to be laid down as of general application. This would cover such instances as those of coal mines and of local provincial undertakings for meeting provincial requirements of social life.

Legislation setting up a Board of Commerce with such powers appears to their Lordships to be beyond the powers conferred by s. 91. They find confirmation of this view in s. 41 of the *Board of Commerce Act*, which enables the Dominion Executive to review and alter the decisions of the Board. It has already been observed that circumstances are conceivable, such as those of war or famine, when the peace, order and good government of the Dominion might be imperilled under conditions so exceptional that they require legislation of a character in reality beyond anything provided for by the enumerated heads in either s. 92 or s. 91 itself. Such a case, if it were to arise would have to be considered closely before the conclusion could properly be reached that it was one which could not be treated as falling under any of the heads enumerated. Still, it is a conceivable case, and although great caution is required in referring to it, even in general terms, it ought not, in the view their Lordships take of the *British North America Act*, read as a whole, to be excluded from what is possible. For throughout the provisions of that Act there is apparent the recognition that subjects which would normally belong exclusively to a specifically assigned class of subject may, under different circumstances and in another aspect, assume a further significance. Such an aspect may conceivably become of paramount importance, and of dimensions that give rise to other aspects. This is a principle which, although recognised in earlier decisions, such as that of *Russell v. The Queen*, both here and in the Courts of Canada, has always been applied with reluctance, and its recognition as relevant can be justified only after scrutiny sufficient to render it clear that the circumstances are abnormal. In the case before them, however important it may seem to the Parliament of Canada, that some such policy as that adopted in the two *Acts* in question should be made general throughout Canada, their Lordships do not find any evidence that the standard of necessity referred to has been reached, or that the attainment of the end sought is practicable, in view of the distribution of legislative powers enacted by the *Constitution Act*, without the co-operation of the Provincial Legislatures. It may well be that it is within the power of the Dominion Parliament to call, for example, for statistical and other information which may be valuable for guidance in questions affecting Canada as a whole. Such information may be required before any power to regulate trade and commerce can be properly exercised, even where such power is construed in a fashion much narrower than that in which it was sought to interpret it in the argument at the Bar for the Attorney-General for Canada. But even this consideration affords no justification for interpreting the words of s. 91, sub-s. 2, in a fashion which would, as was said in the argument on the other side, make them confer capacity to regulate particular trades and businesses.

For the reasons now given their Lordships are of opinion that the first of the questions brought before them must be answered in the negative. As a consequence the second question does not arise.

6 Toronto Electric Commissioners v. Snider, 1925

In *Fort Frances Pulp and Power Co. v. Manitoba Free Press*,[1] a case decided in 1923, the Judicial Committee dealt with a challenge to the federal government's wartime regulations of the price and supply of newsprint that had extended into the postwar period. The regulations were upheld on the basis that the outbreak of a great war was one of those extraordinary circumstances that could justify the federal government, on the basis of its peace, order, and good government power, intervening in matters normally subject to provincial jurisdiction. Viscount Haldane, speaking for the Judicial Committee, said that there would have to be very clear evidence that the crisis had passed away to justify overturning the federal government's decision that exceptional measures were necessary.

In *Snider*, a major piece of national legislation, the *Industrial Disputes Investigation Act, 1907*, was cut down by the Privy Council's restrictive interpretation of the Dominion's peace, order, and good government power. The subject matter of this statute—the establishment of national conciliation services to avoid work stoppages during labour disputes in some of the country's most vital industries, such as mines, transportation and communication agencies, and public service utilities—did not meet Viscount Haldane's "emergency" test. Note that in this particular case the provisions of the *Act* were being applied not to an undertaking that was interprovincial or national in scope, but to a municipal transportation agency.

As a result of this decision, federal legislation providing for the settlement of labour disputes was confined to a much smaller field: industrial activities that are directly subject to federal jurisdiction, such as interprovincial railways or federal Crown agencies. National labour relations legislation limited to these areas was upheld in a reference to the Supreme Court of Canada in 1955.[2]

It appears from the *Snider* case that the Judicial Committee, under Viscount Haldane's leadership, had come to look upon Parliament's general power almost exclusively as an emergency power. The least plausible, but perhaps most entertaining, extension of this approach came in Viscount Haldane's attempt to reconcile the construction of the general power in earlier cases—in particular, in *Russell v. The Queen*—with the emergency doctrine. He was only able to do this by arguing that when the Privy Council decided *Russell v. The Queen* in 1882 it must have looked upon intemperance as a national menace serious enough to justify bringing the *Canada Temperance Act* under the peace, order, and good government clause. ～

---

1   [1923] A.C. 695.

2   *Reference re Validity of Industrial Relations and Disputes Investigation Act*, [1955] S.C.R. 529.

TORONTO ELECTRIC COMMISSIONERS v. SNIDER
[1925] A.C. 396, II Olmsted 394 (Privy Council)

Hearing: November 14, 18, 20, 21, 24, 1924; Judgment: January 20, 1925.

Present: Viscount Haldane, Lord Dunedin, Lord Atkinson, Lord Wrenbury, and Lord Salvesen.

The judgment of the Lordships was delivered by

VISCOUNT HALDANE: It is always with reluctance that their Lordships come to a conclusion adverse to the constitutional validity of any Canadian statute that has been before the public for years as having been validly enacted, but the duty incumbent on the Judicial Committee, now as always, is simply to interpret the *British North America Act* and to decide whether the statute in question has been within the competence of the Dominion Parliament under the terms of s. 91 of that *Act*. In this case the Judicial Committee have come to the conclusion that it was not. To that conclusion they find themselves compelled, alike by the structure of s. 91 and by the interpretation of its terms that has now been established by a series of authorities. They have had the advantage not only of hearing full arguments on the question, but of having before them judgments in the Courts of Ontario [[1924] 2 D.L.R. 761, [1924] 1 D.L.R. 101, 55 O.L.R. 454], from which this appeal to the Sovereign in Council came directly. Some of these judgments are against the view which they themselves take, others are in favour of it, but all of them are of a high degree of thoroughness and ability.

The particular exercise of legislative power with which their Lordships are concerned is contained in a well-known *Act*, passed by the Dominion Parliament in 1907, and known as the *Industrial Disputes Investigation Act*[, *1907* (Can.), c. 20]. As it now stands it has been amended by subsequent *Acts* [1910 (Can.), c. 29; 1918 (Can.), c. 27; 1920 (Can.), c. 29], but nothing turns, for the purposes of the question now raised, on any of the amendments that have been introduced.

The primary object of the *Act* was to enable industrial disputes between any employer in Canada and any one or more of his employees, as to "matters or things affecting or relating to work done or to be done by him or them, or as to the privileges, rights and duties of employers or employees (not involving any such violation thereof as constitutes an indictable offence)," relating to wages or remuneration, or hours of employment; sex, age or qualifications of employees, and the mode, terms and conditions of employment; the employment of children or any person, or classes of persons; claims as to whether preference of employment should be given to members of labour or other organizations; materials supplied or damage done to work; customs or usages, either general or in particular districts; and the interpretation of agreements.

Either of the parties to any such dispute was empowered by the *Act* to apply to the Minister of Labour for the Dominion for the appointment of a Board of Conciliation and Investigation, to which Board the dispute might be referred. The *Act* enabled the Governor in Council to appoint a Registrar of such Boards, with the duty of dealing with all applications for reference, bringing them to the notice of the Minister, and conducting the correspondence necessary for the constitution of the Boards. The Minister was empowered to establish a Board when he thought fit, and no question was to be raised in any Court interfering with his decision. Each Board was to consist of three members, to be appointed by the Minister, one on the recommendation of the employer, one on that of the employees, and the third, who was to be chairman, on the recommendation of the members so chosen. If any of them failed in this duty the Minister was to make the appointment. The department of the Minister of Labour was to provide the staffs required. The application for a Board was to be accompanied by a statutory declaration showing that, failing adjustment, a lock-out or strike would probably occur.

The Board so constituted was to make inquiry and to endeavour to effect a settlement. If the parties came to a settlement the Board was to embody it in a memorandum of recommendation which, if the parties had agreed to it in writing, was to have the effect of an award on a reference to arbitration or one made under the order of a Court of record. In such a case the recommendation could be constituted a Rule of Court and enforced accordingly. If no such settlement was arrived at, then the Board was to make a full report and a recommendation for settlement to the Minister, who was to make it public.

The Boards set up were given powers to summon and to enforce the attendance of witnesses, to administer oaths and to call for business books and other documents, and also to order into custody or subject to fine, in case of disobedience or contempt. The Board was also empowered to enter any premises where anything was taking place which was the subject of the reference and to inspect. This power was also enforceable by penalty. The parties were to be represented before the Board, but no counsel or solicitors were to appeal excepting by consent and subject to the sanction of the Board itself. The proceedings were normally to take place in public.

By s. 56 of the *Act*, in the event of a reference to a Board, it was made unlawful for the employer to lock-out or for the employees to strike on account of any dispute prior to or pending the reference, and any breach of this provision was made punishable by fine. By s. 57, employers and employed were both bound to give at least 30 days' notice of an intended change affecting conditions of employment with respect to wages or hours. In the event of a dispute arising over the intended change, until the dispute had been finally dealt with by a Board and a report had been made, neither employers nor employed were to alter the conditions, or lock-out or strike, or suspend employment or work, and the relationship of employer and employee was to continue uninterrupted. If, in the opinion of the Board, either party were to use this or any other provision of the *Act* for the purpose of unjustly maintaining a given condition of affairs through delay, and the Board were so to report to the Minister, such party was to be guilty of an offence and liable to penalties.

By s. 63(*a*), where a strike or lock-out had occurred or was threatened, the Minister was empowered, although neither of the parties to the dispute had applied for one, to set up a Board. He might also, under the next section, without any application, institute an inquiry.

Whatever else may be the effect of this enactment, it is clear that it is one which could have been passed, so far as any Province was concerned, by the Provincial Legislature under the powers conferred by s. 92 of the *British North America Act*. For its provisions were concerned directly with the civil rights of both employers and employed in the Province. It set up a Board of Inquiry which could summon them before it, administer to them oaths, call for their papers and enter their premises. It did no more than what a Provincial Legislature could have done under head 15 of s. 92, when it imposed punishment by way of penalty in order to enforce the new restrictions on civil rights. It interfered further with civil rights when, by s. 56, it suspended liberty to lock-out or strike during a reference to a Board. It does not appear that there is anything in the *Dominion Act* which could not have been enacted by the Legislature of Ontario, excepting one provision. The field for the operation of the *Act* was made the whole of Canada.

[Viscount Haldane then pointed out the similarities between the provisions of the *Ontario Trade Disputes Act, 1914*, and the Dominion's *Industrial Disputes Investigation Act, 1907*.]

The primary respondents in this appeal are the members of a Board of Conciliation appointed by the Dominion Minister of Labour under the *Act* first referred to. There was a dispute in 1923 between the appellants and a number of the men whom they employed, which dispute was referred to the first respondents, who proceeded to exercise the powers given by the *Dominion Act*. The appellants then commenced an action in the Supreme Court of Ontario for an injunction to restrain these proceedings, on the allegation that the *Dominion Act* was *ultra vires*. The Attorneys-General of Canada and of Ontario were notified and made parties as intervenants.

There was a motion for an interim injunction, which was heard by Orde, J. [(1923), 55 O.L.R. at 455], who, after argument, granted an injunction till the trial. The action was tried by Mowat, J. [[1924] 1 D.L.R. 101, 55 O.L.R. at 464], who intimated his dissent from the view of the *British North America Act* taken by Orde, J., who was co-ordinate in authority

with him, according to which view the *Dominion Act* was *ultra vires*. He, therefore, as he had power by the *Provincial Judicature Act* [R.S.O. 1914, c. 56] to do, directed the action to be heard by a Divisional Court, and it was ultimately heard by the Appellate Division of the Supreme Court of Ontario (Mulock, C.J., Magee, Hodgins, Ferguson and Smith, JJ.A.) [[1924] 2 D.L.R. 761, 55 O.L.R. 454]. The result was that by the majority (Hodgins, J.A., dissenting) the action of the appellants was dismissed.

The broad grounds of the judgment of the majority, which will be referred to later on, was that the *Dominion Act* was not a law relating to matters as to which s. 92 conferred exclusive jurisdiction, but was a law within the competence of the Dominion Parliament, inasmuch as it was directed to the regulation of trade and commerce throughout Canada, and to the protection of the national peace, order and good government, by reason of (*a*) confining, within limits, a dispute which might spread over all the Provinces; (*b*) informing the general public in Canada of the nature of the dispute; and (*c*) bringing public opinion to bear on it. The power of the Dominion Parliament to legislate in relation to criminal law, under head 27 of s. 91 was also considered to apply.

Before referring to these grounds of judgment their Lordships, without repeating at length what has been laid down by them in earlier cases, desire to refer briefly to the construction which, in their opinion, has been authoritatively put on ss. 91 and 92 by the more recent decisions of the Judicial Committee. The Dominion Parliament has, under the initial words of s. 91, a general power to make laws for Canada. But these laws are not to relate to the classes of subjects assigned to the Provinces by s. 92, unless their enactment falls under heads specifically assigned to the Dominion Parliament by the enumeration in s. 91. When there is a question as to which legislative authority has the power to pass an *Act*, the first question must therefore be whether the subject falls within s. 92. Even if it does, the further question must be answered, whether it falls also under an enumerated head in s. 91. If so, the Dominion has the paramount power of legislating in relation to it. If the subject falls within neither of the sets of enumerated heads, then the Dominion may have power to legislate under the general words at the beginning of s. 91.

Applying this principle, does the subject of the legislation in controversy fall fully within s. 92? For the reasons already given their Lordships think that it clearly does. If so, is the exclusive power *prima facie* conferred on the Province trenched on by any of the over-riding powers set out specifically in s. 91? It was, among other things, contended in the argument that the *Dominion Act* now challenged was authorized under head 27, "the Criminal Law, except the Constitution of Courts of Criminal Jurisdiction, but including the Procedure in Criminal Matters." It was further suggested in the argument that the power so conferred is aided by the power conferred on the Parliament of Canada to establish additional Courts for the better administration of the laws of Canada.

But their Lordships are unable to accede to these contentions.

[Viscount Haldane then advanced arguments and authorities rejecting the attempt to bring matters that would normally come under provincial jurisdiction under the criminal law power in section 91 merely by the insertion of penal sanctions in the legislation.]

Nor does the invocation of the specific power in s. 91 to regulate trade and commerce assist the Dominion contention. In *Citizens Ins. Co. v. Parsons* [(1881), 7 App. Cas. 90 at 112] it was laid down that the collocation of this head (No. 2 of s. 91), with classes of subjects enumerated of national and general concern, indicates that what was in the mind of the Imperial Legislature when this power was conferred in 1867 was regulation relating to general trade and commerce. Any other construction would, it was pointed out, have rendered unnecessary the specific mention of certain other heads dealing with banking, bills of exchange and promissory notes, as to which it had been significantly deemed necessary to insert a specific mention. The contracts of a particular trade or business could not, therefore, be dealt with by Dominion legislation so as to conflict with the powers assigned to the Provinces over property and civil rights relating to the regulation of trade and commerce. The Dominion power has a really definite effect when applied in aid of what the Dominion Government are specifically enabled to do independently of the general regulation of trade and commerce, for instance, in the creation of Dominion companies with power to trade throughout the whole of Canada. This was shown in the decision in *John Deere Plow Co. v. Wharton* [[1915] A.C. 330, 340]. The same thing is true of the exercise of an emergency power required as on the occasion of war, in the interest of Canada as a whole, a power which may operate outside the specific enumerations in both ss. 91 and 92. And it was observed in *Attorney General for Canada v. Attorney General for Alberta* [[1916] 1 A.C. 588, 596], in reference to attempted dominion legislation about insurance, that it must now be taken that the authority to legislate for the regulation of trade and commerce does not extend to the regulation, for instance, by a licensing system, of a particular trade in which Canadians would otherwise be free to engage in the Provinces [[1915] A.C. 330, 340]. It is, in their Lordships' opinion, now clear that, excepting so far as the power can be invoked in aid of capacity conferred independently under other words in s. 91, the power to regulate trade and commerce cannot be relied on as enabling the Dominion Parliament to regulate civil rights in the Provinces.

A more difficult question arises with reference to the initial words of s. 91, which enable the Parliament of Canada to make laws for the peace, order and good government of Canada in matters falling outside the provincial powers specifically conferred by s. 92. . . .

It appears to their Lordships that it is not now open to them to treat *Russell v. The Queen* [7 App. Cas. 829] as having established the general principle that the mere fact that Dominion legislation is for the general advantage of Canada or is such that it will meet a mere want which is felt throughout the Dominion, renders it competent if it cannot be brought within the heads enumerated specifically in s. 91. Unless this is so, if the subject-matter falls within any of the enumerated heads in s. 92, such legislation belongs exclusively to provincial competency. No doubt there may be cases arising out of some extraordinary peril to the national life of Canada, as a whole, such as the cases arising out of a war, where legislation is required of an order that passes beyond the heads of exclusive provincial competency. Such cases may be dealt with under the words at the commencement of s. 91, conferring general powers in relation to peace, order and good government, simply because such cases are not otherwise provided for. But instances of this, as was pointed out in the judgment in *Fort Frances Pulp & Paper Co. v. Manitoba Free Press* [[1923] A.C. 695] are highly exceptional. Their Lordships think that the decision in *Russell v. The Queen* can only be supported to-day, not on the footing of having laid down an interpretation, such as has sometimes been invoked of the general words at the beginning of s. 91, but on the assumption of the Board, apparently made at the time of deciding the case of *Russell v. The Queen*, that the evil of intemperance at that time amounted in Canada to one so great and so general that at least for the period it was a menace to the national life of Canada so serious and so pressing that the National Parliament was called on to intervene to protect the nation from disaster. An epidemic of pestilence might conceivably have been regarded as analogous. It is plain from the decision in the *Board of Commerce* case [[1922] 1 A.C. 191] that the evil of profiteering could not have been so invoked, for provincial powers, if exercised, were adequate to it. Their Lordships find it difficult to explain the decision in *Russell v. The Queen* as more than a decision of this order upon facts, considered to have been established at its date rather than upon general law. . . .

Their Lordships have examined the evidence produced at the trial. . . . They are of opinion that it does not prove any emergency putting the national life of Canada in unanticipated peril such as the Board which decided *Russell v. The Queen* may be considered to have had before their minds. . . .

7 In re Regulation and Control of Aeronautics in Canada, 1932

An important issue in any federal system is the way in which the federal state's capacity for participating in international agreements is affected by its internal division of powers between national and local governments. Basic to this question is the distinction between the power of entering into treaties with other states and the power of implementing such treaties through changes in the domestic legal system. In Canada, as in the United States and Australia, the federal government has the power to sign treaties and enter into international agreements on all subjects. It is only in connection with the implementation or enforcement of such international undertakings that the division of legislative powers might impose limitations on the national legislature.

In Canada the only direct reference that the *B.N.A. Act* makes to the field of foreign affairs is section 132, which grants to the national Parliament and government all the powers necessary for carrying out obligations that Canada assumes as a result of treaties concluded between the British Empire and foreign states. Clearly, when this section was drafted in 1867, there was no anticipation of a time when Canada would conduct her own external affairs. All that section 132 provided for was that the Canadian Parliament should have the power of enacting any legislation required in Canada for the implementation of treaties negotiated by the Imperial government. As long as Canada's relations with other states were carried on under the aegis of the Imperial government, the treaty-implementing power raised no serious constitutional problems. It appears that under section 132, Parliament's power of enforcing British Empire treaties could even override the normal division of powers in sections 91 and 92 of the *B.N.A. Act*. For instance, a few years before this *Aeronautics Reference*, both the Supreme Court and the Privy Council had ruled invalid a British Columbia *Act* that barred Japanese and Chinese from certain kinds of employment on the grounds that it violated an *Act* passed by the Dominion Parliament implementing a 1913 treaty made between Great Britain and Japan.[1] But in the 1920s and 1930s, as Canada came to assume the status of an independent nation, the question of treaty implementation emerged in an entirely different context: now that Canada entered into international agreements on her own as an autonomous nation and not as a subordinate part of the British Empire, would the national Parliament find adequate powers under the Constitution for implementing such treaties?

The *Aeronautics Reference* did not force the courts to squarely face this issue. The questions submitted by the federal government to the Supreme Court concerned the validity of the Dominion's *Aeronautics Act* and Air Regulations establishing a comprehensive system of control over aerial navigation in Canada. The main components of this scheme had been enacted with a view to performing Canada's obligations that arose out of a Convention ratified on behalf of the British Empire in 1922. Thus Lord Sankey had no difficulty in finding support in section 132 for the Dominion enactments. It should be noted, however, that the Canadian Supreme Court had not been willing to construe section 132 as granting to the Dominion *exclusively* the power of implementing British Empire treaties and was unanimous in giving a negative answer to the first question in the reference.

---

1 *In re Employment of Aliens* (1922), 63 S.C.R. 293 and *A.-G., B.C. v. A.-G. Canada*, [1924] A.C. 204.

Although Lord Sankey did not deal directly with the effect of Dominion autonomy on the treaty enforcement power, the concluding words of his judgment did point to one possible solution to this problem. He applied the national aspect test to the question, suggesting that the regulation of aerial navigation, the subject matter of an international agreement, was a matter of such general concern to the whole body politic of Canada that it could be brought under Parliament's power of making laws for the peace, order, and good government of Canada.

In a marked departure from the Privy Council's traditional style of constitutional interpretation, Lord Sankey's judgment includes reflections on the historic purposes that inspired the drafting of the *B.N.A. Act*. While acknowledging that one of those purposes was the preservation of the rights of minorities and describing the *B.N.A. Act* as "the charter of the Provinces," he emphasizes that its "real object" was to give the central government the "almost sovereign powers" required to provide legislation on matters of common concern to the whole country. Lord Sankey, who was appointed Lord Chancellor by the Labour government in 1929, introduced this creative approach to the *B.N.A. Act* in a decision in the *Persons* case, which reversed the Supreme Court of Canada and held that women were "persons" and hence eligible to serve in the Canadian Senate.

The 1932 *Radio Reference*[2] also dealt with Parliament's capacity to implement international agreements. However, this case concerned an agreement, the Radio Telegraph Convention, that Canada had signed in 1927 as an independent country, not as part of the British Empire. To implement the Convention, Parliament enacted Canada's first legislation regulating all aspects of radio communications. The Privy Council gave a positive answer to the question whether this legislation was within federal jurisdiction. It cited the power reserved for Parliament in section 92(10)(*a*) over telegraphs, and other works and undertakings connecting the provinces, as one basis for federal jurisdiction over radio broadcasting. But Viscount Dunedin's judgment focused primarily on Parliament's treaty-implementing power as the basis for federal jurisdiction. He stated that with the achievement of autonomy, Canada's obligations to foreign countries could no longer be construed in terms of the British Empire treaties envisaged in section 132. In his view, the implementation of Canadian treaties must be considered a new matter not explicitly provided for in sections 91 and 92 and therefore one that should be brought under Parliament's peace, order, and good government power. ⌐

---

2 *In re Regulation and Control of Radio Communication in Canada*, [1932] A.C. 304.

IN RE REGULATION AND CONTROL OF
AERONAUTICS IN CANADA
[1932] A.C. 54, II Olmsted 709 (Privy Council)

Hearing: July 10, 14, 16, 17, 20, 1931; Judgment: October 22, 1932.

Present: Lord Sankey L.C., Viscount Dunedin, Lord Atkin, Lord Russell of Killowen, and Lord Macmillan.

The judgment of their Lordships was delivered by

LORD SANKEY L.C.: This appeal raises an important question as between the Dominion and the Provinces of Canada regarding the right to control and regulate aeronautics, including the granting of certificates to persons to act as pilots, the inspection and licensing of aircraft, and the inspection and licensing of aerodromes and air-stations. The question is whether the subject is one on which the Dominion Parliament is alone competent to legislate, or whether it is in each Province so related to provincial property and civil rights and local matters as to exclude the Dominion from any (or from more than a very limited) jurisdiction in respect of it.

The Supreme Court of Canada has decided the question in its several branches adversely to the claims of the Dominion, and has held in effect that while the Dominion has a considerable field of jurisdiction in the matter under various heads of s. 91 of the *British North America Act, 1867,* there is also a local field of jurisdiction for the Provinces, and that the Dominion jurisdiction does not extend so far as to permit it to deal with the subject in the broad way in which it has attempted to deal with it in the legislation under consideration.

During the sittings of the Peace Conference in Paris at the close of the European War, a Convention relating to the regulation of aerial navigation, dated October 13, 1919, was drawn up by a Commission constituted by the Supreme Council of the Peace Conference. That Convention was signed by the representatives of the Allied and Associated Powers, including Canada, and was ratified by His Majesty on behalf of the British Empire on June 1, 1922. It is now in force between the British Empire and seventeen other States.

With a view to performing her obligations as part of the British Empire under this Convention, which was then in course of preparation, the Parliament of Canada enacted the *Air Board Act,* c. 11 of the *Statutes of Canada, 1919* (1st session), which, with an amendment thereto, was consolidated in the *Revised Statutes of Canada, 1927,* as c. 43, under the title of the *Aeronautics Act.* It is to be noted, however, that the *Act* does not by reason of its reproduction in the *Revised Statutes* take effect as a new law. The Governor-General in Council, on December 31, 1919, pursuant to the *Air Board Act,* issued detailed "Air Regulations" which, with certain amendments, are now in force. By the *National Defence Act, 1922,* the Minister of National Defence thereafter exercised the duties and functions of the Air Board.

By these statutes and the Air Regulations, and the amendments thereto, provision is made for the regulation and control in a general and comprehensive way of aerial navigation in Canada, and over the territorial waters thereof. In particular, s. 4 of the *Aeronautics Act* purports to give the Minister of National Defence a general power to regulate and control, subject to approval by the Governor in Council (with statutory force and under the sanction of penalties on summary conviction), aerial navigation over Canada and her territorial waters, including power to regulate the licensing of pilots, aircraft, aerodromes, and commercial services; the conditions under which aircraft may be used for goods, mails and passengers, or their carriage over any part of Canada; the prohibition (absolute or conditional) of flying over prescribed areas; aerial routes, and provision for safe and proper flying.

Their Lordships were told during the course of the argument that no provincial Legislature had passed any such legislation, but this had not prevented the progress of aeronautical development in the Provinces. It appears, for example, that in Ontario there has been established subject to these Regulations one of the most complete survey services in the Empire, and that it is working most harmoniously. Their Lordships are not aware that any practical difficulty has arisen in consequence of the general control of flying being in the hands of the Dominion, but at a conference at Ottawa between representatives of the Dominion Government and of the several provincial Governments in November, 1927, a question was raised by the representatives of the Province of Quebec as to the legislative authority of the Parliament of Canada to sanction regulations for the control of aerial navigation generally within Canada—at all events in their application to flying operations carried on within a Province—and it was agreed that the question so raised was proper to be determined by the Supreme Court of Canada. Thereupon four questions were referred by His Excellency, the Governor-General in Council, under an Order dated April 15, 1929, to the Supreme Court for hearing and consideration, pursuant to s. 55 of the *Supreme Court Act,* R.S.C. 1927, c. 35, touching the respective powers under the *British North America Act, 1867,* of the Parliament and Government of Canada and of the Legislatures of the Provinces in relation to the regulation and control of aeronautics in Canada.

The determination of these questions depends upon the true construction of ss. 91, 92 and 132 of the *British North America Act.* Section 132 provides as follows: "The Parliament and Government of Canada shall have all powers necessary or proper for performing the obligations of Canada or of any

Province thereof as part of the British Empire towards foreign countries arising under treaties between the Empire and such foreign countries." It is not necessary to set out at length the familiar ss. 91 and 92 which deal with the distribution of legislative powers. Sect. 91 tabulates the subjects to be dealt with by the Dominion, and s. 92 the subjects to be dealt with exclusively by the Provincial Legislatures, but it will not be forgotten that s. 91, in addition, authorizes The King by and with the advice and consent of the Senate and House of Commons of Canada to make laws for the peace, order and good government of Canada in relation to all matters not coming within the classes of subjects by this *Act* assigned exclusively to the Legislatures of the Provinces, and further provides that any matter coming within any of the classes of subjects enumerated in the section shall not be deemed to come within the classes of matters of a local and private nature comprised in the enumeration of classes of subjects assigned by s. 92 exclusively to the Legislatures of the provinces.

The four questions addressed to the Court are as follows:

1. Have the Parliament and Government of Canada exclusive legislative and executive authority for performing the obligations of Canada, or of any Province thereof, under the Convention entitled "Convention relating to the Regulation of Aerial Navigation?"
2. Is legislation of the Parliament of Canada providing for the regulation and control of aeronautics generally within Canada, including flying operations carried on entirely within the limits of a Province, necessary or proper for performing the obligations of Canada, or of any Province thereof, under the Convention aforementioned within the meaning of s. 132 of the *British North America Act, 1867*?
3. Has the Parliament of Canada legislative authority to enact, in whole or in part, the provisions of s. 4 of the *Aeronautics Act*, R.S.C. 1927, c. 3?
4. Has the Parliament of Canada legislative authority to sanction the making and enforcement, in whole or in part, of the regulations contained in the Air Regulations, 1920, respecting: (*a*) The granting of certificates or licences authorizing persons to act as pilots, navigators, engineers or inspectors of aircraft and the suspension or revocation of such licences; (*b*) The regulation, identification, inspection, certification, and licensing of all aircraft; and (*c*) The licensing, inspection and regulation of all aerodromes and air stations? ...

To question 1, and retaining the word "exclusive," the Board's answer is "Yes."

[The Judicial Committee was not asked to review the Supreme Court's answer to question 2.]

To question 3, their answer is also "Yes."
To question 4, their answer is again "Yes."

Before discussing the several questions individually, it is desirable to make some general observations upon ss. 91 and 92, and 132.

With regard to ss. 91 and 92, the cases which have been decided on the provisions of these sections are legion. Many inquests have been held upon them, and many great lawyers have from time to time dissected them.

Under our system, decided cases effectively construe the words of an Act of Parliament and establish principles and rules whereby its scope and effect may be interpreted. But there is always a danger that in the course of this process the terms of the statute may come to be unduly extended and attention may be diverted from what has been enacted to what has been judicially said about the enactment.

To borrow an analogy; there may be a range of sixty colours, each of which is so little different from its neighbour that it is difficult to make any distinction between the two, and yet at the one end of the range the colour may be white, and at the other end of the range black. Great care must therefore be taken to consider each decision in the light of the circumstances of the case in view of which it was pronounced, especially in the interpretation of an Act such as the *British North America Act*, which was a great constitutional charter, and not to allow general phrases to obscure the underlying object of the *Act*, which was to establish a system of government upon essentially federal principles. Useful as decided cases are, it is always advisable to get back to the words of the *Act* itself and to remember the object with which it was passed.

Inasmuch as the *Act* embodies a compromise under which the original Provinces agreed to federate, it is important to keep in mind that the preservation of the rights of minorities was a condition on which such minorities entered into the federation, and the foundation upon which the whole structure was subsequently erected. The process of interpretation as the years go on ought not to be allowed to dim or to whittle down the provisions of the original contract upon which the federation was founded, nor is it legitimate that any judicial construction of the provisions of ss. 91 and 92 should impose a new and different contract upon the federating bodies.

But while the Courts should be jealous in upholding the Charter of the Provinces as enacted in s. 92 it must no less be borne in mind that the real object of the *Act* was to give the central Government those high functions and almost sovereign powers by which uniformity of legislation might be secured on all questions which were of common concern to all the Provinces as members of a constituent whole.

While the decisions which the Board has pronounced in the many constitutional cases which have come under their consideration from the Dominion must each be regarded in the light of the facts involved in it, their Lordships recognize that there has grown up round the *British North America Act* a body of precedents of high authority and value as guides to its interpretation and application. The useful and essential task of taking stock of this body of authority and reviewing it in relation to the original text has been undertaken by this Board from time to time and notably, for example, in the cases of *Attorney-General for Ontario v. Attorney-General for Canada* [[1896] A.C. 348]; *Attorney-General for Canada v. Attorney-General for Ontario* [[1898] A.C. 700]; *Montreal v. Montreal Street R. Co.* [[1912] A.C. 333, (1911), 1 D.L.R. 681]; and in the same year, *Attorney-General for Ontario, Quebec, etc. v. Attorney-General for Canada* [[1912] A.C. 571, (1911), 3 D.L.R. 509]. In all these four cases the scope of the two sections was carefully considered, but it is not necessary to cite them at length because so recently as last year this Board reviewed them in the case of *Attorney-General for Canada v. Attorney-General for British Columbia* [[1930] A.C. 111, 118, 1 D.L.R. 194], and laid down four propositions relative to the legislative competence of Canada and the Provinces respectively as established by the decisions of the Judicial Committee. These propositions are as follows [pp. 196-97]:

1. The legislation of the Parliament of the Dominion, so long as it strictly relates to subjects of legislation expressly enumerated in s. 91, is of paramount authority, even though it trenches upon matters assigned to the provincial legislature by s. 92.
2. The general power of legislation conferred upon the Parliament of the Dominion by s. 91 of the *Act* in supplement of the power to legislate upon the subjects expressly enumerated must be strictly confined to such matters as are unquestionably of national interest and importance, and must not trench on any of the subjects enumerated in s. 92, as within the scope of provincial legislation, unless these matters have attained such dimensions as to affect the body politic of the Dominion.
3. It is within the competence of the Dominion Parliament to provide for matters which though otherwise within the legislative competence of the Provincial legislature, are necessarily incidental to effective legislation by the Parliament of the Dominion upon a subject of legislation expressly enumerated in s. 91.
4. There can be a domain in which Provincial and Dominion legislation may overlap, in which case, neither legislation will be *ultra vires* if the field is clear, but if the field is not clear and the two regulations meet, the Dominion legislation must prevail.

Their Lordships particularly emphasize the second and third of these categories, and refer to the remarks made by Lord Watson in *Attorney-General for Ontario v. Attorney-General for Canada* [*supra* at 361], where he says: "Their Lordships do not doubt that some matters, in their origin local and provincial, might attain such dimensions as to affect the body politic of the Dominion and to justify the Canadian Parliament in passing laws for their regulation or abolition in the interests of the dominion but great caution must be observed in distinguishing between that which is local and provincial and therefore within the jurisdiction of the Provincial Legislatures and that which has ceased to be merely local or provincial, and has become matter of national concern in such sense as to bring it within the jurisdiction of the Parliament of Canada." Further, their Lordships desire to refer to the case of *Fort Frances Pulp & Paper Co. v. Manitoba Free Press Co.* [[1923] A.C. 695, 704, 706, 3 D.L.R. 629], where it was held that the Canadian *War Measures Act, 1914,* and certain Orders in Council made thereunder during the War were *intra vires* of the Dominion. Lord Haldane there said at p. 631: "The general control of property and civil rights for normal purposes remains with the Provincial Legislatures. But questions may arise by reason of the special circumstances of the national emergency which concern nothing short of the peace, order and good government of Canada as a whole." These remarks must again be taken subject to the situation then prevailing, for he adds on p. 635: "It may be that it has become clear that the crisis which arose is wholly at an end, and that there is no justification for the continued exercise of an exceptional interference which becomes *ultra vires* when it is no longer called for. In such a case, the law as laid down for the distribution of powers in the ruling instrument would have to be invoked."

It is obvious, therefore, that there may be cases of emergency where the Dominion is empowered to act for the whole. There may also be cases where the Dominion is entitled to speak for the whole, and this not because of any judicial interpretation of ss. 91 and 92, but by reason of the plain terms of s. 132, where Canada as a whole, having undertaken an obligation, is given the power necessary and proper for performing such obligation.

During the course of the argument, learned counsel on either side endeavoured respectively to bring the subject of aeronautics within s. 91 or s. 92. Thus, the appellant referred to s. 91, item 2 (the regulation of trade and commerce; item 5 (postal services); item 9 (beacons); item 10 (navigation and shipping). Their Lordships do not think that aeronautics can be brought within the subject of navigation and shipping, although undoubtedly to a large extent, and in some respects, it might be brought under the regulation of trade and commerce, or the postal services. On the other hand, the respondents contended that aeronautics as a class of subject came within item 13 of s. 92 (property and civil rights in the Provinces) or item 16 (generally all matters of a merely local and private nature in the Provinces). Their Lordships do not think that aeronautics is a class of subject within property and civil rights in the Provinces, although here again, ingenious arguments may show that some small part of it might be so included.

In their Lordships' view, transport as a subject is dealt with in certain branches both of s. 91 and of s. 92, but neither of those sections deals specially with that branch of transport which is concerned with aeronautics.

Their Lordships are of opinion that it is proper to take a broader view of the matter rather than to rely on forced analogies or piecemeal analysis. They consider the governing section to be s. 132, which gives to the Parliament and Government of Canada all powers necessary and proper for performing the obligations towards foreign countries arising under treaties between the Empire and such foreign countries. As far as s. 132 is concerned, their Lordships are not aware of any decided case which is of assistance on the present occasion. It will be observed, however, from the very definite words of the section, that it is the Parliament and Government of Canada who are to have all powers necessary or proper for performing the obligations of Canada, or any Province thereof. It would therefore appear to follow that any Convention of the character under discussion necessitates Dominion legislation in order that it may be carried out. It is only necessary to look at the Convention itself to see what wide powers are necessary for performing the obligations arising thereunder. By article 1 the high contracting parties recognize that every Power (which includes Canada) has complete and exclusive sovereignty over the air space above its territory; by article 40, the British Dominions and India are deemed to be States for the purpose of the Convention.

[Lord Sankey then listed the principal obligations undertaken by Canada as part of the British Empire under the stipulations of the Convention.]

It is therefore obvious that the Dominion Parliament, in order duly and fully to "perform the obligations of Canada or of any Province thereof" under the Convention, must make provision for a great variety of subjects. Indeed, the terms of the Convention include almost every conceivable matter relating to aerial navigation, and we think that the Dominion Parliament not only has the right, but also the obligation, to provide by statute and by regulation that the terms of the Convention shall be duly carried out. With regard to some of them, no doubt, it would appear to be clear that the Dominion has power to legislate, for example, under s. 91, item 2, for the regulation of trade and commerce, and under item 5 for the postal services, but it is not necessary for the Dominion to piece together its powers under s. 91 in an endeavour to render them co-extensive with its duty under the Convention when s. 132 confers upon it full power to do all that is legislatively necessary for the purpose.

To sum up, having regard (*a*) to the terms of s. 132; (*b*) to the terms of the Convention which covers almost every conceivable matter relating to aerial navigation; and (*c*) to the fact that further legislative powers in relation to aerial navigation reside in the Parliament of Canada by virtue of s. 91, items 2, 5 and 7, it would appear that substantially the whole field of legislation in regard to aerial navigation belongs to the Dominion. There may be a small portion of the field which is not by virtue of specific words in the *British North America Act* vested in the Dominion; but neither is it vested by specific words in the Provinces. As to such small portion it appears to the Board that it must necessarily belong to the Dominion under its power to make laws for the peace, order and good government of Canada. Further their Lordships are influenced by the facts that the subject of aerial navigation and the fulfilment of Canadian obligations under s. 132 are matters of national interest and importance; and that aerial navigation is a class of subject which has attained such dimensions as to affect the body politic of the Dominion.

For these reasons their Lordships have come to the conclusion that it was competent for the Parliament of Canada to pass the *Act* and authorize the Regulations in question, and that questions 1, 3 and 4, which alone they are asked to answer, should be answered in the affirmative.

Attorney General of Canada v. Attorney General of Ontario (Employment and Social Insurance Act Reference), 1937

The *Employment and Social Insurance Act, 1935,* which the Privy Council ruled *ultra vires* in this case, was the first measure of the Conservative government's social reform program (the so-called New Deal legislation), which was introduced by Prime Minister R.B. Bennett at the beginning of the 1935 session of Parliament. The Liberal opposition under Mackenzie King's leadership, while approving the principle of the social legislation, contended that it was beyond Parliament's jurisdiction. Accordingly, following the defeat of the Bennett government in the general election of October 1935, the King administration referred the question of the validity of eight of the reform measures of the 1935 session to the Supreme Court of Canada and then, on appeal, to the Judicial Committee of the Privy Council. While the adversaries in all these reference cases represented the two levels of government, in some of the cases provincial representatives supported the validity of the federal legislation. In this case, for instance, the province of Ontario supported the federal government's side of the case, while New Brunswick alone maintained the other side.

The Privy Council's decisions in these cases were a grave disappointment to those in Canada who had hoped that the powers assigned by the Constitution to the central government would be sufficiently broad to enable it to deal effectively with the nationwide consequences of a severe economic depression. The invalidation of five of the eight federal statutes submitted to the courts in this series of reference cases dashed the hopes raised by the Privy Council's recent decisions in the *Aeronautics* and *Radio* references, which had pointed to a much broader construction of the Dominion's legislative capacities. Among those who wished to strengthen the powers of the central government, the immediate response was to turn to formal amendment of the *B.N.A. Act* to overcome what was regarded as the inappropriate division of powers being shaped by judicial review. The only real fruit of this renewal of interest in constitutional amendment was the amendment secured in 1940, which, with the unanimous consent of the provinces, assigned unemployment insurance to the exclusive jurisdiction of the federal Parliament.

Mr. Louis St. Laurent, who acted as legal counsel for the Dominion in this case, admitted that a scheme of unemployment insurance designed to have permanent effect could not be justified on emergency grounds. Instead, the case for bringing the legislation under the peace, order, and good government power rested on both the residual aspect of that power and its application to matters of national concern. Council for the Dominion argued that the legislation attacked a problem that had not existed when the *B.N.A. Act* was drawn up and hence was not specifically provided for in any of the enumerated heads of sections 91 and 92. Further, they urged that the problem of unemployment was one that threatened the well-being of the whole Dominion. Lord Atkin, speaking for the Judicial Committee, did not accept this reasoning. His reference to the lack of any special emergency sufficient to justify invoking the federal government's general power suggests an absorption of the residual and national importance phases of that power in the emergency power approach.

Lord Atkin also rejected the federal spending power as a constitutional basis for the unemployment insurance scheme. In doing so, he indicated one significant constitutional limit on the federal government's power to spend federal revenues. A federal spending program cannot take the form of a regulatory scheme that in pith and substance constitutes a regulation of civil rights in the province.

While the legislation considered in this case and in the two companion cases that follow was found unconstitutional, this was not the fate of all the New Deal legislation referred to the courts. A section of the *Criminal Code* prohibiting unfair competition, the *Farmers' Creditors Arrangements Act* reducing the mortgage liabilities of insolvent farmers, and legislation establishing a national trademark for products conforming to the requirements of government-established "Canada Standards" all survived judicial review. In upholding the last piece of legislation, the Judicial Committee reversed the Supreme Court of Canada and showed that some use could be made of the federal trade and commerce power as a basis for general regulations of trade affecting the whole Dominion. ⌒

ATTORNEY GENERAL OF CANADA v. ATTORNEY GENERAL OF ONTARIO
[1937] A.C. 355, III Olmsted 207 (Privy Council)

Hearing: November 5, 6, 9, 1936; Judgment: January 28, 1937.

Present: Lord Atkin, Lord Thankerton, Lord Macmillan, Lord Wright M.R., and Sir Sidney Rowlatt.

The judgment of their Lordships was delivered by

LORD ATKIN: This is an appeal from the judgment of the Supreme Court, delivered on June 17, 1936, in the matter of a reference by the Governor-General in Council dated November 5, 1935, asking whether the *Employment and Social Insurance Act, 1935* [(Can.), c. 38], was *ultra vires* of the Parliament of Canada. The majority of the Supreme Court, Rinfret, Cannon, Crocket and Kerwin, JJ., answered the question in the affirmative, the Chief Justice and Davis, J., dissenting. The *Act* in its preamble recited art. 23 of the *Treaty of Peace*, by which in the covenant of the League of Nations the members of the league agreed that they would endeavour to maintain fair and humane conditions of labour (omitting, however, in the recital that this agreement was subject to and in accordance with the provisions of international conventions existing or hereafter to be agreed), and art. 427 of the said treaty, by which it was declared that the well-being, physical, moral and intellectual, of industrial wage earners, was of supreme international importance. It then recited that it was desirable to discharge the obligations to Canadian labour assumed under the provisions of the said treaty; and that it was essential for the peace, order and good government of Canada to provide for a national employment service and insurance against unemployment, etc. It consists of five parts, Employment and Social Insurance Commission, (ss. 4-9), Employment Service (ss. 10-14), Unemployment Insurance (ss. 15-38), National Health, (ss. 39-41) and General (ss. 42-48). In substance the *Act* provides for a system of compulsory unemployment insurance.

Part I sets up a commission charged with administering the *Act* and obtaining information and making proposals to the Governor in Council for making provision for the assistance of persons during unemployment who would not be entitled to unemployment insurance benefit under Part III. Part II provides for the organization by the commission of employment offices similar to the labour exchanges in the United Kingdom. Part III provides for unemployment insurance, while Part IV merely provides that the commission shall co-operate with other authorities in the Dominion or Provinces and shall collect information concerning any plan for providing medical care or compensation in cases of ill health. Part V provides for regulations and reports. There are three schedules. The first defines employment within the meaning of Part III and excepted employments which include employments in agriculture and forestry, in fishing, and in lumbering and logging. The second enacts the weekly rates of contribution and rules as to payment and recovery of contributions paid by employers on behalf of employed persons. The third enacts the rates of unemployment benefit and supplementary provisions concerning the payment of unemployment benefit.

The substance of the *Act* is contained in the sections constituting Part III. They set up a now familiar system of unemployment insurance under which persons engaged in employment as defined in the *Act* are insured against unemployment. The funds required for making the necessary payments are to be provided partly from money provided by Parliament, partly from contributions by employed persons and partly from contributions by the employers of those persons. The two sets of contributions are to be paid by revenue stamps. Every employed person and every employer is to be liable to pay contributions in accordance with the provisions of the second schedule, the employer being liable to pay both contributions in the first instance, recovering the employed person's share by deduction from his wages, or if necessary in certain cases by action.

There can be no doubt that *prima facie* provisions as to insurance of this kind, especially where they affect the contract of employment, fall within the class of property and civil rights in the Province, and would be within the exclusive competence of the Provincial Legislature. It was sought, however, to justify the validity of Dominion legislation on grounds which their Lordships on consideration feel compelled to reject. Counsel did not seek to uphold the legislation on the ground of the treaty-making power. There was no treaty or labour convention which imposed any obligation upon Canada to pass this legislation and the decision on this question in the reference on the three labour *Acts* [reported below in case 9] does not apply. A strong appeal, however, was made on the ground of the special importance of unemployment insurance in Canada at the time of and for some time previous to the passing of the *Act*. On this point it becomes unnecessary to do more than to refer to the judgment of this Board in the reference on the three labour *Acts*, and to the judgment of the Chief Justice in the *Natural Products Marketing Act* which, on this matter, the Board have approved and adopted. It is sufficient to say that the present *Act* does not purport to deal with any special emergency. It founds itself in the preamble on general world-wide conditions referred to in the Treaty of Peace: it is an *Act* whose operation is intended to be permanent: and there is agreement between all the members of the Supreme Court that it could not be supported upon the suggested existence of any special emergency. Their Lordships find themselves unable to differ from this view.

It only remains to deal with the argument which found favour with the Chief Justice and Davis, J., that the legislation can be supported under the enumerated heads, 1 and 3 of s. 91 of the *British North America Act, 1867*: (1). The public debt and property, namely, (3). The raising of money by any mode or system of taxation. Shortly stated the argument is that the obligation imposed upon employers and persons employed is a mode of taxation: that the money so raised becomes public property and that the Dominion have then complete legislative authority to direct that the money so raised, together with assistance from money raised by general taxation, shall be applied in forming an insurance fund and generally in accordance with the provisions of the *Act*.

That the Dominion may impose taxation for the purpose of creating a fund for special purposes and may apply that fund for making contributions in the public interest to individuals, corporations or public authorities could not as a general proposition be denied. Whether in such an Act as the present, compulsion applied to an employed person to make a contribution to an insurance fund out of which he will receive benefit for a period proportionate to the number of his contributions is in fact taxation, it is not necessary finally to decide. It might seem difficult to discern how it differs from a form of compulsory insurance, or what the difference is between a statutory obligation to pay insurance premiums to the state, or to an insurance company. But assuming that the Dominion has collected by means of taxation a fund, it by no means follows that any legislation which disposes of it is necessarily within Dominion competence.

It may still be legislation affecting the classes of subjects enumerated in s. 92, and, if so, would be *ultra vires*. In other words, Dominion legislation, even though it deals with Dominion property, may yet be so framed as to invade civil rights within the Province: or encroach upon the classes of subjects which are reserved to Provincial competence. It is not necessary that it should be a colourable device, or a pretence. If on the true view of the legislation it is found that in reality in pith and substance the legislation invades civil rights within the Province or in respect of other classes of subjects otherwise encroaches upon the provincial field, the legislation will be invalid. To hold otherwise would afford the Dominion an easy passage into the Provincial domain. In the present case their Lordships agree with the majority of the Supreme Court in holding that in pith and substance this *Act* is an insurance *Act* affecting the civil rights of employers and employed in each Province, and as such is invalid. The other parts of the *Act* are so inextricably mixed up with the insurance provisions of Part III that it is impossible to sever them. It seems obvious also that in its truncated form, apart from Part III, the *Act* would never have come into existence. It follows that the whole *Act* must be pronounced *ultra vires*, and in accordance with the view of the majority of the Supreme Court their Lordships will humbly advise His Majesty that this appeal be dismissed.

Attorney General of Canada v. Attorney General of Ontario (Labour Conventions Case), 1937

The Canadian government first faced the question of whether it could "invade" provincial jurisdiction in order to carry out international labour conventions when Canada became a member of the International Labour Organization after World War I. At that time, it took the cautious course and, following the advice of the federal Department of Justice, left the implementation of five of the six conventions adopted at the first session of the International Labour Conference to the provinces. This procedure was approved by the Supreme Court in 1925 when it was asked to review the proper method of implementing Canada's obligations as a participant in the International Labour Conference.[1] But in 1935, the Bennett government, emboldened by the outcome of the *Radio* case, tried to base an integral part of its New Deal program on the treaty-implementing capacity of Parliament. Early in the 1935 session, Parliament ratified Draft Conventions of the International Labour Organization dealing with hours of work, weekly rest, and minimum wages and, later in the session, to give effect to these Conventions it passed the three *Acts* referred to in this case.

The Privy Council refused to accept the treaty-implementing power as a constitutional support for the impugned labour legislation. Section 132 was ruled out on the ground that even though the Treaty of Versailles was without question a British Empire treaty it had not obliged Canada to accede to the Conventions authorized by the labour part of the treaty. The Canadian government had acted on its own in deciding to ratify these Conventions. Lord Atkin, who delivered the judgment, also denied the interpretation of the *Radio* case that would justify characterizing the enforcement of independently negotiated treaties as a novel class of legislative matter and therefore subject to the Dominion's residual power. The regulation of radio communications as a new subject might rightly be regarded as falling under the residual power, but legislation implementing Canadian treaties was not to be treated in the same way. On the contrary, the proper authority for enforcing a Canadian treaty would depend entirely on the subject matter of the treaty. If the treaty dealt with a subject that was normally under section 92, then legislation giving effect to it could be enacted only by the provincial legislatures.

Lord Atkin's judgment dealt a lethal blow to the doctrine that the national Parliament had a plenary power of implementing treaties. The federal legislature emerged from this decision subject to far more severe limitations on its power of performing international obligations than the federal constitutions of the United States or Australia impose on their central legislatures. Lord Atkin's approach in essence rendered the power of enforcing treaties thoroughly subject to the general division of powers in Canadian federalism. In effect, this means that Canada cannot become a party to an international agreement that requires legislative action beyond the ambit of section 91 unless the prior approval of the provinces is first secured. While this has not prevented the Canadian government from participating in such important and extensive international undertakings as the United Nations Charter, still, when an international arrangement such as the Universal Declaration of Rights has

---

1   *In re Legislative Jurisdiction over Hours of Labour*, [1925] S.C.R. 505.

referred to matters that clearly come under section 92 of the *B.N.A. Act*, Canadian representatives have had to set appropriate qualifications to Canadian participation.

Most of those who have studied this area of Canadian constitutional law have found it difficult, if not impossible, to square Lord Atkin's judgment in the *Labour Conventions* case with Viscount Dunedin's in the *Radio* case. Certainly the fact that the composition of the Judicial Committee was completely different in the two cases did not contribute to continuity. Further, there is some evidence of a serious cleavage within the Judicial Committee on this case: In a speech published in 1955, Lord Wright, who had been a member of the Board that decided the *Labour Conventions* case, in a rare disclosure of dissent within the Privy Council, reported that there had been opposition to Lord Atkin's treatment of the treaty-implementing power.[2] ∼

---

2   (1955) 33 *Canadian Bar Review* 1123.

ATTORNEY GENERAL OF CANADA v. ATTORNEY GENERAL OF ONTARIO
[1937] A.C. 327, III Olmsted 180 (Privy Council)

Hearing: November 13, 16, 17, 19, 20, 23, 1936; Judgment: January 28, 1937.

Present: Lord Atkin, Lord Thankerton, Lord Macmillan, Lord Wright M.R., and Sir Sidney Rowlatt.

The judgment of the Lordships was delivered by

LORD ATKIN: This is one of a series of cases brought before this Board on appeal from the Supreme Court of Canada on references by the Governor-General in Council to determine the validity of certain statutes of Canada passed in 1934 and 1935. Their Lordships will deal with all the appeals in due course, but they propose to begin with that involving the *Weekly Rest in Industrial Undertakings Act*, the *Minimum Wages Act*, and the *Limitation of Hours of Work Act*, both because of the exceptional importance of the issues involved, and because it affords them an opportunity of stating their opinion upon some matters which also arise in the other cases. At the outset they desire to express their appreciation of the valuable assistance which they have received from counsel, both for the Dominion and for the respective Provinces. No pains have been spared to place before the Board all the material both as to the facts and the law which could assist the Board in their responsible task. The arguments were cogent and not diffuse. The statutes in question in the present case were passed, as their titles recite, in accordance with conventions adopted by the International Labour Organization of the League of Nations in accordance with the Labour Part of the Treaty of Versailles of June 28, 1919. It was admitted at the bar that each statute affects property and civil rights

within each Province; and that it was for the Dominion to establish that nevertheless the statute was validly enacted under the legislative powers given to the Dominion Parliament by the *British North America Act, 1867*. It was argued for the Dominion that the legislation could be justified either: (1) under s. 132 of the *British North America Act* as being legislation "necessary or proper for performing the Obligations of Canada or any Province thereof, as part of the British Empire, towards foreign countries, arising under treaties between the Empire and such foreign countries," or (2) under the general powers, sometimes called the residuary powers, given by s. 91 to the Dominion Parliament to make Laws for the peace, order and good government of Canada in relation to all matters not coming within the classes of subjects by this *Act* assigned exclusively to the Legislatures of the Provinces.

The Provinces contended:

As to (1)—(*a*) That the obligations, if any, of Canada under the labour conventions did not arise under a treaty or treaties made between the Empire and foreign countries: and that therefore s. 132 did not apply. (*b*) That the Canadian Government had no executive authority to make any such treaty as was alleged. (*c*) That the obligations said to have been incurred and the legislative powers sought to be exercised by the Dominion were not incurred and exercised in accordance with the terms of the Treaty of Versailles.

As to (2) that if the Dominion had to rely only upon the powers given by s. 91, the legislation was invalid, for it related to matters which came within the classes of subjects exclusively assigned to the Legislatures of the Provinces, *viz.*, Property and Civil Rights in the Province.

In order to indicate the opinion of the Board upon these contentions it will be necessary briefly to refer to the Treaty of Versailles, Part XIII, Labour: to the procedure prescribed by it for bringing into existence labour conventions: and to the procedure adopted in Canada in respect thereto. The Treaty of Peace signed at Versailles on June 28, 1919, was made between the Allied and Associated Powers of the one part and Germany of the other part. The British Empire was described as one of the Principal Allied and Associated Powers, and the high contracting party for the British Empire was His Majesty the King, represented generally by certain of his English Ministers and represented for the Dominion of Canada by the Minister of Justice and the Minister of Customs, and for the other Dominions by their respective Ministers. The treaty began with Part I of the covenant of the League of Nations by which the high contracting parties agreed to the covenant, the effect of which was that the signatories named in the annex to the covenant were to be the original members of the League of Nations. The Dominion of Canada was one of the signatories and so became an original member of the League. The treaty then proceeds in a succession of parts to deal with the agreed terms of peace, stipulations of course entered into not between members of the League but between the high contracting parties, i.e., for the British Empire His Majesty the King. Part XIII, entitled "Labour," after reciting that the object of the League of Nations is the establishment of universal peace, and such a peace can only be established if it is based on social justice and that social justice requires the improvement of conditions of labour throughout the world, provides that the high contracting parties agree to the establishment of a permanent organization for the promotion of the desired objects and that the original and future members of the League of Nations shall be the members of this organization. The organization is to consist of a general conference of representatives of the members and an International Labour Office. After providing for meetings of the conference and for its procedure the treaty contains arts. 405 and 407:

[Lord Atkin then set out the two articles.]

In accordance with the provisions of Part XIII, draft conventions were adopted by general conferences of the International Labour Organization as follows:

October 29—November 29, 1919, Conference.
 Draft Convention limiting the hours of work in industrial undertakings.

October 25—November 19, 1921, Conference.
 Draft Convention concerning the application of the weekly rest in industrial undertakings.

May 30—June 16, 1928, Conference.
 Draft Convention concerning the creation of minimum wage-fixing machinery.

Each of the conventions included stipulations purporting to bind members who ratified it to carry out its provisions, the first two conventions by named dates, viz., July 1, 1921, and January 1, 1924, respectively. These three conventions were in fact ratified by the Dominion of Canada, Hours of Work on March 1, 1935, Weekly Rest on March 1, 1935, and Minimum Wages on April 12, 1935.

In each case in February and March, 1935, there had been passed resolutions of the Senate and House of Commons of Canada approving them. The ratification was approved by order of the Governor-General in Council, was recorded in an instrument of ratification executed by the Secretary of State for External Affairs for Canada, Mr. Bennett, and was duly communicated to the Secretary-General of the League of Nations. The statutes, which in substance give effect to the draft conventions, were passed by the Parliament of Canada and received the Royal Assent, "Hours of Work," on July 5, 1935, to come into force three months after assent; "Weekly Rest," on April 4, 1935, to come into force three months after assent; "Minimum Wage," on July 28, 1935, to come into force, so far as the convention provisions are concerned, when proclaimed by the Governor in Council, an event which has not yet happened.

In 1925 the Governor-General in Council referred to the Supreme Court questions as to the obligations of Canada under the provisions of Part XIII of the Treaty of Versailles and as to whether the Legislatures of the Provinces were the authorities within whose competence the subject-matter of the conventions lay. The answers to the reference, which are to be found in *In Re Legislative Jurisdiction over Hours of Labour* [[1925] Can. S.C.R. 505, 3 D.L.R. 1114], were that the Legislatures of the Provinces were the competent authorities to deal with the subject-matter, save in respect of Dominion servants, and the parts of Canada not within the boundaries of any Province: and that the obligation of Canada was to bring the convention before the Lieutenant-Governor of each Province to enable him to bring the appropriate subject-matter before the Legislature of his Province, and to bring the matter before the Dominion Parliament in respect of so much of the convention as was within their competence. This advice appears to have been accepted, and no further steps were taken until those which took place as stated above in 1935.

Their Lordships, having stated the circumstances leading up to the reference in this case, are now in a position to discuss the contentions of the parties which were summarized earlier in this judgment. It will be essential to keep in mind the distinction between (1) the formation, and (2) the performance, of the obligations constituted by a treaty, using that word as comprising any agreement between two or more sovereign States. Within the British Empire there is a well-established rule that the making of a treaty is an executive act, while the performance of its obligations, if they entail alteration of the existing domestic law, requires legislative action. Unlike some other countries, the stipulations of a treaty duly ratified do not within the Empire, by virtue of the treaty alone, have the force of law. If the national executive, the government of the day, decide to incur the obligations of a treaty which involve alteration of law they have to run the risk of obtaining the assent of Parliament to the necessary statute or statutes. To make themselves as secure as possible they will often in such cases before final ratification seek to obtain from Parliament an expression of approval. But it has never been suggested, and it is not the law, that such an expression of approval operates as law, or that in law it precludes the assenting Parliament or any subsequent Parliament from refusing to give its sanction to any legislative proposals that may subsequently be brought before it. Parliament, no doubt, as the Chief Justice points out, has a constitutional control over the executive; but it cannot be disputed that the creation of the obligations undertaken in treaties and the assent to their form and quality are the function of the executive alone. Once they are created, while they bind the state as against the other contracting parties, Parliament may refuse to perform them and so leave the state in default. In a unitary State whose Legislature possesses unlimited powers the problem is simple. Parliament will either fulfil or not treaty obligations imposed upon the state by its executive. The nature of the obligations does not affect the complete authority of the Legislature to make them law if it so chooses. But in a state where the Legislature does not possess absolute authority, in a federal State where legislative authority is limited by a constitutional document, or is divided up between different Legislatures in accordance with the classes of subject-matter submitted for legislation, the problem is complex. The obligations imposed by treaty may have to be performed, if at all, by several Legislatures; and the executive have the task of obtaining the legislative assent not of the one Parliament to whom they may be responsible, but possibly of several Parliaments to whom they stand in no direct relation. The question is not how is the obligation formed, that is the function of the executive; but how is the obligation to be performed and that depends upon the authority of the competent Legislature or Legislatures. . . .

The first ground upon which counsel for the Dominion sought to base the validity of the legislation was s. 132. So far as it is sought to apply this section to the conventions when ratified the answer is plain. The obligations are not obligations of Canada as part of the British Empire, but of Canada, by virtue of her new status as an international person, and do not arise under a treaty between the British Empire and foreign countries. This was clearly established by the decision in

the *Radio* case [[1932] A.C. 304, 2 D.L.R. 81], and their Lordships do not think that the proposition admits of any doubt. It is unnecessary, therefore, to dwell upon the distinction between legislative powers given to the Dominion to perform obligations imposed upon Canada as part of the Empire by an Imperial executive responsible to and controlled by the Imperial Parliament, and the legislative power of the Dominion to perform obligations created by the Dominion executive responsible to and controlled by the Dominion Parliament. While it is true, as was pointed out in the *Radio* case, that it was not contemplated in 1867 that the Dominion would possess treaty-making powers, it is impossible to strain the section so as to cover the uncontemplated event.

A further attempt to apply the section was made by the suggestion that while it does not apply to the conventions, yet it clearly applies to the Treaty of Versailles itself, and the obligations to perform the conventions arise "under" that treaty because of the stipulations in Part XIII. It is impossible to accept this view. No obligation to legislate in respect of any of the matters in question arose until the Canadian executive, left with an unfettered discretion of their own volition, acceded to the conventions, a *novus actus* not determined by the treaty. For the purposes of this legislation the obligation arose under the conventions alone. It appears that all the members of the Supreme Court rejected the contention based on s. 132 and their Lordships are in full agreement with them.

If, therefore, s. 132 is out of the way the validity of the legislation can only depend upon ss. 91 and 92. Now it had to be admitted that normally this legislation came within the classes of subjects by s. 92 assigned exclusively to the Legislatures of the Provinces, namely—property and civil rights in the Province. This was in fact expressly decided in respect of these same conventions by the Supreme Court in 1925. How then can the legislation be within the legislative powers given by s. 91 to the Dominion Parliament? It is not within the enumerated classes of subjects in s. 91: and it appears to be expressly excluded from the general powers given by the first words of the section. It appears highly probable that none of the members of the Supreme Court would have departed from their decision in 1925 had it not been for the opinion of the Chief Justice that the judgments of the Judicial Committee in the *Aeronautics* case [[1932] A.C. 54, 1 D.L.R. 58], and the *Radio* case [*supra*] constrained them to hold that jurisdiction to legislate for the purpose of performing the obligation of a treaty resides exclusively in the Parliament of Canada. Their Lordships cannot take this view of those decisions.

The *Aeronautics* case [*supra*] concerned legislation to perform obligations imposed by a treaty between the Empire and foreign countries. Sect. 132 therefore clearly applied, and but for a remark at the end of the judgment, which in view of the stated ground of the decision was clearly obiter, the case could not be said to be an authority on the matter now under discussion.

The judgment in the *Radio* case [*supra*] appears to present more difficulty. But when that case is examined it will be found that the true ground of the decision was that the convention in that case dealt with classes of matters which did not fall within the enumerated classes of subjects in s. 92 or even within the enumerated classes in s. 91. Part of the subject-matter of the convention, namely—broadcasting, might come under an enumerated class, but if so it was under a heading "Inter-provincial Telegraphs," expressly excluded from s. 92. Their Lordships are satisfied that neither case affords a warrant for holding that legislation to perform a Canadian treaty is exclusively within the Dominion legislative power.

For the purposes of ss. 91 and 92, i.e., the distribution of legislative powers between the Dominion and the Provinces, there is no such thing as treaty legislation as such. The distribution is based on classes of subjects; and as a treaty deals with a particular class of subjects so will the legislative power of performing it be ascertained. No one can doubt that this distribution is one of the most essential conditions, probably the most essential condition, in the inter-provincial compact to which the *British North America Act* gives effect. If the position of Lower Canada, now Quebec, alone were considered, the existence of her separate jurisprudence as to both property and civil rights might be said to depend upon loyal adherence to her constitutional right to the exclusive competence of her own Legislature in these matters. Nor is it of less importance for the other Provinces, though their law may be based on English jurisprudence, to preserve their own right to legislate for themselves in respect of local conditions which may vary by as great a distance as separates the Atlantic from the Pacific. It would be remarkable that while the Dominion could not initiate legislation however desirable which affected civil rights in the Provinces, yet its Government not responsible to the Provinces nor controlled by Provincial Parliaments need only agree with a foreign country to enact such legislation, and its Parliament would be forthwith clothed with authority to affect Provincial rights to the full extent of such agreement. Such a result would appear to undermine the constitutional safeguards of Provincial constitutional autonomy.

It follows from what has been said that no further legislative competence is obtained by the Dominion from its accession to international status, and the consequent increase in the scope of its executive functions. It is true, as pointed out in the judgment of the Chief Justice, that as the executive is now clothed with the powers of making treaties so the Parliament of Canada, to which the executive is responsible, has imposed

upon it responsibilities in connection with such treaties, for if it were to disapprove of them they would either not be made or the Ministers would meet their constitutional fate. But this is true of all executive functions in their relation to Parliament. There is no existing constitutional ground for stretching the competence of the Dominion Parliament so that it becomes enlarged to keep pace with enlarged functions of the Dominion executive. If the new functions affect the classes of subjects enumerated in s. 92 legislation to support the new functions is in the competence of the provincial Legislatures only. If they do not, the competence of the Dominion Legislature is declared by s. 91 and existed *ab origine*. In other words the Dominion cannot merely by making promises to foreign countries clothe itself with legislative authority inconsistent with the constitution which gave it birth.

But the validity of the legislation under the general words of s. 91 was sought to be established not in relation to the treaty-making power alone, but also as being concerned with matters of such general importance as to have attained "such dimensions as to affect the body politic," and to have "ceased to be merely local or provincial and to have become matters of national concern." . . . It is only necessary to call attention to the phrases in the various cases, "abnormal circumstances," "exceptional conditions," "standard of necessity" (*Board of Commerce* case [[1922] 1 A.C.191, (1921), 60 D.L.R. 513], "some extraordinary peril to the material life of Canada," "highly exceptional," "epidemic of pestilence" (*Snider's* case [[1925] A.C. 396, 2 D.L.R. 5]), to show how far the present case is from the conditions which may override the normal distinction of powers in ss. 91 and 92. . . .

It must not be thought that the result of this decision is that Canada is incompetent to legislate in performance of treaty obligations. In totality of legislative powers, Dominion and provincial together, she is fully equipped. But the legislative powers remain distributed, and if in the exercise of her new functions derived from her new international status Canada incurs obligations they must, so far as legislation be concerned when they deal with Provincial classes of subjects, be dealt with by the totality of powers, in other words by co-operation between the Dominion and the Provinces. While the ship of state now sails on larger ventures and into foreign waters she still retains the water-tight compartments which are an essential part of her original structure. The Supreme Court was equally divided and therefore the formal judgment could only state the opinions of the three Judges on either side. Their Lordships are of opinion that the answer to the three questions should be that the *Act* in each case is *ultra vires* of the Parliament of Canada, and they will humbly advise His Majesty accordingly.

10 Attorney General of Ontario v. Attorney General of Canada (Reference re Abolition of Privy Council Appeals), 1947

In this decision, the Judicial Committee of the Privy Council upheld the federal Parliament's power to abolish all Canadian appeals to the Privy Council and to make the Supreme Court of Canada Canada's highest court of appeal. Legislation to accomplish this purpose had been introduced in the House of Commons in 1939. The legislation took the form of an amendment to the *Supreme Court Act* under which the Supreme Court would exercise "exclusive ultimate appellate civil and criminal jurisdiction within and for Canada."

When the original *Supreme Court Act* was enacted in 1875, Sir John A. Macdonald's Conservatives had opposed severing Canada's judicial link with the Empire. But, by the 1930s, with the growth of Canadian nationalism and the acquisition of Dominion autonomy, the abolition of appeals was supported by all three national political parties. The antagonism aroused among English Canada's political and legal elite by the Privy Council's interpretation of the *B.N.A. Act*, especially its decisions on the New Deal legislation, further fuelled the fires of judicial nationalism. However, this factor was not publicly acknowledged as a reason for abolition by federal political leaders as they did not wish to arouse provincial sensitivities by implying that they hoped the Supreme Court of Canada would adopt a more centralist approach to constitutional interpretation.

The passage of the *Statute of Westminster* in 1931 meant that the power to abolish appeals to Britain now rested in Canada. The Privy Council's decision in the *British Coal Corporation*[1] case in 1935 upholding a section of the *Criminal Code* cutting off Privy Council appeals in criminal cases made it clear that Parliament could abolish appeals with respect to cases involving federal laws. The only major constitutional doubt that remained was whether the federal Parliament could also abolish appeals concerning provincial laws. This issue was referred to the Supreme Court in 1940 and, in a 4-to-2 decision, resolved in the federal Parliament's favour. This decision was appealed to the Privy Council by four provinces (British Columbia, New Brunswick, Ontario, and Quebec), while two provinces (Manitoba and Saskatchewan) supported the federal government. The hearing of the appeal was postponed until after the war.

Lord Jowitt's opinion upholding federal power under section 101 of the *B.N.A. Act* to abolish appeals in all matters of law is remarkable for the connection it makes between Canada's becoming independent of Great Britain in 1931 and the powers of the federal level of government within Canada. One reason Jowitt advanced for holding that the federal Parliament should control appeals in cases relating to provincial laws as well as in cases relating to federal laws was that being able "to secure through its own courts of justice that the law should be one and the same for all citizens" is a "prime element in the self-government of the Dominion." This holding also indicates how far the Judicial Committee would go in attributing a unitary judicial structure to Canada in contrast to its solicitude for the division of legislative powers.

---

1 [1935] A.C. 500.

The amendment making the Supreme Court Canada's ultimate court of appeal was finally enacted in 1949. No cases instituted after that date could be appealed to the Privy Council. However, cases that had commenced prior to that date could be appealed, so that nearly a decade elapsed before Canada's judicial self-government was in fact complete. ⌒

ATTORNEY GENERAL OF ONTARIO v. ATTORNEY GENERAL OF CANADA
[1947] A.C. 128, III Olmsted 508 (Privy Council)

Hearing: October 24, 25, 28, 29, 31, November 1, 1946; Judgment: January 13, 1947.

Present: Lord Jowitt L.C., Viscount Simon, Lord Macmillan, Lord Wright, Lord Greene M.R., Lord Simonds, and Lord Goddard C.J.

The judgment of their Lordships was delivered by

LORD JOWITT L.C.: This appeal is brought from the judgment of the Supreme Court of Canada, given on January 19, 1940, on a question which was referred to that court under provisions of s. 55 of the *Supreme Court Act*, R.S.C. 1927, ch. 35. From the recitals contained in the order of reference, which was made by the Governor-General in Council on April 21, 1939, it appears that, at the Fourth Session of the Eighteenth Parliament of Canada, Bill 9, entitled, "*An Act to amend the Supreme Court Act*," was introduced and received first reading in the House of Commons on January 23, 1939, and that on April 14 of the same year the debate on the motion for the second reading of the Bill was adjourned in order that steps might be taken to obtain a judicial determination of the legislative competence of the Parliament of Canada to enact the provisions of the said Bill in whole or in part. The following question was accordingly referred to the Supreme Court of Canada for hearing and consideration:

> Is said Bill 9, entitled, "*An Act to amend the Supreme Court Act*," or any of the provisions thereof, and in what particular or particulars or to what extent, *intra vires* of the Parliament of Canada?

The contents of the Bill, a short, but pregnant, one, must be stated in full. [His Lordship read the provisions of the Bill, and continued:] On January 19, 1940, the Supreme Court certified that the opinions in respect of the question referred to it were as follows: "By the Court: The Parliament of Canada is competent to enact the Bill referred in its entirety. By Crocket J.: The Bill referred is wholly *ultra vires* of the Parliament of Canada. By Davis J.: The Bill referred if enacted would be within the authority of the Dominion Parliament if amended to provide that nothing therein contained shall alter

or affect the rights of any province in respect of any action or other civil proceedings commenced in any of the provincial courts and solely concerned with some subject matter, legislation in relation to which is within the exclusive legislative competence of the legislature of such province."

From this judgment of the Court the Attorneys General of Ontario, British Columbia and New Brunswick have by special leave brought this appeal, which the Attorney General of Quebec has intervened to support. The Attorneys General of Canada and of Manitoba and Saskatchewan are respondents to the appeal. The hearing of the appeal was postponed until the conclusion of the war. Their Lordships think it worth while to observe that H.M. Attorney General in England took no part in the controversy, which has throughout been between the Dominion of Canada and certain of the provinces on the one hand and others of the provinces on the other hand. The single issue has been whether, as the appellants contend, the subject matter of Bill 9 falls within the exclusive powers committed to the provincial legislatures of the Provinces of Canada under s. 92 of the *British North America Act, 1867*, or, as the respondents contend, is within the powers of the Parliament of Canada under s. 101 or, alternatively, under s. 91 of that *Act*. An alternative argument was faintly addressed to their Lordships by counsel for the appellants, that the Bill lay within the powers of neither provinces nor Dominion, but H.M. Attorney-General in England did not intervene to support this view and their Lordships see no valid reason for accepting it.

[His Lordship then recited sections 91, 92, 101, and 129 of the *B.N.A. Act*.]

It is convenient shortly to restate what at all times until the passing of the *Statute of Westminster* (to which reference will shortly be made) was the constitutional bar to legislation whether by Dominion or province in regard to appeals to His Majesty in Council. In the first place, it must be remembered that by the *Colonial Laws Validity Act, 1865*, any colonial law which was repugnant to the provisions of an Act of the United Kingdom extending to the colony either by express words or necessary intendment was void and inoperative to the extent of such repugnancy. It followed that neither Dominion nor province could then validly legislate so as to abolish a right of appeal to the King in Council which was provided by imperial

Acts. In the second place, the doctrine which imposed a territorial limitation on the powers of colonial legislatures, might be regarded as a fetter on the legislative competence of Dominion or province to deal with the so-called "prerogative" right of appeal. In the third place, the express terms of the exception in s. 129 of the *Act*, to which reference has been made, precluded any alteration of imperial *Acts*.

It is now necessary to return to s. 101 of the *Act*. Acting under its authority the Parliament of Canada in the year 1875 passed the *Supreme Court of Canada Act*, which has from time to time been amended and, as amended, is now R.S.C. 1927, ch. 35. Under the *Act* a Supreme Court of Appeal was established which, under s. 35, was to have, hold and exercise, an appellate civil and criminal jurisdiction within and throughout Canada. It prescribed the limits within, and the terms on which, an appeal might be brought from the courts of the provinces, and by s. 54 provided that the judgment of the Court should in all cases be final and conclusive and that no appeal should be brought from any judgment or order of the Court to any court of appeal established by the Parliament of Great Britain and Ireland by which appeals or petitions to His Majesty in Council might be ordered to be heard, saving any right which His Majesty might be graciously pleased to exercise by virtue of His royal prerogative. It is this s. 54 which the Bill now challenged seeks to amend, and two things may be noticed about the section as originally enacted. In the first place, it is silent, as is the whole *Act*, about appeals from the provincial courts to His Majesty in Council. In the second place, so far as appeals from the Supreme Court are concerned, it expressly saves the prerogative while denying any appeal as of right.

Such being the position before the year 1931, in that year was passed the *Statute of Westminster, 1931*, an *Act* of the Imperial Parliament, which has as its subtitle "An Act to give effect to certain resolutions passed by imperial Conferences held in the years 1926 and 1930." The recitals in the preamble of this *Act*, after referring to the reports of the Conferences, affirm that it is proper to set out that, inasmuch as the Crown is the symbol of the free association of the members of the British Commonwealth of Nations, and as they are united by a common allegiance to the Crown, it would be in accord with the established constitutional position of all the members of the Commonwealth in relation to one another that any alteration in the law touching the succession to the Throne or the Royal Style and Titles should thenceforth require the assent as well of the Parliament of all the Dominions as of the Parliament of the United Kingdom, and that it is in accord with the established constitutional position that no law hereafter made by the Parliament of the United Kingdom shall extend to any of the said Dominions as part of the law of that Dominion

otherwise than at the request and with the consent of that Dominion. By s. 2, sub-s. 1, it is provided that the *Colonial Laws Validity Act, 1865*, shall not apply to any law made after the commencement of the *Act* by the Parliament of a Dominion (which, by definition, includes the Dominion of Canada), and by s. 2, sub-s. 2, that no law and no provision of any law made after the commencement of the *Act* by the Parliament of a Dominion shall be void or inoperative on the ground that it is repugnant to the law of England, or to the provisions of any existing or future *Act* of Parliament of the United Kingdom, or to any order, rule or regulation made under any such *Act*, and the powers of the Parliament of a Dominion shall include the power to repeal or amend any such *Act*, order, rule or regulation in so far as the same is part of the law of the Dominion. By s. 3, it is declared and enacted that the Parliament of a Dominion has full power to make laws having extra-territorial operation. (It may be noticed that this power is not given to the legislature of a province.) By s. 4, it is provided that no *Act* of Parliament of the United Kingdom passed after the commencement of the *Act* shall extend or be deemed to extend to a Dominion as part of the law of that Dominion, unless it is expressly declared in that *Act* that that Dominion has requested, and consented to, the enactment thereof. It remains only to refer to s. 7, which deals with Canada only. By that section it is provided (by sub-s.1) that nothing in the *Act* shall be deemed to apply to the repeal, amendment or alteration of the *British North America Acts*, 1867 to 1930, or any order, rule or regulation made thereunder; (by sub-s. 2) that the provisions of s. 2 and the *Act* shall extend to laws made by any of the provinces of Canada and to the powers of the legislatures of such provinces, and (by sub-s. 3) that the powers conferred by the *Act* upon the Parliament of Canada or upon the legislatures of the provinces shall be restricted to the enactment of laws in relation to matters within the competence of the Parliament of Canada or of any of the legislatures of the provinces respectively.

It is in the light of this *Act* of transcendent constitutional importance that the question must now be considered whether it is competent for the Parliament of Canada to enact not only that the Supreme Court of the Dominion shall have appellate civil and criminal jurisdiction within and for Canada, but also that jurisdiction shall be "exclusive" and "ultimate." This question must be considered under two heads, first, in regard to appeals from the Supreme Court itself, and, secondly, in regard to appeals direct from the provincial courts to His Majesty in Council. First, then, as to appeals from the Supreme Court itself. Here the question is whether under sub-s. 1, of the substituted s. 54, the jurisdiction can validly be made "ultimate," by which, as the subsequent new sub-sections make clear, is intended the abolition of appeal from the

Supreme Court to His Majesty in Council. On this question their Lordships can entertain no doubt. The power vested in the Dominion Parliament by s. 101 of the *British North America Act* to establish a general court of appeal for Canada was necessarily subject to the prerogative right of His Majesty, since that right was not expressly or by necessary intendment excluded, and this limitation was recognized in the first words of s. 54 of the *Supreme Court Act.* But that was a restriction or fetter on the legislative power of the Dominion which could be removed, and has been removed, by an *Act* of the Imperial Parliament, and, since it has been removed, it must be within the power of the Dominion Parliament to enact that the jurisdiction of its Supreme Court shall be ultimate. No other solution is consonant with the status of a self-governing Dominion.

Secondly, as to appeal direct from provincial courts to His Majesty in Council. It is in regard to these appeals that the validity of the Bill has been more strenuously challenged; and their Lordships have felt the familiar difficulty of determining which of two alternative meanings is to be given an instrument, the authors of which did not contemplate the possibility of wither meaning. For how could it be supposed in 1867, only two years after the passing of the *Colonial Laws Validity Act,* that the competence of either the Dominion or the provincial legislatures to pass laws directly repugnant to Acts of Parliament of the United Kingdom and to the common law relating to the prerogative could be the subject of judicial determination? Yet this is the question which must now be decided. In its solution their Lordships have the advantage of two recent pronouncements of the Board, *Nadan v. The King* [1926] A.C. 482 and *British Coal Corporation v. The King* [1935] A.C. 500, the first before, the second after, the passing of the *Statute of Westminster,* and it will be convenient to see what these cases decided.

In *Nadan's* case, the question was as to the validity of s. 1025 of the *Criminal Code* of Canada if and so far as it is purported to prevent the King in Council from giving effective leave to appeal against an order of a Canadian court in a criminal case. Criminal law, including the procedure in criminal matters, was, it will be remembered, one of the subjects to which, under s. 91 of the *Act,* the exclusive authority of the Parliament of Canada extended. It was argued that the legislative power so conferred was complete, and included power to limit the royal prerogative to entertain an appeal. The Board, after a review of the prerogative and of the manner in which the Judicial Committee had been in effect established as a court of appellate jurisdiction, rejected the argument, holding that however widely the powers conferred by s. 91 were construed they were confined to action to be taken in the Dominion and did not authorize the Dominion Parliament to annul the prerogative right of the King in Council to grant special

leave to appeal, and further holding that s. 1025 of the *Criminal Code,* if and so far as it was intended to have that effect, was repugnant to the *Judicial Committee Acts* and therefore void and inoperative by virtue of the *Colonial Laws Validity Act, 1865.*

In 1935 there came before the Board the *British Coal Corporation* case in which the same question was raised, but with this vital difference, that in the meantime the *Statute of Westminster* had been passed. The section of the *Criminal Code* then in force purported in unambiguous terms to abolish the appeal to His Majesty in Council; "Notwithstanding any royal prerogative or anything contained in the *Interpretation Act* or in the *Supreme Court Act,* no appeal shall be brought in any criminal case from any judgment or order of any court in Canada to any court of appeal or authority in which the United Kingdom appeals or petitions to His Majesty may be heard." The validity of this provision was challenged by certain persons who sought leave to appeal in a criminal case from a judgment of the court of King's Bench (Appeal Side) of the Province of Quebec. But it was challenged in vain. The Board, after once more expounding the nature of appeals to His Majesty in Council, explained the decision in *Nadan's* case [[1926] A.C. 482] thus: "Their Lordships are of opinion that the judgment was based on two grounds only: (1) that s. 1025 was repugnant to the *Privy Council Acts* of 1833 and 1844 and was therefore void under the *Colonial Laws Validity Act, 1865*; (2) that it could only be effective if construed as having an extra-territorial operation, whereas according to the law as it was in 1926 a Dominion statute could not have extra-territorial operation. These two difficulties as the law then stood could only be overcome by an Imperial Statute. . . . The Board proceeded to consider the question whether the difficulties had been overcome. Recalling the words used by Lord Loreburn L.C., in delivering the judgment of the Judicial Committee in *Attorney-General for Ontario v. Attorney-General for Canada* [[1912] A.C. 571, 581]: "Now, there can be no doubt that under this organic instrument the powers distributed between the Dominion on the one hand and the provinces on the other hand, cover the whole area of self-government within the whole area of Canada. It would be subversive of the entire scheme and policy of the *Act* to assume that any point of internal self-government was withheld from Canada" (words that their Lordships reiterate in regards to the present appeal), the Board concluded that both difficulties had been removed by the *Statute of Westminster.* "There now remain," it was said "only such limitations as flow from the *Act* itself, the operation of which as affecting the competence of Dominion legislation was saved by s. 7 of the statute, a section which excludes the competence of the Dominion and provincial Parliaments any power of 'repeal, amendment or alteration' of the *Act*" [[1935]

A.C. 520]. It has been properly urged on behalf of the appellants that at the conclusion of their judgment the Board observed that they were dealing only with the legal position in Canada in regard to that type of appeal in criminal matters, and that it was there neither necessary nor desirable to touch on the position as regards civil cases. It was this consideration that led Davis J. in the present case to give the qualified opinion already cited in regard to the validity of the referred Bill. This opinion rightly recognizes whether or not the reasoning of the Board in the *British Coal Corporation* case [[1935] A.C. 500] extends beyond the subject matter of legislation which was by s. 91 of the *Act* confided to the Dominion Parliament, at any rate it cannot be limited to one only of the twenty-nine classes of subject matter enumerated in that section, and that just as an appeal to His Majesty in Council may by Dominion legislation be abrogated in respect of "the criminal law ... including the procedure in criminal matters," so it may be abrogated in respect of, e.g., class 21 "bankruptcy and insolvency" or class 22 "patents of invention and discovery."

But the conclusion reached by Davis J. involves a distinction which their Lordships would not willingly adopt. For if, as he holds, the subject matter provides the test whether the right of appeal may be abrogated by Dominion legislation so that it may not be abrogated in respect of classes of subjects assigned exclusively to the provinces under s. 92, a strange result would follow. It must be remembered that in the provincial courts the subject matter of litigation may arise as well under Dominion as under provincial legislation. The judicial and legislative spheres are not coterminous, provincial courts determining all questions except those for which a special court is set up under s. 101, whether the rights of the parties spring from the common law or Dominion or provincial statutes. Thus, if the right of the Dominion Parliament to prohibit appeals to His Majesty in Council from a provincial court depended on the subject matter in suit, the result would be that from the same court an appeal might lie in one suit to the Supreme Court of Canada only but in another to that court or to His Majesty in Council, nor is it impossible that in the same suit two or more questions might be raised in respect of which different rights of appeal would arise. This result is yet more remarkable when it is remembered how wide is the scope of those classes of subjects which, falling within s. 91 of the *Act*, can on this hypothesis be excluded from appeal to His Majesty in Council. Only the residue of civil cases, in which the rights of the parties were determinable by reference to other than Dominion legislation, would remain the subject of such appeal.

Therefore, while their Lordships give full weight to the observation with which the judgment in the *British Coal Corporation* case [[1935] A.C. 500] concluded and do not doubt

that that case rightly decided that the Dominion Parliament was competent to exclude appeals in criminal cases for the reasons therein appearing, they must observe that that decision can be supported on wider grounds which cover not only criminal cases and not only civil cases falling within the subject matter of s. 91, but also every other case which can be brought before any provincial court in Canada. In coming to this conclusion their Lordships do not think it useful to embark on a nice discrimination between the legislative powers contained in ss. 91 and 92 respectively of the *Act*. Nor, as it appears to them, is it necessary to determine whether the words of head 14 of s. 92, "The administration of justice in the province" would, if they were disembarrassed of any context, be apt to embrace legislation in regard to appeals to His Majesty in Council. There appear to be cogent reasons for thinking that they would not. But their Lordships do not make this the ground of their decision; for it is elsewhere, it is in s. 101 of the *Act* that the solution lies.

In his judgment in the case under appeal, the former Chief Justice of Canada, Sir Lyman Duff, used these words: "Assuming even that s. 92 gives some authority to the legislatures [of the provinces] in respect of appeals to the Privy Council, that cannot detract from the power of Parliament under s. 101. Whatever is granted by the words of the section, read and applied as *prima facie* intended to endow Parliament with power to affect high political objects concerning the self-government of the Dominion (s. 3 of the *B.N.A. Act*) in the matter of judicature, is to be held and exercised as a plenary power in that behalf with all ancillary powers necessary to enable Parliament to attain its objects fully and completely. So read it imports authority to establish a court having supreme and final appellate jurisdiction in Canada" [[1940] S.C.R. (Can.) 63]. The vital words in the passage cited, with which their Lordships are in full agreement, are the words in the last line "and final." But in the opinion of their Lordships the same considerations lead to the conclusion that the court so established must have not only "final," or "ultimate" but also exclusive appellate jurisdiction. They would emphasize that s. 101 confers a legislative power on the Dominion Parliament which by its terms overrides any power conferred by s. 92 on the provinces or preserved by s. 129. "Notwithstanding anything in this *Act*" are words in s. 101 which cannot be ignored. They vest in the Dominion a plenary authority to legislate in regard to appellate jurisdiction, which is qualified only by that which lies outside the *Act*, namely, the sovereign power of the Imperial Parliament. This was fully recognized in *Crown Grain Co. v. Day* [[1908] A.C. 504].

What, then, is the power of the Dominion Parliament since the *Statute of Westminster* has come into operation? It is useful to examine what the position would be if now, for the first time, the Dominion legislature thought fit to exercise its power under s. 101. Nor is this a fanciful or inept mode of examination, for the power is to provide "from time to time" for a general court of appeal. To their Lordships it appears reasonably plain that, since, in the words used by Lord Robertson in delivering the opinion of the Board in the *Crown Grain Co.* case [*ibid.* 507 (A.C.)]: "the subject in conflict belongs primarily to the subject matter committed to the Dominion Parliament, namely, the establishment of the Court of Appeal for Canada," to that Parliament also must belong the power not only to determine in what cases and under what conditions the appellate jurisdiction of that court may be invoked, but also to deny appellate to any other court. The natural attribute of sovereign power was no doubt qualified by an external constitutional limitation, namely, the existence of imperial statutes, but, given the power to abrogate such statutes, the authority conferred by s. 101 stands unqualified and absolute.

It is possible to regard this matter from a somewhat wider point of view.... The regulation of appeals is, to use the words of Lord Sankey in the *British Coal Corporation* case [[1935] A.C. 500] a "prime element in Canadian sovereignty," which would be impaired if at the will of its citizens recourse could be had to a tribunal, in the constitution of which it had no voice. It is, as their Lordships think, irrelevant that the question is one that might have seemed unreal at the date of the *British North America Act.* To such an organic statute the flexible interpretation must be given which changing circumstances require, and it would be alien to the spirit, with which the preamble to the *Statute of Westminster* is instinct, to concede anything less than the widest amplitude of power to the Dominion legislature under s. 101 of the *Act.*

In this connection some argument was addressed to their Lordships on the importance of uniformity of legal decision, which, it was urged, could not be secured if appeal lay indifferently to the Supreme Court of Canada or to His Majesty in Council. For a decision of the Supreme Court would at least be final, though its jurisdiction would not on this hypothesis be exclusive. Against this it was contended that the *British North America Act* contained in s. 94 a provision whereby the postulated uniformity of law could be obtained. In their Lordships' opinion this section provides an imperfect remedy for a state of affairs in which an important Dominion Act might be finally interpreted in one way by the Supreme Court for a province which did not admit appeals to His Majesty in Council and in another way by the Judicial Committee for a province which did admit such appeals, neither tribunal admitting the authority of the other. But it is the possibility of such a conflict, creating a different law for different provinces out of the same Dominion *Act,* which points the way to a truer interpretation of the *British North America Act* in the light of the *Statute of Westminster.* It is, in fact, a prime element in the self-government of the Dominion, that it should be able to secure through its own courts of justice that the law should be one and the same for all its citizens. This result is attainable only if s. 101 now authorizes the establishment of a court with final and exclusive appellate jurisdiction....

It is right to conclude with some observations on s. 7 of the *Statute of Westminster* on which counsel for the appellants strongly relied. Sub-section 1 of s. 7 is in general terms, and it was urged that to interpret the *Statute* as vesting in the Dominion Parliament a power which it did not before possess was in effect to repeal or amend or, at least, to alter the *British North America Act.* But their Lordships cannot accept this reasoning. Necessarily the effect of the statute is to amend and alter the *Act* in so far as from the operation of the statute there arises a new power in the legislatures of both the Dominion and the provinces. The question is, in which legislature the power is vested in regard to this particular subject matter. That is a question of construction on which their Lordships have stated their opinion. Sub-section 2 does not call for further comment here. In regard to sub-s. 3 the same observations appear to apply as to sub-s. 1. If on the true construction of the *British North America Act* the conclusion had been that the power to legislate for abrogation of Appeals to His Majesty in Council was vested under s. 92 in a provincial legislature, that would have been an end of the matter. It is just because their Lordships have come to a different conclusion that sub-s. 3 does not assist the appellants.

Their Lordships are of opinion that this appeal fails, and that it ought to be declared that *Bill 9* of the Fourth Session of the Eighteenth Parliament of Canada, entitled "*An Act to amend the Supreme Court Act,*" is wholly *intra vires* of the Parliament of Canada, and they will humbly advise His Majesty accordingly.

B: THE SUPREME COURT SINCE 1949

 **11** Johannesson v. West St. Paul, 1952

This is the first case following the abolition of Privy Council appeals that provided an occasion for the Supreme Court to indicate the direction in which it might develop Canadian constitutional law in relation to two major issues: the peace, order, and good government power and the power to implement Canadian treaties.

The case originated in private litigation between Johannesson, the operator of a commercial aviation enterprise in Western Canada and the Manitoba town of West St. Paul, which had passed a bylaw preventing Johannesson from establishing an aerodrome in a location he had chosen in that municipality. Johannesson challenged the validity of the provincial *Municipal Act*, which had delegated to the municipality the power to make the bylaw in question. Both the trial judge and a majority of the Manitoba Court of Appeal had ruled the Manitoba legislation *intra vires*. On the appeal to the Supreme Court of Canada, the Attorney General of Manitoba and the Attorney General of Canada intervened to support their respective sides of the case. The Supreme Court was unanimous in reversing the decision of the lower courts and finding that the Dominion's power in relation to aeronautics left no room for a province to regulate the location of aerodromes. Six of the seven judges who took part in the decision supported the validity of the federal *Aeronautics Act* and Air Regulations as an exercise of the peace, order, and good government power. It is significant that in doing so, the Supreme Court justices used the approach to peace, order, and good government that they found in *A.G. Ontario v. Canadian Temperance Federation*,[1] one of the Judicial Committee's last decisions on Canada's Constitution. In that case, Viscount Simon put forward "inherent national importance" as a test of when peace, order, and good government power can be used. That is clearly a much broader understanding of Parliament's general power than Viscount Haldane's emergency doctrine. Justice Locke's opinion demonstrates the policy considerations that judges might take into account in deciding whether legislation relates to a subject which from its inherent nature must be the concern of the Dominion as a whole.

While the decision in this case points to a more expansive treatment of Parliament's general power, its implications for the treaty-implementing power were less clear. The Court was divided on the question whether section 132, which gives Parliament the power of implementing any obligations arising from treaties entered into by Canada as part of the British Empire, could be used, as it had been in the *Aeronautics Reference*,[2] to support the validity of the federal *Aeronautics Act*. The International Convention in support of which the *Aeronautics Act* had originally been enacted was ratified on behalf of the British Empire. But this Convention had been abrogated by the Civil Aviation Convention that Canada had

---

1 [1946] A.C. 193.

2 *In re Regulation and Control of Aeronautics in Canada*, [1932] A.C. 54. See case 7.

signed in her own right at Chicago in 1944. In the light of these facts, three of the judges were of the opinion that section 132 could no longer be used to sustain the Dominion's aeronautics legislation, while three others took the view that even though the Chicago Convention was not, strictly speaking, a British Empire treaty still "it comes to the same thing."[3] The seventh, Justice Locke, does not appear to have committed himself on this point. ⌐

---

3   This was the phrase used by Viscount Dunedin in *In re Regulation and Control of Radio Communication in Canada*, [1932] A.C. 304 at 312. See the introduction to case 7.

JOHANNESSON v. WEST ST. PAUL
[1952] 1 S.C.R. 292

Present: Rinfret C.J. and Cartwright, Estey, Kellock, Kerwin, Locke, and Taschereau JJ.

KERWIN J.: This is an appeal by Mr. and Mrs. Johannesson against a judgment of the Court of Appeal for Manitoba affirming an order of Campbell J. dismissing their application for an order declaring that s. 921 of *The Municipal Act*, R.S.M. 1940, c. 141, was *ultra vires* as not being within the legislative competence of the Legislature, and that by-law 292 of the rural municipality of West St. Paul, passed May 27, 1948, in pursuance of such section, was, therefore, null and void.

Section 921 of *The Municipal Act* appears in Division II "Public Safety and Amenity" under the sub-head "Aerodromes" and reads as follows:

> 921. Any municipal corporation may pass by-laws for licensing, regulating, and, within certain defined areas, preventing the erection, maintenance and continuance of aerodromes or places where aeroplanes are kept for hire or gain.

[Justice Kerwin then reviewed the history of the legislation. He also set out the provisions of the West St. Paul bylaw 292, which banned aerodromes from the area in which Johannesson wished to locate his airport. This bylaw was authorized by section 921 of Manitoba's *Municipal Act*.]

The circumstances which give rise to the present dispute are important as showing the far-reaching effect of the provisions of the section. The appellant Johannesson had been engaged in commercial aviation since 1928 and held an air transport licence, issued by the Air Transport Board of Canada, to operate an air service at Winnipeg and Flin Flon. The charter service which he operated under this licence covers territory in central and northern Manitoba and northern Saskatchewan, and had substantially increased in volume over

the years. This service was operated with light and medium weight planes, which in the main were equipped in summer with floats and in winter with skis in order to permit landing on the numerous lakes and rivers in this territory, and these planes had to be repaired and serviced in Winnipeg, which was the only place within the territory where the necessary supplies and any facilities were available for that purpose. The use by small planes of a large airfield, such as Stevenson Airport near Winnipeg which was maintained for the use of large transcontinental airplanes, was impractical and would eventually be prohibited. No facilities existed on the Red River in Winnipeg for the repairing and servicing of planes equipped with floats, and repairs could only be made to such planes by dismantling them at some private dock and transporting them, by truck, through Winnipeg to Stevenson Airport. After a long search by Johannesson in the suburbs of Winnipeg for a site that would combine an area of level land of sufficient area and dimensions and location to comply with the regulations of the Civil Aviation Branch of the Canadian Department of Transport relating to a licensed air strip with access to a straight stretch of the Red River of sufficient length to be suitable for the landing of airplanes equipped with floats, he found such a location (but one only) in the rural municipality of West St. Paul and acquired an option to purchase it but, before the transaction was completed By-law 292 was passed. Title to the land was subsequently taken in the name of both appellants and these proceedings ensued. The Attorney General of Canada and the Attorney General of Manitoba were notified but only the latter was represented before the judge of first instance and the Court of Appeal. Leave to appeal to this Court was granted by the latter.

On behalf of the appellants and the Attorney General of Canada, reliance is placed upon the decision of the Judicial Committee in the *Aeronautics* case [[1932] A.C. 54]. Irrespective of later judicial comments upon this case, in my view it is a decision based entirely upon the fact that the Dominion *Aeronautics Act* there in question had been enacted pursuant to an International Convention of 1919 to which the British Empire was a party and, therefore, within s. 132 of the *British North America Act, 1867*:

> 132. The Parliament and Government of Canada shall have all Powers necessary or proper for performing the obligations of Canada or of any Province thereof, as part of the British Empire, towards foreign countries arising under treaties between the Empire and such foreign countries.

However, in the subsequent decision in the *Labour Conventions* case [[1937] A.C. 326], Lord Atkin, who had been a member of the Board in the *Aeronautics* case, said with reference to the judgment therein:

> The *Aeronautics* case [[1932] A.C. 54 at 351] concerned legislation to perform obligations imposed by a treaty between the Empire and foreign countries. Sect. 132, therefore, clearly applied, and but for a remark at the end of the judgment, which in view of the stated ground of the decision was clearly obiter, the case could not be said to be an authority on the matter now under discussion.

The remarks of Viscount Simon in *A.G. for Ontario v. Canada Temperance Federation* [[1946] A.C. 193] must be read when considering the words of Lord Sankey in the *Aeronautics* case in another connection. At the moment all I am concerned with emphasizing is that the *Aeronautics* case decided one thing and one thing only, and that is that the matter there discussed fell within the ambit of s. 132 of the *British North America Act*.

At this stage it is necessary to refer to a matter that was not explained to the Courts below. According to a certificate from the Under-Secretary of State for Foreign Affairs, the Convention of 1919 was denounced by Canada, which denunciation became effective in 1947. This was done because [in] February 13, 1947, Canada had deposited its Instrument of Ratification of the Convention on International Civil Aviation signed at Chicago December 8, 1944, and which Convention came into force on April 4, 1947. With the exception of certain amendments that are not relevant to the present discussion, the *Aeronautics Act* remains on the statute books of Canada in the same terms as those considered by the Judicial Committee in the *Aeronautics* case. Section 132 of the *B.N.A. Act*, therefore, ceased to have any efficacy to permit Parliament to legislate upon the subject of aeronautics.

Nevertheless the fact remains that the Convention of 1919 was a treaty between the Empire and foreign countries and that pursuant thereto the *Aeronautics Act* was enacted. It continues as c. 3 of the *Revised Statutes of Canada, 1927*, as amended. Under s. 4 of that *Act*, as it stood when these proceedings were

commenced, the Minister, with the approval of the Governor in Council, had power to regulate and control aerial navigation over Canada and the territorial waters of Canada, and in particular but not to restrict the generality of the foregoing, he might make regulations with respect to . . . (*c*) the licensing, inspection and regulation of all aerodromes and air stations. Pursuant thereto regulations have been promulgated dealing with many of the matters mentioned in the section, including provisions for the licensing of airports. If, therefore, the subject of aeronautics goes beyond local or provincial concern because it has attained such dimensions as to affect the body politic of Canada, it falls under the "Peace, Order and Good Government" clause of s. 91 of the *B.N.A. Act* since aeronautics is not a subject-matter confined to the provinces by s. 92. It does not fall within head 8, "Municipal Institutions," as that head "simply gives the provincial legislature the right to create a legal body for the management of municipal affairs. . . . The extent and nature of the functions" the provincial legislature "can commit to a municipal body of its own creation must depend upon the legislative authority which it derives from the provisions of s. 92 other than No. 8": *Attorney General for Ontario v. Attorney General for Canada* [[1896] A.C. 348 at 364]. Nor, on the authority of the same decision is it within head 9: "shop, saloon, tavern, auctioneer, and other licences in order to the raising of a revenue for provincial, local, or municipal purposes." Once it is held that the subject-matter transcends "Property and Civil Rights in the Province" (head 13) or "Generally all matters of a merely local or private nature in the Province" (head 16), these two heads of s. 92 have no relevancy.

Now, even at the date of the *Aeronautics* case, the Judicial Committee was influenced (i.e. in the determination of the main point) by the fact that in their opinion the subject of air navigation was a matter of national interest and importance and had attained such dimensions. That that is so at the present time is shown by the terms of the Chicago Convention of 1944 and the provisions of the Dominion *Aeronautics Act* and the regulations thereunder referred to above. The affidavit of the appellant Johannesson, from which the statement of facts was culled, also shows the importance that the subject of air navigation has attained in Canada. To all of which may be added those matters of everyday knowledge of which the Court must be taken to be aware.

It is with reference to this phase of the matter that Viscount Simon's remarks in *A.G. for Canada v. Canada Temperance Federation* [[1946] A.C. 193 at 205], must be read. What was there under consideration was the Canada *Temperance Act*, originally enacted in 1878, and Viscount Simon stated: "In their Lordships' opinion, the true test must be found in the real subject matter of the legislation: if it is such that it goes beyond local or provincial concern or interests and must from its inherent nature be the concern of the Dominion as a whole (as, for example, in the *Aeronautics* case [[1932] A.C. 54] and the *Radio* case [[1932] A.C. 304], then it will fall within the competence of the Dominion Parliament as a matter affecting the peace, order and good government of Canada, though it may in another aspect touch on matters specially reserved to the provincial legislatures." This statement is significant because, while not stating that the *Aeronautics* case was a decision on the point, it is a confirmation of the fact that the Board in the *Aeronautics* case considered that the subject of aeronautics transcended provincial legislative boundaries.

The appeal should be allowed, the orders below set aside, and judgment should be entered declaring s. 921 of the *Act ultra vires* and By-law 292 of the rural municipality of West St. Paul null and void.

LOCKE J.: . . . In my opinion, the position taken by the province and by the municipality in this matter cannot be maintained. Whether the control and direction of aeronautics in all its branches be one which lies within the exclusive jurisdiction of Parliament, and this I think to be the correct view, or whether it be a domain in which Provincial and Dominion legislation may overlap, I think the result must be the same. It has been said on behalf of the respondents that the by-law is merely a zoning regulation passed in exercise of the powers vested in the municipality elsewhere in the *Municipal Act*. . . . The by-law, in so far as it prohibits the erection, maintenance or continuation of aerodromes, must depend for its validity upon s. 921: subsec. 3 is apparently based upon subsec. (*h*) of s. 896. . . . The powers sought to be conferred upon the Municipal Council appear to me to be in direct conflict with those vested in the Minister of National Defence by the *Aeronautics Act*. Section 3(*a*) of that statute imposes upon the Minister the duty of supervising all matters connected with aeronautics and prescribing aerial routes and by s. 4 he is authorized, with the approval of the Governor in Council, to make regulations with respect to, *inter alia*, the areas within which aircraft coming from any place outside of Canada are to land and as to aerial routes, their use and control. The power to prescribe the aerial routes must include the right to designate where the terminus of any such route is to be maintained, and the power to designate the area within which foreign aircraft may land, of necessity includes the power to designate such area, whether of land or water, within any municipality in any province of Canada deemed suitable for such purpose.

If the validity of the *Aeronautics Act* and the Air Regulations be conceded, it appears to me that this matter must be determined contrary to the contentions of the respondent. It is, however, desirable, in my opinion, that some of the reasons

for the conclusion that the field of aeronautics is one exclusively within Federal jurisdiction should be stated. There has been since the First World War an immense development in the use of aircraft flying between the various provinces of Canada and between Canada and other countries. There is a very large passenger traffic between the provinces and to and from foreign countries, and a very considerable volume of freight traffic not only between the settled portions of the country but between those areas and the northern part of Canada, and planes are extensively used in the carriage of mails. That this traffic will increase greatly in volume and extent is undoubted. While the largest activity in the carrying of passengers and mails east and west is in the hands of a government controlled company, private companies carry on large operations, particularly between the settled parts of the country and the North and mails are carried by some of these lines. The maintenance and extension of this traffic, particularly to the North, is essential to the opening up of the country and the development of the resources of the nation. It requires merely a statement of these well recognized facts to demonstrate that the field of aeronautics is one which concerns the country as a whole. It is an activity, which to adopt the language of Lord Simon in the *Attorney General for Ontario v. Canada Temperance Federation* [[1946] A.C. 193 at 205], must from its inherent nature be a concern of the Dominion as a whole. The field of legislation is not, in my opinion, capable of division in any practical way. If, by way of illustration, it should be decided that it was in the interests of the inhabitants of some northerly part of the country to have airmail service with centres of population to the south and that for that purpose some private line, prepared to undertake such carriage, should be licensed to do so and to establish the southern terminus for their route at some suitable place in the Municipality of West St. Paul where, apparently, there is an available and suitable field and area of water where planes equipped in a manner enabling them to use the facilities of such an airport might land, it would be intolerable that such a national purpose might be defeated by a rural municipality, the Council of which decided that the noise attendant on the operation of airplanes was objectionable. Indeed, if the argument of the respondents be carried to its logical conclusion the rural municipalities of Manitoba through which the Red River passes between Emerson and Selkirk, and the City of Winnipeg and the Town of Selkirk might prevent the operation of any planes equipped for landing upon water by denying them the right to use the river for that purpose. . . .

While the statement of Lord Sankey in the *Aeronautics Reference* that aerial navigation is a class of subjects which has attained such dimensions as to affect the body politic of the Dominion as a whole, and that of Lord Simon in the *Canada*

Temperance matter in referring to that case and the *Radio* case, were perhaps unnecessary to the decision of those matters, they support what I consider to be the true view of this matter that the whole subject of aeronautics lies within the field assigned to Parliament as a matter affecting the peace, order and good government of Canada. *Municipal Act* [R.S.M. 1940 c. 141] clearly trespasses upon that field and must be declared *ultra vires* the province. As to the by-law I am unable, with respect, to agree with the contention that it is a mere zoning regulation or that, even if it were, it could be sustained. On the contrary, I consider it to be a clear attempt to prevent the carrying on of the operation of commercial aerodromes within the municipality. As the right to do this must depend upon s. 921, the by-law must also be declared *ultra vires*. . . .

[Chief Justice Rinfret and Justice Kellock and Estey wrote opinions in which they concluded that the provincial legislation in question was *ultra vires*. Justice Cartwright concurred with Justice Kellock and Justice Taschereau concurred with Justice Estey.]

Attorney General of Manitoba v. Manitoba Egg and Poultry Association (Chicken and Egg Reference), 1971

In the 1950s, the Supreme Court showed signs of breathing new life into the federal Parliament's trade and commerce power, which, along with the peace, order, and good government power, had been severely limited by the Privy Council. The Privy Council's decisions took a mechanical approach to dividing power over trade and commerce. Transactions that crossed provincial boundaries fell under the federal trade and commerce power, but transactions completed within the province fell under provincial power over property and civil rights. The Judicial Committee's application of this mechanical approach in the New Deal reference case on regulating agricultural marketing appeared to create an insurmountable obstacle to either level of government being able to regulate the marketing of a product at the point where the part of it that will be sold and consumed within a province is not separated from the part that is destined for interprovincial or international markets.[1] In two 1950s cases, several Supreme Court justices, though not a majority, took a much more functional approach, indicating that federal legislation, whose primary purpose was the regulation of the interprovincial and international aspects of a commercial activity, would be valid under the trade and commerce power even though some of the regulated transactions might take place within a province.[2]

In *Carnation*,[3] the only 1960s case involving the trade and commerce power, the Court dealt with the defensive use of that power to prevent provinces from adopting protectionist policies that impinge on Canada's foreign trade. But in this case, the federal trade and commerce power was rejected as a ground for overturning such provincial policies. The Quebec legislation in question authorized the province's Agricultural Marketing Board to fix the price of milk sold by Quebec dairy farmers to the Carnation Company, most of whose products were exported from the province. Justice Martland, writing for a unanimous Court, ruled that this indirect effect of the province's economic regulations on export trade did not constitute an invasion of federal jurisdiction over interprovincial and international trade.

But early in the 1970s the Supreme Court rendered two decisions, both of which expressed an inclination toward strengthening trade and commerce as a significant source of federal power. Both cases brought the Supreme Court as the nation's constitutional arbiter to the centre of major conflicts in federal–provincial politics.

At stake in the *Caloil*[4] case was a clash between a major element in the federal government's national energy policy and the economic development ambitions of Quebec. Caloil Inc. of Montreal had been importing petroleum from Algeria and Spain and selling its products through gasoline stations in Ontario and Quebec. But in May 1970, the National

---

1 *A.G. British Columbia v. A.G. Canada*, [1937] A.C. 377.

2 *Re The Farm Products Marketing Act*, [1957] S.C.R. 198; *Murphy v. C.P.R.*, [1958] S.C.R. 626.

3 *Carnation Co. Ltd. v. The Quebec Agricultural Marketing Board et al.*, [1968] S.C.R. 238.

4 *Caloil Inc. v. Attorney General of Canada*, [1971] S.C.R. 543.

Energy Board, with the aim of preserving the key Ontario market for petroleum produced in Western Canada, moved to keep Caloil out of the Ontario market.

Regulations were promulgated that would, in effect, have denied Caloil a licence to import petroleum if it sold *any* gasoline west of a line running down the Ontario–Quebec border and through the Ottawa valley. Caloil successfully challenged the constitutional validity of these regulations before the Exchequer Court. Immediately, the federal authorities amended the regulations so that the conditions required for obtaining a licence to import petroleum were more explicitly stated and any restriction on selling oil within provincial markets applied only to imported petroleum. The Exchequer Court reviewed these amended regulations and found them valid. The Supreme Court "in view of the urgency of a matter involving an interference with important business operations"[5] heard the appeal from this judgment a few weeks later and also found the Energy Board regulations valid.

In the *Caloil* case, the Supreme Court was again unanimous. Justice Pigeon, the newest Quebec appointee, wrote the principal opinion. He found the Supreme Court's earlier decision in the *Murphy* case[6] an apt precedent for bringing the impugned legislation within the federal trade and commerce power. In his view, "the true character" of the enactment was the control of imports as part of the administration of an extraprovincial marketing scheme; in these circumstances the federal government could validly interfere with local trade in a province. Immediately following the decision, at a press conference in Montreal, Quebec economist Jacques Parizeau announced that some of Caloil's 1,200 workers might lose their jobs and the Montreal refinery close as a result of the Supreme Court decision.[7]

The second decision, the *Chicken and Egg Reference*, reported below, was an episode in another economic struggle involving Quebec, this time with neighbouring provinces. Quebec, a major importer of eggs, had granted powers to FEDCO, the province's egg-marketing agency, enabling it to restrict egg imports in order to protect Quebec producers. The major provinces affected by the regulations were Ontario and Manitoba, which supply most of Quebec's egg imports. On the chicken side, the situation was reversed: here Quebec, a major exporter of broilers, soon found that a number of provinces were retaliating against it by restricting the importation of broilers into their provinces. Manitoba, the province most hurt by Quebec's restrictions on egg imports and least assisted by the retaliatory measures protecting broilers, propelled the chicken-and-egg war into the courts by initiating a reference case in its own Court of Appeal. The regulations referred to the court were drawn up to resemble Quebec's egg marketing scheme. The question of their constitutional validity was hypothetical in the extreme: not only were they not put into force, but Manitoba, in fact, is not an importer of eggs. Nonetheless, the Manitoba court found the regulations beyond provincial competence and this decision was upheld on appeal by the Supreme Court of Canada.

Justice Martland, whose decision was supported by five other justices, considered that a scheme such as that drafted by Manitoba must be designed to protect Manitoba egg producers from imported eggs. Hence it could be characterized as legislation made primarily in

---

5   *Ibid.* at 547.

6   *Murphy v. C.P.R. and Attorney General of Canada*, [1958] S.C.R. 626.

7   *The Globe and Mail* (26 November 1970).

relation to interprovincial trade, a field reserved to the federal legislature under the trade and commerce power, section 91. The case also provided the occasion for Justice Bora Laskin's first major decision on the Canadian Constitution. Justice Laskin's concurring opinion carefully reviewed the recent tendency in judicial interpretation to overcome the earlier "attenuation of the federal power in relation to s. 91(2)" and establish a more balanced understanding of trade and commerce as a positive basis of federal power in regulating and integrating national economic life. Although Justice Laskin expressed his dismay at being asked to decide such a constitutional case without any of the relevant empirical data, still he was able to find that the Manitoba scheme was aimed primarily at the regulation of imports and as such constituted an invasion of the federal trade and commerce power. But he, like all the judges who participated in the case, refused to answer the final part of the reference question, which called on the Court to define the degree to which a provincial marketing scheme could affect interprovincial trade without becoming unlawful.

This decision appeared to bolster the Canadian common market by preventing provinces from using marketing schemes to protect local producers from out-of-province competition. Subsequent developments, however, demonstrated that this policy outcome could be substantially reversed through the workings of cooperative federalism. In 1972, the two levels of government agreed to establish the Canadian Egg Marketing Agency (C.E.M.A.), a federal board to coordinate the activities of provincial boards. Under this arrangement, each province was assigned a share of the national market and the quotas of producers in each province were adjusted to the provincial quotas. The constitutional validity of the federal and provincial legislation establishing this scheme was considered by the Supreme Court in 1978. Except for one provision, the Court upheld the legislative scheme, which relied heavily on the interdelegation device approved by the Court in the 1952 *Willis* case.[8] The Court considered that federal legislation delegating to provincial boards the power to restrict imports from other provinces did not violate the requirement of section 121 of the *B.N.A. Act* that "[a]ll Articles of the Growth, Produce or Manufacture of anyone of the Provinces shall . . . be admitted free into each of the other Provinces." Chief Justice Laskin stated that the application of section 121 may differ according to whether it is provincial or federal legislation that is involved because "what may amount to a tariff or customs duty under a provincial regulatory statute may not have that character at all under a federal regulatory statute."[9] ⌐

---

8   See case 44.

9   *Reference re Agricultural Products Marketing*, [1978] 2 S.C.R. 1198 at 1267.

ATTORNEY GENERAL OF MANITOBA v. MANITOBA EGG AND POULTRY ASSOCIATION ET AL.

[1971] S.C.R. 689

Present: Fauteux C.J. and Abbott, Hall, Judson, Laskin, Martland, Pigeon, Ritchie, and Spence J.J.

The judgment of Fauteux C.J. and of Abbott, Martland, Judson, Ritchie, and Spence J.J. was delivered by

MARTLAND J.: This is an appeal from an opinion pronounced, unanimously, by the Court of Appeal for Manitoba [[1971] 18 D.L.R. (3d) 326] on a matter referred to it by an Order of the Lieutenant-Governor-in-Council, dated November 5, 1970, as amended by a further Order-in-Council dated December 18, 1970. An appeal to this Court is permitted by s. 37 of the *Supreme Court of Canada Act*.

The Order-in-Council approved a recommendation of the Attorney-General for Manitoba of the submission to the Court of Appeal for its consideration of certain questions. The relevant portions of the Order-in-Council, as amended, are reproduced, as follows, with the answers given by the Court of Appeal to each of questions:

[The Order in Council refers to efforts by certain provinces to regulate the marketing of agricultural products imported from other provinces. It then asks the Court to consider the constitutional validity of Manitoba legislation authorizing a marketing scheme that would require all eggs sold in the province to be marketed through a board elected by Manitoba producers. This board could, among other things, establish quotas or prohibit the sale "of a particular regulated product." The Manitoba Court of Appeal held it was not within the legislative competence of Manitoba to authorize such a plan.]

... The Plan ... contemplates that it shall be applicable to all eggs marketed in Manitoba, whether or not they are produced in that province. While the provincial Legislature could not control, or permit the Producer Board (hereinafter referred to as "the Board") to control the production of eggs in another province, the terms of the Plan are applicable to the produce of another province once it is within Manitoba and available for marketing. ...

We have, therefore, a Plan which is intended to govern the sale in Manitoba of all eggs, wherever produced, which is to be operated by and for the benefit of the egg producers of Manitoba, to be carried out by a Board armed with the power to control the sale of eggs in Manitoba, brought in from outside Manitoba, by means of quotas, or even outright prohibition.

The issue which has to be considered in this appeal is as to whether the Plan is *ultra vires* of the Manitoba Legislature because it trespasses upon the exclusive legislative authority of the Parliament of Canada to legislate on the matter of the regulation of trade and commerce conferred by s. 91(2) of the *British North America Act*.

When the Privy Council first addressed itself to the meaning of that provision it was stated that it included "regulation of trade in matters of interprovincial concern" (*Citizens Insurance Company of Canada v. Parsons* [(1881), 7 App. Cas. 96 at 113]). That proposition has not since been challenged. However, the case went on to hold that the provision did not include the regulation of the contracts of a particular business or trade in a single province. ...

The earlier authorities on the matter of provincial marketing regulation were considered by various members of this Court in the *Reference Respecting The Farm Products Marketing Act* [[1957] S.C.R. 198], which case, as well as some of those authorities, was reviewed in the judgment of this Court in *Carnation Company Limited v. The Quebec Agricultural Marketing Board* [[1968] S.C.R. 238]. It was said, in that case, at p. 253:

> While I agree with the view of the four judges in the *Ontario Reference* that a trade transaction, completed in a province, is not necessarily, by that fact alone, subject only to provincial control, I also hold the view that the fact that such a transaction incidentally has some effect upon a company engaged in interprovincial trade does not necessarily prevent its being subject to such control.

Our conclusion was that each transaction and regulation had to be examined in relation to its own facts, and that, in determining the validity of the regulatory legislation in issue in that appeal, the issue was not as to whether it might affect the interprovincial trade of the appellant company, but whether it was made in relation to the regulation of interprovincial trade and commerce. There was cited the following passage from the reasons of Kerwin C.J. in the *Ontario Reference* (at p. 204):

> Once a statute aims at "regulation of trade in matters of interprovincial concern" it is beyond the competence of a Provincial Legislature.

It is my opinion that the Plan now in issue not only affects interprovincial trade in eggs, but that it aims at the regulation of such trade. It is an essential part of this scheme, the purpose of which is to obtain for Manitoba producers the most advantageous marketing conditions for eggs, specifically to control and regulate the sale in Manitoba of imported eggs. It is designed to restrict or limit the free flow of trade between provinces as such. Because of that, it constitutes an invitation of the exclusive legislative authority of the Parliament of Canada over the matter of the regulation of trade and commerce.

That being so, I would hold that the Regulation and Order are not ones which are within the legislative competence of the Manitoba Legislature to authorize. . . .

The judgment of Hall and Laskin JJ. was delivered by

LASKIN J.: The utility of the *Reference* as a vehicle for determining whether actual or proposed legislation is competent under the allocations of power made by the *British North America Act* is seriously affected in the present case because there is no factual underpinning for the issues that are raised by the Order of *Reference*. Marketing data to illuminate those issues might have been set out in the order itself (as was done, for example, in the *Margarine Reference* [[1949] S.C.R. 1], or in an agreed statement of facts, or, indeed, might have been offered to the court to indicate the circumstances which prompted the questions addressed to it.

As it is, I know nothing of the nature of the market for eggs in Manitoba or outside of it, nothing of the production of eggs in that province, nothing of the uses to which the production is put, nothing of the number of producers in Manitoba, nothing of any problems that may have been created in relation of quality, price or otherwise by the entry of out-of-province eggs. I know only, and then in the broad terms set out in the first two recitals in the Order of *Reference* (and of which matters I could, in any event, have taken judicial notice) that (to quote them) "many Provinces of Canada, including the Province of Manitoba, have enacted legislation pertaining to the regulation and control of marketing of agricultural products" and "certain of the marketing agencies established under the afore-mentioned legislation in some of the Provinces assert the right to prohibit, regulate and control the marketing within a Province of agricultural products produced outside that Province."

A knowledge of the market in Manitoba, the extent to which it is supplied by Manitoba producers, and of the competition among them as it is reflected in supply, quality and price, would be of assistance in determining the application of the proposed legislative scheme. Thus, if out-of-province eggs were, to put an example, insignificant in the Manitoba market, this would be a factor bearing on a construction of the scheme as operative only in respect of Manitoba producers, retailers and consumers in production, distribution and consumption in Manitoba. Conversely, if such eggs were significant in the Manitoba market, the legislative scheme, not being expressly confined to production, distribution and consumption in Manitoba, could properly be regarded as directed to the out-of-province eggs. In this respect, the issue would be one of its validity or invalidity, and not one of construing it to be applicable only to the distribution and consumption within the province of eggs produced in the province.

The absence of what I regard as relevant data leaves the position as one where, on the face of the legislative scheme and in the light of the arguments thereon addressed to the court, the contemplated regulations and order purport to embrace out-of-province eggs sent or brought into the province. Moreover, the embrace would extend to out-of-province eggs of whatever quantity, and to whatever extent they might engulf the Manitoba retailer and consumer market. On this view of the situation, there is the naked constitutional question to be faced, namely; there being no federal regulatory legislation in force with the same thrust, is the proposed scheme offensive to the legislative power of Parliament in relation to "the regulation of trade and commerce" under s. 91(2) of the *B.N.A. Act*; and, if not or if so, is it, in any event, offensive to the prescriptions of s. 121 of that *Act*?

Previous cases which have been concerned with the validity of provincial regulatory legislation as tested by the scope of s. 91(2) alone (and not also by the concurrent presence of federal regulatory legislation) cannot be dissociated from cases which have been concerned with the validity of federal regulatory legislation and which, accordingly, have dealt affirmatively with the scope of s. 91(2). These two classes are not necessarily opposite sides of the same coin, and hence, the frame of the legislation in each situation has central importance. On the provincial side, a comparison is apt of *Lawson v. Interior Tree Fruit and Vegetable Committee of Direction* [[1931] S.C.R. 357] with *Shannon v. Lower Mainland Dairy Products Board* [[1938] A.C. 708]; and on the federal side, a comparison may be made of *Reference re Natural Products Marketing Act* [[1937] A.C. 377] with *Murphy v. C.P.R.* [[1958] S.C.R. 626].

I adopt the position put by Rand J. in *Reference re Ontario Farm Products Marketing Act* [[1957] S.C.R. 198 at 208-209], that there is a field of trade within provincial power, such power being a subtraction from that comprehended within s. 91(2). The subtraction is, to me, quite rational under the scheme of the *B.N.A. Act*, although stronger terms, referable to a necessary degree of provincial autonomy, have been used in the cases to support it. That there is such subtraction if a provincial regulatory field is to be recognized was obvious to this court in its earliest years. In the very first reported case on the distribution of legislative power, *Severn v. The Queen* [(1878), 2 S.C.R. 70], Strong J., in a dissenting judgment which favoured the validity of the provincial state that was successfully challenged, pointed out (at p. 104) that, literally, "the regulation of trade and commerce in the Provinces, domestic and internal, as well as foreign and external, [was] by the *British North America Act* exclusively conferred upon the Parliament of the Dominion." A reduction of this all-embracing authority was effected by this Court in *Citizens*

Insurance Co. v. Parsons [(1880), 4 S.C.R. 215], a decision affirmed by the Privy Council [(1881), 7 App. Cas. 96] but with *obiter* remarks that led over the years to almost as much an attenuation of the federal power in relation to s. 91(2) as its literal construction would have led to its aggrandizement. A necessary balance has been coming into view over the past two decades, as is evident from the judgments of this court in *Murphy v. C.P.R.*, already cited (and emphasized by the refusal of leave to appeal in *Regina v. Klassen* [(1959), 20 D.L.R. (2d) 406, [1959] S.C.R. IX] and *Carnation Company Ltd. v. Quebec Agricultural Marketing Board* [[1968] S.C.R. 238].

What this balance points to is a more particular understanding of the meaning of the terms "trade" and "trade and commerce" as they relate respectively to the areas of provincial and federal competence. In *Montreal v. Montreal Street Railway* [[1912] A.C. 333 at 344], the Judicial Committee referred to s. 91(2) as expressing "two of the matters enumerated in s. 91. The provision is perhaps better seen as specifying a single class of subject in words that indicate a stronger source of authority than would be found if "trade" alone was used or "commerce" alone. This view is strengthened by the fact that it is unnecessary here to rely on s. 91(2) for transportation authority (having regard to ss. 92(10)(*a*)(*b*), 91(10) and 91(29)), in contradistinction to the judicial history of the commerce power in the United States under clause 3 of Article I of its Constitution and to the evolution of the power of the commonwealth Parliament under s. 51(i) of the Australian Constitution to make laws with respect to "trade and commerce with other countries and among the states." Etymologically, commerce refers to the buying and selling of goods, and trade has among its meanings (other than commerce) that of mercantile occupation. Although literal application is unthinkable, these meanings do indicate the capacity which inheres in s. 91(2).

Not too often in the history of the interaction of provincial and federal legislation with s. 91(2) have there been attempts to define its terms.... It has been put beyond doubt that Parliament's power under s. 91(2) is exclusive so far as concerns the prohibition or regulation of exports to and imports from other countries, and that a province may not, as legislator, prohibit or regulate the export of goods therefrom. This last-mentioned proposition ... does not, however, mean that, in the absence of federal legislation, a province is incompetent to impose any regulation upon transactions in goods produced therein and between persons therein simply because the regulation may have an effect upon ultimate export of the goods from the province, whether in their original or in some processed form.

The stage of dealing at which the regulation is imposed and its purpose, on which economic data would be relevant, are important considerations in assessing provincial competence. This emerges clearly from *Carnation Milk Company Ltd. v. Quebec Agricultural Marketing Board, supra,* where this court rejected a contention that the regulatory scheme, as reflected in three challenged orders, constituted an unlawful invasion of federal power in relation to export. What was there involved was the fixing of prices, by arbitration if agreement could not otherwise be reached, at which milk and dairy products produced in the province were to be sold by provincial producers, operating under a joint marketing plan, to a distributor and processor in the province. The fact that the processed products were largely distributed and sold outside the province did not react upon the validity of the scheme whose purpose was to improve the bargaining position in the province of provincial producers in their dealings with manufacturers or processors in the province. The regulatory scheme under attack did not involve a marketing control which extended through the various stages or production, distribution and consumption.

What was raised in the *Carnation Milk* case was the meaning, for constitutional purposes, of an intra-provincial transaction where the issue was seen in the context of goods leaving the province. The present *Reference* raises this question in the context of goods entering the province and their subjection, in consequence, to the same regulatory scheme that operates upon like goods produced in the province. This was a matter which had been considered in the *Shannon* case, *supra,* and in *Home Oil Distributors Ltd. v. Attorney-General of British Columbia* [[1940] S.C.R. 444], in both of which the impugned schemes were held to be within provincial legislative competence.

There is a passage in the reasons of the Judicial Committee in the *Shannon* case which has a bearing on this Reference. Lord Atkin said this (at pp. 718-719 of [1938] A.C.):

> It is sufficient to say upon the first ground that it is apparent that the legislation in question is confined to regulating transactions that take place wholly within the Province, and are therefore within the sovereign powers granted to the legislature in that respect by s. 92 of the *British North America Act*. Their Lordships do not accept the view that natural products as defined in the *Act* are confined to natural products produced in British Columbia. There is no such restriction in the *Act*, and the limited construction would probably cause difficulty if it were sought at some future time to co-operate with a valid Dominion scheme. But the *Act* is clearly confined to dealings with such products as are situate within the Province.

The second sentence in this passage must be read in the light of the history of marketing legislation as it evolved in that period. Parliament and provincial legislatures had enacted what they though was dovetailing legislation only to find that the central piece, the federal enactment, had over-reached in attempting to encompass purely intra-provincial transactions in products grown and marketed in the province, this element of the scheme being founded on the fact that some portion of the product might be exported: see *Attorney-General of British Columbia v. Attorney-General of Canada* [[1937] A.C. 377]. The Privy Council appeared to think in the *Shannon* case that effective co-operation in marketing could better be ensured if the small extra-provincial element was an appendage of provincial legislation. The decision did not foresee the later developments in this area through such legislation as the *Motor Vehicle Transport Act, 1954* (Can.), c. 59 and the *Agricultural Products Marketing Act*, R.S.C. 1952, c. 6, as amended by 1957 (Can.), c. 15.

In my opinion, the *Shannon* case cannot today have the effect which a literal application of the second sentence of the quoted passage would suggest. Moreover, the fourth and last sentence indicates that the legislation did not purport to apply to out-of-province producers. However, I find this difficult to reconcile with the second sentence unless it be taken that the marketing scheme did not apply to out-of-province products on their mere entry into the province or that any such application was *de minimis* and not an aim of the scheme. If so, the scheme in the *Shannon* case differs from that involved in this Reference.

Home Oil Distributors Ltd. v. Attorney-General of British Columbia [[1940] S.C.R. 444] concerned not a marketing scheme of the type involved in the *Shannon* case or in the present case, but rather a price fixing scheme, embracing both maximum and minimum prices for coal and petroleum products sold at wholesale or retail in the province or for use in the province. It was urged that the legislation was intended to protect local industry from outside competition and, indeed, was aimed at extra-territorial sources of supply and at an integrated interprovincial and international industry. The challenge to the validity of the legislation was made by companies operating refineries in the province who sold to persons in the province, but whose raw supplies came from outside. There was no attempt to control the entry of their oil which, when refined in the province, was marketed therein, save as that control resulted from the price fixing authority. In these circumstances, the legislation was upheld on the principle of the *Shannon* case.

I cannot see in the *Home Oil* case any parallel with the marketing scheme which the Order of *Reference* put before the Manitoba Court of Appeal. In saying this, I reserve my opinion on a question not dealt with in the reasons of this court in the *Home Oil* case; that is, whether it would have made any difference if under the power given to "fix schedules of prices for different qualities, quantities, standards, grades and kinds of coal and petroleum products" imported goods were treated discriminatorily simply because they were imported....

The *Ontario Farm Products Marketing Act Reference*, although refining the meaning of an intra-provincial transaction, did not expressly address itself to the position of an extra-provincial producer, or a purchaser from him, seeking to bring his production into a province free of a regulatory scheme applicable to local produce. Fauteux J., as he then was, noted in that *Reference* that the hog marketing scheme which was the subject of the court's concern did not cover hogs produced outside the province nor were producers outside the province affected thereby. "In the result," he said, "any one in Ontario is free to import therein and one beyond its boundaries to export thereto the regulated product" [at p. 254 of [1957] S.C.R.]. This is, however, precisely the issue that must be faced in the present *Reference*.

It must be faced under a scheme which, as set out in the proposed measures attached to the Order of *Reference*, has the following elements:

1. A Producer Board is established through which all eggs to be marketed in Manitoba must be sold.
2. All such eggs must go to grading and packing stations which are to be operated by persons under contract with the Board.
3. All such eggs must be graded, packed and marked in the grading and packing stations.
4. They are to be packed in containers provided by the Board which are to bear inscriptions of the grade, station number, grading date, place of origin of the eggs and the Board trade mark.
5. Only authorized collectors may take delivery of eggs from a producer.
6. Production and marketing quotas may be allotted to producers by the Board.
7. The Board may establish quotas for production and sale and also fix the time and place of marketing and, equally, may prohibit marketing otherwise or in violation of established quotas or standards.
8. The Board may contract with distributors as its intermediaries in sales to retailers.
9. Weekly prices for each grade of egg are to be set by the Board and distributors are entitled to buy at those prices.

Although the emphasis is on control of the Manitoba producers and distributors in order (as stated in the proposed measures) "to obtain for producers the most advantageous marketing conditions" and "to avoid overproduction," the scheme brings into its grasp "persons" as well as producers, that is, those outside the province who are either producers or distributors seeking to enter the Manitoba market, or those inside the province who are not themselves producers but who bring in out-of-province eggs for disposition in Manitoba. This view is reinforced by the provision for indicating the origin of eggs, including eggs other than those produced in Manitoba.

There may be a variety of reasons which impel a province to enact regulatory legislation for the marketing of various products. For example, it may wish to secure the health of the inhabitants by establishing quality standards; it may wish to protect consumers against exorbitant prices; it may wish to equalize the bargaining of competitive position of producers or distributors or retailers, or all three classes; it may wish to ensure an adequate supply of certain products. These objects may not all nor always be realizable through legislation which fastens on the regulated product as being within the province. That is no longer, if it ever was, the test of validity. Just as the province may not, as a general rule, prohibit an owner of goods from sending them outside the province, so it may not be able to subject goods to a regulatory scheme upon their entry into the province. This is not to say that goods that have come into a province may not, thereafter, be subject to the same controls in, for example, retail distribution to consumers as apply to similar goods produced in the province.

Assuming such controls to be open to a province, the scheme before this court is not so limited. It embraces products where are in the current of interprovincial trade and, as noted at the beginning of these reasons, it embraces them in whatever degree they seek to enter the provincial market. It begs the question to say that out-of-province producers who come in voluntarily (certainly they cannot be compelled by Manitoba) must not expect to be treated differently from local producers. I do not reach the question of discriminatory standards applied to out-of-province producers or distributors (that is, the question of a possibly illegal administration of the scheme as bearing on its validity) because I am of opinion that the scheme is on its face an invasion of federal power in relation to s. 91(2).

There are several grounds upon which I base this conclusion. The proposed scheme has as a direct object the regulation of the importation of eggs, and it is not saved by the fact that the local market is under the same regime. Anglin J. said in *Gold Seal Ltd. v. Dominion Express Co.* [(1921), 62 S.C.R. 424 at 465] that "it is common ground that the prohibition of importation is beyond the legislative jurisdiction of the province." Conversely, the general limitation upon provincial authority to exercise of its powers within or in the province precludes it from intercepting either goods moving into the province or goods moving out, subject to possible exceptions, as in the case of danger to life or health. Again, the Manitoba scheme cannot be considered in isolation from similar schemes in other provinces; and to permit each province to seek its own advantage, so to speak, through a figurative sealing of its borders to entry of goods from others would be to deny one of the objects of Confederation, evidence by the catalogue of federal powers and by s. 121, namely, to form an economic unit of the whole of Canada: see the *Lawson* case [[1931] S.C.R. 357 at 373]. The existence of egg marketing schemes in more than one province, with objectives similar to the proposed Manitoba scheme, makes it clear that interprovincial trade in eggs is being struck at by the provincial barriers to their movement into various provincial markets. If it be thought necessary or desirable to arrest such movement at any provincial border then the aid of the Parliament of Canada must be sought, as was done through Part V of the *Canada Temperance Act*, R.S.C. 1952, c. 30, in respect of provincial regulation of the sale of intoxicating liquor.

I do not find it necessary in this case to invoke s. 121, and hence say nothing about its applicability to the marketing scheme under review. . . .

[Justice Pigeon also wrote a brief concurring opinion and agreed with Justice Martland's opinion.]

13 Reference re Anti-Inflation Act, 1976

In the fall of 1975, the federal government launched a comprehensive program of wage and price controls. The *Anti-Inflation Act* authorized the federal government to control the level of incomes, prices, and profits in key sectors of the private sector (firms with 500 or more employees, construction firms with 20 or more employees, and professionals). It applied directly to the federal public sector and to government employees of provinces that opted into the scheme. The authority could be exercised for up to three years and could be extended by an Order in Council with the approval of both Houses of Parliament.

The scope of the legislation was not confined to interprovincial and international commerce. It regulated activities that the courts had long regarded as matters of property and civil rights in the province. In enacting the legislation the federal government was relying on its general power. It hoped that if there was a court challenge the Supreme Court would apply the national-dimensions test and find that the national importance of combatting inflation made the subject of the legislation a matter concerning the peace, order, and good government of Canada. The government was careful to refrain from declaring that inflation was an emergency and, in Parliament, denied that it was counting on the emergency doctrine as a basis for the legislation.

But the government did not rely solely on constitutional law. Before moving ahead with such a contentious economic policy, it obtained the agreement of all the provinces that they would support the program. Thus the provinces did not initiate a court challenge. However, the program was attacked in the courts by several Ontario public employees' unions. These groups were particularly concerned that Ontario had brought its public sector into the program without having enabling legislation passed through the provincial legislature. To resolve legal doubts that had begun to be aired in the lower courts, the federal government decided in March 1976 to refer the question of the *Anti-Inflation Act*'s constitutional validity, as well as the question of the validity of Ontario's opting-in agreement, to the Supreme Court.

By a 7-to-2 majority, the Supreme Court upheld the *Anti-Inflation Act* as emergency legislation. But a majority of the judges rejected inherent national importance or national dimensions as the criterion for determining whether such a broad subject matter as combatting inflation can be brought under the peace, order, and good government power. On this point, Justice Beetz's opinion was decisive. In his view the general power could be used in two ways. In extraordinary circumstances amounting to a national emergency it could be used even if it meant Parliament would be legislating on subjects normally falling under provincial jurisdiction. But the normal use of peace, order, and good government was to legislate in relation to narrowly defined subject matters—for example, the incorporation of national companies, radio, aeronautics, or the development of the national capital region—which clearly constitute gaps in the distribution of powers and are matters of national concern. A subject such as combatting inflation did not qualify for this normal use because it was far too broad and encompassed matters clearly subject to provincial jurisdiction. This part of Justice Beetz's opinion was supported by five of the nine judges. It represented a victory for those provinces which, like Quebec, British Columbia, and Saskatchewan, although willing to support the emergency doctrine, had opposed the national-dimensions test.

On the other hand, the Court's willingness to sustain the *Anti-Inflation Act* as emergency legislation had frightening implications for the provinces. When the federal Parliament exercises its emergency powers, the normal rule of law governing the distribution of powers in Canadian federalism is set aside. This was the first time that the judiciary invoked the emergency doctrine as the constitutional basis for peacetime economic regulation.[1] The Court's decision indicated that the onus of proof as to the existence of an emergency lies with those who challenge the legislation. A brief before the Court supported by 39 of the country's leading economists denying the existence of an emergency was given little weight by the judges. Nor was the majority impressed by the fact that the government had deliberately avoided declaring an emergency when the legislation was before Parliament. It was on this point that Justices Beetz and de Grandpré dissented. In their view, a clear indication by Parliament that a national emergency existed was a necessary, although not sufficient, condition for the valid exercise of the emergency power. The ease with which the Court's decision suggested that the federal government could have access to emergency powers stimulated provincial interest in giving a reformed federal Upper House representing provincial governments a veto over the exercise of federal emergency powers.

Although the Court ruled against the Ontario Agreement on the ground that change in provincial labour laws required an act of the legislature, the practical import of this part of the decision was soon negated. The Liberal opposition party in the Ontario legislature withdrew its opposition to the anti-inflation program, permitting the Ontario government, despite its minority position, to have retroactive enabling legislation enacted. ～

---

1 For decisions rejecting the emergency argument as a basis for federal economic legislation in peacetime, see cases 5, 6, and 8. But note that the legislation in these earlier cases was not cast in the form of temporary legislation.

REFERENCE RE ANTI-INFLATION ACT
[1976] 2 S.C.R. 373

Hearing: May 31, June 1, 2, 3, and 4, 1976; Judgment: July 12, 1976.

Present: Laskin C.J. and Martland, Judson, Ritchie, Spence, Pigeon, Dickson, Beetz, and de Grandpré JJ.

The judgment of Laskin C.J. and of Judson, Spence, and Dickson JJ. was delivered by

LASKIN C.J.: Although it is conceded that the Parliament of Canada could validly legislate as it has done if it had limited the legislation to the federal public service and to enterprises or undertakings which are within exclusive federal legislative authority, such as interprovincial transportation and communication services, radio operations, aerial navigation, atomic energy enterprises, banks and works declared to be for the general advantage of Canada, the *Anti-Inflation Act* embraces sectors of industry and of services, including employers and employees therein, which are admittedly sub-

ject in respect of their intraprovincial operation to provincial regulatory authority. I take it as undeniable that it would have been open to each Province to impose price and wage restraints in those sectors, to the extent to which there was no invasion of federal powers such as that in relation to the regulation of trade and commerce. It is equally undeniable that each Province could have validly dealt with restraint of salaries and wages of persons in its public service....

In founding himself upon the federal general power to make laws for the peace, order and good government of Canada, the Attorney-General in his primary submission takes its scope to be that expounded by Viscount Simon in *Attorney-General of Ontario v. Canada Temperance Federation* [[1946] A.C. 193]. That case was a re-run, at a distance of more than sixty years, of the very issue brought before the Privy Council in *Russell v. The Queen* [(1882), 7 App. Cas. 829]....

[The Chief Justice then reviewed the decision of the Privy Council and the Supreme Court dealing with peace, order, and good government from the *Russell* case to the *Snider* case in 1925.]

What emerges from the lines of cases up to the *Snider* case are differences more of degree than of kind about the scope of the federal general power. It is true that neither the *Russell* case nor, indeed, Lord Watson's observations in the *Local Prohibition* case fitted into Viscount Haldane's emphasis on the need for exceptional circumstances, but even on that standard there was no preclusion against finding that a peace-time crisis would warrant resort to the general power in support of federal legislation.

Lord Watson's "national dimensions" proposition, which appears to have been studiously ignored by the Privy Council through to the *Snider* case, was mentioned by it in the *Labour Conventions* case [[1937] A.C. 326], where Lord Atkin said of Lord Watson's words that "they laid down no principle of constitutional law, and were cautious words intended to safeguard possible eventualities which no one at the time had any interest or desire to define" (at p. 353). It is my view that a similar approach of caution is demanded even today, both against a loose and unrestricted scope of the general power and against a fixity of its scope that would preclude resort to it in circumstances now unforeseen. Indeed, I do not see how this Court can, consistently with its supervisory function in respect of the distribution of legislative power, preclude in advance and irrespective of any supervening situations a resort to the general power or, for that matter, to any other head of legislative authority. This is not to say that clear situations are to be unsettled, but only that a Constitution designed to serve this country in years ahead ought to be regarded as a resilient instrument capable of adaptation to changing circumstances. . . .

Chief Justice Duff attempted in his extensive reasons in the *Natural Products Marketing Reference* a synthesis of the preceding case law touching the general power but, significantly, he began his discussion with the following prelude (at p. 416):

> . . . There is no dispute now that the exception which excludes from the ambit of the general power all matters assigned to the exclusive authority of the legislatures must be given its full effect. Nevertheless, it has been laid down that matters normally comprised within the subjects enumerated in section 92 may, in extraordinary circumstances, acquire aspects of such paramount significance as to take them outside the sphere of that section.

What followed was a reconciliation of Lord Watson's national dimensions approach with Viscount Haldane's notion of the extraordinary, by requiring that there be some crisis or peril to support federal legislation for the peace, order and good government of Canada, of which war, present or apprehended, was an example. This did not exclude peacetime crises. . . .

I come, finally, to the *Canada Temperance Federation* case. The Privy Council was fully entitled to overrule the *Russell* case and could have marshalled intervening observations in various cases to support it in doing so. But it felt, to use its own words, that "the decision now sought to be over-ruled has stood for over sixty years . . . and [it] must be regarded as firmly embedded in the constitutional law of Canada and it is impossible now to depart from it" (at p. 206). The importance of Viscount Simon's reasons in the *Canada Temperance Federation* case lies not only in his rejection of the explanation of the *Russell* case given in the *Snider* case but also in his restatement of the scope of the federal general power without advertence either to the *Board of Commerce* case or to the *Fort Frances* case and even without reference to Lord Watson's observations in the *Local Prohibition* case. Of course, as I have already noted, general propositions must be viewed in the context of the facts and issues out of which they arise, and I emphasize again the point made earlier that it would be unwise to nail down any head of Legislative power in such firm fashion as to make it incapable of application to situations as yet unforeseen. . . .

The Attorney-General of Canada, supported by the Attorney-General of Ontario, put his position in support of the *Anti-Inflation Act* on alternative bases. He relied, primarily, on the *Canada Temperance Federation* case, contending that the *Act*, directed to containment and reduction of inflation, concerned a matter which went beyond local or private or provincial concern and was of a nature which engaged vital national interests, among them the integrity of the Canadian monetary system which was unchallengeably within exclusive federal protection and control. He urged, in the alternative, that there was an economic crisis amounting to an emergency or exceptional peril to economic stability sufficient to warrant federal intervention, and, if not an existing peril, there was a reasonable apprehension of an impending one that justified federal intervention through the legislation in question which was designed to support measures and policies of a fiscal and monetary character which were undoubtedly within Parliament's legislative authority. . . .

Since there was, in general, a concession by those opposing the legislation that it would be valid if it were what I may call crisis legislation, and since the proponents of the legislation urged this as an alternative ground on which its validity should be sustained, it appears to me to be the wise course to consider first whether the *Anti-Inflation Act* can be supported on that footing. If it is sustainable as crisis legislation, it becomes necessary to consider the broader ground advanced in its support, and this because, especially in constitutional cases, Courts should not, as a rule, go any farther than is necessary to determine the main issue before them.

The competing arguments on the question whether the *Act* is supportable as crisis legislation raised four main issues: (1) Did the *Anti-Inflation Act* itself belie the federal contention because of the form of the *Act* and, in particular, because of the exclusion of the provincial public sector from its imperative scope, notwithstanding that it is framed as a temporary measure albeit subject to extension of its operation? (2) Is the federal contention assisted by the preamble to the statute? (3) Does the extrinsic evidence put before the Court, and other matters of which the Court can take judicial notice without extrinsic material to back it up, show that there was a rational basis for the *Act* as a crisis measure? (4) Is it a tenable argument that exceptional character could be lent to the legislation as rising beyond local or provincial concerns because Parliament could reasonably take the view that it was a necessary measure to fortify action in other related areas of admittedly federal authority, such as that of monetary policy?

I have referred to the first of these issues earlier in these reasons. It goes to the form of the *Anti-Inflation Act* and to the question whether the scope of the compulsory application of the *Anti-Inflation Act* may be taken to indicate that the Parliament of Canada did not act through any sense of crisis or urgency in enacting it. I note that the federal public service, a very large public service, is governed by the *Act* and the Guidelines, that private employers of five hundred or more persons are subject to the *Act* and Guidelines, that the construction industry is particularly dealt with by making those who employ twenty or more persons in that industry subject to the *Act* and Guidelines and that the *Act* and Guidelines apply also to persons in various professions including architects, accountants, dentists, engineers, lawyers, doctors and management consultants. Again, the *Act* provides for bringing within the *Act* and Guidelines businesses, irrespective of numbers employed, which are declared by order in council to be of strategic importance to the containment and reduction of inflation in Canada. Having regard to the enormous administrative problems which the programme entails, the coverage is comprehensive indeed in its immediately obligatory provisions. What is left out of compulsory coverage is the provincial public sector, including the municipal public sector, but provision is made for bringing this area into the programme under the Guidelines by agreements under s. 4(3) or s. 4(4) or s. 5.

I do not regard the provisions respecting the provincial public sector as an indicator that the Government and Parliament of Canada were not seized with urgency or manifested a lack of any sense of crisis in the establishment of the programme. Provincial government concern about rising inflation and concurrent unemployment was a matter of public record prior to the inauguration of the programme, and this Court

was provided with copies of agreements that eight of the ten Provinces had made with the federal Government or the application therein of the federal Guidelines. Only British Columbia and Saskatchewan had not entered into agreements. With private industry and private services bound to the extent that they are, and with the federal public service also bound, I see it as a reasonable policy from the standpoint of administration to allow the Provinces to contract into the programme in respect of the provincial public sector under their own administration if this was their preference rather than by simply accepting, as they could, the federal administration. Since the "contracting in" is envisaged on the basis of the federal Guidelines the national character of the programme is underlined. . . .

The Attorney-General of Canada relied upon the preamble to the *Anti-Inflation Act* both in respect of his primary argument and in respect of his alternative argument. He emphasized the words therein "that the containment and reduction of inflation has become a matter of *serious* national concern" and as well the following words that "to accomplish such containment and reduction of inflation it is *necessary* to restrain profit margins, prices, dividends and compensation" (the underlined words were especially emphasized). I do not regard it as telling against the Attorney-General's alternative position that the very word "emergency" was not used. Forceful language would not carry the day for the Attorney-General of Canada if the circumstances attending its use did not support the constitutional significance sought to be drawn from it. Of course, the absence of any preamble would weaken the assertion of crisis conditions, and I have already drawn attention to the fact that no preamble suggesting a critical economic situation, indeed no preamble at all was included in the legislation challenged in the *Board of Commerce* case.

The preamble in the present case is sufficiently indicative that Parliament was introducing a far-reaching programme prompted by what in its view was a serious national condition. The validity of the *Anti-Inflation Act* does not, however, stand or fall on that preamble, but the preamble does provide a base for assessing the gravity of the circumstances which called forth the legislation.

This brings me to the third of the four issues abovementioned, namely, the relevancy and weight of the extrinsic evidence and the assistance to be derived from judicial notice. When, as in this case, an issue is raised that exceptional circumstances underlie resort to a legislative power which may properly be invoked in such circumstances, the Court may be asked to consider extrinsic material bearing on the circumstances alleged, both in a support of and in denial of the lawful exercise of legislative authority. In considering such material and assessing its weight, the Court does not look at it in terms of whether it provides proof of the exceptional circumstances as a matter of fact. The matter concerns social and economic policy and hence governmental and legislative judgment. It may be that the existence of exceptional circumstances is so notorious as to enable the Court, of its own motion, to take judicial notice of them without reliance on extrinsic material to inform it. Where this is not so evident, the extrinsic material need go only so far as to persuade the Court that there is a rational basis for the legislation which it is attributing to the head of power invoked in this case in support of its validity.

There is before this Court material from Statistics' Canada, upon which the Court is justified in relying, which, proceeding from a base of 100 in 1971, shows that the purchasing power of the dollar dropped to 0.78 by September, 1974 and 0.71 in September, 1975. On the same base, the cost of living index rose to 127.9 by September, 1974 and to 141.5 by September, 1975, with food, taken alone, and weighted at 28 per cent of all the items taken into calculation, showing a rise to 147.3 in September, 1974 and 166.6 in September, 1975. These are figures from the Consumer Price Index monitored by Statistics Canada. . . .

There have been inflationary periods before in our history but, again referring to Professor Lipsey's study, "the problem of the coexistence of high unemployment and high inflation rates was not, however, encountered before the late 1960s." These twin conditions continued to the time that the Government and Parliament acted in establishing policy under its prices and incomes policy under the *Anti-Inflation Act* and Guidelines, and were the prime reason for the policy. . . .

There is another consideration that arises from the submissions, particularly those of the Canadian Labour Congress, in opposition to the validity of the *Anti-Inflation Act* as a measure justified by crisis circumstances. The consideration I refer to is based on Professor Lipsey's study and on his conclusion that the policy adopted in the *Anti-Inflation Act* is not one that can, on the basis of experience elsewhere and on his appraisal as an economist, be expected to reduce the rate of inflation by more than one or two per cent. The answer to this submission is simple, and it is an answer that has been consistently given by the Courts, namely, that the wisdom or expediency or likely success of a particular policy expressed in legislation is not subject to judicial review. Hence, it is not for the Court to say in this case that because the means adopted to realize a desirable end, i.e., the containment and reduction of inflation in Canada, may not be effectual, those means are beyond the legislative power of Parliament.

I would not exclude the possibility that the means chosen to deal with an alleged evil may be some indicator of whether that evil exists as a foundation for legislation. Professor Lipsey

is candid enough to say in his study that whether "a problem is serious enough to be described as a crisis must be partly a matter of judgment." The general question to which his study is directed is, to use his words, "could an economist say that the Canadian economy faced an economic crisis, or was in a critical situation, in October 1975?" He answers this question in the negative on the basis, *inter alia*, of comparative assessment of different periods, and he is supported in this view by many other economists. The Court cannot, however, be concluded by the judgment of an economist, distinguished as he is in the opinion of his peers, on a question of the validity of the exercise of the legislative power invoked in this case. The economic judgment can be taken into account as an element in arriving at an answer to the question whether there is a rational basis for the governmental and legislative judgment exercised in the enactment of the *Anti-Inflation Act*. It cannot determine the answer.

In my opinion, this Court would be unjustified in concluding, on the submissions in this case and on all the material put before it, that the Parliament of Canada did not have a rational basis for regarding the *Anti-Inflation Act* as a measure which, in its judgment, was temporarily necessary to meet a situation of economic crisis imperilling the well-being of the people of Canada as a whole and requiring Parliament's stern intervention in the interests of the country as a whole. That there may have been other periods of crisis in which no similar action was taken is beside the point.

The rationality of the judgment so exercised is, in my view, supported by a consideration of the fourth of the issues which I enumerated above. The fact that there had been rising inflation at the time federal action was taken, that inflation is regarded as a monetary phenomenon and that monetary policy is admittedly within exclusive federal jurisdiction persuades me that the Parliament of Canada was entitled, in the circumstances then prevailing and to which I have already referred, to act as it did from the springboard of its jurisdiction over monetary policy and, I venture to add, with additional support from its power in relation to the regulation of trade and commerce. The Government White Paper refers to a prices and incomes policy as one element in a four-pronged programme of which the first engages its fiscal and monetary authority; and although the White Paper states that the Government rejects the use of severe monetary and fiscal restraints to stop inflation because of the alleged heavy immediate cost in unemployment and foregone output, it could seek to blend policies in those areas with a prices and incomes policy under the circumstances revealed by the extrinsic material.

Since no argument was addressed to the trade and commerce power I content myself with observing only that it provides the Parliament of Canada with a foothold in respect of "the general regulation of trade affecting the whole dominion," to use the words of the Privy Council in *Citizens Insurance Co. v. Parsons* (1881), 7 App. Cas. 96, at p. 113. The *Anti-Inflation Act* is not directed to any particular trade. It is directed to suppliers of commodities and services in general and to the public services of governments, and to the relationship of those suppliers and of the public services to those employed by and in them, and to their overall relationship to the public. With respect to some of such suppliers and with respect to the federal public service, federal legislative power needs no support from the existence of exceptional circumstances to justify the introduction of a policy of restraint to combat inflation.

The economic interconnection with other suppliers and with provincial public services, underlined by collective bargaining conducted by, or under the policy umbrella of trade unions with Canada-wide operations and affiliations, is a matter of public general knowledge of which the Court can take judicial notice. The extrinsic material does not reveal any distinction in the operation and effect of inflation in respect of those economic areas which are ordinarily within and those ordinarily outside of effective federal regulatory control. In enacting the *Anti-Inflation Act* as a measure for the peace, order and good government of Canada, Parliament is not opening an area of legislative authority which would otherwise have no anchorage at all in the federal catalogue of legislative powers but, rather, it is proceeding from legislative power bases which entitle it to wage war on inflation through monetary and fiscal policies and entitle it to embrace within the *Anti-Inflation Act* some of the sectors covered thereby but not all. The circumstances recounted above justify it in invoking its general power to extend its embrace as it has done.

For all the foregoing reasons, I would hold that the *Anti-Inflation Act* is valid legislation for the peace, order and good government of Canada and does not, in the circumstances under which it was enacted and having regard to its temporary character, invade provincial legislative jurisdiction. It is open to this Court to say, at some future time, as it in effect said in the *Margarine* case [[1949] S.C.R. 1; aff'd [1951] A.C. 179], that a statutory provision valid in its application under circumstances envisaged at the time of its enactment can no longer have a constitutional application to different circumstances under which it would, equally, not have been sustained had they existed at the time of its enactment.

[On question 2, Chief Justice Laskin found that the agreement between the federal government and Ontario was not effective to render the *Anti-Inflation Act* and its Guidelines binding on the provincial public sector in Ontario. This part of the Chief Justice's opinion was concurred in by the other eight judges.]

The judgment of Martland, Ritchie, and Pigeon JJ. was delivered by

RITCHIE J.: I have had the privilege of reading the reasons for judgment of the Chief Justice and his comprehensive review of the authorities satisfies me that the answer to the question of whether or not the *Anti-Inflation Act*, hereinafter referred to as the "*Act*," is *ultra vires* the Parliament of Canada, must depend upon whether or not the legislation was enacted to combat a national economic emergency. I use the phrase "national emergency" in the sense in which I take it to have been used by Lord Wright in *Co-operative Committee on Japanese Canadians v. Attorney General of Canada* [[1947] A.C. 87], and accepted by this Court in the *Reference as to the Validity of the Wartime Leasehold Regulations* [[1950] S.C.R. 124]. In those cases the "emergency" was occasioned by war and the aftermath of war, but I see nothing to exclude the application of the principles there enunciated from a situation created by highly exceptional economic conditions prevailing in times of peace.

In my opinion such conditions exist where there can be said to be an urgent and critical situation adversely affecting all Canadians and being of such proportions as to transcend the authority vested in the Legislatures of the Provinces and thus presenting an emergency which can only be effectively dealt with by Parliament in the exercise of the powers conferred upon it by s. 91 of the *British North America Act* "to make laws for the peace, order and good government of Canada." The authority of Parliament in this regard is, in my opinion, limited to dealing with critical conditions and the necessity to which they give rise and must perforce be confined to legislation of a temporary character.

I do not consider that the validity of the *Act* rests upon the constitutional doctrine exemplified in earlier decisions of the Privy Council, to all of which the Chief Justice has made reference, and generally known as the "national dimension" or "national concern" doctrine. It is not difficult to envisage many different circumstances which could give rise to national concern, but at least since the *Japanese Canadians* case, I take it to be established that unless such concern is made manifest by circumstances amounting to a national emergency, Parliament is not endowed under the cloak of the "peace, order and good government" clause with the authority to legislate in relation to matters reserved to the Provinces under s. 92 of the *British North America Act*. In this regard I am in full agreement with the reasons for judgment prepared for delivery by my brother Beetz which I have had the advantage of reading, and I have little to add to what he has said.

I should also say, however, that I cannot find that the authority of Parliament to pass legislation such as the present

Act stems from any of the enumerated classes of subjects referred to in s. 91. The source of the federal power in relation to the *Anti-Inflation Act* must, in my opinion, be found in the "peace, order and good government" clause, and the aura of federal authority to which that clause relates can in my view only be extended so as to invade the provincial area when the legislation is directed to coping with a genuine emergency in the sense to which I have made reference.

In order to determine whether the legislation here in question was enacted to combat such an emergency, it is necessary to examine the legislation itself, but in so doing I think it not only permissible but essential to give consideration to the material which Parliament had before it at the time when the statute was enacted for the purpose of disclosing the circumstances which prompted its enactment. The most concrete source of this information is, in my opinion, the White Paper tabled in the House by the Minister of Finance and made a part of the case which was submitted on behalf of the Attorney General of Canada.

The preamble to the *Anti-Inflation Act* is quoted in full in the reasons for judgment of the Chief Justice and it is unnecessary for me to repeat it. It is enough to say that it manifests a recognition of the fact "that inflation in Canada at current levels is contrary to the interests of all Canadians" and that it has become a matter of such serious national concern as to make it necessary to enact this legislation. Neither the terms of the preamble nor any provisions of the *Act* specifically declare the existence of a national emergency, nor is there anything in the *Act* which could of itself be characterized as a proclamation that such a situation exists, but when the language of the preamble is read as I have suggested in conjunction with the White Paper, it does not appear to me that it was necessary for Parliament to use any particular form of words in order to disclose its belief that an emergency existed. The "Introduction" and "Conclusion" of the White Paper appear to me to be descriptive of the conditions with which Parliament purported to cope in enacting the legislation. The "Introduction" contains the following statement:

> Canada is in the grip of serious inflation.
>
> If this inflation continues or gets worse there is a grave danger that economic recovery will be stifled, unemployment increased and the nation subjected to mounting stresses and strains.
>
> It has thus become absolutely essential to undertake a concerted national effort to bring inflation under control.
>
> There are no simple or easy remedies for quickly resolving this critical problem. The inflationary process in Canada is so deeply entrenched that it can be brought under control only by a broad and comprehensive program of action on a national scale.

The "Conclusion" contains the following passage:

> As a first essential, it is imperative that we take determined action as a nation to halt and reverse the spiral of costs and prices that jeopardizes the whole fabric of our economy and of our society.

When the words "serious national concern" are read against the background of these excerpts from the White Paper it becomes apparent that they were employed by Parliament in recognition of the existence of a national Emergency.

The provisions of the *Act* quite clearly reveal the decision of Parliament that exceptional measures were considered to be required to combat this emergency and it has not been seriously suggested that these provisions were colourably enacted for any other purpose.

I am accordingly satisfied that the record discloses that in enacting the *Anti-Inflation Act* the Parliament of Canada was motivated by a sense of urgent necessity created by highly exceptional circumstances and that a judgment declaring the *Act* to be *ultra vires* could only be justified by reliance on very clear evidence that an emergency had not arisen when the statute was enacted. In this regard I reiterate what was said by Lord Wright in the *Japanese Canadians* case, supra, at p. 101, in the following passage:

> Again, if it be clear that an emergency has not arisen, or no longer exists, there can be no justification for the exercise or continued exercise of the exceptional powers. The rule of law as to the distribution of powers between the Parliaments of the Dominion and the Parliaments of the Provinces comes into play. But very clear evidence that an emergency has not arisen, or that the emergency no longer exists, is required to justify the judiciary, even though the question is one of *ultra vires*, in overruling the decision of the Parliament of the Dominion that exceptional measures were required or were still required. To this may be added as a corollary that it is not pertinent to the judiciary to consider the wisdom or the propriety of the particular policy which is embodied in the emergency legislation.

In my opinion, the evidence presented to the Court by those opposed to the validity of the legislation did not meet the requirements set by Lord Wright and I am unable to say that the exceptional measures contained in the *Act* were not required.

It is for these reasons I am in agreement with the Chief Justice that the first question posed by this Reference should be answered in the negative.

As to the second question posed by the Reference, I am in complete agreement with the reasons for judgment of the Chief Justice.

The judgment of Beetz and de Grandpré JJ. was delivered by

BEETZ J.: ... The *Anti-Inflation Act* authorizes the imposition of guidelines for the restraint of prices, profit margins, dividends and compensation in those sectors of the economy which it specifies and which may be described as the federal public sector, the federal private sector and the provincial private sector. With provincial consent, the guidelines can be extended, in whole or in part, to the provincial public sector. It is conceded that the Parliament of Canada has legislative competence to enact such legislation with respect to both the public and private federal sectors and to regulate prices, profit margins, dividends and compensation for commodities and services supplied by the federal government and its agencies or by private institutions or undertakings coming within exclusive federal jurisdiction such as banks, railways, bus lines and other transportation undertakings extending beyond the limits of a province, navigation and shipping undertakings and the like.

However, the *Anti-Inflation Act* is not confined to the federal public and private sectors. It extends compellingly to a substantial part of the provincial private sector, which is the most important one in quantitative terms and which comprises, for instance manufacturers of commodities such as automobiles and clothes, department stores and other large retailers, hotels, insurance companies, trust companies, all large suppliers of services, professionals such as doctors, dentists and lawyers.

The control and regulation of local trade and of commodity pricing and of profit margins in the provincial sectors have consistently been held to lie, short of a national emergency, within exclusive provincial jurisdiction....

The *Anti-Inflation Act*, therefore, and the Guidelines directly and ostensibly interfere with classes of matters which have invariably been held to come within exclusive provincial jurisdiction, more particularly property and civil rights and the law of contract....

Two submissions have been made in support of the validity of the *Anti-Inflation Act*. The first submission relates to a constitutional doctrine founded on judicial decisions and known as the national dimension or national concern doctrine. The second submission relates to another constitutional doctrine also founded on judicial decisions and known as the national emergency doctrine.

I

The first submission made by Counsel for Canada and for Ontario is that the subject matter of the *Anti-Inflation Act* is the containment and the reduction of inflation. This subject matter, it is argued, goes beyond local provincial concern or interest and is from its inherent nature the concern of Canada as a whole and falls within the competence of Parliament as a matter affecting the peace, order and good government of Canada....

Some of the extremely far reaching consequences of this submission must be underlined with respect to the so-called subject matter of inflation or its containment as well as in relation to the principles underlying the distribution of powers between Parliament and the Provincial Legislatures.

If the first submission is to be accepted, then it must be conceded that the *Anti-Inflation Act* could be compellingly extended to the provincial public sector. Parliament has not done so in this case as a matter of legislative policy but, it could decide to control and regulate at least the maximum salaries paid to all provincial public servants notwithstanding any provincial appropriations, budgets and laws. Parliament could also regulate wages paid by municipalities, educational institutions, hospitals and other provincial services as well as tuition or other fees charged by some of these institutions for their services. Parliament could occupy the whole field of rent controls. Since in time of inflation there can be a great deal of speculation in certain precious possessions such as land or works of arts, Parliament could move to prevent or control that speculation not only in regulating the trade or the price of those possessions but by any other efficient method reasonably connected with the control of inflation. For example Parliament could presumably enact legislation analogous to mortmain legislation and even extend it to individuals. Parliament could control all inventories in the largest as in the smallest undertakings, industries and trades. Parliament could ration not only food but practically everything else in order to prevent hoarding and unfair profits. One could even go further and argue that since inflation and productivity are greatly interdependent, Parliament could regulate productivity, establish quotas and impose the output of goods or services which corporations, industries, factories, groups, areas, villages, farmers, workers, should produce in any given period. Indeed, since practically any activity or lack of activity affects the gross national product, the value of the Canadian dollar and, therefore, inflation, it is difficult to see what would be beyond the reach of Parliament. Furthermore, all those powers would belong to Parliament permanently; only a constitutional amendment could reduce them. Finally, the power to regulate and control inflation as such would belong to Parliament to the exclusion of the Legislatures if, as is contended, that power were to vest in Parliament in the same manner as the power to control and regulate aeronautics or radio communication or the power to develop and conserve the national capital (*Aeronautics, Radio, Johannesson* and *Munro* cases)....

If the first submission is correct, then it could also be said that the promotion of economic growth or the limits to growth or the protection of the environment have become global problems and now constitute subject matters of national concern going beyond local provincial concern or interest and coming within the exclusive legislative authority of Parliament. It could equally be argued that older subjects such as the business of insurance or labour relations, which are not specifically listed in the enumeration of federal and provincial powers and have been held substantially to come within provincial jurisdiction have outgrown provincial authority whenever the business of insurance or labour have become national in scope. It is not difficult to speculate as to where this line of reasoning would lead: a fundamental feature of the Constitution, its federal nature, the distribution of powers between Parliament and the Provincial Legislatures, would disappear not gradually but rapidly.

I cannot be persuaded that the first submission expresses the state of the law. It goes against the persistent trend of the authorities. It is founded upon an erroneous characterization of the *Anti-Inflation Act.* As for the cases relied upon by Counsel to support the submission, they are quite distinguishable and they do not, in my view, stand for what they are said to stand. . . .

[Justice Beetz then reviewed the major cases dealing with peace, order, and good government.]

This submission is predicated upon the proposition that the subject matter of the *Anti-Inflation Act*, its pith and substance, is inflation or the containment and reduction of inflation.

To characterize a law is but to give a name to its content or subject matter in order to classify it into one or the other of the classes of matters mentioned in s. 91 or s. 92 of the Constitution. These classes of matters are themselves so many labels bearing a more or less specific name, except the general power of Parliament to make laws in relation to matters not coming within the classes of matters exclusively assigned to the Provinces—a label specific only in a negative way—and except the power of the Provinces in relation to all matters of a merely local or private nature—a label unspecific except mainly with regard to dimensions. This leaves some forty-six specific labels, thirty-one of which are in the federal list and fifteen of which are in the provincial list.

But there are in language a great many expressions other than those used for the labels in the federal and the provincial lists. Those innumerable other expressions, often broader and more extensive than those of s. 91 and s. 92, may . . . be employed in the title of a statute or to describe a statute. The expression "inflation" or "the containment and reduction of inflation" are of that nature. Needless to say, their use in the title of a statute or as an attempt to characterize a statute does not suffice by far in disposing of the characterization or in taking the matter with which in fact they deal outside the ambit of provincial jurisdiction. It is necessary to look at the reality of the matter or of the matters with which in effect they deal.

It is possible to invent such matters by applying new names to old legislative purposes. There is an increasing tendency to sum up a wide variety of legislative purposes in single, comprehensive designations. Control of inflation, environmental protection, and preservation of the national identity or independence are examples.

Many matters within provincial jurisdiction can be transformed by being treated as part of a larger subject or concept for which no place can be found within that jurisdiction. This perspective has a close affinity to the notion that there must be a single, plenary power to deal effectively and completely with any problem. The future of the general power, in the absence of emergency, will depend very much on the approach that the courts adopt to this issue of characterization.

"Sir Lyman Duff and the Constitution" by Professor Gerald LeDain, Q.C., as he then was (1974), 12 *Osgoode Hall Law Journal*, 261 at p. 293. See also "Unity and Diversity in Canadian Federalism" by Professor W.R. Lederman, Q.C. (1975), 53 *Canadian Bar Review* 596. I am much indebted to these two articles.

The "containment and reduction of inflation" can be achieved by various means including monetary policies—a federal field—the reduction of public expenditures, federal, provincial and municipal—and the restraint of profits, prices and wages—a federal or a provincial field depending on the sector.

I have no reason to doubt that the *Anti-Inflation Act* is part of a more general program aimed at inflation and which may include fiscal and monetary measures and government expenditure policies. I am prepared to accept that inflation was the occasion or the reason for its enactment. But I do not agree that inflation is the subject matter of the *Act*. In order to characterize an enactment, one must look at its operation, at its effects and at the scale of its effects rather than at its ultimate purpose where the purpose is practically all embracing. If for instance Parliament is to enact a tax law or a monetary law as a part of an anti-inflation program no one will think that such laws have ceased to be a tax law or a monetary law and that they have become subsumed into their ultimate purpose so that they should rather be characterized as "anti-inflation laws," an expression which, in terms of actual content, is not meaningful. They plainly remain and continue to be called a tax law or a monetary law, although they have been enacted by reason of an inflationary situation. . . .

. . . Similarly, the *Anti-Inflation Act* is, as its preamble states, clearly a law relating to the control of profit margins, prices, dividends and compensation, that is, with respect to the provincial private sector, a law relating to the regulation of local trade, to contract and to property and civil rights in the provinces, enacted as part of a program to combat inflation. Property and civil rights in the provinces are, for the greater part, the pith and substance or the subject matter of the *Anti-Inflation Act*. According to the Constitution, Parliament may fight inflation with the powers put at its disposal by the specific heads enumerated in s. 91 or by such powers as are outside of s. 92. But it cannot, apart from a declaration of national emergency or from a constitutional amendment, fight inflation with powers exclusively reserved to the provinces, such as the power to make laws in relation to property and civil rights. . . .

The authorities relied upon by Counsel for Canada and Ontario in support of the first submission are connected with the constitutional doctrine that became known as the national concern doctrine or national dimension doctrine. . . .

In my view, the incorporation of companies for objects other than provincial, the regulation and control of aeronautics and of radio, the development, conservation and improvement of the National Capital Region are clear instances of distinct subject matters which do not fall within any of the enumerated heads of s. 92 and which, by nature, are of national concern.

I fail to see how the authorities which so decide lend support to the first submission. They had the effect of adding by judicial process new matters or new classes of matters to the federal list of powers. However, this was done only in cases where a new matter was not an aggregate but had a degree of unity that made it indivisible, an identity which made it distinct from provincial matters and a sufficient consistence to retain the bounds of form. The scale upon which these new matters enabled Parliament to touch on provincial matters had also to be taken into consideration before they were recognized as federal matters: if an enumerated federal power designated in broad terms such as the trade and commerce power had to be construed so as not to embrace and smother provincial powers (*Parsons* case) and destroy the equilibrium of the Constitution, the Courts must be all the more careful not to add hitherto unnamed powers of a diffuse nature to the list of federal powers.

The "containment and reduction of inflation" does not pass muster as a new subject matter. It is an aggregate of several subjects some of which form a substantial part of provincial jurisdiction. It is totally lacking in specificity. It is so pervasive that it knows no bounds. Its recognition as a federal head of power would render most provincial powers nugatory.

I should add that inflation is a very ancient phenomenon, several thousands years old, as old probably as the history of currency. The Fathers of Confederation were quite aware of it.

It was argued that other heads of power enumerated in s. 91 of the Constitution and which relate for example to the regulation of trade and commerce, to currency and coinage, to banking, incorporation of banks and the issue of paper money may be indicative of the breadth of Parliament's jurisdiction in economic matters. They do not enable Parliament to legislate otherwise than in relation to their objects and it was not argued that the *Anti-Inflation Act* was in relation to their objects. The *Act* does not derive any assistance from those powers any more than the legislation found invalid in the *Board of Commerce* case.

For those reasons, the first submission fails.

II

The second submission made in support of the validity of the *Anti-Inflation Act* is that the inflationary situation was in October of 1975 and still is such as to constitute a national emergency of the same significance as war, pestilence or insurrection and that there is in Parliament an implied power to deal with the emergency for the safety of Canada as a whole. . . .

Before I deal with this second submission I should state at the outset that I am prepared to assume the validity of the following propositions:

- the power of Parliament under the national emergency doctrine is not confined to war situations or to situations of transition from war to peace; an emergency of the nature contemplated by the doctrine may arise in peace time;
- inflation may constitute such an emergency;
- Parliament may validly exercise its national emergency powers before an emergency actually occurs; a state of apprehended emergency or crisis suffices to justify parliament in taking preventive measures including measures to contain and reduce inflation where inflation amounts to [a] state of apprehended crisis.

In order to decide whether the *Anti-Inflation Act* is valid as a national emergency measure, one must first consider the way in which the emergency doctrine operates in the Canadian Constitution; one must find, in the second place whether the *Anti-Inflation Act* was in fact enacted on the basis that it was a measure to deal with a national emergency in the constitutional sense.

In referring to the emergency doctrine, the Judicial Committee has sometimes used expressions which would at first appear to indicate that there is no difference between the national dimension or national concern doctrine and the emergency doctrine, the latter being but an instance of the first, or that the distribution of powers between Parliament and the provincial legislatures is not altered by a state of emergency, or again that when Parliament deals with a matter which in normal times would be an exclusively provincial matter, it does so under a federal aspect or in a new relation which lies outside of s. 92 of the Constitution.

Counsel for Canada and for Ontario have relied upon them for the proposition that the difference between the national concern doctrine and the emergency doctrine is one of semantics, which perhaps explains why the Ontario factum does not support the validity of the *Anti-Inflation Act* on the basis of an emergency although Counsel for Ontario said that his position did not, because of that reason of semantics, differ from that of Counsel for Canada. The latter insisted that the difference between the two doctrines is only one of form but made two separate submissions based on each of the two doctrines.

I disagree with the proposition that the national concern or national dimension doctrine and the emergency doctrine amount to the same. Even if it could be said that "where an emergency exists it is the emergency which gives the matter its dimension of national concern or interest" (LeDain, *op. cit.* p. 291) the emergency does not give the matter the same dimensions as the national concern doctrine applied for instance in the *Aeronautics* case, in the *Johannesson* case or in the *Munro* case. The national concern doctrine illustrated by these cases applies in practice as if certain heads such as aeronautics or the development and conservation of the national capital were added to the categories of subject matters enumerated in s. 91 of the Constitution when it is found by the Courts that, in substance, a class of subjects not enumerated in either s. 91 or s. 92 lies outside the first fifteen heads enumerated in s. 92 and is not of a merely local or private nature. Whenever the national concern theory is applied, the effect is permanent although it is limited by the identity of the subject newly recognized to be of national dimensions. By contrast, the power of Parliament to make laws in a great crisis knows no limits other than those which are dictated by the nature of the crisis. But one of those limits is the temporary nature of the crisis. . . .

In my view, the verbal precautions taken by the Judicial Committee in the *Fort Frances* case, pp. 704 to 706, and in other cases reflect its concern over the fact that a power of such magnitude as the national emergency power had to be inferred. But further passages, some of which are even to be found in the very judgments which in other parts appear to say the contrary, make clear that, in practice, the emergency

doctrine operates as a partial and temporary alteration of the distribution of powers between Parliament and the Provincial Legislatures. . . .

. . . [I]f one looks at the practical effects of the exercise of the emergency power, one must conclude that it operates so as to give to Parliament for all purposes necessary to deal with the emergency, concurrent and paramount jurisdiction over matters which would normally fall within exclusive provincial jurisdiction. To that extent, the exercise of that power amounts to a temporary *pro tanto* amendment of a federal Constitution by the unilateral action of Parliament. The legitimacy of that power is derived from the Constitution: when the security and the continuation of the Constitution and of the nation are at stake, the kind of power commensurate with the situation "is only to be found in that part of the Constitution which establishes power in the State as a whole." (Viscount Haldane in the *Fort Frances* case, p. 704).

The extraordinary nature and the constitutional features of the emergency power of Parliament dictate the manner and form in which it should be invoked and exercised. It should not be an ordinary manner and form. At the very least, it cannot be a manner and form which admits of the slightest degree of ambiguity to be resolved by interpretation. In cases where the existence of an emergency may be a matter of controversy, it is imperative that Parliament should not have recourse to its emergency power except in the most explicit terms indicating that it is acting on the basis of that power. Parliament cannot enter the normally forbidden area of provincial jurisdiction unless it gives an unmistakable signal that it is acting pursuant to its extraordinary power. Such a signal is not conclusive to support the legitimacy of the action of Parliament but its absence is fatal. It is the duty of the courts to uphold the Constitution, not to seal its suspension, and they cannot decide that a suspension is legitimate unless the highly exceptional power to suspend it has been expressly invoked by Parliament. Also, they cannot entertain a submission implicitly asking them to make findings of fact justifying even a temporary interference with the normal constitutional process unless Parliament has first assumed responsibility for affirming in plain words that the facts are such as to justify the interference. The responsibility of the Courts begins after the affirmation has been made. If there is no such affirmation, the Constitution receives its normal application. Otherwise, it is the Courts which are indirectly called upon to proclaim the state of emergency whereas it is essential that this be done by a politically responsible body.

We have not been referred to a single judicial decision, and I know of none, ratifying the exercise by Parliament of its national emergency power where the constitutional foundation for the exercise of that power had not been given clear utterance to. And, apart from judicial decisions, I know of no precedent where it could be said that parliament had attempted to exercise such an extraordinary power by way of suggestion or innuendo. . . .

. . . What is required from Parliament when it purports to exercise its extraordinary emergency power in any situation where a dispute could arise as to the existence of the emergency and as to the constitutional foundation of its action, is an indication, I would even say a proclamation, in the title, the preamble or the text of the instrument, which cannot possibly leave any doubt that, given the nature of the crisis, Parliament in fact purports to act on the basis of that power. The statutes of Canada and the *Canada Gazette* contain several examples of laws, proclamations and orders-in-council which leave room for no doubt that they have been enacted pursuant to the exceptional emergency power of Parliament. . . .

The preamble has been much relied upon:

WHEREAS the Parliament of Canada recognizes that inflation in Canada at current levels is contrary to the interests of all Canadians and that the containment and a reduction of inflation has become a matter of serious national concern;

AND WHEREAS to accomplish such containment and reduction of inflation it is necessary to restrain profit margins, prices, dividends and compensation;

The words "a matter of serious national concern" have been emphasized.

I remain unimpressed.

The death penalty is a matter of national concern. So is abortion. So is the killing or maiming of innumerable people by impaired drivers. So is the traffic in narcotics and drugs. One can conceive of several drastic measures, all coming within the ordinary jurisdiction of the Parliament of Canada, and which could be preceded by a preamble reciting that a given situation had become a matter of serious national concern. I fail to see how the adding of the word "serious" can convey the meaning that Parliament has decided to embark upon an exercise of its extraordinary emergency power. The *Canada Water Act, 1969-70* (Can.), c. 52 on the constitutionality of which, again, I refrain from expressing any view, contains a preamble where it is stated that pollution of the water resources of Canada has become "a matter of urgent national concern." Is the *Canada Water Act* an emergency measure in the constitutional sense? It does not seem to present itself as such. How is a matter of serious national concern to be distinguished from a matter of urgent national concern? I cannot read the preamble of the *Anti-Inflation Act* as indicating that the act was passed to deal with a national emergency in the constitutional sense.

Counsel for Canada has also insisted upon the temporary nature of the *Anti-Inflation Act*. I note that the duration of the act could, under s. 46, be extended by order-in-council with the approval of both Houses of Parliament, although I am not inclined to attach undue importance to this point. Nonetheless, while it would be essential to the validity of a measure enacted under the national emergency power of Parliament that it be not permanent, still the temporary character of an act is hardly indicative and in no way conclusive that it constitutes a measure passed to deal with a national emergency: Parliament can and often does enact temporary measures relating to matters coming within its normal jurisdiction.

I have dealt with the arguments based on the preamble and the limited, duration (s. 46) of the *Anti-Inflation Act*.

There is nothing in the rest of the *Act* and in the Guidelines to show that they have been passed to deal with a national emergency. There is much, on the other hand, within the *Act* and the Guidelines, in terms of actual or potential exemptions which is inconsistent with the nature of a global war launched on inflation considered as a great emergency. . . .

[Justice Beetz noted that farmers and employers of fewer than 500 persons are excluded and the provinces have the option of keeping their public sectors out of the scheme.]

We were provided with a wealth of extrinsic material the consideration of which, it was expected, would enable us to make a finding of fact as to whether or not inflation had reached a level which justified Parliament's reliance on its extraordinary power or as to whether or not there was a rational basis for Parliament to judge that it could rely upon that power. I do not reach that point, of course, since I hold the view that Parliament did not rely upon its extraordinary power. It seems to me however that, if we are entitled to look at extrinsic material such as a policy statement tabled in the House of Commons by the Minister of Finance, statistics, an economic study, a speech delivered by the Governor of the Bank of Canada, it is not improper for us to read *Hansard* in this case, in order not to construe and apply the provisions of the *Anti-Inflation Act*, but to ascertain its constitutional pivot. A perusal of the Debates reveals that between October 14, 1975, when the policy statement was tabled—the *Anti-Inflation Bill* C-73 was read for the first time in the Commons on October 16, 1975—and the third reading and the passing of the bill in the Senate on December 10, 1975, the question was raised repeatedly in both Houses and in Committee as to what was the constitutional foundation of the bill and as to whether it was not necessary expressly to declare a state of emergency in order to insure its constitutionality. The replies vary but slightly; their general tenor is to the effect that Parliament has jurisdiction to pass the bill as drafted under the peace, order and good government power—which is rather unrevealing—in addition to other specific federal powers enumerated in s. 91 of the Constitution. . . .

Reliance upon those statements is not essential to my conclusions. However, they reinforce my opinion that the *Anti-Inflation Act* was enacted in this form because it was believed, erroneously, that Parliament had the ordinary power to enact it under the national concern or national dimension doctrine, that is, a basis which coincides identically with the first submission made to us by Counsel for Canada. Parliament did not purport to enact it under the extraordinary power which it possesses in time of national crisis.

The *Anti-Inflation Act* is in my opinion *ultra vires* of Parliament in so far at least as it applies to the provincial private sector; but severability having not been pleaded by Counsel for Canada, I would declare the *Act ultra vires* of Parliament in whole.

Canadian Industrial Gas and Oil Ltd. v. Government of Saskatchewan, 1978

In the 1970s, jurisdiction over natural resources became a focal point of constitutional conflict between Ottawa and those provinces well endowed with natural resources, especially scarce energy resources such as oil and natural gas. The *C.I.G.O.L.* case in 1978 and the *Central Canada Potash* case the following year plunged the Supreme Court into this area of controversy. Both cases originated in private litigation between private companies and the government of Saskatchewan, but, given the important constitutional issues involved, several provinces intervened on Saskatchewan's side while the federal government intervened to support the corporate challenge. The Supreme Court's decision in both cases went against the provinces and provoked demands from Alberta and Saskatchewan for changes in the structure of the Supreme Court as well as for constitutional amendments to strengthen provincial control over natural resources.

At issue in the *C.I.G.O.L.* case was legislation designed by Saskatchewan's NDP government to capture for the provincial treasury 100 percent of the windfall gains resulting from the 1973 OPEC increases in the world price of oil. The legislation expropriated virtually all the petroleum- and natural-gas-producing tracts in the province and imposed a royalty surcharge on production from Crown-owned land equal to the difference between the current international price for oil and the price before the OPEC increases.

In a 7-to-2 decision, the Court found the legislation unconstitutional. All nine judges agreed that the "royalty surcharge," because it lacked the voluntary character of royalty payments, was not a royalty (which under section 109 of the *B.N.A. Act* belongs to the provinces), but a tax. Justice Martland (incidentally, an Albertan), writing for the majority, held that the tax was indirect because the oil producers passed it on in the form of higher prices to their customers. The power that the legislation gave the Minister to specify the market price for the purpose of calculating the surcharge and to prevent producers from undercutting that price convinced the majority that the provincial tax could increase the price paid by the ultimate purchaser. They concluded that the tax, in essence, was an export tax, a category of taxation that in earlier cases had been considered unconstitutional. Further, because 98 percent of Saskatchewan's crude oil is exported to the United States and Eastern Canada, they considered such an attempt to regulate the price of an export commodity to be an unconstitutional encroachment on exclusive federal jurisdiction over interprovincial and international trade and commerce.

Justice Dickson's dissenting opinion stressed the plenary power of the provinces over their natural resources "subject to limits imposed by the Canadian constitution." He contended that in terms of economic realities the surcharge would not determine the export price of oil nor require buyers of Saskatchewan crude to pay more than they would have paid without the surcharge. The Minister's price-setting powers were simply a device to ensure that companies did not evade the tax by selling oil to related international companies below fair market value. Justice Dickson insisted that "the tax does not set the price. Price sets the tax." Nor was there any evidence that the legislation was impeding the flow of interprovincial and international trade. On the contrary, export sales continued at their pre-tax level.

Although Premier Blakeney complained bitterly about this decision, he was able to overcome its immediate impact on the provincial budget by imposing an oil-well income tax, which, presumably, as a direct tax, can survive constitutional challenge. This tax had retroactive effect and recovered for the province the half billion dollars (plus interest) raised by the unconstitutional royalty surcharge.

Soon after this decision, the Prime Minister agreed in principle to a constitutional amendment giving the provinces some capacity to apply indirect taxes to their natural resources. In 1981, the Trudeau government, in order to secure the support of the national New Democratic Party for its package of constitutional proposals that were then before Parliament, tacked onto the package a proposal to add section 92A to the *B.N.A. Act*, confirming and expanding provincial jurisdiction in relation to natural resources. One part of this section, by giving the provinces the right to levy "any mode or system of taxation" on non-renewable natural resources, forestry resources, and electrical energy, "whether or not such production is exported in whole or in part from the province," would reverse the main implications of the Supreme Court's decision in the *C.I.G.O.L.* case. This natural resource amendment was included in the *Constitution Act, 1982*.

The following year, in *Central Canada Potash*,[1] the Supreme Court overturned Saskatchewan's efforts to manage its huge reserves of potash, over 99 percent of which is exported from the province—mostly to fertilizer companies in the United States. In order to maximize returns and not flood the US market, the Blakeney NDP government set production quotas for potash producers in the province. In a unanimous decision, written by Chief Justice Laskin, the Court ruled that while ordinarily provinces can control production of their natural resources, they cannot do so if the pith and substance of their legislation is to control the marketing of a commodity in international trade. It should be noted that the additional power over natural resources that the provinces acquired in 1982 applies only to interprovincial trade and commerce. The federal Parliament's exclusive power over international trade remained intact, and provided a firm constitutional basis for negotiating and implementing the Free Trade Agreement with the United States. ~

---

1   *Central Canada Potash Co. Ltd. and A.G. Canada v. Government of Saskatchewan*, [1979] 1 S.C.R. 42.

CANADIAN INDUSTRIAL GAS & OIL LTD. v. GOVERNMENT OF SASKATCHEWAN
[1978] 2 S.C.R. 545

Hearing: November 8, 9, 10, 1976; Judgment: November 23, 1976.

Present: Laskin C.J. and Martland, Judson, Ritchie, Spence, Pigeon, Beetz, Dickson, and de Grandpré JJ.

The judgment of Laskin C.J. and Martland, Judson, Ritchie, Spence, Pigeon, and Beetz JJ. was delivered by

MARTLAND J.: The question in issue in this appeal is as to the constitutional validity of certain statutes enacted by the Legislature of the Province of Saskatchewan and regulations enacted pursuant thereto, to which reference will be made hereafter. Their validity was challenged by the appellant, a corporation engaged in the exploration for, drilling for and production of oil and natural gas in Saskatchewan and owning freehold leases, Crown leases and royalty interests in that Province. The respondents are the Government of the Province of Saskatchewan and the Attorney General of that Province. The appellant was unsuccessful in seeking to obtain a declaration of their invalidity, both at trial and on appeal to the Court of Appeal for Saskatchewan. It appeals, with leave, to this Court from the judgment of the Court of Appeal.

The legislation was enacted following the sharp rise in the price of oil on the world market which occurred in 1973. The effect of the legislation has been summarized in the reasons of my brother Dickson, which I have had the advantage of reading. For purposes of convenience I substantially repeat that summary here:

First, production revenues from freehold lands were subjected to what was called a "mineral income tax." The tax was one hundred per cent of the difference between the price received at the well-head and the "basic well-head price," a statutory figure approximately equal to the price per barrel received by producers prior to the energy crisis. The owner's interest in oil and gas rights in producing tracts of less than 1,280 acres were exempted from tax. Deductions approved by the Minister of Mineral Resources were allowed in respect of increases in production costs and extraordinary transportation costs. Provision was made for the Minister to determine the well-head value of the oil where he was of the opinion that oil had been disposed of at less than its fair value.

Secondly, all petroleum and natural gas in all producing tracts within the Province were expropriated and subjected to what was called a "royalty surcharge." Oil and gas rights owned by one person in producing tracts not exceeding 1,280 acres were exempted. Although introduced by regulation rather than statute, the royalty surcharge is calculated in the same manner as the mineral income tax. For all practical purposes they are the same, save one exception. The well-head value for the purposes of royalty surcharge is the higher of the price received at the well-head and the price per barrel listed in the Minister's order.

The statutes and regulations under consideration are:

1. *The Oil and Gas Conservation, Stabilization and Development Act, 1973,* S.S. 1973-74, hereinafter referred to as "Bill 42";
2. *An Act to amend the foregoing Act,* being Chapter 73, S.S. 1973-74, hereinafter referred to as "Bill 128";
3. *An Act to amend The Mineral Resources Act,* Chapter 64, S.S. 1973-74, hereinafter referred to as "Bill 127";
4. Amendments to The Petroleum and Natural Gas Regulations, 1969, made under [t]he *Mineral Resources Act* as made by:
   (a) Order in Council 95/74, made pursuant to Section 18 of Bill 42 and confirmed by Section 1(*a*) of Bill 127;
   (b) Order in Council 1238/74, made pursuant to Section 2 of Bill 127.

In summary, Bill 42 imposes a mineral income tax on the income received on oil produced in Saskatchewan in respect to producing properties. The royalty surcharge is made applicable in respect to production from Crown lands. In each case

the determination of the basic well-head price is the same; that is, by the Minister. In the case of the mineral income tax, the basic well-head price is set out in the schedules to the legislation. In the case of the royalty surcharge, the basic well-head price is set out in the regulations. The method of calculation is the same in each case. As the basic well-head price has been set at the same figure, whether by statute or by regulation, and as the well-head value had been set by the Minister at the same figure for the purposes of both the mineral income tax and the royalty surcharge, the calculation of the mineral income tax and the royalty surcharge has been the same. When effect is given to the expropriation provision of Bill 42, the mineral income tax would apply only to those tracts exempted by s. 27(2) of Bill 42. The royalty surcharge applies both to Crown-owned land, owned by the Crown prior to the enactment of Bill 42, and to oil rights vested in the Crown under the expropriation provisions of Bill 42.

The practical consequence of the application of this legislation is that the Government of Saskatchewan will acquire the benefit of all increases in the value of oil produced in that Province above the set basic well-head price fixed by the statute and regulations, which is approximately the same as that which existed in 1973 before the increase in world prices for oil. In this connection, there is the important fact that 98 per cent of all crude oil produced in Saskatchewan is destined for export from the Province either to Eastern Canada or the United States of America.

The appellant's attack upon the legislation is made upon two grounds:

1. It is contended that both the mineral income tax and the royalty surcharge constitute indirect taxation, and are therefore beyond the power of the Province to impose, the provincial legislative powers being limited to direct taxation within the Province under s. 92(2) of the *British North America Act.*
2. It is contended that the legislation relates to the regulation of interprovincial and international trade and commerce, a matter over which the Federal Parliament has exclusive legislative power under s. 91(2) of the *British North America Act.*

Direct or Indirect Taxation

My brother Dickson has reviewed the leading authorities dealing with the distinction between direct and indirect taxation. It is not necessary for me to repeat that review here. He has pointed out that it has been settled that:

The dividing line between a direct and an indirect tax is referable to and ascertainable by the "general tendencies of the tax and the common understanding of men as to those tendencies. The general tendency of a tax is the relevant criterion."

He has also pointed out that certain well understood categories of taxation have been generally established as falling within one or other of these classes. Thus custom levies are recognized as being indirect taxes, whereas income and property taxes have been recognized as being direct taxes. Similarly, a commodity tax has, as a general rule, been regarded as an indirect tax. The appellant submits that the levies here in question are commodity taxes, and refers to the Privy Council decision in *R. v. Caledonian Collieries, Limited* [[1928] A.C. 358].... In that case the tax was imposed upon the gross revenue of every mine owner, at a rate not to exceed 2 per cent. The Privy Council considered that the general tendency of the tax would be for a mine owner to seek to recover the tax from his purchasers.

A sales tax, imposed upon vendors of goods, has been generally regarded as an indirect tax. On the other hand, where the tax, although collected through the vendor is actually paid by the ultimate consumer, the tax has been held to be direct. (*Atlantic Smoke Shops Ltd. v. Conlon* [[1943] A.C. 550]; *Cairns Construction Limited v. Government of Saskatchewan* [[1960] S.C.R. 619]). However, in the present case the tax is imposed upon and payable by the producer in relation to the sale price of the oil which is produced. It is a sales tax, but the contention of the respondents is that it is not an indirect tax because the legislation does not contemplate and seeks to preclude the recovery of the tax from the purchaser.

The respondent contends that the mineral income tax is, as its name implies, an income tax, and so, a direct tax. I agree with the reasons of my brother Dickson for holding that that tax is not an income tax as that term is understood in the authorities which say that an income tax is a direct tax.

The respondent submits, with respect to the royalty surcharge, that it is not a tax, but that it is a genuine royalty payable to the Crown, as the owner of mineral rights, by its lessees who have been authorized to extract minerals from Crown lands. To determine the validity of this contention it is necessary to consider the nature of the legal relationship between the Crown and the persons from whom payment of the royalty surcharge is demanded. . . .

[Justice Martland found that, because producers on expropriated tracts were required to pay the royalty surcharge as a condition of preserving their leases, the levy imposed by the royalty surcharge was actually not a royalty but a tax.]

In my opinion the royalty surcharge made applicable to these Crown leases was not a royalty for which provision was made in the lease agreement. It was imposed as a levy upon the share of production to which, under the lease, the lessee was entitled, and was a tax upon production.

I agree with the reasons of my brother Dickson for concluding that the royalty surcharge is a tax imposed upon Crown lessees of the same nature as the mineral income tax imposed upon lessees holding leases from freehold owners. . . .

The reasons given by the Court of Appeal for concluding that the mineral income tax was a direct tax are summarized in the following extract from the judgment:

> I think it must be concluded that the tax is one which is demanded from the very persons whom it is intended and desired should pay it. It is not one which is demanded from persons in the expectation and intent that they shall indemnify themselves at the expense of others. In my view, the language of the sections under which the tax is imposed, calculated and payment directed, leaves no doubt but the legislators intended the tax to be paid by the persons upon whom it was imposed and from whom payment is demanded.
>
> If there were any doubt as to this view, I think that doubt would be resolved by an appreciation of the situation that would result if the persons taxed attempted to indemnify themselves at the expense of the purchasers of the oil. If the tax paid pursuant to Bill 42 was added to the sale price of the crude at the well-head, then to the extent it was so passed on, it would increase the well-head price. The effect, therefore, would simply be to increase the tax by the amount which the well-head price was so increased. In other words, such action by the taxpayers would result in no benefit to themselves, but could, if the selling price were increased by the total amount of the tax, substantially increase the tax collected by the Government. Surely such a result following from an attempt to pass on the tax clearly indicates that the Legislature intended the tax to be paid by those upon whom it was imposed and from whom payment was demanded.

With respect, my consideration of the real substance and intent of the legislation under review leads me to a different conclusion.

Both the mineral income tax and the royalty surcharge are taxes upon the production of oil virtually all of which is produced for export from the Province of Saskatchewan. Section 3 of Bill 42 imposes the mineral income tax upon every person having an interest in the oil produced from a well in a producing tract. Section 63(1) of The Petroleum and Natural Gas Regulations, 1969, requires payment of the royalty surcharge upon oil produced or deemed to be produced from Crown lands.

Section 4(1) of Bill 42 as originally enacted fixed the tax payable as being the amount of the difference between the basic well-head price and the international well-head price determined by the Minister. Bill 128 repealed that subsection and substituted the formula of the well-head price received for each barrel of oil produced and sold in each month less the basic well-head price. The operation of the new subsection was made subject to a new section, 4A.

Section 4A provides that where the Minister is of the opinion that oil, income from which is subject to tax, has been disposed of in any month at less than its fair value, he shall determine the well-head value of the oil sold, being the price which he determines should have been obtained, and it is that price, so determined by him, which governs in the computation of the tax and not the actual price received. The purpose of this important provision was twofold. First it enabled the Minister to prevent a reduction in the tax payable by reason of a sale at less than what he considered to be the fair value of the oil. Second it provided a basis for the computation of tax where oil produced from a Saskatchewan well had not been sold at the well-head but had been shipped out by the producer to be refined and sold.

Under this section it is the Minister who has power to determine what he considers to be the fair value of the oil produced, which figure will be applicable in the computation of the tax payable. His determination of fair value is final and conclusive. Section 11 of Bill 42 so provides and also states that his determination is not subject to review by any court of law or by any *certiorari, mandamus*, prohibition, injunction or other proceeding whatsoever.

With respect to the computation of royalty surcharge, I have referred earlier to s. 63(1) of The Petroleum and Natural Gas Regulations, as finally amended, which imposes a royalty surcharge calculated as follows:

> (oil produced less Crown royalty oil, less Road Allowance Crown levy) times (well-head value, as established by the minister less basic well-head price).

The effect of this provision is that the royalty surcharge is determined by subtracting from one figure (well-head value) established by the Minister, another figure (basic well-head price) established by the Crown in the regulations.

These taxing provisions, *i.e.*, both mineral income tax and royalty surcharge, have the following impact upon the Saskatchewan oil producer. In the first place he is effectively precluded from recovering in respect of the oil which he produces any return greater than the basic well-head price per barrel. He is subjected to an income freeze at that figure and can obtain no more than that. In the second place, he is compelled to sell his product at a price which will equal what the Minister determines to be the fair value of the oil which he produces. He must do this, because his production of oil is subject to a

tax per barrel representing the difference between fair value and basic well-head price. If he is the lessee of mineral rights in lands in respect of which the mineral rights were expropriated by the Crown, he does not even have the option to discontinue production. Discontinuance of production without ministerial consent is subject to a heavy penalty.

The tax under consideration is essentially an export tax imposed upon oil production. In the past a tax of this nature has been considered to be an indirect tax. . . .

The mineral income tax and the royalty surcharge are taxes imposed in a somewhat unusual manner. The mineral income tax purports to be a direct tax upon income imposed upon the taxpayer, which he cannot pass on to his purchaser. The royalty surcharge, while carrying a different title, is the same in nature. What differentiates this legislation from other legislation imposing export taxes is that the true effect of the legislation is to impose a freeze upon the actual income which the producer exporter can derive from the sale of his product. All that he is permitted to retain on the sale of each barrel of oil is the basic well-head price. In addition to being subjected to an income freeze, he is compelled to sell his product at a price equivalent to what the Minister considers to be its fair value in order to obtain the funds necessary to meet the tax. This amount per barrel over and above the basic well-head price he must obtain from his purchaser as a part of the purchase price. In essence the producer is a conduit through which the increased value of each barrel of oil above the basic well-head price is channeled into the hands of the Crown by way of tax. The increase in value is itself the tax and it is paid by the purchaser of the oil.

It is contended that the imposition of these taxes will not result in an increase in the price paid by oil purchasers, who would have been required to pay the same market price even if the taxes had not been imposed, and so there could be no passing on of the tax by the Saskatchewan producer to his purchaser. On this premise it is argued that the tax is not indirect. This, however, overlooks the all important fact that the scheme of the legislation under consideration involves the fixing of the maximum return of the Saskatchewan producers at the basic well-head price per barrel, while at the same time compelling him to sell at a higher price. There are two components in the sale price, first the basic well-head price and second the tax imposed. Both are intended by the legislation to be incorporated into the price payable by the purchaser. The purchaser pays the amount of the tax as a part of the purchase price.

For these reasons it is my opinion that the taxation scheme comprising the mineral income tax and the royalty surcharge does not constitute direct taxation within the Province and is therefore outside the scope of the provincial power under s. 92(2) of the *British North America Act.*

Regulation of Trade and Commerce

In considering this issue the important fact is, of course, that practically all of the oil to which the mineral income tax or the royalty surcharge becomes applicable is destined for interprovincial or international trade. Some of this oil is sold by producers at the well-head and thereafter transported from the Province by pipeline. Some of the oil is not sold at the well-head, but is produced by companies for their own purposes, and is likewise transported out of the Province by pipeline. In either case the levy becomes applicable. The producer in the first case must, if he is to avoid pecuniary loss, sell at the well-head at the well-head value established. The company which has its own oil production transported from the Province must, if it is to avoid pecuniary loss, ultimately dispose of the refined product at a price which will recoup the amount of the levy. Thus, the effect of the legislation is to set a floor price for Saskatchewan oil purchased for export by the appropriation of its potential incremental value in interprovincial and international markets, or to ensure that the incremental value is not appropriated by persons outside the Province.

Chief Justice Kerwin in the *Reference re The Farm Products Marketing Act* [[1957] S.C.R. 198] said at p. 204:

Once a statute aims at "regulation of trade in matters of inter-provincial concern" it is beyond the competence of a Provincial Legislature.

At p. 205 he said:

The concept of trade and commerce, the regulation of which is confided to Parliament, is entirely separate and distinct from the regulation of mere sale and purchase agreements. Once an article enters into the flow of inter-provincial or external trade, the subject-matter and all its attendant circumstances cease to be a mere matter of local concern.

The purpose of the legislation under review was accurately defined by Chief Justice Culliton in the Court of Appeal:

There is no doubt in my mind that both the Mineral Income tax and the royalty surcharge were imposed for one purpose, and one purpose only—to drain off substantial benefits that would have accrued to the producers due to the sudden and unprecedented price of crude oil.

The means used to achieve this end are to compel a Saskatchewan oil producer to effect the sale of the oil at a price determined by the Minister. The mineral income tax is defined as the difference between the basic well-head price and the price at which the oil is sold, but with the important proviso that if the Minister is of the opinion that the oil has been sold at less than its fair value, he can determine the price at which

it should have been sold, and that price governs in determining the amount of the tax. The royalty surcharge, as provided under the Regulations requires the payment of the surcharge on oil produced on the basis of the difference between its well-head value, as established by the Minister, less the basic well-head price. In either case the Minister is empowered to determine the well-head value of the oil which is produced which will govern the price at which the producer is compelled to sell the oil which he produces. In an effort to obtain for the provincial treasury the increases in the value of oil exported from Saskatchewan which began in 1973, in the form of a tax upon the production of oil in Saskatchewan, the legislation gave power to the Minister to fix the price receivable by Saskatchewan oil producers on their export sales of a commodity that has almost no local market in Saskatchewan. Provincial legislative authority does not extend to fixing the price to be charged or received in respect of the sale of goods in the export market. It involves the regulation of interprovincial trade and trenches upon s. 91(2) of the *British North America Act*.

This is not a case similar to *Carnation Co. Ltd. v. Quebec Agricultural Marketing Board* [[1968] S.C.R. 238], where the effect of the Regulations was to increase the cost of the milk purchased by Carnation in Quebec and processed there, mostly for sale outside Quebec. The legislation there indirectly affected Carnation's export trade in the sense that its costs of production were increased, but was designed to establish a method for determining the price of milk sold by Quebec milk producers, to a purchaser in Quebec, who processed it there. Here the legislation is directly aimed at the production of oil destined for export and has the effect of regulating the export price, since the producer is effectively compelled to obtain that price on the sale of his product.

For these reasons, in my opinion, the statutory provisions, and the Regulations and orders enacted and made relating to the imposition of the mineral income tax and the royalty surcharge, are ultra vires of the Legislature of the Province of Saskatchewan. . . .

The judgment of Dickson and de Grandpré JJ. was delivered by

DICKSON J. (dissenting): The question raised in this appeal is whether a complex of legislation, enacted by the Legislature of Saskatchewan, following the onset in late 1973 of what has been called the "energy crisis," is *intra vires* the Legislature of Saskatchewan.

I

Virtually all of the crude oil produced in Saskatchewan is exported from the Province. In 1973, only 1.8 per cent of

Saskatchewan crude was used in Saskatchewan refineries; 43.9 per cent was used in provinces of Canada other than Saskatchewan; and 54.3 per cent was exported to the United States. This is attributable in part to the fact that most of the oil produced in the Province is medium or heavy crude which, when refined, produces a heavy residue of bunker oil suitable only for use in heavy industry, which is not present in Saskatchewan. Another contributing factor is the fact that the flow of the pipeline through which the oil leaves the Province is from west to east. Light and medium crudes, suitable for use in Saskatchewan, are produced in the south eastern part of the Province, far from the refineries at Regina and Moose Jaw. These refineries are served by oil from the Province of Alberta.

The appellant, Canadian Industrial Gas & Oil Ltd., is a producer of crude oil in Saskatchewan and sells its entire production at the well site. Virtually all of its product leaves the Province by pipeline for refining by others in more easterly provinces of Canada or in the United States. The appellant owns a variety of interests including freehold leases, Crown leases (granted to the appellant or to its predecessor in title, as lessee, subject to Crown royalty); non-operator interests under freehold leases and under Crown leases; royalty interests on freehold leases and on Crown leases; royalty trust certificates; freehold subject to leases to others. The total acreage involved for all types of interest is 156,011 acres, producing 46,000 to 51,000 barrels of oil per month. Prior to the enactment of the legislation, the validity of which is questioned in these proceedings, the appellant's weighted average receipt per barrel for the Province amounted to $3.10, with direct field costs of 58 cents per barrel, exclusive of administrative overhead, depreciation, depletion and taxes.

Since the legislation came into force there have been no significant changes in the marketing of Saskatchewan crude oil. The levels of production and exports of oil have continued at a constant or slightly increased tempo, close to production capacity.

II

The appellant's attack upon the legislative scheme is made on two broad grounds. The first claim of invalidity rests on the submission that the mineral income tax and royalty surcharge are indirect taxes and hence beyond s. 92, Head 2, of the *British North America Act, 1867*, which empowers a Legislature to "make laws in relation to matters coming within . . . direct taxation within the Province in order to the raising of a revenue for provincial purposes." The second submission is that the legislation, as a whole, is in relation to the regulation of trade and commerce and thus within the exclusive jurisdiction of the federal parliament under s. 91, Head 2, of the *Act*. Section 121 is not relied upon.

Notwithstanding very able argument by Mr. Robinette, counsel for the appellant, and by Mr. Smith, counsel for the Attorney General of Canada, I have reached the conclusion that the appeal must fail. After reading and re-reading the legislation, the evidence and what appear to be the relevant authorities, I adjudge:

1. That the mineral income tax is not an income tax; it is, however, a direct tax, and therefore within provincial competence.
2. That the royalty surcharge is not a royalty; it too is a tax but also a direct tax.
3. That the entire legislative scheme is aimed at taxation and its effect, if any, upon extraprovincial trade and commerce is incidental and non-disabling.

III

Before considering in detail the legislation, one or two observations of a general nature are warranted. This Court is sensitive to the freedom of action which must be allowed to the Legislatures to safeguard their legitimate interests as in their wisdom they see fit. It presumes that they have acted constitutionally. The onus of rebutting that presumption is upon the appellant. Before the Court concludes that the Province has transcended its constitutional powers the evidence must be clear and unmistakable; more than conjecture or speculation is needed to underpin a finding of constitutional incompetence.

On March 20, 1930, an agreement was entered into between the Government of Canada and the Government of Saskatchewan whereby the Government of Canada covenanted and agreed that the Province of Saskatchewan should own all public lands and mines and minerals and should administer and control natural resources within the Province from its entry into Confederation in 1905 and should be placed in a position of equality with the other Provinces of Confederation with respect to administration and control of its natural resources. The agreement effecting the natural resource transfer recited that:

> [i] in order that the Province may be in the same position as the original Provinces of Confederation are in virtue of section one hundred and nine of the *British North America Act, 1867*, the interest of the Crown in all Crown lands, mines, minerals (precious and base) and royalties derived therefrom within the Province . . . shall . . . belong to the Province . . . and the said lands shall be administered by the Province for the purposes thereof. . . .

The agreement was confirmed by federal and provincial legislation as well as the *B.N.A. Act, 1930*, 21 Geo. V, c. 26 (Imp.).

Subject to the limits imposed by the Canadian Constitution, the power of the Province to tax, control and manage its natural resources is plenary and absolute.

IV

[In this portion of his opinion Justice Dickson reviewed the salient features of the legislation.]

V

Direct or Indirect Taxation

The appellant claims that the mineral income tax and the royalty surcharge are indirect taxes and hence beyond the power of a provincial Legislature. The established guide for determining the validity of this submission is the classical formulation of John Stuart Mill (*Principles of Political Economy*, Book V, c. 3):

> Taxes are either direct or indirect. A direct tax is one which is demanded from the very person who it is intended or desired should pay it. Indirect taxes are those which are demanded from one person in the expectation and intention that he shall indemnify himself at the expense of another; such are the excise or customs.
>
> The producer or importer of a commodity is called upon to pay a tax on it not with the intention to levy a peculiar contribution upon him, but to tax through him the consumers of the commodity, from whom it is supposed that he will recover the amount by means of an advance in price.

Mill's well-known writings appeared not long before the drafting of the *British North America Act, 1867,* and were presumed by the Privy Council to be familiar to the Fathers of Confederation. . . . Mill's test became firmly established in *Bank of Toronto v. Lambe* [(1887), 12 App. Cas. 575]. In that case Lord Hobhouse said that while it was proper and, indeed, necessary to have regard to the opinion of economists, the question is a legal one, *viz.* what the words mean as used in the statute. The problem is primarily one of law rather than of refined economic analysis. The dividing line between a direct and an indirect tax is referable to and ascertainable by the "general tendencies of the tax and the common understanding of men as to those tendencies." . . .

There can be no doubt that by the words "direct and indirect taxation" the Fathers of Confederation contemplated certain distinct categories of taxation, as well as a general test of directness. Only certain of such categories, such as income and property taxes, were to be available to the Legislatures. There were two reasons for this. The first was based on arcane political economy. It was thought that a direct tax would be more perceived than an indirect tax. The effect was thought to provide for greater scrutiny and resistance by the electorate with a resulting parsimony in public expenditure. The second reason proved wrong from the start. It was thought that provincial activities would be limited and revenue needs would be slim; the Legislatures, therefore, would have no necessity to resort to most tax pools. . . .

Historically well-understood categories of taxation have a known jurisprudential fate. Thus, a customs levy cannot be made by the Legislature whereas a property tax or income tax falls unquestionably within their competence. Careful constitutional analysis is required in respect of any unusual or hybrid form of taxation. A hybrid form of taxation may well have aspects which are direct and others which are indirect. By nineteenth century political economy, any element of indirectness was a stigma as tending to obfuscate the actions of the Legislature. That consideration is of minor importance today. In assessing the policy of a new a form of taxation the jurisprudence offers no certain guide. One begins with the *British North America Act, 1867,* in which there are two additional criteria (1) that the taxation be within the Province and (2) that it be in order to the raising of a revenue for provincial purposes. Implicit in this, and more important than a vestige of indirectness, is the prohibition of the imposition by a province of any tax upon citizens beyond its borders. Additionally, a province cannot, through the ostensible use of its power to tax, invade prohibited fields. It cannot by way of taxation regulate trade and commerce or prohibit the free admission of produce or manufactured goods from other provinces. It must confine itself to the raising of a revenue for provincial purposes.

VI

Argument was directed to the Court to the effect that the tax here in question is a commodity tax and, as such, the general tendency would be for the tax to be passed on and therefore categorized as indirect. It is true that a tax on any one commodity whether laid on its production, its importation, its carriage from place to place, or its sale will, as a general rule, raise the value and price of the commodity by at least the amount of the tax. Mill, Vol. II (1893 ed.) at p. 435. That is very old doctrine and for that reason a commodity tax is traditionally conceived as an indirect tax. The Courts have taken that as one criterion in characterizing the tax. . . .

It is hard to see that the mineral income tax fits snugly into the commodity tax category. There are several rough edges. First, the tax falls upon a holder of certain rights in respect of part of the amount received. Secondly, unlike a true commodity tax—*i.e.,* a fixed imposition or a percentage of the commodity—s. 6 of the *Act* contemplates an imposition varying with production costs. If production costs rise, the share of the Province by taxation falls. Thirdly, the tax is not an "add-to-the-price" impost but rather a "take-from-the-owner" levy.

Finally, the tax does not fall on the product but only on certain entitled holders. Owners of rights having an aggregate area of less than 1,280 acres in producing tracts are exempted.

For these reasons, the tax resists classification as a commodity tax in so far as constitutional jurisprudence knows that term. It must be subject, therefore, to further constitutional scrutiny. . . .

It should be clear from the foregoing that neat constitutional categories are of marginal assistance in the present case. The tax resists such classification; it is a hybrid. It must be assessed in the light of constitutional analysis, keeping in mind the *indicia* to which I have above referred.

Can it be said, then, that the tax is one which is demanded from the very person who it is intended or desired should pay it, or can it be said, rather, that it is demanded from the oil producer in the expectation and intention that he shall indemnify himself at the expense of another? The question is not easily answered. An example might assist. If we assume a basic well-head price of $3 per barrel and a sale at $7 per barrel, the tax would amount to $4 per barrel. If basic well-head price and production costs remain constant but the selling price increases to $11 per barrel, the tax would amount to $8 per barrel. It is quite obvious that the oil producer will not be in a position to bear the tax of $4 or $8 out of the basic well-head price of $3 per barrel which he retains. On this view it is arguable that the tax is passed on to the purchaser as a component of price. I do not think, however, that this can be said to be the true view. An indirect tax is an amount which is added to what would otherwise be the price of the commodity or service. This appears from Mill's formulation. He says that tax is indirect when the producer is called upon to pay a tax not with the intention of levying a contribution upon him, but to tax through him the consumers of the commodity, from whom it is supposed that he will recover the amount "by means of an advance in price," *i.e.* as an "add-on." In *Attorney-General of British Columbia v. Esquimalt and Nanaimo Railway Company* [[1950] A.C. 87 (P.C.)], Lord Greene pointed out that in order to constitute an indirect tax the tax itself must have a general tendency to be passed on. If an article selling for $10 is subjected to a ten per cent customs duty, the general tendency would be simply to add the amount of the tax or more to the price of the commodity. The purchaser would then pay one dollar or more in excess of the amount he would have paid in the absence of the tax. In *Security Export Co. v. Hetherington* [[1923] S.C.R. 539], at p. 558, Duff J. adopted the following definition of a direct tax, taken from the *Oxford Dictionary*:

> One levied immediately upon the persons who are to bear the burden, as opposed to indirect taxes levied upon commodities, of which *the price is thereby increased* so that the persons on whom the incidence ultimately falls pay indirectly a proportion of taxation included in the price of the article. (Emphasis added.)

If the price is increased by reason of the tax, the tendency will be to have the consumer bear the increase. If the price is not increased, the tendency will be to have the producer bear the tax.

For myself, I can find nothing in the language of the *Act* nor in the oral or documentary evidence to suggest that the price of Saskatchewan oil was increased by the addition of the "mineral income tax" levied, or that the purchaser of Saskatchewan crude paid more per barrel than he would have paid in the absence of the tax. Nor can I discover anything which leads me to conclude that the Legislature of Saskatchewan acted on any view other than that of collecting maximum tax from the persons who are by the statute made liable to pay it, namely Saskatchewan oil producers.

There is a further consideration which should not be overlooked. If it had been intended that those subject to the tax would pass it on to others the inclusion of the "farmers' section," exempting tracts not exceeding 1,280 acres, would have been quite unnecessary.

The "farmers' section" highlights the essential axis on which the present litigation revolves. It is a dispute concerning who, as between the producers and the Government of Saskatchewan, will reap the benefit of a fortuitous rise in the price of oil. In the case of producers holding rights in producing tracts in excess of 1,280 acres, the Legislature has determined the benefit shall accrue to provincial coffers; in the case of a producer in a smaller tract, the Legislature has abstained from imposition leaving the benefit in the producer's pocket. The ultimate position of the final consumer is unaffected. It is also patent that any attempt by an oil producer to pass on an amount additional to the selling price would be self-defeating. Every increase in selling price will be reflected by an equal increase in tax as, according to the formula, tax equals well-head price received minus basic well-head price.

Reference was made in the Saskatchewan Courts, and in argument in this Court, to the international or "world" price of oil and the effect of such upon the pricing of Saskatchewan crude. It has been contended on behalf of the Province that the world price would place a ceiling on the price of Saskatchewan crude and, therefore, the Saskatchewan producer could not pass on the mineral income tax to the purchaser. Again, to take an example, if world price were $11 per barrel and basic well-head price $3 per barrel, the mineral income tax would amount to $8 per barrel. The producer could not recover this amount by increasing the price to $19 per barrel and for good reasons (i) his oil could not command that price in the market, and (ii) he would be deprived of the additional revenue by the mechanics of the *Act.* . . .

If Saskatchewan oil is sold in the market at prevailing market prices, as I understand to be the case, then I do not think it can properly be said that the Eastern Canadian oil consumer pays more by reason of imposition of the tax. There is no added "burden" to "cling" to the commodity unit. See Rand J. in *C.P.R. v. A.-G. Saskatchewan, supra.*

One of the cornerstones upon which appellant's case rests is the contention that there resides in the Minister a general power to fix the price at which oil is sold, and that the oil producer, if he is to avoid pecuniary loss, must sell at the ministerially predetermined price. That is simply not the case. The power of the Minister to determine well-head value in respect of mineral income tax is not an unrestrained and unrestricted general power; it is exercisable only when oil is disposed of at less than fair value, and then, only *after* the sale has taken place. The purpose of s. 4A of Bill 42 is obviously to prevent such practices as sale of oil between related companies at artificially low prices. Well-head value is not arbitrarily set by the Minister; it is set by world and national forces determining the market price at the well-head. No evidence was adduced that the Minister has ever set a figure above market price, thus forcing producers into a loss position if unable to sell at the artificially high figure set. In the normal course of events the tax is the difference between basic well-head price and the market price received by the producer in the course of trade. If the producer seeks to evade tax by undercutting the price his product would command at fair market value, then the possibility of ministerial determination arises, but only then. The tax does not set the price. Price sets the tax. . . .

I would hold that, in its true nature and effect, the mineral income tax constitutes direct taxation within the Province in order to the raising of a revenue for provincial purposes.

IX

The Province seeks to sustain the constitutionality of the royalty surcharge imposed by The Oil and Natural Gas Regulations, 1969, on the basis that it is a "variable" royalty. The right of the Crown, in respect of Crown lands, to impose contractually a royalty and to vary such royalty is undisputed. . . .

The first question to be determined in respect of royalty surcharge, therefore, is whether the royalty surcharge is a royalty or a tax. The answer to that question turns on whether the Province, in imposing royalty surcharge, was acting *qua* lessor or *qua* taxing authority. In other words, was the relationship of the Legislature vis-à-vis the oil producer that of lessor–lessee, or was the true character of the relationship that of sovereign taxing authority-taxpayer. . . .

In my view, although in name a royalty, the royalty surcharge is, in substance, a tax. Except as affecting lessees under pre-existing Crown leases, it is a levy compulsorily imposed on previously existing contractual rights by a public authority for public purposes. It is patent that the consensual agreement

and mutuality ordinarily found in a lessor–lessee relationship is entirely absent in the relationship between the Crown and persons subjected to the royalty surcharge. Royalty surcharge is the same one hundred per cent levy as is imposed in other terms as mineral income tax. That it is a tax is not fatal. In object and purpose and mode of exaction it is congruent with mineral income tax. It is therefore direct and falls within provincial competence.

X

Counsel for appellant urged the Court to strike down the legislation as an infringement of Parliament's exclusive authority respecting the regulation of trade and commerce. Appellant says: "[T]he tax and surcharge are established in a way which enables the Province of Saskatchewan to control the minimum price at which Saskatchewan crude oil is sold. This control is imposed on a commodity almost exclusively consumed outside of Saskatchewan, either in the Canadian or international marketplace. This imposition of a minimum price by the Province to be passed on to consumers outside of the Province is an interference with the free flow of trade between provinces . . . so as to prevent producers in Saskatchewan from dealing unhampered with purchasers outside of Saskatchewan."

Section 91, Head 2 of the *British North America Act, 1867*, has undergone a jurisprudential renaissance during the past fifty years. Appellant asks the Court to extend that revivification to an unprecedented degree. . . .

The notion that a Province may incidentally affect goods in interprovincial or international trade was developed in *Carnation Company Ltd. v. Quebec Agricultural Marketing Board* [[1968] S.C.R. 238]. In that case it was held that a Province could obliquely affect much goods by increasing their cost if the legislation in object and purpose was in relation to a valid head of provincial power. . . .

The argument that the orders of the marketing board might have impact upon interprovincial trade was disposed of in these words, at p. 253:

> I am not prepared to agree that, in determining that aim, the fact that these orders may have some impact upon the appellant's interprovincial trade necessarily means that they constitute a regulation of trade and commerce within s. 91(2) and thus renders them invalid. The fact of such impact is a matter which may be relevant in determining their true aim and purpose, but it is not conclusive.

It is now well established that incidental effect is not a quantum measurement. It is tested by the design or aim of the legislation. That was held in *Brant Dairy Company Limited v. Milk Commission of Ontario* [[1973] S.C.R. 131], where Mr. Justice Judson said, at p. 166:

The test that determines whether a marketing plan or its administration is *ultra vires* the province is the test applied in the *Manitoba Reference* (Mr. Justice Martland at p. 703). Is it "designed to restrict or limit the free flow of trade between provinces as such"? . . .

The conceptual tool of a "flow," or "current," or "stream" of commerce has been referred to by the Court in a number of subsequent cases, the most recent being *MacDonald v. Vapor Canada Ltd.* [(1976), 22 C.P.R. (2d) 1], at p. 27. The real question, unsettled in the jurisprudence, is the determination of when the product enters the export stream marking the start of the process of exportation. American jurisprudence has held that the distinguishing mark of an export product is shipment or entry with a common carrier for transportation to another jurisdiction. . . . Implicit in the argument of the appellant is the assumption that federal regulatory power pursuant to s. 91(2) follows the flow of oil backward across provincial boundaries, back through provincial gathering systems and finally to the well-head. A secondary assumption is that sale at the well-head marks the start of the process of exportation. In the view I take of the case it is unnecessary to reach any conclusion as to the validity of either of these assumptions. It is, however, worth noting that neither American nor Canadian jurisprudence has ever gone that far.

I can find nothing in the present case to lead me to conclude that the taxation measures imposed by the Province of Saskatchewan were merely a colourable device for assuming control of extraprovincial trade. The language of the impugned statutes does not disclose an intention on the part of the Province to regulate, or control, or impede the marketing or export of oil from Saskatchewan. "Oil produced and sold" means produced and sold within the provinces. "Well-head price" by definition means the price at the well-head of a barrel of oil produced in Saskatchewan. The mineral income tax and the royalty surcharge relate only to oil produced within Saskatchewan. The transactions are well-head transactions. There are no impediments to the free movement of goods as were found objectionable in *Attorney-General for Manitoba v. Manitoba Egg and Poultry Association* [[1971] S.C.R. 689], and in *Burns Foods. Ltd. v. Attorney-General for Manitoba* [[1975] 1 S.C.R. 494].

Nor is there anything in the extraneous evidence to form the basis of an argument that the impugned legislation in its effect regulated interprovincial or international trade. The evidence is all to the contrary and that evidence comes entirely from witnesses called on behalf of the appellant. Production and export of oil increased after the legislative scheme was implemented. Sales of oil by the appellant were continued in 1974 as in 1973 and previously.

The trial judge, Hughes J., made the following finding of fact:

> I do emphasize that nothing has happened to suggest any intrusion or invasion on the part of the defendant with respect to the export of crude oil from this Province unless it is to be suggested that it is to be found in price regulation.

Chief Justice Culliton, speaking for a unanimous Court of Appeal, made a further finding:

> Neither of the charges [*i.e.* mineral income tax and royalty surcharge] have any effect on price. As a matter of fact, the true situation is that the tax does not influence the price but rather, the price determines the tax.

On the basis of such concurrent findings it is hard to say that the flow of commerce was in any way impeded, unless it can be said to relate to price.

It was contended in argument that the effect was to place a floor price under Saskatchewan oil and thereby interfere with interprovincial trade. So far as mineral income tax is concerned the incidence of taxation is pegged to the price received for the oil at the well-head. Section 4A is an "after-the-event" provision which comes into play only if there was a sale at less than fair value. The emphasis on fair value ensures that the tax will not change the export oil price. The price of oil subject to the tax and the price of oil free of the tax, *i.e.* from the exempted 1,280-acre tracts, will be the same as the product crosses the provincial border. The ultimate position of consumers is unaffected. The only way in which extraprovincial consumers could have benefited would have been in the event of the Province freezing the price of oil, assuming constitutional competence to do so.

One is free to speculate that, to the extent producers would be prepared to undercut the fair market value of their oil, the legislation discourages them from doing so by virtue of the constant tax liability. The possibility of price-cutting is highly theoretical, unsupported by evidence and in view of the inelasticity of demand for petroleum products, highly unlikely.

In *Burns Foods Limited v. Attorney-General for Manitoba, supra,* in striking down a regulation under [t]he *Natural Products Marketing Act* of Manitoba which required packers in Manitoba to buy hogs only from the Manitoba Hog Producers Marketing Board, Mr. Justice Pigeon said this, at pp. 504-5:

> It is a case of directly regulating extra-provincial trade operations in their essential aspects namely, the price and all the other conditions of sale. . . . The situation here is totally unlike that which obtained in *Brant Dairy Co. v. Milk Commission of Ontario*, [1973] S.C.R. 131, 30 D.L.R.

(3d) 559. In that case, the challenge on constitutional grounds was dismissed because there was no evidence that the orders had any extra-provincial effect.

The key word is "directly" for it leaves open the possibility for a scheme to affect incidentally inter-provincial trade, so long as the scheme is not in pith and substance in relation to inter-provincial trade. This last proposition, while obvious in other areas of constitutional law, was remarkably absent in the cases respecting trade and commerce decided in the first half of this century.

The Province of Saskatchewan had a *bona fide*, legitimate and reasonable interest of its own to advance in enacting the legislation in question, as related to taxation and natural resources, out of all proportion to the burden, if there can be said to be a burden, imposed on the Canadian free trade economic unit through the legislation. The effect, if any, on the extraprovincial trade in oil is merely indirectly and remotely incidental to the manifest revenue-producing object of the legislation under attack.

 **Labatt v. Attorney General of Canada, 1980**

In the *Labatt* case, the Supreme Court rejected the trade-and-commerce power as a basis for federal consumer-protection legislation. This decision indicated that the Court's majority was inclined to set tight limits on exercises of federal regulatory power not aimed primarily at interprovincial or international trade.

In 1881, in the *Parsons*[1] case, Sir Montague Smith referred to "general regulation of trade affecting the whole Dominion" as another possible application of the trade-and-commerce power in addition to the regulation of interprovincial and international activities. The modern Supreme Court's reluctance to give much scope to this "general regulation of trade" dimension of trade and commerce first became evident in the Court's 1977 decision in *MacDonald v. Vapor Canada Ltd.*[2] There, the Court unanimously ruled that a part of the federal *Trade-marks Act* establishing a national code of fair business practice was *ultra vires*. The application of the legislation to business throughout the Dominion did not, in the Court's view, justify federal legislation that, by embracing civil wrongs covered by the law of torts, encroached on provincial jurisdiction over property and civil rights. This was the first time since the abolition of Privy Council appeals in 1949 that the Supreme Court had found federal legislation unconstitutional.

The *Vapor Canada* case was followed by some further federal losses and provincial gains. In two cases decided shortly after *Vapor Canada*, the Court held that federal legislation giving the Federal Court of Canada jurisdiction to try suits in which the federal government is a plaintiff exceeded Parliament's power under section 101 of the *B.N.A. Act* to establish courts "for the better Administration of the Laws of Canada."[3] In one of these cases, *McNamara Construction v. The Queen*, the Court explicitly overruled an earlier Supreme Court decision made in 1894. In the same year, in *Canada Indemnity Co. v. The Queen*,[4] the Court found that the interprovincial effects of B.C. legislation giving a provincial corporation a monopoly on the automobile insurance business in the province did not constitute a ground for holding the legislation *ultra vires*. In *Dominion Stores Ltd. v. The Queen*,[5] decided immediately before the *Labatt* case, the Supreme Court, in a 5-to-4 decision, held that federal legislation establishing a grading system for apples could not validly apply to transactions that are entirely intraprovincial.

The cases cited above, taken together with the cases in which the Court has upheld provincial incursions into the domain of criminal law, demonstrate a considerable balance in the Supreme Court's approach to the division of powers. These cases have not, however, attracted nearly as much political attention as those favouring the federal government.

---

1 See case 1.

2 [1977] 2 S.C.R. 134.

3 *McNamara Construction v. The Queen*, [1977] 2 S.C.R. 655 and *Quebec Northshore Ltd. v. C.P. Ltd.*, [1977] 2 S.C.R. 1054.

4 [1977] 2 S.C.R. 504.

5 [1980] 1 S.C.R. 139.

At issue in the *Labatt* case were regulations passed under the federal *Food and Drugs Act* requiring brewers using the generic term "light beer" to meet certain prescribed standards—for example, an alcoholic content of 1.2 to 2.5 percent. The Court decided, six to three, that the legislation was unconstitutional. None of the judges considered that the legislation could be based on the criminal law or the peace, order, and good government powers. Justice Estey's majority opinion focused on his finding that the legislation did not in its pith and substance apply to international and interprovincial trade, but to a particular industry that appeared to be essentially local in character.[6] Justice Pigeon's dissent, concurred in by Justice McIntyre, was based primarily on the Privy Council's decision in one of the 1937 *New Deal* references, which upheld federal legislation permitting the use of a national trademark for products meeting the requirements of a Canada Standard.[7] Chief Justice Laskin's dissent went further. He defended Parliament's power to equalize competitive advantages in the national market by enforcing commodity standards. In his view, section 121's prohibition of interprovincial trade barriers provided a constitutional "reinforcement" of such a power by indicating a constitutional intention of "marking Canada as a whole as an economic union."

The aftermath of *Labatt* shows how limited the practical impact of a ruling of *ultra vires* can be. Observers originally thought this decision, along with *Dominion Stores*, would undermine a coherent system of national product standards to the detriment of the consumer, but this has not happened. The food industry has an interest in maintaining such standards because common standards facilitate a differential price structure for degrees of quality that are not evident to visual inspection. The industry has thus continued to support the standards. In addition, the impulse to cheat has been kept in check by alternative enforcement possibilities. *Labatt* struck down section 6 of the *Act*, which enforced the product standards directly, but left in place prohibitions of "false, misleading or deceptive" packaging and labelling. The latter prohibitions have been used to enforce the standards indirectly.[8] ∼

---

6   Note that the Justice W.Z. Estey who wrote this opinion is the son of J.W. Estey who served on the Court from 1944 to 1956.

7   *Dominion Trade and Industry Reference*, [1937] A.C. 405.

8   See Patrick Monahan, *Politics and the Constitution: The Charter, Federalism, and the Supreme Court of Canada* (Toronto: Carswell/Methuen, 1987) 228-34.

LABATT v. ATTORNEY GENERAL OF CANADA
[1980] 1 S.C.R. 914

Hearing: June 27, 28, 1979; Judgment: December 1, 1979.

Present: Laskin C.J. and Martland, Dickson, Beetz, Estey, Ritchie, Pratte, McIntyre, and Pigeon JJ.

THE CHIEF JUSTICE (dissenting): I agree with Mr. Justice Pigeon that the appeal should be dismissed with costs to the respondent. ... The constitutional issue which Justice Pigeon resolved in favour of federal power, raises for me more extended considerations than those on which he was content

to proceed and I wish to state my position briefly on what I regard as a highly important issue.

I do not think that the *Dominion Trade and Industry Commission* [[1937] A.C. 405] case is conclusive here. That was a case involving non-compulsory regulation whereas the *Food and Drugs Act* and the relevant Regulations thereunder operate compulsorily. I do not think that anything is added by reference to *Dominion Stores Limited v. The Queen* [[1980] 1 S.C.R. 844] in which judgment was handed down by this Court on December 13, 1979. Insofar as it turned on dealing with local marketing it does not touch the present case. ...

The matter therefore comes down to whether this Court views the federal trade and commerce power as a sufficient support for the legislation and Regulations which are attacked in the present case. I would hold that it does, and, in so doing I would adopt the statement in the *Parsons* case, at p. 113, which envisages competent federal legislation by way of "general regulation of trade affecting the whole Dominion." . . .

In the *Board of Commerce* case, at p. 201, the Privy Council indicated that it might be open to Parliament "to call . . . for statistical and other information which may be valuable for guidance in questions affecting Canada as a whole. Such information may be required before any power to regulate trade and commerce can be properly exercised. . . ." I do not press any perfect analogy to the prescription of common standards for an article of food which is produced throughout the country and which is also imported from abroad, but it does appear to me that if Parliament can set up standards for required returns for statistical purposes, it should be able to fix standards that are common to all manufacturers of foods, including beer, drugs, cosmetics and therapeutic devices, at least to equalize competitive advantages in the carrying on of businesses concerned with such products. I find some reinforcement in this view of the scope of the federal trade and commerce power in s. 121 of the *British North America Act* which precluded interprovincial tariffs, marking Canada as a whole as an economic union.

The operations of Labatt Breweries and of other brewers of beer extend throughout Canada, and would not attenuate the federal trade and commerce power any further than has already been manifested in judicial decisions by denying Parliament authority to address itself to uniform prescriptions for the manufacture of food, drugs, cosmetics, therapeutic devices in the way, in the case of beer, of standards for its production and distribution according to various alcoholic strengths under labels appropriate to the governing regulations.

The judgment of Martland, Dickson, Beetz, and Estey JJ. was delivered by

ESTEY J.: The appellant seeks a declaration that its product "Labatt's Special Lite" as labelled, packaged and sold "is not likely to be mistaken for a 'light beer' within the standards set out . . ." in the regulations under the *Food and Drugs Act*, R.S.C. 1970, c. F-27. . . .

Two issues arise by reason of the marketing of this product under the label set out above. Firstly, the appellant takes the position that this product when so advertised is not likely to be mistaken for a light beer within the applicable regulation. This regulation, being s. B.02.134 of the Food and Drug Regulations, C.R.C., c. 870, was enacted pursuant to s. 25(1) of the *Act* to which I will return shortly. Section 6 of the *Act* states as follows:

> Where a standard has been prescribed for a food, no person shall label, package, sell or advertise any article in such a manner that it is likely to be mistaken for such food, unless the article complies with the prescribed standard.

The second position taken by the appellant is that s. 6 of the *Act* and regulation B.02.134 are *ultra vires* the Parliament of Canada, and to the extent that it authorizes such regulation, s. 25 is likewise *ultra vires*.

[Justice Estey found that the Labatt's "Special Lite" could be mistaken for light beer and therefore had to meet the light beer standards set out in the regulation if the regulations were constitutionally valid.]

I turn now to the constitutional issue. The appellant challenges the constitutional validity of s. 6 and s. 25(1)(c) of the *Food and Drugs Act* and the regulations promulgated thereunder with reference to the production and sale of beer. Before embarking on a discussion of the constitutional considerations, let us examine the form and thrust of the *Act* and its regulations.

Part I of the *Act* is entitled "Foods, Drugs, Cosmetics and Devices." Under the heading "Food" we find four sections creating offences such as the sale of harmful substances, adulterated food and food unfit for human consumption and food manufactured under unsanitary conditions. There is a prohibition against the labelling, packaging, selling or advertising of food in any manner that is false and misleading or deceptive; and there is a general provision applicable to the whole of Part I making it an offence to advertise food, drugs, cosmetics or devices to the general public as a treatment, preventative or cure for any disease. Then we come to s. 6 in the "Food" portion of Part I of the *Act* which has already been set out above. . . .

. . . In Part II of the statute, provision is made for the "administration and enforcement" of the *Act*, including the powers of inspectors, the power of forfeiture, the right to make analysis of substances. Section 25(1)(c) appears in this part and establishes the authority in the Governor-in-Council to pass regulations under the statute

> . . . for carrying the purposes and provisions of this *Act* into effect, and, in particular, but not so as to restrict the generality of the foregoing . . .
>
> (c) prescribing standards of composition, strength, potency, purity, quality or other property of any article of food, drug, cosmetic or device;

The regulatory authority under sub. (c) appears to extend to the four classes of goods or articles regulated under Part I which include "foods" with which we are here concerned.

Under the authority of s. 25(1)(c), there has been produced an elaborate set of regulations dealing with the preparation, manufacture and sale of the four articles or commodities dealt with in Part I of the *Act*. ... The part of the regulations pertaining to alcoholic beverages with which this proceeding is concerned commences under the heading "Malt Liquors" with regulation B.02.130, already reproduced above, which prescribes the nature of "beer," its alcoholic content, and permitted additives. The other malt liquors described by these regulations are ale, stout, porter, light beer, and malt liquor. The only difference between these various malt liquors appears to be the alcoholic content, and "the aroma, taste and character commonly attributed to" them. As we have seen, the alcoholic content for beer shall be not less than 2.6 per cent and not more than 5.5 per cent by volume, and in the case of light beer shall be not less than 1.2 per cent and not more than 2.5 per cent alcohol by volume. It may be observed that s. 6 was introduced into the *Act* in 1953 and s. 25(1)(c) was expanded at the same time to its present form. ...

What then is the constitutional basis for the enactment of the contested portions of this statute by Parliament? The possible origins of this sovereign power include the federal authority under s. 91 of the *British North America Act* in respect of criminal law, trade and commerce, and peace, order and good government. I turn first to the criminal jurisdiction. ...

That there are limits to the extent of the criminal authority is obvious and these limits were pointed out by this Court in The *Reference as to the Validity of Section 5(a) of the Dairy Industry Act* (*Margarine Reference*), where Rand J. looked to the object of the statute to find whether or not it related to the traditional field of criminal law, namely public peace, order, security, health and morality. In that case, the Court found that the object of the statute was economic:

> ... to give trade protection to the dairy industry in the production and sale of butter; to benefit one group of persons as against competitors in business in which, in the absence of the legislation, the latter would be free to engage in the province. To forbid manufacture and sale for such an end is *prima facie* to deal directly with the civil rights of individuals in relation to particular trade within the provinces.

(*per* Rand J., at p. 50.)

The test is one of substance, not form, and excludes from the criminal jurisdiction legislative activity not having the prescribed characteristics of criminal law.

> A crime is an act which the law, with appropriate penal sanctions, forbids; but as prohibitions are not enacted in a vacuum, we can properly look for some evil or injurious or undesirable effect upon the public against which the law is directed. That effect may be in relation to social, economic or political interests; and the legislature has had in mind to suppress the evil or to safeguard the interest threatened.

(*per* Rand J., at p. 49.)

This approach to the federal authority in the field of criminal law was relied upon by this Court in *Dominion Stores v. The Queen* (judgment rendered December 13, 1979). That there is an area of legitimate regulations in respect of trade practices contrary to the interest of the community such as misleading, false or deceptive advertising and misbranding, is not under debate. In the statute now before us, the question of mislabelling arises only after the category of "light beer" is created and the specifications for its production are assigned. When all this has been ordained, the use of the words "Special Lite" by the appellant may be said to be misleading to the beer buying public. The contest, however, is not in respect of this second stage, but rather the first stage, that is the right in the Federal Parliament and the Federal Government to establish the standards of production and content of this product. In any case, the first stage of the process does not come within the criminal law reach as traditionally described in the authorities. I can find no basis, therefore, for this detailed regulation of the brewing industry in the production and sale of its product as a proper exercise of the federal authority in criminal law.

The jurisdiction of Parliament in matters related to health similarly has no application here. Parliament may make laws in relation to health for the peace, order and good government of Canada: quarantine laws come to mind as one example. The Privy Council hinted that legislation enacted by Parliament to deal with an "epidemic of pestilence" would be valid in *Toronto Electric Commissioners v. Snider*. But we are not concerned with such matters here. Where health is an aspect of criminal law, as in the case of adulteration provisions in the statute, the answer is clear but here not helpful. The appellant discussed succinctly in its submission to this Court another aspect of the "health" jurisdiction.

> Furthermore the regulations under consideration do not on their face purport to be, nor can they be, connected or related to the protection of health since any such beverage regardless of its name having an alcoholic content by volume of not less than 1.2% and not more than 8.5% and otherwise brewed in accordance with the process common to all "Malt Liquors" is presumptively not a hazard to health.

One cannot successfully ground the contested elements of this legislation in the field of the federal health power.

By s. 91(2) of the *British North America Act*, authority with reference to "the regulation of Trade and Commerce" was assigned without qualification or explanation to Parliament. Without judicial restraint in the interpretation of this provision, the provincial areas of jurisdiction would be seriously truncated. It is not surprising, therefore, to find the Privy Council stating within 15 years of Confederation:

The words "regulation of trade and commerce," in their unlimited sense are sufficiently wide, *if uncontrolled by the context and other parts of the Act, to include every regulation of trade ranging from political arrangements in regard to trade with foreign governments, requiring the sanction of parliament, down to minute rules for regulating particular trades.* But a consideration of the *Act* shews that the words were not used in this unlimited sense. In the first place the collocation of No. 2 with classes of subjects of national and general concern affords an indication that regulations relating to general trade and commerce were in the mind of the legislature, when conferring this power on the dominion parliament. If the words had been intended to have the full scope of which in their literal meaning they are susceptible, the specific mention of several of the other classes of subjects enumerated in sect. 91 would have been unnecessary; as, 15, banking; 17, weights and measures; 18, bills of exchange and promissory notes; 19, interest; and even 21, bankruptcy and insolvency.

per Sir Montague Smith at p. 112 in *Citizens Insurance Company of Canada v. Parsons*. (Emphasis added.)

Thus it is clear that "minute rules for regulating particular trades" are not within the trade and commerce competence. The statute and regulation with which we are here concerned purport to establish such a detailed single industry regulatory pattern. The judgment of the Privy Council continues:

Construing therefore the words "regulation of trade and commerce" by the various aids to their interpretation above suggested, they would include political arrangements in regard to trade requiring the sanction of parliament, regulation of trade in matters of inter-provincial concern, and it may be that they would include general regulation of trade affecting the whole dominion. Their Lordships abstain on the present occasion from any attempt to define the limits of the authority of the dominion parliament in this direction. It is enough for the decision of the present case to say that, in their view, its authority to legislate for the regulation of trade and commerce does not comprehend the power to regulate by legislation the contracts of a particular business or trade, such as the business of fire insurance in a single province, and therefore that its legislative authority does not in the present case conflict or compete with the power over property and civil rights assigned to the legislature of Ontario by No. 13 of sect. 92.

[*per* Sir Montague Smith, *supra*, at p. 113.]

. . . Reverting to the *Parsons* case, *supra*, the trade and commerce head was there described as consisting of two branches. The first in the words of the judgment includes "political arrangements in regard to trade requiring the sanction of Parliament, regulation of trade in matters of interprovincial concern. . . ." The second branch is said to ". . . include general regulation of trade affecting the whole Dominion." The first branch is illustrated in the succession of cases dealing with the marketing of natural products commencing with *R. v. Eastern Terminal Elevator Co.* [[1925] S.C.R. 434] and continuing to the recent egg marketing judgment in *Reference Re Agricultural Products Marketing Act* [[1978] 2 S.C.R. 1198]. . . .

The principles developed in the natural products marketing judgments only obliquely deal with the second branch of the *Parsons* description of trade and commerce, *supra*, and hence are not of direct application here. The impugned regulations in and under the *Food and Drugs Act* are not concerned with the control and guidance of the flow of articles of commerce through the distribution channels, but rather with the production and local sale of the specified products of the brewing industry. There is no demonstration by the proponent of these isolated provisions in the *Food and Drugs Act* and its regulations of any interprovincial aspect of this industry. The labels in the record reveal that the appellant produces these beverages in all provinces but Quebec and Prince Edward Island. From the nature of the beverage, it is apparent, without demonstration, that transportation to distant markets would be expensive, and hence the local nature of the production operation. . . .

The first successful attempt to breathe life into the second branch of the *Parsons* trade and commerce description, *supra*, is found in *John Deere Plow Co. v. Wharton* [[1915] A.C. 330]. The provincial legislature had attempted to establish regulation in a limited sense of federally incorporated companies within the provincial boundaries. The Court determined that such provincial action was *ultra vires* as being an invasion of the power of Parliament to regulate the exercise by federal companies of their powers throughout the Dominion. This subject should not be left without adding that the Court there found the constitutional basis for legislation authorizing the establishment of federal incorporations in the peace, order and good government clause while the regulation of their activities fell into the trade and commerce category. Viscount Haldane, speaking in the *Wharton* case, *supra*, stated at p. 340:

. . . [T]he power to regulate trade and commerce at all events enables the Parliament of Canada to prescribe to what extent the powers of companies the objects of which extend to the entire Dominion should be exercisable, and what limitations should be placed on such powers. For if it be established that the Dominion Parliament can create such companies, then it becomes a *question of general interest throughout the Dominion* in what fashion they should be permitted to trade. (Emphasis added.)

To this date this is still the test in determining whether the second branch of the trade and commerce power applies; *vide* Laskin C.J. in *Reference re the Anti-Inflation Act*, at p. 426.

What clearly is not of general national concern is the regulation of a single trade or industry. *Vide In Re Insurance Act, 1910*, at pp. 308-9; *Eastern Terminal Elevator Co., supra*.

The section of the *Act* before the Court in *In Re Insurance Act 1910* provided:

> 3. The provisions of this *Act* shall not apply— . . .
>
> (*b*) to any company incorporated by an *Act* of the legislature of the late province of Canada, or by an *Act* of the legislature of any province now forming part of Canada, which carries on the business of insurance wholly within the limits of the province by the legislature of which it was incorporated, and which is within the exclusive control of the legislature of such province;

Nevertheless the statute was struck down as an attempt to regulate a trade within a particular province whether or not the trade was also carried on in all the provinces. The businesses before the Court were national concerns operating in several provinces under a statute which exempted from its application wholly intraprovincial businesses. Thus it is clear that neither national ownership of a trade or undertaking or even national advertising of its products will alone suffice to authorize the imposition of federal trade and commerce regulation.

In more modern times, this Court in *MacDonald v. Vapor Canada Ltd.* struck down that part of the *Trade-marks Act* of Canada purporting to create a cause of action in connection with "any business practice contrary to honest industrial or commercial usage in Canada." Unrestricted geographic play of the provision was not sufficient to find legislative authority under the trade and commerce heading. *Vide* Chief Justice Laskin at pp. 156 and 159. . . .

. . . As we have seen, the trade and commerce head cannot be applied to the regulation of a single trade, even though it be on a national basis, and in the *Board of Commerce* disposition, *supra*, the invocation of the trade and commerce head of federal jurisdiction is forbidden in the regulation of elements of commerce such as contracts, in an individual trade or concern even though the control was imposed in a series of separate regulatory codes each purporting to regulate a separate trade or industry. . . .

In the result, the trade and commerce power has been rescued from near oblivion following the *Citizens Insurance* case, *supra*, by the extension or development of the *obiter* or afterthought of Sir Montague Smith in that case. The application of the power to this stage in our constitutional development finds illustration firstly in general regulation of an element of trade such as the regulation of federal incorporations. With respect to legislation relating to the support, control or regulation of the various levels or components in the marketing cycle of natural products, the provincial authority is *prima facie* qualified to legislate with reference to production (*vide* Pigeon J. in the *Reference Re Agricultural Products Marketing Act, supra*, at p. 1296), and the federal Parliament with reference to marketing in the international and interprovincial levels of trade. In between, the success or failure of the legislator depends upon whether the pith and substance or primary objective of the statute or regulation is related to the heads of power of the legislative authority in question. Incidental effect on the other legislative sphere will no longer necessarily doom the statute to failure. Several *indicia* of the proper tests have evolved. For example, if contractual rights within the province are the object of the proposed regulation, the province has the authority. On the other hand, if regulation of the flow in extraprovincial channels of trade is the object, then the federal statute will be valid. Between these spectrum ends, the shadings cannot be foretold in anything approaching a constitutional formula. The majority of the illustrated tests thus far encountered are largely in the distribution, and not the production, of farm products. Here, however, we are concerned with the proper regulatory authority in connection with the production process of a single industry and, to some extent, with the sale of its products, the latter being concerned largely with the use of labels or identification. Nowhere are the impugned statutory regulations or provisions concerned with the control or regulation of the extraprovincial distribution of these products or their movement through any channels of trade. On the contrary, their main purpose is the regulation of the brewing process itself by means of a "legal recipe," as counsel for the appellant put it. Indeed if the industry is substantially local in character, as seems to be the case from the sparse record before the court (as noted above), the regulations are, in fact, confined to the regulation of a trade within a province.

In the end, the effort of the respondent here is simply to build into these regulations a validity essentially founded upon the embryonic definition of the application of the trade and commerce heading in the *Citizens Insurance* case, *supra*. That observation and the subsequent references thereto are all predicated upon the requirement that the purported trade and commerce legislation affected industry and commerce at large or in a sweeping, general sense. In the context of the *Food and Drugs Act,* it follows that even if this statute were to cover a substantial portion of Canadian economic activity, one industry or trade at a time, by a varying array of regulations or trade codes applicable to each individual sector, there would not, in the result, be at law a regulation of trade and commerce in the sweeping general sense contemplated in the *Citizens Insurance* case, *supra.* That, in my view, is the heart and core of the problem confronting the respondent in this appeal. Thus the provisions regulating malt liquors relate either to a single industry or a sector thereof, while other regulations appear to concern themselves in a similar way with other individual industries; the former being condemned by the *Citizens Insurance* case, *supra,* and the latter does not rescue the malt liquor regulations by reason of the *Board of Commerce* case, *supra.*

I conclude, therefore, in this part, that the impugned sections as they relate to malt liquors cannot be founded in the trade and commerce head of jurisdiction.

There remains to be examined the peace, order and good government clause in s. 91 as the basis for these federal regulations. This subject has already been adverted to above in connection with the health aspect of this statute. The principal authorities dealing with the range of the federal jurisdiction under this heading are illustrated by:

1. *Fort Frances Pulp and Paper Co. v. Manitoba Free Press,* basing the federal competence on the existence of a national emergency;
2. The *Radio Reference,* and the *Aeronautics Reference,* wherein the federal competence arose because the subject matter did not exist at the time of Confederation and clearly cannot be put into the class of matters of merely local or private nature; and,
3. Where the subject matter "goes beyond local or provincial concern or interest and must, from its inherent nature, be the concern of the Dominion as a whole." *Attorney General of Ontario v. Canada Temperance Federation,* at p. 205.

The brewing and labelling of beer and light beer has not been said to have given rise either to a national emergency or a new problem not existing at the time of Confederation, nor to a matter of national concern transcending the local authorities' power to meet and solve it by legislation. This latter concept is the subject of analysis and review by P.W. Hogg, *Constitutional Law of Canada,* 1977 at pp. 259-261. That learned author concludes at p. 261:

These cases suggest that the most important element of national dimension or national concern is a need for one national law which cannot realistically be satisfied by cooperative provincial action because the failure of one province to cooperate would carry with it grave consequences for the residents of other provinces. A subject-matter of legislation which has this characteristic has the necessary national dimension or concern to justify invocation of the p.o.g.g. power.

I see no basis for advancing the proposition that the impugned statutory provisions and regulations as they relate to malt liquor find their basis in law in the peace, order and good government clause of s. 91.

For these reasons, I would therefore answer the following question in the negative:

Is it within the Competence of the Parliament of Canada to enact sections 6 and 25(1)(c) of the *Food and Drugs Act* R.S.C. 1970, c. F-27, and are regulations B.02-130 to B.02-135 inclusive thereunder validly made?

The reasons of Pigeon and McIntrye JJ. were delivered by

PIGEON J. (dissenting): ... [I]n a reference concerning the validity of the *Dominion Trade and Industry Commission Act 1935,* Lord Atkin said (at pp. 417-418):

Sect. 18, sub-s. 1, provides that "the words 'Canada Standard' or the initials 'C.S.' shall be a national trade-mark and the exclusive property in and the right to the use of such trade-mark is thereby declared to be vested in His Majesty in the right of the Dominion ..." By sub-s. 2 such national trade mark as applied to any commodity pursuant to the provisions of that *Act* or any other *Act* of the Parliament of Canada is to constitute a representation that such commodity conforms to the requirements of a specification of a commodity standard established under the provisions of any Dominion Act. ...

There exists in Canada a well established code relating to trade marks created by the Dominion statutes, to be found now in *Trade-marks and Designs Act,* R.S.C., 1927, c. 201, amended by S.C., 1928, c. 10. It gives to the proprietor of a registered trade mark the exclusive right to use the trade mark to designate articles manufactured or sold by him. It creates, therefore, a form of property in each Province and the rights that flow therefrom. No one has challenged the competence of the Dominion to pass such legislation. If challenged one obvious source of authority would appear to be the class of subjects enumerated in s. 91(2), the Regulation of trade and commerce, referred to by the Chief Justice. There could hardly be a more appropriate form of the exercise of this power than the creation and regulation of a uniform law of trade marks. But if the Dominion has power to create trade mark rights for individual traders, it is difficult to see why the power should not extend to that which is now a usual feature of national and international commerce—a national mark.

In my view, the enactments and regulations under attack in the present case are essentially for the same legislative purpose as the sections considered by Lord Atkin. This purpose is to provide that some specific trade designations will guarantee compliance with what the 1935 statute called a "commodity standard" and is known in the present statute and regulations as a "specification" for a "food." The 1935 statute would have such effect only if the producer, manufacturer or merchant chose to apply the trade mark "Canada Standard" or the initials "C.S." The present scheme controls whenever a defined designation is applied to a food for which a specification has been established. I fail to see how this difference can be significant from a constitutional point of view....

... In my view, the federal enactments under attack provide for no more than what might be called "labelling regulations." These state what specifications must be met if some specific designations are used on food labels. In my view this does not go beyond a proper concept of trade mark legislation and I fail to see any invasion of provincial jurisdiction as was found in *MacDonald v. Vapor Canada Ltd.* in respect of s. 7(*e*) of the *Trade-marks Act*.

I would, therefore, answer the constitutional question in the affirmative....

[Justice Ritchie wrote a short opinion concurring with Justice Estey. Justice Pratte also held that the appeal should be allowed.]

The Queen v. Crown Zellerbach Canada Ltd., 1988

Constitutional interpretation never stands still for long. In the *Anti-Inflation Reference*, the Court's majority supported Justice Beetz's view that the peace, order, and good government power could serve as a constitutional basis only for (1) temporary legislation dealing with a national emergency, or (2) legislation dealing with "distinct subject matters which do not fall within any of the enumerated heads of s. 92 and which, by nature, are of national concern."[1] Subsequent decisions indicated that this second use of peace, order, and good government might be wide enough to accommodate a "provincial inability" test that would justify federal legislation if it could be established that a particular problem required national treatment unobtainable through provincial cooperation.[2] In *Crown Zellerbach*, the Court, for the first time, used this test to uphold federal legislation.

The issue in the case was whether federal legislation regulating dumping in the sea could apply to waters well within provincial territory. In defending this application of the legislation, the federal government relied primarily not on specific heads of power dealing with matters such as navigation and fisheries but on its general power to legislate for the peace, order, and good government of Canada. The federal government was successful in persuading a plurality of judges (four out of seven) that controlling marine pollution is one of those problems that from a functional point of view is indivisible and therefore a justifiable use of the peace, order, and good government power. The dissenting judges saw no evidence that in order to deal effectively with ocean pollution Parliament had to claim a plenary power to control the dumping of any substance in provincial waters. They are clearly much more cautious about employing a functional test to justify the use of peace, order, and good government in areas normally under provincial jurisdiction.

If the plurality position articulated by Justice Le Dain prevails, the legislative capacity of the national government will be significantly widened. Changes in court personnel will, as they have in the past, have a critical bearing on the outcome. By the time of the *Crown Zellerbach* case, only two of the judges who had participated in the *Anti-Inflation Reference*—Chief Justice Dickson and Justice Beetz—were still on the Court. Chief Justice Dickson, who had been with the minority on the interpretation of peace, order, and good government in the *Anti-Inflation* case, is now with the majority in *Crown Zellerbach*, while Justice Beetz dissents from the expansive interpretation of his majority opinion in the *Anti-Inflation Reference*. Which view will prevail in the future depends very much on the constitutional philosophies of the new appointees to the Supreme Court. ⌒

---

1 See case 13.

2 See, for example, Justice Estey's opinion in *Labatt*, case 15.

THE QUEEN v. CROWN ZELLERBACH CANADA LTD.
[1988] 1 S.C.R. 401

Hearing: June 26, 1986; Judgment: March 24, 1988.

Present: Dickson C.J. and Beetz, McIntyre, Lamer, Wilson, Le Dain, and La Forest JJ.

Interveners: The Attorney General of Quebec and the Attorney General of British Columbia.

The judgment of Dickson C.J. and McIntrye, Wilson, and Le Dain JJ. was delivered by

[1] **LE DAIN J.:** The question raised by this appeal is whether federal legislative jurisdiction to regulate the dumping of substances at sea, as a measure for the prevention of marine pollution, extends to the regulation of dumping in provincial marine waters. In issue is the validity of s. 4(1) of the *Ocean Dumping Control Act*, S.C. 1974-75-76, c. 55, which prohibits the dumping of any substance at sea except in accordance with the terms and conditions of a permit, the sea being defined for the purposes of the *Act* as including the internal waters of Canada other than fresh waters.

[2] The appeal is by leave of this Court from the judgment on January 26, 1984 of the British Columbia Court of Appeal (1984), 51 B.C.L.R. 32, 7 D.L.R. (4th) 449, [1984] 2 W.W.R. 714, 11 C.C.C. (3d) 113, 13 C.E.L.R. 29, dismissing an appeal by way of stated case from the judgment on May 26, 1982 of Schmidt Prov. Ct. J. (1982), 11 C.E.L.R. 151, who dismissed charges against the respondent of unlawfully dumping in the waters of Johnstone Strait near Beaver Cove in the province of British Columbia on the ground that s. 4(1) of the *Ocean Dumping Control Act* is *ultra vires* the Parliament of Canada.

I

[3] The general purpose of the *Ocean Dumping Control Act* is to regulate the dumping of substances at sea in order to prevent various kinds of harm to the marine environment. The *Act* would appear to have been enacted in fulfilment of Canada's obligations under the *Convention on the Prevention of Marine Pollution by Dumping of Wastes and other Matter,* which was signed by Canada on December 29, 1972.

[4] The concerns of the *Act* are reflected in the nature of the prohibited and restricted substances in Schedules I and II and in the factors to be taken into account by the Minister of the Environment in granting permits to dump, which are set out in ss. 9 and 10 of the *Act* and in Schedule III. What these provisions indicate is that the *Act* is concerned with marine pollution and its effect on marine life, human health and the amenities of the marine environment. There is also reference to the effect of dumping on navigation and shipping and other legitimate uses of the sea.

[5] Section 4(1) of the *Act*, with the contravention of which the respondent was charged, reads as follows:

4.(1) No person shall dump except in accordance with the terms and conditions of a permit.

[6] "Dumping" is defined by s. 2(1) of the *Act* as follows:

2.(1)   In this Act, ...
"dumping" means any deliberate disposal from ships, aircraft, platforms or other man-made structures at sea of any substance but does not include
(*a*) any disposal that is incidental to or derived from the normal operations of a ship or an aircraft or of any equipment thereof other than the disposal of substances from a ship or aircraft operated for the purpose of disposing of such substances at sea, and
(*b*) any discharge that is incidental to or derived from the exploration for, exploitation of and associated off-shore processing of sea bed mineral resources;

[7] "The sea" is defined, for the purposes of the *Act*, by s. 2(2) and (3) as follows:

2. . . .
(2) For the purposes of this *Act*, "the sea" means
(*a*) the territorial sea of Canada;
(*b*) the internal waters of Canada other than inland waters;
(*c*) any fishing zones prescribed pursuant to the *Territorial Sea and Fishing Zones Act*;
(*d*) the arctic waters within the meaning of the *Arctic Waters Pollution Prevention Act*;
(*e*) any area of the sea adjacent to the areas referred to in paragraphs (*a*) to (*d*) as may be prescribed;
(*f*) any area of the sea, under the jurisdiction of a foreign state, other than internal waters; and
(*g*) any area of the sea, other than the internal waters of a foreign state, not included in the areas of the sea referred to in paragraphs (*a*) to (*f*).
(3) For the purposes of paragraph (2)(*b*), "inland waters" means all the rivers, lakes and other fresh waters in Canada and includes the St. Lawrence River as far seaward as the straight lines drawn
(*a*) from Cap des Rosiers to the western-most point of Anticosti Island; and
(*b*) from Anticosti Island to the north shore of the St. Lawrence River along the meridian of longitude sixty-three degrees west. . . .

[11] The respondent was charged, in an information consisting of two counts, with contravening s. 4(1) of the *Act*, and thereby committing an offence under s. 13(1)(*c*) as follows:

Count 1: On or about the 16th day of August, A.D. 1980, in the waters of Johnstone Strait near Beaver Cove, Province of British Columbia, did unlawfully dump except in accordance with the terms and conditions of a permit in contravention of Section 4 of the *Ocean Dumping Control Act*, thereby committing an offence under Section 13(1)(*c*) of the said *Act*.

Count 2: On or about the 17th day of August, A.D. 1980, in the waters of Johnstone Strait near Beaver Cove, Province of British Columbia, did unlawfully dump except in accordance with the terms and conditions of a permit in contravention of Section 4 of the *Ocean Dumping Control Act*, thereby committing an offence under Section 13(1)(*c*) of the said *Act*.

[12] The admitted facts concerning the location and nature of the dumping with which the respondent was charged are as follows. The respondent carries on logging operations on Vancouver Island in connection with its forest products business in British Columbia and maintains a log dump on a water lot leased from the provincial Crown for the purpose of log booming and storage in Beaver Cove, off Johnstone Strait, on the northeast side of Vancouver Island. The waters of Beaver Cove are *inter fauces terrae*, or as put in the stated case, "Beaver Cove is of such size that a person standing on the shoreline of either side of Beaver Cove can easily and reasonably discern between shore and shore of Beaver Cove." On August 16 and 17, 1980 the respondent, using an 80-foot crane operating from a moored scow, dredged woodwaste from the ocean floor immediately adjacent to the shoreline at the site of its log dump in Beaver Cove and deposited it in the deeper waters of the cove approximately 60 to 80 feet seaward of where the woodwaste had been dredged. The purpose of the dredging and dumping was to allow a new A-frame structure for log dumping to be floated on a barge to the shoreline for installation there and to give clearance for the dumping of bundled logs from the A-frame structure into the waters of the log dump area. The woodwaste consisted of waterlogged logging debris such as bark, wood and slabs. There is no evidence of any dispersal of the woodwaste or any effect on navigation or marine life. At the relevant time the only permit held by the respondent under the *Act* was one issued on or about July 28, 1980, effective until July 25, 1981, to dump at a site in Johnstone Strait some 2.2 nautical miles from the place where the woodwaste was dumped.

[13] In the Provincial Court of British Columbia, Schmidt Prov. Ct. J. found that the waters of Beaver Cove in which the woodwaste was dumped are within the province of British Columbia. In support of this finding he referred to the judgment of the British Columbia Court of Appeal in *Reference re*

Ownership of the Bed of the Strait of Georgia and Related Areas (1976), 1 B.C.L.R. 97, in which a majority of the Court held that the waters of Johnstone Strait, of which Beaver Cove forms part, are within British Columbia. (An appeal from this judgment was subsequently dismissed by this Court in *Reference re Ownership of the Bed of the Strait of Georgia and Related Areas*, [1984] 1 S.C.R. 388.) Schmidt Prov. Ct. J. held that the regulation of the dumping of woodwaste in the respondent's log dump area in Beaver Cove, as part of the respondent's logging operations, fell within provincial legislative jurisdiction under head 92(5) of the *Constitution Act, 1867*—"The Management and Sale of Public Lands belonging to the Province and of the Timber and Wood thereon." He further held that the regulation of such dumping did not fall within federal legislative jurisdiction under head 91(10)—"Navigation and Shipping"—or under head 91(12)—"Sea Coast and Inland Fisheries." Applying this Court's judgment in *Fowler v. The Queen*, [1980] 2 S.C.R. 213, he concluded that s. 4(1) of the *Act* "makes no attempt to link the proscribed conduct to actual or potential harm to fisheries or to interference with navigation or shipping." . . .

II

[16] As the constitutional question indicates, the issue raised by the appeal is the constitutionality of the application of s. 4(1) of the *Act* to the dumping of waste in waters, other than fresh waters, within a province. The respondent concedes, as it must, that Parliament has jurisdiction to regulate dumping in waters lying outside the territorial limits of any province. It also concedes that Parliament has jurisdiction to regulate the dumping of substances in provincial waters to prevent pollution of those waters that is harmful to fisheries, if the federal legislation meets the test laid down in the *Fowler* and *Northwest Falling* cases. It further concedes, in view of the opinion expressed in this Court in *Interprovincial Co-operatives Ltd. v. The Queen*, [1976] 1 S.C.R. 477, that Parliament has jurisdiction to regulate the dumping in provincial waters of substances that can be shown to cause pollution in extra-provincial waters. What the respondent challenges is federal jurisdiction to control the dumping in provincial waters of substances that are not shown to have a pollutant effect in extra-provincial waters. The respondent contends that on the admitted facts that is precisely the present case. The respondent submits that in so far as s. 4(1) of the *Act* can only be read as purporting to apply to such dumping it is *ultra vires* and, alternatively, that it should be read, if possible, so as not to apply to such dumping. In either case the appeal must fail. The Attorney General of British Columbia, who supported the attack on s. 4(1), as applied to the dumping of waste in Beaver Cove, and with whom the Attorney General

of Quebec agreed, made a similar submission that s. 4(1) should be read down so as not to apply to dumping in provincial waters. . . .

[17] In this Court the Attorney General of Canada did not contend that there was a sufficient connection between the *Act* and navigation to support the validity of s. 4(1) on the basis of federal jurisdiction with respect to navigation and shipping. He did submit, as I understood his argument, that there was a sufficient connection between the *Act* and the protection of fisheries to meet the test laid down in *Fowler* and *Northwest Falling*, but I did not understand him to place very great reliance on this submission. His principal submission in this Court was that the control of dumping in provincial marine waters, for the reasons indicated in the *Act*, was part of a single matter of national concern or dimension which fell within the federal peace, order and good government power. . . .

[18] Before considering the relationship of the subject-matter of the *Act* to the possible bases of federal legislative jurisdiction something more should be said about the characterization of that subject-matter, according to the respective contentions of the parties. As I have indicated, the appellant contends that the *Act* is directed to the control or regulation of marine pollution, the subject-matter of the *Convention on the Prevention of Marine Pollution by Dumping of Wastes and other Matter*. The respondent, on the other hand, contends that by its terms the *Act* is directed at dumping which need not necessarily have a pollutant effect. It prohibits the dumping of *any* substance, including a substance not specified in Schedule I or Schedule II, except in accordance with the terms and conditions of a permit. In my opinion, despite this apparent scope, the *Act*, viewed as a whole, may be properly characterized as directed to the control or regulation of marine pollution, in so far as that may be relevant to the question of legislative jurisdiction. The chosen, and perhaps only effective, regulatory model makes it necessary, in order to prevent marine pollution, to prohibit the dumping of any substance without a permit. Its purpose is to require a permit so that the regulatory authority may determine before the proposed dumping has occurred whether it may be permitted upon certain terms and conditions, having regard to the factors or concerns specified in ss. 9 and 10 of the *Act* and Schedule III. The *Act* is concerned with the dumping of substances which may be shown or presumed to have an adverse effect on the marine environment. The Minister and not the person proposing to do the dumping must be the judge of this, acting in accordance with the criteria or factors indicated in ss. 9 and 10 and Schedule III of the *Act*. There is no suggestion that the *Act* purports to authorize the prohibition of dumping without regard to perceived adverse effect or the likelihood of such effect on the marine environment. The nature of the marine environment and its protection from adverse effect from dumping is a complex matter which must be left to expert judgment.

III

[Justice LeDain, after reviewing the Court's decision in *Fowler* and *Northwest Falling*, holding that for legislation to be upheld under the fisheries power there must be a direct connection between the prohibited conduct and harm to fish, concludes.]

[22] I agree with Schmidt Prov. Ct. J. and the British Columbia Court of Appeal that federal legislative jurisdiction with respect to seacoast and inland fisheries is not sufficient by itself to support the constitutional validity of s. 4(1) of the *Act* because that section, viewed in the context of the *Act* as a whole, fails to meet the test laid down in *Fowler* and *Northwest Falling*. While the effect on fisheries of marine pollution caused by the dumping of waste is clearly one of the concerns of the *Act* it is not the only effect of such pollution with which the *Act* is concerned. A basis for federal legislative jurisdiction to control marine pollution generally in provincial waters cannot be found in any of the specified heads of federal jurisdiction in s. 91 of the *Constitution Act, 1867*, whether taken individually or collectively.

IV

[23] It is necessary then to consider the national dimensions or national concern doctrine (as it is now generally referred to) of the federal peace, order and good government power as a possible basis for the constitutional validity of s. 4(1) of the *Act*, as applied to the control of dumping in provincial marine waters.

[24] The national concern doctrine was suggested by Lord Watson in the *Local Prohibition* case (*Attorney-General for Ontario v. Attorney-General for the Dominion*, [1896] A.C. 348) and given its modern formulation by Viscount Simon in *Attorney-General for Ontario v. Canada Temperance Federation*, [1946] A.C. 193. In *Local Prohibition*, Lord Watson said at p. 361:

> Their Lordships do not doubt that some matters, in their origin local and provincial, might attain such dimensions as to affect the body politic of the Dominion, and to justify the Canadian Parliament in passing laws for their regulation or abolition in the interest of the Dominion. But great caution must be observed in distinguishing between that which is local or provincial, and therefore within the jurisdiction of the provincial legislatures, and that which has ceased to be merely local or provincial, and has become matter of national concern, in such sense as to bring it within the jurisdiction of the Parliament of Canada.

In *Canada Temperance Federation*, Viscount Simon said at pp. 205-6:

> In their Lordships' opinion, the true test must be found in the real subject matter of the legislation: if it is such that it goes beyond local or provincial concern or interests and must from its inherent nature be the concern of the Dominion as a whole (as, for example, in the *Aeronautics* case and the *Radio* case), then it will fall within the competence of the Dominion Parliament as a matter affecting the peace, order and good government of Canada, though it may in another aspect touch on matters specially reserved to the provincial legislatures....

[25] This Court's conception of the national concern doctrine of the federal peace, order and good government power, as enunciated in *Canada Temperance Federation*, is to be derived from the consideration or application given to the doctrine in the following cases: *Johannesson v. Municipality of West St. Paul*, [1952] 1 S.C.R. 292; *Munro v. National Capital Commission*, [1966] S.C.R. 663; *Re: Anti-Inflation Act*, [1976] 2 S.C.R. 373; *R. v. Hauser*, [[1979] 1 S.C.R. 984]; *Labatt Breweries of Canada Ltd. v. Attorney General of Canada*, [1980] 1 S.C.R. 914; *Schneider v. The Queen*, [1982] 2 S.C.R. 112; and *R. v. Wetmore*, [1983] 2 S.C.R. 284.

[26] The national concern doctrine, as enunciated in *Canada Temperance Federation*, was referred to with approval by a majority of this Court in *Johannesson* as supporting exclusive federal legislative jurisdiction with respect to the whole field of aeronautics. In *Munro*, where the *National Capital Act* was upheld on the basis of the federal peace, order and good government power, Cartwright J., delivering the unanimous judgment of the Court said that the national concern doctrine had been adopted by this Court in *Johannesson* and that the development of the National Capital Region was "a single matter of national concern" (p. 671).

[27] The national concern doctrine was the subject of important commentary in this Court in the *Anti-Inflation Act* reference. A majority of the Court (Laskin C.J. and Martland, Judson, Ritchie, Spence, Pigeon and Dickson JJ.) upheld the *Act* on the basis of the emergency doctrine of the federal peace, order and good government power as legislation required to meet a "crisis" (the word used by Laskin C.J.) or "national emergency" (the words used by Ritchie J.). In the course of a comprehensive review of the judicial decisions with respect to the federal peace, order and good government power, Laskin C.J., with whom Judson, Spence and Dickson JJ. concurred, referred, with implicit approval, to the dictum of Viscount Simon in *Canada Temperance Federation*, but indicated that if he found, as he did, that the *Act* was valid on the basis of the emergency doctrine, as "crisis" legislation, he did

not intend to express an opinion as to its possible validity on the basis of the national concern doctrine, on which the Attorney General of Canada had principally relied.... He indicated, however, that he did not think it wise to attempt to define the scope of the federal peace, order and good government power in such precise or fixed terms as to make it incapable of application to changing or unforeseen circumstances. There is, moreover, a hint that he was disposed to seek a unified theory of the peace, order and good government power and that he regarded the emergency doctrine as a particular application of the national concern doctrine....

[28] Ritchie J., with whom Martland and Pigeon JJ. concurred, held that the validity of the *Act* could rest only on the emergency doctrine of the peace, order and good government power and that the national concern doctrine, in the absence of national emergency, could not give Parliament jurisdiction with respect to matters which would otherwise fall within provincial legislative jurisdiction. He said that he was in agreement with what was said by Beetz J. with reference to the national concern doctrine. Beetz J., with whom de Grandpré J. concurred, was obliged to consider the contention based on the national concern doctrine because he was of the view that the validity of the *Anti-Inflation Act* could not be supported on the basis of national emergency. He held that the national concern doctrine applied, in the absence of national emergency, to single, indivisible matters which did not fall within any of the specified heads of provincial or federal legislative jurisdiction. He held that the containment and reduction of inflation did not meet the test of singleness or indivisibility....

[29] In *Hauser*, a majority of the Court (Martland, Ritchie, Pigeon and Beetz JJ.) held that the constitutional validity of the *Narcotic Control Act* rested on the peace, order and good government power of Parliament rather than on its jurisdiction with respect to criminal law. Pigeon J., who delivered the judgment of the majority, said that the principal consideration in support of this view was that the abuse of narcotic drugs, with which the *Act* dealt, was a new problem which did not exist at the time of Confederation, and that since it did not come within matters of a merely local or private nature in the province it fell within the "general residual power" in the same manner as aeronautics and radio.

[30] In *Labatt Breweries*, in which a majority of the full Court held that certain provisions of the *Food and Drugs Act* and regulations thereunder were *ultra vires*, Estey J., with whom Martland, Dickson and Beetz JJ. concurred, had occasion to consider the peace, order and good government power as a possible basis of validity. He summed up the doctrine with respect to that basis of federal legislative jurisdiction as falling into three categories: (a) the cases "basing the federal competence on the existence of a national emergency"; (b) the

cases in which "federal competence arose because the subject matter did not exist at the time of Confederation and clearly cannot be put into the class of matters of a merely local or private nature," of which aeronautics and radio were cited as examples; and (c) the cases in which "the subject matter 'goes beyond local or provincial concern or interest and must, from its inherent nature, be the concern of the Dominion as a whole,'" citing *Canada Temperance Federation*. Thus Estey J. saw the national concern doctrine enunciated in *Canada Temperance Federation* as covering the case, not of a new subject matter which did not exist at Confederation, but of one that may have begun as a matter of a local or provincial concern but had become one of national concern. He referred to that category as "a matter of national concern transcending the local authorities' power to meet and solve it by legislation," and quoted in support of this statement of the test a passage from Professor Hogg's *Constitutional Law of Canada* (1977), at p. 261, in which it was said that "the most important element of national dimension or national concern is a need for one national law which cannot realistically be satisfied by cooperative provincial action because the failure of one province to cooperate would carry with it grave consequences for the residents of other provinces."

[31] In *Schneider*, in which the Court unanimously held that the *Heroin Treatment Act* of British Columbia was *intra vires*, Dickson J. (as he then was), with whom Martland, Ritchie, Beetz, McIntyre, Chouinard and Lamer JJ. concurred, indicated, with particular reference to the national concern doctrine and what has come to be known as the "provincial inability" test, why he was of the view that the treatment of heroin dependency, as distinct from the traffic in narcotic drugs, was not a matter falling within the federal peace, order and good government power. He referred to the problem of heroin dependency as follows at pp. 131-32:

> It is largely a local or provincial problem and not one which has become a matter of national concern, so as to bring it within the jurisdiction of the Parliament of Canada under the residuary power contained in the opening words of the *B.N.A. Act* (now, *Constitution Act, 1867*).
>
> There is no material before the Court leading one to conclude that the problem of heroin dependency as distinguished from illegal trade in drugs is a matter of national interest and dimension transcending the power of each province to meet and solve its own way....

[32] In *Wetmore*, where the issue was whether the federal Attorney General was entitled to conduct the prosecution of charges for violation of the *Food and Drugs Act*, Dickson J., dissenting, considered whether the applicable provisions of the *Food and Drugs Act* had their constitutional foundation

in the federal criminal law power, or as was held in *Hauser* with respect to the *Narcotic Control Act*, in the peace, order and good government power. In rejecting the latter basis of jurisdiction, he referred to what was said concerning the national concern doctrine of the peace, order and good government power in the *Anti-Inflation Act* reference, *Labatt* and *Hauser* as follows at pp. 294-95:

> In the *Reference re Anti-Inflation Act*, [1976] 2 S.C.R. 373, Beetz J., whose judgment on this point commanded majority support, reviewed the extensive jurisprudence on the subject and concluded that the peace, order and good government power should be confined to justifying (i) temporary legislation dealing with a national emergency (p. 459) and (ii) legislation dealing with "distinct subject matters which do not fall within any of the enumerated heads of s. 92 and which, by nature, are of national concern" (p. 457). In the *Labatt* case, *supra*, at pp. 944-45, Estey J. divided this second heading into (i) areas in which the federal competence arises because the subject matter did not exist at the time of Confederation and cannot be classified as of a merely local and private nature and (ii) areas where the subject matter "goes beyond local or provincial concern or interests and must from its inherent nature be the concern of the Dominion as a whole." This last category is the one enunciated by Viscount Simon in *Attorney-General for Ontario v. Canada Temperance Federation*, [1946] A.C. 193, at p. 205. The one preceding it formed the basis of the majority decision in *Hauser* that the *Narcotic Control Act*, R.S.C. 1970, c. N-1, came under the peace, order and good government power as dealing with "a genuinely new problem which did not exist at the time of Confederation."

Applying these principles to the subject matter of the *Food and Drugs Act*, Dickson J. noted that there was no question of emergency or of a new matter that did not exist at Confederation and rejected the national concern doctrine of the peace, order and good government as a basis for the constitutional validity of the provisions in question....

[33] From this survey of the opinion expressed in this Court concerning the national concern doctrine of the federal peace, order and good government power I draw the following conclusions as to what now appears to be firmly established:

1. The national concern doctrine is separate and distinct from the national emergency doctrine of the peace, order and good government power, which is chiefly distinguishable by the fact that it provides a constitutional basis for what is necessarily legislation of a temporary nature;

2. The national concern doctrine applies to both new matters which did not exist at Confederation and to matters which, although originally matters of a local or private nature in a province, have since, in the absence of national emergency, become matters of national concern;

3. For a matter to qualify as a matter of national concern in either sense it must have a singleness, distinctiveness and indivisibility that clearly distinguishes it from matters of provincial concern and a scale of impact on provincial jurisdiction that is reconcilable with the fundamental distribution of legislative power under the Constitution;

4. In determining whether a matter has attained the required degree of singleness, distinctiveness and indivisibility that clearly distinguishes it from matters of provincial concern it is relevant to consider what would be the effect on extra-provincial interests of a provincial failure to deal effectively with the control or regulation of the intra-provincial aspects of the matter.

[34] This last factor, generally referred to as the "provincial inability" test and noted with apparent approval in this Court in *Labatt*, *Schneider* and *Wetmore*, was suggested, as Professor Hogg acknowledges, by Professor Gibson in his article, "Measuring 'National Dimensions'" (1976), 7 *Man. L.J.* 15, as the most satisfactory rationale of the cases in which the national concern doctrine of the peace, order and good government power has been applied as a basis of federal jurisdiction. As expounded by Professor Gibson, the test would appear to involve a limited or qualified application of federal jurisdiction. As put by Professor Gibson at pp. 34-35, "By this approach, a national dimension would exist whenever a significant aspect of a problem is beyond provincial reach because it falls within the jurisdiction of another province or of the federal Parliament. It is important to emphasize however that the *entire* problem would not fall within federal competence in such circumstances. Only that aspect of the problem that is beyond provincial control would do so. Since the 'P.O. & G.G.' clause bestows only residual powers, the existence of a national dimension justifies no more federal legislation than is necessary to fill the gap in provincial powers. For example, federal jurisdiction to legislate for pollution of interprovincial waterways or to control 'pollution price-wars' would (in the absence of other independent sources of federal competence) extend only to measures to reduce the risk that citizens of one province would be harmed by the non-co-operation of another province or provinces." To similar effect, he said in his conclusion at p. 36: "Having regard to the

residual nature of the power, it is the writer's thesis that 'national dimensions' are possessed by only those aspects of legislative problems which are beyond the ability of the provincial legislatures to deal because they involve either federal competence or that of another province. Where it would be possible to deal fully with the problem by co-operative action of two or more legislatures, the 'national dimension' concerns only the risk of non-co-operation, and justifies only federal legislation addressed to that risk." This would appear to contemplate a concurrent or overlapping federal jurisdiction which, I must observe, is in conflict with what was emphasized by Beetz J. in the *Anti-Inflation Act* reference—that where a matter falls within the national concern doctrine of the peace, order and good government power, as distinct from the emergency doctrine, Parliament has an exclusive jurisdiction of a plenary nature to legislate in relation to that matter, including its intra-provincial aspects.

As expressed by Professor Hogg in the first and second editions of his *Constitutional Law of Canada*, the "provincial inability" test would appear to be adopted simply as a reason for finding that a particular matter is one of national concern falling within the peace, order and good government power: that provincial failure to deal effectively with the intra-provincial aspects of the matter could have an adverse effect on extra-provincial interests. In this sense, the "provincial inability" test is one of the indicia for determining whether a matter has that character of singleness or indivisibility required to bring it within the national concern doctrine. It is because of the interrelatedness of the intra-provincial and extra-provincial aspects of the matter that it requires a single or uniform legislative treatment. The "provincial inability" test must not, however, go so far as to provide a rationale for the general notion, hitherto rejected in the cases, that there must be a plenary jurisdiction in one order of government or the other to deal with any legislative problem. In the context of the national concern doctrine of the peace, order and good government power, its utility lies, in my opinion, in assisting in the determination whether a matter has the requisite singleness or indivisibility from a functional as well as a conceptual point of view. . . .

V

[37] Marine pollution, because of its predominantly extra-provincial as well as international character and implications, is clearly a matter of concern to Canada as a whole. The question is whether the control of pollution by the dumping of substances in marine waters, including provincial marine waters, is a single, indivisible matter, distinct from the control of pollution by the dumping of substances in other provincial waters. The *Ocean Dumping Control Act* reflects a

distinction between the pollution of salt water and the pollution of fresh water. The question, as I conceive it, is whether that distinction is sufficient to make the control of marine pollution by the dumping of substances a single, indivisible matter falling within the national concern doctrine of the peace, order and good government power.

[38] Marine pollution by the dumping of substances is clearly treated by the *Convention on the Prevention of Marine Pollution by Dumping of Wastes and other Matter* as a distinct and separate form of water pollution having its own characteristics and scientific considerations. This impression is reinforced by the United Nations Report of the Joint Group of Experts on the Scientific Aspects of Marine Pollution, Reports and Studies No. 15, *The Review of the Health of the Oceans* (UNESCO 1982) (hereinafter referred to as the "U.N. Report"), which forms part of the materials placed before the Court in the argument. It is to be noted, however, that, unlike the *Ocean Dumping Control Act*, the Convention does not require regulation of pollution by the dumping of waste in the internal marine waters of a state. Article III, para. 3, of the Convention defines the "sea" as "all marine waters other than the internal waters of the States." The internal marine waters of a state are those which lie landward of the baseline of the territorial sea, which is determined in accordance with the rules laid down in the *United Nations Convention on the Law of the Sea* (1982). The limitation of the undertaking in the Convention, presumably for reasons of state policy, to the control of dumping in the territorial sea and the open sea cannot, in my opinion, obscure the obviously close relationship, which is emphasized in the U.N. Report, between pollution in coastal waters, including the internal marine waters of a state, and pollution in the territorial sea. Moreover, there is much force, in my opinion, in the appellant's contention that the difficulty of ascertaining by visual observation the boundary between the territorial sea and the internal marine waters of a state creates an unacceptable degree of uncertainty for the application of regulatory and penal provisions. This, and not simply the possibility or likelihood of the movement of pollutants across that line, is what constitutes the essential indivisibility of the matter of marine pollution by the dumping of substances.

[39] There remains the question whether the pollution of marine waters by the dumping of substances is sufficiently distinguishable from the pollution of fresh waters by such dumping to meet the requirement of singleness or indivisibility. In many cases the pollution of fresh waters will have a pollutant effect in the marine waters into which they flow, and this is noted by the U.N. Report, but that report, as I have suggested, emphasizes that marine pollution, because of the differences in the composition and action of marine waters and fresh waters, has its own characteristics and scientific

considerations that distinguish it from fresh water pollution. Moreover, the distinction between salt water and fresh water as limiting the application of the *Ocean Dumping Control Act* meets the consideration emphasized by a majority of this Court in the *Anti-Inflation Act* reference—that in order for a matter to qualify as one of national concern falling within the federal peace, order and good government power it must have ascertainable and reasonable limits, in so far as its impact on provincial jurisdiction is concerned.

[40] For these reasons I am of the opinion that s. 4(1) of the *Ocean Dumping Control Act* is constitutionally valid as enacted in relation to a matter falling within the national concern doctrine of the peace, order and good government power of the Parliament of Canada, and, in particular, that it is constitutional in its application to the dumping of waste in the waters of Beaver Cove. I would accordingly allow the appeal, set aside the judgments of the Court of Appeal and Schmidt Prov. Ct. J. and refer the matter back to the Provincial Court judge. The constitutional question should be answered as follows:

> Is section 4(1) of the *Ocean Dumping Control Act*, S.C. 1974-75-76, c. 55, *ultra vires* of the Parliament of Canada, and, in particular, is it *ultra vires* of the Parliament of Canada in its application to the dumping of waste in the waters of Beaver Cove, an area within the province of British Columbia?
>
> Answer: No.

The reasons of Beetz, Lamer, and La Forest JJ. were delivered by

[41] **LA FOREST J.** (dissenting): The issue raised in this appeal involves the extent to which the federal Parliament may constitutionally prohibit the disposal of substances not shown to have a pollutant effect in marine waters beyond the coast but within the limits of a province. . . .

[56] I start with the proposition that what is sought to be regulated in the present case is an activity wholly within the province, taking place on provincially owned land. Only local works and undertakings are involved, and there is no evidence that the substance made subject to the prohibition in s. 4(1) is either deleterious in any way or has any impact beyond the limits of the province. It is not difficult, on this basis, to conclude that the matter is one that falls within provincial legislative power unless it can somehow be established that it falls within Parliament's general power to legislate for the peace, order and good government of Canada.

Peace, Order and Good Government

[57] There are several applications of the peace, order and good government power that may have relevance to the

control of ocean pollution. One is its application in times of emergency. The federal Parliament clearly has power to deal with a grave emergency without regard to the ordinary division of legislative power under the Constitution. The most obvious manifestation of this power is in times of war or civil insurrection, but it has in recent years also been applied in peacetime to justify the control of rampant inflation; see *Re: Anti-Inflation Act, supra*. But while there can be no doubt that the control of ocean pollution poses a serious problem, no one has argued that it has reached such grave proportions as to require the displacement of the ordinary division of legislative power under the Constitution.

[58] A second manner in which the power to legislate respecting peace, order and good government may be invoked in the present context is to control that area of the sea lying beyond the limits of the provinces. The federal government may not only regulate the territorial sea and other areas over which Canada exercises sovereignty, either under its power to legislate respecting its public property, or under the general power respecting peace, order and good government under s. 91 (*Reference re Offshore Mineral Rights of British Columbia*, [1967] S.C.R. 792) or under s. 4 of the *Constitution Act, 1871* (U.K.), 34 & 35 Vict., c. 28. I have no doubt that it may also, as an aspect of its international sovereignty, exercise legislative jurisdiction for the control of pollution beyond its borders; see *Reference re Newfoundland Continental Shelf*, [1984] 1 S.C.R. 86.

[59] In legislating under its general power for the control of pollution in areas of the ocean falling outside provincial jurisdiction, the federal Parliament is not confined to regulating activities taking place within those areas. It may take steps to prevent activities in a province, such as dumping substances in provincial waters that pollute or have the potential to pollute the sea outside the province. Indeed, the exercise of such jurisdiction, it would seem to me, is not limited to coastal and internal waters but extends to the control of deposits in fresh water that have the effect of polluting outside a province. Reference may be made here to *Interprovincial Co-operatives Ltd. v. The Queen*, [1976] 1 S.C.R. 477, where a majority of this Court upheld the view that the federal Parliament had exclusive legislative jurisdiction to deal with a problem that resulted from the depositing of a pollutant in a river in one province that had injurious effects in another province. This is but an application of the doctrine of national dimensions triggering the operation of the peace, order and good government clause.

[60] It should require no demonstration that water moves in hydrologic cycles and that effective pollution control requires regulating pollution at its source. That source may, in fact, be situated outside the waters themselves. It is significant

that the provision of the *Fisheries Act* upheld by this Court in *Northwest Falling Contractors Ltd. v. The Queen*, [[1980] 2 S.C.R. 292], as a valid means of protecting the fisheries not only prohibited the depositing of a deleterious substance in water, but *in any place* where it might enter waters frequented by fish. Given the way substances seep into the ground and the movement of surface and ground waters into rivers and ultimately into the sea, this can potentially cover a very large area. Indeed, since the pollution of the ocean in an important measure results from aerial pollution rather than from substances deposited in waters, similar regulations could be made in respect of substances that so pollute the air as to cause damage to the ocean or generally outside the provinces....

[62] In fact, as I see it, the potential breadth of federal power to control pollution by use of its general power is so great that, even without resort to the specific argument made by the appellant, the constitutional challenge in the end may be the development of judicial strategies to confine its ambit. It must be remembered that the peace, order and good government clause may comprise not only prohibitions, like criminal law, but regulation. Regulation to control pollution, which is incidentally only part of the even larger global problem of managing the environment, could arguably include not only emission standards but the control of the substances used in manufacture, as well as the techniques of production generally, in so far as these may have an impact on pollution. This has profound implications for the federal–provincial balance mandated by the Constitution. The challenge for the courts, as in the past, will be to allow the federal Parliament sufficient scope to acquit itself of its duties to deal with national and international problems while respecting the scheme of federalism provided by the Constitution.

[63] These considerations underline the importance of linking the prohibition to the purpose sought to be achieved. At times, that link can readily be inferred, for example in the case of dumping noxious fluid into coastal waters. In other cases, such as the depositing of noxious solid material inland, cogent proof will be required....

[64] However widely one interprets the federal power to control ocean pollution along the preceding line of analysis, it will not serve to support the provision impugned here, one that, as in the *Fowler* case, *supra*, is a blanket prohibition against depositing *any* substance in waters without regard to its nature or amount, and one moreover where there is, in Martland J.'s words, at p. 226 of that case, "no attempt to link the proscribed conduct to actual or potential harm" to what is sought to be protected; in *Fowler*, the fisheries, here, the ocean. As in *Fowler*, too, there is no evidence to indicate that the full range of activities caught by the provision cause the harm sought to be prevented....

[65] Why Parliament should have chosen to enact a prohibition in such broad terms is a matter upon which one is left to speculate. It may be that, in view of the lack of knowledge about the effects of various substances deposited in water, it may be necessary to monitor all such deposits. We have no evidence on the extent to which it is necessary to monitor all deposits into the sea to develop an effective regime for the prevention of ocean pollution. A system of monitoring that was necessarily incidental to an effective legislative scheme for the control of ocean pollution could constitutionally be justified. But here not only was no material advanced to establish the need for such a system, the *Act* goes much further and prohibits the deposit of any substance in the sea, including provincial internal waters. If such a provision were held valid, why would a federal provision prohibiting the emission of any substance in any quantity into the air, except as permitted by federal authorities, not be constitutionally justifiable as a measure for the control of ocean pollution, it now being known that deposits from the air are a serious source of ocean pollution? . . .

[66] Counsel for the appellant did not, of course, frame the issue in the manner in which I have thus far discussed it. I have examined it in this way, however, to show that on a more traditional approach to the underlying issues than he suggests Parliament has very wide powers to deal with ocean pollution, whether within or outside the limits of the province, but that even if one stretches this traditional approach to its limits, the impugned provision cannot constitutionally be justified. It requires a quantum leap to find constitutional justification for the provision, one, it seems to me, that would create considerable stress on Canadian federalism as it has developed over the years. What he argues for, we saw, is that the dumping of any substance in the sea beginning, apparently, from the coasts of the provinces and the mouths of provincial rivers falls exclusively within the legislative jurisdiction of Parliament as being a matter of national concern or dimension even though the sea-bed is within the province and whether or not the substance is noxious or potentially so.

[67] Le Dain J. has in the course of his judgment discussed the cases relating to the development of the "national concern or dimension" aspect of the peace, order and good government clause, and I find it unnecessary to review that development in any detail. It is sufficient for my purpose to say that this development has since the 1930s particularly been resorted to from time to time to bring into the ambit of federal power a number of matters, such as radio (*In re Regulation and Control of Radio Communication in Canada*, [1932] A.C. 304), aeronautics (*Johannesson v. Municipality of West St. Paul*, [1952] 1 S.C.R. 292), and the national capital region (*Munro v. National Capital Commission*, [1966] S.C.R. 663),

that are clearly of national importance. They do not fit comfortably within provincial power. Both in their workings and in their practical implications they have predominantly national dimensions. Many of these subjects are new and are obviously of extra-provincial concern. They are thus appropriate for assignment to the general federal legislative power. They are often related to matters intimately tied to federal jurisdiction. Radio (which is relevant to the power to regulate interprovincial undertakings) is an example. The closely contested issue of narcotics control (cf. *R. v. Hauser*, [1979] 1 S.C.R. 984, and *Schneider v. The Queen*, [1982] 2 S.C.R. 112, per Laskin C.J.) is intimately related to criminal law and international trade.

[68] The need to make such characterizations from time to time is readily apparent. From this necessary function, however, it is easy but, I say it with respect, fallacious to go further, and, taking a number of quite separate areas of activity, some under accepted constitutional values within federal, and some within provincial legislative capacity, consider them to be a single indivisible matter of national interest and concern lying outside the specific heads of power assigned under the Constitution. By conceptualizing broad social, economic and political issues in that way, one can effectively invent new heads of federal power under the national dimensions doctrine, thereby incidentally removing them from provincial jurisdiction or at least abridging the provinces' freedom of operation. This, as I see it, is the implication of the statement made by my colleague, then Professor Le Dain, in his article, "Sir Lyman Duff and the Constitution" (1974), 12 *Osgoode Hall L.J.* 261. He states, at p. 293:

> As reflected in the *Munro* case, the issue with respect to the general power, where reliance cannot be placed on the notion of emergency, is to determine what are to be considered to be single, indivisible matters of national interest and concern lying outside the specific heads of jurisdiction in sections 91 and 92. It is possible to invent such matters by applying new names to old legislative purposes. There is an increasing tendency to sum up a wide variety of legislative purposes in single, comprehensive designations. Control of inflation, environmental protection, and preservation of the national identity or independence are examples.

[69] Professor Le Dain was there merely posing the problem; he did not attempt to answer it. It seems to me, however, that some of the examples he gives, notably the control of inflation and environmental protection, are all-pervasive, and if accepted as items falling within the general power of Parliament, would radically alter the division of legislative power in Canada. The attempt to include them in the federal general

power seems to me to involve fighting on another plane the war that was lost on the economic plane in the Canadian new deal cases. My colleague Beetz J. has, in *Re: Anti-Inflation Act, supra,* fully supported this way of viewing things in rejecting the control of inflation as a proper subject for incorporation into the peace, order and good government clause under the national dimension doctrine. (His was, we saw, a dissenting judgment, but on this issue too, his views were shared by a majority of the Court.) ...

[70] What was there said by Beetz J. seems to me to apply, *a fortiori,* to the control of the environment, a subject more germane to the present issue. All physical activities have some environmental impact. Possible legislative responses to such activities cover a large number of the enumerated legislative powers, federal and provincial. To allocate the broad subject-matter of environmental control to the federal government under its general power would effectively gut provincial legislative jurisdiction. As I mentioned before, environment protection, of course, encompasses far more than environmental pollution, which is what we are principally concerned with here. To take an example from the present context, woodwaste in some circumstances undoubtedly pollutes the environment, but the very depletion of forests itself affects the ecological balance and, as such, constitutes an environmental problem. But environmental pollution alone is itself all-pervasive. It is a by-product of everything we do. In man's relationship with his environment, waste is unavoidable. The problem is thus not new, although it is only recently that the vast amount of waste products emitted into the atmosphere or dumped in water has begun to exceed the ability of the atmosphere and water to absorb and assimilate it on a global scale. There is thus cause for concern and governments at every level have begun to deal with the many activities giving rise to problems of pollution. In Canada, both federal and provincial levels of government have extensive powers to deal with these matters. Both have enacted comprehensive and specific schemes for the control of pollution and the protection of the environment. Some environmental pollution problems are of more direct concern to the federal government, some to the provincial government. But a vast number are interrelated, and all levels of government actively co-operate to deal with problems of mutual concern; ...

[71] To allocate environmental pollution exclusively to the federal Parliament would, it seems to me, involve sacrificing the principles of federalism enshrined in the Constitution. ...

[72] It is true, of course, that we are not invited to create a general environmental pollution power but one restricted to ocean pollution. But it seems to me that the same considerations apply. I shall, however, attempt to look at it in terms of the qualities or attributes that are said to mark the subjects

that have been held to fall within the peace, order and good government clause as being matters of national concern. Such a subject, it has been said, must be marked by a singleness, distinctiveness and indivisibility that clearly distinguishes it from matters of provincial concern. In my view, ocean pollution fails to meet this test for a variety of reasons. In addition to those applicable to environmental pollution generally, the following specific difficulties may be noted. First of all, marine waters are not wholly bounded by the coast; in many areas, they extend upstream into rivers for many miles. The application of the *Act* appears to be restricted to waters beyond the mouths of rivers (and so intrude less on provincial powers), but this is not entirely clear, and if it is so restricted, it is not clear whether this distinction is based on convenience or constitutional imperative. Apart from this, the line between salt and fresh water cannot be demarcated clearly; it is different at different depths of water, changes with the season and shifts constantly. ... There is a constant intermixture of waters; fresh waters flow into the sea and marine waters penetrate deeply inland at high tide only to return to the sea laden with pollutants collected during their incursion inland. Nor is the pollution of the ocean confined to pollution emanating from substances deposited in water. In important respects, the pollution of the sea results from emissions into the air, which are then transported over many miles and deposited into the sea. ... I cannot, therefore, see ocean pollution as a sufficiently discrete subject upon which to found the kind of legislative power sought here. It is an attempt to create a federal pollution control power on unclear geographical grounds and limited to part only of the causes of ocean pollution. Such a power then simply amounts to a truncated federal pollution control power only partially effective to meet its supposed necessary purpose, unless of course one is willing to extend it to pollution emanating from fresh water and the air, when for reasons already given such an extension could completely swallow up provincial power, no link being necessary to establish the federal purpose. ...

[73] This leads me to another factor considered in identifying a subject as falling within the general federal power as a matter of national domain: its impact on provincial legislative power. Here, it must be remembered that in its supposed application within the province the provision virtually prevents a province from dealing with certain of its own public property without federal consent. A wide variety of activities along the coast or in the adjoining sea involves the deposit of some substances in the sea. In fact, where large cities like Vancouver are situated by the sea, this has substantial relevance to recreational, industrial and municipal concerns of all kinds. As a matter of fact, the most polluted areas of the sea adjoin the coast. ... Among the major causes of this are

various types of construction, such as hotels and harbours, the development of mineral resources and recreational activities. . . . These are matters of immediate concern to the province. They necessarily affect activities over which the provinces have exercised some kind of jurisdiction over the years. Whether or not the "newness" of the subject is a necessary criterion for inventing new areas of jurisdiction under the peace, order and good government clause, it is certainly a relevant consideration if it means removing from the provinces areas of jurisdiction which they previously exercised. As I mentioned, pollution, including coastal pollution, is no new phenomenon, and neither are many of the kinds of activities that result in pollution.

[74] A further relevant matter, it is said, is the effect on extra-provincial interests of a provincial failure to deal effectively with the control of intra-provincial aspects of the matter. I have some difficulty following all the implications of this, but taking it at face value, we are dealing here with a situation where, as we saw earlier, Parliament has extensive powers to deal with conditions that lead to ocean pollution wherever they occur. The difficulty with the impugned provision is that it seeks to deal with activities that cannot be demonstrated either to pollute or to have a reasonable potential of polluting the ocean. The prohibition applies to an inert substance regarding which there is no proof that it either moves or pollutes. The prohibition in fact would apply to the moving of rock from one area of provincial property to another. I cannot accept that the federal Parliament has such wide legislative power over local matters having local import taking place on provincially owned property. . . .

Disposition

[76] I would dismiss the appeal with costs and reply to the constitutional question in the affirmative.

Reference re Canada Assistance Plan, 1991

Federal–provincial relations in Canada are regulated more by intergovernmental agreements reached through political negotiations than by the courts. This is especially the case with fiscal federalism—arrangements between the federal government and the provinces concerning taxes and fiscal transfers. It is only in recent years that this dimension of Canadian federalism has been a subject of litigation or Supreme Court decision making. In its handling of the few cases arising out of federal–provincial agreements that have reached the Supreme Court, the Court has been remarkably restrained. Its decisions have given little encouragement to litigation in this area.

Robert James Finlay was the first to bring a case involving a federal–provincial fiscal agreement before the Supreme Court of Canada. Finlay was a welfare recipient in Manitoba whose income support from the province was funded in part by the *Canada Assistance Plan*[1] (CAP). CAP was a shared-cost program established in 1966 under which Ottawa agreed to pay 50 percent of the costs of eligible provincial social welfare programs. Manitoba had temporarily reduced Finlay's payments to compensate for past overpayments. In 1986, Finlay challenged this reduction on the grounds that it violated CAP, which set out the terms on which the federal government would contribute to provincial expenditures on social assistance and welfare.[2] One of CAP's terms was that the programs it funded must meet "the requirements of a person in need." Finlay contended that the reductions from his payments meant that he could not meet his basic needs.

In 1986, Finlay was successful in getting the Supreme Court of Canada to grant him standing to bring such a suit. The case then returned to the lower courts. The substance of Finlay's claim did not come before the Supreme Court until 1993. Then, in a five-to-four decision overruling the Federal Court of Appeal, the Supreme Court rejected Finlay's claim.[3] Although Finlay did not succeed in getting his welfare payments increased, his case established the principle that an individual citizen who is adversely affected by what he or she has reason to believe is a government's breach of a federal–provincial agreement can seek redress in the courts.

In between the *Finlay* cases, the federal government's effort to reduce its exposure to the open-ended and ever-increasing costs of CAP became the target of a governmental court challenge. Federal legislation enacted in 1990 to reduce budget deficits included a provision that limited increases in its CAP payments to financially stronger provinces to 5 percent a year. British Columbia, one of the "have provinces," challenged this cutback in its CAP payments by referring two questions to the B.C. Court of Appeal. The first question asked whether the government of Canada has the authority to limit its obligation to pay 50 percent of provincial social welfare expenditures as set out in the original legislation authorizing CAP. All five judges of the B.C. Court of Appeal answered this question in the negative. The second question asked whether legislation changing federal payments under CAP without the consent of British Columbia violates the province's "legitimate expectations." To this

---

1   S.C. 1966-67, c. 45.

2   *Finlay v. Canada*, [1986] 2 S.C.R. 260.

3   *Finlay v. Canada*, [1993] 1 S.C.R. 1080.

question, four of the B.C. Court of Appeal judges answered yes and one no. The federal government appealed this decision to the Supreme Court.

Before dealing with the substantive questions, the Supreme Court dealt with the threshold issue of "justiciability." Justice Sopinka, writing for a unanimous Court, rejected the Attorney General of Canada's argument that the matter dealt with in the reference question was too political to be decided by a court. So long as the matter before the court has "a significant legal component," the political controversy surrounding it is no bar to its being adjudicated in the courts. Since both questions in this reference case have a significant legal component, it is appropriate for the Court to answer them. Here, the Supreme Court confirms the position it took in one of its earliest Charter cases, *Operation Dismantle*,[4] that it would not follow the U.S. Supreme Court's "political question" doctrine that rejects some matters for adjudiction because in the Court's view they are more appropriately dealt with in the political process.

The Supreme Court reversed the answers given to both questions by the B.C. Court of Appeal. What is remarkable about the Supreme Court's handling of these questions is the importance it attaches to the principle of parliamentary sovereignty. Justice Sopinka acknowledges a provision in the CAP legislation that requires provincial consent for any change in the Plan. But the Plan must be understood as being subject to legislative amendment. The government of Canada "could not bind Parliament from exercising its powers to legislate amendments to the *Plan*." The contrary view would "negate the sovereignty of Parliament." Similarly, with the common law doctrine of legitimate expectations: "Parliamentary government would be paralyzed if the doctrine of legitimate expectations could be applied to prevent the government from introducing legislation in Parliament."

The government of Manitoba, an intervener in the case, challenged the jurisdiction of the federal Parliament to use its spending power to regulate a matter that is outside its jurisdiction. Although the Court did not have to deal with this constitutional issue, it did. Justice Sopinka denied that withholding federal money that the government had previously agreed to provide amounts to regulation of social welfare, and rejected Manitoba's submission that to protect the autonomy of the provinces the Court should supervise the federal government's exercise of its spending power.

The provinces showed their displeasure with the result of this case in the negotiations that produced the Charlottetown Accord. Section 26 of the Accord called for a constitutional amendment "to provide a mechanism to ensure that designated agreements between governments are protected from unilateral change." The section went on to specify that this new mechanism must apply to the *Canada Assistance Plan*. The Charlottetown Accord went down to defeat in the 1992 constitutional referendum, and proposals to prevent unilateral federal changes to shared-cost programs were not revived.

In the 1990s, fiscal federalism in Canada moved away from conditional shared-cost programs and into major federal cost cutting. In 1996, CAP ended when, along with federal transfers for health and higher education, it was folded into the Canada Health and Social Transfer (CHST). Under CHST, federal transfers, instead of being tied to provincial expenditures, are based on gross national product and population levels. The new arrangements reduce the conditions on federal fiscal transfers to the provinces, make them independent of provincial spending, and significantly reduce their overall value. ⌣

---

4   *Operation Dismantle v. The Queen*, [1985] 1 S.C.R. 441.

REFERENCE RE CANADA ASSISTANCE PLAN (B.C.)
[1991] 2 S.C.R. 525

Hearing: December 11, 12, 1990; Judgment: August 15, 1991.

Present: Lamer C.J. and La Forest, Sopinka, Gonthier, Cory, McLachlin, and Stevenson JJ.

Interveners: The Attorney General for Ontario, the Attorney General of Manitoba, the Attorney General for Alberta, the Attorney General for Saskatchewan, the Native Council of Canada, and the United Native Nations of British Columbia.

The judgment of the Court was delivered by

SOPINKA J.: This is an appeal by the Attorney General of Canada from a decision of the British Columbia Court of Appeal, answering two questions which were referred to it under the *Constitutional Question Act*, R.S.B.C. 1979, c. 63. The issues raised by the questions include whether and in what circumstances a court should answer questions referred to it that have a political connotation, the interpretation and binding effect of federal–provincial agreements, and whether the doctrine of legitimate expectations applies to prevent the Cabinet from introducing a money bill.

The Attorneys General for Ontario, Manitoba and Alberta intervened in the Court of Appeal, as did the Native Council of Canada and the United Native Nations of British Columbia. In addition, the Attorney General for Saskatchewan intervened in this Court.

1. The Background

The *Canada Assistance Plan* (the "*Plan*") was enacted by S.C. 1966-67, c. 45; it is now R.S.C., 1985, c. C-1. By its s. 4, it authorizes the Government of Canada to enter into agreements with the provincial governments to pay them contributions toward their expenditures on social assistance and welfare. Section 5 of the *Plan* authorizes payments to the provinces pursuant to such agreements, and broadly speaking it authorizes contributions amounting to half of the provinces' eligible expenditures. The *Plan* (s. 6(2)) specifies certain prerequisites for eligibility of provincial expenditures, but leaves for the provinces the determination of which programmes will be operated and how much money will be spent. By its s. 8(1), the *Plan* further provides that agreements under it shall continue in force so long as the relevant provincial law remains in operation; but, that they may be terminated by consent or on one year's notice from either party (s. 8(2)). Agreements can also be amended by consent (s. 8(2)). The *Plan* provides (s. 9(1)) for regulations under it to govern such things as how eligible costs are to be calculated; but, regulations affecting the substance of agreements are ineffective unless passed with

the consent of any province affected (s. 9(2)). The *Plan* is silent as to the authority of Parliament to amend the *Plan*.

The Government of Canada entered into agreements with each of the provincial governments in 1967. It entered into an agreement with the Government of British Columbia on March 23, 1967. Amounts paid to the provinces under all agreements rose from $151 million in 1967-68 to an estimated $5.5 billion in 1989-90. The *Plan* itself has never been amended, although the regulations under it have been.

In 1990 the federal government decided to cut expenditures in order to reduce the federal budget deficit. The government has created an Expenditure Control Plan. One feature of this Plan is to limit the growth of payments made to financially stronger provinces under the *Canada Assistance Plan*. Such payments are to grow no more than 5 per cent per annum for fiscal 1991 and fiscal 1992. The provinces affected are those which are not entitled to receive equalization payments from the federal government; currently, this means British Columbia, Alberta and Ontario. This change, and others, were embodied in Bill C-69, *An Act to amend certain statutes to enable restraint of government expenditures*. That Bill was introduced in the House of Commons on March 15, 1990. It received royal assent on February 1, 1991, and is now the *Government Expenditures Restraint Act*, S.C. 1991, c. 9.

On February 27, 1990, Order in Council No. 287 was approved and ordered by the Lieutenant Governor of British Columbia. Via this Order, the Government of British Columbia referred the following questions to the British Columbia Court of Appeal:

(1) Has the Government of Canada any statutory, prerogative or contractual authority to limit its obligation under the *Canada Assistance Plan Act* [*sic*], R.S.C. 1970, c. C-1 and its Agreement with the Government of British Columbia dated March 23, 1967, to contribute 50 per cent of the cost to British Columbia of assistance and welfare services?

(2) Do the terms of the Agreement dated March 23, 1967 between the Governments of Canada and British Columbia, the subsequent conduct of the Government of Canada pursuant to the Agreement and the provisions of the *Canada Assistance Plan Act* [*sic*], R.S.C. 1970, c. C-1, give rise to a legitimate expectation that the Government of Canada would introduce no bill into Parliament to limit its obligation under the Agreement or the *Act* without the consent of British Columbia? ...

5. Justiciability

The *Constitutional Question Act*, like similar enactments of other provincial legislatures, allows the Lieutenant Governor in Council to refer "any matter" to the court. This broad word-ing imposes no limit on the type of question which may be asked. Nevertheless, the court has a discretion to refuse to answer questions which are not justiciable. In *Reference re Resolution to amend the Constitution*, [[1981] 1 S.C.R. 753], the majority in Part I said (at p. 768):

> The scope of the [reference] authority in each case is wide enough to saddle the respective courts with the determina-tion of questions which may not be justiciable and there is no doubt that those courts, and this Court on appeal, have a discretion to refuse to answer such questions.

While there may be many reasons why a question is non-justiciable, in this appeal the Attorney General of Canada submitted that to answer the questions would draw the Court into a political controversy and involve it in the legislative process. In exercising its discretion whether to determine a matter that is alleged to be non-justiciable, the Court's primary concern is to retain its proper role within the constitutional framework of our democratic form of government.... In considering its appropriate role the Court must determine whether the question is purely political in nature and should, therefore, be determined in another forum or whether it has a sufficient legal component to warrant the intervention of the judicial branch. In *Reference re Resolution to amend the Constitution, supra*, at p. 884, the majority in Part II of the judgment said:

> We agree with what Freedman C.J.M. wrote on this sub-ject in the Manitoba Reference [*Reference Re Amendment of the Constitution of Canada* (1981), 117 D.L.R. (3d) 1 (Man. C.A.)] at p. 13:
>
>> In my view, this submission goes too far. Its charac-terization of Question 2 as "purely political" overstates the case. That there is a political element embodied in the question, arising from the contents of the joint address, may well be the case. But that does not end the matter. If Question 2, even if in part political, possesses a constitutional feature, it would legiti-mately call for our reply.
>>
>> In my view, the request for a decision by this Court on whether there is a constitutional convention, in the circumstances described, that the Dominion will not act without the agreement of the Provinces poses a question that it [*sic*], at least in part, constitu-tional in character. It therefore calls for an answer, and I propose to answer it.

This was reiterated in *Reference re Objection by Quebec to a Resolution to amend the Constitution*, [1982] 2 S.C.R. 793, at p. 805. The Court reaffirmed the validity of the above passage

from the judgment of Freedman C.J.M. While the passage speaks to a "constitutional feature," it is equally applicable to a question which possesses a sufficient legal component to warrant a decision by a court. Since only a court can authori-tatively resolve a legal question, its decision will serve to resolve a controversy or it will have some other practical significance.

Applying the foregoing to this appeal, I am of the view that both of the questions posed have a significant legal com-ponent. The first question requires the interpretation of a statute of Canada and an agreement. The second raises the question of the applicability of the legal doctrine of legitimate expectations to the process involved in the enactment of a money bill. Both these matters are in contention between the so-called "have provinces" and the federal government. A decision on these questions will have the practical effect of settling the legal issues in contention and will assist in resolv-ing the controversy. Indeed, there is no other forum in which these legal questions could be determined in an authoritative manner. In my opinion, the questions raise matters that are justiciable and should be answered.

6. The Questions

(a) Question 1

... Before turning to the interpretation of and answers to the question, it is convenient to set out certain basic principles of our Constitution.

The Queen of Canada is our head of state, and under our Constitution she is represented in most capacities within the federal sphere by the Governor General. The Governor Gen-eral's executive powers are of course exercised in accordance with constitutional conventions. For example, after an election he asks the appropriate party leader to form a government. Once a government is in place, democratic principles dictate that the bulk of the Governor General's powers be exercised in accordance with the wishes of the leadership of that gov-ernment, namely the Cabinet. So the true executive power lies in the Cabinet. And since the Cabinet controls the govern-ment, there is in practice a degree of overlap among the terms "government," "Cabinet" and "executive." In these reasons, I have used all of these terms, as one or another may be more appropriate in a given context. The government has the power to introduce legislation in Parliament. In practice, the bulk of the new legislation is initiated by the government. By virtue of s. 54 of the *Constitution Act, 1867*, a money bill, including an amendment to a money bill, can only be introduced by means of the initiative of the government.

The interpretation of the questions does not take place in a vacuum but in the context of the above constitutional facts and the events giving rise to the questions. Of particular signifi-cance is the fact that the Government of Canada introduced

Bill C-69 and the allegation that this was a breach of the Agreement. The question must be given an interpretation that will make the answer of assistance in resolving the dispute.

In the Court of Appeal, this first question was interpreted as asking whether the federal government, in the absence of any new legislation amending the *Plan*, could unilaterally modify its obligations under the *Plan* and the Agreement. With respect, this interpretation has insufficient regard for the facts which gave rise to this dispute, and in particular for the introduction of Bill C-69. Moreover, this interpretation leads to an answer which is of no use in resolving the dispute with which the Court is faced. In my opinion, the first question asks the Court to determine whether the Agreement obliges the Government of Canada to pay to British Columbia the contributions that were authorized when the Agreement was signed, or rather whether the obligation is to pay those contributions which are authorized from time to time. Adopting the terminology of Lambert J.A. in the Court of Appeal, the former may be called a "static" interpretation and the latter an "ambulatory" one. If the former interpretation is correct, the Government of Canada acted contrary to the Agreement in introducing Bill C-69 in Parliament, whereas if the latter is correct the government acted in accordance with the Agreement.

In general, the language of the *Plan* is duplicated in the Agreement. But the contribution formula, which actually authorizes payments to the provinces, does not appear in the Agreement. It is only in s. 5 of the *Plan*. Clause 3(1)(a) of the Agreement provides that "Canada agrees . . . to pay to the province of British Columbia the contributions or advances . . . that Canada is authorized to pay to that province under the *Act* and the Regulations." That means, of course, the contributions or advances authorized by s. 5 of the *Plan*, an instrument that is to be construed as subject to amendment. This is the effect of s. 42(1) of the *Interpretation Act* which states:

> **42.**(1) Every Act shall be so construed as to reserve to Parliament the power of repealing or amending it, and of revoking, restricting or modifying any power, privilege or advantage thereby vested in or granted to any person.

In my view this provision reflects the principle of parliamentary sovereignty. The same results would flow from that principle even in the absence or non-applicability of this enactment. But since the *Interpretation Act* governs the interpretation of the *Plan* and all federal statutes where no contrary intention appears, the matter will be resolved by reference to it.

It is conceded that the government could not bind Parliament from exercising its powers to legislate amendments to the *Plan*. To assert the contrary would be to negate the sover-

eignty of Parliament. This basic fact of our constitutional life was, therefore, present to the minds of the parties when the *Plan* and Agreement were enacted and concluded. . . .

. . . [T]he respondent submitted that the Government of Canada was bound by s. 8 of the *Plan* which is set out above. That section provides that the Agreement is to continue in force so long as the provincial legislation (*Guaranteed Available Income for Need Act*, R.S.B.C. 1979, c. 158) remained in force. It could also be terminated on notice by either party and amended with the consent of the parties. The contention is that the Agreement could only be amended in accordance with s. 8. This submission fails to take into account that the Agreement which is subject to the amending formula in s. 8 obliges Canada to pay the amounts which Parliament has authorized Canada to pay pursuant to s. 5 of the *Plan*. Hence, the payment obligations under the Agreement are subject to change when s. 5 is changed. That provision contains within it its own process of amendment by virtue of the principle of parliamentary sovereignty reflected in s. 42 of the *Interpretation Act*.

If this appears to deprive the Agreement of binding effect or mutuality, which are both features of ordinary contracts, it must be remembered that this is not an ordinary contract but an agreement between governments. Moreover, s. 8 itself contains an amending formula that enables either party to terminate at will. In lieu of relying on mutually binding reciprocal undertakings which promote the observance of ordinary contractual obligations, these parties were content to rely on the perceived political price to be paid for non-performance.

The result of this is that the Government of Canada, in presenting Bill C-69 to Parliament, acted in accordance with the Agreement and otherwise with the law which empowers the Government of Canada to introduce a money bill in Parliament.

The answer to Question 1, therefore, is "Yes."

(b) Question 2

Legitimate Expectations

The doctrine of legitimate expectations was discussed in the reasons of the majority in *Old St. Boniface Residents Assn. Inc. v. Winnipeg (City)*, [1990] 3 S.C.R. 1170. That judgment cites seven cases dealing with the doctrine, and then goes on (at p. 1204):

> The principle developed in these cases is simply an extension of the rules of natural justice and procedural fairness. It affords a party affected by the decision of a public official an opportunity to make representations in circumstances in which there otherwise would be no such opportunity. The court supplies the omission where, based on the conduct of the public official, a party has been led to

believe that his or her rights would not be affected without consultation.

It was held by the majority of the court below, and it was argued before us by the Attorney General of British Columbia, that the federal government acted illegally in invoking the power of Parliament to amend the *Plan* without obtaining the *consent* of British Columbia. The action was illegal because it violated a legitimate expectation of British Columbia. These submissions were adopted by the Attorney General for Alberta. This must be contrasted with a claim that there was a legitimate expectation that the federal government would not act without *consulting* British Columbia. If the doctrine of legitimate expectations required consent, and not merely consultation, then it would be the source of substantive rights; in this case, a substantive right to veto proposed federal legislation.

There is no support in Canadian or English cases for the position that the doctrine of legitimate expectations can create substantive rights. It is a part of the rules of procedural fairness which can govern administrative bodies. Where it is applicable, it can create a right to make representations or to be consulted. It does not fetter the decision following the representations or consultation. . . .

Parliamentary government would be paralyzed if the doctrine of legitimate expectations could be applied to prevent the government from introducing legislation in Parliament. Such expectations might be created by statements during an election campaign. The business of government would be stalled while the application of the doctrine and its effect was argued out in the courts. Furthermore, it is fundamental to our system of government that a government is not bound by the undertakings of its predecessor. The doctrine of legitimate expectations would place a fetter on this essential feature of democracy. . . .

(iii) Jurisdiction

The Attorney General of Manitoba argued that Parliament lacked legislative jurisdiction to make the proposed change to the *Plan*. Again, this is not raised by the questions, but I will consider these submissions briefly. . . .

The written argument of the Attorney General of Manitoba was that the legislation "amounts to" regulation of a matter outside federal authority. I disagree. The Agreement under the *Plan* set up an open-ended cost-sharing scheme, which left it to British Columbia to decide which programmes it would establish and fund. The simple withholding of federal money which had previously been granted to fund a matter within provincial jurisdiction does not amount to the regulation of that matter. Still less is this so where, as in this case, the new legislation simply limits the growth of federal contributions. In oral argument, counsel said that the *Government Expenditures Restraint Act* "impacts upon [a] constitutional interest" outside the jurisdiction of Parliament. That is no doubt true, but it does not make the Act *ultra vires.* "Impact" with nothing more is clearly not enough to find that a statute encroaches upon the jurisdiction of the other level of government.

Finally, I turn to the second branch of this argument of the Attorney General of Manitoba. This was the argument that the "overriding principle of federalism" requires that Parliament be unable to interfere in areas of provincial jurisdiction. It was said that, in order to protect the autonomy of the provinces, the Court should supervise the federal government's exercise of its spending power. But supervision of the spending power is not a separate head of judicial review. If a statute is neither *ultra vires* nor contrary to the *Canadian Charter of Rights and Freedoms,* the courts have no jurisdiction to supervise the exercise of legislative power.

The answer to the second question is "No."

# R. v. Hydro-Québec, 1997

After *Crown Zellerbach*, challenges to federal environmental legislation continued to provide opportunities to test where the Supreme Court would go with its interpretation of the peace, order, and good government (POGG) clause. In the 1990s it became apparent that, even without major changes in the Court's composition, it would be very cautious in using the "provincial inability" approach, which had such potential to expand federal power. The Court's caution in this regard might well reflect its sensitivity to the constitutional battles being waged in the political arena around the Charlottetown Accord and the 1995 Quebec referendum. In other cases decided in this period, division within the court on federalism issues shifted to a sleeping giant of federal jurisdiction—the federal Parliament's criminal law power.

In the 1992 *Friends of the Oldman River* case,[1] the Court considered a challenge to federal legislation requiring an environmental assessment before Alberta could build a dam across a river in the province. The Court upheld the federal legislation, but in an opinion written by Justice La Forest, who had written the dissenting judgment in *Crown Zellerbach*, did so on grounds that had nothing to do with the POGG clause. La Forest emphasized, as he had in *Crown Zellerbach*, that environmental protection is not an independent matter of legislative jurisdiction. Both levels of government can and do legislate in this area. The validity of their laws depends on linking them to particular heads of power. In this case, the Court was satisfied that the challenged regulations were integral to federal jurisdiction over navigable waters, fisheries, Indians and lands belonging to Indians, as well as Parliament's residual power to regulate how its institutions administer their responsibilities.

Five years later, in *Hydro-Québec*, it became even clearer that the expansive "provincial inability" approach to POGG that the majority in *Crown Zellerbach* had adopted to justify federal environmental legislation would not be followed by the contemporary court. At issue in the case was a broad regulatory scheme authorized by the *Canadian Environmental Protection Act* aimed at preventing toxic substances from entering the environment. Hydro-Québec, faced with being charged with a criminal offence for failure to comply with the federal regulations, challenged the constitutional validity of the *Act*. The challenge succeeded in the Quebec courts largely on the basis that the legislation was too broad to meet the criteria set out in *Crown Zellerbach* for the peace, order, and good government power. The Supreme Court of Canada agreed unanimously with the Quebec courts about the inapplicability of POGG, but split 5 to 4 on whether the *Act* was a valid use of the federal criminal law power. The majority decided that it was.

Again, it was Justice La Forest, the dissenter in *Crown Zellerbach*, who wrote the majority opinion. La Forest was adamant about environmental protection being too broad a subject to assign exclusively to either level of government. He laid great emphasis on the importance of the federal and provincial governments cooperating in promoting a clean environment and preventing pollution. And he pointed out the opportunities for such cooperation under

---

1   *Friends of the Oldman River Society v. Canada (Minister of Transport)*, [1992] 1 S.C.R. 3.

the challenged legislation. While La Forest favoured caution in employing the national concern and provincial gap basis for using POGG, he did not call for a similarly cautious approach to Parliament's criminal law power. He drew on earlier cases where the federal criminal law power was used as a basis for legislation dealing with matters not usually associated with criminal law—such as economic protection of dairy farmers in the *Margarine Reference*[2] and legislation requiring health warnings on tobacco packaging in *RJR-MacDonald*.[3] Protecting the environment from toxic pollution is a broad purpose, but because criminal sanctions are used to enforce compliance with the detailed regulations developed under the federal *Environmental Protection Act*, the majority was able to characterize the *Act* as, in pith and substance, criminal law.

The four dissenting judges, in an opinion written by Chief Justice Lamer and Justice Iacobucci, thought it was too big a stretch to characterize the *Canadian Environmental Protection Act* as criminal law. In their view, criminal law can legitimately be aimed at public policy issues outside the normal ambit of criminality, but the legislation must be framed primarily around the specific activities that are prohibited. The *Environmental Protection Act* does not meet this test because, instead of clearly defining the prohibited acts, it leaves the definition of offences to the discretion of an administrative arm of government. The dissenting justices did not want to allow one level of government to become so dominant in the environmental field "as to dwarf the presence of the other."

Since *Hydro-Québec*, there has not been a good test of whether the broad La Forest approach to the criminal law power or the narrower Lamer-Iacobucci view will prevail. In 2000, the Supreme Court was unanimous in invoking the criminal law power to uphold federal legislation requiring the registration of firearms.[4] But this legislation amended the *Criminal Code* and dealt with a matter that is readily associated with criminal law. Of the nine justices who participated in *Hydro-Québec*, only Chief Justice McLachlin is still on the Court. So it remains to be seen whether the criminal law power will become a jurisdictional giant, replacing POGG as the constitutional basis for federal initiatives in environmental protection and other new fields of legislation. ⌁

---

2   *Reference re Validity of Section 5(a) of the Dairy Industry Act*, [1949] S.C.R. 1.

3   *RJR-MacDonald Inc. v. Canada*, [1995] 3 S.C.R. 199. For the *Charter* aspect of this case, see case 31.

4   *Reference re Firearms Act (Can.)*, [2000] 1 S.C.R. 783.

R. v. HYDRO-QUÉBEC
[1997] 3 S.C.R. 213

Hearing: February 10, 1997; Judgment: September 18, 1997.

Present: Lamer C.J. and La Forest, L'Heureux-Dubé, Sopinka, Gonthier, Cory, McLachlin, Iacobucci, and Major JJ.

Interveners: The Attorney General for Saskatchewan, IPSCO Inc., Société pour vaincre la pollution inc. ("S.V.P."), Pollution Probe, Great Lakes United (Canada), Canadian Environmental Law Association, and Sierra Legal Defence Fund.

The judgment of La Forest, L'Heureux-Dubé, Gonthier, Cory, and McLachlin JJ. was delivered by

[85] **LA FOREST J.:** This Court has in recent years been increasingly called upon to consider the interplay between federal and provincial legislative powers as they relate to environmental protection. Whether viewed positively as strategies for maintaining a clean environment, or negatively as measures to combat the evils of pollution, there can be no doubt that these measures relate to a public purpose of superordinate importance, and one in which all levels of government and numerous organs of the international community have become increasingly engaged. In the opening passage of this Court's reasons in what is perhaps the leading case, *Friends of the Oldman River Society v. Canada (Minister of Transport)*, [1992] 1 S.C.R. 3, at pp. 16-17, the matter is succinctly put this way:

> The protection of the environment has become one of the major challenges of our time. To respond to this challenge, governments and international organizations have been engaged in the creation of a wide variety of legislative schemes and administrative structures.

[86] The all-important duty of Parliament and the provincial legislatures to make full use of the legislative powers respectively assigned to them in protecting the environment has inevitably placed upon the courts the burden of progressively defining the extent to which these powers may be used to that end. In performing this task, it is incumbent on the courts to secure the basic balance between the two levels of government envisioned by the Constitution. However, in doing so, they must be mindful that the Constitution must be interpreted in a manner that is fully responsive to emerging realities and to the nature of the subject matter sought to be regulated. Given the pervasive and diffuse nature of the environment, this reality poses particular difficulties in this context.

[87] This latest case in which this Court is required to define the nature of legislative powers over the environment

is of major significance. The narrow issue raised is the extent to and manner in which the federal Parliament may control the amount of and conditions under which Chlorobiphenyls (PCBs)—substances well known to pose great dangers to humans and the environment generally—may enter into the environment. However, the attack on the federal power to secure this end is not really aimed at the specific provisions respecting PCBs. Rather, it puts into question the constitutional validity of its enabling statutory provisions. What is really at stake is whether Part II ("Toxic Substances") of the *Canadian Environmental Protection Act*, R.S.C., 1985, c. 16 (4th Supp.), which empowers the federal Ministers of Health and of the Environment to determine what substances are toxic and to prohibit the introduction of such substances into the environment except in accordance with specified terms and conditions, falls within the constitutional power of Parliament.

Facts

[88] The case arose in this way. The respondent Hydro-Québec allegedly dumped polychlorinated biphenyls (PCBs) into the St. Maurice River in Quebec in early 1990. On June 5, 1990, it was charged with the following two infractions under s. 6(*a*) of the *Chlorobiphenyls Interim Order*, P.C. 1989-296 (hereafter "Interim Order"), which was adopted and enforced pursuant to ss. 34 and 35 of the *Canadian Environmental Protection Act*:

[TRANSLATION]

> [1] From January 1 to January 3, 1990, did unlawfully release more than 1 gram per day of chlorobiphenyls into the environment contrary to s. 6(*a*) of the *Chlorobiphenyls Interim Order*, P.C. 1989-29[6] of February 23, 1989, thereby committing an offence under ss. 113(*i*) and (*o*) of the *Canadian Environmental Protection Act*, R.S.C., 1985, c. 16 (4th Supp.);
>
> [2] On or about January 8, 1990, following the release into the environment, in contravention of s. 6(*a*) of the *Chlorobiphenyls Interim Order*, P.C. 1989-296 of February 23, 1989, of a substance specified in Schedule I to the *Canadian Environmental Protection Act*, R.S.C., 1985, c. 16 (4th Supp.), to wit: chlorobiphenyls . . . did fail to report the matter to an inspector as soon as possible in the circumstances contrary to s. 36(1)(*a*) of the said *Act*, thereby committing an offence under ss. 113(*h*) and (*o*) of the said *Act*.

On July 23, 1990, the respondent pleaded not guilty to both charges before the Court of Québec.

[89] On March 4, 1991, the respondent Hydro-Québec brought a motion before Judge Michel Babin seeking to have ss. 34 and 35 of the *Act* as well as s. 6(*a*) of the Interim Order itself declared *ultra vires* the Parliament of Canada on the

ground that they do not fall within the ambit of any federal head of power set out in s. 91 of the *Constitution Act, 1867*. The Attorney General of Quebec intervened in support of the respondent's position. Judge Babin granted the motion on August 12, 1991 ([1991] R.J.Q. 2736), and an appeal to the Quebec Superior Court was dismissed by Trottier J. on August 6, 1992 ([1992] R.J.Q. 2159). A further appeal to the Court of Appeal of Quebec was dismissed on February 14, 1995: [1995] R.J.Q. 398, 67 Q.A.C. 161, 17 C.E.L.R. (N.S.) 34, [1995] Q.J. No. 143 (QL). Leave to appeal to this Court was granted on October 12, 1995: [1995] 4 S.C.R. vii. . . .

The Issues

[108] In this Court, the appellant Attorney General of Canada seeks to support the impugned provisions of the *Act* on the basis of the national concern doctrine under the peace, order and good government clause of s. 91 or under the criminal law power under s. 91(27) of the *Constitution Act, 1867*. The respondent Hydro-Québec and the *mis en cause* Attorney General of Quebec dispute this. In broad terms, they say that the provisions are so invasive of provincial powers that they cannot be justified either under the national dimensions doctrine or under the criminal law power. The attack on the validity of the provisions under the latter power is also supported, most explicitly by the intervener the Attorney General for Saskatchewan, on the ground that they are, in essence, of a regulatory and not of a prohibitory character. Finally, I repeat that while the Interim Order precipitated the litigation, there is no doubt that the respondent and *mis en cause* as well as their supporting interveners are after bigger game—the enabling provisions.

[109] While both the national concern doctrine and the criminal law power received attention in the course of the argument, it is right to say that the principal focus in this Court was on the national concern issue. This may in fact be owing to the fact that this Court's most recent decision dealing extensively with the criminal law power, *RJR-MacDonald Inc. v. Canada (Attorney General)*, [1995] 3 S.C.R. 199, had not been decided when this case came before the courts whose judgments are under review in this case. Whatever the reason, many of the arguments and concerns seemed at times to be addressed at both legislative powers, and the general effect was to colour and I think at times to distort the approach that, in my view, should properly be taken to the criminal law power. Thus I found much of the discussion relating to the pith and substance of the legislation, as well as other matters to which I shall later refer, not altogether apt to a consideration of the criminal law power.

[110] I make these remarks because, in my view, the impugned provisions are valid legislation under the criminal law power—s. 91(27) of the *Constitution Act, 1867*. It thus becomes unnecessary to deal with the national concern doctrine, which inevitably raises profound issues respecting the federal structure of our Constitution which do not arise with anything like the same intensity in relation to the criminal law power.

[111] In analysing the issues as they relate to the criminal law power, I propose to proceed in the following manner. I shall begin with introductory remarks reviewing the manner in which this Court has approached environmental issues arising under the division of powers under the *Constitution Act, 1867*. I shall then turn to a discussion of the federal criminal law power under s. 91(27) of that *Act*. This will be followed by a closer examination of Part II, Toxic Substances, of the *Act*. This will open the way to a discussion of whether ss. 34 and 35, as well as the Interim Order, are valid exercises of the criminal law power.

Analysis

Introduction

[112] In considering how the question of the constitutional validity of a legislative enactment relating to the environment should be approached, this Court in *Oldman River, supra*, made it clear that the environment is not, as such, a subject matter of legislation under the *Constitution Act, 1867*. As it was put there, "the *Constitution Act, 1867* has not assigned the matter of 'environment' *sui generis* to either the provinces or Parliament" (p. 63). Rather, it is a diffuse subject that cuts across many different areas of constitutional responsibility, some federal, some provincial (pp. 63-64). Thus Parliament or a provincial legislature can, in advancing the scheme or purpose of a statute, enact provisions minimizing or preventing the detrimental impact that statute may have on the environment, prohibit pollution, and the like. In assessing the constitutional validity of a provision relating to the environment, therefore, what must first be done is to look at the catalogue of legislative powers listed in the *Constitution Act, 1867* to see if the provision falls within one or more of the powers assigned to the body (whether Parliament or a provincial legislature) that enacted the legislation (*ibid.* at p. 65). If the provision in essence, in pith and substance, falls within the parameters of any such power, then it is constitutionally valid.

[113] Though pith and substance may be described in different ways, the expressions "dominant purpose" or "true character" used in *R. v. Morgentaler*, [1993] 3 S.C.R. 463, at pp. 481-82, or "the dominant or most important characteristic of the challenged law" used in *Whitbread v. Walley*, [1990] 3 S.C.R. 1273, at p. 1286, and in *Oldman River, supra*, at p. 62, appropriately convey the meaning to be attached to the term. If a provision dealing with the environment is really aimed at

promoting the dominant purpose of the statute or at addressing the impact of a statutory scheme, and the scheme itself is valid, then so is the provision.

[114] In examining the validity of legislation in this way, it must be underlined that the nature of the relevant legislative powers must be examined. Different types of legislative powers may support different types of environmental provisions. The manner in which such provisions must be related to a legislative scheme was, by way of example, discussed in *Oldman River* in respect of railways, navigable waters and fisheries. An environmental provision may be validly aimed at curbing environmental damage, but in some cases the environmental damage may be directly related to the power itself. There is a considerable difference between regulating works and activities, like railways, and a resource like fisheries, and consequently the environmental provisions relating to each of these. Environmental provisions must be tied to the appropriate constitutional source.

[115] Some heads of legislation may support a wholly different type of environmental provision than others. Notably under the general power to legislate for the peace, order and good government, Parliament may enact a wide variety of environmental legislation in dealing with an emergency of sufficient magnitude to warrant resort to the power. But the emergency would, of course, have to be established. So too with the "national concern" doctrine, which formed the major focus of the present case. A discrete area of environmental legislative power can fall within that doctrine, provided it meets the criteria first developed in *Reference re Anti-Inflation Act*, [1976] 2 S.C.R. 373, and thus set forth in *Crown Zellerbach, supra*, at p. 432:

> 3. For a matter to qualify as a matter of national concern in either sense it must have a singleness, distinctiveness and indivisibility that clearly distinguishes it from matters of provincial concern and a scale of impact on provincial jurisdiction that is reconcilable with the fundamental distribution of legislative power under the Constitution;

Thus in the latter case, this Court held that marine pollution met those criteria and so fell within the exclusive legislative power of Parliament under the peace, order and good government clause. While the constitutional necessity of characterizing certain activities as beyond the scope of provincial legislation and falling within the national domain was accepted by all the members of the Court, the danger of too readily adopting this course was not lost on the minority. Determining that a particular subject matter is a matter of national concern involves the consequence that the matter falls within the exclusive and paramount power of Parliament and has obvious impact on the balance of Canadian federalism. In *Crown Zellerbach*, the

minority (at p. 453) expressed the view that the subject of environmental protection was all-pervasive, and if accepted as falling within the general legislative domain of Parliament under the national concern doctrine, could radically alter the division of legislative power in Canada.

[116] The minority position on this point (which was not addressed by the majority) was subsequently accepted by the whole Court in *Oldman River, supra*, at p. 64. The general thrust of that case is that the Constitution should be so interpreted as to afford both levels of government ample means to protect the environment while maintaining the general structure of the Constitution. This is hardly consistent with an enthusiastic adoption of the "national dimensions" doctrine. That doctrine can, it is true, be adopted where the criteria set forth in *Crown Zellerbach* are met so that the subject can appropriately be separated from areas of provincial competence.

[117] I have gone on at this length to demonstrate the simple proposition that the validity of a legislative provision (including one relating to environmental protection) must be tested against the specific characteristics of the head of power under which it is proposed to justify it. For each constitutional head of power has its own particular characteristics and raises concerns peculiar to itself in assessing it in the balance of Canadian federalism. This may seem obvious, perhaps even trite, but it is all too easy (see *Fowler v. The Queen*, [1980] 2 S.C.R. 213) to overlook the characteristics of a particular power and overshoot the mark or, again, in assessing the applicability of one head of power to give effect to concerns appropriate to another head of power when this is neither appropriate nor consistent with the law laid down by this Court respecting the ambit and contours of that other power. In the present case, it seems to me, this was the case of certain propositions placed before us regarding the breadth and application of the criminal law power. There was a marked attempt to raise concerns appropriate to the national concern doctrine under the peace, order and good government clause to the criminal law power in a manner that, in my view, is wholly inconsistent with the nature and ambit of that power as set down by this Court from a very early period and continually reiterated since, notably in specific pronouncements in the most recent cases on the subject.

The Criminal Law Power

[118] Section 91(27) of the *Constitution Act, 1867* confers the exclusive power to legislate in relation to criminal law on Parliament. The nature and ambit of this power has recently been the subject of a detailed analytical and historical examination in *RJR-MacDonald, supra*, where it was again described (p. 240), as it has for many years, as being "*plenary in nature*" (emphasis added). I shall not attempt to repeat the analysis

so recently set forth at length by this Court, or attempt to refer extensively to all of the many authorities there cited, but will confine myself to underlining the findings in that case that are most salient to the issues raised here. . . .

[119] What appears from the analysis in *RJR-MacDonald* is that as early as 1903, the Privy Council, in *Attorney-General for Ontario v. Hamilton Street Railway Co.*, [1903] A.C. 524, at pp. 528-29, had made it clear that the power conferred on Parliament by s. 91(27) is "the criminal law in its *widest sense*" (emphasis added). Consistently with this approach, the Privy Council in *Proprietary Articles Trade Association v. Attorney-General for Canada*, [1931] A.C. 310 (hereafter *PATA*), at p. 324, defined the criminal law power as including any prohibited act with penal consequences. As it put it, at p. 324: "The criminal quality of an act cannot be discerned . . . by reference to any standard but one: Is the act prohibited with penal consequences?" This approach has been consistently followed ever since and, as *RJR-MacDonald* relates, it has been applied by the courts in a wide variety of settings. Accordingly, it is entirely within the discretion of Parliament to determine what evil it wishes by penal prohibition to suppress and what threatened interest it thereby wishes to safeguard, to adopt the terminology of Rand J. in the *Margarine Reference*, [*Reference re Validity of Section 5(a) of the Dairy Industry Act*, [1949] S.C.R. 1] *supra*, at p. 49, cited *infra*.

[120] Contrary to the respondent's submission, under s. 91(27) of the *Constitution Act, 1867*, it is also within the discretion of Parliament to determine the extent of blameworthiness that it wishes to attach to a criminal prohibition. So it may determine the nature of the mental element pertaining to different crimes, such as a defence of due diligence like that which appears in s. 125(1) of the *Act* in issue. This flows from the fact that Parliament has been accorded plenary power to make criminal law in the widest sense. This power is, of course, subject to the "fundamental justice" requirements of s. 7 of the *Canadian Charter of Rights and Freedoms*, which may dictate a higher level of *mens rea* for serious or "true" crimes; cf. *R. v. Wholesale Travel Group Inc.*, [1991] 3 S.C.R. 154, and *R. v. Rube*, [1992] 3 S.C.R. 159, but that is not an issue here.

[121] The *Charter* apart, only one qualification has been attached to Parliament's plenary power over criminal law. The power cannot be employed colourably. Like other legislative powers, it cannot, as Estey J. put it in *Scowby v. Glendinning*, [1986] 2 S.C.R. 226, at p. 237, "permit Parliament, simply by legislating in the proper form, to colourably invade areas of exclusively provincial legislative competence." To determine whether such an attempt is being made, it is, of course, appropriate to enquire into Parliament's purpose in enacting the legislation. As Estey J. noted in *Scowby*, at p. 237, since the

Margarine Reference, it has been "accepted that some legitimate public purpose must underlie the prohibition." Estey J. then cited Rand J.'s words in the *Margarine Reference* (at p. 49) as follows:

> A crime is an act which the law, with appropriate penal sanctions, forbids; but as prohibitions are not enacted in a vacuum, we can properly look for some evil or injurious or undesirable effect upon the public against which the law is directed. That effect may be in relation to social, economic or political interests; and the legislature has had in mind to suppress the evil or to safeguard the interest threatened.

[122] In the *Margarine Reference*, *supra*, at p. 50, Rand J. helpfully set forth the more usual purposes of a criminal prohibition in the following passage:

> Is the prohibition . . . enacted with a view to a public purpose which can support it as being in relation to criminal law? *Public peace, order, security, health, morality: these are the ordinary though not exclusive ends served by that law.* . . . [Emphasis added.] . . .

[123] During the argument in the present case, however, one sensed, at times, a tendency, even by the appellant and the supporting interveners, to seek justification solely for the purpose of the protection of health specifically identified by Rand J. Now I have no doubt that that purpose obviously will support a considerable measure of environmental legislation, as perhaps also the ground of security. But I entertain no doubt that the protection of a clean environment is a public purpose within Rand J.'s formulation in the *Margarine Reference*, cited *supra*, sufficient to support a criminal prohibition. It is surely an "interest threatened" which Parliament can legitimately "safeguard," or to put it another way, pollution is an "evil" that Parliament can legitimately seek to suppress. Indeed, as I indicated at the outset of these reasons, it is a public purpose of superordinate importance; it constitutes one of the major challenges of our time. It would be surprising indeed if Parliament could not exercise its plenary power over criminal law to protect this interest and to suppress the evils associated with it by appropriate penal prohibitions.

[124] This approach is entirely consistent with the recent pronouncement of this Court in *Ontario v. Canadian Pacific Ltd.*, [1995] 2 S.C.R. 1031, where Gonthier J., speaking for the majority, had this to say, at para. 55:

> It is clear that over the past two decades, citizens have become acutely aware of the importance of environmental protection, and of the fact that penal consequences may flow from conduct which harms the environment. . . . Everyone is aware that individually and collectively, we

are responsible for preserving the natural environment. I would agree with the Law Reform Commission of Canada, *Crimes Against the Environment, supra*, which concluded at p. 8 that:

> ... a fundamental and widely shared value is indeed seriously contravened by some environmental pollution, a value which we will refer to as the *right to a safe environment*.
>
> To some extent, this right and value appears to be new and emerging, but in part because it is an extension of existing and very traditional rights and values already protected by criminal law, its presence and shape even now are largely discernible. Among the new strands of this fundamental value are, it may be argued, those such as *quality of life*, and *stewardship* of the natural environment. At the same time, traditional values as well have simply expanded and evolved to include the environment now as an area and interest of direct and primary concern. Among these values fundamental to the purposes and protections of criminal law are the *sanctity of life*, the *inviolability and integrity of persons*, and the *protection of human life and health*. It is increasingly understood that certain forms and degrees of environmental pollution can directly or indirectly, sooner or later, seriously harm or endanger human life and human health.
>
> Not only has environmental protection emerged as a fundamental value in Canadian society, but this has also been recognized in legislative provisions such as s. 13(1)(*a*) EPA. [Italics in original; underlining added.]

[125] It is worthy of note that following Working Paper 44 (1985), from which Gonthier J. cites, the Law Reform Commission of Canada in a subsequent report to Parliament (*Recodifying Criminal Law*, Report 31 (1987)), noted its view of the desirability of using the criminal law to underline the value of respect for the environment itself....

[126] This is, of course, in line with the thinking of various international organisms. The World Commission on Environment and Development (the Brundtland Commission) in its report *Our Common Future* (1987) (see at pp. 219-20, and pp. 224-25) long ago recommended the adoption of appropriate legislation to protect the environment against toxic and chemical substances, including the creation of national standards that could be supplemented by local legislation....

[127] What the foregoing underlines is what I referred to at the outset, that the protection of the environment is a major challenge of our time. It is an international problem, one that requires action by governments at all levels. And, as is stated in the preamble to the *Act* under review, "Canada must be able to fulfil its international obligations in respect of the environ-

ment." I am confident that Canada can fulfil its international obligations, in so far as the toxic substances sought to be prohibited from entering into the environment under the *Act* are concerned, by use of the criminal law power. The purpose of the criminal law is to underline and protect our fundamental values. While many environmental issues could be criminally sanctioned in terms of protection of human life or health, I cannot accept that the criminal law is limited to that because "certain forms and degrees of environmental pollution can directly or indirectly, sooner or later, seriously harm or endanger human life and human health," as the paper approvingly cited by Gonthier J. in *Ontario v. Canadian Pacific, supra*, observes. But the stage at which this may be discovered is not easy to discern, and I agree with that paper that the stewardship of the environment is a fundamental value of our society and that Parliament may use its criminal law power to underline that value. The criminal law must be able to keep pace with and protect our emerging values.

[128] In saying that Parliament may use its criminal law power in the interest of protecting the environment or preventing pollution, there again appears to have been confusion during the argument between the approach to the national concern doctrine and the criminal law power. The national concern doctrine operates by assigning full power to regulate an area to Parliament. Criminal law does not work that way. Rather it seeks by discrete prohibitions to prevent evils falling within a broad purpose, such as, for example, the protection of health. In the criminal law area, reference to such broad policy objectives is simply a means of ensuring that the prohibition is legitimately aimed at some public evil Parliament wishes to suppress and so is not a colourable attempt to deal with a matter falling exclusively within an area of provincial legislative jurisdiction.

[129] The legitimate use of the criminal law I have just described in no way constitutes an encroachment on provincial legislative power, though it may affect matters falling within the latter's ambit. This is made clear from the following passage from *Standard Sausage Co. v. Lee*, [1933] 4 D.L.R. 501 (B.C.C.A.), at pp. 506-7, cited with approval in *RJR-MacDonald, supra*, pp. 254-55:

> ... if the Federal Parliament, to protect the public health against actual or threatened danger, places restrictions on, and limits the number of preservatives that may be used, it may do so under s. 91(27) of the *B.N.A. Act*. This is not in essence an interference with property and civil rights. That may follow as an incident but the real purpose (not colourable and not merely to aid what in substance is an encroachment) is to prevent actual, or threatened injury or the likelihood of injury of the most serious kind to all inhabitants of the Dominion....

The primary object of this legislation is the public safety—protecting it from threatened injury. If that is its main purpose—and not a mere pretence for the invasion of civil rights—it is none the less valid. . . .

I shall have more to say about this later.

[130] I conclude that Parliament may validly enact prohibitions under its criminal law power against specific acts for the purpose of preventing pollution or, to put it in other terms, causing the entry into the environment of certain toxic substances. I quite understand that a particular prohibition could be so broad or all-encompassing as to be found to be, in pith and substance, really aimed at regulating an area falling within the provincial domain and not exclusively at protecting the environment. A sweeping prohibition like this (and this would be equally true of one aimed generally at the protection of health) would, in any case, probably be unworkable. But the attack here ultimately is that the impugned provisions grant such a broad discretion to the Governor in Council as to permit orders that go beyond federal power. I can imagine very nice issues being raised concerning this matter under certain types of legislation, though in such a case one would tend to interpret the legislation narrowly if only to keep it within constitutional bounds. But one need not go so far here. For, it seems to me, as we shall see, when one carefully peruses the legislation, it becomes clear enough that Parliament has stayed well within its power.

[131] Though I shall deal with this issue in more detail once I come to consider the legislation, it is well at this point to recall that the use of the federal criminal law power in no way precludes the provinces from exercising their extensive powers under s. 92 to regulate and control the pollution of the environment either independently or to supplement federal action. The situation is really no different from the situation regarding the protection of health where Parliament has for long exercised extensive control over such matters as food and drugs by prohibitions grounded in the criminal law power. This has not prevented the provinces from extensively regulating and prohibiting many activities relating to health. The two levels of government frequently work together to meet common concerns. The cooperative measures relating to the use of tobacco are fully related in *RJR-MacDonald, supra.* Nor, though it arises under a different technical basis, is the situation, in substance, different as regards federal prohibitions against polluting water for the purposes of protecting the fisheries. Here again there is a wide measure of cooperation between the federal and provincial authorities to effect common or complementary ends. It is also the case in many other areas. The fear that the legislation impugned here would distort the federal-provincial balance seems to me to be overstated. . . .

The Provisions Respecting Toxic Substances

[133] The respondent, the *mis en cause* and their supporting interveners primarily attack ss. 34 and 35 of the *Act* as constituting an infringement on provincial regulatory powers conferred by the Constitution. This they do by submitting that the power to regulate a substance is so broad as to encroach upon provincial legislative jurisdiction. That is because of what they call the broad "definition" given to toxic substances under s. 11, and particularly para. (*a*), thereof which, it will be remembered, provides that:

> **11.** For the purposes of this Part, a substance is toxic if it is entering or may enter the environment in a quantity or concentration or under conditions
> (*a*) having or that may have an immediate or long-term harmful effect on the environment;

This, along with the expansive definitions of "substance" and "environment" in s. 3(1), makes it possible, they say, in effect to regulate any substance that can in any way prove harmful to the environment.

[134] I cannot agree with this submission. As I see it, the argument focusses too narrowly on a specific provision of the *Act* and for that matter only on certain aspects of it, and then applies that provision in a manner that I do not think is warranted by a consideration of the provisions of the *Act* as a whole and in light of its background and purpose. I shall deal with the latter first. Before doing so, however, I shall comment briefly on the concern expressed about the breadth of the phraseology of the *Act.* As Gonthier J. observed in *Ontario v. Canadian Pacific, supra,* this broad wording is unavoidable in environmental protection legislation because of the breadth and complexity of the subject and has to be kept in mind in interpreting the relevant legislation. At para. 43, he stated:

> What is clear from this brief review of Canadian pollution prohibitions is that our legislators have preferred to take a broad and general approach, and have avoided an exhaustive codification of every circumstance in which pollution is prohibited. Such an approach is hardly surprising in the field of environmental protection, given that the nature of the environment (its complexity, and the wide range of activities which might cause harm to it) is not conducive to precise codification. Environmental protection legislation has, as a result, been framed in a manner capable of responding to a wide variety of environmentally harmful scenarios, including ones which might not have been foreseen by the drafters of the legislation.

In light of this, he went on to hold that environmental protection legislation should not be approached with the same rigour as statutes dealing with less complex issues in applying the doctrine of vagueness developed under s. 7 of the *Charter*. The effect of requiring greater precision would be to frustrate the legislature in its attempt to protect the public against the dangers flowing from pollution. . . .

[146] In summary, as I see it, the broad purpose and effect of Part II is to provide a procedure for assessing whether out of the many substances that may conceivably fall within the ambit of s. 11, some should be added to the List of Toxic Substances in Schedule I and, when an order to this effect is made, whether to prohibit the use of the substance so added in the manner provided in the regulations made under s. 34(1) subject to a penalty. These listed substances, toxic in the ordinary sense, are those whose use in a manner contrary to the regulations the *Act* ultimately prohibits. This is a limited prohibition applicable to a restricted number of substances. The prohibition is enforced by a penal sanction and is undergirded by a valid criminal objective, and so is valid criminal legislation. . . .

. . . I observe that in enacting the legislation in issue here, Parliament was alive to the need for cooperation and coordination between the federal and provincial authorities. This is evident throughout the *Act*. In particular, under s. 34(2), (5) and (6), Parliament has made it clear that the provisions of this Part are not to apply where a matter is otherwise regulated under other equivalent federal or provincial legislation.

[154] In *Crown Zellerbach*, I expressed concern with the possibility of allocating legislative power respecting environmental pollution exclusively to Parliament. I would be equally concerned with an interpretation of the Constitution that effectively allocated to the provinces, under general powers such as property and civil rights, control over the environment in a manner that prevented Parliament from exercising the leadership role expected of it by the international community and its role in protecting the basic values of Canadians regarding the environment through the instrumentality of the criminal law power. Great sensitivity is required in this area since, as Professor Lederman has rightly observed, environmental pollution "is no limited subject or theme, [it] is a sweeping subject or theme virtually all-pervasive in its legislative implications"; see W. R. Lederman, "Unity and Diversity in Canadian Federalism: Ideals and Methods of Moderation" (1975), 53 *Can. Bar Rev.* 597, at p. 610. . . .

[156] In sum, then, I am of the view that Part II of the *Act*, properly construed, simply provides a means to assess substances with a view to determining whether the substances are sufficiently toxic to be added to Schedule I of the *Act* (which contains a list of dangerous substances carried over from pre-existing legislation), and provides by regulations under s. 34 the terms and conditions under which they can be used, with provisions under s. 35 for by-passing the ordinary provisions

for testing and regulation under Part II in cases where immediate action is required. I have reached this position independently of the legal presumption that a legislature intends to confine itself to matters within its competence; see *Reference re Farm Products Marketing Act*, [1957] S.C.R. 198, at p. 255; *Nova Scotia Board of Censors v. McNeil*, [1978] 2 S.C.R. 662, at p. 688. However, it follows that the position I have taken would by virtue of the presumption displace a possible reading of the *Act* that would render it unconstitutional.

[157] Since I have found the empowering provisions, ss. 34 and 35, to be *intra vires*, the only attack that could be brought against any action taken under them would be that such action went beyond the authority granted by those provisions; in the present case, for example, such an attack might consist in the allegation that PCBs did not pose "a significant danger to the environment or to human life or health" justifying the making of the Interim Order. This would seem to me to be a tall order. The fact that PCBs are highly toxic substances should require no demonstration. This has become well known to the general public and is supported by an impressive array of scientific studies at both the national and international levels. I list here only a sample of those cited to us . . . .

[158] From what appears in these studies, one can conclude that PCBs are not only highly toxic but long lasting and very slow to break down in water, air or soil. They do dissolve readily in fat tissues and other organic compounds, however, with the result that they move up the food chain through birds and other animals and eventually to humans. They pose significant risks of serious harm to both animals and humans. As well they are extremely mobile. They evaporate from soil and water and are transported great distances through the atmosphere. High levels of PCBs have been found in a variety of arctic animals living thousands of kilometres from any major source of PCBs. The extent of the dangers they pose is reflected in the fact that they were the first substance sought to be controlled in Canada under the *Environmental Contaminants Act*, the predecessor of the present legislation. They were also the first substance regulated in the United States under the *Toxic Substances Control Act*, 15 U.S.C. § 2605(c). And because of the trans-boundary nature of the threat, they were the first substances targeted for joint action by Canada, the United States and Mexico through the Commission for Environmental Cooperation established under the North American Free Trade Agreement; see C.E.C. Council of Ministers, Resolution # 95-5 "Sound Management of Chemicals," Oct. 1995; C.E.C. Secretariat Bulletin, vol. 2, No. 3, Winter/Spring 1996.

[159] I should say that the respondent and *mis en cause* do not contest the toxicity of PCBs but simply argue that their control should not fall exclusively within federal competence. They also note that there is one study (G.J. Farquhar and

J. Sykes, *PCB Behavior in Soils* (1978), at pp. 7, 8, 22, 23, 26, 33 and 34) that indicates that PCBs are absorbed, remain stable and are not mobile. I have already discussed the issue of concurrency. So far as mobility is concerned, whatever weight may be attached to the report in relation to the national concern issue, it has no relevance in considering federal jurisdiction under the criminal law power.

[160] I conclude, therefore, that the Interim Order is also valid under s. 91(27) of the *Constitution Act, 1867*.

Disposition

[161] I would allow the appeal with costs, set aside the judgment of the Court of Appeal of Quebec and order that the matter be returned to the Court of summary convictions to be dealt with in accordance with the *Act*. I would answer the constitutional question as follows:

> Q. Do s. 6(*a*) of the *Chlorobiphenyls Interim Order*, P.C. 1989-296, and the enabling legislative provisions, ss. 34 and 35 of the *Canadian Environmental Protection Act*, R.S.C., 1985, c. 16 (4th Supp.), fall in whole or in part within the jurisdiction of the Parliament of Canada to make laws for the peace, order and good government of Canada pursuant to s. 91 of the *Constitution Act, 1867* or its criminal law jurisdiction under s. 91(27) of the *Constitution Act, 1867* or otherwise fall within its jurisdiction?
>
> A. Yes. They fall wholly within Parliament's power to enact laws under s. 91(27) of the *Constitution Act, 1867*. It is not necessary to consider the first issue.

The reasons of Lamer C.J. and Sopinka, Iacobucci, and Major JJ. were delivered by

The **CHIEF JUSTICE** and **IACOBUCCI J.** (dissenting):

[2] ... We have had the advantage of reading the lucid reasons of La Forest J. While we share his concern for the protection of the environment, we are of the view that the impugned provisions cannot be justified under s. 91 of the *Constitution Act, 1867*, and are therefore *ultra vires* the federal government....

A. The Legislative Structure of the Act

[15] The *Canadian Environmental Protection Act* was adopted by Parliament in 1988. It consolidated and replaced several other laws dealing with various kinds of environmental protection. Part II of the *Act*, which contains ss. 34 and 35, is called "Toxic Substances" and deals with the identification and regulation of substances which could potentially pose a risk to the environment and/or to human health. According to s. 11 of the *Act*, a substance is toxic where "it is entering or may enter the environment" under conditions "having or that

may have an immediate or long-term harmful effect on the environment," "constituting or that may constitute a danger to the environment on which human life depends," *or* "constituting or that may constitute a danger in Canada to human life or health." Section 3 broadly defines a "substance" as "any distinguishable kind of organic or inorganic matter, whether animate or inanimate" and the "environment" as "the components of the Earth." "Harmful effect" and "danger" are not defined.

[16] The *Act* instructs the Ministers of the Environment and Health to compile and maintain four lists: the Domestic Substances List (DSL), the Non-Domestic Substances List (NDSL), the Priority Substances List (PSL) and the List of Toxic Substances (LTS). The DSL includes all substances in use in Canada since 1986 (some 21,700 substances as of January 1991). The NDSL contains all other substances. At present, the NDSL list includes over 41,000 substances. See E.A. Fitzgerald, "The Constitutionality of Toxic Substances Regulation Under the Canadian Environmental Protection Act" (1996), 30 *U.B.C.L. Rev.* 55, at p. 70. There is a blanket restriction on importing NDSL substances into Canada until they are approved (s. 26).

[17] Sections 12 and 13 of the *Act* require the Ministers to compile a "Priority Substances List" specifying those substances to which priority should be given in determining whether or not they should be placed on the List of Toxic Substances. ...

[18] Once a priority listed substance is found to be toxic within the meaning of s. 11, the Ministers may recommend adding it to the List of Toxic Substances. After a federal–provincial advisory committee (established under s. 6) has been given an opportunity to provide its advice, the Governor in Council may add the substance to the list and bring it under the regulatory control of s. 34.

[19] Section 34 provides for the regulation of substances on the List of Toxic Substances. The Governor in Council is given extensive powers to prescribe regulations dealing with every conceivable aspect of the listed substance, including: the quantity or concentration in which it can be released; the commercial or manufacturing activity in the course of which it can be released; the quantity of that substance that can be manufactured, imported, owned, sold, or used—including total prohibitions on its manufacture, importation, ownership, use or sale—and likewise the manner in and purposes for which it can be manufactured, imported, processed, used, offered for sale or sold; the manner and conditions in which the substance may be advertised, stored, displayed, handled, transported or offered for transport; the manner, conditions, places and method of disposal of the substance; the maintenance of books and records in respect of the substance; and the

extent to which reports must be made to the Minister regarding the monitoring of the substance. Section 34(1)(x) allows the Governor in Council to regulate "any other matter necessary to carry out the purposes of this Part." . . .

[22] Finally, the *Act* prescribes a number of civil and criminal penalties. Section 113(*f*), for example, creates an offence of contravening regulations made under s. 34. The punishment ranges from a maximum $300,000 fine or six months imprisonment (or both) on summary conviction to a maximum $1 million fine or three years imprisonment (or both) on indictment. A defence of due diligence is allowed for all offences under the *Act* except those under s. 114 (knowingly providing false or misleading information), s. 115(1)(*a*) (intentionally or recklessly causing an environmental disaster) or s. 115(1)(*b*) (showing wanton or reckless disregard for the lives or safety of other persons). These offences require a higher standard of moral culpability.

B. The Pith and Substance of the Legislation

[23] The manner of analysing matters involving division of powers is well established: see Hogg, [Peter W. Hogg, *Constitutional Law of Canada*, vol. 1, 3d ed. (supplemented) (Scarborough, ON: Carswell, 1992) (looseleaf)] *supra*, at p. 15-6. The law in question must first be characterized in relation to its "pith and substance," that is, its dominant or most important characteristic. One must then see if the law, seen in this light, can be successfully assigned to one of the government's heads of legislative power.

[24] In this case, the Quebec Court of Appeal held that, although one of the effects of Part II of the *Act* is to protect human life and health, its pith and substance lies in the protection of the environment . . . :

[25] The respondent Hydro-Québec and the *mis en cause* the Attorney General of Quebec agree with this characterization and suggest that the true goal of the legislation is the regulation of environmental protection, writ large. The appellant, on the other hand, argues that the true object of Part II of the *Act* is simply the control of pollution caused by toxic substances (like PCBs), which are capable of being dispersed into the environment and whose level of toxicity is such as to pose a serious risk of harm to the environment and to human health and life. . . .

[26] In our view, the dominant characteristic of the impugned legislation is apparent from its plain text. Part II of the *Act* seeks, at first glance, to protect the environment, human health and life from harm owing to the release of toxic substances. As noted above, it seeks to do so through extensive—indeed, comprehensive—regulation of these substances and the ways in which they may come into contact with the environment. That being said, we believe it is also necessary to consider the sweeping definitions given by the *Act* to "environment" and "toxic substance." . . .

> (*g*) any animate matter that is, or any complex mixtures of different molecules that are, contained in effluents, emissions or wastes that result from any work, undertaking or activity;

[28] The *Act* is not, as was suggested by the appellant, aimed specifically at chemical substances; rather, it purports to cover "any distinguishable kind of organic or inorganic matter, whether animate or inanimate." Section 11 determines when a substance will be "toxic," and therefore subject to federal regulation:

> 11. For the purposes of this Part, a substance is toxic if it is entering or may enter the environment in a quantity or concentration or under conditions
> (*a*) having or that may have an immediate or long-term harmful effect on the environment;
> (*b*) constituting or that may constitute a danger to the environment on which human life depends; or
> (*c*) constituting or that may constitute a danger in Canada to human life or health.

[29] Paragraphs 11(*a*) through (*c*) are not cumulative. It will suffice to bring a substance under federal regulatory control that it pose a risk to human life or health, part of the environment upon which human life depends, *or* the environment itself.

[30] In this regard, we note that we cannot, with respect, agree with our colleague, La Forest J., that the criteria found in s. 11 are simply a "drafting tool" or that to speak of s. 11 as a definition is "misleading." The purpose of this section is to delineate from the category of "substances" (as defined by s. 3) those particular substances which qualify for regulation under ss. 34 and 35. It does so by specifying that "toxic" substances are, for the purposes of Part II, those which are capable of posing one of the threats listed above. . . .

[32] Nor are we convinced that the federal–provincial consultative process contemplated in s. 35(4) of the *Act* has the effect of changing the character of the impugned provisions. Although we understand why Parliament might wish to seek the opinion of provincial legislatures before enacting regulations which would affect areas under their supervision, nothing in the *Act* requires that this process be anything other than consultative. That is, once having consulted affected provincial governments, Parliament is left free to pass whatever regulations it sees fit in order to address the threat posed by substances qualifying as "toxic."

[33] In light of these factors, we believe the pith and substance of Part II of the *Act* lies in the wholesale regulation by

federal agents of any and all substances which may harm any aspect of the environment or which may present a danger to human life or health. That is, the impugned provisions are in pith and substance aimed at protecting the environment and human life and health from any and all harmful substances by regulating these substances. It remains to be seen whether this can be justified under any of the heads of power listed in s. 91 of the *Constitution Act, 1867*. In that connection, we will begin by considering s. 91(27), the criminal law power.

C. The Criminal Law Power

[34] Parliament has been given broad and exclusive power to legislate in relation to criminal law by virtue of s. 91(27): *RJR-MacDonald Inc. v. Canada (Attorney General)*, [1995] 3 S.C.R. 199; *Scowby v. Glendinning*, [1986] 2 S.C.R. 226. This power has traditionally been construed generously. As La Forest J. noted in *RJR-MacDonald*, at p. 240, "[i]n developing a definition of the criminal law, this Court has been careful not to freeze the definition in time or confine it to a fixed domain of activity."

[35] Nevertheless, the criminal law power has always been made subject to two requirements: laws purporting to be upheld under s. 91(27) must contain prohibitions backed by penalties; and they must be directed at a "legitimate public purpose" ...

(i) A Legitimate Public Purpose

... [43] To the extent that La Forest J. suggests that this legislation is supportable as relating to health, therefore, we must respectfully disagree. We agree with him, however, that the protection of the environment is itself a legitimate criminal public purpose, analogous to those cited in the *Margarine Reference, supra*. We would not add to his lucid reasoning on this point, save to state explicitly that this purpose does not rely on any of the other traditional purposes of criminal law (health, security, public order, etc.). To the extent that Parliament wishes to deter environmental pollution specifically by punishing it with appropriate penal sanctions, it is free to do so, without having to show that these sanctions are ultimately aimed at achieving one of the "traditional" aims of criminal law. The protection of the environment is itself a legitimate basis for criminal legislation.

[44] However, we still do not feel that the impugned provisions qualify as criminal law under s. 91(27). While they have a legitimate criminal purpose, they fail to meet the other half of the *Maragarine Reference* test. The structure of Part II of the *Act* indicates that they are not intended to prohibit environmental pollution, but simply to regulate it. As we will now explain in further detail, they are not, therefore, criminal law: see *Hauser* [[1979] 1 S.C.R. 984], *supra*, at p. 999.

(ii) Prohibitions Backed by Penalties

[45] Ascertaining whether a particular statute is prohibitive or regulatory in nature is often more of an art than a science.... Some guidelines have, however, emerged from previous jurisprudence....

[48] Determining when a piece of legislation has crossed the line from criminal to regulatory involves, in our view, considering the nature and extent of the regulation it creates, as well as the context within which it purports to apply. A scheme which is fundamentally regulatory, for example, will not be saved by calling it an "exemption." As Professor Hogg suggests, *supra*, at p. 18-26, "the more elaborate [a] regulatory scheme, the more likely it is that the Court will classify the dispensation or exemption as being regulatory rather than criminal." At the same time, the subject matter of the impugned law may indicate the appropriate approach to take in characterizing the law as criminal or regulatory....

[49] Having examined the legislation at issue in this case, we have no doubt that it is essentially regulatory in nature, and therefore outside the scope of s. 91(27). In order to have an "exemption," there must first be a prohibition in the legislation from which that exemption is derived....

[52] ... In fact, the only time the word "prohibition" appears in s. 34(1) is in s. 34(1)(*l*), which provides that the Governor in Council *may*, at his or her discretion, prohibit the manufacture, import, use or sale of a given substance. Clearly, this is not analogous to the broad general prohibitions found in the statutes cited above.

[53] The only other mentions of prohibition in relation to the impugned provisions are in ss. 113(*f*) and 113(*i*) of the Act, which provide that failure to comply with a regulation made under ss. 34 or 35 is an offence. The prohibitions, such as they are, are ancillary to the regulatory scheme, not the other way around. This strongly suggests that the focus of the legislation is regulation rather than prohibition....

[54] Moreover, as Professor Hogg notes, *supra*, at p. 18-24:

> A criminal law ordinarily consists of a prohibition which is to be self-applied by the persons to whom it is addressed. There is not normally any intervention by an administrative agency or official prior to the application of the law. The law is "administered" by law enforcement officials and courts of criminal jurisdiction only in the sense that they can bring to bear the machinery of punishment after the prohibited conduct has occurred.

[55] In this case, there *is* no offence until an administrative agency "intervenes." Sections 34 and 35 do not define an offence at all: which, if any, substances will be placed on the List of Toxic Substances, as well as the norms of conduct regarding these substances, are to be defined on an on-going

basis by the Ministers of Health and the Environment. It would be an odd crime whose definition was made entirely dependent on the discretion of the Executive. This further suggests that the *Act's* true nature is regulatory, not criminal, and that the offences created by s. 113 are regulatory offences, not "true crimes": see *R. v. Wholesale Travel Group Inc.*, [1991] 3 S.C.R. 154, *per* Cory J. Our colleague, La Forest J., would hold that the scheme of the impugned act is an effective means of avoiding unnecessarily broad prohibitions and carefully targeting specific toxic substances. The regulatory mechanism allows the schemes to be changed flexibly, as the need arises. Of course, simply because a scheme is effective and flexible does not mean it is *intra vires* the federal Parliament. . . .

[59] *RJR-MacDonald* may be further distinguished, in our view. The *Tobacco Products Control Act* addressed a narrow field of activity: the advertising and promotion of tobacco products. The impugned provisions here deal with a much broader area of concern: the release of substances into the environment. This Court has unanimously held that the environment is a subject matter of shared jurisdiction, that is, that the Constitution does not assign it exclusively to either the provinces or Parliament: *Oldman River, supra*, at p. 63; see also *Crown Zellerbach, supra*, at pp. 455-56, *per* La Forest J. A decision by the framers of the Constitution not to give one level of government exclusive control over a subject matter should, in our opinion, act as a signal that the two levels of government are meant to operate in tandem with regard to that subject matter. One level should not be allowed to take over the field so as to completely dwarf the presence of the other. This does not mean that *no* regulation will be permissible, but wholesale regulatory authority of the type envisaged by the *Act* is, in our view, inconsistent with the shared nature of jurisdiction over the environment. As La Forest J. noted in his dissenting reasons in *Crown Zellerbach*, at p. 455, "environmental pollution alone [i.e. as a subject matter of legislative authority] is itself all-pervasive. It is a by-product of everything we do. In man's relationship with his environment, waste is unavoidable."

[60] We agree completely with this statement. Almost everything we do involves "polluting" the environment in some way. The impugned provisions purport to grant regulatory authority over all aspects of any substance whose release into the environment "ha[s] or . . . may have an immediate or long-term harmful effect on the environment" (s. 11(*a*)). One wonders just what, if any, role will be left for the provinces in dealing with environmental pollution if the federal government is given such total control over the release of these substances. . . .

[61] For all of the above reasons, we are unable to uphold the impugned provisions of the *Act* under the federal criminal law power. That being said, we wish to add that none of this should be read as foredooming future attempts by Parliament to create an effective national—or, indeed, international—strategy for the protection of the environment. We agree with La Forest J. that achieving such a strategy is a public purpose of extreme importance and one of the major challenges of our time. There are, in this regard, many measures open to Parliament which will not offend the division of powers set out by the Constitution, notably the creation of environmental crimes. Nothing, in our view, prevents Parliament from outlawing certain kinds of behaviour on the basis that they are harmful to the environment. But such legislation must actually seek to *outlaw* this behaviour, not merely regulate it.

[62] Other potential avenues include the power to address interprovincial or international environmental concerns under the peace, order and good government power, which is discussed below. Parliament is not without power to act in pursuit of national policies on environmental protection. But it must do so pursuant to the balance of powers assigned by ss. 91 and 92. Environmental protection must be achieved in accordance with the Constitution, not in spite of it. . . .

[63] The impugned provisions are not justified under s. 91(27) of the *Constitution Act, 1867*. We will now consider the appellant's second argument, namely that the provisions may be upheld under the peace, order and good government power.

D. Peace, Order and Good Government

[64] The appellant argues that ss. 34 and 35 of the *Act* fall within the residual jurisdiction of Parliament under the peace, order and good government (POGG) power to legislate respecting matters of national concern, as provided for in the introductory paragraph of s. 91 of the *Constitution Act, 1867*. No argument is made with respect to the national emergency branch of POGG, and therefore only the national concern doctrine is at issue.

[65] The jurisprudence of this Court with respect to the peace, order and good government provision of the Constitution was thoroughly reviewed by Le Dain J. for the majority in *Crown Zellerbach, supra*. . . .

[66] Assuming that the protection of the environment and of human life and health against any and all potentially harmful substances could be a "new matter" which would fall under the POGG power, we must then determine whether that matter has the required "singleness, distinctiveness and indivisibility that clearly distinguishes it from matters of provincial concern" and whether its "impact on provincial jurisdiction . . . is reconcilable with the fundamental distribution of legislative power under the Constitution." Only if these criteria are satisfied will the matter be one of national concern. . . .

[75] The majority of this Court in *Crown Zellerbach*, *supra*, at pp. 436-37, found marine pollution to constitute a single, distinct, and indivisible subject-matter, on the basis that the *Ocean Dumping Control Act*, S.C. 1974-75-76, c. 55, distinguished between the pollution of salt water and the pollution of fresh water, both types of waters having different compositions and characteristics. In Part II of the *Canadian Environmental Protection Act*, there is no analogous clear distinction between types of toxic substances, either on the basis of degree of persistence and diffusion into the environment and the severity of their harmful effect or on the basis of their extraprovincial aspects. The lack of any distinctions similar to those in the legislation upheld in *Crown Zellerbach* means that the *Act* has a regulatory scope which can encroach widely upon several provincial heads of power, notably, s. 92(13) "property and civil rights," s. 92(16) "matters of a merely local or private nature," and s. 92(10) "local works and undertakings." In our view, this failure to circumscribe the ambit of the *Act* demonstrates that the enabling provisions lack the necessary singleness, distinctiveness and indivisibility.

[76] Another criterion that can be used to determine whether the subject matter sought to be regulated can be sufficiently distinguished from matters of provincial interest is to consider whether the failure of one province to enact effective regulation would have adverse effects on interests exterior to the province. This indicator has also been named the "provincial inability" test (see *Crown Zellerbach*, at pp. 432-34). If the impugned provisions of the *Act* were indeed restricted to chemical substances, like PCBs, whose effects are diffuse, persistent and serious, then a *prima facie* case could be made out as to the grave consequences of any one province failing to regulate effectively their emissions into the environment. However, the s. 11(*a*) threshold of "immediate or long-term harmful effect on the environment" also encompasses substances whose effects may only be temporary or local. Therefore, the notion of "toxic substances" as defined in the *Act* is inherently divisible. Those substances whose harmful effects are only temporary and localized would appear to be well within provincial ability to regulate. To the extent that Part II of the *Act* includes the regulation of "toxic substances" that may only affect the particular province within which they originate, the appellant bears a heavy burden to demonstrate that provinces themselves would be incapable of regulating such toxic emissions. It has not discharged this burden before this Court....

[78] These reasons confirm that the subject matter does not fulfill the characteristics of singleness, distinctiveness and indivisibility required to qualify as a national concern matter.

(ii) Impact on Provincial Jurisdiction

[79] Having concluded that the requirement of singleness, distinctiveness and indivisibility was not satisfied, it is unnecessary to examine the second criterion of the national concern test. The subject matter at issue does not qualify as a national concern matter and, since it was not suggested that it could be upheld as a matter of national emergency, it is therefore not justified by the peace, order and good government power.

E. The Trade and Commerce Power

[80] The interveners Pollution Probe et al. submit, in the alternative, that ss. 34 and 35 of the *Act* as well as the Interim Order can be sustained as an exercise of the federal trade and commerce power under s. 91(2) of the *Constitution Act, 1867*. More specifically, they argue that the "general trade and commerce power" recognized in *General Motors of Canada Ltd. v. City National Leasing*, [1989] 1 S.C.R. 641, can justify the federal regulations, which are aimed at controlling the use and release of toxic substances in the course of commercial activities....

[82] We reject these submissions for two main reasons. First, it is clear that the "pith and substance" of the impugned legislation does not concern trade and commerce, even if trade and commerce *may* be affected by the application of these provisions....

[83] Secondly, even if it could be assumed that certain parts of s. 34(1) of the *Act* were aimed at the regulation of trade and commerce (e.g. those paragraphs dealing with importing and exporting), the remainder of s. 34(1) would, based on the arguments adduced above, be *ultra vires* Parliament and would have to be struck down. Assuming that the "trade and commerce" elements could be saved, therefore, they would have to be "severed" from the paragraphs of s. 34(1) that would be struck down. It is not altogether clear that this could be done, particularly since the portion of the statute remaining after severance must be capable of standing independently of the severed portion. In this case, the paragraphs are too "inextricably bound" to be able to survive independently (see Hogg, *supra*, at p. 15-21). For these reasons, we cannot agree with the interveners' submission that the impugned legislation can be justified as an exercise of the federal trade and commerce power.

6. Conclusions and Disposition

[84] For the above reasons, we find that the impugned provisions are not justified under any of the heads of power granted to Parliament by s. 91. We would therefore declare them *ultra vires* and dismiss the appellant's appeal with costs.

PART TWO

Rights and Freedoms

A: FUNDAMENTAL RIGHTS AND FREEDOMS IN THE B.N.A. ACT

Reference re Alberta Statutes (Alberta Press Case), 1938

Until 1982, the Canadian Constitution, unlike that of the United States, did not contain a comprehensive bill of rights protecting a list of fundamental civil liberties from legislative encroachment. The enactment of the *Canadian Bill of Rights* in 1960 did not change that situation. The *Canadian Bill of Rights* was simply a federal statute, not an amendment to the *B.N.A. Act*. As such, it did not apply to the provinces and, even at the federal level, could be set aside by ordinary federal legislation. Besides, as the *Lavell and Bédard*[1] case shows, the Supreme Court was reluctant to give much weight to its provisions.

The absence of a comprehensive charter of rights in the *B.N.A. Act*, however, did not mean that no entrenched constitutional rights could be found there. The mistake was often made of stating that the powers of self-government had been exhaustively distributed between the two levels of government provided for in the *B.N.A. Act*. According to this "exhaustion theory," the only constitutional limitation on legislative supremacy in Canada prior to 1982 was the division of legislative powers. But this theory was a slight exaggeration. Sections 93 and 133 of the *B.N.A. Act* enshrine minority education and language rights[2] that it would appear cannot be diminished by either federal or provincial legislation without a constitutional amendment. In addition, constitutional safeguards of more fundamental rights may be implied by some of the institutional provisions of the *B.N.A. Act*. For instance, section 99, providing security of tenure for the judges of Superior Courts (Canada's trial courts for the most serious civil and criminal cases), restricts the legislative powers not only of the provinces but of the federal Parliament as well.[3]

In the *Alberta Press* case, constitutional protection of another cluster of rights of fundamental importance to the practice of liberal democracy was first suggested in the reasons given by Chief Justice Duff and Justice Cannon for declaring Alberta's *Accurate News and Information Act* unconstitutional. The federal government had asked the Supreme Court to examine the constitutional validity of this *Act* along with two other Social Credit Bills enacted by the Alberta Legislature in 1937. The other two *Acts* concerned some of the regulations and institutions required for a Social Credit system of credit and exchange. The *Accurate News and Information Act* was designed to ensure that newspaper presentation of Social Credit policy satisfied the government's criterion of accuracy. The Supreme Court unanimously found all three *Acts ultra vires*. Only its decision on the *Bank Taxation Act* was appealed to the Privy Council.

---

1 See case 21.

2 See the introduction to case 27.

3 See *McEvoy v. Attorney General for New Brunswick*, [1983] 1 S.C.R. 704.

Chief Justice Duff's opinion, with which Justice Davis concurred, characterized the *Accurate News and Information Act* as legislation affecting the "right of free public discussion of public affairs." This right, he maintained, is essential for the proper working of the parliamentary system of government called for by those sections of the *B.N.A. Act* vesting legislative power at the national level in a federal parliament and by the reference in the *B.N.A. Act's* preamble to "a constitution similar in Principle to that of the United Kingdom." He considered provincial legislation abrogating this right to be unconstitutional. While he stated that the federal Parliament was empowered to protect this right, he did not suggest that it was beyond Ottawa's power to restrict it. While Justice Cannon also held that the Alberta legislation should be struck down because it interfered with the freedom of discussion essential to a democratic state, he based his opinion on a more conventional division-of-powers ground. Legislation curtailing freedom of the press was traditionally part of the criminal law and therefore could be enacted only by the federal Parliament under its exclusive criminal law power.

If one looks only at the Court's prior decisions, the invocation of an implied bill of rights by three of its members is somewhat surprising, especially since it was unnecessary to invalidating the legislation. As Carl Baar notes, "[t]he Court had no record of support for civil liberties," and Justice Duff himself, a British Columbian, "had written opinions in previous years that reflected the anti-oriental sentiments of the Canadian west coast."[4] The answer to this riddle appears to lie in the political context in which the decision was made. The federal government had already disallowed earlier Social Credit legislation in Alberta and disallowance was seriously considered in this case. One argument in favour of disallowance was that it could be justified on the broad ground of protecting freedom of speech and press, while judicial invalidation was likely to focus on narrow jurisdictional considerations. On the other hand, too frequent resort to disallowance could be seen as an attack on the province by a heavy-handed central government. Ottawa chose a legal reference, but its own factum clearly invited an implied-bill-of-rights interpretation. In addition, most of the public criticism of the Press Bill was based on civil libertarian considerations. Given the widespread consensus on the importance of a free press, "it was both politically safe and politically heroic for the Supreme Court to defend civil liberties."[5] It was an inviting context for a new departure. ⁓

---

4   Carl Baar, "Using Process Theory to Explain Judicial Decision Making" (1986) 1 *Canadian Journal of Law and Society* 73.

5   *Ibid.* at 74.

REFERENCE RE ALBERTA STATUTES
[1938] 2 S.C.R. 100

Hearing: January 11, 12, 13, 14, 17, 1938; Judgment: March 4, 1938.

Present: Duff C.J. and Cannon, Crocket, Davis, Kerwin, and Hudson JJ.

DUFF C.J.:

[The Chief Justice first examined the constitutional validity of the *Bank Taxation Act* and the *Credit of Alberta Regulation Act* and concluded that both of these bills were *ultra vires*.]

We now turn to Bill No. 9.

This Bill contains two substantive provisions. Both of them impose duties upon newspapers published in Alberta which they are required to perform on the demand of "the Chairman," who is, by the interpretation clause, the Chairman of "the Board constituted by section 3 of [t]he *Alberta Social Credit Act*."

The Board, upon the acts of whose Chairman the operation of this statute depends, is, in point of law, a non-existent body (there is, in a word, no "board" in existence "constituted by section 3 of [t]he *Alberta Social Credit Act*") and both of the substantive sections, sections 3 and 4, are, therefore, inoperative. The same, indeed, may be said of sections 6 and 7 which are the enactments creating sanctions. It appears to us, furthermore, that this Bill is a part of the general scheme of Social Credit legislation, the basis of which is [t]he *Alberta Social Credit Act*; the Bill presupposes, as a condition of its operation, that [t]he *Alberta Social Credit Act* is validly enacted; and since that Act is *ultra vires*, the ancillary and dependent legislation must fall with it.

This is sufficient for disposing of the question referred to us but, we think, there are some further observations upon the Bill which may properly be made.

Under the constitution established by [t]he *British North America Act*, legislative power for Canada is vested in one Parliament consisting of the Sovereign, an upper house styled the Senate, and the House of Commons. Without entering in detail upon an examination of the enactments of the *Act* relating to the House of Commons, it can be said that these provisions manifestly contemplate a House of Commons which is to be, as the name itself implies, a representative body; constituted, that is to say, by members elected by such of the population of the united provinces as may be qualified to vote. The preamble of the statute, moreover, shows plainly enough that the constitution of the Dominion is to be similar in principle to that of the United Kingdom. The statute contemplates a parliament working under the influence of public opinion and public discussion. There can be no controversy that such institutions derive their efficacy from the free public discussion of affairs, from criticism and answer and counter-criticism, from attack upon policy and administration and defence and counter-attack; from the freest and fullest analysis and examination from every point of view of political proposals. This is signally true in respect of the discharge by Ministers of the Crown of their responsibility to Parliament, by members of Parliament of their duty to the electors, and by the electors themselves of their responsibilities in the election of their representatives.

The right of public discussion is, of course, subject to legal restrictions; those based upon considerations of decency and public order, and others conceived for the protection of various private and public interests with which, for example, the laws of defamation and sedition are concerned. In a word, freedom of discussion means, to quote the words of Lord Wright in *James v. Commonwealth* [[1936] A.C. 578, at 627], "freedom governed by law."

Even within its legal limits, it is liable to abuse and grave abuse, and such abuse is constantly exemplified before our eyes; but it is axiomatic that the practice of this right of free public discussion of public affairs, notwithstanding its incidental mischiefs, is the breath of life for parliamentary institutions.

We do not doubt that (in addition to the power of disallowance vested in the Governor General) the Parliament of Canada possesses authority to legislate for the protection of this right. That authority rests upon the principle that the powers requisite for the protection of the constitution itself arise by necessary implication from [t]he *British North America Act* as a whole (*Fort Frances Pulp & Power Co. Ltd. v. Manitoba Free Press Co. Ltd.* [[1923] A.C. 695]); and since the subject-matter in relation to which the power is exercised is not exclusively a provincial matter, it is necessarily vested in Parliament.

But this by no means exhausts the matter. Any attempt to abrogate this right of public debate or to suppress the traditional forms of the exercise of the right (in public meeting and through the press) would, in our opinion, be incompetent to the legislatures of the provinces, or to the legislature of any one of the provinces, as repugnant to the provisions of [t]he *British North America Act*, by which the Parliament of Canada is established as the legislative organ of the people of Canada under the Crown, and Dominion legislation enacted pursuant to the legislative authority given by those provisions. The subject matter of such legislation could not be described as a provincial matter purely; as in substance exclusively a matter of property and civil rights within the province, or a matter private or local within the province. It would not be, to quote the words of the judgment of the Judicial Committee in *Great West Saddlery Co. v. The King* [[1921] 2 A.C. 91, at 122], "legislation directed solely to the purposes specified in section 92"; and it would be invalid on the principles enunciated in that judgment and adopted in *Caron v. The King* [[1924] A.C. 999 at 1005-6].

The question, discussed in argument, of the validity of the legislation before us, considered as a wholly independent enactment having no relation to the *Alberta Social Credit Act*, presents no little difficulty. Some degree of regulation of newspapers everybody would concede to the provinces. Indeed, there is a very wide field in which the provinces undoubtedly are invested with legislative authority over newspapers; but the limit, in our opinion, is reached when the legislation effects such a curtailment of the exercise of the right of public discussion as substantially to interfere with the working of the parliamentary institutions of Canada as contemplated by the provisions of [t]he *British North America Act* and the statutes of the Dominion of Canada. Such a limitation is necessary, in our opinion, "in order," to adapt the words quoted above from the judgment in *Bank of Toronto v. Lambe* [(1887), 12 A.C. 575] "to afford scope" for the working of such parliamentary institutions. In this region of constitutional practice, it is not permitted to a provincial legislature to do indirectly what cannot be done directly (*Great West Saddlery Co. v. The King* [[1921] 2 A.C. 91 at 100]).

Section 129 of [t]he *British North America Act* is in these words:

> 129. Except as otherwise provided by this *Act*, all Laws in force in Canada, Nova Scotia or New Brunswick, at the Union, and all Courts of Civil and Criminal Jurisdiction, and all legal Commissions, Powers, and Authorities, and all Officers, Judicial, Administrative, and Ministerial, existing therein at the Union, shall continue in Ontario, Quebec, Nova Scotia, and New Brunswick respectively, as if the Union had not been made; subject nevertheless (except with respect to such as are enacted by or exist under *Acts* of the Parliament of Great Britain or of the Parliament of the United Kingdom of Great Britain and Ireland), to be repealed, abolished, or altered by the Parliament of Canada, or by the Legislature of the respective Province, according to the Authority of the Parliament or of that Legislature under this *Act*.

The law by which the right of public discussion is protected existed at the time of the enactment of [t]he *British North America Act* and, as far as Alberta is concerned, at the date on which the *Alberta Act* came into force, the 1st of September, 1905. In our opinion (on the broad principle of the cases mentioned which has been recognized as limiting the scope of general words defining the legislative authority of the Dominion) the Legislature of Alberta has not the capacity under section 129 to alter that law by legislation obnoxious to the principle stated.

The legislation now under consideration manifestly places in the hands of the Chairman of the Social Credit Commission autocratic powers which, it may well be thought, could, if arbitrarily wielded, be employed to frustrate in Alberta these rights of the Crown and the people of Canada as a whole. We do not, however, find it necessary to express an opinion upon the concrete question whether or not this particular measure is invalid as exceeding the limits indicated above.

The answer to the question concerning this Bill is that it is *ultra vires*.

CANNON J.:

[Justice Cannon first examined the *Bank Taxation Act* and the *Credit of Alberta Regulation Act* and concluded that both were *ultra vires*.]

The third question put to us is the following:

> Is Bill No. 9, entitled *An Act to ensure the Publication of Accurate News and Information*, or any of the provisions thereof and in what particular or particulars or to what extent *intra vires* of the legislature of the province of Alberta?

. . . The preamble of the bill, which I will hereafter call the "Press bill" recites that it is

> expedient and in the public interest that the newspapers published in the Province should furnish to the people of the Province statements made by the authority of the Government of the Province as to the true and exact objects of the policy of the Government and as to the hindrances to or difficulties in achieving such objects to the end that the people may be informed with respect thereto.

Section 3 provides that any proprietor, editor, publisher or manager of any newspaper published in the province shall, when required to do so by the Chairman of the Board constituted by section 3 of the *Alberta Social Credit Act*, publish in that newspaper any statement furnished by the Chairman which has for its object the correction or amplification of any statement relating to any policy or activity of the government of the province published by that newspaper within the next preceding thirty-one days.

And section 4 provides that the proprietor, etc., of any newspaper upon being required by the Chairman in writing shall within twenty-four hours after the delivery of the requirement

> make a return in writing setting out every source from which any information emanated, as to any statement

contained in any issue of the newspaper published within sixty days of the making of the requirement and the names, addresses and occupations of all persons by whom such information was furnished to the newspaper and the name and address of the writer of any editorial, article or news item contained in any such issue of the newspaper.

Section 5 denies any action for libel on account of the publication of any statement pursuant to the *Act*.

Section 6 enacts that in the event of a proprietor, etc., of any newspaper being guilty of any contravention of any of the provisions of the *Act*, the Lieutenant-Governor-in-Council, upon a recommendation of the Chairman, may by order prohibit,

> (a) the publication of such newspaper either for a definite time or until further order;
> (b) the publication in any newspaper of anything written by any person specified in the order;
> (c) the publication of any information emanating from any person or source specified in the order.

Section 7 provides for penalties for contraventions or defaults in complying with any requirement of the *Act*.

The policy referred to in the preamble of the Press bill regarding which the people of the province are to be informed from the government standpoint is undoubtedly the Social Credit policy of the government. The administration of the bill is in the hands of the Chairman of the Social Credit Board who is given complete and discretionary power by the bill. "Social Credit," according to sec. 2(b) of ch. 3, 1937, second session, of [t]he *Alberta Social Credit Amendment Act* is

> the power resulting from the belief inherent within society that its individual members in association can gain the objectives they desire;

and the objectives in which the people of Alberta must have a firm and unshaken belief are the monetization of credit and the creation of a provincial medium of exchange instead of money to be used for the purpose of distributing to Albertans loans without interest, per capita dividends and discount rates to purchase goods from retailers. This free distribution would be based on the unused capacity of the industries and people of the province of Alberta to produce goods and services, which capacity remains unused on account of the lack or absence of purchasing power in the consumers in the province. The purchasing power would equal or absorb this hitherto unused capacity to produce goods and services by the issue of Treasury Credit certificates against a Credit Fund or Provincial credit account established by the Commission each year representing the monetary value of this "unused capacity"—which is also called "Alberta credit."

It seems obvious that this kind of credit cannot succeed unless every one should be induced to believe in it and help it along. The word "credit" comes from the latin: *credere*, to believe. It is, therefore, essential to control the sources of information of the people of Alberta, in order to keep them immune from any vacillation in their absolute faith in the plan of the government. The Social Credit doctrine must become, for the people of Alberta, a sort of religious dogma of which a free and uncontrolled discussion is not permissible. The bill aims to control any statement relating to any policy or activity of the government of the province and declares this object to be a matter of public interest. The bill does not regulate the relations of the newspapers' owners with private individual members of the public, but deals exclusively with expressions of opinion by the newspapers concerning government policies and activities. The pith and substance of the bill is to regulate the press of Alberta from the viewpoint of public policy by preventing the public from being misled or deceived as to any policy or activity of the Social Credit Government and by reducing any opposition to silence or bring upon it ridicule and public contempt.

I agree with the submission of the Attorney-General for Canada that this bill deals with the regulation of the press of Alberta, not from the viewpoint of private wrongs or civil injuries resulting from any alleged infringement or privation of civil rights which belong to individuals, considered as individuals, but from the viewpoint of public wrongs or crimes, i.e., involving a violation of the public rights and duties to the whole community, considered as a community, in its social aggregate capacity.

Do the provisions of this bill, as alleged by the Attorney-General for Canada, invade the domain of criminal law and trench upon the exclusive legislative jurisdiction of the Dominion of this regard?

The object of an amendment of the criminal law, as a rule, is to deprive the citizen of the right to do that [which], apart from the amendment, he could lawfully do. Sections 130 to 136 of the *Criminal Code* deal with seditious words and seditious publications; and sect. 133(a) reads as follows:—

> No one shall be deemed to have a seditious intention only because he intends in good faith,—
> (a) to show that His Majesty has been misled or mistaken in his measures; or
> (b) to point out errors or defect in the government or constitution of the United Kingdom, or of any part of it, or of Canada or any province thereof, or in either House of Parliament of the United Kingdom or of Canada, or in any legislature, or in the administration of justice; or to excite His Majesty's subjects to attempt to procure, by lawful means, the alteration of any matter of state; or

(c) to point out, in order to their removal, matters which are producing or have a tendency to produce feelings of hatred and ill-will between different classes of His Majesty's subjects.

It appears that in England, at first, criticism of any government policy was regarded as a crime involving severe penalties and punishable as such; but since the passing of *Fox's Libel Act* in 1792, the considerations now found in the above article of our criminal code that it is not criminal to point out errors in the Government of the country and to urge their removal by lawful means have been admitted as a valid defence in a trial for libel.

Now, it seems to me that the Alberta legislature by this retrograde Bill is attempting to revive the old theory of the crime of seditious libel by enacting penalties, confiscation of space in newspapers and prohibitions for actions which, after due consideration by the Dominion Parliament, have been declared innocuous and which, therefore, every citizen of Canada can do lawfully and without hindrance or fear of punishment. It is an attempt by the legislature to amend the *Criminal Code* in this respect and to deny the advantage of sect. 133(a) to the Alberta newspaper publishers.

Under the British system, which is ours, no political party can erect a prohibitory barrier to prevent the electors from getting information concerning the policy of the government. Freedom of discussion is essential to enlighten public opinion in a democratic State; it cannot be curtailed without affecting the right of the people to be informed through sources independent of the government concerning matters of public interest. There must be an untrammelled publication of the news and political opinions of the political parties contending for ascendancy. As stated in the preamble of [t]he *British North America Act*, our constitution is and will remain, unless radically changed, "similar in principle to that of the United Kingdom." At the time of Confederation, the United Kingdom was a democracy. Democracy cannot be maintained without its foundation: free public opinion and free discussion throughout the nation of all matters affecting the State within the limits set by the criminal code and the common law. Every

inhabitant in Alberta is also a citizen of the Dominion. The province may deal with his property and civil rights of a local and private nature within the province; but the province cannot interfere with his status as a Canadian citizen and his fundamental right to express freely his untrammelled opinion about government policies and discuss matters of public concern. The mandatory and prohibitory provisions of the Press Bill are, in my opinion, *ultra vires* of the provincial legislature. They interfere with the free working of the political organization of the Dominion. They have a tendency to nullify the political rights of the inhabitants of Alberta, as citizens of Canada, and cannot be considered as dealing with matters purely private and local in that province. The federal parliament is the sole authority to curtail, if deemed expedient and in the public interest, the freedom of the press in discussing public affairs and the equal rights in that respect of all citizens throughout the Dominion. These subjects were matters of criminal law before Confederation, have been recognized by Parliament as criminal matters and have been expressly dealt with by the criminal code. No province has the power to reduce in that province the political rights of its citizens as compared with those enjoyed by the citizens of other provinces of Canada. Moreover, citizens outside the province of Alberta have a vital interest in having full information and comment, favourable and unfavourable, regarding the policy of the Alberta government and concerning events in that province which would, in the ordinary course, be the subject of Alberta newspapers' news items and articles.

I would, therefore, answer the question as to Bill No. 9 in the negative.

[Justice Davis concurred with Chief Justice Duff. Justices Kerwin, Crocket, and Hudson all concluded that the three bills were *ultra vires*. However, their conclusion that the Press Bill was *ultra vires* was based not on the considerations regarding freedom of the press advanced by Chief Justice Duff and Justice Cannon, but on the much narrower ground that the *Act* was ancillary to and dependent on the *Alberta Social Credit Act*, which was itself *ultra vires*.]

20 Saumur v. Quebec and Attorney General of Quebec, 1953

In the 1950s, the Supreme Court decided seven Quebec appeals that raised important civil liberties issues. All involved policies of the Quebec government directed against political or religious minorities in the province. In all seven, the Supreme Court reversed the Quebec Court of Appeal and upheld the claim of the political or religious minority against the Quebec government. Only three of the cases involved a constitutional challenge based on the *B.N.A. Act*.[1] The seven cases indicated that, despite the absence of either a constitutional or statutory bill of rights, the Canadian legal system provided considerable protection for the communicative freedoms of unpopular minorities, at least from attacks by oppressive provincial governments.

In *Saumur*, a Jehovah's Witness challenged the constitutional validity of a Quebec City bylaw passed under the Charter of the city of Quebec, prohibiting the distribution in the streets of any book, pamphlet, or tract without the permission of the chief of police. The significance of this case went far beyond the immediate question of the validity of the Quebec City bylaw. As far as the Jehovah's Witnesses were concerned, it was designed to test the general competence of the provinces to restrict a Canadian citizen's rights to freedom of expression and freedom of religious practice. Saumur claimed that these rights were guaranteed by the Constitution, referring in particular to the preamble of the *B.N.A. Act*, and also by statute, referring here to a number of Acts including the *Freedom of Worship Act*, a pre-Confederation Canadian statute that had been re-enacted by the Quebec legislature in 1941. Saumur's action was rejected in the Superior Court of Quebec and his appeal against this judgment was dismissed by the Quebec Court of Queen's Bench.

Before the Supreme Court of Canada, Saumur was more successful—at least on the immediate issue. By a five-to-four majority the Supreme Court ruled that the bylaw did not operate so as to prevent Saumur from distributing his tracts. Four of the five judges who made up the majority (Justices Rand, Locke, Kellock, and Estey) rested their conclusion on the broad ground that it was beyond the jurisdiction of a province to restrict freedom of religious expression. But the deciding vote was cast by Justice Kerwin, whose decision was based on the very different ground that the bylaw, although *intra vires*, must not conflict with the *Freedom of Worship Act*. Contrary to the view of the other members of the majority, Justice Kerwin held that the matter of religious freedom (as well as freedom of the press) was subject to provincial jurisdiction. His opinion would consequently entitle the Quebec legislature to amend the *Freedom of Worship Act* so as to exclude sects like the Jehovah's Witnesses from its protection. Indeed, under the leadership of Premier Duplessis, the Quebec

---

1 Besides *Saumur*, the other two were *Switzman* and *Birks*, which are discussed later in this introduction. The other four Quebec cases were *Boucher v. The King*, [1951] S.C.R. 265 (interpretation of the seditious libel section of the *Criminal Code*); *Chaput v. Romain*, [1955] S.C.R. 834 (police powers to break up religious meetings); *Roncarelli v. Duplessis*, [1959] S.C.R. 121 (the Premier of Quebec's power to remove a restaurant liquor licence because of his disapproval of the proprietor's political activities); and *Lamb v. Benoit*, [1959] S.C.R. 321 (police powers to detain persons for distributing pamphlets considered by the police to be seditious).

legislature lost little time in taking advantage of the loophole created by Justice Kerwin's opinion and, shortly after this decision, amended the *Freedom of Worship Act* so that it would not apply to the distribution of Jehovah's Witness literature. Saumur initiated an action to have this amendment declared unconstitutional, but the Supreme Court of Canada upheld a decision of the Quebec Court of Appeal dismissing the action on the ground that, since the new legislation had not actually been applied against the Jehovah's Witnesses, the case did not involve a real dispute or *lis*, but only an academic question.

On the larger issue of the constitutional status of civil liberties, the Supreme Court's decision in the *Saumur* case was inconclusive and confusing. Three sharply contrasting views were expressed on the general relationship of civil liberties to the division of powers and not one of these views could command the support of a majority. At one extreme, three judges (Chief Justice Rinfret and Justices Taschereau and Kerwin) adopted the completely novel position that freedom of religious practice was subject to provincial jurisdiction, holding that religious freedom was a "civil right in the province" and hence, as a subject matter of legislation, fell under section 92(13) of the *B.N.A. Act*. In direct contradiction, four judges (Justices Rand, Locke, Kellock, and Estey) denied that the phrase "civil rights" in section 92(13) embraced such rights as the right to the free exercise of one's religion. On a number of grounds, they held that the *B.N.A. Act* removed from the provinces the power of legislating for the purpose of curtailing religious freedom. All four of these judges cited the preamble of the *B.N.A. Act* in support of their conclusion and two of them (Justices Rand and Locke) explicitly associated freedom of religious expression with the rights that Chief Justice Duff in *Reference re Alberta Statutes* had deduced from the preamble. Justices Locke and Estey considered that the power of limiting religious freedom lay exclusively with Parliament under its "criminal law" power. Three members of this group also cited the safeguards provided by section 93 of the *B.N.A. Act* against provincial infringement of the educational rights of religious denominations as implying that the provinces have no jurisdiction in relation to religious freedom. Finally, an intermediate position adopted by Justices Cartwright and Fauteux would deny that a question of civil liberties might be considered to be the main ingredient of a piece of legislation for the purpose of bringing it under one of the heads of power in the *B.N.A. Act*. Restrictions on civil liberties might be incidental effects of laws but not their pith and substance. Thus, both Parliament and the provinces could validly limit freedom of worship, providing they did so in the course of legislating on some other subject that lay within their respective powers.

Saumur was the high tide of the implied-bill-of-rights jurisprudence. Two other Quebec laws restricting civil liberties were struck down by the Supreme Court, but in each case on the ground that they encroached on the federal Parliament's criminal law power. *Birks*[2] dealt with a Quebec statute authorizing municipal bylaws for closing stores on Roman Catholic holy days, and *Switzman*[3] concerned the notorious Padlock law, passed in 1937, authorizing the police to close premises on proof that they were being used to propagate Communism. In these cases, only Justices Rand, Kellock, and Abbott looked on the challenged laws as restrictions of fundamental freedoms. The majority based its opinion on the division of

---

2   *Henry Birks and Sons (Montreal) Ltd. v. the City of Montreal*, [1955] S.C.R. 799.

3   *Switzman v. Elbling and A.G. Quebec*, [1957] S.C.R. 285.

powers and the criminal law power. The denouement of the implied-bill-of-rights doctrine came in 1978, in *Dupond*,[4] when the Court's majority rejected a challenge to a Montreal bylaw and ordinance, passed during a period of FLQ terrorist incidents, that empowered the police to prevent gatherings and demonstrations of all kinds in public places. In dismissing arguments based on the implied bill of rights, Justice Beetz, who wrote the majority opinion, said that "[n]one of the freedoms (speech, assembly and association, press, and religion) is enshrined in the constitution so as to be above the reach of competent legislation." ⁓

---

4   *Attorney General of Canada and Dupond v. City of Montreal*, [1978] 2 S.C.R. 770.

SAUMUR v. CITY OF QUEBEC AND ATTORNEY GENERAL OF QUEBEC
[1953] 2 S.C.R. 299

Hearing: December 9, 10, 11, 12, 15, 16, 17, 1952; Judgment: October 6, 1953.

Present: Rinfret C.J. and Kerwin, Taschereau, Rand, Kellock, Estey, Locke, Cartwright, and Fauteux JJ.

Intervener: The Attorney General for Quebec.

The dissenting judgment of Rinfret C.J. and Taschereau J. was delivered by

RINFRET C.J. (dissenting): Dépouillée de son extravagante mise-en-scène et réduite a sa véritable dimension, cette cause, à mon avis, est vraiment très simple. Elle n'a sûrement pas l'ampleur et l'importance qu'ont tenté de lui donner les Témoins de Jéhovah par le truchement de M. Laurier Saumur, l'appelant, se désignant comme un missionnaire-évangéliste.

Il s'agit de la validité d'un règlement municipal et il y a probablement eu des centaines et des centaines de causes de ce genre depuis la Confédération. Si, par contre, cette catégorie de causes n'a pas été soumise très fréquemment à la Cour Suprême du Canada, c'est uniquement à raison de son peu d'importance relative et de son application restreinte, dans chaque cas, au territoire de la municipalité concernée.

Voici le texte du règlement attaqué:

Règlement n° 184

1° Il est, par le présent règlement, défendu de distribuer dans les rues de la Cité de Québec, aucun livre, pamphlet, brochure, circulaire, fascicule quelconque sans avoir au préalable obtenu pour ce faire la permission par écrit du Chef de Police.

2° Toute personne qui contreviendra au présent règlement sera passible d'une amende avec ou sans les frais, et à défaut du paiement immédiat de ladite amende avec ou sans les frais, selon le cas, d'un emprisonnement, le montant de ladite amende et le terme d'emprisonnement

à être fixé par la Cour du Recorder de la Cité de Québec, à sa discrétion; mais ladite amende ne dépassera pas cent dollars, et l'emprisonnement n'excédera pas trois mois de calendrier; ledit emprisonnement cependant, devant cesser en tout temps avant l'expiration du terme fixé par le paiement de ladite amende et des frais, selon le cas; et si l'infraction est réitérée, cette récidive constituera, jour par jour, après sommation ou arrestation, une offense séparée.

L'appelant, invoquant sa qualité de sujet de Sa Majesté le Roi et de résident dans la Cité de Québec, alléguant en outre qu'il est un missionnaire-évangéliste et l'un des Témoins de Jéhovah, déclare qu'il considère de son devoir de prêcher la Bible, soit oralement, soit en distribuant des publications sous forme de livres, opuscules, périodiques, feuillets, etc., de maison en maison et dans les rues.

Il prétend que le règlement n° 184, reproduit plus haut, a pour effet de rendre illégale cette distribution de littérature sans l'approbation écrite du Chef de Police de la Cité de Québec. Il ajoute qu'en sa qualité de citoyen canadien il a un droit absolu à l'expression de ses opinions et que cela découle de son droit à la liberté de parole, la liberté de la presse et le libre exercice de son culte envers Dieu, tel que garanti par la Constitution britannique non écrite, par l'*Acte de l'Amérique britannique du Nord* généralement, et également par les Statuts de la province de Québec, spécialement la *Loi concernant la liberté des cultes et le bon ordre dans les églises et leurs alentours* (S.R.Q. 1941, c. 307).

Il allègue que la Cité de Québec et la province de Québec n'ont aucune juridiction, soit en loi, soit constitutionnellement, pour adopter un règlement tel que ci-dessus, et que ce dernier est *ultra vires*, inconstitutionnel, illégal et nul. ...

L'intimée, la Cité de Québec, a plaidé que le règlement n° 184 était une loi municipale légalement passée dans l'exercice des pouvoirs de réglementation de la Cité et conforme à son acte d'incorporation; que la loi de la province, en vertu de laquelle le règlement a été adopté, est constitutionnelle, légale et valide; que le règlement concerne la propreté, le bon ordre, la paix et la sécurité publiques, la prévention de troubles et émeutes et se rapporte à l'économie intérieure et au bon gouvernement local de la ville; que le demandeur a systématiquement contrevenu à ce règlement de façon délibérée et s'est obstinément refusé à s'y soumettre; qu'il n'a jamais demandé et, par conséquent, n'a pu obtenir de permis pour distribuer ses pamphlets dans la ville de Québec et qu'il a ignoré d'une manière absolue si le règlement est susceptible de le priver d'aucun de ses droits, ayant préféré y désobéir de son plein gré. . . .

La plaidoirie écrite allège, en outre, que l'appelant n'est pas un ministre du culte et que l'organisation dont il fait partie n'est pas une église ni une religion. Au contraire, les pamphlets ou tracts qu'elle insiste à distribuer sans autorisation ont un caractère provocateur et injurieux, ne sont pas des gestes religieux mais des actes anti-sociaux qui étaient et sont de nature à troubler la paix publique et la tranquillité et la sécurité des paisibles citoyens dans la Cité de Québec, ou ils risquent de provoquer des désordres. Il est malvenu en fait et en droit d'invoquer des libertés de parole, de presse et de culte, qui ne sont aucunement concernées en l'occurrence; il n'a jamais été persécuté et, si la Cité de Québec a mis en vigueur son règlement, ce ne fut que pour remplir ses obligations envers le bien commun, l'ordre public exigeant que le règlement soit dûment appliqué dans la Cité.

Après une longue enquête et la production de quelque chose comme soixante-quinze exhibits, avec en plus des mémoires rédigés par l'abbé Gagné, le très révérend Doyen Evans, le rabbin Frank et M. Damien Jasmin, le juge de première instance a maintenu la défense et rejeté l'action de l'appelant. Ce jugement a été confirmé dans son intégrité par la Cour du Banc de la Reine (en appel). . . .

[The Chief Justice then listed the powers asserted in the *Cities and Towns Act.* These included the power of regulating the distribution of literature in the streets.]

Il est non moins clair que l'*Acte de l'Amérique britannique du Nord 1867*, dans la distribution qu'elle fait des pouvoirs législatifs, aux paragraphes 91 et 92 attribue, dans chaque province, à la Législature, le pouvoir exclusif de faire des lois relatives aux institutions municipales dans la province (par. 8), à la propriété et les droits civils dans la province (par. 13) et généralement à toutes les matières d'une nature purement locale et privée dans la province (par. 16).

Il serait vraiment fantastique de prétendre que quelques-uns des pouvoirs ci-dessus mentionnés et que l'on trouve dans la *Loi des Cités et Villes* de 1a province de Québec, pourraient relever du domaine fédéral. Je ne me représente pas facilement le Parlement fédéral entreprenant d'adopter des lois sur aucune de ces matières (Voir le jugement du Conseil Privé

dans *Hodge v. The Queen* [(1883) 9 App. Cas. 117, 131, 133, 134]).

Je ne comprends pas, d'ailleurs, que le procureur de l'appelant dirige son argumentation à l'encontre de ce principe général. Il demande à la Cour de s'écarter du texte du règlement et il cherche à y trouver un motif qui serait celui, qu'il avait déjà allégué dans sa déclaration, "que ce règlement avait été passé spécialement dans le but de limiter les activités du demandeur et des Témoins de Jéhovah."

Il est à remarquer que le règlement lui-même ne dit rien de tel; il s'applique à tous, quelle que soit leur nationalité, leur doctrine ou leur religion. Mais, en plus, le juge de première instance a décidé en fait qu'il "n'a pas été prouvé que ce règlement avait été passé spécialement dans ce but." D'autre part, en matière d'exces de pouvoirs, c'est toujours au mérite ("*pith and substance*") de la législation qu'il faut s'arrêter. Ce que le règlement vise est uniquement l'usage des rues pour fins de distribution. En outre que, ainsi que l'a décidé le juge de la Cour Supérieure, aucun motif, aucune arrière-pensée n'a été dévoilée par la preuve faite à l'enquête, c'est une idée erronée que de chercher à attribuer un motif à une loi qui n'en mentionne pas. Un règlement peut être valide même si le but du conseil municipal est mauvais. . . .

La seule question que les tribunaux ont à examiner est celle de savoir si la Cité de Québec avait le pouvoir d'adopter ce règlement. Nous n'avons pas à chercher derrière le texte qu'elle a adopté pour voir quel a pu être son but en ce faisant. J'irai même plus loin et je dirai que l'usage des rues d'une municipalité est indiscutablement une question du domaine municipal et une question locale. Je cherche encore en vertu de quoi on pourrait prétendre que cette matière ne tombe pas exclusivement dans la catégorie des sujets attribués aux provinces en vertu de l'article 92 dé l'*Acte de 1'Amérique britannique du Nord*; et, dans ce cas, même s'il est admis que le droit de culte est du domaine fédéral, le pouvoir de contrôle des rues municipales, étant un sujet spécifiquement attribué aux provinces, il aurait préséance sur le pouvoir supposé du Parlement fédéral de légiférer en matière de culte. Il est de jurisprudence constante que du moment qu'un sujet est spécialement attribué au domaine provincial par l'article 92, il a préséance et priorité sur tout pouvoir que prétendrait exercer le fédéral, en vertu des pouvoirs généraux mentionnés dans l'article 91. . . .

Ironie du sort, les Témoins de Jéhovah qui, dans leurs publications, affirment catégoriquement non seulement qu'ils ne constituent pas une religion, mais qu'ils sont opposés à toute religion et que les religions sont une invention du démon, sont maintenant devant les tribunaux du Canada pour demander protection au nom de la religion; et, à cette fin l'encontre de la constitutionnalité des lois municipales de la province de Québec, ils sont contraints d'invoquer une loi de la province de Québec, à savoir: la *Loi concernant la liberté des cultes et du bon ordre dans les églises et leurs alentours* (c. 307, S.R.Q. 1941).

Cette loi, invoquée par eux, contient l'article suivant:

> 2. La jouissance et le libre exercice du culte de toute profession religieuse, sans distinction ni préférence, mais de manière à ne pas servir d'excuse à la licence ni à autoriser des pratiques incompatibles avec la paix et la sûreté de la province, sont permis par la constitution et les lois de cette province à tous les sujets de Sa Majesté qui y vivent. S.R. 1925, c. 198, a. 2.

C'est bien ainsi que l'appelant a posé le problème dans sa déclaration:

> ... *his unqualified right as a Canadian citizen to the expression of his views on the issues of the day and in employing thereby his right of freedom of speech, freedom of the press and free exercise of worship of Almighty God as guaranteed by the unwritten British Constitution, by the provisions of the* British North America Act *generally and, in particular, in its preamble and sections 91, 92 and 129, as well as by the statute of the Province of Quebec generally and in particular, by "An Act Respecting Peddlers," (R.S.Q. 1941, Chapter 230, especially section 8 thereof); and by "An Act Respecting Licences," (R.S.Q. 1941, Chapter 76, especially section 82 thereof); and by "An Act Respecting Freedom of Worship and the Maintenance of Good Order In and Near Places of Public Worship," (R.S.Q. 1941, Chapter 307, especially section 2 thereof);*

Il n'y à pas lieu de s'arrêter à la référence à la *Loi concernant les colporteurs* et à la *Loi des licences*.

Le procureur de l'appelant ne s'est pas non plus expliqué sur ce qu'il entend par *"The unwritten British Constitution"* comme gouvernant les pouvoirs respectifs du Parlement canadien et des Législatures provinciales (tels qu'ils sont définis dans les articles 91 et 92 de l'*Acte de l'Amérique britannique du Nord*). C'est cette loi qui contient la Constitution du Canada et le Conseil Privé, à plusieurs reprises, a déclaré que les pouvoirs ainsi distribués entre le Parlement et les législatures convraient absolument tous les pouvoirs que pouvait exercer le Canada comme entité politique. Mais l'appelant prétend que la question de l'exercice du culte est exclusivement de la juridiction du Parlement fédéral et, en particulier, que les prescriptions du règlement attaqué seraient couvertes par le début de l'article 91 qui autorise l'adoption de "lois pour la paix, l'ordre et le bon gouvernement du Canada," ou la *Loi criminelle*.

Au sujet de la première prétention, il suffit de poursuivre la lecture de l'article 91 pour constater que le pouvoir du

Parlement fédéral relativement à la paix, l'ordre et le bon gouvernement du Canada se bornent à toutes les matières ne tombant pas dans les "catégories de sujets exclusivement assignés par le présent acte aux Législatures des provinces." Comme il à été invariablement décidé par le Conseil Privé et conformément, d'ailleurs, au texte précis que nous venons de citer, des que la matière est couverte par l'un des paragraphes de l'article 92, elle devient du domaine exclusif des législatures de chaque province et elle est soustraite à la juridiction du Parlement fédéral. Naturellement, nous ne parlons plus ici du contrôle des rues municipales, car il est évident que, dans ce cas, les paragraphes 8, 13 et 16 de l'article 92 (comme d'ailleurs nous l'avons vu plus haut) attribuent cette juridiction exclusivement aux législatures. Mais, si nous comprenons bien la prétention, c'est que la garantie de l'exercice du culte doit venir du Parlement fédéral et n'appartient pas aux législatures. Nous disons bien qu'elle doit venir, car il est très certain que, pour le moment, elle n'existe pas ailleurs que dans la *Loi concernant la liberté des culte*s invoquée par l'appelant dans sa déclaration (S.R.Q. 1941, c. 307).

La difficulté qu'éprouve ici l'appelant résulte de plusieurs raisons:

Premièrement:—Son droit de distribuer des pamphlets religieux ne constitue pas l'exercice d'un culte d'une profession religieuse.

Deuxièmement:—A tout événement, la jouissance et le libre exercice du culte d'une profession religieuse ne jouit pas, en vertu du chapitre 307, S.R.Q. 1941, d'une autorisation absolue, mais il faut que ce culte s'exerce "de manière a ne pas servir d'excuse a la licence, ni à autoriser des pratiques incompatibles avec la paix et la sûreté de la province."

Troisièmement:—L'exercice du culte est un droit civil et, par conséquent, tombe sous le paragraphe 13 de l'article 92 de l'*Acte de l'Amérique britannique du Nord*. Il est donc du domaine provincial.

Le premier point ci-dessus dépend d'une question de fait. Or, l'appelant a fait entendre comme témoin un monsieur Hayden C. Covington, qui s'est décrit comme *"ordained minister of the gospel, and lawyer, 124 Columbia Heights, Brooklyn, New York."* Au cours de ce témoignage, ce témoin a identifié un nombre considérable de publications dont il a déclaré qu'elles contenaient la doctrine des Témoins de Jéhovah, en ajoutant: *"They comprise the official view, doctrines and principles advocated and taught by Jehovah's Witnesses at the date of publication of each of such books."* Or, dans toutes ces publications, il est affirmé que les Témoins de Jéhovah ne sont pas une religion; que, au contraire, leur but est de combattre toutes les religions et que la religion est une invention du démon....

Pour ce qui est du deuxième point ci-dessus mentionné, il faut réitérer que l'article 2 du chapitre 307 ne permet pas la jouissance et le libre exercise du culte d'une profession religieuse d'une façon absolue. Il faut que cela ne "serve pas d'excuse à la licence, ni a des pratiques incompatibles avec la paix et la sûreté de la province." C'est le texte même de la loi.

Si donc, a l'encontre de la preuve, il fallait décider que les Témoins de Jéhovah pratiquent un culte, il n'en faudrait pas moins, en vertu du texte de la *Loi concernant la liberté des cultes*, que la province ou la municipalité ait le droit de contrôler cet exercice "de manière à ne pas servir d'excuse a la licence, ni a autoriser des pratiques incompatibles avec la paix et la sûreté de la province."

Puisque les Témoins de Jéhovah prétendent que leur profession religieuse consiste a distribuer des tracts religieux, il s'ensuit que la province ou la municipalité, a laquelle la province délègue ce pouvoir, a le droit d'examiner les pamphlets religieux que l'on entend distribuer, de façon à en autoriser ou non la distribution.

A cet égard, je le répète, les Témoins de Jéhovah, ayant pris la position qu'ils ne demanderaient pas l'autorisation et qu'ils ne soumettraient pas la littérature qu'ils voulaient distribuer, nous n'avons aucune preuve au dossier susceptible de nous permettre de savoir si cette littérature tombait ou non dans les exceptions prévues par l'article 2 du chapitre 307. Mais, si nous croyions justifiés de prendre pour acquit que cette littérature serait de la même nature que les livres et les tracts qui ont été produits au dossier, ou encore qu'elle contiendrait les déclarations faites par le vice-président Covington, il serait inconcevable qu'une municipalité ne put empêcher la circulation dans ses rues de cette littérature que son conseil pourrait certainement considérer comme constituant de la licence ou des pratiques incompatibles avec la paix et la sûreté de la province; et, des lors, comme tombant dans l'exception exprimée dans l'article 2.

Voici, en effet, ce qu'on trouve dans le témoignage de M. Covington:

> Q. Are you informed that the religion of a greater part of the people in this province and in this city is Roman Catholic?—A. Yes, I have that information.

En fait, il est notoire que 90 pour cent de la population de la Cité de Québec est catholique romaine et 45 pour cent de la population du Canada appartient à la même religion.

On lui demande alors de lire les passages suivants des publications des Témoins de Jéhovah:

> ... Religion is the adulteress and idolatress that befriends and commits religious fornication with the political and commercial elements. She is the lover of this world and blesses the world from the balcony of the Vatican and in the pulpits. Religion, whose most powerful representative has ruled from Rome for sixteen centuries, traces her origin all the way back to Babylon of Nimrod's founding, and organized religion deservedly bears the name Babylon ... I will shew unto thee the judgment of the great whore (or idolatress) that sitteth upon many waters: with whom the kings of the earth have committed fornication, and the inhabitants of the earth have been made drunk with the wine of her fornication ... full of abominations and filthiness of her fornication; and upon her forehead was a name written, MYSTERY, BABYLON THE GREAT, THE MOTHER OF HARLOTS AND ABOMINATIONS OF THE EARTH.

Les citations qui précèdent sont tirées de l'exhibit D-49, aux pages 345 et 346.

Après avoir mis le témoin Covington en présence des extraits ci-dessus, l'avocat de la Cité de Québec lui demande:

> Q. Do you consider that writing such books with such insults against another religion, in fact the religion practised by the people of this province or city, a proper means of preaching the gospel?—A. I do.

Et au cours de cette réponse, il dit:

> ... history abundantly attests to the fact that the Roman Catholic Hierarchy has had relationship with the world and has had part tacitly in the wars between the nations and the destruction of nations.

Un peu plus loin:

> Q. Do you consider [it] necessary for your organization to attack the other religions, in fact, the Catholic, the Protestant and the Jews?—A. Indeed. The reason for that is because the Almighty God commands that error shall be exposed and not persons or nations. ...

Qui oserait prétendre que des pamphlets contenant les déclarations qui précèdent, distribués dans une cité comme celle de Québec, ne constitueraient pas une pratique incompatible avec la paix et la sûreté de la Cité ou de la province? Quel tribunal condamnerait un conseil municipal qui empêcherait la circulation de pareilles déclarations? Et je n'ai choisi que quelques passages dans des livres et des tracts qui fourmillent de semblables affirmations. La décence, d'ailleurs, me commanderait de ne pas en citer davantage. Et cela ne me paraît pas nécessaire pour démontrer qu'une municipalité, dont 90 pour cent de la population est catholique, a non seulement le droit, mais le devoir, d'empêcher la dissémination de pareilles infamies.

Enfin, le dernier point c'est la question que l'exercice des cultes est un droit civil qui relève de la juridiction des législatures provinciales. C'est ainsi que l'ont considéré les provinces de la Saskatchewan et de l'Alberta, qui ont adopté des lois intitulées: *An Act to Protect Certain Civil Rights* (1947, 11 Geo. VI, c. 35). L'objet de la loi est déclaré dans le préambule comme étant "to protect certain civil rights" et l'article 3 de la Loi stipule:

> ... *Every person and every class of persons shall enjoy the right to freedom of conscience, opinion and belief, and freedom of religious association, teaching, practice and worship.*

La province de l'Alberta a un statut semblable.

Il est intéressant, sur ce point, de référer à l'interprétation donnée par le Conseil Privé de l'expression "*civil rights*" dans l'*Acte de Québec* de 1774, dans la cause de *Citizens Insurance Company of Canada v. Parsons* [(1881) 7 App. Cas. 96]:

> ... *It is to be observed that the same words, "[c]ivil rights" are employed in the* Act *of 14 Geo. 3, c. 83, which made provision for the Government of the province of Quebec, Sect. 8 of that* Act *enacted that His Majesty's Canadian subjects within the province of Quebec should enjoy their property, usages, and other civil rights, as they had before done, and that in all matters of controversy relative to property and civil rights resort should be had to the laws of Canada, and be determined agreeably to the said laws. In this statute the words "property" and "civil rights" are plainly used in their largest sense; and there is no reason for holding that in the statute under discussion they are used in a different and narrower one.*

Il suffit de signaler la contradiction de l'argumentation du procureur de l'appelant qui, d'une part, allègue l'inconstitutionnalité de la Charte de Québec, en invoquant, d'autre part, qu'elle est en conflit avec la *Loi concernant la liberté des cultes* (S.R.Q. 1941, c. 307) de cette même province de Québec. Il est indiscutable que la législature qui a adopté le chapitre 307 avait la compétence voulue pour adopter la Charte de la Cité de Québec, en vertu de laquelle le règlement 184 a été édicté....

Sur le tout, je n'ai donc aucune hésitation à dire que le règlement attaqué est légal, valide et constitutionnel et que les jugements qui l'ont déclaré tel doivent être confirmés, avec dépens.

KERWIN J.: ... Counsel for the appellant declined to contend that the by-law was invalid because a discretion was delegated to the Chief of Police. Counsel for the respondent, the City of Quebec, and for the intervenant, the Attorney General of Quebec, did not deal with the point and nothing is therefore said about it. However, an argument was advanced based upon a pre-Confederation statute of 1852 of the old Province of Canada, 14-15 Vict. c. 175, the relevant part of which provides:—

the free exercise and enjoyment of Religious Profession and Worship, without discrimination or preference, so as the same be not made an excuse for acts of licentiousness, or a justification of practices inconsistent with the peace and safety of the Province, is by the constitution and laws of this Province allowed to all Her Majesty's subjects within the same.

Section 129 of the *British North America Act, 1867,* enacts:—

129. Except as otherwise provided by this *Act,* all Laws in force in Canada, Nova Scotia, or New Brunswick at the Union, and all Courts of Civil and Criminal Jurisdiction, and all legal Commissions, Powers, and Authorities, and all Officers, Judicial, Administrative and Ministerial, existing therein at the Union, shall continue in Ontario, Quebec, Nova Scotia, and New Brunswick respectively, as if the Union had not been made; subject nevertheless (except with respect to such as are enacted by or exist under Acts of the Parliament of Great Britain or of the Parliament of the United Kingdom of Great Britain and Ireland) to be repealed, abolished, or altered by the Parliament of Canada, or by the Legislature of the respective Province, according to the Authority of the Parliament or of that Legislature under this *Act.*

By virtue of this section that part of the pre-Confederation statute extracted above continued to operate in the Province of Quebec at the time of the coming into force of the *British North America Act.* Since then the Quebec Legislature enacted legislation practically in the same words, and certainly to the same effect, which legislation has been continued from time to time and is now found in section 2 of R.S.Q. 1941, c. 307, *The Freedom of Worship Act.* Whether or not such legislation be taken to supersede the pre-Confederation enactment, no statutes such as the Quebec City Charter, in the general terms in which they are expressed, and whenever originally enacted, have the effect of abrogating the specific terms of the enactment providing for freedom of worship.

It appears from the material filed on behalf of the appellant that Jehovah's Witnesses not only do not consider themselves as belonging to a religion but vehemently attack anything that may ordinarily be so termed but in my view they are entitled to "the free exercise and enjoyment of (their) Religious Profession and Worship." The Witnesses attempt to spread their views by way of the printed and written word as well as orally and state that such attempts are part of their belief. Their attacks on religion generally, or on one in particular, do not bring them within the exception "so as the same be not made an excuse for licentiousness or a justification of practices inconsistent with the peace and safety of the Province." While several definitions of "licentious" appear in standard dictionaries, the prevailing sense of that term is said to be "libertine, lascivious, lewd." To certain biblical expressions the pamphlets, etc., of Jehovah's Witnesses which they desire to distribute attach a meaning which is offensive to a great majority of the inhabitants of the Province of Quebec. But, if they have a legal right to attempt to spread their beliefs, as I think they have, the expressions used by them in so doing, as exemplified in the exhibits filed, do not fall within the first part of the exception. Nor in my opinion are their attacks "inconsistent with the peace and safety of the Province" even where they are directed particularly against the religion of most of the Province's residents. The peace and safety of the Province will not be endangered if that majority do not use the attacks as a foundation for breaches of the peace.

Confined to the argument now under consideration, the above reasons do not justify a declaration that the by-law is *ultra vires* the City of Quebec since, if not otherwise objectionable, the by-law may have its effect in other cases and under other circumstances; but they do warrant a declaration that the by-law does not extend so as to prohibit the appellant as a member of Jehovah's Witnesses from distributing in the streets of Quebec any book, pamphlet, booklet, circular or tract of Jehovah's Witnesses included in the exhibits and an injunction restraining the City, its officers and agents from in any way interfering with such actions of the appellant.

The appellant further contended that the by-law should be declared illegal on the ground that the Provincial Legislature has no power to authorize the Council of the City of Quebec to pass a general by-law prohibiting the distribution of books, pamphlets, etc., in the City streets. At first he argued that the subject-matter of any such legislation and by-law falls under section 91 of the *British North America Act* and not section 92, but later changed his position by arguing that neither Parliament nor the Provincial Legislatures possessed the requisite power. I am unable to agree with either of these submissions. I do not find it helpful to refer to rights conferred by early treaties or sanctioned by Imperial Statutes dealing with the old colonies and subdivisions of what is now Canada since it is well-settled that the *British North America Act* has conferred all powers of legislation either upon Parliament or the Legislatures of the Provinces and that there is no field in which the one or the others may not operate . . . .

In my view the right to practise one's religion is a civil right in the Province under head 13 of section 92 of the *British North America Act* just as much as the right to strike or lockout dealt with by the Judicial Committee in *Toronto Electric Commissioners v. Snider* [[1925] A.C. 396] . . . .

For the same reason I also think that freedom of the press is a civil right in the Province. *In Re Alberta Information Act* [[1938] S.C.R. 100], Sir Lyman Duff stated a short ground considered by him (and Davis J.) sufficient to dispose of the question as to whether Bill No. 9 of the Legislative Assembly of Alberta, "*An Act to Ensure the Publication of Accurate News and Information*" was *intra vires* the Legislature of that Province. With the greatest respect I am unable to agree with that part of his ensuing reasons for judgment commencing at the foot of page 132 and continuing to the end of page 135, and particularly the following statement:—"Any attempt to abrogate this right of public debate or to express the traditional forms of the exercise of the right (in public meeting and through the press), would, in our opinion be incompetent to the Legislature of the Province." Also, with respect, I must dissent from the views of Cannon J. upon this topic as expressed in the same report.

We have not a Bill of Rights such as is contained in the United States Constitution and decisions on that part of the latter are of no assistance. While it is true that, as recited in the preamble to the *British North America Act* the three Provinces expressed a desire to be federally united with a constitution similar in principle to that of the United Kingdom, a complete division of legislative powers being effected by the *Act*, I assume as it was assumed in *Re Adoption Act* [[1938] S.C.R. 398], (with reference, it is true, to entirely different matters) that Provincial Legislatures are willing and able to deal with matters of importance and substance that are within their legislative jurisdiction. It is perhaps needless to say that nothing in the foregoing has reference to matters that are confined to Parliament. . . .

RAND J.: . . . As in all controversies of this nature, the first enquiry goes to the real nature and character of the by-law; in what substance and aspect of legislative matter is it enacted? and we must take its objects and purposes to be what its language fairly embraces. The by-law places no restriction on the discretion of the officer and none has been suggested. If, under cover of such a blanket authority, action may be taken which directly deals with matters beyond provincial powers, can the fact that the language may, at the same time, encompass action on matters within provincial authority preserve it from the taint of *ultra vires*? May a court enter upon a delineation of the limits and contours of the valid and invalid areas within it? Must the provision stand or fall as one or can it be severed or otherwise dealt with? These are the subsidiary questions to be answered.

What the practice under the by-law demonstrates is that the language comprehends the power of censorship. From its inception, printing has been recognized as an agency of tremendous possibilities, and virtually upon its introduction into Western Europe it was brought under the control and license of government. At that time, as now in despotisms, authority viewed with fear and wrath the uncensored printed word: it is and has been the *bête noire* of dogmatists in every field of thought; and the seat of its legislative control in this country becomes a matter of the highest moment.

The Christian religion, its practices and profession, exhibiting in Europe and America an organic continuity, stands in the first rank of social, political and juristic importance. The Articles of Capitulation in 1760, the Treaty of Paris in 1763, and the *Quebec Act of 1774*, all contain special provisions placing safeguards against restrictions upon its freedom, which were in fact liberations from the law in force at the time in England. The *Quebec Act*, by sec. 5, declared that His Majesty's subjects,

> professing the religion of the Church of Rome of and in the said province of Quebec, may have, hold and enjoy, the free exercise of the religion of the Church of Rome, subject to the King's supremacy....

and, by sec. 15, that

> no ordinance touching religion ... shall be of any force or effect until the same shall have received His Majesty's approbation.

This latter provision, in modified form, was continued by sec. 42 of the *Constitutional Act of 1791*:

> whenever any act or acts shall ... in any manner relate to or affect the enjoyment of or exercise of any religious form or mode of worship

the proposed *Act* was to be laid before both Houses of Parliament and the assent of the Sovereign could be given only if within thirty days thereafter no address from either House to withhold assent had been presented. The *Union Act of 1840*, sec. 42, contained a like provision. In each of the latter *Acts* existing laws were continued by secs. 33 and 46 respectively. From 1760, therefore, to the present moment religious freedom has, in our legal system, been recognized as a principle of fundamental character; and although we have nothing in the nature of an established church, that the untrammelled affirmations of religious belief and its propagation, personal or institutional, remain as of the greatest constitutional significance throughout the Dominion is unquestionable....

The only powers given by sec. 92 of the *Confederation Act* which have been suggested to extend to legislation in relation to religion are nos. 13, Property and Civil Rights, and 16, Matters of a merely local or private nature in the province. The statutory history of the expression "Property and Civil Rights" already given exhibiting its parallel enactment with special provisions relating to religion shows indubitably that such matters as religious belief, duty and observances were never intended to be included within that collocation of pow-

ers. If it had not been so, the exceptional safeguards to Roman Catholics would have been redundant.

Strictly speaking, civil rights arise from positive law; but freedom of speech, religion and the inviolability of the person, are original freedoms which are at once the necessary attributes and modes of self-expression of human beings and the primary conditions of their community life within a legal order. It is in the circumscription of these liberties by the creation of civil rights in persons who may be injured by their exercise, and by the sanctions of public law, that the positive law operates. What we realize is the residue inside that periphery. Their significant relation to our law lies in this, that under its principles to which there are only minor exceptions, there is no prior or antecedent restraint placed upon them: the penalties, civil or criminal, attach to results which their exercise may bring about, and apply as consequential incidents. So we have the civil rights against defamation, assault, false imprisonment and the like, and the punishments of the criminal law; but the sanctions of the latter lie within the exclusive jurisdiction of the Dominion. Civil rights of the same nature arise also as protection against infringements of these freedoms.

That legislation "in relation" to religion and its profession is not a local or private matter would seem to me to be self-evident: the dimensions of this interest are nationwide; it is even today embodied in the highest level of the constitutionalism of Great Britain; it appertains to a boundless field of ideas, beliefs and faiths with the deepest roots and loyalties; a religious incident reverberates from one end of this country to the other, and there is nothing to which the "body politic of the Dominion" is more sensitive.

There is, finally, the implication of sec. 93 of the *Confederation Act* which deals with education. In this section appear the only references in the statute to religion. Subsec. (i) speaks of "Denominational Schools" and preserves their existing rights and privileges. Subsec. (ii) extends to the separate schools "of the Queen's Protestant and Roman Catholic subjects" in Quebec the same "powers, privileges and duties" then conferred and imposed upon the separate schools of the "Queen's Roman Catholic subjects" in Upper Canada. Subsec. (iii) provides for an appeal to the Governor-General in Council from any act or decision of a provincial authority "affecting any right or privilege of the Protestant or Roman Catholic minority of the Queen's subjects in relation to education." Subsec. (iv) declares that in the event of any failure on the part of the provincial authority to observe or enforce the provincial laws contemplated by the section, Parliament may provide for the execution of the provisions of the section. On the argument advanced, and apart from the question of criminal law, these vital constitutional provisions could be written off by the simple expedient of abolishing, as civil rights and by provincial legislation, the religious freedoms of minorities, and so, in legal contemplation, the minorities themselves.

So is it with freedom of speech. The *Confederation Act* recites the desire of the three provinces to be federally united into one Dominion "with a constitution similar in principle to that of the United Kingdom. Under that constitution, government is by parliamentary institutions, including popular assemblies elected by the people at large in both provinces and Dominion: government resting ultimately on public opinion reached by discussion and the interplay of ideas. If that discussion is placed under license, its basic condition is destroyed: the government, as licensor, becomes disjoined from the citizenry. The only security is steadily advancing enlightenment, for which the widest range of controversy is the *sine qua non.*

In the *Reference re The Accurate News and Information Act of Alberta* [[1938] S.C.R. 100], Sir Lyman Duff deals with this matter. The proposed legislation did not attempt to prevent discussion of affairs in newspapers but rather to compel the publication of statements as to the true and exact objects of governmental policy and as to the difficulties of achieving them....

[Justice Rand then quoted the reasons given by Chief Justice Duff and Justice Cannon in *Reference re Alberta Statutes* for ruling that the provinces cannot abrogate the right of public debate.]

What is proposed before us is that a newspaper, just as a religious, political or other tract or handbill, for the purposes of sale or distribution through use of streets, can be placed under the uncontrolled discretion of a municipal officer; that is, that the province, while permitting all others, could forbid a newspaper or any writing of a particular colour from being so disposed of. That public ways, in some circumstances the only practical means available for any appeal to the community generally, have from the most ancient times been the avenues for such communications, is demonstrated by the Bible itself: in the 6th verse of ch. xi of Jeremiah these words appear: "Proclaim all these words in the cities of Judah, and in the streets of Jerusalem"; and more objectionable interference, short of complete suppression, with that dissemination which is the "breath of life" of the political institutions of this country than that made possible by the by-law can scarcely be imagined.

But it is argued that the by-law relates not to religion or free speech at all but to the administration of streets. Undoubtedly the city may pass regulations for that purpose but within the general and neutral requirement of license by the by-law a number of equally plausible objects may be conjectured. No purpose whatever is indicated much less specified by the language; its sole effect is to create and vest in a functionary a power, to be exercised for any purpose or reason he sees fit, disclosed or undisclosed....

It was urged by Mr. Beaulieu that the city as proprietor of the streets has authority to forbid or permit as it chooses, in the most unlimited and arbitrary manner, any action or conduct that takes place on them. The possibilities of such a proposition can be easily imagined. But it misconceives the relation of the province to the public highways. The public entitled to use them is that of the Dominion, whose citizens are not of this or that province but of Canada. What has been confided to the provinces is the regulation of their use by that public.

Conceding, as in the Alberta Reference, that aspects of the activities of religion and free speech may be affected by provincial legislation, such legislation, as in all other fields, must be sufficiently definite and precise to indicate its subject matter.... Where the language is sufficiently specific and can fairly be interpreted as applying only to matter within the enacting jurisdiction, that attribution will be made; and where the requisite elements are present, there is the rule of severability. But to authorize action which may be related indifferently to a variety of incompatible matters by means of the device of a discretionary license cannot be brought within either of these mechanisms; and the Court is powerless, under general language that overlaps exclusive jurisdictions, to delineate and preserve valid power in a segregated form. If the purpose is street regulation, taxation, registration or other local object, the language must, with sufficient precision, define the matter and mode of administration; and by no expedient which ignores that requirement can constitutional limitations be circumvented.

I would, therefore, allow the appeal, direct judgment declaring the by-law invalid, and enjoin the respondent City from acting upon it. The costs will be as proposed by my brother Kerwin....

LOCKE J.: The preamble to chapter 175 of the Statutes of the Province of Canada for the year 1851 reads as follows:

Whereas the recognition of legal equality amongst all Religious Denominations is an admitted principle of Colonial Legislation: And whereas in the state and condition of this Province, to which such a principle is peculiarly applicable, it is desirable that the same should receive the sanction of direct Legislative Authority recognizing and declaring the same as a fundamental principle of our civil polity: Be it therefore declared and enacted by the Queen's Most Excellent Majesty, by and with the advice and consent of the Legislative Council and of the Legislative Assembly of the Province of Canada constituted and assembled by virtue of and under the authority of an *Act* passed in the Parliament of the United Kingdom of Great Britain and Ireland, and intituled, *An Act to re-unite the Provinces of Upper and Lower Canada,* and for the Government of Canada, and it is hereby declared and enacted by the authority of the same, That the free exercise and enjoyment of Religious Profession and Worship, without discrimination or preference, so as the same be not made an excuse for acts of licentiousness, or a justification of practices inconsistent with the peace and safety of the Province, is by constitution and laws of this Province allowed to all Her Majesty's subjects within the same.

The statute was reserved for the signification of Her Majesty's pleasure and the Royal assent given by Her Majesty in Council on May 15th, 1852.

This statute was in force when the *British North America Act of 1867* was passed by the Imperial Parliament. It could not, in my opinion, be repealed by the Province of Quebec or by the Legislature of any other province of Canada (*Dobie v. Temporalities Board* [(1882), 7 App. Cas. 136]). Whether it would be *intra vires* Parliament to repeal the *Act,* in view of the language of the preamble to the *British North America Act,* is a matter to be decided when that question arises. It does not arise in the present case. Parliament has passed no legislation purporting to repeal the *Act.* . . .

On behalf of the intervenant it has been contended before us that, assuming the belief of the Jehovah's Witnesses is one entitled otherwise to the protection of the Statute of 1852 or the Provincial Statute, he may de deprived of that right by or under the authority of a statute of the Provincial Legislature. The argument is based on the contention that the rights so given to the people of Canada to complete freedom in these matters is a civil right of which they may be deprived by appropriate legislation by the Province. It is further contended, though rather faintly, that the legislation may be justified under Head 16 as being a matter of a merely local or private nature in the province.

In the factum of the intervenant the matter is thus expressed:—

Under our constitution there is no religious freedom except within the limits determined by the competent legislative authority. No such authority is known other than the provincial authority; religious teaching as a matter of fact is part of the realm of education reserved to the provinces; besides, religious freedom is one of the civil rights also reserved to the provinces.

The reference to rights reserved to the provinces in respect of religious teaching refers, of course, to the provisions of section 93 of the *British North America Act.* If the argument is sound, then the holding of religious services by the adherents of any faith designated by the Legislature may be prohibited.

This argument put forward, so far as I am aware, for the first time in any reported case in Canada since Confederation raises questions which are of profound importance to all of the people of this country. Not only the right of freedom of worship would be affected but the exercise of other fundamental rights, such as that of free speech on matters of public interest and to publicly disseminate news, subject only to the restraints imposed by the *Criminal Code* and to such civil liability as may attach to the publication of libelous matters, might be restrained or prohibited. The language of the by-law is perfectly general and if this contention of the intervenants be right the Chief of Police might forbid the distribution in the streets of circulars or pamphlets published by one political party while allowing such distribution by that party which he personally favoured. It is well, in my opinion, that it be made clear that this right is involved in the decision of this case. Once a right of censorship of the contents of religious publications is established, the dissemination of the political views of writers by circulars or pamphlets delivered on the streets may equally be prohibited or restrained. . . .

The purpose of this by-law is to establish a censorship upon the distribution of written publications in the City of Quebec. It is not the distribution of all pamphlets, circulars or other publications in the streets which is prohibited but of those in respect of which the written permission of the Chief of Police has not been obtained.

In the preamble to the *British North America Act* the opening paragraph says:—

Whereas the Provinces of Canada, Nova Scotia and New Brunswick have expressed their desire to be federally united into one Dominion under the Crown of the United Kingdom of Great Britain and Ireland with a constitution similar in principle to that of the United Kingdom.

and, after reciting that such a union would conduce to the welfare of the provinces, it is said that it is expedient not only that the constitution of the legislative authority in the Dominion be provided for but also that the nature of the Executive Government therein be declared. At the time this *Act* was passed, the *Act of 1852* declaring the right to freedom of religious belief and worship was in force in Canada and gave to the inhabitants of the provinces the same rights in that respect as were then enjoyed by the people of the United Kingdom.

It has, I think, always been accepted throughout Canada that, while the exercise of this right might be restrained under the provisions of the saving clause of the statute of 1852 by criminal legislation passed by Parliament under Head 27 of section 91, it was otherwise a constitutional right of all the inhabitants of this country. . . .

Whether the right to religious freedom and the right to free public discussion of matters of public interest and the right to disseminate news, subject to the restrictions to which I have above referred to, differ in their nature, it is unnecessary to decide. The former of these rights is, however, certainly not the lesser of them in Canada. Unless they differ, had the powers of censorship vested by the by-law in the Chief of Police of the City of Quebec been exercised by preventing the distribution of the written views of a political party (and they may be so used) rather than the religious views of Saumur, the opinion of Sir Lyman Duff, C.J. in the *Reference as to The Accurate News and Information Act of the Province of Alberta* [[1938] S.C.R. 100 at 132], would be directly to the contrary of the argument advanced on behalf of the intervenant.

[Justice Locke then quoted at length Chief Justice Duff's reasons for ruling the *Accurate News and Information Act* invalid in the *Alberta Press* case.[5]]

With this opinion in its entirety I respectfully agree and I have heard no reasoned argument against any of its conclusions. It may be said, with at least equal and I think greater force, that the right to the free exercise and enjoyment of religious profession and worship without discrimination or preference, subject to the limitations expressed in the concluding words of the first paragraph of the *Statute of 1852*, existed at the time of the enactment of the *British North America Act* and was not a civil right of the nature referred to under Head 13 of section 92 of the *British North America Act*. . . .

The dissenting judgment of Cartwright and Fauteux JJ. was delivered by:—

CARTWRIGHT J.: . . . It is first necessary to determine the proper construction of the by-law. In doing so we must give to the words used their plain meaning in everyday language and when this is done I think it clear that what is prohibited is the distribution, without the permission of the Chief of Police, of printed matter of the kind described in the by-law in the streets of the City. The distribution of such matter anywhere else, as for example in private houses is not affected by the by-law. There is evidence in the record to indicate that the officials charged with the enforcement of the by-law have not so construed it and have instituted proceedings against persons, as for an infraction of the by-law, on the ground that such persons had distributed written matter at private residences in the City. Such evidence does not seem to me to be

relevant to the proper construction of the by-law. It is only if the words of the by-law are ambiguous that we may resort to extraneous aids in its interpretation and the words used appear to me to be clear and unambiguous. The fact, if be the fact, that the by-law has been misinterpreted, can affect neither its proper construction nor the question of its validity.

In my view, legislation authorizing the city to pass this by-law is *prima facie*, in relation to either or both of two subjects within the provincial power which may be conveniently described as (i) the use of highways, and (ii) police regulations and the suppression of conditions likely to cause disorder.

[Justice Cartwright then cited a number of cases that in his view supported both grounds (1) and (2) for finding the bylaw valid.]

It follows from these authorities that it is within the competence of the Legislature of the Province to prohibit or regulate the distribution, in the streets of the municipalities in the Province, of written matter having a tendency to insult or annoy the recipients thereof with the possible result of giving rise to disorder, and perhaps violence, in the streets.

It is said, however, if I have correctly apprehended the argument for the appellant, that even if the legislation in question appears *prima facie* to fall within the powers of the Provincial Legislature under the two heads with which I have dealt above it is in reality an enactment destructive of the freedom of the press and the freedom of religion both of which are submitted to be matters as to which the Province has no power to legislate. In support of such submission counsel referred to a large number of cases decided in the Courts of the United States of America but I am unable to derive any assistance from them as they appear to be founded on provisions in the Constitution limiting the power to make laws in relation to such matters. Under the *British North America Act*, on the other hand, the whole range of legislative power is committed either to Parliament or the Provincial Legislatures and competence to deal with any subject matter must exist in one or other of such bodies. There are thus no rights possessed by the citizens of Canada which cannot be modified by either Parliament or the Legislature, but it may often be a matter of difficulty to decide which of such bodies has the legislative power in a particular case.

It will be convenient to first examine the appellant's argument in so far as it deals with the freedom of the press. In Blackstone's *Commentaries* (1769) Vol. 4, at pages 151 and 152 it is said:

The liberty of the press is indeed essential to the nature of a free state: but this consists in laying no previous restraints upon publications, and not in freedom from

---

5   For a discussion of *Alberta Press*, see case 19.

censure for criminal matter when published. Every freeman has an undoubted right to lay what sentiments he pleases before the public: to forbid this, is to destroy the freedom of the press: but if he publishes what is improper, mischievous, or illegal, he must take the consequence of his own temerity. To subject the press to the restrictive power of a licenser, as was formerly done, both before and since the revolution, is to subject all freedom of sentiment to the prejudices of one man, and make him the arbitrary and infallible judge of all controverted points in learning, religion, and government. But to punish (as the law does at present) any dangerous or offensive writings, which, when published, shall on a fair and impartial trial be adjudged of a pernicious tendency, is necessary for the preservation of peace and good order, of government and religion, the only solid foundations of civil liberty.

Accepting this as an accurate description of what is commonly understood by the expression "the liberty of the press," as heretofore enjoyed by the inhabitants of Canada, it is clear that By-law No. 184 does infringe such liberty to a limited extent. It does, to adapt the words of Blackstone, lay some previous restraint upon publication. So far as the by-law is concerned every individual is left free to print and publish any matter he pleases except that one particular method of publication is conditionally denied to him. He is forbidden to publish such matter by distributing it in the streets of the City of Quebec without having previously obtained for so doing the written permission of the Chief of Police. I will assume, as is argued for the appellant, that the by-law contemplates that the Chief of Police will examine the written matter in respect of which he is asked to grant a permit and that his decision, whether to grant or refuse it, will be based on the view which he takes of the contents of such matter; that if he regards it as harmless, he will grant the permit, and that if he thinks it is calculated to provoke disorder by annoying or insulting those to whom it is distributed he will refuse the permit. It is urged that power to restrict the liberty of the press even to the limited extent provided in the by-law, is committed exclusively to Parliament under the opening words of section 91 or under head 27 of that section and further that Parliament has fully occupied the field by enacting those provisions of the *Criminal Code* which deal with blasphemous libel, seditious libel, speaking seditious words, spreading false news, defamatory libel, and publishing obscene matter. If I have followed the argument correctly, it is that as Parliament has enacted that certain publications are to be deemed criminal it has by implication declared that all other publications are lawful and that consequently the Legislature has no power to deal with any other type of publication. I am unable to accept this conclusion.

In my view, freedom of the press is not a separate subject matter committed exclusively to either Parliament or the Legislatures. In some respects, Parliament, and in others, the Legislatures may validly deal with it. In some aspects it falls within the field of criminal law, but in others it has been dealt with by Provincial legislation, the validity of which is not open to question, as for example "*The Libel and Slander Act*" R.S.O. 1950 Cap. 204, and the similar acts in the other provinces. If the subject matter of a Provincial enactment falls within the class of subjects enumerated in section 92 of the *British North America Act* such enactment does not, in my opinion, cease to be *intra vires* of the legislature by reason of the fact that it has the effect of cutting down the freedom of the press. . . .

It is next necessary to consider the argument that the by-law is invalid because, as it is alleged, it interferes with freedom of religion. While it was questioned before us, I will, for the purposes of this argument, assume that the system of faith and worship professed by the body to which the plaintiff belongs is a religion, and that the distribution of printed matter in the streets is a practice directed by its teachings.

It may well be that Parliament alone has power to make laws in relation to the subject of religion as such, that that subject is, in its nature, one which concerns Canada as a whole and so cannot be regarded as of a merely local or private nature in any province or as a civil right in any province; but we are not called upon to decide that question in this appeal and I express no opinion upon it. I think it clear that the provinces, legislating within their allotted sphere, may affect the carrying on of activities connected with the practice of religion. For example, there are many municipal by-laws in force in cities in Ontario, passed pursuant to powers conferred by the Provincial Legislature, which provide that no buildings other than private residences shall be erected on certain streets. Such by-laws are, in my opinion, clearly valid although they prevent any religious body from building a church or similar edifice on such streets. Another example of Provincial Legislation which might be said to interfere directly with the free exercise of religious profession is that under which the by-law considered in *Re Cribbin v. The City of Toronto* [(1891), 21 O.R. 325] was passed. That was a by-law of the City of Toronto which provided in part:

> No person shall on the Sabbath-day, in any public park, square, garden, or place for exhibition in the city of Toronto, publicly preach lecture or declaim.

The by-law was attacked on the ground, *inter alia*, that it was unconstitutional but it was upheld by Galt C.J. and in my opinion, his decision was right. No useful purpose would be served by endeavouring to define the limits of the provincial power to pass legislation affecting the carrying on of activities connected with the practice of religion. The better course is, I think, to deal only with the particular legislation now before us.

For the appellant, reliance was placed upon the Statute of Canada (1851) 14-15 Victoria, Chapter 175, re-enacted in substantially identical terms as R.S.Q. 1941 Cap. 307. I will assume, for the purposes of the argument, that counsel for the appellant is right in his submission that it is to the pre-Confederation Statute that we should look. In the relevant portion of that statute it is enacted:—

> That the free exercise and enjoyment of Religious Profession and Worship, without discrimination or preference, so as the same be not made an excuse for acts of licentiousness, or a justification of practices inconsistent with the peace and safety of the Province, is by the constitution and laws of this Province allowed to all Her Majesty's subjects within the same.

I do not think that, on a proper construction, this statute absolves a religious body or an individual member thereof from obedience to any Act of Parliament or of the Legislature which happens to conflict with the teachings of such body....

To summarize, I am of opinion that it was within the competence of the Legislature to authorize the passing of the by-law in question under its power to legislate in relation to (i) the use of highways, and (ii) police regulations and the suppression of conditions likely to cause disorder; and that such legislation is not rendered invalid because it interferes to the limited extents indicated above with either the freedom of the press or the freedom of religion. It follows that I would dismiss the appeal....

[Justices Kellock and Estey gave reasons similar to those advanced by Justices Rand and Locke for finding the bylaw *ultra vires*. Justice Taschereau concurred with Chief Justice Rinfret, and Justice Fauteux concurred with Justice Cartwright.]

B: THE CANADIAN BILL OF RIGHTS

 **Attorney General of Canada v. Lavell and Bédard, 1974**

A new chapter in Canadian civil liberties was inaugurated in 1960 with the enactment of the *Canadian Bill of Rights*. Technically, the new *Bill of Rights* was not an addition to Canada's formal Constitution. It was passed as an ordinary *Act* of the federal Parliament. As such it did not apply to the provinces and could be set aside by subsequent federal legislation. The *Act* had two main clauses. Section 1 declared that in Canada certain fundamental rights and freedoms "have existed and shall continue to exist without discrimination by reason of race, national origin, colour, religion or sex." It listed such fundamental rights as the right to life, liberty, security of the person, and enjoyment of property and the right not to be deprived thereof except by due process of law; the individual's right to equality before the law and protection of the law; and freedom of religion, speech, assembly, association, and the press. Section 2 provided that unless the *Bill of Rights* was explicitly set aside, every federal law shall "be so construed and applied as not to abrogate, abridge or infringe" the rights and freedoms set out in the Bill. It added to the rights listed in section 1 a list of procedural rights, including the right of arrested persons to legal counsel, *habeas corpus*, the presumption of innocence, the right to an interpreter, and the right to a fair hearing when a person's rights or duties are being determined. The final section of the Bill provided that the *Bill of Rights* would not apply to anything done under the *War Measures Act*.

The first real test of the Supreme Court's treatment of the *Bill of Rights* came in 1963 in the *Robertson and Rosetanni* case.[1] Robertson and Rosetanni had been charged with an offence under the federal *Lord's Day Act*, namely, operating a bowling alley on Sunday. On appeal their main defence was that the *Lord's Day Act* conflicted with the *Canadian Bill of Rights* and was therefore inoperative. Justice Ritchie (supported by the three Quebec justices, Taschereau, Fauteux, and Abbott) wrote the majority's opinion, dismissing the appeal. His approach to the *Bill of Rights* was basically conservative. He interpreted it not as a charter designed to enlarge the fundamental rights and freedoms of Canadians, but as a means of conserving these rights in their 1960 form. The *Canadian Bill of Rights*, he argued, "is not concerned with 'human rights and fundamental freedoms' in any abstract sense, but rather with such 'rights and freedoms' as they existed in Canada immediately before the statute was enacted." His review of Canadian history and jurisprudence revealed that the concept of religious freedom was well enshrined in Canadian law as was Lord's Day observance legislation long before 1960. Thus he concluded that the freedom of religion guaranteed by the *Bill of Rights* was not infringed by the *Lord's Day Act*. Justice Cartwright, the sole dissenter, rejected the implication in the majority's position that the *Bill of Rights* could have no effect on laws enacted before the *Bill of Rights*. In his view, section 5 made it clear that the Bill was "to apply to all laws of Canada already in existence at the time it came into force as well as those thereafter enacted."

---

1 [1963] S.C.R. 651.

If Canadian civil libertarians were dismayed by the Court's decision in *Robertson and Rosetanni*, they found new ground for hope in the Court's next major decision on the *Bill of Rights*. This did not occur until 1970 in the *Drybones* decision, which concerned the compatibility of provisions in the *Indian Act* restricting the drinking rights of Indians with the egalitarian provisions of the *Bill of Rights*. Ironically, on this occasion, the positions of Cartwright and Ritchie were completely reversed. Justice Ritchie still spoke for the majority, but this time it was an "activist" majority willing to use the *Bill of Rights* to invalidate a long-established piece of federal legislation. Cartwright, now Chief Justice, along with Justices Abbott and Pigeon, refused to give the Bill such a wide-reaching effect.

The Supreme Court's decision in the *Lavell and Bédard* case indicated that a majority of the judges felt the Court had gone too far in an "activist" direction in *Drybones*. The majority opinion did not retreat from the position established in *Drybones* that the *Bill of Rights* can render inoperative legislation that clearly violates rights enshrined in the Bill, but it did considerably water down the significance of the right to equality before the law.

The decision dealt with appeals in two cases involving Indian women who claimed that section 12(1)(*b*) of the *Indian Act* infringed their right to equality before the law under the *Bill of Rights*. Section 12(1)(*b*) denied an Indian woman who married a non-Indian her Indian status, including her right to hold property and live on an Indian reserve. A male Indian who married a non-Indian could retain his Indian status. Thus, Mrs. Lavell and Mrs. Bédard argued that section 12(1)(*b*) constituted discrimination by reason of sex. While they were supported by the Native Council of Canada representing non-status Indians and by several non-Indian women's organizations, most of the organizations representing status Indians, including eight provincial and two territorial organizations and the National Indian Brotherhood, intervened to oppose Mrs. Lavell and Mrs. Bédard.

The Supreme Court decided, 5 to 4, that section 12(1)(*b*) did not constitute a violation of equality before the law. Again, Justice Ritchie wrote the majority opinion. Just as it is difficult to reconcile his opinion in *Drybones* with the position he had taken earlier in *Robertson and Rosetanni*, it is a daunting task to trace a thread of consistency between his approach to equality before the law in *Lavell and Bédard* and his treatment of that concept in *Drybones*. Citing A.V. Dicey, the 19th-century English constitutional writer, as his authority, Justice Ritchie now defined equality before the law not as a substantive requirement of the law itself, but as a requirement of the way in which laws are administered. The *Indian Act* might well discriminate against women, but so long as it was applied equally to all whom it affected there would be no violation of equality before the law. To this argument Justice Ritchie added the concern expressed by Justice Pigeon in his dissenting opinion in *Drybones*: it would be unreasonable to extend the *Bill of Rights* so far as to make it impossible for Parliament to enact special legislation concerning the property and civil rights of Indians.

Justice Laskin, as was so often the case in civil liberties cases, wrote a vigorous dissent. He could not reconcile the majority's interpretation of equality before the law with the Court's decision in *Drybones*. The opening paragraph of section 1 of the *Canadian Bill of Rights*, in his view, amounted to a prohibition of legal classifications based on race, national origin, colour, religion, or sex. In this sense, the *Canadian Bill of Rights* was more specific and categorical than the equal protection of laws clause in the American Constitution, which did not prohibit any specific form of discrimination, leaving it to the judiciary to distinguish reasonable and unreasonable forms of discrimination. Laskin could not see why laws based on Parliament's power under section 91(24) of the *B.N.A. Act* to legislate in relation to

Indians should enjoy any special immunity from the *Bill of Rights*. To decide otherwise in this case would, in his view, compound racial inequality with sexual inequality. Justice Laskin's dissent was supported by Justices Spence, Hall, and Abbott. Justice Abbott had dissented in *Drybones*, but regarded that decision as now requiring him to support Justice Laskin's dissent. Justice Pigeon, on the other hand, who also dissented in *Drybones*, this time joined the majority and appeared to regard the results of this case as supportive of the position that he had taken in *Drybones*.

The most promising explanation for the logical difficulties posed by the majority opinion is political, not jurisprudential. The judges had been made aware that ruling section 12(1)(*b*) inoperative would cause political and policy difficulties not posed by the *Drybones* decision, and they drew back in an attempt to avoid the political thicket Justice Cartwright had warned them about in *Drybones*.

The central question was whether a broad interpretation of the *Bill of Rights* equality guarantee would undermine the entire *Indian Act*. This concern had been expressed by Justice Pigeon in his dissenting opinion in *Drybones*. By the time of the *Lavell and Bédard* case, the Indian community had become alerted to the threat posed to the *Indian Act* by this jurisprudence and had mobilized to oppose it. Although Indians were not happy with all aspects of the *Act* and its administration, they were not prepared to abandon the idea of special status as such. Not long before, they had successfully resisted the Trudeau government's 1969 proposal to dismantle the *Indian Act* in favour of an individualized concept of equal Canadian citizenship, and they worried that their political victory might now be judicially undone.

In addition to the implicit challenge to the idea of special status, serious political problems were raised by the possible invalidation of section 12(1)(*b*) itself. The liquor provisions of the *Indian Act* struck down in *Drybones* were relatively unimportant parts of the *Act*, with few implications for the system of special status established there. Their invalidation did not really change anything. To the contrary, in most of the country they had already been repealed under local option provisions of the *Indian Act* and they were nowhere actively supported. Thus, in *Drybones*, the "Supreme Court was invited to strike down the feeble remnants of 19th century Indian liquor laws."[2] To do so, moreover, would create no legal gap and pose no policy dilemmas; the relevant laws for the rest of the population would now simply apply to Indians as well.

The same could not be said of the status-defining provisions of section 12(1)(*b*). Some way of determining status was required, and if these rules were invalidated what would replace them? The Court, which could invalidate them, could not itself fill the legal gap that would ensue. Furthermore, what would be the practical, particularly the financial, implications of returning status to women who had lost it? Through the Minister of Indian Affairs, the National Indian Brotherhood expressed strong opposition "to the principles contained in the *Lavell* decision [in the Federal Court] and, in particular, to the effects which they fear it will have on their already overcrowded reserves and their already overcrowded schools." For example, the Minister estimated that it would cost $1 million to reimburse women like

---

2   Douglas Sanders, "The Bill of Rights and the Indian Act" in Anne Bayefsky and Mary Eberts, eds., *Equality Rights and the Charter* (Toronto: Carswell, 1985) 539.

Lavell for the share of band funds they did not receive following their marriages to non-Indians, "even if the principle of the *Lavell* case only applies to marriages which have taken place since the *Canadian Bill of Rights* was enacted."[3]

The existence of major political problems and the extent of the opposition to the invalidation of section 12(1)(*b*) was underlined for the Supreme Court by the number of aspiring interveners clamouring at its door. Whereas in *Drybones* the judges were faced with an antiquated and insignificant section of the *Act* that nobody was willing to defend, in *Lavell and Bédard* they saw the federal government and all the status Indian organizations lining up in vigorous support of the status quo. Indeed, "the provincial Indian Associations, along with the National Indian Brotherhood, joined together in support of a single submission to the Court in support of section 12(1)(*b*), a rare show of unity and organization."[4] In this context, the concerns Justice Cartwright expressed in *Drybones* about the dangers of the political thicket must have loomed much larger for the Court as a whole.

After *Lavell and Bédard* the Supreme Court rejected a series of attacks on discriminatory provisions in federal legislation. In *Burnshine*,[5] the Court dismissed an attack on provisions of the *Prisons and Reformatories Act* under which young offenders in British Columbia and Ontario may serve longer periods of detention than adults or youths in other provinces. In the *Canard* case,[6] the Court held that provisions of the *Indian Act* giving a federal minister the power to administer the estates of Indians did not infringe the right of Indians to equality before the law. Justice Laskin (who between these two cases had been elevated to the Chief Justiceship) wrote dissents in both cases.

The *Bliss* case[7] concerned amendments to the *Unemployment Insurance Act* that created a special pregnancy benefit, but made it conditional on serving a much longer employment period than required for other benefits and denied a woman who left the workforce because of pregnancy access to the ordinary benefits. The Court unanimously (Chief Justice Laskin did not participate in this decision) held that these provisions involved no denial of equality before the law. Justice Ritchie, who authored the Court's opinion, contended that they were "an integral part of a legislative scheme enacted for valid federal objectives and they are concerned with conditions from which men are excluded. Any inequality between the sexes in this area is not created by legislation but by nature." The idea that so long as legislation serves "a valid federal objective" it is a justifiable discrimination was enunciated three years earlier in the *Prata* case,[8] in which the Court unanimously rejected the contention that provisions of the *Immigration Act* restricting the rights of persons deemed to be security risks constituted a denial of equality before the law.

However, there was still no clear consensus among the members of the Supreme Court as to whether the test of "serving a valid federal objective" means more than that legislation

---

3   *Ibid.* at 543.

4   Carl Baar, "Using Process Theory to Explain Judicial Decision Making" (1986) 1 *Canadian Journal of Law and Society* 86.

5   *The Queen v. Burnshine*, [1975] 1 S.C.R. 693.

6   *A.G. of Canada v. Canard*, [1976] 1 S.C.R. 170.

7   *Bliss v. Canada (Attorney General)*, [1979] 1 S.C.R. 183.

8   *Prata v. Minister of Manpower and Immigration*, [1976] 1 S.C.R. 376.

should be in relation to a matter constitutionally within the federal Parliament's jurisdiction. The *MacKay* case, decided in 1980, provided a good test of the justices' position on this question. The case concerned provisions of the *National Defence Act*, under which a member of the armed forces had been convicted by a court martial for a number of drug offences committed at a military base. While the Court decided, 7 to 2, that in these circumstances there was no denial of equality before the law, two of the judges who supported the majority (Justices McIntyre and Dickson) took the position that equality before the law would be violated by the broad provisions of the *Act* that subjected members of the armed forces to military trials for *all* criminal offences, even those having no relationship to a military context. In reaching this conclusion, Justice McIntyre held that, in determining whether a discriminatory classification in federal legislation served a valid federal objective and therefore did not violate equality before the law, the Court must decide whether the inequality "has been created rationally in the sense that it is not arbitrary or capricious and not based upon any ulterior motive . . . and whether it is a necessary departure from the general principle of universal application of the law for the attainment of some necessary and desirable social objective."[9] The two dissenting judges, Chief Justice Laskin and Justice Estey, also appeared to accept the view that discriminatory laws must be based on reasonable classifications. Still, this test of the rationality of legislative classifications, borrowed from American constitutional law, was endorsed by a majority of Supreme Court judges.

The equality clause of the *Charter of Rights*, section 15, was certainly meant to have a more significant effect than the equality provisions in the *Canadian Bill of Rights*. Indeed, the section contains wording explicitly intended to counteract the *Lavell and Bédard* and *Bliss* cases. In addition to equality before the law and the equal protection of the law, section 15 protects equality under the law (to overrule *Lavell and Bédard*) and equal benefit of the law (to overrule *Bliss*). The section stipulates that these rights are to be enjoyed "without discrimination and, in particular, without discrimination based on race, national or ethnic origin, colour, religion, sex, age or mental or physical disability." An interpretation imposed on the equal protection of laws by the U.S. Supreme Court is explicitly overcome by providing that affirmative action laws that discriminate in order to improve the condition of disadvantaged individuals or groups shall not be regarded as violating the equality rights.

Indian women did not have to wait for the *Charter* to overcome the *Indian Act*'s discrimination against them. In 1977, Sandra Lovelace took her case to a hearing before the United Nation's Human Rights Committee. The committee ruled that the section of Canada's *Indian Act* that had been upheld in *Lavell and Bédard* violated the United Nations Convention on Civil and Political Rights.[10] Although this decision was not legally binding on Canada, it was a key factor in putting political pressure on the federal government to amend the *Act*. In 1985, section 12(1)(*b*) was removed from the *Act*, restoring the status of an estimated 22,000 Indian women who had lost it under that provision. The status of the children of these women was left to be determined by Indian bands, which were given power to determine their own membership systems.

---

9   *MacKay v. The Queen*, [1980] 2 S.C.R. 370 at 407.

10   *Lovelace v. Canada*, No. 24/1977. Selected Decisions of the Human Rights Committee Under the Optional Protocol, U.N. Doc. CCPR/OP/1 (1988), 86-90.

The *Charter of Rights and Freedoms* has clear constitutional status and is much more comprehensive in its rights coverage than the *Canadian Bill of Rights*. It has eclipsed the Bill as an instrument for litigating civil rights in Canada. The Supreme Court's sterile and inconsistent jurisprudence interpreting the *Bill of Rights* stands as a marker of where *Charter* jurisprudence will not go. However, the *Canadian Bill of Rights* remains on the statute book. The one point where it might have practical significance is its recognition of a right to property and the right not to be deprived thereof except by due process of law. The *Charter* contains no right of property. ~

ATTORNEY GENERAL OF CANADA
v. LAVELL AND BÉDARD
[1974] S.C.R. 1349

Judgment: August 27, 1973.

Present: Fauteux C.J. and Abbott, Martland, Judson, Ritchie, Hall, Spence, Pigeon, and Laskin JJ.

Interveners: Six Nations Band of Indians of the County of Brant; Native Council of Canada; Rose Wilhelm, Alberta Committee on Indian Rights for Indian Women Inc., Viola Shannacaffo, University Women's Club of Toronto, University Women Graduates Ltd., North Toronto Business and Professional Women's Club Inc., and Monica Agnes Turner; Treaty Voice of Alberta, Anishnarvbekwek of Ontario Inc.; Indian Association of Alberta, the Union of British Columbia Indian Chiefs, the Manitoba Indian Brotherhood Inc., the Union of New Brunswick Indians, the Indian Brotherhood of the Northwest Territories, the Union of Nova Scotia Indians, the Union of Ontario Indians, the Federation of Saskatchewan Indians, the Indian Association of Quebec, the Yukon Native Brotherhood, and the National Indian Brotherhood.

The judgment of Fauteux C.J. and Martland, Judson, and Ritchie JJ. was delivered by

RICHIE J.: ... These appeals, which were heard together, are from two judgments holding that the provisions of s. 12(1)(*b*) of the *Indian Act*, R.S.C. 1970, c. I-6, are rendered inoperative by s. 1(*b*) of the *Canadian Bill of Rights*, 1960 (Can.), c. 44, as denying equality before the law to the two respondents.

Both respondents were registered Indians and "Band" members within the meaning of s. 11(*b*) of the *Indian Act* when they elected to marry non-Indians and thereby relinquished their status as Indians in conformity with the said s. 12(1)(*b*) which reads as follows:

12.(1) The following persons are not entitled to be registered, namely,
   (*b*) a woman who married a person who is not an Indian, unless that woman is subsequently the wife or widow of a person described in section 11.

It is contended on behalf of both respondents that s. 12(1)(*b*) of the *Act* should be held to be inoperative as discriminating between Indian men and women and as being in conflict with the provisions of the *Canadian Bill of Rights* and particularly s. 1 thereof which provides:

1. It is hereby recognized and declared that in Canada there have existed and shall continue to exist without discrimination by reason of race, national origin, colour, religion or sex, the following human rights and fundamental freedoms, namely, ...
   (*b*) the right of the individual to equality before the law and the protection of the law; ...

... The contention which formed the basis of the argument submitted by both respondents was that they had been denied equality before the law by reason of sex, and I propose to deal with the matter on this basis. ...

In my opinion the exclusive legislative authority vested in Parliament under s. 91(24) could not have been effectively exercised without enacting laws establishing the qualifications required to entitle persons to status as Indians and to the use and benefit of Crown "lands reserved for Indians." The legislation enacted to this end was, in my view, necessary for the implementation of the authority so vested in Parliament under the constitution.

To suggest that the provisions of the *Bill of Rights* have the effect of making the whole *Indian Act* inoperative as discriminatory is to assert that the Bill has rendered Parliament powerless to exercise the authority entrusted to it under the constitution of enacting legislation which treats Indians living on Reserves differently from other Canadians in relation to their property and civil rights. The proposition that such a wide effect is to be given to the *Bill of Rights* was expressly reserved by the majority of this Court in the case of *The Queen v. Drybones* [[1970] S.C.R. 282], at 298, to which reference will hereafter be made, and I do not think that it can be sustained.

What is at issue here is whether the *Bill of Rights* is to be construed as rendering inoperative one of the conditions imposed by Parliament for the use and occupation of Crown lands reserved for Indians. These conditions were imposed as a necessary part of the structure created by Parliament for the internal administration of the life of Indians on reserves and their entitlement to the use and benefit of Crown lands situate thereon, they were thus imposed, in discharge of Parliament's constitutional function under s. 91(24) and in my view can only be changed by plain statutory language expressly enacted for the purpose. It does not appear to me that Parliament can be taken to have made or intended to make such a change by the use of broad general language directed at the statutory proclamation of the fundamental rights and freedoms enjoyed by all Canadians, and I am therefore of opinion that the *Bill of Rights* had no such effect. . . .

The contention that the *Bill of Rights* is to be construed as overriding all of the special legislation imposed by Parliament under the *Indian Act* is, in my view, fully answered by Pigeon J. in his dissenting opinion in the *Drybones* case where he said, at p. 304:

> If one of the effects of the *Canadian Bill of Rights* is to render inoperative all legal provisions whereby Indians as such are not dealt with in the same way as the general public, the conclusion is inescapable that Parliament, by the enactment of the Bill, has not only fundamentally altered the status of the Indians in that indirect fashion but has also made any future use of federal legislative authority over them subject to the requirement of expressly declaring every time "that the law shall operate notwithstanding the *Canadian Bill of Rights.*" I find it very difficult to believe that Parliament so intended when enacting the Bill. If a virtual suppression of federal legislation over Indians as such was meant, one would have expected this important change to be made explicitly not surreptitiously so to speak. . . .

In considering the meaning to be given to section 1(*b*) of the *Bill of Rights*, regard must of course be had to what was said by Mr. Justice Laskin, speaking in this regard for the whole of the Court in *Curr v. The Queen* [[1972] S.C.R. 889, at pp. 896 and 897], where he interpreted sections 1(*a*) and 1(*b*) of the Bill in the following passage:

> In considering the reach of s. 1(*a*) and s. 1(*b*), and, indeed, of s. 1 as a whole, I would observe, first, that the section is given its controlling force over federal law by its referential incorporation into s. 2; and, second, that I do not read it as making the existence of any of the forms of prohibited discrimination, a *sine qua non* of its operation. Rather, the prohibited discrimination is an additional lever to which federal legislation must respond. Putting the matter another way, federal legislation which does not offend s. 1 in respect of any of the prohibited kinds of discrimination may nonetheless be offensive to s. 1 if it is violative of what is specified in any of the clauses (*a*) to

(*f*) of s. 1. It is, *a fortiori*, offensive if there is discrimination by reason of race so as to deny equality before the law. That is what this Court decided in *Regina v. Drybones* and I need say no more on this point.

> It is, therefore, not an answer to reliance by the appellant on s. 1(*a*) and s. 1(*b*) of the *Canadian Bill of Rights* that s. 223 does not discriminate against any person by reason of race, national origin, colour, religion or sex. The absence of such discrimination still leaves open the question whether s. 223 can be construed and applied without abrogating, abridging or infringing the rights of the individual listed in s. 1(*a*) and s. 1(*b*).

My understanding of this passage is that the effect of s. 1 of the *Bill of Rights* is to guarantee to all Canadians the rights specified in paragraphs (*a*) to (*f*) of that section, irrespective of race, national origin, colour or sex. This interpretation appears to me to be borne out by the French version which reads:

> 1. *Il est par les présentes reconnu et déclaré que les droits de l'homme et les libertés fondamentales ci-après énoncés ont existé et continueront à exister pour tout individu au Canada quels que soient sa race, son origine nationale, sa couleur, sa religion ou son sexe:*

It was stressed on behalf of the respondents that the provisions of s. 12(1)(*b*) of the *Indian Act* constituted "discrimination by reason of sex" and that the section could be declared inoperative on this ground alone even if such discrimination did not result in the infringement of any of the rights and freedoms specifically guaranteed by s. 1 of the Bill.

I can find no support for such a contention in the *Curr* case in which, in any event, no question of any kind of discrimination was either directly or indirectly involved. My own understanding of the passage which I have quoted from that case was that it recognized the fact that the primary concern evidenced by the first two sections of the *Bill of Rights* is to ensure that the rights and freedoms thereby recognized and declared shall continue to exist for all Canadians, and it follows, in my view, that those sections cannot be invoked unless one of the enumerated rights and freedoms has been denied to an individual Canadian or group of Canadians. Section 2 of the *Bill of Rights* provides for the manner in which the rights and freedoms which are recognized and declared by s. 1 are to be enforced and the effect of this section is that every law of Canada shall "be so construed and applied as not to abrogate, abridge or infringe or authorize the abrogation, abridgment or infringement of any of the rights and freedoms herein recognized and declared . . . ," (*i.e.* by s. 1). There is no language anywhere in the *Bill of Rights* stipulating that the laws of Canada are to be construed without discrimination unless that discrimination involves the denial of one of the guaranteed rights and freedoms, but when, as in the case of *The Queen v. Drybones, supra,* denial of one of the enumerated rights is occasioned by reason of discrimination, then, as Mr. Justice Laskin has said, the discrimination affords an "additional lever to which federal legislation must respond."

The opening words of s. 2 of the *Bill of Rights* are, in my view, determinative of the test to be applied in deciding whether the section here impugned is to be declared inoperative. The words to which I refer are:

> 2. Every law of Canada shall, unless it is expressly declared by an act of the Parliament of Canada that it shall operate notwithstanding the *Canadian Bill of Rights,* be so construed and applied as not to abrogate, abridge or infringe or authorize the abrogation, abridgement or infringement of the freedoms herein recognized and declared ...

In the course of the reasons for judgment rendered on behalf of the majority of this Court in *The Queen v. Drybones, supra,* this language was interpreted in the following passage at p. 294:

> It seems to me that a more realistic meaning must be given to the words in question and they afford, in my view, the clearest indication that s. 2 is intended to mean and does mean that if a law of Canada cannot be "sensibly construed and applied" so that it does not abrogate, abridge or infringe one of the rights and freedoms, recognized and declared by the *Bill,* then such law is inoperative "unless it is expressly declared by an Act of the Parliament of Canada that it shall operate notwithstanding the *Canadian Bill of Rights.*"

Accordingly, in my opinion, the question to be determined in these appeals is confined to deciding whether the Parliament of Canada in defining the prerequisites of Indian status so as not to include women of Indian birth who have chosen to marry non-Indians, enacted a law which cannot be sensibly construed and applied without abrogating, abridging or infringing the rights of such women to equality before the law.

In my view the meaning to be given to the language employed in the *Bill of Rights* is the meaning which it bore in Canada at the time when the *Bill* was enacted, and it follows that the phrase "equality before the law" is to be construed in light of the law existing in Canada at that time.

In considering the meaning to be attached to "equality before the law" as those words occur in section 1(*b*) of the *Bill,* I think it important to point out that in my opinion this phrase is not effective to invoke the egalitarian concept exemplified by the 14th Amendment of the U.S. Constitution as interpreted by the courts of that country. (See *Smythe v. The*

Queen [[1971] S.C.R. 680 *per* Fauteux C.J. at pp. 683 and 686]). I think rather that, having regard to the language employed in the second paragraph of the preamble to the *Bill of Rights,* the phrase "equality before the law" as used in s. 1 is to be read in its context as a part of "the rule of law" to which overriding authority is accorded by the terms of that paragraph.

In this connection I refer to Stephens *Commentaries on the Laws of England,* 21st Ed. 1950, where it is said in Vol. III at p. 337:

> Now the great constitutional lawyer Dicey writing in 1885 was so deeply impressed by the absence of arbitrary governments present and past, that he coined the phrase "the rule of law" to express the regime under which Englishmen lived; and he tried to give precision to it in the following words which have exercised a profound influence on all subsequent thought and conduct.
>
>> That the "rule of law" which forms a fundamental principle of the constitution has three meanings or may be regarded from three different points of view....

The second meaning proposed by Dicey is the one with which we are here concerned and it was stated in the following terms:

> It means again equality before the law or the equal subjection of all classes to the ordinary law of the land administered by the ordinary courts; the "rule of law" in this sense excludes the idea of any exemption of officials or others from the duty of obedience to the law which governs other citizens or from the jurisdiction of the ordinary courts.

"Equality before the law" in this sense is frequently invoked to demonstrate that the same law applies to the highest official of government as to any other ordinary citizen, and in this regard Professor F.R. Scott, in delivering the Plaunt Memorial Lectures on Civil Liberties and Canadian Federalism in 1959, speaking of the case of *Roncarelli v. Duplessis* [[1959] S.C.R. 121], had occasion to say:

> It is always a triumph for the law to show that it is applied equally to all without fear or favour. This is what we mean when we say that all are equal before the law.

The relevance of these quotations to the present circumstances is that "equality before the law" as recognized by Dicey as a segment of the rule of law, carries the meaning of equal subjection of all classes to the ordinary law of the land *as administered by the ordinary courts,* and in my opinion the phrase "equality before the law" as employed in section 1(*b*) of the *Bill of Rights* is to be treated as meaning equality in the administration or application of the law by the law enforcement authorities and the ordinary courts of the land. This construction is, in my view, supported by the provisions of subsections (*a*) to (*g*) of s. 2 of the *Bill* which clearly indicate to me that it was equality in the administration and enforcement of the law with which Parliament was concerned when it guaranteed the continued existence of "equality before the law."

Turning to the *Indian Act* itself, it should first be observed that by far the greater part of that *Act* is concerned with the internal regulation of the lives of Indians on Reserves and that the exceptional provisions dealing with the conduct of Indians off Reserves and their contacts with other Canadian citizens fall into an entirely different category. . . .

A careful reading of the *Act* discloses that section 95 (formerly 94) is the only provision therein made which creates an offence for any behaviour of an Indian *off* a Reserve and it will be plain that there is a wide difference between legislation such as s. 12(1)(*b*) governing the civil rights of designated persons living on Indian Reserves to the use and benefit of Crown lands, and criminal legislation such as s. 95 which creates an offence punishable at law for Indians to act in a certain fashion when *off* a Reserve. The former legislation is enacted as a part of the plan devised by Parliament, under s. 91(24) for the regulation of the internal domestic life of Indians on Reserves. The latter is criminal legislation exclusively concerned with behaviour of Indians off a Reserve. . . .

The *Drybones* case can, in my opinion, have no application to the present appeals as it was in no way concerned with the internal regulation of the lives of Indians *on* Reserves or their right to the use and benefit of Crown lands thereon, but rather deals exclusively with the effect of the *Bill of Rights* on a section of the *Indian Act* creating a crime with attendant penalties for the conduct by Indians *off* a Reserve in an area where non-Indians, who were also governed by federal law, were not subject to any such restriction.

The fundamental distinction between the present case and that of *Drybones*, however, appears to me to be that the impugned section in the latter case could not be enforced without denying equality of treatment in the administration and enforcement of the law before the ordinary courts of the land to a racial group, whereas no such inequality of treatment between Indian men and women flows as a necessary result of the application of s. 12(1)(*b*) of the *Indian Act*.

To summarize the above, I am of opinion:

1. That the *Bill of Rights* is not effective to render inoperative legislation, such as s. 12(1)(*b*) of the *Indian Act*, passed by the Parliament of Canada in discharge of its constitutional function under s. 91(24) of the *B.N.A. Act*, to specify how and by whom Crown lands reserved for Indians are to be used;

2. that the *Bill of Rights* does not require federal legislation to be declared inoperative unless it offends against one of the rights specifically guaranteed by section 1, but where legislation is found to be discriminatory, this affords an added reason for rendering it ineffective;

3. that equality before the law under the *Bill of Rights* means equality of treatment in the enforcement and application of the laws of Canada before the law enforcement authorities and the ordinary courts of the land, and no such inequality is necessarily entailed in the construction and application of s. 12(1)(*b*). . . .

ABBOTT J. (dissenting): The facts which are not in dispute are set out in the reasons of Ritchie and Laskin JJ. which I have had the advantage of reading. I am in agreement with the reasons of Laskin J. and wish to add only a few observations.

I share his view that the decision of this Court in *The Queen v. Drybones* [[1970] S.C.R. 282] cannot be distinguished from the two cases under appeal although in these two appeals the consequences of the discrimination by reason of sex under s. 12(1)(*b*) of the *Indian Act* are more serious than the relatively minor penalty for the drinking offence under s. 94 of the *Act* which was in issue in *Drybones*.

In that case, this Court rejected the contention that s. 1 of the *Canadian Bill of Rights* provided merely a canon of construction for the interpretation of legislation existing when the *Bill* was passed. With respect I cannot interpret "equality before the law" as used in s. 1(*b*) of the *Bill* as meaning simply "the equal subjection of all classes to the ordinary law of the land as administered by the ordinary courts" to use the language of Dicey which is quoted in the reasons of Ritchie J.

Unless the words "without discrimination by reason of race, national origin, colour, religion or sex" used in s. 1 are to be treated as mere rhetorical window dressing, effect must be given to them in interpreting the section. I agree with Laskin J. that s. 1(*b*) must be read as if those words were recited therein.

In my view the *Canadian Bill of Rights* has substantially affected the doctrine of the supremacy of Parliament. Like any other statute it can of course be repealed or amended, or a particular law declared to be applicable notwithstanding the provisions of the *Bill*. In form the supremacy of Parliament is maintained but in practice I think that it has been substantially curtailed. In my opinion that result is undesirable, but that is a matter for consideration by Parliament not the courts.

Ritchie J. said in his reasons for judgment in *Drybones* that the implementation of the *Bill of Rights* by the courts can give rise to great difficulties and that statement has been borne out in subsequent litigation. Of one thing I am certain, the *Bill* will continue to supply ample grist to the judicial mills for some time to come. . . .

The judgment of Hall, Spence, and Laskin JJ. was delivered by

LASKIN J. (dissenting): . . . In my opinion, unless we are to depart from what was said in *Drybones*, both appeals now before us must be dismissed. I have no disposition to reject what was decided in *Drybones*; and on the central issue of prohibited discrimination as catalogued in s. 1 of the *Canadian Bill of Rights*, it is, in my opinion, impossible to distinguish *Drybones* from the two cases in appeal. If, as in *Drybones*, discrimination by reason of race makes certain statutory provisions inoperative, the same result must follow as to statutory provisions which exhibit discrimination by reason of sex. . . .

In both cases, which were argued together, leave was given to various bodies and organizations and to a number of individuals to intervene by representation and by submissions to this Court. The position of the Attorney General of Canada in the *Lavell* case was supported by counsel appearing on behalf of The Indian Association of Alberta, The Union of British Columbia Indian Chiefs, The Manitoba Indian Brotherhood Inc., The Union of New Brunswick Indians, The Indian Brotherhood of the Northwest Territories, The Union of Nova Scotia Indians, The Union of Ontario Indians, The Federation of Saskatchewan Indians, The Indian Association of Quebec, The Yukon Native Brotherhood and The National Indian Brotherhood, by counsel appearing on behalf of the Six Nations Band and by counsel appearing on behalf of the Treaty Voice of Alberta Association. The position of the respondent was supported by counsel appearing for the Native Council of Canada, by counsel appearing for Rose Wilhelm, Alberta Committee on Indian Rights for Indian Women Inc., Viola Shannacappo, University Women's Club of Toronto and University Women Graduates Limited, The North Toronto Business and Professional Women's Club Inc. and Monica Agnes Turner, and by counsel for Anishnawbekwek of Ontario Incorporated. There was the same division of support for the appellants and the respondent in the *Bédard* case, in which the Attorney General of Canada also intervened to support the position of the appellants. . . .

The contentions of the appellants in both cases in appeal, stripped of their detail, amount to a submission that the *Canadian Bill of Rights* does not apply to Indians on a Reserve, nor to Indians in their relations to one another whether or not on a Reserve. This submission does not deny that the effect of s. 12(1)(*b*) of the *Indian Act* is to prescribe substantive discrimination by reason of sex, a differentiation in the treatment of Indian men and Indian women when they marry non-Indians, this differentiation being exhibited in the loss

by the women of their status as Indians under the *Act*. It does, however, involve the assertion that the particular discrimination upon which the two appeals are focused is not offensive to the relevant provisions of the *Canadian Bill of Rights*; and it also involves the assertion that the *Drybones* case is distinguishable or, if not, that it has been overcome by the re-enactment of the *Indian Act* in the Revised Statutes of Canada, 1970, including the then s. 94 (now s. 95) which was in issue in that case. I regard this last-mentioned assertion, which is posited on the fact that the *Canadian Bill of Rights* was not so re-enacted, as simply an oblique appeal for the overruling of the *Drybones* case.

The *Drybones* case decided two things. It decided first—and this decision was a necessary basis for the second point in it—that the *Canadian Bill of Rights* was more than a mere interpretation statute whose terms would yield to a contrary intention; it had paramount force when a federal enactment conflicted with its terms, and it was the incompatible federal enactment which had to give way. This was the issue upon which the then Chief Justice of this Court, Chief Justice Cartwright, and Justices Abbott and Pigeon, dissented. Pigeon J. fortified his view on this main point by additional observations, bringing into consideration, *inter alia*, s. 91(24) of the *British North America Act*. The second thing decided by *Drybones* was that the accused in that case, an Indian under the *Indian Act*, was denied equality before the law, under s. 1(*b*) of the *Canadian Bill of Rights*, when it was made a punishable offence for him, on account of his race, to do something which his fellow Canadians were free to do without being liable to punishment for an offence. Ritchie J., who delivered the majority opinion of the Court, reiterated this basis of decision by concluding his reasons as follows:

> It appears to me to be desirable to make it plain that these reasons for judgment are limited to a situation in which, under the laws of Canada, it is made an offence punishable at law on account of race, for a person to do something which all Canadians who are not members of that race may do with impunity.

It would be unsupportable in principle to view the *Drybones* case as turning on the fact that the challenged s. 94 of the *Indian Act* created an offence visited by punishment. The gist of the judgment lay in the legal disability imposed upon a person by reason of his race when other persons were under no similar restraint. If for the words "on account of race" there are substituted the words "on account of sex" the result must surely be the same where a federal enactment imposes disabilities or prescribes disqualifications for members of the female sex which are not imposed upon members of the male sex in the same circumstances.

It is said, however, that although this may be so as between males and females in general, it does not follow where the distinction on the basis of sex is limited as here to members of the Indian race. This, it is said further, does not offend the guarantee of "equality before the law" upon which the *Drybones* case proceeded. I wish to deal with these two points in turn and to review, in connection with the first point, the legal consequences for an Indian woman under the *Indian Act* when she marries a non-Indian.

It appears to me that the contention that a differentiation on the basis of sex is not offensive to the *Canadian Bill of Rights* where that differentiation operates only among Indians under the *Indian Act* is one that compounds racial inequality even beyond the point that the *Drybones* case found unacceptable. In any event, taking the *Indian Act* as it stands, as a law of Canada whose various provisions fall to be assessed under the *Canadian Bill of Rights*, I am unable to appreciate upon what basis the command of the *Canadian Bill of Rights*, that laws of Canada shall operate without discrimination by reason of sex, can be ignored in the operation of the *Indian Act*.

The *Indian Act* defines an Indian as a person who is registered as an Indian pursuant to the *Act* or is entitled to be so registered. It is registration or registrability upon a Band list or upon a general list that is the key to the scheme and application of the *Act*. The Registrar, charged with keeping the membership records, is the person to whom protests may be made by a Band Council or by an affected person respecting the inclusion or deletion of a name from the Indian Register. By s. 9(2) his decision on a protest is final subject to a reference to a judge under s. 9(3). The *Lavell* case arose in this way. Section 11 of the *Act* enumerates the persons entitled to be registered, and it is common ground that both Mrs. Lavell and Mrs. Bédard were so entitled prior to their respective marriages. Section 12 lists the classes of persons not entitled to be registered, and the only clause thereof relevant here is subsection 1(b) which I have already quoted. Section 14 has a peripheral relevance to the present case in its provision that a woman member of a Band who marries a person outside that Band ceases to be a member thereof but becomes a member of the Band of which her husband is a member. There is no absolute disqualification of an Indian woman from registrability on the Indian Register (that is, as a member on the general list) by marrying outside a Band unless the marriage is to a non-Indian.

Registration or registrability entitles an Indian as a member of a Band (and that was the status of both Mrs. Lavell and Mrs. Bédard prior to their respective marriages) to the use and benefit of the Reserve set aside for the Band. This may take the form of possession or occupation of particular land in the Reserve under an allotment by the Council of the Band

with the approval of the responsible Minister, and it may be evidenced by a certificate of possession or a certificate of occupation, the latter representing possession for a limited period only. Indians may make wills disposing of their property, and it may also pass on intestacy, in either case subject to approval or control of the Minister or of a competent court; and in the case of a devise or descent of land in a Reserve the claimant's possession must be approved by the Minister under s. 49. Section 50 has only a remote bearing on the *Bédard* case in providing that a person who is not entitled to reside on a Reserve does not by devise or descent acquire a right to possession or occupation of land in that Reserve. It begs the question in that the issue here is whether or not Mrs. Bédard became disentitled to reside on the land in the Reserve which was left to her by her mother upon the latter's death in 1969. The fact that the respondent's brother now holds a certificate of possession of all the land formerly possessed by the mother, that certificate having been issued after the respondent transferred her interest to her brother in February, 1971, does not affect the overriding question of the respondent's right to reside on the land, having her brother's consent to residence thereon.

Indians entitled to be registered and to live on a Reserve are members of a society in which, through Band Councils, they share in the administration of the Reserve subject to overriding governmental authority. There is provision for election of councillors by Band members residing on a Reserve, and I note that there is no statutory discrimination between Indian men and women either as qualified electors or as qualified candidates for election as councillors. Other advantages that come from membership in the social unit relate to farm operations and to eligibility for governmental loans for various enumerated purposes.

Section 12(1)(b) effects a statutory excommunication of Indian women but not of Indian men. Indeed, as was pointed out by counsel for the Native Council of Canada, the effect of ss. 11 and 12(1)(b) is to excommunicate the children of a union of an Indian woman with a non-Indian. There is also the invidious distinction, invidious at least in the light of the *Canadian Bill of Rights*, that the *Indian Act* creates between brothers and sisters who are Indians and who respectively marry non-Indians. The statutory banishment directed by s. 12(1)(b) is not qualified by the provision in s. 109(2) for a governmental order declaring an Indian woman who has married a non-Indian to be enfranchised. Such an order is not automatic and no such order was made in relation to Mrs. Bédard; but when made the woman affected is, by s. 110, deemed not to be an Indian within the *Indian Act* or any other statute or law. It is, if anything, an additional legal instrument of separation of an Indian woman from her native society and from her kin, a separation to which no Indian man who marries a non-Indian is exposed.

It was urged, in reliance in part on history, that the discrimination embodied in the *Indian Act* under s. 12(1)(*b*) is based upon a reasonable classification of Indians as a race, that the *Indian Act* reflects this classification and that the paramount purpose of the *Act* to preserve and protect the members of the race is promoted by the statutory preference for Indian men. Reference was made in this connection to various judgments of the Supreme Court of the United States to illustrate the adoption by that Court of reasonable classifications to square with the due process clause of the Fifth Amendment and with due process and equal protection under the Fourteenth Amendment. Those cases have at best a marginal relevance because the *Canadian Bill of Rights* itself enumerates prohibited classifications which the judiciary is bound to respect; and, moreover, I doubt whether discrimination on account of sex, where as here it has no biological or physiological rationale, could be sustained as a reasonable classification even if the direction against it was not as explicit as it is in the *Canadian Bill of Rights*.

I do not think it is possible to leap over the telling words of s. 1, "without discrimination by reason of race, national origin, colour, religion or sex," in order to explain away any such discrimination by invoking the words "equality before the law" in clause (*b*) and attempting to make them alone the touchstone of reasonable classification. That was not done in the *Drybones* case; and this Court made it clear in *Curr v. The Queen*, that federal legislation, which might be compatible with the command of "equality before the law" taken alone, may nonetheless be inoperative if it manifests any of the prohibited forms of discrimination. In short, the proscribed discriminations in s. 1 have a force either independent of the subsequently enumerated clauses (*a*) to (*f*) or, if they are found in any federal legislation, they offend those clauses because each must be read as if the prohibited forms of discrimination were recited therein as a part thereof.

This seems to me an obvious construction of s. 1 of the *Canadian Bill of Rights*. When that provision states that the enumerated human rights and fundamental freedoms shall continue to exist "without discrimination by reason of race, national origin, colour, religion or sex," it is expressly adding these words to clauses (*a*) to (*f*). Section 1(*b*) must read therefore as "the right of the individual to equality before the law and the protection of the law without discrimination by reason of race, national origin, colour, religion or sex." It is worth repeating that this is what emerges from the *Drybones* case and what is found in the *Curr* case.

There is no clear historical basis for the position taken by the appellants, certainly not in relation to Indians in Canada as a whole, and this was in effect conceded during the hearing in this Court. In any event, history cannot avail against the clear words of ss. 1 and 2 of the *Canadian Bill of Rights*. It is s. 2 that gives this enactment its effective voice, because without it s. 1 would remain a purely declaratory provision. Section 2 brings the terms of s. 1 into its orbit, and its reference to "every law of Canada" is a reference, as set out in s. 5(2), to any Act of the Parliament of Canada enacted before or after the effective date of the *Canadian Bill of Rights*. Pre-existing Canadian legislation as well as subsequent Canadian legislation is expressly made subject to the commands of the *Canadian Bill of Rights*, and those commands, where they are as clear as the one which is relevant here, cannot be diluted by appeals to history. Ritchie J. in his reasons in the *Drybones* case touched on this very point when he rejected the contention that the terms of s. 1 of the *Canadian Bill of Rights* must be circumscribed by the provisions of Canadian statutes in force at the date of the enactment of the *Canadian Bill of Rights*: see [1970] S.C.R. 282, at pp. 295-296. I subscribe fully to the rejection of that contention. Clarity here is emphasized by looking at the French version of the *Canadian Bill of Rights* which speaks in s. 1 of the enumerated human rights and fundamental freedoms "*pour tout individu au Canada quels que soient sa race, son origine nationale, sa couleur, sa religion ou son sexe.*"

In my opinion, the appellants' contentions gain no additional force because the *Indian Act*, including the challenged s. 12(1)(*b*) thereof, is a fruit of the exercise of Parliament's exclusive legislative power in relation to "Indians, and Lands reserved for the Indians" under s. 91(24) of the *British North America Act*. Discriminatory treatment on the basis of race or colour or sex does not inhere in that grant of legislative power. The fact that its exercise may be attended by forms of discrimination prohibited by the *Canadian Bill of Rights* is no more a justification for a breach of the *Canadian Bill of Rights* than there would be in the case of the exercise of any other head of federal legislative power involving provisions offensive to the *Canadian Bill of Rights*. The majority opinion in the *Drybones* case dispels any attempt to rely on the grant of legislative power as a ground for escaping from the force of the *Canadian Bill of Rights*. The latter does not differentiate among the various heads of legislative power; it embraces all exercises under whatever head or heads they arise. Section 3 which directs the Minister of Justice to scrutinize every Bill to ascertain whether any of its provisions are inconsistent with ss. 1 and 2 is simply an affirmation of this fact which is evident enough from ss. 1 and 2.

There was an intimation during the argument of these appeals that the *Canadian Bill of Rights* is properly invoked only to resolve a clash under its terms between two federal statutes, and the *Drybones* case was relied on in that connection. It is a spurious contention, if seriously advanced, because the *Canadian Bill of Rights* is itself the indicator to which any Canadian statute or any provision thereof must yield unless Parliament has declared that the statute or the particular provision is to operate notwithstanding the *Canadian Bill of Rights*. A statute may in itself be offensive to the *Canadian Bill of Rights*, or it may be by relation to another statute that it is so offensive.

I would dismiss both appeals with costs.

PIGEON J.: I agree in the result with Ritchie J. I certainly cannot disagree with the view I did express in *The Queen v. Drybones* [at p. 304] that the enactment of the *Canadian Bill of Rights* was not intended to effect a virtual suppression of federal legislation over Indians. My difficulty is Laskin J.'s strongly reasoned opinion that, unless we are to depart from what was said by the majority in *Drybones*, these appeals should be dismissed because, if discrimination by reason of race makes certain statutory provisions inoperative, the same result must follow as to statutory provisions which exhibit discrimination by reason of sex. In the end, it appears to me, that, in the circumstances, I need not reach a firm conclusion on that point. Assuming the situation is such as Laskin J. says, it cannot be improper for me to adhere to what was my dissenting view, when a majority of those who did not agree with it in respect of a particular section of the *Indian Act*, now adopt it for the main body of this important statute.

I would observe that this result does not conflict with any of our decisions subsequent to *Drybones*. In no case was the *Canadian Bill of Rights* given an invalidating effect over prior legislation.

In *Lowry and Lepper v. The Queen* [(1972), 26 D.L.R. (3d) 224] and in *Brownridge v. The Queen* [[1972] S.C.R. 926], the application of criminal legislation, past and subsequent, was held to be subject to provisions respecting a "fair hearing" and "the right to retain and instruct counsel." These decisions are important illustrations of the effectiveness of the *Bill* without any invalidating effect.

In *Smythe v. The Queen* [[1971] S.C.R. 680] it was held that provisions for stiffer penalties depending on the method of prosecution were not rendered inoperative by the *Canadian Bill of Rights* as infringing equality before the law, although the choice of the method of prosecution always depends on executive discretion.

In *Curr v. The Queen* [[1972] S.C.R. 889] recent *Criminal Code* provisions for compulsory breath analysis were held not to infringe the right to the "protection of the law" any more than the right to the "protection against self-crimination."

Finally, in *Duke v. The Queen* [[1972] S.C.R. 917] these same provisions were said not to deprive the accused of a "fair trial" although proclaimed without some paragraphs contemplating a specimen being offered and given on request to the suspect.

C. THE CHARTER OF RIGHTS AND FREEDOMS

 **The Queen v. Big M Drug Mart Ltd., 1985**

*B*ig M Drug Mart was among the first *Charter* cases to be decided by the Supreme Court. It clearly demonstrates the contrast between the Supreme Court's treatment of the *Charter of Rights and Freedoms* and its treatment two decades earlier of the *Canadian Bill of Rights*. In 1963 in *Robertson and Rosetanni*[1] the Court, with only one dissent, found that the federal *Lord's Day Act* did not contravene the right to freedom of religion in the *Canadian Bill of Rights*. Twenty-two years later, in *Big M*, the Court struck down the federal *Lord's Day Act* on the ground that it violated the right to freedom of conscience and religion in section 2 of the Charter.

In its initial approach to the *Bill of Rights*, the Court had adopted the view that the rights and freedoms in that document must be no wider than what was provided for under Canadian law at the time the Bill was adopted. There was no trace of that "frozen rights" thesis in the Court's early treatment of the *Charter*. The fact that the *Lord's Day Act* had been on the statute book since 1906 had no bearing on whether it violated the *Charter*'s guarantee of religious freedom. In *Robertson and Rosetanni*, the majority considered the effect, not the purpose, of the legislation, and held that because compulsory Sunday closing did not actually force anyone to worship in a Christian manner it did not affect freedom of religion. In *Big M*, for all of the justices except Justice Wilson, analysis of the challenged legislation began with the purpose behind the legislation at the time of its enactment. In the Court's view, that purpose in 1906 was clearly religious—to secure the observance by all of the Christian Sabbath. Legislation passed for such a purpose, in the Court's view, clearly violated the right to freedom of religion.

The majority and Justice Wilson differed on whether the assessment of challenged legislation should begin with its purpose or effect, while agreeing that if either the purpose or effect of legislation violates the *Charter* the legislation must be considered unconstitutional. Perhaps the majority's preference for beginning with the purpose of legislation was to avoid, if possible, the extensive examination of the practical consequences of legislation. Justice Wilson was less diffident about the judiciary's capacity for this kind of policy analysis.

Central to the Court's "purposive" approach to *Charter* interpretation was Chief Justice Dickson's inquiry into the meaning of "freedom of religion." The purpose he looks for here is not the stated intent of the *Charter*'s drafters, but the broad historical reasons for this freedom becoming a cherished ideal in western civilization. While this "purposive" approach may yield a fairly generous interpretation of *Charter* rights and freedoms, the Chief Justice was careful to point out that it must not be pushed so far as to "overshoot the actual purpose of the right or freedom in question." The Chief Justice was laying the groundwork for a moderate activism.

---

1   [1963] S.C.R. 651. For a discussion of this case, see case 21.

The Court's decision in *Big M* by no means settled the Sunday-closing issue in Canada. By ruling out a religious or moral rationale for Sunday-closing legislation, it eliminated the criminal law power, the only basis for federal legislation, thereby leaving this controversial policy issue to the provinces. All the provinces had developed more contemporary and secular legislation regulating commercial activities on Sundays. The following year, in *Edwards Books*,[2] the Court upheld Ontario's *Retail Business Holiday Act*, which prohibited most retailing on Sundays, but exempted the owners of small businesses whose religion required them to close their stores on Saturdays.

The Supreme Court's decision in *Big M Drug Mart* recognizes that a major transformation has taken place in Canadian society. Canada was no longer to be considered, in any official or legal sense, a Christian society. Chief Justice Dickson's opinion brought into play, for the first time, section 27 of the *Charter*, directing the courts to interpret the *Charter* "in a manner consistent with the preservation and enhancement of the multicultural heritage of Canadians." The Chief Justice cited this section as a further reason for interpreting the right to freedom of religion as excluding laws enacted for the purpose of enforcing the precepts of the Christian religion. Religious pluralism is to be an essential ingredient of the cultural pluralism of the modern Canadian state. ⁓

---

2   *R. v. Edwards Books and Art Ltd.*, [1986] 2 S.C.R. 713.

HER MAJESTY THE QUEEN v. BIG M DRUG MART LTD.
[1985] 1 S.C.R. 295

Hearing: March 6, 7, 1984; Judgment: April 24, 1985.

Present: Dickson C.J. and Ritchie,* Beetz, McIntyre, Chouinard, Lamer, and Wilson JJ.

Interveners: The Attorney General of Canada, the Attorney General of New Brunswick, and the Attorney General of Saskatchewan.

* Ritchie J. took no part in the judgment.

The judgment of Dickson C.J. and Beetz, McIntyre, Chouinard, and Lamer JJ. was delivered by

[1]   **DICKSON C.J.:** Big M Drug Mart Ltd. was charged with unlawfully carrying on the sale of goods, on Sunday, May 30, 1982 in the City of Calgary, Alberta, contrary to the *Lord's Day Act*, R.S.C. 1970, c. L-13.

[2]   Big M has challenged the constitutionality of the *Lord's Day Act*, both in terms of the division of powers and the *Canadian Charter of Rights and Freedoms*. Such challenge places in issue before this Court, for the first time, one of the fundamental freedoms protected by the *Charter*, the guarantee of "freedom of conscience and religion" entrenched in s. 2.

[3]   The constitutional validity of Sunday observance legislation has in the past been tested largely through the division of powers provided in ss. 91 and 92 of the *Constitution Act, 1867*. Freedom of religion has been seen to be a matter falling within federal legislative competence. Today, following the advent of the *Constitution Act, 1982*, we must address squarely the fundamental issues raised by individual rights and freedoms enshrined in the *Charter*, as well as those concerned with legislative powers....

V. The Characterization of the Lord's Day Act

... [48]   There are obviously two possible ways to characterize the purpose of Lord's Day legislation, the one religious, namely securing public observance of the Christian institution of the Sabbath and the other secular, namely providing a uniform day of rest from labour. It is undoubtedly true that both elements may be present in any given enactment, indeed it is almost inevitable that they will be, considering that such laws combine a prohibition of ordinary employment for one day out of seven with a specification that this day of rest shall be the Christian Sabbath—Sunday. In the Anglo-Canadian tradition this intertwining is to be seen as far back as early Saxon times in such laws as that promulgated by Ine, King of Wessex from 688–725....

[51]   Historically, there seems little doubt that it was religious purpose which underlay the enactment of English Lord's Day legislation. From early times the moral exhortation found in the Fourth Commandment (Exodus 20: 8-11) "Remember the Sabbath day, to keep it holy" increasingly

became a legislative imperative. The first major piece of legislation, *The Sunday Fairs Act*, 27 Hen. 6, c. 5, prefaced its prohibition of fairs and markets on Sunday with a recital of "abomenable injuries and offences done to Almighty God and to his Saints" because of bodily labour, deceitful bargaining, drunkenness and religious non-observance associated with fairs. Following the Reformation under Henry VIII, religious observance acquired an added political significance and a number of statutes aimed at securing religious conformity were promulgated. . . .

[52] Under Charles I the first modern Sunday observance statutes were enacted and their religious purpose is reflected in their titles, *An Act for punishing divers Abuses committed on the Lord's Day, called Sunday*, 1 Car. 1, c. 1 and *An Act for the further Reformation of sundry Abuses committed on the Lord's Day, commonly called Sunday*, 3 Car. 1, c. 2. During the Commonwealth or Interregnum period, the Puritan Parliament passed strict laws prohibiting the profanation of the Lord's Day by any form of marketing, travel, worldly labour, sports or recourse to taverns, tobacco shops or restaurants. With the Restoration came *An Act for the better Observation of the Lord's Day commonly called Sunday*, 29 Car. 2, c. 7, also known as the *Sunday Observance Act*. As its full title indicates, the primary object of this legislation, like that of its predecessors, was clearly religious rather than secular. . . .

[53] The *Sunday Observance Act* of 1677 served as a model for Canadian pre-Confederation legislation, especially *An Act to prevent the Profanation of the Lord's Day, commonly called Sunday, in Upper Canada*, 1845 (Can.), c. 45, which substantially re-enacted the English law with only minor alterations designed to suit it to the specific conditions and activities of Upper Canada. It was this statute, as re-enacted by the post-Confederation legislature of Ontario (R.S.O. 1897, c. 246), that the Privy Council found to be beyond the competence of the province to enact in *Attorney-General for Ontario v. Hamilton Street Railway Co.*, [1903] A.C. 524, a decision which lay behind the passage in 1906 of the federal *Lord's Day Act*. Like the Ontario *Act*, the federal *Act* embodied the basic framework and much of the language of the English *Sunday Observance Act* of 1677. After four consolidations, it still exhibits these same essential characteristics in its present form. . . .

[54] From the time of Confederation until the Privy Council decision in 1903 in *Hamilton Street Railway, supra*, it was the widely-held view that Sunday observance legislation fell within provincial purview under the *Constitution Act, 1867* as being a matter falling under either s. 92(13), property and civil rights within the province, or s. 92(16), a matter of merely local or private nature in the Province. Several of the provinces passed laws prohibiting Sunday activities. In the *Hamilton*

Street Railway case the Ontario statute fell to be considered. Aylesworth K.C. argued before the Privy Council that the primary object of the *Act* under consideration was the promotion of public order, safety and morals, and not the regulation of civil rights as between subject and subject. That view would seem to have prevailed, as their Lordships held that the *Act* as a whole was beyond the competence of the Ontario Legislature to enact. . . .

[55] . . . The Parliament of Canada passed the federal *Lord's Day Act*, 1906 (Can.), c. 27, with what would appear to have been some degree of reluctance because, firstly, s. 14 provided that nothing in the *Act* should be construed to repeal or in any way affect "any provisions of any Act or law relating in any way to the observance of the Lord's Day in force in any province of Canada when this *Act* comes into force." Sunday observance legislation in force in a province at the time it entered Confederation was expressly preserved. Secondly, while the *Act* prohibited a very few activities unconditionally, such as shooting in such a manner as to disturb public worship or observance of the day, or selling foreign newspapers, the most important sections of the *Act* made other activities unlawful only to the extent that provincial legislation did not provide otherwise.

[56] Acting under the authority of the federal *Lord's Day Act*, the provinces have enacted legislation such as the *Lord's Day (Ontario) Act*, R.S.O. 1980, c. 253, and *The Lord's Day (Saskatchewan) Act*, R.S.S. 1978, c. L-34. Provincial legislation of this nature was upheld by the Judicial Committee of the Privy Council in *Lord's Day Alliance of Canada v. Attorney-General for Manitoba*, [1925] A.C. 384, and more recently by this Court in *Lord's Day Alliance of Canada v. Attorney General of British Columbia*, [1959] S.C.R. 497. . . .

[65] We come now to the case of *Robertson and Rosetanni* [(1963) S.C.R. 651], *supra*, to which much attention was directed during argument. The appellants were convicted on a charge of operating a bowling alley on a Sunday, contrary to the *Lord's Day Act*. They contended that the *Canadian Bill of Rights*, R.S.C. 1970, App. III, had in effect repealed s. 4 of the *Lord's Day Act* or, in any event, rendered it inoperative. The Court, Cartwright J. dissenting, rejected the contention and dismissed the appeal. . . .

[73] The United States Supreme Court has sustained the constitutionality of Sunday observance legislation against First Amendment challenges: *McGowan v. Maryland*, 366 U.S. 420 (1961); *Braunfeld v. Brown*, 366 U.S. 599 (1961), *Gallagher v. Crown Kosher Super Market of Massachusetts, Inc.*, 366 U.S. 617 (1961), and *Two Guys from Harrison-Allentown, Inc. v. McGinley*, 366 U.S. 582 (1961). Despite the undoubted religious motivation of the state laws in question at the time of their passage and their clear origin in the religiously coercive

statutes of Stuart England, Chief Justice Warren, writing for the majority, found that those statutes had evolved to become purely secular labour regulation. In his view, none of the impugned state statutes violated the First Amendment guarantee of freedom of religion. Whatever religious terminology still appeared in the legislation (such as the use of the term "Lord's Day" in the Maryland statute) was to be seen simply as a historical curiosity. . . .

[77] It is somewhat ironic that the United States courts upheld the validity of Sunday observance laws, characterizing them as secular in order not to run afoul of the religion clauses of the First Amendment, while in contrast, in *Robertson v. Rosetanni, supra,* the Court found in the same type of legislation, a religious purpose in order to sustain its *vires* as criminal law. At the same time it accorded to the legislation a secular effect in order not to bring it into conflict with the religious freedom recognized and declared in the *Canadian Bill of Rights.* . . .

VI. Purpose and Effect of Legislation

[78] A finding that the *Lord's Day Act* has a secular purpose is, on the authorities, simply not possible. Its religious purpose, in compelling sabbatical observance, has been long-established and consistently maintained by the courts of this country.

[79] The Attorney General for Alberta concedes that the *Act* is characterized by this religious purpose. He contends, however, that it is not the purpose but the effects of the *Act* which are relevant. In his submission, *Robertson and Rosetanni, supra,* is support for the proposition that it is effects alone which must be assessed in determining whether legislation violates a constitutional guarantee of freedom of religion.

[80] I cannot agree. In my view, both purpose and effect are relevant in determining constitutionality; either an unconstitutional purpose or an unconstitutional effect can invalidate legislation. All legislation is animated by an object the legislature intends to achieve. This object is realized through the impact produced by the operation and application of the legislation. Purpose and effect respectively, in the sense of the legislation's object and its ultimate impact, are clearly linked, if not indivisible. Intended and actual effects have often been looked to for guidance in assessing the legislation's object and thus, its validity.

[81] Moreover, consideration of the object of legislation is vital if rights are to be fully protected. The assessment by the courts of legislative purpose focuses scrutiny upon the aims and objectives of the legislature and ensures they are consonant with the guarantees enshrined in the *Charter.* The declaration that certain objects lie outside the legislature's power checks governmental action at the first stage of uncon-

stitutional conduct. Further, it will provide more ready and more vigorous protection of constitutional rights by obviating the individual litigant's need to prove effects violative of *Charter* rights. It will also allow courts to dispose of cases where the object is clearly improper, without inquiring into the legislation's actual impact. . . .

[88] In short, I agree with the respondent that the legislation's purpose is the initial test of constitutional validity and its effects are to be considered when the law under review has passed or, at least, has purportedly passed the purpose test. If the legislation fails the purpose test, there is no need to consider further its effects, since it has already been demonstrated to be invalid. Thus, if a law with a valid purpose interferes by its impact, with rights or freedoms, a litigant could still argue the effects of the legislation as a means to defeat its applicability and possibly its validity. In short, the effects test will only be necessary to defeat legislation with a valid purpose; effects can never be relied upon to save legislation with an invalid purpose.

[89] A second related submission is made by the Attorney General of Saskatchewan with respect to the characterization of the *Lord's Day Act.* Both Stevenson, Prov. Ct. J., at trial, and the American Supreme Court, in its quartet on Sunday observance legislation, suggest that the purpose of legislation may shift, or be transformed over time by changing social conditions. . . . A number of objections can be advanced to this "shifting purpose" argument.

[90] First, there are the practical difficulties. No legislation would be safe from a revised judicial assessment of purpose. Laws assumed valid on the basis of persuasive and powerful authority could, at any time, be struck down as invalid. Not only would this create uncertainty in the law, but it would encourage re-litigation of the same issues and, it could be argued, provide the courts with a means by which to arrive at a result dictated by other than legal considerations. . . .

[91] Furthermore, the theory of a shifting purpose stands in stark contrast to fundamental notions developed in our law concerning the nature of "Parliamentary intention." Purpose is a function of the intent of those who drafted and enacted the legislation at the time, and not of any shifting variable. . . .

[93] While the effect of such legislation as the *Lord's Day Act* may be more secular today than it was in 1677 or in 1906, such a finding cannot justify a conclusion that its purpose has similarly changed. In result, therefore, the *Lord's Day Act* must be characterized as it has always been, a law the primary purpose of which is the compulsion of sabbatical observance.

VII. Freedom of Religion

[94] A truly free society is one which can accommodate a wide variety of beliefs, diversity of tastes and pursuits, customs

and codes of conduct. A free society is one which aims at equality with respect to the enjoyment of fundamental freedoms and I say this without any reliance upon s. 15 of the *Charter*. Freedom must surely be founded in respect for the inherent dignity and the inviolable rights of the human person. The essence of the concept of freedom of religion is the right to entertain such religious beliefs as a person chooses, the right to declare religious beliefs openly and without fear of hindrance or reprisal, and the right to manifest religious belief by worship and practice or by teaching and dissemination. But the concept means more than that.

[95] Freedom can primarily be characterized by the absence of coercion or constraint. If a person is compelled by the state or the will of another to a course of action or inaction which he would not otherwise have chosen, he is not acting of his own volition and he cannot be said to be truly free. One of the major purposes of the *Charter* is to protect, within reason, from compulsion or restraint. Coercion includes not only such blatant forms of compulsion as direct commands to act or refrain from acting on pain of sanction, coercion includes indirect forms of control which determine or limit alternative courses of conduct available to others. Freedom in a broad sense embraces both the absence of coercion and constraint, and the right to manifest beliefs and practices. Freedom means that, subject to such limitations as are necessary to protect public safety, order, health, or morals or the fundamental rights and freedoms of others, no one is to be forced to act in a way contrary to his beliefs or his conscience.

[96] What may appear good and true to a majoritarian religious group, or to the state acting at their behest, may not, for religious reasons, be imposed upon citizens who take a contrary view. The *Charter* safeguards religious minorities from the threat of "the tyranny of the majority."

[97] To the extent that it binds all to a sectarian Christian ideal, the *Lord's Day Act* works a form of coercion inimical to the spirit of the *Charter* and the dignity of all non-Christians. In proclaiming the standards of the Christian faith, the *Act* creates a climate hostile to, and gives the appearance of discrimination against, non-Christian Canadians. It takes religious values rooted in Christian morality and, using the force of the state, translates them into a positive law binding on believers and non-believers alike. The theological content of the legislation remains as a subtle and constant reminder to religious minorities within the country of their differences with, and alienation from, the dominant religious culture.

[98] Non-Christians are prohibited for religious reasons from carrying out activities which are otherwise lawful, moral and normal. The arm of the state requires all to remember the Lord's day of the Christians and to keep it holy. The protection of one religion and the concomitant non-protection of others imports disparate impact destructive of the religious freedom of the collectivity.

[99] I agree with the submission of the respondent that to accept that Parliament retains the right to compel universal observance of the day of rest preferred by one religion is not consistent with the preservation and enhancement of the multicultural heritage of Canadians. To do so is contrary to the expressed provisions of s. 27....

[100] If I am a Jew or a Sabbatarian or a Muslim, the practice of my religion at least implies my right to work on a Sunday if I wish. It seems to me that any law purely religious in purpose, which denies me that right, must surely infringe my religious freedom....

[103] Much of the argument before this Court on the issue of the meaning of freedom of conscience and religion was in terms of "free exercise" and "establishment." These categories derive from the guarantee of freedom of religion in the First Amendment to the Constitution of the United States. The relevant part of the First Amendment reads:

> Congress shall make no law respecting an establishment
> of religion, or prohibiting the free exercise thereof; ...

[104] It is the appellant's argument that unlike the American *Bill of Rights*, the *Canadian Charter of Rights and Freedoms* does not include an "establishment clause." He urged therefore that the protection of freedom of conscience and religion extends only to the "free exercise" of religion....

[105] In my view this recourse to categories from the American jurisprudence is not particulary helpful in defining the meaning of freedom of conscience and religion under the *Charter*. The adoption in the United States of the categories "establishment" and "free exercise" is perhaps an inevitable consequence of the wording of the First Amendment. The cases illustrate, however, that these are not two totally separate and distinct categories, but rather, as the Supreme Court of the United States has frequently recognized, in specific instances "the two clauses may overlap." ...

[106] Thus while it is true that in its four Sunday closing cases the United States Supreme Court does categorize compulsory religious observance as a potential violation of the "anti-establishment" principle, more frequently and more typically these same words signify the very different principle of the prohibition of preferential treatment of, or state financial support to, particular religions or religious institutions.

[107] In further support for this line of argument the appellant cites s. 29 of the *Charter* quoted earlier, and s. 93 of the *Constitution Act, 1867*. These provisions were cited as proof of the non-existence of an anti-establishment principle because they guarantee existing rights to financial support from the state for denominational schools. The respondent

replies that these express provisions constitute specific and limited exceptions to the general principle of religious freedom which would otherwise prohibit any support or preference to denominational schools. Subsequent cases will decide the extent to which the *Charter* allows for state financial support for, or preferential treatment of, particular religions or religious institutions. That issue is not before us in the present case. . . .

[115] It is not necessary to reopen the issue of the meaning of freedom of religion under the *Canadian Bill of Rights*, because whatever the situation under that document, it is certain that the *Canadian Charter of Rights and Freedoms* does not simply "recognize and declare" existing rights as they were circumscribed by legislation current at the time of the *Charter's* entrenchment. The language of the *Charter* is imperative. It avoids any reference to existing or continuing rights but rather proclaims in the ringing terms of s. 2 that:

Everyone has the following fundamental freedoms:
(*a*) Freedom of conscience and religion.

I agree with the submission of the respondent that the *Charter* is intended to set a standard upon which *present as well as future* legislation is to be tested. . . .

[116] This Court has already, in some measure, set out the basic approach to be taken in interpreting the *Charter*. In *Hunter v. Southam Inc.*, [1984] 2 S.C.R. 145, this Court expressed the view that the proper approach to the definition of the rights and freedoms guaranteed by the *Charter* was a purposive one. The meaning of a right or freedom guaranteed by the *Charter* was to be ascertained by an analysis of the *purpose* of such a guarantee; it was to be understood, in other words, in the light of the interests it was meant to protect.

[117] In my view this analysis is to be undertaken, and the purpose of the right or freedom in question is to be sought by reference to the character and the larger objects of the *Charter* itself, to the language chosen to articulate the specific right or freedom, to the historical origins of the concepts enshrined, and where applicable, to the meaning and purpose of the other specific rights and freedoms with which it is associated within the text of the *Charter*. The interpretation should be, as the judgment in *Southam* emphasizes, a generous rather than a legalistic one, aimed at fulfilling the purpose of the guarantee and securing for individuals the full benefit of the *Charter's* protection. At the same time it is important not to overshoot the actual purpose of the right or freedom in question, but to recall that the *Charter* was not enacted in a vacuum, and must therefore, as this Court's decision in *Law Society of Upper Canada v. Skapinker*, [1984] 1 S.C.R. 357, illustrates, be placed in its proper linguistic, philosophic and historical contexts.

[118] With regard to freedom of conscience and religion, the historical context is clear. As they are relevant to the *Charter*, the origins of the demand for such freedom are to be found in the religious struggles in post-Reformation Europe. The spread of new beliefs, the changing religious allegiance of kings and princes, the shifting military fortunes of their armies and the consequent repeated redrawing of national and imperial frontiers led to situations in which large numbers of people—sometimes even the majority in a given territory—found themselves living under rulers who professed faiths different from, and often hostile to, their own and subject to laws aimed at enforcing conformity to religious beliefs and practices they did not share.

[119] English examples of such laws, passed during the Tudor and Stuart periods have been alluded to in the discussion above of the criminal law character of Sunday observance legislation. Opposition to such laws was confined at first to those who upheld the prohibited faiths and practices, and was designed primarily to avoid the disabilities and penalties to which these specific adherents were subject. As a consequence, when history or geography put power into the hands of these erstwhile victims of religious oppression the persecuted all too often became the persecutors.

[120] Beginning, however, with the Independent faction within the Parliamentary party during the Commonwealth or Interregnum, many, even among those who shared the basic beliefs of the ascendent religion, came to voice opposition to the use of the State's coercive power to secure obedience to religious precepts and to extirpate non-conforming beliefs. The basis of this opposition was no longer simply a conviction that the State was enforcing the wrong set of beliefs and practices but rather the perception that belief itself was not amenable to compulsion. Attempts to compel belief or practice denied the reality of individual conscience and dishonoured the God that had planted it in His creatures. It is from these antecedents that the concepts of freedom of religion and freedom of conscience became associated, to form, as they do in s. 2(*a*) of our *Charter*, the single integrated concept of "freedom of conscience and religion."

[121] What unites enunciated freedoms in the American First Amendment, s. 2(*a*) of the *Charter* and in the provisions of other human rights documents in which they are associated is the notion of the centrality of individual conscience and the inappropriateness of governmental intervention to compel or to constrain its manifestation. In *Hunter v. Southam Inc.*, *supra*, the purpose of the *Charter* was identified, at p. 155, as "the unremitting protection of individual rights and liberties." It is easy to see the relationship between respect for individual conscience and the valuation of human dignity that motivates such unremitting protection.

[122] It should also be noted, however, that an emphasis on individual conscience and individual judgment also lies at the heart of our democratic political tradition. The ability of each citizen to make free and informed decisions is the absolute prerequisite for the legitimacy, acceptability, and efficacy of our system of self-government. It is because of the centrality of the rights associated with freedom of individual conscience both to basic beliefs about human worth and dignity and to a free and democractic political system that American jurisprudence has emphasized the primacy or "firstness" of the First Amendment. It is this same centrality that in my view underlies their designation in the *Canadian Charter of Rights and Freedoms* as "fundamental." They are the *sine qua non* of the political tradition underlying the *Charter.*

[123] Viewed in this context, the purpose of freedom of conscience and religion becomes clear. The values that underlie our political and philosophic traditions demand that every individual be free to hold and to manifest whatever beliefs and opinions his or her conscience dictates, provided *inter alia* only that such manifestations do not injure his or her neighbours or their parallel rights to hold and manifest beliefs and opinions of their own. Religious belief and practice are historically prototypical and, in many ways, paradigmatic of conscientiously-held beliefs and manifestations and are therefore protected by the *Charter.* Equally protected, and for the same reasons, are expressions and manifestations of religious non-belief and refusals to participate in religious practice. It may perhaps be that freedom of conscience and religion extends beyond these principles to prohibit other sorts of governmental involvement in matters having to do with religion. For the present case it is sufficient in my opinion to say that whatever else freedom of conscience and religion may mean, it must at the very least mean this: government may not coerce individuals to affirm a specific religious belief or to manifest a specific religious practice for a sectarian purpose....

[133] In my view, the guarantee of freedom of conscience and religion prevents the government from compelling individuals to perform or abstain from performing otherwise harmless acts because of the religious significance of those acts to others. The element of religious compulsion is perhaps somewhat more difficult to perceive (especially for those whose beliefs are being enforced) when, as here, it is non-action rather than action that is being decreed, but in my view compulsion is nevertheless what it amounts to.

[134] I would like to stress that nothing in these reasons should be read as suggesting any opposition to Sunday being spent as a religious day; quite the contrary. It is recognized that for a great number of Canadians, Sunday is the day when their souls rest in God, when the spiritual takes priority over the material, a day which, to them, gives security and meaning because it is linked to Creation and the Creator. It is a day which brings a balanced perspective to life, an opportunity for man to be in communion with man and with God. In my view, however, as I read the *Charter,* it mandates that the legislative preservation of a Sunday day of rest should be secular, the diversity of belief and non-belief, the diverse socio-cultural backgrounds of Canadians make it constitutionally incompetent for the federal Parliament to provide legislative preference for any one religion at the expense of those of another religious persuasion.

[135] In an earlier time, when people believed in the collective responsibility of the community toward some deity, the enforcement of religious conformity may have been a legitimate object of government, but since the *Charter,* it is no longer legitimate. With the *Charter,* it has become the right of every Canadian to work out for himself or herself what his or her religious obligations, if any, should be and it is not for the state to dictate otherwise. The state shall not use the criminal sanctions at its disposal to achieve a religious purpose, namely, the uniform observance of the day chosen by the Christian religion as its day of rest.

[136] On the authorities and for the reasons outlined, the true purpose of the *Lord's Day Act* is to compel the observance of the Christian Sabbath and I find the *Act,* and especially s. 4 thereof, infringes upon the freedom conscience and religion guaranteed in s. 2(*a*) of the *Charter....*

VIII. Section 1 of the Charter

...[138] The appellant submits that even if the *Lord's Day Act* does involve a violation of freedom of conscience and religion as guaranteed by s. 2(*a*) of the *Charter,* the provisions of the *Act* constitute a reasonable limit, demonstrably justifiable in a free and democratic society on that right and that therefore the *Act* can be saved pursuant to s. 1 of the *Charter....*

[140] Two reasons have been advanced to justify the legislation here in issue as a reasonable limit. It can be urged that the choice of the day of rest adhered to by the Christian majority is the most practical. This submission is really no more than an argument of convenience and expediency and is fundamentally repugnant because it would justify the law upon the very basis upon which it is attacked for violating s. 2(*a*).

[141] The other more plausible argument is that everyone accepts the need and value of a universal day of rest from all work, business and labour and it may as well be the day traditionally observed in our society. I accept the secular justification for a day of rest in a Canadian context and the reasonableness of a day of rest has been clearly enunciated by the courts in the United States of America. The first and fatal difficulty with this argument is, as I have said, that it asserts an objective which has never been found by this Court to be the motivation

for the legislation. It seems disingenuous to say that the legislation is valid criminal law and offends s. 2(*a*) because it compels the observance of a Christian religious duty, yet is still a reasonable limit demonstrably justifiable because it achieves the secular objective the legislators did not primarily intend. The appellant can no more assert under s. 1 a secular objective to validate legislation which in pith and substance involves a religious matter than it could assert a secular objective as the basis for the argument that the legislation does not offend s. 2(*a*). While there is no authority on this point, it seems clear that Parliament cannot rely upon an *ultra vires* purpose under s. 1 of the *Charter*. This use of s. 1 would invite colourability, allowing Parliament to do indirectly what it could not do directly....

IX. Classification

[144] The third question put in issue by this Court is this:

Is the *Lord's Day Act*, R.S.C. 1970, c. L-13, and especially s. 4 thereof enacted pursuant to the criminal law power under s. 91(27) of the *Constitution Act, 1867*?

[145] All members of the Alberta Court of Appeal agreed that settled authority compelled the conclusion that the *Lord's Day Act* was competent to Parliament pursuant to its power to legislate in relation to criminal law under s. 91(27). The appellant and his supporting interveners submit that the Court of Appeal was correct in their conclusion and the respondent concedes the point....

[149] It should be noted, however, that this conclusion as to the federal Parliament's legislative competence to enact the *Lord's Day Act* depends on the identification of the purpose of the *Act* as compelling observance of Sunday by virtue of its religious significance. Were its purpose not religious but rather the secular goal of enforcing a uniform day of rest from labour, the *Act* would come under s. 92(13), property and civil rights in the province and, hence, fall under provincial rather than federal competence....

WILSON J.: ...

[153] In his reasons for judgment Dickson J. (Chief Justice at the date of the judgment) has canvassed in a most thorough fashion all the substantive questions entailed in the analysis of constitutionality and has come to the conclusion that the *Lord's Day Act* is validly enacted pursuant to the federal criminal law power under s. 91(27) of the *Constitution Act, 1867*. He has concluded, however, that it infringes upon the right to freedom of religion in s. 2(*a*) of the *Charter* and that such infringement cannot be justified under s. 1 of the *Charter*. I agree with those conclusions and the only issue I wish to address in these reasons is the appropriate analytic

approach to a *Charter* case, in a word, the distinction between the analysis demanded by the *Charter* and the analysis traditionally pursued in resolving division of powers litigation under ss. 91 and 92 of the *Constitution Act, 1867*.

[154] It is, of course, trite law that the analytic starting point in a division of powers case is the determination of the "pith and substance" of the challenged enactment. In the words of Professor Bora Laskin (as he then was) the court endeavours to achieve a "distillation of the 'constitutional value' represented by the challenged legislation . . . and its attribution to a head of power." . . .

[156] The division of powers jurisprudence is repleat with instances where the analytic focal point in determining whether a given piece of legislation is *ultra vires* the enacting legislature is the purpose or primary function of the legislation. Only when the effects of the legislation so directly impinge on some other subject matter as to reflect some alternative or ulterior purpose do the effects themselves take on analytic significance....

[158] In my view, the constitutional entrenchment of civil liberties in the *Canadian Charter of Rights and Freedoms* necessarily changes the analytic approach the courts must adopt in such cases. As Chief Justice Burger indicated in the celebrated anti-discrimination case of *Griggs v. Duke Power Co.*, 401 U.S. 424 (1970), at p. 432, the starting point for any analysis of a civil rights violation is "the *consequences* of [discriminatory] employment practices, not simply the motivation." Speaking in the context of equality rights as they pertain to employment, Burger C.J. stated at p. 432:

. . . good intent or absence of discriminatory intent does not redeem employment procedures or testing mechanisms that operate as "built-in headwinds" for minority groups. . . .

While it remains perfectly valid to evaluate the purpose underlying a particular enactment in order to determine whether the legislature has acted within its constitutional authority in division of powers terms, the *Charter* demands an evaluation of the impingement of even *intra vires* legislation on the fundamental rights and freedoms of the individual. It asks not whether the legislature has acted for a purpose that is within the scope of the authority of that tier of government, but rather whether in so acting it has had the effect of violating an entrenched individual right. It is, in other words, first and foremost an effects-oriented document....

[161] Applying such reasoning to the case at bar, one can agree with Dickson J. at p. 337, that in enacting the *Lord's Day Act* "[t]he arm of the state requires all to remember the Lord's day of the Christians and to keep it holy," and that "[t]he protection of one religion and the concomitant non-protection

of others imports disparate impact destructive of the religious freedom of the collectivity." Accordingly, the *Act* infringes upon the freedom of conscience and religion guaranteed in s. 2(*a*) of the *Charter*. This is not, however, because the statute was enacted for this *purpose* but because it has this *effect*. In my view, so long as a statute has such an actual or potential effect on an entrenched right, it does not matter what the purpose behind the enactment was. . . .

[164] Accordingly, I agree with Dickson J. that the appeal in this case must be dismissed. The *Lord's Day Act* is in pith and substance legislation with a criminal law purpose and is therefore enacted by Parliament pursuant to the federal criminal law power in s. 91(27) of the *Constitution Act, 1867*. In so far as the *Charter of Rights* is concerned, however, I believe that the appropriate analytic starting point is the effect rather than the purpose of the enactment. . . .

# Re B.C. Motor Vehicle Act, 1985

The *B.C. Motor Vehicle Reference* is an example of a case that is relatively unimportant with respect to the policy issue at stake, but very significant in terms of its impact on constitutional interpretation and development. While the fate of section 94(2) of B.C.'s *Motor Vehicle Act* was quickly forgotten, the Supreme Court's decision in this case has gone on to be one of the Court's most frequently cited judgments.

Section 94(1) of B.C.'s *Motor Vehicle Act* made it an offence for a person to drive if his licence had been revoked or he had been legally prohibited from driving. Section 94(2) made it an absolute liability offence—that is, guilt was established by proof of driving, whether or not the driver knew of the prohibition or suspension. The offence was punishable by a fine and a minimum term of imprisonment. Shortly after the adoption of the *Charter*, the B.C. government had doubts about the compatibility of section 94(2) with the *Charter*, and so referred the question to the provincial Court of Appeal. The latter found that the provision violated the *Charter*, and there was an automatic appeal to the Supreme Court of Canada.

At issue was whether the absolute liability provision violated the "principles of fundamental justice" set forth in section 7 of the *Charter*. The Attorney-General of British Columbia argued that the meaning of section 7 was limited to "procedural fairness" alone, and that section 7 did not authorize judges to pass judgment on the fairness of the "substance" of impugned legislation.

The notion of "substantive due process" had a long and checkered history in American constitutional law. Between 1900 and 1937, the American Supreme Court had used the due-process clause of the American Constitution to strike down numerous progressive laws that imposed new social and economic regulations on American business. In effect, the American Court had used substantive due process to protect the laissez-faire economic system and conservative economic interests from the emerging welfare state. This culminated in the New Deal "court crisis" of 1937, after which the substantive-due-process precedents were abandoned and discredited. However, substantive due process re-emerged in American jurisprudence in the 1970s, most notably in the abortion decision.[1] As the *Charter* was being drafted, the term "fundamental justice" replaced "due process" in order to avoid the substantive connotations the latter term had acquired in American law.

Speaking for a unanimous court, Justice Lamer rejected a strict dichotomy between "substantive" and "procedural" interpretations of section 7. The two could not be so easily separated. The entire array of procedural safeguards enumerated in sections 8 through 14 of the *Charter* constitute the substance of principles of fundamental justice articulated in section 7. More to the point, Justice Lamer wrote: "A law that has the potential to convict a person who has not really done anything wrong offends the principles of fundamental justice. . . . In other words, absolute liability and imprisonment cannot be combined."

Justice Lamer was well aware that attributing substantive meaning to the concept of principles of fundamental justice could unduly widen the scope of judicial review under

---

1 *Roe v. Wade*, 410 U.S. 113 (1973). See the introduction to *Morgentaler v. The Queen*, case 25.

section 7, resulting in what he called a "super judicial legislature." To discourage this, he stressed that a substantive interpretation of section 7 was limited to the field of criminal law and legal rights, "the inherent domain of the judiciary," and would not be applied "in the realm of general public policy." However, several subsequent decisions by lower courts extended this doctrine to areas of economic and social policy. The closest the Supreme Court of Canada has come to applying a substantive interpretation of section 7 outside the criminal law area was its decision in *Chaoulli*, where it split, 3 to 3, on whether a ban on private medical insurance for services covered by medicare is "arbitrary" and therefore a violation of section 7.[2] If the Supreme Court were to use section 7 to review the reasonableness of social and economic policy, the scope of the *Charter* and thus the power of the judges would expand considerably.

Of equal significance was Justice Lamer's handling of the historical evidence of the "framers' intent" to limit section 7 to a narrow procedural meaning. While conceding the admissibility of the framers' intent as relevant to determining the proper interpretation of *Charter* rights, Justice Lamer cautioned against granting such extrinsic evidence anything more than "minimal weight." To attach any more significance to the "original understanding" of *Charter* rights, he cautioned, "would in effect be assuming a fact which is nearly impossible of proof, i.e., the intention of the legislative bodies which adopted the *Charter*." Moreover, it would reintroduce the much criticized "frozen concepts" doctrine, as opposed to a "large and liberal" interpretation of the *Charter* mandated by the frequently cited "living tree" approach.[3]

By freeing constitutional law from the drafters' intentions, the Court has granted itself and all other Canadian judges the discretion to read new meaning into the *Charter* sections other than what the framers' understood and intended those sections to mean. Future litigants can now invoke the symbol of the *Charter* as a living tree and argue that, even if the meaning they attribute to a *Charter* right was not part of its original meaning, the judge is still free to add the new meaning.[4]

This aspect of the *B.C. Motor Vehicle Reference* is best illustrated by an anecdote from the *Borowski* anti-abortion case.[5] The very day the Supreme Court handed down its decision in the *Motor Vehicle Reference*—December 17, 1985—pro-life crusader Joe Borowski began his hearing before the Court of Appeal of Saskatchewan. Borowski's lawyer, Morris Schumiatcher, argued that the sections of the *Criminal Code* allowing therapeutic abortions violate the "right to life" of the unborn child/foetus as protected by section 7 of the *Charter*. The history of the drafting of the *Charter* clearly indicates that the government rejected requests to include either a right to abortion for women or a right to life for the unborn. The Crown attorney had effectively used this evidence of the framers' intent to rebut Schumiatcher's arguments. The court would be unjustified, the Crown argued, to give a meaning to the *Charter* that had been explicitly rejected by the people who wrote it.

On the third and last day of the hearing, Schumiatcher was making his closing statement when one of his assistants hurriedly arrived clutching a document. After a brief huddle,

---

2 See case 36.

3 See the introduction to this book.

4 See case 43.

5 Transcript of Appeal Proceedings on October 3 and 4, 1988, *Borowski v. Canada (Attorney General)*, [1989] 1 S.C.R. 342.

Schumiatcher excitedly announced to the Court that he had just received a copy of a Supreme Court decision handed down in Ottawa the previous day. The case was the *B.C. Motor Vehicle Reference.* Schumiatcher triumphantly quoted Justice Lamer's comments about the non-binding character of the "original intent." The three judges were now free, Schumiatcher exhorted them, to adopt the living-tree approach and to expand the meaning of section 7 to include the unborn. Ironically, but not surprisingly, Dr. Henry Morgentaler, Borowski's counterpart in the legal battle over Canada's abortion law, subsequently made extensive use of the *B.C. Motor Vehicle* precedent, but for the opposite purpose—to urge the Supreme Court to find a right to abortion in section 7 of the *Charter.*[6]

Note that the Supreme Court has not been consistent on this matter. In other cases it has relied heavily on the use of the original understanding of *Charter* text to bolster the authority of its decisions. The most important judicial use of original understanding was the *Quebec Association of Protestant School Boards* decision[7] striking down the education provisions of Bill 101. Referring to the "Canada clause" of section 23 of the *Charter,* the Court declared:

> This set of constitutional provisions was not enacted by the legislator in a vacuum. . . . the legislator knew, and clearly had in mind the regimes governing Anglophone and Francophone linguistic minorities in various provinces in Canada . . . and their intention was to remedy the perceived defects of these regimes by uniform corrective measures, namely those contained in s. 23 of the *Charter.* ⌐

---

6   See case 25.

7   *A.G. Quebec v. Quebec Association of Protestant School Boards,* [1984] 2 S.C.R. 66.

RE B.C. MOTOR VEHICLE ACT
[1985] 2 S.C.R. 486

Hearing: November 15, 1984; Judgment: December 17, 1985.

Present: Dickson C.J. and Beetz, McIntyre, Chouinard, Lamer, Wilson, and Le Dain JJ.

Interveners: the Attorney General of Canada, the Attorney General for Ontario, the Attorney General for Saskatchewan, the Attorney General for Alberta, the British Columbia Branch of the Canadian Bar Association.

The judgment of Dickson, Beetz, Chouinard, Le Dain, and Lamer JJ. was delivered by

[1]   **LAMER J.:**

Introduction

[2]   A law that has the potential to convict a person who has not really done anything wrong offends the principles of fundamental justice and, if imprisonment is available as a penalty, such a law then violates a person's right to liberty under s. 7 of the *Charter of Rights and Freedoms* (*Constitution Act, 1982,* as enacted by the *Canada Act 1982,* 1982 (U.K.), c. 11).

[3]   In other words, absolute liability and imprisonment cannot be combined.

The Facts

[4]   On August 16, 1982, the Lieutenant-Governor in Council of British Columbia referred the following question to the Court of Appeal of that province, by virtue of s. 1 of the *Constitutional Question Act,* R.S.B.C. 1979, c. 63:

> Is s. 94(2) of the *Motor Vehicle Act,* R.S.B.C. 1979, as amended by the *Motor Vehicle Amendment Act, 1982,* consistent with the *Canadian Charter of Rights and Freedoms?*

[5]   On February 3, 1983, the Court of Appeal handed down reasons in answer to the question in which it stated that s. 94(2) of the *Act* is inconsistent with the *Canadian Charter of Rights and Freedoms. . .*

The Legislation

[6]   *Motor Vehicle Act,* R.S.B.C. 1979, c. 288, s. 94, as amended by the *Motor Vehicle Amendment Act, 1982,* 1982 (B.C.), c. 36, s. 19:

> 94.(1) A person who drives a motor vehicle on a highway or industrial road while
>   (a) he is prohibited from driving a motor vehicle under sections 90, 91, 92 or 92.1, or

(b) his driver's licence or his right to apply for or obtain a driver's licence is suspended under section 82 or 92 as it was before its repeal and replacement came into force pursuant to the *Motor Vehicle Amendment Act, 1982,*

commits an offence and is liable,

(c) on a first conviction, to a fine of not less than $300 and not more than $2 000 and to imprisonment for not less than 7 days and not more than 6 months, and

(d) on a subsequent conviction, regardless of when the contravention occurred, to a fine of not less than $300 and not more than $2 000 and to imprisonment for not less than 14 days and not more than one year.

(2) Subsection (1) creates an absolute liability offence in which guilt is established by proof of driving, whether or not the defendant knew of the prohibition or suspension. . . .

Section 7

1. Introduction

[10] The issue in this case raises fundamental questions of constitutional theory, including the nature and the very legitimacy of constitutional adjudication under the *Charter* as well as the appropriateness of various techniques of constitutional interpretation. . . .

[12] The novel feature of the *Constitution Act* . . . is not that it has suddenly empowered courts to consider the content of legislation. This the courts have done for a good many years when adjudicating upon the *vires* of legislation. . . .

[13] The truly novel features of the *Constitution Act, 1982* are that it has sanctioned the process of constitutional adjudication and has extended its scope so as to encompass a broader range of values. Content of legislation has always been considered in constitutional adjudication. Content is now to be equally considered as regards new constitutional issues. Indeed, the values subject to constitutional adjudication now pertain to the rights of individuals as well as the distribution of governmental powers. In short, it is the scope of constitutional adjudication which has been altered rather than its nature, at least, as regards the right to consider the content of legislation.

[14] In neither case, be it before or after the *Charter*, have the courts been enabled to decide upon the appropriateness of policies underlying legislative enactments. In both instances, however, the courts are empowered, indeed required, to measure the content of legislation against the guarantees of the Constitution. . . .

[15] In this respect, s. 7 is no different than other *Charter* provisions. As the Attorney General for Ontario has noted in his factum:

Section 7, like most of the other sections in the *Charter*, limits the bounds of legislative action. It is the function of the Court to determine whether the challenged legislation has honoured those boundaries. This process necessitates judicial review of the content of the legislation.

Yet, in the context of s. 7, and in particular, of the interpretation of "principles of fundamental justice," there has prevailed in certain quarters an assumption that all but a narrow construction of s. 7 will inexorably lead the courts to "question the wisdom of enactments," to adjudicate upon the merits of public policy.

[16] From this have sprung warnings of the dangers of a judicial "super-legislature" beyond the reach of Parliament, the provincial legislatures and the electorate. The Attorney General for Ontario, in his written argument, stated that,

. . . the judiciary is neither representative of, nor responsive to the electorate on whose behalf, and under whose authority policies are selected and given effect in the laws of the land.

This is an argument which was heard countless times prior to the entrenchment of the *Charter* but which has in truth, for better or for worse, been settled by the very coming into force of the *Constitution Act, 1982*. It ought not to be forgotten that the historic decision to entrench the *Charter* in our Constitution was taken not by the courts but by the elected representatives of the people of Canada. It was those representatives who extended the scope of constitutional adjudication and entrusted the courts with this new and onerous responsibility. Adjudication under the *Charter* must be approached free of any lingering doubts as to its legitimacy.

[17] The concerns with the bounds of constitutional adjudication explain the characterization of the issue in a narrow and restrictive fashion, *i.e.*, whether the term "principles of fundamental justice" has a substantive or merely procedural content. In my view, the characterization of the issue in such fashion preempts an open-minded approach to determining the meaning of "principles of fundamental justice."

[18] The substantive/procedural dichotomy narrows the issue almost to an all-or-nothing proposition. Moreover, it is largely bound up in the American experience with substantive and procedural due process. It imports into the Canadian context American concepts, terminology and jurisprudence, all of which are inextricably linked to problems concerning the nature and legitimacy of adjudication under the U.S. Constitution. That Constitution, it must be remembered, has no s. 52 nor has it the internal checks and balances of ss. 1 and 33. We would, in my view, do our own Constitution a disservice to simply allow the American debate to define the issue for us,

all the while ignoring the truly fundamental structural differences between the two constitutions. Finally, the dichotomy creates its own set of difficulties by the attempt to distinguish between two concepts whose outer boundaries are not always clear and often tend to overlap. Such difficulties can and should, when possible, be avoided.

[19] The overriding and legitimate concern that courts ought not to question the wisdom of enactments, and the presumption that the legislator could not have intended same, have to some extent distorted the discussion surrounding the meaning of "principles of fundamental justice." This has led to the spectre of a judicial "super-legislature" without a full consideration of the process of constitutional adjudication and the significance of ss. 1 and 33 of the *Charter* and s. 52 of the *Constitution Act, 1982*. This in turn has also led to a narrow characterization of the issue and to the assumption that only a procedural content to "principles of fundamental justice" can prevent the courts from adjudicating upon the merits or wisdom of enactments. If this assumption is accepted, the inevitable corollary, with which I would have to then agree, is that the legislator intended that the words "principles of fundamental justice" refer to procedure only.

[20] But I do not share that assumption. Since way back in time and even recently the courts have developed the common law beyond procedural safeguards without interfering with the "merits or wisdom" of enactments....

[21] The task of the Court is not to choose between substantive or procedural content *per se* but to secure for persons "the full benefit of the *Charter*'s protection" (Dickson J. (as he then was) in *R. v. Big M Drug Mart Ltd.*, [1985] 1 S.C.R. 295, at p. 344), under s. 7, while avoiding adjudication of the merits of public policy. This can only be accomplished by a purposive analysis....

[22] I propose therefore to approach the interpretation of s. 7 in the manner set forth by Dickson J. in *Hunter v. Southam Inc.*, [1984] 2 S.C.R. 145, and *R. v. Big M Drug Mart Ltd.*, *supra*, and by Le Dain J. in *R. v. Therens*, [1985] 1 S.C.R. 613. In *R. v. Big M Drug Mart Ltd.*, Dickson J. wrote at p. 344:

> In *Hunter v. Southam Inc.*, [1984] 2 S.C.R. 145, this Court expressed the view that the proper approach to the definition of the rights and freedoms guaranteed by the *Charter* was a purposive one. The meaning of a right or freedom guaranteed by the *Charter* was to be ascertained by an analysis of the *purpose* of such a guarantee; it was to be understood, in other words, in the light of the interests it was meant to protect....

[23] ... [Section 7] states "and the right not to be deprived thereof except in accordance with the principles of fundamental justice." On the facts of this case it is not necessary to decide whether the section gives any greater protection, such as deciding whether, absent a breach of the principles of fundamental justice, there still can be, given the way the section is structured, a violation of one's rights to life, liberty and security of the person under s. 7. Furthermore, because of the fact that only deprivation of liberty was considered in these proceedings and that no one took issue with the fact that imprisonment is a deprivation of liberty, my analysis of s. 7 will be limited, as was the course taken by all, below and in this Court, to determining the scope of the words "principles of fundamental justice." I will not attempt to give any further content to liberty nor address that of the words life or security of the person.

[24] In the framework of a purposive analysis, designed to ascertain the purpose of the s. 7 guarantee and "the interests it was meant to protect" (*R. v. Big M Drug Mart Ltd.*, *supra*), it is clear to me that the interests which are meant to be protected by the words "and the right not to be deprived thereof except in accordance with the principles of fundamental justice" of s. 7 are the life, liberty and security of the person. The principles of fundamental justice, on the other hand, are not a protected interest, but rather a qualifier of the right not to be deprived of life, liberty and security of the person....

[26] ... As a qualifier, the phrase serves to establish the parameters of the interests but it cannot be interpreted so narrowly as to frustrate or stultify them. For the narrower the meaning given to "principles of fundamental justice" the greater will be the possibility that individuals may be deprived of these most basic rights....

[26] For these reasons, I am of the view that it would be wrong to interpret the term "fundamental justice" as being synonymous with natural justice as the Attorney General of British Columbia and others have suggested. To do so would strip the protected interests of much, if not most, of their content and leave the "right" to life, liberty and security of the person in a sorely emaciated state....

[28] Sections 8 to 14 ... address specific deprivations of the "right" to life, liberty and security of the person in breach of the principles of fundamental justice, and as such, violations of s. 7. They are designed to protect, in a specific manner and setting, the right to life, liberty and security of the person set forth in s. 7. It would be incongruous to interpret s. 7 more narrowly than the rights in ss. 8 to 14....

[29] ... Clearly, some of those sections embody principles that are beyond what could be characterized as "procedural."

[30] Thus, ss. 8 to 14 provide an invaluable key to the meaning of "principles of fundamental justice." Many have been developed over time as presumptions of the common law, others have found expression in the international conventions on human rights. All have been recognized as essential elements of a system for the administration of justice which is

founded upon a belief in "the dignity and worth of the human person" (preamble to the *Canadian Bill of Rights*, R.S.C. 1970, App. III) and on "the rule of law" (preamble to the *Canadian Charter of Rights and Freedoms*).

[31] It is this common thread which, in my view, must guide us in determining the scope and content of "principles of fundamental justice." In other words, the principles of fundamental justice are to be found in the basic tenets of our legal system. They do not lie in the realm of general public policy but in the inherent domain of the judiciary as guardian of the justice system. . . .

[32] Thus, it seems to me that to replace "fundamental justice" with the term "natural justice" misses the mark entirely. It was, after all, clearly open to the legislator to use the term natural justice, a known term of art, but such was not done. We must, as a general rule, be loath to exchange the terms actually used with terms so obviously avoided.

[33] Whatever may have been the degree of synonymy between the two expressions in the past . . . as of the last few decades this country has given a precise meaning to the words natural justice for the purpose of delineating the responsibility of adjudicators (in the wide sense of the word) in the field of administrative law.

[34] It is, in my view, that precise and somewhat narrow meaning that the legislator avoided, clearly indicating thereby a will to give greater content to the words "principles of fundamental justice." . . .

[35] A number of courts have placed emphasis upon the Minutes of the Proceedings and Evidence of the Special Joint Committee of the Senate and of the House of Commons on the Constitution in the interpretation of "principles of fundamental justice." . . .

[36] In particular, the following passages dealing with the testimony of federal civil servants from the Department of Justice, have been relied upon:

Mr. Strayer (Assistant Deputy Minister, Public Law):
Mr. Chairman, it was our belief that the words "fundamental justice" would cover the same thing as what is called procedural due process, that is the meaning of due process in relation to requiring fair procedure. However, it in our view does not cover the concept of what is called substantive due process, which would impose substantive requirements as to policy of the law in question.

This has been most clearly demonstrated in the United States in the area of property, but also in other areas such as the right to life. The term due process has been given the broader concept of meaning both the procedure and substance. Natural justice or fundamental justice in our view does not go beyond the procedural requirements of fairness. . . .

The term "fundamental justice" appears to us to be essentially the same thing as natural justice.

Mr. Tassé (Deputy Minister) also said of the phrase "principles of fundamental justice" in testimony before the Committee:

We assume that the Court would look at that much like a Court would look at the requirements of natural justice. . . .

[37] The Honourable Jean Chrétien, then federal Minister of Justice, also indicated to the Committee that, while he thought "fundamental justice marginally more appropriate than natural justice" in s. 7, either term was acceptable to the Government. . . .

[38] The first issue which arises is whether the Minutes of the Proceedings and Evidence of the Special Joint Committee may even be considered admissible as extrinsic aids to the interpretation of *Charter* provisions. Such extrinsic materials were traditionally excluded from consideration in constitutional adjudication. . . .

[39] In *Reference re Upper Churchill Water Rights Reversion Act*, [1984] 1 S.C.R. 297, at p. 317, however, McIntyre J. stated that,

The general exclusionary rule formerly considered to be applicable in dealing with the admissibility of extrinsic evidence in constitutional cases has been set aside or at least greatly modified and relaxed.

[40] Indeed, in the reference *Re: Anti-Inflation Act*, [1976] 2 S.C.R. 373, Laskin C.J. stated, at p. 389:

. . . [N]o general principle of admissibility or inadmissibility can or ought to be propounded by this Court, and . . . the questions of resort to extrinsic evidence and what kind of extrinsic evidence may be admitted must depend on the constitutional issues on which it is sought adduce such evidence.

[41] This approach was adopted by Dickson J. in the reference *Re Residential Tenancies Act, 1979* [[1981] 1 S.C.R. 714]. . . .

[42] It is to be noted, however, that McIntyre J.'s remarks are in relation to the interpretation of the challenged statutory enactment rather than the interpretation of the Constitution itself. The same is true of the remarks of Laskin C.J. and Dickson J.

[43] With respect to the interpretation of the Constitution, however, such extrinsic materials were considered, in at least two cases, by this Court.

[44] In *Re: Authority of Parliament in relation to the Upper House*, [1980] 1 S.C.R. 54, the Court stated, at p. 66:

It is, we think, proper to consider the historical background which led to the provision which was made in the *Act* for the creation of the Senate as a part of the apparatus for the enactment of federal legislation. In the debates which occurred at the Quebec Conference in 1864, considerable time was occupied in discussing the provisions respecting the Senate. Its important purpose is stated in the following passages in speeches delivered in the debates on Confederation in the parliament of the province of Canada. . . .

[45] The other case is *Attorney General of Canada v. Canadian National Transportation, Ltd.*, [1983] 2 S.C.R. 206. Laskin C.J., in that case, referred to the pre-Confederation debates in the course of interpreting ss. 91(27) and 92(14) of the *Constitution Act, 1867* (at p. 225).

[46] I would adopt this approach when interpreting the *Charter*. Consequently, the Minutes of the Proceedings and Evidence of the Special Joint Committee on the Constitution should, in my view, be considered. . . .

[47] Having said that, however, I nonetheless believe that the logic underlying the reluctance to allow the use of materials such as speeches in Parliament carries considerable force with respect to the Minutes of the Committee as well.

[48] In *Reference re Upper Churchill Water Rights Reversion Act, supra*, McIntyre J. wrote at p. 319:

> . . . I would say that the speeches and public declarations by prominent figures in the public and political life of Newfoundland on this question should not be received as evidence. They represent, no doubt, the considered views of the speakers at the time they were made, but cannot be said to be expressions of the intent of the Legislative Assembly.

[50] If speeches and declarations by prominent figures are inherently unreliable (*per* McIntyre J. in *Reference re Upper Churchill Water Rights Reversion Act, supra*, at p. 319) and "speeches made in the legislature at the time of enactment of the measure are inadmissible as having little evidential weight" (*per* Dickson J. in the reference *Re: Residential Tenancies Act 1979, supra*, at p. 721), the Minutes of the Proceedings of the Special Joint Committee, though admissible, and granted somewhat more weight than speeches should not be given too much weight. The inherent unreliability of such statements and speeches is not altered by the mere fact that they pertain to the *Charter* rather than a statute.

[51] Moreover, the simple fact remains that the *Charter* is not the product of a few individual public servants, however distinguished, but of a multiplicity of individuals who played major roles in the negotiating, drafting and adoption of the *Charter*. How can one say with any confidence that within this enormous multiplicity of actors, without forgetting the role of the provinces, the comments of a few federal civil servants can in any way be determinative?

[52] Were this Court to accord any significant weight to this testimony, it would in effect be assuming a fact which is nearly impossible of proof, *i.e.*, the intention of the legislative bodies which adopted the *Charter*. In view of the indeterminate nature of the data, it would in my view be erroneous to give these materials anything but minimal weight.

[53] Another danger with casting the interpretation of s. 7 in terms of the comments made by those heard at the Special Joint Committee Proceedings is that, in so doing, the rights, freedoms and values embodied in the *Charter* in effect become frozen in time to the moment of adoption with little or no possibility of growth, development and adjustment to changing societal needs. . . . If the newly planted "living tree" which is the *Charter* is to have the possibility of growth and adjustment over time, care must be taken to ensure that historical materials, such as the Minutes of Proceedings and Evidence of the Special Joint Committee, do not stunt its growth. . . .

[54] The appellant states that s. 7 "is a blend of s. 1(*a*) and s. 2(*e*) of the *Canadian Bill of Rights*." Considerable emphasis is then placed upon the case of *Duke v. The Queen*, [1972] S.C.R. 917, in which this Court interpreted the words "principles of fundamental justice" in s. 2(*e*) of the *Canadian Bill of Rights*. Fauteux C.J. noted, at p. 923:

> Without attempting to formulate any final definition of those words, I would take them to mean, generally, that the tribunal which adjudicates upon his rights must act fairly, in good faith, without bias, and in a judicial temper, and must give to him the opportunity adequately to state his case.

[55] However, as Le Dain J. has written in *R. v. Therens, supra*, with the implicit support of the majority . . .

> In considering the relationship of a decision under the *Canadian Bill of Rights* to an issue arising under the *Charter*, a court cannot, in my respectful opinion, avoid bearing in mind an evident fact of Canadian judicial history, which must be squarely and frankly faced: that on the whole, with some notable exceptions, the courts have felt some uncertainty or ambivalence in the application of the *Canadian Bill of Rights* because it did not reflect a clear constitutional mandate to make judicial decisions having the effect of limiting or qualifying the traditional sovereignty of Parliament. . . .

[58] In section 2(*e*) of the *Canadian Bill of Rights*, the words "principles of fundamental justice" were placed explicitly in the context of, and qualify a "right to a fair hearing."

Section 7 of the *Charter* does not create the same context. In section 7, the words "principles of fundamental justice" are placed in the context of, and qualify much more fundamental rights, the "right to life, liberty and security of the person." The distinction is important. . . .

[66] Whether any given principle may be said to be a principle of fundamental justice within the meaning of s. 7 will rest upon an analysis of the nature, sources, *rationale* and essential role of that principle within the judicial process and in our legal system, as it evolves.

[67] Consequently, those words cannot be given any exhaustive content or simple enumerative definition, but will take on concrete meaning as the courts address alleged violations of s. 7.

[68] I now turn to such an analysis of the principle of *mens rea* and absolute liability offences in order to determine the question which has been put to the Court in the present Reference.

Absolute Liability and Fundamental Justice in Penal Law

[69] It has from time immemorial been part of our system of laws that the innocent not be punished. This principle has long been recognized as an essential element of a system for the administration of justice which is founded upon a belief in the dignity and worth of the human person and on the rule of law. It is so old that its first enunciation was in Latin *actus non facit reum nisi mens sit rea.*

[70] As Glanville Williams said:

There is no need here to go into the remote history of *mens rea*; suffice it to say that the requirement of a guilty state of mind (at least for the more serious crimes) had been developed by the time of Coke, which is as far back as the modern lawyer needs to go. "If one shoot at any wild fowl upon a tree, and the arrow killeth any reasonable creature afar off, without any evil intent in him, this is *per infortunium.*" . . .

[72] This view has been adopted by this Court in unmistakable terms in many cases, amongst which the better known are *Beaver v. The Queen*, [1957] S.C.R. 531, and the most recent and often quoted judgment of Dickson J. writing for the Court in *R. v. City of Sault Ste. Marie, supra.*

[73] This Court's decision in the latter case is predicated upon a certain number of postulates one of which, given the nature of the rules it elaborates, has to be to the effect that absolute liability in penal law offends the principles of fundamental justice. Those principles are, to use the words of Dickson J., to the effect that "there is a generally held revulsion against punishment of the morally innocent." He also stated that the argument that absolute liability "violates fundamental

principles of penal liability" was the most telling argument against absolute liability and one of greater force than those advanced in support thereof. . . .

[75] A law enacting an absolute liability offence will violate s. 7 of the *Charter* only if and to the extent that it has the potential of depriving of life, liberty, or security of the person.

[76] Obviously, imprisonment (including probation orders) deprives persons of their liberty. An offence has that potential as of the moment it is open to the judge to impose imprisonment. There is no need that imprisonment, as in s. 94(2), be made mandatory.

[77] I am therefore of the view that the combination of imprisonment and of absolute liability violates s. 7 of the *Charter* and can only be salvaged if the authorities demonstrate under s. 1 that such a deprivation of liberty in breach of those principles of fundamental justice is, in a free and democratic society, under the circumstances, a justified reasonable limit to one's rights under s. 7. . . .

[79] . . . I would not want us to be taken by this conclusion as having inferentially decided that absolute liability may not offend s. 7 as long as imprisonment or probation orders are not available as a sentence. The answer to that question is dependant upon the content given to the words "security of the person." That issue was and is a live one. . . .

[83] . . . In penal law, absolute liability always offends the principles of fundamental justice irrespective of the nature of the offence; it offends s. 7 of the *Charter* if as a result, anyone is deprived of his life, liberty or security of the person, irrespective of the requirement of public interest. In such cases it might only be salvaged for reasons of public interest under s. 1.

[84] In this latter regard, something might be added.

[85] Administrative expediency, absolute liability's main supportive argument, will undoubtedly under s. 1 be invoked and occasionally succeed. Indeed, administrative expediency certainly has its place in administrative law. But when administrative law chooses to call in aid imprisonment through penal law, indeed sometimes criminal law and the added stigma attached to a conviction, exceptional, in my view, will be the case where the liberty or even the security of the person guaranteed under s. 7 should be sacrificed to administrative expediency. Section 1 may, for reasons of administrative expediency, successfully come to the rescue of an otherwise violation of s. 7, but only in cases arising out of exceptional conditions, such as natural disasters, the outbreak of war, epidemics, and the like.

[86] Of course I understand the concern of many as regards corporate offences, specially, as was mentioned by the Court of Appeal, in certain sensitive areas such as the preservation of our vital environment and our natural resources.

This concern might well be dispelled were it to be decided, given the proper case, that s. 7 affords protection to human persons only and does not extend to corporations.

[87] Even if it be decided that s. 7 does extend to corporations, I think the balancing under s. 1 of the public interest against the financial interests of a corporation would give very different results from that of balancing public interest and the liberty or security of the person of a human being.

[88] Indeed, the public interest as regards "air and water pollution offences" requires that the guilty be dealt with firmly, but the seriousness of the offence does not in my respectful view support the proposition that the innocent *human* person be open to conviction, quite the contrary. . . .

Section 1

[94] Having found that s. 94(2) offends s. 7 of the *Charter* there remains the question as to whether the appellants have demonstrated that the section is salvaged by the operation of s. 1 of the *Charter*. No evidence was adduced in the Court of Appeal or in this Court. . . .

[95] I do not take issue with the fact that it is highly desirable that "bad drivers" be kept off the road. I do not take issue either with the desirability of punishing severely bad drivers who are in contempt of prohibitions against driving. The bottom line of the question to be addressed here is: whether the Government of British Columbia has demonstrated as justifiable that the risk of imprisonment of a few innocent is, given the desirability of ridding the roads of British Columbia of bad drivers, a reasonable limit in a free and democratic society. That result is to be measured against the offence being one of strict liability open to a defence of due diligence, the success of which does nothing more than let those few who did nothing wrong remain free.

[96] As did the Court of Appeal, I find that this demonstration has not been satisfied, indeed, not in the least.

[97] In the result, I would dismiss the appeal and answer the question in the negative, as did the Court of Appeal, albeit for somewhat different reasons, and declare s. 94(2) of the *Motor Vehicle Act*, R.S.B.C. 1979, as amended by the *Motor Vehicle Amendment Act, 1982*, inconsistent with s. 7 of the *Canadian Charter of Rights and Freedoms*.

[98] Having come to this conclusion, I choose, as did the Court of Appeal, not to address whether the section violates the rights guaranteed under ss. 11(*d*) and 12 of the *Charter*.

[Justice McIntyre wrote a short concurring opinion.]

[101] **WILSON J.** (concurring): I agree with my colleague, Mr. Justice Lamer, that s. 94(2) of the *Motor Vehicle Act* violates s. 7 of the *Charter* and is not saved by s. 1. I reach that result, however, by a somewhat different route.

[102] I start with a consideration of statutory "offences." These are divisible into offences for which *mens rea* is required and those for which it is not. Statutory offences are subject to a presumption in favour of a *mens rea* requirement as a matter of interpretation, but the courts have increasingly come to accept the proposition that legislatures may create non *mens rea* offences provided they make it clear that the *actus reus* itself is prohibited. This is typically so in the case of the so-called "regulatory" or "public welfare" offences. There is no moral delinquency involved in these offences. They are simply designed to regulate conduct in the public interest.

[103] Two questions, therefore, have to be answered on this appeal. The first is do absolute liability offences created by statute *per se* offend the *Charter*? The second is, assuming they do not, can they be attended by mandatory imprisonment or can such a sanction only be attached to true *mens rea* offences? Certainly, in the absence of the *Charter*, legislatures are free to create absolute liability offences and to attach to them any sanctions they please. Does s. 7 of the *Charter* circumscribe their power in this regard?

Absolute Liability Offenses

[104] Section 7 affirms the right to life, liberty and security of the person while at the same time indicating that a person may be deprived of such a right if the deprivation is effected "in accordance with the principles of fundamental justice." I do not view the latter part of the section as a qualification on the right to life, liberty and security of the person in the sense that it limits or modifies that right or defines its parameters. Its purpose seems to me to be the very opposite, namely to protect the right against deprivation or impairment unless such deprivation or impairment is effected in accordance with the principles of fundamental justice.

[105] Section 7 does not, however, affirm a right to the principles of fundamental justice *per se*. There must first be found an impairment of the right to life, liberty or security of the person. It must then be determined whether that impairment has been effected in accordance with the principles of fundamental justice. If it has, it passes the threshold test in s. 7 itself but the Court must go on to consider whether it can be sustained under s. 1 as a limit prescribed by law on the s. 7 right which is both reasonable and justified in a free and democratic society. If, however, the limit on the s. 7 right has been effected through a violation of the principles of fundamental justice, the enquiry, in my view, ends there and the limit cannot be sustained under s. 1. I say this because I do not believe that a limit on the s. 7 right which has been imposed in violation of the principles of fundamental justice can be either "reasonable" or "demonstrably justified in a free and democratic society." . . .

[106] Assuming that I am correct in my analysis of s. 7 and its relationship to s. 1, an absolute liability offence cannot violate s. 7 unless it impairs the right to life, liberty or security of the person. It cannot violate s. 7 because it offends the principles of fundamental justice because they are not protected by s. 7 absent an impairment of the s. 7 right. Leaving aside for the moment the mandatory imprisonment sanction, I cannot find an interference with life, liberty or security of the person in s. 94 of the *Motor Vehicle Act*. It is true that the section prevents citizens from driving their vehicles when their licences are suspended. Citizens are also prevented from driving on the wrong side of the road. Indeed, all regulatory offences impose some restriction on liberty broadly construed. But I think it would trivialize the *Charter* to sweep all those offences into s. 7 as violations of the right to life, liberty and security of the person even if they can be sustained under s. 1. It would be my view, therefore, that absolute liability offences of this type do not *per se* offend s. 7 of the *Charter*.

2. Absolute Liability Plus Mandatory Imprisonment

[107] The real question, as I see it, is whether s. 7 of the *Charter* is violated by the attachment of a mandatory imprisonment sanction to an absolute liability offence. Clearly a s. 7 right is interfered with here in that a person convicted of such an offence automatically loses his liberty. . . . Given that we can have statutory non *mens rea* offences, what is repugnant to fundamental justice in imprisoning someone for their commission? . . . I believe we must turn to the theory of punishment for the answer.

3. Punishment and Fundamental Justice

[126] It is now generally accepted among penologists that there are five main objectives of a penal system: see Nigel Walker, *Sentencing in a Rational Society*, 1969. They are:

(1) to protect offenders and suspected offenders against unofficial retaliation;
(2) to reduce the incidence of crime;
(3) to ensure that offenders atone for their offences;
(4) to keep punishment to the minimum necessary to achieve the objectives of the system; and
(5) to express society's abhorrence of crime.

Apart from death, imprisonment is the most severe sentence imposed by the law and is generally viewed as a last resort i.e., *as appropriate only when it can be shown that no other sanction can achieve the objectives of the system.*

[127] The Law Reform Commission of Canada in its Working Paper 11, "Imprisonment and Release," in *Studies on Imprisonment* (1976), states at p. 10:

Justice requires that the sanction of imprisonment not be disproportionate to the offence, and humanity dictates

that it must not be heavier than necessary to achieve its objective.

[128] Because of the absolute liability nature of the offence created by s. 94(2) of the *Motor Vehicle Act* a person can be convicted under the section even although he was unaware at the time he was driving that his licence was suspended and was unable to find this out despite the exercise of due diligence. While the legislature may as a matter of government policy make this an offence, and we cannot question its wisdom in this regard, the question is whether it can make it mandatory for the courts to deprive a person convicted of it of his liberty without violating s. 7. This, in turn, depends on whether attaching a mandatory term of imprisonment to an absolute liability offence such as this violates the principles of fundamental justice. I believe that it does. I think the conscience of the court would be shocked and the administration of justice brought into disrepute by such an unreasonable and extravagant penalty. It is totally disproportionate to the offence and quite incompatible with the objective of a penal system referred to in paragraph (4) above.

[129] It is basic to any theory of punishment that the sentence imposed bear some relationship to the offence; it must be a "fit" sentence proportionate to the seriousness of the offence. Only if this is so can the public be satisfied that the offender "deserved" the punishment he received and feel a confidence in the fairness and rationality of the system. This is not to say that there is an inherently appropriate relationship between a particular offence and its punishment but rather that there is a scale of offences and punishments into which the particular offence and punishment must fit. Obviously this cannot be done with mathematical precision and many different factors will go into the assessment of the seriousness of a particular offence for purposes of determining the appropriate punishment but it does provide a workable conventional framework for sentencing. Indeed, judges in the exercise of their sentencing discretion have been employing such a scale for over a hundred years.

[130] I believe that a mandatory term of imprisonment for an offence committed unknowingly and unwittingly and after the exercise of due diligence is grossly excessive and inhumane. It is not required to reduce the incidence of the offence. It is beyond anything required to satisfy the need for "atonement." And society, in my opinion, would not be abhorred by an unintentional and unknowing violation of the section. I believe, therefore, that such a sanction offends the principles of fundamental justice embodied in our penal system. Section 94(2) is accordingly inconsistent with s. 7 of the *Charter* and must, to the extent of the inconsistency, be declared of no force and effect under s. 52. . . .

The Queen v. Oakes, 1986

The Charter has "judicialized politics and politicized the judiciary" in part because interpretive controversies over the meaning of vaguely formulated rights are political as well as legal controversies, with policy consequences extending well beyond the confines of the particular case. Giving concrete meaning to broad constitutional standards, however, does not exhaust the political aspects of the judicial task. If a right, having been defined, is found to be violated, the court must ask whether the violation is saved by section 1 of the *Charter*, which permits such "reasonable limits prescribed by law as are demonstrably justified in a free and democratic society." This question makes the political nature of *Charter* jurisprudence even more transparent; it is clearly not a traditionally legal question, as the Supreme Court has itself admitted. Despite the ritual judicial denial of the claim that constitutional review involves second-guessing the wisdom of legislative choices, many observers think that this is precisely what section 1 requires.

In the *Oakes* case, the Supreme Court attempted a comprehensive articulation of the standards it would use in addressing the section 1 question. The case involved a "reverse onus" provision in the *Narcotic Control Act*, under which someone found guilty of "possession" was deemed also to be guilty of "trafficking" unless he could prove otherwise. Having been found guilty of the first charge, Oakes claimed that the reverse onus violated his section 11(*d*) right to be presumed innocent (of trafficking) until proven guilty. The Court agreed, and thereby set aside the established interpretation of a similar guarantee of the presumption of innocence in the *Canadian Bill of Rights*. The fact that there might be a "rational connection" between the "basic fact" (possession) and the "presumed fact" (trafficking) was considered irrelevant to establishing the violation because "a basic fact may rationally tend to prove a presumed fact, but not prove its existence beyond a reasonable doubt," as required in criminal cases. Justice Dickson was careful to add, however, that such a rational connection could be used as part of a section 1 defence.

To establish a section 1 defence, the onus is on the state to demonstrate to a "very high degree of probability" that the *Charter* violation is justified by a "pressing and substantial" objective, and that the means used are "proportional" to that objective. Proportional means have three characteristics: (1) they are not arbitrary and thus actually achieve the objective—that is, they are "rationally connected" to the objective; (2) they impair the right as little as possible; and (3) their costs are proportional to their benefits—that is, "the more severe the deleterious effects, the more [pressing and substantial] the objective must be."

The Court readily conceded that controlling drug trafficking was a sufficiently compelling purpose to justify a violation of *Charter* rights. The means, however, were not proportional to this end because the reverse onus applied to all cases of possession and there was no "rational connection" between trafficking and possession of small quantities of illegal drugs.

The Court's deference regarding the objective of the policy characterizes most, though not all, forays by the Court into section 1 analysis. This is perhaps not surprising. Challenging the very purpose of a policy would most obviously place the Court in a naked political confrontation with the legislature. On the other hand, if the Court accepts the purpose of the law, and limits its scrutiny to the means chosen to achieve that purpose, it might be easier to sustain the claim that it is not second-guessing the wisdom of legislative policy.[1] In *Oakes*, for example, the Court's judgment may be read as saying no more than that the legislature had been somewhat insensitive or careless in determining how to achieve its legitimate end. Indeed, having conceded the legitimacy of some violation of *Charter* rights to control trafficking, the Court implied that more carefully tailored and hence less intrusive means were possible—perhaps a reverse onus that applied only to possession of sufficiently "large" quantities.

As subsequent cases show,[2] however, the Court cannot consistently hide the political nature of section 1 jurisprudence by concentrating on the question of means. To reject legislative means, the Court must compare them, more or less explicitly, to "better" alternatives. But political controversy is often about means as it is about ends, and the legislative choice of means may be carefully, rather than carelessly, deliberated. In such cases, some will consider the judicial evaluation of alternative means to be no less a matter of second-guessing policy wisdom than is the evaluation of objectives. ⌣

---

1   See Patrick Monahan, *Politics and the Constitution: The Charter, Federalism, and the Supreme Court of Canada* (Toronto: Carswell/Methuen, 1987) 67-68.

2   See, for example, the discussion of *Edwards Books* in case 22.

THE QUEEN v. DAVID EDWIN OAKES
[1986] 1 S.C.R. 103

Hearing: March 12, 1985; Judgment: February 28, 1986.

Present: Dickson C.J. and Estey, McIntyre, Chouinard, Lamer, Wilson, and Le Dain JJ.

The judgment of Dickson C.J., Chouinard, Lamer, Wilson, and Le Dain JJ. was delivered by

[1] **DICKSON C.J.:** This appeal concerns the constitutionality of s. 8 of the *Narcotic Control Act*, R.S.C. 1970, c. N-1. The section provides, in brief, that if the Court finds the accused in possession of a narcotic, he is presumed to be in possession for the purpose of trafficking. Unless the accused can establish the contrary, he must be convicted of trafficking. The Ontario Court of Appeal held that this provision constitutes a "reverse onus" clause and is unconstitutional because it violates one of the core values of our criminal justice system, the presumption of innocence, now entrenched in s. 11(*d*) of the *Canadian Charter of Rights and Freedoms*. The Crown has appealed. . . .

[3] The respondent, David Edwin Oakes, was charged with unlawful possession of a narcotic for the purpose of trafficking, contrary to s. 4(2) of the *Narcotic Control Act*. He elected trial by magistrate without a jury. At trial, the Crown adduced evidence to establish that Mr. Oakes was found in possession of eight one gram vials of *cannabis* resin in the form of hashish oil. Upon a further search conducted at the police station, $619.45 was located. Mr. Oakes told the police that he

had bought ten vials of hashish oil for $150 for his own use, and that the $619.45 was from a workers' compensation cheque. He elected not to call evidence as to possession of the narcotic. Pursuant to the procedural provisions of s. 8 of the *Narcotic Control Act*, the trial judge proceeded to make a finding that it was beyond a reasonable doubt that Mr. Oakes was in possession of the narcotic.

[4] Following this finding, Mr. Oakes brought a motion to challenge the constitutional validity of s. 8 of the *Narcotic Control Act*, which he maintained imposes a burden on an accused to prove that he or she was not in possession for the purpose of trafficking. He argued that s. 8 violates the presumption of innocence contained in s. 11(*d*) of the *Charter*. . . .

[15] Before examining the presumption of innocence contained in s. 11(*d*) of the *Charter*, it is necessary to clarify the meaning of s. 8 of the *Narcotic Control Act*. The procedural steps contemplated by s. 8 were clearly outlined by Branca J.A. in *R. v. Babcock and Auld*.

[Justice Branca observed that the trial of an accused charged with trafficking was divided into two parts. First, the trial "proceeds as if it was a prosecution . . . on a simple charge of possession," with the burden of proof resting on the Crown. Second, if simple possession is proven, the onus shifts to the accused to prove that he was not in possession for the purposes of trafficking.]

[26] I conclude that s. 8 of the *Narcotic Control Act* contains a reverse onus provision imposing a legal burden on an

accused to prove on a balance of probabilities that he or she was not in possession of a narcotic for the purpose of trafficking. It is therefore necessary to determine whether s. 8 of the *Narcotic Control Act* offends the right to be "presumed innocent until proven guilty" as guaranteed by s. 11(*d*) of the *Charter*....

[28] To interpret the meaning of s. 11(*d*), it is important to adopt a purposive approach.... To identify the underlying purpose of the *Charter* right in question ... it is important to begin by understanding the cardinal values it embodies.

[29] The presumption of innocence is a hallowed principle lying at the very heart of criminal law. Although protected expressly in s. 11(*d*) of the *Charter*, the presumption of innocence is referable and integral to the general protection of life, liberty and security of the person contained in s. 7 of the *Charter* (see *Re B.C. Motor Vehicle Act* ...). The presumption of innocence protects the fundamental liberty and human dignity of any and every person accused by the State of criminal conduct. An individual charged with a criminal offence faces grave social and personal consequences, including potential loss of physical liberty, subjection to social stigma and ostracism from the community, as well as other social, psychological and economic harms. In light of the gravity of these consequences, the presumption of innocence is crucial. It ensures that until the State proves an accused's guilt beyond all reasonable doubt, he or she is innocent. This is essential in a society committed to fairness and social justice. The presumption of innocence confirms our faith in humankind; it reflects our belief that individuals are decent and law-abiding members of the community until proven otherwise.

[30] The presumption of innocence has enjoyed longstanding recognition at common law. In the leading case, *Woolmington v. Director of Public Prosecutions*, [1935] A.C. 462 (H.L.), Viscount Sankey wrote at pp. 481-82:

> Throughout the web of the English Criminal Law one golden thread is always to be seen, that it is the duty of the prosecution to prove the prisoner's guilt subject to what I have already said as to the defence of insanity and subject also to any statutory exception. If, at the end of and on the whole of the case, there is a reasonable doubt, created by the evidence given by either the prosecution or the prisoner, as to whether the prisoner killed the deceased with a malicious intention, the prosecution has not made out the case and the prisoner is entitled to an acquittal. No matter what the charge or where the trial, the principle that the prosecution must prove the guilt of the prisoner is part of the common law of England and no attempt to whittle it down can be entertained....

[32] In light of the above, the right to be presumed innocent until proven guilty requires that s. 11(*d*) have, at a minimum, the following content. First, an individual must be proven guilty beyond a reasonable doubt. Second, it is the State which must bear the burden of proof.... Third, criminal prosecutions must be carried out in accordance with lawful procedures and fairness. The latter part of s. 11(*d*), which requires the proof of guilt "according to law in a fair and public hearing by an independent and impartial tribunal," underlines the importance of this procedural requirement....

[33] Having considered the general meaning of the presumption of innocence, it is now, I think, desirable to review briefly the authorities on reverse onus clauses in Canada and other jurisdictions....

[34] Section 2(*f*) of the *Canadian Bill of Rights*, which safeguards the presumption of innocence, provides:

> ... no law of Canada shall be construed or applied so as to ...
>
> (f) deprive a person charged with a criminal offence of the right to be presumed innocent until proved guilty according to law in a fair and public hearing by an independent and impartial tribunal....

The wording of this section closely parallels that of s. 11(*d*). For this reason, one of the Crown's primary contentions is that the *Canadian Bill of Rights* jurisprudence should be determinative of the outcome of the present appeal.

[35] The leading case decided under s. 2(*f*) of the *Canadian Bill of Rights* and relied on by the Crown, is *R. v. Appleby* [[1972] S.C.R. 303], *supra*. In that case, the accused had challenged s. 224A(1)(*a*) (now s. 237(1)(*a*)) of the *Criminal Code*, R.S.C. 1970, c. C-34, which imposes a burden upon an accused to prove that he or she, though occupying the driver's seat, did not enter the vehicle for the purpose of setting it in motion and did not, therefore, have care and control. This Court rejected the arguments of the accused that s. 2(*f*) had been violated; it relied on the *Woolmington* case which held that the presumption of innocence was subject to "statutory exceptions." As Ritchie J. stated in his judgment for the majority at pp. 315-16:

> It seems to me, therefore, that if Woolmington's case is to be accepted, the words "presumed innocent until proved guilty according to law ..." as they appear in s. 2(*f*) of the *Bill of Rights*, must be taken to envisage a law which recognizes the existence of statutory exceptions reversing the onus of proof with respect to one or more ingredients of an offence in cases where certain specific facts have been proved by the Crown in relation to such ingredients....

[38] Although there are important lessons to be learned from the *Canadian Bill of Rights* jurisprudence, it does not constitute binding authority in relation to the constitutional

interpretation of the *Charter*. As this Court held in *R. v. Big M Drug Mart Ltd.* [[1985] 1 S.C.R. 295], *supra*, the *Charter*, as a constitutional document, is fundamentally different from the statutory *Canadian Bill of Rights*, which was interpreted as simply recognizing and declaring existing rights. (See also *Singh v. Minister of Employment and Immigration*, [1985] 1 S.C.R. 177 *per* Wilson J.; *R. v. Therens*, [1985] 1 S.C.R. 613, *per* Le Dain J.)....

[39] With this in mind, one cannot but question the appropriateness of reading into the phrase "according to law" in s. 11(*d*) of the *Charter* the statutory exceptions acknowledged in *Woolmington* and in *Appleby*. The *Woolmington* case was decided in the context of a legal system with no constitutionally entrenched human rights document. In Canada, we have tempered parliamentary supremacy by entrenching important rights and freedoms in the Constitution. Viscount Sankey's statutory exception proviso is clearly not applicable in this context and would subvert the very purpose of the entrenchment of the presumption of innocence in the *Charter*. I do not, therefore, feel constrained in this case by the interpretation of s. 2(*f*) of the *Canadian Bill of Rights* presented in the majority judgment in *Appleby*. Section 8 of the *Narcotic Control Act* is not rendered constitutionally valid simply by virtue of the fact that it is a statutory provision....

[59] As we have seen, the potential for a rational connection between the basic fact and the presumed fact to justify a reverse onus provision has been elaborated in some of the cases discussed above and is now known as the "rational connection test." In the context of s. 11(*d*), however, the following question arises: if we apply the rational connection test to the consideration of whether s. 11(*d*) has been violated, are we adequately protecting the constitutional principle of the presumption of innocence? ... A basic fact may rationally tend to prove a presumed fact, but not prove its existence beyond a reasonable doubt. An accused person could thereby be convicted despite the presence of a reasonable doubt. This would violate the presumption of innocence.

[60] I should add that this questioning of the constitutionality of the "rational connection test" as a guide to interpreting s. 11(*d*) does not minimize its importance. The appropriate stage for invoking the rational connection test, however, is under s. 1 of the *Charter*. This consideration did not arise under the *Canadian Bill of Rights* because of the absence of an equivalent to s. 1. At the Court of Appeal level in the present case, Martin J.A. sought to combine the analysis of s. 11(*d*) and s. 1 to overcome the limitations of the *Canadian Bill of Rights* jurisprudence. To my mind, it is highly desirable to keep s. 1 and s. 11(*d*) analytically distinct. Separating the analysis into two components is consistent with the approach this Court has taken to the *Charter* to date....

[61] To return to s. 8 of the *Narcotic Control Act*, I am in no doubt whatsoever that it violates s. 11(*d*) of the *Charter* by requiring the accused to prove on a balance of probabilities that he was not in possession of the narcotic for the purpose of trafficking. Mr. Oakes is compelled by s. 8 to prove he is *not* guilty of the offence of trafficking. He is thus denied his right to be presumed innocent and subjected to the potential penalty of life imprisonment unless he can rebut the presumption. This is radically and fundamentally inconsistent with the societal values of human dignity and liberty which we espouse, and is directly contrary to the presumption of innocence enshrined in s. 11(*d*). Let us turn now to s. 1 of the *Charter*....

[63] It is important to observe at the outset that s. 1 has two functions: first, it constitutionally guarantees the rights and freedoms set out in the provisions which follow; and, second, it states explicitly the exclusive justificatory criteria (outside of s. 33 of the *Constitution Act, 1982*) against which limitations on those rights and freedoms must be measured. Accordingly, any s. 1 inquiry must be premised on an understanding that the impugned limit violates constitutional rights and freedoms—rights and freedoms which are part of the supreme law of Canada....

[64] A second contextual element of interpretation of s. 1 is provided by the words "free and democratic society." Inclusion of these words as the final standard of justification for limits on rights and freedoms refers the Court to the very purpose for which the *Charter* was originally entrenched in the Constitution: Canadian society is to be free and democratic. The Court must be guided by the values and principles essential to a free and democratic society which I believe embody, to name but a few, respect for the inherent dignity of the human person, commitment to social justice and equality, accommodation of a wide variety of beliefs, respect for cultural and group identity, and faith in social and political institutions which enhance the participation of individuals and groups in society. The underlying values and principles of a free and democratic society are the genesis of the rights and freedoms guaranteed by the *Charter* and the ultimate standard against which a limit on a right or freedom must be shown, despite its effect, to be reasonable and demonstrably justified.

[65] The rights and freedoms guaranteed by the *Charter* are not, however, absolute. It may become necessary to limit rights and freedoms in circumstances where their exercise would be inimical to the realization of collective goals of fundamental importance. For this reason, s. 1 provides criteria of justification for limits on the rights and freedoms guaranteed by the *Charter*. These criteria impose a stringent standard of justification, especially when understood in terms of the two

contextual considerations discussed above, namely, the violation of a constitutionally guaranteed right or freedom and the fundamental principles of a free and democratic society.

[66] The onus of proving that a limit on a right or freedom guaranteed by the *Charter* is reasonable and demonstrably justified in a free and democratic society rests upon the party seeking to uphold the limitation. It is clear from the text of s. 1 that limits on the rights and freedoms enumerated in the *Charter* are exceptions to their general guarantee. The presumption is that the rights and freedoms are guaranteed unless the party invoking s. 1 can bring itself within the exceptional criteria which justify their being limited. This is further substantiated by the use of the word "demonstrably" which clearly indicates that the onus of justification is on the party seeking to limit. . . .

[67] The standard of proof under s. 1 is the civil standard, namely, proof by a preponderance of probability. The alternative criminal standard, proof beyond a reasonable doubt, would, in my view, be unduly onerous on the party seeking to limit. Concepts such as "reasonableness," "justifiability" and "free and democratic society" are simply not amenable to such a standard. Nevertheless, the preponderance of probability test must be applied rigorously. Indeed, the phrase "demonstrably justified" in s. 1 of the *Charter* supports this conclusion. Within the broad category of the civil standard, there exist different degrees of probability depending on the nature of the case. . . .

[68] Having regard to the fact that s. 1 is being invoked for the purpose of justifying a violation of the constitutional rights and freedoms the *Charter* was designed to protect, a very high degree of probability will be, in the words of Lord Denning, "commensurate with the occasion." Where evidence is required in order to prove the constituent elements of a s. 1 inquiry, and this will generally be the case, it should be cogent and persuasive and make clear to the Court the consequences of imposing or not imposing the limit. . . . A court will also need to know what alternative measures for implementing the objective were available to the legislators when they made their decisions. I should add, however, that there may be cases where certain elements of the s. 1 analysis are obvious or self-evident.

[69] To establish that a limit is reasonable and demonstrably justified in a free and democratic society, two central criteria must be satisfied. First, the objective, which the measures responsible for a limit on a *Charter* right or freedom are designed to serve, must be "of sufficient importance to warrant overriding a constitutionally protected right or freedom": *R. v. Big M Drug Mart Ltd., supra,* at p. 352. The standard must be high in order to ensure that objectives which are trivial or discordant with the principles integral to a free and democratic society do not gain s. 1 protection. It is necessary, at a mini-

mum, that an objective relate to concerns which are pressing and substantial in a free and democratic society before it can be characterized as sufficiently important.

[70] Second, once a sufficiently significant objective is recognized, then the party invoking s. 1 must show that the means chosen are reasonable and demonstrably justified. This involves "a form of proportionality test": *R. v. Big M Drug Mart Ltd., supra,* at p. 352. Although the nature of the proportionality test will vary depending on the circumstances, in each case courts will be required to balance the interests of society with those of individuals and groups. There are, in my view, three important components of a proportionality test. First, the measures adopted must be carefully designed to achieve the objective in question. They must not be arbitrary, unfair or based on irrational considerations. In short, they must be rationally connected to the objective. Second, the means, even if rationally connected to the objective in this first sense, should impair "as little as possible" the right or freedom in question: *R. v. Big M Drug Mart Ltd., supra,* at p. 352. Third, there must be a proportionality between the *effects* of the measures which are responsible for limiting the *Charter* right or freedom, and the objective which has been identified as of "sufficient importance."

[71] With respect to the third component, it is clear that the general effect of any measure impugned under s. 1 will be the infringement of a right or freedom guaranteed by the *Charter;* this is the reason why resort to s. 1 is necessary. The inquiry into effects must, however, go further. A wide range of rights and freedoms are guaranteed by the *Charter,* and an almost infinite number of factual situations may arise in respect of these. Some limits on rights and freedoms protected by the *Charter* will be more serious than others in terms of the nature of the right or freedom violated, the extent of the violation, and the degree to which the measures which impose the limit trench upon the integral principles of a free and democratic society. Even if an objective is of sufficient importance, and the first two elements of the proportionality test are satisfied, it is still possible that, because of the severity of the deleterious effects of a measure on individuals or groups, the measure will not be justified by the purposes it is intended to serve. The more severe the deleterious effects of a measure, the more important the objective must be if the measure is to be reasonable and demonstrably justified in a free and democratic society.

[72] Having outlined the general principles of a s. 1 inquiry, we must apply them to s. 8 of the *Narcotic Control Act.* Is the reverse onus provision in s. 8 a reasonable limit on the right to be presumed innocent until proven guilty beyond a reasonable doubt as can be demonstrably justified in a free and democratic society?

[73] The starting point for formulating a response to this question is, as stated above, the nature of Parliament's interest or objective which accounts for the passage of s. 8 of the *Narcotic Control Act*. According to the Crown, s. 8 of the *Narcotic Control Act* is aimed at curbing drug trafficking by facilitating the conviction of drug traffickers. In my opinion, Parliament's concern that drug trafficking be decreased can be characterized as substantial and pressing. The problem of drug trafficking has been increasing since the 1950s at which time there was already considerable concern. . . . Throughout this period, numerous measures were adopted by free and democratic societies, at both the international and national levels. . . .

[76] The objective of protecting our society from the grave ills associated with drug trafficking, is, in my view, one of sufficient importance to warrant overriding a constitutionally protected right or freedom in certain cases. Moreover, the degree of seriousness of drug trafficking makes its acknowledgement as a sufficiently important objective for the purposes of s. 1, to a large extent, self-evident. The first criterion of a s. 1 inquiry, therefore, has been satisfied by the Crown.

[77] The next stage of inquiry is a consideration of the means chosen by Parliament to achieve its objective. The means must be reasonable and demonstrably justified in a free and democratic society. As outlined above, this proportionality test should begin with a consideration of the rationality of the provision: is the reverse onus clause in s. 8 rationally related to the objective of curbing drug trafficking? At a minimum, this requires that s. 8 be internally rational; there must be a rational connection between the basic fact of possession and the presumed fact of possession for the purpose of trafficking. Otherwise, the reverse onus clause could give rise to unjustified and erroneous convictions for drug trafficking of persons guilty only of possession of narcotics.

[78] In my view, s. 8 does not survive this rational connection test. As Martin J.A. of the Ontario Court of Appeal concluded, possession of a small or negligible quantity of narcotics does not support the inference of trafficking. In other words, it would be irrational to infer that a person had an intent to traffic on the basis of his or her possession of a very small quantity of narcotics. The presumption required under s. 8 of the *Narcotic Control Act* is overinclusive and could lead to results in certain cases which would defy both rationality and fairness. In light of the seriousness of the offence in question, which carries with it the possibility of imprisonment for life, I am further convinced that the first component of the proportionality test has not been satisfied by the Crown.

[79] Having concluded that s. 8 does not satisfy this first component of proportionality, it is unnecessary to consider the other two components. . . .

[Justices Estey and McIntyre concurred in the reasons of Chief Justice Dickson with respect to the relationship of section 11(*d*) and section 1 of the *Charter*, but adopted the reasons of Justice Martin in the court below for the disposition of all other issues.]

25   Morgentaler v. The Queen, 1988

The *Morgentaler* decision is one of the most publicized and controversial *Charter* decisions to date, due in part to the emotional and divisive character of its subject matter—abortion. *Morgentaler* also reflects the flamboyant personality of its appellant. Pro-choice crusader Dr. Henry Morgentaler's victory culminated almost 20 years of civil disobedience in protest of Canada's abortion law. In the early 1970s, Morgentaler openly defied the abortion law by performing unauthorized abortions in his Montreal clinic. In three successive trials, juries refused to convict him. However, in 1974, the Quebec Court of Appeal overturned his first jury acquittal and took the unprecedented step of directly convicting him rather than returning the case for retrial. In 1975, the Supreme Court of Canada rejected Morgentaler's appeal, and he was sentenced to 18 months in prison.

Ironically, Morgentaler's legal defeat laid the basis for a subsequent political victory. In response to protests, Parliament amended the *Criminal Code* to withdraw the power to convict from appeal courts. In the light of what was immediately dubbed "the Morgentaler amendment," the federal Attorney General granted Morgentaler a new trial. After his third jury acquittal, Morgentaler was released from prison. The newly elected Parti Québécois government of René Lévesque dropped outstanding charges against Morgentaler, and announced that it would no longer enforce section 251 (the abortion section) of the *Criminal Code* in Quebec. The Lévesque government subsequently supported the creation of community health clinics that included abortion services. By 1980, Morgentaler had achieved his objective of easy and inexpensive access to abortion services in Quebec. In the rest of Canada, however, the section 251 regime was still in effect.

In 1983, Morgentaler renewed his campaign of civil disobedience. With financial backing from the Canadian Abortion Rights Action League (CARAL), he opened abortion clinics in Toronto and Winnipeg. Once again he was brought to trial and acquitted by a jury, and once again he saw his acquittal overturned by a court of appeal. This time, however, armed with the new *Charter of Rights*, Morgentaler prevailed in the Supreme Court of Canada.

The contrast between the Supreme Court's handling of the first *Morgentaler* appeal and its 1988 decision reveals just how much the *Charter* changed the Court's willingness to use the power of judicial review. In his 1975 appeal, Morgentaler used the 1960 *Bill of Rights* to challenge the validity of section 251 of the *Criminal Code*. At oral argument before the Supreme Court, Morgentaler's lawyers argued that section 251 violated women's right to liberty and also "equality before the law." After hearing these arguments, the Court recessed briefly and then announced that section 251 did not violate the *Bill of Rights*. The Crown was told it need not even argue the *Bill of Rights* issues.

In its written judgment six months later, the six-judge majority did not even address the *Bill of Rights* issues. Chief Justice Laskin dissented for other reasons, but explained why the Court was unwilling to accept Morgentaler's *Bill of Rights* arguments. In distinguishing the *Morgentaler* case from the then recently decided American abortion decision, *Roe v. Wade* (1973), the Chief Justice observed, "how foreign to our constitutional traditions, to our constitutional law and to our conceptions of judicial review was any interference by a Court with the substantive content of legislation." This difference, Laskin explained, stemmed from the fact that the *Canadian Bill of Rights* was not constitutionally entrenched:[1]

> It cannot be forgotten that it is a statutory instrument, illustrative of Parliament's primacy within the limits of its assigned legislative authority, and this is a relevant consideration in determining how far the language of the *Canadian Bill of Rights* should be taken in assessing the quality of federal enactments which are challenged under s. 1(a).

The constitutional status of the *Charter* appears to have erased whatever doubts the Court had about the legitimacy of its power to review and nullify Parliament's laws. However, the *Morgentaler* decision was much narrower than was generally reported. The Supreme Court did not declare a constitutional right to abortion or "freedom of choice." Only Justice Wilson took this position, and even she acknowledged a legitimate state interest in protecting the life of the foetus/unborn child at some point in the second trimester of a pregnancy. The other six carefully and explicitly avoided this "substantive" policy issue.

The two dissenters, McIntyre and La Forest, looked behind the text of the *Charter* to the framers' understanding of its meaning. They found that the legislative history of the *Charter* in 1980-81 indicated that it was intentionally neutral on the abortion issue. They concluded that when the *Charter* is purposely silent on an issue, so too must be the judges.

The other four judges who ruled against the abortion law did so because they said that it violated the "procedural fairness" required by section 7, not because there is any independent right to abortion. These four further disagreed among themselves on just how serious even the procedural violations were. Two, Dickson and Lamer, suggested that certain elements of the current law—such as removal of the decision-making power for the abortion decision from the pregnant woman—violated the "security of the person." The other two judges— Beetz and Estey—defined the procedural problems more narrowly and thus as remediable. While certain requirements as currently written—such as approval by a therapeutic abortion committee (TAC)—created unfair delays and burdens, a revised version of the TAC might be acceptable. Unlike Dickson and Lamer, Beetz and Estey ruled that in principle there was no legal problem with the requirement of the current law that abortions be permitted only when the continuation of a pregnancy "would threaten the life or health of the mother," or with the requirement that an independent and impartial third party be the judge of this issue.

A significant aspect of the three plurality opinions was their extensive reliance on "social facts" or "extrinsic evidence." In 1975, Chief Justice Laskin rejected similar evidence that indicated unequal access to abortion services across the country. "This is a reach for equality by judicially unmanageable standards," declared Laskin. "It would mean that the Court would have to come to . . . decide how large or small an area must be within which an acceptable distribution of physicians and hospitals must be found."[2] Thirteen years later, in the second *Morgentaler* appeal, the dissenters, McIntyre and La Forest, were still skeptical about the use of extrinsic evidence to support the "unequal access" argument. McIntyre declared that he would prefer to rely on "evidence given under oath in my consideration of factual matters." He also noted that there had been no first-hand testimony by doctors or patients that supported the lack-of-access argument.

---

1   *Morgentaler v. The Queen*, [1976] 1 S.C.R. 616 at 632.

2   *Ibid.* at 653.

Justices Wilson, Dickson, and Beetz had no such qualms. They cited at length from the Badgley Report to support the lack-of-access claim. The Badgley Report had been commissioned in 1976 by the Trudeau government in response to the first *Morgentaler* case. It was intended to serve as the basis for possible legislative reform of the abortion law, but Parliament had never acted on it. Now, 10 years later, the Badgley Report was being used by judges to strike down the same abortion law. This extensive use of and reliance on extrinsic evidence is a clear indicator of the greater policy-making role the Court has accepted under the *Charter*.

Despite similarities, the *Morgentaler* decision differs significantly from the 1973 American abortion decision. In *Roe v. Wade*, the American Supreme Court declared that there was an implied "right to privacy" in the American Constitution and that it included a woman's right to determine for herself whether to continue or terminate a pregnancy. The Court effectively precluded any legislative response to protect the interests of the unborn or the father except in the last trimester of a pregnancy. By contrast, in the *Morgentaler* decision, by limiting their ruling to procedural requirements of the criminal law, the majority left the door open for Parliament to respond with an amended abortion law.

Six months later, in July 1988, the Mulroney government introduced a motion in the House of Commons for a reformed abortion law. The motion proposed easy access to abortions during the "early stages" of a pregnancy, but in "subsequent stages" an abortion would be permitted only if two doctors found that continuation of the pregnancy would "endanger the woman's life or seriously endanger her health." After two days of almost around-the-clock debate, the government motion was defeated in a "free vote" (147 to 76). Both "pro-life" and "pro-choice" MPs voted against the compromise measure. Both sides offered their own amendments that would have greatly restricted or eased access to abortion, but these too were defeated. The "pro-life" amendment came closest to adoption, losing 118 to 105.

After the 1988 election, the Mulroney government introduced Bill C-43, yet another attempt to retain some criminal sanction against abortion. Bill C-43 would have made abortion at any time an offence, punishable by up to two years in jail, unless performed by a doctor who was of the opinion that without an abortion the life or health of the pregnant woman would be threatened. The vote on Bill C-43 was not a free vote. It passed the House of Commons by a vote of 140 to 131. But in the Senate, for the first time ever, there was a tied vote, so the Bill died. The Mulroney government had no appetite for reviving it. Indeed, no federal government since has touched this highly divisive issue.[3]

The *Morgentaler* decision pulled the legal rug out from under a parallel challenge to Canada's abortion law brought by Joe Borowski, a former Manitoba Cabinet minister and prominent pro-life activist. Borowski was to Canada's pro-life movement what Morgentaler was to the pro-choice camp—a hero, a symbol, and an opportunity to win in the courts what they could not win in Parliament. Whereas Morgentaler's challenge had emphasized the rights of women to "liberty" and "security of the person" under section 7 of the *Charter*, Borowski's challenge argued that the human foetus was included in the "everyone" entitled to the section 7 "right to life." While Morgentaler claimed section 251 placed too many restrictions on abortions, Borowski maintained that it too easily permitted them.

---

3 Thomas Flanagan, "The Staying Power of the Status Quo: Collective Choice in Canada's Parliament after Morgentaler" (1999) 30 *Canadian Journal of Political Science* 31.

Like Morgentaler, Borowski had been travelling the long route to an ultimate Supreme Court decision for many years.[4] When the Supreme Court heard his case in October 1988, however, it had already declared section 251 unconstitutional in *Morgentaler*, creating a serious problem for Borowski. How could he challenge the constitutionality of a law that no longer existed? In legal parlance, Borowski's case had become moot—no longer a live controversy—with the death of section 251. The Court dismissed his case for precisely this reason on March 9, 1989. Although the Court had agreed to hear Borowski's substantive arguments, it did not address them. To do so, wrote Justice Sopinka for a unanimous Court, would be to create a new kind of "private reference," a procedure that would intrude on the prerogative of the executive and possibly pre-empt Parliament's policy options on the abortion issue.

Similar compunctions about mootness did not trouble the Court in its consideration of another abortion case that burst onto the scene in the summer of 1989, close on the heels of the *Borowski* decision. When Chantal Daigle broke up with her boyfriend, Jean-Guy Tremblay, she decided to abort the foetus she had conceived with him. Tremblay persuaded a Quebec Superior Court judge to issue an injunction preventing the abortion because the foetus was a "human being" protected under the Quebec *Charter of Human Rights*. After this decision was hurriedly confirmed by the Quebec Court of Appeal, the Supreme Court agreed to interrupt its summer vacation to hear an expedited final appeal in August 1989. Before the Court could hear Daigle's appeal, however, she slipped across the border to have an abortion in the United States, making her case as moot as Borowski's had been. Nevertheless, the Court heard the substantive issues and decided that if the Quebec legislature had intended to include the foetus in the category of "human beings" guaranteed the right to life under the Quebec *Charter*, it would have done so more explicitly. *Daigle* was based on the Quebec rather than the Canadian *Charter of Rights*, but it had obvious implications for the latter and was widely portrayed as a major legal victory for the pro-choice side in the abortion controversy. ⌐

---

4   For a full account of both sagas, see F.L. Morton, *Morgentaler v. Borowski: Abortion, the Charter, and the Courts* (Toronto: McClelland & Stewart, 1992).

DR. HENRY MORGENTALER, ET AL. v. THE QUEEN
[1988] 1 S.C.R. 30

Hearing: October 7, 8, 9, 10, 1986; Judgment: January 28, 1988.

Present: Dickson C.J. and Beetz, Estey, McIntyre, Lamer, Wilson, and La Forest JJ.

Intervener: The Attorney General of Canada.

The judgment of Dickson C.J. and Lamer J. was delivered by

DICKSON C.J.: The principal issue raised by this appeal is whether the abortion provisions of the *Criminal Code*, R.S.C. 1970, c. C-34, infringe the "right to life, liberty and security of the person and the right not to be deprived thereof except in accordance with the principles of fundamental justice" as

formulated in s. 7 of the *Canadian Charter of Rights and Freedoms*. The appellants, Dr. Henry Morgentaler, Dr. Leslie Frank Smoling and Dr. Robert Scott, have raised thirteen distinct grounds of appeal. During oral submissions, however, it became apparent that the primary focus of the case was upon the s. 7 argument. It is submitted by the appellants that s. 251 of the *Criminal Code* contravenes s. 7 of the *Canadian Charter of Rights and Freedoms* and that s. 251 should be struck down. Counsel for the Crown admitted during the course of her submissions that s. 7 of the *Charter* was indeed "the key" to the entire appeal. . . . In view of my resolution of the s. 7 issue, it will not be necessary for me to address the appellants' other *Charter* arguments and I expressly refrain from commenting upon their merits.

During argument before this Court, counsel for the Crown emphasized repeatedly that it is not the role of the judiciary in Canada to evaluate the wisdom of legislation enacted by our democratically elected representatives, or to second-guess difficult policy choices that confront all governments. In *Morgentaler v. The Queen*, [1976] 1 S.C.R. 616, at p. 671, [hereinafter "*Morgentaler (1975)*"] I stressed that the Court had "not been called upon to decide, or even to enter, the loud and continuous public debate on abortion." Eleven years later, the controversy persists, and it remains true that this Court cannot presume to resolve all of the competing claims advanced in vigorous and healthy public debate. Courts and legislators in other democratic societies have reached completely contradictory decisions when asked to weigh the competing values relevant to the abortion question....

But since 1975, and the first *Morgentaler* decision, the Court has been given added responsibilities. I stated in *Morgentaler (1975)*, at p. 671, that:

The values we must accept for the purposes of this appeal are those expressed by Parliament which holds the view that the desire of a woman to be relieved of her pregnancy is not, of itself, justification for performing an abortion.

Although no doubt it is still fair to say that courts are not the appropriate forum for articulating complex and controversial programmes of public policy, Canadian courts are now charged with the crucial obligation of ensuring that the legislative initiatives pursued by our Parliament and legislatures conform to the democratic values expressed in the *Canadian Charter of Rights and Freedoms*. As Justice McIntyre states in his reasons for judgment, at p. 138, "the task of the Court in this case is not to solve nor seek to solve what might be called the abortion issue, but simply to measure the content of s. 251 against the *Charter*." It is in this latter sense that the current *Morgentaler* appeal differs from the one we heard a decade ago....

The Criminal Code

251. (1) Every one who, with intent to procure the miscarriage of a female person, whether or not she is pregnant, uses any means for the purpose of carrying out his intention is guilty of an indictable offence and is liable to imprisonment for life.

(2) Every female person who, being pregnant, with intent to procure her own miscarriage, uses any means or permits any means to be used for the purpose of carrying out her intention is guilty of an indictable offence and is liable to imprisonment for two years.

(3) In this section, "means" includes

(*a*) the administration of a drug or other noxious thing,

(*b*) the use of an instrument, and

(*c*) manipulation of any kind.

(4) Subsections (1) and (2) do not apply to

(*a*) a qualified medical practitioner, other than a member of a therapeutic abortion committee for any hospital, who in good faith uses in an accredited or approved hospital any means for the purpose of carrying out his intention to procure the miscarriage of a female person, or

(*b*) a female person who, being pregnant, permits a qualified medical practitioner to use in an accredited or approved hospital any means described in paragraph (*a*) for the purpose of carrying out her intention to procure her own miscarriage, if, before the use of those means, the therapeutic abortion committee for that accredited or approved hospital, by a majority of the members of the committee and at a meeting of the committee at which the case of such female person has been reviewed,

(*c*) has by certificate in writing stated that in its opinion the continuation of the pregnancy of such female person would or would be likely to endanger her life or health, and

(*d*) has caused a copy of such certificate to be given to the qualified medical practitioner....

Section 7 of the Charter

In his submissions, counsel for the appellants argued that the Court should recognize a very wide ambit for the rights protected under s. 7 of the *Charter*. Basing his argument largely on American constitutional theories and authorities, Mr. Manning submitted that the right to "life, liberty and security of the person" is a wide-ranging right to control one's own life and to promote one's individual autonomy. The right would therefore include a right to privacy and a right to make unfettered decisions about one's own life.

In my opinion, it is neither necessary nor wise in this appeal to explore the broadest implications of s. 7 as counsel would wish us to do. I prefer to rest my conclusions on a narrower analysis than that put forward on behalf of the appellants. I do not think it would be appropriate to attempt an all-encompassing explication of so important a provision as s. 7 so early in the history of *Charter* interpretation. The Court should be presented with a wide variety of claims and factual situations before articulating the full range of s. 7 rights. I will therefore limit my comments to some interpretive principles already set down by the Court and to an analysis of only two aspects of s. 7, the right to "security of the person" and "the principles of fundamental justice."

The goal of *Charter* interpretation is to secure for all people "the full benefit of the *Charter*'s protection": *R. v. Big M Drug Mart Ltd.*, [1985] 1 S.C.R. 295, at p. 344. To attain that goal, this Court has held consistently that the proper technique for the interpretation of *Charter* provisions is to pursue a "purposive" analysis of the right guaranteed. A right recognized in the *Charter* is "to be understood, in other words, in the light of the interests it was meant to protect": *R. v. Big M Drug Mart Ltd.*, at p. 344. (See also *Hunter v. Southam Inc.*, [1984] 2 S.C.R. 145; and *R. v. Therens*, [1985] 1 S.C.R. 613.)

In *Singh v. Minister of Employment and Immigration*, [1985] 1 S.C.R. 177, at p. 204, Justice Wilson emphasized that there are three distinct elements to the s. 7 right, that "life, liberty, and security of the person" are independent interests, each of which must be given independent significance by the Court (p. 205). This interpretation was adopted by a majority of the Court, *per* Justice Lamer, in *Re B.C. Motor Vehicle Act*, [1985] 2 S.C.R. 486, at p. 500. It is therefore possible to treat only one aspect of the first part of s. 7 before determining whether any infringement of that interest accords with the principles of fundamental justice. (See *Singh, Re B.C. Motor Vehicle Act*, and *R. v. Jones*, [1986] 2 S.C.R. 284.)

With respect to the second part of s. 7, in early academic commentary one of the principal concerns was whether the reference to "principles of fundamental justice" enables the courts to review the substance of legislation. . . . In *Re B.C. Motor Vehicle Act*, Lamer J. noted at p. 497 that any attempt to draw a sharp line between procedure and substance would be ill-conceived. He suggested further that it would not be beneficial in Canada to allow a debate which is rooted in United States constitutional dilemmas to shape our interpretation of s. 7. . . .

Lamer J. went on to hold that the principles of fundamental justice referred to in s. 7 can relate both to procedure and to substance, depending upon the circumstances presented before the Court.

I have no doubt that s. 7 does impose upon courts the duty to review the substance of legislation once it has been determined that the legislation infringes an individual's right to "life, liberty and security of the person." The section states clearly that those interests may only be impaired if the principles of fundamental justice are respected. Lamer J. emphasized, however, that the courts should avoid "adjudication of the merits of public policy" (p. 499). In the present case, I do not believe that it is necessary for the Court to tread the fine line between substantive review and the adjudication of public policy. As in the *Singh* case, it will be sufficient to investigate whether or not the impugned legislative provisions meet the procedural standards of fundamental justice. First it is necessary to determine whether s. 251 of the *Criminal Code* impairs the security of the person.

The law has long recognized that the human body ought to be protected from interference by others. At common law, for example, any medical procedure carried out on a person without that person's consent is an assault. Only in emergency circumstances does the law allow others to make decisions of this nature. Similarly, art. 19 of the *Civil Code of Lower Canada* provides that "[t]he human person is inviolable" and that "[n]o person may cause harm to the person of another without his consent or without being authorized by law to do so." "Security of the person," in other words, is not a value alien to our legal landscape. With the advent of the *Charter*, security of the person has been elevated to the status of a constitutional norm. This is not to say that the various forms of protection accorded to the human body by the common and civil law occupy a similar status. "Security of the person" must be given content in a manner sensitive to its constitutional position. The above examples are simply illustrative of our respect for individual physical integrity. . . .

The case law leads me to the conclusion that state interference with bodily integrity and serious state-imposed psychological stress, at least in the criminal law context, constitute a breach of security of the person. It is not necessary in this case to determine whether the right extends further, to protect either interests central to personal autonomy, such as a right to privacy, or interests unrelated to criminal justice. . . .

At the most basic, physical and emotional level, every pregnant woman is told by the section that she cannot submit to a generally safe medical procedure that might be of clear benefit to her unless she meets criteria entirely unrelated to her own priorities and aspirations. Not only does the removal of decision-making power threaten women in a physical sense; the indecision of knowing whether an abortion will be granted inflicts emotional stress. Section 251 clearly interferes with a woman's bodily integrity in both a physical and emotional sense. Forcing a woman, by threat of criminal sanction, to carry a foetus to term unless she meets certain criteria unrelated to her own priorities and aspirations, is a profound interference with a woman's body and thus a violation of security of the person. Section 251, therefore, is required by the *Charter* to comport with the principles of fundamental justice.

Although this interference with physical and emotional integrity is sufficient in itself to trigger a review of s. 251 against the principles of fundamental justice, the operation of the decision-making mechanism set out in s. 251 creates additional glaring breaches of security of the person. The evidence indicates that s. 251 causes a certain amount of delay for women who are successful in meeting its criteria. In the context of abortion, any unnecessary delay can have profound consequences on the woman's physical and emotional well-being. . . .

[Chief Justice Dickson here quotes relevant findings of the 1977 Badgley Report. The Badgley Report was commissioned by the federal government in the wake of the first *Morgentaler* case (1973-75). It found uneven access to and delays in access to abortion since the 1969 reforms. The delays were linked to increased threat to the health of the mother in later-stage abortions.]

The above physical interference caused by the delays created by s. 251, involving a clear risk of damage to the physical well-being of a woman, is sufficient, in my view, to warrant inquiring whether s. 251 comports with the principles of fundamental justice. However, there is yet another infringement of security of the person. It is clear from the evidence that s. 251 harms the psychological integrity of women seeking abortions. A 1985 report of the Canadian Medical Association, discussed in the Powell Report, at p. 15, emphasized that the procedure involved in s. 251, with the concomitant delays, greatly increases the stress levels of patients and that this can lead to more physical complications associated with abortion....

In its supplementary factum and in oral submissions, the Crown argued that evidence of what could be termed "administrative inefficiency" is not relevant to the evaluation of legislation for the purposes of s. 7 of the *Charter*. The Crown argued that only evidence regarding the purpose of legislation is relevant. The assumption, of course, is that any impairment to the physical or psychological interests of individuals caused by s. 251 of the *Criminal Code* does not amount to an infringement of security of the person because the injury is caused by practical difficulties and is not intended by the legislator.

The submission is faulty on two counts. First, as a practical matter it is not possible in the case of s. 251 to erect a rigid barrier between the purposes of the section and the administrative procedures established to carry those purposes into effect....

Secondly, were it nevertheless possible in this case to dissociate purpose and administration, this Court has already held as a matter of law that purpose is not the only appropriate criterion in evaluating the constitutionality of legislation under the *Charter*....

Even if the purpose of legislation is unobjectionable, the administrative procedures *created by law* to bring that purpose into operation may produce unconstitutional effects, and the legislation should then be struck down....

In summary, s. 251 is a law which forces women to carry a foetus to term contrary to their own priorities and aspirations and which imposes serious delay causing increased physical and psychological trauma to those women who meet its criteria. It must, therefore, be determined whether that infringement is accomplished in accordance with the principles of fundamental justice, thereby saving s. 251 under the second part of s. 7....

My discussion will ... be limited to various aspects of the administrative structure and procedure set down in s. 251 for access to therapeutic abortions....

The procedure surrounding the defence is rather complex. A pregnant woman who desires to have an abortion must apply to the "therapeutic abortion committee" of an "accredited or approved hospital." Such a committee is empowered to issue a certificate in writing stating that in the opinion of a majority of the committee, the continuation of the pregnancy would be likely to endanger the pregnant woman's life or health. Once a copy of the certificate is given to a qualified medical practitioner who is not a member of the therapeutic abortion committee, he or she is permitted to perform an abortion on the pregnant woman and both the doctor and the woman are freed from any criminal liability....

As is so often the case in matters of interpretation, however, the straightforward reading of this statutory scheme is not fully revealing. In order to understand the true nature and scope of s. 251, it is necessary to investigate the practical operation of the provisions. The Court has been provided with a myriad of factual submissions in this area. One of the most useful sources of information is the Badgley Report....

The Badgley Report contains a wealth of detailed information which demonstrates, however, that many of the most serious problems with the functioning of s. 251 are created by procedural and administrative requirements established in the law.... [For example], the seemingly neutral requirement of s. 251(4) that at least four physicians be available to authorize and to perform an abortion meant in practice that abortions would be absolutely unavailable in almost one quarter of all hospitals in Canada.

Other administrative and procedural requirements of s. 251(4) reduce the availability of therapeutic abortions even further. For the purposes of s. 251, therapeutic abortions can only be performed in "accredited" or "approved" hospitals. As noted above, an "approved" hospital is one which a provincial minister of health has designated as such for the purpose of performing therapeutic abortions. The minister is under no obligation to grant any such approval. Furthermore, an "accredited" hospital must not only be accredited by the Canadian Council on Hospital Accreditation, it must also provide specified services. Many Canadian hospitals do not provide all of the required services, thereby being automatically disqualified from undertaking therapeutic abortions. The Badgley Report stressed the remarkable limitations created by these requirements, especially when linked with the four-physician rule discussed above (p. 105):

Of the total of 1,348 non-military hospitals in Canada in 1976, 789 hospitals, or 58.5 percent, were ineligible in terms of their major treatment functions, the size of their medical staff, or their type of facility to establish therapeutic abortion committees.

Moreover, even if a hospital is eligible to create a therapeutic abortion committee, there is no requirement in s. 251 that the hospital need do so. The Badgley Committee discovered that in 1976, of the 559 general hospitals which met the procedural requirements of s. 251, only 271 hospitals in Canada, or only 20.1 per cent of the total, had actually established a therapeutic abortion committee (p. 105).

Even though the Badgley Report was issued ten years ago, the relevant statistics do not appear to be out of date. Indeed, Statistics Canada reported that in 1982 the number of hospitals with therapeutic abortion committees had actually fallen to 261....

A further flaw with the administrative system established in s. 251(4) is the failure to provide an adequate standard for therapeutic abortion committees which must determine when a therapeutic abortion should, as a matter of law, be granted. Subsection (4) states simply that a therapeutic abortion committee may grant a certificate when it determines that a continuation of a pregnancy would be likely to endanger the "life or health" of the pregnant woman. It was noted above that "health" is not defined for the purposes of the section....

Various expert doctors testified at trial that therapeutic abortion committees apply widely differing definitions of health. For some committees, psychological health is a justification for therapeutic abortion; for others it is not. Some committees routinely refuse abortions to married women unless they are in physical danger, while for other committees it is possible for a married woman to show that she would suffer psychological harm if she continued with a pregnancy, thereby justifying an abortion. It is not typically possible for women to know in advance what standard of health will be applied by any given committee....

It is no answer to say that "health" is a medical term and that doctors who sit on therapeutic abortion committees must simply exercise their professional judgment. A therapeutic abortion committee is a strange hybrid, part medical committee and part legal committee [in the words of Parker A.C.J.H.C.]....

When the decision of the therapeutic abortion committee is so directly laden with legal consequences, the absence of any clear legal standard to be applied by the committee in reaching its decision is a serious procedural flaw.

The combined effect of all of these problems with the procedure stipulated in s. 251 for access to therapeutic abortions is a failure to comply with the principles of fundamental justice. In *Re B.C. Motor Vehicle Act*, Lamer J. held, at p. 503, that "the principles of fundamental justice are to be found in the basic tenets of our legal system." One of the basic tenets of our system of criminal justice is that when Parliament creates a defence to a criminal charge, the defence should not be illusory or so difficult to attain as to be practically illusory. The criminal law is a very special form of governmental regulation, for it seeks to express our society's collective disapprobation of certain acts and omissions. When a defence is provided, especially a specifically-tailored defence to a particular charge, it is because the legislator has determined that the disapprobation of society is not warranted when the conditions of the defence are met.

Consider then the case of a pregnant married woman who wishes to apply for a therapeutic abortion certificate because she fears that her psychological health would be impaired seriously if she carried the foetus to term. The uncontroverted evidence reveals that there are many areas in Canada where such a woman would simply not have access to a therapeutic abortion....

The Crown argues in its supplementary factum that women who face difficulties in obtaining abortions at home can simply travel elsewhere in Canada to procure a therapeutic abortion. That submission would not be especially troubling if the difficulties facing women were not in large measure created by the procedural requirements of s. 251 itself. If women were seeking anonymity outside their home town or were simply confronting the reality that it is often difficult to obtain medical services in rural areas, it might be appropriate to say "let them travel." But the evidence establishes convincingly that it is the law itself which in many ways *prevents* access to local therapeutic abortion facilities.... Parliament must be given room to design an appropriate administrative and procedural structure for bringing into operation a particular defence to criminal liability. But if that structure is "so manifestly unfair, having regard to the decisions it is called upon to make, as to violate the principles of *fundamental* justice," that structure must be struck down. In the present case, the structure—the system regulating access to therapeutic abortions—is manifestly unfair. It contains so many potential barriers to its own operation that the defence it creates will in many circumstances be practically unavailable to women who would *prima facie* qualify for the defence, or at least would force such women to travel great distances at substantial expense and inconvenience in order to benefit from a defence that is held out to be generally available.

I conclude that the procedures created in s. 251 of the *Criminal Code* for obtaining a therapeutic abortion do not comport with the principles of fundamental justice. It is not necessary to determine whether s. 7 also contains a substantive content leading to the conclusion that, in some circumstances at least, the deprivation of a pregnant woman's right to security of the person can never comport with fundamental justice. Simply put, assuming Parliament can act, it must do so properly....

V. Section 1 Analysis

Section 1 of the *Charter* can potentially be used to "salvage" a legislative provision which breaches s. 7.... A statutory provision which infringes any section of the *Charter* can only be saved under s. 1 if the party seeking to uphold the provision can demonstrate first, that the objective of the provision is "of sufficient importance to warrant overriding a constitutionally protected right or freedom" (*R. v. Big M Drug Mart Ltd.*, at p. 352) and second, that the means chosen in overriding the right or freedom are reasonable and demonstrably justified in a free and democratic society. This second aspect ensures that the legislative means are proportional to the legislative ends (*Oakes*, at pp. 139-40). In *Oakes*, at p. 139, the Court referred to three considerations which are typically useful in assessing the proportionality of means to ends. First, the means chosen to achieve an important objective should be rational, fair and not arbitrary. Second, the legislative means should impair as little as possible the right or freedom under consideration. Third, the effects of the limitation upon the relevant right or freedom should not be out of proportion to the objective sought to be achieved.

The appellants contended that the sole purpose of s. 251 of the *Criminal Code* is to protect the life and health of pregnant women. The respondent Crown submitted that s. 251 seeks to protect not only the life and health of pregnant women, but also the interests of the foetus. On the other hand, the Crown conceded that the Court is not called upon in this appeal to evaluate any claim to "foetal rights" or to assess the meaning of "the right to life." I expressly refrain from so doing. In my view, it is unnecessary for the purpose of deciding this appeal to evaluate or assess "foetal rights" as an independent constitutional value. Nor are we required to measure the full extent of the state's interest in establishing criteria unrelated to the pregnant woman's own priorities and aspirations. What we must do is evaluate the particular balance struck by Parliament in s. 251, as it relates to the priorities and aspirations of pregnant women and the government's interests in the protection of the foetus.

Section 251 provides that foetal interests are not to be protected where the "life or health" of the woman is threatened. Thus, Parliament itself has expressly stated in s. 251 that the "life or health" of pregnant women is paramount. The procedures of s. 251(4) are clearly related to the pregnant woman's "life or health" for that is the very phrase used by the subsection. As McIntyre J. states in his reasons (at p. 155), the aim of s. 251(4) is "to restrict abortion to cases where the continu-

ation of the pregnancy would, or would likely, be injurious to the life or health of the woman concerned, not to provide unrestricted access to abortion." I have no difficulty in concluding that the objective of s. 251 as a whole, namely, to balance the competing interests identified by Parliament, is sufficiently important to meet the requirements of the first step in the *Oakes* inquiry under s. 1. I think the protection of the interests of pregnant women is a valid governmental objective, where life and health can be jeopardized by criminal sanctions. Like Beetz and Wilson JJ., I agree that protection of foetal interests by Parliament is also a valid governmental objective. It follows that balancing these interests, with the lives and health of women a major factor, is clearly an important governmental objective. As the Court of Appeal stated at p. 366, "the contemporary view [is] that abortion is not always socially undesirable behavior."

I am equally convinced, however, that the means chosen to advance the legislative objectives of s. 251 do not satisfy any of the three elements of the proportionality component of *R. v. Oakes*. The evidence has led me to conclude that the infringement of the security of the person of pregnant women caused by s. 251 is not accomplished in accordance with the principles of fundamental justice. It has been demonstrated that the procedures and administrative structures created by s. 251 are often arbitrary and unfair. The procedures established to implement the policy of s. 251 impair s. 7 rights far more than is necessary because they hold out an illusory defence to many women who would *prima facie* qualify under the exculpatory provisions of s. 251(4). In other words, many women whom Parliament professes not to wish to subject to criminal liability will nevertheless be forced by the practical unavailability of the supposed defence to risk liability or to suffer other harm such as a traumatic late abortion caused by the delay inherent in the s. 251 system. Finally, the effects of the limitation upon the s. 7 rights of many pregnant women are out of proportion to the objective sought to be achieved. Indeed, to the extent that s. 251(4) is designed to protect the life and health of women, the procedures it establishes may actually defeat that objective. The administrative structures of s. 251(4) are so cumbersome that women whose health is endangered by pregnancy may not be able to gain a therapeutic abortion, at least without great trauma, expense and inconvenience.

I conclude, therefore, that the cumbersome structure of subs. (4) not only unduly subordinates the s. 7 rights of pregnant women but may also defeat the value Parliament itself has established as paramount, namely, the life and health of the pregnant woman. As I have noted, counsel for the Crown did contend that one purpose of the procedures required by subs. (4) is to protect the interests of the foetus. State protection of foetal interests may well be deserving of constitutional recognition under s. 1. Still, there can be no escape from the fact that Parliament has failed to establish either a standard or a procedure whereby any such interests might prevail over those of the woman in a fair and non-arbitrary fashion.

Section 251 of the *Criminal Code* cannot be saved, therefore, under s. 1 of the *Charter*. . . .

The judgment of Estey and Beetz JJ. was delivered by

BEETZ J.: . . . Access to abortion without risk of criminal penalty under the *Criminal Code* is expressed by Parliament in subss. (4), (5), (6) and (7) of s. 251 as relieving provisions in respect of the indictable offences defined at s. 251(1) and (2). According to Laskin C.J. (dissenting) in *Morgentaler v. The Queen*, [1976] . . . these relieving provisions "simply permit a person to make conduct lawful which would otherwise be unlawful" (at p. 631). In the same case, Pigeon J. said that in 1969 "an explicit and specific definition was made of the circumstances under which an abortion could lawfully be performed" (at p. 660). . . .

Given that it appears in a criminal law statute, s. 251(4) cannot be said to create a "right," much less a constitutional right, but it does represent an exception decreed by Parliament pursuant to what the Court of Appeal aptly called "the contemporary view that abortion is not always socially undesirable behaviour." Examining the content of the rule by which Parliament decriminalizes abortion is the most appropriate first step in considering the validity of s. 251 as against the constitutional right to abortion alleged by the appellants in argument. . . .

That abortions are recognized as lawful by Parliament based on a specific standard under its ordinary laws is important, I think, to a proper understanding of the existence of a right of access to abortion founded on rights guaranteed by s. 7 of the *Charter*. The constitutional right does not have its source in the *Criminal Code*, but, in my view, the content of the standard in s. 251(4) that Parliament recognized in the *Criminal Law Amendment Act, 1968-69* was for all intents and purposes entrenched at least as a minimum in 1982 when a distinct right in s. 7 became part of Canadian constitutional law.

The Right to Security of the Person in Section 7

. . . A pregnant woman's person cannot be said to be secure if, when her life or health is in danger, she is faced with a rule of criminal law which precludes her from obtaining effective and timely medical treatment. . . .

If a rule of criminal law precludes a person from obtaining appropriate medical treatment when his or her life or health is in danger, then the state has intervened and this intervention constitutes a violation of that man's or that woman's security of the person. "Security of the person" must include a right of access to medical treatment for a condition representing a danger to life or health without fear of criminal sanction. If an act of Parliament forces a person whose life or health is in danger to choose between, on the one hand, the commission of a crime to obtain effective and timely medical treatment and, on the other hand, inadequate treatment or no treatment at all, the right to security of the person has been violated.

This interpretation of s. 7 of the *Charter* is sufficient to measure the content of s. 251 of the *Criminal Code* against that of the *Charter* in order to dispose of this appeal. While I agree with McIntyre J. that a breach of a right to security must be "based upon an infringement of some interest which would be of such nature and such importance as to warrant constitutional protection," I am of the view that the protection of life or health is an interest of sufficient importance in this regard. Under the *Criminal Code*, the only way in which a pregnant woman can legally secure an abortion when the continuation of the pregnancy would or would be likely to endanger her life or health is to comply with the procedure set forth in s. 251(4). Where the continued pregnancy does constitute a danger to life or health, the pregnant woman faces a choice: (1) she can endeavour to follow the s. 251(4) procedure, which, as we shall see, creates an additional medical risk given its inherent delays and the possibility that the danger will not be recognized by the state-imposed therapeutic abortion committee; or (2) she can secure medical treatment without respecting s. 251(4) and subject herself to criminal sanction under s. 251(2).

Delays Caused by Section 251 Procedure

[Justice Beetz's treatment of the causes of delay is similar to that of Chief Justice Dickson. He then goes on to consider whether the delays violate the section 7 right to security of the person.]

The delays which a pregnant woman may have to suffer as a result of the requirements of s. 251(4) must undermine the security of her person in order that there be a violation of this element of s. 7 of the *Charter*. As I said earlier, s. 7 cannot be invoked simply because a woman's pregnancy amounts to a medically dangerous condition. If, however, the delays occasioned by s. 251(4) of the *Criminal Code* result in an additional danger to the pregnant woman's health, then the state has intervened and this intervention constitutes a violation of that woman's security of the person. By creating this additional risk, s. 251 prevents access to effective and timely medical treatment for the continued pregnancy which would or would be likely to endanger her life or health. If an effective and timely therapeutic abortion may only be obtained by committing a crime, then s. 251 violates the pregnant woman's right to security of the person.

The evidence reveals that the delays caused by s. 251(4) result in at least three broad types of additional medical risks. The risk of post-operative complications increases with delay. Secondly, there is a risk that the pregnant woman require a more dangerous means of procuring a miscarriage because of the delay. Finally, since a pregnant woman knows her life or health is in danger, the delay created by the s. 251(4) procedure may result in an additional psychological trauma....

The delays mean therefore that the state has intervened in such a manner as to create an additional risk to health, and consequently this intervention constitutes a violation of the woman's security of the person.

The Principles of Fundamental Justice

I turn now to a consideration of the manner in which pregnant women are deprived of their right to security of the person by s. 251. Section 7 of the *Charter* states that everyone has the right not to be deprived of security of the person except in accordance with the principles of fundamental justice. As I will endeavour to demonstrate, s. 251(4) does not accord with the principles of fundamental justice.

I am of the view, however, that certain elements of the procedure for obtaining a therapeutic abortion which counsel for the appellants argued could not be saved by the second part of s. 7 are in fact in accordance with the principles of fundamental justice. The expression of the standard in s. 251(4)(c), and the requirement for some independent medical opinion to ascertain that the standard has been met as well as the consequential necessity of some period of delay to ascertain the standard are not in breach of s. 7 of the *Charter*.

Counsel for the appellants argued that the expression of the standard in s. 251(4)(c) is so imprecise that it offends the principles of fundamental justice. He submits that pregnant women are arbitrarily deprived of their s. 7 right by reason of the different meanings that can be given to the word "health" in s. 251(4)(c) by therapeutic abortion committees.

I agree with McIntyre J. and the Ontario Court of Appeal that the expression "the continuation of the pregnancy of such female person would or would be likely to endanger her life or health" found in s. 251(4)(c) does provide, as a matter of law, a sufficiently precise standard by which therapeutic abortion committees can determine when therapeutic abortions should be granted....

Laskin C.J. held in *Morgentaler (1975)*, at p. 634, that s. 251(4)(c) was not so vague so as to constitute a violation of "security of the person" without due process of law under s. 1(a) of the *Canadian Bill of Rights*....

I agree with Laskin C.J. that the standard is manageable because it is addressed to a panel of doctors exercising medical judgment on a medical question. This being the case, the standard must necessarily be flexible. Flexibility and vagueness are not synonymous. Parliament has set a medical standard to be determined over a limited range of circumstances. With the greatest of respect, I cannot agree with the view that the therapeutic abortion committee is a "strange hybrid, part medical committee and part legal committee" as the Chief Justice characterizes it (at p. 69). In section 251(4) Parliament has only given the committee the authority to make a medical determination regarding the pregnant woman's life or health. The committee is not called upon to evaluate the sufficiency of the state interest in the foetus as against the woman's health. This evaluation of the state interest is a question of law already decided by Parliament in its formulation of s. 251(4). Evidence has been submitted that many committees fail to apply the standard set by Parliament by requiring the consent of the pregnant woman's spouse, by refusing to authorize second abortions or by refusing all abortions to married women. In so far as these and other requirements fall outside s. 251(4)(c), they constitute an unfounded interpretation of the plain terms of the *Criminal Code*. These patent excesses of authority do not, however, mean that the standard of s. 251 is vague....

Just as the expression of the standard in s. 251(4)(c) does not offend the principles of fundamental justice, the requirement that an independent medical opinion be obtained for a therapeutic abortion to be lawful also cannot be said to constitute a violation of these principles when considered in the context of pregnant women's right to security of the person....

As I noted in my analysis of s. 251(4), by requiring that a committee state that the medical standard has been met for the criminal sanction to be lifted, Parliament seeks to assure that there is a reliable, independent and medically sound opinion that the continuation of the pregnancy would or would be likely to endanger the woman's life or health. Whatever the failings of the current system, I believe that the purpose pursuant to which it was adopted does not offend the principles of fundamental justice. As I shall endeavour to explain, the current mechanism in the *Criminal Code* does not accord with the principles of fundamental justice. This does not preclude, in my view, Parliament from adopting another system, free of the failings of s. 251(4), in order to ascertain that the life or health of the pregnant woman is in danger, by way of a reliable, independent and medically sound opinion.

Parliament is justified in requiring a reliable, independent and medically sound opinion in order to protect the state interest in the foetus. This is undoubtedly the objective of a rule which requires an independent verification of the practising physician's opinion that the life or health of the pregnant woman is in danger. It cannot be said to be simply a mechanism designed to protect the health of the pregnant woman. While this latter objective clearly explains the requirement that the practising physician be a "qualified medical practitioner" and that the abortion take place in a safe place, it cannot explain the necessary intercession of an in-hospital committee of three physicians from which is excluded the practising physician.

While a second medical opinion is very often seen as necessary in medical circles when difficult questions as to a patient's life or health are at issue, the independent opinion called for by the *Criminal Code* has a different purpose. Parliament requires this independent opinion because it is not only the woman's interest that is at stake in a decision to authorize an abortion. The Ontario Court of Appeal alluded to this at p. 378 when it stated that "One cannot overlook the fact that the situation respecting a woman's right to control her own person becomes more complex when she becomes pregnant, and that some statutory control may be appropriate." The presence of the foetus accounts for this complexity. By requiring an independent medical opinion that the pregnant woman's life or health is in fact endangered, Parliament seeks to ensure that, in any given case, only therapeutic reasons will justify the decision to abort. The amendments to the *Criminal Code* in 1969 amounted to a recognition by Parliament, as I have said, that the interest in the life or health of the pregnant woman takes precedence over the interest of the state in the protection of the foetus when the continuation of the pregnancy would or would be likely to endanger the pregnant woman's life or health. Parliament decided that it was necessary to ascertain this from a medical point of view before the law would allow the interest of the pregnant woman to indeed take precedence over that of the foetus and permit an abortion to be performed without criminal sanction.

I do not believe it to be unreasonable to seek independent medical confirmation of the threat to the woman's life or health when such an important and distinct interest hangs in the balance. I note with interest that in a number of foreign jurisdictions, laws which decriminalize abortions require an opinion as to the state of health of the woman independent from the opinion of her own physician. . . .

This said, the practising physician must, according to s. 251(4)(*a*), be in "good faith" and, consequently, have no reason to believe that the standard in s. 251(4)(*c*) has not been met. The practising physician is, however, properly excluded from the body giving the independent opinion. I believe that Parliament is justified in requiring what is no doubt an extraordinary medical practice in its regulation of the criminal law of abortion in accordance with the various interests at stake.

The assertion that an independent medical opinion, distinct from that of the pregnant woman and her practising physician, does not offend the principles of fundamental justice would need to be reevaluated if a right of access to abortion is founded upon the right to "liberty" in s. 7 of the *Charter*. I am of the view that there would still be circumstances in which the state interest in the protection of the foetus would require an independent medical opinion as to the danger to the life or health of the pregnant woman. Assuming without deciding that a right of access to abortion can be founded upon the right to "liberty," there would be a point in time at which the state interest in the foetus would become compelling. From this point in time, Parliament would be entitled to limit abortions to those required for therapeutic reasons and therefore require an independent opinion as to the health exception. The case law reveals a substantial difference of opinion as to the state interest in the protection of the foetus as against the pregnant woman's right to liberty. Wilson J., for example, in her discussion of s. 1 of the *Charter* in the case at bar, notes the following, at p. 183:

> The precise point in the development of the foetus at which the state's interest in its protection becomes "compelling" I leave to the informed judgment of the legislature which is in a position to receive guidance on the subject from all the relevant disciplines. It seems to me, however, that it might fall somewhere in the second trimester.

This view as to when the state interest becomes compelling may be compared with that of O'Connor J. of the United States Supreme Court in her dissenting opinion in *City of Akron v. Akron Center for Reproductive Health, Inc.*, 462 U.S. 416 (1983), at pp. 460-61:

> In *Roe* [*Roe v. Wade*, 410 U.S. 113 (1973)], the Court held that although the State had an important and legitimate interest in protecting potential life, that interest could not become compelling until the point at which the fetus was viable. The difficulty with this analysis is clear: potential life is no less potential in the first weeks of pregnancy than it is at viability or afterward. At any stage in pregnancy, there is the potential for human life. Although the Court refused to "resolve the difficult question of when life begins," *id.*, at 159, the Court chose the point of viability—when the foetus is capable of life independent of its mother—to permit the complete proscription of abortion. The choice of viability as the point at which state interest in potential life becomes compelling is no less arbitrary than choosing any point before viability or any point afterward. Accordingly, I believe that the State's interest in protecting potential human life exists throughout the pregnancy.

As I indicated at the outset of my reasons, it is nevertheless possible to resolve this appeal without attempting to delineate the right to "liberty" in s. 7 of the *Charter*. The violation of the right to "security of the person" and the relevant principles of fundamental justice are sufficient to invalidate s. 251 of the *Criminal Code*.

Some delay is inevitable in connection with any system which purports to limit to therapeutic reasons the grounds upon which an abortion can be performed lawfully. . . .

One . . . example of a rule which is unnecessary is the requirement in s. 251(4) that therapeutic abortions must take place in an eligible hospital to be lawful. I have observed that s. 251(4) directs that therapeutic abortions take place in accredited or approved hospitals, with at least four physicians, and that, because of the lack of such hospitals in many parts of Canada, this often causes delay for women seeking treatment. . . .

Experts testified at trial that the principal justification for the in-hospital rule is the problem of post-operative complications. There are of course instances in which the danger to life or health observed by the therapeutic abortion committee will constitute sufficient grounds for the procedure to take place in a hospital. There are other instances in which the circumstances of the procedure itself requires that it be performed in hospital, such as certain abortions performed at an advanced gestational age or cases in which the patient is particularly vulnerable to what might otherwise be a simple procedure.

In many cases, however, there is no medical justification that the therapeutic abortion take place in a hospital. Experts testified at trial, that many first trimester therapeutic abortions may be safely performed in specialized clinics outside of hospitals because the possible complications can be handled, and in some cases better handled, by the facilities of a specialized clinic. . . .

The substantial increase in the percentage of abortions performed on an out-patient basis since 1975 underscores the view that the in-hospital requirement, which may have been justified when it was first adopted, has become exorbitant. . . .

. . . Although the protection of health of the woman is the objective which the in-hospital rule is intended to serve, the requirement that all therapeutic abortions be performed in eligible hospitals is unnecessary to meet that objective in all cases. In this sense, the rule is manifestly unfair and offends the principles of fundamental justice. I appreciate that the precise nature of the administrative solution may be complicated by the constitutional division of powers between Parliament and the provinces. There is no doubt that Parliament could allow the criminal law exception to operate in all hospitals, for example, though the provinces retain the power to establish these hospitals under s. 92(7) of the *Constitution Act, 1867*.

On the other hand, if Parliament decided to allow therapeutic abortions to be performed in provincially licensed clinics, it is possible that both Parliament and the provinces would be called upon to collaborate in the implementation of the plan.

An objection can also be raised in respect of the requirement that the committee come from the accredited or approved hospital in which the abortion is to be performed. It is difficult to see a connection between this requirement and any of the practical purposes for which s. 251(4) was enacted. It cannot be said to have been adopted in order to promote the safety of therapeutic abortions or the safety of the pregnant woman. Nor is the rule designed to preserve the state interest in the foetus. The integrity of the independent medical opinion is no better served by a committee within the hospital than a committee from outside the hospital as long as the practising physician remains excluded in both circumstances as part of a proper state participation in the choice of the procedure necessary to secure an independent opinion. . . .

. . . [I]t is plain that the requirement that the therapeutic abortion committee come from the hospital in which the abortion will be performed serves no real purpose. The risk resulting from the delay caused by s. 251(4) in this respect is unnecessary. Consequently, this requirement violates the principles of fundamental justice.

Other aspects of the committee requirement in s. 251(4) add to the manifest unfairness of the administrative structure. These include requirements which are at best only tenuously connected to the purpose of obtaining independent confirmation that the standard in s. 251(4)(*c*) has been met and which do not usefully contribute to the realization of that purpose. Hospital boards are entitled to appoint committees made up of three or more qualified medical practitioners. As I observed earlier, if more than three members are appointed, precious time can be lost when quorum cannot be established because members are absent. . . .

Similarly, the exclusion of all physicians who practise therapeutic abortions from the committees is exorbitant. This rule was no doubt included in s. 251(4) to promote the independence of the therapeutic abortion committees' appreciation of the standard. As I have said, the exclusion of the practising physician, although it diverges from usual medical practice, is appropriate in the criminal context to ensure the independent opinion with respect to the life or health of that physician's patient. The exclusion of all physicians who perform therapeutic abortions from committees, even when they have no connection with the patient in question, is not only unnecessary but potentially counterproductive. There are no reasonable grounds to suspect bias from a physician who has no connection with the patient simply because, in the course of his or her medical practice, he or she performs *lawful* abortions. Furthermore, physicians who perform therapeutic abortions have useful expertise which would add to the precision and the integrity of the independent opinion itself. Some state control is appropriate to ensure the independence of the opinion. However, this rule as it now stands is excessive and can increase the risk of delay because fewer physicians are qualified to serve on the committees.

The foregoing analysis of the administrative structure of s. 251(4) is by no means a complete catalogue of all the current systems' strengths and failings. It demonstrates, however, that the administrative structure put in place by Parliament has enough shortcomings so that s. 251(4), when considered as a whole, violates the principles of fundamental justice. These shortcomings stem from rules which are not necessary to the purposes for which s. 251(4) was established. These unnecessary rules, because they impose delays which result in an additional risk to women's health, are manifestly unfair.

Section 1 of the Charter

I agree with Wilson J.'s characterization of s. 251, explained in the following terms, at p. 181:

> In my view, the primary objective of the impugned legislation must be seen as the protection of the foetus. It undoubtedly has other ancillary objectives, such as the protection of the life and health of pregnant women, but I believe that the main objective advanced to justify a restriction on the pregnant woman's s. 7 right is the protection of the foetus.

The primary objective of the protection of the foetus is the main objective relevant to the analysis of s. 251 under the first test of *Oakes*. With the greatest respect, I believe the Chief Justice incorrectly identifies (at p. 75) the objective of *balancing* foetal interests and those of pregnant women, "with the lives and health of women a major factor," as "sufficiently important to meet the requirements of the first step in the *Oakes* inquiry under s. 1."

The focus in *Oakes* is the objective "which the measures responsible for a limit on a *Charter* right or freedom are designed to serve" (*supra*, at p. 138). In the context of the criminal law of abortion, the objective, which the measures in s. 251 responsible for a limit on the s. 7 *Charter* right are designed to serve, is the protection of the foetus. The narrow aim of s. 251(4) should not be confused with the primary objective of s. 251 as a whole.…

Does the objective of protecting the foetus in s. 251 relate to concerns which are pressing and substantial in a free and democratic society? The answer to the first step of the *Oakes*

test is yes. I am of the view that the protection of the foetus is and, as the Court of Appeal observed, always has been, a valid objective in Canadian criminal law. I have already elaborated on this objective in my discussion of the principles of fundamental justice. I think s. 1 of the *Charter* authorizes reasonable limits to be put on a woman's right having regard to the state interest in the protection of the foetus.

I turn now to the second test in *Oakes*. The Crown must show that the means chosen in s. 251 are reasonable and demonstrably justified. In *Oakes, supra*, at p. 139, the Chief Justice outlined three components of the proportionality test.…

For the purposes of the first component of proportionality, I observe that it was necessary, in my discussion of s. 251(4) and the principles of fundamental justice, to explain my view that certain of the rules governing access to therapeutic abortions free from criminal sanction are unnecessary in respect of the objectives which s. 251 is designed to serve. A rule which is unnecessary in respect of Parliament's objectives cannot be said to be "rationally connected" thereto or to be "carefully designed to achieve the objective in question." Furthermore, not only are some of the rules in s. 251 unnecessary to the primary objective of the protection of the foetus and the ancillary objective of the protection of the pregnant woman's life or health, but their practical effect is to undermine the health of the woman which Parliament purports to consider so important. Consequently, s. 251 does not meet the proportionality test in *Oakes*.

There is no saving s. 251 by simply severing the offending portions of s. 251(4). The current rule expressed in s. 251, which articulates both Parliament's principal and ancillary objectives, cannot stand without the exception in s. 251(4). The violation of pregnant women's security of the person would be greater, not lesser, if s. 251(4) was severed leaving the remaining subsections of s. 251 as they are in the *Criminal Code*.

Given my conclusion in respect of the first component of the proportionality test, it is not necessary to address the questions as to whether the means in s. 251 "impair as little as possible" the s. 7 *Charter* right and whether there is a proportionality between the effects of s. 251 and the objective of protecting the foetus. Thus, I am not required to answer the difficult question concerning the circumstances in which there is a proportionality between the effects of s. 251 which limit the right of pregnant women to security of the person and the objective of the protection of the foetus. I do feel bound, however, to comment upon the balance which Parliament sought to achieve between the interest in the protection of the foetus and the interest in the life or health of the pregnant woman in adopting the amendments to the *Criminal Code* in 1969.…

The gist of s. 251(4) is, as I have said, that the objective of protecting the foetus is not of sufficient importance to defeat the interest in protecting pregnant women from pregnancies which represent a danger to life or health. I take this parliamentary enactment in 1969 as an indication that, in a free and democratic society, it would be unreasonable to limit the pregnant woman's right to security of the person by a rule prohibiting abortions in all circumstances when her life or health would or would likely be in danger. This decision of the Canadian Parliament to the effect that the life or health of the pregnant woman takes precedence over the state interest in the foetus is also reflected in legislation in other free and democratic societies....

I note that the laws in some of these foreign jurisdictions, unlike s. 251 of the *Criminal Code*, require a higher standard of danger to health in the latter months of pregnancy, as opposed to the early months, for an abortion to be lawful. Would such a rule, if it was adopted in Canada, constitute a reasonable limit on the right to security of the person under s. 1 of the *Charter*? As I have said, given the actual wording of s. 251, pursuant to which the standard necessary for a lawful abortion does not vary according to the stage of pregnancy, this Court is not required to consider this question under s. 1 of the *Charter*. It is possible that a future enactment by Parliament along the lines of the laws adopted in these jurisdictions could achieve a proportionality which is acceptable under s. 1. As I have stated, however, I am of the view that the objective of protecting the foetus would not justify the *complete* removal of the exculpatory provisions from the *Criminal Code*.

Finally, I wish to stress that we have not been asked to decide nor is it necessary, given my own conclusion that s. 251 contains rules unnecessary to the protection of the foetus, to decide whether a foetus is included in the word "everyone" in s. 7 so as to have a right to "life, liberty and security of the person" under the *Charter*.

WILSON J.: ... My colleagues, the Chief Justice and Justice Beetz, have attacked [the law's procedural] requirements in reasons which I have had the privilege of reading. They have found that the requirements do not comport with the principles of fundamental justice in the procedural sense and have concluded that, since they cannot be severed from the provisions creating the substantive offence, the whole of s. 251 must fall.

With all due respect, I think that the Court must tackle the primary issue first. A consideration as to whether or not the procedural requirements for obtaining or performing an abortion comport with fundamental justice is purely academic if such requirements cannot as a constitutional matter be imposed at all.... Moreover, it would, in my opinion, be an exercise in futility for the legislature to expend its time and energy in attempting to remedy the defects in the procedural requirements unless it has some assurance that this process will, at the end of the day, result in the creation of a valid criminal offence. I turn, therefore, to what I believe is the central issue that must be addressed....

It seems to me ... that to commence the analysis with the premise that the s. 7 right encompasses only a right to physical and psychological security and to fail to deal with the right to liberty in the context of "life, liberty and security of the person" begs the central issue in the case. If either the right to liberty or the right to security of the person or a combination of both confers on the pregnant woman the right to decide for herself (with the guidance of her physician) whether or not to have an abortion, then we have to examine the legislative scheme not only from the point of view of fundamental justice in the procedural sense but in the substantive sense as well. I think, therefore, that we must answer the question: what is meant by the right to liberty in the context of the abortion issue? Does it, as Mr. Manning suggests, give the pregnant woman control over decisions affecting her own body? ...

In order to ascertain the content of the right to liberty we must, as Dickson C.J. stated in *R. v. Big M Drug Mart Ltd.*, [1985] 1 S.C.R. 295, commence with an analysis of the purpose of the right....

The *Charter* is predicated on a particular conception of the place of the individual in society. An individual is not a totally independent entity disconnected from the society in which he or she lives. Neither, however, is the individual a mere cog in an impersonal machine in which his or her values, goals and aspirations are subordinated to those of the collectivity. The individual is a bit of both. The *Charter* reflects this reality by leaving a wide range of activities and decisions open to legitimate government control while at the same time placing limits on the proper scope of that control. Thus, the rights guaranteed in the *Charter* erect around each individual, metaphorically speaking, an invisible fence over which the state will not be allowed to trespass. The role of the courts is to map out, piece by piece, the parameters of the fence.

The *Charter* and the right to individual liberty guaranteed under it are inextricably tied to the concept of human dignity.

The idea of human dignity finds expression in almost every right and freedom guaranteed in the *Charter*. Individuals are afforded the right to choose their own religion and their own philosophy of life, the right to choose with whom they will associate and how they will express themselves, the right to choose where they will live and what occupation they will pursue. These are all examples of the basic theory underlying the *Charter*, namely that the state will respect choices made by individuals and, to the greatest extent possible, will avoid subordinating these choices to any one conception of the good life.

Thus, an aspect of the respect for human dignity on which the *Charter* is founded is the right to make fundamental personal decisions without interference from the state. This right is a critical component of the right to liberty. Liberty, as was noted in *Singh*, is a phrase capable of a broad range of meaning. In my view, this right, properly construed, grants the individual a degree of autonomy in making decisions of fundamental personal importance.

This view is consistent with the position I took in the case of *R. v. Jones*, [1986] 2 S.C.R. 284. One issue raised in that case was whether the right to liberty in s. 7 of the *Charter* included a parent's right to bring up his children in accordance with his conscientious beliefs. In concluding that it did I stated at pp. 318-19:

> I believe that the framers of the Constitution in guaranteeing "liberty" as a fundamental value in a free and democratic society had in mind the freedom of the individual to develop and realize his potential to the full, to plan his own life to suit his own character, to make his own choices for good or ill, to be non-conformist, idiosyncratic and even eccentric—to be, in to-day's parlance, "his own person" and accountable as such. John Stuart Mill described it as "pursuing our own good in our own way." This, he believed, we should be free to do "so long as we do not attempt to deprive others of theirs or impede their efforts to obtain it." He added: "Each is the proper guardian of his own health, whether bodily or mental and spiritual. Mankind are greater gainers by suffering each other to live as seems good to themselves than by compelling each to live as seems good to the rest."

Liberty in a free and democratic society does not require the state to approve the personal decisions made by its citizens; it does, however, require the state to respect them.

This conception of the proper ambit of the right to liberty under our *Charter* is consistent with the American jurisprudence on the subject....

For our purposes the most interesting development in this area of American law are the decisions of the Supreme Court in *Roe v. Wade*, 410 U.S. 113 (1973), and its sister case *Doe v. Bolton*, 410 U.S. 179 (1973). In *Roe v. Wade* the Court held that a pregnant woman has the right to decide whether or not to terminate her pregnancy. This conclusion, the majority stated, was mandated by the body of existing law ensuring that the state would not be allowed to interfere with certain fundamental personal decisions such as education, child-rearing, procreation, marriage and contraception. The Court concluded that the right to privacy found in the Fourteenth Amendment guarantee of liberty "...is broad enough to encompass a woman's decision whether or not to terminate her pregnancy."...

This right was not, however, to be taken as absolute. At some point the legitimate state interests in the protection of health, proper medical standards, and pre-natal life would justify its qualification. Lawrence H. Tribe, Professor of Law at Harvard University, in his work entitled *American Constitutional Law* (1978), conveniently summarizes the limits the Court found to be inherent in the woman's right. I quote from pp. 924-25:

> Specifically, the Court held that, because the woman's right to decide whether or not to end a pregnancy is fundamental, only a compelling interest can justify state regulation impinging in any way upon that right. During the first trimester of pregnancy, when abortion is less hazardous in terms of the woman's life than carrying the child to term would be, the state may require only that the abortion be performed by a licensed physician; no further regulations peculiar to abortion as such are compellingly justified in that period.
>
> After the first trimester, the compelling state interest in the mother's health permits it to adopt reasonable regulations in order to promote safe abortions—but requiring abortions to be performed in hospitals, or only after approval of another doctor or committee in addition to the woman's physician, is impermissible, as is requiring that the abortion procedure employ a technique that, however preferable from a medical perspective, is not widely available.
>
> Once the fetus is viable, in the sense that it is capable of survival outside the uterus with artificial aid, the state interest in preserving the fetus becomes compelling, and the state may thus proscribe its premature removal (i.e., its abortion) except to preserve the mother's life or health.

... In my opinion, the respect for individual decision-making in matters of fundamental personal importance reflected in the American jurisprudence also informs the Canadian *Charter*. Indeed, as the Chief Justice pointed out in *R. v. Big M Drug Mart Ltd.*, beliefs about human worth and dignity "are the *sine qua non* of the political tradition underlying the *Charter*." I would conclude, therefore, that the right to liberty contained in s. 7 guarantees to every individual a degree of personal autonomy over important decisions intimately affecting their private lives.

The question then becomes whether the decision of a woman to terminate her pregnancy falls within this class of protected decisions. I have no doubt that it does. This decision is one that will have profound psychological, economic and social consequences for the pregnant woman. The circumstances giving rise to it can be complex and varied and there may be, and usually are, powerful considerations militating in opposite directions. It is a decision that deeply reflects the way the woman thinks about herself and her relationship to others and to society at large. It is not just a medical decision; it is a profound social and ethical one as well. Her response to it will be the response of the whole person. . . .

Given then that the right to liberty guaranteed by s. 7 of the *Charter* gives a woman the right to decide for herself whether or not to terminate her pregnancy, does s. 251 of the *Criminal Code* violate this right? Clearly it does. The purpose of the section is to take the decision away from the woman and give it to a committee. Furthermore, as the Chief Justice correctly points out, at p. 56, the committee bases its decision on "criteria entirely unrelated to [the pregnant woman's] own priorities and aspirations." The fact that the decision whether a woman will be allowed to terminate her pregnancy is in the hands of a committee is just as great a violation of the woman's right to personal autonomy in decisions of an intimate and private nature as it would be if a committee were established to decide whether a woman should be allowed to continue her pregnancy. Both these arrangements violate the woman's right to liberty by deciding for her something that she has the right to decide for herself.

Section 7 of the *Charter* also guarantees everyone the right to security of the person. Does this, as Mr. Manning suggests, extend to the right of control over one's own body?

I agree with the Chief Justice and with Beetz J. that the right to "security of the person" under s. 7 of the *Charter* protects both the physical and psychological integrity of the individual. . . . I agree with my colleague and I think that his comments are very germane to the instant case because, as the Chief Justice and Beetz J. point out, the present legislative scheme for the obtaining of an abortion clearly subjects pregnant women to considerable emotional stress as well as to unnecessary physical risk. I believe, however, that the flaw in the present legislative scheme goes much deeper than that. In essence, what it does is assert that the woman's capacity to reproduce is not to be subject to her own control. It is to be subject to the control of the state. She may not choose whether to exercise her existing capacity or not to exercise it. This is not, in my view, just a matter of interfering with her right to liberty in the sense (already discussed) of her right to personal autonomy in decision-making, it is a direct interference with her physical "person" as well. She is truly being treated as a means—a means to an end which she does not desire but over which she has no control. She is the passive recipient of a decision made by others as to whether her body is to be used to nurture a new life. Can there be anything that comports

less with human dignity and self-respect? How can a woman in this position have any sense of security with respect to her person? I believe that s. 251 of the *Criminal Code* deprives the pregnant woman of her right to security of the person as well as her right to liberty.

2. The Scope of Rights Under Section 7

I turn now to a consideration of the degree of personal autonomy the pregnant woman has under s. 7 of the *Charter* when faced with a decision whether or not to have an abortion or, to put it into the legislative context, the degree to which the legislature can deny the pregnant woman access to abortion without violating her s. 7 right. This involves a consideration of the extent to which the legislature can "deprive" her of it under the second part of s. 7 and the extent to which it can put "limits" on it under s. 1. . . .

(a) The Principles of Fundamental Justice

. . . I believe . . . that a deprivation of the s. 7 right which has the effect of infringing a right guaranteed elsewhere in the *Charter* cannot be in accordance with the principles of fundamental justice.

In my view, the deprivation of the s. 7 right with which we are concerned in this case offends s. 2(*a*) of the *Charter*. I say this because I believe that the decision whether or not to terminate a pregnancy is essentially a moral decision, a matter of conscience. I do not think there is or can be any dispute about that. The question is: whose conscience? Is the conscience of the woman to be paramount or the conscience of the state? I believe, for the reasons I gave in discussing the right to liberty, that in a free and democratic society it must be the conscience of the individual. Indeed, s. 2(*a*) makes it clear that this freedom belongs to "everyone," i.e., to each of us individually. . . .

In *R. v. Big M Drug Mart Ltd.*, *supra*, Dickson C.J. made some very insightful comments about the nature of the right enshrined in s. 2(*a*) of the *Charter* at pp. 345-47:

> It should also be noted, however, that an emphasis on individual conscience and individual judgment also lies at the heart of our democratic political tradition. *The ability of each citizen to make free and informed decisions is the absolute prerequisite for the legitimacy, acceptability, and efficacy of our system of self-government.* It is because of the centrality of the rights associated with freedom of individual conscience both to basic beliefs about human worth and dignity and to a free and democratic political system that American jurisprudence has emphasized the primacy or "firstness" of the First Amendment. It is this same centrality that in my view underlies their designation in the *Canadian Charter of Rights and Freedoms* as "fundamental." They are the *sine qua non* of the political tradition underlying the *Charter*. . . .

Viewed in this context, the purpose of freedom of conscience and religion becomes clear. *The values that underlie our political and philosophic traditions demand that every individual be free to hold and to manifest whatever beliefs and opinions his or her conscience dictates, provided inter alia only that such manifestations do not injure his or her neighbours or their parallel rights to hold and manifest beliefs and opinions of their own....*

The Chief Justice sees religious belief and practice as the paradigmatic example of conscientiously-held beliefs and manifestations and as such protected by the *Charter*. But I do not think he is saying that a personal morality which is not founded in religion is outside the protection of s. 2(*a*). Certainly, it would be my view that conscientious beliefs which are not religiously motivated are equally protected by freedom of conscience in s. 2(*a*). In so saying I am not unmindful of the fact that the *Charter* opens with an affirmation that "Canada is founded upon principles that recognize the supremacy of God ...." But I am also mindful that the values entrenched in the *Charter* are those which characterize a free and democratic society....

It seems to me, therefore, that in a free and democratic society "freedom of conscience and religion" should be broadly construed to extend to conscientiously-held beliefs, whether grounded in religion or in a secular morality. Indeed, as a matter of statutory interpretation, "conscience" and "religion" should not be treated as tautologous if capable of independent, although related, meaning. Accordingly, for the state to take sides on the issue of abortion, as it does in the impugned legislation by making it a criminal offence for the pregnant woman to exercise one of her options, is not only to endorse but also to enforce, on pain of a further loss of liberty through actual imprisonment, one conscientiously-held view at the expense of another. It is to deny freedom of conscience to some, to treat them as means to an end, to deprive them, as Professor MacCormick puts it, of their "essential humanity."...

Legislation which violates freedom of conscience in this manner cannot, in my view, be in accordance with the principles of fundamental justice within the meaning of s. 7.

(b) Section 1 of the Charter
... In my view, the primary objective of the impugned legislation must be seen as the protection of the foetus. It undoubtedly has other ancillary objectives, such as the protection of the life and health of pregnant women, but I believe that the main objective advanced to justify a restriction on the pregnant woman's s. 7 right is the protection of the foetus. I think this is a perfectly valid legislative objective.

Miss Wein submitted on behalf of the Crown that the Court of Appeal was correct in concluding at p. 378 that "the situa-tion respecting a woman's right to control her own person becomes more complex when she becomes pregnant, and that some statutory control may be appropriate." I agree. I think s. 1 of the *Charter* authorizes reasonable limits to be put upon the woman's right having regard to the fact of the developing foetus within her body. The question is: at what point in the pregnancy does the protection of the foetus become such a pressing and substantial concern as to outweigh the fundamental right of the woman to decide whether or not to carry the foetus to term? At what point does the state's interest in the protection of the foetus become "compelling" and justify state intervention in what is otherwise a matter of purely personal and private concern? ...

It would be my view, and I think it is consistent with the position taken by the United States Supreme Court in *Roe v. Wade*, that the value to be placed on the foetus as potential life is directly related to the stage of its development during gestation. The undeveloped foetus starts out as a newly fertilized ovum; the fully developed foetus emerges ultimately as an infant. A developmental progression takes place in between these two extremes and, in my opinion, this progression has a direct bearing on the value of the foetus as potential life. It is a fact of human experience that a miscarriage or spontaneous abortion of the foetus at six months is attended by far greater sorrow and sense of loss than a miscarriage or spontaneous abortion at six days or even six weeks. This is not, of course, to deny that the foetus is potential life from the moment of conception. Indeed, I agree with the observation of O'Connor J., dissenting in *City of Akron v. Akron Center for Reproductive Health, Inc., supra*, at p. 461,... that the foetus is potential life from the moment of conception. It is simply to say that in balancing the state's interest in the protection of the foetus as potential life under s. 1 of the *Charter* against the right of the pregnant woman under s. 7 greater weight should be given to the state's interest in the later stages of pregnancy than in the earlier. The foetus should accordingly, for purposes of s. 1, be viewed in differential and developmental terms....

...A developmental view of the foetus, on the other hand, supports a permissive approach to abortion in the early stages of pregnancy and a restrictive approach in the later stages. In the early stages the woman's autonomy would be absolute; her decision, reached in consultation with her physician, not to carry the foetus to term would be conclusive. The state would have no business inquiring into her reasons. Her reasons for having an abortion would, however, be the proper subject of inquiry at the later stages of her pregnancy when the state's compelling interest in the protection of the foetus would justify it in prescribing conditions. The precise point in the development of the foetus at which the state's interest in its protection becomes "compelling" I leave to the informed judgment of the legislature which is in a position to receive guidance on the subject from all the relevant disciplines. It seems to me, however, that it might fall somewhere in the second trimester. Indeed, . . . a differential abortion policy with a time limit in the second trimester is already in operation in the United States, Great Britain, France, Italy, Sweden, the Soviet Union, China, India, Japan and most of the countries of Eastern Europe although the time limits vary in these countries from the beginning to the end of the second trimester. . . .

The judgment of McIntyre and La Forest JJ. was delivered by

McINTYRE J. (dissenting): . . . I would say at the outset that it may be thought that this case does not raise the *Charter* issues which were argued and which have been addressed in the reasons of my colleagues. The charge here is one of conspiracy to breach the provisions of s. 251 of the *Criminal Code*. There is no doubt, and it has never been questioned, that the appellants adopted a course which was clearly in defiance of the provisions of the *Code* and it is difficult to see where any infringement of their rights, under s. 7 of the *Charter*, could have occurred. There is no female person involved in the case who has been denied a therapeutic abortion and, as a result, the whole argument on the right to security of the person, under s. 7 of the *Charter*, has been on a hypothetical basis. The case, however, was addressed by all the parties on that basis and the Court has accepted that position.

Section 251(1) and (2) of the *Criminal Code* make it an indictable offence for a person to use any means to procure the miscarriage of a female person. . . . Subsection (4) provides that subss. (1) and (2) shall not apply where an abortion is performed in accordance with paras. (*a*), (*b*), (*c*) and (*d*). . . . It is clear from the foregoing that abortion is prohibited and that subs. (4) provides relieving provisions allowing an abortion in certain limited circumstances. It cannot be said that s. 251 of the *Criminal Code* confers any general right to have or to procure an abortion. On the contrary, the provision is aimed at protecting the interests of the unborn child and only lifts the criminal sanction where an abortion is necessary to protect the life or health of the mother.

In considering the constitutionality of s. 251 of the *Criminal Code*, it is first necessary to understand the background of this litigation and some of the problems which it raises. Section 251 of the *Code* has been denounced as ill-conceived and inadequate by those at one extreme of the abortion debate and as immoral and unacceptable by those at the opposite extreme. There are those, like the appellants, who assert that on moral and ethical grounds there is a simple solution to the problem: the inherent "right of women to control their own bodies" requires the repeal of s. 251 in favour of the principle

of "abortion on demand." Opposing this view are those who contend with equal vigour, and also on moral and ethical grounds, for a clear and simple solution: the inherent "right to life of the unborn child" requires the repeal of s. 251(4), (5), (6) and (7) in order to leave an absolute ban on abortions. The battle lines so drawn are firmly held and the attitudes of the opposing parties admit of no compromise. From the submission of the Attorney General of Canada (set out in his factum at paragraph 6), however, it may appear that a majority in Canada do not see the issue in such black and white terms. Paragraph 6 is in these words:

> The evidence of opinion surveys indicates that there is a surprising consistency over the years and in different survey groups in the spectrum of opinions on the issue of abortion. Roughly 21 to 23% of people at one end of the spectrum are of the view, on the one hand, that abortion is a matter solely for the decision of the pregnant woman and that any legislation on this subject is an unwarranted interference with a woman's right to deal with her own body, while about 19 to 20% are of the view, on the other hand, that destruction of the living fetus is the killing of human life and tantamount to murder. The remainder of the population (about 60%) are of the view that abortion should be prohibited in some circumstances.

Parliament has heeded neither extreme. Instead, an attempt has been made to balance the competing interests of the unborn child and the pregnant woman. Where the provisions of s. 251(4) are met, the abortion may be performed without legal sanction. Where they are not, abortion is deemed to be socially undesirable and is punished as a crime. In *Morgentaler v. The Queen*, [1976] 1 S.C.R. 616 [hereinafter *Morgentaler (1975)*], Laskin C.J. said (in dissent, but not on this point), at p. 627:

> What is patent on the face of the prohibitory portion of s. 251 is that Parliament has in its judgment decreed that interference by another, or even by the pregnant woman herself, with the ordinary course of conception is socially undesirable conduct subject to punishment. That was a judgment open to Parliament in the exercise of its plenary criminal law power, and the fact that there may be safe ways of terminating a pregnancy or that any woman or women claim a personal privilege to that end, becomes immaterial. I need cite no authority for the proposition that Parliament may determine what is not criminal as well as what is, and may hence introduce dispensations or exemptions in its criminal legislation.

Parliament's view that abortion is, in its nature, "socially undesirable conduct" is not new. Parliament's policy, as expressed by s. 251 of the *Code*, is consistent with that which has governed Canadian criminal law since Confederation and before....

Scope of Judicial Review Under the Charter

Before the adoption of the *Charter*, there was little question of the limits of judicial review of the criminal law. For all practical purposes it was limited to a determination of whether the impugned enactment dealt with a subject which could fall within the criminal law power in s. 91(27) of the *Constitution Act, 1867*. There was no doubt of the power of Parliament to say what was and what was not criminal and to prohibit criminal conduct with penal sanctions, although from 1960 onwards legislation was subject to review under the *Canadian Bill of Rights*: see *Morgentaler (1975), supra*. The adoption of the *Charter* brought a significant change. The power of judicial review of legislation acquired greater scope but, in my view, that scope is not unlimited and should be carefully confined to that which is ordained by the *Charter*. I am well aware that there will be disagreement about what was ordained by the *Charter* and, of course, a measure of interpretation of the *Charter* will be required in order to give substance and reality to its provisions. But the courts must not, in the guise of interpretation, postulate rights and freedoms which do not have a firm and a reasonably identifiable base in the *Charter*....

While I differ with the Chief Justice in the disposition of this appeal, I would accept his words, referred to above, which describe the role of the Court, but I would suggest that in "ensuring that the legislative initiatives pursued by our Parliament and legislatures conform to the democratic values expressed in the *Canadian Charter of Rights and Freedoms*" the courts must confine themselves to such democratic values as are clearly found and expressed in the *Charter* and refrain from imposing or creating other values not so based.

It follows, then, in my view, that the task of the Court in this case is not to solve nor seek to solve what might be called the abortion issue, but simply to measure the content of s. 251 against the *Charter*. While this may appear to be self-evident, the distinction is of vital importance. If a particular interpretation enjoys no support, express or reasonably implied, from the *Charter*, then the Court is without power to clothe such an interpretation with constitutional status. It is not for the Court to substitute its own views on the merits of a given question for those of Parliament. The Court must consider not what is, in its view, the best solution to the problems posed; its role is confined to deciding whether the solution enacted by Parliament offends the *Charter*. If it does, the provision must be struck down or declared inoperative, and Parliament may then enact such different provisions as it may decide. I adopt the words of Holmes J., which were referred to in *Ferguson v. Skrupka*, 372 U.S. 726 (1963), at pp. 729-30:

There was a time when the Due Process Clause was used by this Court to strike down laws which were thought unreasonable, that is, unwise or incompatible with some particular economic or social philosophy. In this manner the Due Process Clause was used, for example, to nullify laws prescribing maximum hours for work in bakeries, *Lochner v. New York*, ... outlawing "yellow dog" contracts, *Coppage v. Kansas*, ... setting minimum wages for women, *Adkins v. Children's Hospital*, ... and fixing the weight of loaves of bread, *Jay Burns Baking Co. v. Bryan* ....

This intrusion by the judiciary into the realm of legislative value judgments was strongly objected to at the time, particularly by Mr. Justice Holmes and Mr. Justice Brandeis. Dissenting from the Court's invalidating a state statute which regulated the resale price of theatre and other tickets, Mr. Justice Holmes said: "I think the proper course is to recognize that a state legislature can do whatever it sees fit to do unless it is restrained by some express prohibition in the Constitution of the United States or of the State, and that Courts should be careful not to extend such prohibitions beyond their obvious meaning by reading into them conceptions of public policy that the particular Court may happen to entertain."

And in an earlier case he had emphasized that, "The criterion of constitutionality is not whether we believe the law to be for the public good."

The doctrine that prevailed in *Lochner, Coppage, Adkins, Burns*, and like cases—that due process authorizes courts to hold laws unconstitutional when they believe the legislature has acted unwisely—has long since been discarded. We have returned to the original constitutional proposition that courts do not substitute their social and economic beliefs for the judgment of legislative bodies, who are elected to pass laws.

Holmes J. wrote in 1927, but his words have retained their force in American jurisprudence.... In my view, although written in the American context, the principle stated is equally applicable in Canada.

It is essential that this principle be maintained in a constitutional democracy. The Court must not resolve an issue such as that of abortion on the basis of how many judges may favour "pro-choice" or "pro-life." To do so would be contrary to sound principle and the rule of law affirmed in the preamble to the *Charter* which must mean that no discretion, including a judicial discretion, can be unlimited. But there is a problem, for the Court must clothe the general expression of rights and freedoms contained in the *Charter* with real substance and vitality. How can the courts go about this task without imposing at least some of their views and predilections upon the law? This question has been the subject of much discussion and comment. Many theories have been postulated but few have had direct reference to the problem in the Canadian context. In my view, this Court has offered guidance in this matter. In such cases as *Hunter v. Southam Inc.*, [1984] 2 S.C.R. 145, at pp. 155-56, and *R. v. Big M Drug Mart Ltd.*, [1985] 1 S.C.R. 295, at p. 344, it has enjoined what has been termed a "purposive approach" in applying the *Charter* and its provisions. I take this to mean that the Courts should interpret the *Charter* in a manner calculated to give effect to its provisions, not to the idiosyncratic view of the judge who is writing. This approach marks out the limits of appropriate *Charter* adjudication. It confines the content of *Charter* guaranteed rights and freedoms to the purposes given expression in the *Charter*. Consequently, while the courts must continue to give a fair, large and liberal construction to the *Charter* provisions, this approach prevents the Court from abandoning its traditional adjudicatory function in order to formulate its own conclusions on questions of public policy, a step which this Court has said on numerous occasions it must not take. That *Charter* interpretation is to be purposive necessarily implies the converse: it is not to be "non-purposive." A court is not entitled to define a right in a manner unrelated to the interest which the right in question was meant to protect. I endeavoured to formulate an approach to the problem in *Reference Re Public Service Employee Relations Act*, [1987] 1 S.C.R. 313, in these words, at p. 394:

> It follows that while a liberal and not overly legalistic approach should be taken to constitutional interpretation, the *Charter* should not be regarded as an empty vessel to be filled with whatever meaning we might wish from time to time. The interpretation of the *Charter*, as of all constitutional documents, is constrained by the language, structure and history of the constitutional text, by constitutional tradition, and by the history, traditions, and underlying philosophies of our society.

The approach, as I understand it, does not mean that judges may not make some policy choices when confronted with competing conceptions of the extent of rights or freedoms. Difficult choices must be made and the personal views of judges will unavoidably be engaged from time to time. The decisions made by judges, however, and the interpretations that they advance or accept must be plausibly inferable from something in the *Charter*. It is not for the courts to manufacture a constitutional right out of whole cloth. I conclude on this question by citing and adopting the following words, although spoken in dissent, from the judgment of Harlan J. in *Reynolds v. Sims*, 377 U.S. 533 (1964), which, in my view, while stemming from the American experience, are equally applicable in a consideration of the Canadian position. Harlan J. commented, at pp. 624-25, on the

... current mistaken view of the Constitution and the constitutional function of this Court. This view, in a nutshell, is that every major social ill in this country can find its cure in some constitutional "principle," and that this Court should "take the lead" in promoting reform when other branches of government fail to act. The Constitution is not a panacea for every blot upon the public welfare, nor should this Court, ordained as a judicial body, be thought of as a general haven for reform movements. The Constitution is an instrument of government, fundamental to which is the premise that in a diffusion of governmental authority lies the greatest promise that this Nation will realize liberty for all its citizens. This Court, limited in function in accordance with that premise, does not serve its high purpose when it exceeds its authority, even to satisfy justified impatience with the slow workings of the political process. For when, in the name of constitutional interpretation, the Court adds something to the Constitution that was deliberately excluded from it, the Court in reality substitutes its view of what should be so for the amending process.

The Right to Abortion and Section 7 of the Charter

The judgment of my colleague, Wilson J., is based upon the proposition that a pregnant woman has a right, under s. 7 of the *Charter*, to have an abortion. The same concept underlies the judgment of the Chief Justice....

All laws, it must be noted, have the potential for interference with individual priorities and aspirations. In fact, the very purpose of most legislation is to cause such interference. It is only when such legislation goes beyond interfering with priorities and aspirations, and abridges rights, that courts may intervene. If a law prohibited membership in a lawful association it would be unconstitutional, not because it would interfere with priorities and aspirations, but because of its interference with the guaranteed right of freedom of association under s. 2(*d*) of the *Charter*. Compliance with the *Income Tax Act* has, no doubt, frequently interfered with priorities and aspirations. The taxing provisions are not, however, on that basis unconstitutional, because the ordinary taxpayer enjoys no right to be tax free. Other illustrations may be found. In my view, it is clear that before it could be concluded that any enactment infringed the concept of security of the person, it would have to infringe some underlying right included in or protected by the concept. For the appellants to succeed here, then, they must show more than an interference with priorities and aspirations; they must show the infringement of a right which is included in the concept of security of the person.

The proposition that women enjoy a constitutional right to have an abortion is devoid of support in the language of s. 7 of the *Charter* or any other section. While some human rights documents . . . expressly address the question of abortion, the *Charter* is entirely silent on the point. It may be of some significance that the *Charter* uses specific language in dealing with other topics, such as voting rights, religion, expression and such controversial matters as mobility rights, language rights and minority rights, but remains silent on the question of abortion which, at the time the *Charter* was under consideration, was as much a subject of public controversy as it is today. Furthermore, it would appear that the history of the constitutional text of the *Charter* affords no support for the appellants' proposition. A reference to the Minutes of the Special Joint Committee of Senate and House of Commons on the Constitution of Canada (Proceedings 32nd. Parl., Sess. 1 (1981), vol. 46, p. 43) reveals the following exchange:

> **Mr. Crombie:** . . . And I ask you then finally, what effect will the inclusion of the due process clause have on the question of marriage, procreation, or the parental care of children? . . .
>
> **Mr. Chrétien:** The point, Mr. Crombie, that it is important to understand the difference is that we pass legislation here on abortion, criminal code, and we pass legislation on capital punishment; parliament [*sic*] has the authority to do that, and the court at this moment, because we do not have the due process of law written there, cannot go and see whether we made the right decision or the wrong decision in Parliament.
>
> If you write down the words, "due process of law" here, the advice I am receiving is the court could go behind our decision and say that their decision on abortion was not the right one, their decision on capital punishment was not the right one, and it is a danger, according to legal advice I am receiving, that it will very much limit the scope of the power of legislation by the Parliament and we do not want that; and it is why we do not want the words "due process of law." These are the two main examples that we should keep in mind.
>
> You can keep speculating on all the things that have never been touched, but these are two very sensitive areas that we have to cope with as legislators and my view is that Parliament has decided a certain law on abortion and a certain law on capital punishment, and it should prevail and we do not want the courts to say that the judgment of Parliament was wrong in using the constitution.

This passage, of course, revolves around the second and not the first limb of s. 7, but it offers no support for the suggestion that it was intended to bring the question of abortion into the *Charter*.

It cannot be said that the history, traditions and underlying philosophies of our society would support the proposition that a right to abortion could be implied in the *Charter*. . . .

History of the Law of Abortion

[At English common law, abortion before quickening was not a criminal offence. Quickening occurred when the pregnant woman could feel the foetus in her womb—usually around four months. In 1803, the law of criminal abortion was codified in England. In 1861, the distinction between pre- and post-quickening was abolished. All abortions were treated as felony offences. In *R. v. Bournei* (1939), the crime of abortion was held to be subject to the defence of necessity—viz. saving the mother's life. In Canada, abortion was first made a statutory crime in 1869, and has continued to be so under the various revisions of the *Criminal Code*. In 1969, Parliament significantly reformed the abortion law by adding the exculpatory provisions of section 251(4).]

The historical review of the legal approach in Canada taken from the judgment of the Court of Appeal serves, as well, to cast light on the underlying philosophies of our society and establishes that there has never been a general right to abortion in Canada. There has always been clear recognition of a public interest in the protection of the unborn and there has been no evidence or indication of any general acceptance of the concept of abortion at will in our society. It is to be observed as well that at the time of adoption of the *Charter* the sole provision for an abortion in Canadian law was that to be found in s. 251 of the *Criminal Code*. It follows then, in my view, that the interpretive approach to the *Charter*, which has been accepted in this Court, affords no support for the entrenchment of a constitutional right of abortion.

As to an asserted right to be free from any state interference with bodily integrity and serious state-imposed psychological stress, I would say that to be accepted, as a constitutional right, it would have to be based on something more than the mere imposition, by the State, of such stress and anxiety. It must, surely, be evident that many forms of government action deemed to be reasonable, and even necessary in our society, will cause stress and anxiety to many, while at the same time being acceptable exercises of government power in pursuit of socially desirable goals. The very facts of life in a modern society would preclude the entrenchment of such a constitutional right. . . .

To invade the s. 7 right of security of the person, there would have to be more than state-imposed stress or strain. A breach of the right would have to be based upon an infringement of some interest which would be of such nature and such importance as to warrant constitutional protection. This, it would seem to me, would be limited to cases where the state-action complained of, in addition to imposing stress and strain, also infringed another right, freedom or interest which was deserving of protection under the concept of security of the person. For the reasons outlined above, the right to have an abortion—given the language, structure and history of the *Charter* and given the history, traditions and underlying philosophies of our society—is not such an interest....

It is for these reasons I would conclude, that save for the provisions of the *Criminal Code*, which permit abortion where the life or health of the woman is at risk, no right of abortion can be found in Canadian law, custom or tradition, and that the *Charter*, including s. 7, creates no further right. Accordingly, it is my view that s. 251 of the *Code* does not in its terms violate s. 7 of the *Charter*. Even accepting the assumption that the concept of security of the person would extend to vitiating a law which would require a woman to carry a child to the completion of her pregnancy at the risk of her life or health, it must be observed that this is not our case. As has been pointed out, s. 251 of the *Code* already provides for abortion in such circumstances.

Procedural Fairness

I now turn to the appellant's argument regarding the procedural fairness of s. 251 of the *Criminal Code*.... Because abortions are not generally available to all women who seek them, the argument goes, the defence is illusory, or practically so, and the section therefore fails to comport with the principles of fundamental justice.

Precise evidence on the questions raised is, of course, difficult to obtain and subject to subjective interpretation depending upon the views of those adducing it. Much evidence was led at trial based largely on the Ontario experience. Additional material in the form of articles, reports and studies was adduced, from which the Court was invited to conclude that access to abortion is not evenly provided across the country and that this could be the source of much dissatisfaction. While I recognize that in constitutional cases a greater latitude has been allowed concerning the reception of such material, I would prefer to place principal reliance upon the evidence given under oath in court in my considerations of the factual matters. Evidence was adduced from the chairman of a therapeutic abortion committee at a hospital in Hamilton, where in 1982 eleven hundred and eighty-seven abortions were performed, who testified that of all applications received by his committee in that year less than a dozen were ultimately refused. Refusal in each case was based upon the fact that a majority of the committee was not convinced that "the continuation of the pregnancy would be detrimental to the woman's health." All physicians who performed abortions under the *Criminal Code* provisions admitted in cross-examination that they had never had an application for a therapeutic abortion on behalf of the patient ultimately refused by an abortion committee. No woman testified that she personally had applied for an abortion anywhere in Canada and had been refused, and no physician testified to his participation in such an application.... In all, the extent to which the statutory procedure contributes to the problems connected with procuring an abortion is anything but clear. Accordingly, even if one accepts that it would be contrary to the principles of fundamental justice for Parliament to make available a defence which, by reason of its terms, is illusory or practically so, it cannot, in my view, be said that s. 251 of the *Code* has had that effect.

It would seem to me that a defence created by Parliament could only be said to be illusory or practically so when the *defence is not available in the circumstances in which it is held out as being available*. The very nature of the test assumes, of course, that it is for Parliament to define the defence and, in so doing, to designate the terms and conditions upon which it may be available....

... I would suggest it is apparent that the Court's role is not to second-guess Parliament's policy choice as to how broad or how narrow the defence should be. The determination of when "the disapprobation of society is not warranted" is in Parliament's hands....

It was further argued that the defence in s. 251(4) is procedurally unfair in that it fails to provide an adequate standard of "health" to guide the abortion committees which are charged with the responsibility for approving or disapproving applications for abortions. It is argued that the meaning of the word "health" in s. 251(4) is so vague as to render the sub-section unconstitutional. This argument was ... dealt with fully and effectively in the Court of Appeal ...:

> ... In this case, however, from a reading of s. 251 with its exception, there is no difficulty in determining what is proscribed and what is permitted. It cannot be said that no sensible meaning can be given to the words of the section. Thus, it is for the courts to say what meaning the statute will bear. Counsel was unable to give the Court any authority for holding a statute void for uncertainty. In any event, there is no doubt the respondents knew that the acts they proposed and carried out were in breach of the section. The fact that they did not approve of the law in this regard does not make it "uncertain."...

Finally, this Court has dealt with the matter. Dickson J. (as he then was), speaking for the majority in *Morgentaler (1975)*, *supra*, in concluding a discussion of s. 251(4) of the *Criminal Code*, said, at p. 675:

> Whether one agrees with the Canadian legislation or not is quite beside the point. Parliament has spoken unmistakably in clear and unambiguous language.

In the same case, Laskin C.J., while dissenting on other grounds, said at p. 634:

> The contention under point 2 is equally untenable as an attempt to limit the substance of legislation in a situation which does not admit of it. In submitting that the standard upon which therapeutic abortion committees must act is uncertain and subjective, counsel who make the submission cannot find nourishment for it even in *Doe v. Bolton.* There it was held that the prohibition of abortion by a physician except when "based upon his best clinical judgment that an abortion is necessary" did not prescribe a standard so vague as to be constitutionally vulnerable. *A fortiori,* under the approach taken here to substantive due process, the argument of uncertainty and subjectivity fails. It is enough to say that Parliament has fixed a manageable standard because it is addressed to a professional panel, the members of which would be expected to bring a practised judgment to the question whether "the continuation of the pregnancy . . . would or would be likely to endanger . . . life or health."

In my opinion, then, the contention that the defence provided in s. 251(4) of the *Criminal Code* is illusory cannot be supported

Conclusion

Before leaving this case, I wish to make it clear that I express no opinion on the question of whether, or upon what conditions, there should be a right for a pregnant woman to have an abortion free of legal sanction. No valid constitutional objection to s. 251 of the *Criminal Code* has, in my view, been raised and, consequently, if there is to be a change in the law concerning this question it will be for Parliament to make. Questions of public policy touching on this controversial and divisive matter must be resolved by the elected Parliament. It does not fall within the proper jurisdiction of the courts. Parliamentary action on this matter is subject to judicial review but, in my view, nothing in the *Canadian Charter of Rights and Freedoms* gives the Court the power or duty to displace Parliament in this matter involving, as it does, general matters of public policy. . . .

. . . The solution to this question in this country must be left to Parliament. It is for Parliament to pronounce on and to direct social policy. This is not because Parliament can claim all wisdom and knowledge but simply because Parliament is elected for that purpose in a free democracy and, in addition, has the facilities—the exposure to public opinion and information—as well as the political power to make effective its decisions. . . .

For all of these reasons, I would dismiss the appeal.

26 Quebec v. Ford et al. (Quebec Sign Case), 1988

The decision that the Supreme Court of Canada rendered on December 15, 1988 striking down Quebec's French-only sign law is one of the Court's most important *Charter* decisions. The decision moved constitutional jurisprudence in two different directions simultaneously: while it embraced a wide interpretation of "freedom of expression" as a constitutional right, it also established a broad basis for legislatures to use the power they have under section 33 of the *Charter* to override constitutional rights and freedoms. In addition to these important developments in the interpretation of the *Charter*, the decision had a major impact on constitutional politics in Canada.

This was by no means the first Supreme Court decision overturning sections of Bill 101, the *Charter of the French Language*, introduced by the PQ government in 1977. In 1979, the Court struck down provisions of Bill 101 making French the official language of the province's legislature and courts. Another decision in 1984 forced Quebec to open its English schools to Canadians moving to Quebec from other provinces.[1] Both decisions were based on entrenched constitutional language rights to which the legislative override in the *Charter* did not apply. But the attack on sections of Bill 101 making French the exclusive language for commercial signs and firm names was based not on specific language rights but on the right to freedom of expression—a right found in section 2(*b*) of the *Canadian Charter* (a section to which the override does apply) as well as in Quebec's *Charter of Human Rights and Freedoms*.

In June 1982, just two months after the *Charter* was proclaimed, Quebec's National Assembly, in a defiant gesture against the constitutional settlement of 1982 to which Quebec had not consented, passed a law re-enacting all laws passed prior to the *Charter*, but adding to each a section invoking the override.[2] After five years, in 1987, this omnibus use of the override lapsed and was not renewed. However, Quebec had used the override a second time: in February 1984, a law came into force applying the override just to the French-only sign provision of Bill 101. This override, if valid, was still in force when the Supreme Court was deciding the sign case. But the section of Bill 101 requiring French-only firm names had not been protected from judicial review by the override clause. Also, the Quebec *Charter of Human Rights* contained a right to freedom of expression, and it had not been overridden. Thus, whether or not an override was still in force, the Supreme Court had to consider the compatibility of French-only commercial regulations with the right to freedom of expression.

In the 1985 election campaign in which the Liberals, led by Robert Bourassa, threw the Parti Québécois out of office, the Liberals indicated that they would lift restrictions on the use of bilingual commercial signs. This promise was important in attracting some outstanding representatives of Quebec's English-speaking minority to the Liberal team. On the other

---

1 These cases are discussed in the introduction to case 27.

2 For a discussion of the "notwithstanding clause," or "override," as it is often called, see the introduction to this book.

hand, it threatened to alienate many Quebec Francophones who regarded the French-only sign policy as essential for ensuring that the public face of Quebec would be French.

After the election, Premier Bourassa decided not to act on this controversial issue until the constitutional litigation under way had run its course. A number of firms had challenged provisions of Bill 101 requiring French-only commercial signs and firm names.[3] A challenge had also been brought by Alan Singer, the owner of a stationery shop in an English-speaking district of Montreal, against provisions of Bill 101 that, for some commercial activities—for instance, the publication of catalogues and the signs of firms employing less than four persons or specializing in foreign products—required the use of French, but also permitted the use of another language.[4] Like other politicians in Charterland, Bourassa hoped that the Court might take a deeply divisive issue off his hands.

The litigation may have given the Premier a temporary reprieve, but when the Court's decision finally came down it did not make his political burden any lighter. On the contrary, the Supreme Court's finding that laws prohibiting the use of any language other than French violated the right to freedom of expression in both the *Canadian Charter* and the Quebec *Charter* deepened the resentment of the English-speaking community. The right to advertise in the language of one's choice could now be referred to as "a fundamental right." On the other hand, the Court's argument that a French-only policy was not necessary to preserve the French face of Quebec failed to make much impression on the Francophone majority.

The Court took a remarkably liberal approach to the concept of "freedom of expression." It built into this freedom a new, universal language right—a right to communicate in one's own language, a right, it argued, that is essential to personal identity. The Court rejected arguments that commercial speech should be excluded from freedom of expression. It recognized that when consumer-protection regulations of advertising are under review consideration would have to be given to competing policy interests. But the Court took the position that this kind of balancing was to be done not by narrowly defining freedom of expression but by considering the justification for limits on the right under section 1 of the *Charter*. Applying section 1 to the cases at hand, the Court felt that the objective of maintaining the predominantly French character of Quebec could justify requiring the use of French on a joint-use basis and even a law requiring the "marked predominance" of the French language. However, it saw no evidence justifying the exclusive use of French. Hence it struck down the French-only provisions attacked in *Ford*, but upheld bilingual requirements attacked by Singer.

While the Court's expansive interpretation of freedom of expression expanded the basis for judicial review, the Court in this same decision made it easier for legislatures to use section 33 of the *Charter*, the override clause, to immunize their laws from judicial review. Quebec's Court of Appeal had found Quebec's broad-brush use of the override to be unconstitutional, insisting that to fulfill its democratic purpose the override must be used in an accountable way with the legislature indicating precisely which rights and freedoms it was overriding. But here in *Ford* the Supreme Court rejected this argument: it would come too

---

3   Only one of the five businesses raising the challenge—Valerie Ford's wool shop—was not incorporated. Her name appears to have been used for the citation in this case because equality rights arguments were also made in the case and the Supreme Court had not yet decided whether equality rights extend to corporations.

4   The citation for the Supreme Court decision in this case is *Devine v. Quebec.*

close to requiring "a *prima facie* justification of the decision to exercise the override." The Supreme Court made it clear that it wished to minimize judicial review of the use of the override.

And use the override is exactly what Premier Bourassa did in response to the Court's decision. After agonizing for 48 hours, Bourassa announced his decision to bring in legislation permitting bilingual signs indoors but requiring French-only signs outside. To fend off a court challenge, the override clause was applied to this legislation. The new law, Bill 178, cost Bourassa the services of three of his Anglophone ministers and aroused the ire of English-speaking Quebecers. From the other side it was attacked by the opposition PQ party and by many Quebec Francophones who resented compromising the French-only program of Bill 101.

In the arena of constitutional politics Bourassa's action was a bombshell. By December 1988, there remained only two provinces, Manitoba and New Brunswick, whose legislatures had not approved the Meech Lake package of constitutional amendments. On the day after the Supreme Court decision, the Premier of Manitoba, Gary Filmon, introduced the Meech Lake Accord in the Manitoba legislature. But a few days later, following Premier Bourassa's decision to use the override and restore a unilingual French policy for outdoor signs, Filmon announced that he was suspending legislative consideration of the Meech Lake Accord. Legislative hearings, he said, "may invite a very negative anti-Quebec backlash."[5]

So at this stage the Meech Lake Accord, with its controversial clause recognizing Quebec as a "distinct society," was stalled if not dead. Although this meant that the prospects of a constitutional reconciliation with Quebec were dimmed, the French majority in Quebec learned through these events that the 1982 constitutional changes had left them with considerable power to protect their distinctive culture. For all Canadians the really ominous implication of these events was that they pointed to a deep gulf between the French majority in Quebec and the non-French majority in Canada over what should be regarded as fundamental in Canadian constitutionalism. ⁓

---

5   *The Globe and Mail* (20 December 1988).

QUEBEC v. FORD, ET AL.
[1988] 2 S.C.R. 712

Hearing: November 16, 17, 18, 1987; Judgment: December 15, 1988.

Present: Dickson C.J. and Beetz, Estey,* McIntyre, Lamer, Wilson, and Le Dain* JJ.

Interveners: The Attorney General of Canada, the Attorney General for Ontario, and the Attorney General for New Brunswick. 1987: November 16, 17, 18; 1988: December 15.

* Estey and Le Dain JJ. took no part in the judgment.

[1] **THE COURT:**[1] The principal issue in this appeal is whether ss. 58 and 69 of the Quebec *Charter of the French Language*, R.S.Q., c. C-11, which require that public signs and posters and commercial advertising shall be in the French language only and that only the French version of a firm name may be used, infringe the freedom of expression guaranteed by s. 2(*b*) of the *Canadian Charter of Rights and Freedoms* and s. 3 of the Quebec *Charter of Human Rights and Freedoms*, R.S.Q., c. C-12. There is also an issue as to whether ss. 58 and 69 of the *Charter of the French Language* infringe the guarantee against discrimination based on language in s. 10 of the Quebec *Charter of Human Rights and Freedoms*. The application of the *Canadian Charter of Rights and Freedoms* turns initially on whether there is a valid and applicable override provision, enacted pursuant to s. 33 of the Canadian *Charter*, that ss. 58 and 69 of the *Charter of the French Language* shall operate notwithstanding s. 2(*b*) of the Canadian *Charter*.

[2] The appeal is by leave of this Court from the judgment of the Quebec Court of Appeal on December 22, 1986, [1987] R.J.Q. 80, 5 Q.A.C. 119, 36 D.L.R. (4th) 374, dismissing the appeal of the Attorney General of Quebec from the judgment of Boudreault J. in the Superior Court for the District of Montreal on December 28, 1984, [1985] C.S. 147, 18 D.L.R. (4th) 711, which, on an application for a declaratory judgment, declared s. 58 of the *Charter of the French Language* to be inoperative to the extent that it prescribes that public signs and posters and commercial advertising shall be solely in the French language. The appeal is also from the judgment of the Court of Appeal in so far as it allowed the incidental appeal

of the respondents from the judgment of Boudreault J. and declared s. 69 of the *Charter of the French Language* to be inoperative to the extent that it prescribes that only the French version of a firm name may be used. In allowing the incidental appeal the Court of Appeal also declared ss. 205 to 208 of the *Charter of the French Language* respecting offences, penalties and other sanctions for a contravention of any of its provisions to be inoperative in so far as they apply to ss. 58 and 69.

I. The Respondents' Application for a Declaratory Judgment

[3] On February 15, 1984 the respondents brought a motion for a declaratory judgment pursuant to art. 454 of the Quebec *Code of Civil Procedure* and s. 24(1) of the *Canadian Charter of Rights and Freedoms*. The commercial advertising and signs displayed by the five respondents are described in paragraphs 1 to 5 of their petition as follows:

1. La Chaussure Brown's Inc. ("Brown's") operates a business of retail shoe stores throughout the Province of Quebec, and since at least September 1, 1981, it has used and displayed within and on its premises of its store situated in the Fairview Shopping Centre, 6801 Trans-Canada Highway, Pointe-Claire, commercial advertising containing the following words:

BRAVO	BRAVO
"Brown's quality Bravo's price"	"la qualité a tout prix."

2. Valerie Ford, carrying on business under the firm name and style of Les Lainages du Petit Mouton Enr. ("Ford"), operates a retail store selling, *inter alia*, wool, and since at least September 1, 1981, she has used and displayed on her premises at 311 St. Johns Boulevard, Pointe-Claire, an exterior sign containing the following words:

"laine   wool"

3. Nettoyeur et Tailleur Masson Inc. ("Nettoyeur Masson") carries on the business of a tailor and dry cleaner, and since at least September 1, 1981, it has used and displayed on its premises at 3259 Masson Street, Montreal an exterior sign containing the following words:

NETTOYEURS	Masson inc.	CLEANERS
TAILLEUR	TAILOR	
SERVICE	ALTERATIONS	
	REPAIRS	
1 HEURE	1 HOUR	

4. McKenna Inc. ("McKenna") carries on business as a florist in the City of Montreal and since at least September 1, 1981, it has used and displayed on its premises at

---

1   Chief Justice Dickson and Justices Beetz, Estey, McIntyre, Lamer, Wilson, and Le Dain heard the case when it was argued in November 1987. But Estey and Le Dain did not participate in the decision— Estey because he resigned soon after the hearing and Le Dain because he was too ill.

4509 Côte Des Neiges Road, Montreal, an exterior sign containing the following words:

"Fleurs   McKENNA   Flowers"

5. La Compagnie de Fromage Nationale Ltée ("Fromage Nationale") carries on the business of a cheese distributor and since at least September 1, 1981, it has used and displayed on its premises at 9001 Salley Street, Ville LaSalle, exterior signs containing the following words:

"NATIONAL CHEESE Co Ltd.
La Cie de FROMAGE NATIONALE Ltée"

[4] The petition further alleges that the respondents La Chaussure Brown's Inc., Valerie Ford and La Compagnie de Fromage Nationale Ltée received a *mise en demeure* from the Commission de surveillance de la langue française advising them that their signs were not in conformity with the provisions of the *Charter of the French Language* and calling on them to conform to such provisions and that the respondents McKenna Inc. and Nettoyeur et Tailleur Masson Inc. were charged with violation of the *Charter of the French Language*.

[5] The respondents conclude in their petition for a declaration that they have the right, notwithstanding ss. 58, 69 and 205 to 208 of the *Charter of the French Language*, to use the signs, posters and commercial advertising described in their petition and a declaration that ss. 58 and 69 and ss. 205 to 208, as they apply to ss. 58 and 69 of the *Charter of the French Language*, are inoperative and of no force or effect.

II. The Relevant Legislative and Constitutional Provisions

[6] To facilitate an understanding of the issues in the appeal, as they are reflected in the reasons for judgment of the Superior Court and the Court of Appeal and in the constitutional questions and submissions of the parties in this Court, it is desirable at this point to set out the relevant legislative and constitutional provisions.

A. The Charter of the French Language

[7] Sections 1, 58, 69, 89, 205, 206 . . . of the *Charter of the French Language*, R.S.Q., c. C-11, provide:

1. French is the official language of Québec.
58. Public signs and posters and commercial advertising shall be solely in the official language.

Notwithstanding the foregoing, in the cases and under the conditions or circumstances prescribed by regulation of the Office de la langue française, public signs and posters and commercial advertising may be both in French and in another language or solely in another language.

69. Subject to section 68, only the French version of a firm name may be used in Québec.
89. Where this act does not require the use of the official language exclusively, the official language and another language may be used together.
205. Every person who contravenes a provision of this act other than section 136 or of a regulation made under this act by the Gouvernement or by the Office de la langue française is guilty of an offence and liable, in addition to costs,

    (a) for each offence, to a fine of $30 to $575 in the case of a natural person, and of $60 to $1150 in the case of an artificial person.

    (b) for any subsequent offence within two years of a first offence, to a fine of $60 to $1150 in the case of a natural person, and of $575 to $5750 in the case of an artificial person.

206. A business firm guilty of an offence contemplated in section 136 is liable, in addition to costs, to a fine of $125 to $2300 for each day during which it carries on its business without a certificate.

B. The Quebec Charter of Human Rights and Freedoms

[8] Sections 3, 9.1 and 10 of the *Quebec Charter of Human Rights and Freedoms*, R.S.Q., c. C-12, provide:

3. Every person is the possessor of the fundamental freedoms, including freedom of conscience, freedom of religion, freedom of opinion, freedom of expression, freedom of peaceful assembly and freedom of association.
9.1 In exercising his fundamental freedoms and rights, a person shall maintain a proper regard for democratic values, public order and the general well-being of the citizens of Québec.

In this respect, the scope of the freedoms and rights, and limits to their exercise, may be fixed by law.

10. Every person has a right to full and equal recognition and exercise of his human rights and freedoms, without distinction, exclusion or preference based on race, colour, sex, pregnancy, sexual orientation, civil status, age except as provided by law, religion, political convictions, language, ethnic or national origin, social condition, a handicap or the use of any means to palliate a handicap.

Discrimination exists where such a distinction, exclusion or preference has the effect of nullifying or impairing such right.

[9] Sections 51 and 52 of the *Quebec Charter of Human Rights and Freedoms*, R.S.Q., c. C-12, provide:

51. The Charter shall not be so interpreted as to extend, limit or amend the scope of a provision of law except to the extent provided in section 52.

52. No provision of any Act, even subsequent to the Charter, may derogate from sections 1 to 38, except so far as provided by those sections, unless such Act expressly states that it applies despite the Charter.

[10] Prior to its amendment by s. 16 of *An Act to amend the Charter of Human Rights and Freedoms*, S.Q. 1982, c. 61, s. 52 of the Quebec *Charter* read as follows:

52. Sections 9 to 38 prevail over any provision of any subsequent act which may be inconsistent therewith unless such act expressly states that it applies despite the Charter. . . .

IV. The Constitutional Questions and the Issues in the Appeal

[20] On the appeal to this Court the following constitutional questions were stated by Lamer J. in his order of May 11, 1987:

1. Are section 214 of the *Charter of the French Language*, R.S.Q. 1977, c. C-11, as enacted by S.Q. 1982, c. 21, s. 1, and s. 52 of *An Act to amend the Charter of the French Language*, S.Q. 1983, c. 56, inconsistent with s. 33(1) of the *Constitution Act, 1982* and therefore inoperative and of no force or effect under s. 52(1) of the latter Act?
2. If the answer to question 1 is affirmative, to the extent that they require the exclusive use of the French language, are ss. 58 and 69, and ss. 205 to 208 to the extent they apply thereto, of the *Charter of the French Language*, R.S.Q. 1977, c. C-11, as amended by S.Q. 1983, c. 56, inconsistent with the guarantee of freedom of expression under s. 2(b) of the *Canadian Charter of Rights and Freedoms*?
3. If the answer to question 2 is affirmative in whole or in part, are ss. 58 and 69, and ss. 205 to 208 to the extent they apply thereto, of the *Charter of the French Language*, R.S.Q. 1977, c. C-11, as amended by S.Q. 1983, c. 56, justified by the application of s. 1 of the *Canadian Charter of Rights and Freedoms* and therefore not inconsistent with the *Constitution Act, 1982*?

[21] The issues in the appeal, as reflected in the above constitutional questions, the reasons for judgment of the Superior Court and the Court of Appeal and the submissions in this Court, may be summarized as follows:

1. Is section 58 or s. 69 of the *Charter of the French Language* protected from the application of s. 2(b) of the *Canadian Charter of Rights and Freedoms* by a

valid and applicable override provision enacted in conformity with s. 33 of the Canadian *Charter*?
2. What are the dates from which s. 3 of the Quebec *Charter of Human Rights and Freedoms* took precedence, in case of conflict, over ss. 58 and 69 of the *Charter of the French Language*?
3. Does the freedom of expression guaranteed by s. 2(b) of the Canadian *Charter* and by s. 3 of the Quebec *Charter* include the freedom to express oneself in the language of one's choice?
4. Does the freedom of expression guaranteed by s. 2(b) of the Canadian *Charter* and s. 3 of the Quebec *Charter* extend to commercial expression?
5. If the requirement of the exclusive use of French by ss. 58 and 69 of the *Charter of the French Language* infringes the freedom of expression guaranteed by s. 2(b) of the Canadian *Charter* and s. 3 of the Quebec *Charter*, is the limit on freedom of expression imposed by ss. 58 and 69 justified under s. 1 of the Canadian *Charter* and s. 9.1 of the Quebec *Charter*?
6. Do sections 58 and 69 of the *Charter of the French Language* infringe the guarantee against discrimination based on language in s. 10 of the Quebec *Charter of Human Rights and Freedoms*?

[22] Submissions with respect to the validity and application of the override provisions in issue, as well as the content of freedom of expression and the effect of s. 1 of the Canadian *Charter* and s. 9.1 of the Quebec *Charter*, were also made in the appeals in *Devine v. Quebec (Attorney General)*, [1988] 2 S.C.R. 790, and *Irwin Toy Ltd. v. Quebec (Attorney General)*, S.C.C., No. 20074, which were heard at the same time as this appeal. They will necessarily be taken into consideration in disposing of the issues in this appeal.

V. Is Section 58 or Section 69 of the Charter of the French Language Protected from the Application of Section 2(b) of the Canadian Charter of Rights and Freedoms by a Valid and Applicable Override Provision Enacted in Conformity with Section 33 of the Canadian Charter?

[23] . . . [T]here are two override provisions in issue: (a) s. 214 of the *Charter of the French Language*, which was enacted by s. 1 of *An Act respecting the Constitution Act, 1982*, S.Q. 1982, c. 21; and (b) s. 52 of *An Act to amend the Charter of the French Language*, S.Q. 1983, c. 56. The two override provisions are in identical terms, reading as follows: "This Act shall operate notwithstanding the provisions of sections 2 and 7 to 15 of the *Constitution Act, 1982* (Schedule B of the *Canada Act*,

chapter 11 in the 1982 volume of *Acts of Parliament of the United Kingdom*)." The issue of validity that is common to both s. 214 and s. 52 is whether a declaration in this form is one that is made in conformity with the override authority conferred by s. 33 of the *Canadian Charter of Rights and Freedoms*. There are additional issues of validity applicable to s. 214 of the *Charter of the French Language* arising from the manner of its enactment, that is, the "omnibus" character of the Act which enacted it, and from the retrospective effect given to s. 214 by s. 7 of the Act, which has been quoted above.

[24] Section 214 of the *Charter of the French Language* ceased to have effect by operation of s. 33(3) of the *Canadian Charter of Rights and Freedoms* five years after it came into force, and it was not re-enacted pursuant to s. 33(4) of the *Charter*. If the retrospective effect to April 17, 1982 given to s. 214 by s. 7 of *An Act respecting the Constitution Act, 1982*, was valid, s. 214 ceased to have effect on April 17, 1987. If not, it ceased to have effect on June 23, 1987, which was five years after the enacting Act came into force on the day of its sanction. In either case the question of the validity of s. 214 is moot, on the assumption, which was the one on which the appeal was argued, that on an application for a declaratory judgment in a case of this kind the Court should declare the law as it exists at the time of its judgment. We were, nevertheless, invited by the parties in this appeal and the appeals that were heard at the same time to rule on the validity of the standard override provision as enacted by *An Act respecting the Constitution Act, 1982*, because of the possible significance of that issue in cases pending before other tribunals. Before considering how the Court should respond to that invitation we propose to consider the other override provision in issue which, as we have said, raises a common question of validity.

[25] Section 52 of *An Act to amend the Charter of the French Language*, which was proclaimed in force on February 1, 1984, will not cease to have effect by operation of s. 33(3) of the *Canadian Charter of Rights and Freedoms* until February 1, 1989. It is therefore necessary to consider its validity since the Attorney General of Quebec contends that it protects s. 58 of the *Charter of the French Language* from the application of s. 2(*b*) of the *Canadian Charter of Rights and Freedoms*....

[27] Those who challenged the constitutionality of the override provisions in s. 214 of the *Charter of the French Language* and s. 52 of *An Act to amend the Charter of the French Language* placed particular reliance on the judgment of the Quebec Court of Appeal in *Alliance des professeurs de Montréal v. Procureur général du Québec, supra*, in which the Court of Appeal held that the standard override provision was *ultra vires* and null as not being in conformity with the authority conferred by s. 33 of the *Canadian Charter of Rights and Freedoms*....

[28] In that case the petitioners, Alliance des professeurs de Montréal, sought declarations that s. 1 and other provisions of *An Act respecting the Constitution Act, 1982*, which purported to add the standard override provision to all provincial legislation enacted up to June 23, 1982, and the standard override provisions enacted in some forty-nine statutes after that date were *ultra vires* and null as not being in conformity with s. 33 of the *Canadian Charter of Rights and Freedoms*. Thus the petitioners put in issue not only the validity of the standard override provision as enacted by the "omnibus" *Act respecting the Constitution Act, 1982*, but also its validity as separately enacted in particular statutes....

[29] The essential contention in *Alliance des professeurs*, as in the present appeals, against the validity of the standard override provision, which was rejected by the Superior Court but upheld by the Court of Appeal, was that the provision did not sufficiently specify the guaranteed rights or freedoms which the legislation intended to override. In support of this contention reliance was placed not only on the wording of s. 33(1) and (2) of the *Charter* but on general considerations concerning the effectiveness of the democratic process. For convenience the standard override provision that is in issue, as well as s. 33(1) and (2) of the *Charter*, are quoted again:

This Act shall operate notwithstanding the provisions of sections 2 and 7 to 15 of the *Constitution Act, 1982* (Schedule B of the *Canada Act*, chapter 11 in the 1982 volume of the *Acts of the Parliament of the United Kingdom*).

33.(1) Parliament or the legislature of a province may expressly declare in an Act of Parliament or of the legislature, as the case may be, that the Act or a provision thereof shall operate notwithstanding a provision included in section 2 or sections 7 to 15 of this *Charter*.

(2) An Act or a provision of an Act in respect of which a declaration made under this section is in effect shall have such operation as it would have but for the provision of this *Charter* referred to in the declaration.

[30] It was contended that the words "a provision included in section 2 or sections 7 to 15 of this *Charter*" in s. 33(1) and the words "but for the provision of this *Charter* referred to in the declaration" in s. 33(2) indicate that in order to be valid, a declaration pursuant to s. 33 must specify the particular provision within a section of the *Charter* which Parliament or the legislature of a province intends to override. That is, the specific guaranteed right or freedom to be overridden must be referred to in the words of the *Charter* and not merely by the number of the section or paragraph in which it appears. The rationale underlying this contention is that the nature of the guaranteed right or freedom must be sufficiently drawn

to the attention of the members of the legislature and of the public so that the relative seriousness of what is proposed may be perceived and reacted to through the democratic process. As the Attorney General for Ontario, who argued against the constitutionality of the standard override provision, put it, there must be a "political cost" for overriding a guaranteed right or freedom....

[33] In the course of argument different views were expressed as to the constitutional perspective from which the meaning and application of s. 33 of the *Canadian Charter of Rights and Freedoms* should be approached: the one suggesting that it reflects the continuing importance of legislative supremacy, the other suggesting the seriousness of a legislative decision to override guaranteed rights and freedoms and the importance that such a decision be taken only as a result of a fully informed democratic process. These two perspectives are not, however, particularly relevant or helpful in construing the requirements of s. 33. Section 33 lays down requirements of form only, and there is no warrant for importing into it grounds for substantive review of the legislative policy in exercising the override authority in a particular case. The requirement of an apparent link or relationship between the overriding Act and the guaranteed rights or freedoms to be overridden seems to be a substantive ground of review. It appears to require that the legislature identify the provisions of the Act in question which might otherwise infringe specified guaranteed rights or freedoms. That would seem to require a *prima facie* justification of the decision to exercise the override authority rather than merely a certain formal expression of it. There is, however, no warrant in the terms of s. 33 for such a requirement. A legislature may not be in a position to judge with any degree of certainty what provisions of the *Canadian Charter of Rights and Freedoms* might be successfully invoked against various aspects of the Act in question. For this reason it must be permitted in a particular case to override more than one provision of the *Charter* and indeed all of the provisions which it is permitted to override by the terms of s. 33. The standard override provision in issue in this appeal is, therefore, a valid exercise of the authority conferred by s. 33 in so far as it purports to override all of the provisions in s. 2 and ss. 7 to 15 of the *Charter*. The essential requirement of form laid down by s. 33 is that the override declaration must be an express declaration that an Act or a provision of an Act shall operate notwithstanding a provision included in s. 2 or ss. 7 to 15 of the *Charter*. With great respect for the contrary view, this Court is of the opinion that a s. 33 declaration is sufficiently express if it refers to the number of the section, subsection or paragraph of the *Charter* which contains the provision or provisions to be overridden. Of course, if it is intended to override only a part of the provision

or provisions contained in a section, subsection or paragraph then there would have to be a sufficient reference in words to the part to be overridden. ...

[34] Therefore, s. 52 of *An Act to amend the Charter of the French Language* is a valid and subsisting exercise of the override authority conferred by s. 33 of the *Canadian Charter of Rights and Freedoms* that protects s. 58 of the *Charter of the French Language* from the application of s. 2(*b*) of the Canadian *Charter*. Section 69 of the *Charter of the French Language* is not so protected since it was not affected by *An Act to amend the Charter of the French Language*. In the result, as indicated in the following Part VI of these reasons, s. 58 is subject to s. 3 of the Quebec *Charter of Human Rights and Freedoms* while s. 69 is subject to both s. 2(*b*) of the Canadian *Charter* and s. 3 of the Quebec *Charter*.

[35] Before leaving Part V of these reasons, it remains to be considered whether the Court should exercise its discretion to rule on the other aspects of the validity of the standard override provision as enacted by *An Act respecting the Constitution Act, 1982*: the "omnibus" character of the enactment; and the retrospective effect given to the override provision. These issues affect both s. 214 of the *Charter of the French Language*, which is in issue in this appeal and in the *Devine* appeal and s. 364 of the *Consumer Protection Act*, R.S.Q., c. P-40.1, in the *Irwin Toy* appeal. The Court has concluded that although both of these provisions have ceased to have effect it is better that all questions concerning their validity should be settled in these appeals because of their possible continuing importance in other cases. Given the conclusion that the enactment of the standard override provision in the form indicated above is a valid exercise of the authority conferred by s. 33 of the *Canadian Charter of Rights and Freedoms*, this Court is of the opinion that the validity of its enactment is not affected by the fact that it was introduced into all Quebec statutes enacted prior to a certain date by a single enactment. That was an effective exercise of legislative authority that did not prevent the override declaration so enacted in each statute from being an express declaration within the meaning of s. 33 of the Canadian *Charter*. Counsel referred to this form of enactment as reflecting an impermissibly "routine" exercise of the override authority or even a "perversion" of it. It was even suggested that it amounted to an attempted amendment of the *Charter*. These are once again essentially submissions concerning permissible legislative policy in the exercise of the override authority rather than what constitutes a sufficiently express declaration of override. As has been stated, there is no warrant in s. 33 for such considerations as a basis of judicial review of a particular exercise of the authority conferred by s. 33. The Court is of a different view, however, concerning the retrospective effect given to the standard override provision by s. 7

of *An Act respecting the Constitution Act, 1982*. . . . In providing that s. 1, which re-enacted all of the Quebec statutes adopted before April 17, 1982 with the addition in each of the standard override provision, should have effect from that date, s. 7 purported to give retrospective effect to the override provision. . . .

[36] . . . In *Gustavson Drilling (1964) Ltd. v. Minister of National Revenue*, [1977] 1 S.C.R. 271, Dickson J. (as he then was) wrote, for the majority (at p. 279):

> The general rule is that statutes are not to be construed as having retrospective operation unless such a construction is expressly or by necessary implication required by the language of the Act.

Where, as here, an enabling provision is ambiguous as to whether it allows for retroactive legislation, the same rule of construction applies. In this case, s. 33(1) admits of two interpretations; one that allows Parliament or a legislature to enact retroactive override provisions, the other that permits prospective derogation only. We conclude that the latter and narrower interpretation is the proper one, and that s. 7 cannot give retrospective effect to the override provision. Section 7 of *An Act respecting the Constitution Act, 1982*, is to the extent of this inconsistency with s. 33 of the Canadian *Charter*, of no force or effect, with the result that the standard override provisions enacted by s. 1 of that *Act* came into force on June 23, 1982 in accordance with the first paragraph of s. 7. . . .

VII. Whether the Freedom of Expression Guaranteed by Section 2(b) of the Canadian Charter of Rights and Freedoms and by Section 3 of the Quebec Charter of Human Rights and Freedoms Includes the Freedom to Express Oneself in the Language of One's Choice

[39] In so far as this issue is concerned, the words "freedom of expression" in s. 2(*b*) of the Canadian *Charter* and s. 3 of the Quebec *Charter* should be given the same meaning. As indicated above, both the Superior Court and the Court of Appeal held that freedom of expression includes the freedom to express oneself in the language of one's choice. After indicating the essential relationship between expression and language by reference to dictionary definitions of both, Boudreault J. in the Superior Court said that in the ordinary or general form of expression there cannot be expression without language. Bisson J.A. in the Court of Appeal said that he agreed with the reasons of Boudreault J. on this issue and expressed his own view in the form of the following question: "Is there a purer form of freedom of expression than the spoken language and written language?" He supported his conclusion by quotation of the following statement of this Court in *Reference re Manitoba Language Rights*, [1985] 1 S.C.R. 721, at p. 744: "The

importance of language rights is grounded in the essential role that language plays in human existence, development and dignity. It is through language that we are able to form concepts; to structure and order the world around us. Language bridges the gap between isolation and community, allowing humans to delineate the rights and duties they hold in respect of one another, and thus to live in society."

[40] The conclusion of the Superior Court and the Court of Appeal on this issue is correct. Language is so intimately related to the form and content of expression that there cannot be true freedom of expression by means of language if one is prohibited from using the language of one's choice. Language is not merely a means or medium of expression; it colours the content and meaning of expression. It is, as the preamble of the *Charter of the French Language* itself indicates, a means by which a people may express its cultural identity. It is also the means by which the individual expresses his or her personal identity and sense of individuality. That the concept of "expression" in s. 2(*b*) of the Canadian *Charter* and s. 3 of the Quebec *Charter* goes beyond mere content is indicated by the specific protection accorded to "freedom of thought, belief [and] opinion" in s. 2 and to "freedom of conscience" and "freedom of opinion" in s. 3. That suggests that "freedom of expression" is intended to extend to more than the content of expression in its narrow sense.

[41] The Attorney General of Quebec made several submissions against the conclusion reached by the Superior Court and the Court of Appeal on this issue, the most important of which may be summarized as follows: (a) in determining the meaning of freedom of expression the Court should apply the distinction between the message and the medium which must have been known to the framers of the Canadian and Quebec *Charters*; (b) the express provision for the guarantee of language rights in ss. 16 to 23 of the Canadian *Charter* indicate that it was not intended that a language freedom should result incidentally from the guarantee of freedom of expression in s. 2(*b*); (c) the recognition of a freedom to express oneself in the language of one's choice under s. 2(*b*) of the Canadian *Charter* and s. 3 of the Quebec *Charter* would undermine the special and limited constitutional position of the specific guarantees of language rights in s. 133 of the *Constitution Act, 1867* and ss. 16 to 23 of the Canadian *Charter* that was emphasized by the Court in *MacDonald v. City of Montreal*, [1986] 1 S.C.R. 460, and *Société des Acadiens du Nouveau-Brunswick Inc. v. Association of Parents for Fairness in Education*, [1986] 1 S.C.R. 549; and (d) the recognition that freedom of expression includes the freedom to express oneself in the language of one's choice would be contrary to the views expressed on this issue by the European Commission of Human Rights and the European Court of Human Rights.

[42] The distinction between the message and the medium was applied by Dugas J. of the Superior Court in *Devine v. Procureur général du Québec, supra,* in holding that freedom of expression does not include freedom to express oneself in the language of one's choice. It has already been indicated why that distinction is inappropriate as applied to language as a means of expression because of the intimate relationship between language and meaning. As one of the authorities on language quoted by the appellant Singer in the *Devine* appeal, J. Fishman, *The Sociology of Language* (1972), at p. 4, puts it: "... language is not merely a *means* of inter-personal communication and influence. It is not merely a *carrier* of content, whether latent or manifest. Language itself *is* content, a reference for loyalties and animosities, an indicator of social statuses and personal relationships, a marker of situations and topics as well as of the societal goals and the large-scale value-laden arenas of interaction that typify every speech community." ...

[43] The second and third of the submissions of the Attorney General of Quebec which have been summarized above, with reference to the implications for this issue of the express or specific guarantees of language rights in s. 133 of the *Constitution Act, 1867,* and ss. 16 to 23 of the *Canadian Charter of Rights and Freedoms,* are closely related and may be addressed together. These special guarantees of language rights do not, by implication, preclude a construction of freedom of expression that includes the freedom to express oneself in the language of one's choice.... The central unifying feature of all of the language rights given explicit recognition in the Constitution of Canada is that they pertain to governmental institutions and for the most part they oblige the government to provide for, or at least tolerate, the use of both official languages. In this sense they are more akin to rights, properly understood, than freedoms. They grant entitlement to a specific benefit from the government or in relation to one's dealing with the government. Correspondingly, the government is obliged to provide certain services or benefits in both languages or at least permit use of either language by persons conducting certain affairs with the government.... In contrast, what the respondents seek in this case is a freedom as that term was explained by Dickson J. (as he then was) in *R. v. Big M Drug Mart Ltd.,* [1985] 1 S.C.R. 295, at p. 336: "Freedom can primarily be characterized by the absence of coercion or constraint. If a person is compelled by the state or the will of another to a course of action or inaction which he would not otherwise have chosen, he is not acting of his own volition and he cannot be said to be truly free. One of the major purposes of the *Charter* is to protect, within reason, from compulsion or restraint." The respondents seek to be free of the state imposed requirement that their commercial signs

and advertising be in French only, and seek the freedom, in the entirely private or non-governmental realm of commercial activity, to display signs and advertising in the language of their choice as well as that of French. Manifestly the respondents are not seeking to use the language of their choice in any form of direct relations with any branch of government and are not seeking to oblige government to provide them any services or other benefits in the language of their choice. In this sense the respondents are asserting a freedom, the freedom to express oneself in the language of one's choice in an area of non-governmental activity, as opposed to a language right of the kind guaranteed in the Constitution. The recognition that freedom of expression includes the freedom to express oneself in the language of one's choice does not undermine or run counter to the special guarantees of official language rights in areas of governmental jurisdiction or responsibility....

[44] The decisions of the European Commission of Human Rights and the European Court of Human Rights on which the Attorney General of Quebec relied are all distinguishable on the same basis, apart from the fact that, as Bisson J.A. observed in the Court of Appeal, they arose in an entirely different constitutional context. They all involved claims to language rights in relations with government that would have imposed some obligation on government....

VIII. Whether the Guarantee of Freedom of Expression Extends to Commercial Expression

[45] In argument there arose a question whether the above issue is an issue in this appeal. The Attorney General of Quebec contended that if the guarantee of freedom of expression included the freedom to express oneself in the language of one's choice the respondents must still show that the guarantee extends to commercial expression. The respondents disputed this on the ground that the challenged provisions are directed to the language used and not to regulation of the substantive content of the expression. At the same time they made alternative submissions that the guarantee extended to commercial expression. The Attorney General of Quebec is correct on this issue: there cannot be a guaranteed freedom to express oneself in the language of one's choice in respect of a form or kind of expression that is not covered by the guarantee of freedom of expression. The question whether the guarantee of freedom of expression in s. 2(*b*) of the Canadian *Charter* and s. 3 of the Quebec *Charter* extends to the kind of expression contemplated by ss. 58 and 69 of the *Charter of the French Language,* which for convenience is referred to as commercial expression, is therefore an issue in this appeal. The submissions that were made on the question of commercial expression in the *Devine* and *Irwin Toy* appeals will be considered in determining that issue in this appeal.

[46] It was not disputed that the public signs and posters, the commercial advertising, and the firm name referred to in ss. 58 and 69 of the *Charter of the French Language* are forms of expression, and it was also assumed or accepted in argument that the expression contemplated by these provisions may be conveniently characterized or referred to as commercial expression. Sections 58 and 69 appear in Chapter VII of the *Charter of the French Language*, entitled "The Language of Commerce and Business." It must be kept in mind, however, that while the words "commercial expression" are a convenient reference to the kind of expression contemplated by the provisions in issue, they do not have any particular meaning or significance in Canadian constitutional law, unlike the corresponding expression "commercial speech," which in the United States has been recognized as a particular category of speech entitled to First Amendment protection of a more limited character than that enjoyed by other kinds of speech. The issue in the appeal is not whether the guarantee of freedom of expression in s. 2(*b*) of the Canadian *Charter* and s. 3 of the Quebec *Charter* should be construed as extending to particular categories of expression, giving rise to difficult definitional problems, but whether there is any reason why the guarantee should not extend to a particular kind of expression, in this case the expression contemplated by ss. 58 and 69 of the *Charter of the French Language*. Because, however, the American experience with the First Amendment protection of "commercial speech" was invoked in argument, as it has been in other cases, both for and against the recognition in Canada that the guarantee of freedom of expression extends to the kinds of expression that may be described as commercial expression, it is convenient to make brief reference to it at this point.

[47] In *Valentine v. Chrestensen*, 316 U.S. 52 (1942), the Supreme Court of the United States declined to afford First Amendment protection to speech which did no more than propose a commercial transaction. Some thirty-four years later, in *Virginia State Board of Pharmacy v. Virginia Citizens Consumer Council Inc.*, 425 U.S. 748 (1976), the Supreme Court affirmed a repudiation of the notion that commercial speech constituted an unprotected exception to the First Amendment guarantee. *Virginia Pharmacy* concerned a Virginia statute which prohibited pharmacists from advertising prices for prescription drugs. The statute was challenged by customers who asserted a First Amendment right to receive drug price information that the pharmacist wished to communicate. The speech at issue was purely commercial in that it simply proposed a commercial transaction. By holding that price advertising was not outside the First Amendment, the Court rejected the central premise of the commercial speech doctrine—that is, that business advertising which merely

solicits a commercial transaction is susceptible to government regulation on the same terms as any other aspect of the market place. The reasons of Blackmun J., writing for the Court, focus on the informative function of the speech from the point of view of the listener whose interest, it was said, "may be as keen, if not keener by far, than his interest in the day's most urgent political debate" (p. 763). The rationale stated by the Court for a First Amendment protection of commercial speech was the interest of the individual consumer and the society generally in the free flow of commercial information as indispensable to informed economic choice. The reasons are careful to note, however, that although commercial speech is protected it is entitled to a lesser degree of protection than that afforded to other forms of speech. . . .

[48] By 1980, when the Court decided *Central Hudson Gas & Electric Corp. v. Public Service Commission of New York*, 447 U.S. 557 (1980), it was apparent that some control of truthful advertising was legitimate as long as the regulation directly advanced a substantial state interest. Powell J., writing for the Court, formulated a four-part analysis for determining whether a particular regulation of commercial speech is consistent with the First Amendment, which he summed up as follows at p. 566:

> In commercial speech cases, then, a four-part analysis has developed. At the outset, we must determine whether the expression is protected by the First Amendment. For commercial speech to come within that provision, it at least must concern lawful activity and not be misleading. Next, we ask whether the asserted governmental interest is substantial. If both inquiries yield positive answers, we must determine whether the regulation directly advances the governmental interest asserted, and whether it is not more extensive than is necessary to serve that interest.

. . . It has been observed that this test is very similar to the test that was adopted by this Court in *R. v. Oakes*, [1986] 1 S.C.R. 103, for justification under s. 1 of the *Charter*. The *Central Hudson* test has been described as "an uneasy compromise" between competing strains of commercial speech theory. It is an attempt to balance the legitimacy of government regulations intended to protect consumers from harmful commercial speech with the belief that a free market in ideas and information is necessary to an informed and autonomous consumer.

[49] In *Posadas de Puerto Rico Associates v. Tourism Co. of Puerto Rico*, 106 S.Ct. 2968 (1986), the Court applied the *Central Hudson* test in a manner that attracted much criticism as reflecting, in the opinion of some commentators, an excessively deferential attitude to government regulation in the face of little or no demonstration by the state that the legislative

means it had adopted either directly advanced the asserted substantial interest or minimally restricted first amendment interests. See, for example, Philip B. Kurland, "*Posadas de Puerto Rico v. Tourism Company*: 'Twas Strange, 'Twas Passing Strange; 'Twas Pitiful, 'Twas Wondrous Pitiful," [1986] *Sup. Ct. Rev.* 1; and "The Supreme Court—Leading Cases" (1986), 100 *Harv. L. Rev.* 100, at p. 172. *Posadas* reflects how differences of view or emphasis in the application of the *Central Hudson* test can determine the effective extent of the protection of commercial speech from legislative limitation or restriction. It reveals the tension between two values: the value of the free circulation of commercial information and the value of consumer protection against harmful commercial speech. The American experience with the constitutional protection of commercial speech further indicates the difficulties inherent in its application, in particular the degree to which the courts are involved in the evaluation of regulatory policy in the field of consumer protection. The American jurisprudence with respect to commercial speech has been the subject of much scholarly analysis and criticism. Among the leading articles are the following: Jackson and Jeffries, "Commercial Speech: Economic Due Process and the First Amendment" (1979), 65 *Va. L. Rev.* 1; Weinberg, "Constitutional Protection of Commercial Speech" (1982), 82 *Colum. L. Rev.* 720; and Lively, "The Supreme Court and Commercial Speech: New Words with an Old Message" (1987), 72 *Minn. L. Rev.* 289. There is also an analysis of the American jurisprudence in the very helpful article on commercial expression by Professor Robert J. Sharpe, "Commercial Expression and the Charter" (1987), 37 *U. of T.L.J.* 229.

[50] In the case at bar Boudreault J. in the Superior Court held that the guarantee of freedom of expression in s. 3 of the Quebec *Charter* extended to commercial expression. He relied particularly on the reasoning in the American decisions, quoting at length from the judgment of Blackmun J. in *Virginia Pharmacy* for the rationale underlying the protection of commercial speech in the United States. He emphasized, as does that case, that it is not only the speaker but the listener who has an interest in freedom of expression. In the Court of Appeal, Bisson J.A. applied the judgment of the majority of the Court on this issue in *Irwin Toy Ltd. v. Procureur général du Québec*, [1986] R.J.Q. 2441, and quoted from the opinions of Jacques J.A. and Vallerand J.A. in that case. In *Irwin Toy*, Jacques J.A. held that there was no basis on the face of s. 2(*b*) of the Canadian *Charter* for distinguishing, in respect of the guarantee of freedom of expression, between different kinds of expression, whether they be of a political, artistic, cultural or other nature. He held that commercial expression was as much entitled to protection as other kinds of expression because of the important role played by it in assisting persons to make informed economic choices. He added, however, that commercial expression might be subject to reasonable limits under s. 1 of the Canadian *Charter* of a kind that would not be reasonable in the case of political expression. . . .

[51] In the course of argument reference was made to two other Canadian decisions which reflect the contrasting positions on the question whether freedom of expression should extend to commercial expression: the majority decision of the Ontario Divisional Court in *Re Klein and Law Society of Upper Canada* (1985), 16 D.L.R. (4th) 489, and the unanimous decision of the Alberta Court of Appeal in *Re Grier and Alberta Optometric Association* (1987), 42 D.L.R. (4th) 327. In *Klein*, on which the Attorney General of Quebec and those who supported his contention that freedom of expression should not extend to commercial expression placed particular reliance, the relevant issue was whether the Rules of Professional Conduct of the Law Society of Upper Canada prohibiting fee advertising by solicitors infringed the guarantee of freedom of expression in s. 2(*b*) of the *Charter*. After referring to the pre-*Charter* decisions on freedom of speech and the American jurisprudence on commercial speech, Callaghan J., with whom Eberle J. concurred, concluded that the guarantee of freedom of expression in s. 2(*b*) should not extend to commercial expression. He held that commercial expression was unrelated to political expression, which in his view was the principal if not exclusive object of the protection afforded by s. 2(*b*). He said at p. 532: "The *Charter* reflects a concern with the political rights of the individual and does not, in my view, reflect a similar concern with the economic sphere nor with its incidents such as commercial speech" and "*Prima facie* then, the freedom of expression guaranteed by s. 2(*b*) of the *Charter* would appear to apply to the expression of ideas relating to the political and governmental domains of the country. (I leave aside the question of whether or not artistic expression falls within s. 2(*b*))." After a very full discussion of American jurisprudence and experience with respect to the First Amendment protection of commercial speech Callaghan J. expressed the view that there were good reasons for not following it, among them the extent to which such protection involved the courts in a difficult case-by-case review of regulatory policy. He concluded as follows at p. 539: "I would conclude that there is no reason to expand the meaning of the word 'expression' in s. 2(*b*) of the *Charter* to cover pure commercial speech. Commercial speech contributes nothing to democratic government because it says nothing about how people are governed or how they should govern themselves. It does not relate to government policies or matters of public concern essential to a democratic process. It pertains to the economic realm and is a matter appropriate to regulation by the Legislature." . . .

[52] In *Grier*, the Alberta Court of Appeal (Lieberman, Kerans and Irving JJ.A.) held that a brochure mailed by a licensed optometrist to patients and others quoting prices for various services was protected expression within the meaning of s. 2(*b*) of the *Charter*. It declined to follow *Klein* on the question of commercial expression and expressed agreement with the decision of the Quebec Court of Appeal in *Irwin Toy* on that question....

[53] The submissions of the Attorney General of Quebec and those who supported him on this issue may be summarized as follows. The scope of a guaranteed freedom must be determined, as required by *R. v. Big M Drug Mart Ltd.*, *supra*, in the light of the character and larger objects of the Canadian *Charter* and the linguistic, philosophic and historical context of the particular freedom. There is no historical basis for a guarantee of freedom of commercial expression in pre-*Charter* jurisprudence, in which recognition was given, on the basis of the division of powers and the "implied bill of rights," to freedom of political expression. Freedom of expression appears in both the Canadian *Charter* and the Quebec *Charter* under the heading of "Fundamental Freedoms"; there is nothing fundamental about commercial expression. A guarantee of freedom of expression which embraces commercial advertising would be the protection of an economic right, when both the Canadian *Charter* and the Quebec *Charter* clearly indicate that they are not concerned with the protection of such rights. The American decisions recognizing a limited First Amendment protection for commercial speech must be seen in the context of a constitution that protects the right of property, whereas that right was deliberately omitted from the protection afforded by s. 7 of the Canadian *Charter*. This Court, in refusing to constitutionalize the right to strike, has recognized that the Canadian *Charter* does not extend to economic rights or freedoms. To extend freedom of expression beyond political expression, and possibly artistic and cultural expression, would trivialize that freedom and lead inevitably to the adoption of different justificatory standards under s. 1 according to the kind of expression involved. The terms of s. 1, as interpreted and applied by the courts, do not permit of such differential application. Freedom of commercial expression, and in particular commercial advertising, does not serve any of the values that would justify its constitutional protection. Commercial advertising is manipulative and seeks to condition or control economic choice rather than to provide the basis of a truly informed choice. As the American experience shows, the recognition of a limited protection for commercial expression involves an evaluation of regulatory policy that is better left to the legislature. Academic criticism of the American approach to commercial speech and judicial expression of misgivings concerning it provide sufficient reason for declining to follow it.

[54] It is apparent to this Court that the guarantee of freedom of expression in s. 2(*b*) of the Canadian *Charter* and s. 3 of the Quebec *Charter* cannot be confined to political expression, important as that form of expression is in a free and democratic society. The pre-*Charter* jurisprudence emphasized the importance of political expression because it was a challenge to that form of expression that most often arose under the division of powers and the "implied bill of rights," where freedom of political expression could be related to the maintenance and operation of the institutions of democratic government. But political expression is only one form of the great range of expression that is deserving of constitutional protection because it serves individual and societal values in a free and democratic society.

[55] The post-*Charter* jurisprudence of this Court has indicated that the guarantee of freedom of expression in s. 2(*b*) of the *Charter* is not to be confined to political expression. In holding, in *RWDSU v. Dolphin Delivery Ltd.*, [1986] 2 S.C.R. 573, that secondary picketing was a form of expression within the meaning of s. 2(*b*) the Court recognized that the constitutional guarantee of freedom of expression extended to expression that could not be characterized as political expression in the traditional sense but, if anything, was in the nature of expression having an economic purpose....

[56] Various attempts have been made to identify and formulate the values which justify the constitutional protection of freedom of expression. Probably the best known is that of Professor Thomas I. Emerson in his article, "Toward a General Theory of the First Amendment" (1963), 72 *Yale L.J.* 877, where he sums up these values as follows at p. 878:

> The values sought by society in protecting the right to freedom of expression may be grouped into four broad categories. Maintenance of a system of free expression is necessary (1) as assuring individual self-fulfillment, (2) as a means of attaining the truth, (3) as a method of securing participation by the members of the society in social, including political, decision-making, and (4) as maintaining the balance between stability and change in society.

The third and fourth of these values would appear to be closely related if not overlapping. Generally the values said to justify the constitutional protection of freedom of expression are stated as three-fold in nature, as appears from the article by Professor Sharpe referred to above on "Commercial Expression and the Charter," where he speaks of the three "rationales" for such protection as follows at p. 232:

> The first is that freedom of expression is essential to intelligent and democratic self-government.... The second theory is that freedom of expression protects an open exchange of views, thereby creating a competitive

market-place of ideas which will enhance the search for the truth. . . .

The third theory values expression for its own sake. On this view, expression is seen as an aspect of individual autonomy. Expression is to be protected because it is essential to personal growth and self-realization.

[57] While these attempts to identify and define the values which justify the constitutional protection of freedom of expression are helpful in emphasizing the most important of them, they tend to be formulated in a philosophical context which fuses the separate questions of whether a particular form or act of expression is within the ambit of the interests protected by the value of freedom of expression and the question whether that form or act of expression, in the final analysis, deserves protection from interference under the structure of the Canadian *Charter* and the Quebec *Charter*. These are two distinct questions and call for two distinct analytical processes. The first, at least for the Canadian *Charter*, is to be determined by the purposive approach to interpretation set out by this Court in *Hunter v. Southam Inc.*, [1984] 2 S.C.R. 145, and *Big M Drug Mart Ltd.*, *supra*. The second, the question of the limitation on the protected values, is to be determined under s. 1 of the *Charter* as interpreted in *Oakes*, *supra*, and *R. v. Edwards Books and Art Ltd.*, [1986] 2 S.C.R. 713. The division between the two analytical processes has been established by this Court in the above decisions. First, consideration will be given to the interests and purposes that are meant to be protected by the particular right or freedom in order to determine whether the right or freedom has been infringed in the context presented to the court. If the particular right or freedom is found to have been infringed, the second step is to determine whether the infringement can be justified by the state within the constraints of s. 1. It is within the perimeters of s. 1 that courts will in most instances weigh competing values in order to determine which should prevail.

[58] In order to address the issues presented by this case it is not necessary for the Court to delineate the boundaries of the broad range of expression deserving of protection under s. 2(*b*) of the Canadian *Charter* or s. 3 of the Quebec *Charter*. It is necessary only to decide if the respondents have a constitutionally protected right to use the English language in the signs they display, or more precisely, whether the fact that such signs have a commercial purpose removes the expression contained therein from the scope of protected freedom.

[59] In our view, the commercial element does not have this effect. Given the earlier pronouncements of this Court to the effect that the rights and freedoms guaranteed in the Canadian *Charter* should be given a large and liberal interpretation, there is no sound basis on which commercial

expression can be excluded from the protection of s. 2(*b*) of the *Charter*. It is worth noting that the courts below applied a similar generous and broad interpretation to include commercial expression within the protection of freedom of expression contained in s. 3 of the Quebec *Charter*. Over and above its intrinsic value as expression, commercial expression which, as has been pointed out, protects listeners as well as speakers plays a significant role in enabling individuals to make informed economic choices, an important aspect of individual self-fulfillment and personal autonomy. The Court accordingly rejects the view that commercial expression serves no individual or societal value in a free and democratic society and for this reason is undeserving of any constitutional protection.

[60] Rather, the expression contemplated by ss. 58 and 69 of the *Charter of the French Language* is expression within the meaning of both s. 2(*b*) of the Canadian *Charter* and s. 3 of the Quebec *Charter*. This leads to the conclusion that s. 58 infringes the freedom of expression guaranteed by s. 3 of the Quebec *Charter* and s. 69 infringes the guaranteed freedom of expression under both s. 2(*b*) of the Canadian *Charter* and s. 3 of the Quebec *Charter*. Although the expression in this case has a commercial element, it should be noted that the focus here is on choice of language and on a law which prohibits the use of a language. We are not asked in this case to deal with the distinct issue of the permissible scope of regulation of advertising (for example to protect consumers) where different governmental interests come into play, particularly when assessing the reasonableness of limits on such commercial expression pursuant to s. 1 of the Canadian *Charter* or to s. 9.1 of the Quebec *Charter*. It remains to be considered whether the limit imposed on freedom of expression by ss. 58 and 69 is justified under either s. 1 of the Canadian *Charter* or s. 9.1 of the Quebec *Charter*, as the case may be.

IX. Whether the Limit Imposed on Freedom of Expression by Sections 58 and 69 of the Charter of the French Language Is Justified Under Section 9.1 of the Quebec Charter of Human Rights and Freedoms and Section 1 of the Canadian Charter of Rights and Freedoms

[61] The issues raised in this part are as follows: (a) the meaning of s. 9.1 of the Quebec *Charter* and whether its role and effect are essentially different from that of s. 1 of the Canadian *Charter*; (b) whether the requirement of the exclusive use of French by ss. 58 and 69 of the *Charter of the French Language* is a limit within the meaning of s. 9.1 and s. 1; (c) whether the material (hereinafter referred to as the s. 1 and s. 9.1 materials) relied on by the Attorney General of Quebec in justification

of the limit is properly before the Court; and (d) whether the material justifies the prohibition of the use of any language other than French.

A. The Meaning of Section 9.1 of the Quebec Charter of Human Rights and Freedoms

[62] The issue here is whether s. 9.1 is a justificatory provision similar in its purpose and effect to s. 1 of the Canadian *Charter* and if so what is the test to be applied under it. Section 9.1 is worded differently from s. 1, and it is convenient to set out the two provisions again for comparison, as well as the test under s. 1. Section 9.1 of the Quebec *Charter of Human Rights and Freedoms*, which was added to the *Charter* by *An Act to amend the Charter of Human Rights and Freedoms*, S.Q. 1982, c. 61, s. 2 and entered into force by proclamation on October 1, 1983, reads as follows:

> 9.1. In exercising his fundamental freedoms and rights, a person shall maintain a proper regard for democratic values, public order and the general well-being of the citizens of Québec.
>
> In this respect, the scope of the freedoms and rights, and limits to their exercise, may be fixed by law.

Section 1 of the Canadian *Charter* provides:

> 1. The *Canadian Charter of Rights and Freedoms* guarantees the rights and freedoms set out in it subject only to such reasonable limits prescribed by law as can be demonstrably justified in a free and democratic society.

The test under s. 1 of the Canadian *Charter* was laid down by this Court in *R. v. Oakes, supra,* and restated by the Chief Justice in *R. v. Edwards Books and Art Ltd., supra,* as follows at pp. 768-69:

> Two requirements must be satisfied to establish that a limit is reasonable and demonstrably justified in a free and democratic society. First, the legislative objective which the limitation is designed to promote must be of sufficient importance to warrant overriding a constitutional right. It must bear on a "pressing and substantial concern." Second, the means chosen to attain those objectives must be proportional or appropriate to the ends. The proportionality requirement, in turn, normally has three aspects: the limiting measures must be carefully designed, or rationally connected, to the objective; they must impair the right as little as possible; and their effects must not so severely trench on individual or group rights that the legislative objective, albeit important, is nevertheless outweighed by the abridgment of rights. The Court stated that the nature of the proportionality test would vary depending on the circumstances. Both in articulating the

standard of proof and in describing the criteria comprising the proportionality requirement the Court has been careful to avoid rigid and inflexible standards.

[63] It was suggested in argument that because of its quite different wording s. 9.1 was not a justificatory provision similar to s. 1 but merely a provision indicating that the fundamental freedoms and rights guaranteed by the Quebec *Charter* are not absolute but relative and must be construed and exercised in a manner consistent with the values, interests and considerations indicated in s. 9.1—"democratic values, public order and the general well-being of the citizens of Québec." In the case at bar the Superior Court and the Court of Appeal held that s. 9.1 was a justificatory provision corresponding to s. 1 of the Canadian *Charter* and that it was subject, in its application, to a similar test of rational connection and proportionality. This Court agrees with that conclusion....

B. Whether the Prohibition of the Use of Any Language Other than French by Sections 58 and 69 of the Charter of the French Language Is a "Limit" on Freedom of Expression Within the Meaning of Section 1 of the Canadian Charter and Section 9.1 of the Quebec Charter

[64] The respondents contended that ss. 58 and 69 of the *Charter of the French Language* were not subject to justification under s. 1 of the *Canadian Charter of Rights and Freedoms* because they prescribe a denial or negation of freedom of expression rather than a limit on it within the meaning of that provision. In support of this contention they referred to the opinion to this effect of Deschênes C.J. in the Superior Court and of a majority of the Court of Appeal in *Quebec Association of Protestant School Boards v. Procureur général du Québec,* [1982] C.S. 673, at pp. 689-93; [1983] C.A. 77, at p. 78. They submitted that while this Court did not rule on the general question whether a denial or negation of a guaranteed right or freedom could be a limit within s. 1, it did not expressly or implicitly disavow the opinion expressed by the Superior Court and the Court of Appeal (*Attorney General of Quebec v. Quebec Association of Protestant School Boards,* [1984] 2 S.C.R. 66, at p. 78)....

[65] In the *Quebec Association of Protestant School Boards* case, the minority language educational rights created by s. 23 of the Canadian *Charter* were, as the Court observed, of a very specific, special and limited nature, unlike the fundamental rights and freedoms guaranteed by other provisions. They were well defined rights for specific classes of persons. In the opinion of the Court, the effect of ss. 72 and 73 of Bill 101 was to create an exception to s. 23 for Quebec, that is, to make it inapplicable as a whole in Quebec. There was thus what

amounted to a complete denial in Quebec of the rights created by s. 23. The extent of the denial was co-extensive with the potential exercise of the very specific and limited rights created by s. 23. Such an exception to s. 23, as the Court characterized it, was tantamount to an impermissible attempt to override or amend s. 23. An exception of such effect could not be a limit within the meaning of s. 1 of the *Charter*. Thus in so far as the distinction between a complete denial of a right or freedom and a limitation of it is concerned, the *Quebec Association of Protestant School Boards* is a rather unique example of a truly complete denial of guaranteed rights—a denial that is co-extensive with the complete scope of the potential exercise of the rights. The decision is thus not authority for the proposition that where the effect of a legislative provision is to deny or prohibit the exercise of a guaranteed right or freedom in a limited area of its potential exercise that provision cannot be a limit on the right or freedom subject to justification under s. 1.

[66] In the opinion of this Court, apart from the rare case of a truly complete denial of a guaranteed right or freedom in the sense indicated above, the distinction between the negation of a right or freedom and the limitation of it is not a sound basis for denying the application of s. 1 of the *Charter*. Many, if not most, legislative qualifications of a right or freedom in a particular area of its potential exercise will amount to a denial of the right or freedom to that limited extent. If this effect were to mean that s. 1 could have no application in such a case, the section could have little application in practice....

C. The Admissibility of the Section 1 and Section 9.1 Materials Submitted in Justification of the Limit Imposed on Freedom of Expression by Sections 58 and 69 of the Charter of the French Language

[68] In the Court of Appeal the Attorney General of Quebec attached to his factum certain material of a justificatory nature which Bisson J.A. referred to as linguistic and sociological studies from Quebec and elsewhere and which the respondents describe in their factum in this Court as "numerous sociological, demographic and linguistic studies." The respondents moved to have this material struck from the record as not being in conformity with art. 507 of the *Code of Civil Procedure* and art. 10 of the Rules of Practice of the Court of Appeal respecting the parts of the record that must be attached to or form part of a factum. The ground of attack was presumably that the material did not form part of the record before the trial judge....

[71] In view of the fact that the parties did not appear to be taken by surprise or placed at an unfair disadvantage by the submission of the s. 1 and s. 9.1 materials in this Court, but showed themselves fully prepared to argue the merits of the material, which they did, this Court is of the opinion that the material should be considered as properly before the Court and should be considered by it. The material is of the kind that has been invited and considered by the Court in other cases involving the application of s. 1 of the *Charter*, without having been subjected to the evidentiary testing of the adversary process. It is material that is treated similarly to treatises and articles in other judicial contexts. Due regard should be given, however, to the submissions of the appellant Singer in *Devine* concerning some of the statistical material.

D. Whether the Section 1 and Section 9.1 Materials Justify the Prohibition of the Use of Any Language Other than French

[72] The section 1 and s. 9.1 materials consist of some fourteen items ranging in nature from the general theory of language policy and planning to statistical analysis of the position of the French language in Quebec and Canada. The material deals with two matters of particular relevance to the issue in the appeal: (a) the vulnerable position of the French language in Quebec and Canada, which is the reason for the language policy reflected in the *Charter of the French Language*; and (b) the importance attached by language planning theory to the role of language in the public domain, including the communication or expression by language contemplated by the challenged provisions of the *Charter of the French Language*. As to the first, the material amply establishes the importance of the legislative purpose reflected in the *Charter of the French Language* and that it is a response to a substantial and pressing need. Indeed, this was conceded by the respondents both in the Court of Appeal and in this Court. The vulnerable position of the French language in Quebec and Canada was described in a series of reports by commissions of inquiry beginning with the Report of the Royal Commission on Bilingualism and Biculturalism in 1969 and continuing with the Parent Commission and the Gendron Commission. It is reflected in statistics referred to in these reports and in later studies forming part of the materials, with due adjustment made in the light of the submissions of the appellant Singer in *Devine* with respect to some of the later statistical material. The causal factors for the threatened position of the French language that have generally been identified are: (a) the declining birth rate of Quebec francophones resulting in a decline in the Quebec francophone proportion of the Canadian population as a whole; (b) the decline of the francophone population outside Quebec as a result of assimilation; (c) the greater rate of assimilation of immigrants to Quebec by the anglophone community of Quebec; and (d) the continuing dominance of English at the higher levels of the economic sector. These factors have favoured the use of the English

language despite the predominance in Quebec of a franco-phone population. Thus, in the period prior to the enactment of the legislation at issue, the "*visage linguistique*" of Quebec often gave the impression that English had become as significant as French. This "*visage linguistique*" reinforced the concern among francophones that English was gaining in importance, that the French language was threatened and that it would ultimately disappear. It strongly suggested to young and ambitious francophones that the language of success was almost exclusively English. It confirmed to anglophones that there was no great need to learn the majority language. And it suggested to immigrants that the prudent course lay in joining the anglophone community. The aim of such provisions as ss. 58 and 69 of the *Charter of the French Language* was, in the words of its preamble, "to see the quality and influence of the French language assured." The threat to the French language demonstrated to the government that it should, in particular, take steps to assure that the "*visage linguistique*" of Quebec would reflect the predominance of the French language.

[73] The section 1 and s. 9.1 materials establish that the aim of the language policy underlying the *Charter of the French Language* was a serious and legitimate one. They indicate the concern about the survival of the French language and the perceived need for an adequate legislative response to the problem. Moreover, they indicate a rational connection between protecting the French language and assuring that the reality of Quebec society is communicated through the "*visage linguistique*." The section 1 and s. 9.1 materials do not, however, demonstrate that the requirement of the use of French only is either necessary for the achievement of the legislative objective or proportionate to it. That specific question is simply not addressed by the materials. Indeed, in his factum and oral argument the Attorney General of Quebec did not attempt to justify the requirement of the exclusive use of French. He concentrated on the reasons for the adoption of the *Charter of the French Language* and the earlier language legislation, which, as was noted above, were conceded by the respondents. The Attorney General of Quebec relied on what he referred to as the general democratic legitimacy of Quebec language policy without referring explicitly to the requirement of the exclusive use of French. In so far as proportionality is concerned, the Attorney General of Quebec referred to the American jurisprudence with respect to commercial speech, presumably as indicating the judicial deference that should be paid to the legislative choice of means to serve an admittedly legitimate legislative purpose, at least in the area of commercial expression. He did, however, refer in justification of the requirement of the exclusive use of French to the attenuation of this requirement reflected in ss. 59 to 62 of the *Charter of the French Language* and the regulations. He submitted that these

exceptions to the requirement of the exclusive use of French indicate the concern for carefully designed measures and for interfering as little as possible with commercial expression. The qualifications of the requirement of the exclusive use of French in other provisions of the *Charter of the French Language* and the regulations do not make ss. 58 and 69 any less prohibitions of the use of any language other than French as applied to the respondents. The issue is whether any such prohibition is justified. In the opinion of this Court it has not been demonstrated that the prohibition of the use of any language other than French in ss. 58 and 69 of the *Charter of the French Language* is necessary to the defence and enhancement of the status of the French language in Quebec or that it is proportionate to that legislative purpose. Since the evidence put to us by the government showed that the predominance of the French language was not reflected in the "*visage linguistique*" of Quebec, the governmental response could well have been tailored to meet that specific problem and to impair freedom of expression minimally. Thus, whereas requiring the predominant display of the French language, even its marked predominance, would be proportional to the goal of promoting and maintaining a French "*visage linguistique*" in Quebec and therefore justified under the Quebec *Charter* and the Canadian *Charter*, requiring the exclusive use of French has not been so justified. French could be required in addition to any other language or it could be required to have greater visibility than that accorded to other languages. Such measures would ensure that the "*visage linguistique*" reflected the demography of Quebec: the predominant language is French. This reality should be communicated to all citizens and non-citizens alike, irrespective of their mother tongue. But exclusivity for the French language has not survived the scrutiny of a proportionality test and does not reflect the reality of Quebec society. Accordingly, we are of the view that the limit imposed on freedom of expression by s. 58 of the *Charter of the French Language* respecting the exclusive use of French on public signs and posters and in commercial advertising is not justified under s. 9.1 of the Quebec *Charter*. In like measure, the limit imposed on freedom of expression by s. 69 of the *Charter of the French Language* respecting the exclusive use of the French version of a firm name is not justified under either s. 9.1 of the Quebec *Charter* or s. 1 of the Canadian *Charter*....

X. Do Sections 58 and 69 of the Charter of the French Language Infringe the Guarantee Against Discrimination Based on Language in Section 10 of the Quebec Charter of Human Rights and Freedoms?

[74] In view of the above conclusion it is not necessary to the disposition of the appeal that the Court should pronounce

on the contention of the respondents that ss. 58 and 69 of the *Charter of the French Language* are inoperative as infringing the guarantee against discrimination based on language in s. 10 of the Quebec *Charter of Human Rights and Freedoms*. In view, however, of the fact that this issue is also raised in the *Devine* appeal and the Superior Court and the Court of Appeal addressed it in both cases it is probably desirable that this Court should do so as well because of the general importance of the question.

[75] For convenience s. 10 of the Quebec *Charter* is quoted again:

> 10. Every person has a right to full and equal recognition and exercise of his human rights and freedoms, without distinction, exclusion or preference based on race, colour, sex, pregnancy, sexual orientation, civil status, age except as provided by law, religion, political convictions, language, ethnic or national origin, social condition, a handicap or the use of any means to palliate a handicap.
>
> Discrimination exists where such a distinction, exclusion or preference has the effect of nullifying or impairing such right. . . .

[82] Thus in addressing the question whether s. 58 of the *Charter of the French Language* infringes the guarantee against discrimination based on language in s. 10 of the Quebec *Charter of Human Rights and Freedoms* we are obliged to consider the effect of s. 58, in so far as that may be ascertained. The second observation to be made here is that in order for a distinction based on a prohibited ground to constitute discrimination within the meaning of s. 10 it must have the effect of nullifying or impairing the right to full and equal recognition and exercise of a human right or freedom, which must mean a human right or freedom recognized by the Quebec *Charter of Human Rights and Freedoms*. With these observations in mind we turn to the question whether s. 58 infringes s. 10. It purports, as was said by the Superior Court and the Court of Appeal, to apply to everyone, regardless of their language of use, the requirement of the exclusive use of French. It has the effect, however, of impinging differentially on different classes of persons according to their language of use. Francophones are permitted to use their language of use while anglophones and other non-francophones are prohibited from doing so. Does this differential effect constitute a distinction based on language within the meaning of s. 10 of the Quebec *Charter*? In this Court's opinion it does. Section 58 of the *Charter of the French Language*, because of its differential effect or impact on persons according to their language of use, creates a distinction between such persons based on language of use. It is then necessary to consider whether this distinction has the effect of nullifying or impairing the right to full and equal

recognition and exercise of a human right or freedom recognized by the Quebec *Charter*. The human right or freedom in issue in this case is the freedom to express oneself in the language of one's choice, which has been held to be recognized by s. 3 of the Quebec *Charter*. In this case, the limit imposed on that right was not a justifiable one under s. 9.1 of the Quebec *Charter*. The distinction based on language of use created by s. 58 of the *Charter of the French Language* thus has the effect of nullifying the right to full and equal recognition and exercise of this freedom. Section 58 is therefore also of no force or effect as infringing s. 10 of the Quebec *Charter*. The same conclusion must apply to s. 69 of the *Charter of the French Language*. We note that since one of the respondents, Valerie Ford, is an individual and not a corporation, it is unnecessary in this case to decide whether corporations are entitled to claim the benefit of equality guarantees and we do not do so.

[83] For these reasons the appeal is dismissed with costs and the constitutional questions are answered as follows:

> 1. Are section 214 of the *Charter of the French Language*, R.S.Q. 1977, c. C-11, as enacted by S.Q. 1982, c. 21, s. 1, and s. 52 of *An Act to amend the Charter of the French Language*, S.Q. 1983, c. 56, inconsistent with s. 33(1) of the *Constitution Act, 1982* and therefore inoperative and of no force or effect under s. 52(1) of the latter *Act*?

Answer: No, except in so far as s. 214 is given retrospective effect by s. 7 of *An Act respecting the Constitution Act, 1982*, S.Q. 1982, c. 21.

> 2. If the answer to question 1 is affirmative, to the extent that they require the exclusive use of the French language, are ss. 58 and 69, and ss. 205 to 208 to the extent they apply thereto, of the *Charter of the French Language*, R.S.Q. 1977, c. C-11, as amended by S.Q. 1983, c. 56, inconsistent with the guarantee of freedom of expression under s. 2(b) of the *Canadian Charter of Rights and Freedoms*?

Answer: In so far as s. 214 of the *Charter of the French Language* has ceased to have effect but s. 52 of *An Act to amend the Charter of the French Language* remains in effect, s. 58 of the *Charter of the French Language* is protected from the application of the *Canadian Charter of Rights and Freedoms* but it is inoperative as infringing the guarantee of freedom of expression in s. 3 of the Quebec *Charter of Human Rights and Freedoms* and the guarantee against discrimination based on language in s. 10 of the Quebec *Charter*. In so far as s. 214 of the *Charter of the French Language* has ceased to have effect, s. 69 thereof is inconsistent with the guarantee of freedom of expression under s. 2(b) of the *Canadian Charter of Rights and*

Freedoms. Sections 205 to 208 of the *Charter of the French Language* to the extent they apply to s. 69 thereof are inconsistent with the guarantee of freedom of expression under s. 2(b) of the *Canadian Charter of Rights and Freedoms.* Section 69 of the *Charter of the French Language*, and ss. 205 to 208 thereof, to the extent they apply to ss. 58 and 69, are also inconsistent with the guarantee of freedom of expression under s. 3 of the Quebec *Charter of Human Rights and Freedoms.*

3. If the answer to question 2 is affirmative in whole or in part, are ss. 58 and 69, and ss. 205 to 208 to the extent they apply thereto, of the *Charter of the French Language*, R.S.Q. 1977, c. C-11, as amended by S.Q. 1983, c. 56, justified by the application of s. 1 of the *Canadian Charter of Rights and Freedoms* and therefore not inconsistent with the *Constitution Act, 1982*?

Answer: Section 58 of the *Charter of the French Language* is not justified under s. 9.1 of the Quebec *Charter of Human Rights and Freedoms.* Section 69 of the *Charter of the French Language*, and ss. 205 to 208 thereof, to the extent they apply to s. 69, are not justified under s. 1 of the *Canadian Charter of Rights and Freedoms* and are therefore inconsistent with the *Constitution Act, 1982.* Nor is s. 69 of the *Charter of the French Language*, or ss. 205 to 208 thereof, to the extent they apply to ss. 58 and 69, justified under s. 9.1 of the Quebec *Charter of Human Rights and Freedoms.*

27 Mahe v. Alberta, 1990

The *Constitution Act, 1867* contains only two sections explicitly recognizing rights. These sections confer rights on groups rather than individuals. These are section 93, which sets out school rights for the Protestant minority in Quebec and the Roman Catholic minority in other provinces, and section 133, which sets out rights to use French in the federal Parliament and courts and reciprocal rights to use English in the Quebec legislature and courts. When Manitoba became a province of Canada, a similar provision enshrined the right to use English and French in its legislature and courts. These rights sections in Canada's founding Constitution are specific to the Canadian historical experience. They reflect the accommodation of European cultures upon which Confederation was based.

Section 93 guaranteed that Quebec Protestants would have the same rights to separate schools that Catholics enjoyed in Ontario. It protected not only any school rights enjoyed by Protestant and Catholic minorities in any province at the time of Confederation but any rights that might be established thereafter. This guarantee of denominational schools was varied slightly for the prairie provinces when they became part of Canada and a more extensive guarantee was included in Newfoundland's terms of union in 1949.

The provisions of section 93 show how little the Fathers of Confederation looked to the courts to enforce constitutional rights. Appeals against provinces for denying section 93 rights were to go to the federal Cabinet, and if a province failed to comply with the federal government's instructions, the federal Parliament could pass remedial legislation. The first and only time a federal government threatened to use these remedial powers was when Charles Tupper introduced a Remedial Bill in response to an appeal by Manitoba Catholics in 1895. The proposed Remedial Bill was a major reason for defeat of Tupper's Conservative government by Wilfrid Laurier's Liberals in the 1896 federal election. Laurier favoured provincial rights over the rights of Manitoba's Catholic minority. Since then, appeals against denials of section 93 rights have been dealt with in the courts.

In the years when the most important section 93 cases were heard, Canada's highest court was the Judicial Committee of the Privy Council, and it was remarkably restrained in interpreting section 93. In 1892, it reversed the Supreme Court of Canada and upheld Manitoba legislation establishing a secular school system and withdrawing public funding for Roman Catholic separate schools.[1] In 1917, it upheld an Ontario regulation prohibiting the use of French in all schools, including Roman Catholic separate schools, even though in some parts of the province most of the separate school students at that time were French-speaking.[2] These JCPC decisions were a major factor in preventing Canada west of Quebec from developing along bicultural lines.

Section 29 of the *Charter* stipulates that nothing in the *Charter* can abrogate the historic section 93 denominational school rights. In 1984, the Supreme Court rejected a section 15

---

1   *Barrett v. The City of Winnipeg* (1892), A.C. 445.

2   *Ottawa Roman Catholic Separate School v. Mackell* (1917), A.C. 62.

Charter challenge to Ontario legislation extending public funding to the full secondary-school program of the province's Roman Catholic Separate Schools.[3] The Court based its decision not so much on section 29 of the *Charter* as on the plenary authority section 93 gives provinces to develop a system of denominational schools.

Section 93 came up in a peripheral way in *Mahe*. The central issues in the case were whether the right to minority-language education facilities included the minority's right to manage and control its educational facilities, and whether that right to management and control could be met in Edmonton by including minority-language trustees on the city's Roman Catholic Separate School Board. This raised the side issue whether the denominational school rights would be violated by this arrangement. The Court ruled that because the Separate School Board would lose no power over religious aspects of its schools there was no abrogation of denominational school rights.

Although the Supreme Court has made it clear that the "new Constitution" is not to invalidate fundamental provisions of the "old Constitution," the rights sections of the old Constitution have been changing, reflecting the secularization of Canadian society and an emphasis on minority language rights over minority faith-based rights. In 1997, in response to a unanimous resolution of Quebec's National Assembly, the federal Parliament supported a constitutional amendment making the section 93 guarantee of denominational school rights inapplicable in Quebec. This amendment reflects the desire of English-speaking and French-speaking Quebecers to organize their schools around language communities rather than religious communities. The following year, Newfoundlanders voted by a 73 percent majority to scrap their faith-based school system.[4]

Fundamental to Pierre Trudeau and his government in pressing for a *Charter of Rights* was a vision of Canada in which French-speaking Canadians would feel at home in all parts of the country and English-speaking Canadians would feel secure in Quebec. This vision is reflected in sections 16 to 23 of the *Charter*. The fact that the *Charter*'s legislative override clause does not apply to these sections is indicative of their importance to the *Charter*'s framers. These sections of the *Charter* extend the language rights in section 133 of the Constitution in four ways. First, section 16 states, for the first time, that English and French are "the official languages of Canada." Second, the right to use English or French is extended to communications with all federal head offices and all other offices "where there is significant demand." Third, New Brunswick becomes Canada's first province in which English and French are official languages, and the right to use both languages is extended to its legislature, provincial courts, and governmental services. Fourth, section 23 establishes a complex set of minority-language education rights. This section gives citizens who are members of the English-speaking minority in Quebec or the French-speaking minority in the other provinces the right to have their children receive their primary- and secondary-school instruction in the minority language in that province. The minority-language instruction is to be supported by public funds where numbers warrant. A similar numbers-warrant qualification applies to the right to have the instruction provided through "minority language educational facilities."

3   *Reference Re Bill 30, An Act to Amend the Education Act (Ont.)*, [1987] 1 S.C.R. 1148.

4   For details, see Peter H. Russell, *Constitutional Odyssey: Can Canadians Become a Sovereign People?*, 3d ed. (Toronto: University of Toronto Press, 2004) at 249.

In interpreting constitutional language rights, the Supreme Court's performance has been virtually the polar opposite of the Judicial Committee's treatment of denominational school rights. With one notable exception, it has given these rights, both the old rights in the *Constitution Act, 1867* and the new rights in the *Charter*, a broad and liberal interpretation. This trend was evident before the *Charter* in 1979 when, after decades in which there was virtually no litigation based on the historic language rights, two cases came before the Court. *Blaikie*[5] involved a collision between Bill 101, Quebec's *Charter of the French Language*, the most important legislative initiative of Quebec's recently elected Parti Québécois government, and section 133 in the *Constitution Act, 1867*. The other case, *Forest*,[6] involved a challenge, based on Manitoba's equivalent of section 133, to that province's *Official Language Act*, which had been enacted nearly a century earlier, and that had made English the official language of Manitoba.

The Supreme Court vigorously applied the constitutional guarantees in both the 1979 cases. In *Blaikie*, the Court held that the provision in section 133 that the Acts of Quebec's legislature "shall be printed and published in both English and French" required more than providing an English translation of Quebec's laws. It required that the legislation be actually enacted in both languages so that, contrary to Bill 101, the English version had the same legal status as the French version. Moreover, the Court required that not just Acts, but all regulations and subordinate legislation be available in English as well as French, and that the right to use both languages in the courts of Quebec apply to all administrative agencies exercising adjudicative responsibilities. The Court applied similar guarantees of bilingualism just as vigorously in *Forest*—except that here it was applying them to a regime that had been much more extreme in its unilingualism than Quebec has ever been. The 1890 Manitoba *Act* actually forbade the use of French in the records and journals of the legislature and in court proceedings and provided that Acts of the legislature be printed and published in English only. This legislation had remained in force since its enactment—despite several *successful* challenges at the lower-court level. Now it was found to be unconstitutional by Canada's highest court and in an era when judicial decisions, no matter how challenging and counter-majoritarian they may be, cannot simply be ignored.

There was a remarkable sequel to *Forest*. Even with a brigade of translators, 90 years of legislation cannot be translated overnight. Are statutes and regulations that have not been translated into French unconstitutional? In 1985, this question was referred to the Supreme Court in a highly charged political context. In 1983, a referendum in the city of Winnipeg, where over half of Manitoba's population live, resulted in a 4-to-1 majority against proceeding with a constitutional amendment that would give the province time to translate its laws. In the 1985 reference case, the Supreme Court seemed to be between a rock and a hard place.[7] If it ruled that Manitoba's English-only laws were valid, it would make a mockery of its decision in *Forest*. If it made the opposite ruling and rendered nearly the entire provincial statute book null and void, it would plunge the province into the dark sea of legal anarchy. The Court's solution was to draw on international experience in upholding the laws of unconstitutional regimes and in order to safeguard the rule of law give temporary validity

---

5   *Attorney General of Quebec v. Blaikie*, [1979] 2 S.C.R. 1016.

6   *Attorney General of Manitoba v. Forest*, [1979] 2 S.C.R. 1032.

7   *Reference re Manitoba Language Rights*, [1985] 2 S.C.R. 347.

to the English-only laws while they were being translated into French. "The Constitution," said the Court, "will not suffer a province without laws." It gave Manitoba five years to get the job done, and it gave the world a new contribution to constitutional theory.

One of the Supreme Court's very first *Charter* decisions was the Association of Quebec Protestant School Boards' *Charter*-based challenge to Quebec's Bill 101.[8] In effect, the case pitted the "Quebec Clause" in Bill 101 against the *Charter*'s "Canada Clause." Sections 72-73 of Bill 101 restricted access to publicly funded English-language schools to the children of Anglophone parents already living in Quebec. It was called the "Quebec Clause" because it was designed to stem the growth of English-speaking Quebec. Section 23(1)(*b*) of the *Charter* gave the right to instruction in English to children of parents who had received their primary education in English outside Quebec and at any time in the future moved to Quebec.[9] It applied in a reciprocal way to French-speaking Quebecers who moved to other provinces. It was called the "Canada Clause" because it was designed to enable English-speaking and French-speaking Canadians to move anywhere in Canada with assurance that their children could be educated in their parents' mother tongue. In a unanimous unsigned *per curiam* decision, the Court struck down sections 72-73 of Bill 101. It refused to consider the section 1 arguments advanced by Quebec showing demographic data about the decline in the percentage of French speakers in the province. Because the "Quebec Clause," in the judges' view, was a complete denial of the *Charter* right, it could not be considered as a reasonable limit. In no subsequent case has the Court made this distinction between a denial of a right and a limit on a right. Coming on the heels of Quebec's loss in the *Quebec Veto* case,[10] this decision contributed to Quebec's sense of alienation from the rest of Canada and fueled its agitation for constitutional change.

In a trio of cases decided in 1986, the Supreme Court seemed to be applying the breaks to its language-rights express. Two of the cases, one from Quebec[11] and the other from Manitoba,[12] involved challenges to unilingual summonses issued for traffic violations. In both cases, the Court's majority rejected the challenge on the ground that section 133 states that English or French "may be used" in any process issuing from a court in these provinces so that in this context the minority language is optional, not mandatory. The third case was initiated by New Brunswick Acadians who sought a ruling that their right to use French in New Brunswick's courts implied a right to be understood in French. Again, the Court's majority, which included all of the Court's Francophone justices, rejected the language-rights claim. Justice Beetz's majority opinion recognized that there is a common law right to be heard and understood in court, which, as one aspect of a universal right to a fair hearing, should be interpreted in a broad and liberal way. But, he argued, the language rights in Canada's Constitution are founded on political compromise and should be interpreted narrowly. The

---

8   *Attorney General of Quebec v. Association of Quebec Protestant School Boards*, [1984] 2 S.C.R. 66.

9   Section 23(1)(*a*) confers the right to minority-language education to new Canadians whose first language is English or French. As a last minute concession to Quebec, section 59 was added to the *Constitution Act, 1982*, suspending the enforcement of section 23(1)(*a*) until such time as the legislative assembly or government of Quebec brings it into force.

10   See case 47.

11   *MacDonald v. City of Montreal*, [1986] 1 S.C.R. 460.

12   *Bilodeau v. Attorney General of Manitoba*, [1986] 1 S.C.R. 449.

development of such a right should be left primarily to legislatures and the political process. Justice Wilson took the opposite view, contending that there was a "principle of growth" in the language-rights provisions of the Constitution and that, if these rights are to be developed to their full potential, courts must go beyond the literal words of these provisions.

The Court's decision in *Mahe* indicates that, for now, Justice Wilson's approach appears to have won out over Justice Beetz's. The case was the culmination of a struggle by French-speaking minority communities across Canada, in the words of Michael Behiels, to "infuse s. 23 (of the *Charter*) with real power."[13] On the other side of the struggle were provincial governments (five of them were interveners in the case) concerned that their control over education might be diluted by judicial interpretation of the *Charter*'s section 23. The key issue in the case was whether the right to receive instruction in "minority language education facilities" includes the right to control and manage such facilities. The Court, in a unanimous opinion written by Chief Justice Dickson, answered this question in the affirmative. Early in his analysis, the Chief Justice backed the Court away from Justice Beetz's position, stating that "it must be open to the Court to breathe new life into a compromise that is clearly expressed."

While the case was certainly seen as a victory for the various associations of Francophone parents that brought it on, the Court did not give them all that they were after. In their submissions, these groups argued that the management and control of minority education facilities required that the direction of such facilities be exercised by an independent Francophone school board. Dickson did not think that the number of students likely to attend Francophone schools in Edmonton was sufficient to justify such an independent board. It would suffice to guarantee Francophone representation on the Separate School Board and give these representatives full control over all aspects of French-language instruction. He put forward the idea of a sliding scale of entitlement based on the number of children who qualify for minority-language education as the methodology for applying section 23(3). One additional point that he granted to the Francophone parents was to hold that an Alberta education regulation requiring no less than 300 minutes per week of instruction in the English language in all schools, including Francophone schools, infringed section 23 and was invalid until and unless such a limitation was justified under section 1 of the *Charter*.

Three years later, in *Re Public School Act (Man.)* (1993),[14] the Court struck down Manitoba legislation respecting French-language schools because it made no provision for Francophone parents to control and manage French-language education. In a 2000 case, the Court ruled that Prince Edward Island must provide a school in the community of Summerside for the 49 students enrolled there for French-language education, rather than bus those students to a French-language school 28 kilometres away.[15] The Court's liberal and vigorous treatment of the *Charter*'s language of education rights has certainly qualified the province's exclusive jurisdiction over education much more than the denominational education rights in section 93 ever did. Indeed, this may be the *Charter*'s most significant impact on the federal division of powers. ∽

---

13   Michael D. Behiels, *Canada's Francophone Minority Communities: Constitutional Renewal and the Winning of School Governance* (Montreal and Kingston: McGill-Queen's University Press, 2004) at 169.

14   [1993] 1 S.C.R. 839.

15   *Arsenault-Cameron v. Prince Edward Island*, [2000] 1 S.C.R. 3.

MAHE v. ALBERTA
[1990] 1 S.C.R. 342

Hearing: June 14, 1989; Judgment: March 15, 1990.

Present: Dickson C.J. and Wilson, La Forest, L'Heureux-Dubé, Sopinka, Gonthier, and Cory JJ.

Interveners: The Attorney General of Canada, the Attorney General for Ontario, the Attorney General of Quebec, the Attorney General for New Brunswick, the Attorney General of Manitoba, the Attorney General of Manitoba, the Attorney General for Saskatchewan, the Association canadienne-française de l'Alberta, the Commissioner of Official Languages for Canada, Alliance Quebec, Alliance for Languages Communities in Quebec, the Association canadienne-française de l'Ontario, the Association française des conseils scolaires de l'Ontario, the Association des enseignantes et des enseignantes franco-ontariens, the Quebec Association of Protestant School Boards, the Edmonton Roman Catholic Separate School District No. 7, and the Alberta School Trustees' Association.

The judgment of the Court was delivered by

THE CHIEF JUSTICE: In this appeal the Court is asked to determine whether the educational system in the city of Edmonton satisfies the demands of s. 23 of the *Canadian Charter of Rights and Freedoms*. . . .

Section 23 is one component in Canada's constitutional protection of the official languages. The section is especially important in this regard, however, because of the vital role of education in preserving and encouraging linguistic and cultural vitality. It thus represents a linchpin in this nation's commitment to the values of bilingualism and biculturalism.

The appellants claim that their rights under s. 23 are not satisfied by the existing educational system in Edmonton nor by the legislation under which it operates, resulting in an erosion of their cultural heritage, contrary to the spirit and intent of the *Charter*. In particular, the appellants argue that s. 23 guarantees the right, in Edmonton, to the "management and control" of a minority-language school—that is, to a Francophone school run by a Francophone school board. Our task then is to determine the meaning of s. 23 of the *Charter*.

Constitutional Questions

The following constitutional questions, stated by order of the Court, indicate the range of the issues which this appeal raises:

1. Have the rights of the linguistic minority population in metropolitan Edmonton to minority language educational facilities pursuant to s. 23(3)(*b*) of the *Canadian Charter of Rights and Freedoms* been infringed or denied?

2. Does the right to minority language instruction and educational facilities pursuant to s. 23(3)(*a*) and s. 23(3)(*b*) of the *Charter* include management and control by the minority of:
   (a) the instruction?
   (b) the educational facilities?
   If so, what is the nature and extent of such management and control?

3. (a) Are the *School Act*, R.S.A. 1980, c. S-3, and the regulations passed thereunder inconsistent with or in contravention of s. 23 of the *Charter*?
   (b) If so, is such inconsistency or contravention justified under s. 1 of the *Charter*?

4. Are the rights guaranteed by s. 23 of the *Charter* affected by the provisions of s. 93 of the *Constitution Act, 1867*, s. 29 of the *Charter* and s. 17 of the *Alberta Act*? If so, how?

The Parties and Interveners

The appellants Jean-Claude Mahe and Paul Dubé are parents whose first language learned and still understood is French. The appellant Angeline Martel is a parent who received her primary school instruction in French. All three have school age children, and thus qualify under s. 23(1) of the *Charter* as persons who, subject to certain limitations, "have the right to have their children receive primary and secondary school instruction" in the language of the linguistic minority population of the province—in this case, the French language. They may therefore conveniently be called "s. 23 parents," and their children "s. 23 students." The fourth appellant, the Association de l'école Georges et Julia Bugnet, is an incorporated society whose prime objective is the encouragement of French language education in the province of Alberta.

A number of interveners were granted status in this appeal: the Attorneys General of Canada, Ontario, Québec, New Brunswick, Manitoba, and Saskatchewan; Alliance Quebec; the Edmonton Roman Catholic Separate School District No. 7; the Alberta School Trustees' Association; the Association canadienne-française de l'Alberta; the Quebec Association of Protestant School Boards; the Association canadienne-française de l'Ontario; the Association française des conseils scolaires de l'Ontario; the Association des enseignantes et des enseignants franco-ontariens; and, the Commissioner of Official Languages for Canada.

Facts

The appellants were and still are dissatisfied with the provision of French language education in Alberta, particularly in

Edmonton. In 1982 they forwarded a proposal to the Minister of Education of Alberta for a new French-language public elementary school in Edmonton, which would have the following features: (1) it would instruct Francophone children exclusively in the French language and in a totally "French" environment; (2) it would be administered by a Committee of Parents under the structure of an autonomous French School Board; and (3) it would have a programme reflecting the French linguistic culture.

The appellants were advised that it was a policy of the Province, acting through the Department of Education, to *not* create any French school jurisdictions. The appellants were encouraged to take their proposal to either the Edmonton Roman Catholic Separate School Board or to the Edmonton Public School Board. The appellants did this, but both Boards rejected their proposal. The Roman Catholic Separate School Board did decide to conduct a study with respect to whether the needs of Francophone students in Edmonton were being met. As a result of that study, in June of 1983 the Roman Catholic Separate School Board directed that a Francophone school, École Maurice Lavallée, be established in September of 1984 under the direction of the Edmonton Roman Catholic Separate School District No. 7.

The evidence relating to the chronology of the development of École Maurice Lavallée is somewhat sketchy. It appears that prior to September 1984, École Maurice Lavallée had been a French immersion school. After that date it continued to offer an immersion programme in grades 7 and 8, but from kindergarten to grade 6 it became a "French only" school, with admission restricted to students of parents who qualified under s. 23 of the *Charter*. Evidence was presented that as of September 1985, the Roman Catholic Separate School Board District No. 7 intended to commence a Junior High programme at the school and to move its immersion course out of Maurice Lavallée over a two-year period. After this transition period the school would be comprised entirely of "s. 23 students." At about the same time, the Roman Catholic Board also adopted a motion that they would promote and pursue the establishment of a grade 9 to 12 Francophone programme at a school named École J.H. Picard. It appears that as of the date of the hearing before the Court of Appeal, the Roman Catholic Board had in fact established a Francophone high school at École J.H. Picard, although details of the operation of this school have not been provided to us.

At École Maurice Lavallée, French is the language of instruction and administration, the personnel are all Francophone, and the stated aim of the school is "to primarily reflect the cultural heritage of the French linguistic minority in Alberta." The government emphasized in its argument that the school is not a French immersion school. The respondent also pointed out that non-residents are granted admission to the school if they qualify under s. 23 of the *Charter* and that the school has a Parent Advisory Committee which is incorporated pursuant to the *Societies Act*, R.S.A. 1980, c. S-18, and which acts as an advisory body to the Board of Trustees.

As a result of the failure of the government to accede to all of their requests, the appellants commenced the action which has culminated in the present appeal. . . .

At the heart of this appeal is the claim of the appellants that the term "minority language educational facilities" referred to in s. 23(3)(*b*) includes administration by distinct school boards. The respondent takes the position that the word "facilities" means a school building. The respondent submits that the rights of the Francophone minority in metropolitan Edmonton have not been denied because those rights are being met with current Francophone educational facilities. . . .

Analysis

The primary issue raised by this appeal is the degree, if any, of "management and control" of a French language school which should be accorded to s. 23 parents in Edmonton. (The phrase "management and control," it should be noted, is not a term of art: it appears to have been introduced in earlier s. 23 cases and has now gained such currency that it was utilized by all the groups in this appeal.) The appellants appear to accept that, with a few exceptions, the government has provided whatever other services or rights might be mandated in Edmonton under s. 23: their fundamental complaint is that they do not have the exclusive management and control of the existing Francophone schools. The other issues raised by the appellants in their statement of claim are either consequent upon or secondary to this primary issue. . . .

(1) The Purpose of Section 23

The general purpose of s. 23 is clear: it is to preserve and promote the two official languages of Canada, and their respective cultures, by ensuring that each language flourishes, as far as possible, in provinces where it is not spoken by the majority of the population. The section aims at achieving this goal by granting minority language educational rights to minority language parents throughout Canada.

My reference to cultures is significant: it is based on the fact that any broad guarantee of language rights, especially in the context of education, cannot be separated from a concern for the culture associated with the language. Language is more than a mere means of communication, it is part and parcel of the identity and culture of the people speaking it. It is the means by which individuals understand themselves and the world around them. . . .

In my view the appellants are fully justified in submitting that "history reveals that s. 23 was designed to correct, on a national scale, the progressive erosion of minority official language groups and to give effect to the concept of the 'equal partnership' of the two official language groups in the context of education."

The remedial aspect of s. 23 was indirectly questioned by the respondent and several of the interveners in an argument which they put forward for a "narrow construction" of s. 23. The following statements by Beetz J. in a case dealing with s. 16 of the *Charter, Société des Acadiens du Nouveau-Brunswick Inc. v. Association of Parents for Fairness in Education*, [1986] 1 S.C.R. 549, at p. 578, were relied upon in support of this argument:

> Unlike language rights which are based on political compromise, legal rights tend to be seminal in nature because they are rooted in principle. Some of them, such as the one expressed in s. 7 of the *Charter*, are so broad as to call for frequent judicial determination.
>
> Language rights, on the other hand, although some of them have been enlarged and incorporated into the *Charter*, remain nonetheless founded on political compromise.
>
> This essential difference between the two types of rights dictates a distinct judicial approach with respect to each. More particularly, the courts should pause before they decide to act as instruments of change with respect to language rights. This is not to say that language rights provisions are cast in stone and should remain immune altogether from judicial interpretation. But, in my opinion, the courts should approach them with more restraint than they would in construing legal rights.

I do not believe that these words support the proposition that s. 23 should be given a particularly narrow construction, or that its remedial purpose should be ignored. Beetz J. makes it clear in this quotation that language rights are not cast in stone nor immune from judicial interpretation. In *Reference Re Bill 30, An Act to amend the Education Act (Ont.)*, [1987] 1 S.C.R. 1148, at p. 1176, Wilson J. made the following comments in respect of the above quotation:

> While due regard must be paid not to give a provision which reflects a political compromise too wide an interpretation, it must still be open to the Court to breathe life into a compromise that is clearly expressed.

I agree. Beetz J.'s warning that courts should be careful in interpreting language rights is a sound one. Section 23 provides a perfect example of why such caution is advisable. The provision provides for a novel form of legal right, quite different from the type of legal rights which courts have traditionally dealt with. Both its genesis and its form are evidence of the unusual nature of s. 23. Section 23 confers upon a group a right which places positive obligations on government to alter or develop major institutional structures. Careful interpreta-

tion of such a section is wise: however, this does not mean that courts should not "breathe life" into the expressed purpose of the section, or avoid implementing the possibly novel remedies needed to achieve that purpose.

(2) The Context of Section 23(3)(b): An Overview of Section 23

The proper way of interpreting s. 23, in my opinion, is to view the section as providing a general right to minority language instruction. Paragraphs (*a*) and (*b*) of subs. (3) qualify this general right: para. (*a*) adds that the right to instruction is only guaranteed where the "number of children" warrants, while para. (*b*) further qualifies the general right to instruction by adding that where numbers warrant it includes a right to "minority language educational facilities." In my view, subs. (3)(*b*) is included in order to indicate the upper range of possible institutional requirements which may be mandated by s. 23 (the government may, of course, provide more than the minimum required by s. 23).

Another way of expressing the above interpretation of s. 23 is to say that s. 23 should be viewed as encompassing a "sliding scale" of requirement, with subs. (3)(*b*) indicating the upper level of this range and the term "instruction" in subs. (3)(*a*) indicating the lower level. . . .

The sliding scale approach can be contrasted with that which views s. 23 as only encompassing two rights—one with respect to instruction and one with respect to facilities—each providing a certain level of services appropriate for one of two numerical thresholds. On this interpretation of s. 23, which could be called the "separate rights" approach, a specified number of s. 23 students would trigger a particular level of instruction, while a greater, specified number of students would require, in addition, a particular level of minority language educational facilities. Where the number of students fell between the two threshold numbers, only the lower level of instruction would be required.

The sliding scale approach is preferable to the separate rights approach, not only because it accords with the text of s. 23, but also because it is consistent with the purpose of s. 23. The sliding scale approach ensures that the minority group receives the full amount of protection that its numbers warrant. Under the separate rights approach, if it were accepted, for example, that "X" number of students ensured a right to full management and control, then presumably "X − 1" students would not bring about any rights to management and control or even to a school building. Given the variety of possible means of fulfilling the purpose of s. 23, such a result is unacceptable. Moreover, the separate rights approach places parties like the appellants in the paradoxical position of forwarding an argument which, if accepted, might ultimately harm the overall position of minority language students in

Canada. If, for instance, the appellants succeeded in persuading this Court that s. 23 mandates a completely separate school board—as opposed to some sort of representation on an existing board—then other groups of s. 23 parents with slightly fewer numbers might find themselves without a right to *any* degree of management and control—even though their numbers might justify granting them some degree of management and control.

(3) Management and Control Under Section 23(3)(b): Introduction

Both the trial judge and the Court of Appeal found that s. 23(3)(*b*) allows for the possibility of securing to minority language parents a measure of management and control. Purvis J. held that s. 23 bestows "a degree of exclusive management and control over provision and administration of minority language schools" while, as mentioned earlier, Kerans J.A. stated (at p. 539) that:

> ... s. 23(3)(*b*) offers the minority-language group the right, where numbers warrant, to establish and control an independent school system, but that a province shall select the institutional means by which that right will be implemented.

Courts in Ontario, Saskatchewan, Nova Scotia and Prince Edward Island have reached similar conclusions (*Reference Re Education Act of Ontario, supra; Commission des Écoles Fransaskoises v. Saskatchewan* (1988), 48 D.L.R. (4th) 315 (Sask. Q.B.); *Lavoie v. Nova Scotia (Attorney General), supra*; and *Reference Re Minority Language Educational Rights (P.E.I.)* (1988), 69 Nfld. & P.E.I.R. 236 (P.E.I.S.C., App. Div.))....

(4) Management and Control: The Text of Section 23(3)(b)

In my view, the words of s. 23(3)(*b*) are consistent with and supportive of the conclusion that s. 23 mandates, where the numbers warrant, a measure of management and control. Consider, first, the words of subs. (3)(*b*) in the context of the entire section. Instruction must take place somewhere and accordingly the right to "instruction" includes an implicit right to be instructed in facilities. If the term "minority language educational facilities" is not viewed as encompassing a degree of management and control, then there would not appear to be any purpose in including it in s. 23. This common sense conclusion militates against interpreting "facilities" as a reference to physical structures. Indeed, once the sliding scale approach is accepted it becomes unnecessary to focus too intently upon the word "facilities." Rather, the text of s. 23 supports viewing the entire term "minority language educational facilities" as setting out an upper level of management and control....

(5) Management and Control: The Purpose of Section 23

The foregoing textual analysis of s. 23(3)(*b*) is strongly supported by a consideration of the overall purpose of s. 23. That purpose, as discussed earlier, is to preserve and promote minority language and culture throughout Canada. In my view, it is essential, in order to further this purpose, that, where the numbers warrant, minority language parents possess a measure of management and control over the educational facilities in which their children are taught. Such management and control is vital to ensure that their language and culture flourish. It is necessary because a variety of management issues in education, e.g., curricula, hiring, expenditures, can affect linguistic and cultural concerns. I think it incontrovertible that the health and survival of the minority language and culture can be affected in subtle but important ways by decisions relating to these issues. To give but one example, most decisions pertaining to curricula clearly have an influence on the language and culture of the minority students.

(6) The Meaning of the Phrase "Management and Control"

Section 23 clearly encompasses a right to management and control. On its own, however, the phrase "management and control" is imprecise and requires further specification. This can be accomplished by considering what type of management and control is needed in order to fulfill the purpose of s. 23.

The appellants argue for a completely independent Francophone school board. Much is to be said in support of this position and indeed it may be said to reflect the ideal....

Historically, separate or denominational boards have been the principal bulwarks of minority language education in the absence of any provision for minority representation and authority within public or common school boards. Such independent boards constitute, for the minority, institutions which it can consider its own with all this entails in terms of opportunity of working in its own language and of sharing a common culture, interests and understanding and being afforded the fullest measure of representation and control. These are particularly important in setting overall priorities and responding to the special educational needs of the minority.

In some circumstances an independent Francophone school board is necessary to meet the purpose of s. 23. However, where the number of students enrolled in minority schools is relatively small, the ability of an independent board to fulfill this purpose may be reduced and other approaches may be appropriate whereby the minority is able to identify with the school but has the benefit of participating in a larger organization through representation and a certain exclusive authority within the majority school board. Under these circumstances, such an arrangement avoids the isolation of an independent school district from the physical resources which the majority school district enjoys and facilitates the sharing of resources with the majority board, something which can be crucial for smaller minority schools. By virtue of having a larger student population, it can be expected that the majority board would have greater access to new educational developments and resources. Where the number of s. 23 students is not sufficiently large, a complete isolation of the minority schools would tend to frustrate the purpose of s. 23 because, in the long run, it would contribute to a decline in the status of the minority language group and its educational facilities. Graduates of the minority schools would be less well-prepared (thus hindering career opportunities for the minority) and potential students would be disinclined to enter minority language schools. . . .

In my view, the measure of management and control required by s. 23 of the *Charter* may, depending on the numbers of students to be served, warrant an independent school board. Where numbers do not warrant granting this maximum level of management and control, however, they may nonetheless be sufficient to require linguistic minority representation on an existing school board. In this latter case:

(1) The representation of the linguistic minority on local boards or other public authorities which administer minority language instruction or facilities should be guaranteed;

(2) The number of minority language representatives on the board should be, at a minimum, proportional to the number of minority language students in the school district, i.e., the number of minority language students for whom the board is responsible;

(3) The minority language representatives should have exclusive authority to make decisions relating to the minority language instruction and facilities, including:

(a) expenditures of funds provided for such instruction and facilities;

(b) appointment and direction of those responsible for the administration of such instruction and facilities;

(c) establishment of programs of instruction;

(d) recruitment and assignment of teachers and other personnel; and

(e) making of agreements for education and services for minority language pupils.

I do not doubt that in future cases courts will have occasion to expand upon or refine these words. It is impossible at this stage in the development of s. 23 to foresee all of the circumstances relevant to its implementation.

There are a few general comments I wish to add in respect of the above description. First, the matter of the quality of education to be provided to the minority students was not dealt with above because, strictly speaking, it does not pertain to the issue of management and control. It is, of course, an important issue and one which was raised in this appeal. I think it should be self-evident that in situations where the above degree of management and control is warranted the quality of education provided to the minority should in principle be on a basis of equality with the majority. This proposition follows directly from the purpose of s. 23. However, the specific form of educational system provided to the minority need not be identical to that provided to the majority. The different circumstances under which various schools find themselves, as well as the demands of a minority language education itself, make such a requirement impractical and undesirable. It should be stressed that the funds allocated for the minority language schools must be at least equivalent on a per student basis to the funds allocated to the majority schools. Special circumstances may warrant an allocation for minority language schools that exceeds the per capita allocation for majority schools. I am confident that this will be taken into account not only in the enabling legislation, but in budgetary discussions of the board. . . .

Having canvassed the degrees of management and control which s. 23 *might* require, the next step is to determine what degree the numbers in Edmonton warrant granting. Before I approach this task, however, it will be convenient at this point to consider the issue of denominational rights.

(7) Denominational Schools' Rights

Under the terms of s. 29 of the *Charter* any interpretation of s. 23 must be consistent with the rights and privileges of denominational schools. Section 29 reads:

> **29.** Nothing in this *Charter* abrogates or derogates from any rights or privileges guaranteed by or under the Constitution of Canada in respect of denominational, separate or dissentient schools.

The rights of denominational, separate or dissentient schools referred to in s. 29 are generally provided for in s. 93(1) of the *Constitution Act, 1867*:

> **93.** In and for each Province the Legislature may exclusively make Laws in relation to Education, subject and according to the following Provisions:
>
> (1) Nothing in any such Law shall prejudicially affect any Right or Privilege with respect to Denominational Schools which any Class of Persons have by Law in the Province at the Union:

The province of Alberta is governed by a slightly different provision. When Alberta became a province in 1905, it adopted s. 93 of the *British North America Act, 1867* (later renamed the *Constitution Act, 1867*), but with an amendment to s. 93(1). The amendment is set out in s. 17 of the *Alberta Act*:

> Section 93 of the *Constitution Act, 1867*, shall apply to the said province, with the substitution for paragraph (1) of the said section 93, of the following paragraph:
>
> "(1) Nothing in any such law shall prejudicially affect any right or privilege with respect to separate schools which any class of persons have at the date of the passing of this *Act*, under the terms of chapters 29 and 30 of the Ordinances of the North-west Territories, passed in the year 1901, or with respect to religious instruction in any public or separate school as provided for in the said ordinances." . . .

. . . [T]he powers of management and control which s. 23 would accord to minority language groups under the interpretation proposed would not affect any rights in respect of the denominational aspects of education or related non-denominational aspects. The minority language trustees on a denominational school board who are to be given powers over management and control will be, at the same time, denominational trustees: in such instances, the denominational board is not required to cede powers to a non-denominational group of persons, it is only required to give certain of its members authority over minority language education. The proposed regulation would not remove a denominational board's power to manage and control, or alter its denominational character.

The transfer of the powers in respect of management and control thus amounts to the *regulation* of a non-denominational aspect of education, namely, the language of instruction, a form of regulation which the courts have long held to be valid. . . .

(8) The "Numbers Warrant" Provision

What is being considered when a court addresses the "numbers warrant" question—existing demand, potential demand, or something else? The appellants' position was that the *existing* demand for Francophone services is not a reliable indicator of demand because the demand for any service will to some extent follow the provision of that service. The respondent, on the other hand, argued that the courts cannot simply use the total number of *potential* s. 23 students as a gauge, since it is highly unlikely that all of these students will take advantage of a proposed service. There is some force to both of these arguments; accordingly, the approach I have taken mediates between the concerns which they raise. In my view, the relevant figure for s. 23 purposes is the number of persons who will eventually take advantage of the contemplated programme or facility. It will normally be impossible to know this figure

exactly, yet it can be roughly estimated by considering the parameters within which it must fall—the known demand for the service and the total number of persons who potentially could take advantage of the service.

The numbers warrant provision requires, in general, that two factors be taken into account in determining what s. 23 demands: (1) the services appropriate, in pedagogical terms, for the numbers of students involved; and (2) the cost of the contemplated services. The first, pedagogical requirements, recognizes that a threshold number of students is required before certain programmes or facilities can operate effectively. There is no point, for example, in having a school for only ten students in an urban centre. The students would be deprived of the numerous benefits which can only be achieved through studying and interacting with larger numbers of students. The welfare of the students, and thus indirectly the purposes of s. 23, demands that programmes and facilities which are inappropriate for the numbers of students involved should not be required.

Cost, the second factor, is not usually explicitly taken into account in determining whether or not an individual is to be accorded a right under the *Charter*. In the case of s. 23, however, such a consideration is mandated. Section 23 does not, like some other provisions, create an absolute right. Rather, it grants a right which must be subject to financial constraints, for it is financially impractical to accord to every group of minority language students, no matter how small, the same services which a large group of s. 23 students are accorded. I note, however, that in most cases pedagogical requirements will prevent the imposition of unrealistic financial demands upon the state. Moreover, the remedial nature of s. 23 suggests that pedagogical considerations will have more weight than financial requirements in determining whether numbers warrant.

In my view, the phrase "where numbers warrant" does not provide an explicit standard which courts can use to determine the appropriate instruction and facilities (in light of the aforementioned considerations) in every given situation. The standard will have to be worked out over time by examining the particular facts of each situation which comes before the courts, but, in general, the inquiry must be guided by the purpose of s. 23. In particular, the fact that s. 23 is a remedial section is significant, indicating that the section does not aim at merely guaranteeing the status quo.

Thus, a number of complex and subtle factors must be taken into account beyond simply counting the number of students. For example, what is appropriate may differ between rural and urban areas. Another factor to consider is that s. 23 speaks of "wherever in the province" the "numbers warrant." This means that the calculation of the relevant numbers is not restricted to existing school boundaries (although the redrawing of school boundaries will often involve a certain cost which must be taken into account). . . .

(9) The Situation in Edmonton

We can now examine the facts underlying this appeal to determine whether s. 23 parents in Edmonton should be accorded a measure of management and control as contemplated by s. 23.

At the time of the trial, there were approximately 2,948 citizens in Edmonton whose first language learned and still understood was French and who, therefore, qualified under s. 23 of the *Charter*. These citizens had approximately 4,127 children from birth to age 19, of whom 3,750 were between five and 19 years of age. The vast majority of these parents were separate school supporters. The enrollment at the existing Francophone school, École Maurice Lavallée was 242 students from kindergarten to grade 6, with room for more. No one has been turned away for lack of space. The capacity of the school is 720 students. At the time of trial there were 315 in attendance, of whom 73 were in grades 7 and 8 immersion programme.

It does not appear that any financial or pedagogical problems have accompanied the operation of the existing Francophone school, École Maurice Lavallée. In view of the substantial numbers of students involved I do not think that such problems would be likely. It is, no doubt, slightly more expensive on a per student basis to operate a school with 242 students as compared to a school with 1,000 students. However, the remedial nature of s. 23 means that such differences in cost, if not unreasonable, must be accepted. It seems clear that even at the present level of demand, there are sufficient students to justify in both pedagogical and financial terms the creation of an independent school, such as the one presently existing as well as providing for a continuing course of primary and secondary schooling. A recognition of this fact appeared to be common ground between all of the parties involved in this appeal, as well as by both of the Alberta courts.

Having established that the existing Francophone school in Edmonton is required in order to comply with s. 23, I believe it is reasonable to require, in addition, that the minority language parents enjoy the right to representation on the separate school board and the degree of management and control that this entails (as specified above). In general, wherever the numbers of students justify creating a minority language school, these numbers would also justify granting the minority language parents a measure of management and control. Because a Francophone school already exists in Edmonton, the pedagogical and financial effects of granting management and control in the case at hand are not likely to be great. Reorganization of the relevant school board to provide for a

degree of management and control would not significantly change the pedagogical structure, nor would it be very expensive. At the time of the trial there were approximately 424,622 students enrolled in the public or separate school systems in Alberta in some 146 different jurisdictions. These jurisdictions are administered by Boards of Trustees elected by eligible voters within the boundaries of the districts. Forty-seven of these jurisdictions had fewer than 500 students; of these 25 had fewer than 250 students; of these 8 had fewer than 100 students; and of these 4 had 50 students or less. Of these same 47 districts: 35 were separate school districts whose formation was guaranteed by constitutional guarantees under s. 93 of the *Constitution Act, 1867*, s. 17 of the *Alberta Act*, and s. 29 of the *Charter*; three were in National Parks and subject to federal–provincial agreements; two were consolidated school districts formed under now defunct legislation; one was a regional district formed pursuant to an agreement of three other school jurisdictions; and of the remaining six, four were formed in 1937 and the other two in 1966.

In Edmonton there were approximately 116,788 students enrolled in the public and separate school systems in some nine school jurisdictions. Five of these districts had less than 5,000 students (specifically, the numbers of students in these districts were 4,187, 3,043, 2,600, 758, and 381).

. . . Overall, I think it clear that the numbers described above show that requiring a Francophone school, together with a degree of management and control to the parents, is, in respect of a group of students who, at a minimum, number at least 242, a reasonable requirement. At the same time, I am not satisfied on the basis of present evidence that it has been established that numbers of students likely to attend Francophone schools in Edmonton are sufficient to mandate under s. 23 the establishment of an independent Francophone school board. In reaching this conclusion, I have considered the likely demand upon a Francophone school, and have also allowed for additional numbers of students that will come from an extension of the programme to include secondary school grades. If actual experience reveals a larger than anticipated demand, however, it may be necessary to reconsider whether the appropriate degree of management and control mandates the establishment of an independent minority language school board.

To conclude: the numbers of minority language students in Edmonton warrant as a minimum the provision of s. 23 rights by way of minority language representation on school boards administering minority language schools in the manner and with the authority above described. These rights are not provided at the present time. The Province must enact legislation (and regulations, if necessary) that are in all respects consistent with the provisions of s. 23 of the *Charter*.

Remedies

The appellants' statement of claim, as I have indicated, includes requests for a number of declarations. These declarations fall into two general groups: (1) in respect of the alleged invalidity of certain provisions of the *School Act* of Alberta; and (2) in respect of the rights which must be accorded to s. 23 parents in Edmonton.

The appellants did not specify in their statement of claim which provisions of the Alberta legislation they desired to have struck down, but it appears from their arguments that their main concern was with provisions 13, 158, and 159 of the *School Act*, and Regulation 490/82 passed thereunder:

13(1) The Minister may establish any portion of Alberta as a public school district.

158 Subject to section 159, all pupils in school shall be taught in the English language.

159(1) A board may authorize

(a) that French be used as a language of instruction, or

(b) that any other language be used as a language of instruction in addition to the English language, in all or any of its schools....

Regulation 490/82:

2 Where, pursuant to section 159 of the School Act, a board authorizes a program that uses French as a language of instruction,

(a) if the program commences in grade 1, then with respect to grades 1 and 2,

(i) the amount of time French is used as the language of instruction,

(ii) the nature and extent of English language instruction, if any, and

(iii) the point at which the English language arts program, if any, is initiated

is in the discretion of the board;

(b) regardless of when the program commences, after grade 2,

(i) not less than 300 minutes per week of instruction in English language arts shall be provided for each pupil in each of grades 3, 4, 5, and 6,

(ii) not less than 150 hours per year of instruction in English language arts shall be provided for each pupil in each of grades 7, 8 and 9, and

(iii) not less than 125 hours per year or the equivalent of 5 credits per year of instruction in English language arts shall be provided for each pupil in each of grades 10, 11 and 12....

Regulation 490/82, which mandates that a minimum of approximately 20 per cent of class time be spent on English language education, is not "permissive" legislation and is, therefore, on a different footing from the other impugned provisions. In their statement of claim the appellants asked for a declaration to the effect that 100 per cent of their children's instruction should be in French. The appellants' position is that the regulation directly contradicts s. 23. I agree that Regulation 490/82 may impede the achievement of the purpose of s. 23. The appellants' rights under s. 23 include a general right for their children to be instructed entirely in the French language. However, by virtue of s. 1 of the *Charter*, "reasonable" limitations of *Charter* rights are permitted. Both of the Alberta courts held that if Regulation 490/82 does in fact infringe s. 23, it could nevertheless be upheld as a reasonable limitation on s. 23 rights. In support of this finding they referred to evidence that a knowledge of English is required for any student in Alberta.

I am prepared to agree with the Alberta courts that a certain amount of mandatory English language instruction is a reasonable limitation on s. 23. It seems indisputable that some English language education is important for all students in Alberta. It is not self-evident, however, that a full 300 minutes a week of English instruction is necessary in Francophone schools. It is for the respondent to prove that this limit infringes the s. 23 right no more than is necessary, and in the absence of such a demonstration I conclude that the Regulation is not saved by s. 1. This conclusion does not, of course, preclude the respondent from attempting in the future to prove that some mandatory English instruction, perhaps even 300 minutes per week, is a reasonable limit under s. 1....

28 R. v. Keegstra, 1990

In 1984, James Keegstra was charged under the *Criminal Code* with "wilfully promot[ing] hatred" against a group "distinguished by colour, race, religion, ethnic origin, or [since 2004] sexual orientation." Keegstra, a high school teacher in Eckville, Alberta, had taught his students that Jews were "treacherous," "subversive," "sadistic," "money-loving," "power hungry," "child killers," who had "created the Holocaust to gain sympathy." Students who failed to parrot these teachings lost marks. Keegstra defended himself in court by challenging the constitutionality of the "hate speech" provision used to charge him. He maintained that the provision infringed both the *Charter*'s section 2(*b*) guarantee of freedom of expression and the presumption of innocence guaranteed by section 11(*d*). The Court upheld the law by a 4-to-3 margin on the section 2(*b*) issue and a 4-to-2 margin on the section 11(*d*) issue (which Justice La Forest did not find it necessary to address). We reproduce only the freedom-of-expression debate below.

Previous cases had established that, short of violence, any activity "convey[ing] or attempt[ing] to convey a meaning . . . has expressive content and *prima facie* falls within the scope" of the *Charter*'s freedom-of-expression guarantee. Because Keegstra's teaching was obviously covered by this broad interpretation of section 2(*b*), all seven participating judges agreed that the law could be applied to him only if it could be sustained as a section 1 "reasonable limit" on freedom of expression. The judges all agreed, moreover, that the law had the kind of "pressing and substantial" purpose needed under the *Oakes* test to establish a "reasonable limit." They parted company on whether the legislative means were proportional to that purpose.

Chief Justice Dickson, writing for the majority, underlined the fact that Keegstra's anti-Semitism contributed little to three fundamental values previously identified by the Court as underpinning freedom of expression in a liberal democracy: "the quest for truth, the promotion of individual self-development [and] the protection and fostering of a vibrant democracy." Indeed, Keegstra's hate speech was, for Dickson, generally contrary to these central freedom-of-expression principles. Quoting Justice McLachlin's opinion in *Rocket v. Royal College of Dental Surgeons of Ontario*, Dickson concluded that restrictions on expression so distant from the core of section 2(*b*) "might be easier to justify than other infringements of" that section.

Applying this perspective, Chief Justice Dickson found that the hate speech provision was proportional to its pressing and substantial purpose. Justice McLachlin, often on the more libertarian side of freedom-of-expression issues, disagreed. Thus, on the "rational connection" component of *Oakes*, Dickson emphasized the egalitarian educative message sent by the prosecution of racist expression while McLachlin thought such prosecution was more likely to backfire, giving people reason "to believe that there must be some truth in the racist expression because the government is trying to suppress it." Similarly, on the "minimal impairment" question, Dickson considered the wording of the law precise enough to prevent the unjustified prosecution of "merely unpopular or unconventional opinion," while McLachlin, believing such prosecutions to be possible, worried about the "chilling effect" this prospect would have on robust public expression.

Justice McLachlin's willingness to invalidate the hate-speech law on "rational connection" grounds is noteworthy. In the introduction to *Oakes* (case 24), we observed that laws rarely fail the "pressing and substantial purpose" part of the *Oakes* test, partly because judges are reluctant to accuse governments of harbouring completely illegitimate objectives. It is similarly uncommon for judges, under the rational-connection test, to accuse governments of being so obtuse as to choose completely irrational means to their legislative ends—that is, means that don't attain those ends at all or backfire so badly that they achieve the very opposite of what was intended. Accordingly, most invalidated laws pass the rational-connection test and fail on minimal impairment grounds. There are exceptions, however, and Justice McLachlin fell just one vote short of putting *Keegstra* in that category. She would later have more success in striking down legislation on rational-connection grounds (for example, *RJR MacDonald*, case 31, and *Sauvé*, case 34). Indeed, two years after *Keegstra*, in the closely related case of *R. v. Zundel*, Justice McLachlin would strike down legislation for the even more unusual lack of a "pressing and substantial" purpose (for further discussion, see the introduction to *Butler*, case 30).

Among the groups sufficiently concerned with the hate-speech issues in *Keegstra* to intervene in the case was the Women's Legal Education and Action Fund (LEAF). *Keegstra* did not directly concern women's issues, but LEAF understood that it could be an important precedent for cases involving the censorship of obscenity and pornography. LEAF wished to defend such censorship, not on the traditional ground that public sexuality was immoral, but on the egalitarian theory that certain kinds of public sexuality constituted an inegalitarian assault on women—in effect, a kind of "hate expression" toward women. This interpretive goal would obviously have been jeopardized had the hate-speech provision of the *Criminal Code* been ruled unconstitutional in *Keegstra*. Instead, *Keegstra* helped set the stage for LEAF's successful arguments in *Butler*. ⁓

R. v. KEEGSTRA
[1990] 3 S.C.R. 697

Hearing: December 5, 6, 1989; Judgment: December 13, 1990.

Present: Dickson C.J.* and Wilson, La Forest, L'Heureux-Dubé, Sopinka, Gonthier, and McLachlin JJ.

Interveners: The Attorney General of Canada, the Attorney General for Ontario, the Attorney General of Quebec, the Attorney General for New Brunswick, the Attorney General of Manitoba, the Canadian Jewish Congress, the League for Human Rights of B'nai Brith Canada, Interamicus, the Women's Legal Education and Action Fund, and the Canadian Civil Liberties Association.

* Chief Justice at the time of hearing.

The judgment of Dickson C.J. and Wilson, L'Heureux-Dubé, and Gonthier JJ. was delivered by

DICKSON C.J.: This appeal ... raises a delicate and highly controversial issue as to the constitutional validity of s. 319(2)

of the *Criminal Code*, R.S.C., 1985, c. C-46, a legislative provision which prohibits the wilful promotion of hatred, other than in private conversation, towards any section of the public distinguished by colour, race, religion or ethnic origin. In particular, the Court must decide whether this section infringes the guarantee of freedom of expression found in s. 2(*b*) of the *Canadian Charter of Rights and Freedoms* in a manner that cannot be justified under s. 1 of the *Charter*....

The first step in the ... analysis involves asking whether the activity of the litigant who alleges an infringement of the freedom of expression falls within the protected s. 2(*b*) sphere.... Apart from rare cases where expression is communicated in a physically violent form, ... "if the activity conveys or attempts to convey a meaning, it has expressive content and *prima facie* falls within the scope of the guarantee." In other words, the term "expression" as used in s. 2(*b*) of the *Charter* embraces all content of expression irrespective of the particular meaning or message sought to be conveyed (*Reference re ss. 193 and 195.1(1)(c) of the Criminal Code (Man.)*, [[1990] 1 S.C.R. 1123], at p. 1181, *per* Lamer J.).

... I thus find s. 319(2) to constitute an infringement of the freedom of expression guaranteed by s. 2(*b*) of the *Charter*....

VII. Section 1 Analysis of Section 319(2)

... Under the approach in *Oakes*, it must first be established that impugned state action has an objective of pressing and substantial concern in a free and democratic society. Only such an objective is of sufficient stature to warrant overriding a constitutionally protected right or freedom....

In my opinion, it would be impossible to deny that Parliament's objective in enacting s. 319(2) is of the utmost importance. Parliament has recognized the substantial harm that can flow from hate propaganda, and in trying to prevent the pain suffered by target group members and to reduce racial, ethnic and religious tension in Canada has decided to suppress the wilful promotion of hatred against identifiable groups. The nature of Parliament's objective is supported not only by the work of numerous study groups, but also by our collective historical knowledge of the potentially catastrophic effects of the promotion of hatred (*Jones*, [[1986] 2 S.C.R. 284], *per* La Forest J., at pp. 299-300). Additionally, the international commitment to eradicate hate propaganda and the stress placed upon equality and multiculturalism in the *Charter* strongly buttress the importance of this objective. I consequently find that the first part of the test under s. 1 of the *Charter* is easily satisfied and that a powerfully convincing legislative objective exists such as to justify some limit on freedom of expression.

The second branch of the *Oakes* test—proportionality—poses the most challenging questions with respect to the validity of s. 319(2) as a reasonable limit on freedom of expression in a free and democratic society. It is therefore not surprising to find most commentators, as well as the litigants in the case at bar, agreeing that the objective of the provision is of great importance, but to observe considerable disagreement when it comes to deciding whether the means chosen to further the objective are proportional to the ends....

In my opinion ... the s. 1 analysis of a limit upon s. 2(*b*) cannot ignore the nature of the expressive activity which the state seeks to restrict. While we must guard carefully against judging expression according to its popularity, it is equally destructive of free expression values, as well as the other values which underlie a free and democratic society, to treat all expression as equally crucial to those principles at the core of s. 2(*b*)....

At the core of freedom of expression lies the need to ensure that truth and the common good are attained, whether in scientific and artistic endeavors or in the process of determining the best course to take in our political affairs. Since truth and the ideal form of political and social organization can rarely, if at all, be identified with absolute certainty, it is difficult to prohibit expression without impeding the free exchange of potentially valuable information. Nevertheless, the argument from truth does not provide convincing support for the protection of hate propaganda. Taken to its extreme, this argument would require us to permit the communication of all expression, it being impossible to know with *absolute* certainty which factual statements are true, or which ideas obtain the greatest good. The problem with this extreme position, however, is that the greater the degree of certainty that a statement is erroneous or mendacious, the less its value in the quest for truth. Indeed, expression can be used to the detriment of our search for truth; the state should not be the sole arbiter of truth, but neither should we overplay the view that rationality will overcome all falsehoods in the unregulated marketplace of ideas. There is very little chance that statements intended to promote hatred against an identifiable group are true, or that their vision of society will lead to a better world....

Another component central to the rationale underlying s. 2(*b*) concerns the vital role of free expression as a means of ensuring individuals the ability to gain self-fulfillment by developing and articulating thoughts and ideas as they see fit. It is true that s. 319(2) inhibits this process among those individuals whose expression it limits, and hence arguably works against freedom of expression values. On the other hand, such self-autonomy stems in large part from one's ability to articulate and nurture an identity derived from membership in a cultural or religious group. The message put forth by individuals who fall within the ambit of s. 319(2) represents a most extreme opposition to the idea that members of identifiable groups should enjoy this aspect of the s. 2(*b*) benefit. The extent to which the unhindered promotion of this message furthers free expression values must therefore be tempered insofar as it advocates with inordinate vitriol an intolerance and prejudice which view as execrable the process of individual self-development and human flourishing among all members of society.

Moving on to a third strain of thought said to justify the protection of free expression, one's attention is brought specifically to the political realm. The connection between freedom of expression and the political process is perhaps the linchpin of the s. 2(*b*) guarantee, and the nature of this connection is largely derived from the Canadian commitment to democracy. Freedom of expression is a crucial aspect of the democratic commitment, not merely because it permits the best policies to be chosen from among a wide array of proffered options, but additionally because it helps to ensure that participation in the political process is open to all persons. Such open participation must involve to a substantial degree the notion that all persons are equally deserving of respect and dignity. The state therefore cannot act to hinder or condemn a political view without to some extent harming the openness of Canadian democracy and its associated tenet of equality for all.

The suppression of hate propaganda undeniably muzzles the participation of a few individuals in the democratic process, and hence detracts somewhat from free expression values, but the degree of this limitation is not substantial. I am aware that the use of strong language in political and social debate—indeed, perhaps even language intended to promote hatred—is an unavoidable part of the democratic process. Moreover, I recognize that hate propaganda is expression of a type which would generally be categorized as "political," thus putatively placing it at the very heart of the principle extolling freedom of expression as vital to the democratic process. Nonetheless, expression can work to undermine our commitment to democracy where employed to propagate ideas anathemic to democratic values. Hate propaganda works in just such a way, arguing as it does for a society in which the democratic process is subverted and individuals are denied respect and dignity simply because of racial or religious characteristics. This brand of expressive activity is thus wholly inimical to the democratic aspirations of the free expression guarantee.

Indeed, one may quite plausibly contend that it is through rejecting hate propaganda that the state can best encourage the protection of values central to freedom of expression, while simultaneously demonstrating dislike for the vision forwarded by hate-mongers. In this regard, the reaction to various types of expression by a democratic government may be perceived as meaningful expression on behalf of the vast majority of citizens. I do not wish to be construed as saying that an infringement of s. 2(*b*) can be justified under s. 1 merely because it is the product of a democratic process; the *Charter* will not permit even the democratically elected legislature to restrict the rights and freedoms crucial to a free and democratic society. What I do wish to emphasize, however, is that one must be careful not to accept blindly that the suppression of expression must always and unremittingly detract from values central to freedom of expression (L.C. Bollinger, *The Tolerant Society: Freedom of Speech and Extremist Speech in America* (1986), at pp. 87-93). . . .

. . . I am of the opinion that hate propaganda contributes little to the aspirations of Canadians or Canada in either the quest for truth, the promotion of individual self-development or the protection and fostering of a vibrant democracy where the participation of all individuals is accepted and encouraged. While I cannot conclude that hate propaganda deserves only marginal protection under the s. 1 analysis, I can take cognizance of the fact that limitations upon hate propaganda

are directed at a special category of expression which strays some distance from the spirit of s. 2(*b*), and hence conclude that "restrictions on expression of this kind might be easier to justify than other infringements of s. 2(*b*)" (*Royal College*, [[1990] 2 S.C.R. 232], at p. 247). . . .

Having made some preliminary comments as to the nature of the expression at stake in this appeal, it is now possible to ask whether s. 319(2) is an acceptably proportional response to Parliament's valid objective. . . .

[T]he proportionality aspect of the *Oakes* test requires the Court to decide whether the impugned state action: i) is rationally connected to the objective; ii) minimally impairs the *Charter* right or freedom at issue; and iii) does not produce effects of such severity so as to make the impairment unjustifiable. . . .

. . . Those who would uphold the provision argue that the criminal prohibition of hate propaganda obviously bears a rational connection to the legitimate Parliamentary objective of protecting target group members and fostering harmonious social relations in a community dedicated to equality and multiculturalism. I agree, for in my opinion it would be difficult to deny that the suppression of hate propaganda reduces the harm such expression does to individuals who belong to identifiable groups and to relations between various cultural and religious groups in Canadian society.

Doubts have been raised, however, as to whether the actual effect of s. 319(2) is to undermine any rational connection between it and Parliament's objective. As stated in the reasons of McLachlin J., there are three primary ways in which the effect of the impugned legislation might be seen as an irrational means of carrying out the Parliamentary purpose. First, it is argued that the provision may actually promote the cause of hate-mongers by earning them extensive media attention. In this vein, it is also suggested that persons accused of intentionally promoting hatred often see themselves as martyrs, and may actually generate sympathy from the community in the role of underdogs engaged in battle against the immense powers of the state. Second, the public may view the suppression of expression by the government with suspicion, making it possible that such expression—even if it be hate propaganda—is perceived as containing an element of truth. Finally, it is often noted, citing the writings of A. Neier, *Defending My Enemy: American Nazis, the Skokie Case, and the Risks of Freedom* (1979), that Germany of the 1920s and 1930s possessed and used hate propaganda laws similar to those existing in Canada, and yet these laws did nothing to stop the triumph of a racist philosophy under the Nazis. . . .

It is undeniable that media attention has been extensive on those occasions when s. 319(2) has been used. Yet from my perspective, s. 319(2) serves to illustrate to the public the severe reprobation with which society holds messages of hate directed towards racial and religious groups. The existence of a particular criminal law, and the process of holding a trial when that law is used, is thus itself a form of expression, and the message sent out is that hate propaganda is harmful to target group members and threatening to a harmonious society (see Rauf, ["Freedom of Expression, the Presumption of Innocence, and Reasonable Limits: An Analysis of Keegstra and Andrews" (1988), 65 C.R. (3d) 356], at p. 359). As I stated in my reasons in *R. v. Morgentaler*, [1988] 1 S.C.R. 30, at p. 70:

> The criminal law is a very special form of governmental regulation, for it seeks to express our society's collective disapprobation of certain acts and omissions.

The many, many Canadians who belong to identifiable groups surely gain a great deal of comfort from the knowledge that the hate-monger is criminally prosecuted and his or her ideas rejected. Equally, the community as a whole is reminded of the importance of diversity and multiculturalism in Canada, the value of equality and the worth and dignity of each human person being particularly emphasized.

In this context, it can also be said that government suppression of hate propaganda will not make the expression attractive and hence increase acceptance of its content. Similarly, it is very doubtful that Canadians will have sympathy for either propagators of hatred or their ideas. Governmental disapproval of hate propaganda does not invariably result in dignifying the suppressed ideology. Pornography is not dignified by its suppression, nor are defamatory statements against individuals seen as meritorious because the common law lends its support to their prohibition. Again, I stress my belief that hate propaganda legislation and trials are a means by which the values beneficial to a free and democratic society can be publicized. In this context, no dignity will be unwittingly foisted upon the convicted hate-monger or his or her philosophy, and that a hate-monger might see him or herself as a martyr is of no matter to the content of the state's message.

As for the use of hate propaganda laws in pre-World War Two Germany, I am skeptical as to the relevance of the observation that legislation similar to s. 319(2) proved ineffective in curbing the racism of the Nazis. No one is contending that hate propaganda laws can in themselves prevent the tragedy of a Holocaust; conditions particular to Germany made the rise of Nazi ideology possible despite the existence and use of these laws (see A. Doskow and S.B. Jacoby, "Anti-Semitism and the Law in Pre-Nazi Germany" (1940), 3 *Contemporary Jewish Record* 498, at p. 509). Rather, hate propaganda laws are one part of a free and democratic society's bid to prevent the spread of racism, and their rational connection to this objective must be seen in such a context. Certainly West Germany has not

reacted to the failure of pre-war laws by seeking their removal, a new set of criminal offences having been implemented as recently as 1985 (see E. Stein, "History Against Free Speech: The New German Law Against the 'Auschwitz'—and other—'Lies'" (1987), 85 *Mich. L. Rev.* 277). Nor, as has been discussed, has the international community regarded the promulgation of laws suppressing hate propaganda as futile or counter-productive. Indeed, this Court's attention has been drawn to the fact that a great many countries possess legislation similar to that found in Canada....

In sum, having found that the purpose of the challenged legislation is valid, I also find that the means chosen to further this purpose are rational in both theory and operation, and therefore conclude that the first branch of the proportionality test has been met....

The criminal nature of the impugned provision, involving the associated risks of prejudice through prosecution, conviction and the imposition of up to two years imprisonment, indicates that the means embodied in hate propaganda legislation should be carefully tailored so as to minimize impairment of the freedom of expression....

It is ... submitted that the legislation is overbroad, its terms so wide as to include expression which does not relate to Parliament's objective, and also unduly vague, in that a lack of clarity and precision in its words prevents individuals from discerning its meaning with any accuracy. In either instance, it is said that the effect of s. 319(2) is to limit the expression of merely unpopular or unconventional communications. Such communications may present no risk of causing the harm which Parliament seeks to prevent, and will perhaps be closely associated with the core values of s. 2(*b*). This overbreadth and vagueness could consequently allow the state to employ s. 319(2) to infringe excessively the freedom of expression or, what is more likely, could have a chilling effect whereby persons potentially within s. 319(2) would exercise self-censorship....

In assessing the constitutionality of s. 319(2), especially as concerns arguments of overbreadth and vagueness, an immediate observation is that statements made "in private conversation" are not included in the criminalized expression.... [A] conversation or communication intended to be private does not satisfy the requirements of the provision if through accident or negligence an individual's expression of hatred for an identifiable group is made public.

Is s. 319(2) nevertheless overbroad because it captures *all* public expression intended to promote hatred? It would appear not, for the harm which the government seeks to prevent is not restricted to certain mediums and/or locations. To attempt to distinguish between various forms and fora would therefore be incongruent with Parliament's legitimate objective.

A second important element of s. 319(2) is its requirement that the promotion of hatred be "wilful." [T]his mental element . . . is satisfied only where an accused subjectively desires the promotion of hatred or foresees such a consequence as certain or substantially certain to result from an act done in order to achieve some other purpose. . . . This mental element, requiring more than merely negligence or recklessness as to result, significantly restricts the reach of the provision, and thereby reduces the scope of the targeted expression. . . .

It has been argued, however, that even a demanding *mens rea* component fails to give s. 319(2) a constitutionally acceptable breadth. The problem is said to lie in the failure of the offence to require proof of actual hatred resulting from a communication, the assumption being that only such proof can demonstrate a harm serious enough to justify limiting the freedom of expression under s. 1. . . . [However, to] predicate the limitation of free expression upon proof of actual hatred gives insufficient attention to the severe psychological trauma suffered by members of those identifiable groups targeted by hate propaganda. [Moreover], it is clearly difficult to prove a causative link between a specific statement and hatred of an identifiable group. In fact, to require direct proof of hatred in listeners would severely debilitate the effectiveness of s. 319(2) in achieving Parliament's aim. It is well accepted that Parliament can use the criminal law to prevent the risk of serious harms, a leading example being the drinking and driving provisions in the *Criminal Code*. . . . I conclude that proof of actual hatred is not required in order to justify a limit under s. 1.

The next feature of the provision that must be explored is the phrase "promotes hatred against any identifiable group." . . . In "promotes" we . . . have a word that indicates more than simple encouragement or advancement. The hate-monger must intend or foresee as substantially certain a direct and active stimulation of hatred against an identifiable group. As for the term "identifiable group," s. 318(4) states that an "'identifiable group' means any section of the public distinguished by colour, race, religion or ethnic origin." The act to be targeted is therefore the intentional fostering of hatred against particular members of our society, as opposed to any individual.

The meaning of "hatred" remains to be elucidated. Just as "wilfully" must be interpreted in the setting of s. 319(2), so must the word "hatred" be defined according to the context in which it is found. A dictionary definition may be of limited aid to such an exercise, for by its nature a dictionary seeks to offer a panoply of possible usages, rather than the correct meaning of a word as contemplated by Parliament. Noting the purpose of s. 319(2), in my opinion the term "hatred" connotes emotion of an intense and extreme nature that is clearly associated with vilification and detestation. . . . Hatred is predicated on destruction, and hatred against identifiable groups therefore thrives on insensitivity, bigotry and destruction of both the target group and of the values of our society. Hatred in this sense is a most extreme emotion that belies reason; an emotion that, if exercised against members of an identifiable group, implies that those individuals are to be despised, scorned, denied respect and made subject to ill-treatment on the basis of group affiliation. . . .

. . . [T]he sense in which "hatred" is used in s. 319(2) does not denote a wide range of diverse emotions, but is circumscribed so as to cover only the most intense form of dislike. . . .

The factors mentioned above suggest that s. 319(2) does not unduly restrict the s. 2(*b*) guarantee. The terms of the offence, as I have defined them, rather indicate that s. 319(2) possesses definitional limits which act as safeguards to ensure that it will capture only expressive activity which is openly hostile to Parliament's objective, and will thus attack only the harm at which the prohibition is targeted. The specific defences provided are further glosses on the purview of the offence. . . .

[Chief Justice Dickson then considers the defences to "wilful promotion of hatred" that are provided by section 319(3). That section reads as follows:

(3) No person shall be convicted of an offence under subsection (2)

(*a*) if he establishes that the statements communicated were true;

(*b*) if, in good faith, he expressed or attempted to establish by argument an opinion on a religious subject;

(*c*) if the statements were relevant to any subject of public interest, the discussion of which was for the public benefit, and if on reasonable grounds he believed them to be true; or

(*d*) if, in good faith, he intended to point out, for the purpose of removal, matters producing or tending to produce feelings of hatred towards an identifiable group in Canada.]

A careful reading of the s. 319(3) defences shows them to take in examples of expressive activity that generally would not fall within the "wilful promotion of hatred" as I have defined the phrase. . . . [O]nly rarely will one who intends to promote hatred be acting in good faith or upon honest belief. These defences are hence intended to aid in making the scope of the wilful promotion of hatred more explicit. . . .

. . . [I]f a situation arises where an individual uses statements of truth in order to promote hatred against identifiable groups, the accused is acquitted despite the existence of the harm which Parliament seeks to prevent. . . .

It has been forcefully argued before us that the defence of truth is insufficient protection against an overly broad hate propaganda law. In this vein, it is rightly pointed out that many (if not most) of the communications coming within s. 319(2) are not susceptible to a true/false categorization, existing instead as ideas or opinions in the mind of the communicator. The accused could therefore sincerely believe in the worth of his or her viewpoint and yet be unable to utilize the s. 319(3)(*a*) defence. Moreover, it is said that, even where a statement is capable of categorization as true or false, the individual honestly mistaken as to the validity of his or her position (even if innocently so) is left unprotected, a result which dangerously restricts freedom of expression, causing a "chill" on communications as those who fear that their statements may be false exercise self-censorship. Finally, one might wonder if the courts are not on dangerous ground in attempting to distinguish between truthfulness and falsehood. The potential for bias in making such a determination, be it intentional or subconscious, is a danger frequently noted in freedom of expression theory (this potential is equally evident in s. 319(3)(*c*), insofar as ideas are assessed in light of "reasonableness" and the "public benefit").

The way in which I have defined the s. 319(2) offence, in the context of the objective sought by society and the value of the prohibited expression, gives me some doubt as to whether the *Charter* mandates that truthful statements communicated *with an intention to promote hatred* need be excepted from criminal condemnation. Truth may be used for widely disparate ends, and I find it difficult to accept that circumstances exist where factually accurate statements can be used for no other purpose than to stir up hatred against a racial or religious group. It would seem to follow that there is no reason why the individual who intentionally employs such statements to achieve harmful ends must *under the Charter* be protected from criminal censure.

Nevertheless, it is open to Parliament to make a concession to free expression values, whether or not such is required by the *Charter*. Deference to truth as a value central to free expression has thus led Parliament to include the defence in s. 319(3)(*a*), even though the accused has used truthful statements to cause harm of the type falling squarely within the objective of the legislation. When the statement contains no truth, however, this flicker of justification for the intentional promotion of hatred is extinguished, and the harmful malice of the disseminator stands alone.…

Because the presence of truth, though legally a defence to a charge under s. 319(2), does not change the fact that the accused has intended to promote the hatred of an identifiable group, I cannot find excessive impairment of the freedom of expression merely because s. 319(3)(*a*) does not cover negligent or innocent error. Whether or not a statement is susceptible to classification as true or false, my inclination is therefore to accept that such error should not excuse an accused who has wilfully used a statement in order to promote hatred against an identifiable group. That the legislative line is drawn so as to convict the accused who is negligent or even innocent regarding the accuracy of his or her statements is perfectly acceptable, for the mistake is not as to the use to which the information is put, namely, the promotion of hatred against an identifiable group. As for the argument that the courts and legislature should not involve themselves in the evaluation of "truth," "reasonable grounds for finding truth" or "public interest," the same response applies. Where the likelihood of truth or benefit from an idea diminishes to the point of vanishing, and the statement in question has harmful consequences inimical to the most central values of a free and democratic society, it is not excessively problematic to make a judgment that involves limiting expression.

… I should comment on a final argument marshalled in support of striking down s. 319(2) because of overbreadth or vagueness. It is said that the presence of the legislation has led authorities to interfere with a diverse range of political, educational and artistic expression, demonstrating only too well the way in which overbreadth and vagueness can result in undue intrusion and the threat of persecution. In this regard, a number of incidents are cited where authorities appear to have been overzealous in their interpretation of the law, including the arrest of individuals distributing pamphlets admonishing Americans to leave the country and the temporary holdup at the border of a film entitled *Nelson Mandela* and Salman Rushdie's novel *Satanic Verses*.…

… [O]ne can safely say that the incidents mentioned above illustrate not over-expansive breadth and vagueness in the law, but rather actions by the state which cannot be lawfully taken pursuant to s. 319(2). The possibility of *illegal* police harassment clearly has minimal bearing on the proportionality of hate propaganda legislation to legitimate Parliamentary objectives, and hence the argument based on such harassment can be rejected.

… [E]ven though the terms of s. 319(2) and the nature of the available defences expose an individual to conviction only in narrow and clearly defined circumstances, it is said that non-criminal responses can more effectively combat the harm caused by hate propaganda. Most generally, it is said that discriminatory ideas can best be met with information and education programmes extolling the merits of tolerance and cooperation between racial and religious groups. As for the prohibition of hate propaganda, human rights statutes are pointed to as being a less severe and more effective response than the criminal law. Such statutes not only subject the disseminator of hate propaganda to reduced stigma and punishment, but also take a less confrontational approach to the suppression of such expression. This conciliatory tack is said to be preferable to penal sanction because an incentive is offered the disseminator to cooperate with human rights tribunals and thus to amend his or her conduct. . . .

In assessing the proportionality of a legislative enactment to a valid governmental objective, however, s. 1 should not operate in every instance so as to force the government to rely upon only the mode of intervention least intrusive of a *Charter* right or freedom. It may be that a number of courses of action are available in the furtherance of a pressing and substantial objective, each imposing a varying degree of restriction upon a right or freedom. In such circumstances, the government may legitimately employ a more restrictive measure, either alone or as part of a larger programme of action, if that measure is not redundant, furthering the objective in ways that alternative responses could not, and is in all other respects proportionate to a valid s. 1 aim.

. . . At the moment, for example, the state has the option of responding to hate propaganda by acting under either the *Criminal Code* or human rights provisions. In my view, having both avenues of redress at the state's disposal is justified in a free and democratic society. I see no reason to assume that the state will always utilize the most severe tool at hand, namely, the criminal law, to prevent the dissemination of hate propaganda. Where use of the sanction provided by s. 319(2) is imprudent, employing human rights legislation may be the more attractive route to take, but there may equally be circumstances in which the more confrontational response of criminal prosecution is best suited to punish a recalcitrant hate-monger. To send out a strong message of condemnation, both reinforcing the values underlying s. 319(2) and deterring the few individuals who would harm target group members and the larger community by intentionally communicating hate propaganda, will occasionally require use of the criminal law.

To summarize . . . I find that the terms of s. 319(2) create a narrowly confined offence which suffers from neither overbreadth nor vagueness. . . .

The third branch of the proportionality test entails a weighing of the importance of the state objective against the effect of limits imposed upon a *Charter* right or guarantee. Even if the purpose of the limiting measure is substantial and the first two components of the proportionality test are satisfied, the deleterious effects of a limit may be too great to permit the infringement of the right or guarantee in issue.

. . . It will by now be quite clear that I do not view the infringement of s. 2(*b*) by s. 319(2) as a restriction of the most serious kind. The expressive activity at which this provision aims is of a special category, a category only tenuously connected with the values underlying the guarantee of freedom of speech. Moreover, the narrowly drawn terms of s. 319(2) and its defences prevent the prohibition of expression lying outside of this narrow category. Consequently, the suppression of hate propaganda affected by s. 319(2) represents an impairment of the individual's freedom of expression which is not of a most serious nature.

It is also apposite to stress yet again the enormous importance of the objective fueling s. 319(2), an objective of such magnitude as to support even the severe response of criminal prohibition. Few concerns can be as central to the concept of a free and democratic society as the dissipation of racism, and the especially strong value which Canadian society attaches to this goal must never be forgotten in assessing the effects of an impugned legislative measure. When the purpose of s. 319(2) is thus recognized, I have little trouble in finding that its effects, involving as they do the restriction of expression largely removed from the heart of free expression values, are not of such a deleterious nature as to outweigh any advantage gleaned from the limitation of s. 2(*b*). . . .

LA FOREST J. (dissenting): I agree with Justice McLachlin on the issues respecting freedom of expression and I would accordingly dispose of the appeal and answer the first two constitutional questions as she does. I find it unnecessary to consider the issues respecting the right to be presumed innocent and, in consequence, to answer the other constitutional questions.

The reasons of Sopinka and McLachlin JJ. were delivered by

McLACHLIN J. (dissenting):

[Lengthy sections of Justice McLachlin's opinion, in which she essentially agrees with Dickson that the law in question infringes section 2(*b*) of the *Charter* and must be justified under section 1, are omitted. Justice McLachlin agrees, moreover, that the law meets the "pressing and substantial" purpose component of the *Oakes* test. She dissents on all three components of the "proportional means" dimension of the *Oakes* test.]

The first question [under the proportionality test] is whether s. 319(2) of the *Criminal Code* may be seen as carefully designed or rationally connected to the objectives which it is aimed at promoting. . . .

. . . [I]t is clear that the legislation does, at least at one level, further Parliament's objectives. Prosecutions of individuals for offensive material directed at a particular group may bolster its members' beliefs that they are valued and respected in their community, and that the views of a malicious few do not reflect those of the population as a whole. Such a use of the criminal law may well affirm certain values and priorities which are of a pressing and substantial nature.

It is necessary, however, to go further, and consider not only Parliament's intention, but whether, given the actual effect of the legislation, a rational connection exists between it and its objectives. Legislation designed to promote an objective may in fact impede that objective. In *R. v. Morgentaler*, [1988] 1 S.C.R. 30, this Court considered the actual effect of abortion legislation designed to preserve women's life and health and found that it had the opposite effect of the legislative goals by imposing unreasonable procedural requirements and delays. This Court was particularly mindful of the effects that these requirements had in practice of substantially increasing the risks to the health of pregnant women, especially in certain locations. Dickson C.J. treated this in the context of rational connection, stating, "to the extent that s. 251(4) is designed to protect the life and health of women, the procedures it establishes may actually defeat that objective" (pp. 75–76).

This approach recognizes that s. 1 of the *Charter* could easily become diluted if an intention on the part of government to act on behalf of a disadvantaged group sufficed in all cases to establish the necessary rational connection between the legislation and its objective. In some cases the link between the intention of the legislators and the achievement of the goal may be self-evident. In others, there may be doubt about whether the legislation will in fact achieve its ends; in resolving that doubt deference must be paid to the Parliament and the legislatures. But in cases such as *Morgentaler*, where it appears that the legislation not only may fail to achieve its goal but may have a contrary effect, the Court is justified in finding that the rational connection between the measure and the objective is absent....

In my view, s. 319(2) of the *Criminal Code* falls in this class of case. Section 319(2) may well have a chilling effect on defensible expression by law-abiding citizens. At the same time, it is far from clear that it provides an effective way of curbing hate-mongers. Indeed, many have suggested it may promote their cause. Prosecutions under the *Criminal Code* for racist expression have attracted extensive media coverage. Zundel, prosecuted not under s. 319(2) but for the crime of spreading false news (s. 181), claimed that his court battle had given him "a million dollars worth of publicity": *Globe and Mail*, March 1, 1985, p. P1. There is an unmistakable hint of the joy of martyrdom in some of the literature for which Andrews, in the companion appeal, was prosecuted: ...

Not only does the criminal process confer on the accused publicity for his dubious causes—it may even bring him sympathy. The criminal process is cast as a conflict between the accused and the state, a conflict in which the accused may appear at his most sympathetic. Franz Kafka was not being entirely whimsical when he wrote, "If you have the right eye for these things, you can see that accused men are often attractive" (*The Trial* (1976), at p. 203).

The argument that criminal prosecutions for this kind of expression will reduce racism and foster multiculturalism depends on the assumption that some listeners are gullible enough to believe the expression if exposed to it. But if this assumption is valid, these listeners might be just as likely to believe that there must be some truth in the racist expression because the government is trying to suppress it. Theories of a grand conspiracy between government and elements of society wrongly perceived as malevolent can become all too appealing if government dignifies them by completely suppressing their utterance. It is therefore not surprising that the criminalization of hate propaganda and prosecutions under such legislation have been subject to so much controversy in this country.

Historical evidence also gives reason to be suspicious of the claim that hate propaganda laws contribute to the cause of multiculturalism and equality. This evidence is summarized by A.A. Borovoy, *When Freedoms Collide: The Case for our Civil Liberties* (1988), at p. 50:

> Remarkably, pre-Hitler Germany had laws very much like the Canadian anti-hate law. Moreover, those laws were enforced with some vigour. During the fifteen years before Hitler came to power, there were more than two hundred prosecutions based on anti-semitic speech. And, in the opinion of the leading Jewish organization of that era, no more than 10 per cent of the cases were mishandled by the authorities. As subsequent history so painfully testifies, this type of legislation proved ineffectual on the one occasion when there was a real argument for it. Indeed, there is some indication that the Nazis of pre-Hitler Germany shrewdly exploited their criminal trials in order to increase the size of their constituency. They used the trials as platforms to propagate their message.

Viewed from the point of view of actual effect, the rational connection between s. 319(2) and the goals it promotes may be argued to be tenuous. Certainly it cannot be said that there is a strong and evident connection between the criminalization of hate propaganda and its suppression.

The second matter which must be considered in determining whether the infringement represented by the legislation is proportionate to its ends is whether the legislation impairs the right to the minimum extent possible.

... Despite the limitations found in s. 319(2), a strong case can be made that it is overbroad in that its definition of offending speech may catch many expressions which should be protected.

The first difficulty lies in the different interpretations which may be placed on the word "hatred." The *Shorter Oxford English Dictionary* defines "hatred" as: "The condition or state of relations in which one person hates another; the emotion of hate; active dislike, detestation; enmity, ill-will, malevolence." The wide range of diverse emotions which the word "hatred" is capable of denoting is evident from this definition. Those who defend its use in s. 319(2) of the *Criminal Code* emphasize one end of this range—hatred, they say, indicates the most powerful of virulent emotions lying beyond the bounds of human decency and limiting s. 319(2) to extreme materials. Those who object to its use point to the other end of the range, insisting that "active dislike" is not an emotion for the promotion of which a person should be convicted as a criminal. To state the arguments is to make the case; "hatred" is a broad term capable of catching a wide variety of emotion.

It is not only the breadth of the term "hatred" which presents dangers; it is its subjectivity. "Hatred" is proved by inference—the inference of the jury or the judge who sits as trier of fact—and inferences are more likely to be drawn when the speech is unpopular. The subjective and emotional nature of the concept of promoting hatred compounds the difficulty of ensuring that only cases meriting prosecution are pursued and that only those whose conduct is calculated to dissolve the social bonds of society are convicted. . . . It is argued that the requirement of "wilful promotion" eliminates from the ambit of s. 319(2) statements which are made for honest purposes such as telling a perceived truth or contributing to a political or social debate. The difficulty with this argument is that those purposes are compatible with the intention (or presumed intention by reason of foreseeability) of promoting hatred. A belief that what one says about a group is true and important to political and social debate is quite compatible with and indeed may inspire an intention to promote active dislike of that group. Such a belief is equally compatible with foreseeing that promotion of such dislike may stem from one's statements. The result is that people who make statements primarily for non-nefarious reasons may be convicted of wilfully promoting hatred.

The absence of any requirement that actual harm or incitement to hatred be shown further broadens the scope of s. 319(2) of the *Criminal Code*. This, in the view of the Court of Appeal, was the section's main defect. In effect, the provision makes a crime not only of actually inciting others to hatred, but also of attempting to do so. The Court of Appeal accepted the argument that this made the crime, at least potentially, a victimless one. . . .

Though I regard this breadth as a relevant factor, I would be hesitant to treat it as constitutionally determinative. To view hate propaganda as "victimless" in the absence of any proof that it moved its listeners to hatred is to discount the wrenching impact that it may have on members of the target group themselves. For Jews, many of whom have personally been touched by the terrible consequences of the degeneration of a seemingly civilized society into unparalleled barbarism, statements such as Keegstra's may raise very real fears of history repeating itself. Moreover, it is simply not possible to assess with any precision the effects that expression of a particular message will have on all those who are ultimately exposed to it. The process of "proving" that listeners were moved to hatred has a fictitious air about it. These considerations undermine the notion that we can draw a bright line between provisions which are justifiable because they require proof that hatred actually resulted, and provisions which are unjustifiable because they require only an intent to promote hatred.

The breadth of s. 319(2) is narrowed somewhat by the defences. Statements made in good faith on religious subjects and statements on matters of public interest which the accused reasonably believed to be true, as well as statements made for the purpose of removing hatred, are exempted.

Quite apart from the fact that the onus lies on the accused to prove these defences, it is far from clear that in practice they significantly narrow the ambit of s. 319(2) of the *Criminal Code*. The most important defence is truth—if the accused establishes that his statements are true, s. 319(2) is not violated. On the other hand, as already mentioned, conviction may result for true statements given that the onus of proof lies on the accused. Moreover, the concepts of "truth" and "reasonable belief in truth" may not always be applicable. Statements of opinion may be incapable of being classified as true or false, communicating not facts so much as sentiments and beliefs. Polemic statements frequently do not lend themselves to proof of truth or falsity. As for the defence of reasonable belief, how is a court to evaluate the reasonableness of diverse theories, political or otherwise? The defence of statements in the public interest poses similar problems. How is a court to determine what is in the public interest, given the wide range of views which may be held on matters potentially caught by s. 319(2)?

Not only is the category of speech caught by s. 319(2) defined broadly. The application of the definition of offending speech, i.e., the circumstances in which the offending statements are prohibited, is virtually unlimited. Only private conversations are exempt from state scrutiny. Section 319(2) is calculated to prevent absolutely expression of the offending ideas in any and all public forums through any and all mediums. Speeches are caught. The corner soap-box is no longer open. Books, films and works of art—all these fall under the censor's scrutiny because of s. 319(2) of the *Criminal Code*.

The real answer to the debate about whether s. 319(2) is overbroad is provided by the section's track record. Although the section is of relatively recent origin, it has provoked many questionable actions on the part of the authorities. There have been no reported convictions, other than the instant appeals. But the record amply demonstrates that intemperate statements about identifiable groups, particularly if they represent an unpopular viewpoint, may attract state involvement or calls for police action. Novels such as Leon Uris's pro-Zionist novel, *The Haj,* face calls for banning: *Toronto Star,* September 26, 1984, p. A6. Other works, such as Salman Rushdie's *Satanic Verses,* are stopped at the border on the ground that they violate s. 319(2). Films may be temporarily kept out, as happened to a film entitled *Nelson Mandela,* ordered as an educational film by Ryerson Polytechnic Institute in 1986: *Globe and Mail,* December 24, 1986, p. A14. Arrests are even made for distributing pamphlets containing the words "Yankee Go Home": *Globe and Mail,* July 4, 1975, p. 1. Experience shows that many cases are winnowed out due to prosecutorial discretion and other factors. It shows equally, however, that initially quite a lot of speech is caught by s. 319(2).

Even where investigations are not initiated or prosecutions pursued, the vagueness and subjectivity inherent in s. 319(2) of the *Criminal Code* give ground for concern that the chilling effect of the law may be substantial. . . . The danger here is not so much that the legislation will deter those bent on promoting hatred—in so far as it does so (and of this I remain skeptical) it is arguably not overbroad. The danger is rather that the legislation may have a chilling effect on legitimate activities important to our society by subjecting innocent persons to constraints born out of a fear of the criminal process. Given the vagueness of the prohibition of expression in s. 319(2), one may ask how speakers are to know when their speech may be seen as encroaching on the forbidden area. The reaction is predictable. The combination of overbreadth and criminalization may well lead people desirous of avoiding even the slightest brush with the criminal law to protect themselves in the best way they can—by confining their expression to non-controversial matters. Novelists may steer clear of controversial characterizations of ethnic characteristics, such as Shakespeare's portrayal of Shylock in *The Merchant of Venice.* Scientists may well think twice before researching and publishing results of research suggesting difference between ethnic or racial groups. Given the serious consequences of criminal prosecution, it is not entirely speculative to suppose that even political debate on crucial issues such as immigration, educa-tional language rights, foreign ownership and trade may be tempered. These matters go to the heart of the traditional justifications for protecting freedom of expression.

This brings me to the second aspect of minimum impairment. The examples I have just given suggest that the very fact of criminalization itself may be argued to represent an excessive response to the problem of hate propagation. The procedures and sanctions associated with the criminal law are comparatively severe. Given the stigma that attaches and the freedom which is at stake, the contest between the individual and the state imposed by a criminal trial must be regarded as difficult and harrowing in the extreme. The seriousness of the imprisonment which may follow conviction requires no comment. Moreover, the chilling effect of prohibitions on expression is at its most severe where they are effected by means of the criminal law. It is this branch of the law more than any other which the ordinary, law-abiding citizen seeks to avoid. The additional sanction of the criminal law may pose little deterrent to a convinced hate-monger who may welcome the publicity it brings; it may, however, deter the ordinary individual.

Moreover, it is arguable whether criminalization of expression calculated to promote racial hatred is necessary. Other remedies are perhaps more appropriate and more effective. Discrimination on grounds of race and religion is worthy of suppression. Human rights legislation, focusing on reparation rather than punishment, has had considerable success in discouraging such conduct. This is the conclusion of Borovoy, op. cit., at pp. 221-25. After noting the emphasis in human rights codes on amendment of conduct and their general success in effecting settlements before hearing, Borovoy addresses the suggestion that "racial discriminators be prose-cuted or sued without having any opportunity to make amends" (p. 223). He concludes that criminal prosecution is not only unnecessary, but may be counterproductive. It is unnecessary because proceedings under the human rights codes show strong success in achieving their essential purpose, the curtailment of discrimination. It may be counterproduc-tive in that: (1) racial discriminators threatened with prosecu-tion may have little or no incentive to cooperate with human rights boards and voluntarily amend their conduct (p. 223); and (2) it leaves open the argument that "where a prosecutorial remedy exists, the state is obliged to adopt such a route first" (p. 225), thereby eliminating the possibility of voluntary amendment of conduct. For these reasons, Borovoy concludes that: "[a]part from collateral matters such as obstructing com-plaint investigations, the criminal process can safely be elimi-nated from human rights matters" (p. 225).

It is true that the focus of most human rights legislation is acts rather than words. But if it is inappropriate and ineffective to criminalize discriminatory conduct, it must necessarily be unjustifiable to criminalize discriminatory expression falling short of conduct.

Finally, it can be argued that greater precision is required in the criminal law than, for example, in human rights legislation because of the different character of the two types of proceedings. The consequences of alleging a violation of s. 319(2) of the *Criminal Code* are direct and serious in the extreme. Under the human rights process a tribunal has considerable discretion in determining what messages or conduct should be banned and by its order may indicate more precisely their exact nature, all of which occurs before any consequences inure to the alleged violator.

In summary, s. 319(2) of the *Criminal Code* catches a broad range of speech and prohibits it in a broad manner, allowing only private conversations to escape scrutiny. Moreover, the process by which the prohibition is effected—the criminal law—is the severest our society can impose and is arguably unnecessary given the availability of alternate remedies. I conclude that the criminalization of hate statements does not impair free speech to the minimum extent permitted by its objectives.

The third consideration in determining whether the infringement represented by the legislation is proportionate to the ends is the balance between the importance of the infringement of the right in question and the benefit conferred by the legislation. The analysis is essentially a cost-benefit analysis. . . .

I deal first with the significance of the infringement of the constitutionally guaranteed freedom at issue in this case. Viewed from the perspective of our society as a whole, the infringement of the guarantee of freedom of expression before this Court is a serious one. Section 319(2) of the *Criminal Code* does not merely regulate the form or tone of expression—it strikes directly at its content and at the viewpoints of individuals. It strikes, moreover, at viewpoints in widely diverse domains, whether artistic, social or political. It is capable of catching not only statements like those at issue in this case, but works of art and the intemperate statement made in the heat of social controversy. While few may actually be prosecuted to conviction under s. 319(2), many fall within the shadow of its broad prohibition. These dangers are exacerbated by the fact that s. 319(2) applies to all public expression. In short, the limitation on freedom of expression created by s. 319(2) of the *Criminal Code* invokes all of the values upon which s. 2(*b*) of the *Charter* rests—the value of fostering a vibrant and creative society through the marketplace of

ideas; the value of the vigourous and open debate essential to democratic government and preservation of our rights and freedoms; and the value of a society which fosters the self-actualization and freedom of its members.

The consequences of the infringement of freedom of speech imposed by s. 319(2) of the *Criminal Code* considered from the viewpoint of the individual caught within its net are equally serious. The exercise of the right of free speech contrary to its provisions may result in a criminal record and imprisonment of up to two years. No warning, other than the description in s. 319(2) itself (which necessarily includes subjective elements), is given as to what speech is liable to result in prosecution. And those individuals not caught may find their expression restricted by the fear of running afoul of a vague and subjective law.

These considerations establish an infringement of the guarantee of freedom of expression of the most serious nature—much more serious, for example, than that which this Court upheld under s. 1 in *Irwin Toy*. There the only value which could be prayed in aid of free expression was the right to earn a profit. Section 319(2) of the *Criminal Code*, in contrast, touches on values vital to the preservation of democratic government and our fundamental rights and freedoms, as well as our right to individual self-actualization. And its broad sweep makes the infringement it effects not only serious in nature, but in extent. An infringement of this seriousness can only be justified by a countervailing state interest of the most compelling nature.

I turn then to the other side of the scale and the benefit to be gained by maintenance of the limitation on freedom of expression effected by s. 319(2) of the *Criminal Code*. As indicated earlier, there is no question but that the objectives which underlie this legislation are of a most worthy nature. Unfortunately, the claims of gains to be achieved at the cost of the infringement of free speech represented by s. 319(2) are tenuous. It is far from clear that the legislation does not promote the cause of hate-mongering extremists and hinder the possibility of voluntary amendment of conduct more than it discourages the spread of hate propaganda. Accepting the importance to our society of the goals of social harmony and individual dignity, of multiculturalism and equality, it remains difficult to see how s. 319(2) fosters them.

In my opinion, the result is clear. Any questionable benefit of the legislation is outweighed by the significant infringement on the constitutional guarantee of free expression effected by s. 319(2) of the *Criminal Code*. . . .

R. v. Seaboyer, 1991

Few *Charter* decisions have provoked as much opposition as the *Seaboyer* ruling. A 7-to-2 majority ruled unconstitutional what is commonly referred to as rape-shield legislation. The legislation represented Parliament's second attempt to address what it considered to be prejudicial assumptions in how the common law has historically dealt with sexual assaults, which, overwhelmingly, are committed against women. Before the legislation, the common law permitted questioning about the prior sexual conduct of a complainant without proof of how this information was relevant to a specific issue in the trial. This form of questioning would often undermine the credibility of the woman who alleged she had been sexually assaulted, by allowing inferences to be drawn that she was not to be believed and had likely consented to the alleged sexual assault. This legal tactic also had the effect of discouraging many women from pressing or pursuing claims that they had been sexually assaulted.

The legislation subject to the *Charter* challenge in *Seaboyer* was introduced in 1982. It prevented defence lawyers from cross-examining and leading evidence about a complainant's sexual conduct with three exceptions: rebuttal evidence, evidence going to identity, and evidence relating to consent to sexual activity on the same occasion as the trial incident. The Court was seriously divided about whether the excluded information undermines the *Charter* right to make a full answer and defence to the charge of sexual assault. The majority concluded that the impugned legislation had the potential to exclude otherwise admissible evidence that might be highly relevant to the defence. The dissenting judges did not accept that a *Charter* right had been violated because they believed the legislation excluded only irrelevant or prejudicial evidence. Justice L'Heureux-Dubé, who wrote the dissenting judgment, indicated that even if a case could be made that the legislation excludes relevant evidence, this evidence would be so prejudicial that its exclusion would be justified.

The Court's ruling provoked widespread criticism, particularly from women's groups who worried that the ruling would preserve inappropriate stereotypes about women and sexual assault and that it would also discourage the reporting of sexual assault. The decision also generated broad public discussion about when, if ever, a woman's sexual history is relevant in the context of sexual assault trials. Initially, the federal government indicated it would try to address the majority's concerns about the exclusionary rule. But after extensive lobbying by and consultation with women's groups, Kim Campbell, then Minister of Justice, interpreted the situation as an opportunity to fundamentally change the way the law deals with sexual assault, by addressing and defining consent in sexual relations.

The proposed legislation was subject to extensive review by a parliamentary committee created for that specific purpose, in a rare example where *Charter* considerations assumed a prominent part of parliamentary review and debate. The new legislation amended the *Criminal Code* to define consent in sexual relations, and to make it clear that consent cannot be presumed to have been given based on a woman's conduct or her previous sexual history. The legislation now requires that all reasonable steps be taken to ascertain that consent has been given and explicitly states that mistaken belief about consent is not a valid consideration at trial if it arises from situations of intoxication, recklessness, or wilful blindness. Thus, while the earlier law had allowed an accused to be acquitted if able to convince the judge or jury of an honest belief that the victim had consented, the new legislation makes this defence much more difficult to establish.

Despite all-party support for the legislation, the measures were extremely controversial. Many of the critics were defence lawyers, who argued that the legislation would undermine a fair trial, while other critics mocked the new rape-shield provisions as being more consistent with contract law than criminal law, suggesting that the legislation did not reflect a realistic portrayal of sexual relationships between men and women. Many women's groups rejected the claim that innocent men would be convicted under these measures and argued that if a man is uncertain after taking reasonable steps to ensure that his partner has consented to a sexual act, he should simply abstain.

An interesting aspect of the parliamentary response was the extent to which the legislation appears as a conversation initiated by Parliament to the Court (well before the metaphor of dialogue would become a popular way of characterizing the institutional relationship between Parliament and the judiciary). The legislation was presented as Parliament's efforts to balance conflicting *Charter* rights, and not simply as the protection of the right to a fair trial as the majority had framed the issue, and included a preamble that expressed Parliament's assumptions about how the *Charter* appropriately resolves the relevant issues. In the preamble, Parliament expressed its "grave" concerns about sexual violence, its belief that the right to a fair trial coexists with a woman's right to equality and security, and its view (in contradiction to the majority's ruling) that "evidence of the complainant's sexual history is rarely relevant and that its admission should be subject to particular scrutiny, bearing in mind the inherently prejudicial character of such evidence."

The legislation was subsequently challenged, and upheld by a unanimous Supreme Court as consistent with the *Charter* in *R. v. Darrach*.[1] ⁓

---

1   [2000] 2 S.C.R. 443.

R. v. SEABOYER; R. v. GAYME
[1991] 2 S.C.R. 577

Hearing: March 26, 27, 1991; Judgment: August 22, 1991.

Present: Lamer C.J. and La Forest, L'Heureux-Dubé, Sopinka, Gonthier, Cory, McLachlin, Stevenson, and Iacobucci JJ.

Interveners: The Attorney General of Canada, the Attorney General of Quebec, the Attorney General for Saskatchewan, the Canadian Civil Liberties Association, and Women's Legal Education and Action Fund et al.

The judgment of Lamer C.J. and La Forest, Sopinka, Cory, McLachlin, Stevenson, and Iacobucci JJ. was delivered by

McLACHLIN J.: These cases raise the issue of the constitutionality of ss. 276 and 277 of the *Criminal Code*, R.S.C., 1985, c. C-46 (formerly ss. 246.6 and 246.7), commonly known as the "rape-shield" provisions. The provisions restrict the right of the defence on a trial for a sexual offence to cross-examine and lead evidence of a complainant's sexual conduct on other occasions. The question is whether these restrictions offend the guarantees accorded to an accused person by the *Canadian Charter of Rights and Freedoms*.

My conclusion is that one of the sections in issue, s. 276, offends the *Charter*. While its purpose—the abolition of outmoded, sexist-based use of sexual conduct evidence—is laudable, its effect goes beyond what is required or justified by that purpose. At the same time, striking down s. 276 does not imply reversion to the old common law rules, which permitted evidence of the complainant's sexual conduct even though it might have no probative value to the issues on the case and, on the contrary, might mislead the jury. Instead, relying on the basic principles that actuate our law of evidence, the courts must seek a middle way that offers the maximum protection to the complainant compatible with the maintenance of the accused's fundamental right to a fair trial.

A second issue arises as to the procedure to be followed where a constitutional question is raised on a preliminary inquiry to determine if there is sufficient evidence to commit the accused for trial. On this issue I conclude that the preliminary inquiry judges correctly declined to consider the constitutionality of the legislation and that the cases should be remitted for trial in accordance with the principles of evidence as canvassed in these reasons.

The Background

I deal first with *Seaboyer*. The accused was charged with sexual assault of a woman with whom he had been drinking in a bar. On the preliminary inquiry the judge refused to allow the accused to cross-examine the complainant on her sexual conduct on other occasions. The appellant contends that he should have been permitted to cross-examine as to other acts of sexual intercourse which may have caused bruises and other aspects of the complainant's condition which the Crown had put in evidence. While the theory of the defence has not been detailed at this early stage, such evidence might arguably be relevant to consent, since it might provide other explanations for the physical evidence tendered by the Crown in support of the use of force against the complainant.

The *Gayme* case arose in different circumstances. The complainant was 15, the appellant 18. They were friends. The Crown alleges that the appellant sexually assaulted her at his school. The defence, relying on the defences of consent and honest belief in consent, contends that there was no assault and that the complainant was the sexual aggressor. In pursuance of this defence, the appellant at the preliminary inquiry sought to cross-examine and present evidence on prior and subsequent sexual conduct of the complainant. Accordingly, he brought a motion for an order declaring that ss. 276 and 277 of the *Code* were unconstitutional. The judge rejected the motion, on the ground that he lacked jurisdiction to hear it, and committed the appellant for trial.

In neither *Seaboyer* nor *Gayme* did the preliminary inquiry judge consider the questions individually; they ruled that the blanket exclusion in the *Criminal Code* prevented them from considering whether the questions were otherwise relevant and admissible....

Relevant Legislation

Criminal Code, s. 276:

276. (1) In proceedings in respect of an offence under section 271, 272 or 273, no evidence shall be adduced by or on behalf of the accused concerning the sexual activity of the complainant with any person other than the accused unless

    (*a*) it is evidence that rebuts evidence of the complainant's sexual activity or absence thereof that was previously adduced by the prosecution;

    (*b*) it is evidence of specific instances of the complainant's sexual activity tending to establish the identity of the person who had sexual contact with the complainant on the occasion set out in the charge; or

    (*c*) it is evidence of sexual activity that took place on the same occasion as the sexual activity that forms the subject-matter of the charge, where that evidence relates to the consent that the accused alleges he believed was given by the complainant.

(2) No evidence is admissible under paragraph (1)(*c*) unless

    (*a*) reasonable notice in writing has been given to the prosecutor by or on behalf of the accused of his intention to adduce the evidence together with particulars of the evidence sought to be adduced; and

    (*b*) a copy of the notice has been filed with the clerk of the court.

(3) No evidence is admissible under subsection (1) unless the judge, provincial court judge or justice, after holding a hearing in which the jury and the members of the public are excluded and in which the complainant is not a compellable witness, is satisfied that the requirements of this section are met.

Criminal Code, s. 277:

277. In proceedings in respect of an offence under section 271, 272 or 273, evidence of sexual reputation, whether general or specific, is not admissible for the purpose of challenging or supporting the credibility of the complainant....

Discussion

1. Do ss. 276 and 277 of the Criminal Code Infringe Sections 7 and 11(d) of the Charter?

(a) The Approach to ss. 7 and 11(d) of the Charter

Everyone, under s. 7 of the *Charter*, has the right to life, liberty and security of person and the right not to be deprived thereof except in accordance with the principles of fundamental justice.

The first branch of s. 7 need not detain us. It is not disputed that ss. 276 and 277 of the *Criminal Code* have the capacity to deprive a person of his or her liberty. A person convicted of sexual assault may be sentenced to life imprisonment. In so far as ss. 276 and 277 may affect conviction, they may deprive a person of his or her liberty.

The real issue under s. 7 is whether the potential for deprivation of liberty flowing from ss. 276 and 277 takes place in a manner that conforms to the principles of fundamental justice. The principles of fundamental justice are the fundamental tenets upon which our legal system is based. We find them in the legal principles which have historically been reflected in the law of this and other similar states: *R. v. Beare*, [1988] 2 S.C.R. 387. The sections which follow s. 7, like the right to a fair trial enshrined in s. 11(d), reflect particular principles of fundamental justice: *Re B.C. Motor Vehicle Act*, [1985] 2 S.C.R. 486. Thus the discussion of s. 7 and s. 11(d) is inextricably intertwined.

The principles of fundamental justice reflect a spectrum of interests, from the rights of the accused to broader societal concerns. Section 7 must be construed having regard to those interests and "against the applicable principles and policies that have animated legislative and judicial practice in the field" (*Beare, supra*, at pp. 402-3 *per* La Forest J.). The ultimate question is whether the legislation, viewed in a purposive way, conforms to the fundamental precepts which underlie our system of justice. . . .

(b) The Positions of the Parties

(i) The Arguments in Favour of the Legislation

The supporters of the legislation submit that it conforms to, and indeed furthers, the principles of fundamental justice, both in purpose and effect.

The main purpose of the legislation is to abolish the old common law rules which permitted evidence of the complainant's sexual conduct which was of little probative value and calculated to mislead the jury. The common law permitted questioning on the prior sexual conduct of a complainant without proof of relevance to a specific issue in the trial. Evidence that the complainant had relations with the accused and others was routinely presented (and accepted by judges and juries) as tending to make it more likely that the complainant had consented to the alleged assault and as undermining her credibility generally. These inferences were based not on facts, but on the myths that unchaste women were more likely to consent to intercourse and in any event, were less worthy of belief. These twin myths are now discredited. The fact that a woman has had intercourse on other occasions does not in itself increase the logical probability that she consented to intercourse with the accused. Nor does it make her a liar. In an effort to rid the criminal law of these outmoded and illegitimate notions, legislatures throughout the United States and in England, Australia and Canada passed "rape-shield" laws. (I note that the term "rape shield" is less than fortunate; the legislation offers protection not against rape, but against the questioning of complainants in trials for sexual offences.)

Three subsidiary purposes of such legislation may be discerned. The first, and the one most pressed before us, was the preservation of the integrity of the trial by eliminating evidence which has little or no probative force but which unduly prejudices the judge or jury against the complainant. If we accept, as we must, that the purpose of the criminal trial is to get at the truth in order to convict the guilty and acquit the innocent, then it follows that irrelevant evidence which may mislead the jury should be eliminated in so far as possible. There is no doubt that evidence of the complainant's sexual activities has often had this effect. Empirical studies in the United States suggest that juries often misused evidence of unchastity and improperly considered "victim-precipitating" conduct, such as going to a bar or getting into a car with the defendant, to "penalize" those complainants who did not fit the stereotype of the "good woman" either by convicting the defendant of a lesser charge or by acquitting the defendant . . . .

The second rationale cited in support of rape-shield legislation is that it encourages the reporting of crime. Despite the fact that the statistics do not demonstrate with any certainty that reporting of sexual offences has increased in Canada as a consequence of rape-shield provisions, I accept that it is a legitimate legislative goal to attempt to encourage such reporting by eliminating to the greatest extent possible those elements of the trial which cause embarrassment or discomfort to the complainant. As time passes and the existence of such provisions becomes better known, they may well have some effect in promoting reporting. Certainly failure to consider the position of the complainant in the trial process may have the opposite effect.

A third and related reason sometimes offered for rape-shield legislation is protection of the witness's privacy. This is really the private aspect upon which the social interest in encouraging the reporting of sexual offences is based. In addition to furthering reporting, our system of justice has an interest in preventing unnecessary invasion of witnesses' privacy.

The goals of the legislation—the avoidance of unprobative and misleading evidence, the encouraging of reporting and the protection of the security and privacy of the witnesses—conform to our fundamental conceptions of justice. The concern with the legislation is not as to its purpose, which is laudable, but with its effect. The reasons for these concerns emerge from a consideration of the appellants' position, to which I now turn.

(ii) The Arguments Against the Legislation

The appellants contend that the legislation, however laudable its goals, in fact infringes their right to present evidence relevant to their defence and hence violates their right to a fair trial, one of the most important of the principles of fundamental justice.

The precept that the innocent must not be convicted is basic to our concept of justice. One has only to think of the public revulsion felt at the improper conviction of Donald Marshall in this country or the Birmingham Six in the United Kingdom to appreciate how deeply held is this tenet of justice.

Lamer J. (as he then was) put it this way in *Re B.C. Motor Vehicle Act, supra*, at p. 513:

> It has from time immemorial been part of our system of laws that the innocent not be punished. This principle has long been recognized as an essential element of a system for the administration of justice which is founded upon a belief in the dignity and worth of the human person and on the rule of law. . . .

It is this fundamental principle—that the innocent not be punished—that is urged in support of the contention that ss. 276 and 277 violate the *Charter*. The interest is both individual, in that it affects the accused, and societal, for no just society can tolerate the conviction and punishment of the innocent.

The right of the innocent not to be convicted is reflected in our society's fundamental commitment to a fair trial, a commitment expressly embodied in s. 11(d) of the *Charter*. It has long been recognized that an essential facet of a fair hearing is the "opportunity adequately to state [one's] case." . . . This applies with particular force to the accused, who may not have the resources of the state at his or her disposal. Thus our courts have traditionally been reluctant to exclude even tenuous defence evidence. . . .

The right of the innocent not to be convicted is dependent on the right to present full answer and defence. This, in turn, depends on being able to call the evidence necessary to establish a defence and to challenge the evidence called by the prosecution. . . .

In short, the denial of the right to call and challenge evidence is tantamount to the denial of the right to rely on a defence to which the law says one is entitled. The defence which the law gives with one hand, may be taken away with the other. Procedural limitations make possible the conviction of persons who the criminal law says are innocent.

(iii) The Issue Between the Parties

All the parties agree that the right to a fair trial—one which permits the trier of fact to get at the truth and properly and fairly dispose of the case—is a principle of fundamental justice. Nor is there any dispute that encouraging reporting of sexual offences and protection of the complainant's privacy are legitimate goals provided they do not interfere with the primary objective of a fair trial. Where the parties part company is on the issue of whether ss. 276 and 277 of the *Criminal Code* in fact infringe the right to a fair trial. The supporters of the legislation urge that it furthers the right to a fair trial by eliminating evidence of little or no worth and considerable prejudice. The appellants, on the other hand, say that the legislation goes too far and in fact eliminates relevant evidence which should be admitted notwithstanding the possibility of prejudice.

This raises two questions. First, what are the fundamental principles governing the right to introduce relevant defence evidence which may also be prejudicial? Second, does the legislation infringe these principles?

(c) The Principles Governing the Right to Call Defence Evidence

It is fundamental to our system of justice that the rules of evidence should permit the judge and jury to get at the truth and properly determine the issues. . . .

The problem which arises is that a trial is a complex affair, raising many different issues. Relevance must be determined not in a vacuum, but in relation to some issue in the trial. Evidence which may be relevant to one issue may be irrelevant to another issue. What is worse, it may actually mislead the trier of fact on the second issue. Thus the same piece of evidence may have value to the trial process but bring with it the danger that it may prejudice the fact-finding process on another issue.

The law of evidence deals with this problem by giving the trial judge the task of balancing the value of the evidence against its potential prejudice. Virtually all common law jurisdictions recognize a power in the trial judge to exclude evidence on the basis that its probative value is outweighed by the prejudice which may flow from it. . . .

Canadian courts, like courts in most common law jurisdictions, have been extremely cautious in restricting the power of the accused to call evidence in his or her defence, a reluctance founded in the fundamental tenet of our judicial system that an innocent person must not be convicted. It follows from this that the prejudice must substantially outweigh the value of the evidence before a judge can exclude evidence relevant to a defence allowed by law.

These principles and procedures are familiar to all who practise in our criminal courts. They are common sense rules based on basic notions of fairness, and as such properly lie at the heart of our trial process. In short, they form part of the principles of fundamental justice enshrined in s. 7 of the *Charter*. They may be circumscribed in some cases by other rules of evidence, but as will be discussed in more detail below, the circumstances where truly relevant and reliable evidence is excluded are few, particularly where the evidence goes to the defence. In most cases, the exclusion of relevant evidence can be justified on the ground that the potential prejudice to the trial process of admitting the evidence clearly outweighs its value.

This then is the yardstick by which ss. 276 and 277 of the *Code* are to be measured. Do they exclude evidence the probative value of which is not substantially outweighed by its potential prejudice? If so, they violate the fundamental principles upon which our justice system is predicated and infringe s. 7 of the *Charter*.

The parties, as I understand their positions, agree on this view of the principles of fundamental justice. The Attorney General for Ontario, for the respondent, does not assert that the *Charter* permits exclusion of evidence of real value to an accused's defence. Rather, he contends that any evidence which might be excluded by ss. 276 and 277 of the *Code* would be of such trifling value in relation to the prejudice that might flow from its reception that its exclusion would enhance rather than detract from the fairness of the trial. Others who defend the legislation, do so on the ground that it does not exclude evidence relevant to the defence, that the exceptions contained in the provisions "encompass *all* potential situations where evidence of a complainant's sexual history with men other than the accused would be *relevant* to support a legitimate defence" (emphasis in original): see Grant, [Yola Althea Grant, "The Penetration of the Rape Shield: R. v. Seaboyer and R. v. Gayme in the Ontario Court of Appeal" (1989-1990) 3 C.J.W.L. 592], at p. 601. It is to this issue, which I see as the crux of the case, which I now turn.

(d) The Effect of the Legislation: What Evidence Is Excluded?

Section 277 excludes evidence of sexual reputation for the purpose of challenging or supporting the credibility of the plaintiff. The idea that a complainant's credibility might be affected by whether she has had other sexual experience is today universally discredited. There is no logical or practical link between a woman's sexual reputation and whether she is a truthful witness. It follows that the evidence excluded by s. 277 can serve no legitimate purpose in the trial. Section 277, by limiting the exclusion to a purpose which is clearly illegitimate, does not touch evidence which may be tendered for valid purposes, and hence does not infringe the right to a fair trial.

I turn then to s. 276. Section 276, unlike s. 277, does not condition exclusion on use of the evidence for an illegitimate purpose. Rather, it constitutes a blanket exclusion, subject to three exceptions—rebuttal evidence, evidence going to identity, and evidence relating to consent to sexual activity on the same occasion as the trial incident. The question is whether this may exclude evidence which is relevant to the defence and the probative value of which is not substantially outweighed by the potential prejudice to the trial process. To put the matter another way, can it be said *a priori*, as the Attorney General for Ontario contends, that any and all evidence excluded by s. 276 will necessarily be of such trifling weight in relation to the prejudicial effect of the evidence that it may fairly be excluded?

In my view, the answer to this question must be negative. The Canadian and American jurisprudence affords numerous examples of evidence of sexual conduct which would be excluded by s. 276 but which clearly should be received in the interests of a fair trial, notwithstanding the possibility that it may divert a jury by tempting it to improperly infer consent or lack of credibility in the complainant.

Consider the defence of honest belief. It rests on the concept that the accused may honestly but mistakenly (and not necessarily reasonably) have believed that the complainant was consenting to the sexual act. If the accused can raise a reasonable doubt as to his intention on the basis that he honestly held such a belief, he is not guilty under our law and is entitled to an acquittal. The basis of the accused's honest belief in the complainant's consent may be sexual acts performed by the complainant at some other time or place. Yet section 276 would preclude the accused leading such evidence.

Another category of evidence eliminated by s. 276 relates to the right of the defence to attack the credibility of the complainant on the ground that the complainant was biased or had motive to fabricate the evidence....

... Evidence of sexual activity excluded by s. 276 may be relevant to explain the physical conditions on which the Crown relies to establish intercourse or the use of force, such as semen, pregnancy, injury or disease—evidence which may go to consent.... In the case of young complainants where there may be a tendency to believe their story on the ground that the detail of their account must have come from the alleged encounter, it may be relevant to show other activity which provides an explanation for the knowledge....

Even evidence as to pattern of conduct may on occasion be relevant. Since this use of evidence of prior sexual conduct draws upon the inference that prior conduct infers similar subsequent conduct, it closely resembles the prohibited use of the evidence and must be carefully scrutinized.... Yet such evidence might be admissible in non-sexual cases under the similar fact rule. Is it fair then to deny it to an accused, merely because the trial relates to a sexual offence? ...

[Section] 276 has the potential to exclude evidence of critical relevance to the defence. Can it honestly be said, as the Attorney General for Ontario contends, that the value of such evidence will always be trifling when compared with its potential to mislead the jury? I think not. The examples show that the evidence may well be of great importance to getting at the truth and determining whether the accused is guilty or innocent under the law—the ultimate aim of the trial process. They demonstrate that s. 276, enacted for the purpose of helping judges and juries arrive at the proper and just verdict in the particular case, overshoots the mark, with the result that it may have the opposite effect of impeding them in discovering the truth.

The conclusion that s. 276 overreaches is supported by consideration of how it impacts on the justifications for s. 276 set out above. The first and most important justification for s. 276 is that it prevents the judge or jury from being diverted by irrelevant evidence of other sexual conduct of the complainant which will unfairly prejudice them against the complainant and thus lead to an improper verdict. Accepting that evidence that diverts the trier of fact from the real issue and prejudices the chance of a true verdict can properly be excluded even if it possesses some relevance, the fact remains that a provision which categorically excludes evidence without permitting the trial judge to engage in the exercise of whether the possible prejudicial effect of the evidence outweighs its value to the truth-finding process runs the risk of overbreadth. . . .

The argument based on the reporting of sexual offences similarly fails to justify the wide reach of s. 276. . . . [I]t is counterproductive to encourage reporting by a rule which impairs the ability of the trier of fact to arrive at a just result and determine the truth of the report. Reporting is but the first step in the judicial process, not an end in itself. But even if it is assumed that increased reporting will result in increased convictions, the argument is unpersuasive. . . .

[T]he justification of maintaining the privacy of the witness fails to support the rigid exclusionary rule embodied in s. 276 of the *Code*. First, it can be argued that important as it is to take all measures possible to ease the plight of the witness, the constitutional right to a fair trial must take precedence in case of conflict. . . .

Secondly, s. 276 goes further than required to protect privacy because it fails to permit an assessment of the effect on the witness of the evidence—an effect which may be great in some cases and small in others—in relation to the cogency of the evidence.

The failings of s. 276 are inherent in its concept. Commentators have identified two fundamental flaws in rape-shield provisions similar to s. 276. The first is that such provisions fail to distinguish between the different purposes for which evidence may be tendered. The legislation may misdefine the evil to be addressed as evidence of sexual activity, when in fact the evil to be addressed is the narrower evil of the *misuse* of evidence of sexual activity for irrelevant and misleading purposes, namely the inference that the complainant consented to the act or that she is an unreliable witness. The result of this misdefinition of the problem is a blanket prohibition of evidence of sexual activity, regardless of whether the evidence is tendered for an illegitimate purpose or for a valid one. . . .

A second and related criticism of provisions such as s. 276 is that they adopt a "pigeon-hole" approach which is incapable of dealing adequately with the fundamental evidentiary problem at stake, that of determining whether or not the evidence is truly relevant, and not merely irrelevant and misleading. This amounts, in effect, to predicting relevancy on the basis of a series of categories. . . .

Scholars have criticized rape-shield legislation adopting the format of a blanket exclusion supplemented by exceptions on the ground that this approach is inherently incapable of permitting the Court sufficient latitude to properly determine relevance in the individual case. . . .

In short, the problem with legislation like s. 276 . . . is its failure to rely on the governing concept of whether the evidence is being tendered for an irrelevant, illegitimate purpose, and its reliance instead on categories of admissible evidence which can never anticipate the multitude of circumstances which may arise in trials for sexual offences. The failing is summed up succinctly by Doherty . . . where he characterizes s. 276 as calling for "a mechanical 'pigeon-holing' approach to the question of admissibility based on criteria which may in a given case have little to do with the potential value of the evidence."

To summarize, s. 276 has the potential to exclude otherwise admissible evidence which may in certain cases be relevant to the defence. Such evidence is excluded absolutely, without any means of evaluating whether in the circumstances of the case the integrity of the trial process would be better served by receiving it than by excluding it. Accepting that the rejection of relevant evidence may sometimes be justified for policy reasons, the fact remains that s. 276 may operate to exclude evidence where the very policy which imbues the section—finding the truth and arriving at the correct verdict—suggests the evidence should be received. Given the primacy in our system of justice of the principle that the innocent should not be convicted, the right to present one's case should not be curtailed in the absence of an assurance that the curtailment is clearly justified by even stronger contrary considerations. What is required is a law which protects the fundamental right to a fair trial while avoiding the illegitimate inferences from other sexual conduct that the complainant is more likely to have consented to the act or less likely to be telling the truth. . . .

(f) Other Jurisdictions

In support of the contention that s. 276 of the *Code* does not infringe the principles of fundamental justice or the right to a fair trial, it is argued that provisions similar to s. 276 have been upheld in other jurisdictions.

The first point to note is that s. 276 is among the most draconian approaches to the problem of eradicating improper inferences as to consent and credibility from the evidence of the sexual activities of the complainant. . . . Provisions in England, Australia and many of the United States generally allow for some measure of judicial discretion to deal with the impossibility of foreseeing all eventualities and avoiding the unfairness of excluding evidence which may be highly relevant to the defence. . . .

(g) Summary

I conclude that the operation of s. 276 of the *Criminal Code* permits the infringement of the rights enshrined in ss. 7 and 11(*d*) of the *Charter*. In achieving its purpose—the abolition of the outmoded, sexist-based use of sexual conduct evidence —it overshoots the mark and renders inadmissible evidence which may be essential to the presentation of legitimate defences and hence to a fair trial. In exchange for the elimination of the possibility that the judge and jury may draw illegitimate inferences from the evidence, it exacts as a price the real risk that an innocent person may be convicted. The price is too great in relation to the benefit secured, and cannot be tolerated in a society that does not countenance in any form the conviction of the innocent. Support for this conclusion is found in other rules of evidence which have adapted to meet the dangers of arbitrarily excluding valuable evidence, as well as the law in other jurisdictions, which by one means or another rejects the idea that rape-shield legislation, however legitimate its aims, should be cast so widely as to deprive the accused of the tools with which to build a legitimate defence.

Section 277 does not, by contrast, offend the Charter.

2. Is Section 276 Saved by Section 1 of the Charter?

Is s. 276 of the *Criminal Code* justified in a free and democratic society, notwithstanding the fact that it may lead to infringements of the *Charter*?

The first step under s. 1 is to consider whether the legislation addresses a pressing and substantial objective: *R. v. Oakes*, [1986] 1 S.C.R. 103. As already discussed, it does.

The second requirement under s. 1 is that the infringement of rights be proportionate to the pressing objective. This inquiry involves three considerations. The first—whether there exists a rational connection between the legislative measure and the objective—is arguably met; s. 276 does help to exclude unhelpful and potentially misleading evidence of the complainant's prior sexual conduct. The second consideration under proportionality is whether the legislation impairs the right as little as possible. It has been suggested that legislatures must be given some room to manoeuvre, particularly where the legislation is attempting to fix a balance between competing groups in society: *Irwin Toy Ltd. v. Quebec (Attorney General)*, [1989] 1 S.C.R. 927. Assuming that this case, although criminal and as such a contest between the state and the accused, might fall into this class, it still cannot be said that the degree of impairment effected by s. 276 is appropriately restrained. In creating exceptions to the exclusion of

evidence of the sexual activity of the complainant on other occasions, Parliament correctly recognized that justice requires a measured approach, one which admits evidence which is truly relevant to the defence notwithstanding potential prejudicial effect. Yet Parliament at the same time excluded other evidence of sexual conduct which might be equally relevant to a legitimate defence and which appears to pose no greater danger of prejudice than the exceptions it recognizes. To the extent the section excludes relevant defence evidence whose value is not clearly outweighed by the danger it presents, the section is overbroad.

I turn finally to the third aspect of the proportionality requirement—the balance between the importance of the objective and the injurious effect of the legislation. The objective of the legislation, as discussed above, is to eradicate the erroneous inferences from evidence of other sexual encounters that the complainant is more likely to have consented to the sexual act in issue or less likely to be telling the truth. The subsidiary aims are to promote fairer trials and increased reporting of sexual offences and to minimize the invasion of the complainant's privacy. In this way the personal security of women and their right to equal benefit and protection of the law are enhanced. The effect of the legislation, on the other hand, is to exclude relevant defence evidence, the value of which outweighs its potential prejudice. As indicated in the discussion of s. 7, all parties agree that a provision which rules out probative defence evidence which is not clearly outweighed by the prejudice it may cause to the trial strikes the wrong balance between the rights of complainants and the rights of the accused. The line must be drawn short of the point where it results in an unfair trial and the possible conviction of an innocent person. Section 276 fails this test.

I conclude that s. 276 is not saved by s. 1 of the Charter. . . .

[The majority addressed whether the legislation could be saved by applying the doctrine of constitutional exemption, allowing judges to decline to apply section 276 in cases where a constitutional violation would occur, and ruled this would not be appropriate in this case.]

4. What Follows from Striking Down Section 276?

The first question is whether the striking down of s. 276 revives the old common law rules of evidence permitting liberal and often inappropriate reception of evidence of the complainant's sexual conduct. . . .

The answer to this question is no. The rules in question are common law rules. Like other common law rules of evidence, they must be adapted to conform to current reality. As all counsel on these appeals accepted, the reality in 1991 is that evidence of sexual conduct and reputation in itself cannot be regarded as logically probative of either the complainant's credibility or consent. Although they still may inform the thinking of many, the twin myths which s. 276 sought to eradicate are just that—myths—and have no place in a rational and just system of law. It follows that the old rules which permitted evidence of sexual conduct and condoned invalid inferences from it solely for these purposes have no place in our law. . . .

In the absence of legislation, it is open to this Court to suggest guidelines for the reception and use of sexual conduct evidence. Such guidelines should be seen for what they are— an attempt to describe the consequences of the application of the general rules of evidence governing relevance and the reception of evidence—and not as judicial legislation cast in stone.

In my view the trial judge under this new regime shoulders a dual responsibility. First, the judge must assess with a high degree of sensitivity whether the evidence proffered by the defence meets the test of demonstrating a degree of relevance which outweighs the damages and disadvantages presented by the admission of such evidence. . . . The trial judge must ensure that evidence is tendered for a legitimate purpose, and that it logically supports a defence. The fishing expeditions which unfortunately did occur in the past should not be permitted. The trial judge's discretion must be exercised to ensure that neither the *in camera* procedure nor the trial become forums for demeaning and abusive conduct by defence counsel.

The trial judge's second responsibility will be to take special care to ensure that, in the exceptional case where circumstances demand that such evidence be permitted, the jury is fully and properly instructed as to its appropriate use. The jurors must be cautioned that they should not draw impermissible inferences from evidence of previous sexual activity. While such evidence may be tendered for a purpose logically probative of the defence to be presented, it may be important to remind jurors that they not allow the allegations of past sexual activity to lead them to the view that the complainant is less worthy of belief, or was more likely to have consented for that reason. It is hoped that a sensitive and responsive exercise of discretion by the judiciary will reduce and even eliminate the concerns which provoked legislation such as s. 276, while at the same time preserving the right of an accused to a fair trial.

I would summarize the applicable principles as follows:

1. On a trial for a sexual offence, evidence that the complainant has engaged in consensual sexual conduct on other occasions (including past sexual conduct with the accused) is not admissible solely to support the inference that the complainant is by reason of such conduct:
   (a) more likely to have consented to the sexual conduct at issue in the trial;
   (b) less worthy of belief as a witness.

2. Evidence of consensual sexual conduct on the part of the complainant may be admissible for purposes other than an inference relating to the consent or credibility of the complainant where it possesses probative value on an issue in the trial and where that probative value is not substantially outweighed by the danger of unfair prejudice flowing from the evidence.

   By way of illustration only, and not by way of limitation, the following are examples of admissible evidence:
   (A) Evidence of specific instances of sexual conduct tending to prove that a person other than the accused caused the physical consequences of the rape alleged by the prosecution;
   (B) Evidence of sexual conduct tending to prove bias or motive to fabricate on the part of the complainant;
   (C) Evidence of prior sexual conduct, known to the accused at the time of the act charged, tending to prove that the accused believed that the complainant was consenting to the act charged (without laying down absolute rules, normally one would expect some proximity in time between the conduct that is alleged to have given rise to an honest belief and the conduct charged);
   (D) Evidence of prior sexual conduct which meets the requirements for the reception of similar act evidence, bearing in mind that such evidence cannot be used illegitimately merely to show that the complainant consented or is an unreliable witness;
   (E) Evidence tending to rebut proof introduced by the prosecution regarding the complainant's sexual conduct.

3. Before evidence of consensual sexual conduct on the part of a victim is received, it must be established on a *voir dire* (which may be held *in camera*) by affidavit or the testimony of the accused or third parties, that the proposed use of the evidence of other sexual conduct is legitimate.

4. Where evidence that the complainant has engaged in sexual conduct on other occasions is admitted on a

jury trial, the judge should warn the jury against inferring from the evidence of the conduct itself, either that the complainant might have consented to the act alleged, or that the complainant is less worthy of credit....

Conclusion

I would dismiss the appeals and affirm the order of the Court of Appeal that these cases proceed to trial. I would answer the constitutional questions as follows:

1. Whether s. 246.6 [now 276] or 246.7 [now 277] of the *Criminal Code* is inconsistent with s. 7 or s. 11(d) of the *Canadian Charter of Rights and Freedoms*?

    Yes, s. 276 is inconsistent with s. 7 and s. 11(d). Section 277 is not.

2. If s. 246.6 or 246.7 of the *Criminal Code* is inconsistent with either s. 7 or s. 11(d) of the *Canadian Charter of Rights and Freedoms*, whether that inconsistency is justified on the basis of s. 1 thereof. No.

The reasons of L'Heureux-Dubé and Gonthier JJ. were delivered by

L'HEUREUX-DUBÉ J. (dissenting in part):

Introduction

These two appeals are about relevance, myths and stereotypes in the context of sexual assaults. More particularly, is the prior sexual history of a complainant, in the trial of an accused charged with sexual assault, relevant and/or admissible? ...

Analysis

Of tantamount importance in answering the constitutional questions in this case is a consideration of the prevalence and impact of discriminatory beliefs on trials of sexual offences. These beliefs affect the processing of complaints, the law applied when and if the case proceeds to trial, the trial itself and the ultimate verdict. It is my view that the constitutional questions must be examined in their broader political, social and historical context in order to attempt any kind of meaningful constitutional analysis....

[T]he provisions that are the subject of the constitutional challenge in the present case are commonly referred to as "rape shield" provisions. Implicit in this description is a presumption as to their purpose: that it is solely to shield a complainant from the rigours of cross-examination at trial. As I hope to make clear through the course of my reasons, although

protecting the complainant may be one of the purposes of the provisions, it is neither the only one, nor necessarily the most important. As a result, I will not use this inaccurate shorthand in referring to these provisions.

Sexual Assault

Sexual assault is not like any other crime. In the vast majority of cases the target is a woman and the perpetrator is a man (98.7 percent of those charged with sexual assault are men: *Crime Statistics 1986* ....

Conservative estimates inform us that, in Canada, at least one woman in five will be sexually assaulted during her lifetime.... While social scientists agree that the incidence of sexual assault is great, they also agree that it is impossible, for a variety of reasons, to measure accurately the actual rate of victimization.... While there is a large gap between reported incidents and actual victimization, there is a further gap between what researchers tell us are the actual numbers and what the actual numbers are.

There are a number of reasons why women may not report their victimization: fear of reprisal, fear of a continuation of their trauma at the hands of the police and the criminal justice system, fear of a perceived loss of status and lack of desire to report due to the typical effects of sexual assault such as depression, self-blame or loss of self-esteem. Although all of the reasons for failing to report are significant and important, more relevant to the present inquiry are the numbers of victims who choose not to bring their victimization to the attention of the authorities due to their perception that the institutions with which they would have to become involved will view their victimization in a stereotypical and biased fashion....

The woman who comes to the attention of the authorities has her victimization measured against the current rape mythologies, i.e. who she should be in order to be recognized as having been, in the eyes of the law, raped; who her attacker must be in order to be recognized, in the eyes of the law, as a potential rapist; and how injured she must be in order to be believed. If her victimization does not fit the myths, it is unlikely that an arrest will be made or a conviction obtained....

[P]olice rely in large measure upon popular conceptions of sexual assault in order to classify incoming cases as "founded" or "unfounded." It would appear as though most forces have developed a convenient shorthand regarding their decisions to proceed in any given case. This shorthand is composed of popular myth regarding rapists (distinguishing them from men as a whole), and stereotype about women's character and sexuality.... [T]he most common of these myths and stereotypes [are]:

1. *Struggle and Force: Woman As Defender of Her Honor.* There is a myth that a woman cannot be raped against her will, that if she really wants to prevent a rape she can.

> The prosecution attempts to show that she did struggle, or had no opportunity to do so, while the defence attempts to show that she did not. . . .

2. *Knowing the Defendant: The Rapist As a Stranger.* There is a myth that rapists are strangers who leap out of bushes to attack their victims. . . . [T]he view that interaction between friends or between relatives does not result in rape is prevalent. . . .

3. *Sexual Reputation: The Madonna–Whore Complex.* . . . [W]omen . . . are categorized into one-dimensional types. They are maternal or they are sexy. They are good or they are bad. They are madonnas or they are whores.

> The legal rules use these distinctions.

4. *General Character: Anything Not 100 Percent Proper and Respectable.* . . . Being on welfare or drinking or drug use could be used to discredit anyone, but where women are involved, these issues are used to imply that the woman consented to sex with the defendant or that she contracted to have sex for money.

5. *Emotionality of Females.* Females are assumed to be "more emotional" than males. The expectation is that if a woman is raped, she will get hysterical during the event and she will be visibly upset afterward. If she is able to "retain her cool," then people assume that "nothing happened." . . .

6. *Reporting Rape.* Two conflicting expectations exist concerning the reporting of rape. One is that if a woman is raped she will be too upset and ashamed to report it, and hence most of the time this crime goes unreported. The other is that if a woman is raped she will be so upset that she will report it. Both expectations exist simultaneously.

7. *Woman as Fickle and Full of Spite.* Another stereotype is that the feminine character is especially filled with malice. Woman is seen as fickle and as seeking revenge on past lovers.

8. *The Female Under Surveillance: Is the Victim Trying to Escape Punishment?* . . . It is assumed that the female's sexual behavior, depending on her age, is under the surveillance of her parents or her husband, and also more generally of the community. Thus, the defense argues, if a woman says she was raped it must be because she consented to sex that she was not supposed to have. She got caught, and now she wants to get back in the good graces of whomever's surveillance she is under.

9. *Disputing That Sex Occurred.* That females fantasize rape is another common stereotype. Females are assumed to make up stories that sex occurred when in fact nothing happened. . . . Similarly, women are thought to fabricate the sexual activity not as part of a fantasy life, but out of spite.

10. *Stereotype of the Rapist.* One stereotype of the rapist is that of a stranger who leaps out of the bushes to attack his victim and later abruptly leaves her. . . . [S]tereotypes of the rapist can be used to blame the victim. She tells what he did. And because it often does not match what jurors think rapists do, his behavior is held against her.

A corollary of this myth is the belief that rapists are not "normal" and are "mentally ill."

. . . This list of stereotypical conceptions about women and sexual assault is by no means exhaustive. Like most stereotypes, they operate as a way, however flawed, of understanding the world and, like most such constructs, operate at a level of consciousness that makes it difficult to root them out and confront them directly. This mythology finds its way into the decisions of the police regarding their "founded"/"unfounded" categorization, operates in the mind of the Crown when deciding whether or not to prosecute, influences a judge's or juror's perception of guilt or innocence of the accused and the "goodness" or "badness" of the victim, and finally, has carved out a niche in both the evidentiary and substantive law governing the trial of the matter. . . .

Absolutely pivotal to an understanding of the nature and purpose of the provisions and constitutional questions at issue in this case is the realization of how widespread the stereotypes and myths about rape are, notwithstanding their inaccuracy.

The appellants argue that we, as a society, have become more enlightened, that prosecutors, police, judges and jurors can be trusted to perform their tasks without recourse to discriminatory views about women manifested through rape myth. Unfortunately, social science evidence suggests otherwise. Rape myths still present formidable obstacles for complainants in their dealings with the very system charged with discovering the truth. . . .

The Larger Legal Context

. . . The common law has always viewed victims of sexual assault with suspicion and distrust. As a result, unique evidentiary rules were developed. The complainant in a sexual assault trial was treated unlike any other. In the case of sexual offences, the common law "enshrined" prevailing mythology and stereotype by formulating rules that made it extremely difficult for the complainant to establish her credibility and fend off inquiry and speculation regarding her "morality" or "character." . . .

Under the guise of a principled application of the legal concept of relevance, the common law allowed the accused to delve at great length into the moral character of the complainant by adducing "relevant" sexual history. The prejudicial impact of such an inquiry has already been discussed at length. The true nature and purpose of the inquiry into sexual history is revealed by the resulting prejudice and by the fact that these concepts were only applicable in respect of sexual offences and, in addition, were not deemed relevant to the credibility of the male accused.

Application of the relevance concept was not the only way in which the common law integrated stereotype and myth into trials of sexual offences. Also part of the unique body of evidentiary law surrounding sexual offences were, among other things, the doctrine of recent complaint and corroboration rules. These evidentiary concepts were also based upon stereotypes of the female complainant requiring independent evidence to support her evidence and, in addition, evidence that she raised a "hue and cry" after her assault. It is noteworthy that both recent complaint and corroboration rules formed exceptions to general rules of evidence....

Parliament intervened on two notable occasions, both relevant to the inquiry here. In 1976, Parliament repealed the existing s. 142 of the *Criminal Code*, R.S.C. 1970, c. C-34, and enacted a provision designed to alleviate some of the problems caused by the virtually unrestricted inquiry into a complainant's previous sexual history allowed at common law (*Criminal Law Amendment Act, 1975*, S.C. 1974-75-76, c. 93, s. 8)....

Though the motives of Parliament were commendable, judicial interpretation of the section thwarted any benefit that may have accrued to the complainant. In fact, the provision, as judicially interpreted, provided less protection to the complainant than that offered at common law, surely a surprising result considering the obvious mischief Parliament intended to cure in enacting it....

It may be argued that, not only did the Court feel a somewhat misplaced need to "balance" the "protection" of the complainant against "restrictions" placed upon the accused, it tipped the balance further in favour of the accused. This is obviously a curious result given the fact that the infirmities of the common law led Parliament to intervene. That the complainant should walk away with less than she already had is lamentable....

The failure of the courts, as was indicated earlier, both to take cognizance of and to implement the objectives of Parliament in this earlier legislation, combined with further criticism of the manner in which complainants of sexual offences were treated, generated a sweeping set of reforms in 1982. The Honourable Jean Chrétien, then Minister of Justice and Attorney General of Canada, articulated the principles underlying this second, larger reform package in this manner:

> *The inequality of the present law has placed an unfair burden on female victims of sexual assault.* It has added to the trauma, stigma and embarrassment of being sexually assaulted, and has deterred many victims from reporting these serious crimes to the police.... Bill C-53 would alleviate the legal impediment which allows this to occur....

[Justice L'Heureux-Dubé proceeded with a lengthy discussion of Parliament's intentions with respect to reforming how the law deals with sexual assault complaints.]

The literature and case law in this area abound with examples of the supposed relevant evidence that is excluded by s. 276. For the most part, however, the "relevant" evidence provided in these examples is, on a principled inquiry, irrelevant; any semblance of relevance depends in large measure upon acceptance of stereotype about women and rape. Much of the remainder is admissible under the provision. One hesitates, however, to construct an argument around the speculative scenarios offered. Many of the scenarios are pure fantasy and have absolutely no grounding in life or experience....

Many argue that the most convincing support for the argument that the provision is drawn too narrowly is provided by so-called "similar fact evidence," or "pattern of conduct evidence," i.e. that the complainant has had consensual sexual relations in circumstances that look an awful lot like those supporting the assault allegation and, hence, such evidence is probative of consent. I am of the firm opinion that such evidence is almost invariably irrelevant and, in any event, is nothing more than a prohibited propensity argument, besides being highly prejudicial to the integrity and fairness of the trial process....

A second category of so-called relevant evidence is also widely set up as conclusively demonstrating the infirmity of the provision, namely evidence of mistaken belief in consent. Again, I am of the firm opinion that no relevant evidence regarding the defence of honest but mistaken belief in consent is excluded by the provision under attack here....

It is my view that, assuming that both the trier of fact and the trier of law are operating in an intellectual environment that is free of rape myth and stereotype about women, any evidence excluded by this subsection would not satisfy the "air of reality" that must accompany this defence nor would it provide reasonable grounds for the jury to consider in assessing whether the belief was honestly held. The structure of the exception provided for in s. 276(1)(c) is thus not offensive to such a defence.

Evidence of prior acts of prostitution or allegations of prostitution are properly excluded by the provision. In my opinion, this evidence is never relevant and, besides its irrelevance, is hugely prejudicial. I vehemently disagree with the assertion of the appellant Seaboyer that "a prostitute is generally more willing to consent to sexual intercourse and is less credible as a witness because of that mode of life."...

Many also argue that the provision does not allow evidence going to show motive to fabricate or bias. Clearly, most such alleged motives or bias will not be grounded in the complainant's past sexual history. Moreover, much of this evidence depends for its relevance on certain stereotypical visions of women; that they lie about sexual assault, and that women who allege sexual assault often do so in order to get back in the good graces of those who may have her sexual conduct under scrutiny. Thus, again, refutation of stereotype strikes at the heart of the argument. As to evidence that a complainant has made prior false allegations of sexual assault, such evidence is admissible under the existing provision since this evidence does not involve the admission of her previous sexual history.

As I stated at the outset, the evidence which is excluded by the provision is simply irrelevant. It is based upon discriminatory beliefs about women and sexual assault. In addition, the impugned provision provides wide avenues for the introduction of sexual history evidence that is relevant. Paradoxically, some of the exceptions may be cast overly broadly with the unfortunate result that a large body of evidence may still be improperly admitted on the basis of specious relevancy claims.

If I am wrong in concluding that no relevant sexual history evidence is excluded by the contested provision, I am of the view that such exclusion is proper due to its extremely prejudicial effect on the trial of the legal issues....

The Constitutional Questions

... It is my view that neither "fairness" nor "the principles of fundamental justice" mandate the constitutional invalidity of s. 276. Rather, in order to achieve fairness and to conduct trials in accordance with fundamental tenets of criminal law, this provision must be upheld in all of its vigour....

The constitutional question posed by the present case is whether, notwithstanding the already established irrelevance and/or prejudicial nature of the evidence excluded by the impugned provision, an accused, nevertheless, has a constitutional right to adduce such evidence. On my view of the scope of these constitutional guarantees, this question must be answered with a resounding and compelling no.

It is noncontroversial to state that an accused does not have a constitutional right to adduce irrelevant evidence. To the extent that much, if not all, of the evidence excluded by the provision at issue here is irrelevant, there is no constitutional issue. Nor, in my view, does an accused have the right under the *Charter*, whether under the rubric of a right to a fair trial or the right to make full answer and defence, to adduce evidence that prejudices and distorts the fact-finding process at trial. As a corollary, neither do notions of a "fair trial" or "full answer and defence" recognize a right in the accused to adduce any evidence that may lead to an acquittal. Such propositions cast ss. 7 and 11(*d*) in an extremely narrow fashion and deny meaningful content to notions of "fairness" and "principles of fundamental justice."...

[Although not necessary for her findings, Justice L'Heureux-Dubé considered the section 1 question.]

... In the face of a previous legislative provision that was emasculated by the courts and on the heels of this, the continued application of stereotype, Parliament's measured and considered response was to codify those situations wherein sexual history evidence may be both relevant and sufficiently probative such that its admission was warranted. Parliament exhibited a marked, and justifiedly so, distrust of the ability of the courts to promote and achieve a non-discriminatory application of the law in this area. In view of the history of government attempts, the harm done when discretion is posited in trial judges and the demonstrated inability of the judiciary to change its discriminatory ways, Parliament was justified in so choosing. My attempt to illustrate the tenacity of these discriminatory beliefs and their acceptance at all levels of society clearly demonstrates that discretion in judges is antithetical to the goals of Parliament.

While some degree of latitude must be accorded to the legislative choice of Parliament due to the troubled history that informed its choice, the fact that Parliament had to choose between the interests of competing groups also requires such an approach. This is not a typical situation where the government and accused persons have squared off or where the government is "best characterized as the singular antagonist of the individual whose right has been infringed" (*Irwin Toy Ltd. v. Quebec (Attorney General)*) [[1989] 1 S.C.R. 927]. Rather it is plain that Parliament, in coming to its legislative decision, weighed the claims of different groups and attempted to do that which best balanced their concerns. These circumstances of the legislative decision require that the impugned provisions be accorded a special place in the s. 1 analysis:...

Due to the concerns underlying the passage of this legislation and the extensive efforts of Parliament to assess the viability of a number of means, this is not a situation where the courts are better situated than or even as well situated as

Parliament to determine whether the "least drastic means" has been chosen. The appropriate standard of review at this stage of the proportionality inquiry is thus one of reasonableness, i.e. whether the government had a reasonable basis for concluding that the legislative solution they chose impaired the right as little as possible given the government's pressing and substantial objective. It is clear from my reasons to this point that the legislative choice is, at a minimum, in the realm of the reasonable.

... [T]he nature of the problem facing Parliament did not admit of a solution through the exercise of discretion of trial judges. History demonstrates that it was discretion in trial judges that saturated the law in this area with stereotype. My earlier discussion shows that we are not, all of a sudden, a society rid of such beliefs, and hence, discretionary decision making in this realm is absolutely antithetical to the achievement of government's pressing and substantial objective. . . .

Parliament was faced with a historical record which demonstrated that this discretion was abused and exercised in a discriminatory fashion by trial judges and with overwhelming social science research that says things have not changed. In this context, the notion that Parliament could have, in the name of minimal impairment, awarded a discretion to trial judges, loses sight altogether of the objective that has been found to be pressing and substantial. . . .

In summary, sexual history evidence excluded by s. 276 of the *Criminal Code* is mostly irrelevant and, moreover, so prejudicial that its exclusion both at common law and under the *Canadian Charter of Rights and Freedoms* is mandated. Neither s. 7 nor s. 11(*d*), upon a principled inquiry, directs a different conclusion. However, even assuming that s. 276 is unconstitutional in its effect, it is easily justified under s. 1. In my view, once the constitutional questions are viewed within their larger context, the conclusions reached in these reasons are absolutely uncontentious.

Although for me the questions pertaining to the constitutional exemption and the effect of striking down s. 276 do not arise, I will nevertheless, before disposing of these appeals, make some brief remarks in respect of them.

My colleague, McLachlin J., articulates three reasons for her rejection of the "doctrine of constitutional exemption" in this case: namely, (1) it would not substantially uphold the law and the will of the legislature would become increasingly obscured; (2) applying the doctrine would be indistinguishable in result from striking down the legislation; and (3) applying the doctrine in this case would be difficult. It seems to me, however, that the same rationales highlight the infirmity of the guidelines suggested by the majority with respect to the admission of evidence of prior sexual history. More particularly, the objectives of Parliament in enacting the legislation, identified earlier in these reasons, are ill served by the guidelines. The view that the objectives of Parliament and the values of the *Charter* are better served in this fashion ignores the larger context within which the guidelines will be applied. Furthermore, as a full discussion of this context shows, any optimism that the guidelines will be effectively and consistently applied in a manner that is cognizant of both the objectives of Parliament and the infirmities of the common law is badly misplaced. My final objection to the guidelines, as my previous discussion indicates, is that they are entirely too broad and support the very stereotype and myth that they are meant to eradicate. . . .

30 R. v. Butler, 1992

While a narrow 4-to-3 majority upheld the hate speech law in *Keegstra*, all nine Supreme Court judges (via two opinions) voted to uphold the censorship of obscenity in *Butler*. At issue was section 163(8) of the *Criminal Code*, which defined prohibited obscenity as "any publication a dominant characteristic of which is the undue exploitation of sex, or of sex and any one or more of the following subjects, namely, crime, horror, cruelty and violence." As in the case of hate speech, obscenity was expression protected by section 2(*b*) of the *Charter*, meaning that the censorship provision could be sustained only as a section 1 "reasonable limit" on freedom of expression. At the same time, and again like hate speech, obscenity was judged to fall some distance from the core freedom-of-expression values— "the search for truth, participation in the political process, and individual self-fulfilment"— making its restriction "easier to justify [under section 1] than other infringements."

Did the censorship law have the kind of "pressing and substantial" purpose required of a "reasonable limit" under the *Oakes* test? Not if the law's purpose was simply to protect moral sensibilities from the public display of any kind of explicit sexuality. That was indeed the purpose of censorship laws in the past, but "the prevention of 'dirt for dirt's sake,'" wrote Justice Sopinka, "is not a legitimate objective which would justify the violation of one of the most fundamental freedoms enshrined in the *Charter*." A valid objective must emphasize "not moral disapproval but the avoidance of harm to society." Justice Sopinka was careful to reject a strict separation of law and morality. Indeed, he considered "moral corruption and harm to society [not as] distinct, but [as] inextricably linked [because it] is moral corruption of a certain kind which leads to the detrimental effect on society." His point was that while immorality may indeed cause the kind of harm needed for section 1 justification, not everything traditionally considered immoral causes such harm. Whether a depiction of sexuality was harmful was to be determined by "community standards," which had changed over time. No doubt, those who previously prohibited "dirt for dirt's sake" thought they were preventing "harm to society," but "our understanding of the harms caused by these materials has developed considerably."

For Justice Sopinka, this meant that in the *Charter* era a censorship law could not fully cover three common categories of pornography: (1) explicit sex with violence; (2) explicit sex without violence, but which subjects people to treatment that is degrading or dehumanizing; and (3) explicit sex without violence that is neither degrading nor dehumanizing. The first two categories were clearly harmful according to modern "community standards"; the third, with the crucial exception of child pornography, was not. As long as it depicts adults, the third kind of pornography is "good pornography" (or "erotica") that celebrates consensual sexuality based on equality between the participants. Bad pornography, the kind that could legitimately be censored, especially involved harm to women and children. Finding that section 163(8) was indeed targeted at the "harmful" categories of pornography and not at the legitimate "erotica," Justice Sopinka concluded that it met the "pressing and substantial purpose" part of the *Oakes* test.

Justice Sopinka had clearly responded to the request by the Women's Legal Education and Action Fund (LEAF) "to redefine the rationale for the *Criminal Code* obscenity provisions by focusing on its equality implications for women and children."[1] This feminist reading of section 163(8) attracted international attention as a pathbreaking innovation. *The New York Times* reported that the decision made "Canada the first place in the world that says what is obscene is what harms women."[2] The prominent American feminist Catherine MacKinnon, who had helped write LEAF's factum, devoted significant portions of her 1993 book *Only Words* to praising the innovation wrought by *Butler*.[3] Kathleen Mahoney, another co-author of LEAF's factum, called the ruling "world historic."[4]

Had this "world historic" innovation been in the minds of the legislators who enacted section 163 in 1959? It seems unlikely, and that posed a difficulty for Justice Sopinka. In *Big M Drug Mart* (case 22), the Court, rejecting the idea that a "shifting purpose" had transformed the obviously religious *Lord's Day Act* into secular day-of-rest legislation, insisted that the legislative purpose subjected to *Charter* scrutiny had to be what was in the minds of the legislature at the time of enactment. If he wished to respect the *Big M* precedent, as he clearly did, Justice Sopinka had to show that his innovative reading of section 163(8) did not amount to a "shifting purpose." He did so by distinguishing a "permissible shift in emphasis" from a complete shift in purpose. Preventing harm had always been the purpose of section 163; there had simply been a "shift in emphasis" in how we understand harm.[5] LEAF had considered asking the Court "to strike down the *Criminal Code* provisions and [invite] Parliament to introduce new legislation,"[6] but decided to press instead for a significant reinterpretation of the existing law. The former strategy would have required no "shifting purpose"; the latter required at least a "shift in emphasis."

Justice Gonthier (joined by Justice L'Heureux-Dubé) concurred in the result and supported much of the majority's reasoning, but thought that the modern understanding of harm might still reach adult "erotica" in some cases. Gonthier emphasized the distinction between private activity and its public representation in various media. A sexual activity that is good and meaningful in private can be stripped of its human significance when it is represented to the public in ways that do not "reflect the richness of human sexuality, but rather turn it into pure animality." Such misrepresentations of human sexuality can be more or less problematic depending on the kind of media and publicity involved. Thus, a portrayal of explicit "erotica" that would be of little concern in the pages of a book might, "[i]f found on a billboard sign, . . . be an undue exploitation of sex, because the community does not tolerate it, on the basis of its harmfulness." Gonthier worried that Justice Sopinka's liberation of "erotica" might extend too far.

---

1 Karen Busby, "LEAF and Pornography: Litigating on Equality and Sexual Representations" (1994) 9 *Canadian Journal of Law and Society* 169.

2 (28 February 1992).

3 Catherine MacKinnon, *Only Words* (Boston: Harvard University Press, 1993).

4 Stephen Bindman, "Top court upholds anti-pornography law" *Montreal Gazette* (28 February 1992) B1.

5 Not everyone finds the distinction persuasive. See Jonathon Daniels, "Valid Despite Vagueness: The Relationship Between Vagueness and Shifting Objective" (1994) *Saskatchewan Law Review* 58.

6 Busby, *supra* note 1.

In *Keegstra* (case 28), Justice Sopinka (along with Justice La Forest) had joined in Justice McLachlin's opinion that the hate-speech provision was not rationally connected to its objective because, instead of promoting egalitarian sentiments, censorship was more likely to strengthen racist expression. In *Butler*, Sopinka (with the support of McLachlin and La Forest) came to the opposite conclusion about the censorship of obscenity: "In contrast to the hate-monger who may succeed, by the sudden media attention, in gaining an audience, the prohibition of obscene materials does nothing to promote the pornographer's cause." Censorship of obscenity, in other words, does not irrationally produce the opposite of what it intends. But does it actually produce what it intends? What if obscenity is a reflection or symptom of bad attitudes rather than their cause? What if it actually provides a safety valve for the safe release of attitudes that might otherwise be acted out in truly harmful ways? Would censorship not then be irrational? Perhaps, but the social science evidence on whether obscenity is harmful is contradictory and inconclusive. Here, Sopinka reaffirmed the holding of earlier decisions that "in the face of inconclusive social science evidence" legislatures need only a "reasonable basis" for their ameliorative initiatives, a criterion fulfilled in the case of the obscenity provision. Similarly, on the basis of precedents holding that a law need not be perfectly tailored in order to satisfy the "minimal impairment" part of the *Oakes* test, Sopinka found that section 163 met that test and that its "restriction on freedom of expression [did] not outweigh the importance of the legislative objective."

The judicial agreement in *Butler* stands in stark contrast not only to the earlier disagreement in *Keegstra* but also to the subsequent disagreement in *R. v. Zundel*, which was heard and decided at roughly the same time as *Butler*.[7] Ernst Zundel, a Holocaust denier, had been charged under section 181 of the *Criminal Code*, which made it an indictable offence for anyone to "wilfully" publish "a statement, tale or news that he knows is false and that causes or is likely to cause injury or mischief to a public interest." As in *Keegstra*, a 7-judge panel split 4 to 3, but this time Justice McLachlin wrote the majority opinion invalidating the law. She was joined by Justices La Forest and Sopinka, who had supported her *Keegstra* dissent, and by Justice L'Heureux-Dubé, who had been part of the *Keegstra* majority. For McLachlin, the "false news" provision was an unreasonable limit on freedom of expression because its original purpose—dating back to 1275—was to protect the King and the nobles against slander that might undermine their legitimacy and destabilize the state. This could not be the kind of "pressing and substantial purpose" needed to override freedom of expression in the *Charter* era. The dissenting judgment, written by Justice Gonthier, argued that this original purpose had evolved in the same way that the purpose of the obscenity provision at stake in *Butler* had evolved. While the original purpose of the false-news provision may have been to protect the interest of the nobles, it was now targeted at "the dissemination of false information which strikes at important interests of *society as a whole*" (emphasis added). This, for Justice Gonthier, was a "permissible shift in emphasis" rather than the kind of "shifting purpose" rejected in *Big M*. Justice McLachlin's majority, all of whom had agreed in *Butler* to introduce the distinction Gonthier was using, vigorously disagreed. It is by no means uncommon to see a concept unanimously introduced to resolve one case fueling disagreement in others down the road.

---

7   *Butler* was heard on June 6, 1991 and decided on February 27, 1992; *Zundel* was heard on December 10, 1991 and decided on August 27, 1992.

While LEAF and pro-censorship feminists exulted in their victory in *Butler*, others, including libertarian feminists and gay and lesbian activists, opposed the decision. It was argued, for example, that *Butler*'s criminalizing of violent, degrading, and dehumanizing sex would disproportionately affect gay and lesbian pornography, where sado-masochistic portrayals do not involve structured inequality between the sexes and may be strongly related to sexual identity. In this view, the *Butler* definition of illegal pornography was fundamentally "heterosexist" and did not leave enough room for sexual diversity. This issue arrived at the Supreme Court in 2000 in *Little Sisters Book and Art Emporium v. Canada*.[8] Little Sisters is a gay and lesbian bookstore whose imports had indeed been disproportionately targeted at the border by Canada Customs. The Supreme Court agreed that Customs had been applying the law in a discriminatory manner, but rejected the position, supported by LEAF, "that sado-masochism performs an emancipatory role in gay and lesbian culture and should therefore be judged by a different standard from that applicable to heterosexual culture." The *Butler* standard of harm, as determined by "community standards," would apply equally to heterosexual and homosexual pornography.

The Court revisited the issue of obscenity again in 2001 in *R. v. Sharpe*.[9] In the immediate aftermath of *Butler*, the federal government added a new, explicit child-pornography dimension to the *Criminal Code*. Among other things, the new section 163.1 criminalizes not just the "possession" of child pornography for purposes of distribution or sale but also purely private possession of such material. John Robin Sharpe was charged on both counts for possessing such material as "Sam Paloc's Boyabuse—Flogging, Fun and Fortitude: A Collection of Kiddiekink Classics." He did not constitutionally challenge the charge of possession for distribution and sale, but argued that prohibiting mere private possession could not be justified as a reasonable limit on freedom of expression. The trial court and a majority of the Court of Appeal agreed with him, striking down the simple possession provision and bringing its enforcement temporarily to a halt in British Columbia. As soon as the trial court handed down its decision in January 1999 there was an immense public outcry. All parties in the House of Commons severely criticized the decision, though they disagreed about the appropriate response, with the Reform Party opposition advocating the use of section 33 of the *Charter* to immediately restore the provision and the Liberal government expressing its confidence that higher courts, including ultimately the Supreme Court, would overrule the trial court.[10] The Liberals were wrong about the Court of Appeal, but right about the Supreme Court.

The Court heard *Sharpe* on January 18 and 19, 2000, but did not hand down its decision until January 26, 2001. This was two to three times the normal gestation period, leading to speculation that the Court dragged out its ruling until after the 2000 election.[11] In the event,

---

8   [2000] 2 S.C.R. 1120.

9   [2001] 1 S.C.R. 45.

10   See Rainer Knopff, "A Delicate Dance: The Courts and the Chrétien Government, 1993-2000" in Leslie A. Pal, ed., *How Ottawa Spends 2001-2002: Power in Transition* (Toronto: Oxford University Press, 2001).

11   "Analysts speculate judges may be holding back pornography ruling for political reasons" *The National Post* (15 November 2000).

the Court unanimously upheld the prohibition of simple possession of child pornography. Three of the judges—L'Heureux-Dubé, Gonthier, and Bastarache—would have upheld the law without reservation. Writing for the other six, Justice McLachlin read two exceptions into the provision. First, the prohibition of simple possession would not extend to "any written material or visual representation created by the accused alone, and held by the accused alone, exclusively for his or her own personal use." To illustrate, Justice McLachlin used the example of a teenager's confidential diary. Second, the provision would not reach "any visual recording, created by or depicting the accused, provided it does not depict unlawful sexual activity and is held by the accused exclusively for private use." Here the example was "a teenage couple [who created and kept] sexually explicit pictures featuring each other alone, or together engaged in lawful sexual activity, provided these pictures were created together and shared only with one another."

In *Sharpe*, as elsewhere, Justice McLachlin was on the more libertarian side of a freedom-of-expression issue, though this was much more moderate libertarianism than had been exhibited by the lower courts. McLachlin's *Sharpe* decision, in writing new meaning into the legislation, represented important legal innovation in the context of overall deference to a government policy. The same, of course, was true of Justice Sopinka's *Butler* opinion, which, while not activist in the sense of striking down a law, was widely recognized as a dramatic—even "world historic"—interpretive innovation. ⌒

R. v. BUTLER
[1992] 1 S.C.R. 452

Hearing: June 6, 1991; Judgment: February 27, 1992.

Present: Lamer C.J. and La Forest, L'Heureux-Dubé, Sopinka, Gonthier, Cory, McLachlin, Stevenson, and Iacobucci JJ.

Interveners: The Attorney General of Canada, the Attorney General for Ontario, the Attorney General of Quebec, the Attorney General of British Columbia, the Attorney General for Alberta, Canadian Civil Liberties Association, Manitoba Association for Rights and Liberties, British Columbia Civil Liberties Association, Women's Legal Education and Action Fund, and G.A.P. (Group Against Pornography) Inc.

The judgment of Lamer C.J. and La Forest, Sopinka, Cory, McLachlin, Stevenson, and Iacobucci JJ. was delivered by

SOPINKA J.: This appeal calls into question the constitutionality of the obscenity provisions of the *Criminal Code*, R.S.C., 1985, c. C-46, s. 163. They are attacked on the ground that they contravene s. 2(*b*) of the *Canadian Charter of Rights and Freedoms*. . . .

. . .[T]his appeal should be confined to the examination of the constitutional validity of s. 163(8) only. . . .

(8) For the purposes of this Act, any publication a dominant characteristic of which is the undue exploitation of sex, or of sex and any one or more of the following

subjects, namely, crime, horror, cruelty and violence, shall be deemed to be obscene.

. . . Pornography can be usefully divided into three categories: (1) explicit sex with violence, (2) explicit sex without violence but which subjects people to treatment that is degrading or dehumanizing, and (3) explicit sex without violence that is neither degrading nor dehumanizing. Violence in this context includes both actual physical violence and threats of physical violence. Relating these three categories to the terms of s. 163(8) of the *Code*, the first, explicit sex coupled with violence, is expressly mentioned. Sex coupled with crime, horror or cruelty will sometimes involve violence. Cruelty, for instance, will usually do so. But, even in the absence of violence, sex coupled with crime, horror or cruelty may fall within the second category. As for category (3), subject to the exception referred to below, it is not covered.

Some segments of society would consider that all three categories of pornography cause harm to society because they tend to undermine its moral fibre. Others would contend that none of the categories cause harm. Furthermore there is a range of opinion as to what is degrading or dehumanizing. See *Pornography and Prostitution in Canada: Report of the Special Committee on Pornography and Prostitution* (1985) (the Fraser Report), vol. 1, at p. 51. Because this is not a matter that is susceptible of proof in the traditional way and because we do not wish to leave it to the individual tastes of judges, we must have a norm that will serve as an arbiter in determining what amounts to an undue exploitation of sex. That arbiter is the community as a whole.

The courts must determine as best they can what the community would tolerate others being exposed to on the basis of the degree of harm that may flow from such exposure. Harm in this context means that it predisposes persons to act in an anti-social manner as, for example, the physical or mental mistreatment of women by men, or, what is perhaps debatable, the reverse. Anti-social conduct for this purpose is conduct which society formally recognizes as incompatible with its proper functioning. The stronger the inference of a risk of harm the lesser the likelihood of tolerance. The inference may be drawn from the material itself or from the material and other evidence. Similarly evidence as to the community standards is desirable but not essential.

In making this determination with respect to the three categories of pornography referred to above, the portrayal of sex coupled with violence will almost always constitute the undue exploitation of sex. Explicit sex which is degrading or dehumanizing may be undue if the risk of harm is substantial. Finally, explicit sex that is not violent and neither degrading nor dehumanizing is generally tolerated in our society and will not qualify as the undue exploitation of sex unless it employs children in its production.

If material is not obscene under this framework, it does not become so by reason of the person to whom it is or may be shown or exposed nor by reason of the place or manner in which it is shown. The availability of sexually explicit materials in theatres and other public places is subject to regulation by competent provincial legislation. Typically such legislation imposes restrictions on the material available to children. See *Nova Scotia Board of Censors v. McNeil*, [1978] 2 S.C.R. 662.

[It is also necessary to determine whether the] undue exploitation of sex [is] the main object of the work or [whether] this portrayal of sex [is] essential to a wider artistic, literary, or other similar purpose? Since the threshold determination must be made on the basis of community standards, that is, whether the sexually explicit aspect is undue, its impact when considered in context must be determined on the same basis. The court must determine whether the sexually explicit material when viewed in the context of the whole work would be tolerated by the community as a whole. Artistic expression rests at the heart of freedom of expression values and any doubt in this regard must be resolved in favour of freedom of expression. . . .

In light of our recent decision in *R. v. Keegstra*, [1990] 3 S.C.R. 697, the respondent, and most of the parties intervening in support of the respondent, do not take issue with the proposition that s. 163 of the *Criminal Code* violates s. 2(*b*) of the *Charter*. In *Keegstra*, we were unanimous in advocating a generous approach to the protection afforded by s. 2(*b*) of the

Charter. Our Court confirmed the view expressed in *Reference re ss. 193 and 195.1(1)(c) of the Criminal Code (Man.)*, [1990] 1 S.C.R. 1123 (the "*Prostitution Reference*"), that activities cannot be excluded from the scope of the guaranteed freedom on the basis of the content or meaning being conveyed. . . .

Meaning sought to be expressed need not be "redeeming" in the eyes of the court to merit the protection of s. 2(*b*), whose purpose is to ensure that thoughts and feelings may be conveyed freely in non-violent ways without fear of censure.

In this case, both the purpose and effect of s. 163 are specifically to restrict the communication of certain types of materials based on their content. In my view, there is no doubt that s. 163 seeks to prohibit certain types of expressive activity and thereby infringes s. 2(*b*) of the *Charter*.

Before turning to consider whether this infringement is justified under s. 1 of the *Charter*, I wish to address the argument advanced by the Attorney General of B.C. that in applying s. 2(*b*), a distinction should be made between films and written works. It is argued that by its very nature, the medium of the written word is such that it is, when used, inherently an attempt to convey meaning. In contrast, British Columbia argues that the medium of film can be used for a purpose "not significantly communicative." In its factum, British Columbia maintains that if the activity captured in hard core pornographic magazines and videotapes is itself not expression, the fact that they are reproduced by the technology of a camera does not magically transform them into "expression": the appellant cannot hide behind the label "film" to claim protection for the reproduction of activity the sole purpose of which is to arouse or shock.

In my view, this submission cannot be maintained. This position is not far from that taken by the majority of the Court of Appeal, that the depiction of purely physical activity does not convey meaning. First, I cannot agree with the premise that purely physical activity, such as sexual activity, cannot be expression. Second, in creating a film, regardless of its content, the maker of the film is consciously choosing the particular images which together constitute the film. In choosing his or her images, the creator of the film is attempting to convey some meaning. The meaning to be ascribed to the work cannot be measured by the reaction of the audience, which, in some cases, may amount to no more than physical arousal or shock. Rather, the meaning of the work derives from the fact that it has been intentionally created by its author. To use an example, it may very well be said that a blank wall in itself conveys no meaning. However, if one deliberately chooses to capture that image by the medium of film, the work necessarily has some meaning for its author and thereby constitutes expression. The same would apply to the depiction of persons engaged in purely sexual activity.

D. Is Section 163 Justified Under Section 1 of the Charter?

The appellant argues that the provision is so vague that . . . it does not qualify as "a limit prescribed by law"; . . . so imprecise that it is not a reasonable limit. . . .

Standards which escape precise technical definition, such as "undue," are an inevitable part of the law. . . . It is within the role of the judiciary to attempt to interpret these terms. If such interpretation yields an intelligible standard, the threshold test for the application of s. 1 is met. In my opinion, the interpretation of s. 163(8) in prior judgments which I have reviewed, as supplemented by these reasons, provides an intelligible standard. . . .

The respondent argues that there are several pressing and substantial objectives which justify overriding the freedom to distribute obscene materials. Essentially, these objectives are the avoidance of harm resulting from antisocial attitudinal changes that exposure to obscene material causes and the public interest in maintaining a "decent society." On the other hand, the appellant argues that the objective of s. 163 is to have the state act as "moral custodian" in sexual matters and to impose subjective standards of morality.

The obscenity legislation and jurisprudence prior to the enactment of s. 163 were evidently concerned with prohibiting the "immoral influences" of obscene publications and safeguarding the morals of individuals into whose hands such works could fall. . . .

I agree with Twaddle J.A. of the Court of Appeal that this particular objective is no longer defensible in view of the *Charter*. To impose a certain standard of public and sexual morality, solely because it reflects the conventions of a given community, is inimical to the exercise and enjoyment of individual freedoms, which form the basis of our social contract. . . . The prevention of "dirt for dirt's sake" is not a legitimate objective which would justify the violation of one of the most fundamental freedoms enshrined in the *Charter*.

On the other hand, I cannot agree with the suggestion of the appellant that Parliament does not have the right to legislate on the basis of some fundamental conception of morality for the purposes of safeguarding the values which are integral to a free and democratic society. As Dyzenhaus ["Obscenity and the Charter: Autonomy and Equality" (1991), 1 C.R. (4th) 367], at p. 376, writes:

> Moral disapproval is recognized as an appropriate response when it has its basis in *Charter* values.

As the respondent and many of the interveners have pointed out, much of the criminal law is based on moral conceptions of right and wrong and the mere fact that a law is grounded in morality does not automatically render it illegitimate. In this regard, criminalizing the proliferation of materials which undermine another basic *Charter* right may indeed be a legitimate objective.

In my view, however, the overriding objective of s. 163 is not moral disapprobation but the avoidance of harm to society. . . .

The harm was described in the following way in the Report on Pornography by the Standing Committee on Justice and Legal Affairs (MacGuigan Report) (1978), at p. 18:4:

> The clear and unquestionable danger of this type of material is that it reinforces some unhealthy tendencies in Canadian society. The effect of this type of material is to reinforce male–female stereotypes to the detriment of both sexes. It attempts to make degradation, humiliation, victimization, and violence in human relationships appear normal and acceptable. A society which holds that egalitarianism, non-violence, consensualism, and mutuality are basic to any human interaction, whether sexual or other, is clearly justified in controlling and prohibiting any medium of depiction, description or advocacy which violates these principles.

The appellant argues that to accept the objective of the provision as being related to the harm associated with obscenity would be to adopt the "shifting purpose" doctrine explicitly rejected in *R. v. Big M Drug Mart Ltd.*, [1985] 1 S.C.R. 295. This Court concluded in that case that a finding that the *Lord's Day Act* has a secular purpose was not possible given that its religious purpose, in compelling sabbatical observance, has been long-established and consistently maintained by the courts. . . .

I do not agree that to identify the objective of the impugned legislation as the prevention of harm to society, one must resort to the "shifting purpose" doctrine. First, the notions of moral corruption and harm to society are not distinct, as the appellant suggests, but are inextricably linked. It is moral corruption of a certain kind which leads to the detrimental effect on society. Second, and more importantly, I am of the view that with the enactment of s. 163, Parliament explicitly sought to address the harms which are linked to certain types of obscene materials. The prohibition of such materials was based on a belief that they had a detrimental impact on individuals exposed to them and consequently on society as a whole. Our understanding of the harms caused by these materials has developed considerably since that time; however this does not detract from the fact that the purpose of this legislation remains, as it was in 1959, the protection of society from harms caused by the exposure to obscene materials. . . .

A permissible shift in emphasis was built into the legislation when, as interpreted by the courts, it adopted the community standards test. Community standards as to what is harmful have changed since 1959.

This being the objective, is it pressing and substantial? Does the prevention of the harm associated with the dissemination of certain obscene materials constitute a sufficiently pressing and substantial concern to warrant a restriction on the freedom of expression? In this regard, it should be recalled that in *Keegstra, supra*, this Court unanimously accepted that the prevention of the influence of hate propaganda on society at large was a legitimate objective....

This Court has thus recognized that the harm caused by the proliferation of materials which seriously offend the values fundamental to our society is a substantial concern which justifies restricting the otherwise full exercise of the freedom of expression. In my view, the harm sought to be avoided in the case of the dissemination of obscene materials is similar....

In reaching the conclusion that legislation proscribing obscenity is a valid objective which justifies some encroachment on the right to freedom of expression, I am persuaded in part that such legislation may be found in most free and democratic societies. As Nemetz C.J.B.C. aptly pointed out in *R. v. Red Hot Video*, [(1985), 45 C.R. (3d) 36 (B.C.C.A.)], for centuries democratic societies have set certain limits to freedom of expression. He cited (at p. 40) the following passage of Dickson J.A. (as he then was) in *R. v. Great West News Ltd., supra*, at p. 309:

> ... [A]ll organized societies have sought in one manner or another to suppress obscenity. The right of the state to legislate to protect its moral fibre and well-being has long been recognized, with roots deep in history. It is within this frame that the Courts and Judges must work.

The advent of the *Charter* did not have the effect of dramatically depriving Parliament of a power which it has historically enjoyed. It is also noteworthy that the criminalization of obscenity was considered to be compatible with the *Canadian Bill of Rights*....

The enactment of the impugned provision is also consistent with Canada's international obligations (Agreement for the Suppression of the Circulation of Obscene Publications and the Convention for the Suppression of the Circulation of and Traffic in Obscene Publications).

Finally, it should be noted that the burgeoning pornography industry renders the concern even more pressing and substantial than when the impugned provisions were first enacted. I would therefore conclude that the objective of avoiding the harm associated with the dissemination of pornography in this case is sufficiently pressing and substantial to warrant some restriction on full exercise of the right to freedom of expression. The analysis of whether the measure is propor-

tional to the objective must, in my view, be undertaken in light of the conclusion that the objective of the impugned section is valid only in so far as it relates to the harm to society associated with obscene materials. Indeed, the section as interpreted in previous decisions and in these reasons is fully consistent with that objective. The objective of maintaining conventional standards of propriety, independently of any harm to society, is no longer justified in light of the values of individual liberty which underlie the *Charter*....

In assessing whether the proportionality test is met, it is important to keep in mind the nature of expression which has been infringed. In the *Prostitution Reference, supra*, Dickson C.J. wrote, at p. 1136:

> When a *Charter* freedom has been infringed by state action that takes the form of criminalization, the Crown bears the heavy burden of justifying that infringement. Yet, the expressive activity, as with any infringed *Charter* right, should also be analysed in the particular context of the case. Here, the activity to which the impugned legislation is directed is expression with an economic purpose. It can hardly be said that communications regarding an economic transaction of sex for money lie at, or even near, the core of the guarantee of freedom of expression.

The values which underlie the protection of freedom of expression relate to the search for truth, participation in the political process, and individual self-fulfilment. The Attorney General for Ontario argues that of these, only "individual self-fulfilment," and only in its most base aspect, that of physical arousal, is engaged by pornography. On the other hand, the civil liberties groups argue that pornography forces us to question conventional notions of sexuality and thereby launches us into an inherently political discourse. In their factum, the B.C. Civil Liberties Association adopts a passage from R. West, "The Feminist-Conservative Anti-Pornography Alliance and the 1986 Attorney General's Commission on Pornography Report" (1987), 4 *Am. Bar Found. Res. Jo.* 681, at p. 696:

> Good pornography has value because it validates women's will to pleasure. It celebrates female nature. It validates a range of female sexuality that is wider and truer than that legitimated by the non-pornographic culture. Pornography (when it is good) celebrates both female pleasure and male rationality.

A proper application of the test should not suppress what West refers to as "good pornography." The objective of the impugned provision is not to inhibit the celebration of human sexuality. However, it cannot be ignored that the realities of the pornography industry are far from the picture which the B.C.

Civil Liberties Association would have us paint. Shannon J., in *R. v. Wagner*, [(1985), 43 C.R. (3d) 318 (Alta. Q.B.)], described the materials more accurately when he observed, at p. 331:

> Women, particularly, are deprived of unique human character or identity and are depicted as sexual playthings, hysterically and instantly responsive to male sexual demands. They worship male genitals and their own value depends upon the quality of their genitals and breasts.

In my view, the kind of expression which is sought to be advanced does not stand on an equal footing with other kinds of expression which directly engage the "core" of the freedom of expression values.

This conclusion is further buttressed by the fact that the targeted material is expression which is motivated, in the overwhelming majority of cases, by economic profit. This Court held in *Rocket v. Royal College of Dental Surgeons of Ontario*, [1990] 2 S.C.R. 232, at p. 247, that an economic motive for expression means that restrictions on the expression might "be easier to justify than other infringements."

I will now turn to an examination of the three basic aspects of the proportionality test.

... [T]he rational link between s. 163 and the objective of Parliament relates to the actual causal relationship between obscenity and the risk of harm to society at large. On this point, it is clear that the literature of the social sciences remains subject to controversy. ...

In the face of inconclusive social science evidence, the approach adopted by our Court in *Irwin Toy* is instructive. In that case, the basis for the legislation was that television advertising directed at young children is *per se* manipulative. The Court made it clear, at p. 994, that in choosing its mode of intervention, it is sufficient that Parliament had a *reasonable basis*:

> In the instant case, the Court is called upon to assess competing social science evidence respecting the appropriate means for addressing the problem of children's advertising. The question is whether the government had a reasonable basis, on the evidence tendered, for concluding that the ban on all advertising directed at children impaired freedom of expression as little as possible given the government's pressing and substantial objective.

And at p. 990:

> ... [T]he Court also recognized that the government was afforded a margin of appreciation to form legitimate objectives based on somewhat inconclusive social science evidence.

Similarly, in *Keegstra, supra*, the absence of proof of a causative link between hate propaganda and hatred of an identifiable group was discounted as a determinative factor in assessing the constitutionality of the hate literature provisions of the *Criminal Code*. Dickson C.J. stated, at p. 776:

> First, to predicate the limitation of free expression upon proof of actual hatred gives insufficient attention to the severe psychological trauma suffered by members of those identifiable groups targeted by hate propaganda. Second, it is clearly difficult to prove a causative link between a specific statement and hatred of an identifiable group.

McLachlin J. (dissenting) expressed it as follows, at p. 857:

> To view hate propaganda as "victimless" in the absence of any proof that it moved its listeners to hatred is to discount the wrenching impact that it may have on members of the target group themselves.... Moreover, it is simply not possible to assess with any precision the effects that expression of a particular message will have on all those who are ultimately exposed to it.

... Accordingly, I am of the view that there is a sufficiently rational link between the criminal sanction, which demonstrates our community's disapproval of the dissemination of materials which potentially victimize women and which restricts the negative influence which such materials have on changes in attitudes and behaviour, and the objective.

Finally, I wish to distinguish this case from *Keegstra*, in which the minority adopted the view that there was no rational connection between the criminalization of hate propaganda and its suppression. As McLachlin J. noted, prosecutions under the *Criminal Code* for racist expression have attracted extensive media coverage. The criminal process confers on the accused publicity for his or her causes and succeeds even in generating sympathy. The same cannot be said of the kinds of expression sought to be suppressed in the present case. The general availability of the subject materials and the rampant pornography industry are such that, in the words of Dickson C.J. in *Keegstra*, "pornography is not dignified by its suppression." In contrast to the hate-monger who may succeed, by the sudden media attention, in gaining an audience, the prohibition of obscene materials does nothing to promote the pornographer's cause. ...

In determining whether less intrusive legislation may be imagined, this Court stressed in the *Prostitution Reference, supra*, that it is not necessary that the legislative scheme be the "perfect" scheme, but that it be appropriately tailored *in the context of the infringed right* (at p. 1138). Furthermore, in *Irwin Toy, supra*, Dickson C.J., Lamer and Wilson JJ. stated, at p. 999:

> While evidence exists that other less intrusive options reflecting more modest objectives were available to the

government, there is evidence establishing the necessity of a ban to meet the objectives the government had reasonably set. This Court will not, in the name of minimal impairment, take a restrictive approach to social science evidence and require legislatures to choose the least ambitious means to protect vulnerable groups.

There are several factors which contribute to the finding that the provision minimally impairs the freedom which is infringed.

First, the impugned provision does not proscribe sexually explicit erotica without violence that is not degrading or dehumanizing. It is designed to catch material that creates a risk of harm to society. . . .

Second, materials which have scientific, artistic or literary merit are not captured by the provision. As discussed above, the court must be generous in its application of the "artistic defence." For example, in certain cases, materials such as photographs, prints, books and films which may undoubtedly be produced with some motive for economic profit, may nonetheless claim the protection of the *Charter* in so far as their defining characteristic is that of aesthetic expression, and thus represent the artist's attempt at individual fulfilment. The existence of an accompanying economic motive does not, of itself, deprive a work of significance as an example of individual artistic or self-fulfilment.

Third, in considering whether the provision minimally impairs the freedom in question, it is legitimate for the court to take into account Parliament's past abortive attempts to replace the definition with one that is more explicit. In *Irwin Toy*, our Court recognized that it is legitimate to take into account the fact that earlier laws and proposed alternatives were thought to be less effective than the legislation that is presently being challenged. The attempt to provide exhaustive instances of obscenity has been shown to be destined to fail (Bill C-54, 2nd Sess., 33rd Parl.). It seems that the only practicable alternative is to strive towards a more abstract definition of obscenity which is contextually sensitive and responsive to progress in the knowledge and understanding of the phenomenon to which the legislation is directed. In my view, the standard of "undue exploitation" is therefore appropriate. The intractable nature of the problem and the impossibility of precisely defining a notion which is inherently elusive makes the possibility of a more explicit provision remote. In this light, it is appropriate to question whether, and at what cost, greater legislative precision can be demanded.

Fourth, while the discussion in this appeal has been limited to the definition portion of s. 163, I would note that the impugned section, with the possible exception of subs. 1, which is not in issue here, has been held by this Court not to

extend its reach to the private use or viewing of obscene materials. . . .

Accordingly, it is only the public distribution and exhibition of obscene materials which is in issue here.

Finally, I wish to address the arguments of the interveners, the Canadian Civil Liberties Association and Manitoba Association for Rights and Liberties, that the objectives of this kind of legislation may be met by alternative, less intrusive measures. First, it is submitted that reasonable time, manner and place restrictions would be preferable to outright prohibition. I am of the view that this argument should be rejected. Once it has been established that the objective is the avoidance of harm caused by the degradation which many women feel as "victims" of the message of obscenity, and of the negative impact exposure to such material has on perceptions and attitudes towards women, it is untenable to argue that these harms could be avoided by placing restrictions on access to such material. Making the materials more difficult to obtain by increasing their cost and reducing their availability does not achieve the same objective. Once Parliament has reasonably concluded that certain acts are harmful to certain groups in society and to society in general, it would be inconsistent, if not hypocritical, to argue that such acts could be committed in more restrictive conditions. The harm sought to be avoided would remain the same in either case.

It is also submitted that there are more effective techniques to promote the objectives of Parliament. For example, if pornography is seen as encouraging violence against women, there are certain activities which discourage it—counselling rape victims to charge their assailants, provision of shelter and assistance for battered women, campaigns for laws against discrimination on the grounds of sex, education to increase the sensitivity of law enforcement agencies and other governmental authorities. In addition, it is submitted that education is an under-used response.

It is noteworthy that many of the above suggested alternatives are in the form of *responses* to the harm engendered by negative attitudes against women. The role of the impugned provision is to control the dissemination of the very images that contribute to such attitudes. Moreover, it is true that there are additional measures which could alleviate the problem of violence against women. However, given the gravity of the harm, and the threat to the values at stake, I do not believe that the measure chosen by Parliament is equalled by the alternatives which have been suggested. Education, too, may offer a means of combating negative attitudes to women, just as it is currently used as a means of addressing other problems dealt with in the *Code*. However, there is no reason to rely on education alone. It should be emphasized that this is in no way intended to deny the value of other educational and counselling measures to deal with the roots and effects of negative attitudes. Rather, it is only to stress the arbitrariness and unacceptability of the claim that such measures represent the sole legitimate means of addressing the phenomenon. Serious social problems such as violence against women require multi-pronged approaches by government. Education and legislation are not alternatives but complements in addressing such problems. There is nothing in the *Charter* which requires Parliament to choose between such complementary measures.

The final question to be answered in the proportionality test is whether the effects of the law so severely trench on a protected right that the legislative objective is outweighed by the infringement. The infringement on freedom of expression is confined to a measure designed to prohibit the distribution of sexually explicit materials accompanied by violence, and those without violence that are degrading or dehumanizing. As I have already concluded, this kind of expression lies far from the core of the guarantee of freedom of expression. It appeals only to the most base aspect of individual fulfilment, and it is primarily economically motivated.

The objective of the legislation, on the other hand, is of fundamental importance in a free and democratic society. It is aimed at avoiding harm, which Parliament has reasonably concluded will be caused directly or indirectly, to individuals, groups such as women and children, and consequently to society as a whole, by the distribution of these materials. It thus seeks to enhance respect for all members of society, and non-violence and equality in their relations with each other.

I therefore conclude that the restriction on freedom of expression does not outweigh the importance of the legislative objective.

I conclude that while s. 163(8) infringes s. 2(*b*) of the *Charter*, freedom of expression, it constitutes a reasonable limit and is saved by virtue of the provisions of s. 1....

The reasons of L'Heureux-Dubé and Gonthier JJ. were delivered by

GONTHIER J.: I have had the benefit of the reasons of Justice Sopinka and, while I agree both with his disposition of the case and with his reasons generally, I wish to add to them with respect to the judicial interpretation of s. 163 of the *Criminal Code*, R.S.C., 1985, c. C-46, and to its constitutional validity.

Section 163 of the *Code* offers a peculiar structure. Its subject matter, obscene materials, comprises the dual elements of representation and content. Representation here is understood in the sense of public suggestion. A representation is a portrayal, a description meant to evoke something to the mind and senses.... By "content" I mean of course the content of the representation.

It is the combination of the two, the representation and its content, that attracts criminal liability. A representation as such is not enough, of course, to create the subject matter of s. 163, but neither is an act included in the content of s. 163 of the *Code*, without an element of representation....

... The type of scenes vividly described in *R. v. Wagner* (1985), 43 C.R. (3d) 318 (Alta. Q.B.), *R. v. Doug Rankine Co.* (1983), 9 C.C.C. (3d) 53 (Ont. Co. Ct.) or *R. v. Ramsingh* (1984), 14 C.C.C. (3d) 230 (Man. Q.B.), might perhaps be legal if done between consenting adults, but they become obscene when they are represented.

Without launching into a lengthy debate on the reasons why Parliament may have enacted s. 163 of the *Code*... it can be seen that the combination of representation and content that constitutes obscenity leads to many ills.... Obscene materials... convey a distorted image of human sexuality, by making public and open elements of the human nature which are usually hidden behind a veil of modesty and privacy. D. A. Downs, *The New Politics of Pornography* (1989), aptly describes how these materials do not reflect the richness of human sexuality, but rather turn it into pure animality, at p. 183:

> ... the deeper objection to sheer pornography or obscenity ... is that it represents a retreat from the human dilemma and the responsibility of acknowledging the tensions in our nature. Sheer pornography also reduces us to the lower aspects of our natures by stripping away the modesty that arises from our encounter with our animality....

To summarize ... the particular combination of a representation and its content that forms the subject matter of s. 163 of the *Code* was seen by Parliament as putting forward a distorted image of human sexuality, which in turn can induce harmful behavioural changes. This must be kept in mind when interpreting s. 163 of the *Code*....

... Sopinka J. essentially aligns the definition of obscenity in s. 163(8) of the *Code* with the definition of pornography nowadays. He introduces a three-part categorization that has surfaced in contemporary theory, and that had been adopted in some Canadian cases throughout the 80s:

(a) Explicit sex with violence, which generally constitutes "undue exploitation of sex" within the meaning of s. 163(8) of the *Code*, on the basis of demonstrable harm;

(b) Explicit sex that is degrading or dehumanizing, which will be "undue exploitation of sex" if it creates a substantial risk of harm; the risk of harm can be assessed with reference to the tolerance of the community, under the "community standard of tolerance" test; and

(c) Explicit sex that is neither violent nor degrading or dehumanizing, which will not generally fall under s. 163(8) of the *Code*, according to Sopinka J.

I must say at the outset that I differ only with respect to the third category of materials. I am not prepared to affirm as boldly as my colleague Sopinka J. does that it escapes the application of s. 163(8)....

The dual nature, as representation and content, of the subject matter of s. 163 comes into play here. Yet the classification proposed by my colleague Sopinka J. focuses only on content. The content of the first two categories of materials is so likely to harm that the characteristics of the representation do not really matter: if there is violence or degradation or dehumanization, as long as the element of representation is present, harm will probably ensue.

The content of the third category of materials is generally perceived as unlikely to cause harm, as Sopinka J. rightly points out. He mentions as an exception child pornography, i.e. materials in the production of which children were employed. This exception is important, since it obviously flows from the high likelihood of harm ensuing from the production and dissemination of child pornography.

In addition to this exception, it is quite conceivable that the representation may cause harm, even if its content as such may not be seen as harmful....

... After all, it is the element of representation that gives this material its power of suggestion, and it seems quite conceivable that this power may cause harm despite the apparent neutrality of the content. A host of factors could intervene in the manner of representation to affect the characterization of the material, among which are the medium, the type or the use.

The medium provides a good example. Indeed the differences between the various media are not acknowledged often enough in opinions dealing with s. 163 of the *Code*....

Nevertheless it seems natural to me that the likelihood of harm, and the tolerance of the community, may vary according to the medium of representation, even if the content stays the same. Let me take, as an example, an explicit portrayal of "plain" sexual intercourse, where two individuals are making love. This falls within the third category of Sopinka J. If found in words in a book, it is unlikely to be of much concern (if found in a children's book, though, this may be different). If found depicted in a magazine or in a movie, the likelihood of harm increases but remains low. If found on a poster, it is already more troublesome. If found on a billboard sign, then I would venture that it may well be an undue exploitation of sex, because the community does not tolerate it, on the basis of its harmfulness.

The harmfulness, in the billboard sign example, would come from the immediacy of the representation, inasmuch as the sign stands all by itself (as opposed to a passage in a book, a film or a magazine). Its message is at once crude and inescapable. It distorts human sexuality by taking it out of any context whatsoever and projecting it to the public. This example goes to the extreme, of course, but it is meant to show that the element of representation may create a likelihood of harm that may lead to the application of s. 163 of the *Code*, even if the content of the representation as such is not objectionable.

As I mentioned, the medium of representation is but one variable pertaining to representation that may trigger the application of s. 163 to third-category materials. The overall type or use of the representation, be it education, art, advertising, sexual arousal or other, may also be relevant, among other factors. These factors tie in to the "internal necessities" test to some extent. This test, if it is to find a place within the interpretive framework of Sopinka J., must intervene at the representational level, to change the characterization that would ensue from a mere look at the content of the materials.

For these reasons, therefore, I would hold that materials falling within Sopinka J.'s third category (explicit sex with neither violence nor degradation or dehumanization), while generally less likely to cause harm than those of the first two categories, may nevertheless come within the definition of obscene at s. 163(8) of the *Code*, if their content (child pornography) or their representational element (the manner of representation) is found conducive of harm....

The assessment of the risk of harm here depends on the tolerance of the community, as is the case with the second category of materials. This brings me to outline a certain shift in the meaning of "tolerance." In *Towne Cinema*, [[1985] 1 S.C.R. 494], Dickson C.J. formulated the community standard test as follows at p. 508:

> ... it is a standard of *tolerance*, not taste, that is relevant. What matters is not what Canadians think is right for themselves to see. What matters is what Canadians would not abide other Canadians seeing because it would be beyond the contemporary Canadian standard of tolerance to allow them to see it. [Emphasis in original.]

It is unclear from this excerpt what the basis of tolerance is. It seems that tolerance is for taste the conceptual equivalent of the reasonable person to the actual plaintiff: an abstraction, an average perhaps. Tolerance would be some form of enlightened, altruistic taste, which would factor in and sum up the tastes of the whole population.

In the mind of Dickson C.J., there exists no necessary relationship between tolerance and harm, as he mentions at p. 505:

However, as I have noted above, there is no *necessary* coincidence between the undueness of publications which degrade people by linking violence, cruelty or other forms of dehumanizing treatment with sex, and the community standard of tolerance. Even if certain sex related materials were found to be within the standard of tolerance of the community, it would still be necessary to ensure that they were not "undue" in some other sense, for example in the sense that they portray persons in a degrading manner as objects of violence, cruelty, or other forms of dehumanizing treatment. [Emphasis in original.]

Sopinka J. uses the community standard of tolerance to gauge the risk of harm. In this context, tolerance must be related to the harm. It must mean not only tolerance of the materials, but also tolerance of the harm which they may bring about. It is a more complicated and more reflective form of tolerance than what was considered by Dickson C.J. in *Towne Cinema, supra*. Such a development is fully in accordance with the emphasis put by this Court on harm as the central element in the interpretation of s. 163(8).

In the context of the third category, the harm sought to be avoided is the same as in the first two categories, that is attitudinal changes. While this type of harm was clear in the case of the first category and was probable in the case of the second, it is perhaps more remote here, and will likely occur only in a limited number of cases. The main difference between the second and third categories lies in the presumed likelihood of harm: while degrading or dehumanizing materials are likely to cause harm regardless of whether the community may be ready to tolerate such harm, materials which show no violence, no degradation or dehumanization are less likely to cause harm, and the evidence with respect to the lack of tolerance of the community will be central. Still the risk of harm flowing from the content or the representational element of third-category materials is not always so slight as my colleague Sopinka J. pictures it. If the community cannot tolerate this risk of harm, then in my opinion these materials, even though they may offer a non-violent, non-degrading, non-dehumanizing content, will constitute undue exploitation of sex and will fall under the definition of obscenity at s. 163(8) of the *Code*....

With respect to the constitutional aspects of this case, I am in agreement with Sopinka J., and I wish only to complement his reasons on the objective of s. 163 of the *Code*.

In his reasons, Sopinka J. rules out the possibility that "public morality" can be a legitimate objective for s. 163 of the *Code* and, while admitting that Parliament may legislate to protect "fundamental conceptions of morality," he goes on to conclude that the true objective of s. 163 is the avoidance of harm to society.

In my opinion, the distinction between the two orders of morality advanced by my colleague is correct, and the avoidance of harm to society is but one instance of a fundamental conception of morality.

First of all, I cannot conceive that the State could not legitimately act on the basis of morality. Since its earliest *Charter* pronouncements, this Court has acknowledged this possibility. In *R. v. Big M Drug Mart Ltd.*, [1985] 1 S.C.R. 295, Dickson J. (as he then was) wrote for the Court at p. 337:

Freedom means that, subject to such limitations as are necessary to protect public safety, order, health, or morals or the fundamental rights and freedoms of others, no one is to be forced to act in a way contrary to his beliefs or his conscience.

Morality is also listed as one of the grounds for which freedom of expression can be restricted in the *European Convention on Human Rights* at article 10:

1. Everyone has the right to freedom of expression....
2. The exercise of these freedoms, since it carries with it duties and responsibilities, may be subject to such formalities, conditions, restrictions or penalties as are prescribed by law and are necessary in a democratic society, in the interests of national security, territorial integrity or public safety, for the prevention of disorder or crime, for the protection of health or morals, for the protection of the reputation or rights of others, for preventing the disclosure of information received in confidence, or for maintaining the authority and impartiality of the judiciary.

The European Court of Human Rights has recognized the validity of prohibitions of obscene materials in English and Swiss law, respectively, on the basis that they concern morals, in the *Handyside Case*, judgment of 7 December 1976, Series A No. 24 and in the *Case of Müller and Others*, judgment of 24 May 1988, Series A No. 133.

Indeed the problem is not so much to assess whether morality is a valid objective under the *Charter* as to determine under which conditions it is a pressing and substantial objective. Not all moral claims will be sufficient to warrant an override of *Charter* rights. As R. Dworkin wrote in the chapter of *Taking Rights Seriously* (1977) entitled "Liberty and Moralism" at p. 255:

The claim that a moral consensus exists is not itself based on a poll. It is based on an appeal to the legislator's sense of how his community reacts to some disfavored practice. But this same sense includes an awareness of the grounds on which that reaction is generally supported. If there has been a public debate involving the editorial columns, speeches of his colleagues, the testimony of interested groups, and his own correspondence, these will sharpen his awareness of what arguments and positions are in the field. He must sift these arguments and positions, suppose general principles or theories vast parts of the population could not be supposed to accept, and so on.

This task that Dworkin assigns to Parliament is also entrusted to this Court in *Charter* review. Two dimensions are important here, which allow one to distinguish between morality in the general sense and "fundamental conceptions of morality."

First of all, the moral claims must be grounded. They must involve concrete problems such as life, harm, well-being, to name a few, and not merely differences of opinion or of taste. Parliament cannot restrict *Charter* rights simply on the basis of dislike; this is what is meant by the expression "substantial and pressing" concern.

Secondly, a consensus must exist among the population on these claims. They must attract the support of more than a simple majority of people. In a pluralistic society like ours, many different conceptions of the good are held by various segments of the population. The guarantees of s. 2 of the *Charter* protect this pluralistic diversity. However, if the holders of these different conceptions agree that some conduct is not good, then the respect for pluralism that underlies s. 2 of the *Charter* becomes less insurmountable an objection to State action (this argument has recently been rejuvenated and reformulated in S. Gardbaum, "Why the Liberal State Can Promote Moral Ideals After All" (1991), 104 *Harv. L. Rev.* 1350). In this sense a wide consensus among holders of different conceptions of the good is necessary before the State can intervene in the name of morality. This is also comprised in the phrase "pressing and substantial."

The avoidance of harm caused to society through attitudinal changes certainly qualifies as a "fundamental conception of morality." After all, one of the chief aspirations of morality is the avoidance of harm. It is well grounded, since the harm takes the form of violations of the principles of human equality and dignity. Obscene materials debase sexuality. They lead to the humiliation of women, and sometimes to violence against them. This is more than just a matter of taste. Without entering into the examination of the rational connection, some empirical evidence even elucidates the link between these materials and actual violence. Even then, as was said by

this Court in *Irwin Toy Ltd. v. Quebec (Attorney General)*, [1989] 1 S.C.R. 927, in *R. v. Keegstra*, [1990] 3 S.C.R. 697, and as is reiterated by my colleague in his reasons, scientific proof is not required, and reason and common experience will often suffice.

Furthermore, taking into account that people hold different conceptions about good taste and the acceptable level of sexual explicitness, most would agree that these attitudinal changes are serious and warrant State intervention (civil liberty groups who advocated that this Court strike down s. 163 of the *Code* concede that harm can justify State intervention, but they deny that any harm flows from obscene materials; that is a different question).

I agree with Sopinka J. that s. 163 of the *Code* aims at preventing harm to society and I fully endorse his analysis, and as I tried to demonstrate I would not hesitate to affirm that the prevention of harm is a moral objective that is valid under s. 1 of the *Charter*.

I also agree with Sopinka J.'s analysis of the proportionality between the restriction effected by s. 163 of the *Code* and its objectives. I would add a remark, however, on the first factor listed by Sopinka J. under the minimal impairment branch of the proportionality test, that is the exception for materials of the third category. Contrary to Sopinka J., I consider that the third category may sometimes attract criminal liability. The requirement that the impugned materials exceed the community standard of tolerance of harm provides sufficient precision and protection for those whose activities are at stake. This is so as, on the one hand, the field of sexual exploitation is one of first apprehension, directly related to one of the primary aspects of human personality, and well known to all, including particularly those engaged in it. On the other hand, the criterion of tolerance of harm by the community as a whole is one that, by definition, reflects the general level of tolerance throughout all sectors of the community, hence generally of all its members. It is therefore a very demanding criterion to meet as it must be by definition generally known or apprehended. It is indeed not far removed from the domain of public notoriety and, inasmuch as it falls within it, may be the subject of judicial notice not requiring specific proof.

Subject to the foregoing comments, I otherwise concur both with the reasons and the disposition of the case of my colleague Sopinka J.

RJR-MacDonald Inc. v. Canada (Attorney General), 1995

In this case, major tobacco companies claimed that a federal ban on tobacco advertising fell beyond Ottawa's criminal law power and constituted an unreasonable infringement of the *Charter*'s freedom-of-expression guarantee. Speaking through seven separate opinions (most of them short), a substantial majority (7 to 2) of the Court found that the ban was valid criminal law while a narrow majority (5 to 4) voted to strike it down on freedom-of-expression grounds. We reproduce below only the primary majority and dissenting opinions on the *Charter* issue.

The law at issue prohibited the advertising and promotion of tobacco products and required the packaging for those products to display non-attributed warnings about the toxic ingredients and negative health effects of tobacco. As in other freedom-of-expression cases, a *Charter* violation was (mostly) conceded, and the analysis turned mainly on determining whether the law could be justified as a "reasonable limit" under section 1.

The Court has established two ways of determining how much deference is owed to Parliament in the section 1 stage of analysis. First, as we have seen (for example, in *Keegstra*, case 28, and in *Butler*, case 30), the farther the infringed expression falls from the "core" freedom-of-expression values—"the search for political, artistic and scientific truth, the protection of individual autonomy and self-development, and the *promotion of public participation in the democratic process*"—the lower the standard justification. Second, because courts have well-established expertise in matters of criminal law, where the state acts as the "singular antagonist of the individual," they can apply higher levels of scrutiny than when legislation is aimed at "mediating between different groups" or social interests, which requires policy judgments that lie outside traditional judicial expertise.

While both the main opinions in the case—Justice McLachlin's for the majority and Justice La Forest's for the minority—agreed with these distinctions in principle, they applied them very differently. Thus, while La Forest saw the kind of expression at stake in this case—commercial advertising aimed at increasing profits—as falling far from the core of expression values, McLachlin rejected his reliance on the profit motive, pointing out that booksellers and newspaper owners—surely close to the core—were also profit-oriented enterprises. And while La Forest saw the legislation as compromising "among the competing interests of smokers, non-smokers and manufacturers, with an eye to protecting vulnerable groups in society," and thus as "the very type of legislation to which this Court has generally accorded a high degree of deference," McLachlin observed that it was also a criminal law that "pits the state against the offender." In any case, said McLachlin, "[t]o carry judicial deference to the point of accepting Parliament's view simply on the basis that the problem is serious and the solution difficult"—as she clearly thought La Forest had done—"would be to diminish the role of the courts in the constitutional process and to weaken the structure of rights upon which our constitution and our nation is founded."

One of the reasons La Forest considered the problem serious and the solution difficult is that the law was 20 years in the making and that similarly protracted policy processes had led at least 20 other liberal democracies to enact similar laws. Moreover, in countries such as France and the United States, such laws had been upheld as constitutional. Justice McLachlin was unimpressed.

Given their different orientations to the question of deference, the contrasting conclusions of McLachlin and La Forest on the components of the *Oakes* test come as no surprise. While La Forest found the law to pass all parts of the test, McLachlin saw it as failing all parts of the critical proportionality component.

True, both sides conceded that the law had a "pressing and substantial purpose," but McLachlin defined that purpose more narrowly than did La Forest. For La Forest, the compelling purpose of the law was "protecting Canadians from the health risks associated with tobacco use, and informing them about these risks." For McLachlin, this overly broad purpose made it too easy to find the means proportional. Her narrower purpose was to "prevent people in Canada from being persuaded by advertising and promotion to use tobacco products [and] to discourage people who see the package from tobacco use."

Did a total advertising ban actually prevent people from being persuaded to use tobacco products? In addressing this question, McLachlin distinguished between "informational" and "lifestyle" advertising. Informational advertising simply identifies brands and may even provide useful information about different levels of toxins in various brands. Lifestyle advertising, by contrast, associates smoking with attractive people and activities. While McLachlin thought that "lifestyle advertising may, as a matter of common sense, be seen as having a tendency to discourage those who might otherwise cease tobacco use from doing so," she could find no solid connection, either in empirical scientific evidence or in "reason and logic," between a ban on informational advertising and its intended effect. It was "hard to imagine," she wrote, "how the presence of a tobacco logo on a cigarette lighter, for example, would increase consumption; yet, such use is banned." She concluded that a total ban—one that encompassed purely informational advertising—was not rationally connected to its purpose. Similarly, although a limited prohibition of only lifestyle advertising might pass the minimal impairment part of proportionality analysis, a total ban clearly infringed that criterion.

For Justice La Forest it was not nearly as clear that a ban of informational advertising was irrational, even in the light of Justice McLachlin's more narrowly defined purpose. As a "powerful common sense observation," he found it "difficult to believe that Canadian tobacco companies would spend over 75 million dollars every year on advertising if they did not know that advertising increases the consumption of their product." The government, he maintained, was entitled to come to a similar common-sense conclusion. For Justice McLachlin, such "common sense" did not satisfy the section 1 criterion for evidence or logic sufficient to "demonstrate" the need for a total ban. But note that when McLachlin justified her preferred option of a ban limited to "lifestyle" advertising, she did so "as a matter of [her own] common sense." The tension between the standard McLachlin applied to government policy preferences and the standard she applied to her own has not gone unremarked in the literature.[1]

RJR-MacDonald attracted considerable attention and controversy. Perhaps most dramatically, it led Ed Broadbent, former national leader of the New Democratic Party, to change his mind about the *Charter*'s section 33 notwithstanding clause. When the *Charter* was being

---

1   Janet Hiebert, *Charter Conflicts* (Montreal and Kingston: McGill-Queen's University Press, 2002) at 77-78.

drafted and enacted, Broadbent had opposed section 33. At a 20th-anniversary *Charter* conference in Ottawa in 2002, he expressed his outrage that the *RJR* Court had given the economic freedom of corporations priority over public health. He now understood, he announced, why section 33 was a useful *Charter* provision. *RJR* was for him a prime example of a case that deserved a "notwithstanding" response.

In response to the *RJR* decision—subscribing to the then fashionable notion of inter-institutional "dialogue"—the government enacted a new advertising ban, one that carefully followed Justice McLachlin's recommended limitation to "lifestyle" advertising. That law, too, was challenged by tobacco companies in a subsequent case, *JTI-Macdonald*.[2] This time, a unanimous Court, speaking through now Chief Justice McLachlin, upheld the law as a "reasonable limit" on freedom of expression. ⌐

---

2   *Canada (Attorney General) v. JTI-Macdonald Corp.*, 2007 SCC 30.

RJR-MACDONALD INC. v. THE ATTORNEY GENERAL OF CANADA
[1995] 3 S.C.R. 199

Hearing: November 29, 30, 1994; Judgment: September 21, 1995.

Present: Lamer C.J. and La Forest, L'Heureux-Dubé, Sopinka, Gonthier, Cory, McLachlin, Iacobucci, and Major JJ.

Interveners: The Attorney General for Ontario, the Heart and Stroke Foundation of Canada, the Canadian Cancer Society, the Canadian Council on Smoking and Health, the Canadian Medical Association, and the Canadian Lung Association.

The reasons of La Forest, L'Heureux-Dubé, and Gonthier JJ. were delivered by

[2] **LA FOREST J.** (dissenting): The issues in these appeals are whether the *Tobacco Products Control Act*, S.C. 1988, c. 20 (the "Act"), falls within the legislative competence of the Parliament of Canada under s. 91 of the *Constitution Act, 1867*, either as criminal law or under the peace, order and good government clause, and if so whether it constitutes an infringement of freedom of expression under s. 2(*b*) of the *Canadian Charter of Rights and Freedoms* which is not justified under s. 1 of the *Charter*. In broad terms, the Act prohibits, subject to specified exceptions, all advertising and promotion of tobacco products, and prohibits the sale of a tobacco product unless the package containing it sets forth prescribed health warnings and a list of the toxic constituents of the product and of the smoke produced from its combustion. ...

[58] The Attorney General conceded that the prohibition on advertising and promotion under the Act constitutes an infringement of the appellants' right to freedom of expression under s. 2(*b*) of the *Charter*, and directed his submissions solely to justifying the infringement under s. 1 of the *Charter*. In my view, the Attorney General was correct in making this concession. ...

[59] [H]owever, it is appropriate to draw attention to the fact that the Attorney General did not concede that s. 9 of the Act, which requires tobacco manufacturers to place an unattributed health warning on packages of these products, constitutes an infringement of the appellants' right to freedom of expression. In my view, the Attorney General was correct in not making this concession. However, since there is considerable overlap between my discussion of this issue and my discussion of s. 1, I shall for convenience address this distinct issue separately at the conclusion of my general s. 1 analysis. ...

[61] The appellants have conceded that the objective of protecting Canadians from the health risks associated with tobacco use, and informing them about these risks, is pressing and substantial. Rather than focusing upon the objective, the appellants submit that the measures employed under the Act are not proportional to the objective. ...

[63] This Court has on many occasions affirmed that the *Oakes* requirements must be applied flexibly, having regard to the specific factual and social context of each case. The word "reasonable" in s. 1 necessarily imports flexibility. ... This Court has on many occasions stated that the evidentiary requirements under s. 1 will vary substantially depending upon both the nature of the legislation and the nature of the right infringed. ...

[67] It appears ... that there is a significant gap between our understanding of the health *effects* of tobacco consumption and of the root *causes* of tobacco consumption. In my view, this gap raises a fundamental institutional problem that must be taken into account in undertaking the s. 1 balancing.

Simply put, a strict application of the proportionality analysis in cases of this nature would place an impossible onus on Parliament by requiring it to produce definitive social scientific evidence respecting the root causes of a pressing area of social concern every time it wishes to address its effects. This could have the effect of virtually paralyzing the operation of government in the socio-economic sphere. As I noted in *McKinney* [*v. University of Guelph*, [1990] 3 S.C.R. 229], at pp. 304-5, predictions respecting the ramifications of legal rules upon the social and economic order are not matters capable of precise measurement, and are often "the product of a mix of conjecture, fragmentary knowledge, general experience and knowledge of the needs, aspirations and resources of society, and other components." To require Parliament to wait for definitive social science conclusions every time it wishes to make social policy would impose an unjustifiable limit on legislative power by attributing a degree of scientific accuracy to the art of government which, in my view, is simply not consonant with reality....

[68] In several recent cases, this Court has recognized the need to attenuate the *Oakes* standard of justification when institutional constraints analogous to those in the present cases arise.... [For example, i]n drawing a distinction between legislation aimed at "mediating between different groups," where a lower standard of s. 1 justification may be appropriate, and legislation where the state acts as the "singular antagonist of the individual," where a higher standard of justification is necessary, the Court in *Irwin Toy* was drawing upon the more fundamental institutional distinction between the legislative and judicial functions that lies at the very heart of our political and constitutional system. Courts are specialists in the protection of liberty and the interpretation of legislation and are, accordingly, well placed to subject criminal justice legislation to careful scrutiny. However, courts are not specialists in the realm of policy-making, nor should they be. This is a role properly assigned to the elected representatives of the people, who have at their disposal the necessary institutional resources to enable them to compile and assess social science evidence, to mediate between competing social interests and to reach out and protect vulnerable groups. In according a greater degree of deference to social legislation than to legislation in the criminal justice context, this Court has recognized these important institutional differences between legislatures and the judiciary.

[69] ... In enacting this legislation, Parliament was facing a difficult policy dilemma. On the one hand, Parliament is aware of the detrimental health effects of tobacco use, and has a legitimate interest in protecting Canadians from, and in informing them about, the dangers of tobacco use. Health underlies many of our most cherished rights and values, and

the protection of public health is one of the fundamental responsibilities of Parliament. On the other hand, however, it is clear that a prohibition on the manufacture, sale or use of tobacco products is unrealistic. Nearly seven million Canadians use tobacco products, which are highly addictive. Undoubtedly, a prohibition of this nature would lead to an increase in illegal activity, smuggling and, quite possibly, civil disobedience. Well aware of these difficulties, Parliament chose a less drastic, and more incremental, response to the tobacco health problem. In prohibiting the advertising and promotion of tobacco products, as opposed to their manufacture or sale, Parliament has sought to achieve a compromise among the competing interests of smokers, non-smokers and manufacturers, with an eye to protecting vulnerable groups in society. Given the fact that advertising, by its very nature, is intended to influence consumers and create demand, this was a reasonable policy decision. Moreover, ... the Act is the product of a legislative process dating back to 1969, when the first report recommending a full prohibition on tobacco advertising was published; see *Report of the Standing Committee on Health, Welfare and Social Affairs on Tobacco and Cigarette Smoking* [(1969)], *supra*. In drafting this legislation, Parliament took into account the views of Canadians from many different sectors of society, representing many different interests. Indeed, the legislative committee responsible for drafting Bill C-51, which was subsequently adopted by Parliament as the Act, heard from 104 organizations during hearings in 1988 representing a variety of interests, including medicine, transport, advertising, smokers' rights, non-smokers' rights, and tobacco production.

[70] Seen in this way, it is clear that the Act is the very type of legislation to which this Court has generally accorded a high degree of deference. In drafting this legislation, which is directed toward a laudable social goal and is designed to protect vulnerable groups, Parliament was required to compile and assess complex social science evidence and to mediate between competing social interests. Decisions such as these are properly assigned to our elected representatives, who have at their disposal the necessary resources to undertake them, and who are ultimately accountable to the electorate....

[71] Turning now to the nature of the right infringed under the Act, it is once again necessary to place the appellants' claim in context. This Court has recognized, in a line of freedom of expression cases dating back to *Edmonton Journal, supra*, that, depending on its nature, expression will be entitled to varying levels of constitutional protection....

[72] ...In *Keegstra*..., Dickson C.J. identified these fundamental or "core" values as including the search for political, artistic and scientific truth, the protection of individual autonomy and self-development, and the promotion of public

participation in the democratic process. When state action places such values in jeopardy, this Court has been careful to subject it to a searching degree of scrutiny....

[73] In cases where the expression in question is farther from the "core" of freedom of expression values, this Court has applied a lower standard of justification. For example, in *Keegstra*, where a majority of this Court ruled that a prohibition on hate speech under s. 319(2) of the *Criminal Code*, R.S.C., 1985, c. C-46, was a justifiable limitation on freedom of expression, Dickson C.J. found that this limited infringement was justified because hate propaganda was a form of expression that was only remotely related to "core" free expression values....

[74] This Court adopted a similar approach in *R. v. Butler*, [1992] 1 S.C.R. 452, where it found a prohibition upon publications whose dominant characteristic was the "undue exploitation of sex" under s. 163(8) of the *Criminal Code*, R.S.C., 1985, c. C-46, to be a justifiable infringement upon freedom of expression. In so ruling, this Court found it significant, at p. 500, that "the kind of expression which is sought to be advanced does not stand on an equal footing with other kinds of expression which directly engage the 'core' of the freedom of expression values."... The Court has adopted a similar approach with respect to prostitution, which was also accorded a lower level of protection in the *Prostitution Reference*....

[75] In my view, the harm engendered by tobacco, and the profit motive underlying its promotion, place this form of expression as far from the "core" of freedom of expression values as prostitution, hate mongering, or pornography, and thus entitle it to a very low degree of protection under s. 1. It must be kept in mind that tobacco advertising serves no political, scientific or artistic ends; nor does it promote participation in the political process. Rather, its sole purpose is to inform consumers about, and promote the use of, a product that is harmful, and often fatal, to the consumers who use it. The main, if not sole, motivation for this advertising is, of course, profit....

[76] The appellants, both of whom are large multinational corporations, spend millions of dollars every year to promote their products (in 1987 alone, RJR and Imperial spent over $75 million dollars on advertising and promotion).... The sophistication of the advertising campaigns employed by these corporations, in my view, undermines their claim to freedom of expression protection because it creates an enormous power differential between these companies and tobacco consumers in the "marketplace of ideas."... The power differential between advertiser and consumer is even more pronounced with respect to children who, as this Court observed in *Irwin Toy*, at p. 987, are "particularly vulnerable

to the techniques of seduction and manipulation abundant in advertising."... In this respect, it is critical to keep in mind Dickson C.J.'s reminder in *Edwards Books* [[1986] 2 S.C.R. 713], at p. 779:

> In interpreting and applying the *Charter* I believe that the courts must be cautious to ensure that it does not simply become an instrument of better situated individuals to roll back legislation which has as its object the improvement of the condition of less advantaged persons.

[77] I conclude, therefore, that an attenuated level of s. 1 justification is appropriate in these cases.... With these observations firmly in mind, I now proceed to an application of the proportionality test....

[83] ...The appellants...base their argument principally upon the claim that there is no rational connection between the prohibition on advertising and promotion of tobacco products under ss. 4, 5, 6, and 8 and the objective of reducing tobacco consumption. In my view, the appellants' argument fails....

[84] I begin with what I consider to be a powerful common sense observation. Simply put, it is difficult to believe that Canadian tobacco companies would spend over 75 million dollars every year on advertising if they did not know that advertising increases the consumption of their product. In response to this observation, the appellants insist that their advertising is directed solely toward preserving and expanding brand loyalty among smokers, and not toward expanding the tobacco market by inducing non-smokers to start. In my view, the appellants' claim is untenable for two principal reasons. First, brand loyalty alone will not, and logically cannot, maintain the profit levels of these companies if the overall number of smokers declines. A proportionate piece of a smaller pie is still a smaller piece.... Second, even if this Court were to accept the appellants' brand loyalty argument, the appellants have not adequately addressed the further problem that even commercials targeted solely at brand loyalty may also serve as inducements for smokers not to quit....

[86] ... [T]he power of the common-sense connection between advertising and consumption is sufficient to satisfy the rational connection requirement.

[87] However, it is not necessary to rely solely upon common sense to reach this conclusion....

[92] [A] number of reports introduced at trial... attest to the causal connection between tobacco advertising and consumption....

[93] The views expressed in these reports are not, of course, definitive or conclusive. Indeed, there is currently a lively debate in the social sciences respecting the connection between advertising and consumption, a debate that has been

carried on for years and will no doubt persist well into the near future. However, these reports attest, at the very least, to the existence of what LeBel J.A. called a "body of opinion" supporting the existence of a causal connection between advertising and consumption....

[94] ... I conclude that there is a rational connection between the prohibition on advertising and consumption under ss. 4, 5, 6 and 8 of the Act and the reduction of tobacco consumption....

[95] The next step in the proportionality analysis is to determine whether the legislative means chosen impair the right or freedom in question as little as possible. The appellants submit that Parliament has unjustifiably imposed a complete prohibition on tobacco advertising and promotion when it could have imposed a partial prohibition with equal effectiveness. They suggest that Parliament could have instituted a partial prohibition by forbidding "lifestyle" advertising (which seeks to promote an image by associating the consumption of the product with a particular lifestyle) or advertising directed at children, without at the same time prohibiting "brand preference" advertising (which seeks to promote one brand over another based on the colour and design of the package) or "informational" advertising (which seeks to inform the consumer about product content, taste and strength and the availability of different or new brands). According to the appellants, there is no need to prohibit brand preference or informational advertising because both are targeted solely at smokers, and serve a beneficial function by promoting consumer choice.

[96] In my view, the appellants' argument fails.... [T]he minimal impairment requirement does not impose an obligation on the government to employ the least intrusive measures available. Rather, it only requires it to demonstrate that the measures employed were the least intrusive, *in light of both the legislative objective and the infringed right....*

[97] ... It must be kept in mind that the infringed right at issue in these cases is the right of tobacco corporations to advertise the only legal product sold in Canada which, when used precisely as directed, harms and often kills those who use it. As I discussed above, I have no doubt that Parliament could validly have employed the criminal law power to prohibit the manufacture and sale of tobacco products, and that such a prohibition would have been fully justifiable under the *Charter.* There is no right to sell harmful products in Canada, nor should there be. Thus, in choosing to prohibit solely the advertisement of tobacco products, it is clear that Parliament in fact adopted a relatively *unintrusive* legislative approach to the control of tobacco products.... Under the Act, tobacco companies continue to enjoy the right to manufacture and sell their products, to engage in public or private debate concerning the health effects of their products, and to publish consumer information on their product packages pertaining to the content of the products. The prohibition under this Act serves only to prevent these companies from employing sophisticated marketing and social psychology techniques to induce consumers to purchase their products. This type of expression, which is directed solely toward the pursuit of profit, is neither political nor artistic in nature, and therefore falls very far from the "core" of freedom of expression values discussed by this Court in *Keegstra....*

[98] Furthermore, ... the measures adopted under the Act were the product of an intensive 20-year public policy process, which involved extensive consultation with an array of national and international health groups and numerous studies, and educational and legislative programs. Over the course of this 20-year period, the government adopted an incremental legislative approach by experimenting with a variety of less intrusive measures before determining that a full prohibition on advertising was necessary....

[99] ... It is of great significance, in my view, that over 20 democratic nations have, in recent years, adopted complete prohibitions on tobacco advertising similar to those adopted under the Act, including Australia, New Zealand, Norway, Finland and France. It is also of significance that the constitutionality of full advertising prohibitions have been upheld by the French Conseil constitutionnel (Décision No. 90-283 DC (Jan. 8, 1991) declaring the *Loi n° 91-32 relative à la lutte contre le tabagisme et l'alcoolisme,* which prohibits all direct and indirect tobacco advertising), to be constitutionally valid and by American courts (upholding full prohibitions on alcohol advertising and gambling advertising as a reasonable limitation on freedom of expression under the United States Constitution in *Central Hudson* [*Gas & Electric Corp. v. Public Service Commission of New York,* 447 U.S. 557 (1980)]; *Oklahoma Telecasters* [699 F.2d 490 (1983)]; *Metromedia* [453 U.S. 490 (1981)]; *Posadas* [*de Puerto Rico Associates v. Tourism Co. of Puerto Rico,* 478 U.S. 328 (1986)]; *Dunagin* [*v. City of Oxford, Mississippi,* 718 F.2d 738 (1983)]). The decisions of the American courts, which have traditionally been jealous guardians of the right to freedom of expression, are particularly instructive in this context because they demonstrate that the adoption of a full prohibition upon tobacco advertising is perceived as neither novel nor radical in other democratic nations. Given the background of the legislation and the overwhelming acceptance by other democratic countries of this type of prohibition as a reasonable means for combating the serious evils flowing from the sale and distribution of tobacco products, it seems difficult to argue that the impugned legislation is not a reasonable limit on the appellants' rights demonstrably justified in a free and democratic society under s. 1 of the *Charter....*

[103] Moreover, in considering the comparative advantages of partial and full advertising prohibitions, it is also significant that, in countries where governments have instituted partial prohibitions upon tobacco advertising such as those suggested by the appellants, the tobacco companies have developed ingenious tactics to circumvent the restrictions. For example, when France attempted to institute a partial prohibition on tobacco advertising in the 1980s (by prohibiting "lifestyle" tobacco advertising but not informational or brand preference advertising), the tobacco companies devised techniques for associating their product with "lifestyle" images which included placing pictures on the brand name and reproducing those pictures when an advertisement showed the package, and taking out a full-page magazine advertisement and subcontracting three-quarters of the advertisement to Club Med, whose lifestyle advertisements contributed to a lifestyle association for the brand; see Luc Joossens, "Strategy of the Tobacco Industry Concerning Legislation on Tobacco Advertising in some Western European Countries" in *Proceedings of the 5th World Conference on Smoking and Health* (1983).

[104] Thus, it appears that Parliament had compelling reasons for rejecting a partial prohibition on advertising and instituting a full prohibition. In this light, it would be highly artificial for this Court to decide, on a purely abstract basis, that a partial prohibition on advertising would be as effective as a full prohibition. In my view, this is precisely the type of "line drawing" that this Court has identified as being within the institutional competence of legislatures and not courts. . . .

[107] In reaching the conclusion that the Act satisfies the *Oakes* minimal impairment criterion, I am well aware of the statements of this Court in *Ford* [*v. Quebec (Attorney General)*, [1988] 2 S.C.R. 712], and *Rocket* [*v. Royal College of Dental Surgeons of Ontario*, [1990] 2 S.C.R. 232], to the effect that a complete prohibition on a type of expression will be more difficult to justify than a partial prohibition. In my view, however, these decisions are fully distinguishable from the present cases. Once again, I emphasize the importance of context in the minimal impairment analysis. In *Rocket*, this Court found that a prohibition on advertising by dentists under s. 37(39) and (40) of *Regulation 447 of the Health Disciplines Act*, R.R.O. 1980, was an infringement of s. 2(*b*) and could not be justified under s. 1. . . .

[108] . . . [T]he contrast with *Rocket* could not be more striking. Making an informed choice about dentists serves to promote health by allowing patients to seek out the best care; making an informed choice about tobacco simply permits consumers to choose between equally dangerous products. . . .

[109] A similar contrast can be drawn between the present cases and *Ford, supra*. . . . While, in these cases, the Act prohibits only tobacco advertising, in *Ford*, the law prohibited all non-French commercial expression in Quebec. It was therefore much broader in scope than the prohibition under the Act. Moreover, while the Act prohibits expression that has little or no connection with "core" freedom of expression values, the commercial expression in *Ford* was intimately connected with such core values. The impugned law in that case represented an attempt by the government of Quebec to eradicate the commercial use in public of any language other than French. Given the close historical relationship between language, culture and politics in Canada, it cannot seriously be denied that the implications of this prohibition extended well beyond the commercial sphere and impacted upon the dignity of all minority language groups in Quebec. . . .

[112] The third part of the proportionality analysis requires a proportionality between the deleterious and the salutary effects of the measures. . . . For the reasons I have given with respect to both the nature of the legislation and the nature of the right infringed in these cases, it is my view that the deleterious effects of this limitation, a restriction on the rights of tobacco companies to advertise products for profit that are inherently dangerous and harmful, do not outweigh the legislative objective of reducing the number of direct inducements for Canadians to consume these products.

[113] I now turn to the appellants' final argument, namely, that s. 9 of the Act constitutes an unjustifiable infringement of their freedom of expression by compelling them to place on tobacco packages an unattributed health message. I agree, to use Wilson J.'s phrase, that if the effect of this provision is "to put a particular message into the mouth of the plaintiff, as is metaphorically alleged to be the case here," the section runs afoul of s. 2(*b*) of the *Charter*; see *Lavigne* [*v. Ontario Public Service Employees Union*, [1991] 2 S.C.R. 211], at p. 267. . . . [However] it must be remembered that this statement is *unattributed* and I have some difficulty in seeing, in the context in which it was made, that it can in any real sense be considered to be attributed to the appellants. Simply because tobacco manufacturers are required to place unattributed warnings on their products does not mean that they must endorse these messages, or that they are perceived by consumers to endorse them. In a modern state, labelling of products, and especially products for human consumption, are subject to state regulation as a matter of course. It is common knowledge amongst the public at large that such statements emanate from the government, not the tobacco manufacturers. In this respect, there is an important distinction between messages directly *attributed* to tobacco manufacturers, which would create the impression that the message emanates from the appellants and would violate their right to silence, and the *unattributed* messages at issue in these cases, which emanate from the government and create no such impression. Seen in

this way, the mandatory health warnings under s. 9 are no different from unattributed labelling requirements under the *Hazardous Products Act*, under which manufacturers of hazardous products are required to place unattributed warnings, such as "DANGER" or "POISON," and hazard symbols, such as skull and crossbones on their products; see *Consumer Chemicals and Containers Regulations*, SOR/88-556. I should add that the issue has ramifications for many other spheres of activity where individuals may in certain prescribed circumstances be required to place danger signs on facilities used by the public or on construction sites, and so on. This is not really an expression of opinion by the person in control of the facility or the construction site. It is rather a requirement imposed by the government as a condition of participating in a regulated activity.

[116] Even if I were of the view that there was an infringement, I am firmly convinced that it is fully justifiable under s. 1. Once again, I stress the importance of context in the s. 1 analysis. The appellants are large corporations selling a product for profit which, on the basis of overwhelming evidence, is dangerous, yet maintain the right to engage in "counter-speech" against warnings which do nothing more than bring the dangerous nature of these products to the attention of consumers. Given that the objective of the unattributed health message requirement is simply to increase the likelihood that every literate consumer of tobacco products will be made aware of the risks entailed by the use of that product, and that these warnings have no political, social or religious content, it is clear that we are a long way in this context from cases where the state seeks to coerce a lone individual to make political, social or religious statements without a right to respond. I believe a lower level of constitutional scrutiny is justified in this context. These cases seem to me to be a far more compelling situation than *Slaight* [*Communications Inc. v. Davidson*, [1989] 1 S.C.R. 1038], where a majority of the Court held the infringement there was justified under s. 1. The *Charter* was essentially enacted to protect individuals, not corporations. It may, at times it is true, be necessary to protect the rights of corporations so as to protect the rights of the individual. But I do not think this is such a case, and I again draw inspiration from the statement of Dickson C.J. in *Edwards Books, supra*, at p. 779, that the courts must ensure that the *Charter* not become simply an instrument "of better situated individuals to roll back legislation which has as its object the improvement of the condition of less advantaged persons."

[117] In my view, the requirement that health warnings must be unattributed is also proportional to the objective of informing consumers about the risks of tobacco use. Unattributed warnings are rationally connected to this objective because they increase the visual impact of the warning. It is

not difficult to see that bold unattributed messages on a tobacco package (such as, for example, "SMOKING CAN KILL YOU") are more striking to the eye than messages cluttered by subtitles and attributions. Moreover, the attribution of the warnings also tends to dilute the factual impact of the messages. As Brossard J.A. observed, at p. 383:

> . . . [I]t seems to me to leap to the eye that an "attributed" message can quickly become meaningless, or even ridiculous.
>
> As an example, the message that is supposed to come from the "Surgeon-General" remains a message imputed to an abstract entity or a political body which obviously cannot by simple decree make something hazardous that otherwise would not be. This, it seems to me, rationally weakens and attenuates the message.

These considerations are particularly relevant with respect to Parliament's goal of protecting children, who constitute the largest single group of new smokers every year in this country. In a report submitted at trial ("A Report on the Special Vulnerabilities of Children and Adolescents" [(1989)]), Dr. Michael J. Chandler observed that adolescents are apt to disregard or disobey messages from perceived authority figures. On this basis, he concluded that attributed warnings would be less effective in deterring adolescents from smoking. He stated, at p. 19:

> Adolescents are predisposed, as a function of their persistent cognitive immaturity, to view public disagreements between "experts" as evidence that everything is simply a matter of subjective opinion, and a licence to "do their own thing." A warning by Health and Welfare Canada on a publicly advertised product would provide them with just the sort of evidence they feel is required to justify doing whatever impulsive thing occurs to them at the moment.

[118] Thus, although the unattributed health warning requirement precludes large corporations from disseminating on their product packages the view that tobacco products are not harmful, I believe that any concern arising from this technical infringement of their rights is easily outweighed by the pressing health concerns raised by tobacco consumption. As noted by Dickson C.J. in *Edwards Books, supra*, at p. 759, the *Charter* does not require the elimination of "minuscule" constitutional burdens, and legislative action that increases the costs of exercising a right need not be prohibited if the burden is "trivial" or "insubstantial." In these cases, the only cost associated with the unattributed warning requirement is a potential reduction in profits. In my view, this is a cost that manufacturers of dangerous products can reasonably be expected to bear, given the health benefits of effective health

warnings. As I stated in *Thomson Newspapers Ltd. v. Canada (Director of Investigation and Research, Restrictive Trade Practices Commission)*, [1990] 1 S.C.R. 425, at pp. 506-7:

> In a modern industrial society, it is generally accepted that many activities in which individuals can engage must nevertheless to a greater or lesser extent be regulated by the state to ensure that the individual's pursuit of his or her self-interest is compatible with the community's interest in the realization of collective goals and aspirations. . . .

The following is the judgment delivered by

[122] **McLACHLIN J.:** . . .

[124] . . . I agree with La Forest J. that the prohibition on advertising and promotion of tobacco products constitutes a violation of the right to free expression as the Attorney General conceded. Unlike La Forest J., I take the view that s. 9 of the Act, which requires tobacco manufacturers to place an unattributed health warning on tobacco packages, also infringes the right of free expression. As La Forest J. notes in para. 113, this Court has previously held that "freedom of expression necessarily entails the right to say nothing or the right not to say certain things": *Slaight Communications Inc. v. Davidson*, [1989] 1 S.C.R. 1038, at p. 1080, *per* Lamer J. (as he then was). Under s. 9(2), tobacco manufacturers are prohibited from displaying on their packages any writing other than the name, brand name, trade mark, and other information required by legislation. The combination of the unattributed health warnings and the prohibition against displaying any other information which would allow tobacco manufacturers to express their own views, constitutes an infringement of the right to free expression guaranteed by s. 2(*b*) of the *Charter*.

[125] The only remaining question is whether these infringements of the right of free expression are saved under s. 1 of the *Charter*, as being reasonable and "demonstrably justified in a free and democratic society." Acknowledging that the evidence of justification is problematic, La Forest J. concludes that it nevertheless suffices to justify the infringement of the right of free expression, given the importance of the legislative goal, the context of the law and the need to defer to Parliament on such an important and difficult issue. With respect, I cannot agree. . . .

[135] . . . It is established that the deference accorded to Parliament or the legislatures may vary with the social context in which the limitation on rights is imposed. For example, it has been suggested that greater deference to Parliament or the Legislature may be appropriate if the law is concerned with the competing rights between different sectors of society than if it is a contest between the individual and the state: *Irwin Toy* [*Ltd. v. Quebec (Attorney General)*], [1989] 1 S.C.R. 927],

at pp. 993-94; *Stoffman v. Vancouver General Hospital*, [1990] 3 S.C.R. 483, at p. 521. However, such distinctions may not always be easy to apply. For example, the criminal law is generally seen as involving a contest between the state and the accused, but it also involves an allocation of priorities between the accused and the victim, actual or potential. The cases at bar provide a cogent example. We are concerned with a criminal law, which pits the state against the offender. But the social values reflected in this criminal law lead La Forest J. to conclude that "the Act is the very type of legislation to which this Court has generally accorded a high degree of deference" (para. 70). . . .

[136] [H]owever, care must be taken not to extend the notion of deference too far. Deference must not be carried to the point of relieving the government of the burden which the *Charter* places upon it of demonstrating that the limits it has imposed on guaranteed rights are reasonable and justifiable. . . . To carry judicial deference to the point of accepting Parliament's view simply on the basis that the problem is serious and the solution difficult, would be to diminish the role of the courts in the constitutional process and to weaken the structure of rights upon which our constitution and our nation is founded. . . .

[138] [W]hile I agree with La Forest J. that context, deference and a flexible and realistic standard of proof are essential aspects of the s. 1 analysis, these concepts . . . must not be attenuated to the point that they relieve the state of the burden the *Charter* imposes of demonstrating that the limits imposed on our constitutional rights and freedoms are reasonable and justifiable in a free and democratic society. . . .

[142] Against this background, I return to the cases at bar and the factors for s. 1 justification discussed in *Oakes*.

[143] The question at this stage is whether the objective of the infringing measure is sufficiently important to be capable in principle of justifying a limitation on the rights and freedoms guaranteed by the constitution. Given the importance of the *Charter* guarantees, this is not easily done. To meet the test, the objective must be one of pressing and substantial importance.

[144] Care must be taken not to overstate the objective. The objective relevant to the s. 1 analysis is *the objective of the infringing measure*, since it is the infringing measure and nothing else which is sought to be justified. If the objective is stated too broadly, its importance may be exaggerated and the analysis compromised. As my colleague has noted, the *Tobacco Products Control Act* is but one facet of a complex legislative and policy scheme to protect Canadians from the health risks of tobacco use. However, the objective of the impugned measures themselves is somewhat narrower than this. The objective of the advertising ban and trade mark usage restrictions must

be to prevent people in Canada from being persuaded by advertising and promotion to use tobacco products. The objective of the mandatory package warning must be to discourage people who see the package from tobacco use. Both constitute important objectives, although the significance of the targeted decrease in consumption is reduced by the government's estimate that despite the ban, 65 percent of the Canadian magazine market will contain tobacco advertisements, given that the ban applies only to Canadian media and not to imported publications. . . .

[146] While the limited objective of reducing tobacco-associated health risks by reducing advertising-related consumption and providing warnings of dangers is less significant than the broad objective of protecting Canadians generally from the risks associated with tobacco use, it nevertheless constitutes an objective of sufficient importance to justify overriding the right of free expression guaranteed by the *Charter*. Even a small reduction in tobacco use may work a significant benefit to the health of Canadians and justify a properly proportioned limitation of right of free expression. . . .

[153] As a first step in the proportionality analysis, the government must demonstrate that the infringements of the right of free expression worked by the law are rationally connected to the legislative goal of reducing tobacco consumption. It must show a causal connection between the infringement and the benefit sought on the basis of reason or logic. To put it another way, the government must show that the restriction on rights serves the intended purpose. This must be demonstrated on a balance of probabilities.

[154] The causal relationship between the infringement of rights and the benefit sought may sometimes be proved by scientific evidence showing that as a matter of repeated observation, one affects the other. Where, however, legislation is directed at changing human behaviour, as in the case of the *Tobacco Products Control Act*, the causal relationship may not be scientifically measurable. In such cases, this Court has been prepared to find a causal connection between the infringement and benefit sought on the basis of reason or logic, without insisting on direct proof of a relationship between the infringing measure and the legislative objective . . . .

[155] . . . [In fact,] there was no direct evidence of a scientific nature showing a causal link between advertising bans and decrease in tobacco consumption.

[156] This leaves the question of whether there is less direct evidence that suggests as a matter of "reason" or "logic" that advertising bans and package warnings lead to a reduction in tobacco use. The evidence relied upon by La Forest J. in support of rational connection falls into this category. . . .

[157] The question is whether this evidence establishes that it is reasonable or logical to conclude that there is a causal link between tobacco advertising and unattributed health warnings and tobacco use. To use the words of the Meese Commission on Pornography relied on in *Butler*, at p. 502, "would [it] be surprising . . . to find otherwise"? The government argues that it would be "surprising . . . to find otherwise." Why would tobacco companies spend great sums on advertising if not to increase the consumption of tobacco, it asks?

[158] To this the tobacco companies reply that their advertising is directed not at increasing the size of the total market but at obtaining a larger share of the existing market. The evidence indicates that one of the thrusts of the advertising programs of tobacco companies is securing a larger market share, but there is also evidence suggesting that advertising is used to increase the total market. For example, the Court was referred to an Imperial Tobacco Ltd. ("Imperial") document, *Project Viking*, vol. I: *A Behavioural Model of Smoking*, a market research study carried out to determine an advertising strategy for the company. The report suggests that advertising should be directed to "expanding the market, or at the very least, forestalling its decline" by proactively recruiting new smokers and reassuring present smokers who might otherwise quit in response to vigorous anti-smoking publicity. Moreover, while purely informational advertising may not increase the total market, lifestyle advertising may, as a matter of common sense, be seen as having a tendency to discourage those who might otherwise cease tobacco use from doing so. Conversely, package warnings, attributed or not, may be seen as encouraging people to reduce or cease using tobacco. All this taken together with the admittedly inconclusive scientific evidence is sufficient to establish on a balance of probabilities a link based on reason between certain forms of advertising, warnings and tobacco consumption.

[159] On the other hand, there does not appear to be any causal connection between the objective of decreasing tobacco consumption and the absolute prohibition on the use of a tobacco trade mark on articles other than tobacco products which is mandated by s. 8 of the Act. There is no causal connection based on direct evidence, nor is there, in my view, a causal connection based in logic or reason. It is hard to imagine how the presence of a tobacco logo on a cigarette lighter, for example, would increase consumption; yet, such use is banned. I find that s. 8 of the Act fails the rational connection test. . . .

[160] As the second step in the proportionality analysis, the government must show that the measures at issue impair the right of free expression as little as reasonably possible in order to achieve the legislative objective. The impairment must be "minimal," that is, the law must be carefully tailored so that rights are impaired no more than necessary. The tailoring process seldom admits of perfection and the courts must accord some leeway to the legislator. If the law falls within a

range of reasonable alternatives, the courts will not find it overbroad merely because they can conceive of an alternative which might better tailor objective to infringement: see *Reference re ss. 193 and 195.1(1)(c) of the Criminal Code (Man.)*, [1990] 1 S.C.R. 1123, at pp. 1196-97; *R. v. Chaulk*, [1990] 3 S.C.R. 1303, at pp. 1340-41; *Ramsden v. Peterborough (City)*, [1993] 2 S.C.R. 1084, at pp. 1105-06. On the other hand, if the government fails to explain why a significantly less intrusive and equally effective measure was not chosen, the law may fail....

[162] I turn first to the prohibition on advertising contained in s. 4 of the Act. It is, as has been observed, complete. It bans all forms of advertising of Canadian tobacco products while explicitly exempting all foreign advertising of non-Canadian products which are sold in Canada. It extends to advertising which arguably produces benefits to the consumer while having little or no conceivable impact on consumption. Purely informational advertising, simple reminders of package appearance, advertising for new brands and advertising showing relative tar content of different brands—all these are included in the ban. Smoking is a legal activity yet consumers are deprived of an important means of learning about product availability to suit their preferences and to compare brand content with an aim to reducing the risk to their health.

[163] As this Court has observed before, it will be more difficult to justify a complete ban on a form of expression than a partial ban: *Ramsden v. Peterborough (City)*, *supra*, at pp. 1105-06; *Ford v. Quebec (Attorney General)*, *supra*, at pp. 772-73. The distinction between a total ban on expression, as in *Ford* where the legislation at issue required commercial signs to be exclusively in French, and a partial ban such as that at issue in *Irwin Toy*, *supra*, is relevant to the margin of appreciation which may be allowed the government under the minimal impairment step of the analysis. In *Rocket*, *supra*, the law imposed a complete advertising ban on professionals seeking to advertise their services. I concluded that while the government had a pressing and substantial objective, and while that objective was rationally connected to the means chosen, the minimal impairment requirement was not met since the government had exceeded a reasonable margin of appreciation given the need for consumers to obtain useful information about the services provided. A full prohibition will only be constitutionally acceptable under the minimal impairment stage of the analysis where the government can show that only a full prohibition will enable it to achieve its objective. Where, as here, no evidence is adduced to show that a partial ban would be less effective than a total ban, the justification required by s. 1 to save the violation of free speech is not established.

[164] As noted in my analysis of rational connection, while one may conclude as a matter of reason and logic that

lifestyle advertising is designed to increase consumption, there is no indication that purely informational or brand preference advertising would have this effect. The government had before it a variety of less intrusive measures when it enacted the total ban on advertising, including: a partial ban which would allow information and brand preference advertising; a ban on lifestyle advertising only; measures such as those in Quebec's *Consumer Protection Act*, R.S.Q., c. P-40.1, to prohibit advertising aimed at children and adolescents; and labelling requirements only (which Health and Welfare believed would be preferable to an advertising ban: A.J. Liston's testimony). In my view, any of these alternatives would be a reasonable impairment of the right to free expression, given the important objective and the legislative context....

[169] La Forest J. supports his conclusion that Parliament should be permitted to choose such measures as it sees fit by contrasting the importance of Parliament's objective with the low value of the expression at issue. This way of answering the minimal impairment requirement raises a number of concerns. First, to argue that the importance of the legislative objective justifies more deference to the government at the stage of evaluating minimal impairment, is to engage in the balancing between objective and deleterious effect contemplated by the third stage of the proportionality analysis in *Oakes*. While it may not be of great significance where this balancing takes place, care must be taken not to devalue the need for demonstration of minimum impairment by arguing the legislation is important and the infringement of no great moment.

[170] Second, just as care must be taken not to overvalue the legislative objective beyond its actual parameters, so care must be taken not to undervalue the expression at issue. Commercial speech, while arguably less important than some forms of speech, nevertheless should not be lightly dismissed. For example, in *Rocket*, *supra*, this Court struck down restrictions on dental advertising on the ground that the minimal impairment requirement had not been met. The *Health Disciplines Act*, R.S.O. 1980, c. 196, prohibited forms of advertising which far from being unprofessional, might have benefited consumers and contributed to their health. The same may be said here. Tobacco consumption has not been banned in Canada. Yet the advertising ban deprives those who lawfully choose to smoke of information relating to price, quality and even health risks associated with different brands. It is no answer to suggest, as does my colleague, (para. 108) that the tobacco companies have failed to establish the true benefits of such information. Under s. 1 of the *Charter*, the onus rests on the government to show why restrictions on these forms of advertising are required.

[171] Third, in finding that the commercial speech here at issue is entitled "to a very low degree of protection under

s. 1" (para. 75) and that "an attenuated level of s. 1 justification is appropriate in these cases" (para. 77), La Forest J. places a great deal of reliance on the fact that the appellants are motivated by profit. I note that the same may be said for many business persons or corporations that challenge a law as contrary to freedom of expression. While this Court has stated that restrictions on commercial speech may be easier to justify than other infringements, no link between the claimant's motivation and the degree of protection has been recognized. Book sellers, newspaper owners, toy sellers—all are linked by their shareholders' desire to profit from the corporation's business activity, whether the expression sought to be protected is closely linked to the core values of freedom of expression or not. In my view, motivation to profit is irrelevant to the determination of whether the government has established that the law is reasonable or justified as an infringement of freedom of expression.

[172] It remains to consider whether the requirement that the warning be unattributed pursuant to s. 9 of the Act fails to meet the minimum impairment requirement of proportionality. The appellant corporations contend that a warning similar to that used in the United States, which identifies the author as the Surgeon General, would be equally effective while avoiding the inference some may draw that it is the corporations themselves who are warning of the danger. They object not only to being forced to say what they do not wish to say, but also to being required to do so in a way that associates them with the opinion in question. This impairs their freedom of expression, they contend, more than required to achieve the legislative goal.

[173] The government is clearly justified in requiring the appellants to place warnings on tobacco packaging. The question is whether it was necessary to prohibit the appellants from attributing the message to the government and whether it was necessary to prevent the appellants from placing on their packaging any information other than that allowed by the regulations.

[174] As with the advertising ban, it was for the government to show that the unattributed warning, as opposed to an attributed warning, was required to achieve its objective of reducing tobacco consumption among those who might read the warning. Similarly, it was for the government to show why permitting tobacco companies to place additional information on tobacco packaging, such as a statement announcing lower tar levels, would defeat the government's objective. This it has failed to do. . . .

[175] Having found the requirement of minimum impairment is not satisfied for ss. 4 and 9 of the Act, it is unnecessary to proceed to the final stage of the proportionality analysis under s. 1—balancing the negative effects of the infringement of rights against the positive benefits associated with the legislative goal. A finding that the law impairs the right more than required contradicts the assertion that the infringement is proportionate. Neither the fact that commercial expression may be entitled to a lesser degree of protection than certain other forms of expression, nor the importance of reducing tobacco consumption, even to a small extent, negate this proposition. Freedom of expression, even commercial expression, is an important and fundamental tenet of a free and democratic society. If Parliament wishes to infringe this freedom, it must be prepared to offer good and sufficient justification for the infringement and its ambit. This it has not done. . . .

32 Law v. Canada, 1999

In *Law v. Canada*, the Supreme Court consolidated the various strands of its equality-rights jurisprudence that had been articulated in the numerous equality-rights cases it had decided since handing down its first major decision on section 15, 10 years earlier in *Andrews*.[1] Justice Iacobucci wrote the opinion for the full Court of nine judges.[2] Most of the opinion was devoted to setting out the various considerations that guide the Court's judgment in determining whether a claim should be upheld under section 15(1) of the *Charter*. At the end of the decision, Justice Iacobucci applied these guidelines to the section 15 claim brought before the Court by Nancy Law.

Mrs. Law, whose husband had died at the age of 50, claimed survivor's benefits under the Canada Pension Plan (CPP). The CPP denies regular survivor's benefits to surviving spouses under the age of 45 if they are able-bodied and without children. At the time she was widowed, Nancy Law was 30 years old, had no children, and was not disabled. Accordingly, she was denied the benefits that an over-45 surviving spouse would receive immediately. She would be eligible for a survivor's benefit at age 65, but at a reduced rate. Law claimed that these CPP provisions discriminated against her on the basis of age and therefore violated section 15 of the *Charter*. Her claim was rejected by the Pension Appeals Board and the Federal Court of Appeal, and was rejected again here in the first application of the Supreme Court's consolidation of its section 15 jurisprudence.

The thread running throughout Justice Iacobucci's discourse on section 15 is the justices' understanding of section 15's underlying purpose. The justices believe that the *Charter's* equality-rights clause was intended to have a reforming, "ameliorative" effect on Canadian society. Its purpose, as Justice McIntyre stated in *Andrews*, was to promote "a society in which all are secure in the knowledge that they are recognized as human beings equally deserving of concern, respect and consideration." Thus, section 15 is always to be seen as an instrument of social reform aimed at making society more inclusive, combating demeaning stereotypes, and overcoming hurtful and humiliating discrimination. The other general consideration, more methodological than substantive, is the importance of context. In ascertaining whether differential treatment is unconstitutional discrimination, courts must consider such things as whether the differential treatment that is the subject of the *Charter* challenge is associated with a long historical struggle against unequal treatment or whether failure to take into account the special circumstances of a group will result in severe hardship. The Court's section 15 jurisprudence calls for a lot of empirical fact-finding.

The Court's opinion in *Law* was not intended to serve as a set of rules that provide an easily applied litmus test for violations of section 15. However, toward the end of the judgment, Iacobucci set out "guidelines" to the three steps to be taken in deciding whether a challenged law or governmental practice amounts to unconstitutional discrimination. First, there must be a finding of a differential treatment based on some personal characteristic.

---

1 *Andrews v. Law Society of British Columbia*, [1989] 1 S.C.R. 143.

2 The Court's membership at this time, in addition to Iacobucci J., included Lamer C.J., L'Heureux-Dubé, Gonthier, Cory, McLachlin, Major, Bastarache, and Binnie JJ.

Second, that differential treatment must be based on one of the grounds enumerated in section 15 or analogous grounds. Third, the differential treatment must result in placing an extra burden or denying a benefit in a way that has the effect of perpetuating or promoting the view that the person is less worthy of respect than others in society. What courts should be looking for in this third step is what amounts to a denial of the claimant's "human dignity." Several formulations are advanced of what is involved in respecting human dignity, including such things as unfair treatment that does not relate to a person's capacities or needs or that amounts to social marginalization.

It is at the third step—the denial of human dignity—that Nancy Law's claim failed. The challenged section of the CPP certainly involves differential treatment on the basis of age, one of the enumerated grounds in section 15. But the Court did not think the legislation in either purpose or effect violates the human dignity of Nancy Law or others in similar circumstances. It simply reflects the practical reality that people in her situation are more able to replace the income lost from a spouse's death. In a concluding comment, Justice Iacobucci remarked that this is one of the rare cases where differential treatment based on an enumerated ground is not discrimination under section 15(1).

In this case, the Supreme Court was unanimous in supporting the general approach to section 15(1) that Justice Iacobucci elucidated. However, as equality-rights cases continued to come before the Court, it soon became clear that the Court would not be unanimous in applying the generalities of Iacobucci's equality-rights doctrine. In particular, it is the third and crucial stage of his approach, and the notion of human dignity it turns on, that is the key to divisions within the Court, and perhaps also to the difficulties of lower court judges and lawyers as they struggle to apply the Iacobucci doctrine. ⌣

LAW v. CANADA (MINISTER OF EMPLOYMENT AND IMMIGRATION)
[1999] 1 S.C.R. 497

Hearing: January 20, 1998; Rehearing: December 3, 1998; Judgment: March 25, 1999.

Present: Lamer C.J. and L'Heureux-Dubé, Gonthier, Cory, McLachlin, Iacobucci, Major, Bastarache, and Binnie JJ.

The judgment of the Court was delivered by

IACOBUCCI J.:

I. Introduction and Overview

[1] This appeal concerns the constitutionality of ss. 44(1)(*d*) and 58 of the *Canada Pension Plan*, R.S.C., 1985, c. C-8, which draw distinctions on the basis of age with regard to entitlement to survivor's pensions. The issue is whether the provisions infringe s. 15(1) of the *Canadian Charter of Rights and Freedoms* on the ground that they discriminate against persons under the age of 45 on the basis of age and, if so, whether the infringement is justified under s. 1 of the *Charter*. In my view, a purposive reading and application of s. 15(1)

results in the conclusion that the appellant has not established discrimination within the meaning of the *Charter*.

[2] Section 15 of the *Charter* guarantees to every individual the right to equal treatment by the state without discrimination. It is perhaps the *Charter*'s most conceptually difficult provision. In this Court's first s. 15 case, *Andrews v. Law Society of British Columbia*, [1989] 1 S.C.R 143, at p. 164, McIntyre J. noted that, as embodied in s. 15(1) of the *Charter*, the concept of equality is "an elusive concept," and that "more than any of the other rights and freedoms guaranteed in the *Charter*, it lacks precise definition." Part of the difficulty in defining the concept of equality stems from its exalted status. The quest for equality expresses some of humanity's highest ideals and aspirations, which are by their nature abstract and subject to differing articulations. The challenge for the judiciary in interpreting and applying s. 15(1) of the *Charter* is to transform these ideals and aspirations into practice in a manner which is meaningful to Canadians and which accords with the purpose of the provision.

[3] In *Andrews*, McIntyre J., who delivered the unanimous reasons of the Court on the issue of the proper approach to s. 15(1), cautioned at p. 168 that it would be inappropriate to attempt to confine analysis under s. 15(1) to a "fixed and

limited formula." This sentiment has been echoed in subsequent decisions . . . .

[4] Indeed, in the brief history of this Court's interpretation of s. 15(1) of the *Charter*, there have been several important substantive developments in equality law, relating to, among other things, the meaning of adverse effects discrimination, the role of context in identifying discrimination more generally, and the *indicia* of an analogous ground. All of these developments have been guided by the Court's evolving understanding of the purpose of equality protection under s. 15(1). All have augmented and enriched anti-discrimination jurisprudence under the *Charter*.

[5] Throughout these developments, although there have been differences of opinion among the members of this Court as to the appropriate interpretation of s. 15(1), I believe it is fair to say that there has been and continues to be general consensus regarding the basic principles relating to the purpose of s. 15(1) and the proper approach to equality analysis. In my view, the present case is a useful juncture at which to summarize and comment upon these basic principles, in order to provide a set of guidelines for courts that are called upon to analyze a discrimination claim under the *Charter*.

[6] In accordance with McIntyre J.'s caution in *Andrews*, *supra*, I think it is sensible to articulate the basic principles under s. 15(1) as guidelines for analysis, and not as a rigid test which might risk being mechanically applied. Equality analysis under the *Charter* must be purposive and contextual. The guidelines which I review below are just that—points of reference which are designed to assist a court in identifying the relevant contextual factors in a particular discrimination claim, and in evaluating the effect of those factors in light of the purpose of s. 15(1).

[7] The analysis in these reasons proceeds from the general to the more specific. I begin, after describing the background of the case, with a review of general principles regarding the proper approach to be followed in analyzing a discrimination claim. This portion of the reasons is concerned with outlining elements or stages of analysis, whose content and application I then develop. The second portion of my analysis is a discussion of the basic principles which this Court has articulated in past jurisprudence regarding the purpose of s. 15(1), and the fundamentally purposive nature of each stage of analysis under the provision. Next, on the basis of previous cases, I review some of the contextual factors which may assist a court in determining whether the purpose of s. 15(1) has been engaged within the context of a particular case. A summary of the elements of a discrimination claim, the purpose of s. 15(1), and the contextual factors then follows. Finally, I apply the principles articulated in this analysis to the case at bar.

II. Background

A. The Legislation

. . . [8] The Canada Pension Plan (the "CPP") is a compulsory social insurance scheme which was enacted in 1965 in order to provide contributors and their families with reasonable minimum levels of income upon the retirement, disability or death of the wage earner: see *House of Commons Debates*, vol. VI, 2nd Sess., 26th Parl., August 10, 1964, at p. 6636. Among the benefits available under the CPP is the survivor's pension. This monthly benefit is paid to a surviving spouse whose deceased partner has made sufficient contributions to the CPP, and who meets the eligibility criteria specified in s. 44(1)(*d*), namely, an age threshold, responsibility for dependent children or disability.

[9] A claimant who is over the age of 45 at the time of the contributor's death, or is maintaining dependent children of the deceased contributor, or is (or becomes) disabled, is entitled to receive the survivor's pension at the full rate. However, s. 58 gradually reduces that pension for able-bodied surviving spouses without dependent children who are between the ages of 35 and 45 by 1/120th of the full rate for each month that the claimant's age is less than 45 years at the time of the contributor's death. Pursuant to s. 44(1)(*d*), unless they should become disabled, able-bodied surviving spouses without dependent children who are under 35 at the time of the death of the contributor are precluded from receiving a survivor's pension until they reach the age of 65.

B. Facts

[10] The appellant, Nancy Law, married Jason Law in 1980. Mr. Law died in 1991, at the age of 50, having contributed to the CPP for 22 years. At the time of his death, the appellant was 30 years old. Prior to Mr. Law's death, the couple had co-owned a small business. The appellant was responsible for business operations and her husband had the requisite technical knowledge and expertise. The business failed soon after Mr. Law's death.

[11] The appellant applied to receive survivor's benefits under the CPP. Her husband had made sufficient contributions under the CPP such that she would qualify for survivor benefits if she came within the class of persons entitled to receive them. However, her application was refused because she was under 35 years of age at the time of her husband's death, she was not disabled, and she did not have dependent children.

[12] The appellant appealed this decision to the Minister of National Health and Welfare, who rejected the appeal in May, 1992. She then appealed to the Pension Plan Review Tribunal, arguing that the age distinctions in ss. 44(1)(*d*) and 58 of the CPP discriminate against her on the basis of age contrary to s. 15(1) of the *Charter*. The tribunal found that

the legislation discriminates against those who, at the time of the contributor's death, have not reached age 35, have no dependent children and are not disabled. However, the tribunal was unable to reach a consensus regarding s. 1 of the *Charter*. The majority concluded that the discrimination was justified under s. 1 and, although a more precise test of need could have been crafted, the measures adopted were a reasonable attempt by Parliament to achieve the objective of the CPP. The dissenting member of the tribunal found that the age distinctions in the impugned provisions were arbitrary and that Parliament could have targeted needy dependents without discrimination by legislating a test to determine need.

[13] The appellant then appealed to the Pension Appeals Board, which, in a trial *de novo*, concluded that the impugned age distinctions do not violate the appellant's equality rights. The majority of the board also found that, even if the distinctions did infringe s. 15(1) of the *Charter*, they would be justified under s. 1. A subsequent appeal to the Federal Court of Appeal was dismissed largely for the reasons of the Pension Appeals Board....

VI. Analysis

A. Approach to Section 15(1)

[21] ...

(1) Andrews Revisited

[23] McIntyre J. in *Andrews* adopted an approach to s. 15(1) which focuses upon three central elements: (1) whether a law imposes differential treatment between the claimant and others; (2) whether an enumerated or analogous ground of discrimination is the basis for the differential treatment; and (3) whether the law in question has a "discriminatory" purpose or effect....

[24] McIntyre J. began his discussion of the requirement of differential treatment by noting, at p. 164, that equality is a comparative concept, "the condition of which may only be attained or discerned by comparison with the condition of others in the social and political setting in which the question arises." It is impossible to evaluate a s. 15(1) claim without identifying specific personal characteristics or circumstances of the individual or group bringing the claim, and comparing the treatment of that person or group to the treatment accorded to a relevant comparator. This comparison determines whether the s. 15(1) claimant may be said to experience differential treatment, which is the first step in determining whether there is discriminatory inequality for the purpose of s. 15(1).

[25] At the same time, McIntyre J. emphasized that true equality does not necessarily result from identical treatment. Formal distinctions in treatment will be necessary in some contexts in order to accommodate the differences between

individuals and thus to produce equal treatment in a substantive sense: see pp. 164-69. Correspondingly, a law which applies uniformly to all may still violate a claimant's equality rights. The main consideration, McIntyre J. stated, at p. 165, must be the *impact* of the law upon the individual or group to whom it applies, as well as upon those whom it excludes from its application. He explained that the determination of the impact of legislation, by its nature, must be undertaken in a contextual manner, taking into account the content of the law, its purpose, and the characteristics and circumstances of the claimant, among other things. Hence, equality in s. 15 must be viewed as a substantive concept. Differential treatment, in a substantive sense, can be brought about either by a formal legislative distinction, or by a failure to take into account the underlying differences between individuals in society.

[26] Moving on to discuss the requirement that a s. 15(1) claimant show that differential treatment is discriminatory in order to establish a *Charter* violation, McIntyre J. defined "discrimination" in the following terms, at pp. 174-75:

> ... [D]iscrimination may be described as a distinction, whether intentional or not but based on grounds relating to personal characteristics of the individual or group, which has the effect of imposing burdens, obligations, or disadvantages on such individual or group not imposed upon others, or which withholds or limits access to opportunities, benefits, and advantages available to other members of society. Distinctions based on personal characteristics attributed to an individual solely on the basis of association with a group will rarely escape the charge of discrimination, while those based on an individual's merits and capacities will rarely be so classed.

[27] Importantly, McIntyre J. explained that the determination of whether a distinction in treatment imposes a burden or withholds a benefit so as to constitute "discrimination" within the meaning of s. 15(1) is to be undertaken in a purposive way. As he stated, at pp. 180-81, "[t]he words 'without discrimination' require more than a mere finding of distinction between the treatment of groups or individuals."... The protection of equality rights is concerned with distinctions which are truly discriminatory. A discriminatory burden or denial of a benefit, McIntyre J. stated, is to be understood in a substantive sense and in the context of the historical development of Canadian anti-discrimination law, notably the human rights codes: "The words 'without discrimination'... are a form of qualifier built into s. 15 itself and limit those distinctions which are forbidden by the section to those which involve prejudice or disadvantage" (pp. 180-81)....

[29] Finally, regarding the role of the various grounds of discrimination expressly listed in s. 15(1), McIntyre J. stated,

at p. 175, that they "reflect the most common and probably the most socially destructive and historically practised bases of discrimination," but noted that a s. 15(1) claim may also be brought on an analogous ground, in accordance with the provision's wording and with a proper interpretation of its remedial purpose. In her majority reasons elaborating on the specific issue of analogous grounds, Wilson J. explained, at p. 152, that a ground may qualify as analogous to those listed in s. 15(1) if persons characterized by the trait in question are, among other things, "lacking in political power," "vulnerable to having their interests overlooked and their rights to equal concern and respect violated," and "vulnerab[le] to becoming a disadvantaged group" on the basis of the trait. Just as for the other two elements of the s. 15(1) analysis outlined by McIntyre J., Wilson J. emphasized at p. 152 that the determination of whether a ground qualifies as analogous under s. 15(1) is to be undertaken in a contextual manner:

... [T]his is a determination which is not to be made only in the context of the law which is subject to challenge but rather in the context of the place of the group in the entire social, political and legal fabric of our society. While legislatures must inevitably draw distinctions among the governed, such distinctions should not bring about or reinforce the disadvantage of certain groups and individuals by denying them the rights freely accorded to others.

[30] In summary, then, the *Andrews* decision established that there are three key elements to a discrimination claim under s. 15(1) of the *Charter*: differential treatment, an enumerated or analogous ground, and discrimination in a substantive sense involving factors such as prejudice, stereotyping, and disadvantage. Of fundamental importance, as stressed repeatedly by all of the judges who wrote, the determination of whether each of these elements exists in a particular case is always to be undertaken in a purposive manner, taking into account the full social, political, and legal context of the claim.

(2) Post-Andrews Jurisprudence

[31] The general approach adopted in *Andrews* was regularly applied in subsequent decisions of the Court: see, e.g., *Turpin* [[1989] 1 S.C.R. 1296]; *R. v. Hess; R. v. Nguyen*, [1990] 2 S.C.R. 906; *McKinney* [*v. University of Guelph*, [1990] 3 S.C.R. 229]; *Tétreault-Gadoury v. Canada (Employment and Immigration Commission)*, [1991] 2 S.C.R. 22; *Swain* [[1991] 1 S.C.R. 933]; *Symes v. Canada*, [1993] 4 S.C.R. 695; *Egan v. Canada*, [1995] 2 S.C.R. 513; *Miron v. Trudel*, [1995] 2 S.C.R. 418; *Thibaudeau v. Canada*, [1995] 2 S.C.R. 627; *Benner v. Canada (Secretary of State)*, [1997] 1 S.C.R. 358; *Eaton v. Brant County Board of Education*, [1997] 1 S.C.R. 241; *Eldridge v.*

British Columbia (Attorney General), [1997] 3 S.C.R. 624; *Vriend v. Alberta*, [1998] 1 S.C.R. 493....

[39] In my view, the proper approach to analyzing a claim of discrimination under s. 15(1) of the *Charter* involves a synthesis of these various articulations. Following upon the analysis in *Andrews, supra,* and the two-step framework set out in *Egan, supra,* and *Miron, supra,* among other cases, a court that is called upon to determine a discrimination claim under s. 15(1) should make the following three broad inquiries. First, does the impugned law (a) draw a formal distinction between the claimant and others on the basis of one or more personal characteristics, or (b) fail to take into account the claimant's already disadvantaged position within Canadian society resulting in substantively differential treatment between the claimant and others on the basis of one or more personal characteristics? If so, there is differential treatment for the purpose of s. 15(1). Second, was the claimant subject to differential treatment on the basis of one or more of the enumerated and analogous grounds? And third, does the differential treatment discriminate in a substantive sense, bringing into play the *purpose* of s. 15(1) of the *Charter* in remedying such ills as prejudice, stereotyping, and historical disadvantage? The second and third inquiries are concerned with whether the differential treatment constitutes discrimination in the substantive sense intended by s. 15(1).

B. The Purpose of Section 15(1)

... [42] What is the purpose of the s. 15(1) equality guarantee? There is great continuity in the jurisprudence of this Court on this issue. In *Andrews, supra,* all judges who wrote advanced largely the same view. McIntyre J. stated, at p. 171, that the purpose of s. 15 is to promote "a society in which all are secure in the knowledge that they are recognized at law as human beings equally deserving of concern, respect and consideration." The provision is a guarantee against the evil of oppression, he explained at pp. 180-81, designed to remedy the imposition of unfair limitations upon opportunities, particularly for those persons or groups who have been subject to historical disadvantage, prejudice, and stereotyping.

[43] Similarly, La Forest J., concurring with respect to the proper approach to s. 15(1), stated that the equality guarantee was designed to prevent the imposition of differential treatment that was likely to "inhibit the sense of those who are discriminated against that Canadian society is not free or democratic as far as they are concerned," and that was likely to decrease their "confidence that they can freely and without obstruction by the state pursue their and their families' hopes and expectations of vocational and personal development." ...

[51] All of these statements share several key elements. It may be said that the purpose of s. 15(1) is to prevent the

violation of essential human dignity and freedom through the imposition of disadvantage, stereotyping, or political or social prejudice, and to promote a society in which all persons enjoy equal recognition at law as human beings or as members of Canadian society, equally capable and equally deserving of concern, respect and consideration. Legislation which effects differential treatment between individuals or groups will violate this fundamental purpose where those who are subject to differential treatment fall within one or more enumerated or analogous grounds, and where the differential treatment reflects the stereotypical application of presumed group or personal characteristics, or otherwise has the effect of perpetuating or promoting the view that the individual is less capable, or less worthy of recognition or value as a human being or as a member of Canadian society. . . .

[53] What is human dignity? There can be different conceptions of what human dignity means. For the purpose of analysis under s. 15(1) of the *Charter*, however, the jurisprudence of this Court reflects a specific, albeit non-exhaustive, definition. As noted by Lamer C.J. in *Rodriguez v. British Columbia (Attorney General)*, [1993] 3 S.C.R. 519, at p. 554, the equality guarantee in s. 15(1) is concerned with the realization of personal autonomy and self-determination. Human dignity means that an individual or group feels self-respect and self-worth. It is concerned with physical and psychological integrity and empowerment. Human dignity is harmed by unfair treatment premised upon personal traits or circumstances which do not relate to individual needs, capacities, or merits. It is enhanced by laws which are sensitive to the needs, capacities, and merits of different individuals, taking into account the context underlying their differences. Human dignity is harmed when individuals and groups are marginalized, ignored, or devalued, and is enhanced when laws recognize the full place of all individuals and groups within Canadian society. Human dignity within the meaning of the equality guarantee does not relate to the status or position of an individual in society *per se*, but rather concerns the manner in which a person legitimately feels when confronted with a particular law. Does the law treat him or her unfairly, taking into account all of the circumstances regarding the individuals affected and excluded by the law?

[54] The equality guarantee in s. 15(1) of the *Charter* must be understood and applied in light of the above understanding of its purpose. The overriding concern with protecting and promoting human dignity in the sense just described infuses all elements of the discrimination analysis.

[55] In order to determine whether the fundamental purpose of s. 15(1) is brought into play in a particular claim, it is essential to engage in a comparative analysis which takes into consideration the surrounding context of the claim and the claimant. I now propose to comment briefly on the nature of the comparative approach, and then to examine some of the contextual factors that a court should consider in determining whether s. 15(1) has been infringed. Each factor may be more or less relevant depending upon the circumstances of the case.

C. The Comparative Approach

[56] As discussed above, McIntyre J. emphasized in *Andrews, supra*, that the equality guarantee is a comparative concept. Ultimately, a court must identify differential treatment *as compared* to one or more other persons or groups. Locating the appropriate comparator is necessary in identifying differential treatment and the grounds of the distinction. Identifying the appropriate comparator will be relevant when considering many of the contextual factors in the discrimination analysis. . . .

[58] When identifying the relevant comparator, the natural starting point is to consider the claimant's view. It is the claimant who generally chooses the person, group, or groups with whom he or she wishes to be compared for the purpose of the discrimination inquiry, thus setting the parameters of the alleged differential treatment that he or she wishes to challenge. However, the claimant's characterization of the comparison may not always be sufficient. It may be that the differential treatment is not between the groups identified by the claimant, but rather between other groups. Clearly a court cannot, *ex proprio motu*, evaluate a ground of discrimination not pleaded by the parties and in relation to which no evidence has been adduced: see *Symes, supra*, at p. 762. However, within the scope of the ground or grounds pleaded, I would not close the door on the power of a court to refine the comparison presented by the claimant where warranted.

D. Establishing Discrimination in a Purposive Sense: Contextual Factors

. . . [59] . . .

(2) Contextual Factors

[62] . . .

(a) Pre-existing Disadvantage

[63] As has been consistently recognized throughout this Court's jurisprudence, probably the most compelling factor favouring a conclusion that differential treatment imposed by legislation is truly discriminatory will be, where it exists, pre-existing disadvantage, vulnerability, stereotyping, or prejudice experienced by the individual or group: see, e.g., *Andrews, supra*, at pp. 151-53, *per* Wilson J., p. 183, *per* McIntyre J., pp. 195-97, *per* La Forest J.; *Turpin, supra*, at pp. 1331-33; *Swain, supra*, at p. 992, *per* Lamer C.J.; *Miron, supra*, at paras. 147-48,

per McLachlin J.; *Eaton, supra*, at para. 66. These factors are relevant because, to the extent that the claimant is already subject to unfair circumstances or treatment in society by virtue of personal characteristics or circumstances, persons like him or her have often not been given equal concern, respect, and consideration. It is logical to conclude that, in most cases, further differential treatment will contribute to the perpetuation or promotion of their unfair social characterization, and will have a more severe impact upon them, since they are already vulnerable.

[64] One consideration which the Court has frequently referred to with respect to the issue of pre-existing disadvantage is the role of stereotypes. A stereotype may be described as a misconception whereby a person or, more often, a group is unfairly portrayed as possessing undesirable traits, or traits which the group, or at least some of its members, do not possess. In my view, probably the most prevalent reason that a given legislative provision may be found to infringe s. 15(1) is that it reflects and reinforces existing inaccurate understandings of the merits, capabilities and worth of a particular person or group within Canadian society, resulting in further stigmatization of that person or the members of the group or otherwise in their unfair treatment. This view accords with the emphasis placed by this Court ever since *Andrews, supra,* upon the role of s. 15(1) in overcoming prejudicial stereotypes in society....

[65] It should be stressed that, while it is helpful to demonstrate the existence of historic disadvantage, it is of course not *necessary* to show such disadvantage in order to establish a s. 15(1) violation, for at least two distinct reasons. On the one hand, this Court has stated several times that, although a distinction drawn on such a basis is an important *indicium* of discrimination, it is not determinative....

[66] On the other hand, it may be misleading or inappropriate in some cases to speak about "membership" within a group for the purpose of a s. 15(1) claim. The *Charter* guarantees equality rights to individuals. In this respect, it must be made clear that the s. 15(1) claimant is not required to establish membership in a sociologically recognized group in order to be successful. It will always be helpful to the claimant to be able to identify a pattern of discrimination against a class of persons with traits similar to the claimant, i.e., a group, of which the claimant may consider herself or himself a member. Nonetheless, an infringement of s. 15(1) may be established by other means, and may exist even if there is no one similar to the claimant who is experiencing the same unfair treatment.

[67] At the same time, I also do not wish to suggest that the claimant's association with a group which has historically been more disadvantaged will be conclusive of a violation under s. 15(1), where differential treatment has been estab-

lished. This *may* be the result, but whether or not it is the result will depend upon the circumstances of the case and, in particular, upon whether or not the distinction truly affects the dignity of the claimant....

(b) Relationship Between Grounds and the Claimant's Characteristics or Circumstances

[69] What are some factors other than an individual's or a group's pre-existing disadvantage which may be referred to by a s. 15(1) claimant in order to demonstrate a negative effect upon the claimant's dignity? One factor in some circumstances may be the relationship between the ground upon which the claim is based and the nature of the differential treatment. Some of the enumerated and analogous grounds have the potential to correspond with need, capacity, or circumstances....

[71] Examples are prevalent in the jurisprudence of this Court of legislation or other state action which either failed to take into account the actual situation of a claimant, or alternatively quite properly treated a claimant differently on the basis of actual personal differences between individuals. In *Eldridge, supra,* for example, a provincial government's failure to provide limited funding for sign language interpreters for deaf persons when receiving medical services was found to violate s. 15(1), in part on the basis that the government's failure to take into account the actual needs of deaf persons infringed their human dignity. Conversely, in *Weatherall* [*v. Canada (Attorney General),* [1993] 2 S.C.R. 872], it was stated that the decision to permit cross-gender prison searches of male prisoners but not of female prisoners likely did not violate s. 15(1), because such a difference in treatment was appropriate in light of the historical, biological and sociological differences between men and women.

(c) Ameliorative Purpose or Effects

[72] Another possibly important factor will be the ameliorative purpose or effects of impugned legislation or other state action upon a more disadvantaged person or group in society. As stated by Sopinka J. in *Eaton, supra,* at para. 66: "the purpose of s. 15(1) of the *Charter* is not only to prevent discrimination by the attribution of stereotypical characteristics to individuals, but also to ameliorate the position of groups within Canadian society who have suffered disadvantage by exclusion from mainstream society." An ameliorative purpose or effect which accords with the purpose of s. 15(1) of the *Charter* will likely not violate the human dignity of more advantaged individuals where the exclusion of these more advantaged individuals largely corresponds to the greater need or the different circumstances experienced by the disadvantaged group being targeted by the legislation. I emphasize

that this factor will likely only be relevant where the person or group that is excluded from the scope of ameliorative legislation or other state action is more advantaged in a relative sense. Underinclusive ameliorative legislation that excludes from its scope the members of a historically disadvantaged group will rarely escape the charge of discrimination: see *Vriend, supra,* at paras. 94-104, *per* Cory J.

(d) Nature of the Interest Affected

[74] A further contextual factor which may be relevant in appropriate cases in determining whether the claimant's dignity has been violated will be the nature and scope of the interest affected by the legislation. This point was well explained by L'Heureux-Dubé J. in *Egan, supra,* at paras. 63-64. As she noted, at para. 63, "[i]f all other things are equal, the more severe and localized the ... consequences on the affected group, the more likely that the distinction responsible for these consequences is discriminatory within the meaning of s. 15 of the *Charter.*" L'Heureux-Dubé J. explained, at para. 64, that the discriminatory calibre of differential treatment cannot be fully appreciated without evaluating not only the economic but also the constitutional and societal significance attributed to the interest or interests adversely affected by the legislation in question. Moreover, it is relevant to consider whether the distinction restricts access to a fundamental social institution, or affects "a basic aspect of full membership in Canadian society," or "constitute[s] a complete non-recognition of a particular group." ...

(3) The Nature and Extent of the Claimant's Burden Under Section 15(1)

[76] Having emphasized the importance of a claimant demonstrating that impugned legislation infringes s. 15(1) in a purposive sense, it will be useful at this point to review the nature of the claimant's burden as a practical matter. There are three points which should be addressed.

[77] First, I should underline that none of the foregoing discussion implies that the claimant must adduce data, or other social science evidence not generally available, in order to show a violation of the claimant's dignity or freedom. Such materials may be adduced by the parties, and may be of great assistance to a court in determining whether a claimant has demonstrated that the legislation in question is discriminatory. However, they are not required. A court may often, where appropriate, determine on the basis of judicial notice and logical reasoning alone whether the impugned legislation infringes s. 15(1). It is well established that a court may take judicial notice of notorious and undisputed facts. ...

[80] Second, it is equally important to emphasize that the requirement that a claimant establish a s. 15(1) infringement

in this purposive sense does not entail a requirement that the claimant prove any matters which cannot reasonably be expected to be within his or her knowledge. As this Court has previously stated, the s. 15(1) claimant is not required to establish that the *intent* of the legislature in enacting the impugned legislation was discriminatory. ...

[82] Third, it should be stressed that in some cases it may not be necessary as a practical matter for a claimant to focus the purposive analysis upon more than one element of the discrimination claim. ...

E. Summary of Guidelines

[88] Before moving on to apply the principles that I have just discussed to the facts of this case, I believe it would be useful to summarize some of the main guidelines for analysis under s. 15(1) to be derived from the jurisprudence of this Court, as reviewed in these reasons. As I stated above, these guidelines should not be seen as a strict test, but rather should be understood as points of reference for a court that is called upon to decide whether a claimant's right to equality without discrimination under the *Charter* has been infringed. Inevitably, the guidelines summarized here will need to be supplemented in practice by the explanation of these guidelines in these reasons and those of previous cases, and by a full appreciation of the context surrounding the specific s. 15(1) claim at issue. It goes without saying that as our s. 15 jurisprudence evolves it may well be that further elaborations and modifications will emerge.

General Approach

(1) It is inappropriate to attempt to confine analysis under s. 15(1) of the *Charter* to a fixed and limited formula. A purposive and contextual approach to discrimination analysis is to be preferred, in order to permit the realization of the strong remedial purpose of the equality guarantee, and to avoid the pitfalls of a formalistic or mechanical approach.

(2) The approach adopted and regularly applied by this Court to the interpretation of s. 15(1) focuses upon three central issues:

(A) whether a law imposes differential treatment between the claimant and others, in purpose or effect;

(B) whether one or more enumerated or analogous grounds of discrimination are the basis for the differential treatment; and

(C) whether the law in question has a purpose or effect that is discriminatory within the meaning of the equality guarantee.

(3) Accordingly, a court that is called upon to determine a discrimination claim under s. 15(1) should make the following three broad inquiries:

(A) Does the impugned law (a) draw a formal distinction between the claimant and others on the basis of one or more personal characteristics, or (b) fail to take into account the claimant's already disadvantaged position within Canadian society resulting in substantively differential treatment between the claimant and others on the basis of one or more personal characteristics?

(B) Is the claimant subject to differential treatment based on one or more enumerated and analogous grounds?
and

(C) Does the differential treatment discriminate, by imposing a burden upon or withholding a benefit from the claimant in a manner which reflects the stereotypical application of presumed group or personal characteristics, or which otherwise has the effect of perpetuating or promoting the view that the individual is less capable or worthy of recognition or value as a human being or as a member of Canadian society, equally deserving of concern, respect, and consideration? . . .

F. Application to the Case at Bar

(1) Differential Treatment

. . . [90] The CPP grants benefits to surviving spouses over the age of 35 immediately following the death of the contributor. However, these benefits are not available to able-bodied spouses without dependent children who are less than 35 years of age at the time of the death of the contributor, until they reach age 65 or unless they should become disabled in the interim. In addition, while those over age 45 are entitled to receive benefits at the full rate, those between the ages of 35 and 45 receive a reduced sum. Thus, as a result of the ages specified under the CPP, a clear distinction is drawn between claimants over and under age 35, and also between claimants who are over age 45 and those between the ages of 35 and 45. In my view, both the delay in the receipt of benefits and the reduced entitlement to benefits constitute a denial of equal benefit of the law under the first step of the equality analysis.

(2) Distinction on the Basis of Enumerated or Analogous Grounds

[91] Age is one of the enumerated grounds of discrimination in s. 15(1) of the *Charter*. The appellant alleges that she was rendered ineligible for survivor's benefits by virtue of her age and that its use as a distinguishing criterion was

discriminatory. The appellant does not base her discrimination claim upon any ground other than that of age. In answer, the respondent contends that, although age is a factor in determining eligibility, it cannot be said that the appellant was ineligible solely because of this factor. Rather, the respondent argues that entitlement under s. 44(1)(d) of the CPP depends on the interplay of the three factors included therein, namely, age, disability and responsibility for dependent children. This was the position adopted by the Pension Appeals Board. With respect, I cannot accept this view. In my opinion, it does not follow from the fact that any one of several criteria, including age, might determine entitlement to a survivor's pension, that the legislation does not draw a distinction on the basis of age. . . .

[92] As an able-bodied woman without children, the appellant does not suggest that the CPP discriminates by denying her equal benefits as compared to surviving spouses who have disabilities or dependent children. The appellant submits that the issue in dispute is whether age is properly included among the factors which determine eligibility for survivor's benefits and the amount that is provided. Had the appellant been able-bodied, without dependent children, and over age 45 at the time of her spouse's death, she would have been immediately entitled to receive full benefits. However, as an able-bodied, childless woman who was 30 years of age at the time of her spouse's death, she is denied any benefits until she reaches age 65, provided she does not subsequently become disabled. Similarly, for surviving spouses age 35 to 45, it is their age alone that serves to reduce the amount of benefits they receive as compared to those over age 45. In my view, the survivor's pension provisions of the CPP clearly draw distinctions on the basis of the enumerated ground of age. . . .

(3) Discrimination

[95] The central question in the present case is whether the age discrimination drawn by ss. 44(1)(d) and 58 of the CPP impose a disadvantage upon the appellant as a younger adult in a manner which constitutes discrimination under s. 15(1) of the *Charter*. The appellant is asserting her claim solely on the basis of age—specifically, on the basis of being an adult under the age of 45. Relatively speaking, adults under the age of 45 have not been consistently and routinely subjected to the sorts of discrimination faced by some of Canada's discrete and insular minorities. For this reason it will be more difficult as a practical matter for this Court to reason, from facts of which the Court may appropriately take judicial notice, that the legislative distinction at issue violated the human dignity of the appellant.

[96] The appellant argues that the impugned CPP provisions infringe s. 15(1) of the *Charter* in both their purpose

and their effect. She submits that the original intent underlying the distinctions created by ss. 44(1)(*d*) and 58 was to provide benefits to those surviving spouses most in need, based on an assumed correlation between, among other things, increased age and one's ability to enter or re-enter the workforce following the death of one's spouse. The appellant argues that this assumed correlation is faulty because, in fact, young people generally, and the appellant in particular, have difficulty in obtaining employment, and the legislation's assumptions to the contrary are based on false stereotypes regarding the advantages of youth. . . .

[99] The questions, to take up the dignity-related concerns discussed above, may be put in the following terms. Do the impugned CPP provisions, in purpose or effect, violate essential human dignity and freedom through the imposition of disadvantage, stereotyping, or political or social prejudice? Does the law, in purpose or effect, conform to a society in which all persons enjoy equal recognition as human beings or as members of Canadian society, equally capable and equally deserving of concern, respect, and consideration? Does the law, in purpose or effect, perpetuate the view that people under 45 are less capable or less worthy of recognition or value as human beings or as members of Canadian society?

[100] Before answering these questions, it is useful to note that, although the appellant has referred this Court to government reports and other sources which favour extending survivor's pensions to younger spouses on the basis that they suffer immediate financial need, she has not demonstrated that either the purpose or the effect of the impugned legislative provisions violates her human dignity in the sense discussed above so as to constitute discrimination. I agree with the appellant that surviving spouses of all ages are vulnerable, economically and otherwise, immediately following the death of a spouse. However, as both the appellant and respondent acknowledged in their submissions before this Court, the purpose and function of the impugned CPP provisions is not to remedy the *immediate* financial need experienced by widows and widowers, but rather to enable older widows and widowers to meet their basic needs *during the longer term.* . . .

[102] The answers to the questions which I posed above with respect to human dignity thus lie, in part, in the aim and effects of the legislation in providing *long-term* financial security for Canadians who lose a spouse, coupled with the greater flexibility and opportunity of younger people without dependent children or disabilities to achieve long-term security absent their spouse. Yes, the law imposes a disadvantage on younger spouses in this class. But it is unlikely to be a substantive disadvantage, viewed in the long term. The law on its face

treats such younger people differently, but the differential treatment does not reflect or promote the notion that they are less capable or less deserving of concern, respect, and consideration, when the dual perspectives of long-term security and the greater opportunity of youth are considered. Nor does the differential treatment perpetuate the view that people in this class are less capable or less worthy of recognition or value as human beings or as members of Canadian society. . . .

[104] The challenged legislation simply reflects the fact that people in the appellant's position are more able to overcome long-term need because of the nature of a human being's life cycle. Those who are younger when they lose a spouse are more able to replace the income lost from the death of a spouse. . . .

[108] In these circumstances, recalling the purposes of s. 15(1), I am at a loss to locate any violation of human dignity. The impugned distinctions in the present case do not stigmatize young persons, nor can they be said to perpetuate the view that surviving spouses under age 45 are less deserving of concern, respect or consideration than any others. Nor do they withhold a government benefit on the basis of stereotypical assumptions about the demographic group of which the appellant happens to be a member. I must conclude that, when considered in the social, political, and legal context of the claim, the age distinctions in ss. 44(1)(*d*) and 58 of the CPP are not discriminatory.

[109] In finding that the impugned legislative provisions do not infringe s. 15(1) of the *Charter*, I do not wish in any way to minimize the emotional and economic upset which affects surviving dependents when a spouse dies. My analysis herein is not meant to suggest that young people do not suffer following the death of a loved one, but only that the impugned CPP provisions are not discriminatory between younger and older adults within the purpose and meaning of s. 15(1) of the *Charter*.

[110] I conclude, then, that this is one of the rare cases contemplated in *Andrews, supra,* in which differential treatment based on one or more of the enumerated or analogous grounds in s. 15(1) is not discriminatory. It is important to identify such cases through a purposive analysis of s. 15(1), in order to ensure that analysis under s. 15(1) does not become mechanistic, but rather addresses the true social, political and legal context underlying each and every equality claim.

G. Section 1 of the Charter

[111] As I have found no violation of s. 15(1) of the *Charter*, it is not necessary to turn to s. 1.

33 M. v. H., 1999

The 1999 *M. v. H.* decision represented a significant turning point in terms of state recognition of same-sex partners and their relationships in Canada. The decision had enormous implications for provincial and federal governments because it conveyed the following message: social policies oriented toward spouses that deny recognition or benefits to same-sex partners lack constitutional validity. This decision would have been extremely difficult to anticipate at the time of the *Charter*'s adoption.

When the *Charter* was debated, lesbian and gay activists had little reason to assume that it would be a useful resource in their efforts to pressure politicians to undertake substantial social policy changes to redress discrimination on the basis of sexual orientation. At the time, both federal and provincial legislation relied heavily on a heterosexual definition of "spouse" that had the effect of denying entitlements or recognition to same-sex partners and their relationships. But legislatures were not the only obstacle in overcoming this form of discrimination. Courts routinely accepted the validity of these legislative distinctions either by using a heterosexual definition of "spouse" or "marriage" or by ruling that, in the absence of a statutory basis for recognizing same-sex spouses, judges were powerless to disagree with legislation. During the entrenchment debate, Jean Chrétien, who was then the federal Justice Minister, indicated that the federal Liberal government was not prepared to include sexual orientation as a prohibited category of discrimination in the *Charter*. But he did suggest that, in time, courts might interpret equality in a more expansive manner.

A decade after the equality rights came into force (their application was delayed for three years after the *Charter* was adopted to allow legislatures to identify and revise legislation that might be inconsistent with equality), the Supreme Court ruled in *Egan v. Canada*[1] that the *Charter*'s equality rights do indeed protect individuals from discrimination on the basis of sexual orientation. However, because the Court's ruling was heavily qualified, this decision was not immediately helpful to those hoping for swift legislative changes to redress discrimination against gay men or lesbians. Although the Court was unanimous in its conclusion that section 15 equality rights prohibit discrimination on the basis of sexual orientation, it split on the question whether the legislation at issue, the federal *Old Age Security Act* and the allowance it provided for some qualifying spouses of pensioners, actually violated the *Charter*. Five judges ruled that the heterosexual definition of "spouse" in the *Act* violated equality, while four judges ruled it did not. But Justice Sopinka, one of the five who ruled that equality was violated, concluded that the legislation imposed a reasonable limit under section 1. He argued that legislatures needed more time to recognize new social relationships because the idea of interpreting "spouse" to include same-sex partners represented a "novel concept" and the legislative changes would have significant fiscal implications. The result of this section 1 ruling was that a narrow majority upheld the validity of the *Act*, relieving federal or provincial legislatures of the immediate pressure of having to redress this form of discrimination.

---

1   [1995] 2 S.C.R. 513.

However, it was not long before the Court expressed impatience with what it perceived to be inappropriate delays in introducing the necessary social policy reforms. Three years later, the Court indicated judicial fatigue with legislative inaction in addressing discrimination on the basis of sexual orientation. In *Vriend v. Alberta*,[2] the Court categorically rejected the Alberta government's argument for deference to its explicit decision not to include sexual orientation as a protected ground against discrimination in its provincial human rights code. In *Vriend,* lawyers for the Alberta government argued, unsuccessfully, that the omission of sexual orientation as a prohibited ground of discrimination was justified under section 1, reminding the Court that Justice Sopinka had only a few years earlier suggested that legislatures should be given time to develop an incremental approach to reform legislation affecting spouses and families.

M. v. H. was handed down the following year, and this time the Court clearly was not prepared to accept legislative inaction on this issue. At issue was the failure in Ontario's *Family Law Act* to recognize same-sex relationships in its processes for resolving property and other issues that arise when family relationships are dissolved. Government lawyers had argued that same-sex partners had options other than statutory ones, such as contract law, and that the differential treatment was therefore acceptable. The Court rejected this argument, concluding that the denial of access to the court-enforced and court-protected support system available to others whose relationships have dissolved was not justified under section 1. But it was not simply the lack of equal benefit of the law that troubled the Court. The Court also ruled that the legislation violated equality because it promoted a view that those in same-sex relationships are less worthy of state recognition and protection than those in heterosexual unions and that this message perpetuates the disadvantages incurred by those in same-sex relationships because of the continued social prejudices they encounter.

Although the legislation had immediate implications for Ontario, it also had important consequences for the federal and other provincial governments because they similarly based legislative entitlements and obligations on a heterosexual definition of "spouse." In Ontario, the Progressive Conservative government of Mike Harris indicated that, although the Court's view of family did not correspond with his definition, his government would comply with the Court's decision, suggesting that he did not believe that use of the notwithstanding clause was a valid political response to a judicial ruling. But the government's lack of enthusiasm for the legislative changes it introduced was conveyed in the title of its legislation, which suggested grudging acceptance for the ruling: *Amendments Because of the Supreme Court of Canada Decision in M. v. H. Act, 1999*. This legislation amended more than 67 legislative acts by recognizing "same-sex partners" for inclusion in most social policy entitlements. The federal government responded to this ruling in 2000 by introducing the *Modernization of Benefits and Obligations Act*, which introduced a new term, "common-law partner," and expanded the common-law definition of "non-married relationships" to include same-sex partners. The legislation was extremely controversial, as critics argued that it would affect the definition of "marriage." In response to pressure from the Canadian Alliance, the Liberal government agreed to include a preamble in the legislation, stating that the amendments did not affect the definition of "marriage," which remained "the lawful union of one man and one woman to the exclusion of all others." ⁓

---

2   [1998] 1 S.C.R. 493.

M. v. H.
[1999] 2 S.C.R. 3

Hearing: March 18, 1998; Judgment: May 20, 1999.

Present: Lamer C.J. and L'Heureux-Dubé, Gonthier, Cory, McLachlin, Iacobucci, Major, Bastarache, and Binnie JJ.

Interveners: The Foundation for Equal Families, the Women's Legal Education and Action Fund (LEAF), Equality for Gays and Lesbians Everywhere (EGALE), the Ontario Human Rights Commission, the United Church of Canada, the Evangelical Fellowship of Canada, the Ontario Council of Sikhs, the Islamic Society of North America, Focus on the Family, and REAL Women of Canada.

The judgment of Lamer C.J. and L'Heureux-Dubé, Cory, McLachlin, Iacobucci, and Binnie JJ. was delivered by

CORY AND IACOBUCCI JJ.:

I. Introduction and Overview

[1] The principal issue raised in this appeal is whether the definition of "spouse" in s. 29 of the *Family Law Act*, R.S.O. 1990, c. F.3 ("*FLA*") infringes s. 15(1) of the *Canadian Charter of Rights and Freedoms*, and, if so, whether the legislation is nevertheless saved by s. 1 of the *Charter*. In addition, M. was granted leave to cross-appeal on the issue of the appropriate remedy to be granted and also as to costs.

[2] Our view on this principal issue may be summarized as follows. Section 15(1) of the *Charter* is infringed by the definition of "spouse" in s. 29 of the *FLA*. This definition, which only applies to Part III of the *FLA*, draws a distinction between individuals in conjugal, opposite-sex relationships of a specific degree of duration and individuals in conjugal, same-sex relationships of a specific degree of duration.... Essentially, the definition of "spouse" in s. 29 of the *FLA* extends the obligation to provide spousal support, found in Part III of the *FLA*, beyond married persons to include individuals in conjugal opposite-sex relationships of some permanence. Same-sex relationships are capable of being both conjugal and lengthy, but individuals in such relationships are nonetheless denied access to the court-enforced system of support provided by the *FLA*. This differential treatment is on the basis of a personal characteristic, namely sexual orientation, that, in previous jurisprudence, has been found to be analogous to those characteristics specifically enumerated in s. 15(1).

[3] The crux of the issue is that this differential treatment discriminates in a substantive sense by violating the human dignity of individuals in same-sex relationships. As *Law v. Canada (Minister of Employment and Immigration)*, [1999] 1 S.C.R. 497, established, the inquiry into substantive discrimination is to be undertaken in a purposive and contextual manner. In the present appeal, several factors are important to consider. First, individuals in same-sex relationships face significant pre-existing disadvantage and vulnerability, which is exacerbated by the impugned legislation. Second, the legislation at issue fails to take into account the claimant's actual situation. Third, there is no compelling argument that the ameliorative purpose of the legislation does anything to lessen the charge of discrimination in this case. Fourth, the nature of the interest affected is fundamental, namely the ability to meet basic financial needs following the breakdown of a relationship characterized by intimacy and economic dependence. The exclusion of same-sex partners from the benefits of the spousal support scheme implies that they are judged to be incapable of forming intimate relationships of economic interdependence, without regard to their actual circumstances. Taking these factors into account, it is clear that the human dignity of individuals in same-sex relationships is violated by the definition of "spouse" in s. 29 of the *FLA*.

[4] This infringement is not justified under s.1 of the *Charter* because there is no rational connection between the objectives of the spousal support provisions and the means chosen to further this objective. The objectives were accurately identified by Charron J.A., in the court below, as providing for the equitable resolution of economic disputes when intimate relationships between financially interdependent individuals break down, and alleviating the burden on the public purse to provide for dependent spouses. Neither of these objectives is furthered by the exclusion of individuals in same-sex couples from the spousal support regime. If anything, these goals are undermined by this exclusion.

[5] In this case, the remedy of reading in is inappropriate, as it would unduly recast the legislation, and striking down the *FLA* as a whole is excessive. Therefore the appropriate remedy is to declare s. 29 of no force and effect and to suspend the application of the declaration for a period of six months.

[6] In our elaboration of this position in these joint reasons, Cory J. has addressed the issues of mootness and the breach of s. 15(1) of the *Charter*. Iacobucci J. has addressed s. 1 of the *Charter*, the appropriate remedy, costs and the disposition.

CORY J.:

[7] At the outset, it must be stressed that the questions to be answered are narrow and precise in their scope. The *FLA* provides a means whereby designated persons may apply to the court for support from a spouse or, if unmarried, from a man or woman with whom they lived in an opposite-sex conjugal relationship. The Act specifically extends the obligation

for support beyond married persons who, as a result of their married status, have additional rights under the Act.

[8] The question to be resolved is whether the extension of the right to seek support to members of unmarried opposite-sex couples infringes s. 15(1) of the *Charter* by failing to provide the same rights to members of same-sex couples.

II.   Factual Background

[9] M. and H. are women who met while on vacation in 1980. It is agreed that in 1982 they started living together in a same-sex relationship that continued for at least five years. . . .

[13] By September of 1992, M. and H.'s relationship had deteriorated. . . .

[14] The parties did not divide the personal property or household contents. M. alleged that she encountered serious financial problems after the separation. In October 1992, M. sought an order for partition and sale of the house; a declaration that she was the beneficial owner of certain lands and premises owned by H. and by the companies M. named as defendants; and an accounting of the transactions carried out by the companies. By Notice of Cross-Application, H. and the corporate defendants sought damages for slander of title, partition and sale of property, the repayment of certain loans, and other relief. M. then amended her application to include a claim for support pursuant to the provisions of the *FLA*, and served Notice of a Constitutional Question challenging the validity of the definition of "spouse" in s. 29 of the Act. . . .

B. Does Section 29 of the FLA Infringe Section 15(1) of the Charter?

[45] The Attorney General for Ontario, displaying great candour, very fairly conceded that s. 29 of the *FLA* contravenes the provisions of s. 15 of the *Charter*. His entire argument was directed at demonstrating that the section was nonetheless justifiable and saved by s. 1 of the *Charter*. The Court is certainly not bound by this concession. Although, in my view, he was correct in taking this position, it would not be appropriate in this appeal to undertake only a s. 1 analysis without considering whether s. 15 has in fact been violated. The s. 15(1) issue in this case is important not only to the parties but also to many Canadians. It was the subject of extensive submissions by the respondent H. and many of the interveners.

1.   Approach to Section 15(1)

[46] In the recent decision of this Court in *Law, supra*, Iacobucci J. summarized some of the main guidelines for analysis under s. 15(1) to be derived from the jurisprudence of this Court. He emphasized that these guidelines do not represent a strict test, but rather should be understood as points of reference for a court that is called upon to decide

whether a claimant's right to equality without discrimination under the *Charter* has been infringed: see para. 88.

[47] Iacobucci J. explained that the s. 15(1) equality guarantee is to be interpreted and applied in a purposive and contextual manner, in order to permit the realization of the provision's strong remedial purpose, and to avoid the pitfalls of a formalistic or mechanical approach. Following a review of this Court's jurisprudence regarding the fundamental purpose of s. 15(1), he stated this purpose in the following terms, at para. 88:

> In general terms, the purpose of s. 15(1) is to prevent the violation of essential human dignity and freedom through the imposition of disadvantage, stereotyping, or political or social prejudice, and to promote a society in which all persons enjoy equal recognition at law as human beings or as members of Canadian society, equally capable and equally deserving of concern, respect and consideration.

Iacobucci J. stated that the existence of a conflict between the purpose or effect of an impugned law, on the one hand, and this fundamental purpose of the equality guarantee, on the other, is essential in order to found a discrimination claim.

[48] In *Law*, Iacobucci J. reviewed various articulations of the proper approach to be taken in analyzing a s. 15(1) claim, as expressed in the jurisprudence of this Court. At para. 39, he summarized the basic elements of this Court's approach as involving three broad inquiries, in the following terms:

> In my view, the proper approach to analyzing a claim of discrimination under s. 15(1) of the *Charter* involves a synthesis of these various articulations. Following upon the analysis in *Andrews* [*v. Law Society of British Columbia*], [1989] 1 S.C.R. 143, and the two-step framework set out in *Egan, supra*, and *Miron* [*v. Trudel*, [1995] 2 S.C.R. 418], among other cases, a court that is called upon to determine a discrimination claim under s. 15(1) should make the following three broad inquiries. First, does the impugned law (a) draw a formal distinction between the claimant and others on the basis of one or more personal characteristics, or (b) fail to take into account the claimant's already disadvantaged position within Canadian society resulting in substantively differential treatment between the claimant and others on the basis of one or more personal characteristics? If so, there is differential treatment for the purpose of s. 15(1). Second, was the claimant subject to differential treatment on the basis of one or more of the enumerated and analogous grounds? And third, does the differential treatment discriminate in a substantive sense, bringing into play the *purpose* of s. 15(1) of the *Charter* in remedying such ills as prejudice, stereotyping, and historical disadvantage? [Emphasis in original.]

2. The Structure of the Family Law Act

[49] To begin, it may be useful to review briefly the structure of the *FLA* and the rights and obligations it establishes. First and foremost, it is of critical importance to recognize that the *FLA* contains more than one definition of "spouse." The first definition is set out in s. 1(1) and includes only persons who are actually married, or who have entered into a void or voidable marriage in good faith. This definition applies to *all* parts of the Act.

[50] The second definition is found in s. 29, and extends the meaning of "spouse," but only for certain purposes. Specifically, unmarried opposite-sex couples who have cohabited for at least three years, or who are the natural or adoptive parents of a child and have also cohabited in a relationship of "some permanence," bear a mutual obligation of support under Part III of the *FLA*. They also have the right to enter into cohabitation agreements to regulate their relationship under Part IV, and may bring a claim for dependants' relief in tort under Part V.

[51] All these rights and obligations are obviously available to married persons as well. However, married persons have additional rights under the *FLA* that are denied common law cohabitants, even those who meet the requirements of s. 29. Under Part I, a husband or wife may apply for an equal share of the wealth generated during the marriage, and of the matrimonial home. Under Part II, both married spouses have a right to possession of the matrimonial home, regardless of who owns the property. Moreover, the ability of the owner of the matrimonial home to sell or encumber the property without the consent of the other spouse is severely restricted. These mutual rights and obligations are denied *all* unmarried opposite-sex cohabitants.

[52] These observations on the structure of the *FLA* serve to emphasize that this appeal has nothing to do with marriage *per se*. Much of the *FLA* is devoted solely to regulating the relationship that exists between married persons, or persons who intend to be married. They alone are guaranteed certain property rights that are not extended to any unmarried persons. In some specific instances—such as Part III dealing with support obligations—the legislature has seen fit to extend the rights and obligations that arise under the *FLA beyond* married persons to include certain *unmarried* persons as well.

[53] In other words, the *FLA* draws a distinction by specifically according rights to individual members of unmarried cohabiting opposite-sex couples, which by omission it fails to accord to individual members of same-sex couples who are living together. It is this distinction that lies at the heart of the s. 15 analysis. The rights and obligations that exist between married persons play no part in this analysis. The legislature did not extend full marital status, for the purposes of all the

rights and obligations under the *FLA*, to those unmarried cohabitants included in s. 29 of the Act. Rather, the definition of "spouse" in s. 29 only applies for certain purposes. Specifically, it allows persons who became financially dependent in the course of a lengthy intimate relationship some relief from financial hardship resulting from the breakdown of that relationship. It follows that this provision was designed to reduce the demands on the public welfare system. This will be discussed more fully in the s. 1 analysis below.

[54] ... [T]he legislature drafted s. 29 to allow either a man *or* a woman to apply for support, thereby recognizing that financial dependence can arise in an intimate relationship in a context entirely unrelated either to child rearing or to any gender-based discrimination existing in our society....

[55] [I]n this appeal there is no need to consider whether same-sex couples can marry, or whether same-sex couples must, for all purposes, be treated in the same manner as unmarried opposite-sex couples. The only determination that must be made is whether, in extending the spousal support obligations set out in Part III of the *FLA* to include unmarried men or women in certain opposite-sex relationships, the legislature infringed the equality rights of men or women in similar same-sex relationships, and if so, whether that infringement may be saved by s. 1 of the *Charter*....

[57] The definition [of "spouse" in section 29 of the *FLA*] clearly indicates that the legislature decided to extend the obligation to provide spousal support *beyond* married persons. Obligations to provide support were no longer dependent upon marriage. The obligation was extended to include those relationships which:

(i) exist between a man and a woman;

(ii) have a specific degree of permanence;

(iii) are conjugal.

Only individuals in relationships which meet these minimum criteria may apply for a support order under Part III of the *FLA*.

[58] Same-sex relationships are capable of meeting the last two requirements. Certainly same-sex couples will often form long, lasting, loving and intimate relationships. The choices they make in the context of those relationships may give rise to the financial dependence of one partner on the other. Though it might be argued that same-sex couples do not live together in "conjugal" relationships, in the sense that they cannot "hold themselves out" as husband and wife, on this issue I am in agreement with the reasoning and conclusions of the majority of the Court of Appeal....

[60] Certainly an opposite-sex couple may, after many years together, be considered to be in a conjugal relationship although they have neither children nor sexual relations.

Obviously the weight to be accorded the various elements or factors to be considered in determining whether an opposite-sex couple is in a conjugal relationship will vary widely and almost infinitely. The same must hold true of same-sex couples. Courts have wisely determined that the approach to determining whether a relationship is conjugal must be flexible. This must be so, for the relationships of all couples will vary widely. . . .

[61] Since gay and lesbian individuals are capable of being involved in conjugal relationships, and since their relationships are capable of meeting the *FLA*'s temporal requirements, the distinction of relevance to this appeal is between persons in an opposite-sex, conjugal relationship of some permanence and persons in a same-sex, conjugal relationship of some permanence. In this regard, I must disagree with the dissenting opinion in the court below, which characterized the distinction arising in s. 29 as being between opposite-sex and same-sex *couples*. This conclusion would require that the section be scrutinized for any discriminatory impact it may have on same-sex couples, and not on the individual members of that couple. Section 29 defines "spouse" as "*either* of a man and woman" who meet the other requirements of the section. It follows that the definition could not have been meant to define a couple. Rather it explicitly refers to the *individual* members of the couple. Thus the distinction of relevance must be between individual persons in a same-sex, conjugal relationship of some permanence and individual persons in an opposite-sex, conjugal relationship of some permanence.

[62] Thus it is apparent that the legislation has drawn a formal distinction between the claimant and others, based on personal characteristics. As stated in *Law, supra*, the first broad inquiry in the s. 15(1) analysis determines whether there is differential treatment imposed by the impugned legislation between the claimant and others. It is clear that there is differential treatment here. Under s. 29 of the *FLA*, members of opposite-sex couples who can meet the requirements of the statute are able to gain access to the court-enforced system of support provided by the *FLA*. It is this system that ensures the provision of support to a dependent spouse. Members of same-sex couples are denied access to this system entirely on the basis of their sexual orientation.

4. Sexual Orientation Is an Analogous Ground

[63] Not every legislative distinction is discriminatory. Before it can be found that it gives rise to discrimination, it must be shown that an equality right was denied on the basis of an enumerated or analogous ground, and that this differential treatment discriminates "in a substantive sense, bringing into play the *purpose* of s. 15(1) of the *Charter*": *Law, supra*, at para. 39 (emphasis in original).

[64] In *Egan, supra*, this Court unanimously affirmed that sexual orientation is an analogous ground to those enumerated in s. 15(1). Sexual orientation is "a deeply personal characteristic that is either unchangeable or changeable only at unacceptable personal costs" (para. 5). In addition, a majority of this Court explicitly recognized that gays, lesbians and bisexuals, "whether as individuals or couples, form an identifiable minority who have suffered and continue to suffer serious social, political and economic disadvantage" (para. 175, *per* Cory J.; see also para. 89, *per* L'Heureux-Dubé J.).

5. The Existence of Discrimination in a Purposive Sense

[65] The determination of whether differential treatment imposed by legislation on an enumerated or analogous ground is discriminatory within the meaning of s. 15(1) of the *Charter* is to be undertaken in a purposive and contextual manner. The relevant inquiry is whether the differential treatment imposes a burden upon or withholds a benefit from the claimant in a manner that reflects the stereotypical application of presumed group or personal characteristics, or which otherwise has the effect of perpetuating or promoting the view that the individual is less capable or worthy of recognition or value as a human being or as a member of Canadian society, equally deserving of concern, respect, and consideration: *Law, supra*, at para. 88.

[66] The respondent H. has argued that the differential treatment imposed by s. 29 of the *FLA* does not deny the respondent M. the equal benefit of the law since same-sex spouses are not being denied an economic benefit, but simply the opportunity to gain access to a court-enforced process. Such an analysis takes too narrow a view of "benefit" under the law. It is a view this Court should not adopt. The type of benefit salient to the s. 15(1) analysis cannot encompass only the conferral of an economic benefit. It must also include access to a process that could confer an economic or other benefit: *Egan, supra*, at paras. 158-59; *Vriend v. Alberta*, [1998] 1 S.C.R. 493, at para. 87. Further, the spousal support provisions of the *FLA* help protect the economic interests of individuals in intimate relationships. When a relationship breaks down, the support provisions help to ensure that a member of a couple who has contributed to the couple's welfare in intangible ways will not find himself or herself utterly abandoned. This protective aspect of the spousal support provisions is properly considered in relation to s. 15(1). Thus it is appropriate to conclude that s. 29 of the *FLA* creates a distinction that withholds a benefit from the respondent M. The question is whether this denial of a benefit violates the purpose of s. 15(1).

[67] In *Law*, Iacobucci J. explained that there are a variety of contextual factors that may be referred to by a s. 15(1) claimant in order to demonstrate that legislation demeans

his or her dignity. The list of factors is not closed, and there is no specific formula that must be considered in every case. In *Law* itself, Iacobucci J. listed four important contextual factors in particular which may influence the determination of whether s. 15(1) has been infringed. He emphasized, at paras. 59-61, that in examining these contextual factors, a court must adopt the point of view of a reasonable person, in circumstances similar to those of the claimant, who takes into account the contextual factors relevant to the claim.

[68] One factor which may demonstrate that legislation that treats the claimant differently has the effect of demeaning the claimant's dignity is the existence of pre-existing disadvantage, stereotyping, prejudice, or vulnerability experienced by the individual or group at issue. . . .

[69] In this case, there is significant pre-existing disadvantage and vulnerability, and these circumstances are exacerbated by the impugned legislation. The legislative provision in question draws a distinction that prevents persons in a same-sex relationship from gaining access to the court-enforced and protected support system. This system clearly provides a benefit to unmarried heterosexual persons who come within the definition set out in s. 29, and thereby provides a measure of protection for their economic interests. This protection is denied to persons in a same-sex relationship who would otherwise meet the statute's requirements, and as a result, a person in the position of the claimant is denied a benefit regarding an important aspect of life in today's society. Neither common law nor equity provides the remedy of maintenance that is made available by the *FLA*. The denial of that potential benefit, which may impose a financial burden on persons in the position of the claimant, contributes to the general vulnerability experienced by individuals in same-sex relationships.

[70] A second contextual factor that was discussed in *Law* as being potentially relevant to the s. 15(1) inquiry is the correspondence, or the lack of it, between the ground on which a claim is based and the actual need, capacity, or circumstances of the claimant or others: para. 70. Iacobucci J. nonetheless cautioned that the mere fact that the impugned legislation takes into account the claimant's actual situation will not necessarily defeat a s. 15(1) claim, as the focus of the inquiry must always remain upon the central question of whether, viewed from the perspective of the claimant, the differential treatment imposed by the legislation has the effect of violating human dignity. However, the legislation at issue in the current appeal fails to take into account the claimant's actual situation. As I have already discussed, access to the court-enforced spousal support regime provided in the *FLA* is given to individuals in conjugal relationships of a specific degree of permanence. Being in a same-sex relationship does not mean that it is an impermanent or a non-conjugal relationship.

[71] A third contextual factor referred to by Iacobucci J. in *Law, supra,* at para. 72, is the question of whether the impugned legislation has an ameliorative purpose or effect for a group historically disadvantaged in the context of the legislation:

> An ameliorative purpose or effect which accords with the purpose of s. 15(1) of the *Charter* will likely not violate the human dignity of more advantaged individuals where the exclusion of these more advantaged individuals largely corresponds to the greater need or the different circumstances experienced by the disadvantaged group being targeted by the legislation. I emphasize that this factor will likely only be relevant where the person or group that is excluded from the scope of ameliorative legislation or other state action is more advantaged in a relative sense. Underinclusive ameliorative legislation that excludes from its scope the members of an historically disadvantaged group will rarely escape the charge of discrimination: see *Vriend, supra,* at paras. 94-104, *per* Cory J.

In other words, the existence of an ameliorative purpose or effect may help to establish that human dignity is not violated where the person or group that is excluded is more advantaged with respect to the circumstances addressed by the legislation. Gonthier J. argues that the legislation under scrutiny in the present appeal is just such ameliorative legislation—that it is meant to target women in married or opposite-sex relationships. He proceeds to argue that in this legal context, women in same-sex relationships are not similarly disadvantaged. For the reasons expressed elsewhere, we disagree with this characterization of the legislation. Accordingly, we reject the idea that the allegedly ameliorative purpose of this legislation does anything to lessen the charge of discrimination in this case.

[72] A fourth contextual factor specifically adverted to by Iacobucci J. in *Law,* at para. 74, was the nature of the interest affected by the impugned legislation. Drawing upon the reasons of L'Heureux-Dubé J. in *Egan, supra,* Iacobucci J. stated that the discriminatory calibre of differential treatment cannot be fully appreciated without considering whether the distinction in question restricts access to a fundamental social institution, or affects a basic aspect of full membership in Canadian society, or constitutes a complete non-recognition of a particular group. In the present case, the interest protected by s. 29 of the *FLA* is fundamental, namely the ability to meet basic financial needs following the breakdown of a relationship characterized by intimacy and economic dependence. Members of same-sex couples are entirely ignored by the statute, notwithstanding the undeniable importance to them of the benefits accorded by the statute.

[73] The societal significance of the benefit conferred by the statute cannot be overemphasized. The exclusion of

same-sex partners from the benefits of s. 29 of the *FLA* promotes the view that M., and individuals in same-sex relationships generally, are less worthy of recognition and protection. It implies that they are judged to be incapable of forming intimate relationships of economic interdependence as compared to opposite-sex couples, without regard to their actual circumstances. As the intervener EGALE submitted, such exclusion perpetuates the disadvantages suffered by individuals in same-sex relationships and contributes to the erasure of their existence.

[74] Therefore I conclude that an examination of the four factors outlined above, in the context of the present appeal, indicate that the human dignity of individuals in same-sex relationships is violated by the impugned legislation. In light of this, I conclude that the definition of "spouse" in s. 29 of the *FLA* violates s. 15(1).

IACOBUCCI J.:

C. Is Section 29 of the FLA Justified Under Section 1 of the Charter?

1. Stare Decisis and Egan

[75] At the outset, I wish to address the appellant's submission that an independent examination of the s. 1 issues is unnecessary in the present case. The appellant asserts that the principle of *stare decisis* binds this Court to the decision in *Egan, supra*, and that the s. 1 analysis in that case ought to apply with equal force to the case at bar. Although I recognize the fundamental role of precedent in legal analysis, I cannot accept this submission. Granted, *Egan*, like the case now before this Court, was also concerned with the opposite-sex definition of "spouse" in provincial legislation. However, the similar focus of the two cases is not sufficient to bind the Court to the *Egan* decision. The instant case is based on entirely different legislation with its own unique objectives and legislative context. As a result, it must be evaluated on its own merits.

2. Approach to Section 1

[76] The analytical framework for determining whether a law constitutes a "reasonable" limit that can be "demonstrably justified in a free and democratic society" under s. 1 of the *Charter* was first set out by Dickson C.J. in *R. v. Oakes*, [1986] 1 S.C.R. 103....

[77] However, it is important not to lose sight of the underlying principles animating this general approach....

[78] As noted by this Court in *Vriend, supra*, at para. 134, the introduction of the *Charter* brought about "a redefinition of our democracy." Central to this democratic vision is a dialogue of mutual respect between the courts and the legislatures, which includes the idea that [*Vriend*, at para. 136]:

In carrying out their duties, courts are not to second-guess legislatures and the executives; they are not to make value judgments on what they regard as the proper policy choice; this is for the other branches. Rather, the courts are to uphold the Constitution and have been expressly invited to perform that role by the Constitution itself. But respect by the courts for the legislature and executive role is as important as ensuring that the other branches respect each others' role and the role of the courts.

This Court has often stressed the importance of deference to the policy choices of the legislature in the context of determining whether the legislature has discharged its burden of proof under s. 1 of the *Charter*.... However, it is important to note that deference is not a kind of threshold inquiry under s. 1. As a general matter, the role of the legislature demands deference from the courts to those types of policy decisions that the legislature is best placed to make. The simple or general claim that the infringement of a right is justified under s. 1 is not such a decision. As Cory J. stated in *Vriend, supra*, at para. 54: "The notion of judicial deference to legislative choices should not ... be used to completely immunize certain kinds of legislative decisions from *Charter* scrutiny."

[79] Under s. 1, the burden is on the legislature to prove that the infringement of a right is justified. In attempting to discharge this burden, the legislature will have to provide the court with evidence and arguments to support its general claim of justification. Sometimes this will involve demonstrating why the legislature had to make certain policy choices and why it considered these choices to be reasonable in the circumstances. These policy choices may be of the type that the legislature is in a better position than the court to make, as in the case of difficult policy judgments regarding the claims of competing groups or the evaluation of complex and conflicting social science research: *Irwin Toy, supra*, at p. 993, *per* Dickson C.J. and Lamer and Wilson JJ. Courts must be cautious not to overstep the bounds of their institutional competence in reviewing such decisions. The question of deference, therefore, is intimately tied up with the nature of the particular claim or evidence at issue and not in the general application of the s. 1 test; it can only be discussed in relation to such specific claims or evidence and not at the outset of the analysis.

[80] I therefore agree with my colleague, Bastarache J., that an examination of *context* is essential in determining whether deference is appropriate. It may also be the case that a discussion of context is appropriate at the outset of a s. 1 analysis, depending on the nature of the evidence at issue, for ease of reference when later applying the various steps of s. 1: see, for example, *Thomson Newspapers Co. v. Canada (Attorney General)*, [1998] 1 S.C.R. 877, at para. 88, *per* Bastarache J. However, with respect to his reasons in the present appeal, I

am concerned that Bastarache J. implies that the question of *deference* in a general sense should also be determined at the outset of the inquiry. For example, Bastarache J. states that the question to ask in this case is whether the Court can "rewrite the boundary in order to include that smaller number of individuals [in same-sex relationships] who are in such a position [of dependency], or must it defer to legislative determination of the issue?" (para. 304). The question of rewriting boundaries is, to my mind, at most a question of the appropriate remedy should the rights infringement be unjustified. The question of deference to the role of the legislature certainly enters into any discussion of remedy, as discussed in *Vriend, supra,* and can enter into the discussion of whether the legislature has discharged its burden under any of the steps of the s. 1 test. However, the question of deference is not an issue that can be determined prior to engaging in any of these specific inquiries. Nor should it be determined at the outset of the inquiry, given the court's important role in applying s. 1 of the *Charter* to determine whether the infringement of a guaranteed right can be justified in a free and democratic society.

[81] I will therefore not deal with the question of deference at the outset and will instead discuss it, where appropriate, under the various steps of the s. 1 test.

3. Pressing and Substantial Objective

[82] Section 29 of the *FLA* defines "spouse" as being either of a man and woman who are married to each other or cohabiting within the meaning of the Act. Same-sex couples are necessarily excluded from this definition, thereby giving rise to the charge that the legislation is underinclusive. In *Vriend, supra,* at paras. 109-11, this Court found that where a law violates the *Charter* owing to under-inclusion, the first stage of the s. 1 analysis is properly concerned with the object of the legislation as a whole, the impugned provisions of the Act, and the omission itself. . . .

[86] . . . There is considerable disagreement between the parties as to the underlying purpose of [the *FLA*]. . . .

[93] As I see the matter, the objectives of the impugned spousal support provisions were accurately identified by Charron J.A. in the court below . . . [who] identified the objectives of the Part III provisions as both a means to provide "for the equitable resolution of economic disputes that arise when intimate relationships between individuals who have been financially interdependent break down" and to "alleviate the burden on the public purse by shifting the obligation to provide support for needy persons to those parents and spouses who have the capacity to provide support to these individuals" (p. 450). I find support for this position in the legislative debates, the terms of the provisions, as well as the jurisprudence of this Court. . . .

[100] . . . I turn to the objective of the omission. As I have already stated, when dealing with underinclusive legislation it is important also to consider the impugned omission when construing the objective. Often legislation does not simply further one goal but rather strikes a balance among several goals, some of which may be in tension. This balancing exercise may only become apparent after asking whether, in the case of underinclusive legislation, there is any objective being furthered by the impugned omission. A consideration of what is omitted from legislation may also lead a court to refine its interpretation of the objectives of the impugned legislation, perhaps reducing its scope. I agree with my colleague, Bastarache J., at para. 329, that if the omission is not taken into account in construing the objective then it is more likely that the omission will cause the impugned legislation to fail the rational connection step of the proportionality analysis.

[101] However, the concerns just outlined do not imply that the court must find that there is a separate objective being furthered by the omission. Even if there is no such objective the omission must still be evaluated as part of the means chosen to further the objective of the specific provision in question, under the proportionality analysis. Otherwise the court risks collapsing the two stages of the *Oakes* test (pressing and substantial objective and proportionality) into a general question regarding the reasonableness of the omission. There may be exceptions to this general approach, such as when there is evidence of a deliberate omission by the legislature that is "on its face the very antithesis of the principles embodied in the legislation as a whole": *Vriend, supra,* at para. 116.

[102] With these concerns in mind, I turn to the present appeal. The appellant does not argue that a separate objective is furthered by the impugned omission. Rather, the argument is that a proper consideration of the exclusion of same-sex couples from the definition of "spouse" in s. 29 of the *FLA* reduces the apparent scope of the objective furthered by that provision. The appellant made two arguments in this regard. First, the appellant argued that the *FLA* is a remedial statute designed to address the power imbalance that continues to exist in many opposite-sex relationships. Thus, it was submitted that the inclusion of same-sex couples in a scheme established to deal with problems that are not typical of their relationships is inappropriate. Further, the appellant asserted that where persons fall outside the rationale for which a benefit was established, the legislature is justified in withholding it from those persons.

[103] With respect, I disagree with these submissions. As I stated above, I do not believe that the purpose of the *FLA* in general, nor Part III in particular, is to remedy the disadvantages suffered by women in opposite-sex relationships.

[104]   The second objective for the omission advanced by the appellant is the promotion of opposite-sex relationships to ensure the protection of children. Having found that neither the *FLA* as a whole nor the spousal support provisions in Part III of the Act are primarily concerned with the protection of children, I must also reject the submission that this is part of the objective of s. 29 of the *FLA*.

[105]   Finally, I note that Bastarache J. accepts that the rejection of the *Equality Rights Statute Law Amendment Act, 1994* by the Ontario legislature can provide evidence regarding the objective of s. 29 of the *FLA*. In particular, he argues, at para. 349: "It can therefore be inferred that the legislature's purpose was also to exclude all types of relationships not typically characterized by the state of economic dependency apparent in traditional family relationships." With respect, I cannot agree that a failed amendment can provide evidence as to the objective of the legislation that was to have been amended. Section 17 of the *Interpretation Act*, R.S.O. 1990, c. I.11, provides: "The repeal or amendment of an Act shall be deemed not to be or to involve any declaration as to the previous state of the law." If the amendment of an Act may not be used to interpret the meaning of the Act prior to the amendment, then I do not see how a *failed* amendment may be used in this manner.

[106]   Therefore I endorse the description of the objectives of the impugned provisions provided by Charron J.A. in the court below. These objectives are consonant with the overall scheme of the *FLA* and are not plausibly reinterpreted through examining the omission of same-sex spouses. Providing for the equitable resolution of economic disputes when intimate relationships between financially interdependent individuals break down, and alleviating the burden on the public purse to provide for dependent spouses, are to my mind pressing and substantial objectives. These objectives promote both social justice and the dignity of individuals— values Dickson C.J. identified in *Oakes, supra*, at p. 136, as values underlying a free and democratic society.

[107]   In saying this, I wish to note my disagreement with my colleague, Bastarache J., who argues, at para. 354, that s. 29 of the *FLA* "must be respectful of the equality of status and opportunity of all persons" in order to be consistent with *Charter* values and therefore pass this stage of the s. 1 analysis. While I agree that an objective must be consistent with the principles underlying the *Charter* in order to pass the first stage of the s. 1 analysis, I find Bastarache J.'s approach unnecessarily narrow. It may be that a violation of s. 15(1) can be justified because, although not designed to promote equality, it is designed to promote *other* values and principles of a free and democratic society. This possibility must be left open, as the inquiry into *Charter* values under s. 1 is a broad inquiry into the values and principles that, as Dickson C.J. stated in *Oakes, supra*, at p. 136, "are the *genesis* of the rights and freedoms guaranteed by the *Charter*" (emphasis added).

4. Proportionality Analysis

(a) Rational Connection

... [109] ... In my view, it defies logic to suggest that a gender-neutral support system is rationally connected to the goal of improving the economic circumstances of heterosexual women upon relationship breakdown. In addition, I can find no evidence to demonstrate that the exclusion of same-sex couples from the spousal support regime of the *FLA* in any way furthers the objective of assisting heterosexual women....

[112]   The second of the objectives put forth by the appellant, namely, the protection of children, also fails the rational connection test. The appellant submits that the exclusion of same-sex partners from Part III of the *FLA* is rationally connected to this objective as such couples are far less likely to engage in parenting than opposite-sex couples....

[116]   If anything, the goals of the legislation are undermined by the impugned exclusion. Indeed, the *inclusion* of same-sex couples in s. 29 of the *FLA* would better achieve the objectives of the legislation while respecting the *Charter* rights of individuals in same-sex relationships. In these circumstances, I conclude that the exclusion of same-sex couples from s. 29 of the Act is simply not rationally connected to the dual objectives of the spousal support provisions of the legislation.

[117]   Given this lack of a rational connection, s. 29 of the *FLA* is not saved by s. 1 of the *Charter*. Although it is therefore not strictly necessary to consider the other two branches of the second stage of the *Oakes* test, I will discuss them briefly in order to clarify some fundamental misunderstandings advanced in this appeal.

(b) Minimal Impairment

[118]   ... The appellant suggests that the exclusion of same-sex couples from s. 29 of the *FLA* minimally impairs the respondent's s. 15 rights since reasonable alternative remedies are available where economic dependence does occur in such relationships. I cannot accept these submissions.

[119]   The appellant's arguments on this point are based on the remedies available under the equitable doctrine of unjust enrichment (e.g. constructive trust) and the law of contract. Turning first to the equitable remedies, the doctrine of unjust enrichment allows claimants to found an action on indirect or non-financial contributions to the acquisition, maintenance, or preservation of an asset held by the other spouse. However, to be successful, the applicant must demonstrate his or her spouse's enrichment, a corresponding

personal deprivation and the absence of any juristic reason for the enrichment....

[120] Moreover,... equitable common law remedies such as a constructive trust are proprietary in nature and ... not all relationships will give rise to property claims. Indeed, as submitted by LEAF, the *FLA* expressly recognizes that entitlement to the division of property is in addition to, and not in lieu of entitlement to support. Thus, it seems to me that compared to awards of spousal support, the equitable remedies are less flexible, impose more onerous requirements on claimants, and are available under far narrower circumstances. I do not accept that they provide an adequate alternative to spousal support under the *FLA*.

[121] In my view, the law of contract is an equally unacceptable alternative to the spousal support scheme under the *FLA*. The appellant emphasizes that the impugned provisions of the Act do not preclude same-sex partners from contracting for mutual support obligations. However, the voluntary assumption of such obligations is not equivalent to a statutory entitlement to apply for a support order....

[124] In sum, neither the common law equitable remedies nor the law of contract are adequate substitutes for the *FLA*'s spousal support regime. Indeed, if these remedies were considered satisfactory there would have been no need for the spousal support regime, or its extension to unmarried, opposite-sex couples. It must also be remembered that the exclusion of same-sex partners from this support regime does not simply deny them a certain benefit, but does so in a manner that violates their right to be given equal concern and respect by the government. The alternative regimes just outlined do not address the fact that exclusion from the statutory scheme has moral and societal implications beyond economic ones.... Therefore the existence of these remedies fails to minimize sufficiently the denial of same-sex partners' constitutionally guaranteed equality rights.

[125] However, the appellant asserts that the circumstances of this case call for a measure of deference to the decision of the Ontario legislature. In this context, it is argued that it was reasonable for the government to conclude that it had impaired the rights of same-sex partners as little as possible.

[126] As I see the matter, the deferential approach advocated by the appellant is inappropriate in the case at bar. This Court has resorted to such an approach where the impugned legislation involves the balancing of claims of competing groups (see, e.g., *Irwin Toy, supra*, at pp. 999-1000; *McKinney v. University of Guelph*, [1990] 3 S.C.R. 229, at pp. 317-19, *per* La Forest J.; and *Egan, supra*, at para. 29, *per* La Forest J. and at paras. 105-8, *per* Sopinka J.).... This is not such a case. As no group will be disadvantaged by granting members of same-sex couples access to the spousal support scheme under

the *FLA*, the notion of deference to legislative choices in the sense of balancing claims of competing groups has no application to this case....

[128] In addition, the deferential approach is not warranted, as submitted by the appellant, on the basis that Part III of the *FLA* and s. 29 thereof are steps in an incremental process of reform of spousal support. As this Court noted in *Vriend, supra*, government incrementalism, or the notion that government ought to be accorded time to amend discriminatory legislation, is generally an inappropriate justification for *Charter* violations. However, even if I were to accept that such a justification might be suitable in the present case, it seems to me that its application to the facts of the case at bar cannot legitimize the continued exclusion of same-sex couples from the *FLA*'s spousal support regime.

[129] ... [T]here is no evidence of any progress with respect to this group since the inception of the spousal support regime. If the legislature refuses to act so as to evolve towards *Charter* compliance then deference as to the timing of reforms loses its *raison d'être*.

[130] Moreover, in contrast to *Egan, supra*, where Sopinka J. relied in part on incrementalism in upholding the impugned legislation under s. 1 of the *Charter*, there is no concern regarding the financial implications of extending benefits to gay men and lesbians in the case at bar. As already pointed out, rather than increasing the strain on the public coffers, the extension will likely go some way toward alleviating those concerns because same-sex couples as a group will be less reliant on government welfare if the support scheme is available to them. Thus, I conclude that government incrementalism cannot constitute a reason to show deference to the legislature in the present case.

[131] Finally, as this Court has emphasized on other occasions, "[d]eference must not be carried to the point of relieving the government of the burden which the *Charter* places upon it of demonstrating that the limits it has imposed on guaranteed rights are reasonable and justifiable": *RJR-MacDonald, supra*, at para. 136, *per* McLachlin J. See also *Eldridge* [*v. British Columbia (Attorney General)*, [1997] 3 S.C.R. 624]; *Tétreault-Gadoury v. Canada (Employment and Immigration Commission)*, [1991] 2 S.C.R. 22; and *Vriend, supra*.

[132] In the present case, the government has failed to show that it had a reasonable basis for concluding that the rights of same-sex couples were impaired no more than was reasonably necessary to achieve its goals. The exclusion from the s. 29 definition of "spouse," and consequently from the *FLA* spousal support regime, is absolute. No effort has been made to tailor the limiting measure. I conclude that the appellant's case also fails at the minimal impairment stage of the s. 1 analysis.

(c) Proportionality Between the Effect of the Measure and the Objective

[133] ... The damaging effects engendered by the exclusion of same-sex couples from s. 29 of the *FLA*, as noted by Cory J., are numerous and severe. Such harms cannot be justified where the statute has not achieved what it set out to do. Where, as here, the impugned measures actually undermine the objectives of the legislation it cannot be said that the deleterious effects of the measures are outweighed by the promotion of any laudable legislative goals, nor by the salutary effects of those measures.

[134] I therefore conclude that the exclusion of same-sex couples from s. 29 of the *FLA* cannot be justified as a reasonable limit on constitutional rights under s. 1 of the *Charter*. Before turning to a discussion of the appropriate remedy, I wish to emphasize, like Cory J., that the sole issue presented by this case is whether the *Charter* mandates that same-sex couples be accorded the right to apply for spousal support under the *FLA*. This appeal does not challenge traditional conceptions of marriage, as s. 29 of the Act expressly applies to *unmarried* opposite-sex couples. That being said, I do not wish to be understood as making any comment on marriage or indeed on related issues. ...

VI. Remedy

[136] ... In the court below, the words "a man and woman" were read out of the definition of "spouse" in s. 29 of the *FLA* and replaced with the words "two persons." The application of the order was suspended for a period of one year. With respect, I am not convinced that that is a suitable remedy in the circumstances of the present case. ...

[141] If the remedy adopted by the court below is allowed to stand, s. 29 of the *FLA* will entitle members of same-sex couples who otherwise qualify under the definition of "spouse" to apply for spousal support. However, any attempt to opt out of this regime by means of a cohabitation agreement provided for in s. 53 or a separation agreement set out in s. 54 would not be recognized under the Act. Both ss. 53 and 54 extend to common-law cohabitants but apply only to agreements entered into between "a man and woman." Any extension of s. 29 of the Act would have no effect upon these Part IV domestic contract provisions of the *FLA*, which do not rely upon the Part III definition of "spouse." Thus, same-sex partners would find themselves in the anomalous position of having no means of opting out of the default system of support rights. As this option is available to opposite-sex couples, and protects the ability of couples to choose to order their own affairs in a manner reflecting their own expectations, reading in would in effect remedy one constitutional wrong only to create another, and thereby fail to ensure the validity of the legislation.

[142] In addition, reading into the definition of "spouse" in s. 29 of the Act will have the effect of including same-sex couples in Part V of the *FLA* (Dependants' Claim for Damages), as that part of the Act relies upon the definition of "spouse" as it is defined in Part III. In my opinion, where reading in to one part of a statute will have significant repercussions for a separate and distinct scheme under that Act, it is not safe to assume that the legislature would have enacted the statute in its altered form. In such cases, reading in amounts to the making of *ad hoc* choices, which Lamer C.J. in *Schachter* [*v. Canada*, [1992] 2 S.C.R. 679], at p. 707, warned is properly the task of the legislatures, not the courts.

[143] In cases where reading in is inappropriate, the court must choose between striking down the legislation in its entirety and severing only the offending portions of the statute. As noted by Lamer C.J. in *Schachter*, at p. 697, "[w]here the offending portion of a statute can be defined in a limited manner it is consistent with legal principles to declare inoperative only that limited portion. In that way, as much of the legislative purpose as possible may be realized."

[144] In the case at bar, striking down the whole of the *FLA* would be excessive as only the definition of "spouse" in Part III of the Act has been found to violate the *Charter*. This is not a case where the parts of the legislative scheme which do offend the *Charter* are so inextricably bound up with the non-offending portions of the statute that what remains cannot independently survive. As a result, it would be safe to assume that the legislature would have passed the constitutionally sound parts of the statute without the unsound parts. See *Attorney-General for Alberta v. Attorney-General for Canada*, [1947] A.C. 503, at p. 518; *Schachter, supra*, at p. 697.

[145] On the basis of the foregoing, I conclude that severing s. 29 of the Act such that it alone is declared of no force or effect is the most appropriate remedy in the present case. This remedy should be temporarily suspended for a period of six months. ...

[147] ... I note that declaring s. 29 of the *FLA* to be of no force or effect may well affect numerous other statutes that rely upon a similar definition of the term "spouse." The legislature may wish to address the validity of these statutes in light of the unconstitutionality of s. 29 of the *FLA*. On this point, I agree with the majority of the Court of Appeal which noted that if left up to the courts, these issues could only be resolved on a case-by-case basis at great cost to private litigants and the public purse. Thus, I believe the legislature ought to be given some latitude in order to address these issues in a more comprehensive fashion. ...

GONTHIER J. (dissenting): . . .

[268] The *Charter* cannot possibly require the Legislative Assembly to revise the *FLA* to exclude non-procreative opposite-sex couples from its scope. As La Forest J. indicated, the legislative and administrative scheme necessary to do so would be highly intrusive and would likely violate *Charter* privacy guarantees. By contrast, exclusion of same-sex couples, who are inherently, rather than situationally, non-procreative, from the *FLA* support regime raises none of these concerns. . . .

[270] The entire issue in this appeal is whether the distinction drawn by the Legislative Assembly between cohabiting opposite-sex couples and all other relationships is maintainable. My colleagues' implicit suggestion is that the simplest way to render s. 29 constitutionally viable would be to restrict its application to married couples alone. I see no reason to conclude that the *Charter* operates so restrictively. Here, the Legislative Assembly has made a distinction on the basis of a fundamental biological and social reality to address a unique form of disadvantage specific to opposite-sex couples. On the other hand, if the Legislative Assembly is obliged to address all of the manifestations of economic interdependence between individuals, it is difficult to see how drawing the line to include same-sex couples, but to exclude those relationships which are not conjugal (and which can be similarly distinguished on enumerated or analogous grounds), can itself withstand constitutional challenge.

[271] It may be, of course, that extending the definition of "spouse" to include same-sex couples or other relationships or otherwise providing for support obligations based on dependency would be a prudent or reasonable policy decision. My colleague Iacobucci J.'s view, for example, is that to make this extension would advance what he sees as the purpose of the legislation. However, the wisdom or desirability of such an extension is not itself a matter properly within the consideration of this Court. The legislature itself considered the desirability of extending the scope of s. 29 to same-sex couples, but in the end, decided to the contrary. We must take seriously the contention that the legislation violates the *Charter*. Yet we must be careful not to jump from the assertion that a legislative change would be prudent to the contention that such a change is constitutionally mandated. In my view, my colleagues make that jump. For this reason, I respectfully disagree. . . .

[273] One of the fundamental principles in Canadian society is that individuals enjoy freedom and are expected to provide for their own needs. This rule is obviously not absolute. Canadians take pride in our social programs which lend a hand to those who, for differing reasons, cannot provide for themselves. At the same time, these social programs have specific policy goals, and in pursuit of those goals, they target specific groups of people. When the State provides assistance, only those who need the assistance should receive it. In this appeal, the impugned legislation sought to redress a historical fact that individuals in opposite-sex relationships suffer a *systemic* dynamic of dependence, which manifests in a support obligation that exists not only while the two individuals are in the relationship, but also after the relationship breaks down. Usually, it is the female partner who suffers the greatest burden upon marriage or common-law relationship breakdown: *Moge* [*v. Moge*, [1992] 3 S.C.R. 813]. The legislature has, since 1859, used a variety of legislative tools to alleviate this systemic suffering, which is unique to opposite-sex relationships. The statutory language, the preamble, and the legislative debates reveal that this legislation is one of those tools.

[274] In my view, the s. 15(1) claim in this case fails because s. 29 of the *FLA* seeks to ameliorate a historical and structural disadvantage specific to individuals in certain types of opposite-sex relationships, and in so doing, accurately corresponds with the needs, capacity, and circumstances of the claimant and these opposite-sex couples. Although individuals in same-sex relationships suffer pre-existing disadvantage in many areas of life, it has not been shown that this is one of them. In fact, the contrary has been shown: individuals in same-sex relationships generally exhibit less dependency in the relationship; they do not have a structural wage differential between the partners in the relationship; and they do not exhibit the same gendered division of domestic and child-care responsibilities. Although any of these elements may be present in a same-sex relationship, none will have been created by the structural dynamic of dependence which the legislature has seen fit to address, but rather will be attributable to the individual idiosyncrasies of the claimant.

[275] . . . The right to equality in s. 15(1) does not guarantee equality in the abstract; it rests on a comparison with others. This requires us to examine whether the claimant group suffers pre-existing disadvantage, stereotyping, prejudice or vulnerability *as compared with* the selected comparison group, and as related to the subject-matter of the legislation. In this case, individuals in same-sex relationships are not disadvantaged in relation to the dynamic of dependence which the legislation seeks to address. As such, the ameliorative purpose of the *FLA* is not underinclusive of a group which is disadvantaged in relation to that purpose. Moreover, although the claimant is affected by her exclusion from the mandatory support regime, this regime both confers a benefit *and* imposes a burden. Mandatory support restricts personal choice and reduces the concomitant financial advantages. The legislation does not render individuals in same-sex relationships "invisible." They are fully entitled to impose support obligations

upon themselves, if they so choose. However, the circumstances unique to individuals in opposite-sex relationships which warrant the reduction of that group's autonomy do not similarly exist in same-sex relationships.

[276] By analysing all of the contextual factors, it is apparent that the claimant's human dignity is not violated by s. 29 of the *FLA*. A reasonable person in the position of the claimant, having taken into account all of the contextual factors relevant to the claim, would not find their human dignity violated by a provision which appropriately takes into account their actual needs, capacity, and circumstances as compared to those of opposite-sex couples subject to the legislation. For these reasons, it is my view that the s. 15(1) claim must fail. . . .

[Justices Major and Bastarache wrote separate reasons that concurred with the majority's decision. Justice Major reached the result on a more narrow basis than the majority. Justice Bastarache differed with how the majority interpreted the purpose of the legislation.]

Sauvé v. Canada (Chief Electoral Officer), 2002

S ection 3 of the *Charter* gives every Canadian citizen the right to vote. At the same time, section 1 permits such "reasonable limits" on this right as "can be demonstrably justified in a free and democratic society." A variety of historical disqualifications based on such criteria as sex, race, and wealth had already been found to be "unreasonable limits" on the franchise well before the *Charter* came into effect. Others—for example, the traditional disqualification of judges and the mentally disabled—have been abandoned since, and partly because of, the *Charter*'s advent.[1] We know that some reasonable limits remain, however, because age restrictions continue to enjoy almost universal support. Could the traditional disqualification of imprisoned criminals—another persistent holdout against the trend of franchise expansion—be similarly maintained? In *Sauvé* (2002),[2] a narrowly (and intensely) divided Court decided that it could not. The case also raised section 15 equality-rights issues,[3] but these occupied little of the Court's attention[4] and did not affect the outcome.

Several years earlier, the same litigant, Richard Sauvé, had already brought the issue to the Supreme Court. *Sauvé* (1993)[5] considered what was then a blanket prisoner disqualification, under which a petty offender who elected brief imprisonment in lieu of a fine might find himself disenfranchised on voting day while his accomplice paid the fine and voted. By the time *Sauvé* (1993) reached the Supreme Court, the law had been altered to disqualify only criminals imprisoned for terms of two years or more, but the judges preferred not to comment on this change, choosing instead to invalidate only the previous blanket disqualification. For Richard Sauvé this was a pyrrhic victory. As a convicted murderer he was imprisoned for more than two years and thus continued to be disenfranchised by the new law. Undaunted, Sauvé launched a new case.

Writing for the five-judge majority in *Sauvé* (2002), Justice McLachlin doubted that the prisoner disqualification met even the "pressing and substantial purpose" requirement of the *Oakes* test,[6] but she was likely prevented from deciding the case on this basis by the precedent of *Sauvé* (1993). In that earlier case, the nine judges of the Supreme Court, including Justice McLachlin, unanimously invalidated the blanket disqualification in an unusually terse, one-paragraph opinion, the substance of which is contained in a single sentence:

---

1   See *Muldoon v. Canada*, [1988] 3 F.C. 628 (T.D.) and *Canadian Disability Rights Council v. Canada*, [1988] 3 F.C. 622 (T.D.).

2   *Sauvé v. Canada (Chief Electoral Officer)*, [2002] 3 S.C.R. 519.

3   This was either because prisoners deserved the status of an "analogous group" under section 15 or because the impact of the disqualification fell more heavily on Aboriginals, who are disproportionately represented in the prison population.

4   The majority, having found the disqualification unconstitutional under section 3, did not think it necessary to address section 15. In brief reasons, the minority denied that the disqualification infringed section 15.

5   *Sauvé v. Canada (Attorney General)*, [1993] 2 S.C.R. 438.

6   This is usually the easiest hurdle to clear in the *Oakes* test. See the introduction to *Oakes*, case 24.

In our view, [the blanket disqualification] is drawn too broadly and fails to meet the proportionality test, particularly the minimal impairment component of the test, as expressed in the s. 1 jurisprudence of the Court.

In focusing entirely on the proportionality test, *Sauvé* (1993) clearly assumed that even a blanket disqualification of prisoners has the kind of compelling purpose required by the first part of the *Oakes* test. Having agreed to this in the earlier case, Justice McLachlin could not easily find that the less draconian disqualification at issue in *Sauvé* (2002) lacked a compelling purpose. However, grudgingly, she thus conceded a compelling purpose and moved on to the question of proportional means.

Writing for *Sauvé* (2002)'s four-judge minority, Justice Gonthier, who had also participated in *Sauvé* (1993), was happy to focus on proportional means. If the blanket disqualification in *Sauvé* (1993) "particularly" failed "the minimal impairment component" of the *Oakes* test, the government's task was to find more finely tuned means to its end. For Gonthier, this is precisely what the much vaunted concept of "dialogue" between courts and legislatures is all about. In his view, the appropriate legislative response in this particular dialogue was to disqualify only more serious criminals, as defined by the length of their incarceration. But what length, exactly? Just as those who agree in principle on an age-based voting restriction often disagree on what the cut-off age should be, so those who agree on a length-of-sentence criterion for prisoner disqualification can disagree on what the sentence cut-off should be. For example, while the government had chosen two years as the cut-off, the Royal Commission on Electoral Reform and Party Financing (the Lortie Commission) had previously suggested a 10-year sentence as the appropriate threshold for disqualification.[7] Gonthier was not inclined to micromanage this issue. The government's two-year threshold was good enough to meet the minimal impairment standard.

The two-year threshold wasn't good enough for Justice McLachlin. But neither would she agree to a longer sentence as more appropriate. In fact, she made it abundantly clear that no disqualification, no matter how finely tailored, would pass constitutional muster in her view. How is this possible, given that she had agreed to ground her conclusions on the issue of proportional means, as *Sauvé* (1993) requires? Had the cryptic judgment in *Sauvé* (1993) read simply that the disqualification "fails to meet the minimal impairment component" of the *Oakes* test, McLachlin would indeed have been reduced to debating the right length of sentence to use as a threshold for disqualification. But *Sauvé* (1993) speaks of the proportionality test as a whole; indeed, by "particularly" emphasizing its minimal impairment component, it implicitly holds the door open to the possible involvement of the proportionality test's other components.[8]

Justice McLachlin walked through this door, especially with respect to the rational-connection component of proportionality. Rational connection requires that the challenged legislative means must actually achieve the compelling purpose to which they are directed.

---

7   Royal Commission on Electoral Reform and Party Financing, *Final Report* (Ottawa: Minister of Supply and Services, 1991) vol. I at 45.

8   Given the judicial preferences on display in *Sauvé* (2002), it is difficult to escape the conclusion that the key sentence of *Sauvé* (1993) was, in fact, the carefully crafted outcome of a strategic compromise between the contending factions. On the strategic dimensions of *Sauvé* and many other Canadian cases, see Rainer Knopff, Dennis Baker, and Sylvia LeRoy, "Courting Controversy: Strategic Judicial Decision Making" (forthcoming).

Only if they do, does it make sense to proceed to issues of minimal impairment. The judges unanimously agree that conclusive scientific proof is not required to establish such a rational connection between means and ends; the logic and common sense of a "reasonable person" will do. Because McLachlin's "reasonable person" could imagine no prisoner disqualification that achieves any plausible compelling purpose, none could meet the rational-connection test. Nor could there be any room for "dialogue" about "irrational" legislative means. Disagreeing with Gonthier's view that there had been appropriate dialogue about how best to achieve minimal impairment of the right to vote, McLachlin insisted that to apply the concept in this instance would debase it to a rule of "if at first you don't succeed, try, try again." It is not healthy dialogue to keep attempting what is fundamentally irrational.

Wherever McLachlin saw irrationality, Gonthier discerned plausible and defensible positions. Social contract theory, for example, which McLachlin saw as utterly hostile to a prisoner disqualification, was for Gonthier an important justification of the disqualification. In grounding the legitimacy of government on the foundational consent of its citizens (as institutionalized in democracies through public elections), contract theory establishes a "vital symbolic, theoretical and practical connection between having a voice in making the law and being obliged to obey it." Part of consenting to government, in other words, is agreeing to abide by its laws. For McLachlin, this meant that one cannot—as the government claimed to be doing—teach people to be law abiding by depriving them of the pedagogical tool best suited to teaching this lesson—the vote. In support of this position, she quoted John Stuart Mill's claim that "the possession and the exercise of political, and among others of electoral, rights, is one of the chief instruments both of moral and of intellectual training for the popular mind."[9] For Gonthier, by contrast, nothing could be more appropriate from the standpoint of the social contract than to temporarily deprive those who break the law of their law-making role. How else can one effectively teach the "connection between having a voice in making the law and being obliged to obey it"? To do otherwise is symbolically to demean the dignity of the vote. Just as McLachlin found support for her position in J.S. Mill, Gonthier could easily have invoked such contract theorists as Kant in support of his. "In my role as colegislator making the penal law," wrote Kant, "I cannot be the same person who, as a subject, is punished by the law; for, as a subject who is also a criminal, I cannot have a voice in legislation."[10]

This kind of vigorous point and counterpoint characterizes the extensive debate between the majority and dissenting opinions in *Sauvé* (2002); that debate repays careful investigation. ⌐

---

9   This quotation does not, of course, directly address the issue of prisoner voting. When he explicitly considers that question elsewhere, Mill admits that "[a]s far as the direct influence of [prisoners'] votes went, it would scarcely be worthwhile to exclude them," but that "[a]s an aid to the great object of giving a moral character to the exercise of the suffrage, it might be expedient that in the case of crimes evincing a high degree of insensibility to social obligation, the deprivation of this and other civic rights should form part of the sentence." *The Collected Works of John Stuart Mill* (Toronto: University of Toronto Press, 1977) 322n. Mill, moreover, was not a social contract theorist.

10   Immanuel Kant, *The Metaphysical Elements of Justice*, Part 1 of *The Metaphysics of Morals*, trans. John Ladd (Indianapolis: Bobbs-Merrill, 1978) at 105. For a review of how the thought of many other philosophers bears on the question of prisoner voting, see Zdravko Planinc, "Should Imprisoned Criminals Have a Constitutional Right to Vote?" (1987) *Canadian Journal of Law and Society* 2.

SAUVÉ v. CANADA (CHIEF ELECTORAL OFFICER)
2002 SCC 68, [2002] 3 S.C.R. 519

Hearing: December 10, 2001; Judgment: October 31, 2002.

Present: McLachlin C.J. and L'Heureux-Dubé, Gonthier, Iacobucci, Major, Bastarache, Binnie, Arbour, and LeBel JJ.

Interveners: The Attorney General for Alberta, the Attorney General of Manitoba, the Canadian Association of Elizabeth Fry Societies, the John Howard Society of Canada, the British Columbia Civil Liberties Association, the Aboriginal Legal Services of Toronto Inc., and the Canadian Bar Association.

The judgment of McLachlin C.J. and Iacobucci, Binnie, Arbour, and LeBel JJ. was delivered by

THE CHIEF JUSTICE:

[1] The right of every citizen to vote, guaranteed by s. 3 of the *Canadian Charter of Rights and Freedoms*, lies at the heart of Canadian democracy. The law at stake in this appeal denies the right to vote to a certain class of people—those serving sentences of two years or more in a correctional institution. The question is whether the government has established that this denial of the right to vote is allowed under s. 1 of the *Charter* as a "reasonable limit . . . demonstrably justified in a free and democratic society." I conclude that it is not. The right to vote, which lies at the heart of Canadian democracy, can only be trammeled for good reason. Here, the reasons offered do not suffice. . . .

[6] The respondents concede that the voting restriction at issue violates s. 3 of the *Charter*. The restriction is thus invalid unless demonstrably justified under s. 1. I shall therefore proceed directly to the s. 1 analysis. . . .

[8] My colleague Justice Gonthier . . . argues that in justifying limits on the right to vote under s. 1, we owe deference to Parliament because we are dealing with "philosophical, political and social considerations," because of the abstract and symbolic nature of the government's stated goals, and because the law at issue represents a step in a dialogue between Parliament and the courts.

[9] I must, with respect, demur. The right to vote is fundamental to our democracy and the rule of law and cannot be lightly set aside. Limits on it require not deference, but careful examination. This is not a matter of substituting the Court's philosophical preference for that of the legislature, but of ensuring that the legislature's proffered justification is supported by logic and common sense. . . .

[13] The core democratic rights of Canadians do not fall within a "range of acceptable alternatives" among which Parliament may pick and choose at its discretion. Deference may be appropriate on a decision involving competing social and

political policies. It is not appropriate, however, on a decision to limit fundamental rights. This case is not merely a competition between competing social philosophies. It represents a conflict between the right of citizens to vote—one of the most fundamental rights guaranteed by the *Charter*—and Parliament's denial of that right. Public debate on an issue does not transform it into a matter of "social philosophy," shielding it from full judicial scrutiny. It is for the courts, unaffected by the shifting winds of public opinion and electoral interests, to safeguard the right to vote guaranteed by s. 3 of the *Charter*.

[14] *Charter* rights are not a matter of privilege or merit, but a function of membership in the Canadian polity that cannot lightly be cast aside. This is manifestly true of the right to vote, the cornerstone of democracy, exempt from the incursion permitted on other rights through s. 33 override.

[15] The *Charter* charges courts with upholding and maintaining an inclusive, participatory democratic framework within which citizens can explore and pursue different conceptions of the good. While a posture of judicial deference to legislative decisions about social policy may be appropriate in some cases, the legislation at issue does not fall into this category. To the contrary, it is precisely when legislative choices threaten to undermine the foundations of the participatory democracy guaranteed by the *Charter* that courts must be vigilant in fulfilling their constitutional duty to protect the integrity of this system.

[16] Nor can I concur in the argument that the philosophically-based or symbolic nature of the government's objectives in itself commands deference. . . . Parliament cannot use lofty objectives to shield legislation from *Charter* scrutiny. Section 1 requires valid objectives *and* proportionality.

[17] Finally, the fact that the challenged denial of the right to vote followed judicial rejection of an even more comprehensive denial, does not mean that the Court should defer to Parliament as part of a "dialogue." Parliament must ensure that whatever law it passes, at whatever stage of the process, conforms to the Constitution. The healthy and important promotion of a dialogue between the legislature and the courts should not be debased to a rule of "if at first you don't succeed, try, try again."

[18] While deference to the legislature is not appropriate in this case, legislative justification does not require empirical proof in a scientific sense. While some matters can be proved with empirical or mathematical precision, others, involving philosophical, political and social considerations, cannot. In this case, it is enough that the justification be convincing, in the sense that it is sufficient to satisfy the reasonable person looking at all the evidence and relevant considerations, that the state is justified in infringing the right at stake to the degree it has: see *RJR-MacDonald* [*Inc. v. The Attorney General*

of Canada, [1995] 3 S.C.R. 199], at para. 154, *per* McLachlin J.; *R. v. Butler*, [1992] 1 S.C.R. 452, at pp. 502-3, *per* Sopinka J. What is required is "rational, reasoned defensibility": *RJR-MacDonald*, at para. 127. Common sense and inferential reasoning may supplement the evidence: *R. v. Sharpe*, [2001] 1 S.C.R. 45, 2001 SCC 2, at para. 78, *per* McLachlin C.J. However, one must be wary of stereotypes cloaked as common sense, and of substituting deference for the reasoned demonstration required by s. 1.

[19] Keeping in mind these basic principles of *Charter* review, I approach the familiar stages of the *Oakes* test. I conclude that the government's stated objectives of promoting civic responsibility and respect for the law and imposing appropriate punishment, while problematically vague, are capable in principle of justifying limitations on *Charter* rights. However, the government fails to establish proportionality, principally for want of a rational connection between denying the vote to penitentiary inmates and its stated goals. . . .

[21] . . . [T]he government asserts two broad objectives as the reason for this denial of the right to vote: (1) to enhance civic responsibility and respect for the rule of law; and (2) to provide additional punishment, or "enhance the general purposes of the criminal sanction." The record leaves in doubt how much these goals actually motivated Parliament; the Parliamentary debates offer more fulmination than illumination. However, on the basis of "some glimmer of light," the trial judge at p. 878 concluded that they could be advanced as objectives of the denial. I am content to proceed on this basis. . . .

[22] . . . Vague and symbolic objectives such as these almost guarantee a positive answer to this question. Who can argue that respect for the law is not pressing? Who can argue that proper sentences are not important? Who can argue that either of these goals, taken at face value, contradict democratic principles? However, precisely because they leave so little room for argument, vague and symbolic objectives make the justification analysis more difficult. Their terms carry many meanings, yet tell us little about why the limitation on the right is necessary, and what it is expected to achieve in concrete terms. . . .

[23] . . . If Parliament can infringe a crucial right such as the right to vote simply by offering symbolic and abstract reasons, judicial review either becomes vacuously constrained or reduces to a contest of "our symbols are better than your symbols." Neither outcome is compatible with the vigorous justification analysis required by the *Charter*. . . .

[26] Quite simply, the government has failed to identify particular problems that require denying the right to vote, making it hard to say that the denial is directed at a pressing and substantial purpose. Nevertheless, despite the abstract nature of the government's objectives and the rather thin basis upon which they rest, prudence suggests that we proceed to the proportionality analysis, rather than dismissing the government's objectives outright. . . .

[27] At this stage the government must show that the denial of the right to vote will promote the asserted objectives (the rational connection test); that the denial does not go further than reasonably necessary to achieve its objectives (the minimal impairment test); and that the overall benefits of the measure outweigh its negative impact (the proportionate effect test). . . .

[28] Will denying the right to vote to penitentiary inmates enhance respect for the law and impose legitimate punishment? The government must show that this is likely, either by evidence or in reason and logic: *RJR-MacDonald*, *supra*, at para. 153.

[29] The government advances three theories to demonstrate rational connection between its limitation and the objective of enhancing respect for law. First, it submits that depriving penitentiary inmates of the vote sends an "educative message" about the importance of respect for the law to inmates and to the citizenry at large. Second, it asserts that allowing penitentiary inmates to vote "demeans" the political system. Finally, it takes the position that disenfranchisement is a legitimate form of punishment, regardless of the specific nature of the offence or the circumstances of the individual offender. In my respectful view, none of these claims succeed.

[30] The first asserted connector with enhancing respect for the law is the "educative message" or "moral statement" theory. The problem here, quite simply, is that denying penitentiary inmates the right to vote is bad pedagogy. It misrepresents the nature of our rights and obligations under the law, and it communicates a message more likely to harm than to help respect for the law.

[31] Denying penitentiary inmates the right to vote misrepresents the nature of our rights and obligations under the law and consequently undermines them. In a democracy such as ours, the power of lawmakers flows from the voting citizens, and lawmakers act as the citizens' proxies. This delegation from voters to legislators gives the law its legitimacy or force. Correlatively, the obligation to obey the law flows from the fact that the law is made by and on behalf of the citizens. In sum, the legitimacy of the law and the obligation to obey the law flow directly from the right of every citizen to vote. As a practical matter, we require all within our country's boundaries to obey its laws, whether or not they vote. But this does not negate the vital symbolic, theoretical and practical connection between having a voice in making the law and being obliged to obey it. This connection, inherited from social contract theory and enshrined in the *Charter*, stands at the heart of our system of constitutional democracy.

[32] The government gets this connection exactly backwards when it attempts to argue that depriving people of a voice in government teaches them to obey the law. . . . [I]f we accept that governmental power in a democracy flows from the citizens, it is difficult to see how that power can legitimately be used to disenfranchise the very citizens from whom the government's power flows.

[33] Reflecting this truth, the history of democracy is the history of progressive enfranchisement. The universal franchise has become, at this point in time, an essential part of democracy. From the notion that only a few meritorious people could vote (expressed in terms like class, property and gender), there gradually evolved the modern precept that all citizens are entitled to vote as members of a self-governing citizenry. . . . Under s. 3 of the *Charter*, the final vestiges of the old policy of selective voting have fallen, including the exclusion of persons with a "mental disease" and federally appointed judges: see *Canadian Disability Rights Council v. Canada*, [1988] 3 F.C. 622 (T.D.); and *Muldoon v. Canada*, [1988] 3 F.C. 628 (T.D.). The disenfranchisement of inmates takes us backwards in time and retrenches our democratic entitlements. . . .

[35] More broadly, denying citizens the right to vote runs counter to our constitutional commitment to the inherent worth and dignity of every individual. As the South African Constitutional Court said in *August v. Electoral Commission*, 1999 (3) SALR 1, at para. 17, "[t]he vote of each and every citizen is a badge of dignity and of personhood. Quite literally, it says that everybody counts." . . .

[36] In recognition of the seminal importance of the right to vote in the constellation of rights, the framers of the *Charter* accorded it special protections. Unlike other rights, the right of every citizen to vote cannot be suspended under the "notwithstanding clause." . . .

[37] The government's vague appeal to "civic responsibility" is unhelpful, as is the attempt to lump inmate disenfranchisement together with legitimate voting regulations in support of the government's position. The analogy between youth voting restrictions and inmate disenfranchisement breaks down because the type of judgment Parliament is making in the two scenarios is very different. In the first case, Parliament is making a decision based on the experiential situation of all citizens when they are young. It is not saying that the excluded class is unworthy to vote, but regulating a modality of the universal franchise. In the second case, the government is making a decision that some people, whatever their abilities, are not morally worthy to vote—that they do not "deserve" to be considered members of the community and hence may be deprived of the most basic of their constitutional rights. But this is not the lawmakers' decision to make.

The *Charter* makes this decision for us by guaranteeing the right of "every citizen" to vote and by expressly placing prisoners under the protective umbrella of the *Charter* through constitutional limits on punishment. The *Charter* emphatically says that prisoners are protected citizens, and short of a constitutional amendment, lawmakers cannot change this.

[38] The theoretical and constitutional links between the right to vote and respect for the rule of law are reflected in the practical realities of the prison population and the need to bolster, rather than to undermine, the feeling of connection between prisoners and society as a whole. The government argues that disenfranchisement will "educate" and rehabilitate inmates. However, disenfranchisement is more likely to become a self-fulfilling prophecy than a spur to reintegration. Depriving at-risk individuals of their sense of collective identity and membership in the community is unlikely to instill a sense of responsibility and community identity, while the right to participate in voting helps teach democratic values and social responsibility (testimony of Professor Jackson, appellant's record at pp. 2001-2). As J. S. Mill wrote:

> To take an active interest in politics is, in modern times, the first thing which elevates the mind to large interests and contemplations; the first step out of the narrow bounds of individual and family selfishness, the first opening in the contracted round of daily occupations. . . . The possession and the exercise of political, and among others of electoral, rights, is one of the chief instruments both of moral and of intellectual training for the popular mind. . . .
>
> (J. S. Mill, "Thoughts on Parliamentary Reform" (1859), in J.M. Robson, ed., *Essays on Politics and Society*, Vol. XIX (1977), at pp. 322-23)

To deny prisoners the right to vote is to lose an important means of teaching them democratic values and social responsibility. . . .

[42] The government also argues that denying penitentiary inmates the vote will enhance respect for law because allowing people who flaunt the law to vote demeans the political system. . . . But . . . the argument that only those who respect the law should participate in the political process is a variant on the age-old unworthiness rationale for denying the vote. . . .

[43] . . . Until recently, large classes of people, prisoners among them, were excluded from the franchise [on] the assumption that they were not fit or "worthy" of voting—whether by reason of class, race, gender or conduct. . . . We should reject the retrograde notion that "worthiness" qualifications for voters may be logically viewed as enhancing the political process and respect for the rule of law. . . .

[45] This brings us to the government's final argument for rational connection—that disenfranchisement is a legitimate weapon in the state's punitive arsenal against the individual lawbreaker....

[46] The argument, stripped of rhetoric, proposes that it is open to Parliament to add a new tool to its arsenal of punitive implements—denial of constitutional rights. I find this notion problematic. I do not doubt that Parliament may limit constitutional rights in the name of punishment, provided that it can justify the limitation. But it is another thing to say that a particular class of people for a particular period of time will completely lose a particular constitutional right. This is tantamount to saying that the affected class is outside the full protection of the *Charter*. It is doubtful that such an unmodulated deprivation, particularly of a right as basic as the right to vote, is capable of justification under s. 1. Could Parliament justifiably pass a law removing the right of all penitentiary prisoners to be protected from cruel and unusual punishment? I think not. What of freedom of expression or religion? Why, one asks, is the right to vote different?

[47] The social compact requires the citizen to obey the laws created by the democratic process. But it does not follow that failure to do so nullifies the citizen's continued membership in the self-governing polity. Indeed, the remedy of imprisonment for a term rather than permanent exile implies our acceptance of continued membership in the social order. Certain rights are justifiably limited for penal reasons, including aspects of the right to liberty, security of the person, mobility, and security against search and seizure. But whether a right is justifiably limited cannot be determined by observing that an offender has, by his or her actions, withdrawn from the social compact. Indeed, the right of the state to punish and the obligation of the criminal to accept punishment is tied to society's acceptance of the criminal as a person with rights and responsibilities. Other *Charter* provisions make this clear. Thus s. 11 protects convicted offenders from unfair trials, and s. 12 from "cruel and unusual treatment or punishment."

[48] The second flaw in the argument that s. 51(*e*) furthers legitimate punishment is that it does not meet the dual requirements that punishment must not be arbitrary and must serve a valid criminal law purpose. Absence of arbitrariness requires that punishment be tailored to the acts and circumstances of the individual offender: *R. v. Smith*, [1987] 1 S.C.R. 1045, at p. 1073. In the immortal words of Gilbert and Sullivan, the punishment should fit the crime. Section 51(*e*) *qua* punishment bears little relation to the offender's particular crime. It makes no attempt to differentiate among inmates serving sentences of two years and those serving sentences of twenty. It is true that those serving shorter sentences will be deprived of the right to vote for a shorter time. Yet the correlation of the denial with the crime remains weak. It is not only the violent felon who is told he is an unworthy outcast; a person imprisoned for a non-violent or negligent act, or an Aboriginal person suffering from social displacement receives the same message. They are not targeted, but they are caught all the same. For them the message is doubly invidious—not that they are cast out for their apparently voluntary rejection of society's norms, but that they are cast out arbitrarily, in ways that bear no necessary relation to their actual situation or attitude towards state authority.

[49] Punishment must also fulfill a legitimate penal purpose.... These include deterrence, rehabilitation, retribution, and denunciation.... Neither the record nor common sense supports the claim that disenfranchisement deters crime or rehabilitates criminals. On the contrary, as Mill recognized long ago, participation in the political process offers a valuable means of teaching democratic values and civic responsibility.

[50] This leaves retribution and denunciation. Parliament may denounce unlawful conduct. But it must do so in a way that closely reflects the moral culpability of the offender and his or her circumstances.... Denunciation as a symbolic expression of community values must be individually tailored in order to fulfill the legitimate penal purpose of condemning a *particular* offender's conduct (see *M. (C.A.)* [*R. v.*, [1996] 1 S.C.R. 500], at para. 81) and to send an appropriate "educative message" about the importance of law-abiding behavior.

[51] Section 51(*e*) imposes blanket punishment on all penitentiary inmates regardless of the particular crimes they committed, the harm they caused, or the normative character of their conduct. It is not individually tailored to the particular offender's act. It does not, in short, meet the requirements of denunciatory, retributive punishment. It follows that it is not rationally connected to the goal of imposing legitimate punishment....

[53] I conclude that the government has failed to establish a rational connection between s. 51(*e*)'s denial of the right to vote and the objectives of enhancing respect for the law and ensuring appropriate punishment.

[54] If the denial of a right is not rationally connected to the government's objectives, it makes little sense to go on to ask whether the law goes further than is necessary to achieve the objective. I simply observe that if it were established that denying the right to vote sends an educative message that society will not tolerate serious crime, the class denied the vote—all those serving sentences of two years or more—is too broad, catching many whose crimes are relatively minor and who cannot be said to have broken their ties to society. Similarly, if it were established that this denial somehow furthers legitimate

sentencing goals, it is plain that the marker of a sentence of two years or more catches many people who, on the government's own theory, should not be caught....

[57] If a connection could be shown between the denial of the right to vote and the government's objectives, the negative effects of denying citizens the right to vote would greatly outweigh the tenuous benefits that might ensue....

[60] The negative effects of s. 51(*e*) upon prisoners have a disproportionate impact on Canada's already disadvantaged Aboriginal population, whose over-representation in prisons reflects "a crisis in the Canadian criminal justice system": *R. v. Gladue*, [1999] 1 S.C.R. 688, at para. 64, *per* Cory and Iacobucci JJ. To the extent that the disproportionate number of Aboriginal people in penitentiaries reflects factors such as higher rates of poverty and institutionalized alienation from mainstream society, penitentiary imprisonment may not be a fair or appropriate marker of the degree of individual culpability....

The reasons of L'Heureux-Dubé, Gonthier, Major, and Bastarache JJ. were delivered by

GONTHIER J. (dissenting):

[68] ... The Chief Justice and I are in agreement that the right to vote is profoundly important, and ought not to be demeaned. Our differences lie principally in the fact that she subscribes to a philosophy whereby the temporary disenfranchising of criminals does injury to the rule of law, democracy and the right to vote, while I prefer deference to Parliament's reasonable view that it strengthens these same features of Canadian society.

[69] The reasons of the Chief Justice refer to the historical evolution of the franchise in Canada. This evolution has generally involved the weeding out of discriminatory exclusions. It is undeniable and, obviously, to be applauded, that, over time, Canada has been evolving towards the universalization of the franchise in such a manner. The provision in question in the case at bar, however, is strikingly and qualitatively different from these past discriminatory exclusions. It is a temporary suspension from voting based exclusively on the serious criminal *activity* of the offender. It is the length of the sentence, reflecting the nature of the offence and the criminal activity committed, that results in the temporary disenfranchisement during incarceration....

[70] ... While there is little logical correlation between maintaining a "decent and responsible citizenry" and any of the past discriminatory exclusions (such as land-ownership, religion, gender, ethnic background), there clearly is such a logical connection in the case of distinguishing persons who have committed serious criminal offences. "*Responsible* citizenship" does not relate to what gender, race, or religion a person belongs to, but is logically related to whether or not a person engages in serious criminal activity....

[73] The reasons of the Chief Justice express the view that the temporary disenfranchisement of serious criminal offenders necessarily undermines their inherent "worth" or "dignity." I disagree. In fact, it could be said that the notion of punishment is predicated on the dignity of the individual: it recognizes serious criminals as rational, autonomous individuals who have made choices. When these citizens exercise their freedom in a criminal manner, society imposes a concomitant responsibility for that choice....

[74] If there is any negative connotation associated with this temporary disenfranchisement, it arises from the fact that a criminal act was perpetrated, an act for which the criminal offender is consequently being punished. This is not stereotyping. Criminal acts are rightly condemned by society. Serious criminals being punished and temporarily disenfranchised are not in any way of less "worth" or "dignity" because social condemnation is of the criminal acts and its purpose is not to diminish the individual prisoner as a person....

[92] ... [T]here seem generally to be two options available for dealing with the issue at hand. The first, that chosen by the Chief Justice, is to prefer an inclusive approach to democratic participation for serious criminal offenders incarcerated for two years or more. This view locates democratic participation as a central dimension of rehabilitation, insofar as the incarcerated offenders remain citizens with the fullest exercise of their democratic rights. By the same token, the unrestricted franchise enhances democratic legitimacy of government, and confirms or enhances the citizenship or standing of prisoners in society. To do otherwise, it is suggested, undermines the "dignity" or "worth" of prisoners. The alternative view, adopted by Parliament, considers that the temporary suspension of the prisoner's right to vote, in fact, enhances the general purposes of the criminal sanction, including rehabilitation. It does so by underlining the importance of civic responsibility and the rule of law. This approach sees the temporary removal of the vote as a deterrent to offending or re-offending and the return of the vote as an inducement to reject further criminal conduct. In withdrawing for a time one expression of political participation concurrently with personal freedom, the significance of both are enhanced. Rather than undermine the dignity or worth of prisoners, the removal of their vote takes seriously the notion that they are free actors and attaches consequences to actions that violate certain core values as expressed in the *Criminal Code*.

[93] Both of these approaches, however, entail accepting logically prior political or social philosophies about the nature and content of the right to vote. The former approach, that accepted by the reasons of the Chief Justice, entails accepting a

philosophy that preventing criminals from voting does damage to both society and the individual, and undermines prisoners' inherent worth and dignity. The latter approach also entails accepting a philosophy, that not permitting serious incarcerated criminals to vote is a social rejection of serious crime which reflects a moral line which safeguards the social contract and the rule of law and bolsters the importance of the nexus between individuals and the community. Both of these social or political philosophies, however, are *aimed at the same goal*: that of supporting the fundamental importance of the right to vote itself. Further, both of these social or political philosophies are supported by the practices of the various Canadian provinces, the practices of other liberal democracies, and academic writings. Finally, neither position can be proven empirically—rather, the selection of one over the other is largely a matter of philosophical preference. What is *key* to my approach is that the acceptance of one or the other of these social or political philosophies dictates much of the constitutional analysis which ensues, since the reasonableness of any limitation upon the right to vote and the appropriateness of particular penal theories and their relation to the right to vote will logically be related to whether or not the justification for that limitation is based upon an "acceptable" social or political philosophy.

[94] The reasons of the Chief Justice hold ... that the challenge of the Government is to present a justification that is "convincing, in the sense that it is sufficient to satisfy the reasonable person looking at all the evidence and relevant considerations, that the state is justified in infringing the right at stake to the degree it has." ...

[95] The reasons of the Chief Justice apply something seemingly more onerous than the "justification" standard referred to just above. She describes the right to vote as a "core democratic right" and suggests that its exemption from the s. 33 override somehow raises the bar for the government in attempting to justify its restriction (paras. 13 and 14). This altering of the justification standard is problematic in that it seems to be based upon the view that there is only one plausible social or political philosophy upon which to ground a justification for or against the limitation of the right. This approach, however, is incorrect on a basic reading of s. 1 of the *Charter*, which clearly does not constrain Parliament or authorize this Court to prioritize one reasonable social or political philosophy over reasonable others, but only empowers this Court to strike down those limitations which are not reasonable and which cannot be justified in a free and democratic society.

[96] ... It does not follow from the fact that Parliament is denied the authority to remove or qualify the right to vote in its sole discretion under s. 33 that limitations on that right may not be justified under s. 1, or that a more onerous s. 1 analysis must necessarily apply .... It does not behoove the Court to read s. 33 into s. 3 by finding in s. 3, when divorced from s. 1, the statement of a political philosophy which preempts another political philosophy which is reasonable and justified under the latter section. The *Charter* was not intended to monopolize the ideological space....

[100] In her reasons, the Chief Justice claims ... that Parliament is relying on "lofty objectives," and suggests at para. 23 that the presence of "symbolic and abstract" objectives is problematic. However, the reasons of the Chief Justice have the very same objective—to protect the value of the right to vote and the rule of law—and rely on equally vague concepts. Breaking down the meaning and value of the right to vote, one is unavoidably led to abstract and symbolic concepts such as the rule of law, the legitimacy of law and government, and the meaning of democracy. The Chief Justice discusses these concepts at length, along with theories of individual motivation. For instance, relying on the philosopher J.S. Mill, she suggests at para. 38 that "[t]o deny prisoners the right to vote is to lose an important means of teaching them democratic values and social responsibility." This type of statement is as symbolic, abstract and philosophical as the government's claim that denying serious incarcerated criminals the right to vote will strengthen democratic values and social responsibility. ...

[104] Linden J.A., in the Federal Court of Appeal below, stressed the importance of deference to Parliament. In para. 56 of his reasons, he stated:

> This case is another episode in the continuing dialogue between courts and legislatures on the issue of prisoner voting. In 1992 and 1993, two appeal courts and the Supreme Court of Canada held that a blanket disqualification of prisoners from voting, contained in earlier legislation which was challenged, violated section 3 of the Charter and could not be saved by section 1 of the Charter. Parliament responded to this judicial advice by enacting legislation aimed at accomplishing part of its objectives while complying with the Charter. That legislation, which is being challenged in this case, disqualifies from voting only prisoners who are serving sentences of two years or more. [Footnotes omitted.]

This Court has stressed the importance of "dialogue" in *Vriend v. Alberta*, [1998] 1 S.C.R. 493, at paras. 138-39 and in *Mills* [*R. v.*, [1999] 3 S.C.R. 668], at paras. 20, 57 and 125. (See also P.W. Hogg and A.A. Bushell, "The Charter Dialogue Between Courts and Legislatures" (1997), 35 *Osgoode Hall L.J.* 75.) I am of the view that since this case is about evaluating choices regarding social or political philosophies and about shaping, giving expression, and giving practical application to values, especially values that may lie outside the *Charter* but are of fundamental importance to Canadians, "dialogue" is of particular importance. In my view, especially in the context of the case at bar, the heart of the dialogue metaphor is that neither the courts nor Parliament hold a monopoly on the determination of values. Importantly, the dialogue metaphor *does not signal a lowering of the s. 1 justification standard*. It simply suggests that when, after a full and rigorous s. 1 analysis, Parliament has satisfied the court that it has established a reasonable limit to a right that is demonstrably justified in a free and democratic society, the dialogue ends; the court lets Parliament have the last word and does not substitute Parliament's reasonable choices with its own. . . .

[109] What social or political philosophy has motivated Parliament to insist on the temporary disenfranchisement of prisoners? Is it reasonable and rational? I suggest that, in enacting s. 51(*e*) of the Act and in providing a justification of that provision before the courts, Parliament has indicated that it has drawn a line. This line reflects a moral statement about serious crime, and about its significance to and within the community. The core of this moral statement is the denunciation of serious crime, serious antisocial acts. Parliament has indicated that criminal conduct of such severity that it warrants imprisonment for a sentence of two years or more also carries with it the disenfranchisement of the offender for the duration of his or her incarceration. . . .

[115] The denunciation of crime and its effects on society is often explained by reference to the notion of the social contract. The social contract is the theoretical basis upon which the exercise of rights and participation in the democratic process rests. In my view, the social contract necessarily relies upon the acceptance of the rule of law and civic responsibility and on society's need to promote the same. The preamble to the *Charter* establishes that ". . . Canada is founded upon principles that recognize the supremacy of God and the rule of law. . . ." In *Reference re Manitoba Language Rights*, [1985] 1 S.C.R. 721, at p. 750, this Court cited with approval a passage from *The Authority of Law* (1979) by Professor Raz, wherein he states that " 'The rule of law' means literally what it says. . . . It has two aspects: (1) that people should be ruled by the law and obey it, and (2) that the law should be such that people will be able to be guided by it." The important point arising from that passage is the corollary that promoting law-abiding behaviour can be thought to be a dimension of the rule of law as well. Further, the rule of law, as was said in the *Reference re Secession of Quebec*, [1998] 2 S.C.R. 217, at p. 257, "vouchsafes to the citizens and residents of the country a stable, predictable and ordered society in which to conduct their affairs." Given its fundamental importance in our society, it is not surprising that Parliament occasionally insists to take some

action to promote it, to safeguard it. As was stated by Wilson J. in *Operation Dismantle v. The Queen*, [1985] 1 S.C.R. 441, at p. 489: "There is no liberty without law and there is no law without some restriction of liberty: see Dworkin, *Taking Rights Seriously* (1977), p. 267."

[116] Permitting the exercise of the franchise by offenders incarcerated for serious offences undermines the rule of law and civic responsibility because such persons have demonstrated a great disrespect for the community in their committing serious crimes: such persons have attacked the stability and order within our community. Society therefore may choose to curtail temporarily the availability of the vote to serious criminals both to punish those criminals and to insist that civic responsibility and respect for the rule of law, as goals worthy of pursuit, are prerequisites to democratic participation. I say "goals worthy of pursuit" because it is clear that not all those who are otherwise eligible to vote are guaranteed to exercise civic responsibility, since, for example, there may be serious criminal offenders who may have avoided being apprehended and therefore still vote. This does not, however, detract from the laudability of the goal.

[117] Related to the notion of the social contract is the importance of reinforcing the significance of the relationship between individuals and their community when it comes to voting. This special relationship is inherent in the fact that it is only "citizens" who are guaranteed the right to vote within s. 3 of the *Charter*. This limitation of the scope of s. 3 of the *Charter* stands in stark contrast to the protections offered by the fundamental freedoms, legal rights, and equality rights in the *Charter*, which are available to "everyone" or to "every individual." I am of the view that this limitation reflects the special relationship, characterized by entitlements and responsibilities, between citizens and their community. It is this special relationship and its responsibilities which serious criminal offenders have assaulted. . . .

[120] From the perspective of the person whose criminal activity has resulted in their temporary disenfranchisement, their benefiting from society brought with it the responsibility to be subjected to the sanctions which the state decides will be attached to serious criminal activity such as they have chosen to undertake. This understanding is complemented by the rehabilitative view that those who are in jail will hope and expect to regain the exercise of the vote on their release from incarceration, just like they hope and expect to regain the exercise of the fullest expressions of their liberty. Once released from prison, they are on the road to reintegration into the community. Obtaining the vote once released or paroled is a recognition of regaining the nexus with the community that was temporarily suspended during the incarceration. . . .

[135] I now turn to the application of the *Oakes* test. . . .

[139] Parliament's two principal objectives in s. 51(*e*) of the Act, accepted by both the trial judge and the Federal Court of Appeal below, are: the enhancement of civic responsibility and respect for the rule of law, and the enhancement of the general purposes of the criminal sanction. Above, I developed the view that these objectives are based upon a reasonable and rational social or political philosophy. Thus, I am of the view that any provision which seeks to advance such objectives clearly has a pressing and substantial purpose....

[150] This Court has unanimously agreed that "[r]ational connection is to be established, upon a civil standard, through reason, logic or simply common sense": *RJR-MacDonald, supra, per* La Forest J., at para. 86, McLachlin J., at paras. 156-58, and Iacobucci J., at para. 184; referred to in *Thomson Newspapers* [*Co. v. Canada (Attorney General)*, [1998] 1 S.C.R. 877], at para. 39. The existence of scientific proof is simply of probative value in supporting this reason, logic or common sense. In the case at bar, as discussed above, a causal relationship between disenfranchising prisoners and the objectives approved of above is not empirically demonstrable. However, this Court has clearly stated that Parliament must be afforded a margin of appreciation in regard to legitimate objectives which may, nonetheless, be based upon somewhat inconclusive social science evidence: Sopinka J. in *Butler, supra,* at pp. 502-3.... Thus, it is clear that this Court's approach to this dimension of the test demands not the strongest connection, the most convincing rational connection, but a logical or rational connection.

[157] ... [R]eason, logic and common sense, as well as extensive expert evidence support a conclusion that there is a rational connection between disenfranchising offenders incarcerated for serious crimes and the objectives of promoting civic responsibility and the rule of law and the enhancement of the general objectives of the penal sanction. The rational connection between the disenfranchisement and the first objective is explained above, in my discussion of dignity and the fact that removing the right to vote from serious incarcerated criminals does no injury to, but rather recognizes their dignity. It is also explained ... below in my discussion of the salutary effects of the measure [where] I discuss the legislation's expression of societal values and its signalling effect. The Chief Justice prefers a different line of reasoning. Citing J.S. Mill as her authority, she states that "denying penitentiary inmates the right to vote is more likely to send messages that undermine respect for the law and democracy than messages that enhance those values" (para. 41). However, apart from one philosopher, she provides no support for this contention; she simply replaces one reasonable position with another, dismissing the government's position as "unhelpful" (para. 37 of the Chief Justice's reasons).

[158] The rational connection between the legislation and the enhancement of the criminal sanction is also elaborated on elsewhere. Below, ... on minimal impairment, I explain at length that the disenfranchisement is carefully tailored to apply to perpetrators of serious crimes. I therefore disagree with the Chief Justice's statement that denial of the right to vote is insufficiently tailored and therefore not rationally connected to legitimate punishment....

[160] The Crown must demonstrate that the impairment of rights is minimal, i.e. that the law was carefully tailored so that *Charter* rights are impaired no more than is necessary to meet the legislative provision's objectives.... This analysis does not, notably, require the Crown to have adopted the absolutely least intrusive means for promoting the purpose, although it does require that the Crown prefer a significantly less intrusive means if it is of *equal effectiveness*....

[161] I emphasize that it was "particularly" on the ground of minimal impairment that this Court, in the first *Sauvé* case, established that the previous s. 51(*e*) of the Act, which disenfranchised all prisoners regardless of the duration of their incarceration, was contrary to the *Charter* and incapable of being justified under s. 1. Our decision was, at pp. 439-40:

> We are all of the view that these appeals should be dismissed.
>
> The Attorney General of Canada has properly conceded that s. 51(*e*) of the *Canada Elections Act*, R.S.C., 1985, c. E-2, contravenes s. 3 of the *Canadian Charter of Rights and Freedoms* but submits that s. 51(*e*) is saved under s. 1 of the *Charter*. We do not agree. In our view, s. 51(*e*) is drawn too broadly and fails to meet the proportionality test, particularly the minimal impairment component of the test, as expressed in the s. 1 jurisprudence of the Court.

The language of Iacobucci J.'s reasons seem to imply that, while Parliament's complete ban of prisoner voting in the old provision was unconstitutional, Parliament was free to investigate where an appropriate line could be drawn. This is exactly what it was in the process of doing at the time the first *Sauvé* case was heard. It has drawn a line in the form of s. 51(*e*) of the Act.

[162] The appellants and their experts have argued that there are less intrusive means for the Crown to pursue its objectives: disenfranchisement could be left to the discretion of the sentencing judge; as *per* the Lortie Commission, only those convicted of the most serious offences (those punishable by a maximum of life) and the most serious sentences (those punishable by 10 years in jail or more) could lose the vote; an offence-oriented approach could define specific types of crimes which could be seen as bearing a rational connection

to the franchise; or the measure could allow for the vote to be restored if the offender demonstrated good behaviour while incarcerated. To these I add that it is obvious that any higher cutoff line, i.e. 5, 10, or 25 years of incarceration, would also, technically, be less intrusive.

[163] I am of the view that no less intrusive measure would be equally effective. Since Parliament has drawn a line which identifies which incarcerated offenders have committed serious enough crimes to warrant being deprived of the vote, any alternative line will not be of equal effectiveness. Equal effectiveness is a dimension of the analysis that should not be underemphasized, as it relates directly to Parliament's ability to pursue its legitimate objectives effectively. Any other line insisted upon amounts to *second-guessing* Parliament as to what amounts to "serious" crime....

[174] In my view, it is particularly inappropriate, in the case at bar, to find the justification of the limitation of the right to be unconvincing at this phase of the *Oakes* test. First, as was noted above, there is a need for deference to Parliament in its drawing of a line, especially since this Court gave the impression that it was up to Parliament to do exactly that after the first *Sauvé* case was heard in 1993. Second, also as developed above, the analysis of social and political philosophies and the accommodation of values in the context of the *Charter* must be sensitive to the fact that there may be many possible reasonable and rational balances. Developing this point, it is important to note that, given the theoretical nature of the arguments raised by both parties in the case at bar, they do not gain proportionally in strength as the bar is moved higher. Symbolic and theoretical justifications such as employed in this case do not get stronger as the line changes. The fundamental premises underlying the line chosen would be the same if the cutoff was 10 years, or even 25 years. See, for example, *Driskell* [*v. Manitoba (Attorney General)*, [1999] 11 W.W.R. 615], in which similar analytical problems to those in the case at bar arose and resulted in a line of five years being held unconstitutional. Line drawing, amongst a range of acceptable alternatives, is for Parliament....

[175] The final prong of the *Oakes* test demands that the effects of the limiting measure (the impugned provision) must not so severely trench on *Charter* rights that the legislative objective, albeit important, is outweighed by the infringement of the rights....

[178] It is my view that the arguments in this dimension of the analysis are basically either persuasive or not. If the objectives are taken to reflect a moral choice by Parliament which has great symbolic importance and effect and which are based on a reasonable social or political philosophy, then their resulting weight is great indeed. Over all, while the temporary disenfranchisement is clear, the salutary effects and objectives are, in my view, of greater countervailing weight. Generally, I agree with the analysis of Linden J.A. at the Federal Court of Appeal below to this effect....

[181] Linden J.A. found that the primary salutary effect was that the legislation, *intrinsically*, expresses societal values in relation to serious criminal behaviour and the right to vote in our society. He thus concluded ... that it has more than symbolic effect:

> This legislation sends a message signalling Canadian values, to the effect that those people who are found guilty of the most serious crimes will, while separated from society, lose access to one of the levers of electoral power. This is an extremely important message, one which is not sent by incarceration alone. Incarceration is essentially separation from the community. Incarceration alone signals a denunciation of the offender's anti-societal behaviour and indicates society's hope for rehabilitation through separation from the community. Incarceration by itself, however, leaves those convicted of serious crimes free to exercise all the levers of electoral power open to all law-abiding citizens. This maintains a political parity between those convicted of society's worst crimes and their victims. Disqualification from voting, however, signals a denunciation of the criminal's anti-societal behaviour *and* sends the message that those people convicted of causing the worst forms of indignity to others will be deprived of one aspect of the political equality of citizens—the right to vote. It can be said that, in this context, "kindness toward the criminal can be an act of cruelty toward his victims, and the larger community." [Footnotes omitted; emphasis in original.]

Linden J.A. suggested that value emerges from the signal or message that those who commit serious crimes will temporarily lose one aspect of the political equality of citizens. Therefore, "the enactment of the measure is itself a salutary effect." I agree....

[188] When the objectives and the salutary effects are viewed in the totality of the context, they outweigh the temporary disenfranchisement of the serious criminal offender which mirrors the fact of his or her incarceration. In my view, Parliament has enacted a law which is reasonable, and which is justified in a free and democratic society....

[204] The reasons of the Chief Justice, at para. 60, refer to the fact that this Court, in *R. v. Gladue*, [1999] 1 S.C.R. 688, noted that the over-representation of Aboriginal persons in the criminal justice system and the prison population reflects a "crisis in the Canadian criminal justice system." I agree that a sad and pressing social problem exists, but suggest that it is quite a leap to then say that Parliament is incapable of enacting a provision which disenfranchises serious criminal offenders

who have been sentenced to two or more years of incarceration. As noted above, it is not plausible to say that the temporary disenfranchisement is in some way targeted at Aboriginal people: it hinges only upon the commission of serious criminal offences. If there is a problem with the over-representation of Aboriginal people in our criminal justice system and prisons, then that issue must continue to be addressed, by not only continuing to pay attention to the sentencing considerations pursuant to s. 718.2(*e*) of the *Criminal Code*, which are specifically aimed at such a reduction, but also by addressing some of the root causes of the over-representation identified by this Court in *Gladue, supra,* including poverty, substance abuse, lack of education, lack of employment opportunities, and bias against Aboriginal people. The continuing need to address these factors does not, however, preclude the ability of Parliament to address other pressing social problems, including denouncing serious crime, enhancing the meaning of the criminal sanction and promoting civic responsibility and the rule of law, which s. 51(*e*) of the Act is directed to. Also in *Gladue*, at para. 78, this Court stated that it is unreasonable to assume that Aboriginal people do not believe in goals of punishment such as denunciation, deterrence and separation, to which I add, obviously, the principle of rehabilitation. These goals of punishment, as discussed above, are related to the temporary disenfranchisement of serious criminal offenders and are ultimately aimed at the reintegration of offenders, Aboriginal or otherwise, back into the community....

Reference re Same-Sex Marriage, 2004

If *Charter* commentators were to identify the most significant social policy change that can be attributed to the *Charter* in its first quarter century, the definition of marriage would certainly be a leading contender. As of 2005, Canada became one of only a handful of nations that recognizes marriages between same-sex partners.

The federal Parliament has jurisdiction over marriage, but, until 2005, had never actually defined marriage. Instead, Canada relied on a common-law definition of marriage dating back to 1866, which defined marriage "as understood in Christendom" as "the voluntary union for life of one man and one woman, to the exclusion of all others."[1]

The transformation in the definition of marriage has been contentious. In the aftermath of the Supreme Court's ruling in *M. v. H.* (case 33), which declared unconstitutional social policy distinctions that discriminated against same-sex partners, many politicians and religious groups expressed concern that the *Charter* might be interpreted in a manner that alters this traditional definition of marriage. Pressure from the opposition Reform/Alliance parties, as well as criticism within the Liberal caucus, were sufficiently powerful to convince the Liberal government to twice accede to political pressure (in 1999 and, again, in 2000) to declare that the traditional definition of marriage would not be altered by legislative changes being introduced to redress the denial of social policy benefits for same-sex partners.

Despite this attempt to preserve an opposite-sex definition of marriage, many within and outside government believed that Parliament would soon have to change the definition of marriage to include same-sex unions or risk having the courts change the common-law definition. The logic of the Court's approach to equality in *M. v. H.*—that equality requires not only equal benefits in law but also that the state treat same-sex partners with the same degree of respect and recognition given to those in heterosexual relationships—provided strong indication that the Supreme Court might not accept the constitutional validity of a definition of marriage that denies same-sex partners the opportunity to marry. A few years after the *M. v. H.* ruling, provincial courts of appeal in British Columbia, Ontario, and Quebec ruled that the common-law definition of marriage violates equality. In 2003, the Liberal government decided not to appeal one of these rulings, the Ontario Court of Appeal decision in *Halpern v. Canada (Attorney General)*,[2] which not only held that the common-law prohibition on same-sex marriage was unconstitutional, but issued a new definition of marriage to replace the old common-law definition, allowing same-sex partners to marry. Soon after, the government developed draft legislation that changed the definition of marriage to read: "Marriage, for civil purposes, is the lawful union of two persons to the exclusion of all others." However, faced with strong opposition from the Alliance party, as well as substantial opposition from within its own ranks, the government decided to delay the introduction

---

1   *Hyde v. Hyde and Woodmansee* (1866), L.R. 1 P. & D. 130 at 133.

2   (2003), 65 O.R. (3d) 161 (C.A.).

of the legislation until it had asked the Supreme Court to review the draft bill and address several constitutional questions.

These questions addressed whether Ottawa has jurisdictional capacity to define marriage; whether the recognition of same-sex partners' ability to marry is consistent with the *Charter*; and whether the *Charter*'s safeguarding of religious freedom protects religious officials from having to marry same-sex partners, contrary to their beliefs. Omitted from the reference were two related questions central to the ongoing political debate: (1) is the opposite-sex definition of marriage contrary to the *Charter*, and (2) would the creation of a new category of relationship, a civil union for same-sex partners, be acceptable under the *Charter* as an alternative to same-sex marriage?

At the time of the reference, the Liberal government was incurring serious internal strife, as leader Jean Chrétien was under strong pressure from within his own caucus to resign. His likely successor, Paul Martin, indicated his discomfort with the draft legislation and suggested he supported use of the notwithstanding clause should courts force churches to perform same-sex marriages. Martin was chosen as leader of the party soon after the reference case was initiated and, shortly thereafter, his government added a fourth question for the Court to address: is the opposite-sex requirement for civil marriage in the common law consistent with the *Charter*?

The Court's ruling was unanimous and succinct by recent standards. The Court answered the first three questions in the affirmative, which did not surprise most commentators. But it declined to answer the fourth question, which went to the heart of the debate taking place at the time: is same-sex marriage constitutionally required? The Court's refusal suggests reluctance to be drawn into this political debate, particularly as the use of the reference device was broadly seen as a political strategy intended to weaken opposition to the proposed legislation. The Court characterized the circumstances for the reference as "unique," in part because no precedent exists for answering a reference question that "mirrors issues already disposed of in lower courts where an appeal was available but not pursued." The Court further indicated that since the government had stated its intention to address the issue regardless of the Court's opinion, the "hypothetical benefit" Parliament would derive from its advisory opinion on this question did not warrant the Court's answer.

In February 2005, Martin's government introduced a bill defining marriage in a manner inclusive of both heterosexual and same-sex unions. Despite his earlier expressed reluctance about recognizing same-sex marriage, Martin presented the issue as involving fundamental rights, and suggested that any position short of marriage would require use of the notwithstanding clause, a position for which he now indicated his disapproval. In opposing the legislation, Conservative opposition leader Stephen Harper argued against conceiving same-sex marriage as a fundamental human right and recommended amendments to preserve the traditional definition of marriage while allowing provinces to offer civil unions. The legislation passed the House of Commons in June 2005, by a vote of 158 to 133, in which one Cabinet minister resigned for refusing to support the bill.

But the controversy over same-sex marriage did not end. Harper reopened the issue in the 2005 federal election campaign, promising that, if elected, he would hold a free vote on marriage. Upon the election of his government with minority status, Harper carried through with his promise to revisit the marriage issue, but, in December 2006, a motion calling on the government to introduce legislation to restore the traditional definition of marriage was defeated by a vote of 175 to 123. ⌐

REFERENCE RE SAME-SEX MARRIAGE
2004 SCC 79, [2004] 3 S.C.R. 698

Hearing: October 6, 7, 2004; Judgment: December 9, 2004.

Present: McLachlin C.J. and Major, Bastarache, Binnie, LeBel, Deschamps, Fish, Abella, and Charron JJ.

Interveners: The Attorney General of Quebec, the Attorney General of Alberta, the Canadian Human Rights Commission, the Ontario Human Rights Commission, the Manitoba Human Rights Commission, the Canadian Civil Liberties Association, the British Columbia Civil Liberties Association, the Canadian Bar Association, the Canadian Conference of Catholic Bishops, the Ontario Conference of Catholic Bishops, the Seventh-Day Adventist Church in Canada, the United Church of Canada, the Canadian Unitarian Council, the Church of Jesus Christ of Latter-Day Saints, the Metropolitan Community Church of Toronto, Egale Canada Inc. and Egale Couples, the B.C. Couples, the Ontario Couples and the Quebec Couple, the Working Group on Civil Unions, the Association for Marriage and the Family in Ontario, the Canadian Coalition of Liberal Rabbis for same-sex marriage and Rabbi Debra Landsberg, as its nominee, the Foundation for Equal Families, Mouvement laïque québécois, Coalition pour le mariage civil des couples de même sexe, the Interfaith Coalition on Marriage and Family, and the Honourable Anne Cools, Member of the Senate, and Roger Gallaway, Member of the House of Commons.

The following is the opinion delivered by

THE COURT:

I. Introduction

[1] On July 16, 2003, the Governor in Council issued Order in Council P.C. 2003-1055 asking this Court to hear a reference on the federal government's *Proposal for an Act respecting certain aspects of legal capacity for marriage for civil purposes* ("*Proposed Act*"). The operative sections of the *Proposed Act* read as follows:

> **1.** Marriage, for civil purposes, is the lawful union of two persons to the exclusion of all others.
>
> **2.** Nothing in this Act affects the freedom of officials of religious groups to refuse to perform marriages that are not in accordance with their religious beliefs.

It will be noted that s. 1 of the *Proposed Act* deals only with civil marriage, not religious marriage.

[2] The Order in Council sets out the following questions:

> 1. Is the annexed *Proposal for an Act respecting certain aspects of legal capacity for marriage for civil purposes* within the exclusive legislative authority of the Parliament of Canada? If not, in what particular or particulars, and to what extent?
>
> 2. If the answer to question 1 is yes, is section 1 of the proposal, which extends capacity to marry to persons of the same sex, consistent with the *Canadian Charter of Rights and Freedoms*? If not, in what particular or particulars, and to what extent?
>
> 3. Does the freedom of religion guaranteed by paragraph 2(*a*) of the *Canadian Charter of Rights and Freedoms* protect religious officials from being compelled to perform a marriage between two persons of the same sex that is contrary to their religious beliefs?

[3] On January 26, 2004, the Governor in Council issued Order in Council P.C. 2004-28 asking a fourth question, namely:

> 4. Is the opposite-sex requirement for marriage for civil purposes, as established by the common law and set out for Quebec in section 5 of the *Federal Law–Civil Law Harmonization Act, No. 1*, consistent with the *Canadian Charter of Rights and Freedoms*? If not, in what particular or particulars and to what extent?

[4] With respect to Question 1, we conclude that s. 1 of the *Proposed Act* is within the exclusive legislative competence of Parliament, while s. 2 is not.

[5] With respect to Question 2, we conclude that s. 1 of the *Proposed Act*, which defines marriage as the union of two persons, is consistent with the *Canadian Charter of Rights and Freedoms*.

[6] With respect to Question 3, we conclude that the guarantee of freedom of religion in the *Charter* affords religious officials protection against being compelled by the state to perform marriages between two persons of the same sex contrary to their religious beliefs.

[7] For reasons to be explained, the Court declines to answer Question 4.

II. The Reference Questions

[8] Certain interveners suggest that the Court should decline to answer any of the questions posed on this Reference on the ground that they are not justiciable. They argue that the questions are essentially political, should be dealt with in Parliament and lack sufficient precision with respect to the *Proposed Act*'s purpose to permit of *Charter* analysis.

[9] The reference provisions of the *Supreme Court Act*, R.S.C. 1985, c. S-26, are broad. In particular, s. 53(1) provides:

> **53.** (1) The Governor in Council may refer to the Court for hearing and consideration important questions of law or fact concerning . . .

(*d*) the powers of the Parliament of Canada, or of the legislatures of the provinces, or of the respective governments thereof, whether or not the particular power in question has been or is proposed to be exercised.

[10] The Court has recognized that it possesses a residual discretion not to answer reference questions where it would be inappropriate to do so because, for example, the question lacks sufficient legal content, or where the nature of the question or the information provided does not permit the Court to give a complete or accurate answer: see, e.g., *Reference re Canada Assistance Plan (B.C.)*, [1991] 2 S.C.R. 525, at p. 545; *Reference re Objection by Quebec to a Resolution to Amend the Constitution*, [1982] 2 S.C.R. 793, at p. 806; and *Reference re Secession of Quebec*, [1998] 2 S.C.R. 217 (*"Secession Reference"*), at paras. 26-30.

[11] We conclude that none of the questions posed here lack the requisite legal content for consideration on a reference. The political underpinnings of the instant reference are indisputable. However, much as in the *Secession Reference*, these political considerations provide the context for, rather than the substance of, the questions before the Court. Moreover, any lack of precision with respect to the *Proposed Act's* purpose can be addressed in the course of answering the questions.

[12] Question 4 raises other concerns. While it possesses the requisite legal content to be justiciable, it raises considerations that render a response on this reference inappropriate, as discussed more fully below.

A. Question 1: Is the Proposed Act Within the Exclusive Legislative Authority of the Parliament of Canada?

[13] It is trite law that legislative authority under the *Constitution Act, 1867* is assessed by way of a two-step process: (1) characterization of the "pith and substance" or dominant characteristic of the law; and (2) concomitant assignment to one of the heads of power enumerated in ss. 91 and 92 of that Act: see, e.g., *R. v. Hydro-Québec*, [1997] 3 S.C.R. 213, at para. 23, *per* Lamer C.J. and Iacobucci J. (dissenting, but not on this point).

[14] An answer to Question 1 requires that we engage in this process with respect to both operative sections of the *Proposed Act*.

(1) Section 1 of the Proposed Act

[15] Section 1 of the *Proposed Act* provides:

1. Marriage, for civil purposes, is the lawful union of two persons to the exclusion of all others.

(a) Determination of Legislative Competence

[16] The dominant characteristic of s. 1 of the *Proposed Act* is apparent from its plain text: marriage as a civil institution. In saying that marriage for civil purposes is "the lawful union of two persons to the exclusion of all others," this section stipulates the threshold requirements of that institution: "two persons," regardless of gender, are legally capable of being married. In pith and substance, therefore, the section pertains to the capacity for marriage.

[17] Turning to the assignment of this matter to an enumerated head of power, we note that legislative authority in respect of marriage is divided between the federal Parliament and the provincial legislatures. Section 91(26) of the *Constitution Act, 1867* confers on Parliament competence in respect of "Marriage and Divorce" whereas s. 92(12) of that Act confers on the provinces competence in respect of "[t]he Solemnization of Marriage in the Province."

[18] As early as 1912, this Court recognized that s. 91(26) confers on Parliament legislative competence in respect of the capacity to marry, whereas s. 92(12) confers authority on the provinces in respect of the performance of marriage once that capacity has been recognized: see *In Re Marriage Laws* (1912), 46 S.C.R. 132. Subsequent decisions have upheld this interpretation. Thus, the capacity to marry in instances of consanguinity (*Teagle v. Teagle*, [1952] 3 D.L.R. 843 (B.C.S.C.)) or in view of prior marital relationships (*Hellens v. Densmore*, [1957] S.C.R. 768) falls within the exclusive legislative competence of Parliament.

[19] We have already concluded that, in pith and substance, s. 1 of the *Proposed Act* pertains to legal capacity for civil marriage. *Prima facie*, therefore, it falls within a subject matter allocated exclusively to Parliament (s. 91(26)).

(b) Objections: The Purported Scope of Section 91(26)

[20] Some interveners nevertheless suggested that s. 91(26) cannot be interpreted as granting legislative competence over same-sex marriage to Parliament. Any law allowing same-sex marriage is alleged to exceed the bounds of s. 91(26) in two key respects: (i) the meaning of "marriage" is constitutionally fixed, necessarily incorporating an opposite-sex requirement; and (ii) any such law would trench upon subject matters clearly allocated to the provincial legislatures.

(i) The Meaning of Marriage Is Not Constitutionally Fixed

[21] Several interveners say that the *Constitution Act, 1867* effectively entrenches the common law definition of "marriage" as it stood in 1867. That definition was most notably articulated in *Hyde v. Hyde* (1866), L.R. 1 P. & D. 130, at p. 133:

What, then, is the nature of this institution as understood in Christendom? Its incidents may vary in different countries, but what are its essential elements and invariable features? If it be of common acceptance and existence, it must needs (however varied in different countries in its minor incidents) have some pervading identity and universal basis. I conceive that marriage, as understood in Christendom, may for this purpose be defined as the voluntary union for life of one man and one woman, to the exclusion of all others.

[22] The reference to "Christendom" is telling. *Hyde* spoke to a society of shared social values where marriage and religion were thought to be inseparable. This is no longer the case. Canada is a pluralistic society. Marriage, from the perspective of the state, is a civil institution. The "frozen concepts" reasoning runs contrary to one of the most fundamental principles of Canadian constitutional interpretation: that our Constitution is a living tree which, by way of progressive interpretation, accommodates and addresses the realities of modern life. In the 1920s, for example, a controversy arose as to whether women as well as men were capable of being considered "qualified persons" eligible for appointment to the Senate of Canada. Legal precedent stretching back to Roman Law was cited for the proposition that women had always been considered "unqualified" for public office, and it was argued that this common understanding in 1867 was incorporated in s. 24 of the *Constitution Act, 1867* and should continue to govern Canadians in succeeding ages. Speaking for the Privy Council in *Edwards v. Attorney-General for Canada*, [1930] A.C. 124 (P.C.) (the "*Persons*" case), Lord Sankey L.C. said at p. 136:

> Their Lordships do not conceive it to be the duty of this Board—it is certainly not their desire—to cut down the provisions of the [*B.N.A.*] *Act* by a narrow and technical construction, but rather to give it a *large and liberal interpretation* so that the Dominion to a great extent, but within certain fixed limits, may be mistress in her own house, as the Provinces to a great extent, but within certain fixed limits, are mistresses in theirs. [Emphasis added.]

This approach applies to the construction of the powers enumerated in ss. 91 and 92 of the *Constitution Act, 1867.*

[23] A large and liberal, or progressive, interpretation ensures the continued relevance and, indeed, legitimacy of Canada's constituting document. By way of progressive interpretation our Constitution succeeds in its ambitious enterprise, that of structuring the exercise of power by the organs of the state in times vastly different from those in which it was crafted. For instance, Parliament's legislative competence in respect of telephones was recognized on the basis of its authority over interprovincial "undertakings" in s. 92(10)(*a*) even though the telephone had yet to be invented in 1867: *Toronto Corporation v. Bell Telephone Co. of Canada*, [1905] A.C. 52 (P.C.). Likewise, Parliament is not limited to the range

of criminal offences recognized by the law of England in 1867 in the exercise of its criminal law power in s. 91(27): *Proprietary Articles Trade Association v. Attorney-General for Canada*, [1931] A.C. 310 (P.C.), at p. 324. Lord Sankey L.C. noted in the *Persons* case, at p. 135, that early English decisions are not a "secure foundation on which to build the interpretation" of our Constitution. We agree.

[24] The arguments presented to this Court in favour of a departure from the "living tree" principle fall into three broad categories: (1) marriage is a pre-legal institution and thus cannot be fundamentally modified by law; (2) even a progressive interpretation of s. 91(26) cannot accommodate same-sex marriage since it falls outside the "natural limits" of that head of power, a corollary to this point being the objection that s. 15 of the *Charter* is being used to "amend" s. 91(26); and (3) in this instance, the intention of the framers of our Constitution should be determinative. As we shall see, none of these arguments persuade.

[25] First, it is argued, the institution of marriage escapes legislative redefinition. Existing in its present basic form since time immemorial, it is not a legal construct, but rather a supra-legal construct subject to legal incidents. In the *Persons* case, Lord Sankey L.C., writing for the Privy Council, dealt with this very type of argument, though in a different context. In addressing whether the fact that women never had occupied public office was relevant to whether they could be considered "persons" for the purposes of being eligible for appointment to the Senate, he said at p. 134:

> The fact that no woman had served or has claimed to serve such an office is not of great weight when it is remembered that custom would have prevented the claim being made or the point being contested.
>
> Customs are apt to develop into traditions which are stronger than law and remain unchallenged long after the reason for them has disappeared.
>
> The appeal to history therefore in this particular matter is not conclusive.

Lord Sankey L.C. acknowledged, at p. 134, that "several centuries ago" it would have been understood that "persons" should refer only to men. Several centuries ago it would have been understood that marriage should be available only to opposite-sex couples. The recognition of same-sex marriage in several Canadian jurisdictions as well as two European countries belies the assertion that the same is true today.

[26] Second, some interveners emphasize that while Lord Sankey L.C. envisioned our Constitution as a "living tree" in the *Persons* case, he specified that it was "capable of growth and expansion within its natural limits" (p. 136). These natural limits, they submit, preclude same-sex marriage. As a corollary,

some suggest that s. 1 of the *Proposed Act* would effectively amount to an amendment to the *Constitution Act, 1867* by interpretation based on the values underlying s. 15(1) of the *Charter*.

[27] The natural limits argument can succeed only if its proponents can identify an objective core of meaning which defines what is "natural" in relation to marriage. Absent this, the argument is merely tautological. The only objective core which the interveners before us agree is "natural" to marriage is that it is the voluntary union of two people to the exclusion of all others. Beyond this, views diverge. We are faced with competing opinions on what the natural limits of marriage may be.

[28] Lord Sankey L.C.'s reference to "natural limits" did not impose an obligation to determine, in the abstract and absolutely, the core meaning of constitutional terms. Consequently, it is not for the Court to determine, in the abstract, what the natural limits of marriage must be. Rather, the Court's role is to determine whether marriage as defined in the *Proposed Act* falls within the subject matter of s. 91(26).

[29] In determining whether legislation falls within a particular head of power, a progressive interpretation of the head of power must be adopted. The competing submissions before us do not permit us to conclude that "marriage" in s. 91(26) of the *Constitution Act, 1867*, read expansively, excludes same-sex marriage.

[30] Third, it is submitted that the intention of the framers should be determinative in interpreting the scope of the heads of power enumerated in ss. 91 and 92 given the decision in *R. v. Blais*, [2003] 2 S.C.R. 236, 2003 SCC 44. That case considered the interpretive question in relation to a particular constitutional agreement, as opposed to a head of power which must continually adapt to cover new realities. It is therefore distinguishable and does not apply here.

(ii) The Scope Accorded to Section 91(26) Does Not Trench on Provincial Competence

[31] The potential impact on provincial powers of a federal law on same-sex marriage does not undermine the constitutionality of s. 1 of the *Proposed Act*. Arguments to the effect that it does can be met: (1) they ignore the incidental nature of any effect upon provincial legislative competence; and (2) they conflate same-sex relationships with same-sex marriage.

[32] Clearly, federal recognition of same-sex marriage would have an impact in the provincial sphere. For instance, provincial competence over the solemnization of marriage provided for in s. 92(12) would be affected by requiring the issuance of marriage licences, the registration of marriages, and the provision of civil solemnization services to same-sex

couples. Further, provincial competence in relation to property and civil rights provided for in s. 92(13) would be affected in that a host of legal incidents attendant upon marital status would attach to same-sex couples: e.g., division of property upon dissolution of marriage. These effects, however, are incidental and do not relate to the core of the powers over solemnization and property and civil rights. Incidental effects of federal legislation in the provincial sphere are permissible so long as they do not relate, in pith and substance, to a provincial head of power (*Attorney-General of Saskatchewan v. Attorney-General of Canada*, [1949] 2 D.L.R. 145 (P.C.), at p. 152).

[33] Our law has always recognized that some conjugal relationships are based on marital status, while others are not. The provinces are vested with competence in respect of non-marital same-sex relationships, just as they are vested with competence in respect of non-marital opposite-sex relationships (via the power in respect of property and civil rights under s. 92(13)). For instance, the province of Quebec has established a civil union regime as a means for individuals in committed conjugal relationships to assume a host of rights and responsibilities: see the *Act instituting civil unions and establishing new rules of filiation*, S.Q. 2002, c. 6. Marriage and civil unions are two distinct ways in which couples can express their commitment and structure their legal obligations. Civil unions are a relationship short of marriage and are, therefore, provincially regulated. The authority to legislate in respect of such conjugal relationships cannot, however, extend to marriage. If we accept that provincial competence in respect of same-sex relationships includes same-sex marriage, then we must also accept that provincial competence in respect of opposite-sex relationships includes opposite-sex marriage. This is clearly not the case. Likewise, the scope of the provincial power in respect of solemnization cannot reasonably be extended so as to grant jurisdiction over same-sex marriage to the provincial legislatures. Issues relating to solemnization arise only upon conferral of the right to marry. Just as an opposite-sex couple's ability to marry is not governed by s. 92(12), so a same-sex couple's ability to marry cannot be governed by s. 92(12).

[34] The principle of exhaustiveness, an essential characteristic of the federal distribution of powers, ensures that the whole of legislative power, whether exercised or merely potential, is distributed as between Parliament and the legislatures. . . . In essence, there is no topic that cannot be legislated upon, though the particulars of such legislation may be limited by, for instance, the *Charter*. A jurisdictional challenge in respect of any law is therefore limited to determining to which head of power the law relates. Legislative competence over same-sex marriage must be vested in either Parliament or the legislatures. Neither s. 92(12) nor s. 92(13) can accommodate

this matter. Given that a legislative void is precluded, s. 91(26) most aptly subsumes it.

(2) Section 2 of the Proposed Act

[35]   Section 2 of the *Proposed Act* provides:

> **2.** Nothing in this Act affects the freedom of officials of religious groups to refuse to perform marriages that are not in accordance with their religious beliefs.

[36]   Section 2 of the *Proposed Act* relates to those who may (or must) perform marriages. Legislative competence over the performance or solemnization of marriage is exclusively allocated to the provinces under s. 92(12) of the *Constitution Act, 1867*.

[37]   The Attorney General of Canada suggests that s. 2 of the *Proposed Act* is declaratory, merely making clear Parliament's intention that other provisions of the *Proposed Act* not be read in a manner that trenches on the provinces' jurisdiction over the solemnization of marriage. The provision might be seen as an attempt to reassure the provinces and to assuage the concerns of religious officials who perform marriages. However worthy of attention these concerns are, only the provinces may legislate exemptions to existing solemnization requirements, as any such exemption necessarily relates to the "solemnization of marriage" under s. 92(12). Section 2 of the *Proposed Act* is therefore *ultra vires* Parliament.

[38]   While it is true that Parliament has exclusive jurisdiction to enact declaratory legislation relating to the interpretation of its own statutes, such declaratory provisions can have no bearing on the constitutional division of legislative authority. That is a matter to be determined, should the need arise, by the courts. It follows that a federal provision seeking to ensure that the Act within which it is situated is not interpreted so as to trench on provincial powers can have no effect and is superfluous.

[39]   The Court is asked in Question 1 whether s. 2 of the *Proposed Act* is within the *exclusive* legislative competence of Parliament. Because s. 2 of the *Proposed Act* relates to a subject matter allocated to the provinces, it follows that it does not fall within the *exclusive* legislative competence of Parliament. The answer to the second part of the first question must therefore be "no."

B. Question 2: Is Section 1 of the Proposed Act, Which Extends Capacity to Marry to Persons of the Same Sex, Consistent with the Charter?

[40]   To determine whether a provision is consistent with the *Charter*, it is first necessary to ascertain whether its purpose or effect is to curtail a *Charter* right: *R. v. Big M Drug Mart Ltd.*, [1985] 1 S.C.R. 295, at p. 331. If so, the further question arises of whether the curtailment is justified under s. 1 of the *Charter*.

(1) Purpose of Section 1 of the Proposed Act

[41]   The purpose of s. 1 of the *Proposed Act* is to extend the right to civil marriage to same-sex couples. The course of events outlined below in relation to Question 4 suggests that the provision is a direct legislative response to the findings of several courts that the opposite-sex requirement for civil marriage violates the equality guarantee enshrined in s. 15(1) of the *Charter*: see *EGALE Canada Inc. v. Canada (Attorney General)* (2003), 225 D.L.R. (4th) 472, 2003 BCCA 251; *Halpern v. Canada (Attorney General)* (2003), 65 O.R. (3d) 161 (C.A.); and *Hendricks v. Québec (Procureur général)*, [2002] R.J.Q. 2506 (Sup. Ct.).

[42]   The preamble to the *Proposed Act* is also instructive. The Act's stated purpose is to ensure that civil marriage as a legal institution is consistent with the *Charter*:

> WHEREAS, in order to reflect values of tolerance, respect and equality consistent with the *Canadian Charter of Rights and Freedoms*, access to marriage for civil purposes should be extended to couples of the same sex;
>
> AND WHEREAS everyone has the freedom of conscience and religion under the *Canadian Charter of Rights and Freedoms* and officials of religious groups are free to refuse to perform marriages that are not in accordance with their religious beliefs;

[43]   Turning to the substance of the provision itself, we note that s. 1 embodies the government's policy stance in relation to the s. 15(1) equality concerns of same-sex couples. This, combined with the circumstances giving rise to the *Proposed Act* and with the preamble thereto, points unequivocally to a purpose which, far from violating the *Charter*, flows from it.

(2) Effect of Section 1 of the Proposed Act

[44]   Section 1 of the *Proposed Act* was impugned before this Court on the basis that, in its effect, it violates ss. 15(1) and 2(*a*) of the *Charter*.

(a) Section 15(1): Equality

[45]   Some interveners submit that the mere legislative recognition of the right of same-sex couples to marry would have the effect of discriminating against (1) religious groups who do not recognize the right of same-sex couples to marry (religiously) and/or (2) opposite-sex married couples. No submissions have been made as to how the *Proposed Act*, in its effect, might be seen to draw a distinction for the purposes of s. 15, nor can the Court surmise how it might be seen to do so. It withholds no benefits, nor does it impose burdens on a differential basis. It therefore fails to meet the threshold requirement of the s. 15(1) analysis laid down in *Law v.*

Canada (Minister of Employment and Immigration), [1999] 1 S.C.R. 497.

[46] The mere recognition of the equality rights of one group cannot, in itself, constitute a violation of the rights of another. The promotion of *Charter* rights and values enriches our society as a whole and the furtherance of those rights cannot undermine the very principles the *Charter* was meant to foster.

(b) Section 2(a): Religion

[47] The question at this stage is whether s. 1 of the proposed legislation, considered in terms of its effects, is consistent with the guarantee of freedom of religion under s. 2(*a*) of the *Charter*. It is argued that the effect of the *Proposed Act* may violate freedom of religion in three ways: (1) the *Proposed Act* will have the effect of imposing a dominant social ethos and will thus limit the freedom to hold religious beliefs to the contrary; (2) the *Proposed Act* will have the effect of forcing religious officials to perform same-sex marriages; and (3) the *Proposed Act* will create a "collision of rights" in spheres other than that of the solemnization of marriages by religious officials.

[48] The first allegation of infringement says in essence that equality of access to a civil institution like marriage may not only conflict with the views of those who are in disagreement, but may also violate their legal rights. This amounts to saying that the mere conferral of rights upon one group can constitute a violation of the rights of another. This argument was discussed above in relation to s. 15(1) and was rejected.

[49] The second allegation of infringement, namely the allegation that religious officials would be compelled to perform same-sex marriages contrary to their religious beliefs, will be addressed below in relation to Question 3.

[50] This leaves the issue of whether the *Proposed Act* will create an impermissible collision of rights. The potential for a collision of rights does not necessarily imply unconstitutionality. The collision between rights must be approached on the contextual facts of actual conflicts. The first question is whether the rights alleged to conflict can be reconciled: *Trinity Western University v. British Columbia College of Teachers*, [2001] 1 S.C.R. 772, 2001 SCC 31, at para. 29. Where the rights cannot be reconciled, a true conflict of rights is made out. In such cases, the Court will find a limit on religious freedom and go on to balance the interests at stake under s. 1 of the *Charter*: *Ross v. New Brunswick School District No. 15*, [1996] 1 S.C.R. 825, at paras. 73-74. In both steps, the Court must proceed on the basis that the *Charter* does not create a hierarchy of rights (*Dagenais v. Canadian Broadcasting Corp.*, [1994] 3 S.C.R. 835, at p. 877) and that the right to religious freedom enshrined in s. 2(*a*) of the *Charter* is expansive.

[51] Here, we encounter difficulty at the first stage. The *Proposed Act* has not been passed, much less implemented. Therefore, the alleged collision of rights is purely abstract. There is no factual context. In such circumstances, it would be improper to assess whether the *Proposed Act*, if adopted, would create an impermissible collision of rights in as yet undefined spheres. . . .

[52] The right to same-sex marriage conferred by the *Proposed Act* may conflict with the right to freedom of religion if the Act becomes law, as suggested by the hypothetical scenarios presented by several interveners. However, the jurisprudence confirms that many if not all such conflicts will be resolved *within* the *Charter*, by the delineation of rights prescribed by the cases relating to s. 2(*a*). Conflicts of rights do not imply conflict with the *Charter*; rather the resolution of such conflicts generally occurs within the ambit of the *Charter* itself by way of internal balancing and delineation.

[53] The protection of freedom of religion afforded by s. 2(*a*) of the *Charter* is broad and jealously guarded in our *Charter* jurisprudence. We note that should impermissible conflicts occur, the provision at issue will by definition fail the justification test under s. 1 of the *Charter* and will be of no force or effect under s. 52 of the *Constitution Act, 1982*. In this case the conflict will cease to exist.

[54] In summary, the potential for collision of rights raised by s. 1 of the *Proposed Act* has not been shown on this reference to violate the *Charter*. It has not been shown that impermissible conflicts—conflicts incapable of resolution under s. 2(*a*)—will arise.

C. Question 3: Does the Freedom of Religion Guaranteed by Section 2(a) of the Charter Protect Religious Officials from Being Compelled to Perform Same-Sex Marriages Contrary to Their Religious Beliefs?

[55] The *Proposed Act* is limited in its effect to marriage for civil purposes: see s. 1. It cannot be interpreted as affecting religious marriage or its solemnization. However, Question 3 is formulated broadly and without reference to the *Proposed Act*. We therefore consider this question as it applies to the performance, by religious officials, of both religious and civil marriages. We also must consider the question to mean "compelled by the *state*" to perform, since s. 2(*a*) relates only to state action; the protection of freedom of religion against private actions is not within the ambit of this question. We note that it would be for the Provinces, in the exercise of their power over the solemnization of marriage, to legislate in a way that protects the rights of religious officials while providing for solemnization of same-sex marriage. It should also be noted that human rights codes must be interpreted and

applied in a manner that respects the broad protection granted to religious freedom under the *Charter*.

[56] Against this background, we return to the question. The concern here is that if the *Proposed Act* were adopted, religious officials could be required to perform same-sex marriages contrary to their religious beliefs. Absent state compulsion on religious officials, this conjecture does not engage the *Charter*. If a promulgated statute were to enact compulsion, we conclude that such compulsion would almost certainly run afoul of the *Charter* guarantee of freedom of religion, given the expansive protection afforded to religion by s. 2(*a*) of the *Charter*.

[57] The right to freedom of religion enshrined in s. 2(*a*) of the *Charter* encompasses the right to believe and entertain the religious beliefs of one's choice, the right to declare one's religious beliefs openly and the right to manifest religious belief by worship, teaching, dissemination and religious practice: *Big M Drug Mart, supra*, at pp. 336-37. The performance of religious rites is a fundamental aspect of religious practice.

[58] It therefore seems clear that state compulsion on religious officials to perform same-sex marriages contrary to their religious beliefs would violate the guarantee of freedom of religion under s. 2(*a*) of the *Charter*. It also seems apparent that, absent exceptional circumstances which we cannot at present foresee, such a violation could not be justified under s. 1 of the *Charter*.

[59] The question we are asked to answer is confined to the performance of same-sex marriages by religious officials. However, concerns were raised about the compulsory use of sacred places for the celebration of such marriages and about being compelled to otherwise assist in the celebration of same-sex marriages. The reasoning that leads us to conclude that the guarantee of freedom of religion protects against the compulsory celebration of same-sex marriages, suggests that the same would hold for these concerns.

[60] Returning to the question before us, the Court is of the opinion that, absent unique circumstances with respect to which we will not speculate, the guarantee of religious freedom in s. 2(*a*) of the *Charter* is broad enough to protect religious officials from being compelled by the state to perform civil or religious same-sex marriages that are contrary to their religious beliefs.

D. Question 4: Is the Opposite-Sex Requirement for Marriage for Civil Purposes, as Established by the Common Law and Set Out for Quebec in Section 5 of the Federal Law–Civil Law Harmonization Act, No. 1, Consistent with the Charter?

(1) Threshold Issue: Whether the Court Should Answer Question 4

[61] The first issue is whether this Court should answer the fourth question, in the unique circumstances of this refer-

ence. This issue must be approached on the basis that the answer to Question 4 may be positive or negative; the preliminary analysis of the discretion not to answer a reference question cannot be predicated on a presumed outcome. The reference jurisdiction vested in this Court by s. 53 of the *Supreme Court Act* is broad and has been interpreted liberally: see, e.g., *Secession Reference, supra*. The Court has rarely exercised its discretion not to answer a reference question reflecting its perception of the seriousness of its advisory role.

[62] Despite this, the Court may decline to answer reference questions where to do so would be inappropriate, either because the question lacks sufficient legal content (which is not the case here) or because attempting to answer it would for other reasons be problematic.

[63] In the *Secession Reference, supra*, at para. 30, we noted that instances where the Court has refused to answer reference questions on grounds other than lack of legal content tend to fall into two broad categories: (1) where the question is too ambiguous or imprecise to allow an accurate answer: see, e.g., *Reference re Goods and Services Tax*, [1992] 2 S.C.R. 445, at p. 485; and *Reference re Remuneration of Judges of the Provincial Court of Prince Edward Island*, [1997] 3 S.C.R. 3, at para. 256; and (2) where the parties have not provided the Court with sufficient information to provide a complete answer: see, e.g., *Reference re Authority of Parliament in relation to the Upper House*, [1980] 1 S.C.R. 54, at pp. 75-77; and *Reference re Remuneration of Judges of the Provincial Court of Prince Edward Island*, at para. 257. These categories highlight two important considerations, but are not exhaustive.

[64] A unique set of circumstances is raised by Question 4, the combined effect of which persuades the Court that it would be unwise and inappropriate to answer the question.

[65] The first consideration on the issue of whether this Court should answer the fourth question is the government's stated position that it will proceed by way of legislative enactment, regardless of what answer we give to this question. In oral argument, counsel reiterated the government's unequivocal intention to introduce legislation in relation to same-sex marriage, regardless of the answer to Question 4. The government has clearly accepted the rulings of lower courts on this question and has adopted their position as its own. The common law definition of marriage in five provinces and one territory no longer imports an opposite-sex requirement. In addition, s. 5 of the *Federal Law–Civil Law Harmonization Act, No. 1*, S.C. 2001, c. 4, no longer imports an opposite-sex requirement. Given the government's stated commitment to this course of action, an opinion on the constitutionality of an opposite-sex requirement for marriage serves no legal purpose. On the other hand, answering this question may have serious deleterious effects, which brings us to our next point.

[66] The second consideration is that the parties to previous litigation have now relied upon the finality of the judgments they obtained through the court process. In the circumstances, their vested rights outweigh any benefit accruing from an answer to Question 4. Moreover, other same-sex couples acted on the finality of *EGALE*, *Halpern* and *Hendricks* to marry, relying on the Attorney General of Canada's adoption of the result in those cases. While the effects of the *EGALE* and *Hendricks* decisions were initially suspended, the suspensions were lifted with the consent of the Attorney General. As a result of these developments, same-sex marriages have generally come to be viewed as legal and have been regularly taking place in British Columbia, Ontario and Quebec. Since this reference was initiated, the opposite-sex requirement for marriage has also been struck down in the Yukon, Manitoba, Nova Scotia and Saskatchewan: *Dunbar v. Yukon*, [2004] Y.J. No. 61 (QL), 2004 YKSC 54; *Vogel v. Canada (Attorney General)*, [2004] M.J. No. 418 (QL) (Q.B.); *Boutilier v. Nova Scotia (Attorney General)*, [2004] N.S.J. No. 357 (QL) (S.C.); and *N.W. v. Canada (Attorney General)*, [2004] S.J. No. 669 (QL), 2004 SKQB 434. In each of those instances, the Attorney General of Canada conceded that the common law definition of marriage was inconsistent with s. 15(1) of the *Charter* and was not justifiable under s. 1, and publicly adopted the position that the opposite-sex requirement for marriage was unconstitutional.

[67] As noted by this Court in *Nova Scotia (Attorney General) v. Walsh*, [2002] 4 S.C.R. 325, 2002 SCC 83, at para. 43:

> The decision to marry or not is intensely personal and engages a complex interplay of social, political, religious, and financial considerations by the individual.

The parties in *EGALE*, *Halpern* and *Hendricks* have made this intensely personal decision. They have done so relying upon the finality of the judgments concerning them. We are told that thousands of couples have now followed suit. There is no compelling basis for jeopardizing acquired rights, which would be a potential outcome of answering Question 4.

[68] There is no precedent for answering a reference question which mirrors issues already disposed of in lower courts where an appeal was available but not pursued. Reference questions may, on occasion, pertain to already adjudicated disputes: see, e.g., *Reference re Truscott*, [1967] S.C.R. 309; *Reference re Regina v. Coffin*, [1956] S.C.R. 191; *Reference re Minimum Wage Act of Saskatchewan*, [1948] S.C.R. 248; and *Reference re Milgaard (Can.)*, [1992] 1 S.C.R. 866. In those cases, however, no appeal to the Supreme Court was possible, either because leave to appeal had been denied (*Truscott* and *Milgaard*) or because no right of appeal existed (*Coffin* and *Minimum Wage Act of Saskatchewan*). The only instance that we are aware of where a reference was pursued in lieu of appeal is *Reference re Newfoundland Continental Shelf*, [1984]

1 S.C.R. 86. That reference is also distinguishable: unlike the instant reference, it was not a direct response to the findings of a lower appellate court and the parties involved in the prior proceedings had consented to the use of the reference procedure.

[69] The final consideration is that answering this question has the potential to undermine the government's stated goal of achieving uniformity in respect of civil marriage across Canada. There is no question that uniformity of the law is essential. This is the very reason that Parliament was accorded legislative competence in respect of marriage under s. 91(26) of the *Constitution Act, 1867*. However, as discussed, the government has already chosen to address the question of uniformity by means of the *Proposed Act*, which we have found to be within Parliament's legislative competence and consistent with the *Charter*. Answering the fourth question will not assist further. Given that uniformity is to be addressed legislatively, this rationale for answering Question 4 fails to compel.

[70] On the other hand, consideration of the fourth question has the potential to undermine the uniformity that would be achieved by the adoption of the proposed legislation. The uniformity argument succeeds only if the answer to Question 4 is "no." By contrast, a "yes" answer would throw the law into confusion. The decisions of the lower courts in the matters giving rise to this reference are binding in their respective provinces. They would be cast into doubt by an advisory opinion which expressed a contrary view, even though it could not overturn them. The result would be confusion, not uniformity.

[71] In sum, a unique combination of factors is at play in Question 4. The government has stated its intention to address the issue of same-sex marriage by introducing legislation regardless of our opinion on this question. The parties to previous litigation have relied upon the finality of their judgments and have acquired rights which in our view are entitled to protection. Finally, an answer to Question 4 would not only fail to ensure uniformity of the law, but might undermine it. These circumstances, weighed against the hypothetical benefit Parliament might derive from an answer, convince the Court that it should exercise its discretion not to answer Question 4.

(2) The Substance of Question 4

[72] For the reasons set out above, the Court exercises its discretion not to answer this question.

III. Conclusion

[73] The Court answers the reference questions as follows:

1. Is the annexed *Proposal for an Act respecting certain aspects of legal capacity for marriage for civil purposes* within the exclusive legislative authority of the

Parliament of Canada? If not, in what particular or particulars, and to what extent?

   Answer: With respect to s. 1: Yes. With respect to s. 2: No.

2. If the answer to question 1 is yes, is section 1 of the proposal, which extends capacity to marry to persons of the same sex, consistent with the *Canadian Charter of Rights and Freedoms*? If not, in what particular or particulars, and to what extent?

   Answer: Yes.

3. Does the freedom of religion guaranteed by paragraph 2(*a*) of the *Canadian Charter of Rights and Freedoms* protect religious officials from being compelled to perform a marriage between two persons of the same sex that is contrary to their religious beliefs?

   Answer: Yes.

4. Is the opposite-sex requirement for marriage for civil purposes, as established by the common law and set out for Quebec in section 5 of the *Federal Law–Civil Law Harmonization Act, No. 1,* consistent with the *Canadian Charter of Rights and Freedoms*? If not, in what particular or particulars and to what extent?

   Answer: The Court exercises its discretion not to answer this question. . . .

36 Chaoulli v. Quebec (Attorney General), 2005

The *Chaoulli* case involved judicial intervention in a major public policy issue concerning Canada's system of publicly insured health care: did Quebec legislation banning private insurance for services covered by the public health care plan violate the *Canadian Charter of Rights and Freedoms* or the Quebec *Charter of Human Rights and Freedoms*?

The litigation was initiated by George Zeliotis, who had experienced long waiting lists for heart surgery and a hip operation and Jacques Chaoulli, a Montreal physician who had been trying to operate a private hospital. The crux of their case was that the long waiting lists resulting from the public health plan's monopoly of insured medical services violated the right to security of the person under the *Canadian Charter* and to the inviolability of the person under the *Quebec Charter*.

The public policy stakes in this case were large. The *Canada Health Act*, which sets out the conditions under which provinces receive federal funding for health services, does not prohibit private insurance for services available through the public plan. However, there is a widespread perception that Canada's system of comprehensive and universal, publicly administered medicare would be jeopardized if private medical insurance became widely available in the country. In addition to Quebec, five other provinces—Alberta, British Columbia, Manitoba, Ontario, and Prince Edward Island—prohibit private insurance for services offered by the public plan. A sixth province, Nova Scotia, has no such ban, but, like Manitoba and Ontario, prohibits physicians operating in the private sector from charging more than physicians receive from the public plan. Only three provinces—New Brunswick, Newfoundland and Labrador, and Saskatchewan—set no limits on what physicians operating outside the public system can charge and have no ban on private medical insurance. But these are smaller provinces with relatively few physicians operating in the private sector. If the *Canadian Charter* challenge to Quebec's prohibition on private medical insurance were to succeed, similar legislation in provinces containing over 90 percent of Canada's population would be invalid, tipping Canada's health care decisively in the direction of a two-tier system.

Were you to judge the outcome of this case by the media response to the Supreme Court's decision, you would conclude that the challenge had been completely successful and that Quebec's legislation had been found to violate the *Canadian Charter of Rights and Freedoms*, invalidating the ban on private medical insurance all across the country. According to a front page headline in the *Toronto Star*, "The Supreme Court has delivered a hammer-blow to medicare." "The new face of medicare," trumpeted *The Globe and Mail*.[1] But, in fact, the Court did not find that the legislation violated the *Canadian Charter*. The justices split 3 to 3 on that question. The decisive opinion was written by Justice Deschamps, who found that the legislation violated the *Quebec Charter*. Deschamps did not find it necessary to make a

---

1   Quoted in Peter H. Russell, "Chaoulli: The Political Versus the Legal Life of a Judicial Decision" in Colleen M. Flood, Kent Roach, and Lorne Sossin, eds., *Access to Care, Access to Justice: The Legal Debate over Private Health Insurance in Canada* (Toronto: University of Toronto Press, 2005).

ruling on the *Canadian Charter*. The three justices—Bastarache, Major, and McLachlin—who did find that the legislation violated the *Canadian Charter* also found that it violated the *Quebec Charter*. This means that the common denominator of the Court's majority decision was that Quebec's prohibition of private health insurance contravened Quebec's *Charter of Human Rights and Freedoms*. There was no ruling that applied to the rest of Canada. The ban on private health insurance, despite newspaper headlines suggesting the contrary, remained intact elsewhere in the country.

In confining her judgment to the *Quebec Charter*, Justice Deschamps followed a jurisprudential strategy set down by Justice Jean Beetz in the early years of the *Charter* when he suggested that it is best, when possible, to decide cases on the basis of rights-protecting laws that do not have the full constitutional weight of the *Canadian Charter*.[2] Such a strategy Beetz argued will ensure that these statutory, quasi-constitutional instruments continue to play a role in developing the protection of rights and freedoms.

Justice Deschamps accepted the trial judge's finding that the ban on private health care insurance infringed the right to life and security of the person protected in section 7 of the *Canadian Charter*, and since the right to inviolability of the person in the *Quebec Charter* is even wider than the right to security of the person, the ban on private insurance must also violate that right. However, Justice Deschamps rejected the trial judge's finding that the Quebec government's rationale for the ban on private insurance satisfies the standard of justification in the *Quebec Charter* for limiting rights. Justice Deschamps equated that standard of justification with section 1 of the *Canadian Charter*—except that in her view the burden of proof for meeting the standard is on the government. After reviewing the government's reasons for believing that private health insurance would weaken public medicare, she concluded that the government had failed to prove that its ban on private insurance meets the minimal impairment test—that is, that there are not other ways of protecting public medicare which are less intrusive on the inviolability of the person. Thus, she concludes that the Quebec legislation violates a right guaranteed by the *Quebec Charter* and is not a reasonable limit on that right.

The real fireworks in this case were set off by a sharp division among the other six justices who focused their opinions on section 7 of the *Canadian Charter*. Chief Justice McLachlin, Justice Major, and Justice Bastarache found that the ban on private health care violates section 7 and cannot be justified as a reasonable limit under section 1. The other three justices, Binnie, LeBel, and Fish, disagreed. The crux of their disagreement is the interpretation of "principles of fundamental justice" in section 7. All six justices agreed with the trial judge's conclusion that waiting-list delays in the public health system infringe the right to life and security of the person—although the Binnie group underlined that it is some Quebec residents, not all Quebecers, who experience this deprivation. It is on the second part of section 7 that the judges divided: has the deprivation of the rights been done in a way that breaches "principles of fundamental justice"? The judges agreed that these words require that laws which

---

2   In *Singh v. Minister of Employment and Immigration*, [1985] 1 S.C.R. 177, Justice Beetz and two other justices based their decision that refugee applicants were entitled to a hearing on the statutory *Canadian Bill of Rights*. Three other justices based a similar finding on the *Canadian Charter of Rights and Freedoms*.

encroach on the right to life and security must not be "arbitrary," but they differed over what "arbitrary" means. For the Chief Justice's group, if a law encroaching on a section 7 right cannot be shown to be necessary, it breaches principles of fundamental justice. For the Binnie group, the test is whether the law is related to the objective that lies behind it and does not contradict that objective. The Binnie trio's understanding of "principles of fundamental justice" clearly sets a much lower standard for government to meet than the Chief Justice trio's test of necessity.

It is evident that much more lies behind this split in the Court than a technical point of jurisprudence. The two groups of justices appeared to have profoundly different views on the extent to which *Charter*-based judicial review should second-guess the policy decisions of democratic governments. The Chief Justice's group regarded the arguments of government as well as those of the Romanow Commission of Inquiry as unproven assertions of belief. They had confidence in their own assessment of health policy in other jurisdictions, which led them to the observation that public medicare systems can function without prohibitions on private insurance. On that basis they concluded that such a prohibition is unnecessary and therefore arbitrary. The Binnie group was clearly upset by this judicial foray into the field of policy analysis. They were satisfied that the ban on public health insurance is well connected to the government's aim to sustain a high quality, needs-based, public medicare system. They contended that a facts-based debate about the merits of one-tier versus two-tier health systems "does not fit easily within the institutional competence of courts of law."

Echoes of the right-versus-left political debate over medicare can be heard in these conflicting judicial opinions. Justice Deschamps talked somewhat scathingly about the "iconic status" of Canada's medicare program and the emotional way in which its supporters, including her colleagues, Justices Binnie and LeBel, defend it. The Chief Justice's group talked about the medicare program giving the public plan "a virtual monopoly" that effectively limits access to private medicine to the very rich. The opinion of the Binnie group resonates with an opposing ideology. These justices contended that the beneficiaries of removing the ban on private health insurance would be "the more advantaged members of society" and they recalled the admonition of an earlier Chief Justice, Brian Dickson, that the *Canadian Charter* should not become an instrument to be used by the wealthy to "roll back" the benefits of a legislative scheme that helps the poorer members of society.

It would not have been difficult for the Quebec government to bring in legislation overriding this decision. Indeed, this is what the opposition Parti Québécois urged should be done. The Charest Liberal government decided to implement the Court's decision—but in a very limited way. It brought in legislation allowing private health insurance for cataract surgery and knee and hip replacements, but imposing strict restrictions on the expansion of private care.[3]

As for Canada in general, the future of *Charter*-based judicial review of medicare and other legislation encroaching on "the right to life, liberty and security of the person" depends on new appointments to the Court. Shortly before the *Chaoulli* decision was rendered, Justices Abella and Charron filled Ontario vacancies on the Court. In 2006, the Harper government's

---

3   Rheal Seguin, "Quebec tables bill to expand private health coverage: 'Rigid' checks are to oversee clinic care" *The Globe and Mail* (16 June 2006).

first Supreme Court appointee, Justice Marshall Rothstein, filled the Prairie-province vacancy created by Justice Major's retirement from the Court. How these three new members of the Court align themselves with the two opposing interpretations of "the principle of funda-mental justice" in section 7, articulated in *Chaoulli*, will have a major bearing on whether we will witness under the McLachlin court a major increase in judicial activism and the expansion of judicial power. A test is likely to come soon, as *Charter*-based challenges to the prohibition of private health insurance are under way in several provinces. ⌒

CHAOULLI v. QUEBEC (ATTORNEY GENERAL)
2005 SCC 35, [2005] 1 S.C.R. 791

Hearing: June 8, 2004; Judgment: June 9, 2005.*

Present: McLachlin C.J. and Major, Bastarache, Binnie, LeBel, Deschamps, and Fish JJ.

Interveners: Attorney General of Ontario, Attorney General of New Brunswick, Attorney General for Saskatchewan, Augustin Roy, Senator Michael Kirby, Senator Marjory Lebreton, Senator Catherine Callbeck, Senator Joan Cook, Senator Jane Cordy, Senator Joyce Fairbairn, Senator Wilbert Keon, Senator Lucie Pépin, Senator Brenda Robertson and Senator Douglas Roche, Canadian Medical Association and Canadian Orthopaedic Association, Canadian Labour Congress, Charter Committee on Poverty Issues and Canadian Health Coalition, Cambie Surgeries Corp., False Creek Surgical Centre Inc., Delbrook Surgical Centre Inc., Okanagan Plastic Surgery Centre Inc., Specialty MRI Clinics Inc., Fraser Valley MRI Ltd., Image One MRI Clinic Inc., McCallum Surgical Centre Ltd., 4111044 Canada Inc., South Fraser Surgical Centre Inc., Victoria Surgery Ltd., Kamloops Surgery Centre Ltd., Valley Cosmetic Surgery Associates Inc., Surgical Centres Inc., British Columbia Orthopaedic Association, and British Columbia Anesthesiologists Society.

* On August 4, 2005, the Court stayed the judgment for a period of 12 months from the date of the judgment.

English version of the reasons delivered by

[1] **DESCHAMPS J.:** Quebeckers are prohibited from tak-ing out insurance to obtain in the private sector services that are available under Quebec's public health care plan. Is this prohibition justified by the need to preserve the integrity of the plan?

[2] As we enter the 21st century, health care is a constant concern. The public health care system, once a source of national pride, has become the subject of frequent and some-times bitter criticism. This appeal does not question the appropriateness of the state making health care available to all Quebeckers. On the contrary, all the parties stated that they

support this kind of role for the government. Only the state can make available to all Quebeckers the social safety net consisting of universal and accessible health care. The demand for health care is constantly increasing, and one of the tools used by governments to control this increase has been the management of waiting lists. The choice of waiting lists as a management tool falls within the authority of the state and not of the courts. The appellants do not claim to have a solu-tion that will eliminate waiting lists. Rather, they submit that the delays resulting from waiting lists violate their rights under the *Charter of Human Rights and Freedoms*, R.S.Q., c. C-12 ("*Quebec Charter*"), and the *Canadian Charter of Rights and Freedoms* ("*Canadian Charter*"). They contest the validity of the prohibition in Quebec, as provided for in s. 15 of the *Health Insurance Act*, R.S.Q., c. A-29 ("*HEIA*"), and s. 11 of the *Hospital Insurance Act*, R.S.Q., c. A-28 ("*HOIA*"), on private insurance for health care services that are available in the public system. The appellants contend that the prohibi-tion deprives them of access to health care services that do not come with the wait they face in the public system.

[3] The two sections in issue read as follows:

15. No person shall make or renew a contract of insurance or make a payment under a contract of insur-ance under which an insured service is furnished or under which all or part of the cost of such a service is paid to a resident or a deemed resident of Québec or to another person on his behalf.

11. (1) No one shall make or renew, or make a pay-ment under a contract under which

(*a*) a resident is to be provided with or to be reim-bursed for the cost of any hospital service that is one of the insured services;

(*b*) payment is conditional upon the hospitaliza-tion of a resident; or

(*c*) payment is dependent upon the length of time the resident is a patient in a facility maintained by an institution contemplated in section 2.

[4] In essence, the question is whether Quebeckers who are prepared to spend money to get access to health care that

is, in practice, not accessible in the public sector because of waiting lists may be validly prevented from doing so by the state. For the reasons that follow, I find that the prohibition infringes the right to personal inviolability and that it is not justified by a proper regard for democratic values, public order and the general well-being of the citizens of Quebec.

[5] The validity of the prohibition is contested by the appellants, George Zeliotis and Jacques Chaoulli. Over the years, Mr. Zeliotis has experienced a number of health problems and has used medical services that were available in the public system, including heart surgery and a number of operations on his hip. The difficulties he encountered prompted him to speak out against waiting times in the public health care system. Mr. Chaoulli is a physician who has tried unsuccessfully to have his home-delivered medical activities recognized and to obtain a licence to operate an independent private hospital. Mr. Zeliotis and Mr. Chaoulli joined forces to apply to the court by way of motion for a declaration that s. 15 *HEIA* and s. 11 *HOIA* are unconstitutional and invalid....

I. Legislative Context

[16] Although the federal government has express jurisdiction over certain matters relating to health, such as quarantine, and the establishment and maintenance of marine hospitals (s. 91(11) of the *Constitution Act, 1867*), it is in practice that it imposes its views on the provincial governments in the health care sphere by means of its spending power.... In order to receive federal funds, a provincial plan must conform to the principles set out in the *Canada Health Act*, R.S.C. 1985, c. C-6: it must be administered publicly, it must be comprehensive and universal, it must provide for portability from one province to another and it must be accessible to everyone. These broad principles have become the hallmarks of Canadian identity. Any measure that might be perceived as compromising them has a polarizing effect on public opinion. The debate about the effectiveness of public health care has become an emotional one. The Romanow Report stated that the *Canada Health Act* has achieved an iconic status that makes it untouchable by politicians.... The tone adopted by my colleagues Binnie and LeBel JJ. is indicative of this type of emotional reaction. It leads them to characterize the debate as pitting rich against poor when the case is really about determining whether a specific measure is justified under either the *Quebec Charter* or the *Canadian Charter*. I believe that it is essential to take a step back and consider these various reactions objectively. The *Canada Health Act* does not prohibit private health care services, nor does it provide benchmarks for the length of waiting times that might be regarded as consistent with the principles it lays down, and in particular with the principle of real accessibility.

[17] In reality, a large proportion of health care is delivered by the private sector. First, there are health care services in respect of which the private sector acts, in a sense, as a subcontractor and is paid by the state. There are also many services that are not delivered by the state, such as home care or care provided by professionals other than physicians. In 2001, private sector services not paid for by the state accounted for nearly 30 percent of total health care spending (Canadian Institute for Health Information, *National Health Expenditure Trends, 1975–2003* (2003), at p. 16, Figure 13, "Public and Private Shares of Total Health Expenditure, by Use of Funds, Canada, 2001"). In the case of private sector services that are not covered by the public plan, Quebeckers may take out private insurance without the spectre of the two-tier system being evoked. The *Canada Health Act* is therefore only a general framework that leaves considerable latitude to the provinces. In analysing the justification for the prohibition, I will have occasion to briefly review some of the provisions of Canada's provincial plans. The range of measures shows that there are many ways to deal with the public sector/private sector dynamic without resorting to a ban....

III. Priority Given to Arguments Based on the Quebec Charter

[25] The *Canadian Charter* is neither an ordinary statute nor an extraordinary statute like the *Canadian Bill of Rights*, R.S.C. 1985, App. III. It is a part of the Constitution: *Law Society of Upper Canada v. Skapinker*, [1984] 1 S.C.R. 357, at p. 365. As a result, the *Canadian Charter* is different from the *Quebec Charter* in that the *Quebec Charter* is the product of the legislative will of Quebec's National Assembly. In addition, while the *Quebec Charter* has no constitutional dimension, it is also different from ordinary statutes by virtue of its considerably broader purpose: to guarantee respect for human beings (see A. Morel, "La coexistence des Chartes canadienne et québécoise: problèmes d'interaction" (1986), 17 R.D.U.S. 49). The *Quebec Charter* protects not only the fundamental rights and freedoms, but also certain civil, political, economic and social rights. By virtue of s. 52, Quebec courts have the power to review legislation to determine whether it is consistent with the rules set out in the *Quebec Charter*. The *Quebec Charter* has an identity that is independent of the statutes of Quebec.

[26] In the case of a challenge to a Quebec statute, it is appropriate to look first to the rules that apply specifically in Quebec before turning to the *Canadian Charter*, especially where the provisions of the two charters are susceptible of producing cumulative effects, but where the rules are not identical. This is the approach suggested by Beetz J. in *Singh v. Minister of Employment and Immigration*, [1985] 1 S.C.R. 177, at p. 224:

Thus, the *Canadian Bill of Rights* retains all its force and effect, together with the various provincial charters of rights. Because these constitutional or quasi-constitutional instruments are drafted differently, they are susceptible of producing cumulative effects for the better protection of rights and freedoms. But this beneficial result will be lost if these instruments fall into neglect.

[27] In the instant case, s. 7 of the *Canadian Charter* and s. 1 of the *Quebec Charter* have numerous points in common:

Canadian Charter

7. Everyone has the right to life, liberty and security of the person and the right not to be deprived thereof except in accordance with the principles of fundamental justice.

Quebec Charter

1. Every human being has a right to life, and to personal security, inviolability and freedom.

[28] The similarities between these two provisions probably explain in part why the Superior Court and the Court of Appeal considered only the *Canadian Charter* in their decisions. With regard to certain aspects of the two charters, the law is the same. For example, the wording of the right to life and liberty is identical. It is thus appropriate to consider the two together. Distinctions must be made, however, and I believe that it is important to begin by considering the specific protection afforded by the *Quebec Charter* for the reason that it is not identical to the protection afforded by the *Canadian Charter*.

[29] The most obvious distinction is the absence of any reference to the principles of fundamental justice in s. 1 of the *Quebec Charter*. The analysis dictated by s. 7 of the *Canadian Charter* is twofold. Under the approach that is generally taken, the claimant must prove, first, that a deprivation of the right to life, liberty and security of the person has occurred and, second, that the deprivation is not in accordance with the principles of fundamental justice....

[30] According to established principles, the onus is on the claimant to prove a violation of constitutional rights: *R. v. Collins*, [1987] 1 S.C.R. 265, and *Rio Hotel Ltd. v. New Brunswick (Liquor Licensing Board)*, [1987] 2 S.C.R. 59; see also Hogg, at p. 44-3. Under s. 7 of the *Canadian Charter*, the claimant would thus have a dual burden. The effect of placing this burden of proof on the claimant is that it makes his or her task more onerous. There is no such dual burden of proof under the *Quebec Charter* because the principles of fundamental justice are not incorporated into s. 1 of the *Quebec Charter*. For this reason, the *Quebec Charter* has a scope that is potentially broader. This characteristic should not be disregarded.

[31] Ruling on the points in issue by applying the *Quebec Charter* enhances an instrument that is specific to Quebec; this approach is also justified by the rules of Canadian constitutional law....

V. Infringement of the Rights Protected by Section 1 of the Quebec Charter

[37] The appellant Zeliotis argues that the prohibition infringes Quebeckers' right to life. Some patients die as a result of long waits for treatment in the public system when they could have gained prompt access to care in the private sector. Were it not for s. 11 *HOIA* and s. 15 *HEIA*, they could buy private insurance and receive care in the private sector.

[38] The Superior Court judge stated [TRANSLATION] "that there [are] serious problems in certain sectors of the health care system" (p. 823). The evidence supports that assertion. After meticulously analysing the evidence, she found that the right to life and liberty protected by s. 7 of the *Canadian Charter* had been infringed. As I mentioned above, the right to life and liberty protected by the *Quebec Charter* is the same as the right protected by the *Canadian Charter*. Quebec society is no different from Canadian society when it comes to respect for these two fundamental rights. Accordingly, the trial judge's findings of fact concerning the infringement of the right to life and liberty protected by s. 7 of the *Canadian Charter* apply to the right protected by s. 1 of the *Quebec Charter*.

[39] Not only is it common knowledge that health care in Quebec is subject to waiting times, but a number of witnesses acknowledged that the demand for health care is potentially unlimited and that waiting lists are a more or less implicit form of rationing....

[41] The *Quebec Charter* also protects the right to personal inviolability. This is a very broad right. The meaning of "inviolability" is broader than the meaning of the word "security" used in s. 7 of the *Canadian Charter*. In civil liability cases, it has long been recognized in Quebec that personal inviolability includes both physical inviolability and mental or psychological inviolability....

[42] In the instant case, Dr. Eric Lenczner, an orthopaedic surgeon, testified that the usual waiting time of one year for patients who require orthopaedic surgery increases the risk that their injuries will become irreparable. Clearly, not everyone on a waiting list is in danger of dying before being treated. According to Dr. Edwin Coffey, people may face a wide variety of problems while waiting. For example, a person with chronic arthritis who is waiting for a hip replacement may experience considerable pain. Dr. Lenczner also stated that many patients on non-urgent waiting lists for orthopaedic surgery are in pain and cannot walk or enjoy any real quality of life.

[43] Canadian jurisprudence shows support for interpreting the right to security of the person generously in relation

to delays. In *R. v. Morgentaler*, [1988] 1 S.C.R. 30, at p. 59, Dickson C.J. found, based on the consequences of delays, that the procedure then provided for in s. 251 of the *Criminal Code*, R.S.C. 1970, c. C-34, jeopardized the right to security of the person. Beetz J., at pp. 105-6, with Estey J. concurring, was of the opinion that the delay created an additional risk to health and constituted a violation of the right to security of the person.... If the evidence establishes that the right to security of the person has been infringed, it supports, *a fortiori*, the finding that the right to the inviolability of the person has been infringed.

[44] In the opinion of my colleagues Binnie and LeBel JJ., there is an internal mechanism that safeguards the public health system. According to them, Quebeckers may go outside the province for treatment where services are not available in Quebec. This possibility is clearly not a solution for the system's deficiencies. The evidence did not bring to light any administrative mechanism that would permit Quebeckers suffering as a result of waiting times to obtain care outside the province. The possibility of obtaining care outside Quebec is case-specific and is limited to crisis situation.

[45] I find that the trial judge did not err in finding that the prohibition on insurance for health care already insured by the state constitutes an infringement of the right to life and security. This finding is no less true in the context of s. 1 of the *Quebec Charter*. Quebeckers are denied a solution that would permit them to avoid waiting lists, which are used as a tool to manage the public plan. I will now consider the justification advanced under s. 9.1 of the *Quebec Charter*.

VI. Justification for the Prohibition

[46] Section 9.1 of the *Quebec Charter* sets out the standard for justification. It reads as follows:

> **9.1.** In exercising his fundamental freedoms and rights, a person shall maintain a proper regard for democratic values, public order and the general well-being of the citizens of Québec.

In this respect, the scope of the freedoms and rights, and limits to their exercise, may be fixed by law.

[47] The Court had occasion to consider the scope of this provision in *Ford v. Quebec (Attorney General)*, [1988] 2 S.C.R. 712. In its view, in the context of the relationship between citizens and the state, the provision is of the same nature as s. 1 of the *Canadian Charter*....

[48] The interpretation adopted by the Court in that decision still applies today, and the analytical approach developed in *R. v. Oakes*, [1986] 1 S.C.R. 103, must be followed. This approach is well known. First, the court must determine whether the objective of the legislation is pressing and substantial. Next, it must determine whether the means chosen to attain this legislative end are reasonable and demonstrably justifiable in a free and democratic society. For this second part of the analysis, three tests must be met: (1) the existence of a rational connection between the measure and the aim of the legislation; (2) minimal impairment of the protected right by the measure; and (3) proportionality between the effect of the measure and its objective (*Egan v. Canada*, [1995] 2 S.C.R. 513, at para. 182). It is the minimal impairment analysis that has proven to be the most delicate stage in the instant case. The other stages cannot, however, be bypassed.

A. Purpose of the Statute

[49] The prohibitions are set out in the *HOIA* and the *HEIA*. The general objective of these statutes is to promote health care of the highest possible quality for all Quebeckers regardless of their ability to pay....

B. Proportionality

(1) Rational Connection

[57] The next question is whether the prohibition on private insurance has a rational connection with the objective of preserving the public plan. Does this measure assist the state in implementing a public plan that provides high-quality health care services that are accessible to all residents of Quebec?

[58] According to the trial judge, the effect of the measure adopted by the state is to "significantly" limit private health care. Although the effect of a measure is not always indicative of a rational connection between the measure and its objective, in the instant case the consequences show an undeniable connection between the objective and the measure. The public plan is preserved because it has a quasi-monopoly.

(2) Minimal Impairment

[59] The trial judge made certain assertions that suggest she found that the measure met the minimal impairment test. However, her approach was not appropriate to s. 9.1 of the *Quebec Charter*. Her comments must therefore be considered in their context, not only because she failed to address the *Quebec Charter*, but also because she appears to have placed the onus on the appellants to prove that private insurance would provide a solution to the problem of waiting lists....

[60] The burden of proof does not rest on the appellants. Under s. 9.1 of the *Quebec Charter*, the onus was on the Attorney General of Quebec to prove that the prohibition is justified. He had to show that the measure met the minimal impairment test. The trial judge did not consider the evidence on the basis that there was a burden on the Attorney General of Quebec.

[61] To determine whether the Attorney General of Quebec has discharged this burden, I will begin by analysing the

expert evidence submitted to the Superior Court. I will then examine the situations in the other provinces of Canada and in certain countries of the Organization for Economic Cooperation and Development ("OECD"). Finally, I will address the deference the Court must show where the government has chosen among a number of measures that may impair protected rights.

(a) The Experts Who Testified at Trial and Whose Evidence Was Accepted by the Superior Court Judge

[62] As can be seen from the evidence, the arguments made in support of the position that the integrity of the public system could be jeopardized by abolishing the prohibition can be divided into two groups. The first group of arguments relates to human reactions of the various people affected by the public plan, while the second group relates to the consequences for the plan itself.

(i) Human Reactions

[63]

1. Some witnesses asserted that the emergence of the private sector would lead to a reduction in popular support in the long term because the people who had private insurance would no longer see any utility for the public plan....
2. Some witnesses were of the opinion that the quality of care in the public plan would decline because the most influential people would no longer have any incentive to bring pressure for improvements to the plan. Dr. Bergman cited a study by the World Bank in support of his expert report. Dr. Marmor relied on this argument but confirmed that there is no direct evidence to support this view.
3. There would be a reduction in human resources in the public plan because many physicians and other health care professionals would leave the plan out of a motive for profit: Dr. Charles J. Wright cited a study done in the United Kingdom, but admitted that he had read only a summary and not the study itself. Although Dr. Marmor supported the assertion, he testified that there is really no way to confirm it empirically. In his opinion, it is simply a matter of common sense.
4. An increase in the use of private health care would contribute to an increase in the supply of care for profit and lead to a decline in the professionalism and ethics of physicians working in hospitals. No study was cited in support of this opinion that seems to be based only on the witnesses' common sense.

[64] It is apparent from this summary that for each threat mentioned, no study was produced or discussed in the Superior

Court.... The evidence that the existence of the health care system would be jeopardized by human reactions to the emergence of a private system carries little weight.

(ii) Impact on the Public Plan

[65]

1. There would be an increase in overall health expenditures: the alleged increase would come primarily from the additional expenditures incurred by individuals who decide to take out private insurance; the rest of the increase in costs would be attributable to the cost of management of the private system by the state.
2. Insurers would reject the most acute patients, leaving the most serious cases to be covered by the public plan.
3. In a private system, physicians would tend to lengthen waiting times in the public sector in order to direct patients to the private sector from which they would derive a profit.

[66] Once again, I am of the opinion that the reaction some witnesses described is highly unlikely in the Quebec context. First, if the increase in overall costs is primarily attributable to the individual cost of insurance, it would be difficult for the state to prevent individuals who wished to pay such costs from choosing how to manage their own finances. Furthermore, because the public plan already handles all the serious cases, I do not see how the situation could be exacerbated if that plan were relieved of the clientele with less serious health problems....

[69] There is other evidence in the record that might be of assistance in the justification analysis. In this regard, it is useful to observe the approaches of the other Canadian provinces because they also operate within the financial framework established by the *Canada Health Act.*

(b) Overview of Other Provincial Plans

[70] The approach to the role of the private sector taken by the other nine provinces of Canada is by no means uniform. In addition to Quebec, six other provinces have adopted measures to discourage people from turning to the private sector. The other three, in practice, give their residents free access to the private sector.

[71] Ontario (*Health Care Accessibility Act*, R.S.O. 1990, c. H.3, s. 2), Nova Scotia (*Health Services and Insurance Act*, R.S.N.S. 1989, c. 197, s. 29(2)) and Manitoba (*Health Services Insurance Act*, R.S.M. 1987, c. H35, s. 95(1)) prohibit non-participating physicians from charging their patients more than what physicians receive from the public plan. In practice, there is no financial incentive to opt for the private sector. It

is worth noting that Nova Scotia does not prohibit insurance contracts to cover health care obtained in the private sector. Ontario and Manitoba prohibit insurance contracts but refund amounts paid by patients to non-participating physicians.

[72] Alberta (*Alberta Health Care Insurance Act*, R.S.A. 2000, c. A-20, s. 9(1)), British Columbia (*Medicare Protection Act*, R.S.B.C. 1996, c. 286, s. 18(2)) and Prince Edward Island (*Health Services Payment Act*, R.S.P.E.I. 1988, c. H-2, ss. 10, 10.1 and 14.1) have adopted a very different approach. In those provinces, non-participating physicians are free to set the amount of their fees, but the cost of the services is not refunded and contracts for insurance to cover services offered by the public plan are prohibited. This is the same policy as has been adopted by Quebec.

[73] Saskatchewan (*Saskatchewan Medical Care Insurance Act*, R.S.S. 1978, c. S-29, s. 18(1.1)), New Brunswick (*Medical Services Payment Act*, R.S.N.B. 1973, c. M-7, s. 2.01(a), and *General Regulation—Medical Services Payment Act*, N.B. Reg. 84-20, Sch. 2, para. (n.1)), and Newfoundland and Labrador (*Medical Care Insurance Act*, 1999, S.N.L. 1999, c. M-5.1, s. 10(5), and *Medical Care Insurance Insured Services Regulations*, C.N.L.R. 21/96, s. 3) are open to the private sector. New Brunswick allows physicians to set their own fees. In Saskatchewan, this right is limited to non-participating physicians. The cost is not refunded by the public plan, but patients may purchase insurance to cover those costs. Newfoundland and Labrador agrees to reimburse patients, up to the amount covered by the public plan, for fees paid to non-participating physicians. In Newfoundland and Labrador, patients may subscribe to private insurance to cover the difference.

[74] Even if it were assumed that the prohibition on private insurance could contribute to preserving the integrity of the system, the variety of measures implemented by different provinces shows that prohibiting insurance contracts is by no means the only measure a state can adopt to protect the system's integrity. . . .

[75] In the context of s. 9.1 of the *Quebec Charter*, I must conclude that a comparison with the plans of the other Canadian provinces does not support the position of the Attorney General of Quebec.

[76] There are also many reports in the record on which to base an overview of current practices in several OECD countries.

(c) Overview of Practices in Certain OECD Countries

[77] Mr. Chaoulli, echoed by at least one of the witnesses (Dr. Coffey), argued that Canada is the only OECD country to prohibit insurance for health care provided by non-participating physicians. This assertion must be clarified as it relates to Canada: it is true of only six provinces. It must

also be qualified in the international context: while no such prohibition is found in any other OECD country, it should nonetheless be mentioned that measures to protect the public plan have been implemented in a number of countries, even some of the countries whose health care plans have been provided as models. There is no single model; the approach in Europe is no more uniform than in Canada.

[78] In a number of European countries, there is no insurance paid for directly out of public funds. In Austria, services are funded through decentralized agencies that collect the necessary funds from salaries. People who want to obtain health care in the private sector in addition to the services covered by the mandatory social insurance are free to do so, but private insurance may cover no more than 80 percent of the cost billed by professionals practising in the public sector. The same type of plan exists in Germany and the Netherlands, but people who opt for private insurance are not required to pay for the public plan. Only nine percent of Germans opt for private insurance.

[79] Australia's public system is funded in a manner similar to the Quebec system. However, Australia's system is different in that the private and public sectors coexist, and insurance covering private sector health care is not prohibited. The government attempts to balance access to the two sectors by allowing taxpayers to deduct 30 percent of the cost of private insurance. Insurance rates are regulated to prevent insurers from charging higher premiums for higher-risk individuals (C.H. Tuohy, C.M. Flood and M. Stabile, "How Does Private Finance Affect Public Health Care Systems? Marshaling the Evidence from OECD Nations" (2004), 29 *J. Health Pol.* 359)

[80] The United Kingdom does not restrict access to private insurance for health care (*The Health of Canadians—The Federal Role*, vol. 3, *Health Care Systems in Other Countries*, Interim Report (2002), at p. 38). Nor does the United Kingdom limit a physician's ability to withdraw from the public plan. However, physicians working full-time in public hospitals are limited in the amounts that they may bill in the private sector to supplement income earned in the public sector (p. 40). Only 11.5 percent of Britons had taken out private insurance in 1998 (Tuohy, Flood and Stabile, at p. 374), and only 8 percent of hospital beds in the United Kingdom are private (Quebec and France, *Health Indicators: International Comparisons: 15 years of Evolution: Canada, France, Germany, Québec, United Kingdom, United States* (1998), at p. 55). New Zealand has a plan similar to that of the United Kingdom with the difference that 40 percent of New Zealanders have private insurance (Tuohy, Flood and Stabile, at p. 363).

[81] Sweden does not prohibit private insurance, and the state does not refund the cost of health care paid for in the private sector. Private insurance accounts for only two percent

of total health care expenditures and there are only nine private hospitals....

[82] It can be seen from the systems in these various OECD countries that a number of governments have taken measures to protect their public plans from abuse. The measures vary from country to country depending on the nature of their specific systems. For example, in the United Kingdom, there are limits on the amounts physicians may earn in the private sector in addition to what they receive from the public plan. Australia has opted to regulate insurance premiums, but it is alone in this respect....

[84] It cannot therefore be concluded from the evidence relating to the Quebec plan or the plans of the other provinces of Canada, or from the evolution of the systems in place in various OECD countries, that the Attorney General of Quebec has discharged his burden of proof under s. 9.1 of the *Quebec Charter*. A number of measures are available to him to protect the integrity of Quebec's health care plan. The choice of prohibiting private insurance contracts is not justified by the evidence. However, is this a case in which the Court should show deference?

(d)   Level of Deference Required

...[86] Under the charters, the government is responsible for justifying measures it imposes that impair rights. The courts can consider evidence concerning the historical, social and economic aspects, or any other evidence that may be material.

[87] It cannot be said that the government lacks the necessary resources to show that its legislative action is motivated by a reasonable objective connected with the problem it has undertaken to remedy. The courts are an appropriate forum for a serious and complete debate. As G. Davidov said in "The Paradox of Judicial Deference" (2000-2001), 12 *N.J.C.L.* 133, at p. 143, "[c]ourts do not have to define goals, choose means or come up with ideas. They do not have to create social policies; they just have to understand what the other branches have created. No special expertise is required for such an understanding." In fact, if a court is satisfied that all the evidence has been presented, there is nothing that would justify it in refusing to perform its role on the ground that it should merely defer to the government's position. When the courts are given the tools they need to make a decision, they should not hesitate to assume their responsibilities. Deference cannot lead the judicial branch to abdicate its role in favour of the legislative branch or the executive branch....

[89] The courts have a duty to rise above political debate. They leave it to the legislatures to develop social policy. But when such social policies infringe rights that are protected by the charters, the courts cannot shy away from considering them. The judicial branch plays a role that is not played by the legislative branch....

[90] From this perspective, it is through the combined action of legislatures and courts that democratic objectives can be achieved....

[91] The court's reasons for showing deference must always reflect the two guiding principles of justification: the measure must be consistent with democratic values and it must be necessary in order to maintain public order and the general well-being of citizens. The variety of circumstances that may be presented to a court is not conducive to the rigidity of an exhaustive list....

[97] For many years, the government has failed to act; the situation continues to deteriorate. This is not a case in which missing scientific data would allow for a more informed decision to be made. The principle of prudence that is so popular in matters relating to the environment and to medical research cannot be transposed to this case. Under the Quebec plan, the government can control its human resources in various ways, whether by using the time of professionals who have already reached the maximum for payment by the state, by applying the provision that authorizes it to compel even non-participating physicians to provide services (s. 30 *HEIA*) or by implementing less restrictive measures, like those adopted in the four Canadian provinces that do not prohibit private insurance or in the other OECD countries. While the government has the power to decide what measures to adopt, it cannot choose to do nothing in the face of the violation of Quebeckers' right to security. The government has not given reasons for its failure to act. Inertia cannot be used as an argument to justify deference.

[98] In the instant case, the effectiveness of the prohibition has by no means been established. The government has not proved, by the evidence in the record, that the measure minimally impairs the protected rights. Moreover, the evidence shows that a wide variety of measures are available to governments, as can be seen from the plans of other provinces and other countries.

(3)   Proportionality

[99] Having found that s. 15 *HEIA* and s. 11 *HOIA* do not meet the minimal impairment test, I do not need to consider proportionality. If the prohibition is not minimally impairing, it obviously cannot be regarded as a measure that sufficiently addresses the effect of the measure on the protected rights.

VII.   Conclusion

[100] The relief sought by the appellants does not necessarily provide a complete response to the complex problem of waiting lists. However, it was not up to the appellants to find a way to remedy a problem that has persisted for a number of years and for which the solution must come from the state itself. Their only burden was to prove that their right to

life and to personal inviolability had been infringed. They have succeeded in proving this. The Attorney General of Quebec, on the other hand, has not proved that the impugned measure, the prohibition on private insurance, was justified under s. 9.1 of the *Quebec Charter*. Given that this finding is sufficient to dispose of the appeal, it is not necessary to answer the other constitutional questions.

[101] For these reasons, I would allow the appeal with costs throughout and would answer the questions relating to the *Quebec Charter* as follows:

Question 1: Does s. 11 of the *Hospital Insurance Act*, R.S.Q., c. A-28, infringe the rights guaranteed by s. 1 of the *Quebec Charter*?

Answer: Yes.

Question 2: If so, is the infringement a reasonable limit prescribed by law as can be demonstrably justified in a free and democratic society under s. 9.1 of the *Quebec Charter*?

Answer: No.

Question 3: Does s. 15 of the *Health Insurance Act*, R.S.Q., c. A-29, infringe the rights guaranteed by s. 1 of the *Quebec Charter*?

Answer: Yes.

Question 4: If so, is the infringement a reasonable limit prescribed by law as can be demonstrably justified in a free and democratic society under s. 9.1 of the *Quebec Charter*?

Answer: No.

The reasons of McLachlin C.J. and Major and Bastarache JJ. were delivered by

[102] **THE CHIEF JUSTICE AND MAJOR J.:** We concur in the conclusion of our colleague Deschamps J. that the prohibition against contracting for private health insurance violates s. 1 of the *Quebec Charter of Human Rights and Freedoms*, R.S.Q., c. C-12, and is not justifiable under s. 9.1. On the argument that the anti-insurance provision also violates s. 7 of the *Canadian Charter of Rights and Freedoms* ("*Charter*"), we conclude that the provision impermissibly limits the right to life, liberty and security of the person protected by s. 7 of the *Charter* and has not been shown to be justified as a reasonable limit under s. 1 of the *Charter*.

[103] The appellants do not seek an order that the government spend more money on health care, nor do they seek an order that waiting times for treatment under the public health care scheme be reduced. They only seek a ruling that because delays in the public system place their health and security at risk, they should be allowed to take out insurance to permit them to access private services.

[104] The *Charter* does not confer a freestanding constitutional right to health care. However, where the government puts in place a scheme to provide health care, that scheme must comply with the *Charter*. We are of the view that the prohibition on medical insurance in s. 15 of the *Health Insurance Act*, R.S.Q., c. A-29, and s. 11 of the *Hospital Insurance Act*, R.S.Q., c. A-28 (see Appendix), violates s. 7 of the *Charter* because it impinges on the right to life, liberty and security of the person in an arbitrary fashion that fails to conform to the principles of fundamental justice.

[105] The primary objective of the *Canada Health Act*, R.S.C. 1985, c. C-6, is "to protect, promote and restore the physical and mental well-being of residents of Canada and *to facilitate reasonable access* to health services without financial or other barriers" (s. 3). By imposing exclusivity and then failing to provide public health care of a reasonable standard within a reasonable time, the government creates circumstances that trigger the application of s. 7 of the *Charter*.

[106] The *Canada Health Act*, the *Health Insurance Act*, and the *Hospital Insurance Act* do not expressly prohibit private health services. However, they limit access to private health services by removing the ability to contract for private health care insurance to cover the same services covered by public insurance. The result is a virtual monopoly for the public health scheme. The state has effectively limited access to private health care except for the very rich, who can afford private care without need of insurance. This virtual monopoly, on the evidence, results in delays in treatment that adversely affect the citizen's security of the person. Where a law adversely affects life, liberty or security of the person, it must conform to the principles of fundamental justice. This law, in our view, fails to do so. . . .

I. Section 7 of the Charter

[109] Section 7 of the *Charter* guarantees that "[e]veryone has the right to life, liberty and security of the person and the right not to be deprived thereof except in accordance with the principles of fundamental justice." The disposition of this appeal therefore requires us to consider (1) whether the impugned provisions deprive individuals of their life, liberty or security of the person; and (2) if so, whether this deprivation is in accordance with the principles of fundamental justice: see, e.g., *R. v. Malmo-Levine*, [2003] 3 S.C.R. 571, 2003 SCC 74, at para. 83.

A. Deprivation of Life, Liberty, or Security of the Person

[110] The issue at this stage is whether the prohibition on insurance for private medical care deprives individuals of their life, liberty or security of the person protected by s. 7 of the *Charter*.

[111] The appellants have established that many Quebec residents face delays in treatment that adversely affect their security of the person and that they would not sustain but for the prohibition on medical insurance. It is common ground that the effect of the prohibition on insurance is to allow only the very rich, who do not need insurance, to secure private health care in order to avoid the delays in the public system. Given the ban on insurance, most Quebeckers have no choice but to accept delays in the medical system and their adverse physical and psychological consequences.

[112] Delays in the public system are widespread and have serious, sometimes grave, consequences. There was no dispute that there is a waiting list for cardiovascular surgery for life-threatening problems. Dr. Daniel Doyle, a cardiovascular surgeon who teaches and practises in Quebec City, testified that a person with coronary disease is [TRANSLATION] "sitting on a bomb" and can die at any moment. He confirmed, without challenge, that patients die while on waiting lists: A.R., at p. 461. Inevitably, where patients have life-threatening conditions, some will die because of undue delay in awaiting surgery. . . .

[116] In addition to threatening the life and the physical security of the person, waiting for critical care may have significant adverse psychological effects. Serious psychological effects may engage s. 7 protection for security of the person. These "need not rise to the level of nervous shock or psychiatric illness, but must be greater than ordinary stress or anxiety": *New Brunswick (Minister of Health and Community Services) v. G.(J.)*, [1999] 3 S.C.R. 46, at para. 60. . . .

[124] We conclude, based on the evidence, that prohibiting health insurance that would permit ordinary Canadians to access health care, in circumstances where the government is failing to deliver health care in a reasonable manner, thereby increasing the risk of complications and death, interferes with life and security of the person as protected by s. 7 of the *Charter*.

[125] The remaining question is whether this inference is in accordance with the principles of fundamental justice. "[I]f the state [interferes] with security of the person, the *Charter* requires such interference to conform with the principles of fundamental justice": *Morgentaler*, at p. 54, per Dickson C.J.

B. Deprivation in Accordance with the Principles of Fundamental Justice

[126] Having concluded that the ban on private medical insurance constitutes a deprivation of life and security of the person, we now consider whether that deprivation is in accordance with the principles of fundamental justice. Our colleagues Binnie and LeBel JJ. argue that the record here provides no ground for finding that the deprivation violates the principles of fundamental justice. With respect, we cannot agree. . . .

[128] The principle of fundamental justice implicated in this case is that laws that affect the life, liberty or security of the person shall not be arbitrary. We are of the opinion that the evidence before the trial judge supports a finding that the impugned provisions are arbitrary and that the deprivation of life and security of the person that flows from them cannot therefore be said to accord with the principles of fundamental justice.

(1) Laws Shall Not Be Arbitrary: A Principle of Fundamental Justice

[129] It is a well-recognized principle of fundamental justice that laws should not be arbitrary: see, e.g., *Malmo-Levine*, at para. 135; *Rodriguez*, at p. 594. The state is not entitled to arbitrarily limit its citizens' rights to life, liberty and security of the person.

[130] A law is arbitrary where "it bears no relation to, or is inconsistent with, the objective that lies behind [it]." To determine whether this is the case, it is necessary to consider the state interest and societal concerns that the provision is meant to reflect: *Rodriguez*, at pp. 594-95.

[131] In order not to be arbitrary, the limit on life, liberty and security requires not only a theoretical connection between the limit and the legislative goal, but a real connection on the facts. The onus of showing lack of connection in this sense rests with the claimant. The question in every case is whether the measure is arbitrary in the sense of bearing no real relation to the goal and hence being manifestly unfair. The more serious the impingement on the person's liberty and security, the more clear must be the connection. Where the individual's very life may be at stake, the reasonable person would expect a clear connection, in theory and in fact, between the measure that puts life at risk and the legislative goals.

(2) Whether the Prohibition on Private Medical Insurance Is Arbitrary

. . . [135] The government argues that the interference with security of the person caused by denying people the right to purchase private health insurance is necessary to providing effective health care under the public health system. It argues that if people can purchase private health insurance, they will seek treatment from private doctors and hospitals, which are not banned under the Act. According to the government's argument, this will divert resources from the public health system into private health facilities, ultimately reducing the quality of public care.

[136] In support of this contention, the government called experts in health administration and policy. Their conclusions were based on the "common sense" proposition that the improvement of health services depends on exclusivity (R.R., at p. 591). They did not profess expertise in waiting times for

treatment. Nor did they present economic studies or rely on the experience of other countries. They simply assumed, as a matter of apparent logic, that insurance would make private health services more accessible and that this in turn would undermine the quality of services provided by the public health care system.

[137] The appellants, relying on other health experts, disagreed and offered their own conflicting "common sense" argument for the proposition that prohibiting private health insurance is neither necessary nor related to maintaining high quality in the public health care system. Quality public care, they argue, depends not on a monopoly, but on money and management. They testified that permitting people to buy private insurance would make alternative medical care more accessible and reduce the burden on the public system. The result, they assert, would be better care for all. The appellants reinforce this argument by pointing out that disallowing private insurance precludes the vast majority of Canadians (middle-income and low-income earners) from accessing additional care, while permitting it for the wealthy who can afford to travel abroad or pay for private care in Canada.

[138] To this point, we are confronted with competing but unproven "common sense" arguments, amounting to little more than assertions of belief. We are in the realm of theory. But as discussed above, a theoretically defensible limitation may be arbitrary if in fact the limit lacks a connection to the goal.

[139] This brings us to the evidence called by the appellants at trial on the experience of other developed countries with public health care systems which permit access to private health care. The experience of these countries suggests that there is no real connection in fact between prohibition of health insurance and the goal of a quality public health system.

[140] The evidence adduced at trial establishes that many western democracies that do not impose a monopoly on the delivery of health care have successfully delivered to their citizens medical services that are superior to and more affordable than the services that are presently available in Canada. This demonstrates that a monopoly is not necessary or even related to the provision of quality public health care.

[141] In its report *The Health of Canadians—The Federal Role*, the Standing Senate Committee on Social Affairs, Science and Technology discussed in detail the situations in several countries, including Sweden, Germany and the United Kingdom. The following discussion of the health care systems in these three countries is drawn directly from the findings in volume 3 of that report (*The Health of Canadians—The Federal Role*, vol. 3, *Health Care Systems in Other Countries*, Interim Report (2002) ("Kirby Report")).

[142] In Sweden, as in Canada, access to public health care is universal. The public health care system is financed predominantly by the public sector through a combination of general taxation and social insurance (i.e., employer/employee contributions) and employs a user fee mechanism. Unlike in Canada, private health care insurance that covers the same benefits as public insurance is "legal" in Sweden. However, only a small minority of the population purchase private insurance. The result is a system of public health care coverage that provides quality care on a broader basis than in Canada and encompasses physicians, hospital services, drugs and dental care: Kirby Report, vol. 3, at pp. 29-36. In Sweden, the availability of private health care insurance appears not to have harmed the public health care system.

[143] In Germany, public health care insurance is administered by 453 Sickness Funds—private non-profit organizations structured on a regional task or occupational basis. Sickness Fund membership is compulsory for employees with gross incomes lower than approximately $63,000 Canadian, and voluntary for those with gross incomes above that level. Although all Sickness Funds are regulated at the federal level through what is known as the "Social Code Book," they are essentially run by representatives of employees and employers. As in Sweden, public health care coverage is broader in Germany than in Canada, including physician services, hospitals, prescription drugs, diagnostic services, dental care, rehabilitative care, medical devices, psychotherapists, nursing care at home, medical services by non-physicians (physiotherapists, speech therapists, occupational therapists, etc.) and income support during sick leave: Kirby Report, vol. 3, at p. 14.

[144] In Germany, as in Sweden, private health insurance is available to individuals at a certain income level who may voluntarily opt out of the Sickness Funds. Private coverage is currently offered by 52 private insurance companies that are obliged to offer an insurance policy with the same benefits as the Sickness Funds at a premium that is no higher than the average maximum contribution to the Sickness Funds....

[145] Despite the availability of alternatives, 88 percent of the German population are covered by the public Sickness Funds: this includes 14 percent to whom private insurance is available. Of the remaining 12 percent, only 9 percent are covered by private insurance and less than 1 percent have no health insurance at all. The remaining 2 percent are covered by government insurance for military and other personnel: Kirby Report, vol. 3, at p. 15.

[146] The United Kingdom offers a comprehensive public health care system—the National Health Service (NHS)—while also allowing for private insurance. Unlike Canada, the United Kingdom allows people to purchase private health care insurance that covers the same benefits as the NHS if these services are supplied by providers working outside of the NHS. Despite the existence of private insurance, only 11.5 percent of the population have purchased it: Kirby Report, vol. 3, at

pp. 37-44. Again, it appears that the public system has not suffered as a result of the existence of private alternatives.

[147] After reviewing a number of public health care systems, the Standing Senate Committee on Social Affairs, Science and Technology concluded in the Kirby Report that far from undermining public health care, private contributions and insurance improve the breadth and quality of health care for all citizens. . . .

[149] In summary, the evidence on the experience of other western democracies refutes the government's theoretical contention that a prohibition on private insurance is linked to maintaining quality public health care.

[150] Binnie and LeBel JJ. suggest that the experience of other countries is of little assistance. With respect, we cannot agree. This evidence was properly placed before the trial judge and, unless discredited, stands as the best guide with respect to the question of whether a ban on private insurance is necessary and relevant to the goal of providing quality public health care.

[151] Binnie and LeBel JJ. also suggest that the government's continued commitment to a monopoly on the provision of health insurance cannot be arbitrary because it is rooted in reliance on "a series of authoritative reports [that analysed] health care in this country and in other countries." . . . But the conclusions of other bodies on other material cannot be determinative of this litigation. They cannot relieve the courts of their obligation to review government action for consistency with the *Charter* on the evidence before them.

[152] When we look to the evidence rather than to assumptions, the connection between prohibiting private insurance and maintaining quality public health care vanishes. The evidence before us establishes that where the public system fails to deliver adequate care, the denial of private insurance subjects people to long waiting lists and negatively affects their health and security of the person. The government contends that this is necessary in order to preserve the public health system. The evidence, however, belies that contention.

[153] We conclude that on the evidence adduced in this case, the appellants have established that in the face of delays in treatment that cause psychological and physical suffering, the prohibition on private insurance jeopardizes the right to life, liberty and security of the person of Canadians in an arbitrary manner, and is therefore not in accordance with the principles of fundamental justice.

II. Section 1 of the Charter

[154] Having concluded that the prohibition on private health insurance constitutes a breach of s. 7, we must now consider whether that breach can be justified under s. 1 of the *Charter* as a reasonable limit demonstrably justified in a free and democratic society. The evidence called in this case falls short of demonstrating such justification.

[155] The government undeniably has an interest in protecting the public health regime. However, given the absence of evidence that the prohibition on the purchase and sale of private health insurance protects the health care system, the rational connection between the prohibition and the objective is not made out. Indeed, we question whether an arbitrary provision, which by reason of its arbitrariness cannot further its stated objective, will ever meet the rational connection test under *R. v. Oakes*, [1986] 1 S.C.R. 103.

[156] In addition, the resulting denial of access to timely and effective medical care to those who need it is not proportionate to the beneficial effects of the prohibition on private insurance to the health system as a whole. On the evidence here and for the reasons discussed above, the prohibition goes further than necessary to protect the public system: it is not minimally impairing.

[157] Finally, the benefits of the prohibition do not outweigh the deleterious effects. Prohibiting citizens from obtaining private health care insurance may, as discussed, leave people no choice but to accept excessive delays in the public health system. The physical and psychological suffering and risk of death that may result outweigh whatever benefit (and none has been demonstrated to us here) there may be to the system as a whole.

[158] In sum, the prohibition on obtaining private health insurance, while it might be constitutional in circumstances where health care services are reasonable as to both quality and timeliness, is not constitutional where the public system fails to deliver reasonable services. Life, liberty and security of the person must prevail. To paraphrase Dickson C.J. in *Morgentaler*, at p. 73, if the government chooses to act, it must do so properly.

[159] We agree with Deschamps J.'s conclusion that the prohibition against contracting for private health insurance violates s. 1 of the *Quebec Charter of Human Rights and Freedoms* and is not justifiable under s. 9.1. We also conclude that this prohibition violates s. 7 of the *Canadian Charter of Rights and Freedoms* and cannot be saved under s. 1.

[160] We would allow the appeal, with costs to the appellants throughout.

The reasons of Binnie, LeBel, and Fish JJ. were delivered by

BINNIE AND LEBEL JJ. (dissenting):

I. Introduction

[161] The question in this appeal is whether the province of Quebec not only has the constitutional authority to establish a comprehensive single-tier health plan, but to discourage a second (private) tier health sector by prohibiting the purchase and sale of private health insurance. The appellants argue that timely access to needed medical service is not being

provided in the publicly funded system and that the province cannot therefore deny to those Quebeckers (who can qualify) the right to purchase private insurance to pay for medical services whenever and wherever such services can be obtained for a fee, i.e., in the private sector. This issue has been the subject of protracted debate across Canada through several provincial and federal elections. We are unable to agree with our four colleagues who would allow the appeal that such a debate can or should be resolved as a matter of law by judges. We find that, on the *legal* issues raised, the appeal should be dismissed.

[162] Our colleagues the Chief Justice and Major J. state at para. 105:

> By imposing exclusivity and then failing to provide *public health care of a reasonable standard within a reasonable time*, the government creates circumstances that trigger the application of s. 7 of the [*Canadian*] *Charter*. [Emphasis added.]

[163] The Court recently held in *Auton (Guardian ad litem of) v. British Columbia (Attorney General)*, [2004] 3 S.C.R. 657, 2004 SCC 78, that the government was not required to fund the treatment of autistic children. It did not on that occasion address in constitutional terms the scope and nature of "reasonable" health services. Courts will now have to make that determination. What, then, are constitutionally required "reasonable health services"? What is treatment "within a reasonable time"? What are the benchmarks? How short a waiting list is short enough? How many MRIs does the Constitution require? The majority does not tell us. The majority lays down no manageable constitutional standard. The public cannot know, nor can judges or governments know, how much health care is "reasonable" enough to satisfy s. 7 of the *Canadian Charter of Rights and Freedoms* ("*Canadian Charter*") and s. 1 of the *Charter of Human Rights and Freedoms*, R.S.Q. c. C-12 ("*Quebec Charter*"). It is to be hoped that we will know it when we see it.

[164] The policy of the *Canada Health Act*, R.S.C. 1985, c. C-6, and its provincial counterparts is to provide health care based on need rather than on wealth or status. The evidence certainly established that the public health care system put in place to implement this policy has serious and persistent problems. This does not mean that the courts are well placed to perform the required surgery. The resolution of such a complex fact-laden policy debate does not fit easily within the institutional competence or procedures of courts of law. The courts can use s. 7 of the *Canadian Charter* to pre-empt the ongoing public debate only if the current health plan violates an established "principle of fundamental justice." Our colleagues McLachlin C.J. and Major J. argue that Quebec's enforcement of a single-tier health plan meets this legal test

because it is "arbitrary." In our view, with respect, the prohibition against private health insurance is a rational consequence of Quebec's commitment to the goals and objectives of the *Canada Health Act*....

[166] The Quebec government views the prohibition against private insurance as essential to preventing the current single-tier health system from disintegrating into a *de facto* two-tier system. The trial judge found, and the evidence demonstrated, that there is good reason for this fear. The trial judge concluded that a private health sector fuelled by private insurance would frustrate achievement of the objectives of the *Canada Health Act*. She thus found no *legal* basis to intervene, and declined to do so. This raises the issue of *who* it is that *should* resolve these important and contentious issues. Commissioner Roy Romanow makes the following observation in his Report:

> Some have described it as a perversion of Canadian values that they cannot use their money to purchase faster treatment from a private provider for their loved ones. I believe it is a far greater perversion of Canadian values to accept a system where money, rather than need, determines who gets access to care.
>
> (*Building on Values: The Future of Health Care in Canada: Final Report* (2002) ("Romanow Report"), at p. xx)

Whether or not one endorses this assessment, his premise is that the debate is about *social* values. It is not about constitutional law. We agree.

[167] We believe our colleagues the Chief Justice and Major J. have extended too far the strands of interpretation under the *Canadian Charter* laid down in some of the earlier cases, in particular the ruling on abortion in *R. v. Morgentaler*, [1988] 1 S.C.R. 30 (which involved criminal liability, not public health policy). We cannot find in the constitutional law of Canada a "principle of fundamental justice" dispositive of the problems of waiting lists in the Quebec health system. In our view, the appellants' case does not rest on constitutional law but on their disagreement with the Quebec government on aspects of its social policy. The proper forum to determine the social policy of Quebec in this matter is the National Assembly....

II. Analysis

[177] The appellants' principal argument is that the existence of waiting lists in Quebec and the concurrent prohibition on private health insurance violate s. 7 of the *Canadian Charter*, which guarantees everyone the right to life, liberty and security of the person, and the right not to be deprived thereof except in accordance with the principles of fundamental justice.

[178] The legal question raised by our colleagues the Chief Justice and Major J. under the *Canadian Charter* is

whether or not the Quebec health plan violates a principle of fundamental justice and, if so, whether the plan can nevertheless be saved under s. 1.

[179] The reasons of our colleague Deschamps J., on the other hand, are limited to s. 1 of the *Quebec Charter* which protects the right of every human being to life and to personal security, inviolability and freedom. The *Quebec Charter* does not talk explicitly about "principles of fundamental justice." Nevertheless, in our view, the legislative limits fixed by the *Quebec Charter* are no more favourable to the appellants' case than are those fixed by the *Canadian Charter*. Rights under the *Quebec Charter* are to be exercised with "proper" regard to "democratic" values (including those of the electorate) "public order and the general well-being of the citizens of Québec" (including those who cannot afford, or may not qualify for, private health insurance coverage)....

[180] Our colleagues the Chief Justice and Major J. agree with the appellants that there is a violation of s. 7 of the *Canadian Charter*. As mentioned earlier, their opinion rests in substantial part on observations made by various members of this Court in *Morgentaler*. At issue in that case was the criminal liability of doctors and their patients under s. 251 of the *Criminal Code*, R.S.C. 1970, c. C-34, for performing abortions. The nub of the legal challenge was that in creating the abortion offence Parliament had qualified the charge with a "therapeutic abortion" defence, but the defence was not working. The factual and legal issues raised in that criminal law problem are, we think, far removed from the debate over a two-tier health system. *Morgentaler* applied a "manifest unfairness" test which has never been adopted by the Court outside the criminal law, and certainly not in the context of the design of social programs. The *Morgentaler* judgment fastened on *internal* inconsistencies in s. 251 of the Code, which find no counterpart here. In our view, with respect, *Morgentaler* provides no support for the appellants in this case, as we discuss commencing at para. 259....

B. Canadian Charter of Rights and Freedoms

[190] ...

(1) The Application of Section 7 to Matters Not Falling Within the Administration of Justice

... [193] Section 7 gives rise to some of the most difficult issues in *Canadian Charter* litigation. Because s. 7 protects the most basic interests of human beings—life, liberty and security—claimants call on the courts to adjudicate many difficult moral and ethical issues. It is therefore prudent, in our view, to proceed cautiously and incrementally in applying s. 7, particularly in distilling those principles that are so vital to our society's conception of "principles of fundamental justice" as to be constitutionally entrenched....

[196] It will likely be a rare case where s. 7 will apply in circumstances entirely unrelated to adjudicative or administrative proceedings. That said, the Court has consistently left open the possibility that s. 7 may apply outside the context of the administration of justice: *Gosselin v. Quebec (Attorney General)*, [2002] 4 S.C.R. 429, 2002 SCC 84, at paras. 78-80 and 414.

[197] The Court has been moving away from a narrow approach to s. 7, which restricted the scope of the section to legal rights to be interpreted in light of the rights enumerated in ss. 8 to 14.... In *Blencoe v. British Columbia (Human Rights Commission)*, [2000] 2 S.C.R. 307, 2000 SCC 44, the majority held that s. 7 can apply outside of the criminal context. Further, in *Winnipeg Child and Family Services v. K.L.W.*, [2000] 2 S.C.R. 519, 2000 SCC 48, the Court noted that it had held in *B.(R.) v. Children's Aid Society of Metropolitan Toronto*, [1995] 1 S.C.R. 315, that the wardship provisions of the *Child Welfare Act*, R.S.O. 1980, c. 66, denying parents the ability to choose medical treatment for their infants, implicated the s. 7 liberty interests of parents.

[198] Placing s. 7 under the heading "Legal Rights" in the *Canadian Charter* does not narrow or control its scope. Such a result would be unduly formalistic and inconsistent with the large, liberal and purposive interpretation of s. 7 that has been the hallmark of this Court's approach since *Re B.C. Motor Vehicle Act*, [1985] 2 S.C.R. 486. This is evidenced by the refusal of the majority in that case to restrict "principles of fundamental justice" solely to procedural guarantees. Lamer J. observed that "the principles of fundamental justice are to be found in the basic tenets and principles, *not only of our judicial process*, but also of the other components of our legal system" (p. 512 (emphasis added)).

[199] Claimants whose life, liberty or security of the person is put at risk are entitled to relief only to the extent that their complaint arises from a breach of an identifiable principle of fundamental justice. *The real control over the scope and operation of s. 7 is to be found in the requirement that the applicant identify a violation of a principle of fundamental justice.* The further a challenged state action lies from the traditional adjudicative context, the more difficult it will be for a claimant to make that essential link. As will become clear, that is precisely the difficulty encountered by the claimants here: they are unable to demonstrate that any principle of fundamental justice has been contravened.

(2) Which Section 7 Interests Are Engaged?

[200] Section 7 interests are enumerated as life, liberty and security of the person. As stated, we accept the trial judge's finding that the current state of the Quebec health system, linked to the prohibition against health insurance for insured

services, is capable, at least in the cases of *some* individuals on *some* occasions, of putting at risk their life or security of the person.

[201] We do not agree with the appellants, however, that the Quebec Health Plan puts the "liberty" of Quebeckers at risk. The argument that "liberty" includes freedom of contract (in this case to contract for private medical insurance) is novel in Canada, where economic rights are not included in the *Canadian Charter* and discredited in the United States. In that country, the liberty of individuals (mainly employers) to contract out of social and economic programs was endorsed by the Supreme Court in the early decades of the 20th century on the theory that laws that prohibited employers from entering into oppressive contracts with employees violated their "liberty" of contract; see, e.g., *Lochner v. New York*, 198 U.S. 45 (1905), at p. 62:

> . . . a prohibition to enter into any contract of labor in a bakery for more than a certain number of hours a week, is, in our judgment, so wholly beside the matter of a proper, reasonable and fair provision, as to run counter to that liberty of person and of free contract provided for in the Federal Constitution.

Of this line of cases, which was not brought to an end until *West Coast Hotel Co. v. Parrish*, 300 U.S. 379 (1937), Professor L.H. Tribe has written that the Supreme Court of the United States:

> . . . relied on the Fourteenth Amendment's Due Process Clause to strike down economic legislation that the Court saw as improperly *infringing on contractual liberty*, but in which the Court was widely (even if not always correctly) perceived to be substituting its own judgment, in the absence of any actual constitutional mandate, for that of the legislature. [Emphasis added.]

> (*American Constitutional Law* (3rd ed. 2000), vol. 1, at p. 1318)

. . . [207] As stated, the principal legal hurdle to the appellants' *Canadian Charter* challenge is not the preliminary step of identifying a s. 7 interest potentially affected in the case of *some* Quebeckers in *some* circumstances. The hurdle lies in their failure to find a fundamental principle of justice that is violated by the Quebec health plan so as to justify the Court in striking down the prohibition against private insurance for what the government has identified as "insured services."

C. Principles of Fundamental Justice

[208] For a principle to be one of fundamental justice, it must count among the basic tenets of our *legal* system: *Re B.C. Motor Vehicle Act*, at p. 503. It must generally be accepted as

such among reasonable people. As explained by the majority in *Malmo-Levine*, at para. 113:

> The requirement of "general acceptance among reasonable people" enhances the legitimacy of judicial review of state action, and ensures that the values against which state action is measured are not just fundamental "in the eye of the beholder *only*": *Rodriguez*, at pp. 607 and 590. . . .

[209] Thus, the formal requirements for a principle of fundamental justice are threefold. First, it must be a *legal* principle. Second, the reasonable person must regard it as vital to our societal notion of justice, which implies a significant *societal consensus*. Third, it must be capable of being *identified with precision* and applied in a manner that yields *predictable results*. These requirements present insurmountable hurdles to the appellants. The aim of "health care of a reasonable standard within a reasonable time" is not a *legal* principle. There is no "societal consensus" about what it means or how to achieve it. It cannot be "identified with precision." As the testimony in this case showed, a level of care that is considered perfectly reasonable by some doctors is denounced by others. . . .

[210] Much of the argument pursued by the Chief Justice and Major J., as well as by Deschamps J. in her reasons relating to the *Quebec Charter*, revolves around the vexing issue of waiting lists, which have notoriously fuelled major public debates and controversies.

[211] The case history of the appellant Zeliotis illustrates why rationing of health services is necessary and how it works. The trial judge, having heard all the evidence, concluded that the delays Mr. Zeliotis experienced in obtaining hip surgery were caused not by excessive waiting lists but by a number of other factors, including his pre-existing depression and his indecision and unfounded medical complaints. . . .

(a) There Is No Consensus About What Constitutes "Reasonable" Waiting Times

[212] A review of the expert evidence and the medical literature suggests that there is no consensus regarding guidelines for timely medical treatment. Dr. Wright remarked:

> So the issue of defining what is a reasonable waiting list is a very difficult one because if you have a hundred (100) surgeons, you have a hundred (100) opinions, it's very difficult to come to a consensus on these questions. [A.R., at p. 1186] . . .

(b) The Experts Accepted by the Trial Judge Relied on More Than Just "Common Sense"

[214] Our colleagues the Chief Justice and Major J. dismiss the experts accepted by the trial judge as relying on little more than "common sense" (para. 137). Although we agree

that the experts offered "common sense," they offered a good deal more. The experts heard by the trial court included Mr. Claude Castonguay, who was Quebec's Minister of Health in 1970 (the [TRANSLATION] "father of Quebec health insurance") and who chaired the Commission of Inquiry on Health and Social Welfare, as well as a number of other public health experts, including Dr. Fernand Turcotte, a professor of medicine at Laval University, who holds degrees from the University of Montreal and Harvard and has been certified by the Royal College of Physicians and Surgeons of Canada as a specialist in community medicine; Dr. Howard Bergman, Chief of the Division of Geriatric Medicine at Montreal's Jewish General Hospital, Director of the Division of Geriatric Medicine and a professor in the departments of Internal Medicine and Family Medicine at McGill University, a fellow of the American Geriatrics Society and an associate professor at the University of Montreal in the department of health administration; Dr. Charles J. Wright, a physician specialized in surgery, Director of the Centre for Clinical Epidemiology & Evaluation at the Vancouver Hospital & Health Sciences Centre, and a faculty member of the University of British Columbia and of the British Columbia Office of Health Technology Assessment; Professor Jean-Louis Denis, a community health doctor of the University of Montreal's [TRANSLATION] "health services organization"; Professor Theodore R. Marmor, a professor of public policy and management and of political science at Yale University, who holds a PhD from Harvard University in politics and history and is a graduate research fellow at Oxford; and Dr. J. Edwin Coffey, a graduate of McGill University in medicine who specializes in obstetrics and gynecology, a fellow of the Royal College of Physicians and Surgeons of Canada and of the American College of Obstetricians and Gynecologists, and a former associate professor in the McGill University Faculty of Medicine. The respondent's experts testified and were cross-examined. The trial judge found them to be credible and reliable. We owe deference to her findings in this respect

[215] The trial judge, having heard the evidence, concluded as follows:

> [TRANSLATION] ... although some of these specialists indicated a desire to be free to obtain private insurance, none of them gave their full and absolute support to the applicants' proposals, as they explained *that it was neither clear nor obvious that a reorganization of the health system with a parallel private system would solve all the existing problems of delays and access.* On the contrary, the specialists who testified remained quite circumspect about this complex and difficult question. [Emphasis added; p. 796.]

The exception to the consensus was the appellants' expert, Dr. Coffey, who stated that in his opinion the development of a private insurance scheme would not affect the public health scheme. This is the argument accepted by our colleagues the Chief Justice and Major J. However on this point the trial judge observed, as on others, [TRANSLATION] "*that Dr. Coffey stood alone in both his expert evaluation and the conclusions he reached*" (p. 808 (emphasis in original)). ...

(c) The Lack of Accurate Data

[217] How serious is the waiting-list problem? No doubt it is serious; but how serious? The first major evidentiary difficulty for the appellants is the lack of accurate data. The major studies concluded that the real picture concerning waiting lists in Canada is subject to contradictory evidence and conflicting claims (Romanow Report, at p. 139, and the Kirby Report, vol. 4, at p. 41, and vol. 6, at pp. 109-10). This can also be seen from the evidence of the experts who testified at trial in the present case. ...

[226] We have similar concerns about the use made by the appellants of various reports in connection with other OECD countries. These "country" reports were included in an *Interim* Kirby Report but not in its final version. The Final Kirby Report's recommendation was to stick with a single-tier system. We think the Court is sufficiently burdened with conflicting evidence about our own health system without attempting a detailed investigation of the merits of trade-offs made in other countries, for their own purposes. ...

[229] We are not to be taken as disputing the undoubted fact that there are serious problems with the single-tier health plan in Canada. Our point is simply that bits of evidence must be put in context. With respect, it is particularly dangerous to venture selectively into aspects of foreign health care systems with which we, as Canadians, have little familiarity. At the very least such information should be filtered and analysed at trial through an expert witness.

[230] Taking the good with the bad, the Final Kirby Report recommended continuation of a single-tier health system (as did the Romanow Report). The authors of the Kirby Report were fully aware of the extracts from their interim report relied upon by our colleagues the Chief Justice and Major J., yet they specifically rejected two-tier health care. ...

(2) Arbitrariness

[231] Our colleagues the Chief Justice and Major J. take the view that a law which arbitrarily violates life or security of the person is unconstitutional. We agree that this is a principle of fundamental justice. We do not agree that it applies to the facts of this case.

[232] A deprivation of a right will be arbitrary and will thus infringe s. 7 if it bears no relation to, or is inconsistent with, the state interest that lies behind the legislation. ...

[233] We agree with our colleagues the Chief Justice and Major J. that a law is arbitrary if "it bears no relation to, or is inconsistent with, the objective that lies behind [the legislation]" (para. 130). We do not agree with the Chief Justice and Major J. that the prohibition against private health insurance "bears no relation to, or is inconsistent with" the preservation of access to a health system based on need rather than wealth in accordance with the *Canada Health Act*. We also do not agree with our colleagues' expansion of the *Morgentaler* principle to invalidate a prohibition simply because a court believes it to be "unnecessary" for the government's purpose. There must be more than that to sustain a valid objection.

[234] The accepted definition in *Rodriguez* states that a law is arbitrary only where "it bears no relation to, or is inconsistent with, the objective that lies behind the legislation." To substitute the term "unnecessary" for "inconsistent" is to substantively alter the meaning of the term "arbitrary." "Inconsistent" means that the law logically contradicts its objectives, whereas "unnecessary" simply means that the objective could be met by other means. It is quite apparent that the latter is a much broader term that involves a policy choice. If a court were to declare unconstitutional every law impacting "security of the person" that the court considers unnecessary, there would be much greater scope for intervention under s. 7 than has previously been considered by this Court to be acceptable....

[235] Rejecting the findings in the courts below based on their own reading of the evidence, our colleagues the Chief Justice and Major J. state (at para. 128):

> We are of the opinion that the evidence before the trial judge supports a finding that the impugned provisions are arbitrary and that the deprivation of life and security of the person that flows from them cannot therefore be said to accord with the principles of fundamental justice.

We note that our colleagues refer to the evidence *before* the trial judge rather than the view taken of that evidence *by* the trial judge. The trial judge reached a contrary conclusion on the facts, and deference is due to her view of that evidence; see *Housen v. Nikolaisen*, [2002] 2 S.C.R. 235, 2002 SCC 33. In any event, with respect, we accept the contrary conclusions of the trial judge and the Quebec Court of Appeal. We approach the issue of arbitrariness in three steps:

(i) What is the "state interest" sought to be protected?
(ii) What is the relationship between the "state interest" thus identified and the prohibition against private health insurance?
(iii) Have the appellants established that the prohibition bears no relation to, or is inconsistent with, the state interest?

We will address each question in turn.

(a) What Is the "State Interest" Sought to Be Protected?

[236] Quebec's legislative objective is to provide high quality health care, at a reasonable cost, for as many people as possible in a manner that is consistent with principles of efficiency, equity and fiscal responsibility. Quebec (along with the other provinces and territories) subscribes to the policy objectives of the *Canada Health Act*, which include (i) the equal provision of medical services to all residents, regardless of status, wealth or personal insurability, and (ii) fiscal responsibility. An overbuilt health system is seen as no more in the larger public interest than a system that on occasion falls short. The legislative task is to strike a balance among competing interests....

(b) What Is the Relationship Between the "State Interest" Thus Identified and the Prohibition Against Private Health Insurance?

... [239] In *principle*, Quebec wants a health system where access is governed by need rather than wealth or status. Quebec does not want people who are uninsurable to be left behind. To accomplish this objective endorsed by the *Canada Health Act*, Quebec seeks to discourage the growth of private-sector delivery of "insured" services based on wealth and insurability. We believe the prohibition is rationally connected to Quebec's objective and is not inconsistent with it.

[240] In *practical terms*, Quebec bases the prohibition on the view that private insurance, and a consequent major expansion of private health services, would have a harmful effect on the public system....

[242] The trial judge considered all the evidence and concluded that the expansion of private health care would undoubtedly have a negative impact on the public health system (at p. 827):

> [TRANSLATION] The evidence has shown that the right of access to a parallel private health care system claimed by the applicants *would have repercussions on the rights of the population as a whole. We cannot bury our heads in the sand. The effect of establishing a parallel private health care system would be to threaten the integrity, proper functioning and viability of the public system.* ...

(vi) Conclusion on "Arbitrariness"

[256] For all these reasons, we agree with the conclusion of the trial judge and the Quebec Court of Appeal that in light of the legislative objectives of the *Canada Health Act* it is not "arbitrary" for Quebec to discourage the growth of private sector health care. Prohibition of private health insurance is directly related to Quebec's interest in promoting a need-based

system and in ensuring its viability and efficiency. Prohibition of private insurance is not "inconsistent" with the state interest; still less is it "unrelated" to it.

[257] In short, it cannot be said that the prohibition against private health insurance "bears no relation to, or is inconsistent with" preservation of a health system predominantly based on need rather than wealth or status, as required by the *Rodriguez* test, at pp. 594-95.

[258] As to our colleagues' dismissal of the factual basis for Quebec's legislative choice, the public has invested very large sums of money in a series of authoritative reports to analyse health care in this country and in other countries. The reports uniformly recommend the retention of single-tier medicine. People are free to challenge (as do the appellants) the government's reliance on those reports but such reliance cannot be dismissed as "arbitrary." . . .

(4) Conclusion Under Section 7 of the Canadian Charter

[265] For the foregoing reasons, even accepting (as we do) the trial judge's conclusion that the claimants have established a deprivation of the life and security of *some* Quebec residents occasioned in *some* circumstances by waiting list delays, the deprivation would not violate any *legal* principle of fundamental justice within the meaning of s. 7 of the *Canadian Charter*. On that point, too, we share the opinion of the trial judge and the Quebec Court of Appeal, as previously mentioned.

D. The Appellants' Challenge Under the Quebec Charter

[266] The *Quebec Charter* is a major quasi-constitutional instrument. Our colleague Deschamps J. finds a violation of s. 1. . . .

[272] Under s. 1 of the *Quebec Charter*, as at the first stage of a s. 7 analysis, the claimant bears the burden of establishing, on a balance of probabilities, that the impugned law infringes his or her protected rights and interests. If such a claim is made out, the focus of the analysis may shift to s. 9.1 of the *Quebec Charter* in order to determine whether the claimed exercise of the right is made with due regard for "democratic values, public order and the general well-being of the citizens of Québec."

[273] In our view, on the evidence, the exercise by the appellants of their claimed *Quebec Charter* rights to defeat the prohibition against private insurance would not have "proper regard for democratic values" or "public order," as the future of a publicly supported and financed single-tier health plan should be in the hands of elected representatives. Nor

would it have proper regard for the "general well-being of the citizens of Québec," who are the designated beneficiaries of the health plan, and in particular for the well-being of the less advantaged Quebeckers.

[274] Those who seek private health insurance are those who can afford it and can qualify for it. They will be the more advantaged members of society. They are differentiated from the general population, not by their health problems, which are found in every group in society, but by their income status. We share the view of Dickson C.J. that the *Canadian Charter* should not become an instrument to be used by the wealthy to "roll back" the benefits of a legislative scheme that helps the poorer members of society. He observed in *Edwards Books*, at p. 779:

> In interpreting and applying the *Charter* I believe that the courts must be cautious to ensure that it does not simply become an instrument of better situated individuals to roll back legislation which has as its object the improvement of the condition of less advantaged persons.

The concern, of course, is that once the health needs of the wealthier members of society are looked after in the "upper tier," they will have less incentive to continue to pressure the government for improvements to the public system as a whole.

[275] The comments of Dickson C.J. are even more relevant to the *Quebec Charter* given its broad scope and its potential application to a wide range of private relationships.

[276] This is not a case, in our view, where the onus of proof determines the outcome. The evidence amply supports the validity of the prohibition of private insurance under the *Quebec Charter*. The objectives are compelling. A rational connection is demonstrated. The decision boils down to an application of the minimal impairment test. In respect of questions of social and economic policy, this test leaves a substantial margin of appreciation to the Quebec legislature. Designing, financing and operating the public health system of a modern democratic society like Quebec remains a challenging task. It calls for difficult choices. In the end, we find that the choice made a generation ago by the National Assembly of Quebec remains within the range of options that are justifiable under s. 9.1. Shifting the design of the health system to the courts is not a wise choice. . . .

[278] The evidence reviewed above establishes that the impugned provisions were part of a system which is mindful and protective of the interests of all, not only of some.

[279] We would dismiss the appeal.

Health Services and Support—Facilities Subsector Bargaining Assn. v. British Columbia, 2007

*H*ealth Services and Support—Facilities Subsector Bargaining Assn. v. British Columbia is the most explicit reversal of an earlier Supreme Court *Charter* ruling to date. The question for the Court was whether freedom of association in the *Charter* protects collective bargaining for unions. At issue was controversial legislation that granted health care employers absolute power to contract out of collective agreements, and to do so without consultation or giving notice as previously required. The legislation was motivated by governmental concerns about the increasing costs of the public health care system, which were said to have increased in the period from 1991 to 2001 at a rate three times that of the provincial economy. The B.C. government defended this legislation as necessary "to respond to growing demands on services, to reduce structural barriers to patient care, and to improve planning and accountability, so as to achieve long term sustainability."

In its first discussion on whether the *Charter* protects collective bargaining, the Supreme Court decisively rejected this possibility. This occurred in a 1987 ruling[1] in which the majority interpreted freedom of association narrowly, as merely a right to create associations without protection for the activities of the association. It also rejected the idea that freedom of association should be interpreted with consideration for the activities of labour unions, indicating that this right should not be interpreted any differently for organized labour than for any other organization of a political, religious, or social nature. An interesting part of the explanation for the Court's earlier refusal to recognize *Charter* protection for collective bargaining was concern about interfering with legislative responsibilities, particularly on matters for which the Court has no special expertise. In an opinion concurring with the majority ruling, Justice McIntyre explained that if the Court were to recognize a right to collective bargaining, it would then be required to assess any governmental decision to prohibit strikes or lockouts that involve issues that are not "amenable to principled resolution" and therefore permit "no clearly correct answers." He suggested the Court could and should avoid this problem. It could do so, he indicated, by refusing to recognize that a *Charter* right exists, which would ensure that issues of a nature "peculiarly apposite to the function of the Legislature" remain the responsibility of the legislature.[2]

This suggestion that the Court constrain its interpretation of rights to avoid having to render decisions for which no obviously correct answer exists has not generally characterized the Court's approach to the *Charter*. In fact, in *Health Services and Support*, the Court explicitly rejected the idea that it is appropriate to exercise deference to the legislature simply because the subject matter involves the complex issue of regulating labour relations. In this ruling, decided 20 years after the *Alberta Reference*,[3] the Court suggested that its earlier

---

1   *Reference re Public Service Employee Relations Act (Alta.)*, [1987] 1 S.C.R. 313 ("*Alberta Labour Reference*").

2   *Ibid.* at para. 184.

3   *Supra* note 1.

denial of *Charter* protection for collective bargaining can "no longer stand" and that the Court's earlier handling of the relevant issues does not "withstand principled scrutiny." In explaining this clear reversal, the Court explicitly repudiated the following assumptions on which this earlier denial that the *Charter* protects collective bargaining was based: that the rights to strike and to bargain collectively are "modern rights" created by legislation, not "fundamental freedoms"; that recognition of a right to collective bargaining is inconsistent with the principle of judicial restraint in interfering with government regulation of labour relations; and that freedom of association protects only those activities performable by an individual.

Despite the Court's ruling that freedom of association protects collective bargaining, the Court made it clear in *Health Services and Support* that protection for collective bargaining is a limited right. It is a right to a process, not a guarantee of a certain substantive or economic outcome; it is a right to a general process of collective bargaining, not to a particular model of labour relations, nor to a specific bargaining method; and, more important, *Charter* protection is relevant only when interference with this right is so substantial that it undermines the very process that enables workers to pursue these objectives by engaging in meaningful negotiations with the employer.

The ruling came as a considerable surprise to many critics of the *Charter*, particularly those on the left who believed that jurisprudence on the *Charter* had become hostile to the interests of organized labour and who were doubtful that this would soon change. Nevertheless, six years before the *Health Services* decision, the Court had hinted that it was prepared to reassess its narrow interpretation of freedom of association. This occurred in the 2001 ruling, *Dunmore v. Ontario (Attorney General)*,[4] where the Court rejected the earlier view that freedom of association applies only to activities capable of performance by individuals, and left room to recognize a right to collective bargaining in future cases. At issue in *Dunmore* was the exclusion of agricultural workers from Ontario's labour relations legislation, which the Court ruled was unconstitutional.

What remains unclear is whether the Court will also rule that the *Charter* protects the right of organized labour groups to strike and if so, what grounds might be considered a justification for limiting this right. ⌒

---

4   [2001] 3 S.C.R. 1016, 2001 SCC 94.

HEALTH SERVICES AND SUPPORT—
FACILITIES SUBSECTOR BARGAINING
ASSN. v. BRITISH COLUMBIA
2007 SCC 27

Hearing: February 8, 2006; Judgment: June 8, 2007.

Present: McLachlin C.J. and Bastarache, Binnie, LeBel,
Deschamps, Fish, and Abella JJ.

Interveners: Attorney General of Ontario, Attorney General of
New Brunswick, Attorney General of Alberta, Confederation of
National Trade Unions, Canadian Labour Congress, Michael J.
Fraser on his own behalf and on behalf of United Food and
Commercial Workers Union Canada, and British Columbia
Teachers' Federation.

The judgment of McLachlin C.J. and Bastarache, Binnie,
LeBel, Fish, and Abella JJ. was delivered by

THE CHIEF JUSTICE AND LEBEL J.:

I. Introduction

A. Overview

[1] The appellants challenge the constitutional validity of
Part 2 of the *Health and Social Services Delivery Improvement
Act*, S.B.C. 2002, c. 2 ("Act"), as violative of the *Canadian
Charter of Rights and Freedoms* guarantees of freedom of asso-
ciation (s. 2(*d*)) and equality (s. 15).

[2] We conclude that the s. 2(*d*) guarantee of freedom of
association protects the capacity of members of labour unions
to engage in collective bargaining on workplace issues. While
some of the impugned provisions of the Act comply with this
guarantee, ss. 6(2), 6(4) and 9 breach it and have not been
shown to be justified under s. 1 of the *Charter*. We further
conclude that the Act does not violate the right to equal treatment under s. 15 of the *Charter*. . . .

B. The Background

[3] This case requires the Court to balance the need for
governments to deliver essential social services effectively with
the need to recognize the *Charter* rights of employees affected
by such legislation, who were working for health and social
service employers. The respondent government characterizes
the impugned legislation as a crucial element of its response
to a pressing health care crisis, necessary and important to the
well-being of British Columbians. The appellants, unions and
individual workers representing some of the subsectors of the
health care sector affected by the legislation, by contrast, see
the Act as an affront to the fundamental rights of employees
and union members under the *Charter*, which they under-

stand as including a collective right to pursue fundamental
workplace goals through collective bargaining in respect of
terms of employment.

C. The Act

[4] The Act was adopted as a response to challenges facing
British Columbia's health care system. Demand for health care
and the cost of providing needed health care services had been
increasing significantly for years. For example, in the period
from 1991 to 2001, the growth rate of health care costs in
British Columbia was three times that of the provincial economy. As a result, the government of British Columbia found
itself struggling to provide health care services to its citizens.
The government characterized the state of affairs in 2001 as
a "crisis of sustainability" in the health care system. . . .

[5] The goals of the Act were to reduce costs and to facilitate the efficient management of the workforce in the health
care sector. Not wishing to decrease employees' wages, the
government attempted to achieve these goals in more sustainable ways. According to the government, the Act was designed
in particular to focus on permitting health care employers to
reorganize the administration of the labour force and on making operational changes to enhance management's ability to
restructure service delivery (see British Columbia, *Debates of
the Legislative Assembly*, 2nd Sess., 37th Parl., vol. 2, No. 28,
January 25, 2002, at p. 865).

[6] The Act was quickly passed. It came into force three
days after receiving a first reading as Bill 29 before the British
Columbia legislature.

[7] There was no meaningful consultation with unions
before it became law. The government was aware that some
of the areas affected by Bill 29 were of great concern to the
unions and had expressed a willingness to consult. However,
in the end, consultation was minimal. . . .

[8] In British Columbia, the collective bargaining structure in the health services is sectoral. Thus, the Act affects
labour relations between "health sector employers" and their
unionized employees. A "health sector employer," as defined
under the Act, is a member of the Health Employers Association of British Columbia ("HEABC") established under s. 6
of the *Public Sector Employers Act*, R.S.B.C. 1996, c. 384, and
whose employees are unionized (s. 3 of the Act). The HEABC
is an employers' association accredited to act as the representative of its members in the bargaining process with health
sector employees. Members of the HEABC are hospitals and
other employers designated by regulation, including employers in the health sector receiving a substantial amount of
funding from the Ministry of Health (A.R., at p. 212). Therefore, while the Act applies mainly to public sector employers,
it also applies to some private sector employers.

[9] The appellants in the present case are unions and members of the unions representing the nurses, facilities or community subsectors—groups affected by the legislation. Although they were affected by the legislation, other groups like residents and paramedical professionals did not join the litigation.

[10] Only Part 2 of the Act is at issue in the current appeal (see Appendix). It introduced changes to transfers and multi-worksite assignment rights (ss. 4 and 5), contracting out (s. 6), the status of employees under contracting-out arrangements (s. 6), job security programs (ss. 7 and 8), and layoffs and bumping rights (s. 9).

[11] Part 2 gave health care employers greater flexibility to organize their relations with their employees as they see fit, and in some cases, to do so in ways that would not have been permissible under existing collective agreements and without adhering to requirements of consultation and notice that would otherwise obtain. It invalidated important provisions of collective agreements then in force, and effectively precluded meaningful collective bargaining on a number of specific issues. Section 10 invalidated any part of a collective agreement, past or future, which was inconsistent with Part 2, and any collective agreement purporting to modify these restrictions. In the words of the Act, s. 10: "Part [2] prevails over collective agreements." It is not open to the employees (or the employer) to contract out of Part 2 or to rely on a collective agreement inconsistent with Part 2.

[12] ... [W]hile some of the changes were relatively innocuous administrative changes, others had profound effects on the employees and their ability to negotiate workplace matters of great concern to them. ...

III. Analysis

A. Section 2(d) of the Charter

[19] At issue in the present appeal is whether the guarantee of freedom of association in s. 2(*d*) of the *Charter* protects collective bargaining rights. We conclude that s. 2(*d*) of the *Charter* protects the capacity of members of labour unions to engage, in association, in collective bargaining on fundamental workplace issues. This protection does not cover all aspects of "collective bargaining," as that term is understood in the statutory labour relations regimes that are in place across the country. Nor does it ensure a particular outcome in a labour dispute, or guarantee access to any particular statutory regime. What is protected is simply the right of employees to associate in a process of collective action to achieve workplace goals. If the government substantially interferes with that right, it violates s. 2(*d*) of the *Charter*: *Dunmore*. We note that the present case does not concern the right to strike, which was considered in earlier litigation on the scope of the guarantee of freedom of association.

[20] Our conclusion that s. 2(*d*) of the *Charter* protects a process of collective bargaining rests on four propositions. First, a review of the s. 2(*d*) jurisprudence of this Court reveals that the reasons evoked in the past for holding that the guarantee of freedom of association does not extend to collective bargaining can no longer stand. Second, an interpretation of s. 2(*d*) that precludes collective bargaining from its ambit is inconsistent with Canada's historic recognition of the importance of collective bargaining to freedom of association. Third, collective bargaining is an integral component of freedom of association in international law, which may inform the interpretation of *Charter* guarantees. Finally, interpreting s. 2(*d*) as including a right to collective bargaining is consistent with, and indeed, promotes, other *Charter* rights, freedoms and values. ...

[21] ... [I]n applying our analysis to the facts of the case, we find provisions of the Act to be in violation of s. 2(*d*) and not justified by s. 1 of the *Charter*.

(1) Reasons for Excluding Collective Bargaining from Section 2(d) in the Past Require Reconsideration

[22] In earlier decisions, the majority view in the Supreme Court of Canada was that the guarantee of freedom of association did not extend to collective bargaining. *Dunmore* opened the door to reconsideration of that view. We conclude that the grounds advanced in the earlier decisions for the exclusion of collective bargaining from the *Charter*'s protection of freedom of association do not withstand principled scrutiny and should be rejected.

[23] The first cases dealing squarely with the issue of whether collective bargaining is protected under s. 2(*d*) of the *Charter* were a group of three concurrently released appeals known as the labour "trilogy": *Reference re Public Service Employee Relations Act (Alta.)*, [1987] 1 S.C.R. 313 ("*Alberta Reference*"), *PSAC v. Canada*, [1987] 1 S.C.R. 424, and *RWDSU v. Saskatchewan*, [1987] 1 S.C.R. 460. The main reasons were delivered in the *Alberta Reference*, a case involving compulsory arbitration to resolve impasses in collective bargaining and a prohibition on strikes. Of the six justices participating in the case, three held that collective bargaining was not protected by s. 2(*d*); four held that strike activity was not protected. The next case to deal with the issue was *Professional Institute of the Public Service of Canada v. Northwest Territories (Commissioner)*, [1990] 2 S.C.R. 367 ("*PIPSC*"), in which the government of the Northwest Territories refused to enact legislation required in order for the PIPSC union to bargain collectively on behalf of nurses. A majority of four held that collective bargaining was not protected by s. 2(*d*).

[24] In these cases, different members of the majorities put forth five main reasons in support of the contention that collective bargaining does not fall within s. 2(*d*)'s protection.

[25] The first suggested reason was that the rights to strike and to bargain collectively are "modern rights" created by legislation, not "fundamental freedoms" (*Alberta Reference*, *per* Le Dain J., writing on behalf of himself, Beetz and La Forest JJ., at p. 391). The difficulty with this argument is that it fails to recognize the history of labour relations in Canada. . . . [T]he fundamental importance of collective bargaining to labour relations was the very reason for its incorporation into statute. Legislatures throughout Canada have historically viewed collective bargaining rights as sufficiently important to immunize them from potential interference. The statutes they passed did not create the right to bargain collectively. Rather, they afforded it protection. There is nothing in the statutory entrenchment of collective bargaining that detracts from its fundamental nature.

[26] The second suggested reason was that recognition of a right to collective bargaining would go against the principle of judicial restraint in interfering with government regulation of labour relations (*Alberta Reference*, at p. 391). The regulation of labour relations, it is suggested, involves policy decisions best left to government. This argument again fails to recognize the fact that worker organizations historically had the right to bargain collectively outside statutory regimes and takes an overbroad view of judicial deference. It may well be appropriate for judges to defer to legislatures on policy matters expressed in particular laws. But to declare a judicial "no go" zone for an entire right on the ground that it may involve the courts in policy matters is to push deference too far. Policy itself should reflect *Charter* rights and values.

[27] The third suggested reason for excluding collective bargaining from s. 2(*d*) of the *Charter* rested on the view that freedom of association protects only those activities performable by an individual (see *PIPSC*, *per* L'Heureux-Dubé and Sopinka JJ.). . . .

[28] This narrow focus on individual activities has been overtaken by *Dunmore*, where this Court rejected the notion that freedom of association applies only to activities capable of performance by individuals. . . .

[29] The fourth reason advanced for excluding collective bargaining rights from s. 2(*d*) was the suggestion of L'Heureux-Dubé J. that s. 2(*d*) was not intended to protect the "objects" or goals of an association (see *PIPSC*, at pp. 391-93). This argument overlooks the fact that it will always be possible to characterize the pursuit of a particular activity in concert with others as the "object" of that association. Recasting collective bargaining as an "object" begs the question of whether or not the activity is worthy of constitutional protection. L'Heureux-Dubé J.'s underlying concern—that the *Charter* not be used to protect the substantive outcomes of any and all associations—is a valid one. However, "collective bargaining" as a procedure has always been distinguishable from its final out-comes (e.g., the results of the bargaining process, which may be reflected in a collective agreement). . . . In our view, it is entirely possible to protect the "procedure" known as collective bargaining without mandating constitutional protection for the fruits of that bargaining process. Thus, the characterization of collective bargaining as an association's "object" does not provide a principled reason to deny it constitutional protection.

[30] An overarching concern is that the majority judgments in the *Alberta Reference* and *PIPSC* adopted a decontextualized approach to defining the scope of freedom of association, in contrast to the purposive approach taken to other *Charter* guarantees. The result was to forestall inquiry into the purpose of that *Charter* guarantee. The generic approach of the earlier decisions to s. 2(*d*) ignored differences between organizations. Whatever the organization—be it trade union or book club—its freedoms were treated as identical. The unfortunate effect was to overlook the importance of collective bargaining—both historically and currently—to the exercise of freedom of association in labour relations.

[31] We conclude that the reasons provided by the majorities in the *Alberta Reference* and *PIPSC* should not bar reconsideration of the question of whether s. 2(*d*) applies to collective bargaining. This is manifestly the case since this Court's decision in *Dunmore*, which struck down a statute that effectively prohibited farm workers from engaging in collective bargaining by denying them access to the Province's labour relations regime, as violating of s. 2(*d*) of the *Charter*. *Dunmore* clarified three developing aspects of the law: what constitutes interference with the "associational aspect" of an activity; the need for a contextual approach to freedom of association; and the recognition that s. 2(*d*) can impose positive obligations on government. . . .

[36] In summary, a review of the jurisprudence leads to the conclusion that the holdings in the *Alberta Reference* and *PIPSC* excluding collective bargaining from the scope of s. 2(*d*) can no longer stand. None of the reasons provided by the majorities in those cases survive scrutiny, and the rationale for excluding inherently collective activities from s. 2(*d*)'s protection has been overtaken by *Dunmore*.

[37] Our rejection of the arguments previously used to exclude collective bargaining from s. 2(*d*) leads us to a reassessment of that issue, discussed below.

(2) Collective Bargaining Falls Within the Scope of Section 2(d) of the Charter

[38] The question is whether the s. 2(*d*) guarantee of freedom of association extends to the right of employees to join together in a union to negotiate with employers on workplace issues or terms of employment—a process described broadly as collective bargaining.

[39] The general purpose of the *Charter* guarantees and the language of s. 2(*d*) are consistent with at least a measure of protection for collective bargaining. The language of s. 2(*d*) is cast in broad terms and devoid of limitations. However, this is not conclusive. To answer the question before us, we must consider the history of collective bargaining in Canada, collective bargaining in relation to freedom of association in the larger international context, and whether *Charter* values favour an interpretation of s. 2(*d*) that protects a process of collective bargaining. . . .

[41] The respondent argues that the right to collective bargaining is of recent origin and is merely a creature of statute. This assertion may be true if collective bargaining is equated solely to the framework of rights of representation and collective bargaining now recognized under federal and provincial labour codes. However, the origin of a right to collective bargaining in the sense given to it in the present case (i.e., a procedural right to bargain collectively on conditions of employment), precedes the adoption of the present system of labour relations in the 1940s. The history of collective bargaining in Canada reveals that long before the present statutory labour regimes were put in place, collective bargaining was recognized as a fundamental aspect of Canadian society. This is the context against which the scope of the s. 2(*d*) must be considered.

[42] Canadian labour history can be summarized by borrowing words from the 1968 *Report of the Task Force on Labour Relations*. As society entered into the industrialized era, "workers began to join unions and to engage in collective bargaining with their employers. Although employers resisted this development with all the resources at their command, it eventually became apparent that unions and collective bargaining were natural concomitants of a mixed enterprise economy. The state then assumed the task of establishing a framework of rights and responsibilities within which management and organized labour were to conduct their relations" (Task Force on Labour Relations, *Canadian Industrial Relations: The Report of Task Force on Labour Relations* (1968) ("Woods Report"), at p. 13).

[43] Canadian labour law traces its roots to various legal systems, most importantly to British and American law. Prior to the 1940s, British law had a significant influence on the development of our labour law. American law became an influential force when the United States passed the *Wagner Act* in 1935. . . .

[44] The development of labour relations law in Canada may be divided into three major eras: repression, toleration and recognition. . . .

[47] From the beginning, the law was used as a tool to limit workers' rights to unionize. . . .

[51] A major shift in Canadian labour law took place in the aftermath of the Toronto Typographical Unions' strike that occurred in 1872. The strike by the Toronto typographers, inspired by the call for a nine-hour work day, led to numerous arrests and charges against the strikers for common law criminal conspiracy. At that time, Canada had not yet adopted legislation immunizing trade union members from criminal charges for conspiracy or restraint of trade. The criminal charges against the Toronto strikers raised public concern and revealed that Canada was behind the times—at least compared to Britain—on the issue of union protection and recognition.

[52] In consequence, Canada adopted its own legislation copied in part from the British *Trade Union Act* of 1871. The Canadian *Trade Unions Act* of 1872 "made it clear that no worker could be criminally prosecuted for conspiracy solely on the basis of attempting to influence the rate of wages, hours of labour, or other aspects of the work relation." . . . Through this legislative action, the Canadian Parliament recognized the value for the individual of collective actions in the context of labour relations. . . .

[53] By the beginning of the 1900s, the main criminal barriers to unionism in Canada had been brought down. Criminal law no longer prohibited employees from combining for the purposes of ameliorating their working conditions. . . . However, courts continued to apply common law doctrines to restrain union activities. . . . Moreover, nothing in the law required employers to recognize unions or to bargain collectively with them. Employers could simply ignore union demands and even refuse to hire union members. . . .

[54] While employers could refuse to recognize and bargain with unions, workers had recourse to an economic weapon: the powerful tool of calling a strike to force an employer to recognize a union and bargain collectively with it. The law gave both parties the ability to use economic weapons to attain their ends. Before the adoption of the modern statutory model of labour relations, the majority of strikes were motivated by the workers' desire to have an employer recognize a union and bargain collectively with it. . . .

[55] The first few decades of the 20th century saw Parliament's promotion of voluntary collective bargaining. The federal Parliament enacted a series of statutes to promote collective bargaining by conferring on the labour minister the power to impose conciliation on the parties in an attempt to bring them to compromise. . . . This model failed, mainly because employers had no real incentive to participate in the process. . . . In search of a better model, Canadian governments looked at what was happening in the United States.

[56] . . . In 1914, the American Congress immunized unions from the application of antitrust law and adopted a non-interventionist attitude in order to let workers and

employers use their respective economic powers to manage their own labour relations. However, the Depression and resulting industrial tension of the 1930s rendered the old laissez-faire model inappropriate. The result was the *Wagner Act*, which explicitly recognized the right of employees to belong to a trade union of their choice, free of employer coercion or interference, and imposed a duty upon employers to bargain in good faith with their employees' unions....

[58] By the end of the 1930s, most Canadian provinces had passed legislation incorporating the main objectives of the *Wagner Act.* ... However, it is Order in Council P.C. 1003, a regulation adopted by the federal government to rule labour relations in time of war, that firmly implemented the principles of the *Wagner Act* in Canada and triggered further development of provincial labour laws....

[60] P.C. 1003 was a compromise adopted to promote peaceful labour relations. On the one hand, it granted major protections to workers to organize without fear of unfair interference from the employers and guaranteed workers the right to bargain collectively in good faith with their employers without having to rely on strikes and other economic weapons. On the other hand, it provided employers with a measure of stability in their relations with their organized workers, without the spectre of intensive state intervention in the economy.... These elements of P.C. 1003 continue to guide our system of labour relations to this day....

[63] In summary, workers in Canada began forming collectives to bargain over working conditions with their employers as early as the 18th century. However, the common law cast a shadow over the rights of workers to act collectively. When Parliament first began recognizing workers' rights, trade unions had no express statutory right to negotiate collectively with employers. Employers could simply ignore them. However, workers used the powerful economic weapon of strikes to gradually force employers to recognize unions and to bargain collectively with them. By adopting the *Wagner Act* model, governments across Canada recognized the fundamental need for workers to participate in the regulation of their work environment. This legislation confirmed what the labour movement had been fighting for over centuries and what it had access to in the laissez-faire era through the use of strikes—the right to collective bargaining with employers....

[64] At the time the *Charter* was enacted in 1982, collective bargaining had a long tradition in Canada and was recognized as part of freedom of association in the labour context....

[66] Collective bargaining, despite early discouragement from the common law, has long been recognized in Canada. Indeed, historically, it emerges as the most significant collective activity through which freedom of association is expressed in the labour context. In our opinion, the concept of freedom of association under s. 2(*d*) of the *Charter* includes this notion of a procedural right to collective bargaining.

[67] This established Canadian right to collective bargaining was recognized in the Parliamentary hearings that took place before the adoption of the *Charter*. The acting Minister of Justice, Mr. Robert Kaplan, explained why he did not find necessary a proposed amendment to have the freedom to organize and bargain collectively expressly included under s. 2(*d*). These rights, he stated, were already implicitly recognized in the words "freedom of association." ...

[68] The protection enshrined in s. 2(*d*) of the *Charter* may properly be seen as the culmination of a historical movement towards the recognition of a procedural right to collective bargaining....

[The Court discussed Canada's adherence to international documents recognizing a right to collective bargaining, which it indicated supports the recognition of this right being included in section 2(*d*) of the *Charter*.]

(c) Charter Values Support Protecting a Process of Collective Bargaining Under Section 2(d)

[80] Protection for a process of collective bargaining within s. 2(*d*) is consistent with the *Charter*'s underlying values. The *Charter*, including s. 2(*d*) itself, should be interpreted in a way that maintains its underlying values and its internal coherence....

[81] Human dignity, equality, liberty, respect for the autonomy of the person and the enhancement of democracy are among the values that underlie the *Charter*: *R. v. Zundel*, [1992] 2 S.C.R. 731; *Corbiere v. Canada (Minister of Indian and Northern Affairs)*, [1999] 2 S.C.R. 203, at para. 100; *R. v. Oakes*, [1986] 1 S.C.R. 103. All of these values are complemented and indeed, promoted, by the protection of collective bargaining in s. 2(*d*) of the *Charter*.

[82] The right to bargain collectively with an employer enhances the human dignity, liberty and autonomy of workers by giving them the opportunity to influence the establishment of workplace rules and thereby gain some control over a major aspect of their lives, namely their work....

[84] Collective bargaining also enhances the *Charter* value of equality. One of the fundamental achievements of collective bargaining is to palliate the historical inequality between employers and employees....

[85] Finally, a constitutional right to collective bargaining is supported by the *Charter* value of enhancing democracy. Collective bargaining permits workers to achieve a form of workplace democracy and to ensure the rule of law in the workplace. Workers gain a voice to influence the establishment of rules that control a major aspect of their lives....

[86] We conclude that the protection of collective bargaining under s. 2(*d*) of the *Charter* is consistent with and supportive of the values underlying the *Charter* and the purposes of the *Charter* as a whole. Recognizing that workers have the right to bargain collectively as part of their freedom to associate reaffirms the values of dignity, personal autonomy, equality and democracy that are inherent in the *Charter*.

(3) Section 2(d) of the Charter and the Right to Collective Bargaining

[87] The preceding discussion leads to the conclusion that s. 2(*d*) should be understood as protecting the right of employees to associate for the purpose of advancing workplace goals through a process of collective bargaining. The next question is what this right entails for employees, for government employers subject to the *Charter* under s. 32, and for Parliament and provincial legislatures which adopt labour laws. . . .

[89] The scope of the right to bargain collectively ought to be defined bearing in mind the pronouncements of *Dunmore*, which stressed that s. 2(*d*) does not apply solely to individual action carried out in common, but also to associational activities themselves. The scope of the right properly reflects the history of collective bargaining and the international covenants entered into by Canada. Based on the principles developed in *Dunmore* and in this historical and international perspective, the constitutional right to collective bargaining concerns the protection of the ability of workers to engage in associational activities, and their capacity to act in common to reach shared goals related to workplace issues and terms of employment. In brief, the protected activity might be described as employees banding together to achieve particular work-related objectives. Section 2(*d*) does not guarantee the particular objectives sought through this associational activity. However, it guarantees the process through which those goals are pursued. It means that employees have the right to unite, to present demands to health sector employers collectively and to engage in discussions in an attempt to achieve workplace-related goals. Section 2(*d*) imposes corresponding duties on government employers to agree to meet and discuss with them. It also puts constraints on the exercise of legislative powers in respect of the right to collective bargaining, which we shall discuss below.

[90] Section 2(*d*) of the *Charter* does not protect all aspects of the associational activity of collective bargaining. It protects only against "substantial interference" with associational activity, in accordance with a test crafted in *Dunmore* by Bastarache J., which asked whether "excluding agricultural workers from a statutory labour relations regime, without expressly or intentionally prohibiting association, [can] constitute a substantial interference with freedom of association"

(para. 23). . . . It follows that the state must not substantially interfere with the ability of a union to exert meaningful influence over working conditions through a process of collective bargaining conducted in accordance with the duty to bargain in good faith. Thus the employees' right to collective bargaining imposes corresponding duties on the employer. It requires both employer and employees to meet and to bargain in good faith, in the pursuit of a common goal of peaceful and productive accommodation.

[91] The right to collective bargaining thus conceived is a limited right. First, as the right is to a process, it does not guarantee a certain substantive or economic outcome. Moreover, the right is to a general process of collective bargaining, not to a particular model of labour relations, nor to a specific bargaining method. . . . Finally, and most importantly, the interference, as *Dunmore* instructs, must be substantial—so substantial that it interferes not only with the attainment of the union members' objectives (which is not protected), but with the very process that enables them to pursue these objectives by engaging in meaningful negotiations with the employer.

[92] To constitute *substantial interference* with freedom of association, the intent or effect must seriously undercut or undermine the activity of workers joining together to pursue the common goals of negotiating workplace conditions and terms of employment with their employer that we call collective bargaining. Laws or actions that can be characterized as "union breaking" clearly meet this requirement. But less dramatic interference with the collective process may also suffice. In *Dunmore*, denying the union access to the labour laws of Ontario designed to support and give a voice to unions was enough. Acts of bad faith, or unilateral nullification of negotiated terms, without any process of meaningful discussion and consultation may also significantly undermine the process of collective bargaining. The inquiry in every case is contextual and fact-specific. The question in every case is whether the process of voluntary, good faith collective bargaining between employees and the employer has been, or is likely to be, significantly and adversely impacted.

[93] Generally speaking, determining whether a government measure affecting the protected process of collective bargaining amounts to substantial interference involves two inquiries. The first inquiry is into the importance of the matter affected to the process of collective bargaining, and more specifically, to the capacity of the union members to come together and pursue collective goals in concert. The second inquiry is into the manner in which the measure impacts on the collective right to good faith negotiation and consultation.

[94] Both inquiries are necessary. If the matters affected do not substantially impact on the process of collective bargaining,

the measure does not violate s. 2(*d*) and, indeed, the employer may be under no duty to discuss and consult. There will be no need to consider process issues. If, on the other hand, the changes substantially touch on collective bargaining, they will still not violate s. 2(*d*) if they preserve a process of consultation and good faith negotiation.

[95] Turning to the first inquiry, the essential question is whether the subject matter of a particular instance of collective bargaining is such that interfering with bargaining over that issue will affect the ability of unions to pursue common goals collectively. ... The more important the matter, the more likely that there is substantial interference with the s. 2(*d*) right. Conversely, the less important the matter to the capacity of union members to pursue collective goals, the less likely that there is substantial interference with the s. 2(*d*) right to collective bargaining.

[96] ... Laws or state actions that prevent or deny meaningful discussion and consultation about working conditions between employees and their employer may substantially interfere with the activity of collective bargaining, as may laws that unilaterally nullify significant negotiated terms in existing collective agreements. ...

[97] Where it is established that the measure impacts on subject matter important to collective bargaining and the capacity of the union members to come together and pursue common goals, the need for the second inquiry arises: does the legislative measure or government conduct in issue respect the fundamental precept of collective bargaining—the duty to consult and negotiate in good faith? If it does, there will be no violation of s. 2(*d*), even if the content of the measures might be seen as being of substantial importance to collective bargaining concerns, since the process confirms the associational right of collective bargaining. ...

[99] Consistent with this, the *Canada Labour Code* and legislation from all provinces impose on employers and unions the right and duty to bargain in good faith. ... The duty to bargain in good faith under labour codes is essentially procedural and does not dictate the content of any particular agreement achieved through collective bargaining. ...

[100] A basic element of the duty to bargain in good faith is the obligation to actually meet and to commit time to the process. ...

[101] The parties have a duty to engage in meaningful dialogue and they must be willing to exchange and explain their positions. They must make a reasonable effort to arrive at an acceptable contract. ...

[104] In principle, the duty to bargain in good faith does not inquire into the nature of the proposals made in the course of collective bargaining; the content is left to the bargaining forces of the parties. ... However, when the examination of the content of the bargaining shows hostility from one party toward the collective bargaining process, this will constitute a breach of the duty to bargain in good faith. In some circumstances, even though a party is participating in the bargaining, that party's proposals and positions may be "inflexible and intransigent to the point of endangering the very existence of collective bargaining" (*Royal Oak Mines*, at para. 46). ...

[107] In considering whether the legislative provisions impinge on the collective right to good faith negotiations and consultation, regard must be had for the circumstances surrounding their adoption. Situations of exigency and urgency may affect the content and the modalities of the duty to bargain in good faith. Different situations may demand different processes and timelines. Moreover, failure to comply with the duty to consult and bargain in good faith should not be lightly found, and should be clearly supported on the record. Nevertheless, there subsists a requirement that the provisions of the Act preserve the process of good faith consultation fundamental to collective bargaining. That is the bottom line.

[108] Even where a s. 2(*d*) violation is established, that is not the end of the matter; limitations of s. 2(*d*) may be justified under s. 1 of the *Charter*, as reasonable limits demonstrably justified in a free and democratic society. This may permit interference with the collective bargaining process on an exceptional and typically temporary basis, in situations, for example, involving essential services, vital state administration, clear deadlocks and national crisis.

[109] In summary, s. 2(*d*) may be breached by government legislation or conduct that substantially interferes with the collective bargaining process. Substantial interference must be determined contextually, on the facts of the case, having regard to the importance of the matter affected to the collective activity, and to the manner in which the government measure is accomplished. Important changes effected through a process of good faith negotiation may not violate s. 2(*d*). Conversely, less central matters may be changed more summarily, without violating s. 2(*d*). Only where the matter is both important to the process of collective bargaining, and has been imposed in violation of the duty of good faith negotiation, will s. 2(*d*) be breached.

(4) Application of the Law to the Facts at Bar

[110] ... Ultimately, we conclude that ss. 6(2), 6(4) and 9 of the Act are unconstitutional because they infringe the right to collective bargaining protected under s. 2(*d*) and cannot be saved under s. 1. The remainder of Part 2 of the Act (consisting of ss. 3, 4, 5, 7, 8 and 10) does not violate the right to collective bargaining and withstands constitutional scrutiny under s. 2(*d*). ...

(i) Does the Act Interfere with Collective Bargaining?

[113] Sections 4 to 10 of the Act have the potential to interfere with collective bargaining in two ways: first, by invalidating existing collective agreements and consequently undermining the past bargaining processes that formed the basis for these agreements; and second, by prohibiting provisions dealing with specified matters in future collective agreements and thereby undermining future collective bargaining over those matters. Future restrictions on the content of collective agreements constitute an interference with collective bargaining because there can be no real dialogue over terms and conditions that can never be enacted as part of the collective agreement.

[114] We pause to reiterate briefly that the right to bargain collectively protects not just the act of making representations, but also the right of employees to have their views heard in the context of a meaningful process of consultation and discussion. This rebuts arguments made by the respondent that the Act does not interfere with collective bargaining because it does not explicitly prohibit health care employees from making collective representations. While the language of the Act does not technically prohibit collective representations to an employer, the right to collective bargaining cannot be reduced to a mere right to make representations. The necessary implication of the Act is that prohibited matters cannot be adopted into a valid collective agreement, with the result that the process of collective bargaining becomes meaningless with respect to them. This constitutes interference with collective bargaining. . . .

[116] Sections 4 and 5 deal with transfer and reassignment of employees. Their effect was summarized by Garson J. at trial:

> Sections 4 and 5 of [the Act] give health sector employers the right to reorganize the delivery of their services. Pursuant to these sections, employers have the right to transfer functions, services and employees to another health sector employer or within a worksite. The Regulation sets out employee transfer rights and obligations. For example employees must not be transferred outside of their geographic location without their consent. Employees who decline transfers in such circumstances are entitled to lay-off notice and the limited bumping rights available under the Act. Employees who decline transfers within their geographic region, however, will be deemed to have resigned 30 days after the refusal. [para. 38]

. . . [119] . . . [T]he effect of ss. 4 and 5, in conjunction with s. 10, is to render *future* collective bargaining over transfers and reassignments largely meaningless, since collective bargaining cannot alter the employer's right to make transfers

and reassignments. Section 10 of the Act would render void any terms inconsistent with ss. 4 and 5. Because it is meaningless to bargain over an issue which cannot ever be included in a collective agreement, ss. 4 and 5, considered together with s. 10, interfere with future collective bargaining. . . .

[120] Section 6(2) gives the employer increased power to contract out non-clinical services. . . . The effect of s. 6(2), together with s. 10, is to invalidate these provisions in prior collective agreements. Further, s. 6(4), in conjunction with s. 10, invalidates any provision of a collective agreement that requires an employer to consult with a trade union prior to contracting outside the bargaining unit. For example, s. 17.12 of the Facilities Subsector Collective Agreement, which limits the ways in which the employer can contract out, is made void by ss. 6(4) and 10.

[121] The combined effect of ss. 6(2), 6(4) and 10 is to forbid the incorporation into future collective agreements of provisions protecting employees from contracting out, or the inclusion of a provision requiring the employer to consult with the union. . . . The prohibition both repudiates past collective bargaining relating to the issue of contracting out and makes future collective bargaining over this issue meaningless. It follows that ss. 6(2) and 6(4) have the effect of interfering with collective bargaining. . . .

[127] Section 9 made collective bargaining over specified aspects of layoff and bumping meaningless and also invalidated parts of collective agreements dealing with these issues, up to December 31, 2005. This constituted interference with both past and future collective bargaining, albeit an interference limited to the period between the enactment of the Act and December 31, 2005.

[128] We conclude that ss. 4, 5, 6(2), 6(4) and 9, in conjunction with s. 10, interfere with the process of collective bargaining, either by disregarding past processes of collective bargaining, by pre-emptively undermining future processes of collective bargaining, or both. This requires us to determine whether these changes substantially interfere with the associational right of the employees to engage in collective bargaining on workplace matters and terms of employment.

(ii) Was the Interference Substantial, so as to Constitute a Breach of Freedom of Association?

[129] To amount to a breach of the s. 2(*d*) freedom of association, the interference with collective bargaining must compromise the essential integrity of the process of collective bargaining protected by s. 2(*d*). Two inquiries are relevant here. First, substantial interference is more likely to be found in measures impacting matters central to the freedom of association of workers, and to the capacity of their associations (the unions) to achieve common goals by working in concert.

This suggests an inquiry into the nature of the affected right. Second, the manner in which the right is curtailed may affect its impact on the process of collective bargaining and ultimately freedom of association. To this end, we must inquire into the process by which the changes were made and how they impact on the voluntary good faith underpinning of collective bargaining. Even where a matter is of central importance to the associational right, if the change has been made through a process of good faith consultation it is unlikely to have adversely affected the employees' right to collective bargaining. Both inquiries, as discussed earlier, are essential.

1. The Importance of the Provisions

[130] The provisions dealing with contracting out (ss. 6(2) and 6(4)), layoffs (ss. 9(a), 9(b) and 9(c)) and bumping (s. 9(d)) deal with matters central to the freedom of association. Restrictions in collective agreements limiting the employer's discretion to lay off employees affect the employees' capacity to retain secure employment, one of the most essential protections provided to workers by their union. Similarly, limits in collective agreements on the management rights of employers to contract out allow workers to gain employment security. Finally, bumping rights are an integral part of the seniority system usually established under collective agreements, which is a protection of significant importance to the union.... Viewing the Act's interference with these essential rights in the context of the case as a whole, we conclude that its interference with collective bargaining over matters pertaining to contracting out, layoff conditions and bumping constitutes substantial interference with the s. 2(*d*) right of freedom of association.

[131] The same cannot be said of the transfers and reassignments covered under ss. 4 and 5 of the Act. These provisions, as discussed above, are concerned with relatively minor modifications to in-place schemes for transferring and reassigning employees. Significant protections remained in place. It is true that the Act took these issues off the collective bargaining table for the future. However, on balance ss. 4 and 5 cannot be said to amount to a substantial interference with the union's ability to engage in collective bargaining so as to attract the protection under s. 2(*d*) of the *Charter*.

2. The Process of Interference with Collective Bargaining Rights

[132] Having concluded that the subject matter of ss. 6(2), 6(4) and 9 of the Act is of central importance to the unions and their ability to carry on collective bargaining, we must now consider whether those provisions preserve the processes of collective bargaining. Together, these two inquiries will permit us to assess whether the law at issue here constitutes

significant interference with the collective aspect of freedom of association, which *Dunmore* recognized....

[134] It is true that the government was facing a situation of exigency. It was determined to come to grips with the spiralling cost of health care in British Columbia. This determination was fuelled by the laudable desire to provide quality health services to the people of British Columbia. Concerns such as these must be taken into account in assessing whether the measures adopted disregard the fundamental s. 2(*d*) obligation to preserve the processes of good faith negotiation and consultation with unions.

[135] The difficulty, however, is that the measures adopted by the government constitute a virtual denial of the s. 2(*d*) right to a process of good faith bargaining and consultation. The absolute prohibition on contracting out in s. 6(2), as discussed, eliminates any possibility of consultation. Section 6(4) puts the nail in the coffin of consultation by making void any provisions in a collective agreement imposing a requirement to consult before contracting out. Section 9, in like fashion, effectively precludes consultation with the union prior to laying off or bumping.

[136] We conclude that ss. 6(2), 6(4) and 9 of the legislation constitute a significant interference with the right to bargain collectively and hence violate s. 2(*d*) of the *Charter*. The remaining issue is whether these infringements can be saved under s. 1 of the *Charter*, as limits that are reasonable and justifiable in a free and democratic society.

(b) Are the Violations of Section 2(d) Justified Under Section 1?

... [140] In this case, the infringement of the appellants' right to bargain collectively is unquestionably prescribed by law, since the interference with collective bargaining is set out in legislation. The question is whether the remaining elements of the *Oakes* test are made out, such that the law is a reasonable limit on the appellants' right to collective bargaining under s. 2(*d*).

[141] We find that the intrusions on collective bargaining represented by ss. 6(2), 6(4) and 9 are not minimally impairing, and therefore cannot be saved as a reasonable and justifiable limit in a free and democratic society....

[143] The government set out its objectives for enacting the Act as follows:

> The objective of the *Act* is to improve the delivery of health care services by enabling health authorities to focus resources on the delivery of clinical services, by enhancing the ability of health employers and authorities to respond quickly and effectively to changing circumstances, and by enhancing the accountability of decision-makers in public health care....

[144] These are pressing and substantial objectives. We agree with the respondent that the health care crisis in British Columbia is an important contextual factor in support of the conclusion that these objectives are pressing and substantial. ...

[148] The second stage of the *Oakes* analysis requires the government to establish that there is a rational connection between the pressing and substantial objective and the means chosen by the government to achieve the objective. In other words, the government must establish, on the balance of probabilities, that the means adopted in the Act are rationally connected to achieving its pressing and substantial objectives. ...

[149] ... Although the evidence does not conclusively establish that the means adopted by the Act achieve the government's objectives, it is at least logical and reasonable to conclude so. We therefore move to the determinative inquiry of minimal impairment. ...

[150] ... The government need not pursue the least drastic means of achieving its objective. Rather, a law will meet the requirements of the third stage of the *Oakes* test so long as the legislation "falls within a range of reasonable alternatives" which could be used to pursue the pressing and substantial objective (*RJR-MacDonald Inc. v. Canada (Attorney General)*, [1995] 3 S.C.R. 199, at para. 160).

[151] We conclude that the requirement of minimal impairment is not made out in this case. The government provides no evidence to support a conclusion that the impairment was minimal. It contents itself with an assertion of its legislative goal—"to enhance management flexibility and accountability in order to make the health care system sustainable over the long term,"—adding that "the *Act* is a measured, reasonable, and effective response to this challenge, and ... satisfies the minimal impairment requirement" (R.F., at para. 147). In the absence of supportive evidence, we are unable to conclude that the requirement of minimal impairment is made out in this case.

[152] The provisions at issue bear little evidence of a search for a minimally impairing solution to the problem the government sought to address.

[153] Section 6(2) forbids any provision "that in any manner restricts, limits or regulates the right of a health sector employer to contract outside of the collective agreement." It gives the employers absolute power to contract out of collective agreements. There is no need or incentive to consult with the union or the employees before sending the work they normally perform to an outside contractor. To forbid any contracting out clause completely and unconditionally strikes us as not minimally impairing. A more refined provision, for example, permitting contracting out after meaningful consultation with the union, might be envisaged.

[154] Section 6(4) makes void a provision in a collective agreement to consult before contracting out. The bite of s. 6(4) is arguably small; given the employer's absolute power to contract out under s. 6(2), there would appear to be no reason for an employer to agree to such a clause in any event. However, insofar as it hammers home the policy of no consultation under any circumstances, it can scarcely be described as suggesting a search for a solution that preserves collective bargaining rights as much as possible, given the legislature's goal.

[155] Section 9 evinces a similar disregard for the duty to consult the union, in this case before making changes to the collective agreement's layoff and bumping rules. It is true that s. 9 was temporally limited, being in force only to December 31, 2005. However, this is scant comfort to employees who may have been laid off or bumped before this date, without the benefit of a union to represent them on the issue.

[156] An examination of the record as to alternatives considered by the government reinforces the conclusion that the impairment in this case did not fall within the range of reasonable alternatives available to the government in achieving its pressing and substantial objective of improving health care delivery. The record discloses no consideration by the government of whether it could reach its goal by less intrusive measures, and virtually no consultation with unions on the matter.

[157] Legislators are not bound to consult with affected parties before passing legislation. On the other hand, it may be useful to consider, in the course of the s. 1 justification analysis, whether the government considered other options or engaged consultation with the affected parties, in choosing to adopt its preferred approach. The Court has looked at pre-legislative considerations in the past in the context of minimal impairment. This is simply evidence going to whether other options, in a range of possible options, were explored.

[158] In this case, the only evidence presented by the government, including the sealed evidence, confirmed that a range of options were on the table. One was chosen. The government presented no evidence as to why this particular solution was chosen and why there was no consultation with the unions about the range of options open to it. ...

[160] This was an important and significant piece of labour legislation. It had the potential to affect the rights of employees dramatically and unusually. Yet it was adopted with full knowledge that the unions were strongly opposed to many of the provisions, and without consideration of alternative ways to achieve the government objective, and without explanation of the government's choices.

[161] We conclude that the government has not shown that the Act minimally impaired the employees' s. 2(*d*) right

of collective bargaining. It is unnecessary to consider the proportionality between the pressing and substantial government objectives and the means adopted by the law to achieve these objectives. We find that the offending provisions of the Act (ss. 6(2), 6(4) and 9) cannot be justified as reasonable limits under s. 1 of the *Charter* and are therefore unconstitutional.

[The majority concluded that the Act does not violate section 15 equality rights.]

The following are the reasons delivered by

DESCHAMPS J.:

[170] ... I part company with my colleagues over their analysis relating to both the infringement of s. 2(*d*) and the justification of the infringement under s. 1 of the *Charter*.

[171] The interpretation that the Court is now giving to s. 2(*d*) of the *Charter* is a major step forward in the recognition of collective activities. However, the importance of this advance should not overshadow the justification analysis under s. 1 of the *Charter*. . . . I find that ss. 4, 5, 6(2), 6(4) and 9 of the Act infringe s. 2(*d*) of the *Charter*, but in my view only s. 6(4) of the Act is not demonstrably justified in a free and democratic society. . . .

[175] I have concerns with the majority's test for determining whether a government measure amounts to an infringement of s. 2(*d*). According to my colleagues, the test involves two inquiries, the first into the importance of the matter for the union and the employees, and the second into the impact of the measure on the collective right to good faith negotiation and consultation. . . .

[176] The majority focus on "substantial" interference with a collective bargaining process and purport to do so on the basis of this Court's decision in *Dunmore v. Ontario (Attorney General)*, [2001] 3 S.C.R. 1016, 2001 SCC 94 (majority reasons at paras. 19, 35 and 90). However, the "substantial interference" standard cannot be adopted in this case simply because it was mentioned in *Dunmore*. . . .

[177] Since the present appeal does not involve a claim of underinclusive legislation, but an obligation that the state not interfere in a collective bargaining process, I cannot agree with imposing a "substantial interference" standard.

[178] Moreover, the first inquiry of the majority's test ("the importance of the matter affected to the process of collective bargaining" (para. 93)) is focused on the substance of the workplace issue rather than on interference with the collective bargaining process, which is what the constitutionally guaranteed right protects against. Since there is no constitutional protection for the substantive outcome of a collective bargaining process, I consider that the matter affected is not the threshold issue when a claim is being evaluated under

s. 2(*d*) of the *Charter*. Rather, the primary focus of the inquiry should be whether the legislative measures infringe the ability of workers to act in common in relation to workplace issues. . . . I remain unconvinced that the importance of the workplace issue should "play a key role" in the infringement analysis.

[179] With respect to the second inquiry ("the manner in which the measure impacts on the collective right to good faith negotiation and consultation" (para. 93)), I am concerned with the way this test is restated and applied in the majority's reasons. For example, rather than focussing on the impact on the right, the majority refer to "the manner in which the government measure is accomplished" (para. 109), "the process by which the measure was implemented" (para. 112) and "the process by which the changes were made" (para. 129). With respect, these formulations imply a duty to consult that is inconsistent with the proposition that "[l]egislators are not bound to consult with affected parties before passing legislation" (para. 157), one with which I fully agree. Another concern is that the majority consider the "circumstances" surrounding the adoption of the legislative provisions, such as the spiralling health care costs faced by the government, at the stage of determining whether s. 2 (*d*) is infringed. In my view, those considerations are entirely relevant to the s. 1 justification analysis, but are irrelevant where the issue is whether freedom of association is infringed.

[180] Given these concerns, I find it more appropriate to rely on a somewhat different test than the one suggested by the majority, although the test I propose is built on the same foundation as theirs (see majority's reasons, para. 96). I am adjusting their test to take into consideration the fact that what is in issue is a positive infringement, not underinclusiveness, and that what is under scrutiny is legislation, not government action. My test can be stated as follows:

> Laws or state actions that prevent or deny meaningful discussion and consultation about significant workplace issues between employees and their employer may interfere with the activity of collective bargaining, as may laws that unilaterally nullify negotiated terms on significant workplace issues in existing collective agreements.

[181] This test still involves two inquiries. The first is into whether the process of negotiation between employers and employees or their representatives is interfered with in any way, and the second into whether the interference concerns a significant issue in the labour relations context. An approach under which interference with the process is considered first has the merit of focussing attention on the constitutionally protected right itself, rather than having the court indirectly protect the substance of clauses in collective agreements. Only

if the court determines that there has been interference with a process of negotiation should it turn to the second inquiry and consider whether the issues involved are significant, in order to ensure that the scope of s. 2(*d*) is not interpreted so as to exceed its purpose. In this way, not all workplace issues, but only significant ones, are relevant to s. 2(*d*). I agree with the majority that the "protection does not cover all aspects of 'collective bargaining,' as that term is understood in the statutory labour relations regimes that are in place across the country" (para. 19). There may be matters covered by collective agreements that do not warrant constitutional protection—it is not every workplace issue that triggers s. 2(*d*) protection, but only those of significance.

[182] Thus, legislation that alters terms of a collective agreement bearing on significant workplace issues, or that precludes negotiations on significant workplace issues that would normally be negotiable, will interfere with the collective bargaining process. Such legislative measures nullify negotiations that have already taken place or prevent future negotiations on the topics they cover.

[183] Even though I disagree with significant aspects of the majority's test for determining whether an infringement has occurred, I agree ... that certain provisions of the Act infringe s. 2(*d*) of the *Charter*. ...

C. Contextual Approach Required in the Section 1 Analysis

[190] Over the past decade, my colleague Bastarache J. has been at the forefront of articulating the basis for and operation of the contextual approach to s. 1 in a trilogy of judgments of this Court that have garnered majority support. This jurisprudence is a major contribution towards a full and proper understanding of the s. 1 analysis. Several considerations are important to highlight in reviewing this case law. ...

[196] While the majority agree that a contextual approach to s. 1 is appropriate, they do not apply it in their justification analysis. In my view, the majority do not give context the importance it deserves. ...

[209] In my view, the vulnerability of health care users and their constitutionally protected rights are relevant contextual factors to be considered in determining whether the impugned legislative provisions are demonstrably justified under s. 1. ...

[251] In addressing the crisis of sustainability in health care, governments face a difficult public policy challenge with no end in sight in the immediate future. As alternatives are considered, competing rights and interests arise. Government must be accorded deference to enable them to navigate these difficult waters. At the same time, this Court must ensure that the path they take is respectful of the constitutional rights of those who are affected by it, and that any infringement of those rights is demonstrably justified.

[252] In the case at bar, the freedom of association of health care employees has been infringed in several instances, because provisions of the legislation enacted by the government interfere with their right to a process of collective bargaining with the employer. It is the collective bargaining process that is constitutionally protected, not the content of the actual provisions of the collective agreements. In my view, the government has established that four of the five infringements, namely those resulting from ss. 4, 5, 6(2) and 9 of the Act, are constitutionally justified. However, I find that s. 6(4) of the Act fails the minimal impairment and proportionate effects tests and thus is not saved under s. 1 of the *Charter*. ...

PART THREE
Aboriginal Rights

38 R. v. Sparrow, 1990

The package of amendments that patriated Canada's Constitution in 1982 and added a *Charter of Rights and Freedoms* to the Constitution included another important constitutional development—formal recognition of the rights of Canada's Aboriginal peoples.[1] This was done in section 35 of the *Constitution Act, 1982*, which declared that "[t]he existing aboriginal and treaty rights of the aboriginal peoples of Canada are hereby recognized and affirmed."

Aboriginal and treaty rights were not created by the 1982 constitutional amendment. From the earliest days of contact, both British and French relations with indigenous peoples had been regulated by treaties on mutual rights and responsibilities. The *Royal Proclamation of 1963* setting out constitutional arrangements after the cession of New France to Britain declared that the "several Nations or Tribes of Indians" with whom Britain was connected "should not be molested or disturbed in the Possession of such Parts of our Dominions" that had not been formally ceded to the Crown. Though the Proclamation's recognition of Indian nations and their possession of lands continued in theory as Canadian law after Confederation, these rights, as the Supreme Court observes below, for many years were virtually ignored.

The Supreme Court's decision in the 1973 *Calder*[2] case showed signs of a judicial turnaround. Six of the seven justices participating in the case recognized that Aboriginal people had title to the land they occupied and used before European settlers arrived. As members of a court appointed by the settlers' government, these judges were of the view that an Aboriginal people's title to their traditional lands could be extinguished unilaterally by the sovereign power of the British Crown, a power passed on to the government of Canada after Confederation. In the case at hand, the justices split 3 to 3 as to whether the Nisga'a nation's title to their lands in the Nass Valley of northwest British Columbia had been extinguished. This decision convinced the Government of Canada to begin negotiating comprehensive land claims agreements with Aboriginal peoples in Canada who had not entered into land cession treaties.

By the 1970s, indigenous Canadians sought recognition of their rights at the political level by forming Canada-wide organizations and linking up with native groups in other countries. Though section 35 was the first constitutional fruit of this endeavour, it fell far short of Aboriginal aspirations. It was the insertion of the word "existing" in section 35 that caused much of the consternation. The Trudeau government, in its efforts to win provincial approval of its patriation package, dropped the entire Aboriginal rights section. In response to protests for doing this, section 35 was restored but with the word "existing" inserted to win Alberta Premier Peter Lougheed's support for the section. Though Jean Chrétien told

---

1 Aboriginal is capitalized here, as it is in the Royal Commission on Aboriginal Peoples, to recognize that Aboriginal is a political, not a racial, category.

2 *Calder v. Attorney General of British Columbia* (1973), 34 D.L.R. (3d) 145 (SCC).

the House of Commons that the word "existing" did not change the meaning of the section, the impression was left that it may have taken most of the bite out of it. Only one native organization, the Métis Association of Alberta, supported the new wording.

Another part of the 1982 constitutional package committed the First Ministers to meet within a year with Aboriginal representatives to work out a more definitive statement of Aboriginal rights. This conference took place in 1983 and resulted in the first constitutional change under the new patriated amending process. The amendment made it clear that treaty rights recognized in section 35 include rights acquired through existing or future land claims agreements. It also stipulated that section 35 rights are guaranteed equally to male and female persons. This still fell far short of securing the constitutional recognition of the self-government rights sought by the main Aboriginal organizations. Three more attempts to define Aboriginal rights through First Ministers conferences took place in 1984, 1985, and 1987. All three were abortive, the last failure coming just a month before the First Ministers' announcement of their proposed Meech Lake Accord—a set of constitutional proposals that offered nothing to Aboriginal peoples.

The effort to get a clearer definition of constitutionally protected Aboriginal rights now focused on the courts. *Sparrow* was the first of these court actions to reach the Supreme Court of Canada. It arose out of a charge brought against members of the Musqueam Indian Band in British Columbia for fishing with nets wider than those allowed under federal regulations. The Musqueam's defence was that the restriction on their nets violated their Aboriginal right to fish recognized under section 35 of the Constitution. In dealing with this defence, the Supreme Court would give the first indication of whether section 35, as some contended, was "an empty box" or whether it had real content.

The Court's treatment of section 35 in this case firmly rejected the "empty box" theory. That theory had been based on the idea that "existing" Aboriginal rights incorporated all the regulations and limitations that governments had imposed on the activities of native peoples up to 1982. Such a position, in the Court's view, would turn Aboriginal rights into a crazy patchwork and deny them any vigour. Past regulation of an Aboriginal activity is not to be confused with extinguishment of an Aboriginal right. Extinguishment of an Aboriginal right, as three of the Court's justices had held in the 1973 *Calder* case, requires a clear and plain expression of the sovereign legislator's intention to extinguish. The Court accepted the BC Court of Appeal's finding that the Musqueam Indians have an existing Aboriginal right to fish in the area where Sparrow and others were charged. Evidence submitted in the courts below had shown that for the Musqueam the salmon fishery had always been "an integral part of their distinctive culture." After the assertion of British sovereignty and through over a hundred years of Canadian fisheries regulations, the Musqueam had enjoyed the right to fish for subsistence and ceremonial purposes.

Though the Musqueam's right to fish had not been extinguished, it had been regulated. Indeed, the point at issue in this case was whether a regulation limiting the size of their nets violated the Musqueam's Aboriginal fishing right. The Court held that Parliament could regulate such an Aboriginal right even though this right was now "recognized" and "confirmed" in the Constitution. However, precisely because such a right has been incorporated into the Constitution, regulations limiting or interfering with it must meet a very high level of justification. In effect, the Supreme Court at this point read section 1 of the *Charter of Rights and Freedoms*, its general limitation clause, into section 35 of the *Constitution Act, 1982*. If a regulation is found to interfere with an existing Aboriginal right, it can only be upheld if it is shown to be enacted for a valid legislative objective and interferes no more than is necessary.

The Court stressed that this test for a valid restriction of a constitutionally protected Aboriginal right is to be applied with sensitivity to the nature of the special rights at stake. To begin with, the scope and meaning of an existing Aboriginal right are not to be interpreted narrowly. Consideration is to be given to the way the Aboriginal people themselves understand the right. Thus, it would be artificial to draw a sharp distinction between the right to fish and the manner in which that right has been exercised. Further, such rights may come to be exercised in a contemporary manner—they are not frozen in the past. The first consideration in determining whether a regulation that interferes with an existing Aboriginal right is justified is the "special trust responsibility of the government vis-à-vis aboriginals." This fiduciary relationship is based on a long line of precedents in Canadian law. Meeting this fiduciary obligation to Aboriginal peoples does not mean that government must abandon its responsibility for conserving and managing fish stocks, but that its plans must treat Aboriginal peoples "in a way ensuring that their rights are taken seriously." Among other things, this means giving the Aboriginal right priority in any rationing scheme required for conservation and consulting with the Aboriginal people on conservation measures.

The Court did not decide the concrete issue of whether the fishing regulation limiting the size of the Musqueam's net was an unjustifiable restriction of their existing Aboriginal right. Determination of that matter would require a new trial at which pertinent evidence could be adduced and examined. The Musqueam claimants would have to show that the regulation did constitute a *prima facie* infringement of their right to fish for food. If an infringement were found, the Crown would have to show, on the basis of the test set out in this opinion, whether the infringement was justifiable. Though the Supreme Court did not settle the specific question addressed to it in this case, it did lay down some broad principles of interpretation with respect to what it means to affirm and recognize Aboriginal rights in Canada's Constitution. Clearly the Court itself was prepared to take such rights seriously. Yet it was not willing to treat them as absolute rights. Its initial jurisprudence in this area indicated that *Sparrow* would be just the beginning of a long series of cases in which the Court would be called on to balance Aboriginal and treaty rights against other constitutional values. For instance, the Court would not want to extend section 35 rights to a point that rendered provinces incapable of exercising their constitutional responsibility for managing their natural resources. ⁓

R. v. SPARROW
[1990] 1 S.C.R. 1075

Hearing: November 3, 1988; Judgment: May 31, 1990.

Present: Dickson C.J. and McIntyre,* Lamer, Wilson, La Forest, L'Heureux-Dubé, and Sopinka JJ.

Interveners: The National Indian Brotherhood/Assembly of First Nations, the B.C. Wildlife Federation, the Steelhead Society of British Columbia, the Pacific Fishermen's Defence Alliance, Northern Trollers' Association, the Pacific Gillnetters' Association, the Gulf Trollers' Association, the Pacific Trollers' Association, the Prince Rupert Fishing Vessel Owners' Association, the Fishing Vessel Owners' Association of British Columbia, the Pacific Coast Fishing Vessel Owners' Guild, the Prince Rupert Fishermen's Cooperative Association, the Co-op Fishermen's Guild, Deep Sea Trawlers' Association of B.C., the Fisheries Council of British Columbia, the United Fishermen and Allied Workers' Union, the Attorney General for Ontario, the Attorney General of Quebec, the Attorney General of British Columbia, the Attorney General for Saskatchewan, the Attorney General for Alberta and the Attorney General of Newfoundland.

* McIntyre J. took no part in the judgment.

The judgment of the Court was delivered by

THE CHIEF JUSTICE AND LA FOREST J.: This appeal requires this Court to explore for the first time the scope of s. 35(1) of the *Constitution Act, 1982*, and to indicate its strength as a promise to the aboriginal peoples of Canada. Section 35(1) is found in Part II of that Act, entitled "Rights of the Aboriginal Peoples of Canada," and provides as follows:

> **35.** (1) The existing aboriginal and treaty rights of the aboriginal peoples of Canada are hereby recognized and affirmed.

Facts

The appellant, a member of the Musqueam Indian Band, was charged under s. 61(1) of the *Fisheries Act* of the offence of fishing with a drift net longer than that permitted by the terms of the Band's Indian food fishing licence. The fishing which gave rise to the charge took place on May 25, 1984 in Canoe Passage which is part of the area subject to the Band's licence. The licence, which had been issued for a one-year period beginning March 31, 1984, set out a number of restrictions including one that drift nets were to be limited to 25 fathoms in length. The appellant was caught with a net which was 45 fathoms in length. He has throughout admitted the facts alleged to constitute the offence, but has defended the charge on the basis that he was exercising an existing aboriginal right to fish and that the net length restriction contained in the

Band's licence is inconsistent with s. 35(1) of the *Constitution Act, 1982* and therefore invalid. . . .

Analysis

We will address first the meaning of "existing" aboriginal rights and the content and scope of the Musqueam right to fish. We will then turn to the meaning of "recognized and affirmed," and the impact of s. 35(1) on the regulatory power of Parliament.

"Existing"

The word "existing" makes it clear that the rights to which s. 35(1) applies are those that were in existence when the *Constitution Act, 1982* came into effect. This means that extinguished rights are not revived by the *Constitution Act, 1982*. . . .

Further, an existing aboriginal right cannot be read so as to incorporate the specific manner in which it was regulated before 1982. The notion of freezing existing rights would incorporate into the Constitution a crazy patchwork of regulations. . . .

The arbitrariness of such an approach can be seen if one considers the recent history of the federal regulation in the context of the present case and the fishing industry. If the *Constitution Act, 1982* had been enacted a few years earlier, any right held by the Musqueam Band, on this approach, would have been constitutionally subjected to the restrictive regime of personal licences that had existed since 1917. Under that regime, the Musqueam catch had by 1969 become minor or non-existent. In 1978 a system of band licences was introduced on an experimental basis which permitted the Musqueam to fish with a 75 fathom net for a greater number of days than other people. Under this regime, from 1977 to 1984, the number of Band members who fished for food increased from 19 persons using 15 boats, to 64 persons using 38 boats, while 10 other members of the Band fished under commercial licences. Before this regime, the Band's food fish requirement had basically been provided by Band members who were licensed for commercial fishing. Since the regime introduced in 1978 was in force in 1982, then, under this approach, the scope and content of an aboriginal right to fish would be determined by the details of the Band's 1978 licence.

The unsuitability of the approach can also be seen from another perspective. Ninety-one other tribes of Indians, comprising over 20,000 people (compared with 540 Musqueam on the reserve and 100 others off the reserve) obtain their food fish from the Fraser River. Some or all of these bands may have an aboriginal right to fish there. A constitutional patchwork quilt would be created if the constitutional right of these bands were to be determined by the specific regime available to each of those bands in 1982.

Far from being defined according to the regulatory scheme in place in 1982, the phrase "existing aboriginal rights" must be interpreted flexibly so as to permit their evolution over time. To use Professor Slattery's expression, in "Understanding Aboriginal Rights" [(1987), 66 *Can. Bar Rev.* 727], at p. 782, the word "existing" suggests that those rights are "affirmed in a contemporary form rather than in their primeval simplicity and vigour." Clearly, then, an approach to the constitutional guarantee embodied in s. 35(1) which would incorporate "frozen rights" must be rejected.

The Aboriginal Right

We turn now to the aboriginal right at stake in this appeal. The Musqueam Indian Reserve is located on the north shore of the Fraser River close to the mouth of that river and within the limits of the City of Vancouver. There has been a Musqueam village there for hundreds of years. This appeal does not directly concern the reserve or the adjacent waters, but arises out of the Band's right to fish in another area of the Fraser River estuary known as Canoe Passage in the South Arm of the river, some 16 kilometres (about 10 miles) from the reserve. The reserve and those waters are separated by the Vancouver International Airport and the Municipality of Richmond.

The evidence reveals that the Musqueam have lived in the area as an organized society long before the coming of European settlers, and that the taking of salmon was an integral part of their lives and remains so to this day. Much of the evidence of an aboriginal right to fish was given by Dr. Suttles, an anthropologist, supported by that of Mr. Grant, the Band administrator. . . .

While the trial for a violation of a penal prohibition may not be the most appropriate setting in which to determine the existence of an aboriginal right, and the evidence was not extensive, the correctness of the finding of fact of the trial judge "that Mr. Sparrow was fishing in ancient tribal territory where his ancestors had fished from time immemorial in that part of the mouth of the Fraser River for salmon" is supported by the evidence and was not contested. The existence of the right, the Court of Appeal tells us, was "not the subject of serious dispute." . . .

In this Court, however, the respondent contested the Court of Appeal's finding, contending that the evidence was insufficient to discharge the appellant's burden of proof upon the issue. It is true that for the period from 1867 to 1961 the evidence is scanty. But the evidence was not disputed or contradicted in the courts below and there is evidence of sufficient continuity of the right to support the Court of Appeal's finding, and we would not disturb it.

What the Crown really insisted on, both in this Court and the courts below, was that the Musqueam Band's aboriginal right to fish had been extinguished by regulations under the *Fisheries Act.*

The history of the regulation of fisheries in British Columbia is set out in *Jack v. The Queen*, [1980] 1 S.C.R. 294, especially at pp. 308 *et seq.*, and we need only summarize it here. Before the province's entry into Confederation in 1871, the fisheries were not regulated in any significant way, whether in respect of Indians or other people. The Indians were not only permitted but encouraged to continue fishing for their own food requirements. Commercial and sport fishing were not then of any great importance. The federal *Fisheries Act* was only proclaimed in force in the province in 1876 and the first *Salmon Fishery Regulations for British Columbia* were adopted in 1878 and were minimal.

The 1878 regulations were the first to mention Indians. They simply provided that the Indians were at all times at liberty, by any means other than drift nets or spearing, to fish for food for themselves, but not for sale or barter. The Indian right or liberty to fish was thereby restricted, and more stringent restrictions were added over the years. . . .

It is this progressive restriction and detailed regulation of the fisheries which, respondent's counsel maintained, have had the effect of extinguishing any aboriginal right to fish. The extinguishment need not be express, he argued, but may take place where the sovereign authority is exercised in a manner "necessarily inconsistent" with the continued enjoyment of aboriginal rights. For this proposition, he particularly relied on *St. Catherine's Milling and Lumber Co. v. The Queen* (1888), 14 App. Cas. 46 (P.C.); *Calder v. Attorney-General of British Columbia, supra; Baker Lake (Hamlet) v. Minister of Indian Affairs and Northern Development,* [1980] 1 F.C. 518 (T.D.); and *Attorney-General for Ontario v. Bear Island Foundation* [(1984), 49 O.R. (2d) 353 (H.C.)]. The consent to its extinguishment before the *Constitution Act, 1982* was not required; the intent of the Sovereign could be effected not only by statute but by valid regulations. Here, in his view, the regulations had entirely displaced any aboriginal right. . . .

At bottom, the respondent's argument confuses regulation with extinguishment. That the right is controlled in great detail by the regulations does not mean that the right is thereby extinguished. . . .

In the context of aboriginal rights, it could be argued that, before 1982, an aboriginal right was automatically extinguished to the extent that it was inconsistent with a statute. As Mahoney J. stated in *Baker Lake, supra*, at p. 568:

> Once a statute has been validly enacted, it must be given effect. If its necessary effect is to abridge or entirely abrogate a common law right, then that is the effect that the courts must give it. That is as true of an aboriginal title as of any other common law right.

See also *Attorney-General for Ontario v. Bear Island Founda-tion, supra*, at pp. 439-40. That in Judson J.'s view was what had occurred in *Calder, supra*, where, as he saw it, a series of statutes evinced a unity of intention to exercise a sovereignty inconsistent with any conflicting interest, including aboriginal title. But Hall J. in that case stated (at p. 404) that "the onus of proving that the Sovereign intended to extinguish the Indian title lies on the respondent and *that intention must be 'clear and plain'.*" (Emphasis added.) The test of extinguish-ment to be adopted, in our opinion, is that the Sovereign's intention must be clear and plain if it is to extinguish an aboriginal right.

There is nothing in the *Fisheries Act* or its detailed regula-tions that demonstrates a clear and plain intention to extin-guish the Indian aboriginal right to fish. The fact that express provision permitting the Indians to fish for food may have applied to all Indians and that for an extended period permits were discretionary and issued on an individual rather than a communal basis in no way shows a clear intention to extin-guish. These permits were simply a manner of controlling the fisheries, not defining underlying rights.

We would conclude then that the Crown has failed to discharge its burden of proving extinguishment. In our opin-ion, the Court of Appeal made no mistake in holding that the Indians have an existing aboriginal right to fish in the area where Mr. Sparrow was fishing at the time of the charge. This approach is consistent with ensuring that an aboriginal right should not be defined by incorporating the ways in which it has been regulated in the past.

The scope of the existing Musqueam right to fish must now be delineated. The anthropological evidence relied on to establish the existence of the right suggests that, for the Mus-queam, the salmon fishery has always constituted an integral part of their distinctive culture. Its significant role involved not only consumption for subsistence purposes, but also con-sumption of salmon on ceremonial and social occasions. The Musqueam have always fished for reasons connected to their cultural and physical survival. As we stated earlier, the right to do so may be exercised in a contemporary manner. . . .

Government regulations governing the exercise of the Musqueam right to fish, as described above, have only recog-nized the right to fish *for food* for over a hundred years. This may have reflected the existing position. However, historical policy on the part of the Crown is not only incapable of extin-guishing the existing aboriginal right without clear intention, but is also incapable of, in itself, delineating that right. The nature of government regulations cannot be determinative of the content and scope of an existing aboriginal right. Govern-ment policy *can* however regulate the exercise of that right, but such regulation must be in keeping with s. 35(1).

In the courts below, the case at bar was not presented on the footing of an aboriginal right to fish for commercial or livelihood purposes. Rather the focus was and continues to be on the validity of a net length restriction affecting the appel-lant's *food fishing license*. We therefore adopt the Court of Appeal's characterization of the right for the purpose of this appeal, and confine our reasons to the meaning of the consti-tutional recognition and affirmation of the existing aboriginal right to fish for food and social and ceremonial purposes.

"Recognized and Affirmed"

We now turn to the impact of s. 35(1) of the *Constitution Act, 1982* on the regulatory power of Parliament and on the out-come of this appeal specifically.

Counsel for the appellant argued that the effect of s. 35(1) is to deny Parliament's power to restrictively regulate aboriginal fishing rights under s. 91(24) ("Indians and Lands Reserved for the Indians"), and s. 91(12) ("Sea Coast and Inland Fisheries"). The essence of this submission, supported by the intervener, the National Indian Brotherhood/Assembly of First Nations, is that the right to regulate is part of the right to use the resource in the Band's discretion. Section 35(1) is not subject to s. 1 of the *Canadian Charter of Rights and Free-doms* nor to legislative override under s. 33. The appellant submitted that, if the regulatory power continued, the limits on its extent are set by the word "inconsistent" in s. 52(1) of the *Constitution Act, 1982* and the protective and remedial purposes of s. 35(1). This means that aboriginal title entails a right to fish by any non-dangerous method chosen by the aboriginals engaged in fishing. Any continuing governmental power of regulation would have to be exceptional and strictly limited to regulation that is clearly not inconsistent with the protective and remedial purposes of s. 35(1). Thus, counsel for the appellant speculated, "in certain circumstances, neces-sary and reasonable conservation measures *might* qualify" (emphasis added)—where for example such measures were necessary to prevent serious impairment of the aboriginal rights of present and future generations, where conservation could only be achieved by restricting the right and not by restricting fishing by other users, and where the aboriginal group concerned was unwilling to implement necessary con-servation measures. The onus of proving a justification for restrictive regulations would lie with the government by analogy with s. 1 of the *Charter*.

In response to these submissions and in finding the appro-priate interpretive framework for s. 35(1), we start by looking at the background of s. 35(1).

It is worth recalling that while British policy towards the native population was based on respect for their right to occupy their traditional lands, a proposition to which the

Royal Proclamation of 1763 bears witness, there was from the outset never any doubt that sovereignty and legislative power, and indeed the underlying title, to such lands vested in the Crown; see *Johnson v. M'Intosh* (1823), 8 Wheaton 543 (U. S.S.C.); see also the *Royal Proclamation* itself (R.S.C., 1985, App. II, No. 1, pp. 4-6); *Calder, supra, per* Judson J., at p. 328, Hall J., at pp. 383 and 402. And there can be no doubt that over the years the rights of the Indians were often honoured in the breach. . . .

For many years, the rights of the Indians to their aboriginal lands—certainly as *legal* rights—were virtually ignored. The leading cases defining Indian rights in the early part of the century were directed at claims supported by the *Royal Proclamation* or other legal instruments, and even these cases were essentially concerned with settling legislative jurisdiction or the rights of commercial enterprises. For fifty years after the publication of Clement's *The Law of the Canadian Constitution* (3rd ed. 1916), there was a virtual absence of discussion of any kind of Indian rights to land even in academic literature. By the late 1960s, aboriginal claims were not even recognized by the federal government as having any legal status. Thus the *Statement of the Government of Canada on Indian Policy* (1969), although well meaning, contained the assertion (at p. 11) that "aboriginal claims to land . . . are so general and undefined that it is not realistic to think of them as specific claims capable of remedy except through a policy and program that will end injustice to the Indians as members of the Canadian community." In the same general period, the James Bay development by Quebec Hydro was originally initiated without regard to the rights of the Indians who lived there, even though these were expressly protected by a constitutional instrument; see *The Quebec Boundaries Extension Act, 1912*, S.C. 1912, c. 45. It took a number of judicial decisions and notably the *Calder* case in this Court (1973) to prompt a reassessment of the position being taken by government.

In the light of its reassessment of Indian claims following *Calder*, the federal Government on August 8, 1973 issued "a statement of policy" regarding Indian lands. By it, it sought to "signify the Government's *recognition and acceptance* of its continuing responsibility under the *British North America Act* for Indians and lands reserved for Indians," which it regarded "as an historic evolution dating back to the *Royal Proclamation of 1763*, which, whatever differences there may be about its judicial interpretation, stands as a basic declaration of the Indian people's interests in land in this country." (Emphasis added.) See *Statement made by the Honourable Jean Chrétien, Minister of Indian Affairs and Northern Development on Claims of Indian and Inuit People*, August 8, 1973. The remarks about these lands were intended "as an expression of acknowledged responsibility." But the statement went on to express, for the first time, the government's willingness to negotiate regarding claims of aboriginal title, specifically in British Columbia, Northern Quebec, and the Territories, and this without regard to formal supporting documents. "The Government," it stated, "is now ready to negotiate with authorized representatives of these native peoples on the basis that where their traditional interest in the lands concerned can be established, an agreed form of compensation or benefit will be provided to native peoples in return for their interest."

It is obvious from its terms that the approach taken towards aboriginal claims in the 1973 statement constituted an expression of a policy, rather than a legal position; see also *In All Fairness: A Native Claims Policy-Comprehensive Claims* (1981), pp. 11-12; Slattery, "Understanding Aboriginal Rights" op. cit., at p. 730. As recently as *Guerin v. The Queen*, [1984] 2 S.C.R. 335, the federal government argued in this Court that any federal obligation was of a political character.

It is clear, then, that s. 35(1) of the *Constitution Act, 1982*, represents the culmination of a long and difficult struggle in both the political forum and the courts for the constitutional recognition of aboriginal rights. The strong representations of native associations and other groups concerned with the welfare of Canada's aboriginal peoples made the adoption of s. 35(1) possible and it is important to note that the provision applies to the Indians, the Inuit and the Métis. Section 35(1), at the least, provides a solid constitutional base upon which subsequent negotiations can take place. It also affords aboriginal peoples constitutional protection against provincial legislative power. . . .

The approach to be taken with respect to interpreting the meaning of s. 35(1) is derived from general principles of constitutional interpretation, principles relating to aboriginal rights, and the purposes behind the constitutional provision itself. Here, we will sketch the framework for an interpretation of "recognized and affirmed" that, in our opinion, gives appropriate weight to the constitutional nature of these words.

In *Reference re Manitoba Language Rights*, [1985] 1 S.C.R. 721, this Court said the following about the perspective to be adopted when interpreting a constitution, at p. 745:

> The Constitution of a country is a statement of the will of the people to be governed in accordance with certain principles held as fundamental and certain prescriptions restrictive of the powers of the legislature and government. It is, as s. 52 of the *Constitution Act, 1982* declares, the "supreme law" of the nation, unalterable by the normal legislative process, and unsuffering of laws inconsistent with it. The duty of the judiciary is to interpret and apply the laws of Canada and each of the provinces, and it is thus our duty to ensure that the constitutional law prevails.

The nature of s. 35(1) itself suggests that it be construed in a purposive way. When the purposes of the affirmation of aboriginal rights are considered, it is clear that a generous, liberal interpretation of the words in the constitutional provision is demanded. . . .

In *Nowegijick v. The Queen*, [1983] 1 S.C.R. 29, at p. 36, the following principle that should govern the interpretation of Indian treaties and statutes was set out:

> . . . [T]reaties and statutes relating to Indians should be liberally construed and doubtful expressions resolved in favour of the Indians.

In *R. v. Agawa* [(1988), 28 O.A.C. 201], Blair J.A. stated that the above principle should apply to the interpretation of s. 35(1). He added the following principle to be equally applied, at pp. 215-16:

> The second principle was enunciated by the late Associate Chief Justice MacKinnon in *R. v. Taylor and Williams* (1981), 34 O.R. (2d) 360. He emphasized the importance of Indian history and traditions as well as the perceived effect of a treaty at the time of its execution. He also cautioned against determining Indian rights "in a vacuum." The honour of the Crown is involved in the interpretation of Indian treaties and, as a consequence, fairness to the Indians is a governing consideration. . . .
>
> This view is reflected in recent judicial decisions which have emphasized the responsibility of Government to protect the rights of Indians arising from the special trust relationship created by history, treaties and legislation: see *Guerin v. The Queen*, [1984] 2 S.C.R. 335; 55 N.R. 161; 13 D.L.R. (4th) 321.

In *Guerin, supra,* the Musqueam Band surrendered reserve lands to the Crown for lease to a golf club. The terms obtained by the Crown were much less favourable than those approved by the Band at the surrender meeting. This Court found that the Crown owed a fiduciary obligation to the Indians with respect to the lands. The *sui generis* nature of Indian title, and the historic powers and responsibility assumed by the Crown constituted the source of such a fiduciary obligation. In our opinion, *Guerin,* together with *R. v. Taylor and Williams* (1981), 34 O.R. (2d) 360, ground a general guiding principle for s. 35(1). That is, the Government has the responsibility to act in a fiduciary capacity with respect to aboriginal peoples. The relationship between the Government and aboriginals is trust-like, rather than adversarial, and contemporary recognition and affirmation of aboriginal rights must be defined in light of this historic relationship.

We agree with both the British Columbia Court of Appeal below and the Ontario Court of Appeal that the principles outlined above, derived from *Nowegijick, Taylor and Williams*

and *Guerin,* should guide the interpretation of s. 35(1). As commentators have noted, s. 35(1) is a solemn commitment that must be given meaningful content (Lyon ["An Essay on Constitutional Interpretation" (1988), 26 *Osgoode Hall L.J.* 95]; Pentney ["The Rights of the Aboriginal Peoples of Canada in the Constitution Act, 1982, Part II, Section 35: The Substantive Guarantee" (1988), 22 *U.B.C. L. Rev.* 207]; Schwartz, "Unstarted Business: Two Approaches to Defining s. 35— 'What's in the Box?' and 'What Kind of Box?,'" Chapter XXIV, in *First Principles, Second Thoughts: Aboriginal Peoples, Constitutional Reform and Canadian Statecraft*; Slattery, op. cit.; and Slattery, "The Hidden Constitution: Aboriginal Rights in Canada" (1984), 32 *Am. J. of Comp. Law* 361).

In response to the appellant's submission that s. 35(1) rights are more securely protected than the rights guaranteed by the *Charter*, it is true that s. 35(1) is not subject to s. 1 of the *Charter*. In our opinion, this does not mean that any law or regulation affecting aboriginal rights will automatically be of no force or effect by the operation of s. 52 of the *Constitution Act, 1982*. Legislation that affects the exercise of aboriginal rights will nonetheless be valid, if it meets the test for justifying an interference with a right recognized and affirmed under s. 35(1).

There is no explicit language in the provision that authorizes this Court or any court to assess the legitimacy of any government legislation that restricts aboriginal rights. Yet, we find that the words "recognition and affirmation" incorporate the fiduciary relationship referred to earlier and so import some restraint on the exercise of sovereign power. Rights that are recognized and affirmed are not absolute. Federal legislative powers continue, including, of course, the right to legislate with respect to Indians pursuant to s. 91(24) of the *Constitution Act, 1867*. These powers must, however, now be read together with s. 35(1). In other words, federal power must be reconciled with federal duty and the best way to achieve that reconciliation is to demand the justification of any government regulation that infringes upon or denies aboriginal rights. Such scrutiny is in keeping with the liberal interpretive principle enunciated in *Nowegijick, supra*, and the concept of holding the Crown to a high standard of honourable dealing with respect to the aboriginal peoples of Canada as suggested by *Guerin v. The Queen, supra*.

We refer to Professor Slattery's "Understanding Aboriginal Rights," *supra*, with respect to the task of envisioning a s. 35(1) justificatory process. Professor Slattery, at p. 782, points out that a justificatory process is required as a compromise between a "patchwork" characterization of aboriginal rights whereby past regulations would be read into a definition of the rights, and a characterization that would guarantee aboriginal rights in their original form unrestricted by subsequent regulation.

We agree with him that these two extreme positions must be rejected in favour of a justificatory scheme.

Section 35(1) suggests that while regulation affecting aboriginal rights is not precluded, such regulation must be enacted according to a valid objective. Our history has shown, unfortunately all too well, that Canada's aboriginal peoples are justified in worrying about government objectives that may be superficially neutral but which constitute *de facto* threats to the existence of aboriginal rights and interests. By giving aboriginal rights constitutional status and priority, Parliament and the provinces have sanctioned challenges to social and economic policy objectives embodied in legislation to the extent that aboriginal rights are affected. Implicit in this constitutional scheme is the obligation of the legislature to satisfy the test of justification. The way in which a legislative objective is to be attained must uphold the honour of the Crown and must be in keeping with the unique contemporary relationship, grounded in history and policy, between the Crown and Canada's aboriginal peoples. The extent of legislative or regulatory impact on an existing aboriginal right may be scrutinized so as to ensure recognition and affirmation.

The constitutional recognition afforded by the provision therefore gives a measure of control over government conduct and a strong check on legislative power. While it does not promise immunity from government regulation in a society that, in the twentieth century, is increasingly more complex, interdependent and sophisticated, and where exhaustible resources need protection and management, it does hold the Crown to a substantive promise. The government is required to bear the burden of justifying any legislation that has some negative effect on any aboriginal right protected under s. 35(1)....

Section 35(1) and the Regulation of the Fisheries

Taking the above framework as guidance, we propose to set out the test for *prima facie* interference with an existing aboriginal right and for the justification of such an interference....

The first question to be asked is whether the legislation in question has the effect of interfering with an existing aboriginal right. If it does have such an effect, it represents a *prima facie* infringement of s. 35(1). Parliament is not expected to act in a manner contrary to the rights and interests of aboriginals, and, indeed, may be barred from doing so by the second stage of s. 35(1) analysis. The inquiry with respect to interference begins with a reference to the characteristics or incidents of the right at stake. Our earlier observations regarding the scope of the aboriginal right to fish are relevant here. Fishing rights are not traditional property rights. They are rights held by a collective and are in keeping with the culture and existence of that group. Courts must be careful, then, to avoid the

application of traditional common law concepts of property as they develop their understanding of what the reasons for judgment in *Guerin, supra*, at p. 382, referred to as the "*sui generis*" nature of aboriginal rights....

While it is impossible to give an easy definition of fishing rights, it is possible, and, indeed, crucial, to be sensitive to the aboriginal perspective itself on the meaning of the rights at stake. For example, it would be artificial to try to create a hard distinction between the right to fish and the particular manner in which that right is exercised.

To determine whether the fishing rights have been interfered with such as to constitute a *prima facie* infringement of s. 35(1), certain questions must be asked. First, is the limitation unreasonable? Second, does the regulation impose undue hardship? Third, does the regulation deny to the holders of the right their preferred means of exercising that right? The onus of proving a *prima facie* infringement lies on the individual or group challenging the legislation. In relation to the facts of this appeal, the regulation would be found to be a *prima facie* interference if it were found to be an adverse restriction on the Musqueam exercise of their right to fish for food. We wish to note here that the issue does not merely require looking at whether the fish catch has been reduced below that needed for the reasonable food and ceremonial needs of the Musqueam Indians. Rather the test involves asking whether either the purpose or the effect of the restriction on net length unnecessarily infringes the interests protected by the fishing right. If, for example, the Musqueam were forced to spend undue time and money per fish caught or if the net length reduction resulted in a hardship to the Musqueam in catching fish, then the first branch of the s. 35(1) analysis would be met.

If a *prima facie* interference is found, the analysis moves to the issue of justification. This is the test that addresses the question of what constitutes legitimate regulation of a constitutional aboriginal right. The justification analysis would proceed as follows. First, is there a valid legislative objective? Here the court would inquire into whether the objective of Parliament in authorizing the department to enact regulations regarding fisheries is valid. The objective of the department in setting out the particular regulations would also be scrutinized. An objective aimed at preserving s. 35(1) rights by conserving and managing a natural resource, for example, would be valid. Also valid would be objectives purporting to prevent the exercise of s. 35(1) rights that would cause harm to the general populace or to aboriginal peoples themselves, or other objectives found to be compelling and substantial.

The Court of Appeal below held, at p. 331, that regulations could be valid if reasonably justified as "necessary for the proper management and conservation of the resource *or in the public interest."* (Emphasis added.) We find the "public interest" justification to be so vague as to provide no meaningful guidance and so broad as to be unworkable as a test for the justification of a limitation on constitutional rights.

The justification of conservation and resource management, on the other hand, is surely uncontroversial. . . .

While the "presumption" of validity is now outdated in view of the constitutional status of the aboriginal rights at stake, it is clear that the value of conservation purposes for government legislation and action has long been recognized. Further, the conservation and management of our resources is consistent with aboriginal beliefs and practices, and, indeed, with the enhancement of aboriginal rights.

If a valid legislative objective is found, the analysis proceeds to the second part of the justification issue. Here, we refer back to the guiding interpretive principle derived from *Taylor and Williams* and *Guerin, supra.* That is, the honour of the Crown is at stake in dealings with aboriginal peoples. The special trust relationship and the responsibility of the government vis-à-vis aboriginals must be the first consideration in determining whether the legislation or action in question can be justified.

The problem that arises in assessing the legislation in light of its objective and the responsibility of the Crown is that the pursuit of conservation in a heavily used modern fishery inevitably blurs with the efficient allocation and management of this scarce and valued resource. The nature of the constitutional protection afforded by s. 35(1) in this context demands that there be a link between the question of justification and the allocation of priorities in the fishery. The constitutional recognition and affirmation of aboriginal rights may give rise to conflict with the interests of others given the limited nature of the resource. There is a clear need for guidelines that will resolve the allocational problems that arise regarding the fisheries. . . .

The constitutional nature of the Musqueam food fishing rights means that any allocation of priorities after valid conservation measures have been implemented must give top priority to Indian food fishing. If the objective pertained to conservation, the conservation plan would be scrutinized to assess priorities. While the detailed allocation of maritime resources is a task that must be left to those having expertise in the area, the Indians' food requirements must be met first when that allocation is established. The significance of giving the aboriginal right to fish for food top priority can be described as follows. If, in a given year, conservation needs required a reduction in the number of fish to be caught such that the number equalled the number required for food by the Indians, then all the fish available after conservation would go to the Indians according to the constitutional nature of their

fishing right. If, more realistically, there were still fish after the Indian food requirements were met, then the brunt of conservation measures would be borne by the practices of sport fishing and commercial fishing. . . .

We acknowledge the fact that the justificatory standard to be met may place a heavy burden on the Crown. However, government policy with respect to the British Columbia fishery, regardless of s. 35(1), already dictates that, in allocating the right to take fish, Indian food fishing is to be given priority over the interests of other user groups. The constitutional entitlement embodied in s. 35(1) requires the Crown to ensure that its regulations are in keeping with that allocation of priority. The objective of this requirement is not to undermine Parliament's ability and responsibility with respect to creating and administering overall conservation and management plans regarding the salmon fishery. The objective is rather to guarantee that those plans treat aboriginal peoples in a way ensuring that their rights are taken seriously.

Within the analysis of justification, there are further questions to be addressed, depending on the circumstances of the inquiry. These include the questions of whether there has been as little infringement as possible in order to effect the desired result; whether, in a situation of expropriation, fair compensation is available; and, whether the aboriginal group in question has been consulted with respect to the conservation measures being implemented. The aboriginal peoples, with their history of conservation-consciousness and interdependence with natural resources, would surely be expected, at the least, to be informed regarding the determination of an appropriate scheme for the regulation of the fisheries.

We would not wish to set out an exhaustive list of the factors to be considered in the assessment of justification. Suffice it to say that recognition and affirmation requires sensitivity to and respect for the rights of aboriginal peoples on behalf of the government, courts and indeed all Canadians.

Application to This Case—Is the Net Length Restriction Valid?

The Court of Appeal below found that there was not sufficient evidence in this case to proceed with an analysis of s. 35(1) with respect to the right to fish for food. In reviewing the competing expert evidence, and recognizing that fish stock management is an uncertain science, it decided that the issues at stake in this appeal were not well adapted to being resolved at the appellate court level. . . .

According to the Court of Appeal, the findings of fact were insufficient to lead to an acquittal. There was no more evidence before this Court. We also would order a re-trial which would allow findings of fact according to the tests set out in these reasons.

The appellant would bear the burden of showing that the net length restriction constituted a *prima facie* infringement of the collective aboriginal right to fish for food. If an infringement were found, the onus would shift to the Crown which would have to demonstrate that the regulation is justifiable. To that end, the Crown would have to show that there is no underlying unconstitutional objective such as shifting more of the resource to a user group that ranks below the Musqueam. Further, it would have to show that the regulation sought to be imposed is required to accomplish the needed limitation. In trying to show that the restriction is necessary in the circumstances of the Fraser River fishery, the Crown could use facts pertaining to fishing by other Fraser River Indians.

In conclusion, we would dismiss the appeal and the cross-appeal and affirm the Court of Appeal's setting aside of the conviction. We would accordingly affirm the order for a new trial on the questions of infringement and whether any infringement is nonetheless consistent with s. 35(1), in accordance with the interpretation set out here.

For the reasons given above, the constitutional question must be answered as follows:

Question   Is the net length restriction contained in the Musqueam Indian Band Indian Food Fishing Licence dated March 30, 1984, issued pursuant to the *British Columbia Fishery (General) Regulations* and the *Fisheries Act*, R.S.C. 1970, c. F-14, inconsistent with s. 35(1) of the *Constitution Act, 1982*?

Answer   This question will have to be sent back to trial to be answered according to the analysis set out in these reasons.

39 Delgamuukw v. British Columbia, 1997

This case arose from the claim of Delgamuukw and other hereditary chiefs of the Gitksan and Wet'suwet'en on behalf of their peoples to ownership of and jurisdiction over 58,000 square kilometres of the British Columbia interior. The right claimed in this case was to native title, a much broader and more fundamental Aboriginal right than the right to carry on a traditional activity such as the Musqueam's right to fish for salmon that was at issue in *Sparrow*. After *Sparrow*, the Court decided a number of cases involving claims to section 35 rights, but all of them dealt with the right to engage in a specific activity—such as commercial fishing or operating a high stakes casino.[1] Most of these claims were rejected by the Court. The majority took the position that Aboriginal peoples could claim rights only to activities that could be shown to have been integral to their cultures before contact with Europeans.

Though the Supreme Court had recognized the general concept of native title in the 1973 *Calder* case, it did not give a detailed account of the meaning of native title in that case. In *Delgamuukw* it gave a full account of the meaning of native title in Canadian constitutional law and how such a right is established in Canadian courts.

As in *Sparrow*, the Supreme Court's decision did not resolve the particular points at issue in the case—namely, whether the Gitksan and Wet'suwet'en peoples had title to the land in question. Because of technical changes that the native parties made to their claim after trial, and flaws in the trial judge's treatment of important legal issues, the Court decided that a new trial was required. But if the new trial took place it would be guided by the general principles the Court proceeded to set out in its judgment.

The first such principle was one of methodology—the use of oral history. The Supreme Court found that the trial judge had erred in refusing to admit or give independent weight to the oral histories submitted by the Aboriginal claimants. The Court reiterated a point made in previous cases that to reject evidence given by Aboriginal people about their history and culture because of its oral character would defeat the very purpose of Aboriginal rights, which is to reconcile "prior occupation of North America by distinctive aboriginal societies with the assertion of Crown sovereignty over Canadian territory." Such a reconciliation requires that Aboriginal rights achieve a "bridging of aboriginal and non-aboriginal cultures."

The same aspiration of reconciliation permeates the general principles on the nature of Aboriginal title set out by Chief Justice Lamer. Because the common law relating to native title has aimed to reconcile the native peoples' occupation of land with the assertion of Crown sovereignty over it, this title must be understood as a *sui generis* form of land ownership. To begin with, it is a land right that originates not from any grant or act of recognition by the Crown, but from the fact that Aboriginal people possessed the land before the Crown asserted its sovereignty. It follows that an Aboriginal group that claims native title over land must be able to prove that it occupied the land at the time British sovereignty was asserted.

---

1 In 1996, the Supreme Court decided three such cases, *R. v. Van der Peet*, [1996] 2 S.C.R. 507; *R. v. Gladstone*, [1996] 2 S.C.R. 723; and *R. v. Pamajewon*, [1996] 2 S.C.R. 821.

Great Britain did not assert its sovereignty in British Columbia until 1846. Note that this is considerably later than the time of first contact with Europeans, which is the time that, according to the Court in other cases, Aboriginal peoples must go back to when claiming rights to engage in particular activities unrelated to their ownership of land. While prior occupation of land to which title is claimed must be shown to have been exclusive, this test could be satisfied by showing that efforts had been made to exclude others or that members of other nations had been permitted to use the land.

The Court identified two other unique features of Aboriginal title. First, it is a title to land that cannot be held by individuals—"it is a collective right to land held by all members of an aboriginal nation." Second, Aboriginal title is inalienable—that is, Aboriginal title lands cannot be sold to third parties, but can be sold or surrendered only to the Crown.

Unlike specific activity rights that are confined to pre-contact practices, holders of native title, in the majority's view, have rights to use the land in ways that go well beyond traditional activities. For example, Aboriginal title holders have the right to develop the land, including exploitation of its mineral resources, in a non-traditional way. This right to develop the land is subject to just one limitation: the land cannot be used "in a manner that is irreconcilable with the nature of the claimants' attachment to these lands." The Chief Justices gave two examples of forbidden uses: strip-mining a traditional hunting area or converting ceremonial land into a parking lot. The unfreezing of Aboriginal title from strictly traditional pursuits was the main point on which Justice La Forest, supported by Justice L'Heureux-Dubé, differed from the majority. Justice La Forest would have Aboriginal title focus "on the occupation and use of land as part of the aboriginal society's *traditional way of life.*"

Though the Gitksan and Wet'suwet'en had put forward a claim to self-government as well as to native title, the Court declined to deal with that claim in any detail. The parties' submissions to the Court did not provide the Court with enough material to grapple with such a complex issue as the Aboriginal peoples' constitutional right to self-government. Nonetheless, the Court leaves no doubt that Aboriginal title itself confers considerable scope for self-government. For instance, in discussing the exclusive nature of Aboriginal title, the Chief Justice said that "aboriginal people have *the right to choose* to what use lands can be put."

The Court held that Aboriginal title like all constitutionally recognized rights cannot be treated as an absolute. It gave a broad account of the legislative objectives that could be sufficiently "compelling and substantial" to justify infringement of native title by either the federal or provincial governments. The development of agriculture, forestry, mining, hydro-electric power, the "general economic development of the interior of the province, the building of infrastructure, and the settlement of foreign populations"—any of these, in principle, could justify infringement of Aboriginal title. However, the second part of the justification test requires the infringement to be as minimal as possible. This means that government is obliged to give real weight and, in some instances, "priority" to accommodating Aboriginal interests in any development that takes place on their land. At the very least, there is always "a duty of consultation" and, in some cases, the full consent of an Aboriginal nation may be required. Also, there would have to be financial compensation for economic losses resulting from an infringement of Aboriginal title.

The Court dealt with the possibility of going beyond encroachments on native title to full extinguishment. In a section of the judgment that we have not included, the Court found that the province cannot extinguish native title. Jurisdiction to extinguish Aboriginal rights lies exclusively with the federal Parliament under its power in section 91(24) over

"Indians, and Lands reserved for Indians." Not that the Court favoured unilateral extinguishment of native title. Quite to the contrary, all the judges made it clear that they favoured negotiated solutions to this and other claims to native title. The Crown, said Chief Justice Lamer, has a moral, if not a legal, duty to conduct such negotiations in good faith. Only in this way can a genuine reconciliation be achieved. "Let us face it," Lamer concluded, "we are all here to stay."

Ironically, the Supreme Court's elucidation of the constitutional right to native title did not, in the short term, expedite the negotiation of land claims settlements. In negotiating land claims agreements, the federal government continued to insist on Aboriginal peoples consenting to extinguishment of their native title in exchange for ownership in fee simple (the normal common form of land ownership) of a portion of their traditional lands and other economic and political benefits. But Aboriginal peoples, now that they had—thanks to *Delgamuukw*—a clearer understanding of what they were entitled to if they could establish native title in the courts, were reluctant to surrender that entitlement at the negotiating table. The federal government's policy is that First Nations must either litigate or negotiate. Part of the claimant group in *Delgamuukw* continued to litigate.

British Columbia had resisted the treaty process for a very long time. In the colonial period, Governor Douglas had made treaties to settle land issues with native peoples on Vancouver Island. However, when British Columbia entered Confederation, it refused to follow the Canadian practice of obtaining land for settlement by making treaties with its native owners. As the province developed, some lands were set aside for Indians, but these reserves were not based on treaties. In effect, the provincial government took the position that common-law native title did not apply in British Columbia. Even after *Calder*, British Columbia did not agree to negotiate a land settlement with the Nisga'a until the 1990s. In 1993, it also agreed to negotiate modern treaties with other First Nations in the province who, like the Nisga'a, had claims to unceded lands. For this purpose, the British Columbia Treaty Commission, made up of federal, provincial, and Aboriginal representatives, was established to preside over a modern treaty process. Fifty-four First Nations agreed to participate in the process.[2]

In 1999, the Nisga'a finally agreed to a treaty with Canada and British Columbia that left them with ownership of just 10 percent of their traditional lands. It was not until 2007 that the first land settlement treaties were made under the BC Treaty Commission process, when treaties with the Tsawwassen First Nation near Vancouver and with the Maa'nulth people on Vancouver Island were ratified. In November 2007, the Xeni Gwet'in, part of the larger group that were claimants in *Delgamuukw*, finally won a court ruling that they met the legal test for Aboriginal title over roughly 45 percent of the 440,000 hectares they claimed in the Nemiah Valley of British Columbia. But this First Nation may still have to return to court to settle its rights with respect to the remainder of the land. In all of this, we can see that, while the Supreme Court can clarify the constitutional principles that underlie the First Nations' relations with Canada, it cannot settle the concrete issues involved in each case. Settlement involves an ongoing mixture of litigation in the courts and political negotiations. ⌁

---

2   For an account of treaty making in British Columbia, see Tony Penikett, *Reconciliation: First Nations Treaty Making in British Columbia* (Vancouver: Douglas & McIntyre, 2006).

DELGAMUUKW v. BRITISH COLUMBIA
[1997] 3. S.C.R. 1010

Hearing: June 16, 17, 1997; Judgment: December 11, 1997.

Present: Lamer C.J. and La Forest, L'Heureux-Dubé, Sopinka,* Cory, McLachlin, and Major JJ.

Interveners: The First Nations Summit, the Musqueam Nation et al. (as shown in Schedule 2), the Westbank First Nation, the B.C. Cattlemen's Association et al. (as shown in Schedule 3), Skeena Cellulose Inc., and Alcan Aluminum Ltd.

* Sopinka J. took no part in this judgment.

The judgment of Lamer C.J. and Cory and Major JJ. was delivered by

THE CHIEF JUSTICE:

I. Introduction

[1] This appeal is the latest in a series of cases in which it has fallen to this Court to interpret and apply the guarantee of existing aboriginal rights found in s. 35(1) of the *Constitution Act, 1982*. Although that line of decisions, commencing with *R. v. Sparrow*, [1990] 1 S.C.R. 1075, proceeding through the *Van der Peet* trilogy (*R. v. Van der Peet*, [1996] 2 S.C.R. 507, *R. v. N.T.C. Smokehouse Ltd.*, [1996] 2 S.C.R. 672, and *R. v. Gladstone*, [1996] 2 S.C.R. 723), and ending in *R. v. Pamajewon*, [1996] 2 S.C.R. 821, *R. v. Adams*, [1996] 3 S.C.R. 101, and *R. v. Côté*, [1996] 3 S.C.R. 139, have laid down the jurisprudential framework for s. 35(1), this appeal raises a set of interrelated and novel questions which revolve around a single issue—the nature and scope of the constitutional protection afforded by s. 35(1) to common law aboriginal title.

[2] In *Adams*, and in the companion decision in *Côté*, I considered and rejected the proposition that claims to aboriginal rights must also be grounded in an underlying claim to aboriginal title. But I held, nevertheless, that aboriginal title was a distinct species of aboriginal right that was recognized and affirmed by s. 35(1). Since aboriginal title was not being claimed in those earlier appeals, it was unnecessary to say more. This appeal demands, however, that the Court now explore and elucidate the implications of the constitutionalization of aboriginal title. The first is the specific content of aboriginal title, a question which this Court has not yet definitively addressed, either at common law or under s. 35(1). The second is the related question of the test for the proof of title, which, whatever its content, is a right *in land*, and its relationship to the definition of the aboriginal rights recognized and affirmed by s. 35(1) in *Van der Peet* in terms of *activities*. The third is whether aboriginal title, as a right in land, mandates a modified approach to the test of justification first laid down in *Sparrow* and elaborated upon in *Gladstone*.

[3] In addition to the relationship between aboriginal title and s. 35(1), this appeal also raises an important practical problem relevant to the proof of aboriginal title which is endemic to aboriginal rights litigation generally—the treatment of the oral histories of Canada's aboriginal peoples by the courts. In *Van der Peet*, I held that the common law rules of evidence should be adapted to take into account the *sui generis* nature of aboriginal rights. In this appeal, the Court must address what specific form those modifications must take.

[4] Finally, given the existence of aboriginal title in British Columbia, this Court must address, on cross-appeal, the question of whether the province of British Columbia, from the time it joined Confederation in 1871, until the entrenchment of s. 35(1) in 1982, had jurisdiction to extinguish the rights of aboriginal peoples, including aboriginal title, in that province. Moreover, if the province was without this jurisdiction, a further question arises—whether provincial laws of general application that would otherwise be inapplicable to Indians and Indian lands could nevertheless extinguish aboriginal rights through the operation of s. 88 of the *Indian Act*, R.S.C., 1985, c. I-5.

II. Facts

[5] At the British Columbia Supreme Court, McEachern C.J. heard 374 days of evidence and argument. Some of that evidence was not in a form which is familiar to common law courts, including oral histories and legends. Another significant part was the evidence of experts in genealogy, linguistics, archeology, anthropology, and geography.

[6] The trial judge's decision (reported at [1991] 3 W.W.R. 97) is nearly 400 pages long, with another 100 pages of schedules. Although I am of the view that there must be a new trial, I nevertheless find it useful to summarize some of the relevant facts, so as to put the remainder of the judgment into context.

A. The Claim at Trial

[7] This action was commenced by the appellants, who are all Gitksan or Wet'suwet'en hereditary chiefs, who, both individually and on behalf of their "Houses" claimed separate portions of 58,000 square kilometres in British Columbia. For the purpose of the claim, this area was divided into 133 individual territories, claimed by the 71 Houses. This represents all of the Wet'suwet'en people, and all but 12 of the Gitksan Houses. Their claim was originally for "ownership" of the territory and "jurisdiction" over it. (At this Court, this was transformed into, primarily, a claim for aboriginal title over the land in question.) The province of British Columbia counterclaimed for a declaration that the appellants have no right or interest in and to the territory or alternatively, that

the appellants' cause of action ought to be for compensation from the Government of Canada.

B. The Gitksan and Wet'suwet'en Peoples

(1) Demography

[8] The Gitksan consist of approximately 4,000 to 5,000 persons, most of whom now live in the territory claimed, which is generally the watersheds of the north and central Skeena, Nass and Babine Rivers and their tributaries. The Wet'suwet'en consist of approximately 1,500 to 2,000 persons, who also predominantly live in the territory claimed. This territory is mainly in the watersheds of the Bulkley and parts of the Fraser-Nechako River systems and their tributaries. It lies immediately east and south of the Gitksan.

[9] Of course, the Gitksan and Wet'suwet'en are not the only people living in the claimed territory. As noted by both McEachern C.J. at trial (at p. 440) and Lambert J.A. on appeal (at p. 243), there are other aboriginals who live in the claimed territory, notably the Carrier-Sekani and Nishga peoples. Some of these people have unsettled land claims overlapping with the territory at issue here. Moreover, there are also numerous non-aboriginals living there. McEachern C.J. found that, at the time of the trial, the non-aboriginal population in the territory was over 30,000.

(2) History

[10] There were numerous theories of the history of the Gitksan and Wet'suwet'en peoples before the trial judge. His conclusion from the evidence was that their ancestors migrated from Asia, probably through Alaska, and spread south and west into the areas which they found to be liveable. There was archeological evidence, which he accepted, that there was some form of human habitation in the territory and its surrounding areas from 3,500 to 6,000 years ago, and intense occupation of the Hagwilget Canyon site (near Hazelton), prior to about 4,000 to 3,500 years ago. This occupation was mainly in or near villages on the Skeena River, the Babine River or the Bulkley River, where salmon, the staple of their diet, was easily obtainable. The other parts of the territory surrounding and between their villages and rivers were used for hunting and gathering for both food and ceremonial purposes. The scope of this hunting and gathering area depended largely on the availability of the required materials in the areas around the villages. Prior to the commencement of the fur trade, there was no reason to travel far from the villages for anything other than their subsistence requirements.

(3) North American Exploration

[11] There was little European influence in western Canada until the arrival of Capt. Cook at Nootka on Vancouver Island in 1778, which led to the sea otter hunt in the north Pacific. This influence grew with the establishment of the first Hudson's Bay trading post west of the Rockies (although east of the territories claimed) by Simon Fraser in 1805-1806. Trapping for the commercial fur trade was not an aboriginal practice, but rather one influenced by European contact. The trial judge held that the time of direct contact between the Aboriginal Peoples in the claimed territory was approximately 1820, after the trader William Brown arrived and Hudson's Bay had merged with the North West Company.

(4) Present Social Organization

[12] McEachern C.J. set out a description of the present social organization of the appellants. In his opinion, this was necessary because "one of the ingredients of aboriginal land claims is that they arise from long-term communal rather than personal use or possession of land" (at p. 147). The fundamental premise of both the Gitksan and the Wet'suwet'en peoples is that they are divided into clans and Houses. Every person born of a Gitksan or Wet'suwet'en woman is automatically a member of his or her mother's House and clan. There are four Gitksan and four Wet'suwet'en clans, which are subdivided into Houses. Each House has one or more Hereditary Chief as its titular head, selected by the elders of their House, as well as possibly the Head Chief of the other Houses of the clan. There is no head chief for the clans, but there is a ranking order of precedence within communities or villages, where one House or clan may be more prominent than others.

[13] At trial, the appellants' claim was based on their historical use and "ownership" of one or more of the territories. The trial judge held that these are marked, in some cases, by physical and tangible indicators of their association with the territories. He cited as examples totem poles with the Houses' crests carved, or distinctive regalia. In addition, the Gitksan Houses have an "adaawk" which is a collection of sacred oral tradition about their ancestors, histories and territories. The Wet'suwet'en each have a "kungax" which is a spiritual song or dance or performance which ties them to their land. Both of these were entered as evidence on behalf of the appellants (see my discussion of the trial judge's view of this evidence, *infra*).

[14] The most significant evidence of spiritual connection between the Houses and their territory is a feast hall. This is where the Gitksan and Wet'suwet'en peoples tell and retell their stories and identify their territories to remind themselves of the sacred connection that they have with their lands. The feast has a ceremonial purpose, but is also used for making important decisions. The trial judge also noted the *Criminal Code* prohibition on aboriginal feast ceremonies, which existed until 1951....

IV. Issues

[72] The following are the principal issues which must be addressed in this appeal. As will become apparent in my analysis, some of these issues in turn raise a number of sub-issues which I will address as well:

A. Do the pleadings preclude the Court from entertaining claims for aboriginal title and self-government?
B. What is the ability of this Court to interfere with the factual findings made by the trial judge?
C. What is the content of aboriginal title, how is it protected by s. 35(1) of the *Constitution Act, 1982*, and what is required for its proof?
D. Has a claim to self-government been made out by the appellants?
E. Did the province have the power to extinguish aboriginal rights after 1871, either under its own jurisdiction or through the operation of s. 88 of the *Indian Act*?

V. Analysis

A. Do the Pleadings Preclude the Court from Entertaining Claims for Aboriginal Title and Self-Government?

[73] In their pleadings, the appellants, 51 Chiefs representing most of the Houses of the Gitksan and Wet'suwet'en nations, originally advanced 51 individual claims on their own behalf and on behalf of their houses for "ownership" and "jurisdiction" over 133 distinct territories which together comprise 58,000 square kilometres of northwestern British Columbia. On appeal, that original claim was altered in two different ways. First, the claims for ownership and jurisdiction have been replaced with claims for aboriginal title and self-government, respectively. Second, the individual claims by each house have been amalgamated into two communal claims, one advanced on behalf of each nation. However, there were no formal amendments to the pleadings to this effect, and the respondents accordingly argue that claims which are central to this appeal are not properly before the Court....

[76] ...Given the absence of an amendment to the pleadings, I must reluctantly conclude that the respondents suffered some prejudice. The appellants argue that the respondents did not experience prejudice since the collective and individual claims are related to the extent that the territory claimed by each nation is merely the sum of the individual claims of each House; the external boundaries of the collective claims therefore represent the outer boundaries of the outer territories. Although that argument carries considerable weight, it does not address the basic point that the collective claims were simply not in issue at trial. To frame the case in a different

manner on appeal would retroactively deny the respondents the opportunity to know the appellants' case.

[77] This defect in the pleadings prevents the Court from considering the merits of this appeal. However, given the importance of this case and the fact that much of the evidence of individual territorial holdings is extremely relevant to the collective claims now advanced by each of the appellants, the correct remedy for the defect in pleadings is a new trial, where, to quote the trial judge at p. 368, "[i]t will be for the parties to consider whether any amendment is required in order to make the pleadings conform with the evidence." Moreover, as I will now explain, there are other reasons why a new trial should be ordered.

B. What Is the Ability of this Court to Interfere with the Factual Findings Made by the Trial Judge?

(1) General Principles

[78] I recently reviewed the principles governing the appellate review of findings of fact in *Van der Peet, supra*. As a general rule, this Court has been extremely reluctant to interfere with the findings of fact made at trial, especially when those findings of fact are based on an assessment of the testimony and credibility of witnesses. Unless there is a "palpable and overriding error," appellate courts should not substitute their own findings of fact for those of the trial judge....

[80] I recently held, in *Van der Peet*, that these general principles apply to cases litigated under s. 35(1). On the other hand, while accepting the general principle of non-interference, this Court has also identified specific situations in which an appeal court can interfere with a finding of fact made at trial. For example, appellate intervention is warranted "where the courts below have misapprehended or overlooked material evidence": see *Chartier v. Attorney General of Quebec*, [1979] 2 S.C.R. 474, at p. 493. In cases involving the determination of aboriginal rights, appellate intervention is also warranted by the failure of a trial court to appreciate the evidentiary difficulties inherent in adjudicating aboriginal claims when, first, applying the rules of evidence and, second, interpreting the evidence before it. As I said in *Van der Peet*, at para. 68:

> In determining whether an aboriginal claimant has produced evidence sufficient to demonstrate that her activity is an aspect of a practice, custom or tradition integral to a distinctive aboriginal culture, *a court should approach the rules of evidence, and interpret the evidence that exists*, with a consciousness of the special nature of aboriginal claims, and of the evidentiary difficulties in proving a right which originates in times where there were no written records of the practices, customs and traditions engaged in. *The courts must not undervalue the evidence presented by aboriginal claimants simply because that evidence does not*

conform precisely with the evidentiary standards that would be applied in, for example, a private law torts case. [Emphasis added.]

[81] The justification for this special approach can be found in the nature of aboriginal rights themselves. I explained in *Van der Peet* that those rights are aimed at the reconciliation of the prior occupation of North America by distinctive aboriginal societies with the assertion of Crown sovereignty over Canadian territory. They attempt to achieve that reconciliation by "their bridging of aboriginal and non-aboriginal cultures" (at para. 42). Accordingly, "a court must take into account the perspective of the aboriginal people claiming the right . . . while at the same time taking into account the perspective of the common law" such that "[t]rue reconciliation will, equally, place weight on each" (at paras. 49 and 50). . . .

[87] Notwithstanding the challenges created by the use of oral histories as proof of historical facts, the laws of evidence must be adapted in order that this type of evidence can be accommodated and placed on an equal footing with the types of historical evidence that courts are familiar with, which largely consists of historical documents. This is a long-standing practice in the interpretation of treaties between the Crown and aboriginal peoples: *Sioui* [*R. v.*, [1990] 1 S.C.R. 1025], at p. 1068; *R. v. Taylor* (1981), 62 C.C.C. (2d) 227 (Ont. C.A.), at p. 232. . . .

(2) Application of General Principles

(a) General Comments

[89] The general principle of appellate non-interference applies with particular force in this appeal. The trial was lengthy and very complex. There were 318 days of testimony. There were a large number of witnesses, lay and expert. The volume of evidence is enormous. . . . The result was a judgment of over 400 pages in length.

[90] It is not open to the appellants to challenge the trial judge's findings of fact merely because they disagree with them. I fear that a significant number of the appellants' objections fall into this category. . . .

[92] On the other hand, the appellants have alleged that the trial judge made a number of serious errors relating to the treatment of the oral histories of the appellants. Those oral histories were expressed in three different forms: (i) the adaawk of the Gitksan, and the kungax of the Wet'suwet'en; (ii) the personal recollections of members of the appellant nations, and (iii) the territorial affidavits filed by the heads of the individual houses within each nation. The trial judge ruled on both the admissibility of, and the weight to be given to, these various forms of oral history without the benefit of my reasons in *Van der Peet*, as will become evident in the discussion that follows. . . .

(e) Conclusion

[107] The trial judge's treatment of the various kinds of oral histories did not satisfy the principles I laid down in *Van der Peet*. These errors are particularly worrisome because oral histories were of critical importance to the appellants' case. They used those histories in an attempt to establish their occupation and use of the disputed territory, an essential requirement for aboriginal title. The trial judge, after refusing to admit, or giving no independent weight to these oral histories, reached the conclusion that the appellants had not demonstrated the requisite degree of occupation for "ownership." Had the trial judge assessed the oral histories correctly, his conclusions on these issues of fact might have been very different.

[108] In the circumstances, the factual findings cannot stand. However, given the enormous complexity of the factual issues at hand, it would be impossible for the Court to do justice to the parties by sifting through the record itself and making new factual findings. A new trial is warranted, at which the evidence may be considered in light of the principles laid down in *Van der Peet* and elaborated upon here. In applying these principles, the new trial judge might well share some or all of the findings of fact of McEachern C.J.

C. What Is the Content of Aboriginal Title, How Is It Protected by Section 35(1) of the Constitution Act, 1982, and What Is Required for Its Proof?

(1) Introduction

[109] The parties disagree over whether the appellants have established aboriginal title to the disputed area. However, since those factual issues require a new trial, we cannot resolve that dispute in this appeal. But factual issues aside, the parties also have a more fundamental disagreement over the content of aboriginal title itself, and its reception into the Constitution by s. 35(1). In order to give guidance to the judge at the new trial, it is to this issue that I will now turn.

[110] I set out these opposing positions by way of illustration and introduction because I believe that all of the parties have characterized the content of aboriginal title incorrectly. The appellants argue that aboriginal title is tantamount to an inalienable fee simple, which confers on aboriginal peoples the rights to use those lands as they choose and which has been constitutionalized by s. 35(1). The respondents offer two alternative formulations: first, that aboriginal title is no more than a bundle of rights to engage in activities which are themselves aboriginal rights recognized and affirmed by s. 35(1), and that the *Constitution Act, 1982*, merely constitutionalizes those individual rights, not the bundle itself, because the latter has no independent content; and second, that aboriginal title, at most, encompasses the right to exclusive use and occupation

of land in order to engage in those activities which are aboriginal rights themselves, and that s. 35(1) constitutionalizes this notion of exclusivity.

[111] The content of aboriginal title, in fact, lies somewhere in between these positions. Aboriginal title is a right in land and, as such, is more than the right to engage in specific activities which may be themselves aboriginal rights. Rather, it confers the right to use land for a variety of activities, not all of which need be aspects of practices, customs and traditions which are integral to the distinctive cultures of aboriginal societies. Those activities do not constitute the right *per se*; rather, they are parasitic on the underlying title. However, that range of uses is subject to the limitation that they must not be irreconcilable with the nature of the attachment to the land which forms the basis of the particular group's aboriginal title. This inherent limit, to be explained more fully below, flows from the definition of aboriginal title as a *sui generis* interest in land, and is one way in which aboriginal title is distinct from a fee simple.

(2) Aboriginal Title at Common Law

(a) General Features

[112] The starting point of the Canadian jurisprudence on aboriginal title is the Privy Council's decision in *St. Catherine's Milling and Lumber Co. v. The Queen* (1888), 14 A.C. 46, which described aboriginal title as a "personal and usufructuary right" (at p. 54). The subsequent jurisprudence has attempted to grapple with this definition, and has in the process demonstrated that the Privy Council's choice of terminology is not particularly helpful to explain the various dimensions of aboriginal title. What the Privy Council sought to capture is that aboriginal title is a *sui generis* interest in land. Aboriginal title has been described as *sui generis* in order to distinguish it from "normal" proprietary interests, such as fee simple. . . . As with other aboriginal rights, it must be understood by reference to both common law and aboriginal perspectives.

[113] The idea that aboriginal title is *sui generis* is the unifying principle underlying the various dimensions of that title. One dimension is its *inalienability*. Lands held pursuant to aboriginal title cannot be transferred, sold or surrendered to anyone other than the Crown and, as a result, is inalienable to third parties. This Court has taken pains to clarify that aboriginal title is only "personal" in this sense, and does not mean that aboriginal title is a non-proprietary interest which amounts to no more than a licence to use and occupy the land and cannot compete on an equal footing with other proprietary interests: see *Canadian Pacific Ltd. v. Paul*, [1988] 2 S.C.R. 654, at p. 677.

[114] Another dimension of aboriginal title is its *source*. It had originally been thought that the source of aboriginal title in Canada was the *Royal Proclamation, 1763*: see *St. Catherine's Milling*. However, it is now clear that although aboriginal title was recognized by the *Proclamation*, it arises from the prior occupation of Canada by aboriginal peoples. That prior occupation, however, is relevant in two different ways, both of which illustrate the *sui generis* nature of aboriginal title. The first is the physical fact of occupation, which derives from the common law principle that occupation is proof of possession in law: see Kent McNeil, *Common Law Aboriginal Title* (1989), at p. 7. Thus, in *Guerin* [*v. The Queen*, [1984] 2 S.C.R. 335], Dickson J. described aboriginal title, at p. 376, as a "legal right derived from the Indians' historic occupation and possession of their tribal lands." What makes aboriginal title *sui generis* is that it arises from possession *before* the assertion of British sovereignty, whereas normal estates, like fee simple, arise afterwards: see Kent McNeil, "The Meaning of Aboriginal Title," in Michael Asch, ed., *Aboriginal and Treaty Rights in Canada* (1997), 135, at p. 144. . . .

[115] A further dimension of aboriginal title is the fact that it is held *communally*. Aboriginal title cannot be held by individual aboriginal persons; it is a collective right to land held by all members of an aboriginal nation. Decisions with respect to that land are also made by that community. This is another feature of aboriginal title which is *sui generis* and distinguishes it from normal property interests.

(b) The Content of Aboriginal Title

[116] Although cases involving aboriginal title have come before this Court and Privy Council before, there has never been a definitive statement from either court on the *content* of aboriginal title. In *St. Catherine's Milling*, the Privy Council, as I have mentioned, described the aboriginal title as a "personal and usufructuary right," but declined to explain what that meant because it was not "necessary to express any opinion upon the point" (at p. 55). Similarly, in *Calder*, *Guerin*, and *Paul*, the issues were the extinguishment of, the fiduciary duty arising from the surrender of, and statutory easements over land held pursuant to, aboriginal title, respectively; the content of title was not at issue and was not directly addressed.

[117] Although the courts have been less than forthcoming, I have arrived at the conclusion that the content of aboriginal title can be summarized by two propositions: first, that aboriginal title encompasses the right to exclusive use and occupation of the land held pursuant to that title for a variety of purposes, which need not be aspects of those aboriginal practices, customs and traditions which are integral to distinctive aboriginal cultures; and second, that those protected uses must not be irreconcilable with the nature of the group's attachment to that land. For the sake of clarity, I will discuss each of these propositions separately.

Aboriginal Title Encompasses the Right to Use the Land Held Pursuant to that Title for a Variety of Purposes, Which Need Not Be Aspects of Those Aboriginal Practices, Cultures and Traditions Which Are Integral to Distinctive Aboriginal Cultures

[118] The respondents argue that aboriginal title merely encompasses the right to engage in activities which are aspects of aboriginal practices, customs and traditions which are integral to distinctive aboriginal cultures of the aboriginal group claiming the right and, at most, adds the notion of exclusivity; i.e., the exclusive right to use the land for those purposes. However, the uses to which lands held pursuant to aboriginal title can be put are not restricted in this way. This conclusion emerges from three sources: (i) the Canadian jurisprudence on aboriginal title, (ii) the relationship between reserve lands and lands held pursuant to aboriginal title, and (iii) the *Indian Oil and Gas Act.*, R.S.C., 1985, c. I-7. As well, although this is not legally determinative, it is supported by the critical literature. In particular, I have profited greatly from Professor McNeil's article, "The Meaning of Aboriginal Title," *supra.*

(i) Canadian Jurisprudence on Aboriginal Title

[119] Despite the fact that the jurisprudence on aboriginal title is somewhat underdeveloped, it is clear that the uses to which lands held pursuant to aboriginal title can be put is not restricted to the practices, customs and traditions of aboriginal peoples integral to distinctive aboriginal cultures. In *Guerin*, for example, Dickson J. described aboriginal title as an "interest in land" which encompassed "a legal right to occupy and possess certain lands" (at p. 382). The "right to occupy and possess" is framed in broad terms and, significantly, is not qualified by reference to traditional and customary uses of those lands. Any doubt that the right to occupancy and possession encompasses a broad variety of uses of land was put to rest in *Paul*, where the Court went even further and stated that aboriginal title was "more than the right to enjoyment and occupancy" (at p. 678). Once again, there is no reference to aboriginal practices, customs and traditions as a qualifier on that right. Moreover, I take the reference to "more" as emphasis of the broad notion of use and possession.

(ii) Reserve Land

[120] Another source of support for the conclusion that the uses to which lands held under aboriginal title can be put are not restricted to those grounded in practices, customs and traditions integral to distinctive aboriginal cultures can be found in *Guerin*, where Dickson J. stated at p. 379 that the same legal principles governed the aboriginal interest in reserve lands and lands held pursuant to aboriginal title:

It does not matter, in my opinion, that the present case is concerned with the interest of an Indian Band in a reserve rather than with unrecognized aboriginal title in traditional tribal lands. *The Indian interest in the land is the same in both cases....* [Emphasis added.]

[121] The nature of the Indian interest in reserve land is very broad, and can be found in s. 18 of the *Indian Act*, which I reproduce in full:

18. (1) Subject to this Act, reserves are held by Her Majesty for the *use and benefit* of the respective bands for which they were set apart, and subject to this Act and to the terms of any treaty or surrender, the Governor in Council may determine whether any purpose for which lands in a reserve are used or are to be used is for the use and benefit of the band.

(2) The Minister may authorize the use of lands in a reserve for the purpose of Indian schools, the administration of Indian affairs, Indian burial grounds, Indian health projects or, with the consent of the council of the band, *for any other purpose for the general welfare of the band,* and may take any lands in a reserve required for those purposes, but where an individual Indian, immediately prior to the taking, was entitled to the possession of those lands, compensation for that use shall be paid to the Indian, in such amount as may be agreed between the Indian and the Minister, or, failing agreement, as may be determined in such manner as the Minister may direct. [Emphasis added.] ...

(iii) Indian Oil and Gas Act

[122] The third source for the proposition that the content of aboriginal title is not restricted to practices, customs and traditions which are integral to distinctive aboriginal cultures is the *Indian Oil and Gas Act.* The overall purpose of the statute is to provide for the exploration of oil and gas on reserve lands through their surrender to the Crown. The statute presumes that the aboriginal interest in reserve land includes mineral rights, a point which this Court unanimously accepted with respect to the *Indian Act* in *Blueberry River Indian Band v. Canada (Department of Indian Affairs and Northern Development)*, [1995] 4 S.C.R. 344. On the basis of *Guerin*, aboriginal title also encompass mineral rights, and lands held pursuant to aboriginal title should be capable of exploitation in the same way, which is certainly not a traditional use for those lands. ...

[123] Although this is not determinative, the conclusion that the content of aboriginal title is not restricted to those uses with their origins in the practices, customs and traditions integral to distinctive aboriginal societies has wide support in the critical literature. ...

[124] In conclusion, the content of aboriginal title is not restricted to those uses which are elements of a practice, custom or tradition integral to the distinctive culture of the aboriginal group claiming the right. However, nor does aboriginal title amount to a form of inalienable fee simple, as I will now explain.

(c) Inherent Limit: Lands Held Pursuant to Aboriginal Title Cannot Be Used in a Manner That Is Irreconcilable with the Nature of the Attachment to the Land Which Forms the Basis of the Group's Claim to Aboriginal Title

[125] The content of aboriginal title contains an inherent limit that lands held pursuant to title cannot be used in a manner that is irreconcilable with the nature of the claimants' attachment to those lands. This limit on the content of aboriginal title is a manifestation of the principle that underlies the various dimensions of that special interest in land—it is a *sui generis* interest that is distinct from "normal" proprietary interests, most notably fee simple.

[126] I arrive at this conclusion by reference to the other dimensions of aboriginal title which are *sui generis* as well. I first consider the source of aboriginal title. As I discussed earlier, aboriginal title arises from the prior occupation of Canada by aboriginal peoples. That prior occupation is relevant in two different ways: first, because of the physical fact of occupation, and second, because aboriginal title originates in part from pre-existing systems of aboriginal law. However, the law of aboriginal title does not only seek to determine the historic rights of aboriginal peoples to land; it also seeks to afford legal protection to prior occupation in the present-day. Implicit in the protection of historic patterns of occupation is a recognition of the importance of the continuity of the relationship of an aboriginal community to its land over time....

[128] Accordingly, in my view, lands subject to aboriginal title cannot be put to such uses as may be irreconcilable with the nature of the occupation of that land and the relationship that the particular group has had with the land which together have given rise to aboriginal title in the first place. As discussed below, one of the critical elements in the determination of whether a particular aboriginal group has aboriginal title to certain lands is the matter of the occupancy of those lands. Occupancy is determined by reference to the activities that have taken place on the land and the uses to which the land has been put by the particular group. If lands are so occupied, there will exist a special bond between the group and the land in question such that the land will be part of the definition of the group's distinctive culture. It seems to me that these elements of aboriginal title create an inherent limitation on the uses to which the land, over which such title exists, may be put. For example, if occupation is established with reference to the use of the land as a hunting ground, then the group that successfully claims aboriginal title to that land may not use it in such a fashion as to destroy its value for such a use (e.g., by strip mining it). Similarly, if a group claims a special bond with the land because of its ceremonial or cultural significance, it may not use the land in such a way as to destroy that relationship (e.g., by developing it in such a way that the bond is destroyed, perhaps by turning it into a parking lot).

[129] It is for this reason also that lands held by virtue of aboriginal title may not be alienated. Alienation would bring to an end the entitlement of the aboriginal people to occupy the land and would terminate their relationship with it.... What the inalienability of lands held pursuant to aboriginal title suggests is that those lands are more than just a fungible commodity. The relationship between an aboriginal community and the lands over which it has aboriginal title has an important non-economic component. The land has an inherent and unique value in itself, which is enjoyed by the community with aboriginal title to it. The community cannot put the land to uses which would destroy that value....

[131] Finally, what I have just said regarding the importance of the continuity of the relationship between an aboriginal community and its land, and the non-economic or inherent value of that land, should not be taken to detract from the possibility of surrender to the Crown in exchange for valuable consideration. On the contrary, the idea of surrender reinforces the conclusion that aboriginal title is limited in the way I have described. If aboriginal peoples wish to use their lands in a way that aboriginal title does not permit, then they must surrender those lands and convert them into non-title lands to do so.

[132] The foregoing amounts to a general limitation on the use of lands held by virtue of aboriginal title. It arises from the particular physical and cultural relationship that a group may have with the land and is defined by the source of aboriginal title over it. This is not, I must emphasize, a limitation that restricts the use of the land to those activities that have traditionally been carried out on it. That would amount to a legal straitjacket on aboriginal peoples who have a legitimate legal claim to the land. The approach I have outlined above allows for a full range of uses of the land, subject only to an overarching limit, defined by the special nature of the aboriginal title in that land.

(d) Aboriginal Title Under Section 35(1) of the Constitution Act, 1982

[133] Aboriginal title at common law is protected in its full form by s. 35(1). This conclusion flows from the express language of s. 35(1) itself, which states in full: "[t]he *existing*

aboriginal and treaty rights of the aboriginal peoples of Canada are hereby recognized and affirmed" (emphasis added). On a plain reading of the provision, s. 35(1) did not create aboriginal rights; rather, it accorded constitutional status to those rights which were "existing" in 1982. The provision, at the very least, constitutionalized those rights which aboriginal peoples possessed at common law, since those rights existed at the time s. 35(1) came into force. Since aboriginal title was a common law right whose existence was recognized well before 1982 (e.g., *Calder* [*v. Attorney-General of British Columbia*, [1973] S.C.R. 313]), s. 35(1) has constitutionalized it in its full form. . . .

[136] I hasten to add that the constitutionalization of common law aboriginal rights by s. 35(1) does not mean that those rights exhaust the content of s. 35(1). As I said in *Côté, supra*, at para. 52:

> Section 35(1) would fail to achieve its noble purpose of preserving the integral and defining features of distinctive aboriginal societies if it only protected those defining features which were fortunate enough to have received the legal recognition and approval of European colonizers.

I relied on this proposition in *Côté* to defeat the argument that the possible absence of aboriginal rights under French colonial law was a bar to the existence of aboriginal rights under s. 35(1) within the historic boundaries of New France. But it also follows that the existence of a particular aboriginal right at common law is not a *sine qua non* for the proof of an aboriginal right that is recognized and affirmed by s. 35(1). Indeed, none of the decisions of this Court handed down under s. 35(1) in which the existence of an aboriginal right has been demonstrated has relied on the existence of that right at common law. The existence of an aboriginal right at common law is therefore sufficient, but not necessary, for the recognition and affirmation of that right by s. 35(1).

[137] The acknowledgement that s. 35(1) has accorded constitutional status to common law aboriginal title raises a further question—the relationship of aboriginal title to the "aboriginal rights" protected by s. 35(1). I addressed that question in *Adams, supra*, where the Court had been presented with two radically different conceptions of this relationship. The first conceived of aboriginal rights as being "inherently based in aboriginal title to the land" (at para. 25), or as fragments of a broader claim to aboriginal title. By implication, aboriginal rights must rest either in a claim to title or the unextinguished remnants of title. Taken to its logical extreme, this suggests that aboriginal title is merely the sum of a set of individual aboriginal rights, and that it therefore has no independent content. However, I rejected this position for another—that aboriginal title is "simply one manifestation of

a broader-based conception of aboriginal rights" (at para. 25). Thus, although aboriginal title is a species of aboriginal right recognized and affirmed by s. 35(1), it is distinct from other aboriginal rights because it arises where the connection of a group with a piece of land "was of a central significance to their distinctive culture" (at para. 26).

[138] The picture which emerges from *Adams* is that the aboriginal rights which are recognized and affirmed by s. 35(1) fall along a spectrum with respect to their degree of connection with the land. At the one end, there are those aboriginal rights which are practices, customs and traditions that are integral to the distinctive aboriginal culture of the group claiming the right. However, the "*occupation and use of the land*" where the activity is taking place is not "*sufficient to support a claim of title to the land*" (at para. 26 (emphasis in original)). Nevertheless, those activities receive constitutional protection. In the middle, there are activities which, out of necessity, take place on land and indeed, might be intimately related to a particular piece of land. Although an aboriginal group may not be able to demonstrate title to the land, it may nevertheless have a site-specific right to engage in a particular activity. . . . At the other end of the spectrum, there is aboriginal title itself. As *Adams* makes clear, aboriginal title confers more than the right to engage in site-specific activities which are aspects of the practices, customs and traditions of distinctive aboriginal cultures. Site-specific rights can be made out even if title cannot. What aboriginal title confers is the right to the land itself.

[139] Because aboriginal rights can vary with respect to their degree of connection with the land, some aboriginal groups may be unable to make out a claim to title, but will nevertheless possess aboriginal rights that are recognized and affirmed by s. 35(1), including site-specific rights to engage in particular activities. As I explained in *Adams*, this may occur in the case of nomadic peoples who varied "the location of their settlements with the season and changing circumstances" (at para. 27).

(e) Proof of Aboriginal Title

(i) *Introduction*

. . . [41] . . . Since the purpose of s. 35(1) is to reconcile the prior presence of aboriginal peoples in North America with the assertion of Crown sovereignty, it is clear . . . that s. 35(1) must recognize and affirm both aspects of that prior presence—first, the occupation of land, and second, the prior social organization and distinctive cultures of aboriginal peoples on that land. To date the jurisprudence under s. 35(1) has given more emphasis to the second aspect. To a great extent, this has been a function of the types of cases which have come before this Court under s. 35(1)—prosecutions for regulatory offences that, by their very nature, proscribe discrete types of activity. . . .

(ii) The Test for the Proof of Aboriginal Title

[143] In order to make out a claim for aboriginal title, the aboriginal group asserting title must satisfy the following criteria: (i) the land must have been occupied prior to sovereignty, (ii) if present occupation is relied on as proof of occupation pre-sovereignty, there must be a continuity between present and pre-sovereignty occupation, and (iii) at sovereignty, that occupation must have been exclusive.

The Land Must Have Been Occupied Prior to Sovereignty

[144] In order to establish a claim to aboriginal title, the aboriginal group asserting the claim must establish that it occupied the lands in question at the *time at which the Crown asserted sovereignty over the land subject to the title*. The relevant time period for the establishment of title is, therefore, different than for the establishment of aboriginal rights to engage in specific activities. In *Van der Peet*, I held, at para. 60 that "[t]he time period that a court should consider in identifying whether the right claimed meets the standard of being integral to the aboriginal community claiming the right is the period prior to contact. . . ." This arises from the fact that in defining the central and distinctive attributes of pre-existing aboriginal societies it is necessary to look to a time prior to the arrival of Europeans. Practices, customs or traditions that arose solely as a response to European influences do not meet the standard for recognition as aboriginal rights.

[145] On the other hand, in the context of aboriginal title, sovereignty is the appropriate time period to consider for several reasons. First, from a theoretical standpoint, aboriginal title arises out of prior occupation of the land by aboriginal peoples and out of the relationship between the common law and pre-existing systems of aboriginal law. Aboriginal title is a burden on the Crown's underlying title. However, the Crown did not gain this title until it asserted sovereignty over the land in question. Because it does not make sense to speak of a burden on the underlying title before that title existed, aboriginal title crystallized at the time sovereignty was asserted. Second, aboriginal title does not raise the problem of distinguishing between distinctive, integral aboriginal practices, customs and traditions and those influenced or introduced by European contact. Under common law, the act of occupation or possession is sufficient to ground aboriginal title and it is not necessary to prove that the land was a distinctive or integral part of the aboriginal society before the arrival of Europeans. Finally, from a practical standpoint, it appears that the date of sovereignty is more certain than the date of first contact. It is often very difficult to determine the precise moment that each aboriginal group had first contact with European culture. . . . For these reasons, I conclude that aboriginals must establish occupation of the land from the date of the assertion of sovereignty in order to sustain a claim for aboriginal title. McEachern C.J. found, at pp. 233-34, and the parties did not dispute on appeal, that British sovereignty over British Columbia was conclusively established by the Oregon Boundary Treaty of 1846. . . .

[146] There was a consensus among the parties on appeal that proof of historic occupation was required to make out a claim to aboriginal title. However, the parties disagreed on how that occupancy could be proved. The respondents assert that in order to establish aboriginal title, the occupation must be the physical occupation of the land in question. The appellant Gitksan nation argue, by contrast, that aboriginal title may be established, at least in part, by reference to aboriginal law.

[147] This debate over the proof of occupancy reflects two divergent views of the source of aboriginal title. The respondents argue, in essence, that aboriginal title arises from the physical reality at the time of sovereignty, whereas the Gitksan effectively take the position that aboriginal title arises from and should reflect the pattern of land holdings under aboriginal law. However, as I have explained above, the source of aboriginal title appears to be grounded both in the common law and in the aboriginal perspective on land; the latter includes, but is not limited to, their systems of law. It follows that both should be taken into account in establishing the proof of occupancy. . . .

[148] . . . As a result, if, at the time of sovereignty, an aboriginal society had laws in relation to land, those laws would be relevant to establishing the occupation of lands which are the subject of a claim for aboriginal title. Relevant laws might include, but are not limited to, a land tenure system or laws governing land use.

[149] However, the aboriginal perspective must be taken into account alongside the perspective of the common law. Professor McNeil has convincingly argued that at common law, the fact of physical occupation is proof of possession at law, which in turn will ground title to the land: *Common Law Aboriginal Title, supra*, at p. 73; also see *Cheshire and Burn's Modern Law of Real Property* [E.H. Burn, 14th ed. (1988)], at p. 28; and Megarry and Wade, *The Law of Real Property* [4th ed. (1975)], at p. 1006. Physical occupation may be established in a variety of ways, ranging from the construction of dwellings through cultivation and enclosure of fields to regular use of definite tracts of land for hunting, fishing or otherwise exploiting its resources: see McNeil, *Common Law Aboriginal Title*, at pp. 201-2. In considering whether occupation sufficient to

ground title is established, "one must take into account the group's size, manner of life, material resources, and technological abilities, and the character of the lands claimed": Brian Slattery, "Understanding Aboriginal Rights," at p. 758. . . .

If Present Occupation Is Relied on as Proof of Occupation Pre-Sovereignty, There Must Be a Continuity Between Present and Pre-Sovereignty Occupation

[152] In *Van der Peet*, I explained that it is the pre-contact practices, customs and traditions of aboriginal peoples which are recognized and affirmed as aboriginal rights by s. 35(1). But I also acknowledged it would be "next to impossible" (at para. 62) for an aboriginal group to provide conclusive evidence of its pre-contact practices, customs and traditions. What would suffice instead was evidence of post-contact practices, which was "directed at demonstrating which aspects of the aboriginal community and society have their origins pre-contact" (at para. 62). The same concern, and the same solution, arises with respect to the proof of occupation in claims for aboriginal title, although there is a difference in the time for determination of title. Conclusive evidence of pre-sovereignty occupation may be difficult to come by. Instead, an aboriginal community may provide evidence of present occupation as proof of pre-sovereignty occupation in support of a claim to aboriginal title. What is required, in addition, is a *continuity* between present and pre-sovereignty occupation, because the relevant time for the determination of aboriginal title is at the time before sovereignty.

[153] Needless to say, there is no need to establish "an unbroken chain of continuity" (*Van der Peet*, at para. 65) between present and prior occupation. The occupation and use of lands may have been disrupted for a time, perhaps as a result of the unwillingness of European colonizers to recognize aboriginal title. To impose the requirement of continuity too strictly would risk "undermining the very purpose of s. 35(1) by perpetuating the historical injustice suffered by aboriginal peoples at the hands of colonizers who failed to respect" aboriginal rights to land (*Côté, supra,* at para. 53). In *Mabo* [*v. Queensland* (1992), 107 A.L.R. 1 (H.C.)], the High Court of Australia set down the requirement that there must be "substantial maintenance of the connection" between the people and the land. In my view, this test should be equally applicable to proof of title in Canada. . . .

At Sovereignty, Occupation Must Have Been Exclusive

[155] Finally, at sovereignty, occupation must have been exclusive. The requirement for exclusivity flows from the definition of aboriginal title itself, because I have defined aboriginal

title in terms of the right to *exclusive* use and occupation of land. Exclusivity, as an aspect of aboriginal title, vests in the aboriginal community which holds the ability to exclude others from the lands held pursuant to that title. . . .

[156] As with the proof of occupation, proof of exclusivity must rely on both the perspective of the common law and the aboriginal perspective, placing equal weight on each. At common law, a premium is placed on the factual reality of occupation, as encountered by the Europeans. However, as the common law concept of possession must be sensitive to the realities of aboriginal society, so must the concept of exclusivity. . . . For example, it is important to note that exclusive occupation can be demonstrated even if other aboriginal groups were present, or frequented the claimed lands. Under those circumstances, exclusivity would be demonstrated by "the intention and capacity to retain exclusive control" (McNeil, *Common Law Aboriginal Title, supra,* at p. 204). Thus, an act of trespass, if isolated, would not undermine a general finding of exclusivity, if aboriginal groups intended to and attempted to enforce their exclusive occupation. Moreover, as Professor McNeil suggests, the presence of other aboriginal groups might actually reinforce a finding of exclusivity. For example, "[w]here others were allowed access upon request, the very fact that permission was asked for and given would be further evidence of the group's exclusive control" (at p. 204). . . .

[158] In their submissions, the appellants pressed the point that requiring proof of exclusive occupation might preclude a finding of joint title, which is shared between two or more aboriginal nations. The possibility of joint title has been recognized by American courts: *United States v. Santa Fe Pacific Railroad Co.,* 314 U.S. 339 (1941). I would suggest that the requirement of exclusive occupancy and the possibility of joint title could be reconciled by recognizing that joint title could arise from shared exclusivity. The meaning of shared exclusivity is well-known to the common law. Exclusive possession is the right to exclude others. Shared exclusive possession is the right to exclude others except those with whom possession is shared. There clearly may be cases in which two aboriginal nations lived on a particular piece of land and recognized each other's entitlement to that land but nobody else's. . . .

[159] I should also reiterate that if aboriginals can show that they occupied a particular piece of land, but did not do so exclusively, it will always be possible to establish aboriginal rights short of title. These rights will likely be intimately tied to the land and may permit a number of possible uses. However, unlike title, they are not a right to the land itself. Rather, as I have suggested, they are a right to do certain things in connection with that land. . . . Hence, in addition to shared title, it will be possible to have shared, non-exclusive, site-specific

rights. In my opinion, this accords with the general principle that the common law should develop to recognize aboriginal rights (and title, when necessary) as they were recognized by either *de facto* practice or by the aboriginal system of governance. It also allows sufficient flexibility to deal with this highly complex and rapidly evolving area of the law.

(f) Infringements of Aboriginal Title: The Test of Justification

(i) Introduction

[160] The aboriginal rights recognized and affirmed by s. 35(1), including aboriginal title, are not absolute. Those rights may be infringed, both by the federal (e.g., *Sparrow*) and provincial (e.g., *Côté*) governments. However, s. 35(1) requires that those infringements satisfy the test of justification. In this section, I will review the Court's nascent jurisprudence on justification and explain how that test will apply in the context of infringements of aboriginal title.

(ii) General Principles

[161] The test of justification has two parts, which I shall consider in turn. First, the infringement of the aboriginal right must be in furtherance of a legislative objective that is compelling and substantial. I explained in *Gladstone* that compelling and substantial objectives were those which were directed at either one of the purposes underlying the recognition and affirmation of aboriginal rights by s. 35(1), which are (at para. 72):

> ... the recognition of the prior occupation of North America by aboriginal peoples or ... the reconciliation of aboriginal prior occupation with the assertion of the sovereignty of the Crown.

I noted that the latter purpose will often "be most relevant" (at para. 72) at the stage of justification. I think it important to repeat why (at para. 73) that is so:

> Because ... distinctive aboriginal societies exist within, and are a part of, a broader social, political and economic community, over which the Crown is sovereign, there are circumstances in which, in order to pursue objectives of compelling and substantial importance to that community as a whole (taking into account the fact that aboriginal societies are a part of that community), some limitation of those rights will be justifiable. *Aboriginal rights are a necessary part of the reconciliation of aboriginal societies with the broader political community of which they are part; limits placed on those rights are, where the objectives furthered by those limits are of sufficient importance to the broader community as a whole, equally a necessary part of that reconciliation.* [Emphasis added; "equally" emphasized in original.]

The conservation of fisheries, which was accepted as a compelling and substantial objective in *Sparrow*, furthers both of these purposes, because it simultaneously recognizes that fishing is integral to many aboriginal cultures, and also seeks to reconcile aboriginal societies with the broader community by ensuring that there are fish enough for all. But legitimate government objectives also include "the pursuit of economic and regional fairness" and "the recognition of the historical reliance upon, and participation in, the fishery by non-aboriginal groups" (para. 75). By contrast, measures enacted for relatively unimportant reasons, such as sports fishing without a significant economic component (*Adams, supra*) would fail this aspect of the test of justification.

[162] The second part of the test of justification requires an assessment of whether the infringement is consistent with the special fiduciary relationship between the Crown and aboriginal peoples. ...

[163] In addition to variation in the *form* which the fiduciary duty takes, there will also be variation in degree of scrutiny required by the fiduciary duty of the infringing measure or action. The degree of scrutiny is a function of the nature of the aboriginal right at issue. The distinction between *Sparrow* and *Gladstone*, for example, turned on whether the right amounted to the exclusive use of a resource, which in turn was a function of whether the right had an internal limit. In *Sparrow*, the right was internally limited, because it was a right to fish for food, ceremonial and social purposes, and as a result would only amount to an exclusive right to use the fishery in exceptional circumstances. Accordingly, the requirement of priority was applied strictly to mean that (at p. 1116) "any allocation of priorities after valid conservation measures have been implemented must give top priority to Indian food fishing."

[164] In *Gladstone*, by contrast, the right to sell fish commercially was only limited by supply and demand. Had the test for justification been applied in a strict form in *Gladstone*, the aboriginal right would have amounted to an exclusive right to exploit the fishery on a commercial basis. This was not the intention of *Sparrow*, and I accordingly modified the test for justification, by altering the idea of priority in the following way (at para. 62):

> ... [T]he doctrine of priority requires that the government demonstrate that, in allocating the resource, it has taken account of the existence of aboriginal rights and allocated the resource in a manner respectful of the fact that those rights have priority over the exploitation of the fishery by other users. This right is at once both procedural and substantive; at the stage of justification the government must demonstrate both that the process by which it allocated the resource and the actual allocation

of the resource which results from that process reflect the prior interest of aboriginal rights holders in the fishery....

(iii) Justification and Aboriginal Title

[165] The general principles governing justification laid down in *Sparrow*, and embellished by *Gladstone*, operate with respect to infringements of aboriginal title. In the wake of *Gladstone*, the range of legislative objectives that can justify the infringement of aboriginal title is fairly broad. Most of these objectives can be traced to the *reconciliation* of the prior occupation of North America by aboriginal peoples with the assertion of Crown sovereignty, which entails the recognition that "distinctive aboriginal societies exist within, and are a part of, a broader social, political and economic community" (at para. 73). In my opinion, the development of agriculture, forestry, mining, and hydroelectric power, the general economic development of the interior of British Columbia, protection of the environment or endangered species, the building of infrastructure and the settlement of foreign populations to support those aims, are the kinds of objectives that are consistent with this purpose and, in principle, can justify the infringement of aboriginal title. Whether a particular measure or government act can be explained by reference to one of those objectives, however, is ultimately a question of fact that will have to be examined on a case-by-case basis.

[166] The manner in which the fiduciary duty operates with respect to the second stage of the justification test—both with respect to the standard of scrutiny and the particular form that the fiduciary duty will take—will be a function of the nature of aboriginal title....

[167] The exclusive nature of aboriginal title is relevant to the degree of scrutiny of the infringing measure or action. For example, if the Crown's fiduciary duty requires that aboriginal title be given priority, then it is the altered approach to priority that I laid down in *Gladstone* which should apply. What is required is that the government demonstrate (at para. 62) "both that the process by which it allocated the resource and the actual allocation of the resource which results from that process reflect the prior interest" of the holders of aboriginal title in the land....

[168] Moreover, the other aspects of aboriginal title suggest that the fiduciary duty may be articulated in a manner different than the idea of priority. This point becomes clear from a comparison between aboriginal title and the aboriginal right to fish for food in *Sparrow*. First, aboriginal title encompasses within it a right to choose to what ends a piece of land can be put. The aboriginal right to fish for food, by contrast, does not contain within it the same discretionary component. This aspect of aboriginal title suggests that the fiduciary rela-

tionship between the Crown and aboriginal peoples may be satisfied by the involvement of aboriginal peoples in decisions taken with respect to their lands. There is always a duty of consultation.... The nature and scope of the duty of consultation will vary with the circumstances. In occasional cases, when the breach is less serious or relatively minor, it will be no more than a duty to discuss important decisions that will be taken with respect to lands held pursuant to aboriginal title. Of course, even in these rare cases when the minimum acceptable standard is consultation, this consultation must be in good faith, and with the intention of substantially addressing the concerns of the aboriginal peoples whose lands are at issue. In most cases, it will be significantly deeper than mere consultation. Some cases may even require the full consent of an aboriginal nation, particularly when provinces enact hunting and fishing regulations in relation to aboriginal lands.

[169] Second, aboriginal title, unlike the aboriginal right to fish for food, has an inescapably economic aspect, particularly when one takes into account the modern uses to which lands held pursuant to aboriginal title can be put. The economic aspect of aboriginal title suggests that compensation is relevant to the question of justification as well, a possibility suggested in *Sparrow* and which I repeated in *Gladstone*. Indeed, compensation for breaches of fiduciary duty are a well-established part of the landscape of aboriginal rights: *Guerin*. In keeping with the duty of honour and good faith on the Crown, fair compensation will ordinarily be required when aboriginal title is infringed. The amount of compensation payable will vary with the nature of the particular aboriginal title affected and with the nature and severity of the infringement and the extent to which aboriginal interests were accommodated....

D. Has a Claim to Self-Government Been Made Out by the Appellants?

[170] In the courts below, considerable attention was given to the question of whether s. 35(1) can protect a right to self-government, and if so, what the contours of that right are. The errors of fact made by the trial judge, and the resultant need for a new trial, make it impossible for this Court to determine whether the claim to self-government has been made out. Moreover, this is not the right case for the Court to lay down the legal principles to guide future litigation. The parties seem to have acknowledged this point, perhaps implicitly, by giving the arguments on self-government much less weight on appeal....

[171] The broad nature of the claim at trial also led to a failure by the parties to address many of the difficult conceptual issues which surround the recognition of aboriginal self-government. The degree of complexity involved can be

gleaned from the *Report of the Royal Commission on Aboriginal Peoples*, which devotes 277 pages to the issue. That report describes different models of self-government, each differing with respect to their conception of territory, citizenship, jurisdiction, internal government organization, etc. We received little in the way of submissions that would help us to grapple with these difficult and central issues. Without assistance from the parties, it would be imprudent for the Court to step into the breach. In these circumstances, the issue of self-government will fall to be determined at trial. . . .

VI. Conclusion and Disposition

[184] For the reasons I have given above, I would allow the appeal in part, and dismiss the cross-appeal. Reluctantly, I would also order a new trial.

[185] I conclude with two observations. The first is that many aboriginal nations with territorial claims that overlap with those of the appellants did not intervene in this appeal, and do not appear to have done so at trial. This is unfortunate, because determinations of aboriginal title for the Gitksan and Wet'suwet'en will undoubtedly affect their claims as well. This is particularly so because aboriginal title encompasses an *exclusive* right to the use and occupation of land, i.e., to the *exclusion* of both non-aboriginals and members of other aboriginal nations. It may, therefore, be advisable if those aboriginal nations intervened in any new litigation.

[186] Finally, this litigation has been both long and expensive, not only in economic but in human terms as well. By ordering a new trial, I do not necessarily encourage the parties to proceed to litigation and to settle their dispute through the courts. As was said in *Sparrow*, at p. 1105, s. 35(1) "provides a solid constitutional base upon which subsequent negotiations can take place." Those negotiations should also include other aboriginal nations which have a stake in the territory claimed. Moreover, the Crown is under a moral, if not a legal, duty to enter into and conduct those negotiations in good faith. Ultimately, it is through negotiated settlements, with good faith and give and take on all sides, reinforced by the judgments of this Court, that we will achieve what I stated in *Van der Peet, supra*, at para. 31, to be a basic purpose of s. 35(1)—"the reconciliation of the pre-existence of aboriginal societies with the sovereignty of the Crown." Let us face it, we are all here to stay.

The reasons of La Forest and L'Heureux-Dubé JJ. were delivered by

[187] **LA FOREST J.:** I have read the reasons of the Chief Justice, and while I agree with his conclusion, I disagree with various aspects of his reasons and in particular, with the methodology he uses to prove that aboriginal peoples have a general right of occupation of certain lands (often referred to as "aboriginal title"). . . .

[189] In my view, the foundation of "aboriginal title" was succinctly described by Judson J. in *Calder v. Attorney-General of British Columbia*, [1973] S.C.R. 313, where, at p. 328, he stated: "the fact is that when the settlers came, the Indians were there, organized in societies and occupying the land as their forefathers had done for centuries. This is what Indian title means. . . ." Relying in part on Judson J.'s remarks, Dickson J. (as he then was) wrote in *Guerin v. The Queen*, [1984] 2 S.C.R. 335, at p. 382, that aboriginal peoples have a "legal right to occupy and possess certain lands, the ultimate title to which is in the Crown." . . .

[190] It follows from these cases that the aboriginal right of possession is derived from the historic occupation and use of ancestral lands by aboriginal peoples. Put another way, "aboriginal title" is based on the continued occupation and use of the land as part of the aboriginal peoples' traditional way of life. This *sui generis* interest is not equated with fee simple ownership; nor can it be described with reference to traditional property law concepts. The best description of "aboriginal title," as set out above, is a broad and general one derived from Judson J.'s pronouncements in *Calder, supra*. Adopting the same approach, Dickson J. wrote in *Guerin, supra*, that the aboriginal right of occupancy is further characterized by two principal features. First, this *sui generis* interest in the land is personal in that it is generally inalienable except to the Crown. Second, in dealing with this interest, the Crown is subject to a fiduciary obligation to treat aboriginal peoples fairly. Dickson J. went on to conclude, at p. 382, that "[a]ny description of Indian title which goes beyond these two features is both unnecessary and potentially misleading." I share his views and am therefore reluctant to define more precisely the "right [of aboriginal peoples] to continue to live on their lands as their forefathers had lived"; see *Calder*, at p. 328. . . .

[200] I would also add that my approach regarding the nature of aboriginal occupancy is supported by the terms of the *Royal Proclamation, 1763*, R.S.C., 1985, App. II, No. 1. Although the *Proclamation* is not the sole source of "aboriginal title" in this country, it bears witness to the British policy towards aboriginal peoples which was based on respect for their right to occupy their ancestral lands; see *Sparrow, supra*, at p. 1103. Specifically, the *Proclamation* provides:

> And We do further declare it to be Our Royal Will and Pleasure, for the present as aforesaid, to reserve under our Sovereignty, Protection, and Dominion, for the use of the said Indians, all the Lands and Territories not included within the Limits of Our said Three new Governments, or within the Limits of the Territory granted to the Hudson's

Bay Company, as also all the Lands and Territories lying to the Westward of the Sources of the Rivers which fall into the Sea from the West and North West as aforesaid.

In clear terms vast tracts of territory (including large portions of the area now comprising Ontario, Quebec, and the prairie provinces) were reserved for aboriginal peoples. These huge tracts of land were by no means limited to villages or permanent settlements but were reserved more generally as "Hunting Grounds" and "for the use of the said Indians." Aboriginal peoples had the right to possess the lands reserved for them and "not be molested or disturbed in the Possession" of such territory. In essence, the rights set out in the *Proclamation*—which were applied in principle to aboriginal peoples across the country—underlie the view I have taken of aboriginal occupancy....

[201] The analysis thus far has focussed on the nature of the aboriginal right to occupy and possess certain lands—a right recognized and affirmed under s. 35(1) of the *Constitution Act, 1982*. Nonetheless, as Dickson C.J. and I wrote in *Sparrow, supra*, at p. 1109: "Rights that are recognized and affirmed are not absolute." Thus, government regulation can infringe upon aboriginal rights if it meets the test of justification under s. 35(1)....

[202] In the context of the present case, I agree with the Chief Justice that the general economic development of the interior of British Columbia, through agriculture, mining, forestry, and hydroelectric power, as well as the related building of infrastructure and settlement of foreign populations are valid legislative objectives that, in principle, satisfy the first part of the justification analysis.

[203] Under the second part of the justification test, these legislative objectives are subject to accommodation of the aboriginal peoples' interests. This accommodation must always be in accordance with the honour and good faith of the Crown. Moreover, when dealing with a generalized claim over vast tracts of land, accommodation is not a simple matter of asking whether licences have been fairly allocated in one industry, or whether conservation measures have been properly implemented for a specific resource. Rather, the question of accommodation of "aboriginal title" is much broader than this.

Certainly, one aspect of accommodation in this context entails notifying and consulting aboriginal peoples with respect to the development of the affected territory. Another aspect of accommodation is fair compensation....

[204] In summary, in developing vast tracts of land, the government is expected to consider the economic well being of *all* Canadians. But the aboriginal peoples must not be forgotten in this equation. Their legal right to occupy and possess certain lands, as confirmed by s. 35(1) of the *Constitution Act, 1982*, mandates basic fairness commensurate with the honour and good faith of the Crown....

[207] On a final note, I wish to emphasize that the best approach in these types of cases is a process of negotiation and reconciliation that properly considers the complex and competing interests at stake. This point was made by Lambert J.A. in the Court of Appeal, [1993] 5 W.W.R. 97, at pp. 379-80:

> So, in the end, *the legal rights of the Indian people will have to be accommodated within our total society by political compromises and accommodations based in the first instance on negotiation and agreement and ultimately in accordance with the sovereign will of the community as a whole.* The legal rights of the Gitksan and Wet'suwet'en peoples, to which this law suit is confined, and which allow no room for any approach other than the application of the law itself, and the legal rights of all aboriginal peoples throughout British Columbia, form only one factor in the ultimate determination of what kind of community we are going to have in British Columbia and throughout Canada in the years ahead. [Emphasis added.]

(See also *Report of the Royal Commission on Aboriginal Peoples* (1996), vol. 2 (*Restructuring the Relationship*), Part 2, at pp. 561-62.)

[208] Accordingly, I would allow the appeal in part and order a new trial on the basis of the principles set out in these reasons. I would also dismiss the cross-appeal.

The following are the reasons delivered by

[209] **McLACHLIN J.:** I concur with the Chief Justice. I add that I am also in substantial agreement with the comments of Justice La Forest.

R. v. Marshall (First Marshall Decision), 1999

In the early days of contact, European and Aboriginal peoples used treaties to order their relations with one another.[1] France, Great Britain, and Holland all entered into treaty relations with Indian nations. Treaties were used to secure friendly relations, to establish trading partnerships and military alliances, and to delineate the boundaries of European settlement. In the 1800s, Great Britain and the United States, once they no longer needed Indian nations as trading partners or military allies, began to use treaties primarily as a means of purchasing Indian lands for settlement and economic development. While the U.S. Congress, in 1871, terminated the treaty process in that country, the Canadian government at that time embarked on a series of "land cession" treaties with Aboriginal nations in northern Ontario, across the western prairies, in northeast British Columbia, and in the Northwest Territories. This treaty-making process stopped in the 1920s. For several decades, First Nations were prevented from claiming treaty rights in Canadian courts. In 1969, Prime Minister Trudeau proposed the termination of treaty relationships with Aboriginal peoples. But Aboriginal organizations strenuously resisted this policy. In the 1970s, in response to the Supreme Court's decision on *Calder*, the federal government inaugurated the program of negotiating comprehensive land claims with Aboriginal people living on unceded lands. In effect, this was the beginning of a modern treaty process. Treaty rights were given constitutional protection in section 35 of the *Constitution Act, 1982*. In 1983, the Constitution was amended to remove any doubt that modern land claims agreements have the status of constitutionally protected treaties.

In the 1980s and '90s, members of Indian nations who were parties to historic treaties resorted increasingly to the courts to challenge provincial or federal laws on the ground that they violated constitutionally protected treaty rights. *R. v. Marshall* is one such case. When Donald Marshall Jr. was charged with the offence of fishing for eels without a licence in Pomquet Harbour on the south shore of Nova Scotia, his defence was that the fishing regulations violated rights that his people, the Mi'kmaq, had secured through a treaty with Britain in 1760. This defence failed at trial and in the Nova Scotia Court of Appeal, but was upheld by a majority in the Supreme Court of Canada.

From the standpoint of constitutional law, of crucial importance in this decision are the principles of treaty interpretation enunciated by the Supreme Court. Treaty interpretation is particularly challenging in a context where the Aboriginal party at the time the treaty was entered into was a pre-literate society. That was certainly the case here as with many other of the historic treaties. In earlier decisions the Canadian Supreme Court recognized, as had its American counterpart, that it would be unjust to interpret treaties made under these conditions solely on the basis of a strict reading of the written text of a treaty, a text that could only have been understood by one of the parties. The aim, as the Supreme Court put

---

1 For further information on treaties with Aboriginal peoples, see the *Report of the Royal Commission on Aboriginal Peoples*, Volume 2, Part one, chapter 2.

it in the 1990 *Sioui* case,[2] was to use various historical records that would make it possible "to choose from among the various possible interpretations of common intention the one which best reconciles the interests of both parties at the time the treaty was signed." The Court, in these earlier cases, further stated that ambiguities in treaties should be resolved in favour of the Aboriginal signatories and in a manner that is consistent with the honour of the Crown in its dealings with Aboriginal peoples. Though both the majority and minority in *Marshall* endorsed these principles, their application of them to the treaty at issue in this case led them to opposite conclusions.

The Treaty of Peace and Friendship concluded on March 10, 1760 at Halifax by Governor Charles Lawrence, the British Governor, and Paul Laurent, chief of the LaHave Mi'kmaq people, was part of a series of negotiations with communities of Mi'kmaq, Maliseet, and Passamaquoddy peoples across what is now Nova Scotia and New Brunswick. The negotiations were triggered by the fall of the French fortresses at Louisbourg in 1758 and Quebec in 1759. The British wanted to establish friendly relations with native peoples in the region who, in the past, had supported the French. The Aboriginal communities wanted to continue exchanging the products of their hunting, fishing, and gathering for European trade goods. The trial judge found that many of the key issues were first negotiated with the Maliseet and Passamaquoddy and that the Mi'kmaq were offered similar terms. The written text of the March 10 agreement at Halifax covers only the Mi'kmaq's promise to maintain peace, return British prisoners, and trade exclusively at British "truck houses." In *Marshall*, Justice Binnie, writing for the majority, held that the written document must be understood as part of a broader agreement that included not only the right of the Aboriginal parties to trade, but also the right to engage in the harvesting activities, including fishing, which provided them something to trade with. This right extended only to what is needed to furnish "necessaries," which Justice Binnie interpreted as covering what today would be considered "a moderate livelihood."

Justice McLachlin, with Justice Gonthier concurring, while willing to consider the treaty in its broad historical setting, could not support inferring from the treaties a general right to trade or to continue traditional harvesting activities. In her view, the only treaty right secured by the Mi'kmaq was the right to bring goods to British truck houses. In effect, that right lapsed a few years later when the British abandoned the truck house system. She criticized the majority for finding a treaty right "undefined in scope" that would give the government no guidance on how far it could go in trenching on the right "in the collective interest of Canadians."

The majority acknowledged that the Mi'kmaq's harvesting and trading rights could be regulated by the federal government. In the 1996 *Badger* case,[3] the Supreme Court applied to treaty rights the same "justifiable limits" that it had imposed on section 35 Aboriginal rights in *Sparrow*. So long as the federal government's fishing regulations did not impose catch limits that would prevent Marshall or other Mi'kmaq families from earning a moderate livelihood no justification would be required. In the case at hand, the federal government had not offered any justification of the restrictions imposed on Donald Marshall. Absent

---

2   *R. v. Sioui*, [1990] 1 S.C.R. 1025.

3   *R. v. Badger*, [1996] 1 S.C.R. 771.

such justification, given that the regulations prevented Marshall from catching and selling eels to support himself and his family, the regulations as applied to him must be deemed to be unconstitutional. Marshall was therefore entitled to an acquittal.

Donald Marshall Jr. was acquitted but the issues raised by the case were by no means settled. A storm of protest and concern greeted the decision. Non-native fishers in the Atlantic region felt threatened by the prospect of having to comply with regulatory limits that would not apply to native fishers. This uproar led quickly to the Supreme Court's second *Marshall* decision. ⌒

R. v. MARSHALL
[1999] 3 S.C.R. 456

Hearing: November 5, 1998; Judgment: September 17, 1999.

Present: Lamer C.J. and L'Heureux-Dubé, Gonthier, Cory, McLachlin, Iacobucci, and Binnie JJ.

Interveners: The Attorney General for New Brunswick, the West Nova Fishermen's Coalition, the Native Council of Nova Scotia, and the Union of New Brunswick Indians.

The judgment of Lamer C.J. and L'Heureux-Dubé, Cory, Iacobucci, and Binnie JJ. was delivered by

[1] **BINNIE J.:** On an August morning six years ago the appellant and a companion, both Mi'kmaq Indians, slipped their small outboard motorboat into the coastal waters of Pomquet Harbour, Antigonish County, Nova Scotia to fish for eels. They landed 463 pounds, which they sold for $787.10, and for which the appellant was arrested and prosecuted.

[2] On an earlier August morning, some 235 years previously, the Reverend John Seycombe of Chester, Nova Scotia, a missionary and sometime dining companion of the Governor, noted with satisfaction in his diary, "Two Indian squaws brought seal skins and eels to sell." That transaction was apparently completed without arrest or other incident. The thread of continuity between these events, it seems, is that the Mi'kmaq people have sustained themselves in part by harvesting and trading fish (including eels) since Europeans first visited the coasts of what is now Nova Scotia in the 16th century. The appellant says that they are entitled to continue to do so now by virtue of a treaty right agreed to by the British Crown in 1760. As noted by my colleague, Justice McLachlin, the appellant is guilty as charged unless his activities were protected by an existing aboriginal or treaty right. No reliance was placed on any aboriginal right; the appellant chooses to rest his case entirely on the Mi'kmaq treaties of 1760-61.

[3] The trial judge ([1996] N.S.J. No. 246 (QL) (Prov. Ct.)) accepted as applicable the terms of a Treaty of Peace and Friendship signed on March 10, 1760 at Halifax. The parties

disagree about the existence of alleged oral terms, as well as the implications of the "trade clause" written into that document. From this distance, across more than two centuries, events are necessarily seen as "through a glass, darkly." The parties were negotiating in March 1760 in the shadow of the great military and political turmoil following the fall of the French fortresses at Louisbourg, Cape Breton (June 1758) and Quebec (September 1759). The Mi'kmaq signatories had been allies of the French King, and Montreal would continue to be part of New France until it subsequently fell in June 1760. The British had almost completed the process of expelling the Acadians from southern Nova Scotia. Both the Treaty of Paris, ending hostilities, and the Royal Proclamation of 1763 were still three years in the future. Only six years prior to the signing of the treaties, the British Governor of Nova Scotia had issued a Proclamation (May 14, 1756) offering rewards for the killing and capturing of Mi'kmaq throughout Nova Scotia, which then included New Brunswick. The treaties were entered into in a period where the British were attempting to expand and secure their control over their northern possessions. The subtext of the Mi'kmaq treaties was reconciliation and mutual advantage.

[4] I would allow this appeal because nothing less would uphold the honour and integrity of the Crown in its dealings with the Mi'kmaq people to secure their peace and friendship, as best the content of those treaty promises can now be ascertained. In reaching this conclusion, I recognize that if the present dispute had arisen out of a modern commercial transaction between two parties of relatively equal bargaining power, or if, as held by the courts below, the short document prepared at Halifax under the direction of Governor Charles Lawrence on March 10, 1760 was to be taken as being the "entire agreement" between the parties, it would have to be concluded that the Mi'kmaq had inadequately protected their interests. However, the courts have not applied strict rules of interpretation to treaty relationships. In *R. v. Denny* (1990), 55 C.C.C. (3d) 322, and earlier decisions cited therein, the Nova Scotia Court of Appeal has affirmed the Mi'kmaq aboriginal right to fish for food. The appellant says the treaty allows him to fish for trade. In my view, the 1760 treaty does

affirm the right of the Mi'kmaq people to continue to provide for their own sustenance by taking the products of their hunting, fishing and other gathering activities, and trading for what in 1760 was termed "necessaries." This right was always subject to regulation. The Crown does not suggest that the regulations in question accommodate the treaty right. The Crown's case is that no such treaty right exists. Further, no argument was made that the treaty right was extinguished prior to 1982, and no justification was offered by the Crown for the several prohibitions at issue in this case. Accordingly, in my view, the appellant is entitled to an acquittal.

Analysis

[5] The starting point for the analysis of the alleged treaty right must be an examination of the specific words used in any written memorandum of its terms. In this case, the task is complicated by the fact the British signed a series of agreements with individual Mi'kmaq communities in 1760 and 1761 intending to have them consolidated into a comprehensive Mi'kmaq treaty that was never in fact brought into existence. The trial judge, Embree Prov. Ct. J., found that by the end of 1761 all of the Mi'kmaq villages in Nova Scotia had entered into separate but similar treaties. Some of these documents are missing. Despite some variations among some of the documents, Embree Prov. Ct. J. was satisfied that the written terms applicable to this dispute were contained in a Treaty of Peace and Friendship entered into by Governor Charles Lawrence on March 10, 1760, which in its entirety provides as follows:

Treaty of Peace and Friendship concluded by [His Excellency Charles Lawrence] Esq. Govr and Comr. in Chief in and over his Majesty's Province of Nova Scotia or Accadia with Paul Laurent chief of the LaHave tribe of Indians at Halifax in the Province of N.S. or Acadia.

I, Paul Laurent do for myself and the tribe of LaHave Indians of which I am Chief do acknowledge the jurisdiction and Dominion of His Majesty George the Second over the Territories of Nova Scotia or Accadia and we do make submission to His Majesty in the most perfect, ample and solemn manner.

And I do promise for myself and my tribe that I nor they shall not molest any of His Majesty's subjects or their dependents, in their settlements already made or to be hereafter made or in carrying on their Commerce or in any thing whatever within the Province of His said Majesty or elsewhere and if any insult, robbery or outrage shall happen to be committed by any of my tribe satisfaction and restitution shall be made to the person or persons injured.

That neither I nor any of my tribe shall in any manner entice any of his said Majesty's troops or soldiers to desert, nor in any manner assist in conveying them away but on the contrary will do our utmost endeavours to bring them back to the Company, Regiment, Fort or Garrison to which they shall belong.

That if any Quarrel or Misunderstanding shall happen between myself and the English or between them and any of my tribe, neither I, nor they shall take any private satisfaction or Revenge, but we will apply for redress according to the Laws established in His said Majesty's Dominions.

That all English prisoners made by myself or my tribe shall be sett at Liberty and that we will use our utmost endeavours to prevail on the other tribes to do the same, if any prisoners shall happen to be in their hands.

And I do further promise for myself and my tribe that we will not either directly nor indirectly assist any of the enemies of His most sacred Majesty King George the Second, his heirs or Successors, nor hold any manner of Commerce traffick nor intercourse with them, but on the contrary will as much as may be in our power discover and make known to His Majesty's Governor, any ill designs which may be formed or contrived against His Majesty's subjects. *And I do further engage that we will not traffick, barter or Exchange any Commodities in any manner but with such persons or the managers of such Truck houses as shall be appointed or Established by His Majesty's Governor at Lunenbourg or Elsewhere in Nova Scotia or Accadia.*

And for the more effectual security of the due performance of this Treaty and every part thereof I do promise and Engage that a certain number of persons of my tribe which shall not be less in number than two prisoners shall on or before September next reside as Hostages at Lunenburg or at such other place or places in this Province of Nova Scotia or Accadia as shall be appointed for that purpose by His Majesty's Governor of said Province which Hostages shall be exchanged for a like number of my tribe when requested.

And all these foregoing articles and every one of them made with His Excellency C. L., His Majesty's Governor I do promise for myself and on of sd part—behalf of my tribe that we will most strictly keep and observe in the most solemn manner.

In witness whereof I have hereunto putt my mark and seal at Halifax in Nova Scotia this day of March one thousand

Paul Laurent

I do accept and agree to all the articles of the forgoing treaty in Faith and Testimony whereof I have signed these present I have caused my seal to be hereunto affixed this day of march in the 33 year of His Majesty's Reign and in the year of Our lord—1760

Chas Lawrence [Emphasis added.]

[6] The [italicized] portion of the document, the so-called "trade clause," is framed in negative terms as a restraint on the ability of the Mi'kmaq to trade with non-government individuals. A "truckhouse" was a type of trading post. The evidence showed that the promised government truckhouses disappeared from Nova Scotia within a few years and by 1780 a replacement regime of government licensed traders had also fallen into disuse while the British Crown was attending to the American Revolution. The trial judge, Embree Prov. Ct. J., rejected the Crown's argument that the trade clause amounted to nothing more than a negative covenant. He found, at para. 116, that it reflected a grant to the Mi'kmaq of the positive right to "bring the products of their hunting, fishing and gathering to a truckhouse to trade." The Court of Appeal ((1997), 159 N.S.R. (2d) 186) found that the trial judge misspoke when he used the word "right." It held that the trade clause does not grant the Mi'kmaq any rights. Instead, the trade clause represented a "mechanism imposed upon them to help ensure that the peace was a lasting one, by obviating their need to trade with enemies of the British" (p. 208). When the truckhouses disappeared, said the court, so did any vestiges of the restriction or entitlement, and that was the end of it.

[7] The appellant's position is that the truckhouse provision not only incorporated the alleged right to trade, but also the right to pursue traditional hunting, fishing and gathering activities in support of that trade. It seems clear that the words of the March 10, 1760 document, standing in isolation, do not support the appellant's argument. The question is whether the underlying negotiations produced a broader agreement between the British and the Mi'kmaq, memorialized only in part by the Treaty of Peace and Friendship, that would protect the appellant's activities that are the subject of the prosecution. I should say at the outset that the appellant overstates his case. In my view, the treaty rights are limited to securing "necessaries" (which I construe in the modern context, as equivalent to a moderate livelihood), and do not extend to the open-ended accumulation of wealth. The rights thus construed, however, are, in my opinion, treaty rights within the meaning of s. 35 of the *Constitution Act, 1982*, and are subject to regulations that can be justified under the *Badger* test (*R. v. Badger*, [1996] 1 S.C.R 771).

[8] Although the agreed statement of facts does not state explicitly that the appellant was exercising his rights for the purpose of necessaries, the Court was advised in the course of oral argument that the appellant "was engaged in a small-scale commercial activity to help subsidize or support himself and his common-law spouse." The Crown did not dispute this characterization and it is consistent with the scale of the operation, the amount of money involved, and the other surrounding facts. If at some point the appellant's trade and related fishing activities were to extend beyond what is reasonably required for necessaries, as hereinafter defined, he would be outside treaty protection, and can expect to be dealt with accordingly.

Evidentiary Sources

[9] The Court of Appeal took a strict approach to the use of extrinsic evidence when interpreting the Treaties of 1760-61. Roscoe and Bateman JJ.A. stated at p. 194: "While treaties must be interpreted in their historical context, extrinsic evidence cannot be used as an aid to interpretation, in the absence of ambiguity." I think this approach should be rejected for at least three reasons.

[10] Firstly, even in a modern constitutional context, extrinsic evidence is available to show that a written document does not include all of the terms of an agreement. . . .

[11] Secondly, even in the context of a treaty document that purports to contain all of the terms, this Court has made clear in recent cases that extrinsic evidence of the historical and cultural context of a treaty may be received even absent any ambiguity on the face of the treaty. MacKinnon A.C.J.O. laid down the principle in *Taylor and Williams* [*R. v.* (1981), 62 C.C.C. (2d) 227 (Ont. C.A.) (leave to appeal dismissed, [1981] 2 S.C.R. xi)], at p. 236:

> . . . if there is evidence by conduct or otherwise as to how the parties understood the terms of the treaty, then such understanding and practice is of assistance in giving content to the term or terms.

The proposition is cited with approval in *Delgamuukw v. British Columbia*, [1997] 3 S.C.R. 1010, at para. 87, and *R. v. Sioui*, [1990] 1 S.C.R. 1025, at p. 1045.

[12] Thirdly, where a treaty was concluded verbally and afterwards written up by representatives of the Crown, it would be unconscionable for the Crown to ignore the oral terms while relying on the written terms, *per* Dickson J. (as he then was) in *Guerin v. The Queen*, [1984] 2 S.C.R. 335. . . .

[13] The narrow approach applied by the Court of Appeal to the use of extrinsic evidence apparently derives from the comments of Estey J. in *R. v. Horse*, 1 S.C.R. 187, where, at p. 201, he expressed some reservations about the use of extrinsic materials . . . except in the case of ambiguity. (Estey J. went on to consider the extrinsic evidence anyway, at p. 203.) Lamer J. . . . mentioned this aspect of *Horse* in *Sioui, supra*, at p. 1049, but advocated a more flexible approach. . . .

[14] Subsequent cases have distanced themselves from a "strict" rule of treaty interpretation, as more recently discussed by Cory J., in *Badger, supra*, at para. 52:

. . . [W]hen considering a treaty, a court must take into account the context in which the treaties were negotiated, concluded and committed to writing. The treaties, as written documents,

recorded an agreement that had already been reached orally and they did not always record the full extent of the oral agreement: see Alexander Morris, *The Treaties of Canada with the Indians of Manitoba and the North-West Territories* (1880), at pp. 338-42; *Sioui, supra,* at p. 1068; *Report of the Aboriginal Justice Inquiry of Manitoba* (1991); Jean Friesen, *Grant me Wherewith to Make my Living* (1985). The treaties were drafted in English by representatives of the Canadian government who, it should be assumed, were familiar with common law doctrines. Yet, the treaties were not translated in written form into the languages (here Cree and Dene) of the various Indian nations who were signatories. Even if they had been, it is unlikely that the Indians, who had a history of communicating only orally, would have understood them any differently. *As a result, it is well settled that the words in the treaty must not be interpreted in their strict technical sense nor subjected to rigid modern rules of construction.* [Emphasis added.]

"Generous" rules of interpretation should not be confused with a vague sense of after-the-fact largesse. The special rules are dictated by the special difficulties of ascertaining what in fact was agreed to. . . . The bottom line is the Court's obligation is to "choose from among the various possible interpretations of the *common* intention [at the time the treaty was made] the one which best reconciles" the Mi'kmaq interests and those of the British Crown (*Sioui, per* Lamer J. at p. 1069 (emphasis added)). . . .

The 1760 Negotiations

[22] I propose to review briefly the documentary record to emphasize and amplify certain aspects of the trial judge's findings. He accepted in general the evidence of the Crown's only expert witness, Dr. Stephen Patterson, a Professor of History at the University of New Brunswick, who testified at length about what the trial judge referred to (at para. 116) as British encouragement of the Mi'kmaq "hunting, fishing and gathering lifestyle." That evidence puts the trade clause in context, and answers the question whether there was something more to the treaty entitlement than merely the right to bring fish and wildlife to truckhouses.

(i) The Documentary Record

[23] I take the following points from the matters particularly emphasized by the trial judge at para. 90 following his thorough review of the historical background:

> 1. The 1760-61 treaties were the culmination of more than a decade of intermittent hostilities between the British and the Mi'kmaq. Hostilities with the French were also prevalent in Nova Scotia throughout the 1750's, and the Mi'kmaq were constantly allied with the French against the British.

> 2. The use of firearms for hunting had an important impact on Mi'kmaq society. The Mi'kmaq remained dependant on others for gun powder and the primary sources of that were the French, Acadians and the British.

> 3. The French frequently supplied the Mi'kmaq with food and European trade goods. By the mid-18th century, the Mi'kmaq were accustomed to, and in some cases relied on, receiving various European trade goods [including shot, gun powder, metal tools, clothing cloth, blankets and many other things]. . . .

> 6. The British wanted peace and a safe environment for their current and future settlers. Despite their recent victories, they did not feel completely secure in Nova Scotia.

[24] Shortly after the fall of Louisbourg in June 1758, the British commander sent emissaries to the Mi'kmaq, through the French missionary, Father Maillard (who served as translator at the subsequent negotiations), holding out an offer of the enjoyment of peace, liberty, property, possessions and religion:

> . . . my Reverend Father, It is necessary that I make known to you that your Capital Quebec has fallen to the arms of the King, my master, your armies are in flight, thus if you and your people are so reckless to continue [this war] without justification, it is certain that you will perish by starvation since you have no other assistance.

> So you, My Reverend Father, would do well to accept the olive branches that I send to you and to put me in possession of the vessels that your people took from me and return them all to me, *I am commanded to assure you by His Majesty that you will enjoy all your possessions, your liberty, property with the free exercise of your religion as you can see by the declaration that I have the honour of sending you.* [Emphasis added.]

[25] In the harsh winter of 1759-1760, so many Mi'kmaq turned up at Louisbourg seeking sustenance that the British Commander expressed concern that unless their demand for necessaries was met, they would become "very Troublesome" and "entirely putt a Stop to any Settling or fishing all along the Coast" or indeed "the Settlement of Nova Scotia" generally. . . . It is apparent that the British saw the Mi'kmaq trade issue in terms of peace, as the Crown expert Dr. Stephen Patterson testified, "people who trade together do not fight, that was the theory." Peace was bound up with the ability of the Mi'kmaq people to sustain themselves economically. Starvation breeds discontent. The British certainly did not want the Mi'kmaq to become an unnecessary drain on the public purse of the colony of Nova Scotia or of the Imperial purse in London, as the trial judge found. To avoid such a result, it became

necessary to protect the traditional Mi'kmaq economy, including hunting, gathering and fishing. . . .

[26] The trial judge concluded that in 1760 the British Crown entered into a series of negotiations with communities of first nations spread across what is now Nova Scotia and New Brunswick. These treaties were essentially "adhesions" by different Mi'kmaq communities to identical terms because, as stated, it was contemplated that they would be consolidated in a more comprehensive and all-inclusive document at a later date, which never happened. The trial judge considered that the key negotiations took place not with the Mi'kmaq people directly, but with the St. John River Indians, part of the Maliseet First Nation, and the Passamaquody First Nation, who lived in present-day New Brunswick.

[27] The trial judge found as a fact, at para. 108, that the relevant Mi'kmaq treaty did "make peace upon the *same* conditions" (emphasis added) as the Maliseet and Passamaquody. Meetings took place between the Crown and the Maliseet and the Passamaquody on February 11, 1760, twelve days before these bands signed their treaty with the British and eighteen days prior to the meeting between the Governor and the Mi'kmaq representatives, Paul Laurent of LaHave and Michel Augustine of the Richibucto region, where the terms of the Maliseet and Passamaquody treaties were "communicated" and accepted. . . .

[29] The genesis of the Mi'kmaq trade clause is therefore found in the Governor's earlier negotiations with the Maliseet and Passamaquody First Nations. In that regard, the appellant places great reliance on a meeting between the Governor and their chiefs on February 11, 1760 for the purpose of reviewing various aspects of the proposed treaty. The following exchange is recorded in contemporaneous minutes of the meeting prepared by the British Governor's Secretary:

> His Excellency then demanded of them, Whether they were directed by their Tribes, to propose any other particulars to be Treated upon at this time. To which they replied that their Tribes had not directed them to propose any thing further than that *there might be a Truckhouse established, for the furnishing them with necessaries, in Exchange for their Peltry*, and that it might, at present, be at Fort Frederick.
>
> Upon which His Excellency acquainted them *that in case of their now executing a Treaty* in the manner proposed, and its being ratified at the next General Meeting of their Tribes the next Spring, *a Truckhouse should be established at Fort Frederick, agreable to their desire*, and likewise at other Places if it should be found necessary, for furnishing them with such Commodities as shall be necessary for them, in Exchange for their Peltry & and that great care should be taken, that the Commerce at the

said Truckhouses should be managed by Persons on whose Justice and good Treatment, they might always depend; and that it would be expected that the said Tribes should not Trafic or Barter and Exchange any Commodities at any other Place, nor with any other Persons. *Of all which* the Chiefs expressed their entire Approbation. [Emphasis added.]

[31] At a meeting of the Governor's Council on February 16, 1760 (less than a week later), the Council and the representatives of the Indians proceeded to settle the prices of various articles of merchandise including beaver, marten, otter, mink, fox, moose, deer, ermine and bird feathers, etc. Prices of "necessaries" for purchase at the truckhouse were also agreed, e.g., one pound of spring beaver could purchase 30 pounds of flour or 14 pounds of pork. The British took a liberal view of "necessaries." Two gallons of rum cost one pound of spring beaver pelts. The oral agreement on a price list was reflected in an Order in Council dated February 23, 1760, which provided "[t]hat the Prizes of all other kinds of Merchandize not mention'd herein be Regulated according to the Rates of the Foregoing articles." At trial the Crown expert and the defence experts agreed that fish could be among the items that the Mi'kmaq would trade.

[32] In furtherance of this trade arrangement, the British established six truckhouses following the signing of the treaties in 1760 and 1761, including Chignecto, Lunenburg, St. John, Windsor, Annapolis and "the Eastern Battery" along the coast from Halifax. The existence of advantageous terms at the truckhouses was part of an imperial peace strategy . . . the strategy would be effective only if the Mi'kmaq had access *both* to trade *and* to the fish and wildlife resources necessary to provide them with something to trade.

[33] Accordingly, on March 21, 1760, the Nova Scotia House of Assembly passed *An Act to prevent any private Trade or Commerce with the Indians*, 34 Geo. II, c. 11. In July 1761, however, the "Lords of Trade and Plantation" (the Board of Trade) in London objected and the King disallowed the Act as a restraint on trade that disadvantaged British merchants. This coincided with exposure of venality by the local truckhouse merchants. As Dr. Patterson testified:

> . . . the first Indian commissary, Halifax merchant, Benjamin Garrish, managed the system so that it was the Government which lost money while he profited usuriously.

[34] By 1762, Garrish was removed and the number of truckhouses was reduced to three. By 1764, the system itself was replaced by the impartial licensing of private traders approved by the London Board of Trade's "Plan for the Future Management of Indian Affairs," but that eventually died out as well, as mentioned earlier.

[35] In my view, all of this evidence, reflected in the trial judgment, demonstrates the inadequacy and incompleteness of the written memorial of the treaty terms by selectively isolating the restrictive trade covenant. Indeed, the truckhouse system offered such advantageous terms that it hardly seems likely that Mi'kmaq traders had to be compelled to buy at lower prices and sell at higher prices. At a later date, they objected when truckhouses were abandoned. The trade clause would not have advanced British objectives (peaceful relations with a self-sufficient Mi'kmaq people) or Mi'kmaq objectives (access to the European "necessaries" on which they had come to rely) unless the Mi'kmaq were assured at the same time of continuing access, implicitly or explicitly, to wildlife to trade. This was confirmed by the expert historian called by the Crown, as set out below.

(ii) The Expert Evidence

[36] The courts have attracted a certain amount of criticism from professional historians for what these historians see as an occasional tendency on the part of judges to assemble a "cut and paste" version of history. . . .

[37] While the tone of some of this criticism strikes the non-professional historian as intemperate, the basic objection, as I understand it, is that the judicial selection of facts and quotations is not always up to the standard demanded of the professional historian, which is said to be more nuanced. Experts, it is argued, are trained to read the various historical records together with the benefit of a protracted study of the period, and an appreciation of the frailties of the various sources. The law sees a finality of interpretation of historical events where finality, according to the professional historian, is not possible. The reality, of course, is that the courts are handed disputes that require for their resolution the finding of certain historical facts. The litigating parties cannot await the possibility of a stable academic consensus. The judicial process must do as best it can. In this particular case, however, there was an unusual level of agreement amongst all of the professional historians who testified about the underlying expectations of the participants regarding the treaty obligations entered into by the Crown with the Mi'kmaq. I set out, in particular, the evidence of the Crown's expert, Dr. Stephen Patterson, who spent many days of testimony reviewing the minutiae of the historical record. While he generally supported the Crown's narrow approach to the interpretation of the Treaty, which I have rejected on points of law, he did make a number of important concessions to the defence in a relatively lengthy and reflective statement which should be set out in full:

> Q. I guess it's fair to say that the British would have understood that the Micmac lived and survived by hunting and fishing and gathering activities.

> A. Yes, of course.

> Q. And that in this time period, 1760 and '61, fish would be amongst the items they would have to trade. And they would have the right under this treaty to bring fish and feathers and furs into a truckhouse in exchange for commodities that were available.

> A. Well, it's not mentioned but it's not excluded. So I think it's fair to assume that it was *permissible*.

> Q. Okay. It's fair to say that it's an assumption on which the trade truckhouse clause is based.

> A. That the truckhouse clause is based on the *assumption that natives will have a variety of things to trade, some of which are mentioned and some not.* Yes, I think that's fair.

> Q. Yes. And wouldn't be out of line to call that a right to fish and a right to bring the fish or furs or feathers or fowl or venison or whatever they might have, into the truckhouses to trade.

> A. *Ah, a right.* I think the implication here is that there is a *right to trade* under a certain form of regulation—

> Q. Yes.

> A. —that's laid down. And if you're saying *right to fish*, I've assumed that in recognizing the Micmac by treaty, the British were recognizing them as the people they were. They understood how they lived and that that meant that *those people had a right to live in Nova Scotia in their traditional ways.* And, to me, that *implies* that the British were accepting that the Micmac would continue to be a hunting and gathering people, that they would fish, that they would hunt to support themselves. I don't see any problem with that.

> It seems to me that *that's implicit* in the thing. Even though it doesn't say it, and I know that there seems to, in the 20th century, be some reluctance to see the value of the 1760 and 1761 treaties because they're not so explicit on these matters, but I personally don't see the hang-up. Because it strikes me that there is a recognition that the Micmac are a people and they have the right to exist. And that has—carries certain implications with it.

> More than this, the very fact that there is a truckhouse and that the truckhouse does list some of the things that natives are expected to trade, implies that the British are condoning or recognizing that this is the way that natives live. *They do live by hunting and, therefore, this is the produce of their hunting. They have the right to trade it.* . . .

[38] The trial judge gave effect to this evidence in finding a *right* to bring fish to the truckhouse to trade, but he declined to find a treaty right to fish and hunt to obtain the wherewithal to trade, and concluded that the right to trade expired along with the truckhouses and subsequent special arrangements. The Court of Appeal concluded, at p. 207, that Dr. Patterson used the word "right" interchangeably with the

word "permissible," and that the trade clause gave rise to no "rights" at all. I think the view taken by the courts below rather underestimates Dr. Patterson. No reason is given for doubting that Dr. Patterson meant what he said about the common understanding of the parties that he considered at least implicit in this particular treaty arrangement. He initially uses the words "permissible" and "assumption," but when asked specifically by counsel about a "right" to fish and to trade fish, he says, "Ah, a *right*" (emphasis added), then, weighing his words carefully, he addresses a "right to fish" and concludes that "by treaty" the British did recognize that the Mi'kmaq "had a *right* to live in Nova Scotia in their traditional ways" (emphasis added) which included hunting and fishing and trading their catch for necessaries. . . .

[40] In my view, the Nova Scotia judgments erred in concluding that the only enforceable treaty obligations were those set out in the written document of March 10, 1760, whether construed flexibly (as did the trial judge) or narrowly (as did the Nova Scotia Court of Appeal). The findings of fact made by the trial judge taken as a whole demonstrate that the concept of a disappearing treaty right does justice neither to the honour of the Crown nor to the reasonable expectations of the Mi'kmaq people. It is their common intention in 1760—not just the terms of the March 10, 1760 document—to which effect must be given.

Ascertaining the Terms of the Treaty

[41] Having concluded that the written text is incomplete, it is necessary to ascertain the treaty terms not only by reference to the fragmentary historical record, as interpreted by the expert historians, but also in light of the stated objectives of the British and Mi'kmaq in 1760 and the political and economic context in which those objectives were reconciled. . . .

[43] The law has long recognized that parties make assumptions when they enter into agreements about certain things that give their arrangements efficacy. Courts will imply a contractual term on the basis of presumed intentions of the parties where it is necessary to assure the efficacy of the contract, e.g., where it meets the "officious bystander test." . . . Here, if the ubiquitous officious bystander had said, "This talk about truckhouses is all very well, but if the Mi'kmaq are to make these promises, will they have the right to hunt and fish to catch something to trade at the truckhouses?", the answer would have to be, having regard to the honour of the Crown, "of course." If the law is prepared to supply the deficiencies of written contracts prepared by sophisticated parties and their legal advisors in order to produce a sensible result that accords with the intent of both parties, though unexpressed, the law cannot ask less of the honour and dignity of the Crown in its dealings with First Nations. . . .

[44] . . . While I do not believe that in ordinary commercial situations a right to trade implies any right of access to things to trade, I think the honour of the Crown requires nothing less in attempting to make sense of the result of these 1760 negotiations.

Rights of the Other Inhabitants

[45] My colleague, McLachlin J., takes the view that, subject to the negative restriction in the treaty, the Mi'kmaq possessed only the liberty to hunt, fish, gather and trade "enjoyed by other British subjects in the region" (para. 103). The Mi'kmaq were, in effect, "citizens minus" with no greater liberties but with greater restrictions. I accept that in terms of the *content* of the hunting, fishing and gathering activities, this may be true. . . .

[47] . . . The issue here is not so much the content of the rights or liberties as the level of legal protection thrown around them. A treaty could, to take a fanciful example, provide for a right of the Mi'kmaq to promenade down Barrington Street, Halifax, on each anniversary of the treaty. Barrington Street is a common thoroughfare enjoyed by all. There would be nothing "special" about the Mi'kmaq use of a common right of way. The point is that the treaty rights-holder not only has the *right* or liberty "enjoyed by other British subjects" but may enjoy special treaty *protection* against interference with its exercise. So it is with the trading arrangement. On June 25, 1761, following the signing of the Treaties of 1760-61 by the last group of Mi'kmaq villages, a ceremony was held at the farm of Lieutenant Governor Jonathan Belcher, the first Chief Justice of Nova Scotia, who was acting in the place of Governor Charles Lawrence, who had recently been drowned on his way to Boston. In reference to the treaties, including the trade clause, Lieutenant Governor Belcher proclaimed:

> The Laws will be like a great Hedge about your Rights and properties, if any break this Hedge to hurt and injure you, the heavy weight of the Laws will fall upon them and punish their Disobedience.

[48] Until enactment of the *Constitution Act, 1982*, the treaty rights of aboriginal peoples could be overridden by competent legislation as easily as could the rights and liberties of other inhabitants. The hedge offered no special protection, as the aboriginal people learned in earlier hunting cases such as *Sikyea v. The Queen*, [1964] S.C.R. 642, and *R. v. George*, [1966] S.C.R. 267. On April 17, 1982, however, this particular type of "hedge" was converted by s. 35(1) into sterner stuff that could only be broken down when justified according to the test laid down in *R. v. Sparrow*. . . . The fact the *content* of Mi'kmaq rights under the treaty to hunt and fish and trade was no greater than those enjoyed by other inhabitants does not, unless those rights were extinguished prior to April 17,

1982, detract from the higher *protection* they presently offer to the Mi'kmaq people.

The Honour of the Crown

[49] This appeal puts to the test the principle, emphasized by this Court on several occasions, that the honour of the Crown is always at stake in its dealings with aboriginal people. . . .

[52] I do not think an interpretation of events that turns a positive Mi'kmaq trade demand into a negative Mi'kmaq covenant is consistent with the honour and integrity of the Crown. Nor is it consistent to conclude that the Lieutenant Governor, seeking in good faith to address the trade demands of the Mi'kmaq, accepted the Mi'kmaq suggestion of a trading facility while denying any treaty protection to Mi'kmaq access to the things that were to be traded, even though these things were identified and priced in the treaty negotiations. This was not a commercial contract. The trade arrangement must be interpreted in a manner which gives meaning and substance to the promises made by the Crown. In my view, with respect, the interpretation adopted by the courts below left the Mi'kmaq with an empty shell of a treaty promise. . . .

The Limited Scope of the Treaty Right

[57] The Crown expresses the concern that recognition of the existence of a constitutionally entrenched right with, as here, a trading aspect, would open the floodgates to uncontrollable and excessive exploitation of the natural resources. Whereas hunting and fishing for food naturally restricts quantities to the needs and appetites of those entitled to share in the harvest, it is argued that there is no comparable, built-in restriction associated with a trading right, short of the paramount need to conserve the resource. . . . The ultimate fear is that the appellant, who in this case fished for eels from a small boat using a fyke net, could lever the treaty right into a factory trawler in Pomquet Harbour gathering the available harvest in preference to all non-aboriginal commercial or recreational fishermen. (This is indeed the position advanced by the intervener the Union of New Brunswick Indians.) This fear (or hope) is based on a misunderstanding of the narrow ambit and extent of the treaty right.

[58] The recorded note of February 11, 1760 was that "there might be a Truckhouse established, for the furnishing them with *necessaries*" (emphasis added). What is contemplated therefore is not a right to trade generally for economic gain, but rather a right to trade for necessaries. The treaty right is a regulated right and can be contained by regulation within its proper limits.

[59] The concept of "necessaries" is today equivalent to the concept of what Lambert J.A., in *R. v. Van der Peet* (1993),

80 B.C.L.R. (2d) 75, at p. 126, described as a "moderate livelihood." Bare subsistence has thankfully receded over the last couple of centuries as an appropriate standard of life for aboriginals and non-aboriginals alike. A moderate livelihood includes such basics as "food, clothing and housing, supplemented by a few amenities," but not the accumulation of wealth (*Gladstone* [*R. v.*, [1996] 2 S.C.R. 723], at para. 165). It addresses day-to-day needs. This was the common intention in 1760. It is fair that it be given this interpretation today. . . .

[61] Catch limits that could reasonably be expected to produce a moderate livelihood for individual Mi'kmaq families at present-day standards can be established by regulation and enforced without violating the treaty right. In that case, the regulations would accommodate the treaty right. Such regulations would *not* constitute an infringement that would have to be justified under the *Badger* standard.

Application to the Facts of this Case

[62] The appellant is charged with three offences: the selling of eels without a licence, fishing without a licence and fishing during the close season with illegal nets. These acts took place at Pomquet Harbour, Antigonish County. For Marshall to have satisfied the regulations, he was required to secure a licence under either the *Fishery (General) Regulations*, SOR/93-53, the *Maritime Provinces Fishery Regulations*, SOR/93-55, or the *Aboriginal Communal Fishing Licences Regulations*, SOR/93-332.

[63] All of these regulations place the issuance of licences within the absolute discretion of the Minister. . . .

[64] Furthermore, there is nothing in these regulations which gives direction to the Minister to explain how she or he should exercise this discretionary authority in a manner which would respect the appellant's treaty rights. . . .

[66] The appellant caught and sold the eels to support himself and his wife. Accordingly, the close season and the imposition of a discretionary licensing system would, if enforced, interfere with the appellant's treaty right to fish for trading purposes, and the ban on sales would, if enforced, infringe his right to trade for sustenance. In the absence of any justification of the regulatory prohibitions, the appellant is entitled to an acquittal.

Disposition

[67] The constitutional question stated by the Chief Justice on February 9, 1998, as follows:

Are the prohibitions on catching and retaining fish without a licence, on fishing during the close time, and on the unlicensed sale of fish, contained in ss. 4(1)(*a*) and 20 of the *Maritime Provinces Fishery Regulations* and s. 35(2) of the *Fishery (General) Regulations*, inconsistent with the treaty rights of the appellant contained in the Mi'kmaq Treaties of 1760-61 and therefore of no force or effect or application to him, by virtue of ss. 35(1) and 52 of the *Constitution Act, 1982*?

should be answered in the affirmative. I would therefore allow the appeal and order an acquittal on all charges.

The reasons of Gonthier and McLachlin JJ. were delivered by

McLACHLIN J. (dissenting):

A. What Principles of Interpretation Apply to the Interpretation of the Treaty Trade Clause?

[78] This Court has set out the principles governing treaty interpretation on many occasions. They include the following.

1. Aboriginal treaties constitute a unique type of agreement and attract special principles of interpretation: *R. v. Sundown*, [1999] 1 S.C.R 393, at para. 24; *R. v. Badger*, [1996] 1 S.C.R. 771, at para. 78; *R. v. Sioui*, [1990] 1 S.C.R. 1025, at p. 1043; *Simon v. The Queen*, [1985] 2 S.C.R. 387, at p. 404. See also: J. [Sákéj] Youngblood Henderson, "Interpreting *Sui Generis* Treaties" (1997), 36 *Alta. L. Rev.* 46; L.I. Rotman, "Defining Parameters: Aboriginal Rights, Treaty Rights, and the *Sparrow* Justificatory Test" (1997), 36 *Alta. L. Rev.* 149.

2. Treaties should be liberally construed and ambiguities or doubtful expressions should be resolved in favour of the aboriginal signatories: *Simon, supra*, at p. 402; *Sioui, supra*, at p. 1035; *Badger, supra*, at para. 52.

3. The goal of treaty interpretation is to choose from among the various possible interpretations of common intention the one which best reconciles the interests of both parties at the time the treaty was signed: *Sioui, supra*, at pp. 1068-69.

4. In searching for the common intention of the parties, the integrity and honour of the Crown is presumed: *Badger, supra*, at para. 41.

5. In determining the signatories' respective understanding and intentions, the court must be sensitive to the unique cultural and linguistic differences between the parties: *Badger, supra*, at paras. 52-54; *R. v. Horseman*, [1990] 1 S.C.R. 901, at p. 907.

6. The words of the treaty must be given the sense which they would naturally have held for the parties at the time: *Badger, supra*, at paras. 53 *et seq.*; *Nowegijick v. The Queen*, [1983] 1 S.C.R. 29, at p. 36.

7. A technical or contractual interpretation of treaty wording should be avoided: *Badger, supra*; *Horseman, supra*; *Nowegijick, supra*.

8. While construing the language generously, courts cannot alter the terms of the treaty by exceeding what "is possible on the language" or realistic: *Badger, supra*, at para. 76; *Sioui, supra*, at p. 1069; *Horseman, supra*, at p. 908.

9. Treaty rights of aboriginal peoples must not be interpreted in a static or rigid way. They are not frozen at the date of signature. The interpreting court must update treaty rights to provide for their modern exercise. This involves determining what modern practices are reasonably incidental to the core treaty right in its modern context: *Sundown, supra*, at para. 32; *Simon, supra*, at p. 402.

[79] Two specific issues of interpretation arise on this appeal. The answer to each is found in the foregoing summary of principles.

[80] The first issue of interpretation arises from the Court of Appeal's apparent suggestion that peace treaties fall in a different category from land cession treaties for purposes of interpretation, with the result that, when interpreting peace treaties, there is no "presumption" that rights were granted to the aboriginal signatories in exchange for entering into the treaty. This raises the issue of whether it is useful to slot treaties into different categories, each with its own rules of interpretation. The principle that each treaty must be considered in its unique historical and cultural context suggests that this practice should be avoided.

[81] The second issue of interpretation raised on this appeal is whether extrinsic evidence can be used in interpreting aboriginal treaties, absent ambiguity. Again, the principle that every treaty must be understood in its historical and cultural context suggests the answer must be yes. It is true that in *R. v. Horse*, [1988] 1 S.C.R. 187, at p. 201, this Court alluded with approval to the strict contract rule that extrinsic evidence is not admissible to construe a contract in the absence of ambiguity. However, subsequent decisions have made it clear that extrinsic evidence of the historic and cultural context of a treaty may be received absent ambiguity. . . .

[82] The fact that both the words of the treaty and its historic and cultural context must be considered suggests that it may be useful to approach the interpretation of a treaty in two steps. First, the words of the treaty clause at issue should be examined to determine their facial meaning, in so far as this can be ascertained, noting any patent ambiguities and misunderstandings that may have arisen from linguistic and cultural differences. This exercise will lead to one or more possible

interpretations of the clause. As noted in *Badger, supra,* at para. 76, "the scope of treaty rights will be determined by their wording." The objective at this stage is to develop a preliminary, but not necessarily determinative, framework for the historical context inquiry, taking into account the need to avoid an unduly restrictive interpretation and the need to give effect to the principles of interpretation.

[83]   At the second step, the meaning or different meanings which have arisen from the wording of the treaty right must be considered against the treaty's historical and cultural backdrop. A consideration of the historical background may suggest latent ambiguities or alternative interpretations not detected at first reading. Faced with a possible range of interpretations, courts must rely on the historical context to determine which comes closest to reflecting the parties' common intention. This determination requires choosing "from among the various possible interpretations of the common intention the one which best reconciles" the parties' interests: *Sioui, supra,* at p. 1069. Finally, if the court identifies a particular right which was intended to pass from generation to generation, the historical context may assist the court in determining the modern counterpart of that right: *Simon, supra,* at pp. 402-3; *Sundown, supra,* at paras. 30 and 33.

[84]   In the case on appeal, the trial judge heard 40 days of trial, the testimony of three expert witnesses, and was presented with over 400 documents. . . . The trial judge's review of the historical context, the cultural differences between the parties, their different methods of communication, and the pre-treaty negotiations, led him to conclude that there was no misunderstanding or lack of agreement between the British and the Mi'kmaq that trade under the treaties was to be carried out in accordance with the terms of the trade clause. Having come to this conclusion, the trial judge turned again to the historical context to interpret the content of such terms, in accordance with the parties' common intention. In my opinion, the trial judge's approach to the interpretation of the Treaties of 1760-61 is in keeping with the principles governing treaty interpretation. With the greatest respect for the contrary view of my colleague, Justice Binnie, I find no basis for error in the trial judge's approach.

B. Do the Treaties of 1760-61 Grant a General Right to Trade?

[85]   At trial, the appellant argued that the treaty trade clause conferred on the Mi'kmaq a general trading right. The trial judge rejected this submission, finding that the treaties conferred only a limited "right to bring" goods to truckhouses and licensed traders to trade. The Court of Appeal went even further, finding that the treaties conferred no trade right at all. Before this Court, the appellant once again advances the argument that the Treaties of 1760-61 conferred a general trade right on the Mi'kmaq.

[86]   Before addressing whether the words of the treaties, taken in their historic and cultural context support a general treaty right to trade, it is necessary to distinguish between a right to trade under the law applicable to all citizens, and a treaty right to trade. All inhabitants of the province of Nova Scotia or Acadia enjoyed a general right to trade. No treaty was required to confer such a right as it vested in all British subjects. The Mi'kmaq, upon signing the Treaties of 1760-61 and thereby acknowledging the jurisdiction of the British king over Nova Scotia, automatically inherited this general right. This public right must be distinguished from the asserted *treaty* right to trade. Treaty rights are by definition special rights conferred by treaty. They are given protection over and above rights enjoyed by the general populace. Only rights conferred by treaty are protected by s. 35 of the *Constitution Act, 1982.* I note that while rights enjoyed by the general populace can be included in treaties, where this occurs, they become separate and distinct treaty rights subject to a higher level of protection. The appellant in this case must establish a distinct treaty right if he is to succeed.

(1)   The Wording of the Trade Clause

[87]   This brings me to the words of the treaty trade clause. It states:

> And I do further engage that we will not traffick, barter or Exchange any Commodities in any manner but with such persons or the managers of such Truck houses as shall be appointed or Established by His Majesty's Governor at [insert location of closest truck house] or Elsewhere in Nova Scotia or Accadia.

The clause is short, the words simple. The Mi'kmaq covenant that they will "*not* traffick, barter or Exchange any Commodities in any manner *but* with [British agents]" (emphasis added). The core of this clause is the obligation on the Mi'kmaq to trade only with the British. Ancillary to this is the implied promise that the British will establish truckhouses where the Mi'kmaq can trade. These words do not, on their face, confer a general right to trade.

[88]   The next question is whether the historic and cultural context in which the treaties were made establishes a general right to trade, having due regard for the need to interpret treaty rights generously. I will deal first with the linguistic and cultural differences between the parties, then with the historical record generally.

(2)   Cultural and Linguistic Considerations

[89]   The trial judge found that there was no misunderstanding or lack of agreement between the British and the

Mi'kmaq that trade under the treaties was to be carried out in accordance with the terms of the trade clause, and that the Mi'kmaq understood those terms. . . .

(3) The Historical Context and the Scope of the Trade Clause

[90] After a meticulous review of the historical evidence, the trial judge concluded that: (1) the Treaties of 1760-61 were primarily peace treaties, cast against the background of both a long struggle between the British and the French in which the Mi'kmaq were allied with the French, and over a decade of intermittent hostilities between the British and the Mi'kmaq; (2) the French defeat and withdrawal from Nova Scotia left the Mi'kmaq to co-exist with the British without the presence of their former ally and supplier; (3) the Mi'kmaq were accustomed to and in some cases dependent on trade for firearms, gunpowder, food and European trade goods; and (4) the British wanted peace and a safe environment for settlers and, despite recent victories, did not feel completely secure in Nova Scotia.

[91] Considering the wording of the trade clause in this historical context, the trial judge concluded that it was not within the common intention of the parties that the treaties granted a general right to trade. He found that at the time of entering the treaties, the Mi'kmaq wanted to secure peace and continuing access to European trade goods. He described the Mi'kmaq concerns at the time as very focussed and immediate. The British, for their part, wanted peace in the region to ensure the safety of their settlers. While the British were willing to support the costly truckhouse system to secure peace, they did not want the Mi'kmaq to become a long-term burden on the public treasury. To this end, the trial judge found that the British wanted the Mi'kmaq to continue their traditional way of life. The trial judge found that the interpretation of the treaty trade clause which best reconciled the intentions of both parties was that the trade clause imposed an obligation on the Mi'kmaq to trade only at British truckhouses or with licensed traders, as well as a correlative obligation on the British to provide the Mi'kmaq with such trading outlets so long as this restriction on Mi'kmaq trade existed. This correlative obligation on the British gave rise to a limited Mi'kmaq "right to bring" goods to trade at these outlets. When the British ceased to provide trading outlets to the Mi'kmaq, the restriction on their trade fell as did the limited "right to bring" which arose out of the system of mutual obligations. . . .

[93] The desire to establish a secure and successful peace led each party to make significant concessions. The Mi'kmaq accepted that forging a peaceful relationship with the British was essential to ensuring continued access to European trade goods and to their continued security in the region. To this end, the Mi'kmaq agreed to limit their autonomy by trading only with the British and ceasing all trading relations with the French. Agreeing to restricted trade at truckhouses made the limit on Mi'kmaq autonomy more palatable as truckhouses were recognized as vehicles for stable trade at guaranteed and favourable terms. . . .

[96] To achieve the mutually desired objective of peace, both parties agreed to make certain concessions. The Mi'kmaq agreed to forgo their trading autonomy and the general trading rights they possessed as British subjects, and to abide by the treaty trade regime. The British, in exchange, undertook to provide the Mi'kmaq with stable trading outlets where European goods were provided at favourable terms while the exclusive trade regime existed. This is the core of what the parties intended. The wording of the trade clause, taken in its linguistic, cultural and historical context, permits no other conclusion. Both the Mi'kmaq and the British understood that the "right to bring" goods to trade was a limited right contingent on the existence of a system of exclusive trade and truckhouses. On the historical record, neither the Mi'kmaq nor the British intended or understood the treaty trade clause as creating a general right to trade. . . .

[98] The pre-treaty negotiations between the British and the Maliseet and the Passamaquody, indicate that the aboriginal leaders requested truckhouses in response to their accommodation of the British desire for restricted trade. The negotiations also indicate that the British agreed to furnish truckhouses where necessary to ensure that the Maliseet and the Passamaquody could continue to acquire commodities and necessities through trade. The negotiations highlight the concessions that both the aboriginal and the British signatories made in order to secure the mutually desired objective of peace. The negotiations also indicate that both parties understood that the treaties granted a specific, and limited, right to bring goods to truckhouses to trade. . . .

[100] The fall of the licensed trading system marked the fall of the trading regime established under the Treaties. This left the Mi'kmaq free to trade with whomever they wished, like all other inhabitants of the colonies. . . .

[101] The record thus shows that within a few years of the signing of the Treaty, the Mi'kmaq treaty obligation to trade only with the British fell into disuse and with it the correlative British obligation to supply the Mi'kmaq with trading outlets. Both parties contributed to the demise of the system of mutual obligations and, apart from a lament that prices were better regulated under the truckhouse system, neither seems to have mourned it. The exclusive trade and truckhouse system was a temporary mechanism to achieve peace in a troubled region between parties with a long history of hostilities. . . .

[102] The historical context, as the trial judge points out, supports the view that the British wanted the Mi'kmaq to maintain their traditional way of life and that trade was important to the Mi'kmaq. From this, Binnie J. suggests that the purpose of the treaty trading regime was to promote the self-sufficiency of the Mi'kmaq, and finds a treaty right to hunt, to fish, and to trade for sustenance. Yet, with respect, the historical record does not support this inference. The dominant purpose of the treaties was to prevent the Mi'kmaq from maintaining alliances with the French. To this end, the British insisted on a treaty term that the Mi'kmaq trade exclusively with British agents at British trading outlets—the truck-houses. Implicit in this is the expectation that the Mi'kmaq would continue to trade. But it does not support the inference that the treaty clause conveyed a general right to trade and to sustenance. The treaty reference to the right to bring goods to truckhouses was required by and incidental to the obligation of the Mi'kmaq to trade with the British, and cannot be stretched to embrace a general treaty right to trade surviving the exclusive trade and truckhouse regime. To do so is to transform a specific right agreed to by both parties into an unintended right of broad and undefined scope. . . .

[104] I conclude that the trial judge did not err—indeed was manifestly correct—in his interpretation of the historical record and the limited nature of the treaty right that this suggests. . . .

[111] A claimant seeking to rely on a treaty right to defeat a charge of violating Canadian law must first establish *a treaty right that protects, expressly or by inference, the activities in question*, see: *Sioui, supra*, at pp. 1066-67. Only then does the onus shift to the government to show that it has accommodated the right or that its limitations of the right are justified.

[112] To proceed from a right undefined in scope or modern counterpart to the question of justification would be to render treaty rights inchoate and the justification of limitations impossible. How can one meaningfully discuss accommoda-tion or justification of a right unless one has some idea of the core of that right and its modern scope? How is the government, in the absence of such definition, to know how far it may justifiably trench on the right in the collective interest of Canadians? How are courts to judge whether the government that attempts to do so has drawn the line at the right point? Referring to the "right" in the generalized abstraction risks both circumventing the parties' common intention at the time the treaty was signed, and functioning illegitimately to create, in effect, an unintended right of broad and undefined scope.

[113] Instead of positing an undefined right and then requiring justification, a claim for breach of a treaty right should begin by defining the core of that right and seeking its modern counterpart. Then the question of whether the law at issue derogates from that right can be explored, and any justification for such derogation examined, in a meaningful way.

[114] Based on the wording of the treaties and an extensive review of the historical evidence, the trial judge concluded that the only trade right conferred by the treaties was a "right to bring" goods to truckhouses that terminated with the demise of the exclusive trading and truckhouse regime. This led to the conclusion that no Crown breach was established and therefore no accommodation or justification required. The record amply supports this conclusion, and the trial judge made no error of legal principle. I see no basis upon which this Court can interfere.

Justification

[115] Having concluded that the Treaties of 1760-61 confer no general trade right, I need not consider the arguments specifically relating to justification.

Conclusion

[116] There is no existing right to trade in the Treaties of 1760-61 that exempts the appellant from the federal fisheries regulations. It follows that I would dismiss the appeal.

R. v. Marshall (Second Marshall Decision), 1999

Announcement of the Supreme Court's *Marshall* decision on September 18, 1999 brought about immediate howls of outrage from non-native Atlantic fishers who feared that it meant Aboriginal fishers would have unlimited and unregulated access to the entire Atlantic fishery, including the lucrative lobster industry. A spokesman for the West Nova Fishermen's Coalition told the *National Post* that "[i]t's a scary situation here. It's like Ontario losing its automobile industry." Public statements from Aboriginal spokesmen suggesting that the decision extended to timber and mining rights did nothing to assuage such fears.[1] The West Nova Fishermen's Coalition asked the Supreme Court for a "rehearing" to consider the Canadian government's regulatory authority over the east coast fisheries and a new trial for Donald Marshall Jr. at which the government might justify conservation restrictions on the exercise of his treaty right. On November 17, 1999, in response to this request, the Supreme Court rendered its decision in the second *Marshall* case. Six of the seven judges who had participated in the first *Marshall* decision participated in this unanimous opinion of the Court. Justice Cory did not participate because he had retired.

The Court's bottom line was a firm no to the request for a rehearing and a new trial. The Court was unwilling to order a new trial simply because the Crown in the first trial had failed to address the question of justifying restrictions on Marshall's treaty right. A request that the Court review the government's power to regulate fisheries in areas affected by Aboriginal treaty rights was, in effect, a request for a reference case, and only the federal government can initiate a reference case in the Supreme Court. Therefore the Court declined to grant a rehearing. But in elaborating on its reasons, the Court, in effect, came close to providing a reference case opinion on the extent of the treaty rights at issue and the government's power to regulate them. Providing such extensive reasons in these circumstances was an unprecedented event.

The Court spelled out in more detail the extent of the treaty rights recognized in its earlier decision. The treaty rights were confined to the areas traditionally used by each local Aboriginal community. Moreover, these rights belong to communities, not to individuals, and must be exercised according to the authority of the local community. The "gathering" rights dealt with were limited to fish, wildlife, fruit and berries, and to quantities that could be traded for basic necessaries. No arguments had been made that would extend the treaty rights to modern resources such as timber, minerals, or offshore gas. The Court noted that other cases being litigated in the lower courts raised some of these issues. Note that the treaties at issue in *Marshall* were "peace and friendship" treaties that did not deal with land cession. Thus, some of these other resource claims may involve claims based on native title to unceded lands.

As for the government's regulatory power, the Court repeated, for the benefit of those who had either missed or ignored them, passages in the earlier decision where it had recognized

---

1 For an account of these events, see Ken Coates, *The Marshall Decision and Native Rights* (Montreal and Kingston: McGill-Queen's University Press, 2000).

the government's power to regulate the treaty right. Again it cited previous cases—namely, *Sparrow* and *Badger*—in which it set out the test that government must satisfy to justify encroachments on Aboriginal and treaty rights. The Minister of Fisheries could use "the full range of resource management tools" to regulate the fishery, providing he could justify any limits that restricted Aboriginal fishers with treaty rights to less fish than needed to support a moderate livelihood. Such justification might be based on protecting the interests of non-native fishers as well as on the need to conserve fish stocks. Taking into consideration the needs of non-native fishers was especially relevant in a context where the treaty right is exercised "on a commercial scale." But justifiable limits on treaty rights must be developed in consultation with the Aboriginal communities and in a manner that recognized the Crown's special trust relationship with Aboriginal peoples as "the first consideration."

If the Supreme Court's decision in the second *Marshall* case was designed to pour oil on troubled waters, it did not succeed—at least in the short run. In December 1999, a fierce "lobster war" broke out on the New Brunswick coast, with the most violent incidents occurring at Burnt Church where Mi'kmaq lobster traps were vandalized, a prayer tower burned to the ground, and three Mi'kmaq men injured when their pickup truck was rammed. In retaliation, native fishers burned an empty house and rammed two non-native trucks. Attempts by fisheries officials to prevent Mi'kmaq from setting lobster traps in a "closed season" led to further confrontations the following year and a futile attempt at mediation by former Ontario Premier Bob Rae. A more satisfactory outcome may come only when the federal government and the Aboriginal peoples in the areas follow the Supreme Court's suggestion and negotiate a modern agreement, building on the historic treaties. ⌐

R. v. MARSHALL
[1999] 3 S.C.R. 533

Judgment: November 17, 1999.

Present: Lamer C.J. and L'Heureux-Dubé, Gonthier, McLachlin, Iacobucci, and Binnie JJ.

Interveners: The Attorney General for New Brunswick, the West Nova Fishermen's Coalition, the Native Council of Nova Scotia, and the Union of New Brunswick Indians.

The following is the judgment delivered by

[1] **THE COURT:** The intervener, the West Nova Fishermen's Coalition (the "Coalition"), applies for a rehearing to have the Court address the regulatory authority of the Government of Canada over the east coast fisheries together with a new trial to allow the Crown to justify for conservation or other purposes the licensing and closed season restriction on the exercise of the appellant's treaty right, and for an order that the Court's judgment, dated September 17, 1999, [1999] 3 S.C.R. 456, be stayed in the meantime. The application is opposed by the Crown, the appellant Marshall and the other interveners.

[2] Those opposing the motion object in different ways that the Coalition's motion rests on a series of misconceptions about what the September 17, 1999 majority judgment decided and what it did not decide. These objections are well founded. The Court did not hold that the Mi'kmaq treaty right cannot be regulated or that the Mi'kmaq are guaranteed an open season in the fisheries. Justification for conservation or other purposes is a separate and distinct issue at the trial of one of these prosecutions. It is up to the Crown to decide whether or not it wishes to support the applicability of government regulations when prosecuting an accused who claims to be exercising an aboriginal or treaty right.

[3] The Attorney General of Canada, in opposing the Coalition's motion, acknowledges that the Crown did not lead any evidence at trial or make any argument on the appeal that the licensing and closed season regulations which restricted the exercise of the treaty right were justified in relation to the eel fishery. Accordingly, the issue whether these restrictions could have been justified in this case formed no part of the Court's majority judgment of September 17, 1999, and the constitutional question posed in this prosecution was answered on that basis.

The September 17, 1999 Acquittal

[4] In its majority judgment, the Court acquitted the appellant of charges arising out of catching 463 pounds of eel and selling them for $787.10. The acquittal was based on a treaty made with the British in 1760, and more particularly, on the oral terms reflected in documents made by the British at the time of the negotiations but recorded incompletely in the "truckhouse" clause of the written treaty. The treaty right permits the Mi'kmaq community to work for a living through continuing access to fish and wildlife to trade for "necessaries," which a majority of the Court interpreted as "food, clothing and housing, supplemented by a few amenities."

[5] The Coalition argues that the native and non-native fishery should be subject to the same regulations. In fact, as pointed out in the September 17, 1999 majority judgment, natives and non-natives *were* subject to the unilateral regulatory authority of successive governments from 1760-61 to 1982. Until adoption of the *Constitution Act, 1982*, the appellant would clearly have been subject to regulations under the federal *Fisheries Act* and predecessor enactments in the same way and to the same extent as members of the applicant Coalition unless given a regulatory exemption as a matter of government policy.

[6] As further pointed out in the September 17, 1999 majority judgment, the framers of the Constitution caused existing aboriginal and treaty rights to be entrenched in s. 35 of the *Constitution Act, 1982*. This gave constitutional status to rights that were previously vulnerable to unilateral extinguishment. The constitutional language necessarily included the 1760-61 treaties, and did not, on its face, refer expressly to a power to regulate. Section 35(1) simply says that "[t]he existing aboriginal and treaty rights of the aboriginal peoples of Canada are hereby recognized and affirmed." In subsequent cases, some aboriginal peoples argued that, as no regulatory restrictions on their rights were expressed in plain language in the Constitution, none could be imposed except by constitutional amendment. On the other hand, some of the Attorneys General argued that as aboriginal and treaty rights had always been vulnerable to unilateral regulation and extinguishment by government, this vulnerability was itself part of the rights now entrenched in s. 35 of the *Constitution Act, 1982*. In a series of important decisions commencing with *R. v. Sparrow*, [1990] 1 S.C.R. 1075, which arose in the context of the west coast fishery, this Court affirmed that s. 35 aboriginal and treaty rights *are* subject to regulation, provided such regulation is shown by the Crown to be justified on conservation or other grounds of public importance. A series of tests to establish such justification was laid out. These cases were referred to in the September 17, 1999 majority judgment, but the

applicable principles were not elaborated because justification was not an issue which the Crown chose to make part of this particular prosecution, and therefore neither the Crown nor the defence had made submissions respecting the government's continuing powers of regulation. The Coalition recognizes that it is raising a new issue.…

[7] …The Coalition asks the Court in effect to transform the proceeding retroactively into an advisory reference or declaratory action. The Attorney General of Canada objects to this transformation.…

[12] An order suspending the effect of a judgment of this Court is infrequently granted, especially where (as here) the parties have not requested such an order. This was not a reference to determine the general validity of legislative and regulatory provisions, as was the case, for example, in *Reference re Manitoba Language Rights*, [1985] 1 S.C.R. 721, at p. 780, where the Court suspended its declaration of invalidity of Manitoba enactments until "the expiry of the minimum period required for translation, re-enactment, printing and publishing." Nor was this a case where the Court was asked to grant declaratory relief with respect to the invalidity of statutory provisions, as in *M. v. H.*, [1999] 2 S.C.R. 3, where the Court suspended the effect of its declaration of invalidity of the definition of "spouse" for the purpose of s. 29 of the Ontario *Family Law Act*, R.S.O. 1990, c. F.3, for a period of six months to enable the legislature to consider appropriate amendments.…

[14] As stated in para. 56 of the September 17, 1999 majority judgment, the treaty right was "to continue to obtain necessaries through hunting and fishing by trading the products of those traditional activities *subject to restrictions that can be justified under the Badger test*" (emphasis added). The *Badger* test (*R. v. Badger*, [1996] 1 S.C.R. 771) will be discussed below. The Crown, as stated, did not offer any evidence or argument justifying the licensing and closed season restrictions (referred to in the statute and regulations as a "close time") on the appellant's exercise of the collective treaty right, such as (for example) a need to conserve and protect the eel population. The eel population may not in fact require protection from commercial exploitation. Such was the assertion of the Native Council of Nova Scotia in opposition to the Coalition's motion:

> … Mr. Marshall was fishing eels. There are no possible conservation issues involving the eel fishery. They are not an endangered species and there is no significant non-native commercial fishery. They are a traditional harvest species, being harvested by Mr. Marshall in a traditional method and in relatively small quantities. There is simply no justificatory evidence that the Crown could have led.

The Attorney General of Canada's written argument on the appeal to this Court specifically stated that "[s]ince no such treaty rights have been established in this case, then there was no requirement for the Crown to justify its *Fisheries Act* regulations in accordance with ... *R. v. Sparrow* [*supra*] or *R. v. Gladstone* [[1996] 2 S.C.R. 723]." ... The issue of justification was not before the Court and no judgment was made about whether or not such restrictions could have been justified in relation to the eel fishery had the Crown led evidence and argument to support their applicability.

Grounds on Which the Coalition Seeks a Rehearing

1. Whether the Appellant Is Entitled to Have Been Acquitted on a Charge of Unlicensed Sale of Fish, Contrary to Section 35(2) of the Fishery (General) Regulations, in the Absence of a New (or Further) Trial on the Issue of Whether That Regulation Is or Can Be Justified by the Government of Canada

[15] The appellant, as any other citizen facing a prosecution, is entitled to know in a timely way the case he has to meet, and to be afforded the opportunity to answer it. The Coalition seeks a new trial on a new issue. The September 17, 1999 majority decision specifically noted at para. 4 that the treaty right

> *was always subject to regulation.* The Crown does not suggest that the regulations in question accommodate the treaty right. The Crown's case is that no such treaty right exists. Further, no argument was made that the treaty right was extinguished prior to [enactment of the *Constitution Act, 1982*], and *no justification was offered by the Crown for the several prohibitions at issue in this case.* [Emphasis added.]

The Attorney General of Canada affirms in opposition to the Coalition's motion the limited nature of the issues raised at trial:

> In this case, the intervener wishes to contest the appellant's entitlement to an acquittal by raising issues as to whether the regulations under which the appellant was charged could be justified in accordance with the test in *R. v. Sparrow. That would clearly be a new issue in the proceedings.* It is not open to the intervener to raise an issue that did not arise between the parties to the appeal. [Emphasis added.]

In its Reply, the Coalition argues that to require the parties to deal with the issue of regulatory justification in the same trial as treaty entitlement "would be to impose an unreasonable and unworkable burden in aboriginal rights litigation at the trial level." Whatever may be the advantages or disadvantages of splitting these issues into a two-stage trial, no such proposal was made to the trial judge by the parties, and no such procedure was considered, much less adopted, in this case. As stated, the Crown here opposes a rehearing and opposes a new trial. The issues of concern to the Coalition largely relate to the lobster fishery, not the eel fishery, and, if necessary, can be raised and decided in future cases that involve the specifics of the lobster fishery. It is up to the Crown to initiate enforcement action in the lobster and other fisheries if and when it chooses to do so.

2. Whether the Appellant Is Entitled to Have Been Acquitted on a Charge of Out-of-Season Fishing, Contrary to Item 2 of Schedule III of the Maritime Provinces Fishery Regulations, in the Absence of a New (or Further) Trial on the Issue of Whether Those Regulations Are or Can Be Justified by the Government of Canada

[16] The Coalition argues that a rehearing and a further trial are necessary because of "uncertainty" about the authority of the government to manage the fisheries. The Attorney General of Canada, acting on behalf of the federal government which regulates the fisheries, opposes the Coalition's position.

[17] In the event of another prosecution under the regulations, the Crown will (as it did in this case) have the onus of establishing the factual elements of the offence. The onus will then switch to the accused to demonstrate that he or she is a member of an aboriginal community in Canada with which one of the local treaties described in the September 17, 1999 majority judgment was made, and was engaged in the exercise of the community's collective right to hunt or fish in that community's traditional hunting and fishing grounds. The Court's majority judgment noted in para. 5 that no treaty was made by the British with the Mi'kmaq population as a whole:

> ... [T]he British signed a series of agreements with individual Mi'kmaq communities in 1760 and 1761 intending to have them consolidated into a comprehensive Mi'kmaq treaty that was never in fact brought into existence. The trial judge, Embree Prov. Ct. J., found that by the end of 1761 all of the Mi'kmaq villages in Nova Scotia had entered into *separate but similar treaties.* [Emphasis added.]

The British Governor in Halifax thus proceeded on the basis that local chiefs had no authority to promise peace and friendship on behalf of other local chiefs in other communities, or to secure treaty benefits on their behalf. The treaties were local and the reciprocal benefits were local. In the absence of a fresh agreement with the Crown, the exercise of the treaty rights will be limited to the area traditionally used by the local community with which the "separate but similar" treaty was made.

Moreover, the treaty rights do not belong to the individual, but are exercised by authority of the local community to which the accused belongs, and their exercise is limited to the purpose of obtaining from the identified resources the wherewithal to trade for "necessaries." . . .

[19] At the end of the day, it is always open to the Minister (as it was here) to seek to justify the limitation on the treaty right because of the need to conserve the resource in question or for other compelling and substantial public objectives, as discussed below. Equally, it will be open to an accused in future cases to try to show that the treaty right was intended in 1760 by *both* sides to include access to resources other than fish, wildlife and traditionally gathered things such as fruits and berries. The word "gathering" in the September 17, 1999 majority judgment was used in connection with the types of the resources traditionally "gathered" in an aboriginal economy and which were thus reasonably in the contemplation of the parties to the 1760-61 treaties. While treaty rights are capable of evolution within limits, as discussed below, their subject matter (absent a new agreement) cannot be wholly transformed. Certain unjustified assumptions are made in this regard by the Native Council of Nova Scotia on this motion about "the effect of the economic treaty right on forestry, minerals and natural gas deposits offshore." The Union of New Brunswick Indians also suggested on this motion a need to "negotiate an integrated approach dealing with all resources coming within the purview of fishing, hunting and gathering which includes harvesting from the sea, the forests and the land." This extended interpretation of "gathering" is not dealt with in the September 17, 1999 majority judgment, and negotiations with respect to such resources as logging, minerals or offshore natural gas deposits would go beyond the subject matter of this appeal.

[20] The September 17, 1999 majority judgment did not rule that the appellant had established a treaty right "to gather" anything and everything physically capable of being gathered. The issues were much narrower and the ruling was much narrower. No evidence was drawn to our attention, nor was any argument made in the course of this appeal, that trade in logging or minerals, or the exploitation of off-shore natural gas deposits, was in the contemplation of either or both parties to the 1760 treaty; nor was the argument made that exploitation of such resources could be considered a logical evolution of treaty rights to fish and wildlife or to the type of things traditionally "gathered" by the Mi'kmaq in a 1760 aboriginal lifestyle. It is of course open to native communities to assert broader treaty rights in that regard, but if so, the basis for such a claim will have to be established in proceedings where the issue is squarely raised on proper historical evidence, as was done in this case in relation to fish and wildlife.

Other resources were simply not addressed by the parties, and therefore not addressed by the Court in its September 17, 1999 majority judgment. As acknowledged by the Union of New Brunswick Indians in opposition to the Coalition's motion, "there are cases wending their way through the lower courts dealing specifically with some of these potential issues such as cutting timber on Crown lands."

[21] The fact the Crown elected not to try to justify a closed season on the eel fishery at issue in this case cannot be generalized, as the Coalition's question implies, to a conclusion that closed seasons can never be imposed as part of the government's regulation of the Mi'kmaq limited commercial "right to fish." A "closed season" is clearly a potentially available management tool, but its application to treaty rights will have to be justified for conservation or other purposes. In the absence of such justification, an accused who establishes a treaty right is ordinarily allowed to exercise it. . . .

[22] Resource conservation and management and allocation of the permissible catch inevitably raise matters of considerable complexity both for Mi'kmaq peoples who seek to work for a living under the protection of the treaty right, and for governments who seek to justify the regulation of that treaty right. The factual context, as this case shows, is of great importance, and the merits of the government's justification may vary from resource to resource, species to species, community to community and time to time. As this and other courts have pointed out on many occasions, the process of accommodation of the treaty right may best be resolved by consultation and negotiation of a modern agreement for participation in specified resources by the Mi'kmaq rather than by litigation. . . .

3. Whether the Government of Canada Has Power to Regulate the Exercise by Mi'kmaq Persons of Their Treaty Right to Fish Through the Imposition of Licensing Requirements

[24] The government's power to regulate the treaty right is repeatedly affirmed in the September 17, 1999 majority judgment. In addition to the reference at para. 4 of the majority decision, already mentioned, that the treaty right "was always subject to regulation," the majority judgment further stated, at para. 7:

> In my view, the treaty rights are limited to securing "necessaries" (which I construe in the modern context, as equivalent to a moderate livelihood), and do not extend to the open-ended accumulation of wealth. The rights thus construed, however, are, in my opinion, treaty rights within the meaning of s. 35 of the *Constitution Act, 1982, and are subject to regulations that can be justified under the Badger test.* . . . [Emphasis added.]

At para. 38, the majority judgment noted that:

> Dr. Patterson went on to emphasize that the understanding of the Mi'kmaq would have been that these treaty rights were subject to regulation, which I accept.

At para. 58, the limited nature of the right was reiterated:

> What is contemplated therefore is not a right to trade generally for economic gain, but rather a right to trade for necessaries. *The treaty right is a regulated right and can be contained by regulation within its proper limits.* [Emphasis added.]

At para. 64, the majority judgment again referred to regulation permitted by the *Badger* test. The Court was thus most explicit in confirming the regulatory authority of the federal and provincial governments within their respective legislative fields to regulate the exercise of the treaty right subject to the constitutional requirement that restraints on the exercise of the treaty right have to be justified on the basis of conservation or other compelling and substantial public objectives, discussed below.

4. Whether the Government of Canada Has Power to Regulate the Exercise by Mi'kmaq Persons, Including the Appellant, of Their Treaty Right to Fish Through the Imposition of Closed Seasons

[29] The regulatory device of a closed season is at least in part directed at conservation of the resource. Conservation has always been recognized to be a justification of paramount importance to limit the exercise of treaty and aboriginal rights in the decisions of this Court cited in the majority decision of September 17, 1999, including *Sparrow, supra,* and *Badger, supra.* As acknowledged by the Native Council of Nova Scotia in opposition to the Coalition's motion, "[c]onservation is clearly a first priority and the Aboriginal peoples accept this." Conservation, where necessary, may require the complete shutdown of a hunt or a fishery for aboriginal and non-aboriginal alike.

[30] In this case, the prosecution of the appellant was directed to a "closed season" in the eel fishery which the Crown did not try to justify, and that is the precise context in which the majority decision of September 17, 1999 is to be understood. No useful purpose would be served for those like the Coalition who are interested in justifying a closed season in the lobster fishery if a rehearing or a new trial were ordered in this case, which related only to the closed season in the eel fishery.

5. In Any Event, What Is the Scope of Regulatory Power Possessed by the Government of Canada for Purposes of Regulating the Treaty Right?

[31] On the face of it, this question is not raised by the subject matter of the appeal, nor is it capable of being answered on the factual record. As framed, it is so broad as to be incapable of a detailed response. . . .

[33] The majority judgment of September 17, 1999 did not put in doubt the validity of the *Fisheries Act* or any of its provisions. What it said, in para. 66, was that, "the close season and the imposition of a discretionary licensing system would, if enforced, interfere with the appellant's treaty right to fish for trading purposes, and the ban on sales would, if enforced, infringe his right to trade for sustenance. *In the absence of any justification of the regulatory prohibitions, the appellant is entitled to an acquittal*" (emphasis added). Section 43 of the Act sets out the basis of a very broad regulatory authority over the fisheries which may extend to the native fishery where justification is shown. . . .

[35] Despite the limitations on the Court's ability in a prosecution to address broader issues not at issue between the Crown and the defence, the majority judgment of September 17, 1999 nevertheless referred to the Court's principal pronouncements on the various grounds on which the exercise of treaty rights may be regulated. These include the following grounds:

[36] *The treaty right itself is a limited right.* The September 17, 1999 majority judgment referred to the "narrow ambit and extent of the treaty right" (para. 57). In its written argument, the Coalition says that the only regulatory method specified in that judgment was a limit on the quantities of fish required to satisfy the Mi'kmaq need for necessaries. This is not so. What the majority judgment said is that the Mi'kmaq treaty right does not extend *beyond* the quantities required to satisfy the need for necessaries. . . .

[38] Other limitations apparent in the September 17, 1999 majority judgment include the local nature of the treaties, the communal nature of a treaty right, and the fact it was only hunting and fishing resources to which access was affirmed, together with traditionally gathered things like wild fruit and berries. With regard to the Coalition's concern about the fishing rights of its members, para. 38 of the September 17, 1999 majority judgment noted the trial judge's finding that the Mi'kmaq had been fishing to trade with non-natives for over 200 years prior to the 1760-61 treaties. The 1760-61 treaty rights were thus from their inception enjoyed alongside the commercial and recreational fishery of non-natives. Paragraph 42 of the September 17, 1999 majority judgment recognized that, unlike the scarce fisheries resources of today, the view in 1760 was that the fisheries were of "limitless proportions." On this point, it was noted in para. 53 of the September 17, 1999 majority judgment:

> It was established in *Simon* [*Simon v. The Queen,* [1985] 2 S.C.R. 387], at p. 402, that treaty provisions should be interpreted "in a flexible way that is sensitive to the evolution

of changes in normal" practice, and *Sundown* [*R. v. Sundown*, [1999] 1 S.C.R. 393], at para. 32, confirms that courts should not use a "frozen-in-time" approach to treaty rights.

The Mi'kmaq treaty right to participate in the largely unregulated commercial fishery of 1760 has evolved into a treaty right to participate in the largely regulated commercial fishery of the 1990s. The notion of equitable sharing seems to be endorsed by the Coalition, which refers in its written argument on the motion to "the equal importance of the fishing industry to both Mi'kmaq and non-Mi'kmaq persons." In its Reply, the Coalition says that it is engaged in discussions "with representatives of the Acadia and Bear River Bands in southwestern Nova Scotia and takes pride that those discussions have been productive and that there is reason to hope that they will lead to harmonious and mutually beneficial participation in the commercial lobster fishery by members of those Bands." Equally, the Mi'kmaq treaty right to hunt and trade in game is not now, any more than it was in 1760, a *commercial* hunt that must be satisfied before non-natives have access to the same resources for recreational or commercial purposes. The emphasis in 1999, as it was in 1760, is on assuring the Mi'kmaq equitable access to identified resources for the purpose of earning a moderate living. In this respect, a treaty right differs from an aboriginal right which in its origin, by definition, was *exclusively* exercised by aboriginal people prior to contact with Europeans.

[39] Only those regulatory limits that take the Mi'kmaq catch *below* the quantities reasonably expected to produce a moderate livelihood or other limitations that are not inherent in the limited nature of the treaty right itself have to be justified according to the *Badger* test.

[40] (b) *The paramount regulatory objective is the conservation of the resource. This responsibility is placed squarely on the Minister and not on the aboriginal or non-aboriginal users of the resource.* The September 17, 1999 majority decision referred to *Sparrow, supra,* which affirmed the government's paramount authority to act in the interests of conservation. This principle was repeated in *R. v. Gladstone,* [1996] 2 S.C.R. 723, *Nikal* [*R. v.,* [1996] 1 S.C.R. 1013], *Adams* [*R. v.,* [1996] 3 S.C.R. 101], *R. v. Côté,* [1996] 3 S.C.R. 139, and *Delgamuukw* [*v. British Columbia,* [1997] 3 S.C.R. 1010], all of which were referred to in the September 17, 1999 majority judgment.

[41] (c) *The Minister's authority extends to other compelling and substantial public objectives which may include economic and regional fairness, and recognition of the historical reliance upon, and participation in, the fishery by non-aboriginal groups.* The Minister's regulatory authority is not limited to conservation. This was recognized in the submission of the appellant Marshall in opposition to the Coalition's motion. He acknowledges that "it is clear that limits may be imposed to conserve the species/stock being exploited and to protect public safety." Counsel for the appellant Marshall goes on to say: "Likewise, Aboriginal harvesting preferences, *together with non-Aboriginal regional/community dependencies,* may be taken into account in devising regulatory schemes" (emphasis added)....

[42] In the case of any treaty right which may be exercised on a commercial scale, the natives constitute only one group of participants, and regard for the interest of the non-natives, as stated in *Gladstone, supra,* may be shown in the right circumstances to be entirely legitimate. Proportionality is an important factor. In asking for a rehearing, the Coalition stated that it is the lobster fishery "in which the Applicant's members are principally engaged and in which, since release of the Reasons for Judgment, controversy as to exercise of the treaty right has most seriously arisen." In response, the affidavit evidence of Dr. Gerard Hare, a fisheries biologist of some 30 years' experience, was filed. The correctness of Dr. Hare's evidence was not contested in reply by the Coalition. Dr. Hare estimated that the non-native lobster fishery in Atlantic Canada, excluding Newfoundland, sets about 1,885,000 traps in inshore waters each year and "[t]o put the situation in perspective, the recent Aboriginal commercial fisheries appear to be minuscule in comparison." It would be significant if it were established that the combined aboriginal food and limited commercial fishery constitute only a "minuscule" percentage of the non-aboriginal commercial catch of a particular species, such as lobster, bearing in mind, however, that a fishery that is "minuscule" on a provincial or regional basis could nevertheless raise conservation issues on a local level if it were concentrated in vulnerable fishing grounds.

[43] (d) *Aboriginal people are entitled to be consulted about limitations on the exercise of treaty and aboriginal rights.* The Court has emphasized the importance in the justification context of consultations with aboriginal peoples. Reference has already been made to the rule in *Sparrow, supra,* at p. 1114, repeated in *Badger, supra,* at para. 97, that:

> The special trust relationship and the responsibility of the government vis-à-vis aboriginals must be the first consideration in determining whether the legislation or action in question can be justified.

The special trust relationship includes the right of the treaty beneficiaries to be consulted about restrictions on their rights, although, as stated in *Delgamuukw, supra,* at para. 168:

> The nature and scope of the duty of consultation will vary with the circumstances.

This variation may reflect such factors as the seriousness and duration of the proposed restriction, and whether or not the

Minister is required to act in response to unforeseen or urgent circumstances. As stated, if the consultation does not produce an agreement, the adequacy of the justification of the government's initiative will have to be litigated in the courts.

[44] (e) *The Minister has available for regulatory purposes the full range of resource management tools and techniques, provided their use to limit the exercise of a treaty right can be justified.* If the Crown establishes that the limitations on the treaty right are imposed for a pressing and substantial public purpose, after appropriate consultation with the aboriginal community, and go no further than is required, the same techniques of resource conservation and management as are used to control the non-native fishery may be held to be justified. Equally, however, the concerns and proposals of the native communities must be taken into account, and this might lead to different techniques of conservation and management in respect of the exercise of the treaty right.

[45] In its written argument on this appeal, the Coalition also argued that no treaty right should "operate to involuntarily displace any non-aboriginal existing participant in any commercial fishery," and that "neither the authors of the Constitution nor the judiciary which interprets it are the appropriate persons to mandate who shall and shall not have access to the commercial fisheries." The first argument amounts to saying that aboriginal and treaty rights should be recognized only to the extent that such recognition would not occasion disruption or inconvenience to non-aboriginal people. According to this submission, if a treaty right would be disruptive, its existence should be denied or the treaty right should be declared inoperative. This is not a legal principle. It is a political argument. What is more, it is a political argument that was expressly rejected by the political leadership when it decided to include s. 35 in the *Constitution Act, 1982.* The democratically elected framers of the *Constitution Act, 1982* provided in s. 35 that "[t]he existing aboriginal and treaty rights of the aboriginal peoples of Canada are hereby recognized *and affirmed*" (emphasis added). It is the obligation of the courts to give effect to that national commitment. No useful purpose would be served by a rehearing of this appeal to revisit such fundamental and incontrovertible principles. . . .

Disposition

[48] The Coalition's motion is dismissed with costs.

Motion dismissed.

Haida Nation v. British Columbia (Ministry of Forests), 2004

In *Haida Nation*, for the first time, the Supreme Court dealt with government-authorized activity on lands to which a First Nation claims native title, but to which the validity of the title claim has yet to be determined by a Canadian court. The Queen Charlotte Islands, off the west coast of the British Columbia mainland, are the traditional homeland of the Haida people. The Haida call the islands Haida Gwaii. Although the Haida have claimed title to Haida Gwaii for more than a century, their title has not yet been legally recognized under Canadian law. In 1999, the Haida challenged permits granted by British Columbia, without the consent and over the objections of the Haida, to a lumber company to harvest trees on Haida Gwaii. The question in the case was whether there is an obligation to consult and try to accommodate an Aboriginal people's interests before authorizing an activity on lands to which they claim native title.

In a unanimous decision, the Supreme Court ruled that in the circumstances in which the Haida people found themselves, the Crown has a legal obligation to consult and to try to accommodate the First Nation's interests before licensing forestry operations on lands to which they claim native title. This duty is based on the principle of the honour of the Crown. Underlying this principle is the general idea that the Crown's assertion of sovereignty over the Aboriginal peoples must be balanced by honourable dealings with them. Without fair and honourable dealings there is no prospect of reconciling Aboriginal people with the assertion of Crown sovereignty.

Courts in the common-law world have recognized fiduciary obligations of trustees in many different contexts such as parent–child, solicitor–client, and physician–patient relations. In the field of Aboriginal relations, the courts have recognized the Crown's fiduciary duty to act honourably in several different contexts.[1] For instance, because an Aboriginal people can sell its land only to the Crown and not on the private market, the Crown—that is, the federal government—has a duty to deal honourably with any sale or lease of Aboriginal lands and ensure that such transactions are in the best interests of the Aboriginal people.[2] In the context of this case, the duty related to protecting the Aboriginal people's interests in their traditional lands while their legal claim to title over these lands was still in the process of being determined. The Court's decision recognized that, if the government were under no obligation to protect the interests of the Aboriginal people during the long process of validating native title, when the process was finally completed the Aboriginal people might have lost much of what they valued in their lands.

The Court laid out a range of circumstances along which the duty to consult and accommodate lies. At one end are situations where the duty is light because the claim to title is weak and the threat to Aboriginal interests not great. At the other end, where the claim appears to be well grounded and the potential damage to Aboriginal interests severe, the

---

1   See Leonard Ian Rotman, *Parallel Paths: Fiduciary Doctrine and the Crown–Native Relationship in Canada* (Toronto: University of Toronto Press, 1996).

2   The Supreme Court first enunciated the principle in such a context in *Guerin v. The Queen*, [1984] 2 S.C.R. 335.

obligation is heavy. In the case at hand there was a judicial determination in the lower courts indicating a "reasonable probability" of the Haida being able to establish Aboriginal title to "at least some parts" of the lands covered by forestry licences, and the company's activity could deprive the Haida of forests vital to their economy and their culture. In these circumstances, Chief Justice McLachlin, writing the Court's judgment, concluded that the British Columbia government had a duty to consult the Haida and "perhaps accommodate" their interests in issuing the tree farm licences at issue. In reaching this conclusion, the Court overturned the B.C. Court of Appeal's finding that it was the forestry company that owed the Haida people a duty to consult and accommodate. "The honour of the Crown," said the Court, "cannot be delegated."

The point of coupling a duty to consult with a duty to accommodate is to make it clear that consultation means more than warning an Aboriginal people about what is about to take place on their lands, listening to their concerns, and then going ahead with the project without any modifications. "Deep consultation" requires "good faith" efforts to find a way of accommodating Aboriginal interests that may entail Aboriginal participation in decision making, mediation, and other forms of dispute resolution. However, the Court made it clear that the duty to accommodate does not give the Aboriginal people a veto over the proposed development.

The Court acknowledged that the stakes in this case were huge. Much of British Columbia is subject to unsettled native title claims in areas of great importance to the province's resource industries. And British Columbia was by no means the only province concerned about the issues in this case. Five other provinces—Alberta, Nova Scotia, Ontario, Quebec, and Saskatchewan—intervened in the case. The provinces argued that section 109 of the *Constitution Act, 1867* providing that "[a]ll Lands, Mines, Minerals, and Royalties belonging to the several Provinces of Canada . . . at the Union . . . shall belong to the several Provinces of [Canada]" means that the provinces have exclusive right to the land at issue. But the Court countered this argument by observing that section 109 also stipulates that the provinces took over their lands from Great Britain subject to "any Interest other than that of the Province." Among those other interests are those of Aboriginal peoples. Thus, the provinces' ownership of their lands and resources is burdened with the constitutional duty to consult and accommodate Aboriginal peoples.

In a companion decision, *Taku River Tlingit First Nation v. British Columbia,*[3] released the same day as *Haida Nation,* the Supreme Court showed how a province could comply with the duty to consult and accommodate. At issue in *Taku River* was a plan to reopen a mine and build a road to it on land to which the Tlingit Nation claimed native title. Representatives of the Tlingit First Nation participated in the environmental assessment process required as a condition for approving the project. Assistance was provided to enable the First Nation to liaise with relevant decision makers and politicians on issues that went beyond those dealt with in the environmental assessment process. In this case the Court concluded that the duty to consult and accommodate had been met.

Although the Supreme Court's decisions on *Haida Nation* and *Taku River* were greeted by an initial outburst of anger and alarm in the media, government and business in British Columbia have been learning to live with the implications of these decisions. Indeed, the

---

3   [2004] 3 S.C.R. 550.

Campbell Liberal government in British Columbia has turned away from its policy of confrontation with Aboriginal peoples and has adopted a policy of negotiating co-management and resource-sharing agreements with First Nations on lands subject to native title claims. This has led to numerous Interim Agreements with Aboriginal peoples which, though falling short of full comprehensive treaty settlements, facilitate resource development to proceed in ways that serve both Aboriginal and non-Aboriginal interests.[4]

A year later, the Supreme Court's decision in *Mikisew Cree First Nation*[5] demonstrated that the "duty to consult and accommodate" had serious implications for provinces in which most of the land is subject to historic treaties with First Nations. This case involved the federal government's approval for building a winter road through Wood Buffalo National Park in northern Alberta. The road went through lands that the Mikisew Cree had "surrendered" to the Crown under Treaty 8 in 1899. Treaty 8 included a clause found in all the numbered treaties made across the west and in Ontario that recognized the right of members of the signatory First Nation to continue their traditional economic activities of hunting, fishing, and trapping throughout the tract of land ceded to the Crown. But the treaties also stated that the First Nation's access to the ceded lands was subject to the right of government to use any part of these lands for other purposes. The federal government denied that it was under any obligation to consult with the First Nation if it decided to use land in ways that might encroach on its traditional pursuits. The Supreme Court disagreed and held that the principle of the honour of the Crown means that "[t]he Crown was required to solicit and listen carefully to the Mikisew concerns and to attempt to mitigate adverse impacts on the Mikisew hunting, fishing and trapping rights."

Through this series of cases the Supreme Court has carved out an important role for the judiciary in overseeing governmental relations with Aboriginal peoples. ⁓

---

4 See Tony Penikett, *Reconciliation: First Nation Treaty Making in British Columbia* (Vancouver: Douglas & McIntyre, 2006).

5 *Mikisew Cree First Nation v. Canada (Minister of Canadian Heritage)*, [2005] S.C.R. 388.

HAIDA NATION v. BRITISH COLUMBIA (MINISTRY OF FORESTS)
2004 SCC 73, [2004] 3 S.C.R. 511

Hearing: March 24, 2004; Judgment: November 18, 2004.

Present: McLachlin C.J. and Major, Bastarache, Binnie, LeBel, Deschamps, and Fish JJ.

Interveners: Attorney General of Canada, Attorney General of Ontario, Attorney General of Quebec, Attorney General of Nova Scotia, Attorney General for Saskatchewan, Attorney General of Alberta, Squamish Indian Band and Lax-kw'alaams Indian Band, Haisla Nation, First Nations Summit, Dene Tha' First Nation, Tenimgyet, aka Art Matthews, Gitxsan Hereditary Chief, Business Council of British Columbia, Aggregate Producers Association of British Columbia, British Columbia and Yukon Chamber of Mines, British Columbia Chamber of Commerce, Council of Forest Industries, Mining Association of British Columbia, British Columbia Cattlemen's Association, and Village of Port Clements.

The judgment of the Court was delivered by

THE CHIEF JUSTICE:

I. Introduction

[1] To the west of the mainland of British Columbia lie the Queen Charlotte Islands, the traditional homeland of the Haida people. Haida Gwaii, as the inhabitants call it, consists of two large islands and a number of smaller islands. For more than 100 years, the Haida people have claimed title to all the lands of the Haida Gwaii and the waters surrounding it. That title is still in the claims process and has not yet been legally recognized.

[2] The islands of Haida Gwaii are heavily forested. Spruce, hemlock and cedar abound. The most important of these is the cedar which, since time immemorial, has played a central role in the economy and culture of the Haida people. It is from cedar that they made their ocean-going canoes, their clothing, their utensils and the totem poles that guarded their lodges. The cedar forest remains central to their life and their conception of themselves.

[3] The forests of Haida Gwaii have been logged since before the First World War. Portions of the island have been logged off. Other portions bear second-growth forest. In some areas, old-growth forests can still be found.

[4] The Province of British Columbia continues to issue licences to cut trees on Haida Gwaii to forestry companies. The modern name for these licenses are Tree Farm Licences, or T.F.L.'s. Such a licence is at the heart of this litigation. A large forestry firm, MacMillan Bloedel Limited acquired T.F.L. 39 in 1961, permitting it to harvest trees in an area designated as Block 6. In 1981, 1995 and 2000, the Minister replaced T.F.L. 39 pursuant to procedures set out in the *Forest Act*, R.S.B.C. 1996, c. 157. In 1999, the Minister approved a transfer of T.F.L. 39 to Weyerhaeuser Company Limited ("Weyerhaeuser"). The Haida people challenged these replacements and the transfer, which were made without their consent and, since at least 1994, over their objections. Nevertheless, T.F.L. 39 continued.

[5] In January of 2000, the Haida people launched a lawsuit objecting to the three replacement decisions and the transfer of T.F.L. 39 to Weyerhaeuser and asking that they be set aside. They argued legal encumbrance, equitable encumbrance and breach of fiduciary duty, all grounded in their assertion of Aboriginal title.

[6] This brings us to the issue before this Court. The government holds legal title to the land. Exercising that legal title, it has granted Weyerhaeuser the right to harvest the forests in Block 6 of the land. But the Haida people also claim title to the land—title which they are in the process of trying to prove—and object to the harvesting of the forests on Block 6 as proposed in T.F.L. 39. In this situation, what duty if any does the government owe the Haida people? More concretely, is the government required to *consult* with them about decisions to harvest the forests and to *accommodate* their concerns about what if any forest in Block 6 should be harvested before they have proven their title to land and their Aboriginal rights?

[7] The stakes are huge. The Haida argue that absent consultation and accommodation, they will win their title but find themselves deprived of forests that are vital to their economy and their culture. Forests take generations to mature, they point out, and old-growth forests can never be replaced. The Haida's claim to title to Haida Gwaii is strong, as found

by the chambers judge. But it is also complex and will take many years to prove. In the meantime, the Haida argue, their heritage will be irretrievably despoiled.

[8] The government, in turn, argues that it has the right and responsibility to manage the forest resource for the good of all British Columbians, and that until the Haida people formally prove their claim, they have no legal right to be consulted or have their needs and interests accommodated.

[9] The chambers judge found that the government has a moral, but not a legal, duty to negotiate with the Haida people: [2001] 2 C.N.L.R. 83, 2000 BCSC 1280. The British Columbia Court of Appeal reversed this decision, holding that both the government and Weyerhaeuser have a duty to consult with and accommodate the Haida people with respect to harvesting timber from Block 6: (2002), 99 B.C.L.R. (3d) 209, 2002 BCCA 147, with supplementary reasons (2002), 5 B.C.L.R. (4th) 33, 2002 BCCA 462.

[10] I conclude that the government has a legal duty to consult with the Haida people about the harvest of timber from Block 6, including decisions to transfer or replace Tree Farm Licences. Good faith consultation may in turn lead to an obligation to accommodate Haida concerns in the harvesting of timber, although what accommodation if any may be required cannot at this time be ascertained. Consultation must be meaningful. There is no duty to reach agreement. The duty to consult and, if appropriate, accommodate cannot be discharged by delegation to Weyerhaeuser. Nor does Weyerhaeuser owe any independent duty to consult with or accommodate the Haida people's concerns, although the possibility remains that it could become liable for assumed obligations. It follows that I would dismiss the Crown's appeal and allow the appeal of Weyerhaeuser.

[11] This case is the first of its kind to reach this Court. Our task is the modest one of establishing a general framework for the duty to consult and accommodate, where indicated, before Aboriginal title or rights claims have been decided. As this framework is applied, courts, in the age-old tradition of the common law, will be called on to fill in the details of the duty to consult and accommodate.

II. Analysis

A. Does the Law of Injunctions Govern This Situation?

[12] It is argued that the Haida's proper remedy is to apply for an interlocutory injunction against the government and Weyerhaeuser, and that therefore it is unnecessary to consider a duty to consult or accommodate. In *RJR–MacDonald Inc. v. Canada (Attorney General)*, [1994] 1 S.C.R. 311, the requirements for obtaining an interlocutory injunction were reviewed. The plaintiff must establish: (1) a serious issue to be tried; (2) that irreparable harm will be suffered if the injunction

is not granted; and (3) that the balance of convenience favours the injunction.

[13] It is open to plaintiffs like the Haida to seek an interlocutory injunction. However, it does not follow that they are confined to that remedy. If plaintiffs can prove a special obligation giving rise to a duty to consult or accommodate, they are free to pursue these remedies. Here the Haida rely on the obligation flowing from the honour of the Crown toward Aboriginal peoples.

[14] Interlocutory injunctions may offer only partial imperfect relief. First, as mentioned, they may not capture the full obligation on the government alleged by the Haida. Second, they typically represent an all-or-nothing solution. Either the project goes ahead or it halts. By contrast, the alleged duty to consult and accommodate by its very nature entails balancing of Aboriginal and other interests and thus lies closer to the aim of reconciliation at the heart of Crown–Aboriginal relations, as set out in *R. v. Van der Peet*, [1996] 2 S.C.R. 507, at para. 31, and *Delgamuukw v. British Columbia*, [1997] 3 S.C.R. 1010, at para. 186. Third, the balance of convenience test tips the scales in favour of protecting jobs and government revenues, with the result that Aboriginal interests tend to "lose" outright pending a final determination of the issue, instead of being balanced appropriately against conflicting concerns. . . . Fourth, interlocutory injunctions are designed as a stop-gap remedy pending litigation of the underlying issue. Aboriginal claims litigation can be very complex and require years and even decades to resolve in the courts. An interlocutory injunction over such a long period of time might work unnecessary prejudice and may diminish incentives on the part of the successful party to compromise. While Aboriginal claims can be and are pursued through litigation, negotiation is a preferable way of reconciling state and Aboriginal interests. For all these reasons, interlocutory injunctions may fail to adequately take account of Aboriginal interests prior to their final determination.

[15] I conclude that the remedy of interlocutory injunction does not preclude the Haida's claim. We must go further and see whether the special relationship with the Crown upon which the Haida rely gives rise to a duty to consult and, if appropriate, accommodate. In what follows, I discuss the source of the duty, when the duty arises, the scope and content of the duty, whether the duty extends to third parties, and whether it applies to the provincial government and not exclusively the federal government. I then apply the conclusions flowing from this discussion to the facts of this case.

B. The Source of a Duty to Consult and Accommodate

[16] The government's duty to consult with Aboriginal peoples and accommodate their interests is grounded in the honour of the Crown. The honour of the Crown is always at stake in its dealings with Aboriginal peoples: see for example *R. v. Badger*, [1996] 1 S.C.R. 771, at para. 41; *R. v. Marshall*, [1999] 3 S.C.R. 456. It is not a mere incantation, but rather a core precept that finds its application in concrete practices.

[17] The historical roots of the principle of the honour of the Crown suggest that it must be understood generously in order to reflect the underlying realities from which it stems. In all its dealings with Aboriginal peoples, from the assertion of sovereignty to the resolution of claims and the implementation of treaties, the Crown must act honourably. Nothing less is required if we are to achieve "the reconciliation of the pre-existence of aboriginal societies with the sovereignty of the Crown": *Delgamuukw, supra*, at para. 186, quoting *Van der Peet, supra*, at para. 31.

[18] The honour of the Crown gives rise to different duties in different circumstances. Where the Crown has assumed discretionary control over specific Aboriginal interests, the honour of the Crown gives rise to a fiduciary duty: *Wewaykum Indian Band v. Canada*, [2002] 4 S.C.R. 245, 2002 SCC 79, at para. 79. The content of the fiduciary duty may vary to take into account the Crown's other, broader obligations. . . . Here, Aboriginal rights and title have been asserted but have not been defined or proven. The Aboriginal interest in question is insufficiently specific for the honour of the Crown to mandate that the Crown act in the Aboriginal group's best interest, as a fiduciary, in exercising discretionary control over the subject of the right or title.

[19] The honour of the Crown also infuses the processes of treaty making and treaty interpretation. In making and applying treaties, the Crown must act with honour and integrity, avoiding even the appearance of "sharp dealing" (*Badger*, at para. 41). . . .

[20] Where treaties remain to be concluded, the honour of the Crown requires negotiations leading to a just settlement of Aboriginal claims: *R. v. Sparrow*, [1990] 1 S.C.R. 1075, at pp. 1105-6. Treaties serve to reconcile pre-existing Aboriginal sovereignty with assumed Crown sovereignty, and to define Aboriginal rights guaranteed by s. 35 of the *Constitution Act, 1982*. Section 35 represents a promise of rights recognition, and "[i]t is always assumed that the Crown intends to fulfil its promises" (*Badger, supra*, at para. 41). This promise is realized and sovereignty claims reconciled through the process of honourable negotiation. It is a corollary of s. 35 that the Crown act honourably in defining the rights it guarantees and in reconciling them with other rights and interests. This, in turn, implies a duty to consult and, if appropriate, accommodate.

[21] This duty to consult is recognized and discussed in the jurisprudence. In *Sparrow, supra*, at p. 1119, this Court affirmed a duty to consult with west-coast Salish asserting an unresolved right to fish. . . .

[22] The Court affirmed the duty to consult regarding resources to which Aboriginal peoples make claim a few years later in *R. v. Nikal*, [1996] 1 S.C.R. 1013, where Cory J. wrote: "So long as every reasonable effort is made to inform and to consult, such efforts would suffice to meet the justification requirement" (para. 110). . . .

[24] The Court's seminal decision in *Delgamuukw, supra*, at para. 168, in the context of a claim for title to land and resources, confirmed and expanded on the duty to consult, suggesting the content of the duty varied with the circumstances: from a minimum "duty to discuss important decisions" where the "breach is less serious or relatively minor"; through the "significantly deeper than mere consultation" that is required in "most cases"; to "full consent of [the] aboriginal nation" on very serious issues. These words apply as much to unresolved claims as to intrusions on settled claims.

[25] Put simply, Canada's Aboriginal peoples were here when Europeans came, and were never conquered. Many bands reconciled their claims with the sovereignty of the Crown through negotiated treaties. Others, notably in British Columbia, have yet to do so. The potential rights embedded in these claims are protected by s. 35 of the *Constitution Act, 1982*. The honour of the Crown requires that these rights be determined, recognized and respected. This, in turn, requires the Crown, acting honourably, to participate in processes of negotiation. While this process continues, the honour of the Crown may require it to consult and, where indicated, accommodate Aboriginal interests.

C. When the Duty to Consult and Accommodate Arises

[26] Honourable negotiation implies a duty to consult with Aboriginal claimants and conclude an honourable agreement reflecting the claimants' inherent rights. But proving rights may take time, sometimes a very long time. In the meantime, how are the interests under discussion to be treated? Underlying this question is the need to reconcile prior Aboriginal occupation of the land with the reality of Crown sovereignty. Is the Crown, under the aegis of its asserted sovereignty, entitled to use the resources at issue as it chooses, pending proof and resolution of the Aboriginal claim? Or must it adjust its conduct to reflect the as yet unresolved rights claimed by the Aboriginal claimants?

[27] The answer, once again, lies in the honour of the Crown. The Crown, acting honourably, cannot cavalierly run roughshod over Aboriginal interests where claims affecting these interests are being seriously pursued in the process of treaty negotiation and proof. It must respect these potential, but yet unproven, interests. The Crown is not rendered impotent. It may continue to manage the resource in question pending claims resolution. But, depending on the circum-

stances, discussed more fully below, the honour of the Crown may require it to consult with and reasonably accommodate Aboriginal interests pending resolution of the claim. To unilaterally exploit a claimed resource during the process of proving and resolving the Aboriginal claim to that resource, may be to deprive the Aboriginal claimants of some or all of the benefit of the resource. That is not honourable. . . .

[29] The government cites both authority and policy in support of its position. It relies on *Sparrow, supra*, at pp. 1110-13 and 1119, where the scope and content of the right were determined and infringement established, prior to consideration of whether infringement was justified. The government argues that its position also finds support in the perspective of the Ontario Court of Appeal in *TransCanada Pipelines Ltd. v. Beardmore (Township)* (2000), 186 D.L.R. (4th) 403, which held that "what triggers a consideration of the Crown's duty to consult is a showing by the First Nation of a violation of an existing Aboriginal or treaty right recognized and affirmed by s. 35(1)" (para. 120).

[30] As for policy, the government points to practical difficulties in the enforcement of a duty to consult or accommodate unproven claims. If the duty to consult varies with the circumstances from a "mere" duty to notify and listen at one end of the spectrum to a requirement of Aboriginal consent at the other end, how, the government asks, are the parties to agree which level is appropriate in the face of contested claims and rights? And if they cannot agree, how are courts or tribunals to determine this? The government also suggests that it is impractical and unfair to require consultation before final claims determination because this amounts to giving a remedy before issues of infringement and justification are decided.

[31] The government's arguments do not withstand scrutiny. Neither the authorities nor practical considerations support the view that a duty to consult and, if appropriate, accommodate arises only upon final determination of the scope and content of the right.

[32] The jurisprudence of this Court supports the view that the duty to consult and accommodate is part of a process of fair dealing and reconciliation that begins with the assertion of sovereignty and continues beyond formal claims resolution. Reconciliation is not a final legal remedy in the usual sense. Rather, it is a process flowing from rights guaranteed by s. 35(1) of the *Constitution Act, 1982*. This process of reconciliation flows from the Crown's duty of honourable dealing toward Aboriginal peoples, which arises in turn from the Crown's assertion of sovereignty over an Aboriginal people and *de facto* control of land and resources that were formerly in the control of that people. As stated in *Mitchell v. M.N.R.*, [2001] 1 S.C.R. 911, 2001 SCC 33, at para. 9, "*[w]ith this*

assertion [sovereignty] arose an obligation to treat aboriginal peoples fairly and honourably, and to protect them from exploitation" (emphasis added).

[33] To limit reconciliation to the post-proof sphere risks treating reconciliation as a distant legalistic goal, devoid of the "meaningful content" mandated by the "solemn commitment" made by the Crown in recognizing and affirming Aboriginal rights and title: *Sparrow, supra*, at p. 1108. It also risks unfortunate consequences. When the distant goal of proof is finally reached, the Aboriginal peoples may find their land and resources changed and denuded. This is not reconciliation. Nor is it honourable....

[35] But, when precisely does a duty to consult arise? The foundation of the duty in the Crown's honour and the goal of reconciliation suggest that the duty arises when the Crown has knowledge, real or constructive, of the potential existence of the Aboriginal right or title and contemplates conduct that might adversely affect it....

[36] This leaves the practical argument. It is said that before claims are resolved, the Crown cannot know that the rights exist, and hence can have no duty to consult or accommodate. This difficulty should not be denied or minimized. As I stated (dissenting) in *Marshall, supra*, at para. 112, one cannot "meaningfully discuss accommodation or justification of a right unless one has some idea of the core of that right and its modern scope." However, it will frequently be possible to reach an idea of the asserted rights and of their strength sufficient to trigger an obligation to consult and accommodate, short of final judicial determination or settlement. To facilitate this determination, claimants should outline their claims with clarity, focussing on the scope and nature of the Aboriginal rights they assert and on the alleged infringements. This is what happened here, where the chambers judge made a preliminary evidence-based assessment of the strength of the Haida claims to the lands and resources of Haida Gwaii, particularly Block 6.

[37] There is a distinction between knowledge sufficient to trigger a duty to consult and, if appropriate, accommodate, and the content or scope of the duty in a particular case. Knowledge of a credible but unproven claim suffices to trigger a duty to consult and accommodate. The content of the duty, however, varies with the circumstances, as discussed more fully below. A dubious or peripheral claim may attract a mere duty of notice, while a stronger claim may attract more stringent duties. The law is capable of differentiating between tenuous claims, claims possessing a strong *prima facie* case, and established claims....

[38] I conclude that consultation and accommodation before final claims resolution, while challenging, is not impossible, and indeed is an essential corollary to the honourable

process of reconciliation that s. 35 demands. It preserves the Aboriginal interest pending claims resolution and fosters a relationship between the parties that makes possible negotiations, the preferred process for achieving ultimate reconciliation....

D. The Scope and Content of the Duty to Consult and Accommodate

[39] The content of the duty to consult and accommodate varies with the circumstances. Precisely what duties arise in different situations will be defined as the case law in this emerging area develops. In general terms, however, it may be asserted that the scope of the duty is proportionate to a preliminary assessment of the strength of the case supporting the existence of the right or title, and to the seriousness of the potentially adverse effect upon the right or title claimed....

[43] ... In this respect, the concept of a spectrum may be helpful, not to suggest watertight legal compartments but rather to indicate what the honour of the Crown may require in particular circumstances. At one end of the spectrum lie cases where the claim to title is weak, the Aboriginal right limited, or the potential for infringement minor. In such cases, the only duty on the Crown may be to give notice, disclose information, and discuss any issues raised in response to the notice. "'[C]onsultation' in its least technical definition is talking together for mutual understanding": T. Isaac and A. Knox, "The Crown's Duty to Consult Aboriginal People" (2003), 41 *Alta. L. Rev.* 49, at p. 61.

[44] At the other end of the spectrum lie cases where a strong *prima facie* case for the claim is established, the right and potential infringement is of high significance to the Aboriginal peoples, and the risk of non-compensable damage is high. In such cases deep consultation, aimed at finding a satisfactory interim solution, may be required. While precise requirements will vary with the circumstances, the consultation required at this stage may entail the opportunity to make submissions for consideration, formal participation in the decision-making process, and provision of written reasons to show that Aboriginal concerns were considered and to reveal the impact they had on the decision. This list is neither exhaustive, nor mandatory for every case. The government may wish to adopt dispute resolution procedures like mediation or administrative regimes with impartial decision-makers in complex or difficult cases.

[45] Between these two extremes of the spectrum just described, will lie other situations. Every case must be approached individually. Each must also be approached flexibly, since the level of consultation required may change as the process goes on and new information comes to light. The controlling question in all situations is what is required to maintain the honour of the Crown and to effect reconciliation

between the Crown and the Aboriginal peoples with respect to the interests at stake. Pending settlement, the Crown is bound by its honour to balance societal and Aboriginal interests in making decisions that may affect Aboriginal claims. The Crown may be required to make decisions in the face of disagreement as to the adequacy of its response to Aboriginal concerns. Balance and compromise will then be necessary.

[46] Meaningful consultation may oblige the Crown to make changes to its proposed action based on information obtained through consultations. The New Zealand Ministry of Justice's *Guide for Consultation with Māori* (1997) provides insight (at pp. 21 and 31):

> Consultation is not just a process of exchanging information. It also entails testing and being prepared to amend policy proposals in the light of information received, and providing feedback. Consultation therefore becomes a process which should ensure both parties are better informed. . . .

[47] When the consultation process suggests amendment of Crown policy, we arrive at the stage of accommodation. Thus the effect of good faith consultation may be to reveal a duty to accommodate. Where a strong *prima facie* case exists for the claim, and the consequences of the government's proposed decision may adversely affect it in a significant way, addressing the Aboriginal concerns may require taking steps to avoid irreparable harm or to minimize the effects of infringement, pending final resolution of the underlying claim. . . .

[48] This process does not give Aboriginal groups a veto over what can be done with land pending final proof of the claim. The Aboriginal "consent" spoken of in *Delgamuukw* is appropriate only in cases of established rights, and then by no means in every case. Rather, what is required is a process of balancing interests, of give and take.

[49] This flows from the meaning of "accommodate." The terms "accommodate" and "accommodation" have been defined as to "adapt, harmonize, reconcile" . . . "an adjustment or adaptation to suit a special or different purpose . . . a convenient arrangement; a settlement or compromise": *Concise Oxford Dictionary of Current English* (9th ed. 1995), at p. 9. The accommodation that may result from pre-proof consultation is just this—seeking compromise in an attempt to harmonize conflicting interests and move further down the path of reconciliation. A commitment to the process does not require a duty to agree. But it does require good faith efforts to understand each other's concerns and move to address them. . . .

E.   Do Third Parties Owe a Duty to Consult and Accommodate?

[52] The Court of Appeal found that Weyerhaeuser, the forestry contractor holding T.F.L. 39, owed the Haida people a duty to consult and accommodate. With respect, I cannot agree.

[53] It is suggested (*per* Lambert J.A.) that a third party's obligation to consult Aboriginal peoples may arise from the ability of the third party to rely on justification as a defence against infringement. However, the duty to consult and accommodate, as discussed above, flows from the Crown's assumption of sovereignty over lands and resources formerly held by the Aboriginal group. This theory provides no support for an obligation on third parties to consult or accommodate. The Crown alone remains legally responsible for the consequences of its actions and interactions with third parties that affect Aboriginal interests. The Crown may delegate procedural aspects of consultation to industry proponents seeking a particular development; this is not infrequently done in environmental assessments. Similarly, the terms of T.F.L. 39 mandated Weyerhaeuser to specify measures that it would take to identify and consult with "aboriginal people claiming an aboriginal interest in or to the area" (Tree Farm Licence No. 39, Haida Tree Farm Licence, para. 2.09(g)(ii)). However, the ultimate legal responsibility for consultation and accommodation rests with the Crown. The honour of the Crown cannot be delegated. . . .

[56] The fact that third parties are under no duty to consult or accommodate Aboriginal concerns does not mean that they can never be liable to Aboriginal peoples. If they act negligently in circumstances where they owe Aboriginal peoples a duty of care, or if they breach contracts with Aboriginal peoples or deal with them dishonestly, they may be held legally liable. But they cannot be held liable for failing to discharge the Crown's duty to consult and accommodate.

F.   The Province's Duty

[57] The Province of British Columbia argues that any duty to consult or accommodate rests solely with the federal government. I cannot accept this argument.

[58] The Province's argument rests on s. 109 of the *Constitution Act, 1867*, which provides that "[a]ll Lands, Mines, Minerals, and Royalties belonging to the several Provinces of Canada . . . at the Union . . . shall belong to the several Provinces." The Province argues that this gives it exclusive right to the land at issue. This right, it argues, cannot be limited by the protection for Aboriginal rights found in s. 35 of the *Constitution Act, 1982*. To do so, it argues, would "undermine the balance of federalism" (Crown's factum, at para. 96).

[59] The answer to this argument is that the Provinces took their interest in land subject to "any Interest other than that of the Province in the same" (s. 109). The duty to consult and accommodate here at issue is grounded in the assertion of Crown sovereignty which pre-dated the Union. It follows that the Province took the lands subject to this duty. It cannot

therefore claim that s. 35 deprives it of powers it would otherwise have enjoyed. As stated in *St. Catherine's Milling and Lumber Co. v. The Queen* (1888), 14 App. Cas. 46 (P.C.), lands in the Province are "available to [the Province] as a source of revenue whenever the estate of the Crown is disencumbered of the Indian title" (p. 59)....

H. Application to the Facts

(1) Existence of the Duty

[64] The question is whether the Province had knowledge, real or constructive, of the potential existence of Aboriginal right or title and contemplated conduct that might adversely affect them. On the evidence before the Court in this matter, the answer must unequivocally be "yes."

[65] The Haida have claimed title to all of Haida Gwaii for at least 100 years. The chambers judge found that they had expressed objections to the Province for a number of years regarding the rate of logging of old-growth forests, methods of logging, and the environmental effects of logging. Further, the Province was aware since at least 1994 that the Haida objected to replacement of T.F.L. 39 without their consent and without accommodation with respect to their title claims. As found by the chambers judge, the Province has had available evidence of the Haida's exclusive use and occupation of some areas of Block 6 "[s]ince 1994, and probably much earlier." The Province has had available to it evidence of the importance of red cedar to the Haida culture since before 1846 (the assertion of British sovereignty)....

(2) Scope of the Duty

[68] As discussed above, the scope of the consultation required will be proportionate to a preliminary assessment of the strength of the case supporting the existence of the right or title, and to the seriousness of the potentially adverse effect upon the right or title claimed.

(i) Strength of the Case

[69] On the basis of evidence described as "voluminous," the chambers judge found, at para. 25, a number of conclusions to be "inescapable" regarding the Haida's claims. He found that the Haida had inhabited Haida Gwaii continuously since at least 1774, that they had never been conquered, never surrendered their rights by treaty, and that their rights had not been extinguished by federal legislation. Their culture has utilized red cedar from old-growth forests on both coastal and inland areas of what is now Block 6 of T.F.L. 39 since at least 1846.

[70] The chambers judge's thorough assessment of the evidence distinguishes between the various Haida claims relevant to Block 6. On the basis of a thorough survey of the evidence, he found, at para. 47:

(1) a "reasonable probability" that the Haida may establish title to "at least some parts" of the coastal and inland areas of Haida Gwaii, including coastal areas of Block 6. There appears to be a "reasonable possibility" that these areas will include inland areas of Block 6;

(2) a "substantial probability" that the Haida will be able to establish an aboriginal right to harvest old-growth red cedar trees from both coastal and inland areas of Block 6.

The chambers judge acknowledged that a final resolution would require a great deal of further evidence, but said he thought it "fair to say that the Haida claim goes far beyond the mere 'assertion' of Aboriginal title" (para. 50).

[71] The chambers judge's findings grounded the Court of Appeal's conclusion that the Haida claims to title and Aboriginal rights were "supported by a good *prima facie* case" (para. 49). The strength of the case goes to the extent of the duty that the Province was required to fulfill. In this case the evidence clearly supports a conclusion that, pending a final resolution, there was a *prima facie* case in support of Aboriginal title, and a strong *prima facie* case for the Aboriginal right to harvest red cedar.

(ii) Seriousness of the Potential Impact

[72] The evidence before the chambers judge indicated that red cedar has long been integral to Haida culture. The chambers judge considered that there was a "reasonable probability" that the Haida would be able to establish infringement of an Aboriginal right to harvest red cedar "by proof that old-growth cedar has been and will continue to be logged on Block 6, and that it is of limited supply" (para. 48). The prospect of continued logging of a resource in limited supply points to the potential impact on an Aboriginal right of the decision to replace T.F.L. 39.

[73] Tree Farm Licences are exclusive, long-term licences. T.F.L. 39 grants exclusive rights to Weyerhaeuser to harvest timber within an area constituting almost one quarter of the total land of Haida Gwaii. The chambers judge observed that "it [is] apparent that large areas of Block 6 have been logged off" (para. 59). This points to the potential impact on Aboriginal rights of the decision to replace T.F.L. 39.

[74] To the Province's credit, the terms of T.F.L. 39 impose requirements on Weyerhaeuser with respect to Aboriginal peoples. However, more was required. Where the government has knowledge of an asserted Aboriginal right or title, it must consult the Aboriginal peoples on how exploitation of the land should proceed....

[76] I conclude that the Province has a duty to consult and perhaps accommodate on T.F.L. decisions. The T.F.L. decision reflects the strategic planning for utilization of the

resource. Decisions made during strategic planning may have potentially serious impacts on Aboriginal right and title. . . .

[77] The last issue is whether the Crown's duty went beyond consultation on T.F.L. decisions, to accommodation. We cannot know, on the facts here, whether consultation would have led to a need for accommodation. However, the strength of the case for both the Haida title and the Haida right to harvest red cedar, coupled with the serious impact of incremental strategic decisions on those interests, suggest that the honour of the Crown may well require significant accommodation to preserve the Haida interest pending resolution of their claims.

(3) Did the Crown Fulfill its Duty?

[78] The Province did not consult with the Haida on the replacement of T.F.L. 39. The chambers judge found, at para. 42:

[O]n the evidence presented, it is apparent that the Minister refused to consult with the Haida about replacing T.F.L. 39 in 1995 and 2000, on the grounds that he was not required by law to consult, and that such consultation could not affect his statutory duty to replace T.F.L. 39.

. . . [79] It follows, therefore, that the Province failed to meet its duty to engage in something significantly deeper than mere consultation. It failed to engage in any meaningful consultation at all.

III. Conclusion

[80] The Crown's appeal is dismissed and Weyerhaeuser's appeal is allowed. The British Columbia Court of Appeal's order is varied so that the Crown's obligation to consult does not extend to Weyerhaeuser. . . .

PART FOUR
Constitutional Change

Henrietta Muir Edwards v. Attorney-General for Canada (Persons Case), 1930

The Persons Case was triggered by five Alberta women: Emily Murphy, the first female magistrate in the British Empire; Nellie McClung and Louise McKinney, early women legislators in Canada; Irene Parlby, one of the first two female Cabinet ministers in the British Empire; and Henrietta Muir Edwards, who, like McClung, was a well-known author and activist. Having made their individual marks as female pioneers in public life, these women joined forces in the late 1920s to challenge the male-only tradition of Senate appointments. Under the leadership of Murphy, they persuaded Ottawa to refer to the Supreme Court the question whether women were included among the "qualified persons" eligible for Senate appointments under section 24 of the *British North America Act*. When the Supreme Court panel unanimously concluded that women were not included, the group successfully appealed to the Judicial Committee of the Privy Council. Largely because of this success, the "Famous Five," as they have become known, have been commemorated by public statues in both Ottawa and Calgary.

The Judicial Committee's judgment enjoys iconic status in Canada, not only as a feminist landmark but also as "a Constitutional watershed that interpreted the *BNA Act* as . . . dynamic and open to change, and not narrowly bound by the intentions of the original framers."[1] The *B.N.A. Act*, wrote Lord Sankey, "planted in Canada a living tree capable of growth and expansion within its natural limits." Because the *Act* sought "to grant a Constitution to Canada," it deserved not the "narrow and technical construction" that might be appropriate to a "a penal or taxing statute" but rather the "large and liberal interpretation" that would allow "the Dominion to a great extent, but within certain fixed limits, [to] be mistress in her own house, as the Provinces to a great extent, but within certain fixed limits, are mistresses in theirs."

Applying this "large and liberal" interpretation to the term "persons" in section 24 of the *B.N.A. Act*, Lord Sankey noted that on its face the term embraces both sexes. While it may have been understood in "more barbarous" ages to include only men as far as public office was concerned, that older understanding was not written directly into the Constitution in the way that male "persons" under the age of 30 or owning less than a specified value of property are explicitly barred from the Senate.[2] Had the exclusion of women been made similarly explicit, the case "would have present[ed] no difficulty" for Sankey—that is, he would have respected the clear if unpalatable provision—but he denied that an unwritten understanding carries similar weight. If the customs and traditions underlying a restrictive reading of the otherwise general term "persons" have changed, it is open to the judges living

---

1 Catherine Cavanaugh, "Out of the West: History, Memory, and the 'Persons' Case, 1919-2000" in Richard Connors and John M. Law, eds., *Forging Alberta's Constitutional Framework* (Edmonton: University of Alberta Press, 2005) 138. For a book length account of the case and its significance, see Robert Sharpe and Patricia I. McMahon, *The Persons Case: The Origins and Legacy of the Fight for Legal Personhood* (Toronto: University of Toronto Press, 2007).

2 Section 23 of the *B.N.A. Act*.

in less "barbarous" times to read the term in a more inclusive fashion. To those who today "ask why the word should include females," wrote Sankey, "the obvious answer is why should it not?"

Note that the "living tree" approach was used in this case to remove a traditional restriction on government. "No one, either male or female," insisted Lord Sankey, "has a right to be summoned to the Senate. The real point at issue is whether the Governor General has a right to summon women to the Senate." In other words, the Judicial Committee used the "living tree" metaphor to liberate government from a constraint based on inexplicit or unwritten principles, leaving it to government to decide whether and how to use its new-found liberty. Does the metaphor provide an equally compelling justification to judges who use inexplicit and unwritten principles to impose new constraints on governments?[3] That question lies at the heart of the controversy about "judicial activism." ∼

---

3   For example, *Reference Re Remuneration of Judges*, [1997] 3 S.C.R. 3; *Reference re Secession of Quebec*, [1998] 2 S.C.R. 217.

HENRIETTA MUIR EDWARDS v. ATTORNEY-GENERAL FOR CANADA
[1930] 1 A.C. 124 (PC)

Hearing: July 22, 23, 24, 25, 1929; Judgment: October 18, 1929.

Present: Lord Sankey L.C., Lord Darling, Lord Merrivale, Lord Tomlin, and Sir Lancelot Sanderson.

The judgment of their Lordships was delivered by

LORD SANKEY L.C.: By sec. 24 of the *British North America Act, 1867*, it is provided that:

> The Governor General shall from time to time, in the Queen's name, by instrument under the Great Seal of Canada, summon qualified persons to the Senate; and, subject to the provisions of this Act, every person so summoned shall become and be a member of the Senate and a senator.

The question at issue in this appeal is whether the words "qualified persons" in that section include a woman, and consequently whether women are eligible to be summoned to and became members of the Senate of Canada....

Their Lordships are of opinion that the word "persons" in s. 24 does include women, and that women are eligible to be summoned to and become members of the Senate of Canada....

[Their Lordships come to this conclusion despite the fact that historically, both by custom and at common law, women had been mostly excluded from public affairs. Lord Sankey describes such exclusion as a "relic of days more barbarous than ours." After recounting this "barbarous" history, the judgment turns to the question of its relevance to interpreting the *BNA Act*.]

No doubt in any code where women were expressly excluded from public office the problem would present no difficulty, but where instead of such exclusion those entitled to be summoned to or placed in public office are described under the word "person" different considerations arise.

The word is ambiguous, and in its original meaning would undoubtedly embrace members of either sex. On the other hand, supposing in an Act of Parliament several centuries ago it had been enacted that any person should be entitled to be elected to a particular office it would have been understood that the word only referred to males, but the cause of this was not because the word "person" could not include females but because at common law a woman was incapable of serving a public office. The fact that no woman had served or has claimed to serve such an office is not of great weight when it is remembered that custom would have prevented the claim being made or the point being contested.

Customs are apt to develop into traditions which are stronger than law and remain unchallenged long after the reason for them has disappeared.

The appeal to history therefore in this particular matter is not conclusive....

As far back as *Stradling v. Morgan* (1560) 1 Plowd. 199, at 209, 75 E.R. 305, it was laid down that extraneous circumstances may be admitted as an aid to the interpretation of a statute, and in *Herron v. Rathmines and Rathgar Improvement Commrs.*, [1892] A.C. 498, 502, 67 L.T. 658, Lord Halsbury L.C. said: "The subject matter with which the legislature was dealing, and the facts existing at the time with respect to which the legislature was legislating, are legitimate topics to consider in ascertaining what was the object and purpose of the legislature in passing the Act," but the argument must not be pushed too far, and their Lordships are disposed to agree with Farwell L.J. in *Rex v. West Riding of Yorkshire County Council* [1906] 2 K.B. 676, 716, "although it may, perhaps, be legitimate to call history in aid to show what facts existed to bring about a statute, the inferences to be drawn therefrom are extremely slight": see *Craies Statute Law*, 3rd ed., p. 118.

Over and above that, their Lordships do not think it right to apply rigidly to Canada of to-day the decisions and the reasons therefor which commended themselves, probably rightly, to those who had to apply the law in different circumstances, in different centuries, to countries in different stages of development. Referring therefore to the judgment of the Chief Justice and those who agreed with him, their Lordships think that the appeal to Roman law and to early English decisions is not of itself a secure foundation on which to build the interpretation of the *British North America Act* of 1867. . . .

The *British North America Act* planted in Canada a living tree capable of growth and expansion within its natural limits. The object of the *Act* was to grant a Constitution to Canada. "Like all written constitutions it has been subject to development through usage and convention": *Canadian Constitutional Studies*, Sir Robert Borden (1922), p. 55.

Their Lordships do not conceive it to be the duty of this Board—it is certainly not their desire—to cut down the provisions of the *Act* by a narrow and technical construction, but rather to give it a large and liberal interpretation so that the Dominion to a great extent, but within certain fixed limits, may be mistress in her own house, as the Provinces to a great extent, but within certain fixed limits, are mistresses in theirs. "The Privy Council, indeed, has laid down that Courts of law must treat the provisions of the *British North America Act* by the same methods of construction and exposition which they apply to other statutes. But there are statutes and statutes; and the strict construction deemed proper in the case, for example, of a penal or taxing statute or one passed to regulate the affairs of an English parish, would be often subversive of Parliament's real intent if applied to an Act passed to ensure the peace, order and good government of a British Colony": see *Clement's Canadian Constitution*, 3rd ed., p. 347.

The learned author of that treatise quotes from the argument of Mr. Mowat and Mr. Edward Blake before the Privy Council in *St. Catherine's Milling and Lumber Co. v. The Queen* (1888) 14 App. Cas. 46, 50: "That Act should be on all occasions interpreted in a large, liberal and comprehensive spirit, considering the magnitude of the subjects with which it purports to deal in very few words." With that their Lordships agree,

but as was said by the Lord Chancellor in *Brophy v. Attorney-General of Manitoba*, [1895] A.C. 202, 216, the question is not what may be supposed to have been intended, but what has been said.

It must be remembered, too, that their Lordships are not here considering the question of the legislative competence either of the Dominion or its Provinces which arise under ss. 91 and 92 of the *Act* providing for the distribution of legislative powers and assigning to the Dominion and its Provinces their respective spheres of Government. Their Lordships are concerned with the interpretation of an Imperial Act, but an Imperial Act which creates a constitution for a new country. Nor are their Lordships deciding any question as to the rights of women but only a question as to their eligibility for a particular position. No one, either male or female, has a right to be summoned to the Senate. The real point at issue is whether the Governor General has a right to summon women to the Senate. . . .

The word "person," as above mentioned, may include members of both sexes, and to those who ask why the word should include females the obvious answer is why should it not? In these circumstances the burden is upon those who deny that the word includes women to make out their case. . . .

It will be observed that s. 21 provides that the Senate shall consist of seventy-two members, who shall be styled senators. The word "member" is not in ordinary English confined to male persons. Sect. 24 provides that the Governor General shall summon qualified persons to the Senate.

As already pointed out, "persons" is not confined to members of the male sex, but what effect does the adjective "qualified" before the word "persons" have?

In their Lordships' view it refers back to the previous section, which contains the qualifications of a senator. Sub-ss. 2 and 3 appear to have given difficulties to the Supreme Court. Sub-s. 2 provides that the qualification of a senator shall be that he shall be either a natural born subject of the Queen, naturalized by an Act of Parliament of Great Britain or of one of the Provincial Legislatures before the union or of the Parliament of Canada after the union. The Chief Justice in dealing with this says that it does not include those who become subjects by marriage, a provision which one would have looked for had it been intended to include women as being eligible.

The attention of the Chief Justice, however, was not called to the *Aliens Act, 1844* (7 & 8 Vict. ch. 66), s. 16 of which provides that any woman married or who shall be married to a natural born subject or person naturalized shall be deemed and taken to be herself naturalized, and have all the rights and privileges of a natural born subject. The Chief Justice assumed that by common law a wife took her husband's nationality on marriage, but by virtue of that section any woman who marries a natural born or naturalized British subject was deemed and taken to be herself naturalized. Accordingly, s. 23, subs. 2, uses language apt to cover the case of those who become British subjects by marriage.

Their Lordships agree with Duff J. when he says: "I attach no importance to the use of the masculine personal pronoun in s. 23, and, indeed, very little importance to the provision in sec. 23 with regard to nationality," and refer to sec. 1 of the *Interpretation Act, 1889*, which in sec. 1, subsec. 2, provides that words importing the masculine gender shall include females.

The reasoning of the Chief Justice would compel their Lordships to hold that the word "persons" as used in sec. 11 relating to the constitution of the Privy Council for Canada was limited to "male persons," with the resultant anomaly that a woman might be elected a member of the House of Commons but could not even then be summoned by the Governor General as a member of the Privy Council.

Sub-s. 3 of s. 23 provided that the qualification of a senator shall be that he is legally and equitably seised of a freehold for his own use and benefit of lands and tenements of a certain value. This section gave some trouble to Duff J., who says that subsection points to the exclusion of married women, and would have been expressed in a different way if the presence of married women had been contemplated. Their Lordships think that this difficulty is removed by a consideration of the rights of a woman under the *Married Women's Property Acts*. A married woman can possess the property qualification required by this sub-section. Apart from statute a married woman could be equitably seized of freehold property for her own use only, and by an *Act respecting certain separate rights of property of married women*, consolidated statutes of Upper Canada, cap. 73, s. 1, it was provided: "Every woman who has married since May 4, 1859, or who marries after this Act takes effect, without any marriage contract or settlement, shall and may, notwithstanding her coverture, have, hold and enjoy all her real and personal property . . . in as full and ample a matter as if she continued sole and unmarried. . . ."

Their Lordships do not think it possible to interpret the word "persons" by speculating whether the framer of the *British North America Act* purposely followed the system of Legislative Councils enacted in the Acts of 1791 and 1840 rather than that which prevailed in the maritime Province for the model on which the Senate was to be formed, neither do they think that either of these subsections is sufficient to rebut the presumption that the word "persons" includes women. Looking at the sections which deal with the Senate as a whole (ss. 21-36) their Lordships are unable to say that there is anything in those sections themselves upon which the Court could come to a definite conclusion that women are to be excluded from the Senate.

So far with regard to the sections dealing especially with the Senate—are there any other sections in the *Act* which shed light upon the meaning of the word "persons"?

Their Lordships think that there are. For example, s. 41 refers to the qualifications and disqualifications of persons to be elected or to sit or vote as members of the House of Assembly or Legislative Assembly, and by a proviso it is said that until the Parliament of Canada otherwise provides at any election for a member of the House of Commons for the district of Algoma in addition to persons qualified by the law of the Province of Canada to vote every male British subject aged twenty-one or upwards being a householder shall have a vote. This section shows a distinction between "persons" and "males." If persons excluded females it would only have been necessary to say every person who is a British subject aged twenty-one years or upwards shall have a vote.

Again in s. 84, referring to Ontario and Quebec, a similar proviso is found stating that every male British subject in contradistinction to "person" shall have a vote.

Again in s. 133 it is provided that either the English or the French language may be used by any person or in any pleadings in or issuing from any court of Canada established under this *Act* and in or from all of any of the courts of Quebec. The word "person" there must include females, as it can hardly have been supposed that a man might use either the English or the French language but a woman might not.

If Parliament had intended to limit the word "persons" in s. 24 to male persons it would surely have manifested such intention by an express limitation, as it has done in ss. 41 and 84. The fact that certain qualifications are set out in s. 23 is not an argument in favour of further limiting the class, but is an argument to the contrary, because it must be presumed that Parliament has set out in s. 23 all the qualifications deemed necessary for a senator, and it does not state that one of the qualifications is that he must be a member of the male sex. . . .

The history of these sections and their interpretation in Canada is not without interest and significance.

From confederation to date both the Dominion Parliament and the Provincial legislatures have interpreted the word "persons" in ss. 41 and 84 of the *British North America Act* as including female persons, and have legislated either for the inclusion or exclusion of women from the class of persons entitled to vote and to sit in the Parliament and Legislature respectively, and this interpretation has never been questioned.

From confederation up to 1916 women were excluded from the class of persons entitled to vote in both Federal and Provincial elections. From 1916 to 1922 various Dominion and Provincial Acts were passed to admit women to the franchise and to the right to sit as members in both Dominion and Provincial legislative bodies. At the present time women are entitled to vote and to be candidates: (1) At all Dominion elections on the same basis as men; (2) At all Provincial elections save in the Province of Quebec.

From the date of the enactment of the *Interpretation Acts* in the Province of Canada, Nova Scotia and New Brunswick prior to confederation and in the Dominion of Canada since confederation and until the franchise was extended, women have been excluded by express enactment from the right to vote.

Neither is it without interest to record that when upon May 20, 1867, the *Representation of the People Bill* came before a Committee of the House of Commons, John Stuart Mill moved an amendment to secure women's suffrage, and the amendment proposed was to leave out the word "man" in order to insert the word "person" instead thereof: see *Hansard*, 3rd series, vol. clxxxvii., col. 817.

A heavy burden lies on an appellant who seeks to set aside a unanimous judgment of the Supreme Court, and this Board will only set aside such a decision after convincing argument and anxious consideration, but having regard:

1. To the object of the *Act*—namely, to provide a constitution for Canada, a responsible and developing State;
2. that the word "person" is ambiguous, and may include members of either sex;
3. that there are sections in the *Act* above referred to which show that in some cases the word "person" must include females;
4. that in some sections the words "male persons" are expressly used when it is desired to confine the matter in issue to males; and
5. to the provisions of the *Interpretation Act*;

their Lordships have come to the conclusion that the word "persons" in sec. 24 includes members both of the male and female sex, and that, therefore, the question propounded by the Governor General should be answered in the affirmative, and that women are eligible to be summoned to and become members of the Senate of Canada, and they will humbly advise His Majesty accordingly.

P.E.I. Potato Marketing Board v. H.B. Willis Inc., 1952

One of the devices most often canvassed for overcoming rigidities in the division of powers has been the delegation of legislative powers from one level of government to the other. Such a mechanism was recommended in 1939 by the Rowell-Sirois Royal Commission on Dominion–Provincial Relations in order to overcome barriers to effective administration created by strict judicial enforcement of divided jurisdictions. Because of doubts as to whether it was constitutionally valid for the federal Parliament and provincial legislatures to transfer legislative functions to one another, the Royal Commission called for a constitutional amendment to establish such a power of delegation.

It was precisely this technique of voluntary interdelegation that was embodied in the Nova Scotia statute challenged before the Supreme Court in 1951. This Bill would have authorized the provincial government to delegate to the federal Parliament the power to legislate with respect to employment in areas under provincial jurisdiction. Complete flexibility would be achieved by providing for delegation in the opposite direction: the Bill anticipated the Nova Scotia legislature receiving from the national Parliament the power to make laws in relation to employment in industries under federal jurisdiction as well as legislative authority in the indirect tax field. Before proceeding with its enactment, the government of Nova Scotia first submitted the question of the constitutional validity of this delegation procedure to the Supreme Court of Nova Scotia. A majority of the Court ruled that it was unconstitutional for either Parliament or the legislatures to employ the delegation device contemplated in the Nova Scotia legislation.

The appeal from this judgment was dismissed by the Supreme Court of Canada in a unanimous decision.[1] The various members of the Court who wrote opinions insisted upon a fundamental distinction between delegations of power by Parliament or the legislatures to subordinate agencies and delegations of power from one legislative level to the other. There was ample authority to justify the former type of delegation, but the latter was, in their view, clearly unconstitutional. Interdelegation between the national and provincial legislatures would have the effect of altering the basic scheme of Canadian federalism and neither Parliament nor the legislatures were authorized by the *B.N.A. Act* to make what, in the Court's opinion, would be tantamount to *ad hoc* amendments to the division of legislative powers. Here the Supreme Court demonstrated how fully committed it was to federalism as a basic principle of the Canadian Constitution.

Although the Supreme Court's decision in the Nova Scotia Reference put the interdelegation of power between Parliament and the provincial legislatures beyond the pale of the Constitution, it left intact other possible forms of legislative collaboration. Referential and conditional legislation are two such techniques that have been frequently employed in the past and that, in principle, were not affected by this case. In referential legislation, either Parliament or a provincial legislature referentially incorporates in a statute the valid enactments of the other; in conditional legislation, a legislature makes the carrying out of the policy stated in a statute conditional on the act of another governmental agency. But an

---

1 *Attorney General of Nova Scotia v. Attorney General of Canada*, [1951] S.C.R. 31.

additional and far more useful avenue for the advancement of cooperative federalism was to be opened up by the Supreme Court two years after this case in *Willis*.

In *Willis*, the Supreme Court was asked to determine the constitutional validity of a slightly modified version of the delegation device that the Court had ruled unconstitutional in the *Nova Scotia Interdelegation* case. Here it was a question of whether the federal Parliament could validly delegate legislative powers not to a provincial legislature but to an administrative board created by a provincial legislature. This question arose out of another joint effort by the legislature of a province and the Dominion to arm a single provincial marketing board with the power of regulating both intraprovincial and extraprovincial aspects of trade in natural produce. The Prince Edward Island legislature had passed the *Agricultural Products Marketing Act* in 1940 authorizing the Lieutenant-Governor in Council to establish a board for regulating various aspects of trade in natural products within the province. The *Act* also provided that such a board could, with the approval of the Lieutenant-Governor in Council, perform any functions delegated to it by the Dominion. In September 1950, the government of P.E.I., exercising its power under this *Act*, established a Potato Marketing Board to administer a scheme for regulating local trade in potatoes. Meanwhile, at the federal level, Parliament had enacted in 1949 the *Agricultural Products Marketing Act*, the crucial section of which authorized the Governor in Council to delegate the Dominion's jurisdiction over interprovincial and export trade to a provincial board. Following this, the federal government by Order in Council in October 1950 delegated to the P.E.I. Potato Marketing Board the power to regulate the extraprovincial marketing of potatoes from the province.

The validity of this device of Dominion delegation to a provincial board was first challenged successfully before the Supreme Court of Prince Edward Island. The provincial Supreme Court simply followed the Supreme Court of Canada's earlier decision in the *Nova Scotia Interdelegation* case and reasoned that if the *B.N.A. Act* prohibited Parliament from delegating legislative power to a provincial legislature it must also prohibit Parliament from delegating power to a creature of such a legislature. But the federal Supreme Court was able to find a distinction of kind between the type of delegation at issue in this case and that which it had found invalid the year before. Delegation from Parliament to a provincial board did not, apparently, involve a transfer of power across the sacrosanct wall dividing provincial from federal powers. A provincial board, although it might be a thoroughly subordinate offspring of a provincial legislature, could still exist, at least in thought, as an autonomous unit entirely distinct from the provincial legislature that created it. Justice Rand rationalized this point of view by suggesting that it could be regarded as simply a coincidence that both the Dominion and a province had decided to bestow their regulatory powers on the same group of men.

Devious as the Court's logic in this case might seem, its decision to uphold this form of delegation did, in large measure, reverse the consequences of its earlier decision. The power that Parliament could not delegate directly to a provincial legislature could be indirectly delegated to an agency established by such a legislature.

The first application of this valid form of delegation had the ironic purpose of reversing the Privy Council's last decision on the *B.N.A. Act*—a decision that had had an expansionary effect on the Dominion's powers. In the *Winner*[2] case, the Privy Council had ruled that an

---

2   *A.-G. Ont. v. Winner*, [1954] A.C. 541.

interprovincial bus line, even though one phase of its operation was completed entirely within a province, was, for purposes of licensing regulations, entirely within the jurisdiction of the federal Parliament. Shortly after this decision was brought down, the Dominion agreed to enact legislation that would return to the individual provincial transport boards the power of licensing interprovincial carriers. Thus, while the type of delegation validated in the *Willis* case might facilitate greater decentralization in the operation of Canadian federalism, it is doubtful whether it could work in the opposite direction to promote greater administrative uniformity or simplification. On this point, note that the Supreme Court in *Willis* declined to determine whether the indirect delegation procedure could be validly reversed and the provinces delegate regulatory powers to federal agencies.

In 1968, the Supreme Court, by a 5-to-2 majority, turned back a challenge to the federal *Motor Vehicle Transport Act* that delegated regulatory power over extraprovincial carriers to provincial boards.[3] The legislation challenged in this case went even further than that at issue in *Willis* toward a delegation of legislative power from federal to provincial authorities. Here Parliament had delegated authority directly to the provincial boards, authorizing them to apply to extraprovincial carriers not simply existing provincial licensing regulations but also any subsequent changes provincial legislatures might make in provincial regulations. By validating this form of delegation the Supreme Court further reduced the impact of the *Nova Scotia Interdelegation* case and by the same token increased the opportunities for a more flexible working of the Canadian federal system.

The Supreme Court's decision in *Willis* undoubtedly contributed to the era of "co-operative federalism" that flourished in Canada in the 1950s and 1960s. Its approval of delegation to administrative agencies also reinforced an emphasis on "executive federalism." The establishment of the Canadian Egg Marketing Agency (C.E.M.A.)[4] in the 1970s shows that even when federal–provincial relations revert to a more combative style, cooperative interdelegation may still take place, especially when important symbolic issues or economic resources are not at stake.

A proposal to reverse the *Nova Scotia Interdelegation* decision and permit direct delegation between legislatures was included in the "Fulton-Favreau" constitutional proposals that came close to adoption in 1964. However, delegation has not been a feature of the plethora of constitutional proposals considered since then.[5] This may reflect the efficacy of the administrative delegation validated in *Willis* and a diminution of interest in facilitating cooperative federalism. ⌒

---

3   *Coughlin v. Ontario Highway Transport Board et al.,* [1968] S.C.R. 569.

4   For a discussion of the Supreme Court's decision in 1978 upholding *C.E.M.A.*, see case 12.

5   A delegation device was included in the amending formula agreed to on April 16, 1981 by the eight provinces then opposing Ottawa. But this element of the "April accord" was dropped from the amending formula agreed to by the federal government and nine provinces on November 5, 1981 and was not included in the *Constitution Act, 1982*.

P.E.I. POTATO MARKETING BOARD v.
H.B. WILLIS INC.
[1952] 2 S.C.R. 392

Present: Rinfret C.J. and Kerwin, Taschereau, Rand, Kellock, Estey, Locke, Cartwright, and Fauteux JJ.

RINFRET C.J.: In my opinion, the appeal of the Prince Edward Island Potato Marketing Board should be upheld.

The judgment of the Supreme Court of Prince Edward Island *in banco* was delivered on the 31st of January, 1952. The Lieutenant-Governor-in-Council had referred to that Court for hearing and consideration the following questions:

(1) Is it within the jurisdiction and competence of the Parliament of Canada to enact *The Agricultural Products Marketing Act,* (1949) 13 George VI, (1st Session) c. 16?

(2) If the answer to question No. 1 is yes, is it within the jurisdiction and competence of the Governor-General-in-Council to pass P.C. 5159?

(3) Is it within the jurisdiction and competence of the Lieutenant-Governor-in-Council to establish the said Scheme and in particular s. 16 thereof?

(4) Is it within the jurisdiction and competence of the Prince Edward Island Potato Marketing Board to make the Orders made under the said Scheme or any of the Orders so made?

Tweedy J. wrote the main judgment, in which the Chief Justice and MacGuigan J. concurred, the Chief Justice simply adding a few additional reasons.

The main ground of the judgment of Tweedy J. appears to have been that of the Supreme Court of Canada in *A.G. of N.S. v. A.G. of Can.* ([1951] S.C.R. 31.) which held that the Parliament of Canada and each provincial legislature were not capable of delegating one to the other the powers with which it had been vested, nor of receiving from the other the powers with which the other has been vested. In the opinion of the Supreme Court *in banco* of Prince Edward Island that judgment was really decisive with respect to the first two questions in the reference under appeal.

With deference, such is not the effect of the judgment of this Court in the Nova Scotia reference. It was made quite clear in our reasons for judgment that they only applied to the questions as put and which had to deal only with an Act respecting the delegation from the Parliament of Canada to the Legislature of Nova Scotia and *vice versa.* The unanimous opinion of this Court was that each legislature could only exercise the legislative powers respectively given to them by ss. 91 and 92 of the *Act,* that these sections indicated a settled line of demarcation and it did not belong to the Parliament

of Canada or the Legislatures to confer their powers upon the other. At the same time it was pointed out that *In re Gray* ((1918) 57 Can. S.C.R. 150.) and *The Chemical Reference* ([1943] S.C.R. 1.), the delegations there dealt with were delegations to a body subordinate to Parliament and were, therefore, of a character different from the delegation meant by the Bill submitted to the Court in the Nova Scotia reference.

But, on the other hand, the delegations passed upon by this Court in *In Re Gray* and *The Chemical Reference* were along the same lines as those with which we are concerned in the present appeal. It follows that our judgment in the Nova Scotia reference can be no authority for the decision which we have to give in the present instance. It may be added that at bar counsel did not rely upon that ground in this Court.

The first question submitted to the Supreme Court *in banco* of Prince Edward Island had to do with the jurisdiction and competence of the Parliament of Canada to enact *The Agricultural Products Marketing Act* (1949), 13 George VI, (1st Session) c. 16. That *Act* was assented to on the 30th of April, 1949. The preamble, among other things, stated that it was "desirable to co-operate with the provinces and to enact a measure respecting the marketing of agricultural products in interprovincial and export trade." Sec. (2) of the Act reads as follows:

2. (1) The Governor in Council may by order grant authority to any board or agency authorized under the law of any province to exercise powers of regulation in relation to the marketing of any agricultural product locally within the province, to regulate the marketing of such agricultural product outside the province in interprovincial and export trade and for such purposes to exercise all or any powers like the powers exercisable of such board or agency in relation to the marketing of such agricultural product locally within the province.

(2) The Governor in Council may by order revoke any authority granted under subsection one.

The effect of that enactment is for the Governor-in-Council to adopt as its own a board, or agency already authorized under the law of a province, to exercise powers of regulation outside the province in interprovincial and export trade, and for such purposes to exercise all or any powers exercisable by such board, or agency, in relation to the marketing of such agricultural products locally within the province. I cannot see any objection to federal legislation of this nature. Ever since *Valin v. Langlois* ((1879), 5 App. Cas. 115.), when the Privy Council refused leave to appeal from the decision of this Court ((1879), 3 Can. S.C.R. 1.), the principle has been consistently admitted that it was competent for Parliament to "employ its own executive officers for the purpose of carrying out legislation which is within its constitutional authority, as it does regularly in the case of revenue officials and other matters which need not be enumerated." The latter are the words of Lord Atkin, who delivered the judgment of the Judicial Committee in *Proprietary Articles Trade Association et al. v. A.G. for Canada et al.* ([1931] A.C. 310.).

In *The Agricultural Products Marketing Act* of 1949 that is precisely what Parliament has done. Parliament has granted authority to the Governor-in-Council to employ as its own a board, or agency, for the purpose of carrying out its own legislation for the marketing of agricultural products outside the province in interprovincial and export trade, two subject-matters which are undoubtedly within its constitutional authority. Moreover, it may be added, that in doing so Parliament was following the advice of the Judicial Committee in the several judgments which it rendered on similar Acts and, more particularly, on the *Reference concerning the Natural Products Marketing Act,* ([1937] A.C. 377 at 389.) adopted by Parliament in 1934 (S. of C. 24 and 25 George V, c. 57), (1937), that the proper way to carry out legislation of that character in Canada, in view of the distribution of legislative powers under the *British North America Act,* was for Parliament and the Legislatures to act by co-operation.

I would, therefore, answer question (1) in the affirmative....

RAND J.: The validity of the provincial legislation generally was not impugned since its provisions are virtually identical with those of the *Act* of British Columbia which was approved by the Judicial Committee in *Shannon v. Lower Mainland Dairy Products Board* ([1938] A.C. 708.). The Committee there construed the *Act* as a whole to be limited to transactions strictly within the field of local or provincial trade. The administration of the *Act* so circumscribed, apart from co-operative Dominion legislation, may encounter serious practical difficulties if not insuperable obstacles; but that cannot affect its constitutional validity nor its administration conjointly with Dominion powers.

The principal point of attack was the efficacy of the Dominion delegation. Mr. Farris argued that the province was incompetent to confer on the Board capacity to accept such powers from the Governor-in-Council. This question was not involved in *Shannon, supra,* as the administration there was provincial only and s. 7 of the Act was not expressly considered. The Potato Board is not, under the statute, a corporation, and the contention is this: the power to create such an entity and to clothe it with jural attributes and capacities is derived from head 13 of s. 92 of the *Act* of 1867 which deals with property and civil rights within the province; as the incorporation of companies under head 11 has its source in the prerogative, a

body so created may have unlimited "capacities"; the prerogative is not drawn on for a body created under any other head than 11; a board created as here can have, then, only a capacity in relation to local law. From this it follows that the purported grant of authority from the Dominion is inoperative.

The central feature of this argument is the notion of the creation of an "entity." That a group of human beings acting jointly in a certain manner, with certain scope and authority and for certain objects, can be conceived as an entirety, different from that of the sum of the individuals and their actions in severalty, is undoubted; and it is the joint action so conceived that is primarily the external counterpart of the mental concept.

But to imagine that total counterpart as an organic creation fashioned after the nature of a human being with faculties called "capacities" and to pursue a development of it logically, can lead us into absurdities. We might just as logically conceive it as a split personality with co-ordinate creators investing it with two orders of capacities. These metaphors and symbolisms are convenient devices to enable us to aggregate incidents or characteristics but carried too far they may threaten common sense.

What the law in this case has done has been to give legal significance called incidents to certain group actions of five men. That to the same men, acting in the same formality, another co-ordinate jurisdiction in a federal constitution cannot give other legal incidents to other joint actions is negated by the admission that the Dominion by appropriate words could create a similar board, composed of the same persons, bearing the same name, and with a similar formal organization, to execute the same Dominion functions. Twin phantoms of this nature must, for practical purposes, give way to realistic necessities. As related to courts, the matter was disposed of in *Valin v. Langlois* ((1879) 5 App. Cas. 115.). No question of disruption of constitutive provincial features or frustration of provincial powers arises: both legislatures have recognized the value of a single body to carry out one joint, though limited, administration of trade. At any time the Province could withdraw the whole or any part of its authority. The delegation was, then, effective.

[Justice Kerwin (Justice Fauteux concurring), Justices Taschereau and Kellock (Justice Locke concurring), and Justice Estey (Justice Cartwright concurring) all wrote opinions in which they held that the *Agricultural Products Marketing Act, 1949* was *ultra vires.* The answers to the other questions in the reference are not included here as they were not directly concerned with the constitutional question of delegation.]

Reference Re Legislative Authority of Parliament to Alter or Replace the Senate, 1980

As originally enacted in 1867, the *B.N.A. Act* did not include an amending clause. In those days of liberal imperialism, it was accepted that as an Act of the Imperial Parliament it would be amended by that Parliament in response to requests from Canada. In 1949, at the request of the federal Parliament, the United Kingdom Parliament amended the *B.N.A. Act* to give the federal Parliament a limited legislative power, section 91(1), to amend "the Constitution of Canada." Excluded from this power were the jurisdiction of provincial legislatures, the rights and privileges of provincial governments, education and language rights, and some of the requirements of parliamentary government at the federal level (annual sessions of Parliament and an election every five years). Section 91(1) paralleled the power that the provincial legislatures had enjoyed since Confederation to amend the constitution of the province. The federal Parliament exercised its Constitution-amending power five times after 1949: three times to change representation in the House of Commons and twice to alter the Senate (compulsory retirement of senators at age 75 in 1965 and the representation of the Northwest Territories and the Yukon by one member each in 1974).

The *Senate Reference* of 1980 provided the only occasion for judicial scrutiny of the scope of the amending power obtained by the federal Parliament in 1949. The reference was provoked by the two-phase program of constitutional reform initiated by Prime Minister Trudeau in June 1978. Phase I concerned changes that the federal government believed it could accomplish on its own using section 91(1). It included a codification of the position of governor general; changes in the Supreme Court; a constitutional charter of rights applying only to the federal level (provinces could opt in); and replacing the Senate with a new upper house, half of whose members would be chosen by the House of Commons and the other half by the provincial legislatures. The Constitution Amendment Bill (Bill C-60) embodying Phase I was referred to a special Joint Committee of the Senate and House of Commons. In response to a vote of the Committee to seek the Supreme Court's opinion on the constitutional validity of sections of the Bill dealing with the Governor General and the Senate, the federal government decided to submit questions to the Court on Parliament's power to abolish or alter the Senate.

The questions covered a wider range of upper house reforms than the proposals in Bill C-60. Reference was also made to the possibility of an elected upper house or a house composed of provincial government representatives (a proposal favoured by British Columbia, the Quebec Liberal party, and the federal (Pepin-Robarts) Task Force on Canadian Unity). The Supreme Court's answers to these questions were essentially in the negative. It held that under section 91(1) the federal Parliament could not change the essential character of the Senate. Although the Court refused to answer questions that were too broadly phrased, its opinion made it clear that the Senate's essential features were its capacity to represent the various regions of Canada and to function as a non-elected chamber of "sober second thought" in relation to the elected House of Commons.

A remarkable feature of the Court's opinion is the extent to which it goes beyond narrow textual interpretation of the *B.N.A. Act*. The Court's view of the Senate's essential features was based on its understanding of the historical background that led to the creation of the Senate. Its appreciation of the limits of the unilateral federal amending power under section 91(1) was expressed in terms of that power's relationship to the whole constitutional framework of federal government. It is also interesting to observe that this broad statesman-like approach was not associated with the authorship of a particular judge but was a decision of "the Court."

The Court's decision had no immediate practical consequences; by the time it was rendered the Trudeau Liberal government had been replaced by the Clark Conservative government. The new government gave a low priority to constitutional reform and did not wish to proceed with the Constitutional Amendment Bill. However, the decision pointed to possible important longer-term consequences insofar as it suggested that the Supreme Court might be a serious obstacle to unilateral federal restructuring of the Canadian Constitution.

The new all-Canadian constitutional amending formula that came into effect in 1982 gives the provinces a substantial role in Senate reform. Under section 42 of the *Constitution Act, 1982*, amendments concerning the powers of the Senate, the method of selection, and residential qualifications of senators and the distribution of Senate positions among the provinces require the approval of the House of Commons and the legislatures of seven provinces containing 50 percent of the population. The Senate's role in all constitutional amendments (except those few that can still be effected unilaterally by the federal Parliament) has been reduced to a suspensory, six-month veto.

Section 91(1), which was added to the *B.N.A. Act* in 1949, has been replaced by section 44 of the *Constitution Act, 1982*, which, subject to sections 41 and 42 of the amending formula, gives Parliament the power "to make laws amending the Constitution of Canada in relation to the executive government of Canada or the Senate or the House of Commons." This means that Parliament can unilaterally, without the provinces, make changes in the Senate, provided that such changes are not in relation to the powers of the Senate, the method of selecting senators, or the allocation of Senate seats among the provinces.

In 2007, the Harper Conservative government introduced two Senate reform bills— Bill S-4,[1] to limit senators to one eight-year term, and Bill C-43,[2] to authorize the federal Chief Electoral Officer to conduct a "consultation" with provincial voters to choose registered nominees for Senate vacancies. The government believes that both bills can proceed without provincial consent using section 44 of the Constitution amending formula. Provincial leaders have challenged this use of section 44, and the Liberal Opposition in Parliament insists that the Bills not proceed until the Supreme Court has pronounced on their constitutionality. While Bill C-43 does not alter the governor general's power, under section 24 of the *Constitution Act, 1867*, "to summon qualified Persons to the Senate," its aim is arguably to change the way the prime minister selects those he advises the governor general to summon, and might therefore be considered beyond section 44. It is likely that in the near future the Supreme Court will be asked once again to test the limits of Parliament's unilateral power to reform the Senate. ⌐

---

1   *An Act to Amend the Constitution Act, 1862 (Senate Tenure).*

2   *An Act to provide for consultations with electors on their preferences for appointments to the Senate.*

REFERENCE RE LEGISLATIVE AUTHORITY OF PARLIAMENT TO ALTER OR REPLACE THE SENATE
[1980] 1 S.C.R. 54

Hearing: March 20, 21, 1979; Judgment: December 21, 1979.

Present: Laskin C.J. and Martland, Ritchie, Pigeon, Dickson, Estey, Pratte, and McIntyre JJ.

THE COURT: By Order in Council P.C. 1978-3581, dated November 23, 1978, the Governor General in Council, pursuant to s. 55 of the *Supreme Court Act,* referred to this Court for hearing and consideration the following two questions:

1. Is it within the legislative authority of the Parliament of Canada to repeal sections 21 to 36 of the *British North America Act, 1867,* as amended, and to amend other sections thereof so as to delete any reference to an Upper House or the Senate? If not, in what particular or particulars and to what extent?

2. Is it within the legislative authority of the Parliament of Canada to enact legislation altering, or providing a replacement for, the Upper House of Parliament, so as to effect any or all of the following:

(a) to change the name of the Upper House;

(b) to change the numbers and proportions of members by whom provinces and territories are represented in that House;

(c) to change the qualifications of members of that House;

(d) to change the tenure of members of that House;

(e) to change the method by which members of that House are chosen by

(i) conferring authority on provincial legislative assemblies to select, on the nomination of the respective Lieutenant Governors in Council, some members of the Upper House, and, if a legislative assembly has not selected such members within the time permitted, authority on the House of Commons to select those members on the nomination of the Governor General in Council, and

(ii) conferring authority on the House of Commons to select, on the nomination of the Governor General in Council, some members of the Upper House from each province, and, if the House of Commons has not selected such members from a province within the time permitted, authority on the legislative assembly of the province to select those members on the nomination of the Lieutenant Governor in Council,

(iii) conferring authority on the Lieutenant Governors in Council of the provinces or on some other body or bodies to select some or all of the members of the Upper House, or

(iv) providing for the direct election of all or some of the members of the Upper House by the public; or

(f) to provide that Bills approved by the House of Commons could be given assent and the force of law after the passage of a certain period of time notwithstanding that the Upper House has not approved them?

If not, in what particular or particulars and to what extent?

Submissions in respect of these questions were made to the Court on behalf of the Attorney General of Canada and also on behalf of the Attorneys General of Ontario, Nova Scotia, New Brunswick, Prince Edward Island, Saskatchewan, Alberta and Newfoundland.

Question 1

Sections 21 to 36 of the *British North America Act,* hereinafter referred to as "the Act," referred to in Question 1, appear in the Act under the heading "The Senate" and deal with the constitution of that body, including the number of senators; the representation in the Senate of the four divisions, *i.e.,* Ontario, Quebec, the Maritime Provinces and the Western Provinces; the qualifications for appointment to the Senate; the appointment of senators; the age limit for senators; resignation and disqualification of senators. References to the Senate by name, or as a House of Parliament, and references to senators are also to be found in ss. 17, 18, 39, 51A, 55, 56, 57, 59, 73, 74, 91, 128, 133, 146 and 147.

It is clear that Question 1 in essence, although not in terms, asks whether the Parliament of Canada has legislative authority to abolish the Senate. The Attorney General of Canada contends that the question should be answered in the affirmative. All of the Attorneys General of the provinces, represented on the hearing, contended that the question should be answered in the negative.

The Attorney General of Canada bases his submission upon the provisions of Class 1 of the subject matters enumerated in s. 91 of the Act. Section 91, which appears in Part VI of the Act, under the heading "Powers of the Parliament," defines the legislative authority of the Parliament of Canada. The opening words of this section are as follows:

> 91. It shall be lawful for the Queen, by and with the Advice and Consent of the Senate and House of Commons, to make Laws for the Peace, Order, and good Government of Canada, in relation to all Matters not coming within the Classes of Subjects by this Act assigned exclusively to the Legislatures of the Provinces; and for greater

Certainty, but not so as to restrict the Generality of the foregoing Terms of this Section, it is hereby declared that (notwithstanding anything in this Act) the exclusive Legislative Authority of the Parliament of Canada extends to all Matters coming within the Classes of Subjects next herein-after enumerated. . . .

Class 1 of s. 91 was added to it by an amendment to the Act enacted by the British Parliament on December 16, 1949. Section 1 of the amending statute provided as follows:

> 1. Section 91 of the *British North America Act*, 1867 is hereby amended by renumbering Class 1 thereof as Class 1A and by inserting therein immediately before that Class the following as Class 1:
>
> > 1. The amendment from time to time of the Constitution of Canada, except as regards matters coming within the classes of subjects by this Act assigned exclusively to the Legislatures of the provinces, or as regards rights or privileges by this or any other Constitutional Act granted or secured to the Legislature or the Government of a province, or to any class of persons with respect to schools or as regards the use of the English or the French language or as regards the requirements that there shall be a session of the Parliament of Canada at least once each year, and that no House of Commons shall continue for more than five years from the day of the return of the Writs for choosing the House: provided, however, that a House of Commons may in time of real or apprehended war, invasion or insurrection be continued by the Parliament of Canada if such continuation is not opposed by the votes of more than one-third of the members of such House.

Prior to 1949, in most respects, the Act did not provide for its amendment by any legislative authority in Canada. Accordingly, as it was a statute enacted by the British Parliament, any changes in its content had to be made by way of an amending Act enacted by that Parliament. Many amendments have been made in that way. A brief account of them and of other statutes of a constitutional character is found in a White Paper published in 1965 under the authority of the Honourable Guy Favreau, then Minister of Justice for Canada, under the title of "The Amendment of the Constitution of Canada":

> 1. The *Rupert's Land Act, 1868* authorized the acceptance by Canada of the rights of the Hudson's Bay Company over Rupert's Land and the North-Western Territory. It also provided that, on Address from the Houses of Parliament of Canada, the Crown could declare this territory part of Canada and the Parliament of Canada could make laws for its peace, order and good government.

> 2. The *British North America Act* of 1871 ratified the *Manitoba Act* passed by the Parliament of Canada in 1870, creating the province of Manitoba and giving it a provincial constitution similar to those of the other provinces. The *British North America Act* of 1871 also empowered the Parliament of Canada to establish new provinces out of any Canadian territory not then included in a province; to alter the boundaries of any province (with the consent of its legislature), and to provide for the administration, peace and good government of any territory not included in a province.

> 3. The *Parliament of Canada Act* of 1875 amended section 8 of the *British North America Act, 1867,* which set forth the privileges, immunities and powers of each of the House of Parliament.

> 4. The *British North America Act* of 1886 authorized the Parliament of Canada to provide for the representation in the Senate and the House of Commons of any territories not included in any province.

> 5. The *Statute Law Revision Act, 1893* repealed some obsolete provisions of the *British North America Act* of 1867.

> 6. The *Canadian Speaker (Appointment of Deputy) Act, 1895* confirmed an *Act of the Parliament of Canada* which provided for the appointment of a Deputy-Speaker for the Senate.

> 7. The *British North America Act, 1907* established a new scale of financial subsidies to the provinces in lieu of those set forth in section 118 of the *British North America Act* of 1867. While not expressly repealing the original section, it made its provisions obsolete.

> 8. The *British North America Act, 1915* re-defined the Senatorial Divisions of Canada to take into account the provinces of Manitoba, British Columbia, Saskatchewan and Alberta. Although this statute did not expressly amend the text of the original section 22, it did alter its effect.

> 9. The *British North America Act, 1916* provided for the extension of the life of the current Parliament of Canada beyond the normal period of five years.

> 10. The *Statute Law Revision Act, 1927* repealed additional spent or obsolete provisions in the United Kingdom statutes, including two provisions of the *British North America Acts.*

> 11. The *British North America Act, 1930* confirmed the natural resources agreements between the Government of Canada and the Governments of Manitoba, British Columbia, Alberta and Saskatchewan, giving the agreements the force of law notwithstanding anything in the *British North America Acts.*

> 12. The *Statute of Westminster, 1931* while not directly amending the *British North America Acts,* did alter some of their provisions. Thus, the Parliament of Canada was

given the power to make laws having extraterritorial effect. Also, Parliament and the provincial legislatures were given the authority, within their powers under the *British North America Acts*, to repeal any United Kingdom statute that formed part of the law of Canada. This authority, however, expressly excluded the *British North America Act* itself.

13. The *British North America Act, 1940* gave the Parliament of Canada the exclusive jurisdiction to make laws in relation to Unemployment Insurance.

14. The *British North America Act, 1943* provided for the postponement of redistribution of the seats in the House of Commons until the first session of Parliament after the cessation of hostilities.

15. The *British North America Act, 1946* replaced section 51 of the *British North America Act, 1867*, and altered the provisions for the readjustment of representation in the House of Commons.

16. The *British North America Act, 1949* confirmed the Terms of Union between Canada and Newfoundland.

17. The *British North America Act (No. 2), 1949* gave the Parliament of Canada authority to amend the Constitution of Canada with certain exceptions.

18. The *Statute Law Revision Act, 1950* repealed an obsolete section of the *British North America Act, 1867*.

19. The *British North America Act, 1951* gave the Parliament of Canada concurrent jurisdiction with the provinces to make laws in relation to Old Age Pensions.

20. The *British North America Act, 1960* amended section 99 and altered the tenure of office of superior court judges.

21. The *British North America Act, 1964* amended the authority conferred upon the Parliament of Canada by the *British North America Act, 1951*, in relation to benefits supplementary to Old Age Pensions.

22. *Amendment by Order in Council*. Section 146 of the *British North America Act, 1867* provided for the admission of other British North American territories by Order in Council and stipulated that the provisions of any such Order in Council would have the same effect as if enacted by the Parliament of the United Kingdom. Under this section, Rupert's Land and the North-Western Territory were admitted by Order in Council on June 23rd, 1870; British Columbia by Order in Council on May 16th, 1871; Prince Edward Island by Order in Council on June 26th, 1873. Because all of these Orders in Council contained provisions of a constitutional character—adapting the provisions of the *British North America Act* to the new provinces, but with some modifications in each case—they may therefore be regarded as constitutional amendments.

The practice, since 1875, has been to seek amendment of the Act by a joint address of both Houses of Parliament. Con-

sultation with one or more of the provinces has occurred in some instances, The amendment in 1907 was based on resolutions passed at provincial conferences, although opposed by British Columbia. The 1930 amendment respecting the transfer of resources to the four western provinces resulted from agreements with those provinces. The 1949 amendment respecting Newfoundland becoming a province was made after there had been an agreement with that province. The amendments of 1940, 1951, 1960 and 1964, respecting unemployment insurance, old age pensions, the compulsory retirement of judges and adding supplementary benefits to old age pensions all had the unanimous consent of the provinces.

The White Paper, after reviewing the procedures followed in respect of amendments to the Act, went on to state four general principles, as follows:

The first general principle that emerges in the foregoing resume is that although an enactment by the United Kingdom is necessary to amend the *British North America Act*, such action is taken only upon formal request from Canada. No Act of the United Kingdom Parliament affecting Canada is therefore passed unless it is requested and consented to by Canada. Conversely, every amendment requested by Canada in the past has been enacted.

The second general principle is that the sanction of Parliament is required for a request to the British Parliament for an amendment to the *British North America Act*. This principle was established early in the history of Canada's constitutional amendments, and has not been violated since 1895. The procedure invariably is to seek amendments by a joint Address of the Canadian House of Commons and Senate to the Crown.

The third general principle is that no amendment to Canada's Constitution will be made by the British Parliament merely upon the request of a Canadian province. A number of attempts to secure such amendments have been made, but none has been successful. The first such attempt was made as early as 1868, by a province which was at that time dissatisfied with the terms of Confederation. This was followed by other attempts in 1869, 1874 and 1887. The British Government refused in all cases to act on provincial government representations on the grounds that it should not intervene in the affairs of Canada except at the request of the federal government representing all of Canada.

The fourth general principle is that the Canadian Parliament will not request an amendment directly affecting federal–provincial relationships without prior consultation and agreement with the provinces. This principle did not emerge as early as others but since 1907, and particularly since 1930, has gained increasing recognition and acceptance. The nature and the degree of provincial participation in the amending process, however, have not lent themselves to easy definition.

The apparent intention of the 1949 amendment to the Act which enacted s. 91(1) was to obviate the necessity for the enactment of a statute of the British Parliament to effect amendments to the Act which theretofore had been obtained through a joint resolution of both Houses of Parliament and without provincial consent. Legislation enacted since 1949 pursuant to s. 91(1) has not, to quote the White Paper, "affected federal–provincial relationships." The following statutes have been enacted by the Parliament of Canada:

1. The *British North America Act, 1952*, effected a readjustment of representation in the House of Commons. The principle of representation by population was not affected by this legislation.

2. The *British North America Act, 1965*, provided for the compulsory retirement of senators, henceforth appointed, at age seventy-five.

3. The *British North America Act (No. 2), 1974*, repealed the provisions of the Act of 1952 and substituted a new readjustment of representation in the House of Commons. The principle of representation by population was maintained.

4. The *British North America Act, 1975*, increased the representation of the Northwest Territories in the House of Commons from one to two members.

5. The *British North America Act (No. 2), 1975*, increased the total number of senators from 102 to 104, and provided for representation in the Senate for the Yukon Territory and the Northwest Territories by one member each.

All of these measures dealt with what might be described as federal "housekeeping" matters which, according to the practice existing before 1949, would have been referred to the British Parliament by way of a joint resolution of both Houses of Parliament, and without the consent of the provinces. The last two of these statutes were within the power of the Parliament of Canada to enact by virtue of s. 1 of the *British North America Act, 1886*. Like the others they did not in any substantial way affect federal–provincial relationships.

The legislation contemplated in the first question is of an entirely different character. While it does not directly affect federal–provincial relationships in the sense of changing federal and provincial legislative powers, it does envision the elimination of one of the two Houses of Parliament, and so would alter the structure of the federal Parliament to which the federal power to legislate is entrusted under s. 91 of the Act.

The Senate has a vital role as an institution forming part of the federal system created by the Act. The recitals in the Act have some significance:

Whereas the Provinces of Canada, Nova Scotia and New Brunswick have expressed their Desire to be federally united into One Dominion under the Crown of the United Kingdom of Great Britain and Ireland, with a Constitution similar in Principle to that of the United Kingdom:

And whereas such a Union would conduce to the Welfare of the Provinces and promote the Interests of the British Empire:

And whereas on the Establishment of the Union by Authority of Parliament it is expedient, not only that the Constitution of the Legislative Authority in the Dominion be provided for, but also that the Nature of the Executive Government therein be declared:

Under the Constitution of the United Kingdom, to which reference is made in the first recital, legislative power was and is exercised by the Queen, by and with the advice and consent of the House of Lords and the House of Commons. The Upper House was not and is not an elected body, the Lower House was and is.

It is, we think, proper to consider the historical background which led to the provision which was made in the Act for the creation of the Senate as a part of the apparatus for the enactment of federal legislation. In the debates which occurred at the Quebec Conference in 1864, considerable time was occupied in discussing the provisions respecting the Senate. Its important purpose is stated in the following passages in speeches delivered in the debates on Confederation in the parliament of the province of Canada:

Sir John A. Macdonald:

In order to protect local interests and to prevent sectional jealousies, it was found requisite that the three great divisions into which British North America is separated, should be represented in the Upper House on the principle of equality. There are three great sections, having different interests, in this proposed Confederation.... To the Upper House is to be confided the protection of sectional interests: therefore is it that the three great divisions are there equally represented for the purpose of defending such interests against the combinations of majorities in the Assembly.

(Parliamentary Debates on the Subject of the Confederation of the British North American Provinces, Quebec, 1865, pages 35 and 38.)

The Honourable George Brown:

But the very essence of our compact is that the union shall be federal and not legislative. Our Lower Canada friends have agreed to give us representation by population in the Lower House, on the express condition that they shall have equality in the Upper House. On no other condition could we have advanced a step; and, for my part, I am quite willing they should have it. In maintaining the existing sectional boundaries and handing over the control of local matters to local bodies, we recognize, to a certain extent, a diversity of interests; and it is quite natural that the protection for those interests, by equality in the Upper Chamber, should be demanded by the less numerous provinces.

(Parliamentary Debates on the Subject of the Confederation of the British North American Provinces, Quebec, 1865, p. 88.)

A primary purpose of the creation of the Senate, as a part of the federal legislative process, was, therefore, to afford protection to the various sectional interests in Canada in relation to the enactment of federal legislation. The Act, as originally enacted, provided, in s. 22, that in relation to the constitution of the Senate, Canada should be deemed to consist of Three Divisions, to be equally represented, *i.e.* Ontario, Quebec and the Maritime Provinces (Nova Scotia and New Brunswick). This provision was later amended and s. 22 now provides for Four Divisions, the Western Provinces of Manitoba, British Columbia, Saskatchewan and Alberta being added as a Fourth Division. The Act now makes provision for representation of Prince Edward Island (as one of the Maritime Provinces), Newfoundland, the Yukon Territory and the Northwest Territories. Subsection 23(5) of the Act requires that a senator shall be resident in the province for which he is appointed.

The place of the Senate in the exercise of federal legislative powers is determined by ss. 17 and 91 of the Act. The former section provides that:

17. There shall be One Parliament for Canada, consisting of the Queen, an Upper House styled the Senate, and the House of Commons.

The opening words of s. 91, the all important section defining federal legislative powers, have already been quoted. Power to "make laws for the Peace, Order and Good Government of Canada in relation to all Matters not coming within the Classes of Subjects of this Act assigned exclusively: to the Legislatures of the Provinces" was conferred by the British Parliament upon "the Queen, by and with the Advice and Consent of the Senate and the House of Commons."

The creation of a federal system in Canada involved the necessity of effecting a division of legislative powers. This division is made by the provisions of ss. 91 and 92 of the Act. The latter section empowered each provincial legislature generally to make laws, effective within the province, in respect of matters of a local or private nature. Fifteen specific classes of subjects were enumerated. Section 91 provided generally for the making of laws for the peace, order and good government of Canada. Twenty-nine classes of subject matters were enu-

merated. Legislation dealing with those matters might affect local or private matters within a province.

The power to enact federal legislation was given to the Queen by and with the advice and consent of the Senate and the House of Commons. Thus, the body which had been created as a means of protecting sectional and provincial interests was made a participant in this legislative process.

The amendment to the Act made in 1949 added an additional class of subject matters to those which already existed. By that time the classes had been increased to thirty. The amendment was made on a joint resolution of both Houses of Parliament, but without the consent of the provinces. It gave power to the Queen, by and with the advice and consent of the Senate and the House of Commons to amend "the Constitution of Canada." This power was made subject to certain specific exceptions, as follows:

. . . except as regards matters coming within the classes of subjects by this Act assigned exclusively to the Legislatures of the provinces, or as regards rights or privileges by this or any other Constitutional Act granted or secured to the Legislature or the Government of a province, or to any class of persons with respect to schools or as regards the use of the English or the French language or as regards the requirements that there shall be a session of the Parliament of Canada at least one each year, and that no House of Commons shall continue for more than five years from the day of the return of the Writs for choosing the House: provided, however, that a House of Commons may in time of real or apprehended war, invasion or insurrection be continued by the Parliament of Canada if such continuation is not opposed by the votes of more than one-third of the members of such House.

The phrase "Constitution of Canada" does not appear elsewhere in the Act. The word "constitution" appears in various places and in different contexts. The preamble to the Act refers to "a Constitution similar in principle to that of the United Kingdom" and, later, to "the constitution of Legislative Authority in the Dominion." Section 22 refers to "the Constitution of the Senate" as being deemed to consist of four divisions. Part V of the Act is entitled "Provincial Constitutions" and the sections in that Part, 58 to 90, deal with the exercise of executive power and legislative power in the provinces. Section 92(1) refers to the amendment of "the Constitution of the Province." Section 147 refers to "Three Divisions into which Canada is, in relation to the Constitution of the Senate, divided by this Act."

The Attorney General of Canada submitted that the power conferred upon Parliament by s. 91(1) is limited only by the specific exceptions contained in it. He contended that the very specificity of these exceptions pointed to the wide powers being conferred. If this approach were adopted, it would mean that the Federal Parliament, acting unilaterally, could amend any part of the Act, subject only to the exceptions specified in s. 91(1). But s. 91(1) does not give power to amend the Act. Instead, the phrase "Constitution of Canada" is used. In our opinion, the word "Canada" as used in s. 91(1) does not refer to Canada as a geographical unit but refers to the juristic federal unit. "Constitution of Canada" does not mean the whole of the *British North America Act*, but means the constitution of the federal government, as distinct from the provincial governments. The power of amendment conferred by s. 91(1) is limited to matters of interest only to the federal government.

The word "Canada" is used with reference to the juristic federal unit in several sections of the Act, of which the following are examples:

Section 111 provided that "Canada shall be liable for the Debts and Liabilities of each Province existing at the Union."

Section 125 provides that "No Lands or Property belonging to Canada or any Province shall be liable to taxation."

Section 101 refers to "the Laws of Canada," the meaning of which phrase has recently been interpreted by this Court. The section reads as follows:

> 101. The Parliament of Canada may, notwithstanding anything in this Act, from Time to Time provide for the Constitution, Maintenance, and Organization of a General Court of Appeal for Canada, and for the Establishment of any additional Courts for the better Administration of the Laws of Canada.

... In our opinion, the power of amendment given by s. 91(1) relates to the constitution of the federal government in matters of interest only to that government. The statutes enacted by the Federal Parliament since 1949, to which we have previously referred, are illustrations of the exercise of that power.

The next question is whether, in that limited sense, s. 91(1) would permit the Federal Parliament to abolish the Senate.

Bearing in mind the historical background in which the creation of the Senate as a part of the federal legislative process was conceived, the words of Lord Sankey L.C. in *Re the Regulation and Control of Aeronautics in Canada* ([1932] A.C. 54), at p. 70, although they were written in relation to the Act as originally enacted, are apt:

> Inasmuch as the Act embodies a compromise under which the original Provinces agreed to federate, it is important to keep in mind that the preservation of the rights of minorities was a condition on which such minorities entered into the federation, and the foundation upon which the whole structure was subsequently erected. The process of interpretation as the years go on ought not to be allowed to dim or to whittle down the provisions of the original contract upon which the federation was founded, nor is it legitimate that any judicial construction of the provisions of ss. 91 and 92 should impose a new and different contract upon the federating bodies.

In our opinion, the power given to the Federal Parliament by s. 91(1) was not intended to enable it to alter in any way the provisions of ss. 91 and 92 governing the exercise of legislative authority by the Parliament of Canada and the Legislatures of the Provinces. Section 91(1) is a particularization of the general legislative power of the Parliament of Canada. That general power can be exercised only by the Queen by and with the advice and consent of the Senate and the House of Commons. Section 91(1) cannot be construed to confer power to supplant the whole of the rest of the section. It cannot be construed as permitting the transfer of the legislative powers enumerated in s. 91 to some body or bodies other than those specifically designated in it.

This Court, in *Attorney General of Nova Scotia v. Attorney General of Canada and Lord Nelson Hotel Company Limited* ([1951] S.C.R. 31), determined that neither the Parliament of Canada nor a Provincial Legislature could delegate to the other the legislative powers with which it has been vested nor receive from the other the powers with which the other has been vested. The elimination of the Senate would go much further in that it would involve a transfer by Parliament of all its legislative powers to a new legislative body of which the Senate would not be a member. . . .

The continued existence of the Senate as a part of the federal legislative process is implied in the exceptions provided in s. 91(1). One exception to the power conferred by s. 91(1) to amend the Constitution of Canada is "as regards the requirement that there shall be a session of the Parliament of Canada at least once each year." "Parliament" under s. 17 is to consist of the Queen, the Senate and the House of Commons. This exception contemplates that there shall continue to be sessions of the Senate and the House of Commons at least once each year.

The next exception requires that "no House of Commons shall continue for more than five years from the day of the return of the Writs for choosing the House" except in time of real or apprehended war, invasion or insurrection.

These two exceptions clearly indicate that the power to amend "the Constitution of Canada" given by s. 91(1) was not intended to include the power to eliminate the Senate or the House of Commons.

The Attorney General of Canada contended that the power to amend given by s. 91(1) was the equivalent, in the federal field, of s. 92(1) in the provincial field.

He points out that, pursuant to that power, the provinces of Manitoba, New Brunswick, Prince Edward Island, Nova Scotia and Quebec abolished their respective legislative councils.

The two sections are not, however, analogous. Section 92 does not, as does s. 91, particularize the participants in the law making process. Section 91 confers the authority to legislate in respect of matters within that section upon the Queen, with the advice and consent of the Senate and the House of Commons. Section 92 confers the authority to legislate in respect of matters within that section upon "the Legislature."

More importantly, s. 92(1) gives a power to amend the constitution of a province to the legislature, except as regards the office of the Lieutenant Governor, "notwithstanding anything in this Act." Section 91(1) confers a power of amendment subject to specified exceptions which, as we have already pointed out, contemplate the continued existence of both the Senate and the House of Commons.

For the foregoing reasons, we would answer the first question in the negative.

Question 2

The Attorney General of Canada submits that this question, in all its aspects, should be answered in the affirmative. Differing views were expressed by the Attorneys General of the provinces.

All of the provincial Attorneys General, other than the Attorney General of Prince Edward Island, submitted that Question 2(*f*) should be answered in the negative. This sub-question raises the question of the power of Parliament, under s. 91(1), to provide that all bills be given assent and the force of law after a certain time period notwithstanding that they had not been approved by the Upper House. The only provision presently existing, which limits the power of the Senate as compared with the power of the House of Commons, is s. 53 which provides that bills for appropriating any part of the public revenue or for imposing any tax or impost shall originate in the House of Commons.

A provision of the kind contemplated would seriously impair the position of the Senate in the legislative process because it would permit legislation to be enacted under s. 91 without the consent of the Senate. For the reasons already given in respect of Question 1, it is our view that Parliament cannot under s. 91(1) impair the role of the Senate in that process. We would answer this question in the negative.

With respect to the other portions of Question 2, the Attorney General of Ontario and the Attorney General of Nova Scotia submit that these sub-questions cannot be answered categorically in the form in which they are asked. As the Attorney General of Nova Scotia puts it, they cannot

be answered "in the absence of a factual context or actual draft legislation." In our opinion there is merit in this contention. We will deal with the sub-questions seriatim.

Sub-question (*a*) asks whether Parliament could change the name of the Upper House. We would assume that a change of name would be proposed only as a part of some scheme for the alteration of the Senate itself. If that scheme were to be held *ultra vires* of Parliament, then the change of name would probably go with it. We do not think the question can properly be answered in the absence of such a context.

Sub-question (*b*) involves changing the numbers and proportions of members by whom provinces and territories are represented in the Senate. None of the provinces supported the federal submission on this point.

As previously noted, the system of regional representation in the Senate was one of the essential features of that body when it was created. Without it, the fundamental character of the Senate as part of the Canadian federal scheme would be eliminated. In the absence of a factual context, it is not possible to say whether a change contemplated by this question would be in keeping with that fundamental character.

Sub-question (*c*) deals with a change in the qualifications of senators. The difficulty here is that we have not been told what changes are contemplated. Some of the qualifications for senators prescribed in s. 23, such as the property qualifications, may not today have the importance which they did when the Act was enacted. On the other hand, the requirement that a senator should be resident in the province for which he is appointed has relevance in relation to the sectional characteristic of the make-up of the Senate. In our opinion, the question cannot be answered categorically.

Sub-question (*d*) relates to the tenure of senators. At present, a senator, when appointed, has tenure until he attains the age of seventy-five. At some point, a reduction of the term of office might impair the functioning of the Senate in providing what Sir John A. Macdonald described as "the sober second thought in legislation." The Act contemplated a constitution similar in principle to that of the United Kingdom, where members of the House of Lords hold office for life. The imposition of compulsory retirement at age seventy-five did not change the essential character of the Senate. However, to answer this question we need to know what change of tenure is proposed.

Sub-question (*e*), paragraphs (i), (ii) and (iii), contemplates changing the method of appointment of senators, presently the function of the Governor General, by having "some" members selected by provincial legislatures, "some" members by the House of Commons, "some" members selected by the Lieutenant Governor in Council or "some other body or bodies." The selection of senators by a provincial legislature or by the Lieutenant Governor of a province would involve an indirect participation by the provinces in the enactment of federal legislation and is contrary to the reasoning of this Court in the *Lord Nelson Hotel* case previously cited.

Again, we do not feel that we have a factual context in which to formulate a satisfactory answer.

Sub-question (*e*) paragraph (iv) deals with the possible selection of all or some members of the senate by direct election by the public. The substitution of a system of election for a system of appointment would involve a radical change in the nature of one of the component parts of Parliament. As already noted, the preamble to the Act referred to "a constitution similar in principle to that of the United Kingdom," where the Upper House is not elected. In creating the Senate in the manner provided in the Act, it is clear that the intention was to make the Senate a thoroughly independent body which could canvass dispassionately the measures of the House of Commons. This was accomplished by providing for the appointment of members of the Senate with tenure for life. To make the Senate a wholly or partially elected body would

affect a fundamental feature of that body. We would answer this sub-question in the negative.

Dealing generally with Question 2, it is our opinion that while s. 91(1) would permit some changes to be made by Parliament in respect of the Senate as now constituted, it is not open to Parliament to make alterations which would affect the fundamental features, or essential characteristics, given to the Senate as a means of ensuring regional and provincial representation in the federal legislative process. The character of the Senate was determined by the British Parliament in response to the proposals submitted by the three provinces in order to meet the requirement of the proposed federal system. It was that Senate, created by the Act, to which a legislative role was given by s. 91. In our opinion, its fundamental character cannot be altered by unilateral action by the Parliament of Canada and s. 91(1) does not give that power.

We answer Question 1 in the negative. We answer sub-questions 2(*b*), 2(*e*)(iv) and 2(*f*) in the negative. In our opinion, the other sub-questions in Question 2, in the absence of a factual back-ground, cannot be answered categorically.

Re: Resolution to Amend the Constitution (The Patriation Reference), 1981

Under Pierre Trudeau's leadership, the Liberals returned to power in February 1980. It did not take long for Trudeau to renew the momentum of constitutional reform. He and other representatives of the federal government played a prominent role in the Quebec referendum campaign, which took place in the spring of 1980. To persuade Quebecers not to give René Lévesque's government a mandate to negotiate Quebec independence, Trudeau and his colleagues promised to work toward a constitutional restructuring of Canadian federalism. Following the defeat of the independence option in the referendum, the Prime Minister convened a meeting with the provincial premiers. Twelve areas were agreed to as priority items on the agenda of constitutional reform: 6 concerned various aspects of the federal division of powers; 2 were directed toward restructuring federal institutions (the Supreme Court and the Senate); and the remaining 4 dealt with a new preamble, the principle of fiscal equalization, a formula for amending a patriated constitution entirely in Canada, and a charter of fundamental rights and freedoms. A continuing committee of ministers representing the 11 governments was established to develop proposals in these areas. This process culminated in a federal–provincial first ministers conference in September 1980. After a week of discussion, the conference failed to produce a consensus on any combination of proposals in the 12 areas.

At this point the federal government took the initiative that led to the following case. On October 2, 1980, Trudeau announced plans to proceed unilaterally with the federal government's reform priorities, the so-called people's package of patriation with an amending formula, a charter of rights, and recognition of the principle of fiscal equalization. The Constitution Act, 1981 was drafted, containing proposals on these items, and a resolution was placed before the federal Parliament requesting the Queen to lay the Constitution Act before the United Kingdom Parliament.

Most provinces objected strongly to this departure from what they regarded as the well-established constitutional convention of obtaining the agreement of the provinces to amendments affecting provincial powers. Only Ontario and New Brunswick supported the Trudeau constitutional plan. The Prime Minister claimed that the long series of failures to reach a federal–provincial consensus on constitutional reform justified unilateral federal action, and that, in any event, the question whether provincial consent was needed for federal requests to the U.K. Parliament to amend the *B.N.A. Act* was a matter of convention, not law, to be settled in the political, not the judicial, arena. Accordingly, he refused to submit a reference question to the Supreme Court on the validity of his procedure. Once Parliament (in which his party had a clear majority) passed the resolution, it was his intention to have the U.K. Parliament pass the Constitution Act forthwith. His government took the view that constitutional convention required the British Parliament automatically to pass any amendment to the Canadian Constitution requested by the federal Parliament regardless of provincial objections.

Three of the dissident provinces decided to seek the judicial opinion that Trudeau spurned. The governments of Manitoba, Quebec,[1] and Newfoundland submitted questions to their provincial Courts of Appeal on (1) whether the Constitution Act, 1981 affects the federal–provincial relationship or provincial powers; (2) whether there is a convention requiring provincial consent for such an amendment; and (3) whether provincial consent for such an amendment was a "constitutional requirement."[2] The provincial Courts of Appeal were divided in answering the crucial third question. While the Manitoba Court (3 judges to 2) and the Quebec Court (4 to 1) found that provincial consent was not a constitutional requirement, the Newfoundland courts held unanimously (3 to 0) that it was. The Quebec Court, the last of the three to render a decision, released its decision in April 1981. Both sides then prepared to appeal these decisions to the Supreme Court of Canada.

Meanwhile, the resolution continued to be debated by a joint parliamentary committee and, eventually, in both houses of Parliament. The government was able to broaden the base of its parliamentary support by amending the constitutional proposals to accommodate the views of the small left-wing New Democratic Party: the *Charter of Rights* was strengthened (except for property rights, which were removed), and a section enhancing provincial juris-diction over natural resources was added. These changes did not placate the Conservatives, whose opposition focused on the extent to which Trudeau's constitutional plans violated both in substance and procedure the principles and practices of Canadian federalism. In terms of substance, they were particularly concerned about the inclusion of a referendum method of amending the Constitution that could be initiated only by the federal government and would therefore bypass the provincial governments.

By April 1981, the Conservatives had resorted to filibuster tactics in the House of Com-mons as the only way to prevent the government from proceeding unilaterally with its request to the U.K. Parliament. The Conservatives agreed to stop their filibuster when the government agreed not to submit its constitutional package to Britain until the Supreme Court rendered its opinion on the appeals from the Manitoba, Quebec, and Newfoundland courts. The Prime Minister indicated that his government would not proceed with its con-stitutional plans if the Supreme Court found the unilateral procedure unconstitutional. On the other hand, if the Supreme Court decided in his favour he would proceed after no more than two days of parliamentary debate. For their part, the opposition leaders agreed not to submit any additional amendments to the proposal. Thus, the fate of Trudeau's constitu-tional proposals rested, for the moment, with the nine judges of the Supreme Court.

On Monday, September 28, 1981, the Supreme Court of Canada released its decision. On the first question, all the judges agreed that the federal government's constitutional package would affect federal–provincial relationships and the powers of the provincial leg-islatures. But on the second and third questions the Court gave a mixed verdict. The Court held (6 to 3) that there was a constitutional convention requiring "a substantial degree of

---

1   Quebec's questions were somewhat different from those of Manitoba and Newfoundland— see case 47.

2   A fourth question, referred to the Newfoundland Court of Appeal, asked whether Newfound-land's Terms of Union with Canada, or section 3 of the *B.N.A. Act* of 1871, requiring a province's consent to changes in its boundaries could, if the Constitution Act, 1981 were enacted, be amended without the consent of Newfoundland's legislature or a majority of its people.

provincial consent" for federal requests to the U.K. Parliament to amend the *B.N.A. Act* in matters affecting federal–provincial relationships or provincial powers. But the Court also held (7 to 2) that, although this convention was a "constitutional requirement," observance of the convention was not "legally required."

The key to understanding the internal consistency of this judgment is the position of the majority (Justices Martland, Ritchie, Dickson, Beetz, Chouinard, and Lamer)[3] on the nature of constitutional conventions. The majority divided the Constitution of Canada into two categories: conventions and constitutional law. The purpose of conventions "is to ensure that the legal framework of the Constitution will be operated in accordance with the prevailing constitutional values and principles." Because conventions are part of the Constitution, and "some conventions may be more important than some laws," the failure of politicians or officials to observe convention in the way they exercise their legal powers is unconstitutional. However, unlike with violations of constitutional law, the remedy for breaches of convention does not lie with the courts. Conventions, by their very nature, are distinct from the legal system. Unlike common law, the precedents on which constitutional conventions are based are not judge-made rules but those established "by the institutions of government themselves." Courts may describe conventions and, as in this case, answer requests for advisory opinions about conventions, but they do not enforce conventions. The sanctions for enforcing conventions "rest with institutions of government other than courts, such as the Governor General or the Lieutenant-Governor, or the Houses of Parliament, or with public opinion and ultimately with the electorate." In this sense, the remedies for breach of convention are political, not legal.

The majority's finding that a constitutional convention exists requiring substantial provincial consent was based, in part, on an examination of earlier amendments. The majority regarded only 5 of the 22 amendments to the *B.N.A. Act* as meeting its criterion of amendments directly affecting provincial powers: the 1930 amendment confirming the transfer of natural resources to the western provinces; the *Statute of Westminster*; the 1940 unemployment insurance amendment; and the 1951 and 1964 amendments giving the federal Parliament jurisdiction over old-age pensions and supplementary benefits. For the last four, the consent of all the provinces was obtained, while the 1930 amendment was based on explicit agreements with the provinces directly concerned and had received the general approval of all the provinces at a Dominion–provincial conference. While these precedents might be thought to point to a convention of unanimity, the majority pointed to statements of political leaders and the wording of the fourth principle in the 1965 White Paper as evidence for the finding that the unanimity principle was not accepted "by all the actors in the precedents."

The majority did not rest their case solely on relevant precedents or the statements of politicians. They contended that a convention, to be accepted as obligatory, must be based on "principles of the period." The reason for the rule requiring provincial consent for constitutional amendments to their powers was the principle of federalism. In their view, "[t]he

---

3   The judges are listed in order of seniority. No authorship is attributed. While some unanimous decisions have not attributed authorship (see, for example, case 12), this is the first time, of which this author is aware, that no authorship has been attributed to majority and dissenting opinions.

federal principle cannot be reconciled with a state of affairs where the modification of provincial legislative powers could be obtained by the unilateral action of the federal authorities."

The dissenting judges[4] on the convention part of the decision felt that the question submitted to the courts must be interpreted as asking only whether *unanimous* agreement was required. Also, they did not accept the majority's narrowing of the relevant precedents to those that altered the distribution of powers. In their view, the real test was whether amendments sponsored by the federal government provoked a negative reaction from one or more of the provinces. Using this test, they had no difficulty in identifying a number of amendments that were made despite some strenuous provincial opposition—for instance, the 1943 amendment postponing a redistribution of seats in the House of Commons that would have favoured Quebec. This, they held, demonstrated that there was not a consistent practice of obtaining provincial consent. They could not understand how a convention could exist when the degree of provincial participation was a matter of continuing controversy and the requirements of the convention (that is, exactly how many provinces must agree) could not be stated with precision. Finally, they rejected the majority's understanding of the federal principle. They took the position that the overriding powers that the *B.N.A. Act* bestows on the central government deprive the federalism argument of its force.

Justices Dickson, Beetz, Chouinard, and Lamer, who were in the majority on the question of convention, were joined by the three judges who dissented on that issue to form the majority on the question of law. Their opinion examined the English and Canadian cases cited by counsel for the provinces in which courts had referred to constitutional conventions, but concluded that, while conventions may have been used as an aid to interpreting common law and statute law, no case constituted an instance of a convention crystallizing into a rule of law. The opinion of the two dissenting judges, Martland and Ritchie, was not based on this issue. These two judges contended that because the privileges and powers of the House of Commons and Senate, including their right to address resolutions concerning the Constitution to the British Parliament, were limited by statute to activities "consistent with and not repugnant to" the *B.N.A. Act*, neither of the houses of the federal Parliament was legally authorized to pass a resolution striking at what, in their view, was a basic element of the *B.N.A. Act*—the federal system. The majority, on the other hand, held that the content of parliamentary resolutions, unlike legislation, was subject only to the "self-regulating authority of Houses of Parliament" and not subject to court-enforced legal constraints. The majority also rejected provincial arguments to the effect that events leading up to the *Statute of Westminster* and the language of the Statute itself provided a basis in law for requiring provincial agreement to amendments altering provincial powers. Generally, the Court endeavoured to avoid ruling on the powers of the U.K. Parliament. The majority stated that "[t]he authority of the British Parliament or its practices and conventions are not matters upon which this Court would presume to pronounce."

Both the federal government and the eight provinces that opposed its unilateral approach found support in this decision. By undermining the legitimacy of the federal government's unilateralism, the Court's decisions greatly increased the political costs of proceeding without substantial provincial consent. On the other hand, provincial leaders realized now that there was no legal bar to the federal initiative. Consequently, the decision had the immediate effect of renewing interest in reaching a federal–provincial agreement on the terms for

---

4   Chief Justice Laskin and Justices Estey and McIntyre (again listed in order of seniority with no authorship attributed).

patriating the Canadian Constitution. The prospects for reaching an accord were now somewhat increased by virtue of the fact that the Supreme Court had declared that unanimous agreement was not necessarily required.

The effectiveness of the Supreme Court's decision in promoting a federal–provincial accommodation on the Constitution was soon demonstrated. A federal–provincial conference was held five weeks after the decision in November 1981. At this conference, the federal government agreed to replace the amending formula it had favoured with one originally put forward by eight of the provinces (including Quebec). In return, all the provinces except Quebec agreed to accept a modified version of the *Charter of Rights*. The November Accord, with some further amendments agreed to by the federal government and all the provinces except Quebec, served as the basis for the resolution adopted by the federal Parliament on December 9, 1981, requesting the Queen to submit to the United Kingdom Parliament a measure to patriate the Canadian Constitution. On March 25, 1982, the U.K. Parliament passed the *Canada Act*, severing Canada's last remaining legal ties to Britain and making the *Constitution Act, 1982* the law of Canada. The *Constitution Act, 1982* contains an all-Canadian amending formula and the *Charter of Rights*. It was proclaimed in force by the Queen on April 17, 1982. ~

RE: RESOLUTION TO AMEND THE CONSTITUTION
[1981] 1 S.C.R. 753

Hearing: April 28, 29, 30, and May 1 and 4, 1981; Judgment: September 28, 1981.

Present: Laskin C.J. and Martland, Ritchie, Dickson, Beetz, Estey, McIntyre, Chouinard, and Lamer JJ.

Interveners: The Attorney General of Quebec, the Attorney General of Nova Scotia, the Attorney General of Manitoba, the Attorney General of British Columbia, the Attorney General of Prince Edward Island, the Attorney General for Saskatchewan, the Attorney General for Alberta, the Attorney General of Newfoundland, and Four Nations Confederacy Inc., the Attorney General for Ontario and the Attorney General for New Brunswick.

A. THE QUESTIONS OF LAW
CHIEF JUSTICE LASKIN AND DICKSON, BEETZ, MCINTYRE, CHOUINARD, AND LAMER JJ.:

I

Three appeals as of right are before this Court, concerning in the main common issues. They arise out of three References made, respectively, to the Manitoba Court of Appeal, to the Newfoundland Court of Appeal and to the Quebec Court of Appeal by the respective governments of the three provinces.

Three questions were posed in the Manitoba Reference, as follows:

1. If the amendments to the Constitution of Canada sought in the "Proposed Resolution for a Joint Address to Her Majesty the Queen respecting the Constitution of Canada," or any of them, were enacted, would federal–provincial relationships or the powers, rights or privileges granted or secured by the Constitution of Canada to the provinces, their legislatures or governments be affected, and if so, in what respect or respects?

2. Is it a constitutional convention that the House of Commons and Senate of Canada will not request Her Majesty the Queen to lay before the Parliament of the United Kingdom of Great Britain and Northern Ireland a measure to amend the Constitution of Canada affecting federal–provincial relationships or the powers, rights or privileges granted or secured by the Constitution of Canada to the provinces, their legislatures or governments without first obtaining the agreement of the provinces?

3. Is the agreement of the provinces of Canada constitutionally required for amendment to the Constitution of Canada where such amendment affects federal–provincial relationships or alters the powers, rights or privileges granted or secured by the Constitution of Canada to the provinces, their legislatures or governments?

The same three questions were asked in the Newfoundland Reference and, in addition, a fourth question was put in these terms:

4. If Part V of the proposed resolution referred to in question 1 is enacted and proclaimed into force could
   (a) the Terms of Union, including terms 2 and VI, c. 22 (U.K.)), or

(b) section 3 of the *British North America Act, 1871* (34-35 Victoria, c. 28 (U.K.))

be amended directly or indirectly pursuant to Part V without the consent of the Government, Legislature or a majority of the people of the Province of Newfoundland voting in a referendum held pursuant to Part V?

In the Quebec Reference there was a different formulation, two questions being asked which read:

[TRANSLATION]

A. If the *Canada Act* and the *Constitution Act, 1981* should come into force and if they should be valid in all respects in Canada, would they affect:

(i) the legislative competence of the provincial legislatures in virtue of the Canadian Constitution?

(ii) the status or role of the provincial legislatures or governments within the Canadian Federation?

B. Does the Canadian Constitution empower, whether by statute, convention or otherwise, the Senate and the House of Commons of Canada to cause the Canadian Constitution to be amended without the consent of the provinces and in spite of the objection of several of them, in such a manner as to affect:

(i) the legislative competence of the provincial legislatures in virtue of the Canadian Constitution?

(ii) the status or role of the provincial legislatures or governments within the Canadian Federation?

The answers given by the judges of the Manitoba Court of Appeal, each of whom wrote reasons, are as follows:

Freedman C.J.M.:

Question 1—Not answered, because it is tentative and premature.

Question 2—No.

Question 3—No.

Hall J.A.:

Question 1—Not answered because it is not appropriate for judicial response, and, in any event, the question is speculative and premature.

Question 2—Not answered because it is not appropriate for judicial response.

Question 3—No, because there is no legal requirement of provincial agreement to amendment of the Constitution as asserted in the question.

Matas J.A.:

Question 1—Not answered, because it is speculative and premature.

Question 2—No.

Question 3—No.

O'Sullivan J.A.:

Question 1—Yes, as set out in reasons.

Question 2—The constitutional convention referred to has not been established as a matter simply of precedent; it is, however, a constitutional principle binding in law that the House of Commons and Senate of Canada should not request Her Majesty the Queen to lay before the Parliament of the United Kingdom of Great Britain and Northern Ireland any measure to amend the Constitution of Canada affecting federal–provincial relationships or the powers, rights or privileges granted or secured by the Constitution of Canada to the Provinces, their Legislatures or Governments without first obtaining the agreement of the Provinces.

Question 3—Yes, as set out in reasons.

Huband J.A.:

Question 1—Yes.

Question 2—No.

Question 3—Yes.

The Newfoundland Court of Appeal, in reasons of the Court concurred in by all three judges who sat on the Reference, answered all three questions common to the Manitoba Reference in the affirmative. The Court answered the fourth question in this way:

1. By s. 3 of the *British North America Act, 1871*, Term 2 of the Terms of Union cannot now be changed without the consent of the Newfoundland Legislature.

2. By s. 43 of the *Constitution Act, 1981*, as it now reads, none of the Terms of Union can be changed without the consent of the Newfoundland Legislative Assembly.

3. Both of these sections can be changed by the amending formulae prescribed in s. 41 and the Terms of Union could then be changed without the consent of the Newfoundland Legislature.

4. If the amending formula under s. 42 is utilized, both of these sections can be changed by a referendum held pursuant to the provisions of s. 42. In this event, the Terms of Union could then be changed without the consent of the Newfoundland Legislature, but not without the consent of the majority of the Newfoundland people voting in a referendum.

The Quebec Court of Appeal, in reasons delivered by each of five judges who sat on the Reference, answered the two questions submitted to it as follows:

[TRANSLATION]

Question A: i) Yes (unanimously).

ii) Yes (unanimously).

Question B: i) Yes (Bisson J.A., dissenting, would answer no).

ii) Yes (Bisson J.A., dissenting, would answer no).

II

The References in question here were prompted by the opposition of six provinces, later joined by two others, to a proposed Resolution which was published on October 2, 1980 and intended for submission to the House of Commons and as well to the Senate of Canada. It contained an address to be presented to Her Majesty the Queen in right of the United Kingdom respecting what may generally be referred to as the Constitution of Canada. The address laid before the House of Commons on October 6, 1980, was in these terms:

To the Queen's Most Excellent Majesty:
Most Gracious Sovereign:

We, Your Majesty's loyal subjects, the House of Commons of Canada in Parliament assembled, respectfully approach Your Majesty, requesting that you may graciously be pleased to cause to be laid before the Parliament of the United Kingdom a measure containing the recitals and clauses hereinafter set forth:

An Act to give effect to a request by the Senate
and House of Commons of Canada

Whereas Canada has requested and consented to the enactment of an Act of the Parliament of the United Kingdom to give effect to the provisions hereinafter set forth and the Senate and the House of Commons of Canada in Parliament assembled have submitted an address to Her Majesty requesting that Her Majesty may graciously be pleased to cause a Bill to be laid before the Parliament of the United Kingdom for that purpose.

Be it therefore enacted by the Queen's Most Excellent Majesty, by and with the advice and consent of the Lords Spiritual and Temporal, and Commons, in this present Parliament assembled, and by the authority of the same, as follows:

1. *The Constitution Act, 1981* set out in Schedule B to this *Act* is hereby enacted for and shall have the force of law in Canada and shall come into force as provided in that *Act*.
2. No Act of Parliament of the United Kingdom passed after the *Constitution Act, 1981* comes into force shall extend to Canada as part of its law.
3. So far as it is not contained in Schedule B, the French version of this *Act* is set out in Schedule A to this *Act* and has the same authority in Canada as the English version thereof.
4. This *Act* may be cited as the *Canada Act*.

It will be noticed that included in the terms of the address are the words "cause to be laid before the Parliament of the United Kingdom" and that they are reflected in Question B put before the Quebec Court of Appeal. The proposed Resolu-

tion, as the terms of the address indicate, includes a statute which, in turn, has appended to it another statute providing for the patriation of the *British North America Act* (and a consequent change of name), with an amending procedure, and a *Charter of Rights and Freedoms* including a range of provisions (to be entrenched against legislative invasion) which it is unnecessary to enumerate. The proposed Resolution carried the approval of only two provinces, Ontario and New Brunswick, expressed by their respective governments. The opposition of the others, save Saskatchewan, was based on their assertion that both conventionally and legally the consent of all the provinces was required for the address to go forward to Her Majesty with the appended statutes. Although there was general agreement on the desirability of patriation with an amending procedure, agreement could not be reached at conferences preceding the introduction of the proposed Resolution into the House of Commons, either on the constituents of such a procedure or on the formula to be embodied therein, or on the inclusion of a *Charter of Rights*.

The References to the respective courts of appeal were made and the hearings on the questions asked were held before the proposed Resolution was adopted. This fact underlays the unwillingness of judges in the Manitoba Court of Appeal to answer Question I; changes might be made to the proposed Resolution in the course of debate and hence the assertion of prematurity.

The proposed Resolution, as adopted by the House this Court on the three appeals. Indeed, the opinions of the courts in all three References were given and certified before the ultimate adoption of the proposed Resolution. The result of its adoption by the Senate and by the House of Commons was to change the position of the Attorney General of Canada and of his two supporting interveners on the propriety of answering Question 1 in the Manitoba and Newfoundland References. He abandoned his initial contention that the question should not be answered.

III

The reference legislation under which the various questions were put to the three courts of appeal is in wide terms. The Manitoba legislation, *An Act for Expediting the Decision of Constitutional and other Provincial Questions*, R.S.M. 1970, c. C180 provides in s. 1 that the Lieutenant Governor in Council may refer to the Court of Queen's Bench or a judge thereof or to the Court of Appeal or a judge thereof for hearing or consideration "any matter which he thinks fit to refer." The *Judicature Act*, R.S. Nfld. 1970, c. 187, s. 6, as amended, similarly provides for a reference by the Lieutenant Governor in Council to the Court of Appeal of "any matter which he thinks fit to refer." The *Court of Appeal Reference Act*, R.S.Q.

1977, c. R-23, s. 1 authorizes the Government of Quebec to refer to the Court of Appeal for hearing and consideration "any question which it deems expedient." The scope of the authority in each case is wide enough to saddle the respective courts with the determination of questions which may not be justiciable and there is no doubt that those courts, and this Court on appeal, have a discretion to refuse to answer such questions. . . .

IV

A summary of the views expressed in the courts below on the various questions before them may usefully be set out at this point. . . .

V

The reasons which now follow deal with Questions 1 and 3 in the Manitoba and Newfoundland References, with Question 4 in the Newfoundland Reference, with Question A in the Quebec Reference and with Question B in that Reference in its legal aspect. Question 2 in the Manitoba and Newfoundland References and Question B in the Quebec Reference in its comparable conventional aspect are dealt with in separate reasons.

VI

On the footing of the adopted Resolution, the Attorney General of Canada agrees that Question 1 in the Manitoba and Newfoundland References and Question A in the Quebec Reference should be answered in the affirmative as is asserted by the Attorneys General of Manitoba, Newfoundland and Quebec. Certainly, it is plain that under the terms of the enactments proposed in the Resolution, the legislative powers of the provincial legislatures would be affected, indeed, limited by the *Charter of Rights and Freedoms*. The limitations of the proposed *Charter of Rights and Freedoms* on legislative power apply both at the federal level and the provincial level. This does not, however, alter the fact that there is an intended suppression of provincial legislative power. Moreover, the enhancement of provincial legislative authority under some provisions of the proposed enactment, as for example, in respect of resource control, including interprovincial export, (albeit subject to federal paramountcy) and in respect of taxing power does not alter the fact that there is an effect on existing federal–provincial relationships under these and other provisions of the draft statute intended for submission to enactment by the Parliament of the United Kingdom.

The simple answer "yes" to Question 1 and Question A answers both of them sufficiently, even though Question 1 asks also "in what respect or respects" would federal–provincial relationships and provincial powers, rights or privileges be affected. Counsel were agreed that it would carry them and

the Court into considerable exposition of detail if this aspect of Question 1 were to be explored; for the time being, an affirmative answer to the primary issue in the question would satisfy all concerned.

VII

Coming now to Question 3 in the Manitoba and Newfoundland References and Part B (on its legal side) in the Quebec Reference. By reason of the use of the words "constitutionally required" in Question 3, the question imports both legal and conventional issues, and as the latter are dealt with in separate reasons, what follows is concerned only with the legal side of Question 3 in the Manitoba and Newfoundland References and Part B (on its legal side) in the Quebec Reference, which meets the submissions of all counsel on this issue.

There are two broad aspects to the matter under discussion which divide into a number of separate issues: (1) the authority of the two federal Houses to proceed by resolution where provincial powers and federal–provincial relationships are thereby affected and (2) the role or authority of the Parliament of the United Kingdom to act on the Resolution. The first point concerns the need of legal power to initiate the process in Canada; the second concerns legal power or want of it in the Parliament of the United Kingdom to act on the Resolution when it does not carry the consent of the provinces.

The submission of the eight provinces which invites this Court to consider the position of the British Parliament is based on the *Statute of Westminster, 1931* in its application to Canada. The submission is that the effect of the Statute is to qualify the authority of the British Parliament to act on the federal Resolution without previous provincial consent where provincial powers and interests are thereby affected, as they plainly are here. This issue will be examined later in these reasons.

Two observations are pertinent here. First, we have the anomaly that although Canada has international recognition as an independent, autonomous and self-governing state, as, for example, a founding member of the United Nations, and through membership in other international associations of sovereign states, yet it suffers from an internal deficiency in the absence of legal power to alter or amend the essential distributive arrangements under which legal authority is exercised in the country, whether at the federal or provincial level. When a country has been in existence as an operating federal state for more than a century, the task of introducing a legal mechanism that will thereafter remove the anomaly undoubtedly raises a profound problem. Secondly, the authority of the British Parliament or its practices and conventions are not matters upon which this Court would presume to pronounce.

The proposition was advanced on behalf of the Attorney General of Manitoba that a convention may crystallize into law and that the requirement of provincial consent to the kind of resolution that we have here, although in origin political, has become a rule of law. (No firm position was taken on whether the consent must be that of the governments or that of the legislatures.)

In our view, this is not so. No instance of an explicit recognition of a convention as having matured into a rule of law was produced. The very nature of a convention, as political in inception and as depending on a consistent course of political recognition by those for whose benefit and to whose detriment (if any) the convention developed over a considerable period of time is inconsistent with its legal enforcement.

The attempted assimilation of the growth of a convention to the growth of the common law is misconceived. The latter is the product of judicial effort, based on justiciable issues which have attained legal formulation and are subject to modification and even reversal by the courts which gave them birth when acting within their role in the state in obedience to statutes or constitutional directives. No such parental role is played by the courts with respect to conventions.

It was urged before us that a host of cases have given legal force to conventions. This is an over-drawn proposition. One case in which direct recognition and enforcement of a convention was sought is *Madzimbamuto v. Lardner-Burke and George* ([1969]1 A.C. 645). There the Privy Council rejected the assertion that a convention formally recognized by the United Kingdom as established, namely, that it would not legislate for Southern Rhodesia on matters within the competence of the latter's legislature without its government's consent, could not be overridden by British legislation made applicable to Southern Rhodesia after the unilateral declaration of independence by the latter's government. Speaking for the Privy Council, Lord Reid pointed out that although the convention was a very important one, "it had no legal effect in limiting the legal power of Parliament" (at p. 723). And, again (at the same page):

> It is often said that it would be unconstitutional for the United Kingdom Parliament to do certain things, meaning that the moral, political and other reasons against doing them are so strong that most people would regard it as highly improper if Parliament did these things. But that does not mean that it is beyond the power of Parliament to do such things. If Parliament chose to do any of them the courts could not hold the Act of Parliament invalid. . . .

Quite a number of cases were cited on which counsel for Manitoba relied to support his contention of conventions crystallizing into law. The chief support put forward for the "crystallization into law" proposition was the opinion of

Duff C.J. in *References re The Weekly Rest in Industrial Undertakings Act* ([1936] S.C.R. 461), better known as the *Labour Conventions* case. . . .

The following portion of the reasons of Sir Lyman Duff contains the passage relied on, but extends it for more accurate context (at pp. 476-78):

> With reference to the Report of the Conference of 1926, which in explicit terms recognizes treaties in the form of agreements between governments (to which His Majesty is not, in form, a party), it is said that since an Imperial Conference possesses no legislative power, its declarations do not operate to effect changes in the law, and it is emphatically affirmed that, in point of strict law, neither the Governor General nor any other Canadian authority has received from the Crown power to exercise the prerogative.
>
> The argument is founded on the distinction it draws between constitutional convention and legal rule; and it is necessary to examine the contention that, in point of legal rule, as distinct from constitutional convention, the Governor General in Council had no authority to become party by ratification to the convention with which we are concerned.
>
> There are various points of view from which this contention may be considered. First of all, constitutional law consists very largely of established constitutional usages recognized by the Courts as embodying a rule of law. An Imperial Conference, it is true, possesses no legislative authority. But there could hardly be more authoritative evidence as to constitutional usage than the declarations of such a Conference. The Conference of 1926 categorically recognizes treaties in the form of agreements between governments in which His Majesty does not formally appear, and in respect of which there has been no Royal intervention. It is the practice of the Dominion to conclude with foreign countries agreements in such form, and agreements even of a still more informal character—merely by an exchange of notes. Conventions under the auspices of the Labour Organization of the League of Nations invariably are ratified by the Government of the Dominion concerned. As a rule, the crystallization of constitutional usage into a rule of constitutional law to which the Courts will give effect is a slow process extending over a long period of time; but the Great War accelerated the pace of development in the region with which we are concerned, and it would seem that the usages to which I have referred, the practice, that is to say, under which Great Britain and the Dominions enter into agreements with foreign countries in the form of agreements between governments and of a still more informal character, must be recognized by the Courts as having the force of law.

Indeed, agreements between the Government of Canada and other governments in the form of an agreement between Governments, to which His Majesty is not a party, have been recognized by the Judicial Committee of the Privy Council as adequate in international law to create an international obligation binding upon Canada (*Radio Reference*, [1932] A.C. 304.)....

Ratification was the effective act which gave binding force to the convention. It was, as respects Canada, the act of the Government of Canada alone, and the decision mentioned appears, therefore, to negative decisively the contention that, in point of strict law, the Government of Canada is incompetent to enter into an international engagement.

What the learned Chief Justice was dealing with was an evolution which is characteristic of customary international law; the attainment by the Canadian federal executive of full and independent power to enter into international agreements. (Indeed, in speaking of "convention" in the last quoted paragraph, he was referring to an international agreement and, similarly, in the use of the word in the second last line of the second paragraph of the quotation and again in the middle of the third paragraph.) International law perforce has had to develop, if it was to exist at all, through commonly recognized political practices of states, there being no governing constitution, no legislating authority, no executive enforcement authority and no generally accepted judicial organ through which international law could be developed. The situation is entirely different in domestic law, in the position of a state having its own governing legislative, executive and judicial organs and, in most cases, an overarching written constitution.

Chief Justice Duff indicated his view of convention as allegedly maturing into law in a domestic setting in *Reference re Disallowance and Reservation of Provincial Legislation* ([1938] S.C.R. 71). There it was urged that a certain portion of s. 90 of the *British North America Act* (incorporating, in respect of the provinces, ss. 56 and 57, with some modification) had by reason of convention become spent and was suspended by the alleged convention. As to this, the Chief Justice said (at p. 78):

We are not concerned with constitutional usage. We are concerned with questions of law which, we repeat, must be determined by reference to the enactments of the *British North America Acts* of 1867 to 1930, the *Statute of Westminster*, and, it might be, to relevant statutes of the Parliament of Canada if there were any.

Section 90 which, with the changes therein specified, re-enacts sections 55, 56 and 57 of the *B.N.A. Act*, is still

subsisting. It has not been repealed or amended by the Imperial Parliament and it is quite clear that, by force of subsection 1 of section 7 of the *Statute of Westminster*, the Dominion Parliament did not acquire by that statute, any authority to repeal, amend or alter the *British North America Acts*. Whether or not, by force of section 91(29) and section 92(1) of the *B.N.A. Act*, the Dominion Parliament has authority to legislate in respect of reservation, it is not necessary to consider because no such legislation has been passed.

The powers are, therefore, subsisting. Are they subject to any limitation or restriction?

Once more, we are not concerned with constitutional usage or constitutional practice.

There is nothing in the other judgments delivered in the *Labour Conventions* case, either in the Supreme Court or in the Privy Council that takes the matter there beyond its international law setting or lends credence to the crystallization proposition urged by counsel for the Attorney General of Manitoba and, it should be said, supported by other provinces and by observations in the reasons of the Newfoundland Court of Appeal. Other cases cited for the proposition turn out, on examination, to be instances where the courts proceeded on firm statutory or other legal principles. This is as true ... of the denial of injunctive relief in respect of disclosure of the Crossman diaries in *Attorney-General v. Jonathan Cape Ltd.*, [1976] 1 Q.B. 752. The Court pointed out in the latter case that it had the power to restrain breaches of confidence where demanded in the public interest, although the confidence stemmed from a convention respecting cabinet deliberations. However, the need for restraint had gone because of the passage of time. The Court was applying its own legal principles as it might to any question of confidence, however it arose.

A close look at some other cases and issues raised on so-called crystallization reveals no support for the contention....

Finally, there was an appeal to the *Senate Reference* decision of this Court. It is baffling how it can be said that this Court recognized convention as having *per se* grown into law. What was involved was a proposed federal enactment sought to be justified mainly under s. 91(1) of the *British North America Act*. This Court held that the proposal, at least in its main features, was beyond federal competence. Although the Court referred to certain historical background for perspective on the position of the Senate as it was dealt with under the *British North America Act*, its fundamental duty was to examine the validity of a proposed federal measure sought to be justified under a grant of federal power under that *Act*.

As to all the cases cited, it must be said that there is no independent force to be found in selective quotations from a portion of the reasons unless regard is had to issues raised and the context in which the quotations are found.

We were invited to consider academic writings on the matter under discussion. There is no consensus among the author-scholars, but the better and prevailing view is that expressed in an article by Munro, "Laws and Conventions Distinguished" (1975), 91 *Law Q. Rev.* 218 where he says (at p. 228):

> The validity of conventions cannot be the subject of proceedings in a court of law. Reparation for breach of such rules will not be effected by any legal sanction. There are no cases which contradict these propositions. In fact, the idea of a court enforcing a mere convention is so strange that the question hardly arises.

Another passage from this article deserves mention, as follows (at p. 224):

> If in fact laws and conventions are different in kind, as is my argument, then an accurate and meaningful picture of the constitution may only be obtained if this distinction is made. If the distinction is blurred, analysis of the constitution is less complete; this is not only dangerous for the lawyer, but less than helpful to the political scientist....

There is no difference in approach whether the issue arises in a unitary state or in a federal state: see Hogg, *Constitutional Law of Canada* (1977), at pp. 7-11.

A contrary view relied on by the provincial appellants is that expressed by Professor W.R. Lederman in two published articles, one entitled "The Process of Constitutional Amendment in Canada" (1966-67), 12 *McGill Law Journal* 371 and the second entitled "Constitutional Amendment and Canadian Unity" (1978), *Law Society Upper Canada Lectures* 17. As a respected scholar, Professor Lederman's views deserve more than cursory consideration. He himself recognizes that there are contrary views, including those of an equally distinguished scholar, Professor F.R. Scott: see Scott, *Essays on the Constitution* (1977), at pp. 144, 169, 204-5, 245, 370-71, 402. There is also the contrary view of Professor Hogg, already cited.

Professor Lederman relies in part on a line of cases that has already been considered, especially the reasons of Duff C.J. in the *Labour Conventions* case. The leap from convention to law is explained almost as if there was a common law of constitutional law, but originating in political practice. That is simply not so. What is desirable as a political limitation does not translate into a legal limitation, without expression in imperative constitutional text or statute. The position advocated is all the more unacceptable when substantial provincial compliance or consent is by him said to be sufficient. Although Professor Lederman would not give a veto to Prince Edward Island, he would to Ontario or Quebec or British Columbia or Alberta. This is an impossible position for a court to manage. Further reference to this is made later in these reasons.

VIII

Turning now to the authority or power of the two federal Houses to proceed by resolution to forward the address and appended draft statutes to Her Majesty the Queen for enactment by the Parliament of the United Kingdom. There is no limit anywhere in law, either in Canada or in the United Kingdom (having regard to s. 18 of the *British North America Act*, as enacted by 1875 (U.K.), c. 38, which ties the privileges, immunities and powers of the federal Houses to those of the British House of Commons) to the power of the Houses to pass resolutions. Under s. 18 aforesaid, the federal Parliament may by statute define those privileges, immunities and powers, so long as they do not exceed those held and enjoyed by the British House of Commons at the time of the passing of the federal statute....

How Houses of Parliament proceed, how a provincial legislative assembly proceeds is in either case a matter of self-definition, subject to any overriding constitutional or self-imposed statutory or indoor prescription. It is unnecessary here to embark on any historical review of the "court" aspect of Parliament and the immunity of its procedures from judicial review. ... Reference may appropriately be made to art. 9 of the *Bill of Rights* of 1689, undoubtedly in force as part of the law of Canada, which provides that "Proceedings in Parliament ought not to be impeached or questioned in any Court or Place out of Parliament."

It is said, however, that where the resolution touches provincial powers, as the one in question here does, there is a limitation on federal authority to pass it on to Her Majesty the Queen unless there is provincial consent. If there is such a limitation, it arises not from any limitation on the power to adopt resolutions but from an external limitation based on other considerations which will shortly be considered.

Although the *British North America Act* itself is silent on the question of the power of the federal Houses to proceed by resolution to procure an amendment to the *Act* by an address to Her Majesty, its silence gives positive support as much as it may reflect the negative. Quebec Question B suggests in its formulation that there is the necessity of affirmative proof of the power asserted, but it would be equally consistent with constitutional precedent to require disproof. Moreover, if the two federal Houses had the power to proceed by resolution, how is it that they have lost it?

For the moment, it is relevant to point out that even in those cases where an amendment to the *British North America*

Act was founded on a resolution of the federal Houses after having received provincial consent, there is no instance, save in the *British North America Act, 1930* where such consent was recited in the resolution. The matter remained, in short, a conventional one within Canada, without effect on the validity of the resolution in respect of United Kingdom action. The point is underscored in relation to the very first amendment directly affecting provincial legislative power, that in 1940 which added "Unemployment Insurance" to the catalogue of exclusive federal powers. Sir William Jowitt, then Solicitor-General, and later Lord Chancellor, was asked in the British House of Commons about provincial consent when the amendment was in course of passage. The question put to him and his answer are as follows (see 362 U.K. Parl. Deb. 5th Series, H.C. 1177-81):

> Mr. Mander ... In this Bill we are concerned only with the Parliament of Canada, but, as a matter of interest, I would be obliged if the Solicitor-General would say whether the Provincial Canadian Parliaments are in agreement with the proposals submitted by the Dominion Parliament....
>
> Sir William Jowitt ... One might think that the Canadian Parliament was in some way subservient to ours, which is not the fact. The true position is that at the request of Canada this old machinery still survives until something better is thought of, but we square the legal with the constitutional position by passing these Acts only in the form that the Canadian Parliament require and at the request of the Canadian Parliament.
>
> My justification to the House for this Bill—and it is important to observe this—is not on the merits of the proposal, which is a matter for the Canadian Parliament; if we were to embark upon that, we might trespass on what I conceive to be their constitutional position. The sole justification for this enactment is that we are doing in this way what the Parliament of Canada desires to do....
>
> In reply to the hon. Member for East Wolverhampton (Mr. Mander), I do not know what the view of the Provincial Parliaments is. I know, however, that when the matter was before the Privy Council some of the Provincial Parliaments supported the Dominion Parliament. It is a sufficient justification for the Bill that we are morally bound to act on the ground that we have here the request of the Dominion Parliament and that we must operate the old machinery which has been left over at their request in accordance with their wishes.

IX

This Court is being asked, in effect, to enshrine as a legal imperative a principle of unanimity for constitutional amendment to overcome the anomaly—more of an anomaly today than it was in 1867—that the *British North America Act* contained no provision for effecting amendments by Canadian action alone. Although Saskatchewan has, alone of the eight provinces opposing the federal package embodied in the Resolution, taken a less stringent position, eschewing unanimity but without quantifying the substantial support that it advocates, the provinces, parties to the References and to the appeals here, are entitled to have this Court's primary consideration of their views. ...

An important question was raised by the Saskatchewan position which invited this Court to take a severable view of the substance of the Resolution, namely, to "hive off" the *Charter of Rights and Freedoms* and perhaps other elements, save the amending formula and the patriation feature. This was not the position of the Attorney General of Canada nor of any of the other provincial Attorneys General; they were all of the view that it was the whole package that was involved in the legal issue posed by Question 3 and Question B. Indeed, the legal arguments pro and con do not engage the contents of the package, and it is impossible to qualify the issue of legality by considerations of fairness or equity or political acceptability or even judicial desirability.

The stark legal question is whether this Court can enact by what would be judicial legislation a formula of unanimity to initiate the amending process which would be binding not only in Canada but also on the Parliament of the United Kingdom with which amending authority would still remain. It would be anomalous indeed, overshadowing the anomaly of a constitution which contains no provision for its amendment, for this Court to say retroactively that in law we have had an amending formula all along, even if we have not hitherto known it; or, to say, that we have had in law one amending formula, say from 1867 to 1931, and a second amending formula that has emerged after 1931. No one can gainsay the desirability of federal–provincial accord of acceptable compromise. That does not, however, go to legality. As Sir William Jowitt said, and quoted earlier, we must operate the old machinery perhaps one more time.

X

The provincial contentions asserted a legal incapacity in the federal Houses to proceed with the Resolution which is the subject of the References and of the appeals here. Joined to this assertion was a claim that the United Kingdom Parliament had, in effect, relinquished its legal power to act on a resolution such as the one before this Court, and that it could only act in relation to Canada if a request was made by "the proper authorities." The federal Houses would be such authorities if provincial powers or interests would not be affected; if they would be, then the proper authorities would include the provinces. It is not that the provinces must be joined in the federal address to Her Majesty the Queen; that was not argued. Rather their consent (or, as in the Saskatchewan submission, substantial provincial compliance or approval) was required as a condition of the validity of the process by address and Resolution and, equally, as a condition of the valid action thereon by the United Kingdom Parliament....

XI

The Court was invited to regard the Balfour Declaration of 1926 as embracing the provinces of Canada (and, presumably, the states of the sister dominion of Australia) in its reference to "autonomous communities." That well-known statement of principle, a political statement in the context of evolving independence of the dominions in their relations with the United Kingdom, is as follows:

> They are autonomous Communities within the British Empire, equal in status, in no way subordinate one to another in any aspect of their domestic or external affairs, though united by a common allegiance to the Crown, and freely associated as members of the British Common- wealth of Nations.

It is impossible to seek nourishment for the provincial position in these appeals in this Declaration. The provinces did not come into the picture in the march to the *Statute of Westminster, 1931* until after the 1929 Conference on the Oper- ation of Dominion Legislation, although to a degree before the Imperial Conference of 1930. They then made their views known on certain aspects of the looming statute, views which were canvassed in a Dominion–Provincial Conference in 1931. The main concern touched the proposed repeal of the *Colonial Laws Validity Act*, 1865 (U.K.), c. 63 and the effect that this might have on the amendment of the *British North America Act*, a matter to be considered later in these reasons.

Although the Balfour Declaration cannot, of itself, sup- port the assertion of provincial autonomy in the wide sense contended for, it seems to have been regarded as retroactively having that effect by reason of the ultimate enactment of the *Statute of Westminster, 1931*. That statute is put forward not only as signifying an equality of status as between the Domin- ion and the provinces vis-à-vis the United Kingdom Parlia- ment, but also as attenuating the theretofore untrammelled legislative authority of that Parliament in relation to Canada where provincial interests are involved....

[The relevant provisions of the *Statute of Westminster* were then set out.]

There is nothing in the preamble that relates to the prov- inces other than the reference to the Report of the Imperial Conference of 1930. What emerged prior to this Conference was an understandable provincial concern that the effect of the proposed repeal of the *Colonial Laws Validity Act* in favour

of the Parliament of a dominion and, in addition, the effect of what became s. 2(2) of the Statute might enlarge federal power to alter, by its own legislation, provisions of the *British North America Act*. Thus it was that the Conference of 1930 placed on record (Cmd. 3717, at pp. 17-18):

> ... that the sections of the Statute relating to the *Colonial Laws Validity Act* should be so drafted as not to extend to Canada unless the Statute was enacted in response to such requests as are appropriate to an amendment of the *Brit- ish North America Act*. It also seemed desirable to place on record the view that the sections should not subse- quently be extended to Canada except by an Act of the Parliament of the United Kingdom enacted in response to such requests as are appropriate to an amendment of the *British North America Act*.

The *Colonial Laws Validity Act* was intended to be a liberat- ing statute, releasing colonial legislatures from subservience to British common law (subject to Privy Council authority) and from subservience to British statute law unless such statute law applied expressly or by necessary implication to the colony. In the evolution of independence of the dominions, it came to be recognized that the United Kingdom should no longer legislate at its own instance for any dominion; and that the latter should be free to repeal any British legislation that was or would be made applicable to it.... Following the Imperial Conference of 1930 and as a result of the Dominion–Provincial Conference of 1931, the provinces obtained an assurance that they too would benefit by the repeal of the *Colonial Laws Validity Act* and by being empowered to repeal any British legislation made applicable to them. This was achieved by s. 7(2) of the *Statute of Westminster, 1931*....

The most important issue was, however, the position of the Dominion vis-à-vis the *British North America Act*. What s. 7(1), reinforced by s. 7(3), appeared to do was to maintain the *status quo ante*; that is, to leave any changes in the *British North America Act* (that is, such changes which, under its terms, could not be carried out by legislation of the provinces or of the Dominion) to the prevailing situation, namely, with the legislative authority of the United Kingdom Parliament being left untouched....

The argument on the *Statute of Westminster* is untenable, but it leaves for more anxious consideration the effect of the removal of the *British North America Act* from the *Statute of Westminster* and the preservation by s. 7(3) of the existing distribution of legislative powers under the *British North America Act*.

XII

This leads to the submissions made on the sovereignty of the provinces in respect of their powers under the *British North*

America Act, the term "sovereignty" being modified in the course of argument to "supremacy." Allied to this was the contention that Canada cannot do indirectly what it cannot do directly; it could not by an enactment of its own accomplish that which is proposed by the Resolution. Such an enactment would be clearly *ultra vires* as to most of the provisions put forward by the Resolution, and it should not be able to improve its position in law by invoking the aid of the United Kingdom Parliament. Moreover, even if the Parliament of the United Kingdom retained its formal legal authority over the *British North America Act,* as one of its enactments, it was in the words used by the late and at the time, former Justice Rand, "a bare legislative trustee," subject as a matter of law to the direction of the beneficiaries, namely, the Dominion and the provinces, in respect of the Resolution....

The direct-indirect contention, taken by itself, amounts to this: that whether or not the federal Houses can seek to obtain enactment of the draft statute appended to the Resolution, it would, in any event, be illegal to invoke United Kingdom authority to do for Canada what it cannot do itself. The maxim "you cannot do indirectly what you cannot do directly" is a much abused one.... However, it does not preclude a limited legislature from achieving directly under one head of legislative power what it could not do directly under another head. The question, of course, remains whether the two federal Houses may alone initiate and carry through the process to invoke the competence of the United Kingdom Parliament.

At least with regard to the amending formula the process in question here concerns not the amendment of a complete constitution but rather the completion of an incomplete constitution.

We are involved here with a finishing operation, with fitting a piece into the constitutional edifice; it is idle to expect to find anything in the *British North America Act* that regulates the process that has been initiated in this case. Were it otherwise, there would be no need to resort to the Resolution procedure invoked here, a procedure which takes account of the intergovernmental and international link between Canada and Great Britain. There is no comparable link that engages the provinces with Great Britain. Moreover, it is to confuse the issue of process, which is the basic question here, with the legal competence of the British Parliament when resort is had to the direct-indirect argument. The legal competence of that Parliament, for the reasons already given, remains unimpaired, and it is for it alone to determine if and how it will act.

The late Justice Rand used the words "a bare legislative trustee" in the Holmes Lecture delivered at Harvard Law School under the title "Some Aspects of Canadian Constitutionalism" and reproduced in (1960), 38 *Can. Bar Rev.* 135. His use of the phrase came in the course of his discussion of the effect of the *Statute of Westminster, 1931.* He said this (at p. 145):

> Legislatively, a unique situation has been created. The British Parliament has in effect become a bare legislative trustee for the Dominion; the constitutional organ for altering the provisions of the Canadian constitution contained in the *Act* of 1867 remains so far the British Parliament; but the political direction resides in the Parliament of the Dominion; the former has conceded its residue of legislative power vis-à-vis Canada, to be no more than means for effecting the will of Canada.

The Newfoundland Court of Appeal adopted the phrase but decided that Justice Rand should not have limited the suggested trusteeship as being for the Dominion of Canada alone. Moreover, the Court overlooked a central point in the Rand lecture that "the political direction resides in the Parliament of the Dominion." Thus the Court said:

> We adopt that statement fully with the important addition that the Parliament of Great Britain is a "bare legislative trustee" for both the Federal Parliament and the Provincial Legislatures in relation to the matters within their respective legislative competence. Any amendment enacted by the Parliament of Great Britain affecting the legislative competence of either of the parties, without that party's consent, would not only be contrary to the intendment of the *Statute of Westminster,* but it could defeat the whole scheme of the Canadian federal Constitution.

It is enough to counter this assessment of the Newfoundland Court of Appeal by referring to what Gérin-Lajoie said in his seminal text *Constitutional Amendment in Canada* (1950) at p. 138:

> While the Parliament of the United Kingdom is precluded from enacting any constitutional amendment without a proper request from Canada the only competent voice of Canada for this purpose is that of the federal power. The provincial authorities—either executive or legislative—have no *locus standi* to move the British Parliament or Government with a view to securing an amendment to the federal Constitution....

XIII

At bottom, the challenge to the competency in law of the federal Houses to seek enactment by the Parliament of the United Kingdom of the statutes embodied in the Resolution is based on the recognized supremacy of provincial legislatures in relation to the powers conferred upon them under the *British North America Act,* a supremacy *vis-à-vis* the federal Parliament. Reinforcement, or perhaps the foundation of this supremacy is said to lie in the nature or character of Canadian federalism.

The supremacy position, taken alone, needs no further justification that that found in the respective formulations of the powers of Parliament and the provincial legislatures in ss. 91 and 92 of the *British North America Act*. Federal paramountcy is, however, the general rule in the actual exercise of these powers. This notwithstanding, the exclusiveness of the provincial powers (another way of expressing supremacy and more consonant with the terms of the *British North America Act*) cannot be gainsaid. The long list of judicial decisions, beginning with *Hodge v. The Queen* (1883), 9 App. Cas. 117 and carrying through such cases as *Liquidators of the Maritime Bank of Canada v. Receiver-General of New Brunswick*, [1892] A.C. 437 and the *Labour Conventions* case, *supra*, where the Privy Council expressed its "watertight compartments view" of legislative power (at p. 354) provide adequate support for the principle of exclusiveness or supremacy but, of course, within the limits of the *British North America Act*.

Although there are what have been called unitary features in the *British North America Act*, involving overriding powers (to be distinguished from paramountcy of legislation) in the federal Parliament and Government, their modification of exclusive provincial authority does not detract from that authority to any substantial degree. Thus the federal declaratory power under s. 92(10)(c) has a limited operation; reservation and disallowance of provincial legislation, although in law still open, have, to all intents and purposes, fallen into disuse. The fact of appointment of the Lieutenant Governors of the provinces by the central government does not, as a practical matter, have any significance for provincial powers when, under the law, the Lieutenant Governor is as much the personal representative of the Crown as is the Governor General. In each case, the representation is, of course, in respect of the powers respectively assigned to Parliament and the legislatures. Moreover, since there is an international, a foreign relations aspect involved in the relationship of Canada and Great Britain, any formal communication between a province and its Lieutenant Governor with the United Kingdom Government or with the Queen, must be through the federal Government or through the Governor General.

It is important in this connection to emphasize that the Government of Canada had, by 1923, obtained recognition internationally of its independent power to enter into external obligations when it negotiated the Halibut Treaty with the United States. Great Britain understood this by that time as did the United States. The subsequent Imperial Conferences added confirmation, sanctified by the *Statute of Westminster, 1931* which also put internal independence from Great Britain on a legal foundation. The remaining badge of subservience,

the need to resort to the British Parliament to amend the *British North America Act*, although preserved by the *Statute of Westminster, 1931* did not carry any diminution of Canada's legal right in international law, and as a matter of Canadian constitutional law, to assert its independence in external relations, be they with Great Britain or other countries. The matter is emphasized by the judgment of this Court in *Reference Re: Offshore Mineral Rights of British Columbia*, [1967] S.C.R. 792, at p. 816. This is a relevant consideration in the appeals which are before this Court.

What is put forward by the provinces which oppose the forwarding of the address without provincial consent is that external relations with Great Britain in this respect must take account of the nature and character of Canadian federalism. It is contended that a legal underpinning of their position is to be found in the Canadian federal system as reflected in historical antecedents, in the pronouncements of leading political figures and in the preamble to the *British North America Act*.

The arguments from history do not lead to any consistent view or any single view of the nature of the *British North America Act*.... So too, with pronouncements by political figures or persons in other branches of public life. There is little profit in parading them.

Support for a legal requirement of provincial consent to the Resolution that is before this Court, consent which is also alleged to condition United Kingdom response to the Resolution, is, finally, asserted to lie in the preamble of the *British North America Act* itself, and in the reflection, in the substantive terms of the *Act*, of what are said to be fundamental presuppositions in the preamble as to the nature of Canadian federalism. The preamble recites ... the following:

> Whereas the Provinces of Canada, Nova Scotia, and New Brunswick have expressed their Desire to be federally united into One Dominion under the Crown of the United Kingdom of Great Britain and Ireland, with a Constitution similar in Principle to that of the United Kingdom....

What is stressed is the desire of the named provinces "to be federally united ... with a Constitution similar in Principle to that of the United Kingdom." The preamble speaks also of union into "One Dominion" and of the establishment of the Union "by Authority of Parliament," that is the United Kingdom Parliament. What, then, is to be drawn from the preamble as a matter of law? A preamble, needless to say, has no enacting force but, certainly, it can be called in aid to illuminate provisions of the statute in which it appears. Federal union "with a Constitution similar in Principle to that of the United Kingdom" may well embrace responsible government and some common law aspects of the United Kingdom's unitary

constitutionalism, such as the rule of law and Crown prerogatives and immunities. The "rule of law" is a highly textured
expression, importing many things which are beyond the need
of these reasons to explore but conveying, for example, a sense
of orderliness, of subjection to known legal rules and of
executive accountability to legal authority. Legislative changes
may alter common law prescriptions, as has happened with
respect to Crown prerogatives and immunities. There is also
an internal contradiction in speaking of federalism in the light
of the invariable principle of British parliamentary supremacy. Of course, the resolution of this contradiction lies in the
scheme of distribution of legislative power, but this owes
nothing to the preamble, resting rather on its own exposition
in the substantive terms of the *British North America Act.*

There is not and cannot be any standardized federal system
from which particular conclusions must necessarily be drawn.
Reference was made earlier to what were called unitary features
of Canadian federalism and they operate to distinguish Canadian federalism from that of Australia and that of the United
States. Allocations of legislative power differ as do the institutional arrangements through which power is exercised. This
Court is being asked by the provinces which object to the so-
called federal "package" to say that the internal distribution
of legislative power must be projected externally, as a matter of
law, although there is no legal warrant for this assertion. . . .

At bottom, it is this distribution, it is the allocation of
legislative power as between the central Parliament and the
provincial Legislatures that the provinces rely on as preclud-
ing unilateral federal action to seek amendments to the *British
North America Act* that affect, whether by limitation or extension, provincial legislative authority. The Attorney General of
Canada was pushed to the extreme by being forced to answer
affirmatively the theoretical question whether in law the federal government could procure an amendment to the *British
North America Act* that would turn Canada into a unitary
state. That is not what the present Resolution envisages
because the essential federal character of the country is preserved under the enactments proposed by the Resolution.

That, it is argued, is no reason for conceding unilateral
federal authority to accomplish, through invocation of legislation by the United Kingdom Parliament, the purposes of the
Resolution. There is here, however, an unprecedented situation in which the one constant since the enactment of the
British North America Act in 1867 has been the legal authority
of the United Kingdom Parliament to amend it. The law
knows nothing of any requirement of provincial consent,
either to a resolution of the federal Houses or as a condition
of the exercise of United Kingdom legislative power.

In the result, the third question in the Manitoba and Newfoundland cases should, as a matter of law, be answered in the
negative and Question B should, in its legal aspect, be answered
in the affirmative.

XIV

There remains for consideration question 4 in the Newfoundland Reference. . . .

[The Newfoundland Court of Appeal's answer to question 4
is upheld except for the correction that follows.]

. . . It was wrong to say that in a referendum under s. 42
(as it then was) of the proposed statute (now s. 47) the
approval of the majority of the people in each province was
required. The proper view was that only the approval of the
majority of the people voting in a referendum in those provinces, the approval of whose legislatures would be required
under the general amending formula, would be necessary. . . .

In summary, the answers to Questions 1 and 3 common
to the Manitoba and Newfoundland References, should be as
follows:

Question 1: Yes.
Question 3: As a matter of law, no.

The answer to Question 4 in the Newfoundland Reference
should be as expressed in the reasons of the Newfoundland
Court of Appeal, subject to the correction made in the reasons
herein.

The answers to the questions in the Quebec Reference
should be as follows:

Question A   (i): Yes.
                 (ii): Yes.
Question B   (i): As a matter of law, yes.
                 (ii): As a matter of law, yes.

There will be, of course, no order as to costs.

MARTLAND AND RITCHIE JJ. (dissenting): . . . The third question in the Manitoba and the Newfoundland References asks
whether the agreement of the provinces of Canada is "constitutionally required" for amendment to the Constitution of
Canada where such amendment affects federal–provincial
relationships or alters the powers, rights or privileges granted
or secured by the Constitution of Canada to the provinces,
their legislatures or governments. If the second question is
answered in the affirmative, then it is recognized that a constitutional convention exists that the House of Commons and
the Senate will not request an amendment of the *B.N.A. Act*
of the kind contemplated in Question 2 without first obtaining
the agreement of the provinces. If that is so, then the agreement of the provinces is constitutionally required for such an
amendment and the answer to Question 3 should be in the
affirmative and, in our opinion, that answer should be given.

However, there is a further issue which requires consideration in that in the courts below and in the arguments submitted by counsel before this Court, the answer to Question 3 was debated as though the words "constitutionally required" were to be considered as meaning "legally required."

In the Quebec Reference the question is phrased differently in Question B. What is asked is whether the Senate and the House of Commons are empowered by the Canadian Constitution, whether by statute, convention or otherwise, to cause the Canadian Constitution to be amended without the consent of the provinces, and in spite of the objection of several of them, in such a manner as to affect the legislative competence of provincial legislatures, or the status or role of provincial legislatures or governments within the Canadian Federation.

We were not referred to any statute which confers such a power. The answer to Question 2, if answered in the affirmative, denies that such a power exists by convention. The remaining issue is whether such a power has been conferred on the two Houses otherwise than by statute or convention.

We think Question B of the Quebec Reference more clearly raises the legal issue than does Question 3 in the other two References and we shall deal with that issue in these reasons.

At the outset, we would point out that we are not concerned with the matter of legality or illegality in the sense of determining whether or not the passage of the Resolution under consideration involves a breach of the law. The issue is as to the existence of a power to do that which is proposed to be done. The question is whether it is *intra vires* of the Senate and the House of Commons to cause the proposed amendments to the *B.N.A. Act* to be made by the Imperial Parliament by means of the Resolution now before the Court, in the absence of provincial agreement.

This issue is unique because in the one hundred and fourteen years since Confederation the Senate and House of Commons of Canada have never sought, without the consent of the provinces, to obtain such an amendment nor, apparently, has that possibility ever been contemplated.

The *British North America Act, 1867* (herein the *B.N.A. Act*) commences with the following significant recitals:

Whereas the Provinces of Canada, Nova Scotia, and New Brunswick have expressed their Desire to be federally united into One Dominion under the Crown of the United Kingdom of Great Britain and Ireland, with a Constitution similar in Principle to that of the United Kingdom: ...

... The first recital makes it clear that this statute was passed at the behest of the named provinces and that what was sought was a federal union. ...

... This *Act* became the Constitution of Canada. It created a federal union of provinces and it carefully defined the respective spheres of the Canadian Parliament and the provincial legislatures in matters of legislative jurisdiction and property rights.

The status of the provinces under the Constitution was determined by the Privy Council in two important cases which arose not long after the enactment of the *B.N.A. Act*.

It was contended in *Hodge v. The Queen*, ((1883), 9 App. Cas. 117) that a provincial legislature could not delegate its legislative powers to License Commissioners, for it was itself merely a delegate of the Imperial Parliament. The Judicial Committee of the Privy Council rejected this argument in the following terms, at p. 132:

It appears to their Lordships, however, that the objection thus raised by the appellants is founded on an entire misconception of the true character and position of the provincial legislatures. They are in no sense delegates of or acting under any mandate from the Imperial Parliament. When the *British North America Act* enacted that there should be a legislature for Ontario, and that its legislative assembly should have exclusive authority to make laws for the Province and for provincial purposes in relation to the matters enumerated in sect. 92, it conferred powers not in any sense to be exercised by delegation from or as agents of the Imperial Parliament, but authority as plenary and as ample within the limits prescribed by sect. 92 as the Imperial Parliament in the plenitude of its power possessed and could bestow. Within these limits of subjects and area the local legislature is supreme, and has the same authority as the Imperial Parliament, or the Parliament of the Dominion, would have had under like circumstances to confide to a municipal institution or body of its own creation authority to make by-laws or resolutions as to subjects specified in the enactment, and with the object of carrying the enactment into operation and effect.

In *Liquidators of the Maritime Bank of Canada v. Receiver-General of New Brunswick* ([1892] A.C. 437) it was argued that the province enjoyed no part of the Crown prerogative, and accordingly the Province of New Brunswick could not claim priority in respect of the Bank's assets for a debt owed to the province. The argument also involved the proposition that the federal government did not share this constitutional incompetence.

Lord Watson spoke for the Judicial Committee and, at p. 441, had this to say:

... Their Lordships do not think it necessary to examine, in minute detail, the provisions of the *Act* of 1867, which nowhere profess to curtail in any respect the rights and privileges of the Crown, or to disturb the relations then subsisting between the Sovereign and the provinces. The object of the *Act* was neither to weld the provinces into one, nor to subordinate provincial governments to a central authority, but to create a federal government in which they should all be represented, entrusted with the exclusive administration of affairs in which they had a common interest, each province retaining its independence and autonomy....

The assignment of powers by the *Act* to the Parliament of Canada and to the provincial legislatures covered the whole area of self government. This was recognized by the Privy Council in *Attorney-General for Ontario v. Attorney-General for Canada,* [1912] A.C. 571, at p. 581....

The foregoing review shows that the enactment of the *B.N.A. Act* created a federal constitution of Canada which confided the whole area of self-government within Canada to the Parliament of Canada and the provincial legislatures each being supreme within its own defined sphere and area. It can fairly be said, therefore, that the dominant principle of Canadian constitutional law is federalism. The implications of that principle are clear. Each level of government should not be permitted to encroach on the other, either directly or indirectly. The political compromise achieved as a result of the Quebec and London Conferences preceding the passage of the *B.N.A. Act* would be dissolved unless there were substantive and effective limits on unconstitutional action.

The *B.N.A. Act* did not make any specific provision as to the means of determining the constitutionality of any federal or provincial legislation. That task has been assumed and performed by the courts, with supreme authority initially resting with the Judicial Committee of the Privy Council and, since 1949, with this Court.

In performing this function, the courts, in addition to dealing with cases involving alleged excesses of legislative jurisdiction, have had occasion to develop legal principles based on the necessity of preserving the integrity of the federal structure. We will be dealing with these later in this judgment. We will, however, at this point cite one instance of the performance of this task in the following case by the Privy Council.

In *Attorney-General for Canada v. Attorney-General for Ontario,* [1937] A.C. 326 (the *Labour Conventions* case) the issue was as to the constitutional validity of three federal statutes enacted in 1935 dealing with labour matters, such as weekly rest in industrial undertakings, hours of work and minimum wages. In substance, they gave effect to draft conventions adopted by the International Labour Organization of the League of Nations in accordance with the Labour Pact of the Treaty of Versailles, 1919, ratified by Canada. For the Attorney General of Canada it was argued that the legislation

was valid because it was for the purpose of performing Canadian treaty obligations....

There are several features of the *Labour Conventions* case which require emphasis. The federal government was in that case asserting the right to enact legislation which was within provincial authority in order to carry out the treaty obligations which it had assumed. No question was raised as to the validity of the federal government's authority to negotiate and ratify international treaties. What was held unconstitutional by the Privy Council was the use of that lawful procedure to legislate indirectly beyond the powers invested in the federal Parliament by s. 91 of the *B.N.A. Act.*

In these appeals this Court is equally concerned with the exercise of a valid power, namely, the power of the federal Houses of Parliament to pass resolutions requesting amendments to the *B.N.A. Act.* That power has historic foundation, but we note that it has never before been exercised for the purpose of curtailing provincial legislative authority without provincial consent. In the context of the *Labour Conventions* case, the issue in these appeals is whether the established incompetence of the federal government to encroach on provincial powers can be avoided through the use of the resolution procedure to effect a constitutional amendment passed at the behest of the federal government by the Parliament of the United Kingdom.

The only provisions of the *B.N.A. Act* dealing with amendments to the Constitution are as follows. Head 1 of s. 92 empowered a provincial legislature to make laws in relation to:

> 1. The Amendment from Time to Time, notwithstanding anything in this *Act,* of the Constitution of the Province, except as regards the Office of Lieutenant Governor.

Section 146, already cited, made provision for the admission of other colonies and territories into the Union.

By an amendment made in 1949 to s. 91 of the *B.N.A. Act,* a limited power of amendment was given to the federal Parliament. Head 1 of s. 91 enabled it to legislate in relation to:

> 1. The amendment from time to time of the Constitution of Canada, except as regards matters coming within the classes of subjects by this *Act* assigned exclusively to the Legislatures of the provinces, or as regards rights or privileges by this or any other Constitutional Act granted or secured to the Legislature or the Government of a province, or to any class of persons with respect to schools or as regards the use of the English or the French language or as regards the requirements that there shall be a session of the Parliament of Canada at least once each year, and that no House of Commons shall continue for more than five years from the day of the return of the Writs for

choosing the House: Provided, however, that a House of Commons may in time of real or apprehended war, invasion or insurrection be continued by the Parliament of Canada if such continuation is not opposed by the votes of more than one-third of the members of such House.

This provision specifically excepted from its operation, *inter alia*, matters coming within the classes of subjects assigned exclusively to the provinces. The scope of s. 91(1) was considered by this Court in *Re: Authority of Parliament in relation to the Upper House*, [1980] 1 S.C.R. 54 (herein the *Senate Reference*). In that case, this Court unanimously held that the federal government could not, acting under s. 91(1), abolish the Senate. The term "Constitution of Canada" found in s. 91(1) was held in its context to refer only to the federal juristic unit. It is significant that when, as recently as 1949, the Houses of Parliament sought and obtained a provision permitting the federal Parliament to amend the Constitution by legislation, specific provision was made to ensure that this power was not capable of implying any right to interfere with those powers assigned to the provinces by the *B.N.A. Act*.

Because the Canadian Constitution was created by the *B.N.A. Act* in the form of an Imperial statute, it followed that in the absence of a provision for amendment within it, its amendment could only be effected by the enactment of an Imperial statute. Over the years many amendments have occurred in this way. The practice has developed, since 1895, to have the formal approach to the Imperial Parliament made by means of a joint address of both Houses of Parliament....

[Justices Martland and Ritchie then set out statements from the 1965 White Paper describing the procedure followed with respect to the 14 important amendments to the *B.N.A. Act* passed by the Imperial Parliament since 1867.]

In no instance has an amendment to the *B.N.A. Act* been enacted which directly affected federal–provincial relationships in the sense of changing provincial legislative powers, in the absence of federal consultation with and the consent of all the provinces. Notably, this procedure continued to be followed in the four instances which occurred after the enactment of the *Statute of Westminster, 1931.*

This history of amendments reveals the operation of constitutional constraints. While the choice of the resolution procedure is itself a matter of internal parliamentary responsibility, the making of the addresses to the Sovereign falls into two areas. Resolutions concerning the federal juristic unit and federal powers were made without reference to any but the members of the federal Houses. Resolutions abridging provincial authority have never been passed without the concurrence of the provinces. In other words, the normal constitutional

principles recognizing the inviolability of separate and exclusive legislative powers were carried into and considered an integral part of the operation of the resolution procedure.

The history of constitutional amendments also parallels the development of Canadian sovereignty. The *B.N.A. Act* did not have among its purposes the severance of Canada from the British Commonwealth. However, the vital role of Canadian consent as an expression of Canadian sovereignty is revealed in the fact that no constitutional amendment has been passed without that consent....

The *Statute of Westminster, 1931* was passed on December 11, 1931. Earlier that year, Mr. Louis St. Laurent, then President of the Canadian Bar Association, and a distinguished constitutional lawyer, referred in his presidential address, reported in (1931), 9 *Can. Bar Rev.* 525, to the resolutions of the House of Commons and the Senate requesting the enactment of the Statute. This speech was not delivered in a political context. At that time he did not hold any political office. It was some years later that he became a Member of the House of Commons and a Minister of the Crown. The following passage from that speech is relevant to the issue now before the Court:

> Now, it may be that while both the Dominion and the Provinces remained subject to the legislative jurisdiction of His Majesty's Parliament of the United Kingdom, that Parliament had, in theory, full power to vary the distribution of legislative jurisdiction between them. But after the declaration of 1926 that both the United Kingdom and the Dominions are autonomous communities equal in status, in no way subordinate one to another in any aspect of their domestic or external affairs it would hardly seem probable that the Parliament of the United Kingdom would undertake to legislate for the territory of any one of those Dominions, unless it be expressly declared in the Act that that Dominion had requested and consented to the enactment of the proposed legislation. And if the United Kingdom and the Dominions are equal in status and in no way subordinate one to another in any aspect of their domestic or external affairs, does not the provision of section 92 of the Act of 1867, that in each province the legislature may exclusively make laws in relation to the amendment from time to time of its constitution, except as regards the office of Lieutenant-Governor, seem to indicate that the Houses of the Dominion Parliament would have no jurisdiction to request or to consent to enactments that might extend or abridge Provincial legislative autonomy?

The *Statute of Westminster* gave statutory recognition to the independent sovereign status of Canada as a nation. However, while Canada, as a nation, was recognized as being sovereign, the government of the nation remained federal in character and the federal Parliament did not acquire sole control of the exercise of that sovereignty. Section 2 of the *Statute of Westminster, 1931,* standing alone, could be construed as giving that control to the federal Parliament, but the enactment of s. 7, at the instance of the provinces, was intended to preclude that exercise of power by the federal Parliament. Section 7(3) in particular gave explicit recognition to the continuation of the division of powers created by the *B.N.A. Act.* The powers conferred on the Parliament of Canada by the *Statute of Westminster, 1931* were restricted to the enactment of laws in relation to matters within the competence of the Parliament of Canada.

The effect of s. 7(1) was to preserve the Imperial Parliament as the legal instrument for enacting amendments to the *B.N.A. Acts, 1867-1930.* This clearly had no effect on the existing procedure which had been used to obtain the amendment of the *B.N.A. Act.* The resolution procedure, which, after 1895, had produced all the constitutional amendments until 1931, has been followed in respect of all the constitutional amendments passed since 1931.

The Attorney General of Canada presented a deceptively simple argument in support of the legality of the Resolution at issue in these appeals. It was argued that the Resolution is not a law, and therefore not a proper subject for judicial consideration and, further, that the two Houses can legally pass any resolution which they desire. The Imperial Parliament has full legal authority to amend the *B.N.A. Act* by enacting a statute, and its power to do so cannot be questioned. If, therefore, the Imperial Parliament enacts such a statute in response to a resolution of the Senate and the House of Commons, there can be no question of illegality.

However, it was also submitted that while the Imperial Parliament has full legal authority to amend the *B.N.A. Act,* there exists a "firm and unbending" convention that such an amendment will only be enacted in response to a resolution of the two Houses requesting it, and, further, that it will enact any amendment to the *B.N.A. Act* which is so requested.

In the result, if this process is examined from the point of view of substance rather than of form, what is being asserted is the existence of a power in the Senate and the House of Commons to cause any amendment to the *B.N.A. Act* which they desire to be enacted, even though that amendment subtracts, without provincial consent, from the legislative powers of the provinces granted to them by the *B.N.A. Act.* . . .

The power of the Senate and the House of Commons to pass resolutions of any kind, and to use such resolutions for any purpose, was stated by the Attorney General to have been recognized in s. 18 of the *B.N.A. Act* and s. 4 of the *Senate and House of Commons Act,* R.S.C. 1970, c. S-8. Section 18 of the *B.N.A. Act* provides:

18. The privileges, immunities, and powers to be held, enjoyed, and exercised by the Senate and by the House of Commons, and by the members thereof respectively, shall be such as are from time to time defined by Act of the Parliament of Canada, but so that any Act of the Parliament of Canada defining such privileges, immunities, and powers shall not confer any privileges, immunities, or powers exceeding those at the passing of such Act held, enjoyed, and exercised by the Commons House of Parliament of the United Kingdom of Great Britain and Ireland, and by the members thereof.

. . . Section 18 did not, in itself, create or recognize the existence of the privileges, immunities and powers of the Senate and the House of Commons. It provided that their privileges, immunities and powers should be such as are, from time to time, defined by act of the Parliament of Canada, subject to the limitation that Parliament could not by statute, give to the Senate or the House of Commons any privileges, immunities or powers which exceeded those enjoyed by the House of Commons of the United Kingdom Parliament. Parliament could not grant legislative powers to its two Houses. Furthermore, because, unlike the Parliament of the United Kingdom, Parliament's power to legislate was limited in extent, it could not grant to the Senate and the House of Commons powers which it did not itself possess.

In the exercise of the power granted to it by s. 18 of the *B.N.A. Act,* the Parliament of Canada, in 1868, passed *An Act to define the privileges, immunities and powers of the Senate and House of Commons,* 1868 (Can.), c. 23. . . .

The essential provisions . . . now appear in ss. 4 and 5 of the *Senate and House of Commons Act, supra,* as follows:

4. The Senate and the House of Commons respectively, and the members thereof respectively, hold, enjoy and exercise,

(a) such and the like privileges, immunities and powers as, at the time of the passing of the *British North America Act, 1867,* were held, enjoyed and exercised by the Commons House of Parliament of the United Kingdom, and by the members thereof, so far as the same are consistent with and not repugnant to that *Act;* and

(b) such privileges, immunities and powers as are from time to time defined by Act of the Parliament of Canada, not exceeding those at the time of the passing of such Act held, enjoyed and exercised by the Commons House of Parliament of the United Kingdom and by the members thereof respectively.

5. Such privileges, immunities and powers are part of the general and public law of Canada, and it is not necessary to plead the same, but the same shall, in all courts in Canada, and by and before all judges, be taken notice of judicially.

Parliament did not confer upon the Senate and the House of Commons all of the privileges, immunities and powers held, enjoyed and exercised by the House of Commons of the United Kingdom, but only conferred them "so far as the same are consistent with and not repugnant to that *Act*," i.e. the *B.N.A. Act, 1867*. It thus recognized that some powers enjoyed by the House of Commons of the United Kingdom might not be consistent with the provisions of the *B.N.A. Act*.

In our opinion this very important proviso took into account the fact that, whereas the House of Commons in the United Kingdom was one of the Houses in the Parliament of a unitary state, the Canadian Senate and House of Commons were Houses in a Parliament in a federal state, whose powers were not all embracing, but were specifically limited by the *Act* which created it.

In order to pass the Resolution now under consideration the Senate and the House of Commons must purport to exercise a power. The source of that power must be found in s. 4(*a*) of the *Senate and House of Commons Act*, since there has been no legislation enacted to date, other than s. 4(*a*) which actually defines the privileges, immunities and powers upon the two Houses of Parliament. The Resolution now before us was passed for the purpose of obtaining an amendment to the *B.N.A. Act*, the admitted effect of which is to curtail provincial legislative powers under s. 92 of the *B.N.A. Act*. In our opinion that power is not consistent with the *B.N.A. Act* but is repugnant to it. It is a power which is out of harmony with the very basis of the *B.N.A. Act*. Therefore paragraph (*a*) of s. 4, because of the limitations which it contains, does not confer that power. The Senate and the House of Commons are purporting to exercise a power which they do not possess.

The effect of the position taken by the Attorney General of Canada is that the two Houses of Parliament have unfettered control of a triggering mechanism by means of which they can cause the *B.N.A. Act* to be amended in any way they desire. It was frankly conceded in argument that there were no limits of any kind upon the type of amendment that could be made in this fashion. In our opinion, this argument in essence maintains that the provinces have since, at the latest 1931, owed their continued existence not to their constitutional powers expressed in the *B.N.A. Act*, but to the federal Parliament's sufferance. While the federal Parliament was throughout this period incompetent to legislate in respect of matters assigned to the provinces by s. 92, its two Houses could at any time have done so by means of a resolution to the Imperial Parliament, procuring an amendment to the *B.N.A. Act*.

The Attorney General of Canada, in substance, is asserting the existence of a power in the two Houses of Parliament to obtain amendments to the *B.N.A. Act* which could disturb and even destroy the federal system of constitutional government in Canada. We are not aware of any possible legal source for such a power. . . .

. . . In our opinion, the two Houses lack legal authority, of their own motion, to obtain constitutional amendments which would strike at the very basis of the Canadian federal system, *i.e.* the complete division of legislative powers between the Parliament of Canada and the provincial legislatures. It is the duty of this Court to consider this assertion of rights with a view to the preservation of the Constitution.

This Court, since its inception, has been active in reviewing the constitutionality of both federal and provincial legislation. This role has generally been concerned with the interpretation of the express terms of the *B.N.A. Act*. However, on occasions, this Court has had to consider issues for which the *B.N.A. Act* offered no answer. In each case, this Court has denied the assertion of any power which would offend against the basic principles of the Constitution.

In *Amax Potash Ltd. et al. v. Government of Saskatchewan*, [1977] 2 S.C.R. 576, the plaintiff sued for a declaration that certain sections of *The Mineral Taxation Act*, R.S.S. 1965, c. 64, and certain regulations made pursuant to that *Act*, were *ultra vires* and sought the recovery of moneys paid by way of tax under the regulations. The Government of Saskatchewan disputed the contention that these provisions were *ultra vires*, but also contended that no cause of action was disclosed because s. 5(7) of *The Proceedings against the Crown Act*, R.S.S. 1965, c. 87, was a bar to the recovery of moneys paid to the Crown. . . .

In the course of his reasons, Dickson J., who delivered the judgment of the Court, said at p. 590:

> A state, it is said, is sovereign and it is not for the Courts to pass upon the policy or wisdom of legislative will. As a broad statement of principle that is undoubtedly correct, but the general principle must yield to the requisites of the constitution in a federal state. By it the bounds of sovereignty are defined and supremacy circumscribed. . . .

In *British Columbia Power Corp. v. British Columbia Electric Co. et al.*, [1962] S.C.R. 642 this Court had to decide whether a receivership order could be made to preserve assets pending a decision as to the constitutionality of certain legislation in British Columbia which litigation would determine whether the Crown had title to the common shares of British Columbia Electric Company Limited which the legislation gave to the Crown.

It was contended that a receivership order could not be made by virtue of the Crown's prerogative of immunity. Chief Justice Kerwin, who delivered the judgment of the Court, said at pp. 644-45:

In a federal system, where legislative authority is divided, as are also the prerogatives of the Crown, as between the Dominion and the Provinces, it is my view that it is not open to the Crown, either in right of Canada or of a Province, to claim a Crown immunity based upon an interest in certain property, where its very interest in that property depends completely and solely on the validity of the legislation which it has itself passed, if there is a reasonable doubt as to whether such legislation is constitutionally valid. To permit it to do so would be to enable it, by the assertion of rights claimed under legislation which is beyond its powers, to achieve the same results as if the legislation were valid. In a federal system it appears to me that, in such circumstances, the Court has the same jurisdiction to preserve assets whose title is dependant on the validity of the legislation as it has to determine the validity of the legislation itself.

In *Attorney General of Nova Scotia v. Attorney General of Canada*, [1951] S.C.R. 31 the Court had to consider the validity of legislation which contemplated a delegation of legislative powers by the Provincial Legislature to the Parliament of Canada, and by Parliament to the Provincial Legislature. Chief Justice Rinfret said, at p. 34:

> The constitution of Canada does not belong either to Parliament, or to the Legislatures; it belongs to the country and it is there that the citizens of the country will find the protection of the rights to which they are entitled. It is part of that protection that Parliament can legislate only on the subject matters referred to it by section 91 and that each Province can legislate exclusively on the subject matters referred to it by section 92....

In *Reference re Alberta Statutes*, [1938] S.C.R. 100 the Court considered, *inter alia*, the constitutional validity of *The Accurate News and Information Act* which imposed certain duties of publication upon newspapers published in Alberta. Chief Justice Duff (Davis J. concurring) referred to the right of public discussion and the authority of Parliament to protect that right and said at pp. 133-34:

> That authority rests upon the principle that the powers requisite for the protection of the constitution itself arise by necessary implication from *The British North America Act* as a whole (*Fort Frances Pulp & Power Co. Ltd. v. Manitoba Free Press Co. Ltd.*, [1923] A.C. 695); and since the subject-matter in relation to which the power is exercised is not exclusively a provincial matter, it is necessarily vested in Parliament.

It may be noted that the above instances of judicially developed legal principles and doctrines share several char-

acteristics. *First*, none is to be found in express provisions of the *British North America Acts* or other constitutional enactments. *Second*, all have been perceived to represent constitutional requirements that are derived from the federal character of Canada's Constitution. *Third*, they have been accorded full legal force in the sense of being employed to strike down legislative enactments. *Fourth*, each was judicially developed in response to a particular legislative initiative in respect of which it might have been observed, as it was by Dickson J. in the *Amax (supra)* case at p. 591, that: "There are no Canadian constitutional law precedents addressed directly to the present issue...."

In our opinion the accession of Canada to sovereign international status did not enable the federal Parliament, whose legislative authority is limited to the matters defined in s. 91 of the *B.N.A. Act*, unilaterally by means of a resolution of its two Houses, to effect an amendment to the *B.N.A. Act* which would offend against the basic principle of the division of powers created by that *Act*. The assertion of such a right, which has never before been attempted, is not only contrary to the federal system created by the *B.N.A. Act*, but also runs counter to the objective sought to be achieved by s. 7 of the *Statute of Westminster*.

The federal position in these appeals can be summarized in these terms. While the federal Parliament lacks legal authority to achieve the objectives set out in the Resolution by the enactment of its own legislation, that limitation upon its authority can be evaded by having the legislation enacted by the Imperial Parliament at the behest of a resolution of the two Houses of the federal Parliament. This is an attempt by the federal Parliament to accomplish indirectly that which it is legally precluded from doing directly by perverting the recognized resolution method of obtaining constitutional amendments by the Imperial Parliament for an improper purpose. In our opinion, since it is beyond the power of the federal Parliament to enact such an amendment, it is equally beyond the power of its two Houses to effect such an amendment through the agency of the Imperial Parliament.

Conclusions

... The fact that the status of Canada became recognized as a sovereign state did not alter its federal nature. It is a sovereign state, but its government is federal in character with a clear division of legislative powers. The Resolution at issue in these appeals could only be an effective expression of Canadian sovereignty if it had the support of both levels of government.

The two Houses of the Canadian Parliament claim the power unilaterally to effect an amendment to the *B.N.A. Act* which they desire, including the curtailment of provincial legislative powers. This strikes at the basis of the whole federal system. It asserts a right by one part of the Canadian governmental system to curtail, without agreement, the powers of the other part.

There is no statutory basis for the exercise of such a power. On the contrary, the powers of the Senate and the House of Commons, given to them by s. 4(*a*) of the *Senate and House of Commons Act*, excluded the power to do anything inconsistent with the *B.N.A. Act*. The exercise of such a power has no support in constitutional convention. The constitutional convention is entirely to the contrary. We see no other basis for the recognition of the existence of such a power. This being so, it is the proper function of this Court, in its role of protecting and preserving the Canadian constitution, to declare that no such power exists. We are, therefore, of the opinion that the Canadian Constitution does not empower the Senate and the House of Commons to cause the Canadian Constitution to be amended in respect of provincial legislative powers without the consent of the provinces.

Question B in the Quebec Reference raises the issue as to the power of the Senate and the House of Commons of Canada to cause the Canadian Constitution to be amended "without the consent of the provinces and in spite of the objection of several of them." The Attorney General of Saskatchewan when dealing with Question 3 in the Manitoba and Newfoundland References submitted that it was not necessary in these proceedings for the Court to pronounce on the necessity for the unanimous consent of all the provinces to the constitutional amendments proposed in the Resolution. It was sufficient, in order to answer the question, to note the opposition of eight of the provinces which contained a majority of the population of Canada.

We would answer Question B in the negative. We would answer Question 3 of the Manitoba and Newfoundland References in the affirmative without deciding, at this time, whether the agreement referred to in that question must be unanimous.

B. THE QUESTION OF CONVENTION

MARTLAND, RITCHIE, DICKSON, BEETZ, CHOUINARD AND LAMER JJ.:

The second question in the Manitoba Reference and Newfoundland Reference is the same:

> 2. Is it a constitutional convention that the House of Commons and Senate of Canada will not request Her Majesty the Queen to lay before the Parliament of the United Kingdom of Great Britain and Northern Ireland a measure to amend the Constitution of Canada affecting federal–provincial relationships or the powers, rights or privileges granted or secured by the Constitution of Canada to the provinces, their legislatures or governments without first obtaining the agreement of the provinces?

As for Question B in the Quebec Reference, it reads in part as follows:

> [TRANSLATION]
> B. Does the Canadian Constitution empower ... by ... convention ... the Senate and the House of Commons of Canada to cause the Canadian Constitution to be amended without the consent of the provinces and in spite of the objection of several of them, in such a manner as to affect:
>> (i) the legislative competence of the provincial legislatures in virtue of the Canadian Constitution?
>> (ii) the status or role of the provincial legislatures or governments within the Canadian Federation?

In these questions, the phrases "Constitution of Canada" and "Canadian Constitution" do not refer to matters of interest only to the federal government or federal juristic unit. They are clearly meant in a broader sense and embrace the global system of rules and principles which govern the exercise of constitutional authority in the whole and in every part of the Canadian state. They will be used in the same broad sense in these reasons.

The meaning of the second question in the Manitoba and Newfoundland References calls for further observations.

As will be seen later, counsel for several provinces strenuously argued that the convention exists and requires the agreement of all the provinces. However, we did not understand any of them to have taken the position that the second question in the Manitoba and Newfoundland References should be dealt with and answered as if the last part of the question read

> ... without obtaining the agreement of all the provinces?

Be that as it may, the question should not in our view be so read.

It would have been easy to insert the word "all" into the question had it been intended to narrow its meaning. But we do not think it was so intended. The issue raised by the question is essentially whether there is a constitutional convention that the House of Commons and Senate of Canada will not proceed alone. The thrust of the question is accordingly on whether or not there is a conventional requirement for provincial agreement, not on whether the agreement should be unanimous assuming that it is required. Furthermore, this manner of reading the question is more in keeping with the wording of Question B in the Quebec Reference which refers to something less than unanimity when it says:

> ... without the consent of the provinces and in spite of the objection of several of them ...

I The Nature of Constitutional Conventions

A substantial part of the rules of the Canadian constitution are written. They are contained not in a single document called a constitution but in a great variety of statutes some of which have been enacted by the Parliament at Westminster, such as the *British North America Act, 1867,* (the *B.N.A. Act*) or by the Parliament of Canada, such as *The Alberta Act, The Saskatchewan Act,* the *Senate and House of Commons Act,* or by the provincial legislatures, such as the provincial electoral acts. They are also to be found in orders in council like the Imperial Order in Council of May 16, 1871 admitting British Columbia into the Union, and the Imperial Order in Council of June 26, 1873, admitting Prince Edward Island into the Union.

Another part of the Constitution of Canada consists of the rules of the common law. These are rules which the courts have developed over the centuries in the discharge of their judicial duties. An important portion of these rules concerns the prerogative of the Crown. Sections 9 and 15 of the *B.N.A. Act* provide:

> 9. The Executive Government and Authority of and over Canada is hereby declared to continue and be vested in the Queen.
> 15. The Commander-in-Chief of the Land and Naval Militia, and of all Naval and Military Forces, of and in Canada, is hereby declared to continue and be vested in the Queen.

But the *Act* does not otherwise say very much with respect to the elements of "Executive Government and Authority" and one must look at the common law to find out what they are, apart from authority delegated to the executive by statute.

The common law provides that the authority of the Crown includes for instance the prerogative of mercy or clemency and the power to incorporate by charter. . . .

Those parts of the Constitution of Canada which are composed of statutory rules and common law rules are generically referred to as the law of the constitution. In cases of doubt or dispute, it is the function of the courts to declare what the law is and since the law is sometimes breached, it is generally the function of the courts to ascertain whether it has in fact been breached in specific instances and, if so, to apply such sanctions as are contemplated by the law, whether they be punitive sanctions or civil sanctions such as a declaration of nullity. Thus, when a federal or a provincial statute is found by the courts to be in excess of the legislative competence of the legislature which has enacted it, it is declared null and void and the courts refuse to give effect to it. In this sense it can be said that the law of the constitution is administered or enforced by the courts.

But many Canadians would perhaps be surprised to learn that important parts of the constitution of Canada, with which they are the most familiar because they are directly involved when they exercise their right to vote at federal and provincial elections, are nowhere to be found in the law of the constitution. For instance it is a fundamental requirement of the constitution that if the opposition obtains the majority at the polls, the government must tender its resignation forthwith. But fundamental as it is, this requirement of the constitution does not form part of the law of the constitution.

It is also a constitutional requirement that the person who is appointed prime minister or premier by the Crown and who is the effective head of the government should have the support of the elected branch of the legislature; in practice this means in most cases the leader of the political party which has won a majority of seats at a general election. Other ministers are appointed by the Crown on the advice of the prime minister or premier when he forms or reshuffles his cabinet. Ministers must continuously have the confidence of the elected branch of the legislature, individually and collectively. Should they lose it, they must either resign or ask the Crown for a dissolution of the legislature and the holding of a general election. Most of the powers of the Crown under the prerogative are exercised only upon the advice of the prime minister of the cabinet which means that they are effectively exercised by the latter, together with the innumerable statutory powers delegated to the Crown in council.

Yet none of these essential rules of the constitution can be said to be a law of the constitution. It was apparently Dicey who, in the first edition of his *Law of the Constitution,* in 1885, called them the "conventions of the constitution," an expression which quickly became current. What Dicey described under these terms are the principles and rules of responsible government, several of which are stated above and which regulate the relations between the Crown, the prime minister, the cabinet and the two Houses of Parliament. These rules developed in Great Britain by way of custom and precedent during the nineteenth century and were exported to such British colonies as were granted self-government.

Dicey first gave the impression that constitutional conventions are a peculiarly British and modern phenomenon. But he recognized in later editions that different conventions are found in other constitutions. As Sir William Holdsworth wrote:

> In fact conventions must grow up at all times and in all places where the powers of government are vested in different persons or bodies—where in other words there is a mixed constitution. "The constituent parts of a state," said Burke, [French Revolution, 28.] "are obliged to hold their public faith with each other, and with all those who derive any serious interest under their engagements, as much as the whole state is bound to keep its faith with

separate communities." Necessarily conventional rules spring up to regulate the working of the various parts of the constitution, their relations to one another, and to the subject.

Within the British Empire, powers of government were vested in different bodies which provided a fertile ground for the growth of new constitutional conventions unknown to Dicey and from which self-governing colonies acquired equal and independent status within the Commonwealth. Many of these culminated in the *Statute of Westminster, 1931.*

A federal constitution provides for the distribution of powers between various legislatures and governments and may also constitute a fertile ground for the growth of constitutional conventions between those legislatures and governments. It is conceivable for instance that usage and practice might give birth to conventions in Canada relating to the holding of federal–provincial conferences, the appointment of lieutenant governors, the reservation and disallowance of provincial legislation. . . .

The main purpose of constitutional conventions is to ensure that the legal framework of the constitution will be operated in accordance with the prevailing constitutional values or principles of the period. For example, the constitutional value which is the pivot of the conventions stated above and relating to responsible government is the democratic principle: the powers of the state must be exercised in accordance with the wishes of the electorate; and the constitutional value or principle which anchors the conventions regulating the relationship between the members of the Commonwealth is the independence of the former British colonies.

Being based on custom and precedent, constitutional conventions are usually unwritten rules. Some of them, however, may be reduced to writing and expressed in the proceedings and documents of imperial conferences, or in the preamble of statutes such as the *Statute of Westminster, 1931,* or in the proceedings and documents of federal–provincial conferences. They are often referred to and recognized in statements made by members of governments.

The conventional rules of the constitution present one striking peculiarity. In contradistinction to the laws of the constitution, they are not enforced by the courts. One reason for this situation is that, unlike common law rules, conventions are not judge-made rules. They are not based on judicial precedents but on precedents established by the institutions of government themselves. Nor are they in the nature of statutory commands which it is the function and duty of the courts to obey and enforce. Furthermore, to enforce them would mean to administer some formal sanction when they are breached. But the legal system from which they are distinct does not contemplate formal sanctions for their breach.

Perhaps the main reason why conventional rules cannot be enforced by the courts is that they are generally in conflict with the legal rules which they postulate and the courts are bound to enforce the legal rules. The conflict is not of a type which would entail the commission of any illegality. It results from the fact that legal rules create wide powers, discretions and rights which conventions prescribe should be exercised only in a certain limited manner, if at all.

Some examples will illustrate this point.

As a matter of law, the Queen, or the Governor General or the Lieutenant Governor could refuse assent to every bill passed by both Houses of Parliament or by a Legislative Assembly as the case may be. But by convention they cannot of their own motion refuse to assent to any such bill on any ground, for instance because they disapprove of the policy of the bill. We have here a conflict between a legal rule which creates a complete discretion and a conventional rule which completely neutralizes it. But conventions, like laws, are sometimes violated. And if this particular convention were violated and assent were improperly withheld, the courts would be bound to enforce the law, not the convention. They would refuse to recognize the validity of a vetoed bill. This is what happened in *Gallant v. The King* ([1949] 2 D.L.R. 425) . . . a case in keeping with the classic case of *Stockdale v. Hansard* ((1839), 9 Ad. and E. 1) where the English Court of Queen's Bench held that only the Queen and both Houses of Parliament could make or unmake laws. The Lieutenant Governor who had withheld assent in *Gallant* apparently did so towards the end of his term in office. Had it been otherwise, it is not inconceivable that his witholding of assent might have produced a political crisis leading to his removal from office which shows that if the remedy for a breach of a convention does not lie with the courts, still the breach is not necessarily without a remedy. The remedy lies with some other institutions of government; furthermore it is not a formal remedy and it may be administered with less certainty or regularity than it would be by a court.

Another example of the conflict between law and convention is provided by a fundamental convention already stated above: if after a general election where the opposition obtained the majority at the polls the government refused to resign and clung to office, it would thereby commit a fundamental breach of convention, one so serious indeed that it could be regarded as tantamount to a *coup d'état.* The remedy in this case would lie with the Governor General or the Lieutenant Governor as the case might be who would be justified in dismissing the ministry and in calling on the opposition to form the government. But should the Crown be slow in taking this course, there is nothing the courts could do about it except at the risk of creating a state of legal discontinuity, that is, a form of revolution. An order or a regulation passed by a minister under statutory authority and otherwise valid could not be invalidated on the ground that, by convention, the minister ought no longer be a minister. A writ of *quo warranto* aimed at ministers, assuming that *quo warranto* lies against a minister of the Crown, which is very doubtful, would be of no avail to remove them from office. Required to say by what warrant they occupy their ministerial office, they would answer that they occupy it by the pleasure of the Crown under a commission issued by the Crown and this answer would be a complete one at law, for at law the government is in office by the pleasure of the Crown although by convention it is there by the will of the people.

This conflict between convention and law which prevents the courts from enforcing conventions also prevents conventions from crystallizing into laws, unless it be by statutory adoption.

It is because the sanctions of convention rest with institutions of government other than courts, such as the Governor General or the Lieutenant Governor, or the Houses of Parliament, or with public opinion and ultimately, with the electorate, that it is generally said that they are political.

We respectfully adopt the definition of a convention given by the learned Chief Justice of Manitoba, Freedman C.J.M., in the Manitoba Reference, *supra*, at pp. 13-14:

> What is a constitutional convention? There is a fairly lengthy literature on the subject. Although there may be shades of difference among the constitutional lawyers, political scientists, and Judges who have contributed to that literature, the essential features of a convention may be set forth with some degree of confidence. Thus there is general agreement that a convention occupies a position somewhere in between a usage or custom on the one hand and a constitutional law on the other. There is general agreement that if one sought to fix that position with greater precision he would place convention nearer to law than to usage or custom. There is also general agreement that "a convention is a rule which is regarded as obligatory by the officials to whom it applies." Hogg, *Constitutional Law of Canada* (1977), p. 9. There is, if not general agreement, at least weighty authority, that the sanction for breach of a convention will be political rather than legal.

It should be borne in mind however that, while they are not laws, some conventions may be more important than some laws. Their importance depends on that of the value or principle which they are meant to safeguard. Also they form an integral part of the constitution and of the constitutional system. They come within the meaning of the word "Constitution" in the preamble of the *British North America Act, 1867*:

> Whereas the Provinces of Canada, Nova Scotia, and New Brunswick have expressed their Desire to be federally united ... with a Constitution similar in Principle to that of the United Kingdom:

That is why it is perfectly appropriate to say that to violate a convention is to do something which is unconstitutional although it entails no direct legal consequence. But the words "constitutional" and "unconstitutional" may also be used in a strict legal sense, for instance with respect to a statute which is found *ultra vires* or unconstitutional. The foregoing may perhaps be summarized in an equation: constitutional conventions plus constitutional law equal the total constitution of the country.

II   Whether the Questions Should Be Answered

It was submitted by counsel for Canada and for Ontario that the second question in the Manitoba and Newfoundland References and the conventional part of Question B in the Quebec Reference ought not be answered because they do not raise a justiciable issue and are accordingly not appropriate for a court. It was contended that the issue whether a particular convention exists or not is a purely political one. The existence of a definite convention is always unclear and a matter of debate. Furthermore conventions are flexible, somewhat imprecise and unsuitable for judicial determination.

The same submission was made in substance to the three courts below and, in our respectful opinion, rightfully dismissed by all three of them, Hall J.A. dissenting in the Manitoba Court of Appeal.

We agree with what Freedman C.J.M. wrote on this subject in the Manitoba Reference at p. 13:

> In my view, this submission goes too far. Its characterization of Question 2 as "purely political" overstates the case. That there is a political element embodied in the question, arising from the contents of the joint address, may well be the case. But that does not end the matter. If Question 2, even if in part political, possesses a constitutional feature, it would legitimately call for our reply.
>
> In my view, the request for a decision by this Court on whether there is a constitutional convention, in the circumstances described, that the Dominion will not act without the agreement of the Provinces poses a question that is, at least in part, constitutional in character. It therefore calls for an answer, and I propose to answer it.

Question 2 is not confined to an issue of pure legality but it has to do with a fundamental issue of constitutionality and legitimacy. Given the broad statutory basis upon which the Governments of Manitoba, Newfoundland and Quebec are empowered to put questions to their three respective courts of appeal, they are in our view entitled to an answer to a question of this type. . . .

Finally, we are not asked to hold that a convention has in effect repealed a provision of the *B.N.A. Act*, as was the case in the *Reference re Disallowance and Reservation of Provincial Legislation (supra)*. Nor are we asked to enforce a convention. We are asked to recognize it if it exists. Courts have done this very thing many times in England and the Commonwealth to provide aid for and background to constitutional or statutory construction. Several such cases are mentioned in the reasons of the majority of this Court relating to the question whether constitutional conventions are capable of crystallizing into law. There are many others . . . . This Court did the same in the recent case of *Arseneau v. The Queen* ([1979] 2 S.C.R. 136 at p. 149) and in the still unreported judgment rendered on April 6, 1981 after the re-hearing of *Attorney General of Quebec v. Blaikie et al.*

In so recognizing conventional rules, the courts have described them, sometimes commented upon them and given them such precision as is derived from the written form of a judgment. They did not shrink from doing so on account of the political aspects of conventions, nor because of their supposed vagueness, uncertainty or flexibility.

In our view, we should not, in a constitutional reference, decline to accomplish a type of exercise that courts have been doing of their own motion for years.

III Whether the Convention Exists

It was submitted by counsel for Canada, Ontario and New Brunswick that there is no constitutional convention, that the House of Commons and Senate of Canada will not request Her Majesty the Queen to lay before the Parliament at Westminster a measure to amend the Constitution of Canada affecting federal–provincial relationships, etc., without first obtaining the agreement of the provinces.

It was submitted by counsel for Manitoba, Newfoundland, Quebec, Nova Scotia, British Columbia, Prince Edward Island and Alberta that the convention does exist, that it requires the agreement of all the provinces and that the second question in the Manitoba and Newfoundland References should accordingly be answered in the affirmative.

Counsel for Saskatchewan agreed that the question be answered in the affirmative but on a different basis. He submitted that the convention does exist and requires a measure of provincial agreement. Counsel for Saskatchewan further submitted that the Resolution before the Court has not received a sufficient measure of provincial consent.

We wish to indicate at the outset that we find ourselves in agreement with the submissions made on this issue by counsel for Saskatchewan.

1. The Class of Constitutional Amendments Contemplated by the Question

Constitutional amendments fall into three categories: (1) amendments which may be made by a provincial legislature acting alone under s. 92(1) of the *B.N.A. Act*; (2) amendments which may be made by the Parliament of Canada acting alone under s. 91(1) of the *B.N.A. Act*; (3) all other amendments.

The first two categories are irrelevant for the purposes of these References. While the wording of the second and third questions of the Manitoba and Newfoundland References may be broad enough to embrace all amendments in the third category, it is not necessary for us to consider those amendments which affect federal–provincial relationships only indirectly. In a sense, most amendments of the third category are susceptible of affecting federal–provincial relationships to some extent. But we should restrict ourselves to the consideration of amendments which

> . . . directly affect federal–provincial relationships in the sense of changing federal and provincial legislative powers . . . (the *Senate Reference, supra*, at p. 65.)

The reason for this is that the second and third questions of the Manitoba and Newfoundland References must be read in the light of the first question. They must be meant to contemplate the same specific class of constitutional amendments as the ones which are sought in the "Proposed Resolution for a Joint Address to Her Majesty the Queen respecting the Constitution of Canada." More particularly, they must be meant to address the same type of amendments as the *Charter of Rights*, which abridges federal and provincial legislative powers, and the amending formula, which would provide for the amendment of the Constitution including the distribution of legislative powers.

These proposed amendments present one essential characteristic: they directly affect federal–provincial relationships in changing legislative powers and in providing for a formula to effect such change.

Therefore, in essence although not in terms, the issue raised by the second question in the Manitoba and Newfoundland References is whether there is a constitutional convention for agreement of the provinces to amendments which change legislative powers and provide for a method of effecting such change. The same issue is raised by Question B of the Quebec Reference above quoted in part.

2. Requirements for Establishing a Convention

The requirements for establishing a convention bear some resemblance with those which apply to customary law. Precedents and usage are necessary but do not suffice. They must be normative. We adopt the following passage of Sir W. Ivor

Jennings, *The Law and the Constitution* (5th ed., 1959), at p. 136:

> We have to ask ourselves three questions: first, what are the precedents; secondly, did the actors in the precedents believe that they were bound by a rule; and thirdly, is there a reason for the rule? A single precedent with a good reason may be enough to establish the rule. A whole string of precedents without such a reason will be of no avail, unless it is perfectly certain that the persons concerned regarded them as bound by it.

i) The Precedents

An account of the statutes enacted by the Parliament at Westminster to modify the Constitution of Canada is found in a White Paper published in 1965 under the authority of the Honourable Guy Favreau, then Minister of Justice for Canada, under the title of "The Amendment of the Constitution of Canada" (the White Paper). This account is quoted in the *Senate Reference* (*supra*) but we find it necessary to reproduce it here for convenience: ....

Of these twenty-two amendments or groups of amendments, five directly affected federal–provincial relationships in the sense of changing provincial legislative powers: they are the amendment of 1930, the *Statute of Westminster, 1931*, and the amendments of 1940, 1951 and 1964.

Under the agreements confirmed by the 1930 amendment, the western provinces were granted ownership and administrative control of their natural resources so as to place these provinces in the same position vis-à-vis natural resources as the original confederating colonies. The western provinces, however, received these natural resources subject to some limits on their power to make laws relating to hunting and fishing rights of Indians. Furthermore, the agreements did provide a very substantial object for the provincial power to make laws relating to "The Management and Sale of the Public Lands belonging to the Province and of the Timber and Wood thereon" under s. 92(5) of the *B.N.A. Act.* ...

The preamble of the *Act* recites that "each of the said agreements has been duly approved by the Parliament of Canada and by the Legislature of the Province to which it relates." The other provinces lost no power, right or privilege in consequence. In any event, the proposed transfer of natural resources to the western provinces had been discussed at the 1927 Dominion–Provincial Conference and had met with general approval (Paul Gérin-Lajoie, *Constitutional Amendment in Canada* (1950), at pp. 91-92).

All the provinces agreed to the passing of the *Statute of Westminster, 1931*. It changed legislative powers: Parliament and the legislatures were given the authority, within their powers, to repeal any United Kingdom statute that formed part of the law of Canada; Parliament was also given the power to make laws having extraterritorial effect.

The 1940 amendment is of special interest in that it transferred an exclusive legislative power from the provincial legislatures to the Parliament of Canada.

In 1938, the Speech from the Throne stated:

> The cooperation of the provinces has been sought with a view to an amendment of the *British North America Act*, which would empower the parliament of Canada to enact forthwith a national scheme of unemployment insurance. My ministers hope the proposal may meet with early approval, in order that unemployment insurance legislation may be enacted during the present session of parliament.
>
> (Commons Debates, 1938, at p. 2.)

In November 1937, the Government of Canada had communicated with the provinces and asked for their views in principle. A draft amendment was later circulated. By March 1938, five of the nine provinces had approved the draft amendment. Ontario bad agreed, in principle, but Alberta, New Brunswick and Quebec had declined to join in. The proposed amendment was not proceeded with until June 1940 when Prime Minister King announce to the House of Commons that all nine provinces had assented to the proposed amendment.

The 1951 and 1964 amendments changed the legislative powers: areas of exclusive provincial competence became areas of concurrent legislative competence. They were agreed upon by all the provinces.

These five amendments are the only ones which can be viewed as positive precedents whereby federal–provincial relationships were directly affected in the sense of changing legislative powers.

Every one of these five amendments was agreed upon by each province whose legislative authority was affected.

In negative terms, no amendment changing provincial legislative powers has been made since Confederation when agreement of a province whose legislative powers would have been changed was withheld.

There are no exceptions.

Furthermore, in even more telling negative terms, in 1951, an amendment was proposed to give the provinces a limited power of indirect taxation. Ontario and Quebec did not agree and the amendment was not proceeded with (see *Commons Debates*, 1951, at pp. 2682 and 2726-2743).

The Constitutional Conference of 1960 devised a formula for the amendment of the Constitution of Canada. Under this formula, the distribution of legislative powers could have been modified. The great majority of the participants found the formula acceptable but some differences remained and the proposed amendment was not proceeded with.

In 1964, a conference of first ministers unanimously agreed on an amending formula that would have permitted the modification of legislative powers. Quebec subsequently withdrew its agreement and the proposed amendment was not proceeded with (see Senate House of Commons Special Joint Committees on Constitution of Canada, issue No. 5, August 23, 1978, at p. 14, Professor Lederman).

Finally, in 1971, proposed amendments which included an amending formula were agreed upon by the federal government and eight of the ten provincial governments. Quebec disagreed and Saskatchewan which had a new government did not take a position because it was believed the disagreement of Quebec rendered the question academic. The proposed amendments were not proceeded with.

The accumulation of these precedents, positive and negative, concurrent and without exception, does not of itself suffice in establishing the existence of the convention; but it unmistakably points in its direction. Indeed, if the precedents stood alone, it might be argued that unanimity is required. . . .

We do not think it is necessary to deal with classes of constitutional amendments other than those which change legislative powers or provide for a method to effect such change. But we will briefly comment on two amendments about which much has been made to support the argument against the existence of the convention. These are the amendment of 1907 increasing the scale of financial subsidies to the provinces and the amendment of 1949 confirming the Terms of Union between Canada and Newfoundland.

It was contended that British Columbia objected to the 1907 amendment which had been agreed upon by all the other provinces.

Even if it were so, this precedent would at best constitute an argument against the unanimity rule.

But the fact is that British Columbia did agree in principle with the increase of financial subsidies to the provinces. It wanted more and objected to the proposed finality of the increase. The finality aspect was deleted from the amendment by the United Kingdom authorities. Mr. Winston Churchill, Under-Secretary of State for the Colonies made the following comment in the House of Commons:

> In deference to the representations of British Columbia the words "final and unalterable" applying to the revised scale had been omitted from the Bill.
> (Commons Debates, (U.K.), June 13, 1907, at p. 1617.)

In the end, the Premier of British Columbia did not refuse to agree to the Act being passed.

With respect to the 1949 amendment, it was observed by Turgeon J.A. in the Quebec Reference that, without Quebec's consent, this amendment confirmed the Quebec-Labrador boundary as delimited in the report delivered by the Judicial Committee of the Privy Council on March 1, 1927.

The entry of Newfoundland into Confederation was contemplated from the beginning by s. 146 of the *B.N.A. Act.* It was at the request of Quebec in 1904 that the dispute relating to the boundary was ultimately submitted to the Judicial Committee (see Minute of Privy Council (Canada), P.C. 82 of M. April 18, 1904). Quebec participated in the litigation, being represented by counsel appointed and paid by the province, although the province did not intervene separately from Canada. When the 1949 amendment was passed, the Premier of Quebec is reported to have stated at a press conference simply that the province should have been "consulted" or "advised" as a matter of "courtesy." He is not reported as having said that the consent of the province was required. (See Luce Patenaude, *Le Labrador l'heure de la contestation.*) The Premier of Nova Scotia spoke to the same effect. Neither premier made any formal demand or protest.

We fail to see how this precedent can affect the convention.

It was also observed by Turgeon J.A. in the Quebec Reference that the *Charter of Rights* annexed to the proposed Resolution for a Joint Address does not alter the distribution of powers between the Parliament of Canada and the provincial legislatures.

This observation may be meant as an argument to the effect that the five positive precedents mentioned above should be distinguished and ought not to govern the situation before the Court since in those five cases the distribution of legislative powers was altered.

To this argument we would reply that if provincial consent was required in those five cases, it would be *a fortiori* required in the case at bar.

Each of those five constitutional amendments effected a limited change in legislative powers, affecting one head of legislative competence such as unemployment insurance. Whereas, if the proposed *Charter of Rights* became law, every head of provincial (and federal) legislative authority could be affected. Furthermore, the *Charter of Rights* would operate retrospectively as well as prospectively with the result that laws enacted in the future as well as in the past, even before Confederation, would be exposed to attack if inconsistent with the provisions of the *Charter of Rights.* This *Charter* would thus abridge provincial legislative authority on a scale exceeding the effect of any previous constitutional amendment for which provincial consent was sought and obtained.

Finally, it was noted in the course of argument that in the case of four of the five amendments mentioned above where provincial consent effectively had been obtained, the statutes enacted by the Parliament at Westminster did not refer to this consent. This does not alter the fact that consent was obtained.

ii) The Actors Treating the Rule as Binding

In the White Paper, one finds this passage at pp. 10-11:

> Procedures Followed in the Past in Securing
> Amendments to the British North America Act
>
> The procedures for amending a constitution are normally a fundamental part of the laws and conventions by which a country is governed. This is particularly true if the constitution is embodied in a formal document, as is the case in such federal states as Australia, the United States and Switzerland. In these countries, the amending process forms an important part of their constitutional law.
>
> In this respect, Canada has been in a unique constitutional position. Not only did the *British North America Act* not provide for its amendment by Canadian legislative authority, except to the extent outlined at the beginning of this chapter, but it also left Canada without any clearly defined procedure for securing constitutional amendments from the British Parliament. As a result, procedures have varied from time to time, with recurring controversies and doubts over the conditions under which various provisions of the Constitution should be amended.
>
> Certain rules and principles relating to amending procedures have nevertheless developed over the years. They have emerged from the practices and procedures employed in securing various amendments to the *British North America Act* since 1867. Though not constitutionally binding in any strict sense, they have come to be recognized and accepted in practice as part of the amendment process in Canada.
>
> In order to trace and describe the manner in which these rules and principles have developed, the approaches used to secure amendments through the Parliament of the United Kingdom over the past 97 years are described in the following paragraphs. Not all the amendments are included in this review, but only those that have contributed to the development of accepted constitutional rules and principles.

There follows a list of fourteen constitutional amendments thought to "have contributed to the development of accepted constitutional rules and principles." The White Paper then goes on to state these principles, at p. 15:

> The first general principle that emerges in the foregoing resumé is that although an enactment by the United Kingdom is necessary to amend the *British North America Act*, such action is taken only upon formal request from Can-

ada. No Act of the United Kingdom Parliament affecting Canada is therefore passed unless it is requested and consented to by Canada. Conversely, every amendment requested by Canada in the past has been enacted.

> The second general principle is that the sanction of Parliament is required for a request to the British Parliament for an amendment to the *British North America Act*. This principle was established early in the history of Canada's constitutional amendments, and has not been violated since 1895. The procedure invariably is to seek amendments by a joint Address of the Canadian House of Commons and Senate to the Crown.

> The third general principle is that no amendment to Canada's Constitution will be made by the British Parliament merely upon the request of a Canadian province. A number of attempts to secure such amendments have been made, but none has been successful. The first such attempt was made as early as 1868, by a province which was at that time dissatisfied with the terms of Confederation. This was followed by other attempts in 1869, 1874 and 1887. The British Government refused in all cases to act on provincial government representations on the grounds that it should not intervene in the affairs of Canada except at the request of the federal government representing all of Canada.

> The fourth general principle is that the Canadian Parliament will not request an amendment directly affecting federal–provincial relationships without prior consultation and agreement with the provinces. This principle did not emerge as early as others but since 1907, and particularly since 1930, has gained increasing recognition and acceptance. The nature and the degree of provincial participation in the amending process, however, have not lent themselves to easy definition.

The text which precedes the four general principles makes it clear that it deals with conventions. It refers to the laws and conventions by which a country is governed and to constitutional rules which are not binding in any strict sense (that is in a legal sense) but which have come to be recognized and accepted in practice as part of the amendment process in Canada. The first three general principles are statements of well-known constitutional conventions governing the relationships between Canada and the United Kingdom with respect to constitutional amendments.

In our view, the fourth general principle equally and unmistakably states and recognizes as a rule of the Canadian constitution the convention referred to in the second question of the Manitoba and Newfoundland References as well as in Question B of the Quebec Reference, namely that there is a requirement for provincial agreement to amendments which change provincial legislative powers.

This statement is not a casual utterance. It is contained in a carefully drafted document which had been circulated to all the provinces prior to its publication and had been found satisfactory by all of them (see *Commons Debates*, 1965, at p. 11574). . . . It was published as a white paper, that is as an official statement of government policy, under the authority of the federal Minister of Justice as member of a government responsible to Parliament, neither House of which, so far as we know, has taken issue with it. This statement is a recognition by all the actors in the precedents that the requirement of provincial agreement is a constitutional rule.

In the Manitoba Reference, Freedman C.J.M. took the view that the third sentence in the fourth general principle stated in the White Paper contradicted, and therefore negated, the first sentence.

With the greatest respect, this interpretation is erroneous. The first sentence is concerned with the existence of the convention, and the third sentence, not with its existence, but with the measure of provincial agreement which is necessary with respect to this class of constitutional amendment. It seems clear that while the precedents taken alone point at unanimity, the unanimity principle cannot be said to have been accepted by all the actors in the precedents.

This distinction is illustrated by statements made by Prime Minister King in the House of Commons in 1938 and 1940 with respect to the unemployment insurance amendment.

In 1938, some provinces had not yet assented to the unemployment insurance amendment and one finds the following exchange in the Commons Debates:

> Right Hon. R.B. BENNETT (Leader of the Opposition): Perhaps the Prime Minister would not object to a supplementary question: Does he conceive it necessary or desirable that all the provinces should agree before action is taken?
>
> Mr. MACKENZIE KING: I do not think this is the moment to answer that question. We had better wait and see what replies we get in the first instance.
> (Commons Debates, 1938, p. 1747)

In 1940, Mr. J.T. Thorson, not then a member of the government, took issue with the contention that it was necessary to obtain the consent of the provinces before an application is made to amend the *B.N.A. Act.* Mr. Lapointe replied:

> May I tell my hon. friend that neither the Prime Minister nor I have said that it is necessary, but it may be desirable.
> (Commons Debates, 1940, at p. 1122.)

But what the Prime Minister had said in fact was this:

> We have avoided anything in the nature of coercion of any of the provinces. Moreover we have avoided the raising of a very critical constitutional question, namely, whether or not in amending the *British North America Act* it is absolutely necessary to secure the consent of all the provinces, or whether the consent of a certain number of provinces would of itself be sufficient. That question may come up but not in reference to unemployment insurance at some time later on.
> (Commons Debates, 1940, at p. 1117.)

This statement expressed some uncertainty as to whether unanimity is a necessity, but none as to whether substantial provincial support is required.

As for Mr. Lapointe's reply, it is non-committal and must be qualified by several other statements he made indicating the necessity of provincial consent. . . .

Most declarations made by statesmen favour the conventional requirement of provincial consent. We will quote only two such declarations.

In discussing the 1943 amendment, Mr. St. Laurent argued that the amendment did not alter the allocation of federal and provincial powers. He said:

> Hon. L.S. ST. LAURENT (Minister of Justice): . . . I would readily concede to hon. members that if there were to be any suggested amendment to change the allocation of legislative or administrative jurisdiction as between the provinces, on the one hand, and the federal parliament, on the other, it could not properly be done without the consent of the organism that was set up by the constitution to have powers that would assumedly be taken from that organism. . . .
>
> I submit that it would have been quite improper to take away from the provinces without their consent anything that they had by the constitution.
> (Commons Debates, 1943, at p. 4366.)

The statement is addressed at constitutional propriety which is the terminology ordinarily used for conventions.

In 1960, it was suggested to Prime Minister Diefenbaker that his proposed *Canadian Bill of Rights* be entrenched in the Constitution and made binding on the provinces as would be the *Charter of Rights* annexed to the proposed Resolution for a Joint Address. Here is how he dealt with this suggestion:

> They say, if you want to make this effective it has to cover the provinces too. Any one advocating that must realize the fact that there is no chance of securing the consent of all the provinces. . . .
>
> As far as constitutional amendment is concerned, it is impossible of attainment at this time.
>
> Mr. Winch: Why?
>
> Mr. Diefenbaker: Simply because of the fact that the consent of the provinces to any interference with property and civil rights cannot be secured. . . .

I also want to add that if at any time the provinces are prepared to give their consent to a constitutional amendment embodying a bill of rights comprising these freedoms, there will be immediate co-operation from this government. We will forthwith introduce a constitutional amendment covering not only the federal, but the provincial jurisdictions when and if there is consent by the provinces everywhere in this country.

(Commons Debates, 1960, at pp. 5648-49.)

Prime Minister Diefenbaker was clearly of the view that the *Canadian Bill of Rights* could not be entrenched in the Constitution and made to apply to the provinces without the consent of all of them. We have also indicated that while the precedents point at unanimity, it does not appear that all the actors in the precedents have accepted the unanimity rule as a binding one.

In 1965, the White Paper had stated that

[t]he nature and the degree of provincial participation in the amending process . . . have not lent themselves to easy definition.

Nothing has occurred since then which would permit us to conclude in a more precise manner.

Nor can it be said that this lack of precision is such as to prevent the principle from acquiring the constitutional status of a conventional rule. If a consensus had emerged on the measure of provincial agreement, an amending formula would quickly have been enacted and we would no longer be in the realm of conventions. To demand as much precision as if this were the case and as if the rule were a legal one is tantamount to denying that this area of the Canadian constitution is capable of being governed by conventional rules.

Furthermore, the Government of Canada and the governments of the provinces have attempted to reach a consensus on a constitutional amending formula in the course of ten federal–provincial conferences held in 1927, 1931, 1935, 1950, 1960, 1964, 1971, 1978, 1979 and 1980 (see Gerald A. Beaudoin [*Le partage des pouvoirs* (1980)], at p. 346). A major issue at these conferences was the quantification of provincial consent. No consensus was reached on this issue. But the discussion of this very issue for more than fifty years postulates a clear recognition by all the governments concerned of the principle that a substantial degree of provincial consent is required.

It would not be appropriate for the Court to devise in the abstract a specific formula which would indicate in positive terms what measure of provincial agreement is required for the convention to be complied with. Conventions by their nature develop in the political field and it will be for the political actors, not this Court, to determine the degree of provincial consent required.

It is sufficient for the Court to decide that at least a substantial measure of provincial consent is required and to decide further whether the situation before the Court meets with this requirement. The situation is one where Ontario and New Brunswick agree with the proposed amendments whereas the eight other provinces oppose it. By no conceivable standard could this situation be thought to pass muster. It clearly does not disclose a sufficient measure of provincial agreement. Nothing more should be said about this.

iii) A Reason for the Rule

The reason for the rule is the federal principle. Canada is a federal union. The preamble of the *B.N.A. Act* states that

. . . the Provinces of Canada, Nova Scotia, and New Brunswick have expressed their Desire to be federally united . . .

The federal character of the Canadian Constitution was recognized in innumerable judicial pronouncements. We will quote only one, that of Lord Watson in *Liquidators of the Maritime Bank of Canada v. Receiver-General of New Brunswick, supra*, at pp. 441-42:

The object of the *Act* was neither to weld the provinces into one, nor to subordinate provincial governments to a central authority, but to create a federal government in which they should all be represented, entrusted with the exclusive administration of affairs in which they had a common interest, each province retaining its independence and autonomy.

The federal principle cannot be reconciled with a state of affairs where the modification of provincial legislative powers could be obtained by the unilateral action of the federal authorities. It would indeed offend the federal principle that "a radical change to . . . [the] constitution [be] taken at the request of a bare majority of the members of the Canadian House of Commons and Senate." (Report of Dominion-Provincial Conference of 1931, p. 3.)

This is an essential requirement of the federal principle which was clearly recognized by the Dominion-Provincial Conference of 1931. . . .

Furthermore, as was stated in the fourth general principle of the White Paper, the requirement of provincial consent did not emerge as early as other principles, but it has gained increasing recognition and acceptance since 1907 and particularly since 1930. This is clearly demonstrated by the proceedings of the Dominion–Provincial Conference of 1931.

Then followed the positive precedents of 1940, 1951 and 1964 as well as the abortive ones of 1951, 1960 and 1964, all discussed above. By 1965, the rule had become recognized as a binding constitutional one formulated in the fourth general principle of the White Paper already quoted reading in part as follows:

> The fourth general principle is that the Canadian Parliament will not request an amendment directly affecting federal–provincial relationships without prior consultation and agreement with the provinces.

The purpose of this conventional rule is to protect the federal character of the Canadian Constitution and prevent the anomaly that the House of Commons and Senate could obtain by simple resolutions what they could not validly accomplish by statute.

It was contended by counsel for Canada, Ontario and New Brunswick that the proposed amendments would not offend the federal principle and that, if they became law, Canada would remain a federation. The federal principle would even be reinforced, it was said, since the provinces would as a matter of law be given an important role in the amending formula.

It is true that Canada would remain a federation if the proposed amendments became law. But it would be a different federation made different at the instance of a majority in the Houses of the federal Parliament acting alone. It is this process itself which offends the federal principle.

It was suggested by counsel for Saskatchewan that the proposed amendments were perhaps severable; that the proposed *Charter of Rights* offended the federal principle in that it would unilaterally alter legislative powers whereas the proposed amending formula did not offend the federal principle.

To this suggestion we cannot accede. Counsel for Canada (as well as counsel for other parties and all interveners) took the firm position that the proposed amendment formed an unseverable package. Furthermore, and to repeat, whatever the result, the process offends the federal principle. It was to guard against this process that the constitutional convention came about.

IV Conclusion

We have reached the conclusion that the agreement of the provinces of Canada, no views being expressed as to its quantification, is constitutionally required for the passing of the "Proposed Resolution for a Joint Address to Her Majesty the Queen respecting the Constitution of Canada" and that the passing of this Resolution without such agreement would be unconstitutional in the conventional sense.

We would, subject to these reasons, answer Question 2 of the Manitoba and Newfoundland References and that part of Question B in the Quebec Reference which relates to conventions as follows:

> 2. Is it a constitutional convention that the House of Commons and Senate of Canada will not request Her

Majesty the Queen to lay before the Parliament of the United Kingdom of Great Britain and Northern Ireland a measure to amend the Constitution of Canada affecting federal–provincial relationships or the powers, rights or privileges granted or secured by the Constitution of Canada to the provinces, their legislatures or governments without first obtaining the agreement of the provinces?
>   YES.

[TRANSLATION]
> B. Does the Canadian Constitution empower ... by convention ... the Senate and the House of Commons of Canada to cause the Canadian Constitution to be amended without the consent of the provinces and in spite of the objection of several of them, in such a manner as to affect:
>   (i) the legislative competence of the provincial legislatures in virtue of the Canadian Constitution?
>   (ii) the status or role of the provincial legislatures or governments within the Canadian Federation?
>   NO.

THE CHIEF JUSTICE AND ESTEY AND MCINTYRE JJ. (dissenting): These reasons are addressed solely to Question 2 in the Manitoba and Newfoundland References and the conventional segment of Question B in the Quebec Reference. Our views upon the other questions raised in the three References are expressed in another judgment. As will be pointed out later, no legal question is raised in the questions under consideration in these reasons and, ordinarily, the Court would not undertake to answer them for it is not the function of the Court to go beyond legal determinations. Because of the unusual nature of these References and because the issues raised in the questions now before us were argued at some length before the Court and have become the subject of the reasons of the majority, with which, with the utmost deference, we cannot agree, we feel obliged to answer the questions notwithstanding their extra-legal nature....

At the outset it should be observed that the convention referred to in the above questions, and contended for by all objecting provinces except Saskatchewan, is a constitutional convention which requires that before the two Houses of the Canadian Parliament will request Her Majesty the Queen to lay before the Parliament of the United Kingdom a measure to amend the Constitution of Canada, affecting federal–provincial relationships, it will obtain agreement thereto from the provinces. From the wording of the questions and from the course of argument it is clear that the questions mean the consent of all the provinces. This then is the question which must be answered on this part of the References. An affirmative answer would involve a declaration that such a convention, requiring the consent of all the provinces, exists, while a negative answer would, of course, deny its existence. No other answers can be open to the Court for, on a reference of this nature, the Court may answer only the questions put and may not conjure up questions of its own. . . .

Where there is ambiguity, or where questions are phrased in such general terms that a precise answer is difficult or impossible to give, the Court may qualify the answers, answer in general terms, or refuse to answer: see *Reference re Waters and Water-Powers* [[1929] S.C.R. 200]. No such considerations apply here. There is no ambiguity in the questions before the Court. Question 2 in the Manitoba and Newfoundland References refers without qualification to the "agreement of the provinces." Question B in the Quebec Reference uses the words "the consent of the provinces," also without qualification. The expressions "of the provinces" or "of the provinces of Canada" in this context and in general usage mean in plain English *all* of the provinces of Canada, and our consideration of the questions must be upon this basis. . . .

What are conventions and, particularly, what are constitutional conventions? While our answers to Question 2 in the Manitoba and Newfoundland References and the conventional segment of Question B in the Quebec Reference will differ from those of the majority of the Court, we are in agreement with much of what has been said as to the general nature of constitutional conventions in the reasons for judgment by the majority, which we have had the advantage of reading. We are in agreement, as well, with the words of Freedman C.J.M. in his reasons for judgment in the Manitoba Reference, referred to with approval and quoted by the majority. We cannot, however, agree with any suggestion that the non-observance of a convention can properly be termed unconstitutional in any strict or legal sense, or that its observance could be, in any sense, a constitutional requirement within the meaning of Question 3 of the Manitoba and Newfoundland References. In a federal state where the essential feature of the constitution must be the distribution of powers between the two levels of government, each supreme in its own legislative sphere, constitutionality and legality must be synonymous, and conventional rules will be accorded less significance than they may have in a unitary state such as the United Kingdom. . . . [C]onstitutionalism in a unitary state and practices in the national and regional political units of a federal state must be differentiated from constitutional law in a federal state. Such law cannot be ascribed to informal or customary origins, but must be found in a formal document which is the source of authority, legal authority, through which the central and regional units function and exercise their powers.

The constitution of Canada, as has been pointed out by the majority, is only in part written, i.e. contained in statutes which have the force of law and which include, in addition to the *British North America Act* (hereinafter called the *B.N.A. Act*), the various other enactments which are listed in the reasons of the majority. Another, and indeed highly important, part of the constitution has taken the form of custom and usage, adopting in large part the practices of the Parliament of the United Kingdom and adapting them to the federal nature of this country. These have evolved with time to form with the statutes referred to above and certain rules of the common law a constitution for Canada. This constitution depends then on statutes and common law rules which declare the law and have the force of law, and upon customs, usages and conventions developed in political science which, while not having the force of law in the sense that there is a legal enforcement process or sanction available for their breach, form a vital part of the constitution without which it would be incomplete and unable to serve its purpose.

As has been pointed out by the majority, a fundamental difference between the legal, that is the statutory and common law rules of the constitution, and the conventional rules is that, while a breach of the legal rules, whether of statutory or common law nature, has a legal consequence in that it will be restrained by the courts, no such sanction exists for breach or non-observance of the conventional rules. The observance of constitutional conventions depends upon the acceptance of the obligation of conformance by the actors deemed to be bound thereby. When this consideration is insufficient to compel observance no court may enforce the convention by legal action. The sanction for non-observance of a convention is political in that disregard of a convention may lead to political defeat, to loss of office, or to other political consequences, but it will not engage the attention of the courts which are limited to matters of law alone. Courts, however, may recognize the existence of conventions and that is what is asked of us in answering the questions. The answer, whether affirmative or negative however, can have no legal effect, and acts performed or done in conformance with the law, even though in direct contradiction of well-established conventions, will not be enjoined or set aside by the courts. . . .

There are different kinds of conventions and usages, but we are concerned here with what may be termed "constitutional" conventions or rules of the constitution. They were described by Professor Dicey in the tenth edition of his *Law of the Constitution* (1959), at pp. 23-24, in the following passage:

> The one set of rules are in the strictest sense "laws," since they are rules which (whether written or unwritten, whether enacted by statute or derived from the mass of custom, tradition, or judge-made maxims known as the common law) are enforced by the courts; these rules

constitute "constitutional law" in the proper sense of that term, and may for the sake of distinction be called collectively "the law of the constitution."

The other set of rules consist of conventions, understandings, habits, or practices which, though they may regulate the conduct of the several members of the sovereign power, of the Ministry, or of other officials, are not in reality laws at all since they are not enforced by the courts. This portion of constitutional law may, for the sake of distinction, be termed the "conventions of the constitution," or constitutional morality.

Later, at p. 27, after discussing examples from English practice, he said:

Under the English constitution they have one point in common: they are none of them "laws" in the true sense of that word, for if any or all of them were broken, no court would take notice of their violation. ...

This view has been adopted by Canadian writers, e.g. Professor Peter W. Hogg in *Constitutional Law of Canada* (1977), dealt with the matter in these terms, at p. 7:

Conventions are rules of the constitution which are not enforced by the law courts. Because they are not enforced by the law courts they are best regarded as non-legal rules, but because they do in fact regulate the working of the constitution they are an important concern of the constitutional lawyer. What conventions do is to prescribe the way in which legal powers shall be exercised. Some conventions have the effect of transferring effective power from the legal holder to another official or institution. Other conventions limit an apparently broad legal power, or even prescribe that a legal power shall not be exercised at all.

At page 8, he said:

If a convention is disobeyed by an official, then it is common, especially in the United Kingdom, to describe the official's act or omission as "unconstitutional." But this use of the term unconstitutional must be carefully distinguished from the case where a legal rule of the constitution has been disobeyed. Where unconstitutionality springs from a breach of law, the purported act is normally a nullity and there is a remedy available in the courts. But where "unconstitutionality" springs merely from a breach of convention, no breach of the law has occurred and no legal remedy will be available. If a court did give a remedy for a breach enacted by both houses of Parliament, then we would have to change our language and describe the rule which used to be thought of as a convention as a rule of the common law. In other words a judicial decision could have the effect of transforming a conventional rule into a legal rule. A convention may also be transformed into law by being enacted as a statute.

It will be noted that Professor Hogg, in the quotation immediately above, has expressed the view that a judicial decision could have the effect of transforming a conventional rule into a legal rule, as could the enactment of a convention in statutory form. There can be no doubt that a statute, by enacting the terms of a convention, could create positive law, but it is our view that it is not for the Courts to raise a convention to the status of a legal principle. As pointed out above, courts may recognize the existence of conventions in their proper sphere. That is all that may be properly sought from the Court in answering Question 2 in the Manitoba and Newfoundland References and the conventional part of Question B in the Quebec Reference: an answer by the Court recognizing the existence of the convention or denying its existence. For the Court to postulate some other convention requiring less than unanimous provincial consent to constitutional amendments would be to go beyond the terms of the References and in so doing to answer a question not posed in the References. It would amount, in effect, to an attempt by judicial pronouncement to create an amending formula for the Canadian constitution which, in addition to being beyond the Court's power to declare, not being raised in a question posed in any of the References before the Court, would be incomplete for failure to specify the degree or percentage of provincial consent required. Furthermore, all the provinces, with the exception of Saskatchewan, oppose such a step. Those favouring the position of the federal Parliament, Ontario and New Brunswick, do so because they say no convention exists and those attacking the federal position, Quebec, Nova Scotia, Prince Edward Island, Manitoba, Alberta and British Columbia, do so because they say provincial participation is already fixed by what may be called "the rule of unanimity."

Conventions, while frequently unwritten, may nonetheless be reduced to writing. They may be reached by specific agreement between the parties to be bound, or they may more commonly arise from practice and usage. It is true, as well, that conventions can become law but this, in our view, would require some formal legal step such as enactment in statutory form. The *Statute of Westminster, 1931* affords an example of the enactment of conventions concerning constitutional relations between the United Kingdom and the various Dominions. However a convention may arise or be created, the essential condition for its recognition must be that the parties concerned regard it as binding upon them. While a convention, by its very nature, will often lack the precision and clearness of expression of a law, it must be recognized, known and understood with sufficient clarity that conformance is possible and a breach of conformance immediately discernible. It must play as well a necessary constitutional role.

There are many such conventions of the Canadian constitution and while at different periods they may have taken different forms, and while change and development have been observable and are, no doubt, continuing processes, they have been recognized nonetheless as rules or conventions of the Canadian constitution, known and observed at any given time in Canadian affairs. As the reasons of the majority point out, there are many examples. The general rule that the Governor General will act only according to the advice of the Prime Minister is purely conventional and is not to be found in any legal enactment. In the same category is the rule that after a general election the Governor General will call upon the leader of the party with the greatest number of seats to form a government. The rule of responsible government that a government losing the confidence of the House of Commons must itself resign, or obtain a dissolution, the general principles of majority rule and responsible government underlying the daily workings of the institutions of the executive and legislative branches of each level of government, and a variety of other such conventional arrangements, serve as further illustrations. These rules have an historical origin and bind, and have bound, the actors in constitutional matters in Canada for generations. No one can doubt their operative force or the reality of their existence as an effective part of the Canadian constitution. They are, nonetheless, conventional and, therefore, distinct from purely legal rules. . . .

These then are recognized conventions; they are definite, understandable and understood. They have the unquestioned acceptance not only of the actors in political affairs but of the public at large. Can it be said that any convention having such clear definition and acceptance concerning provincial participation in the amendment of the Canadian Constitution has developed? It is in the light of this comparison that the existence of any supposed constitutional convention must be considered. It is abundantly clear, in our view, that the answer must be no. The degree of provincial participation in constitutional amendments has been a subject of lasting controversy in Canadian political life for generations. It cannot be asserted, in our opinion, that any view on this subject has become so clear and so broadly accepted as to constitute a constitutional convention. It should be observed that there is a fundamental difference between the convention in the Dicey concept and the convention for which some of the provinces here contend. The Dicey convention relates to the functioning of individuals and institutions within a parliamentary democracy in unitary form. It does not qualify or limit the authority or sovereignty of Parliament or the Crown. The convention sought to be advanced here would truncate the functioning of the executive and legislative branches at the federal level. This would impose a limitation on the sovereign body itself within the Constitution. Surely such a convention would require for its recognition, even in the non-legal, political sphere, the clearest signal from the plenary unit intended to be bound, and not simply a plea from the majority of the beneficiaries of such a convention, the provincial plenary units.

An examination of the Canadian experience since Confederation will, bearing in mind the considerations above described, serve to support our conclusion on this question. It may be observed here that it was not suggested in argument before this Court that there was any procedure for amendment now available other than by the addresses of both Houses of Parliament to Her Majesty the Queen. It was argued, however, that this was a procedural step only and that before it could be undertaken by Parliament the consent of the provinces would be required. It is with the frequency with which provincial consents were obtained or omitted, with the circumstances under which consent was or was not sought, with the nature of the amendments involved, and with provincial attitudes towards them that we must concern ourselves. As has been pointed out in other judgments on these References, here and in the other courts, there have been since Confederation some twenty-two amendments to the *B.N.A. Act*. . . .

In examining these amendments it must be borne in mind that all do not possess the same relevance or force for the purpose of this inquiry. Question 2 of the Manitoba and Newfoundland References and the conventional segment of Question B in the Quebec Reference raise the issue of the propriety of non-consensual amendments which affect federal–provincial relationships and the powers, rights and privileges of the provinces. The questions do not limit consideration to those amendments which affected the distribution of legislative powers between the federal Parliament and the provincial legislatures. Since the distribution of powers is the very essence of a federal system, amendments affecting such distribution will be of especial concern to the provinces. Precedents found in such amendments will be entitled to serious consideration. It does not follow, however, that other amendments which affected federal–provincial relationships without altering the distribution of powers should be disregarded in this inquiry. Consideration must be given in according weight to the various amendments, to the reaction they provoked from the provinces. This is surely the real test of relevance in this discussion. On many occasions provinces considered that amendments not affecting the distribution of legislative power were sufficiently undesirable to call for strenuous opposition. The test of whether the convention exists, or has existed, is to be found by examining the results of such opposition. . . .

Prior to the amendment effected by the *B.N.A. Act* of 1930 there were at least three amendments, those of 1886, 1907 and 1915, which substantially affected the provinces and which were procured without the consent of all the provinces. The amendment of 1886 gave power to Parliament to provide for parliamentary representation in the Senate and House of Commons for territories not forming part of any province, and therefore altered the provincial balance of representation. That of 1907 changed the basis of federal subsidies payable to the provinces and thus directly affected the provincial interests. That of 1915 redefined territorial divisions for senatorial representation, and therefore had a potential for altering the provincial balance. Those of 1886 and 1915 were passed without provincial consultation or consent, and that of 1907 had the consent of all provinces save British Columbia, which actively opposed its passage both in Canada and in the United Kingdom. The amendment was passed with minor changes. These precedents, it may be said, should by themselves have only a modest influence in the consideration of the question before the Court. It is clear, however, that no support whatever for the convention may be found on an examination of the amendments made up to 1930. None had full provincial approval.

The *B.N.A. Act* of 1930 provided for the transfer of natural resources within the provincial territories to the Provinces of Manitoba, Saskatchewan and Alberta. It also provided for the re-conveyance of certain railway lands to British Columbia. In effecting this amendment the consent of the provinces directly concerned, *i.e.* the four western provinces only, was obtained, although the arrangement had received the general approval of the other provinces as expressed at a conference in 1927. This is a precedent of modest weight, but it is worthy of note that despite the fact that the interests of all non-involved provinces were affected by the alienation of the assets formerly under federal control, it was not considered necessary to procure any formal consent from them. It is of more than passing interest to note that in the amending procedure provided for in the 1930 *British North America Act* amendment there is no requirement for consent or participation by any of the other five provinces (as they then were) although their indirect interest in federal resources might be affected.

The amendments of 1943, 1946, 1949, 1949(2), 1950 and 1960 were not considered of great significance on this issue by the parties and little comment was made upon them but all, save that of 1960, were achieved without full provincial consent. This, subject to what is later said concerning the 1943 amendment, leaves for consideration the *Statute of Westminster, 1931* and the amendments of 1940, 1951 and 1964. The *Statute of Westminster, 1931* and the amendments of 1940, 1951 and 1964 affected the provinces directly. Canadian participation in the settlement of the provisions of the *Statute* and the said amendments had the consent of all provinces. These examples were heavily relied upon by the objecting

provinces to support an affirmative answer to Question 2 of the Manitoba and Newfoundland References and the negative answer to the conventional part of Question B of the Quebec Reference. As to the *Statute of Westminster, 1931*, it freed federal and provincial legislation from the restrictions imposed by the *Colonial Laws Validity Act* of 1865 and gave statutory recognition to certain conventions which had grown up with the development of self-government in the former colonies. The pre-existing division of legislative power between federal and provincial legislatures in Canada was not, however, in any way affected and it did not recognize or give statutory form to any convention requiring provincial consent to the amendment of the *B.N.A. Act.* . . .

The amendment of 1940 transferring legislative power over unemployment insurance to the federal Parliament also had full provincial consent. It must be observed here, however, that when questioned in the House of Commons on this point Mr. Mackenzie King, then Prime Minister, while acknowledging that consents had been obtained, specifically stated that this course had been followed to avoid any constitutional issue on this point and he disclaimed any necessity for such consent. . . .

It is clear, we suggest, that he procured the consent of the provinces on that occasion in order to avoid raising any question on the subject and as a measure of good politics rather than as a constitutional requirement. It is surely obvious that the federal government would always prefer to have, as a political matter, provincial approval, but the position of the federal authorities as expressed in the foregoing parliamentary exchange does not support the proposition that they considered that they were bound by any convention.

We are aware, of course, that other declarations have been made upon this subject by persons of high political rank as well as academics of high standing. Many such pronouncements were cited in argument before us. We do not propose to deal with them in detail. It is sufficient to say that many favour the existence of the convention; many deny its existence. . . . The continuation of controversy on the subject among political and academic figures only adds additional weight to the contention that no convention of provincial consent has achieved constitutional recognition to this day.

The amendment of 1951 had full approval from the provinces, as did that of 1964. The 1951 amendment gave power relating to old age pensions to the federal Parliament and the 1964 amendment was merely a supplementary tidying-up of the original 1951 provisions. In our view, they dealt with the same matter and can stand as only one precedent favouring the existence of the convention.

After examining the amendments made since Confederation, and after observing that out of the twenty-two amendments listed above only in the case of four was unanimous provincial consent sought or obtained and, even after according special weight to those amendments relied on by the provinces, we cannot agree that history justifies a conclusion that the convention contended for by the provinces has emerged.

Great weight was put upon the 1940 *Unemployment Insurance Act* amendment as a precedent favouring the existence of the convention. Despite the obtaining of provincial consent for the 1940 amendment, the federal government proceeded three years later to the completion of the amendment of 1943 without provincial consent and in the face of the strong protests of the Province of Quebec. This amendment did not touch provincial powers. It dealt with the postponement of redistribution of seats in the House of Commons. Nevertheless, it was deemed of sufficient importance by Quebec because its interest was particularly affected to arouse active opposition which was overborne by the federal government in procuring the amendment. . . .

In summary, we observe that in the one hundred and fourteen years since Confederation Canada has grown from a group of four somewhat hesitant colonies into a modern, independent state, vastly increased in size, power and wealth, and having a social and governmental structure unimagined in 1867. It cannot be denied that vast change has occurred in Dominion–provincial relations over that period. Many factors have influenced this process and the amendments to the *B.N.A. Act*—all the amendments—have played a significant part and all must receive consideration in resolving this question. Only in four cases has full provincial consent been obtained and in many cases the federal government has proceeded with amendments in the face of active provincial opposition. In our view, it is unrealistic in the extreme to say that the convention has emerged.

As a further support for the convention argument, the White Paper referred to above was cited and relied upon. . . . It is the fourth principle which is stressed by the objecting provinces. In our view, they have attributed too much significance to this statement of the four principles. The author of the White Paper was at pains to say, at p. 11:

> Certain rules and principles relating to amending procedures have nevertheless developed over the years. They have emerged from the practices and procedures employed in securing various amendments to the *British North America Act* since 1867. *Though not constitutionally binding in any strict sense,* they have come to be recognized and accepted in practice as part of the amendment process in Canada. (Emphasis added.)

It would not appear that he was satisfied that the principles had become so well-established that they had acquired strict constitutional force. Furthermore, we are unable to accord to the fourth principle the significance given to it by the objecting provinces. The first sentence pronounces strongly in favour of the existence of the convention. If it stopped there, subject to what the author had said earlier, it would constitute a statement of great weight. However, the third sentence contradicts the first and, in fact, cancels it out. By suggesting the possibility of a requirement of partial provincial consent it answers Question 2 in the Manitoba and Newfoundland References and the conventional segment of Question B in the Quebec Reference against the provinces. "Increasing recognition," that is "partial" but not "complete" recognition, is all that is claimed by the author of the White Paper. A convention requires universal recognition by the actors in a scheme and this is certainly so where, as here, acceptance of a convention involves the surrender of a power by a sovereign body said to be a party to the convention. Furthermore, in recognizing uncertainty in specifying the degree of provincial participation, it denies the existence of any convention including that suggested by the Province of Saskatchewan. If there is difficulty in defining the degree of provincial participation, which there surely is, it cannot be said that any convention on the subject has been settled and recognized as a constitutional condition for the making of an amendment. It is the very difficulty of fixing the degree of provincial participation which, while it remains unresolved, prevents the formation or recognition of any convention. It robs any supposed convention of that degree of definition which is necessary to allow for its operation. . . .

It was also argued that Canada was formed as a federal union and that the existence of a legal power of the central government to unilaterally change the Constitution was inimical to the concept of federalism. The convention then, it was argued, arose out of the necessity to restrain such unilateral conduct and preserve the federal nature of Canada. In this connection, it must be acknowledged at once that, in a federal union, the powers and rights of each of the two levels of government must be protected from the assault of the other. The whole history of constitutional law and constitutional litigation in Canada since Confederation has been concerned with this vital question. We are asked to say whether the need for the preservation of the principles of Canadian federalism dictates the necessity for a convention, requiring consent from the provinces as a condition of the exercise by the federal government of its legal powers, to procure amendment to the Canadian Constitution. If the convention requires only partial consent, as is contended by Saskatchewan, it is difficult to see how the federal concept is thereby protected for, while those provinces favouring amendment would be pleased, those refusing consent could claim coercion. If unanimous consent is required (as contended by the other objecting provinces), while it may be said that in general terms the concept of federalism would be protected it would only be by overlooking the special nature of Canadian federalism that this protection would be achieved. The *B.N.A. Act* has not created a perfect or ideal federal state. Its provisions have accorded a measure of paramountcy to the federal Parliament. Certainly this has been done in a more marked degree in Canada than in many other federal states. For example, one need only look to the power of reservation and disallowance of provincial enactments; the power to declare works in a province to be for the benefit of all Canada and to place them under federal regulatory control; the wide powers to legislate generally for the peace, order and good government of Canada as a whole; the power to enact criminal law of the entire country; the power to create and admit provinces out of existing territories and, as well, the paramountcy accorded federal legislation. It is this special nature of Canadian federalism which deprives the federalism argument described above of its force. This is particularly true when it involves the final settlement of Canadian constitutional affairs with an external government, the federal authority being the sole conduit for communication between Canada and the Sovereign and Canada alone having the power to deal in external matters. We therefore reject the argument that the preservation of the principles of Canadian federalism requires the recognition of the convention asserted before us.

While it may not be necessary to do so in dealing with Question 2, we feel obliged to make a further comment related to the federalism argument. It was argued that the federal authorities were assuming a power to act without restraint in disregard of provincial wishes which could go so far as to convert Canada into a unitary state by means of a majority vote in the Houses of Parliament. A few words will suffice to lay that argument at rest. What is before the Court is the task of answering the questions posed in three References. As has been pointed out, the Court can do no more than that. The questions all deal with the constitutional validity of precise proposals for constitutional amendment and they form the complete subject-matter of the Court's inquiry and our comments must be made with reference to them. It is not for the Court to express views on the wisdom or lack of wisdom of these proposals. We are concerned solely with their constitutionality. In view of the fact that the unitary argument has been raised, however, it should be noted, in our view, that the federal constitutional proposals, which preserve a federal state without disturbing the distribution or balance of power, would create an amending formula which would enshrine provincial rights on the question of amendments on a secure, legal and constitutional footing, and would extinguish, as well, any presently existing power on the part of the federal Parliament to act unilaterally in constitutional matters. In so doing, it may be said that the parliamentary resolution here under examination does not, save for the enactment of the *Charter of Rights*, which circumscribes the legislative powers of both the federal and provincial legislatures, truly amend the Canadian Constitution. Its effect is to complete the formation of an incomplete constitution by supplying its present deficiency, *i.e.* an amending formula, which will enable the Constitution to be amended in Canada as befits a sovereign state. We are not here faced with an action which in any way has the effect of transforming this federal union into a unitary state. The *in terrorem* argument raising the spectre of a unitary state has no validity.

For the above reasons we answer the questions posed in the three References as follows:

Manitoba and Newfoundland References:
    Question 2: No.

Quebec Reference:
    Question B (i): Yes.
    (ii): Yes.

Re: Objection to a Resolution to Amend the Constitution (Quebec Veto Reference), 1982

On November 25, 1981, just three weeks after Prime Minister Trudeau and the premiers of all the provinces except Quebec reached an accord on the terms of patriation, the Quebec National Assembly passed a resolution objecting to making these changes in Canada's Constitution without Quebec's consent. At that time, the government of Quebec also referred to Quebec's Court of Appeal the question whether proceeding with these amendments without Quebec's consent was "unconstitutional in the conventional sense." On April 7, 1982, the Quebec Court of Appeal brought down its decision, holding unanimously that, as a matter of constitutional convention, Quebec's consent was not required. On April 13, 1982, just four days before the changes to which Quebec objected were proclaimed in force in Canada, this decision was appealed to the Supreme Court of Canada. On December 6, 1982, the Supreme Court of Canada rendered its decision upholding the verdict of the Quebec Court of Appeal.

In dealing with this reference case, the Supreme Court was in a peculiar position. Because the question at issue was entirely one of convention, the Court's answer could have no legal consequences. But it would have been a political bombshell for the Supreme Court to find that Canada's so-called new Constitution had been obtained in a manner that violates a convention of the Canadian Constitution. Such a ruling would certainly detract from the new Constitution's legitimacy and bolster the political fortunes of René Lévesque's Parti Québécois government. To nobody's great surprise, the Supreme Court did not render such a decision.

It was easy for the Court to reject Quebec's argument that, under the unpatriated Constitution, a convention had developed requiring the unanimous consent of the provinces to amend the Constitution in matters affecting the powers or status of the provinces. A year earlier, the entire Court had rejected the claim that there existed a conventional rule of unanimity and the majority had found that only "a substantial degree of provincial consent" was required. The Court, composed of the same nine judges who had participated in the *Patriation Reference*, simply invoked that ruling here. Quebec, however, had a second argument that virtually contradicted the first—namely, that Quebec was not a province like the others; as the home province of one of the country's two founding peoples, it forms a "distinct society within the Canadian federation" and, under the principle of "Canadian duality," it had a power of veto over constitutional changes affecting its position in Confederation.

The Court, through an anonymous and unanimous decision, managed to reject this second argument without addressing the principle on which it rests. It did so by concentrating on one of Sir Ivor Jennings's three tests for the existence of a constitutional convention—recognition of the convention by the political actors involved in the precedents. The Court took the view that such recognition must be explicit and rejected Quebec's argument because it had not been presented with any evidence that politicians outside Quebec had explicitly acknowledged such a convention. This may not have been an entirely convincing performance, but it was perhaps the best the Court could do under the circumstances.[1]

---

1   For a critical appraisal of the Court's argument, see Marc E. Gold, "The Mask of Objectivity: Politics and Rhetoric in the Supreme Court of Canada" (1985) 7 *Supreme Court Review* 455.

The subsequent course of constitutional politics demonstrated widespread recognition among leading politicians throughout Canada of the need to secure Quebec's support for the changes made to the Constitution in 1982. With the Mulroney Conservatives replacing the Trudeau Liberals in Ottawa in 1984, and the Bourassa Liberals taking over from the Parti Québécois in Quebec City a year later, the prospects improved of working out terms on which Quebec could accept the 1982 changes. On April 30, 1987, at a federal government retreat on Meech Lake, Prime Minister Mulroney and the premiers of all 10 provinces reached an agreement in principle on a package of proposed constitutional amendments. The Meech Lake Accord was based on proposals brought forward by Premier Bourassa as Quebec's minimal conditions for accepting the *Constitution Act, 1982*.[2] The first and, as it has turned out, most controversial of these proposals is constitutional recognition of Quebec as a "distinct society"—the very principle on which Quebec based its challenge to the earlier constitutional process.

Under the new amending system that came into effect in 1982, constitutional changes do not flow automatically from agreement at the executive level. Formal approval of the federal and provincial legislatures must be obtained. For the Meech Lake package, all the provincial legislatures and the federal House of Commons had to approve the amendments. There is a three-year time limit on obtaining the necessary legislative approvals. When the end of that three-year period was reached in June 1990, without approval of the Meech Lake Accord by the legislatures of Manitoba and Newfoundland, the Accord died.

Quebec eventually obtained a veto in the Constitution-amending process, but through politics rather than litigation. In 1996, Prime Minister Chrétien introduced legislation to honour the commitment he had made in the 1995 Quebec referendum to restore Quebec's constitutional veto. This legislation commits the federal Parliament to support amendments under the 7-provinces/50 percent of the population rule only when they are supported by legislatures or referendums in British Columbia; Ontario; Quebec; at least two of the Prairie provinces, with 50 percent of that region's population; and at least two of the Atlantic provinces, with 50 percent of that region's population. In effect, this legislation gives each of Canada's five regions a veto over constitutional amendments. Although the federal legislation adding the 5-region veto to the 7/50 rule is not constitutionally entrenched, it would take a very bold federal government to override it.[3] ⁓

---

2   For an account and analysis of the Accord, see Peter W. Hogg, *Meech Lake Constitutional Accord Annotated* (Toronto: Carswell, 1988).

3   S.C. 1996, c. 1.

RE: OBJECTION BY QUEBEC TO A RESOLUTION TO AMEND THE CONSTITUTION
[1982] 2 S.C.R. 793

Present: Laskin C.J. and Dickson, Beetz, McIntyre, Chouinard, Lamer, Martland, Estey, and Ritchie JJ.

THE COURT:

I: The Facts

This is an appeal from the opinion pronounced on April 7, 1982, by the Quebec Court of Appeal on a question referred to it by the Government of Quebec regarding the Resolution to amend the Constitution....

The reference is the second one on this subject. The first reference also gave rise to an appeal to this Court in which judgment was delivered on September 28, 1981 at the same time as in two other appeals arising from a reference by the Government of Manitoba and a reference by the Government of Newfoundland: *Re: Resolution to amend the Constitution*, [1981] 1 S.C.R. 753, hereinafter referred to as the *First Reference*.

Following the judgment in the *First Reference*, the Government of Canada and the governments of the ten provinces held a Constitutional Conference, on November 2 to 5, 1981, to seek agreement on the patriation of the Constitution together with a charter of rights and an amending formula. On November 5, 1981 Canada and nine of the ten provinces signed an agreement to this effect. Quebec was the dissenting province....

On November 18, 1981 the Minister of Justice of Canada laid before the House of Commons a resolution which contained a joint address of the Senate and the House of Commons to be presented to her Majesty the Queen in right of the United Kingdom. While in substance the joint address reflected the agreement of November 5, 1981 it was similar in form to the one quoted in the *First Reference*, at p. 766. It included a draft United Kingdom statute the short title of which was *The Canada Act* which, in turn, had appended to it another draft statute entitled the *Constitution Act, 1981*, later designated as the *Constitution Act, 1982*. The latter statute provided for the entrenchment of a *Canadian Charter of Rights and Freedoms* and it contained the new procedure for amending the Constitution of Canada. The *Constitution Act, 1982*, also contained a range of other provisions which it is necessary to enumerate....

On November 25, 1981 the Government of Quebec expressed its formal opposition to the proposed Resolution in Decree No. 3214-81:

[TRANSLATION]

DECREE
GOVERNMENT OF QUEBEC

CONCERNING the objection by Quebec to the proposed patriation and amendment of the Constitution of Canada ...

WHEREAS on November 18, 1981 the federal government tabled in the House of Commons a motion regarding the patriation and amendment of the Constitution of Canada;

WHEREAS if implemented, this motion would have the effect of substantially reducing the powers and rights of Quebec and of its National Assembly without its consent;

WHEREAS it has always been recognized that no change of this kind could be made without the consent of Quebec.

BE IT RESOLVED, on the motion of the Premier:

THAT this objection be officially communicated to the federal government and the governments of the other provinces.

> AUTHENTIC COPY
> DEPUTY CLERK OF THE
> EXECUTIVE COUNCIL
> Jean-Pierre Vaillancourt

On the same date, the Government of Quebec ordered the present reference in Decree No. 3215-81....

The joint address was adopted by the House of Commons on December 2, 1981 and by the Senate on December 8, 1981. It included further amendments agreed upon by Canada and all the provinces except Quebec.

On December 8, 1981 the Governor General of Canada received the text of the joint address and, pursuant to the advice of Her Majesty's Privy Council for Canada, transmitted it to Her Majesty on December 9, 1981.

On the same date, the Government of Quebec re-ordered the present reference in Decree No. 3367-81:

[TRANSLATION] WHEREAS the Senate and House of Commons of Canada adopted a Resolution regarding the Constitution of Canada;

WHEREAS this Resolution requests the introduction in the Parliament of the United Kingdom of a bill entitled the *Canada Act* which, if adopted by the Parliament of the United Kingdom, will most notably have the effect of enacting for Canada the *Constitution Act, 1981*;

WHEREAS the proposed legislation has the effect of making significant changes in the status and role of Quebec within the Canadian federal system;

WHEREAS Quebec forms a distinct society within the Canadian federation;

WHEREAS the Supreme Court of Canada stated on September 28, 1981 that the consent of the provinces is constitutionally necessary for the adoption of this proposal;

WHEREAS Quebec has not agreed and has objected to the proposed changes;

WHEREAS no change of a similar significance to that proposed in this Resolution has to date been made without the consent and over the objection of Quebec;

WHEREAS it is expedient to submit to the Court of Appeal for hearing and consideration, pursuant to the *Court of Appeal Reference Act* the question herein below set out.

ACCORDINGLY, it is ordered, upon the proposal of the Minister of Justice, that the following question be submitted to the Court of Appeal for hearing and consideration:

Is the consent of the Province of Quebec constitutionally required, by convention, for the adoption by the Senate and the House of Commons of Canada a resolution the purpose of which is to cause the Canadian Constitution to be amended in such a manner as to affect:

i) the legislative competence of the Legislature of the Province of Quebec in virtue of the Canadian Constitution

ii) the status or role of the Legislature or Government of the Province of Quebec within the Canadian federation;

and, does the objection of the Province of Quebec render the adoption of such resolution unconstitutional in the conventional sense?

On December 22, 1981 the Government of the United Kingdom introduced in the Parliament of Westminster a bill known as "A Bill to Give Effect to a Request of the Senate and House of Commons of Canada" which was to become the *Canada Act 1982*.

The Quebec Court of Appeal heard counsel in argument on the reference on March 15, 16 and 17, 1982.

The bill introduced at Westminster was passed on March 25, 1982 and received royal assent on March 29, 1982. The *Canada Act 1982* came into force on this date.

On April 7, 1982 the Quebec Court of Appeal rendered its unanimous opinion answering in the negative the question referred to it.

On April 13, 1982 the Attorney General of Quebec appealed to this Court and on April 15, 1982 at the request of the appellant, Lamer J. stated a constitutional question pursuant to Rule 17 of this Court. The terms of this question are identical to those of the question referred to the Quebec Court of Appeal.

On April 17, 1982 the *Constitution Act, 1982* was proclaimed in force by the Queen under the Great Seal of Canada and has been in force since that date.

II. The Opinion of the Court of Appeal

The unanimous opinion of the Quebec Court of Appeal, answering the question in the negative, is a collective one. It has been signed as a multiple-author opinion by the five judges who participated in the reference, Crête C.J.Q., and Montgomery, Turgeon, Monet and Jacques JJ.A.

The Court of Appeal first observed that at the time of the hearing, on March 15, 16 and 17, 1982 the process of constitutional amendment had not yet been completed. Although it had been conceded by counsel for the Attorney General for Quebec that an affirmative answer to the question could have political consequences but no legal ones, the Court of Appeal took the view that, given the broad terms of the *Court of Appeal Reference Act*, R.S.Q. 1977, c. R-23, it should answer a question which had to do with the "legitimacy" if not the "legality" of the patriation process.

The Court of Appeal was asked by the Attorney General for Quebec to answer the question in the affirmative on the basis of two alternative submissions. According to the first submission, there was a convention requiring the unanimous consent of the ten provinces to any constitutional amendment of the type in issue. According to the second submission, because of the principle of duality, Quebec had by convention a power of veto over any constitutional amendment affecting the legislative competence of the Province or the status or role of its legislature or government within the Canadian federation.

The Court of Appeal rejected the first submission as it found that this Court had already ruled it out in the *First Reference*. It rejected the second submission on the following grounds: at law, all the provinces are fundamentally equal and the Attorney General of Quebec had failed to establish that either the Government of Canada or the other provinces had conventionally recognized in Quebec any special power of veto over constitutional amendment not possessed by the other provinces. . . .

III. The Position of the Parties

Before coming to the submissions made by the parties, it should be said at the outset that the Attorney General of Canada concede that the *Canadian Charter of Rights and Freedoms* contained in the *Constitution Act, 1982* affects the legislative competence of all the provinces including Quebec.

To the question whether the status or role of the Legislature or Government of the Province of Quebec within the Canadian federation is affected by the *Constitution Act, 1982* the factum of the Attorney General of Canada makes the following answer:

> As for the role and status of Quebec within the Canadian federation, this *Act* provides Quebec a constitutionally guaranteed right to participate in the amendment of the constitution and to opt out of amendments that derogate from its legislative powers, its proprietary rights or any other rights or privileges of its legislature or government (section 38(2)) under reserve of its constitutionally guaranteed right to financial compensation when the amendment involves a transfer of provincial legislative competence to Parliament in relation to education or other cultural matters (section 40).

The answer is a qualified admission, but an admission nonetheless, that the role and status of Quebec within the Canadian federation are modified by the procedure for amending the Constitution. . . .

The position of the appellant was that the appeal should be allowed and the constitutional question answered in the affirmative on the basis of the same two submissions which he had made to the Court of Appeal, the first relating to a conventional rule of unanimity and the second to a conventional power of veto said to have been held by Quebec. (Actually, the submission relating to unanimity was made in the second place, but it will be dealt with first, as was done in the Court of Appeal.)

While both submissions seek the same answer to the constitutional question, they are alternative ones, as they have to be, for not only are they quite distinct from each other, they actually contradict one another: the rule of unanimity is predicated on the fundamental equality of all the provinces as it would give a power of veto to each of them whereas an exclusive power of veto for Quebec negates the rule of unanimity as well as the principle of fundamental equality. Also, and as will be seen below, the reason which is said to anchor the conventional rule is a different one in each submission. . . .

At page 888 of the *First Reference*, the majority opinion adopted the following passage of Sir W. Ivor Jennings, *The Law and the Constitution* (5th ed., 1959), at p. 136:

> We have to ask ourselves three questions: first, what are the precedents; secondly, did the actors in the precedents believe that they were bound by a rule; and thirdly, is there a reason for the rule? A single precedent with a good reason may be enough to establish the rule. A whole string of precedents without such a reason will be of no avail, unless it is perfectly certain that the persons concerned regarded them as bound by it.

The main purpose of constitutional conventions is to ensure that the legal framework of the constitution will be operated in accordance with generally accepted principles. It should be borne in mind however that conventional rules, although quite distinct from legal ones, are nevertheless to be distinguished from rules of morality, rules of expediency and subjective rules. Like legal rules, they are positive rules the existence of which has to be ascertained by reference to objective standards. In being asked to answer the question whether the convention did or did not exist, we are called upon to say whether or not the objective requirements for establishing a convention had been met. But we are in no way called upon to say whether it was desirable that the convention should or should not exist and no view is expressed on the matter.

Subject to an important qualification which will be dealt with in due course, appellant accepted the above stated requirements for establishing conventions and made his two submissions within the framework defined by this Court in the *First Reference*.

With respect to the precedents, positive and negative, the appellant invoked for the purposes of his two submissions the same precedents as had been relied upon by the majority opinion in the *First Reference*, at pp. 891 to 894.

The positive precedents are the constitutional amendments leading to the *Constitution Act, 1930*, the *Statute of Westminster, 1931*, the *Constitution Act, 1940*, the *British North America Act, 1951* and the *Constitution Act, 1964*, all of which directly affected federal–provincial relationships in the sense of changing legislative powers and each of which was agreed upon by each province whose legislative authority was affected.

The negative precedents are the failure of a proposed amendment relating to indirect taxation in 1951 and the failure of the Constitutional Conferences of 1960, 1964 and 1971. The precedents also comprise, in negative terms, the fact that no amendment changing provincial legislative powers had been made when agreement of a province whose legislative power would have been changed was withheld.

It was further pointed out by the appellant that no relevant constitutional amendment had been passed without the consent of Quebec and that with respect to one of them, the *Constitution Act, 1964* Quebec alone had delayed the amendment already agreed upon by the nine other provinces as early as 1962. Quebec finally gave its consent in 1964 and the amendment was passed.

The appellant also underlined that the *Constitution Act, 1940* had been delayed because three provinces, Quebec, New Brunswick and Alberta had not yet consented to it; that the lack of agreement of two provinces, Ontario and Quebec, had prevented a proposed constitutional amendment relating to indirect taxation in 1951; and that the lack of agreement of the sole Province of Quebec had caused the failure of the

Constitutional Conference of 1964, relating to the Fulton-Favreau formula as well, in practice, as the failure of the Constitutional Conference of 1971 relating to the Victoria Charter, although in the latter case, Saskatchewan did not make its position known.

It was recognized by the appellant that there must be a reason for the alleged conventional rule.

The reason for the unanimity rule, he argued, was the federal principle within the meaning given to this principle by the majority opinion in the *First Reference*.

The reason for the conventional rule giving to Quebec a power of veto was said to be the principle of duality, the meaning and nature of which will be discussed in more detail below.

Finally, as to the requirements that the actors in the precedents believe that they were bound by the rule, the appellant submitted that it had been met. But his counsel substantially qualified this submission by pleading in his factum and in oral argument that the precedents and the reason for the rule suffice to establish a constitutional convention and, accordingly, that the recognition of the actors in the precedents is not required or alternatively that recognition can be tacit and inferred from the precedents.

The respondent submitted that the Court should refuse to answer the question. He also submitted that if the Court should answer the question it should answer in the negative on the basis of the *First Reference*. He submitted alternatively that, if the Court should answer the question, it should answer that the political leaders had complied with the convention recognized by this Court in the *First Reference*.

The interveners generally supported the position of the appellant.

IV. Whether the Question Should Be Answered

The respondent advanced two reasons why the Court should refuse to answer the question: it was a purely political question and it had become academic.

The first objection had also been raised in the *First Reference* and dismissed in the majority opinion as well as in the dissenting opinion. The majority opinion adopted the view of Freedman C.J.M. on this point, at p. 884:

> In my view, this submission goes too far. Its characterization of Question 2 as "purely political" overstates the case. That there is a political element embodied in the question, arising from the contents of the joint address, may well be the case. But that does not end the matter. If Question 2, even if in part political, possesses a constitutional feature, it would legitimately call for our reply.
>
> In my view, the request for a decision by this Court on whether there is a constitution convention, in the cir-

cumstances described, that the Dominion will not act without the agreement of the Provinces poses a question that is, at least in part, constitutional in character. It therefore calls for an answer, and I propose to answer it.

This view is still valid and ought to prevail in the case at bar.

On the other hand, counsel for the respondent is right in asserting that the constitutional question has become moot. The *Constitution Act, 1982* is now in force. Its legality is neither challenged nor assailable. It contains a new procedure for amending the Constitution of Canada which entirely replaces the old one in its legal as well as in its conventional aspects. *Even assuming therefore that there was a conventional requirement for the consent of Quebec under the old system, it would no longer have any object or force.*

However, when the reference was ordered, when it was argued before the Court of Appeal and when the Court of Appeal delivered its certified opinion on April 7, 1982 it could not be said that the question was moot since the process of constitutional amendment had not been completed, the *Constitution Act, 1982* having not yet been proclaimed....

While this Court retains its discretion to entertain or not to entertain an appeal as of right where the issue has become moot, it may, in the exercise of its discretion, take into consideration the *importance of the constitutional* issue determined by a court of appeal judgment which would remain unreviewed by this Court.

In the circumstances of this case, it appears desirable that the constitutional question be answered in order to dispel any doubt over it and it accordingly will be answered.

V. Whether There Exists a Conventional Rule of Unanimity

It was the appellant's contention that the majority opinion in the *First Reference* has left open the question whether there existed a conventional rule of unanimity. His main argument for so contending was that the majority opinion did not limit the meaning of the questions relating to convention solely to determining whether there existed a convention which required the unanimous consent of the provinces.

It is quite true that the majority opinion in the *First Reference* gave to the constitutional questions a wider scope than did the dissenting opinion, but this enabled the majority to consider all arguments, including the one related to unanimity, which it clearly rejected....

At page 905 of the *First Reference*, the majority decided that "a substantial degree of provincial consent" was required. A "substantial degree of provincial consent" means less than unanimity. This is what the dissenting judges understood that the majority was deciding: the dissenting opinion contains the following statement at p. 856:

For the Court to postulate some other convention requiring less than unanimous provincial consent to constitutional amendments would be to go beyond the terms of the References and in so doing to answer a question not posed in the References.

The dissenting opinion was based on the understanding of the dissenting judges that the constitutional questions relating to conventions meant the consent of all the provinces. The dissenting judges held that there existed no convention requiring any such consent.

This Court was therefore unanimous in the *First Reference* in rejecting the conventional rule of unanimity.

The appellant advanced no compelling reason why this unanimous opinion should be modified. . . .

VI. Whether Quebec Has a Conventional Power of Veto

It has already been indicated, with respect to the precedents which are said to establish the conventional rule of a power of veto for Quebec, that the appellant relied upon those which had been invoked by the majority opinion in the *First Reference*, at pp. 891 and 894.

The reason advanced by the appellant for the existence of a conventional rule of a power of veto for Quebec is the principle of duality, this principle being however understood in a special sense.

The expression "Canadian duality" is frequently used to refer to the two larger linguistic groups in Canada and to the constitutional protection afforded to the official languages by provisions such as s. 133 of the *Constitution Act, 1867* and s. 23 of the *Manitoba Act, 1870*.

Counsel for the appellant characterized this aspect of the Canadian duality as the "federal" aspect and recognized that the central government had a role to play in this respect within the framework of federal institutions as well as outside Quebec. But he also made it clear that what he meant by the principle of duality embraced much more than linguistic or cultural differences. What was meant by the principle of duality was what counsel called its "Quebec" aspect which he defined more precisely in his factum at pp. 8 and 16:

[TRANSLATION] In the context of this reference, the word "duality" covers all the circumstances that have contributed to making Quebec a distinct society, since the foundation of Canada and long before, and the range of guarantees that were made to Quebec in 1867, as a province which the Task Force on Canadian Unity has described as "the stronghold of the French-Canadian people" and the "living heart of the French presence in North America." These circumstances and these guarantees extend far beyond matters of language and culture

alone: the protection of the British North America Act was extended to all aspects of Quebec society—language, certainly, but also the society's values, its law, religion, education, territory, natural resources, government and the sovereignty of its legislative assembly over everything which was at the time of a "local" nature. . . .

In 1867, the French Canadian minority became a majority within the Quebec Legislature. This is what accounts for the special nature of this province, and it is the reason underlying the convention that the powers of its Legislature cannot be reduced without consent.

One finds another expression of the principle of duality understood in this sense in the preamble of the above quoted Decree No. 3367-81, dated December 9, 1981, the fourth paragraph of which states in concise terms:

[TRANSLATION] WHEREAS Quebec forms a distinct society within the Canadian federation;

Another more elaborate expression of the principle of duality understood in the special sense urged by counsel for the appellant is to be found in a resolution passed by the Quebec National Assembly on December 1, 1981, and more particularly in condition no. 1 of the Resolution:

[TRANSLATION] . . . that the National Assembly of Quebec, having in mind the right of the people of Quebec to self-determination and exercising its historical right to be a party to and approve any change in the Constitution of Canada which might affect the rights and powers of Quebec, states that it cannot approve the proposal to patriate the constitution unless it includes the following conditions:

1. It shall be recognized that the two founding people of Canada are fundamentally equal, and that within the Canadian federation Quebec forms a society distinct by its language, culture and institutions, one which possesses all the attributes of a distinct national community;

2. The constitutional amending formula:
   a) shall either preserve Quebec's right of veto, or
   b) shall be the one approved in the constitutional agreement signed by Quebec on April 16, 1981, affirming the right of Quebec not to have imposed on it any change which would reduce its powers or rights, and if such a reduction were to take place, to be given reasonable compensation as a matter of right; . . .

These then are the precedents and the reason for the rule, according to counsel for the appellant.

It will not be necessary in our view to look further into these matters because this submission must in any event be rejected, the appellant having failed completely to demonstrate compliance with the most important requirement for establishing a convention that is, acceptance or recognition by the actors in the precedents.

We have been referred to an abundance of material, speeches made in the course of parliamentary debates, reports of royal commissions, opinions of historians, political scientists, constitutional experts which endorse in one way or another the principle of duality within the meaning assigned to it by the appellant, and there can be no doubt that many Canadian statesmen, politicians and experts favoured this principle.

But neither in his factum nor in oral argument did counsel for the appellant quote a single statement made by any representative of the federal authorities recognizing either explicitly or by necessary implication that Quebec had a conventional power of veto over certain types of constitutional amendments. The statement made by Minister Favreau on November 20, 1964, and the passage to be found at pp. 46 and 47 of the White Paper have been quoted twice in the appellant's factum, as if they supported the veto rule as well as the unanimity one, but they refer only to unanimity and have been above dealt with in this respect.

Furthermore, a convention such as the one now asserted by Quebec *would have to be recognized by other provinces*. We have not been referred to and we are not aware of any statement by the actors in any of the other provinces acknowledging such a convention. Not only have we not been given any evidence of the acquiescence of other provinces but in the *First Reference*, three of them, Manitoba, Prince Edward Island and Alberta, explicitly pleaded in favour of the unanimity rule in their factums, a position compatible only with the principle of equality among the provinces and incompatible with a special power of veto for Quebec. It should also be noted that in the *First Reference*, Ontario and New Brunswick had taken the position that the constitutional amending process was not regulated by conventions involving the provinces.

In order to make up for these fundamental flaws in his submission, counsel for the appellant argued as follows in his factum:

> [TRANSLATION] In the opinion of the Attorney General, custom and a reason suffice by themselves to establish the normative nature of the rule.

Counsel for the appellant also referred to Ivor Jennings' test, adopted by the Court in the *First Reference*, and more particularly to the last part of this test:

> A single precedent with good reason may be enough to establish the rule. A whole string of precedents without

such a reason will be of no avail, unless it is perfectly certain that the persons concerned regarded them as bound by it.

As we understand it, the *contention was that recognition by the actors in the precedents is not an absolutely* essential requirement for establishing a convention and that the last part of Jennings' test is an authority for that proposition.

This contention is based on two sentences taken out of context and is an oversimplified and erroneous view of Jennings' test. In these two sentences, Jennings is merely expanding on what he said in the sentence immediately preceding them about the three requirements and illustrating the interrelation between them. He is not doing away with the requirement that the actors in the precedents believe that they were bound by a rule. Indeed Jennings insists in several passages of his book, *The Law and the Constitution*, that recognition or acquiescence is an essential ingredient of constitutional conventions. Thus, he writes, at p. 81:

> "Convention" implies some form of agreement, whether expressed or implied....

And at page 117:

> The conventions are like most fundamental rules of any constitution in that they rest essentially upon general acquiescence.

And at page 135:

> ... if the authority itself and those connected with it believe that they ought to do so, then the convention does not exist. This is the ordinary rule applied to customary law. Practice alone is not enough. It must be normative.

In the *First Reference*, at pp. 852, 857 and 883, these views were approved by all the members of this Court who adopted the definition of convention given by Freedman C.J.M. in the Manitoba Reference, including, at p. 883, the following quotation of Hogg, *Constitutional Law of Canada* (1977), at p. 9:

> [A] convention is a rule which is regarded as obligatory by the officials to whom it applies.

Recognition by the actors in the precedents is not only an essential element of conventions. In our opinion, it is the most important element since it is the normative one, the formal one which enables us unmistakably to distinguish a constitutional rule from a rule of convenience or from political expediency.

Counsel for the appellant also contended in reply that recognition by the actors in the precedents need not be explicit, and this contention appears to be supported by the following statement of Jennings already quoted above:

"Convention" implies some form of agreement, whether expressed or implied....

Again, Jennings' assertion must be qualified. Some conventions have been formulated in writing, for instance in the Reports of Imperial Conferences or in the preamble of the *Statute of Westminster, 1931.* Such conventions can be said to have been expressly agreed upon in authoritative or official form.

The majority of constitutional conventions however have not so been reduced to writing. Does this mean that they are based on implied agreements strictly so-called in that they have never been the object of any form of utterance? We do not think so.

Conventions are commonly asserted or claimed by some political actors in more or less informal statements, while the other actors similarly acknowledge them in principle if not always in their application to particular facts. Conventions are analysed, dissected, commented upon and sometimes criticized albeit not to the point of rejection. But, in our view, a convention could not have remained wholly inarticulate, except perhaps at the inchoate stage when it has not yet been accepted as a binding rule. We know of no example of a convention being born while remaining completely unspoken, and none was cited to us....

In our view, the Quebec Court of Appeal was correct in holding that the appellant had failed to establish that Quebec had a conventional power of veto over constitutional amendments such as those in issue in the present Reference.

VII. Conclusion

For these reasons, we would answer "No" to the constitutional question, and we would dismiss the appeal. There should be no order as to costs.

Reference re Secession of Quebec, 1998

In 1985, the Liberal government of Quebec set five conditions to be satisfied in exchange for Quebec's political assent to the 1982 patriation package of constitutional changes. Among those conditions was a constitutional recognition that Quebec constitutes within Canada a "distinct society" and that Quebec has a veto over any significant constitutional changes affecting that province. These conditions formed the basis of the Meech Lake Accord of 1987. After the death of the Accord, in 1990, and the failure of the 1992 Charlottetown Accord, which also would have granted key Quebec constitutional demands, many Quebecers were convinced that independence from Canada was the only route to political autonomy and broad recognition that Quebec is a nation.[1]

In 1994, the Parti Québécois, under Jacques Parizeau, formed the provincial government and soon after declared that a referendum on sovereignty would be held in 1995. The question put to Quebecers on October 30 was:

> Do you agree that Quebec should become sovereign after having made a formal offer to Canada for a new economic and political partnership within the scope of the bill respecting the future of Quebec and of the agreement signed on June 12, 1995?

The government did ask Quebecers to agree to Quebec becoming sovereign after certain steps were followed. But, referring as it did to an offer yet to be made, a bill, and an "agreement," the question could be considered unclear.

The Quebec referendum campaign became a highly emotional affair and was almost won by the charismatic—indeed, messianic—Bloc Québécois leader Lucien Bouchard, whose appeal to ordinary Quebecers surpassed that of Parizeau and provincial Liberal leader Daniel Johnson.[2] On October 30, 1995, 49.42 percent of Quebecers voted "Oui," just shy of a stunning victory.

Prime Minister Jean Chrétien, confident all along that the "Non" forces would prevail, and appearing to assume that a 50 + 1 percent "Non" vote was all that was needed to defeat the "Oui" forces, was criticized for almost having lost the country by his inaction. Ottawa responded to the vote with a sympathetic "Plan A" and, later, with a tougher "Plan B." Plan A granted Quebec a constitutional veto: the federal government would commit itself by non-constitutional means not to ratify any amendment to the Constitution arising under the 7/50 rule[3] without first being assured of Quebec's assent to the amendment. It also had the House of Commons pass a resolution recognizing Quebec as a distinct society.

---

1 For a general discussion of the constitutional politics of the period, see Peter H. Russell, *Constitutional Odyssey: Can Canadians Become a Sovereign People?*, 3d ed. (Toronto: University of Toronto Press, 2004) cc. 9 to 12.

2 Mario Cardinal, *Breaking Point Quebec/Canada: The 1995 Referendum*, trans. Ferdinanda Van Gennip with Mark Stout (Montreal: CBC/Bayard Canada Books, 2005) cc. 8 and 9.

3 Under the general "7/50" rule set out in section 38 of the *Constitution Act, 1982*, proposed constitutional amendments must be ratified by the House of Commons, Senate, and at least seven provincial assemblies representing 50 percent of the Canadian population.

But Plan B was in the works. In the summer of 1995, Quebec lawyer (and former separatist) Guy Bertrand had attempted to get a Quebec court to stop the sovereignty referendum. The Quebec Superior Court granted his claim that a successful referendum result leading to the rupture of Canada would infringe Bertrand's rights under the *Canadian Charter*, but refused to grant an injunction that would have halted the referendum.[4] After the referendum, he was back at it. The federal government then decided to take over Bertrand's legal action and convert it into a reference directly to the Supreme Court of Canada. The government's position was clear and now firmer: if Quebec were to leave, it would either have to do so in contravention of the Canadian Constitution (and risk losing the support of the international community) or it would have to negotiate secession and comply with the amendment procedures of the Canadian Constitution. The government put three questions to the Court:

1. Under the Constitution of Canada, can the National Assembly, legislature, or government of Quebec effect the secession of Quebec from Canada unilaterally?
2. Does international law give the National Assembly, legislature, or government of Quebec the right to effect the secession of Quebec from Canada unilaterally? In this regard, is there a right to self-determination under international law that would give the National Assembly, legislature, or government of Quebec the right to effect the secession of Quebec from Canada unilaterally?
3. In the event of a conflict between domestic and international law on the right of the National Assembly, legislature or government of Quebec to effect the secession of Quebec from Canada unilaterally, which would take precedence in Canada?

Courts are free to refrain from answering reference questions. Indeed, counsel appointed by the Court to argue against the federal government (the Quebec government refused to participate in the reference proceedings) suggested that the questions were too vague, political, or hypothetical to merit the Court's attention. Noting that its primary concern in exercising its discretion in references is "to retain its proper role within the framework of our democratic form of government," the Court concluded that the reference questions raise questions of importance, are precise enough to permit a proper legal answer, and do not drag the Court into matters beyond the judicial role.

The Court's opinion reads more like an essay than a legal decision, containing references to studies and academic papers, but few legal precedents. This should not be a surprise. The Canadian Constitution contains no reference to secession. The Court, as a result, offered a legal opinion on a fundamental constitutional matter on which there was no domestic legal provision or precedent for it to rely. In the absence of black letter law, the Court referred to "basic constitutional principles" and the "structure" or "architecture" of the Constitution. The four key principles are federalism, democracy, rule of law and constitutionalism, and the protection of minority rights. Quebec's strongest argument in secession politics has always been that democracy is a bedrock principle in Quebec and Canada and that a popular vote to secede itself confers legitimacy on secession. By nesting democratic principle in a set of equally fundamental constitutional principles, the Court was able to suggest that "[i]t would be a grave mistake to equate legitimacy with the 'sovereign will' or majority rule alone, to the exclusion of other constitutional values."

---

4   *Bertrand v. Quebec (Procureur General)* (1995), 127 D.L.R. (4th) 408 (Quebec Sup. Ct.).

In an ingenious resolution to the explosive questions put to it, the Court held in a unanimous, unsigned opinion that Quebec does not have a constitutional right to unilateral secession. This also is unsurprising. How could Canada's highest law court affirm Quebec's secession from Canada outside the terms of the Constitution? The Court's *raison d'être* is to uphold the Constitution. This basic principle gave the federal government every confidence in the answers to its questions. More surprising is how the Court fashioned a series of compelling constitutional requirements from a set of vague constitutional principles. Its answer to question 1 was that, if a clear majority of Quebec voters approved a clear question on secession, the rest of Canada would assume a constitutional obligation to negotiate the amendments to the Constitution that would effect Quebec secession. "The referendum result, if it is to be taken as an expression of the democratic will, must be free of ambiguity both in terms of the question asked and in terms of the support it receives."

The *Quebec Secession* opinion proved attentive to the dynamics of Quebec secession politics: the vaguer the referendum question on sovereignty, the higher the popular support it would garner; the clearer the question, the lower the support. According to the Supreme Court, the Canadian Constitution requires that Quebec separatists would need both a clear majority and a clear question. To get both is much harder than getting one or the other. For Canadians whose Canada includes Quebec, this is good news. For the Court, its legitimacy in Quebec was tested by a reference opinion so cleverly engineered as to make separation by constitutional means unlikely. After the release of the opinion, separatists took heart that the Court recognized formally that Canada is divisible.[5] The Court escaped with its authority intact.

The Court refused to specify what counts as a clear majority and a clear question. "It will be for the political actors," the Court held, "to determine what constitutes a 'a clear majority on a clear question.'" Having laid out the principles in play in a secession scenario, the Court left the controversial details to the legislature, effectively replacing the prospect of popular revolution with popular constitutionalism.[6] Parliament responded to the reference opinion by enacting the *Clarity Act* (2000). Its preamble recognizes the Court's "determination" of the central issues in secession referenda. The *Act* requires the House of Commons to pronounce on the clarity of a sovereignty referendum question within 30 days of its publication. Section 1(3) requires the House to consider, among other things, "whether the question would result in a clear expression of the will of the population of a province on whether the province should cease to be part of Canada and become an independent state." After a referendum is held, the House is required to determine "whether . . . there has been a clear expression of a will by a clear majority of the population" of the province. In determining the clarity of the question and of the majority in favour sufficient to trigger negotiations, the House is required to take into account a variety of factors including the views of other parties in the legislature of the province in which the referendum will take place. If the

---

5 For reactions to the Secession Reference, see David Schneiderman, ed., *The Quebec Decision: Perspectives on the Supreme Court's Ruling on Secession* (Toronto: Lorimer, 1999), and David Cameron, ed., *The Referendum Papers: Essays on Secession and National Unity* (Toronto: University of Toronto Press, 1999).

6 Sujit Choudhry, "Popular Revolution or Popular Constitutionalism? Reflections on the Constitutional Politics of Quebec Secession" in Richard W. Bauman and Tsvi Kahana, eds., *The Least Examined Branch: The Role of Legislatures in the Constitutional State* (New York: Cambridge University Press, 2006) 480-98.

House determines that a clear majority voted in favour of a clear question on secession, then the Government of Canada and the provinces must enter into negotiations on amendments to the Constitution to effect secession. All parties are instructed to consider the rights and interests of Aboriginal peoples and minority groups.

In putting legislative flesh on the bones of the Court's opinion, the *Clarity Act* leaves the decision to negotiate secession to a chamber whose Quebec members constitute 24.4 percent of the whole. And the decisions to be made on the clarity of the question and the majority voting in favour—both highly debatable—are left to that chamber. The *Clarity Act*'s power may depend on its provisions never having to be tested in a secession crisis.[7]

Politicians are attracted to references in part because the courts can be given difficult issues to address while sparing the politicians the unhappy political consequences of addressing those issues themselves. Furthermore, a court's opinion on a reference gives the answer a patina of authority it might lack coming from the mouth of a prime minister. The key for governments is not to ask the Court questions whose answers they do not already know. Here the reference strategy worked perfectly for the federal government. ⌁

---

7   In defiance of the terms of the *Clarity Act*, the Quebec National Assembly in 2000 passed *An Act respecting the Exercise of the fundamental rights and prerogatives of the Québec people and the Québec State*, which, among other things, declares that "[n]o other parliament or government may reduce the powers, authority, sovereignty or legitimacy of the National Assembly, or impose constraint on the democratic will of the Québec people to determine its own future."

REFERENCE RE SECESSION OF QUEBEC
[1998] 2 S.C.R. 217

Hearing: February 16, 17, 18, 19, 1998; Judgment: August 20, 1998.

Present: Lamer C.J. and L'Heureux-Dubé, Gonthier, Cory, McLachlin, Iacobucci, Major, Bastarache, and Binnie JJ.

Interveners: The Attorney General of Manitoba; the Attorney General for Saskatchewan; the Minister of Justice of the Northwest Territories; the Minister of Justice for the Government of the Yukon Territory; Kitigan Zibi Anishinabeg; the Grand Council of the Crees (Eeyou Estchee); the Makivik Corporation; the Chiefs of Ontario; the Minority Advocacy and Rights Council; the Ad Hoc Committee of Canadian Women on the Constitution; Guy Bertrand; Roopnarine Singh, Keith Owen Henderson, Claude Leclerc, Kenneth O'Donnell, and Van Hoven Petteway; and Vincent Pouliot.

The following is the judgment delivered by

THE COURT:

I. Introduction

[1] This Reference requires us to consider momentous questions that go to the heart of our system of constitutional government. . . .

[2] The [question] posed by the Governor in Council . . . reads as follows:

Under the Constitution of Canada, can the National Assembly, legislature or government of Quebec effect the secession of Quebec from Canada unilaterally? . . .

A. [The] Question

[32] . . . In order to endure over time, a constitution must contain a comprehensive set of rules and principles which are capable of providing an exhaustive legal framework for our system of government. Such principles and rules emerge from an understanding of the constitutional text itself, the historical context, and previous judicial interpretations of constitutional meaning. In our view, there are four fundamental and organizing principles of the Constitution which are relevant to addressing the question before us (although this enumeration is by no means exhaustive): federalism; democracy; constitutionalism and the rule of law; and respect for minorities. . . .

(3) Analysis of Constitutional Principles

[49] . . . Our Constitution is primarily a written one, the product of 131 years of evolution. Behind the written word is an historical lineage stretching back through the ages, which aids in the consideration of the underlying constitutional principles. These principles inform and sustain the constitutional

text: they are the vital unstated assumptions upon which the text is based. The following discussion addresses the four foundational constitutional principles that are most germane for resolution of this Reference: federalism, democracy, constitutionalism and the rule of law, and respect for minority rights. These defining principles function in symbiosis. No single principle can be defined in isolation from the others, nor does any one principle trump or exclude the operation of any other.

[50] ... The individual elements of the Constitution are linked to the others, and must be interpreted by reference to the structure of the Constitution as a whole. As we recently emphasized in the *Provincial Judges Reference*, [1997], certain underlying principles infuse our Constitution and breathe life into it. Speaking of the rule of law principle in the *Manitoba Language Rights Reference*, [1985] ... we held that "the principle is clearly implicit in the very nature of a Constitution." The same may be said of the other three constitutional principles we underscore today.

[51] Although these underlying principles are not explicitly made part of the Constitution by any written provision, other than in some respects by the oblique reference in the preamble to the *Constitution Act, 1867*, it would be impossible to conceive of our constitutional structure without them. The principles dictate major elements of the architecture of the Constitution itself and are as such its lifeblood.

[52] The principles assist in the interpretation of the text and the delineation of spheres of jurisdiction, the scope of rights and obligations, and the role of our political institutions. Equally important, observance of and respect for these principles is essential to the ongoing process of constitutional development and evolution of our Constitution as a "living tree" .... Canadians have long recognized the existence and importance of unwritten constitutional principles in our system of government.

[53] ... [T]here are compelling reasons to insist upon the primacy of our written constitution. A written constitution promotes legal certainty and predictability, and it provides the foundation and a touchstone for the exercise of constitutional judicial review. However ... the effect of the preamble to the *Constitution Act, 1867* was to incorporate certain constitutional principles by reference. ...

[54] Underlying constitutional principles may in certain circumstances give rise to substantive legal obligations ... which constitute substantive limitations upon government action. These principles may give rise to very abstract and general obligations, or they may be more specific and precise in nature. The principles are not merely descriptive, but are also invested with a powerful normative force, and are binding upon both courts and governments. ... It is to a discussion of those underlying constitutional principles that we now turn.

(b) Federalism

... [56] In a federal system of government such as ours, political power is shared by two orders of government: the federal government on the one hand, and the provinces on the other. Each is assigned respective spheres of jurisdiction by the *Constitution Act, 1867* .... In interpreting our Constitution, the courts have always been concerned with the federalism principle, inherent in the structure of our constitutional arrangements, which has from the beginning been the lodestar by which the courts have been guided. ...

[58] The principle of federalism recognizes the diversity of the component parts of Confederation, and the autonomy of provincial governments to develop their societies within their respective spheres of jurisdiction. The federal structure of our country also facilitates democratic participation by distributing power to the government thought to be most suited to achieving the particular societal objective having regard to this diversity. The scheme of the *Constitution Act, 1867*, it was said in *Re the Initiative and Referendum Act*, [1919] ... was

> not to weld the Provinces into one, nor to subordinate Provincial Governments to a central authority, but to establish a central government in which these Provinces should be represented, entrusted with exclusive authority only in affairs in which they had a common interest. Subject to this each Province was to retain its independence and autonomy and to be directly under the Crown as its head. ...

[59] The principle of federalism facilitates the pursuit of collective goals by cultural and linguistic minorities which form the majority within a particular province. This is the case in Quebec, where the majority of the population is French-speaking, and which possesses a distinct culture. This is not merely the result of chance. The social and demographic reality of Quebec explains the existence of the province of Quebec as a political unit and indeed, was one of the essential reasons for establishing a federal structure for the Canadian union in 1867. The experience of both Canada East and Canada West under the *Union Act, 1840*, had not been satisfactory. The federal structure adopted at Confederation enabled French-speaking Canadians to form a numerical majority in the province of Quebec, and so exercise the considerable provincial powers conferred by the *Constitution Act, 1867* in such a way as to promote their language and culture. It also made provision for certain guaranteed representation within the federal Parliament itself.

[60] Federalism was also welcomed by Nova Scotia and New Brunswick, both of which also affirmed their will to protect their individual cultures and their autonomy over local matters. All new provinces joining the federation sought to achieve similar objectives, which are no less vigorously

pursued by the provinces and territories as we approach the new millennium.

(c) Democracy

[61] Democracy is a fundamental value in our constitutional law and political culture. While it has both an institutional and an individual aspect, the democratic principle was also argued before us in the sense of the supremacy of the sovereign will of a people, in this case potentially to be expressed by Quebecers in support of unilateral secession. It is useful to explore in a summary way these different aspects of the democratic principle.

[62] ... [T]he democracy principle can best be understood as a sort of baseline against which the framers of our Constitution, and subsequently, our elected representatives under it, have always operated. It is perhaps for this reason that the principle was not explicitly identified in the text of the *Constitution Act, 1867* itself. To have done so might have appeared redundant, even silly, to the framers. As [we] explained in the *Provincial Judges Reference*, [1997] ... it is evident that our Constitution contemplates that Canada shall be a constitutional democracy. Yet this merely demonstrates the importance of underlying constitutional principles that are nowhere explicitly described in our constitutional texts. The representative and democratic nature of our political institutions was simply assumed....

[64] Democracy is not simply concerned with the process of government. On the contrary, as suggested in *Switzman v. Elbling*, [1957] ... democracy is fundamentally connected to substantive goals, most importantly, the promotion of self-government. Democracy accommodates cultural and group identities.... Put another way, a sovereign people exercises its right to self-government through the democratic process. In considering the scope and purpose of the *Charter*, the Court in *R. v. Oakes*, [1986] articulated some of the values inherent in the notion of democracy ...:

> The Court must be guided by the values and principles essential to a free and democratic society which I believe to embody, to name but a few, respect for the inherent dignity of the human person, commitment to social justice and equality, accommodation of a wide variety of beliefs, respect for cultural and group identity, and faith in social and political institutions which enhance the participation of individuals and groups in society....

[66] ... It is, of course, true that democracy expresses the sovereign will of the people. Yet this expression, too, must be taken in the context of the other institutional values we have identified as pertinent to this Reference. The relationship between democracy and federalism means, for example, that in Canada there may be different and equally legitimate

majorities in different provinces and territories and at the federal level. No one majority is more or less "legitimate" than the others as an expression of democratic opinion, although, of course, the consequences will vary with the subject matter. A federal system of government enables different provinces to pursue policies responsive to the particular concerns and interests of people in that province. At the same time, Canada as a whole is also a democratic community in which citizens construct and achieve goals on a national scale through a federal government acting within the limits of its jurisdiction. The function of federalism is to enable citizens to participate concurrently in different collectivities and to pursue goals at both a provincial and a federal level.

[67] The consent of the governed is a value that is basic to our understanding of a free and democratic society. Yet democracy in any real sense of the word cannot exist without the rule of law. It is the law that creates the framework within which the "sovereign will" is to be ascertained and implemented. To be accorded legitimacy, democratic institutions must rest, ultimately, on a legal foundation. That is, they must allow for the participation of, and accountability to, the people, through public institutions created under the Constitution. Equally, however, a system of government cannot survive through adherence to the law alone. A political system must also possess legitimacy, and in our political culture, that requires an interaction between the rule of law and the democratic principle. The system must be capable of reflecting the aspirations of the people. But there is more. Our law's claim to legitimacy also rests on an appeal to moral values, many of which are imbedded in our constitutional structure. It would be a grave mistake to equate legitimacy with the "sovereign will" or majority rule alone, to the exclusion of other constitutional values.

[68] Finally, we highlight that a functioning democracy requires a continuous process of discussion. The Constitution mandates government by democratic legislatures, and an executive accountable to them, "resting ultimately on public opinion reached by discussion and the interplay of ideas" (*Saumur v. City of Quebec*, [1953]. . . .) At both the federal and provincial level, by its very nature, the need to build majorities necessitates compromise, negotiation, and deliberation. No one has a monopoly on truth, and our system is predicated on the faith that in the marketplace of ideas, the best solutions to public problems will rise to the top. Inevitably, there will be dissenting voices. A democratic system of government is committed to considering those dissenting voices, and seeking to acknowledge and address those voices in the laws by which all in the community must live.

[69] *The Constitution Act, 1982* gives expression to this principle, by conferring a right to initiate constitutional change on each participant in Confederation. In our view, the existence

of this right imposes a corresponding duty on the participants in Confederation to engage in constitutional discussions in order to acknowledge and address democratic expressions of a desire for change in other provinces. This duty is inherent in the democratic principle which is a fundamental predicate of our system of governance.

(d) Constitutionalism and the Rule of Law

[70] ... At its most basic level, the rule of law vouchsafes to the citizens and residents of the country a stable, predictable and ordered society in which to conduct their affairs. It provides a shield for individuals from arbitrary state action....

[72] The constitutionalism principle bears considerable similarity to the rule of law, although they are not identical. The essence of constitutionalism in Canada is embodied in s. 52(1) of the *Constitution Act, 1982*, which provides that "[t]he Constitution of Canada is the supreme law of Canada, and any law that is inconsistent with the provisions of the Constitution is, to the extent of the inconsistency, of no force or effect." Simply put, the constitutionalism principle requires that all government action comply with the Constitution. The rule of law principle requires that all government action must comply with the law, including the Constitution....

[73] An understanding of the scope and importance of the principles of the rule of law and constitutionalism is aided by acknowledging explicitly why a constitution is entrenched beyond the reach of simple majority rule. There are three overlapping reasons.

[74] First, a constitution may provide an added safeguard for fundamental human rights and individual freedoms which might otherwise be susceptible to government interference. Although democratic government is generally solicitous of those rights, there are occasions when the majority will be tempted to ignore fundamental rights in order to accomplish collective goals more easily or effectively. Constitutional entrenchment ensures that those rights will be given due regard and protection. Second, a constitution may seek to ensure that vulnerable minority groups are endowed with the institutions and rights necessary to maintain and promote their identities against the assimilative pressures of the majority. And third, a constitution may provide for a division of political power that allocates political power amongst different levels of government. That purpose would be defeated if one of those democratically elected levels of government could usurp the powers of the other simply by exercising its legislative power to allocate additional political power to itself unilaterally.

[75] The argument that the Constitution may be legitimately circumvented by resort to a majority vote in a province-wide referendum is superficially persuasive, in large measure because it seems to appeal to some of the same principles that underlie the legitimacy of the Constitution itself, namely, democracy and self-government.... However, closer analysis reveals that this argument is unsound, because it misunderstands the meaning of popular sovereignty and the essence of constitutional democracy.

[76] Canadians have never accepted that ours is a system of simple majority rule. Our principle of democracy, taken in conjunction with the other constitutional principles discussed here, is richer. Constitutional government is necessarily predicated on the idea that the political representatives of the people of a province have the capacity and the power to commit the province to be bound into the future by the constitutional rules being adopted. These rules are "binding" not in the sense of frustrating the will of a majority of a province, but as defining the majority which must be consulted in order to alter the fundamental balances of political power (including the spheres of autonomy guaranteed by the principle of federalism), individual rights, and minority rights in our society. Of course, those constitutional rules are themselves amenable to amendment, but only through a process of negotiation which ensures that there is an opportunity for the constitutionally defined rights of all the parties to be respected and reconciled.

[77] In this way, our belief in democracy may be harmonized with our belief in constitutionalism. Constitutional amendment often requires some form of substantial consensus precisely because the content of the underlying principles of our Constitution demand it. By requiring broad support in the form of an "enhanced majority" to achieve constitutional change, the Constitution ensures that minority interests must be addressed before proposed changes which would affect them may be enacted.

[78] It might be objected, then, that constitutionalism is therefore incompatible with democratic government. This would be an erroneous view. Constitutionalism facilitates—indeed, makes possible—a democratic political system by creating an orderly framework within which people may make political decisions. Viewed correctly, constitutionalism and the rule of law are not in conflict with democracy; rather, they are essential to it. Without that relationship, the political will upon which democratic decisions are taken would itself be undermined.

(e) Protection of Minorities

[79] The fourth underlying constitutional principle we address here concerns the protection of minorities. There are a number of specific constitutional provisions protecting minority language, religion and education rights....

[81] The concern of our courts and governments to protect minorities has been prominent in recent years, particularly following the enactment of the *Charter*. Undoubtedly, one of the key considerations motivating the enactment of the

Charter, and the process of constitutional judicial review that it entails, is the protection of minorities. However, it should not be forgotten that the protection of minority rights had a long history before the enactment of the *Charter*. Indeed, the protection of minority rights was clearly an essential consideration in the design of our constitutional structure even at the time of Confederation . . . .

[82] Consistent with this long tradition of respect for minorities, which is at least as old as Canada itself, the framers of the *Constitution Act, 1982* included in s. 35 explicit protection for existing aboriginal and treaty rights, and in s. 25, a non-derogation clause in favour of the rights of aboriginal peoples. The "promise" of s. 35, as it was termed in *R. v. Sparrow*, [1990] . . . recognized not only the ancient occupation of land by aboriginal peoples, but their contribution to the building of Canada, and the special commitments made to them by successive governments. The protection of these rights, so recently and arduously achieved, whether looked at in their own right or as part of the larger concern with minorities, reflects an important underlying constitutional value.

(4) The Operation of the Constitutional Principles in the Secession Context

[83] Secession is the effort of a group or section of a state to withdraw itself from the political and constitutional authority of that state, with a view to achieving statehood for a new territorial unit on the international plane. In a federal state, secession typically takes the form of a territorial unit seeking to withdraw from the federation. Secession is a legal act as much as a political one. By the terms of [the question] of this Reference, we are asked to rule on the legality of unilateral secession "[u]nder the Constitution of Canada." This is an appropriate question, as the legality of unilateral secession must be evaluated, at least in the first instance, from the perspective of the domestic legal order of the state from which the unit seeks to withdraw. . . .

[84] The secession of a province from Canada must be considered, in legal terms, to require an amendment to the Constitution, which perforce requires negotiation. The amendments necessary to achieve a secession could be radical and extensive. Some commentators have suggested that secession could be a change of such a magnitude that it could not be considered to be merely an amendment to the Constitution. We are not persuaded by this contention. It is of course true that the Constitution is silent as to the ability of a province to secede from Confederation but, although the Constitution neither expressly authorizes nor prohibits secession, an act of secession would purport to alter the governance of Canadian territory in a manner which undoubtedly is inconsistent with our current constitutional arrangements. The fact that those changes would be profound, or that they would purport to have a significance with respect to international law, does not negate their nature as amendments to the Constitution of Canada. . . .

[86] The "unilateral" nature of [Quebec secession] is of cardinal importance and we must be clear as to what is understood by this term. In one sense, any step towards a constitutional amendment initiated by a single actor on the constitutional stage is "unilateral." We do not believe that this is the meaning contemplated by [the reference question], nor is this the sense in which the term has been used in argument before us. Rather, what is claimed by a right to secede "unilaterally" is the right to effectuate secession without prior negotiations with the other provinces and the federal government. At issue is not the legality of the first step but the legality of the final act of purported unilateral secession. The supposed juridical basis for such an act is said to be a clear expression of democratic will in a referendum in the province of Quebec. This claim requires us to examine the possible juridical impact, if any, of such a referendum on the functioning of our Constitution, and on the claimed legality of a unilateral act of secession.

[87] Although the Constitution does not itself address the use of a referendum procedure, and the results of a referendum have no direct role or legal effect in our constitutional scheme, a referendum undoubtedly may provide a democratic method of ascertaining the views of the electorate on important political questions on a particular occasion. The democratic principle identified above would demand that considerable weight be given to a clear expression by the people of Quebec of their will to secede from Canada, even though a referendum, in itself and without more, has no direct legal effect, and could not in itself bring about unilateral secession. Our political institutions are premised on the democratic principle, and so an expression of the democratic will of the people of a province carries weight, in that it would confer legitimacy on the efforts of the government of Quebec to initiate the Constitution's amendment process in order to secede by constitutional means. In this context, we refer to a "clear" majority as a qualitative evaluation. The referendum result, if it is to be taken as an expression of the democratic will, must be free of ambiguity both in terms of the question asked and in terms of the support it achieves.

[88] The federalism principle, in conjunction with the democratic principle, dictates that the clear repudiation of the existing constitutional order and the clear expression of the desire to pursue secession by the population of a province would give rise to a reciprocal obligation on all parties to Confederation to negotiate constitutional changes to respond to that desire. The amendment of the Constitution begins with a political process undertaken pursuant to the Constitution

itself. In Canada, the initiative for constitutional amendment is the responsibility of democratically elected representatives of the participants in Confederation. Those representatives may, of course, take their cue from a referendum, but in legal terms, constitution-making in Canada, as in many countries, is undertaken by the democratically elected representatives of the people. The corollary of a legitimate attempt by one participant in Confederation to seek an amendment to the Constitution is an obligation on all parties to come to the negotiating table. The clear repudiation by the people of Quebec of the existing constitutional order would confer legitimacy on demands for secession, and place an obligation on the other provinces and the federal government to acknowledge and respect that expression of democratic will by entering into negotiations and conducting them in accordance with the underlying constitutional principles already discussed.

[89] What is the content of this obligation to negotiate? . . .

[90] The conduct of the parties in such negotiations would be governed by the same constitutional principles which give rise to the duty to negotiate: federalism, democracy, constitutionalism and the rule of law, and the protection of minorities. Those principles lead us to reject two absolutist propositions. One of those propositions is that there would be a legal obligation on the other provinces and federal government to accede to the secession of a province, subject only to negotiation of the logistical details of secession. This proposition is attributed either to the supposed implications of the democratic principle of the Constitution, or to the international law principle of self-determination of peoples.

[91] The For both theoretical and practical reasons, we cannot accept this view. We hold that Quebec could not purport to invoke a right of self-determination such as to dictate the terms of a proposed secession to the other parties: that would not be a negotiation at all. As well, it would be naive to expect that the substantive goal of secession could readily be distinguished from the practical details of secession. The devil would be in the details. The democracy principle, as we have emphasized, cannot be invoked to trump the principles of federalism and rule of law, the rights of individuals and minorities, or the operation of democracy in the other provinces or in Canada as a whole. No negotiations could be effective if their ultimate outcome, secession, is cast as an absolute legal entitlement based upon an obligation to give effect to that act of secession in the Constitution. Such a foregone conclusion would actually undermine the obligation to negotiate and render it hollow.

[92] However, we are equally unable to accept the reverse proposition, that a clear expression of self-determination by the people of Quebec would impose no obligations upon the other provinces or the federal government. The continued existence and operation of the Canadian constitutional order cannot remain indifferent to the clear expression of a clear majority of Quebecers that they no longer wish to remain in Canada. This would amount to the assertion that other constitutionally recognized principles necessarily trump the clearly expressed democratic will of the people of Quebec. Such a proposition fails to give sufficient weight to the underlying constitutional principles that must inform the amendment process, including the principles of democracy and federalism. The rights of other provinces and the federal government cannot deny the right of the government of Quebec to pursue secession, should a clear majority of the people of Quebec choose that goal, so long as in doing so, Quebec respects the rights of others. Negotiations would be necessary to address the interests of the federal government, of Quebec and the other provinces, and other participants, as well as the rights of all Canadians both within and outside Quebec.

[93] Is the rejection of both of these propositions reconcilable? Yes, once it is realized that none of the rights or principles under discussion is absolute to the exclusion of the others. This observation suggests that other parties cannot exercise their rights in such a way as to amount to an absolute denial of Quebec's rights, and similarly, that so long as Quebec exercises its rights while respecting the rights of others, it may propose secession and seek to achieve it through negotiation. The negotiation process precipitated by a decision of a clear majority of the population of Quebec on a clear question to pursue secession would require the reconciliation of various rights and obligations by the representatives of two legitimate majorities, namely, the clear majority of the population of Quebec, and the clear majority of Canada as a whole, whatever that may be. There can be no suggestion that either of these majorities "trumps" the other. A political majority that does not act in accordance with the underlying constitutional principles we have identified puts at risk the legitimacy of the exercise of its rights.

[94] In such circumstances, the conduct of the parties assumes primary constitutional significance. The negotiation process must be conducted with an eye to the constitutional principles we have outlined, which must inform the actions of *all* the participants in the negotiation process.

[95] Refusal of a party to conduct negotiations in a manner consistent with constitutional principles and values would seriously put at risk the legitimacy of that party's assertion of its rights, and perhaps the negotiation process as a whole. Those who quite legitimately insist upon the importance of upholding the rule of law cannot at the same time be oblivious to the need to act in conformity with constitutional principles and values, and so do their part to contribute to the

maintenance and promotion of an environment in which the rule of law may flourish.

[96] No one can predict the course that such negotiations might take. The possibility that they might not lead to an agreement amongst the parties must be recognized. Negotiations following a referendum vote in favour of seeking secession would inevitably address a wide range of issues, many of great import. After 131 years of Confederation, there exists, inevitably, a high level of integration in economic, political and social institutions across Canada. The vision of those who brought about Confederation was to create a unified country, not a loose alliance of autonomous provinces. Accordingly, while there are regional economic interests, which sometimes coincide with provincial boundaries, there are also national interests and enterprises (both public and private) that would face potential dismemberment. There is a national economy and a national debt. Arguments were raised before us regarding boundary issues. There are linguistic and cultural minorities, including aboriginal peoples, unevenly distributed across the country who look to the Constitution of Canada for the protection of their rights. Of course, secession would give rise to many issues of great complexity and difficulty. These would have to be resolved within the overall framework of the rule of law, thereby assuring Canadians resident in Quebec and elsewhere a measure of stability in what would likely be a period of considerable upheaval and uncertainty. Nobody seriously suggests that our national existence, seamless in so many aspects, could be effortlessly separated along what are now the provincial boundaries of Quebec. As the Attorney General of Saskatchewan put it in his oral submission:

> A nation is built when the communities that comprise it make commitments to it, when they forego choices and opportunities on behalf of a nation, ... when the communities that comprise it make compromises, when they offer each other guarantees, when they make transfers and perhaps most pointedly, when they receive from others the benefits of national solidarity. The threads of a thousand acts of accommodation are the fabric of a nation. ...

[97] In the circumstances, negotiations following such a referendum would undoubtedly be difficult. While the negotiators would have to contemplate the possibility of secession, there would be no absolute legal entitlement to it and no assumption that an agreement reconciling all relevant rights and obligations would actually be reached. It is foreseeable that even negotiations carried out in conformity with the underlying constitutional principles could reach an impasse. We need not speculate here as to what would then transpire. Under the Constitution, secession requires that an amendment be negotiated.

[98] The respective roles of the courts and political actors in discharging the constitutional obligations we have identified follows ineluctably from the foregoing observations. ...

[100] The role of the Court in this Reference is limited to the identification of the relevant aspects of the Constitution in their broadest sense. We have interpreted the questions as relating to the constitutional framework within which political decisions may ultimately be made. Within that framework, the workings of the political process are complex and can only be resolved by means of political judgments and evaluations. The Court has no supervisory role over the political aspects of constitutional negotiations. Equally, the initial impetus for negotiation, namely a clear majority on a clear question in favour of secession, is subject only to political evaluation, and properly so. A right and a corresponding duty to negotiate secession cannot be built on an alleged expression of democratic will if the expression of democratic will is itself fraught with ambiguities. Only the political actors would have the information and expertise to make the appropriate judgment as to the point at which, and the circumstances in which, those ambiguities are resolved one way or the other.

[101] If the circumstances giving rise to the duty to negotiate were to arise, the distinction between the strong defence of legitimate interests and the taking of positions which, in fact, ignore the legitimate interests of others is one that also defies legal analysis. The Court would not have access to all of the information available to the political actors, and the methods appropriate for the search for truth in a court of law are ill-suited to getting to the bottom of constitutional negotiations. To the extent that the questions are political in nature, it is not the role of the judiciary to interpose its own views on the different negotiating positions of the parties, even were it invited to do so. Rather, it is the obligation of the elected representatives to give concrete form to the discharge of their constitutional obligations which only they and their electors can ultimately assess. The reconciliation of the various legitimate constitutional interests outlined above is necessarily committed to the political rather than the judicial realm, precisely because that reconciliation can only be achieved through the give and take of the negotiation process. Having established the legal framework, it would be for the democratically elected leadership of the various participants to resolve their differences.

[102] The non-justiciability of political issues that lack a legal component does not deprive the surrounding constitutional framework of its binding status, nor does this mean that constitutional obligations could be breached without incurring serious legal repercussions. Where there are legal rights there are remedies, but ... the appropriate recourse in some circumstances lies through the workings of the political process rather than the courts.

[103] To the extent that a breach of the constitutional duty to negotiate in accordance with the principles described above undermines the legitimacy of a party's actions, it may have important ramifications at the international level. Thus, a failure of the duty to undertake negotiations and pursue them according to constitutional principles may undermine that government's claim to legitimacy which is generally a precondition for recognition by the international community. Conversely, violations of those principles by the federal or other provincial governments responding to the request for secession may undermine their legitimacy. Thus, a Quebec that had negotiated in conformity with constitutional principles and values in the face of unreasonable intransigence on the part of other participants at the federal or provincial level would be more likely to be recognized than a Quebec which did not itself act according to constitutional principles in the negotiation process. Both the legality of the acts of the parties to the negotiation process under Canadian law, and the perceived legitimacy of such action, would be important considerations in the recognition process. In this way, the adherence of the parties to the obligation to negotiate would be evaluated in an indirect manner on the international plane.

[104] Accordingly, the secession of Quebec from Canada cannot be accomplished by the National Assembly, the legislature or government of Quebec unilaterally, that is to say, without principled negotiations, and be considered a lawful act. Any attempt to effect the secession of a province from Canada must be undertaken pursuant to the Constitution of Canada, or else violate the Canadian legal order. However, the continued existence and operation of the Canadian constitutional order cannot remain unaffected by the unambiguous expression of a clear majority of Quebecers that they no longer wish to remain in Canada. The primary means by which that expression is given effect is the constitutional duty to negotiate in accordance with the constitutional principles that we have described herein. In the event secession negotiations are initiated, our Constitution, no less than our history, would call on the participants to work to reconcile the rights, obligations and legitimate aspirations of all Canadians within a framework that emphasizes constitutional responsibilities as much as it does constitutional rights. . . .

[The Court answered the second reference question— whether international law recognizes Quebec's right to self-determination, which justifies unilateral secession from Canada—in the negative. International law, the Court held, supports secession when a people is oppressed and denied meaningful opportunities for self-determination within the polities from which they want to secede. Assuming, without

deciding, that Quebec constitutes a "people" for the purposes of international law, the Court held that Quebec is not oppressed and denied meaningful self-determination within Canada. It elects officers to the national government, enjoys constitutionally protected jurisdiction over matters assigned to provinces, and can participate in amendment of the Constitution. Because the answers to the first and second questions both fail to affirm Quebec's right to unilateral secession, the Court did not have to answer the third reference question.]

IV. Summary of Conclusions

. . . [149] The Reference requires us to consider whether Quebec has a right to *unilateral* secession. Those who support the existence of such a right found their case primarily on the principle of democracy. Democracy, however, means more than simple majority rule. As reflected in our constitutional jurisprudence, democracy exists in the larger context of other constitutional values such as those already mentioned. In the 131 years since Confederation, the people of the provinces and territories have created close ties of interdependence (economically, socially, politically and culturally) based on shared values that include federalism, democracy, constitutionalism and the rule of law, and respect for minorities. A democratic decision of Quebecers in favour of secession would put those relationships at risk. The Constitution vouchsafes order and stability, and accordingly secession of a province "under the Constitution" could not be achieved unilaterally, that is, without principled negotiation with other participants in Confederation within the existing constitutional framework.

[150] The Constitution is not a straitjacket. Even a brief review of our constitutional history demonstrates periods of momentous and dramatic change. Our democratic institutions necessarily accommodate a continuous process of discussion and evolution, which is reflected in the constitutional right of each participant in the federation to initiate constitutional change. This right implies a reciprocal duty on the other participants to engage in discussions to address any legitimate initiative to change the constitutional order. While it is true that some attempts at constitutional amendment in recent years have faltered, a clear majority vote in Quebec on a clear question in favour of secession would confer democratic legitimacy on the secession initiative which all of the other participants in Confederation would have to recognize. . . .

[153] The task of the Court has been to clarify the legal framework within which political decisions are to be taken "under the Constitution," not to usurp the prerogatives of the political forces that operate within that framework. The obligations we have identified are binding obligations under the Constitution of Canada. However, it will be for the political

actors to determine what constitutes "a clear majority on a clear question" in the circumstances under which a future referendum vote may be taken. Equally, in the event of demonstrated majority support for Quebec secession, the content and process of the negotiations will be for the political actors to settle. The reconciliation of the various legitimate constitutional interests is necessarily committed to the political rather than the judicial realm precisely because that reconciliation can only be achieved through the give and take of political negotiations. To the extent issues addressed in the course of negotiation are political, the courts, appreciating their proper role in the constitutional scheme, would have no supervisory role. . . .

[155] Although there is no right, under the Constitution or at international law, to unilateral secession . . . this does not rule out the possibility of an unconstitutional declaration of secession leading to a *de facto* secession. The ultimate success of such a secession would be dependent on recognition by the international community, which is likely to consider the legality and legitimacy of secession having regard to, amongst other facts, the conduct of Quebec and Canada, in determining whether to grant or withhold recognition. Such recognition, even if granted, would not, however, provide any retroactive justification for the act of secession, either under the Constitution of Canada or at international law.

APPENDIX 1

The Constitution Act, 1867

30 & 31 Victoria, c. 3 (U.K.)

VI. DISTRIBUTION OF LEGISLATIVE POWERS

Powers of the Parliament

91. It shall be lawful for the Queen, by and with the Advice and Consent of the Senate and House of Commons, to make Laws for the Peace, Order, and good Government of Canada, in relation to all Matters not coming within the Classes of Subjects by this Act assigned exclusively to the Legislatures of the Provinces; and for greater Certainty, but not so as to restrict the Generality of the foregoing Terms of this Section, it is hereby declared that (notwithstanding anything in this Act) the exclusive Legislative Authority of the Parliament of Canada extends to all Matters coming within the Classes of Subjects next hereinafter enumerated; that is to say,

Legislative Authority of Parliament of Canada

1. Repealed.
1A. The Public Debt and Property.
2. The Regulation of Trade and Commerce.
2A. Unemployment insurance.
3. The raising of Money by any Mode or System of Taxation.
4. The borrowing of Money on the Public Credit.
5. Postal Service.
6. The Census and Statistics.
7. Militia, Military and Naval Service, and Defence.
8. The fixing of and providing for the Salaries and Allowances of Civil and other Officers of the Government of Canada.
9. Beacons, Buoys, Lighthouses, and Sable Island.
10. Navigation and Shipping.
11. Quarantine and the Establishment and Maintenance of Marine Hospitals.
12. Sea Coast and Inland Fisheries.
13. Ferries between a Province and any British or Foreign Country or between Two Provinces.
14. Currency and Coinage.
15. Banking, Incorporation of Banks, and the Issue of Paper Money.
16. Savings Banks.
17. Weights and Measures.
18. Bills of Exchange and Promissory Notes.
19. Interest.
20. Legal Tender.
21. Bankruptcy and Insolvency.

22. Patents of Invention and Discovery.
23. Copyrights.
24. Indians, and Lands reserved for the Indians.
25. Naturalization and Aliens.
26. Marriage and Divorce.
27. The Criminal Law, except the Constitution of Courts of Criminal Jurisdiction, but including the Procedure in Criminal Matters.
28. The Establishment, Maintenance, and Management of Penitentiaries.
29. Such Classes of Subjects as are expressly excepted in the Enumeration of the Classes of Subjects by this Act assigned exclusively to the Legislatures of the Provinces.

And any Matter coming within any of the Classes of Subjects enumerated in this Section shall not be deemed to come within the Class of Matters of a local or private Nature comprised in the Enumeration of the Classes of Subjects by this Act assigned exclusively to the Legislatures of the Provinces.

Exclusive Powers of Provincial Legislatures

Subjects of exclusive Provincial Legislation

92. In each Province the Legislature may exclusively make Laws in relation to Matters coming within the Classes of Subjects next hereinafter enumerated; that is to say,

1. Repealed.
2. Direct Taxation within the Province in order to the raising of a Revenue for Provincial Purposes.
3. The borrowing of Money on the sole Credit of the Province.
4. The Establishment and Tenure of Provincial Offices and the Appointment and Payment of Provincial Officers.
5. The Management and Sale of the Public Lands belonging to the Province and of the Timber and Wood thereon.
6. The Establishment, Maintenance, and Management of Public and Reformatory Prisons in and for the Province.
7. The Establishment, Maintenance, and Management of Hospitals, Asylums, Charities, and Eleemosynary Institutions in and for the Province, other than Marine Hospitals.
8. Municipal Institutions in the Province.
9. Shop, Saloon, Tavern, Auctioneer, and other Licences in order to the raising of a Revenue for Provincial, Local, or Municipal Purposes.
10. Local Works and Undertakings other than such as are of the following Classes:
    (a) Lines of Steam or other Ships, Railways, Canals, Telegraphs, and other Works and Undertakings connecting the Province with any other or others of the Provinces, or extending beyond the Limits of the Province:
    (b) Lines of Steam Ships between the Province and any British or Foreign Country:
    (c) Such Works as, although wholly situate within the Province, are before or after their Execution declared by the Parliament of Canada to be for the general Advantage of Canada or for the Advantage of Two or more of the Provinces.

11. The Incorporation of Companies with Provincial Objects.
12. The Solemnization of Marriage in the Province.
13. Property and Civil Rights in the Province.
14. The Administration of Justice in the Province, including the Constitution, Maintenance, and Organization of Provincial Courts, both of Civil and of Criminal Jurisdiction, and including Procedure in Civil Matters in those Courts.
15. The Imposition of Punishment by Fine, Penalty, or Imprisonment for enforcing any Law of the Province made in relation to any Matter coming within any of the Classes of Subjects enumerated in this Section.
16. Generally all Matters of a merely local or private Nature in the Province.

Non-Renewable Natural Resources, Forestry Resources and Electrical Energy

92A. (1) In each province, the legislature may exclusively make laws in relation to

   (a) exploration for non-renewable natural resources in the province;

   (b) development, conservation and management of non-renewable natural resources and forestry resources in the province, including laws in relation to the rate of primary production therefrom; and

   (c) development, conservation and management of sites and facilities in the province for the generation and production of electrical energy.

(2) In each province, the legislature may make laws in relation to the export from the province to another part of Canada of the primary production from non-renewable natural resources and forestry resources in the province and the production from facilities in the province for the generation of electrical energy, but such laws may not authorize or provide for discrimination in prices or in supplies exported to another part of Canada.

(3) Nothing in subsection (2) derogates from the authority of Parliament to enact laws in relation to the matters referred to in that subsection and, where such a law of Parliament and a law of a province conflict, the law of Parliament prevails to the extent of the conflict.

(4) In each province, the legislature may make laws in relation to the raising of money by any mode or system of taxation in respect of

   (a) non-renewable natural resources and forestry resources in the province and the primary production therefrom, and

   (b) sites and facilities in the province for the generation of electrical energy and the production therefrom,

whether or not such production is exported in whole or in part from the province, but such laws may not authorize or provide for taxation that differentiates between production exported to another part of Canada and production not exported from the province.

(5) The expression "primary production" has the meaning assigned by the Sixth Schedule.

(6) Nothing in subsections (1) to (5) derogates from any powers or rights that a legislature or government of a province had immediately before the coming into force of this section.

Laws respecting non-renewable natural resources, forestry resources and electrical energy

Export from provinces of resources

Authority of Parliament

Taxation of resources

"Primary production"

Existing powers or rights

Education ·

Legislation respecting Education

93. In and for each Province the Legislature may exclusively make Laws in relation to Education, subject and according to the following Provisions:

(1) Nothing in any such Law shall prejudicially affect any Right or Privilege with respect to Denominational Schools which any Class of Persons have by Law in the Province at the Union:

(2) All the Powers, Privileges, and Duties at the Union by Law conferred and imposed in Upper Canada on the Separate Schools and School Trustees of the Queen's Roman Catholic Subjects shall be and the same are hereby extended to the Dissentient Schools of the Queen's Protestant and Roman Catholic Subjects in Quebec:

(3) Where in any Province a System of Separate or Dissentient Schools exists by Law at the Union or is thereafter established by the Legislature of the Province, an Appeal shall lie to the Governor General in Council from any Act or Decision of any Provincial Authority affecting any Right or Privilege of the Protestant or Roman Catholic Minority of the Queen's Subjects in relation to Education:

(4) In case any such Provincial Law as from Time to Time seems to the Governor General in Council requisite for the due Execution of the Provisions of this Section is not made, or in case any Decision of the Governor General in Council on any Appeal under this Section is not duly executed by the proper Provincial Authority in that Behalf, then and in every such Case, and as far only as the Circumstances of each Case require, the Parliament of Canada may make remedial Laws for the due Execution of the Provisions of this Section and of any Decision of the Governor General in Council under this Section.

Quebec

93A. Paragraphs (1) to (4) of section 93 do not apply to Quebec.

Uniformity of Laws in Ontario, Nova Scotia, and New Brunswick

Legislation for Uniformity of Laws in Three Provinces

94. Notwithstanding anything in this Act, the Parliament of Canada may make Provision for the Uniformity of all or any of the Laws relative to Property and Civil Rights in Ontario, Nova Scotia, and New Brunswick, and of the Procedure of all or any of the Courts in those Three Provinces, and from and after the passing of any Act in that Behalf the Power of the Parliament of Canada to make Laws in relation to any Matter comprised in any such Act shall, notwithstanding anything in this Act, be unrestricted; but any Act of the Parliament of Canada making Provision for such Uniformity shall not have effect in any Province unless and until it is adopted and enacted as Law by the Legislature thereof.

Old Age Pensions

Legislation respecting old age pensions and supplementary benefits

94A. The Parliament of Canada may make laws in relation to old age pensions and supplementary benefits, including survivors' and disability benefits irrespective of age, but no such law shall affect the operation of any law present or future of a provincial legislature in relation to any such matter.

Agriculture and Immigration

95. In each Province the Legislature may make Laws in relation to Agriculture in the Province, and to Immigration into the Province; and it is hereby declared that the Parliament of Canada may from Time to Time make Laws in relation to Agriculture in all or any of the Provinces, and to Immigration into all or any of the Provinces; and any Law of the Legislature of a Province relative to Agriculture or to Immigration shall have effect in and for the Province as long and as far only as it is not repugnant to any Act of the Parliament of Canada.

Concurrent Powers of Legislation respecting Agriculture, etc.

VII. JUDICATURE

96. The Governor General shall appoint the Judges of the Superior, District, and County Courts in each Province, except those of the Courts of Probate in Nova Scotia and New Brunswick.

Appointment of Judges

97. Until the Laws relative to Property and Civil Rights in Ontario, Nova Scotia, and New Brunswick, and the Procedure of the Courts in those Provinces, are made uniform, the Judges of the Courts of those Provinces appointed by the Governor General shall be selected from the respective Bars of those Provinces.

Selection of Judges in Ontario, etc.

98. The Judges of the Courts of Quebec shall be selected from the Bar of that Province.

Selection of Judges in Quebec

99. (1) Subject to subsection two of this section, the Judges of the Superior Courts shall hold office during good behaviour, but shall be removable by the Governor General on Address of the Senate and House of Commons.

Tenure of office of Judges

(2) A Judge of a Superior Court, whether appointed before or after the coming into force of this section, shall cease to hold office upon attaining the age of seventy-five years, or upon the coming into force of this section if at that time he has already attained that age.

Termination at age 75

100. The Salaries, Allowances, and Pensions of the Judges of the Superior, District, and County Courts (except the Courts of Probate in Nova Scotia and New Brunswick), and of the Admiralty Courts in Cases where the Judges thereof are for the Time being paid by Salary, shall be fixed and provided by the Parliament of Canada.

Salaries, etc., of Judges

101. The Parliament of Canada may, notwithstanding anything in this Act, from Time to Time provide for the Constitution, Maintenance, and Organization of a General Court of Appeal for Canada, and for the Establishment of any additional Courts for the better Administration of the Laws of Canada.

General Court of Appeal, etc.

. . .

IX. MISCELLANEOUS PROVISIONS

General

. . .

132. The Parliament and Government of Canada shall have all Powers necessary or proper for performing the Obligations of Canada or of any Province thereof, as Part of the British Empire, towards Foreign Countries, arising under Treaties between the Empire and such Foreign Countries.

Treaty Obligations

Use of English and French Languages

133. Either the English or the French Language may be used by any Person in the Debates of the Houses of the Parliament of Canada and of the Houses of the Legislature of Quebec; and both those Languages shall be used in the respective Records and Journals of those Houses; and either of those Languages may be used by any Person or in any Pleading or Process in or issuing from any Court of Canada established under this Act, and in or from all or any of the Courts of Quebec.

The Acts of the Parliament of Canada and of the Legislature of Quebec shall be printed and published in both those Languages.

APPENDIX 2

The Constitution Act, 1982

Schedule B
Constitution Act, 1982

Enacted as Schedule B to the *Canada Act 1982* (U.K.), 1982,
c. 11, which came into force on April 17, 1982

PART I

Canadian Charter of Rights and Freedoms

Whereas Canada is founded upon principles that recognize the supremacy of God
and the rule of law:

Guarantee of Rights and Freedoms

1. The *Canadian Charter of Rights and Freedoms* guarantees the rights and freedoms
set out in it subject only to such reasonable limits prescribed by law as can be demonstrably justified in a free and democratic society.

Rights and freedoms in Canada

Fundamental Freedoms

2. Everyone has the following fundamental freedoms:
    (*a*) freedom of conscience and religion;
    (*b*) freedom of thought, belief, opinion and expression, including freedom of the
press and other media of communication;
    (*c*) freedom of peaceful assembly; and
    (*d*) freedom of association.

Fundamental freedoms

Democratic Rights

3. Every citizen of Canada has the right to vote in an election of members of the
House of Commons or of a legislative assembly and to be qualified for membership
therein.

Democratic rights of citizens

4. (1) No House of Commons and no legislative assembly shall continue for longer
than five years from the date fixed for the return of the writs of a general election of its
members.

Maximum duration of legislative bodies

(2) In time of real or apprehended war, invasion or insurrection, a House of Commons
may be continued by Parliament and a legislative assembly may be continued by the
legislature beyond five years if such continuation is not opposed by the votes of more
than one-third of the members of the House of Commons or the legislative assembly,
as the case may be.

Continuation in special circumstances

Annual sitting of
legislative bodies

5. There shall be a sitting of Parliament and of each legislature at least once every twelve months.

Mobility Rights

Mobility of citizens

Rights to move and
gain livelihood

6. (1) Every citizen of Canada has the right to enter, remain in and leave Canada.

(2) Every citizen of Canada and every person who has the status of a permanent resident of Canada has the right

(*a*) to move to and take up residence in any province; and

(*b*) to pursue the gaining of a livelihood in any province.

Limitation

(3) The rights specified in subsection (2) are subject to

(*a*) any laws or practices of general application in force in a province other than those that discriminate among persons primarily on the basis of province of present or previous residence; and

(*b*) any laws providing for reasonable residency requirements as a qualification for the receipt of publicly provided social services.

Affirmative action
programs

(4) Subsections (2) and (3) do not preclude any law, program or activity that has as its object the amelioration in a province of conditions of individuals in that province who are socially or economically disadvantaged if the rate of employment in that province is below the rate of employment in Canada.

Legal Rights

Life, liberty and security
of person

7. Everyone has the right to life, liberty and security of the person and the right not to be deprived thereof except in accordance with the principles of fundamental justice.

Search or seizure

8. Everyone has the right to be secure against unreasonable search or seizure.

Detention or imprisonment

9. Everyone has the right not to be arbitrarily detained or imprisoned.

Arrest or detention

10. Everyone has the right on arrest or detention

(*a*) to be informed promptly of the reasons therefor;

(*b*) to retain and instruct counsel without delay and to be informed of that right; and

(*c*) to have the validity of the detention determined by way of *habeas corpus* and to be released if the detention is not lawful.

Proceedings in criminal
and penal matters

11. Any person charged with an offence has the right

(*a*) to be informed without unreasonable delay of the specific offence;

(*b*) to be tried within a reasonable time;

(*c*) not to be compelled to be a witness in proceedings against that person in respect of the offence;

(*d*) to be presumed innocent until proven guilty according to law in a fair and public hearing by an independent and impartial tribunal;

(*e*) not to be denied reasonable bail without just cause;

(*f*) except in the case of an offence under military law tried before a military tribunal, to the benefit of trial by jury where the maximum punishment for the offence is imprisonment for five years or a more severe punishment;

(*g*) not to be found guilty on account of any act or omission unless, at the time of the act or omission, it constituted an offence under Canadian or international law or was criminal according to the general principles of law recognized by the community of nations;

(*h*) if finally acquitted of the offence, not to be tried for it again and, if finally found guilty and punished for the offence, not to be tried or punished for it again; and

(*i*) if found guilty of the offence and if the punishment for the offence has been varied between the time of commission and the time of sentencing, to the benefit of the lesser punishment.

12. Everyone has the right not to be subjected to any cruel and unusual treatment or punishment.

Treatment or punishment

13. A witness who testifies in any proceedings has the right not to have any incriminating evidence so given used to incriminate that witness in any other proceedings, except in a prosecution for perjury or for the giving of contradictory evidence.

Self-crimination

14. A party or witness in any proceedings who does not understand or speak the language in which the proceedings are conducted or who is deaf has the right to the assistance of an interpreter.

Interpreter

Equality Rights

15. (1) Every individual is equal before and under the law and has the right to the equal protection and equal benefit of the law without discrimination and, in particular, without discrimination based on race, national or ethnic origin, colour, religion, sex, age or mental or physical disability.

Equality before and under law and equal protection and benefit of law

(2) Subsection (1) does not preclude any law, program or activity that has as its object the amelioration of conditions of disadvantaged individuals or groups including those that are disadvantaged because of race, national or ethnic origin, colour, religion, sex, age or mental or physical disability.

Affirmative action programs

Official Languages of Canada

16. (1) English and French are the official languages of Canada and have equality of status and equal rights and privileges as to their use in all institutions of the Parliament and government of Canada.

Official languages of Canada

(2) English and French are the official languages of New Brunswick and have equality of status and equal rights and privileges as to their use in all institutions of the legislature and government of New Brunswick.

Official languages of New Brunswick

(3) Nothing in this Charter limits the authority of Parliament or a legislature to advance the equality of status or use of English and French.

Advancement of status and use

16.1. (1) The English linguistic community and the French linguistic community in New Brunswick have equality of status and equal rights and privileges, including the right to distinct educational institutions and such distinct cultural institutions as are necessary for the preservation and promotion of those communities.

English and French linguistic communities in New Brunswick

(2) The role of the legislature and government of New Brunswick to preserve and promote the status, rights and privileges referred to in subsection (1) is affirmed.

Role of the legislature and government of New Brunswick

Proceedings of Parliament

17. (1) Everyone has the right to use English or French in any debates and other proceedings of Parliament.

Proceedings of New Brunswick legislature

(2) Everyone has the right to use English or French in any debates and other proceedings of the legislature of New Brunswick.

Parliamentary statutes and records

18. (1) The statutes, records and journals of Parliament shall be printed and published in English and French and both language versions are equally authoritative.

New Brunswick statutes and records

(2) The statutes, records and journals of the legislature of New Brunswick shall be printed and published in English and French and both language versions are equally authoritative.

Proceedings in courts established by Parliament

19. (1) Either English or French may be used by any person in, or in any pleading in or process issuing from, any court established by Parliament.

Proceedings in New Brunswick courts

(2) Either English or French may be used by any person in, or in any pleading in or process issuing from, any court of New Brunswick.

Communications by public with federal institutions

20. (1) Any member of the public in Canada has the right to communicate with, and to receive available services from, any head or central office of an institution of the Parliament or government of Canada in English or French, and has the same right with respect to any other office of any such institution where

(*a*) there is a significant demand for communications with and services from that office in such language; or

(*b*) due to the nature of the office, it is reasonable that communications with and services from that office be available in both English and French.

Communications by public with New Brunswick institutions

(2) Any member of the public in New Brunswick has the right to communicate with, and to receive available services from, any office of an institution of the legislature or government of New Brunswick in English or French.

Continuation of existing constitutional provisions

21. Nothing in sections 16 to 20 abrogates or derogates from any right, privilege or obligation with respect to the English and French languages, or either of them, that exists or is continued by virtue of any other provision of the Constitution of Canada.

Rights and privileges preserved

22. Nothing in sections 16 to 20 abrogates or derogates from any legal or customary right or privilege acquired or enjoyed either before or after the coming into force of this Charter with respect to any language that is not English or French.

Minority Language Educational Rights

Language of instruction

23. (1) Citizens of Canada

(*a*) whose first language learned and still understood is that of the English or French linguistic minority population of the province in which they reside, or

(*b*) who have received their primary school instruction in Canada in English or French and reside in a province where the language in which they received that instruction is the language of the English or French linguistic minority population of the province,

have the right to have their children receive primary and secondary school instruction in that language in that province.

Continuity of language instruction

(2) Citizens of Canada of whom any child has received or is receiving primary or secondary school instruction in English or French in Canada, have the right to have all their children receive primary and secondary school instruction in the same language.

(3) The right of citizens of Canada under subsections (1) and (2) to have their children receive primary and secondary school instruction in the language of the English or French linguistic minority population of a province

    (*a*) applies wherever in the province the number of children of citizens who have such a right is sufficient to warrant the provision to them out of public funds of minority language instruction; and

    (*b*) includes, where the number of those children so warrants, the right to have them receive that instruction in minority language educational facilities provided out of public funds.

Application where numbers warrant

Enforcement

24. (1) Anyone whose rights or freedoms, as guaranteed by this Charter, have been infringed or denied may apply to a court of competent jurisdiction to obtain such remedy as the court considers appropriate and just in the circumstances.

Enforcement of guaranteed rights and freedoms

(2) Where, in proceedings under subsection (1), a court concludes that evidence was obtained in a manner that infringed or denied any rights or freedoms guaranteed by this Charter, the evidence shall be excluded if it is established that, having regard to all the circumstances, the admission of it in the proceedings would bring the administration of justice into disrepute.

Exclusion of evidence bringing administration of justice into disrepute

General

25. The guarantee in this Charter of certain rights and freedoms shall not be construed so as to abrogate or derogate from any aboriginal, treaty or other rights or freedoms that pertain to the aboriginal peoples of Canada including

    (*a*) any rights or freedoms that have been recognized by the Royal Proclamation of October 7, 1763; and

    (*b*) any rights or freedoms that now exist by way of land claims agreements or may be so acquired.

Aboriginal rights and freedoms not affected by Charter

26. The guarantee in this Charter of certain rights and freedoms shall not be construed as denying the existence of any other rights or freedoms that exist in Canada.

Other rights and freedoms not affected by Charter

27. This Charter shall be interpreted in a manner consistent with the preservation and enhancement of the multicultural heritage of Canadians.

Multicultural heritage

28. Notwithstanding anything in this Charter, the rights and freedoms referred to in it are guaranteed equally to male and female persons.

Rights guaranteed equally to both sexes

29. Nothing in this Charter abrogates or derogates from any rights or privileges guaranteed by or under the Constitution of Canada in respect of denominational, separate or dissentient schools.

Rights respecting certain schools preserved

30. A reference in this Charter to a Province or to the legislative assembly or legislature of a province shall be deemed to include a reference to the Yukon Territory and the Northwest Territories, or to the appropriate legislative authority thereof, as the case may be.

Application to territories and territorial authorities

31. Nothing in this Charter extends the legislative powers of any body or authority.

Legislative powers not extended

Application of Charter

Application of Charter

32. (1) This Charter applies

(*a*) to the Parliament and government of Canada in respect of all matters within the authority of Parliament including all matters relating to the Yukon Territory and Northwest Territories; and

(*b*) to the legislature and government of each province in respect of all matters within the authority of the legislature of each province.

Exception

(2) Notwithstanding subsection (1), section 15 shall not have effect until three years after this section comes into force.

Exception where express declaration

33. (1) Parliament or the legislature of a province may expressly declare in an Act of Parliament or of the legislature, as the case may be, that the Act or a provision thereof shall operate notwithstanding a provision included in section 2 or sections 7 to 15 of this Charter.

Operation of exception

(2) An Act or a provision of an Act in respect of which a declaration made under this section is in effect shall have such operation as it would have but for the provision of this Charter referred to in the declaration.

Five year limitation

(3) A declaration made under subsection (1) shall cease to have effect five years after it comes into force or on such earlier date as may be specified in the declaration.

Re-enactment

(4) Parliament or the legislature of a province may re-enact a declaration made under subsection (1).

Five year limitation

(5) Subsection (3) applies in respect of a re-enactment made under subsection (4).

Citation

Citation

34. This Part may be cited as the *Canadian Charter of Rights and Freedoms.*

Suggestions for Further Reading

GENERAL

The Constitutional Law Group, *Canadian Constitutional Law*, 3d ed. (Toronto: Emond Montgomery, 2002).

Hogg, Peter W. *Constitutional Law of Canada*, 5th ed., 2 vols. (Toronto: Thomson Carswell, 2007).

Jackson, Donald W., and C. Neal Tate, eds. *Comparative Judicial Review and Public Policy* (Westport, CT: Greenwood Press, 1992).

James, Matt. *Misrecognized Materialists: Social Movements and Canadian Constitutional Politics* (Vancouver: University of British Columbia Press, 2006).

Laforest, Guy. *Trudeau and the End of a Canadian Dream* (Montreal and Kingston: McGill-Queen's University Press, 1995).

LaSelva, Samuel. *The Moral Foundations of Canadian Federalism: Paradoxes, Achievements and Tragedies of Nationhood* (Montreal and Kingston: McGill-Queen's University Press, 1996).

Lederman, W.R., ed. *The Courts and the Canadian Constitution* (Toronto: McClelland & Stewart, 1964).

McWhinney, Edward. *Judicial Review in the English-Speaking World*, 4th ed. (Toronto: University of Toronto Press, 1968).

Reesor, Bayard. *The Canadian Constitution in Historical Perspective* (Scarborough, ON: Prentice-Hall, 1992).

Russell, Peter H. *The Judiciary in Canada: The Third Branch of Government* (Toronto: McGraw-Hill Ryerson, 1987).

Smith, Jennifer. "The Origins of Judicial Review in Canada" (1983) 16 *Canadian Journal of Political Science* 115.

Strayer, Barry L. *The Canadian Constitution and the Courts*, 2d ed. (Toronto: Butterworths, 1983).

Supreme Court of Canada website: <http://www.scc-csc.gc.ca/welcome/index_e.asp>.

Tate, C. Neal, and Torbjorn Vallinder, eds. *The Global Expansion of Judicial Power* (New York: New York University Press, 1995).

Taylor, Charles. "Shared and Divergent Values" in Guy Laforest, ed., *Reconciling the Solitudes: Essays on Canadian Federalism and Nationalism* (Montreal and Kingston: McGill-Queen's University Press, 1992).

Vaughn, Frederick. *The Canadian Federalist Experiment: From Defiant Monarchy to Reluctant Republic* (Montreal and Kingston: McGill-Queen's University Press, 2003).

Vipond, Robert. *Liberty and Community: Canadian Federalism and the Failure of the Constitution* (Albany, NY: SUNY Press, 1991).

THE JUDICIAL COMMITTEE OF THE PRIVY COUNCIL

Cairns, Alan C. "The Judicial Committee and Its Critics" (1971) 3 *Canadian Journal of Political Science* 301.

Greenwood, F. Murray. "Lord Watson, Institutional Self-Interest and the Decentralization of Canadian Federalism in the 1890s" (1974) 9 *University of British Columbia Law Review* 244.

Haldane, Viscount. "The Work for the Empire of the Judicial Committee of the Privy Council" (1922) 1 *Cambridge Law Journal* 143.

O'Connor, William Francis. *Report Pursuant to Resolution of the Senate to the Honourable the Speaker by the Parliamentary Counsel, relating to: The Enactment of the British North America act, 1867, Any Lack of Consonance Between Its Terms and Judicial Construction of Them and Cognate Matters* (Ottawa: Queen's Printer, 1939).

Saywell, John. *The Lawmakers: Judicial Power and the Shaping of Canadian Federalism* (Toronto: University of Toronto Press, 2002).

Scott, F.R. "The Consequences of the Privy Council Decisions" (1937) 15 *Canadian Bar Review* 485.

Smith, Miriam. "Ghosts of the Judicial Committee of the Privy Council" (2002) 35 *Canadian Journal of Political Science* 1.

Vaughan, Frederick. "Critics of the Judicial Committee: The New Orthodoxy and an Alternative Explanation" and Replies by Alan Cairns and Peter Russell (1986) 19 *Canadian Journal of Political Science* 495.

Vipond, Robert C. "Constitutional Politics and the Legacy of the Provincial Rights Movement in Canada" (1985) 18 *Canadian Journal of Political Science* 271.

THE SUPREME COURT OF CANADA

Flemming, Roy B. *Tournament of Appeals: Granting Judicial Review in Canada* (Vancouver: University of British Columbia Press, 2004).

Fouts, Donald E. "Policy-Making in the Supreme Court of Canada, 1950-1960" in Glendon Schubert and David J. Danelski, eds., *Comparative Judicial Behaviour* (Toronto: Oxford University Press, 1969).

Greene, Ian, Carl Baar, Peter McCormick, George Szablowski, and Martin Thomas. *Final Appeal, Decision-Making in Canadian Courts of Appeal* (Toronto: Lorimer, 1998).

Hogg, Peter W. "Appointment of Justice Marshall Rothstein to the SCC" (2006) 44 *Osgoode Hall Law Journal* 527.

Laskin, Bora. "The Supreme Court of Canada: A Final Court of and for Canadians" (1951) 29 *Canadian Bar Review* 1038. Also in W.R. Lederman, ed., *The Courts and the Canadian Constitution* (Toronto: McClelland & Stewart, 1964) 125.

Mackinnon, Frank. "The Establishment of the Supreme Court of Canada" (1946) 27 *Canadian Historical Review* 258. Also in W.R. Lederman, ed., *The Courts and the Canadian Constitution* (Toronto: McClelland & Stewart, 1964) 106.

Monahan, Patrick. *Politics and the Constitution: The Charter, Federalism and the Supreme Court of Canada* (Toronto: Carswell/Methuen, 1987).

Muttart, Daved. *The Empirical Gap in Jurisprudence: A Comprehensive Study of the Supreme Court of Canada* (Toronto: University of Toronto Press, 2007).

Ostberg, G.T., and Mathew E. Wetstein. *Attitudinal Decision Making in the Supreme Court of Canada* (Vancouver: University of British Columbia Press, 2007).

Russell, Peter H. *The Supreme Court of Canada as a Bilingual and Bicultural Institution* (Ottawa: Queen's Printer, 1969).

———. "The Supreme Court Proposals in the Meech Lake Accord" (1988) 14 *Canadian Public Policy* S81.

Sauvageau, Florian, David Schneiderman, and David Taras. *The Last Word: Media Coverage of the Supreme Court of Canada* (Vancouver: University of British Columbia Press, 2005).

Snell, James, and Frederick Vaughan. *The Supreme Court of Canada: History of the Institution* (Toronto: University of Toronto Press, 1985).

Songer, Donald R. *The Transformation of the Supreme Court of Canada: An Empirical Examination* (Toronto: University of Toronto Press, 2008).

Tate, C. Neal, and Panu Sittiwong. "Decision-making in the Supreme Court of Canada" (1989) 59 *Journal of Politics* 900.

Weiler, Paul C. *In the Last Resort* (Toronto: Carswell/Methuen, 1974).

THE DIVISION OF POWERS

Baier, Gerald. *Courts and Federalism: Judicial Doctrine in the United States, Australia, and Canada* (Vancouver: University of British Columbia Press, 2006).

Bakvis, Herman, and Grace Skogstad, eds. *Canadian Federalism: Performance, Effectiveness, and Legitimacy* (Toronto: Oxford University Press, 2002).

Gagnon, Alain-G., ed. *Contemporary Canadian Federalism: Quebec Perspectives* (Toronto: University of Toronto Press, 2008).

Hogg, Peter W. "Is the Supreme Court of Canada Biased in Constitutional Cases?" (1979) 57 *Canadian Bar Review* 721.

L'Ecuyer, Gilbert. *La Court Suprême du Canada et la partage des compétences, 1949-78* (Québec: Gouvernement du Québec, 1978).

Laskin, Bora. " 'Peace, Order and Good Government' Re-examined" (1947) 25 *Canadian Bar Review* 1054. Also in W.R. Lederman, ed., *The Courts and the Canadian Constitution* (Toronto: McClelland & Stewart, 1964) 66.

Lederman, W.R. "Unity and Diversity in Canadian Federalism: Ideals and Methods of Moderation" (1975) 53 *Canadian Bar Review* 597.

Mallory, J.R. *Social Credit and the Federal Power in Canada* (Toronto: University of Toronto Press, 1954).

Mcconnell, W.H. "The Judicial Review of Prime Minister Bennett's 'New Deal'" (1968) 6 *Osgoode Hall Law Review* 39.

McWhinney, Edward. *Comparative Federalism* (Toronto: University of Toronto Press, 1962).

Morton, F.L. "The Constitutional Division of Powers with Respect to Environment in Canada" in Kenneth M. Holland, F.L. Morton, and Brian Galligan, eds., *Federalism and Environmental Policy-making in Australia, Canada and the United States* (Westport, CT: Greenwood Press, 1996).

Pigeon, Louis-Philippe. "The Meaning of Provincial Autonomy" (1951) 29 *Canadian Bar Review* 1126. Also in W.R. Lederman, ed., *The Courts and the Canadian Constitution* (Toronto: McClelland & Stewart, 1964) 35.

Remillard, Gil. *Fédéralisme Canadien* (Montreal: Québec/Amérique, 1980).

Russell, Peter H. "The Anti-Inflation Case: The Anatomy of a Constitutional Decision" (1977) 20 *Canadian Public Administration* 632.

———. "The Supreme Court and Federal-Provincial Relations: The Political Use of Legal Resources" (1985) 11 *Canadian Public Policy* 161.

Smith, Alexander. *The Commerce Power in Canada and the United States* (Toronto: Butterworths, 1963).

Stevenson, Garth. *Federalism in Canada: Selected Readings* (Toronto: McClelland & Stewart, 1989).

Swinton, Katherine E. *The Supreme Court and Canadian Federalism: The Laskin-Dickson Years* (Toronto: Carswell, 1990).

Tremblay, Guy. "The Supreme Court of Canada: Final Arbiter of Political Disputes" in Ivan Bernier and Andree Lajoie, eds., *The Supreme Court of Canada as an Instrument of Political Change* (Toronto: University of Toronto Press, 1985).

RIGHTS AND FREEDOMS

Baker, Dennis, and Rainer Knopff. "Charter Checks and Parliamentary Balances" (2007) 16 *Constitutional Forum* 71.

Baker, Dennis, and Rainer Knopff. "Minority Retort: A Parliamentary Power to Resolve Judicial Disagreement in Close Cases" (2002) 21 *Windsor Yearbook of Access to Justice* 348.

Bayefsky, Anne F., and Mary Eberts, eds. *Equality Rights and the Canadian Charter of Rights and Freedoms* (Toronto: Carswell, 1985).

Beckton, Clare F., and A. Wayne Mackay. *The Courts and the Charter* (Toronto: University of Toronto Press, 1985).

Brodie, Ian. *Friends of the Court: The Privileging of Interest Group Litigants in Canada* (Albany, NY: State University of New York Press, 2002).

Cairns, Alan C. *Charter versus Federalism: The Dilemmas of Constitutional Reform* (Montreal and Kingston: McGill-Queen's University Press, 1992).

Cavalluzzo, Paul. "Judicial Review and the Bill of Rights: Drybones and Its Aftermath" (1971) 9 *Osgoode Hall Law Journal* 511.

Choudhry, Sujit, and Claire E. Hunter. "Measuring Judicial Activism on the Supreme Court of Canada: A Comment on Newfoundland (Treasury Board) v. NAPE" (2003) 48 *McGill Law Journal* 525.

Choudhry, Sujit. "So What Is the Real Legacy of Oakes? Two Decades of Proportionality Analysis Under the Canadian Charter's Section 1" (2006) 34 *Supreme Court Law Review* (2d) 501.

Clarke, Jeremy. "Beyond the Democratic Dialogue, and Towards a Federalist One: Provincial Arguments and Supreme Court Responses in Charter Litigation" (2006) 39 *Canadian Journal of Political Science* 293.

Epp, Charles R. *The Rights Revolution* (Chicago: University of Chicago Press, 1998).

Fudge, Judy. "Legally Speaking: Courts, Democracy, and the Market" (2003) 19 *Supreme Court Law Review* (2d) 111.

Gaudreault-Desbiens, Jean-François. "La Charte canadienne des droits et libertés et le fédéralisme: quelques remarques sur les vingt premières années d'une relation amigugé" (2003) *Revue du Barreau* 271.

Hennigar, Mathew. "Expanding the 'Dialogue' Debate: Canadian Federal Government Responses to Lower Court Charter Decisions" (2004) 37 *Canadian Journal of Political Science* 3.

Hiebert, Janet L. *Charter Conflicts: What Is Parliament's Role?* (Montreal and Kingston: McGill-Queen's University Press, 2002).

———. *Limiting Rights: The Dilemma of Judicial Review* (Montreal and Kingston: McGill-Queen's University Press, 1996).

Hirschl, Ran. *Towards Juristocracy: The Origins and Consequences of the New Constitutionalism* (Cambridge, MA: Harvard University Press, 2004).

Hogg, Peter W., and A.A. Bushell. "The Charter Dialogue Between Courts and Legislatures (Or Perhaps the Charter of Rights Isn't Such a Bad Thing After All)" (1997) 35 *Osgoode Hall Law Journal* 75.

Howe, Paul, and Peter H. Russell, eds. *Judicial Power and Canadian Democracy* (Montreal and Kingston: McGill-Queen's University Press, 2001).

Huscroft, Grant A. "'Thank God We're Here': Judicial Exclusivity in Charter Interpretation and Its Consequences" (2004) 25 *Supreme Court Law Review* (2d) 239.

Hutchinson, Allan, and Andrew Petter. "Private Rights/Public Wrongs: The Liberal Lie of the Charter" (1988) 38 *University of Toronto Law Journal* 278.

James, Patrick, Donald E. Abelson, and Michael Lusztig, eds. *The Myth of the Sacred: The Charter, the Courts, and the Politics of the Constitution in Canada* (Montreal and Kingston: McGill-Queen's University Press, 2002).

Kahana, Tsvi. "The Notwithstanding Mechanism and Public Discussion: Lessons from the Ignored Practice of Section 33 of the Charter" (2001) 44 *Canadian Public Administration* 255.

Kelly, James B. "Bureaucratic Activism and the Charter of Rights and Freedoms: The Department of Justice and Its Entry into the Centre of Government" (1999) 42 *Canadian Public Administration* 476.

―――. *Governing with the Charter: Legislative and Judicial Activism and Framers' Intent* (Vancouver: University of British Columbia Press, 2005).

Knopff, Rainer. "How Democratic Is the Charter? And Does It Matter?" (2003) 19 *Supreme Court Law Review* (2d) 199.

―――. "Populism and the Politics of Rights: The Dual Attack on Representative Democracy" (1998) 31 *Canadian Journal of Political Science* 683.

―――. "What Do Constitutional Equality Rights Protect Canadians Against?" (1987) 20 *Canadian Journal of Political Science* 265.

Knopff, Rainer, and F.L. Morton. *Charter Politics* (Scarborough, ON: Nelson Canada, 1992).

LaSelva, Samuel V. *The Moral Foundations of Canadian Federalism* (Montreal and Kingston: McGill-Queen's University Press, 1996).

Laskin, Bora. "Our Civil Liberties—The Role of the Supreme Court" (1955) 41 *Queen's Quarterly* 445.

Leeson, Howard. "Section 33, The Notwithstanding Clause: A Paper Tiger?" in Paul Howe and Peter H. Russell, eds., *Judicial Power and Canadian Democracy* (Montreal and Kingston: McGill-Queen's University Press, 2001).

MacIvor, Heather. *Canadian Politics and Government in the Charter Era* (Toronto: Thomson-Nelson, 2006).

―――. "The Charter of Rights and Party Politics" (2004) 10 *Choices* 1.

MacLennan, Christopher. *Toward the Charter: Canadians and the Demand for a National Bill of Rights, 1929-1960* (Montreal and Kingston: McGill-Queen's University Press, 2003).

Manfredi, Christopher P. "The Day the Dialogue Died: A Comment on Sauvé v. Canada" (2007) 45 *Osgoode Hall Law Journal* 105.

―――. *Feminist Activism in the Supreme Court* (Vancouver: University of British Columbia Press, 2004).

―――. *Judicial Power and the Charter: Canada and the Paradox of Liberal Constitutionalism*, 2d ed. (Don Mills, ON: Oxford University Press, 2001).

Manfredi, Christopher, and Mark Rush. *Judging Democracy* (Peterborough, ON: Broadview Press, 2008).

Morton, F.L. "Dialogue or Monologue" in Paul Howe and Peter H. Russell, eds., *Judicial Power and Canadian Democracy* (Montreal and Kingston: McGill-Queen's University Press, 2001).

―――. "The Political Impact of the Canadian Charter of Rights and Freedoms" (1987) 20 *Canadian Journal of Political Science* 31.

―――. "The Politics of Rights: What Canadians Should Know About the American Bill of Rights" (1988) 1 *Windsor Review of Legal and Social Issues* 61.

Morton, F.L., and Rainer Knopff. *The Charter Revolution and the Court Party* (Peterborough, ON: Broadview Press, 2000).

Morton, F.L., Peter H. Russell, and Troy Riddell. "The Canadian Charter of Rights and Freedoms: A Descriptive Analysis of the First Decade, 1982-1992" (1995) 5 *National Journal of Constitutional Law* 1.

Petter, Andrew. "The Politics of the Charter" (1986) 8 *Supreme Court Law Review* 473.

———. "Taking Dialogue Theory Much Too Seriously (Or Perhaps Charter Dialogue Isn't Such a Good Thing After All" (2007) 45 *Osgoode Hall Law Journal* 147.

Pinard, Danielle. "Une Malheureuse celebration de la Charte des droits et libertés de la personne par la Cour suprême du Canada: l'arrête Chaoulli" in *La Charter Québécoise: origines, enjeux et perspectives,* Revue du Barreau du Québec 2006.

Roach, Kent. *The Supreme Court on Trial: Judicial Activism or Democratic Dialogue?* (Toronto: Irwin Law, 2001).

Russell, Peter H. "The Political Purposes of the Canadian Charter of Rights and Freedoms" (1983) 61 *Canadian Bar Review* 30.

———. "Standing Up for Notwithstanding" (1991) 29 *Alberta Law Review* 293.

Schmeiser, D.A. *Civil Liberties in Canada* (Toronto: Oxford University Press, 1964).

Scott, F.R. *Civil Liberties and Canadian Federalism* (Toronto: University of Toronto Press, 1959).

———. "The Privy Council and Minority Rights" (1930) *Queen's Quarterly* 668.

Sharpe, Robert J. *Charter Litigation* (Toronto: Butterworths, 1987).

Smith, Miriam. *Lesbian and Gay Rights in Canada: Social Movements and Equality-Seeking, 1971-1995* (Toronto: University of Toronto Press, 1999).

———. *Political Institutions and Lesbian and Gay Rights in the United States and Canada* (New York: Routledge, 2008).

Sniderman, Paul M., Joseph F. Fletcher, Peter H. Russell, and Philip E. Tetlock. *The Clash of Rights: Liberty, Equality and Legitimacy in Pluralist Democracy* (New Haven, CT: Yale University Press, 1997).

Strayer, Barry. "Life Under the Charter: Adjusting the Balance Between Legislatures and Courts" (1988) *Public Law* 347.

Stuart, Don. *Charter Justice in Canadian Criminal Law*, 4th ed. (Toronto: Thomson Carswell, 2005).

Tarnopolsky, W.S. *The Canadian Bill of Rights* (Toronto: McClelland & Stewart, 1975).

Weiler, Paul. "Rights and Judges in a Democracy: A New Canadian Version" (1984) 18 *University of Michigan Journal of Law Reform* 51.

Whyte, John D. "On Not Standing for Notwithstanding" (1990) 28 *Alberta Law Review* 347.

Wilson, Bertha. "The Making of a Constitution: Approaches to Judicial Interpretation" (1988) *Public Law* 370.

ABORIGINAL RIGHTS

Asch, Michael. *Home and Native Land: Aboriginal Rights and the Canadian Constitution* (Toronto: Methuen, 1984).

———. ed. *Aboriginal and Treaty Rights in Canada: Essays on Law, Equality and Respect for Difference* (Vancouver: University of British Columbia Press, 1997).

Borrows, John. *Recovering Canada: The Resurgence of Indigenous Law* (Toronto: University of Toronto Press, 2002).

Coates, Kenneth. *The Marshall Decision and Native Rights* (Montreal and Kingston: McGill-Queen's University Press, 2000).

Henderson, James Youngblood. *First Nations Jurisprudence and Aboriginal Rights* (Saskatoon: Native Law Centre, University of Saskatchewan, 2006).

Kulchyski, Peter. *Unjust Relations: Aboriginal Rights in Canadian Courts* (Toronto: Oxford University Press, 1994).

Macklem, Patrick. *Indigenous Difference and the Constitution of Canada* (Toronto: University of Toronto Press, 2001).

Mercredi, Ovide, and Mary Ellen Turpel. *In the Rapids: Navigating the Future of First Nations* (Toronto: Penguin Books, 1994).

Penikett, Tony. *Reconciliation: First Nations Treaty Making in British Columbia* (Vancouver: Douglas & McIntyre, 2006).

Russell, Peter H. "High Courts and the Rights of Aboriginal Peoples: The Limits of Judicial Independence" (1998) 61 *Saskatchewan Law Review* 247.

Slattery, Brian. "Understanding Aboriginal Rights" (1987) 66 *Canadian Bar Review* 727.

Tully, James. *Strange Multiplicity: Constitutionalism in an Age of Diversity* (Cambridge, UK: University of Cambridge Press, 1995).

Wilkins, Kerry, ed. *Advancing Aboriginal Claims: Visions/Strategies/Directions* (Saskatoon: Purich, 2004).

CONSTITUTIONAL CHANGE

Banting, Keith, and Richard Simeon, eds. *And No One Cheered: Federalism, Democracy and the Constitution Act* (Toronto: Methuen, 1983).

Cameron, David R., ed. *The Referendum Papers: Essays on Secession and National Unity* (Toronto: University of Toronto Press, 1999).

Cook, Curtis, ed. *Constitutional Predicament: Canada After the Referendum of 1992* (Montreal and Kingston: McGill-Queen's University Press, 1994).

Favreau, Guy. *The Amendment of the Constitution of Canada* (Ottawa: Queen's Printer, 1965).

Gerin-Lajoie, Paul. *Constitutional Amendment in Canada* (Toronto: University of Toronto Press, 1950).

Knopff, Rainer. "Legal Theory and the 'Patriation' Debate" (1981) 7 *Queen's Law Journal* 41.

Lederman, W.R. *Continuing Constitutional Dilemmas* (Toronto: Butterworths, 1981).

McRoberts, Kenneth, and Patrick Monahan. *The Charlottetown Accord, the Referendum, and the Future of Canada* (Toronto: University of Toronto Press, 1993).

Milne, David. *The New Canadian Constitution* (Toronto: James Lorimer, 1982).

Monahan, Patrick. *Meech Lake: The Inside Story* (Toronto: University of Toronto Press, 1991).

Peach, Ian, Graeme Mitchell, David Smith, and John Whyte, eds. *A Living Tree: The Legacy of 1982 in Canada's Political Evolution* (Markham, ON: LexisNexis, 2007).

Romanow, Roy, John White, and Howard Leeson. *Canada Notwithstanding: The Making of the Constitution, 1976-1982* (Toronto: Carswell/Methuen, 1984).

Russell, Peter H. *Constitutional Odyssey: Can Canadians Become a Sovereign People?*, 3d ed. (Toronto: University of Toronto Press, 2004).

Russell, Peter H., et al. *The Court and the Constitution* (Kingston: Institute of Intergovernmental Relations, Queen's University, 1982).

Thomas, David M. *Whistling Past the Graveyard: Constitutional Abeyance, Quebec and the Future of Canada* (Toronto: Oxford University Press, 1997).